Higher Education
AND THE
Law

by

Harry T. Edwards
PROFESSOR OF LAW
UNIVERSITY OF MICHIGAN

and

Virginia Davis Nordin
ASSISTANT PROFESSOR OF EDUCATIONAL ADMINISTRATION
UNIVERSITY OF WISCONSIN - MADISON

IEM

INSTITUTE FOR EDUCATIONAL MANAGEMENT
HARVARD UNIVERSITY
CAMBRIDGE, MASSACHUSETTS

Higher Education *AND THE* Law

HIGHER EDUCATION AND THE LAW

Copyright © 1979 by:

HARRY T. EDWARDS
Professor of Law
University of Michigan Law School
Ann Arbor, Michigan 48104

VIRGINIA DAVIS NORDIN
Assistant Professor of Educational Administration
University of Wisconsin
Madison, Wisconsin 53706

International Standard Book Number: 0-934222-00-2
Library of Congress Catalogue Card Number: 79-88195

Published by:
INSTITUTE FOR EDUCATIONAL MANAGEMENT
HARVARD UNIVERSITY
CAMBRIDGE, MASSACHUSETTS 02138

PREFACE

The study of "higher education and the law" is really about "the law" as it affects the higher education community. There are relatively few significant laws, administrative regulations or judicial opinions that have been written solely for higher education. It is true that the past decade has witnessed an extraordinary proliferation in legislation and judicial opinions impacting higher education. Nevertheless, even when university and college administrators are heard to complain about this recent proliferation, it must be understood that many of these same laws, regulations and opinions being complained about affect not only academia but other institutions in society as well.

The real issue, therefore, is not simply the proliferation of laws, regulations and judicial opinions affecting higher education, but rather the *nature of the impact* of these laws, regulations and opinions on the academic community. It seems to us that one of the few really good reasons to justify a book of this sort is the serious concern within the academic community, and some significant evidence to support the concern, that institutions of higher education may now be struggling under the excess weight of these new (and sometimes ill-conceived) statutes, regulations and opinions. This struggling has been caused by laws which may alter the educational mission of institutions of higher education, adversely affect relationships between faculty, students and administrators on campus, and substantially increase the operating costs of colleges and universities. The other side of the coin, however, is that the increase in laws, regulations and judicial opinions has often produced greater protections for the rights of individual faculty members and students, and even for the public-at-large. Therefore, in considering the materials in this volume, the reader should always be prepared to weigh the cost of regulation against the substantive protection secured. Some of these issues are discussed in greater detail in Chapter 13.

The book is divided into four parts: The University and College as a Legal Entity; Faculty Rights; Student Rights; and Federal Regulation of Higher Education. There are several topical chapters within each part and numerous topical headings within each chapter. The first three parts involve a number of constitutional as well as statutory issues affecting higher education. Part Four, however, is mostly concerned with federal statutory and administrative regulations affecting the academic community.

A careful review of the detailed Table of Contents will give the reader a good understanding of the design and substantive coverage of the book. There are several subjects covered in the book that could properly have been included under a number of different headings. A good example of this is "Procedural Due Process for Faculty," which we have elected to place as the last section in the chapter on Faculty Tenure. Some may disagree with our subject ordering; therefore, materials have been carefully segregated under appropriate sub-headings so that they may be easily taught or studied out of the order in which they appear in this volume.

Every effort has been made to make the book useful for both students and practitioners. The "case method" design predominates, primarily because we are wedded to the belief that law cases still furnish the best sources for study and review of legal developments. However, there are substantial discussions, in both original and reprinted text and in "Notes" following cases, offered to give historical and theoretical perspectives, to raise questions about case opinions and to analyze legal developments.

Although the subject coverage is intended to be extensive, it does not purport to be comprehensive in every subject area; such a goal would be impossible to achieve in a single volume. In addition, certain subjects (such as matters falling within the compass of traditional tort law) are given at best only sparse treatment. Rather, we have tried to concentrate on areas of greatest significance and concern to the higher education community.

Apart from the judicial opinions cited, there are a number of scholarly writings listed within each chapter. The reader may wish to consider certain of these works in connection with further study in any given subject area.

Given the nature of the laws and regulations affecting higher education, the "law" in this area will be subject to significant refinements and changes in the years to come. Indeed, as this book goes to press, there are three major cases (dealing with Title IX, the Rehabilitation Act and Title VII) pending decision by the United States Supreme Court. To deal with such legal refinements and changes, Supplements to the book will be published on an annual basis. These Supplements will update material appearing in this volume.

Judicial opinions appearing in the book (and in later Supplements) will often be edited by the authors to facilitate study. Where footnotes have been retained from a case opinion, the original number will appear in brackets. Otherwise, footnotes will appear in successive numerical order in each chapter, with a new set of footnotes appearing in each new chapter.

Much of the research that has gone into this work has been sponsored by grants from the Institute for Educational Management at Harvard University and the Sloan Commission on Government and Higher Education. The authors are extremely grateful for this support. A special note of thanks goes to Professors Richard Chait and Frederic Jacobs, the Academic and Administrative directors of the Institute for Educational Management, who have given strong encouragement to the authors to complete the publication effort.

The preparation of these materials has consumed a significant period of time and involved some invaluable aid from several research assistants. For their help at various stages of this work, thanks go to Phoebe Salten (Harvard Law School), Robert Varco and Kathy Weinman (University of Michigan Law School), Mary Rinne, Esq. (Ann Arbor, Michigan), David Nordin (University of Illinois Law School), Clare Alschuler, Judy Brindley and David Dabroski (University of Wisconsin Law School) and Arthur C. Perez and William Lloyd Turner (University of Wisconsin). Our appreciation is also extended to Evelyn Otterback and Francine Fein for their assistance in the preparation of the manuscript.

Our sincerest words of thanks are saved for Jan Abbs, Loretta Anderson, Nancy Martin and Susan Segal (University of Michigan Law School), whose outstanding research assistance helped to make possible the timely completion of this volume, and Debra Jackson, who worked tirelessly and unselfishly for countless hours to complete the preparation of the final manuscript. We are truly indebted to them for their special efforts.

Harry T. Edwards
Ann Arbor, Michigan

Virginia Davis Nordin
Madison, Wisconsin

March 1, 1979

SUMMARY TABLE OF CONTENTS

CONTENTS

REFERENCE MATERIALS

The following list of reference materials and organizations may be helpful to readers who are pursuing special research efforts in higher education and the law. Certain of the references are used to cite materials in the book.

Academe: Bulletin of the AAUP: published by the American Association of University Professors, One Dupont Circle, N.W., Washington, D.C. 20036.

The Chronicle of Higher Education: newspaper published weekly by The Chronicle of Higher Education, Inc., 1333 New Hampshire Avenue, N.W., Washington, D.C. 20036. The *Chronicle* contains a wealth of information about current affairs, legal developments, fiscal data, enrollment figures, job opportunities for faculty members, and other like matters, in higher education.

The College Administrator and the Courts: published by the College Administration Publications, Inc., P.O. Box 8492, Asheville, North Carolina 28804. Looseleaf service summarizing the major court cases and legislation affecting college administrators.

The College Student and the Courts: published by the College Administration Publications, Inc., P.O. Box 8492, Asheville, North Carolina 28804. Looseleaf service summarizing the major court cases and legislation affecting college students.

College and University Law by Alexander and Solomon. Published by the Michie Company, Charlottesville, Virginia, 1972.

The Condition of Education: published annually by the National Center for Education Statistics, Dept. of Health, Education, and Welfare, Washington, D.C.

The Constitution and American Education by Arval A. Morris. Published by West Publishing Company, St. Paul, Minnesota, 1974.

Employee Relations Law Journal: published quarterly by Executive Enterprises Publications Co., 10 Columbus Circle, New York, N.Y. 10019.

F.E.P. Cas.: designates Fair Employment Practice Cases, published by the Bureau of National Affairs, Inc., Washington, D.C. The FEP service reports a large number of state and federal opinions dealing with employment discrimination cases.

F.2d: refers to the *Federal Reporter* service, second series, published by West Publishing Company, St. Paul, Minnesota. The *Federal Reporter* includes all of the cases decided by the United States Courts of Appeals.

F.Supp.:   refers to *Federal Supplement*, published by West Publishing Company, St. Paul, Minnesota. The *Federal Supplement* service reports the opinions of the United States District Courts.

Higher Education and National Affairs: weekly newsletter published by the American Council on Education, Suite 800, One Dupont Circle, N.W., Washington, D.C. 20036.

Higher Education Daily: published by Capitol Publications, Inc., Suite G-12, 2430 Pennsylvania Ave. N.W., Washington, D.C. 20037.

IRRA: designates the Industrial Relations Research Association, 7226 Social Science Building, University of Wisconsin, Madison, Wisconsin 53706.

Journal of College and University Law: published by the National Association of College and University Attorneys, Suite 510, One Dupont Circle, N.W., Washington, D.C. 20036.

Journal of Law and Education: published quarterly by the Jefferson Law Book Company, 646 Main Street, Cincinnati, Ohio 45201.

LRRM: designates *Labor Relations Reference Manual*, published by the Bureau of National Affairs, Inc., Washington, D.C.   The LRRM service brings together decisions of the NLRB and courts in cases involving labor-management relations.

The Law of Higher Education: Legal Implications of Administrative Decision Making by William A. Kaplin. Published by Jossey-Bass Publishers, Inc., San Francisco, California, 1978.

Law Reviews: law review articles are cited as follows: "Adams, The Integrity of the Arbitral Process, 76 Mich. L. Rev. 231 (1977)," indicating the author's name, the article name, the volume, the place where the law review is published, page number and year of publication. Law review articles can be found in the libraries of any major law school.

Legal Handbook for Educators: by Patricia Hollander. Published by Westview Press, 5500 Central Avenue, Boulder, Colorado, 1978.

NOLPE Notes: published monthly by the National Organization on Legal Problems of Education, 5401 S.W. 7th Avenue, Topeka, Kansas 66606. This publication summarizes important legal developments affecting higher education.

NOLPE School Law Journal: published semiannually by the National Organization on Legal Problems of Education, 5401 S.W. 7th Avenue, Topeka, Kansas 66606.

NOLPE School Law Reporter: published bimonthly by the National Organization on Legal Problems of Education, 5401 S.W. 7th Avenue, Topeka, Kansas 66606.

Professional Women and Minorities: A Manpower Data Resource Service: published by the Scientific Manpower Commission, 1776 Massachusetts Avenue, N.W., Washington, D.C. 20036. The book is designed to provide current and historical statistics about the professional segment of the United States population and particularly the participation and availability of women and minorities in professional areas which generally require formal education to at least the baccalaureate level. Looseleaf service that is updated periodically.

School Law News: published biweekly by Capitol Publications, Inc., Suite G-12, 2430 Pennsylvania Ave. N.W., Washington, D.C. 20037.

S.Ct.:   designates *Supreme Court Reporter*, published by West Publishing Company, St. Paul, Minnesota 55102. The *Supreme Court Reporter* includes the full text of all United States Supreme Court opinions.

The Yearbook of Higher Education Law: published annually by the National Organization on Legal Problems of Education, 5401 S.W. 7th Avenue, Topeka, Kansas 66606.

TABLE OF CASES

PART ONE

THE COLLEGE OR UNIVERSITY
AS A LEGAL ENTITY

CHAPTER I

THE COLLEGE OR UNIVERSITY AS A LEGAL ENTITY

I. Introduction

The exact nature of the university as an organization and its precise place in the societal structure is often studied yet rarely clearly defined. There are many ways to describe a college or university. In recent years students of higher education have discussed whether such institutions are essentially academic, social, political or some other form of organization. Whatever their organizational form, all colleges or universities are legal entities of one kind or another. The form of legal organization of an institution of higher learning gives it distinct powers and capacities which directly affect its essential academic nature. In contemporary American society, in which the rule of law has never been more dominant, the legal nature of any institution is extremely important.

Most importantly, legal structure directly affects the ability of the funding source—the legislature, the church or other—to control or regulate the institution. The importance of autonomy to a strong university has been recognized in the recent establishment of constitutional autonomy for several state universities. (See Chapter 3, *infra*.)

The ideological concept of autonomy for universities was established at the very beginning of their formations in the twelfth and thirteenth centuries when "[t]hey appealed to king or council against pope, to pope against king or bishop, and to kings and popes alike against truculent town governments." Hofstadter and Metzger, The Development of Academic Freedom in the United States (New York: Columbia University Press, 1955), at 8. At that time university power was more parallel to the powers of other social institutions. Universities through "cessation" (strike) or migration to another location, were able to exert considerable pressure, and to establish the ideal of an autonomous society-within-society with its own rules, and responsibility for its own members. See Ross, The University: The Anatomy of Academe (New York: McGraw-Hill, 1976), Chapter 1, "The Beginning."

Although in later historical periods (Ross defines an "interim period" as 1500–1850), the universities were not always able to maintain the complete independence of their earliest days against increasingly strong church and state institutions, the ideal persisted both within and without the university. Perhaps the strongest legal protection for this position was found in the Prussian Constitution of 1850 which provided succinctly that "[s]cience and teaching shall be free."

Today, the concepts of academic freedom and institutional autonomy reflect this position. In the United States as elsewhere the nature of the

3

university as it relates to society is defined more in custom, usage and scholarly comment than in formalized legal relationships. However, since America is a nation founded on law and legal process, the position of higher education is also reflected in court cases, as well as statutes and regulations. Historically, American courts have adhered fairly consistently to the doctrine of academic abstention in order to avoid excess judicial oversight of academic institutions. The courts have also frequently stepped in to prevent the intrusion by other governmental agencies into the affairs of institutions of higher education, particularly with respect to issues pertaining to intellectual freedom.

Even though the case law indicates a greater growth of individual academic freedom as a "penumbra" right under the First Amendment (see Griswold v. Connecticut, 381 U.S. 479 (1965)) than much judicial recognition of institutional autonomy, there has been substantial dicta on the importance of institutional freedom, as well as some direct consideration. During the McCarthy era, Justice Frankfurter wrote:

> Political power must abstain from intrustion into this activity of freedom, pursued in the interest of wise government and the people's well-being, except for the reasons that are exigent and obviously compelling. . . .
>
> These pages need not be burdened with proof, based on the testimony of a cloud of impressive witnesses, of the dependence of a free society on free universities. This means the exclusion of governmental intervention in the intellectual life of a university. It matters little whether such intervention occurs avowedly or through action that inevitably tends to check the ardor and fearlessness of scholars, qualities at once so fragile and so indispensable for fruitful academic labor. [Sweezy v. New Hampshire, 354 U.S. 234, 262 (1957), concurring opinion.]

See also Justice Frankfurter's concurring opinion in Wieman v. Updegraff, 344 U.S. 183 (1952). More recently, Justice Powell made a strong statement for university autonomy in University of California Regents v. Bakke, 98 S.Ct. 2733 (1978) where he wrote, "The freedom of a university to make its own judgments as to education includes the selection of its student body." (See Chapter 14, *infra*.) Additional cases which consider direct institutional autonomy include Haverford College v. Reeher, 329 F.Supp. 1196 (E. D. Pa. 1971) (student scholarships and campus violence reports); Wayne State University v. Cleland, —F.2d—(6th Cir. 1978) (Veterans Administration supervision of university classes); and Regents of the University of Minnesota v. N.C.A.A., 422 F.Supp. 1158 (1976), *rev'd*, 560 F.2d 352 (7th Cir. 1977).

Since there is no clear case law on institutional autonomy, the legal rights and responsibilities of universities have historically been primarily defined by the charters, deeds of trust, state statutes or state constitutional provisions establishing them. Cases construing these documents have been few in number. However, in recent years the courts seem to have overcome their reluctance to hear cases concerning academic institutions, so that an increasing number of decisions are beginning to define legal rights and responsibilities of the university and its constituent parts. In 1972–1974, for example, the Supreme Court decided four highly significant cases in higher education, more decisions on higher education than it had made in the previous two decades (and for an even longer period if the academic freedom cases are excepted): Healy v. James, 408 U.S. 169 (1972; Board of Regents v. Roth, 408 U.S. 564 (1972); Perry v. Sinderman, 408 U.S. 593 (1972); Vlandis v. Kline, 412 U.S. 441 (1973).

Several factors probably have caused this increasing interaction. (1) The general increase in litigiousness in today's society. Americans are tending to want to resolve all social and personal problems in the courts and college problems are no exception. (2) The civil rights movement. Increased regard for individual rights has encouraged the filing of complaints against all institutions including private organizations and public entities. The funding of legal service offices has added to the ability and willingness of individuals to file suits against large organizations. (3) The tight academic job market and the increase of unions on campus. Union activity has undoubtedly supported the formal filing of more employment grievances. The gentlemanly tradition of moving elsewhere when you disagree with your institution is no longer always possible. Unions may provide financial and organizational support for filing actual lawsuits as well as for handling internal grievances. (4) The student protest movement. Student activism has caused both universities and students to become more familiar with the uses of legal process. (5) Increased government regulation. The desire to resist over-regulation has caused administrators to look for ways in which the law, among other sources, can be used to defend their independence, and regulatory agencies have used the courts to enforce their laws and regulations. As a result of these factors, the university's existence as a legal entity is becoming more and more precisely defined; legal definitions may yet supercede scholarly analysis and social consensus as the source of the university's status in contemporary society.

As American universities and colleges are extremely diverse in their individual characters, so their legal formations also tend to be diverse. While these different legal formulations generally reflect the same attempt by each institution to define its powers as against funding sources and the seat of governmental authority, it is interesting to study the significance of the differences in legal organizations and attributes of different universities. For example, it can be argued that the high academic status of the University of Michigan and the University of California at Berkeley, two great public universities, can be traced to their histories of legal autonomy, guaranteed by their respective state constitutions.

Legally, there are distinctly different types of institutions of higher education. The major forms are: the private institution incorporated as a nonprofit corporation with a corporate charter; the public institution which has constitutional status carrying with it a strong degree of autonomy; the public institution which is created by statute and which consequently has a lesser degree of autonomy; the public institution operating primarily as a government agency with no strong legal basis for autonomy; and the two-year institution, which is often a creature of local government entities, falling somewhere between the state statutory college and the public school district.

The early American legal forms were not so clearly drawn. Many of our major private institutions originally had a number of members of the legislature as members of the board of governors as well as state administrators. Usually additional spaces were filled by members of the clergy, but these members often had quasi-public status. In fact, church, state and school were public and integrated functions. Even today the distinction between public and private universities is not as clear as one might like to think. The blurring of private and public lines now arises in the context of the Fourteenth Amendment state action issues; only recently a Fourteenth Amendment challenge was made to the private nature of Harvard University, based partly on its historical origins. Krohn v. Harvard Law School, 552 F.2d 21 (1st Cir. 1977).

Under the common law system the configuration of the university as a legal entity is outlined by specific case decisions. Thus, questions concerning the essential nature of the university may run the gamut from whether it is part of the university function to provide student housing, raised in 1899 in Yale University v. Town of New Haven, 71 Conn. 316, 42 A.87, to whether the university can operate a television station, raised in Illinois in Turkovich v. University of Illinois, 143 N.E.2d 229 (1957). The extent of the legislative oversight of a public university is an extensive issue as is the ability of the state auditor to control public universities' finances. Student-faculty rights define the responsibilities of the university as do the current extensive government regulations. All these issues, and others, will be covered in subsequent chapters, but all the issues will help define the university as a legal entity.

Final notice should be taken of the distinctive legal position of religiously affiliated institutions whose status stems in part from the First Amendment. The Free Exercise clause is the clearest Constitutional authority which any university can invoke to resist government intervention and maintain its autonomy, but the protection runs only to the religious, not the academic, nature of the institution.

II. Historical Notes

J. HERBST, THE FIRST THREE AMERICAN COLLEGES: SCHOOLS OF THE REFORMATION, in VIII, PERSPECTIVES IN AMERICAN HISTORY, 7-11 (1974)*

The first three colleges founded in the English-speaking colonies in North America—Harvard, William and Mary, and Yale—have one feature of their early existence in common: they did *not* begin their careers as incorporated colleges or universities as such institutions were then known in Europe. Rather, they were created as unincorporated provincial Latin grammar boarding schools governed by trustees, and as such they are more closely related in conception and in governmental practice to the contemporary academic institutions of Reformed Europe—*gymnasia illustria*, academies, or *Gelehrtenschulen* on the Continent and the independent grammar schools of Elizabethan England or the dissenting academies after 1662—than to the medieval universities. If one is to understand the origins and early development of American higher education this fact must first of all be understood, though it runs counter to much of what has been written on the subject. It is the purpose of this essay to establish the evidence for this statement and to explore its implications.

Only the first three colleges in the American colonies will be considered. For the later collegiate institutions—in New Jersey (the college later known as Princeton, 1746), in New York (King's, later known as Columbia, 1754), and in Pennsylvania (the College of Philadelphia, later the University of Pennsylvania, 1755)—came into being under conditions of sectarian rivalry and strife, whereas the earlier ones existed in colonies dominated and governed by the representatives of an established Protestant denomination: Puritan in New England and Anglican in Virginia. These first three American collegiate foundations were establishments of the Protestant Reformation. The schools, colleges, and universities of Protestant Europe had themselves been founded under conditions of officially sanctioned or prescribed religious homogeneity and could thus serve as examples for the inhabitants of seventeenth-century New England and Virginia in which a similar religious homogeneity prevailed. And in their foundings the first three colleges illustrate the lack of clear and inflexible lines of demarcation between schools and colleges on the one hand, and colleges and universities on the other. Harvard is first mentioned in the records of the General Court of the Massachusetts Bay Colony in 1636 as "a school or college" to which the Court agreed it would give £400. But it was not until fourteen years later that the school was formally chartered

---

* Reprinted by permission of the President and Fellows of Harvard College, Cambridge, Massachusetts. (Volume VIII of Perspectives in American History was published by the Charles Warren Center for Studies in American History and edited by D. Fleming and B. Bailyn.)

as a college. In Virginia the College of William and Mary carried on its operations for the first thirty-six years as a grammar school and an English petty
school for Indian boys and neighborhood children. It was not until 1729
that the college corporation of president and six masters took over the college property. At Yale formal incorporation of the collegiate school had to
wait from 1701 to 1745. Only then did Yale College come into legal existence as a formally incorporated body politic. All Protestant reformers were
concerned with learning and schooling as aids to faith, and institutional
arrangements and legal nomenclature were matters of convenience and
accommodation to circumstance.

During the first five years of its nominal existence Harvard, the first
institution of higher learning to be founded in the original thirteen English-
speaking colonies on the North American continent, was placed under the
care of a government committee. In November 1637, one year after the
General Court of the Massachusetts Bay Colony had first agreed "to give
400 lbs. towards a school or college," the Court appointed the governor,
deputy-governor, and the treasurer of the colony together with three additional magistrates and six ministers as inspectors, governors, or trustees of
this new school. The committee assumed the oversight of the institution's
affairs and appointed Nathaniel Eaton as its first professor, only to lose
him again in 1639 when the General Court dismissed him for "cruel and
barbarous beatings . . . and for other neglecting and misusing of his scholars. . . ." The committee of inspectors apparently did not take an active
part in the next chapter of the story when assorted members of the General
Court took the initiative in appointing Henry Dunster as president in 1640.
The General Court as the colony's highest legislative and judicial forum kept
tight reins on the college's affairs and did not always delegate its authority
to its committee. But in 1642, four days after Dunster's first commencement, it reconstituted the inspectors as a permanent board of overseers,
now consisting of governor, deputy-governor, college president, all nine
assistants of the Court, and the nine pastors and teachers of the six adjoin-
ing towns. These twenty-one men were to administer the college funds and
property, were obliged to hear appeals concerning rules and decisions affecting the college, and were themselves held accountable to the General Court
which served as the general supervisory agency for all such public trusts. At
the same time the new Board of Overseers had received and took on the
characteristics of a quasi-corporation, that is, of a body which, while lacking
formal incorporation, showed the governmental powers and other attributes
of corporate status. It was self-perpetuating; it made laws and statutes for
the college by majority vote; it promulgated a set of "Laws, Liberties, and
Orders," and it ordered the casting of a college seal. It obviously exercised
far greater authority than had ever been allowed to its predecessor, the
government committee of inspectors.

In Virginia, James Blair, the commissary of the Anglican Church and
representative of the Bishop of London, took the initiative and moved
toward the establishment of a grammar school and a college for the training

of a native Episcopalian ministry. To accomplish this he succeeded in 1693 in obtaining a royal charter which established an unincorporated board of eighteen Virginia gentlemen as trustees over the new institution and its property, he himself among them as president of the school. The same eighteen gentlemen and their successors were also to serve as governors and visitors of the college to be established. But it took another thirty-six years until the full corporate body of the college consisting of a president and six masters could be assembled. In the meantime a grammar school opened in 1694 under the trusteeship, and an Indian school began its operations in 1711. In 1729 the two surviving trustees could finally hand over the property to the college corporation, and the initial stage in the existence of the College of William and Mary had come to an end. During the period both of trusteeship and of the college corporation the charter provided for a royal cash grant out of the Virginia quitrents, for a portion of the tobacco revenue, for the patronage and income of the office of surveyor-general, and for twenty thousand acres of land. Funded with royal gifts, the College of William and Mary survived its infancy under the benevolent oversight of its trustees before it emerged as a fully incorporated collegiate body.

In Connecticut, finally, the General Court's authorization of 1701 granted "full liberty, right, and privilege" to a number of ministers and their successors "to stand as trustees, partners, or undertakers" for a collegiate school. They were to erect it and to improve and encourage it in the future. It was assumed in this document of 1701 that such a school for instructing youth in the arts and sciences and for fitting them for public employment in church and state had already been funded and endowed. The trustees, for such is the implication, were to take charge of this project, and the charter was only to provide the proper legal framework within which the school could grow and thrive. As an added encouragement the document committed the Assembly to an annual contribution of £120 "until this Court order otherwise," and empowered the trustees to accept other funds already bequeathed or expected to be received from private persons in the future. As at Harvard and at William and Mary earlier, the legal form provided for the school was the trust. As a trust Yale lived through its first forty-four years until in 1745 the Connecticut Assembly saw fit to incorporate it as a college. . . .

YALE UNIVERSITY v. TOWN OF NEW HAVEN
Supreme Court of Errors of Connecticut
71 Conn. 316, 42 A 87 (1899)

HAMERSLEY, J. In 1887 the corporation of the President and Fellows of Yale College in New Haven was authorized to use the title "Yale University," and gifts received and contracts made under either of said names were declared to be valid. The powers of the corporation were not otherwise changed. 10 Sp. Laws, p. 467. In October, 1895, the university filed with the assessors of the town of New Haven a list of the property owned by it subject to taxation for the year 1896. The list contained seven pieces of land, valued at $57,680. To this list the assessors added certain buildings used for dormitories and dining hall, with the land on which they stood, valued at $214,990, and also added certain vacant building lots, dwelling houses, and factories, valued at $167,112. The plaintiff appealed to the board of relief, which confirmed the action of the assessors. This appeal is an application to the superior court, alleging that the board of relief acted illegally in confirming the action of the assessors, and praying for appropriate relief. The alleged illegality depends on the meaning given to two statutes, viz. section 3820 of the General Statutes, and the act of 1834, amending the charter of the college, which appears also in section 3822 of the General Statutes.

1. Section 3820 of the General Statutes provides that "buildings or portions of buildings exclusively occupied as colleges, academies, churches or public school houses, or infirmaries" shall be exempt from taxation. If buildings used by the college exclusively as dormitories and dining halls for its students are buildings exclusively occupied as a college, then the action complained of, in adding to the list dormitories and dining hall, was illegal; if such use is not a college occupation, then said action was legal. The word "college," used to denote a constituent of or the equivalent of "university," has acquired a definite meaning. As first used, "college" indicated a place of residence for students, and occasionally a "universitas," or "studium generale." The expressions "universitas studii" and "universitatis collegium" occur in early official documents. A suggestion of the modern university appears in the College and Library of Alexandria, founded and endowed by Ptolemy Soter. Here the Museum provided from [for] the first lodgings and refectory for the professors, and later similar provisions were made for the students. A writer of the twelfth century speaks of the "handsome pile of buildings, which has twenty colleges, whither students betake themselves from all parts of the world." The university in Europe developed about the year 1200. It was a community organized for the study of all branches of knowledge, and authorized by pope, king, or emperor to confer degrees upon those found competent to instruct others. At Bologna—perhaps the earliest organized university—we find colleges almost from the beginning. Such college was a separate house, with a fund for the maintenance of a specified number of poor students. Similar colleges existed in Paris, Oxford, and other universities. At first little more than lodging rooms and refectory, they grew, especially in England, to be the home of the students for all purposes. The instruction and discipline of the university were through the colleges. The conditions of the early universities were peculiar. Vast throngs of students were gathered at one place. They were divided into "nations," each—as at Paris—with its own proctor or procurator. They were further divided among faculties, each with its dean. The divisions into nations and faculties were cross divisions; and another cross division was that into colleges and halls (hall sometimes meaning an unorganized college, and

sometimes used as synonymous with college). With changes in conditions, the college was largely eliminated from the continental universities, while in England the university became practically the associated colleges. Merton College, Oxford, founded in 1264, was the prototype of the English college. That college consisted of the chapel, refectory, and dormitories. Here the scholars, called "fellows," in token of the spirit of equality and companionship, lived under one government, educational and moral, and prepared to take the degree granted by the university. As the colleges increased, all noncollegiate students were driven away. The vagabonds or chamberdekyns—i.e. camera degens,—living in lodgings, as opposed to those who lived in a college, disappeared. Each student in a college must belong to the university, and each student of the university must be attached to a college; and the heads of the colleges administered the university. Thus was developed the English theory of the university, where the honors and influence of the studium generale are gained and enjoyed by students living and working under the government of their respective colleges. As Newman says, the university, to enforce discipline, developed itself into colleges, and so the term "college" "was taken to mean a place of residence for the university student, who would there find himself under the guidance and instructions of superiors and tutors, bound to attend to his personal interest, moral and intellectual." See, passim, 3 Newman, Hist. Sketches; Lyte's History of University of Oxford; 1 and 2 Huber's English Universities; Enc. Brit. "Universities." The college and university, however, were sometimes united in one corporation. Newman says, "The University of Toulouse was founded in a college; so was Orleans." Trinity College, Dublin, styled in its charter (1591) "The College of the Holy Undivided Trinity of Queen Elizabeth, near Dublin," is both university and college. It was founded by the queen as a "mater universitatis"; but the hope was not realized, and the university and college have ever since remained one, called in common speech indiscriminately "Trinity College, Dublin," "Dublin University," "The University of Trinity College, Dublin." Marischal College, Aberdeen, was founded in 1593 as a college and a university, with power of conferring degrees. And so at the beginning of the seventeenth century the students of an English university lived in colleges; were instructed and governed through colleges, whether the university included a number of colleges or a single college; and among the buildings indispensable for every college were the great hall, or dining room, and the living rooms, or dormitories.

In establishing universities in the new world the limitations of the people compelled the founders to follow the example of Trinity College, Dublin, and Marischal College, Aberdeen, and not that of Oxford and Cambridge. Upon the same corporation was conferred the power of the university in granting degrees and of the college in government, and such community and the buildings required for its use were known as "the college." The first appropriation to endow a university in Virginia was made in 1607. In 1660 an act of the colonial legislature endowed "The College," and in 1693 William III. established the university, described in the charter as "a certain place of universal study, or perpetual college of divinity, philosophy, languages, and other good arts and sciences," and named it "The College of William and Mary in Virginia." The settlers of New England early felt the need of a local university, and the first step was the erection of a college, i.e. a building where the students were to be lodged, fed, and instructed while pursuing the university studies and qualifying for its degrees. In 1630 the general court at Boston advanced £400 for this purpose, and subsequently appointed Newtown as the seat of the university, and for this reason changed the name of the town to Cambridge. 2 Mather's Magnalia, pp. 7-9, 19, 20; Quincy's History of Harvard. In 1642, the court established overseers of "a college founded in Cambridge," and in 1650 the charter was granted. The statutes immediately adopted provided that all students admitted to the college "must board at the commons," and also provided for conferring the first and second degrees in arts. While the college exercised some of the privileges of a university, doubt was felt as to the power of the general court to confer such privileges. The colonial charter of 1692 was construed as authorizing the court to erect a university, and immediately, as Mather says, the general assembly granted "a charter to this university," authorizing it to grant degrees "as in the universities in England." This charter expired within three years, from failure to receive the royal approval, and the college was subsequently reorganized under the charter of 1650. The degree of D. D. was conferred by the college in 1693 on Increase Mather, its president, who, in conferring the degrees at the first commencement after the new charter, maintained that "the right of establishing universities (academias) is reserved to all those, and to those only, who hold the sovereignty in the state," and that the general court, under the charter of 1692, possessed such sovereignty. No other degree of doctorate was conferred until 1771, when Nathaniel Appleton was made doctor of divinity; a few years later George Washington was made doctor of laws. The Massachusetts constitution of 1779 recognized "the University at Cambridge," and ratified and confirmed all the rights and privileges it had been accustomed to exercise.

The colonies of Connecticut and New Haven were at first unable to erect a college by themselves, and for some years contributed to that of Cambridge. The plan of a college at New Haven was early mooted, and in 1654 steps were taken towards its consummation. Davenport wished to direct the benefaction of Gov. Hopkins to the founding of a college, and the court of that colony acceded to that plan. The difficulties attending the union of the colonies of New Haven and Connecticut obstructed the execution of the plan, and eventually the funds were appropriated to the Hopkins Grammar School. In 1698 the plan was revived, and ten of the principal ministers agreed to stand as trustees to found, erect, and govern a college. They formed themselves into a society at New Haven in 1700, and the same year, at a meeting at Branford, they (in the language of Trumbull) "founded the University of Yale College." 1 Trum. Hist. Conn. 402. In 1701 the general court of Connecticut granted to said trustees the privilege of founding, endowing, and ordering a "collegiate school," and authorized them to acquire and hold real estate, not exceeding the value of £500 per annum, and personal property to any amount, for the use of said school, and for erecting and endowing the same. 4 Col. Rec. 363. The act did not purport to establish a college and university, unless by indirection; but the trustees, following the example of Harvard, proceeded at once to grant degrees in arts. Until 1716 the school was migratory. The trustees then decided that it should be established at New Haven, and this decision was confirmed by the legislature the following year. 6 Col. Rec. 30. In pursuance of this authority, aided by appropriations by the colonial government, as well as by gifts from Gov. Yale and other benefactors, a college house "for the entertainment of the scholars" was so far finished in 1718 as "to be fit for the reception and accommodation of all the students." It contained nearly 50 studies, and was furnished with a convenient hall, library, and kitchen. At the commencement for that year, in the presence of the authorities of the colony, the trustees did, "with one consent, agree, determine, and ordain that our college house shall be called by the name of its munificent patron, and shall be named Yale College." * * * The "college" and the buildings for entertaining the students under college government were inseparable. In 1818, Yale College consisted of three college buildings for housing the officers and students, a lyceum, a chapel, a kitchen, and large dining room; and it was this college whose charter was confirmed by our constitution of 1818.

The settled meaning of "college" as a building or group of buildings in which scholars are housed, fed, instructed, and governed under college discipline, while qualifying for their university degree, whether the university includes a number of colleges or a single college, is now attacked. We have deemed it proper to trace this meaning with sufficient detail to demonstrate the utter unreason of the attack. This peculiar function of a college is inherent in the best conception of the university. This meaning has been attached to the English word for 800 years; it was the only meaning known at the time our first American colleges were founded; it was recognized and distinctly affirmed in the charter of Yale College; it has since been affirmed by repeated acts of legislation, and has received the sanction of constitutional confirmation. It was impossible for the legislature to express its meaning more clearly than in the language of section 3820, "buildings occupied as colleges." If it had said, "dormitories, dining halls, and other buildings occupied as colleges," the meaning would have been the same, and the amplification would have added nothing to the precise certainty of the language used. * * *

The fact that certain sums are paid for use of the rooms occupied does not alter the character of the occupation. A church is none the less a church because the worshipers contribute to the support of services by way of pew rent. A hospital is none the less a hospital because the beneficiaries contribute something towards its maintenance. And a college is none the less a college because its beneficiaries share the cost of maintenance; and it is immaterial whether such contribution is lumped in one sum, or apportioned to sources of expense, as tuition, room rent, lecture fee, dining hall, etc. . . .

III. The Doctrine of Academic Abstention

While there are many cases in which judges refuse to hold colleges or universities accountable in court due to some facet of the particular institution's legal identity, there are also numerous cases in which the courts, as a matter of common law, refuse to intrude on the academic process. The courts have traditionally refused to interfere in the basic academic process of the university, particularly in the evaluation of students or faculty. Most recently, the Supreme Court in Board of Curators of the University of Missouri v. Horowitz, 98 S.Ct. 948 (1978), a case involving academic dismissal of a medical student, said:

> We decline to further enlarge the judicial presence in the academic community and thereby risk deterioration of many beneficial aspects of the faculty-student relationship. We recognize, as did the Massachusetts Supreme Judicial Court over 60 years ago, that a hearing may be "useless or even harmful in finding out the truth as to scholarship". . . .
> "Judicial interposition in the operation of the public school system of the Nation raises problems requiring care and restraint. . . .
> By and large public education in our Nation is committed to the control of state and local authorities." Epperson v. Arkansas. . . .

Earlier, Chief Justice Burger, in his concurring opinion in the SDS students' rights case, stated:

> It is within [the college administrative] structure and within the academic community that problems such as these should be resolved. The courts, state and federal, should be a last resort. [Healy v. James, 408 U.S. 169, 195 (1972).]

The doctrine of academic abstention has probably had one of its clearest statements, and its most dramatic impact, in the area of academic sex discrimination, where none of the first thirty-odd cases reported have been decided in favor of the plaintiff faculty member. The classic statement of the doctrine is found in Faro v. N.Y.U., 502 F.2d 1229, 1231-32 (2nd Cir. 1974). The court stated:

> Of all fields, which the federal courts should hesitate to invade and take over, education and faculty appointments at a University level are probably the least suited for federal court supervision. Dr. Faro would remove any subjective judgments by her faculty colleagues in the decision-making process by having the courts examine "the university's recruitment, compensation, promotion and termination and by analyzing the way these procedures are applied to the claimant personally" (Applt's Br. p. 26). All this information she would obtain "through extensive discovery, either by the EEOC or the litigant herself" (Id.). This argument

might well lend itself to a *reductio ad absurdum* rebuttal. Such a procedure, in effect, would require a faculty committee charged with recommending or withholding advancements or tenure appointments to subject itself to a court inquiry at the behest of unsuccessful and disgruntled candidates as to why the unsuccessful was not as well qualified as the successful. This decision would then be passed on by a Court of Appeals or even the Supreme Court. The process might be simplified by a legislative enactment that no faculty appointment or advancement could be made without the committee obtaining a declaratory judgment naming the successful candidate after notice to all contending candidates to present their credentials for court inspection and decision. This would give "due process" to all contenders, regardless of sex, to advance their "I'm just as good as you are" arguments. But such a procedure would require a discriminating analysis of the qualifications of each candidate for hiring or advancement, taking into consideration his or her educational experience, the specifications of the particular position open and, of great importance, the personality of the candidate.

In Johnson v. University of Pittsburgh, 435 F. Supp. 1328, 1355, 1371 (W.D. Pa. 1977), a case in which the court granted a preliminary injunction to the plaintiff, the court ultimately decided in favor of the university, primarily on the basis of academic abstention. (This conclusion was reached after an exhaustive review of the facts.) The court said:

The federal courts cannot of course allow the faculty or university to use facially proper criteria for promotion and tenure to be used as window dressing to disguise what is actually a case of invidious sex discrimination. To do so would completely wipe out the provisions of the act of Congress in this field which Congress has expressly mandated to be applicable to appointments in educational institutions. We hold in this case however that the defendants have presented substantial reasons for the failure to promote plaintiff to the rank of associate professor and give her tenure and that plaintiff has not shown by the weight of the evidence that such reasons are so insubstantial and irrational as to serve as a mask for what is forbidden by the law. . . .

On the one hand we have the important problem as to whether sex discrimination is operating to the detriment of women in the halls of academia. If so Congress has mandated that it must be eradicated. Colleges and universities must understand this and guide themselves accordingly. On the other hand we also have the important question as to whether the federal courts are to take over the matter of promotion and tenure for college professors when experts in the academic field agree that such should not occur. In determining qualifications in such circumstances the court is way beyond its field of expertise and in the absence of a clear carrying of the burden of proof by the plaintiff, we must leave such decisions to the PhDs in academia.

The leading countervailing view was first presented by Judge Tuttle, a distinguished jurist in the civil rights area, in Sweeney v. Trustees of Keene State College, 569 F.2d 169 (1st Cir. 1978): [1]

However, we voice misgivings over one theme recurrent in those opinions: the notion that courts should keep "hands off" the salary, promotion, and hiring decisions of colleges and universities. This reluctance no doubt arises from the courts' recognition that hiring, promotion, and tenure decisions require subjective evaluation most appropriately made by persons thoroughly familiar with the academic setting. Nevertheless, we caution against permitting judicial deference to result in judicial abdication of a responsibility entrusted to the courts by Congress. That responsibility is simply to provide a forum for the litigation of complaints of sex discrimination in institutions of higher learning as readily as for other Title VII suits.

In Powell v. Syracuse University, 580 F.2d 1150, 1153-4 (2nd Cir. 1978), even though, once again the plaintiff did not prevail, the Second Circuit modified its earlier position in *Faro*, stating:

We fear, however, that the common-sense position we took in *Faro*, namely that courts must be ever-mindful of relative institutional competences, has been pressed beyond all reasonable limits, and may be employed to undercut the explicit legislative intent of the Civil Rights Act of 1964. In affirming here, we do not rely on any such policy of self-abnegation where colleges are concerned....

It is our task, then, to steer a careful course between excessive intervention in the affairs of the university and the unwarranted tolerance of unlawful behavior. Faro does not, and was never intended to, indicate that academic freedom embraces the freedom to discriminate.

Lowenthal v. Vanderbilt, an unreported case discussed in Chapter 11, recognized the doctrine of academic abstention stating that:

A court must abstain from substituting its judgment for that of the university faculty on such matters as degree requirements and academic dismissals of students. . . . As has been repeatedly held, these are matters for determination by the university and courts must not interfere absent a clear showing that decisions are arbitrary, capricious, and made in bad faith. *Depperman v. University of Kentucky*, 371 F. Supp. 73 (E. D. Ky. 1974); *Lai v. Board of Trustees of East Carolina University*, 330 F. Supp. 904

---

1. Although the plaintiff was successful in the Court of Appeals, the U.S. Supreme Court reversed and remanded for reconsideration using a less difficult burden of proof for the college. 99 S.Ct. 295 (1978). On remand the district court again found for the plaintiff, Sweeney, _____ F.Supp.___ (D.N.H. 1979).

(E. D. N.C. 1971); *Cieboter v. O'Connell*, 236 So.2d 470 (Fla. App. 1970); *Militana v. University of Miami*, 236 So.2d 162 (Fla. App. 1970); and *Connelly v. The University of Vermont*, 244 F. Supp. 156 (D. Vt. 1965). Tennessee has recently adopted the academic abstention rule in a suit by a Memphis State University law student who filed suit over a grade he received on a research paper. *Horne v. Cox*, 551 S.W.2d 690 (Tenn. 1977).

The court found, however, that the doctrine of academic abstention was not a defense to a student contract action.

IV. Institutional Autonomy

The other side of the coin of academic abstention is the idea of institutional autonomy. At the present time the concept of autonomy for the institution is more an ideological expression of academic custom and usage than a specifically enunciated legal doctrine even though academic abstention is implicitly based on judicial recognition of institutional autonomy. The legal protections for the independence of academia, such as they are, run to the protection of the individual through the extension of First Amendment concepts to cover academic freedom for the faculty member or student.

The only case in which the issue of institutional freedom was directly considered was ultimately decided on other grounds. In Haverford College v. Reeher, 329 F. Supp. 1196 (E.D. Pa. 1977) the college challenged a statute directing it to report violations of campus rules by students for the purpose of withdrawing state scholarship aid. The statute was declared unconstitutional, with a ruling that the government could not indirectly deny a benefit to students based on their exercise of First Amendment rights, when it could not take that action against them directly. Thus any institutional rights established by this decision were derivative, based on students' constitutional rights rather than institutional autonomy.

The issue of institutional autonomy is presently being considered on remand by the district court in Wayne State University v. Cleland___F.2d __(6 Cir. 1978). The Sixth Circuit overturned summary judgment by the district court in favor of Wayne State on the grounds that certain Veteran's Administration regulations governing educational benefits were promulgated without statutory authority. The circuit court found the regulations valid, but remanded for further consideration of the argument that the regulations constituted an unconstitutional interference with academic procedures.

It is argued in the *Wayne State* case that the V.A. regulations are not consistent with the freedoms afforded academic policy and educational programs by the due process clause of the Fifth Amendment and the First Amendment, citing Meyer v. Nebraska, 262 U.S. 390 (1923) in which a state statute forbidding teaching in any language but German was struck down, and Pierce v. Society of Sisters, 268 U.S. 510 (1925) which allowed private schools to successfully challenge a statutory requirement that all grammar schools be public. These cases, it is argued, establish an institutional, as opposed to individual, right to academic freedom. Reference is also made to Supreme Court language in *Sweezy v. New Hampshire* and *Keyishian v. Board of Regents, infra,* Chapter 6, as well as *Healy v. James, infra,* Chapter 9. No doubt Justice Powell's holding in *Bakke, infra,* Chapter 14, that a university has an institutional right of academic freedom will also be cited.

Although a number of distinguished lawyer-presidents have argued strongly for institutional autonomy, and in particular for freedom from federal government regulations, the only effective legal argument to date is based on the Free Exercise clause of the First Amendment and applies only to genuinely religious institutions. *See* Oaks, "A Private University Looks at Government Regulations," 4 J. Col. U. L. 1 (1976) NACUA, 1976; Oaks, "Government Regulation of Higher Education," an address before the Opening General Session of the Pennsylvania Association of Colleges and Universities, Hershey, Pennsylvania, Sept. 25, 1978. *See also,* Bok, The President's Report (Cambridge: Harvard University, 1975) and Brewster, The Report of the President (New Haven: Yale University, 1974–75). And *see* O'Neil, *God and Government at Yale: The Limits of Federal Regulation of Higher Education,* 44 U. Cin. L. Rev. 525 (1975).

Since courts have not yet fashioned a legal doctrine clearly defining a concept of institutional autonomy, except as implied by the doctrine of academic abstention, institutions of higher education have had to rely on a wide variety of rules and constructions to secure institutional autonomy. The next three chapters outline the ways by which various types of public and private universities seek to legally protect the autonomy vital to their operation as independent academic institutions.

CHAPTER 2

LEGAL ATTRIBUTES OF PRIVATE UNIVERSITIES

I.   The College Charter as Contract

THE TRUSTEES OF DARTMOUTH COLLEGE
v. WOODWARD
Supreme Court of the United States
4 Wheat (U.S.) 518 (1819)

MARSHALL, C. J., delivered the opinion of the court, as follows:—

This is an action of trover, brought by the Trustees of Dartmouth College, against William H. Woodward, in the state court of New Hampshire, for the book of records, corporate seal, and other corporate property, to which the plaintiffs allege themselves to be entitled. . . .

[T]he American people have said, in the constitution of the United States, that "no State shall pass any bill of attainder, *ex post facto* law, or law impairing the obligation of contracts." In the same instrument they have also said, "that the judicial power shall extend to all cases in law and equity arising under the constitution." On the judges of this court, then, is imposed the high and solemn duty of protecting, from even legislative violation, those contracts which the constitution of our country has placed beyond legislative control; and, however irksome the task may be, this is a duty from which we dare not shrink.

The title of the plaintiffs originates in a charter, dated the 13th day of December, in the year 1769, incorporating twelve persons therein mentioned, by the name of "The Trustees of Dartmouth College," granting to them and their successors the usual corporate privileges and powers, and authorizing the trustees, who are to govern the college, to fill up all vacancies which may be created in their own body.

The defendant claims under three acts of the legislature of New Hampshire, the most material of which was passed on the 27th of June, 1816, and is entitled, "An act to amend the charter, and enlarge and improve the corporation of Dartmouth College." Among other alterations in the charter, this act increases the number of trustees to twenty-one, gives the appointment of the additional members to the executive of the State, and creates a board of overseers, with power to inspect and control the most important acts of the trustees. This board consists of twenty-five persons. The president of the senate, the speaker of the house of representatives of New Hampshire, and the governor and lieutenant governor of Vermont, for the time being, are to be members *ex officio*. The board is to be completed by the governor and council of New Hampshire, who are also empowered to fill all vacancies

19

which may occur. The acts of the 18th and 26th of December are supplemental to that of the 27th of June, and are principally intended to carry that act into effect.

The majority of the trustees of the college have refused to accept this amended charter, and have brought this suit for the corporate property, which is in possession of a person holding by virtue of the acts which have been stated.

It can require no argument to prove, that the circumstances of this case constitute a contract. An application is made to the crown for a charter to incorporate a religious and literary institution. In the application it is stated, that large contributions have been made for the object, which will be conferred on the corporation, as soon as it shall be created. The charter is granted, and on its faith the property is conveyed. Surely, in this transaction, every ingredient of a complete and legitimate contract is to be found.

The points for consideration are,

1.   Is this contract protected by the constitution of the United States?

2.   Is it impaired by the acts under which the defendant holds? * * *

It becomes then the duty of the court most seriously to examine this charter, and to ascertain its true character.

From the instrument itself, it appears, that about the year 1754, the Rev. Eleazer Wheelock established, at his own expense, and on his own estate, a charity school for the instruction of Indians in the Christian religion. The success of this institution inspired him with the design of soliciting contributions in England, for carrying on and extending his undertaking. In this pious work, he employed the Rev. Nathaniel Whitaker, who, by virtue of a power of attorney from Dr. Wheelock, appointed the Earl of Dartmouth and others, trustees of the money which had been and should be contributed; which appointment Dr. Wheelock confirmed by a deed of trust authorizing the trustees to fix on a site for the college. They determined to establish the school on Connecticut River, in the western part of New Hampshire; that situation being supposed favorable for carrying on the original design among the Indians, and also for promoting learning among the English; and the proprietors in the neighborhood having made large offers of land, on condition that the college should there be placed. Dr. Wheelock then applied to the crown for an act of incorporation; and represented the expediency of appointing those whom he had, by his last will, named as trustees in America, to be members of the proposed corporation. "In consideration of the premises," "for the education and instruction of the youth of the Indian tribes," &c., "and also of English youth, and any others," the charter was granted, and the Trustees of Dartmouth College were by that name created a body corporate, with power, for the use of the said college, to acquire real and personal property, and to pay the president, tutors, and other officers of the college, such salaries as they shall allow. * * *

This charter was accepted, and the property, both real and personal, which has been contributed for the benefit of the college, was conveyed to, and vested in, the corporate body.

From this brief review of the most essential parts of the charter, it is apparent that the funds of the college consisted entirely of private donations. It is, perhaps, not very important, who were the donors. The probability is, that the Earl of Dartmouth, and the other trustees in England, were, in fact, the largest contributors. Yet the legal conclusion, from the facts recited in the charter, would probably be, that Dr. Wheelock was the founder of the college.

The origin of the institution was, undoubtedly, the Indian charity school, established by Dr. Wheelock, at his own expense. It was at his instance, and to enlarge this school, that contributions were solicited in England. The person soliciting these contributions was his agent; and the trustees, who received the money, were appointed by, and act under, his authority. It is not too much to say, that the funds were obtained by him, in trust, to be applied by him to the purposes of his enlarged school. The charter of incorporation was granted at his instance. The persons named by him in his last will, as the trustees of his charity school, compose a part of the corporation, and he is declared to be the founder of the college, and its president for life. Were the inquiry material, we should feel some hesitation in saying, that Dr. Wheelock was not, in law, to be considered as the founder (1 Bl. Com. 481) of this institution, and as possessing all the rights appertaining to that character. But be this as it may, Dartmouth College is really endowed by private individuals, who have bestowed their funds for the propagation of the Christian religion among the Indians, and for the promotion of piety and learning generally. From these funds the salaries of the tutors are drawn; and these salaries lessen the expense of education to the students. It is then an eleemosynary, (1 Bl. Com. 471) and, as far as respects its funds, a private corporation.

Do its objects stamp on it a different character? Are the trustees and professors public officers, invested with any portion of political power, partaking in any degree in the administration of civil government, and performing duties which flow from the sovereign authority?

That education is an object of national concern, and a proper subject of legislation, all admit. That there may be an institution founded by government, and placed entirely under its immediate control, the officers of which would be public officers, amenable exclusively to government, none will deny. But is Dartmouth College such an institution? Is education altogether in the hands of government? Does every teacher of youth become a public officer, and do donations for the purpose of education necessarily become public property, so far that the will of the legislature, not the will of the donor, becomes the law of the donation? These questions are of serious moment to society, and deserve to be well considered.

Doctor Wheelock, as the keeper of his charity school, instructing the Indians in the art of reading, and in our holy religion; sustaining them at his own expense, and on the voluntary contributions of the charitable, could scarcely be considered as a public officer, exercising any portion of those duties which belong to government; nor could the legislature have supposed, that his private funds, or those given by others, were subject to legislative management, because they were applied to the purposes of education. When afterwards, his school was enlarged, and the liberal contributions made in England and in America, enabled him to extend his cares to the education of the youth of his own country, no change was wrought in his own character, or in the nature of his duties. Had he employed assistant tutors with the funds contributed by others, or had the trustees in England established a school, with Dr. Wheelock at its head, and paid salaries to him and his assistants, they would still have been private tutors; and the fact that they were employed in the education of youth, could not have converted them into public officers, concerned in the administration of public duties, or have given the legislature a right to interfere in the management of the fund. The trustees, in whose care that fund was placed by the contributors, would have been permitted to execute their trust, uncontrolled by legislative authority.

Whence, then, can be derived the idea, that Dartmouth College has become a public institution, and its trustees public officers, exercising powers conferred by the public, for public objects? Not from the source whence its funds were drawn; for its foundation is purely private and eleemosynary. Not from the application of those funds; for money may be given for education, and the persons receiving it do not, by being employed in the education of youth, become members of the civil government. Is it from the act of incorporation? Let this subject be considered.

A corporation is an artificial being, invisible, intangible, and existing only in contemplation of law. Being the mere creature of law, it possesses only those properties which the charter of its creation confers upon it, either expressly, or as incidental to its very existence. These are such as are supposed best calculated to effect the object for which it was created. Among the most important are immortality, and, if the expression may be allowed, individuality; properties by which a perpetual succession of many persons are considered as the same, and may act as a single individual. They enable a corporation to manage its own affairs, and to hold property without the perplexing intricacies, the hazardous and endless necessity of perpetual conveyances, for the purpose of transmitting it from hand to hand. It is chiefly for the purpose of clothing bodies of men, in succession, with these qualities and capacities, that corporations were invented, and are in use. By these means a perpetual succession of individuals are capable of acting for the promotion of the particular object, like one immortal being. But this being does not share in the civil government of the country, unless that be the purpose for which it was created. Its immortality no more confers on it political power, or a political character, than immortality would confer such power or character on a natural person. It is no more a State instrument, than a natural person exercising the same powers would be. If, then, a natural person employed by individuals in the education of youth, or for the government of a seminary in which youth is educated, would not become a public officer, or be considered as a member of the civil government, how is it that this artificial being, created by law, for the purpose of being employed by the same individuals for the same purposes, should become a part of the civil government of the country? Is it because its existence, its capacities, its powers, are given by law? Because the government has given it the power to take and to hold property in a particular form, and for particular purposes, has the government a consequent right substantially to change that form, or to vary the purposes to which the property is to be applied? This principle has never been asserted or recognized, and is supported by no authority. Can it derive aid from reason?

The objects for which a corporation is created are universally such as the government wishes to promote. They are deemed beneficial to the country; and this benefit constitutes the consideration, and, in most cases, the sole consideration, of the grant. In most eleemosynary institutions, the object would be difficult, perhaps unattainable, without the aid of a charter of incorporation. Charitable, or public spirited individuals, desirous of making permanent appropriations for charitable or other useful purposes, find it impossible to effect their design, securely and certainly, without an incorporating act. They apply to the government, state their beneficent object, and offer to advance the money necessary for its accomplishment, provided the government will confer on the instrument, which is to execute their designs, the capacity to execute them. The proposition is considered and approved. The benefit to the public is considered as an ample compensation for the faculty it confers, and the corporation is created. If the advantages to the public constitute a full compensation for the faculty it gives, there can be no reason for exacting a further compensation, by claiming a right to exercise over this artificial being a power which changes its nature, and touches the fund, for the security and application of which it was created. There can be no reason for implying in a charter, given for a valuable consideration, a power which is not only not expressed, but is in direct contradiction to its express stipulations.

From the fact, then, that a charter of incorporation has been granted, nothing can be inferred which changes the character of the institution, or transfers to the government any new power over it. The character of civil institutions does not grow out of their incorporation, but out of the manner in which they are formed, and the objects for which they are created. The right to change them is not founded on their being incorporated, but on their being the instruments of government, created for its purposes. The same institutions, created for the same objects, though not incorporated, would be public institutions, and, of course, be controllable by the legislature. The incorporating act neither gives nor prevents this control. Neither, in reason, can the incorporating act change the character of a private eleemosynary institution. . . .

We are next led to the inquiry, for whose benefit the property given to Dartmouth College was secured? The counsel for the defendant have insisted, that the beneficial interest is in the people of New Hampshire. The charter, after reciting the preliminary measures which had been taken, and the application for an act of incorporation, proceeds thus: "Know ye, therefore, that we, considering the premises and being willing to encourage the laudable and charitable design of spreading Christian knowledge among the savages of our American wilderness, and, also, that the best means of education be established, in our province of New Hampshire, for the benefit of said province, do, of our special grace," &c. Do these expressions bestow on New Hampshire any exclusive right to the property of the college, any exclusive interest in the labors of the professors? Or do they merely indicate a willingness that New Hampshire should enjoy these advantages which result to all from the establishment of a seminary of learning in the neighborhood? On this point we think it impossible to entertain a serious doubt. The words themselves, unexplained by the context, indicate, that the "benefit intended for the province" is that which is derived from "establishing the best means of education therein," that is, from establishing in the province Dartmouth College, as constituted by the charter. But if these words, considered alone, could admit of doubt, that doubt is completely removed by an inspection of the entire instrument.

The particular interests of New Hampshire never entered into the mind of the donors, never constituted a motive for their donation. The propagation of the Christian religion among the savages, and the dissemination of useful knowledge among the youth of the country, were the avowed and the sole objects of their contributions. * * * The clause which constitutes the incorporation, and expresses the objects for which it was made, declares those objects to be the instruction of the Indians, "and also of English youth, and any others." So that the objects of the contributors, and the incorporating act, were the same; the promotion of Christianity, and of education generally, not the interests of New Hampshire particularly.

From this review of the charter, it appears, that Dartmouth College is an eleemosynary institution, incorporated for the purpose of perpetuating the application of the bounty of the donors, to the specified objects of that bounty; that its trustees or governors were originally named by the founder, and invested with the power of perpetuating themselves; that they are not public officers, nor is it a civil institution, participating in the administration of government; but a charity school, or a seminary of education, incorporated for the preservation of its property, and the perpetual application of that property to the objects of its creation. * * *

This is plainly a contract to which the donors, the trustees, and the crown, (to whose rights and obligations New Hampshire succeeds,) were the original parties. It is a contract made on a valuable consideration. It is a contract for the security and disposition of property. It is a contract, on the faith of which, real and personal estate has been conveyed to the corporation. It is then a contract within the letter of the constitution, and within its spirit also, unless the fact that the property is invested by the donors in trustees, for the promotion of religion and education, for the benefit of persons who are perpetually changing, though the objects remain the same, shall create a particular exception, taking this case out of the prohibition contained in the constitution. * * *

The opinion of the court, after mature deliberation, is, that this is a contract, the obligation of which cannot be impaired, without violating the constitution of the United States. This opinion appears to us to be equally supported by reason, and by the former decisions of this court.

2. We next proceed to the inquiry, whether its obligation has been impaired by those acts of the legislature of New Hampshire, to which the special verdict refers.

From the review of this charter, which has been taken, it appears that the whole power of governing the college, of appointing and removing tutors, of fixing their salaries, of directing the course of study to be pursued by the students, and of filling up vacancies created in their own body, was vested in the trustees. On the part of the crown, it was expressly stipulated that this corporation, thus constituted, should continue forever; and that the number of trustees should forever consist of twelve, and no more. By this contract, the crown was bound, and could have made no violent alteration in its essential terms, without impairing its obligation.

By the Revolution, the duties as well as the powers of government devolved on the people of New Hampshire. It is admitted, that among the latter was comprehended the transcendent power of parliament, as well as that of the executive department. It is too clear to require the support of argument, that all contracts and rights, respecting property, remained unchanged by the Revolution. The obligations, then, which were created by the charter to Dartmouth College, were the same in the new that they had been in the old government. The power of the government was also the same. A repeal of this charter at any time prior to the adoption of the present constitution of the United States, would have been an extraordinary and unprecedented act of power, but one which could have been contested only by the restrictions upon the legislature, to be found in the constitution of the State. But the constitution of the United States has imposed this additional limitation, that the legislature of a State shall pass no act "impairing the obligation of contracts."

It has been already stated, that the act "to amend the charter, and enlarge and improve the corporation of Dartmouth College," increases the number of trustees to twenty-one, gives the appointment of the additional members to the executive of the State, and creates a board of overseers, to consist of twenty-five persons, of whom twenty-one are also appointed by the executive of New Hampshire, who have power to inspect and control the most important acts of the trustees.

On the effect of this law, two opinions cannot be entertained. Between acting directly, and acting through the agency of trustees and overseers, no essential difference is perceived. The whole power of governing the college is transferred from trustees, appointed according to the will of the founder,

expressed in the charter, to the executive of New Hampshire. The management and application of the funds of this eleemosynary institution, which are placed by the donors in the hands of trustees named in the charter, and empowered to perpetuate themselves, are placed by this act under the control of the government of the State. The will of the State is substituted for the will of the donors, in every essential operation of the college. This is not an immaterial change. The founders of the college contracted, not merely for the perpetual application of the funds which they gave, to the objects for which those funds were given; they contracted also, to secure that application by the constitution of the corporation. They contracted for a system, which should, as far as human foresight can provide, retain forever the government of the literary institution they had formed, in the hands of persons approved by themselves. This system is totally changed. The charter of 1769 exists no longer. It is reorganized; and reorganized in such a manner, as to convert a literary institution, moulded according to the will of its founders, and placed under the control of private literary men, into a machine entirely subservient to the will of government. This may be for the advantage of this college in particular, and may be for the advantage of literature in general; but it is not according to the will of the donors, and is subversive of that contract, on the faith of which their property was given.
* * *

It results from this opinion, that the acts of the legislature of New Hampshire, which are stated in the special verdict found in this cause, are repugnant to the constitution of the United States, and that the judgment on this special verdict ought to have been for the plaintiffs. The judgment of the state court must, therefore, be reversed.

NOTES

1. In the *Dartmouth* case, Justice Marshall implies that one of the factors to be considered in deciding whether a college is public or private, is whether the funds originally used to start the college were public property or from some other source. Suppose a privately funded college incorporated by a state had been granted land by the federal government. Would it be public or private? See Vincennes University v. Indiana, 55 U.S. 268 (1852), wherein the Court said:

> The donation in no sense proceeded from the State. It was made by the federal government, and is no more subject to state power than if it had been given by an individual for the same purpose. An act of incorporation being necessary, would not be withheld to give effect to a private donation of land, for the purpose of establishing a literary institution. Its benefits would be enjoyed by the public generally, but this would not make it a public corporation. Id. at 277.

2. What is the nature of the contract between the state and the college in *Dartmouth*? Can it be enforced by third parties? Suppose the current trustees decided that, in view of the statement of purpose in the Dartmouth College charter, a certain minimum number of places in each incoming class should be reserved for Native American students. Would such a provision be legal? See *Bakke v. University of California, Chapter 14, infra.* Suppose a Native American was denied admission to Dartmouth and sued, alleging that the college was failing to operate as directed by the terms of its charter and thereby had impaired its contractual obligation to the state. What result?

II.   The College Charter as a Basis for Tax Exemption

NABISCO, INC. v. KORZEN
Supreme Court of Illinois
369 N.E.2d 829 (1977)

GOLDENHERSH, Justice:

In 1855 Northwestern University's corporate charter, granted in 1851, was amended to provide "That all property of whatever kind or description belonging to or owned by said corporation shall be forever free from taxation for any and all purposes." (1855 Ill.Laws 483, 484.) In earlier litigation (see *Northwestern University v. People ex rel. Miller*, 99 U.S. 309, 25 L.Ed. 387; *In re Assessment of Northwestern University*, 206 Ill. 64, 69 N.E. 75; *Northwestern University v. Hanberg*, 237 Ill. 185, 86 N.E. 734; and *People ex rel. County Collector v. Northwestern University*, 51 Ill.2d 131, 281 N.E.2d 334) attacks on the exemption were rejected. These appeals arise out of the efforts of the taxing authorities of Cook County to assess and tax leasehold estates under the provisions of section 26 of the Revenue Act of 1939 (Ill.Rev.Stat. 1967, ch. 120, par. 507), which provides: "When real estate which is exempt from taxation is leased to another whose property is not exempt, and the leasing of which does not make the real estate taxable, the leasehold estate and the appurtenances shall be listed as the property of the lessee thereof, or his assignee, as real estate." . . .

Although our earlier cases established that Northwestern's tax exemption constitutes a contract between the State and the University which cannot be impaired by subsequent legislation imposing taxes upon its property whether that property be directly used for school purposes or leased to others and the proceeds used for school purposes, we have not heretofore considered the question whether a property tax assessed to the lessees under section 26, upon the value of their leasehold estates in property owned by Northwestern is a constitutionally impermissible impairment of the contract.

We consider first defendants' contention that plaintiffs are not third party beneficiaries of the charter contract entered into between Northwestern and the State, and are therefore without standing to challenge the tax upon their leasehold estates as being an unconstitutional impairment of Northwestern's contract. We do not agree. Whether the leasehold estates are taxable depends upon the scope of the tax exemption granted in the charter, and the right to pass on to Northwestern as lessor the amount of any taxes which they are called upon to pay is in dispute. Under these circumstances plaintiffs clearly have standing to invoke the charter exemption as a ground for holding the tax invalid. *Mutual Tobacco Co. v. Halpin*, 414 Ill. 226, 229, 111 N.E.2d 155.

Nabisco contends that the exemption to Northwestern is in the nature of "a broad subsidy exemption" and that therefore *La Salle County Manufacturing Co. v. City of Ottawa*, 16 Ill. 418, *Chicago v. University of Chicago*, 302 Ill. 455, 134 N.E.723, *Goodyear Tire and Rubber Co. v. Tierney*, 411 Ill. 421, 104 N.E.2d 222, *cert. denied*, 344 U.S. 825, 73 S.Ct. 24, 97 L.Ed.

642, and *People ex rel. Korzen v. American Airlines*, 39 Ill.2d 11, 233 N.E. 2d 568, which upheld the taxation of leasehold interests in land owned by governmental bodies are distinguishable. We do not agree. The leading case of *Jetton v. University of the South*, 208 U.S. 489, 28 S.Ct. 375, 52 L.Ed. 584, presented a factual situation similar to this case. The charter granted by the State of Tennessee authorized the University of the South to own 10,000 acres of land "one thousand of which, including buildings and other effects and property of said corporation, shall be exempt from taxation as long as said lands belong to said university." The university leased some of its exempt land and the county taxing official sought to tax the leasehold interest of one lessee, and announced the intent to tax "all lessees similarly situated." In holding the leasehold interest was not exempt from taxation, the Supreme Court stated the rule, as follows:

> "As long as different interests may exist in the same land, we think it plain that an exemption granted to the owner of the land in fee does not extend to an exemption from taxation of an interest in the same land, granted by the owner of the fee to another person as a lessee for a term of years. The two interests are totally distinct, and the exemption of one from taxation plainly does not thereby exempt the other." 208 U.S. 489, 500, 28 S.Ct. 375, 377, 52 L.Ed. 584, 589.

Plaintiffs argue that *Jetton* is distinguishable in that the purposes of Northwestern's charter tax exemption is to subsidize the university (see *People ex rel. County Collector v. Northwestern University*, 51 Ill.2d 131, 281 N.E.2d 334), while the purpose of the charter tax exemption of 1,000 acres to the University of the South was "to protect said institution and the students thereof from the intrusion of evil-minded persons who may settle near said institution" and to "maintain a buffer zone around the campus." They argue, too, that the taxation of the leasehold interest of the lessee of the University of the South "did not interfere with the purpose of the charter." The court did not rest its decision in *Jetton* on the ground that taxing the university's lessee would not interfere with the purpose of the charter. The rationale of the decision is that unless the consent of the legislature is given in clear and unmistakable terms the exemption of the fee from taxation does not serve to exempt the leasehold. Furthermore, the court treated the exemption as a "subsidy exemption" and rejected the argument which plaintiffs here advance, that the taxing of the leasehold interest diminished the university's income from the lease property and, therefore, impaired the exemption contract. The court said:

> "If the university could lease its lands and could also effectually provide that the interest of the lessee in the land so leased should be exempt from taxation, it may readily be seen that the amount of rent which it would receive would be larger than if no such exemption could be obtained, but that is a matter which is wholly immaterial upon the question of the impairment of the contract of exemption that was really made. That contract cannot be extended

simply because it would, as so construed, add value to the exemption. The language used does not include the exemption claimed."
208 U.S. 489, 501, 28 S.Ct. 375, 378, 52 L.Ed. 584, 589. . . .

We hold that Northwestern's charter tax exemption does not proscribe
the taxing of plaintiffs' leasehold estates as real estate under section 26 of
the Revenue Act of 1939. *Jetton v. University of the South*, 208 U.S. 489,
28 S.Ct. 375, 52 L.Ed. 584; *People v. International Salt Co.*, 233 Ill. 223,
84 N.E. 278. . . .

In its *amicus* brief Northwestern contends that "The real issue in this
case * * * is whether Section 26 of the Revenue Act * * * may be applied
* * * to tax a lessee for property which belongs not to the lessee but to the
lessor, the owner of the fee." Simply stated, its position is that the lessees'
interests may indeed be taxed, but that the only valuation, for assessment
purposes, which may be placed on a leasehold estate is that which results in
the appreciation of its value. In view of the conclusions reached we need not
further consider its arguments.

In its *amicus curiae* brief Lake Forest College urges that if we find the
leasehold estates under consideration to be taxable, we make our ruling
prospective in application and not retroactive as to existing leases. We have
limited the retroactive effect of a decision to those situations where a change
in the law would impose undue hardship upon those who had relied upon
the prior law. (See, *e.g., Molitor v. Kaneland Community Unit District No.
302*, 18 Ill.2d 11, 163 N.E.2d 89.) Where no change in prior Illinois law is
effected by the decision we have refused to limit its retroactive application.
(*Baier v. State Farm Insurance Co.*, 66 Ill.2d 119, 5 Ill.Dec. 572, 361 N.E.2d
1100.) Lake Forest, while conceding that the limiting of the retroactive effect of a decision has been confined to those cases in which a prior decision
is overruled, argues that the "state of the law under which such leaseholds
could in no way have fairly been foreseen as taxable prior to a decision of
this court" requires a different result. We do not agree. . . .

III.   State Action

If the public purpose of education does not make a private corporation
public in nature, does contemporary receipt of substantial government funds
change the legal nature of a private university? Can the use of state funds
make the recipient college into a state agency? These questions have been
posed most directly in cases considering whether actions taken by a private
university may constitute "state action" for purposes of the due process and
equal protection clauses of the Fourteenth Amendment and derivative civil
rights legislation. Under the "state action" doctrine as it has more generally
evolved, a private institution may retain its intrinsic private nature, but because of various governmental nexi, usually financial or regulatory, the
private institution can be deemed to be acting under the "color of state
law." This determination means that the requirements of the Fourteenth
Amendment and derivative civil rights legislation can be applied to private

institutions deemed to be taking state action. The degree to which receipt and expenditure of public funds causes a private university to act "under color of state law" (Const. XIV) is currently at issue in the courts in a number of different contexts.

KROHN v. HARVARD LAW SCHOOL
First Circuit Court of Appeals
552 F.2d 21 (1977)

BOWNES, District Judge.

Plaintiff-appellant appeals from the dismissal of his civil rights suit against Harvard Law School in which he alleged that the rejection of his application to the defendant law school was the result of an arbitrary selection process which violated his rights to due process and equal protection of the laws under the Fourteenth Amendment of the United States Constitution. . . .

Plaintiff-appellant bases the presence of the requisite "state action" on two major theories: first, that Harvard University is a public institution by virtue of its historic connections with the Massachusetts Bay Colony and the supposed control exercised over it in the early days of the Commonwealth of Massachusetts; and, second, that there presently exists a sufficient nexus between the Commonwealth and Harvard Law School to imbue the law school's activities with "color of state law."

While appellant has written a fascinating historical review of the founding of Harvard University, we agree with the district court that he has failed to show a sufficient present day relationship between Harvard and the Commonwealth to treat the school as a public institution subject to federal jurisdiction in a 42 U.S.C. § 1983 suit. To hold otherwise would serve only to disrupt the less anciently established balance of rights and duties Harvard assumes as a private educational institution in Massachusetts. *See, e.g., Grueninger v. President and Fellows of Harvard College*, 343 Mass. 338, 178 N.E.2d 917 (1961) (Harvard is entitled to raise the limited defense of charitable immunities); *Attorney General v. President and Fellows of Harvard College,* 350 Mass. 125, 137, 213 N.E.2d 840, 847 (1966) (some gifts to Harvard are "public charitable trusts in private educational hands"). This court will not enter into a historical debate with appellant; suffice it to say that Harvard has been for at least one hundred years and continues to be treated as a private educational institution in the whole range of its legal and educational relations and activities by both the private and public sectors in Massachusetts. It is considered by all reasonable persons to be a private educational institution and "[w]hile legitimate public belief is scarcely enough to determine that the acts of an avowedly private institution are state action, it is a factor to be weighed in the scales. . . ." *Grafton v. Brooklyn Law School,* 478 F.2d 1137, 1143 (2d Cir. 1973). As a private entity, Harvard Law School is not subject to suit brought under 42 U.S.C. § 1983. *Civil Rights Cases*, 109 U.S. 3, 3 S.Ct. 18, 27 L.Ed. 835 (1883). . . .

In order to determine whether or not "private action" is "so inter-twined with the state" we must look to

> whether there is a sufficiently close nexus between the State and the challenged action of the regulated entity so that the action of the latter may be fairly treated as that of the State itself. *Jackson v. Metropolitan Edison Co.*, 419 U.S. 345, 351, 95 S.Ct. 449, 453, 42 L.Ed.2d 477 (1974).

Accord, Moose Lodge No. 107 v. Irvis, 407 U.S. 163, 92 S.Ct. 1965, 32 L.Ed.2d 627 (1972).

This court has held, in another context, that the receipt by a private university of state financial assistance through tax exemptions and a student aid program, regulation of the university by a public accreditation council and the authority of that council to oversee university disciplinary procedures, either individually or together, were insufficient attributes of governmental involvement to render the university's disciplinary proceedings "state action" for section 1983 purposes. *Berrios, supra*, 535 F.2d at 1332. Here, plaintiff has alleged no more than the Supreme Judicial Court rule, and

> the mere fact that a school is giving instruction the successful completion of which affords one, and the more generally desired, path to the taking of a state bar examination, does not make its functions any more governmental than the imparting of the pre-legal instruction which is also required, ... *Grafton, supra*, 478 F.2d at 1141. (Footnote omitted.)

There is not, in this case, an intertwining of state and private action suffi-cient for a section 1983 cause of action.

Further, it is clear that the mere offering of an education, regulated by the State, does not imbue defendant's activities with sufficient "public interest" to render defendant's activities governmental in nature. *See Evans v. Newton*, 382 U.S. 296, 86 S.Ct. 486, 15 L.Ed.2d 373 (1966). The Su-preme Court has said:

> It is difficult to imagine a regulated activity more essential or more "clothed with the public interest" than the maintenance of schools, yet we stated in *Evans v. Newton*, 382 U.S. 296, 300, 86 S.Ct. 486, 489, 15 L.Ed.2d 373 (1966):
> "The range of governmental activities is broad and varied, and the fact that government has engaged in a particular activity does not necessarily mean that an individual entrepreneur or manager of the same kind of undertaking suffers the same con-stitutional inhibitions. While a State may not segregate public schools so as to exclude one or more religious groups, those sects may maintain their own parochial educational systems."
> *Jackson, supra* 419 U.S. at 354 n. 9, 95 S.Ct. at 455 n. 9.

Finally, plaintiff has failed to allege any connection whatsoever be-tween defendant's allegedly discriminatory admissions policy and any activity on the part of the Commonwealth. In order to subject the activities of private entities to a section 1983 claim, a plaintiff must allege that the acts of the state are in some way involved in the private discriminatory conduct in that they were "intended either overtly or covertly to encourage discrimination," *Moose Lodge, supra* 407 U.S. at 173, 92 S.Ct. at 1972, or that they affirmatively promoted the discriminatory conduct. *See id.* at 175 n. 3, 92 S.Ct. 1965. Here, plaintiff alleges no nexus whatsoever between the Supreme Judicial Court rule or any other rule, regulation or conduct on the part of the Commonwealth of Massachusetts and defendant's admissions policy. Therefore, plaintiff has not stated a cause of action against the defendant under 42 U.S.C. § 1983.

We have carefully read plaintiff's complaint in light of the Supreme Court's recent decisions concerning 42 U.S.C. § 1981 which provides in part that "[a]ll persons . . . shall have the same right in every State and Territory to make and enforce contracts . . . as is enjoyed by white citizens . . . ."

In *Runyon v. McCrary*, 427 U.S. 160, 96 S.Ct. 2586, 49 L.Ed.2d 415 (1976), the Court held that section 1981 prohibits private, commercially operated schools from denying admission to prospective students on the basis of race. It also decided that section 1981 forbids racial discrimination against white persons as well as against non-whites. *McDonald v. Santa Fe Trail Transp. Co.*, 427 U.S. 273, 96 S.Ct. 2574, 49 L.Ed.2d 493 (1976).

In the instant case, plaintiff has alleged too few facts for this court to infer that he claims that the denial of his application was based upon racial discrimination. He alleges, upon information and belief, that in its selection process the defendant "routinely accords preference to members of certain racial minority groups (notably blacks), women, young applicants, applicants from wealthy families or with personal or political 'connections'. . .," paragraph 17, Verified Amended Complaint, and that the admissions process is "biased by considerations of race, age, sex and place of origin." Paragraph 33D, Verified Amended Complaint. The thrust of these claims is not to allege "reverse discrimination" in the sense that plaintiff's application was denied due to racial bias, but to show the preference accorded "currently fashionable or exotic characteristics wholly unrelated to academic or professional merit or aptitude" and to demonstrate that "few if any places are awarded primarily on the basis of academic merit." Paragraph 17, Verified Amended Complaint. Plaintiff concedes that he "does not know whether he was discriminated against on the basis of his age, religion or race . . . ."

We find that plaintiff has not claimed that he was denied the opportunity to contract with the defendant because of his race. His claim is based on an assumption that, because of his academic credentials, he is entitled to, but has been denied, the opportunity to enter Harvard Law School. This does not state a cause of action under 42 U.S.C. section 1981.

The dismissal of the section 1983 claim is affirmed; any claim the plaintiff may have under § 1981 should be dismissed without prejudice.

So ordered.

BRADEN v. THE UNIVERSITY OF PITTSBURGH
United States Court of Appeals, Third Circuit
552 F.2d 948 (1977)

*   *   *   *

STATE ACTION

Having decided that this Court had the power to entertain the inter-locutory appeal, we now turn to the obdurate question of state action.

Because every claim based on § 1983 requires state action as a juris-dictional prerequisite, we must determine whether the district court erred in refusing to dismiss the complaint on the ground that the University of Pittsburgh was not acting "under color of" state law. . . .

A.

At the inception of our analysis of the state action issue, we recog-nize the consequences of sustaining the refusal by the trial judge to declare that Pitt is not clothed with the mantle of the Commonwealth. Should this case be allowed to proceed, and state action ultimately be held to exist, then the University may be subjected to some of the constitutional and statutory strictures ordinarily applied to the state. Not only may Pitt have to answer for alleged violations of portions of the Bill of Rights and the 14th Amendment, but it may be liable under the statutory counterparts to such constitutional provisions as well. Because the burdens that may radi-ate from a decision upholding the district court may be potentially quite far-reaching, this issue should be dealt with in a full and thoughtful fashion.

Also, it should be observed that the difficulties of drawing a line between state and private action are by now well-recognized. This is so because the realms of the government and the private sector are not as clearly defined as they were during the epoch in which the 14th and 15th Amendments—the sources of the statutory claim in question—were adopted. Today, the federal courts, with ever-increasing frequency, are called upon to judge whether the conduct of ostensibly nongovernmental entities is such as to warrant the application of constitutional and statutory requirements to them.

It becomes our task to consider whether, given the legal precedents and factual setting at hand, the relationship between the University of Pittsburgh and the Commonwealth supports the decision of the trial judge that, at least on the available record, the activities of that educational institution cannot be deemed to be devoid of state action. In undertaking such a consideration, we must, of course, be aware that, although we are required to decide the controversy before us, this does not mean that the present case may be dis-associated from the past or unrelated to the future.

B.

On several occasions, the Supreme Court has endeavored to decide when the participation of a state in an otherwise private activity is so sig-

nificant that the acts of the seemingly private enterprise are to be considered
state action. While the leading cases may serve as guidelines for our inquiry
here, no attempt has been made by the Supreme Court, as of yet, to reconcile what may appear to be conflicting pronouncements on state action. Nor
has the Court thus far sought to delineate a unitary theory of state action.

Although the Supreme Court frequently has written on the subject of
state action, the two opinions most pertinent to the case at bar are *Burton v.
Wilmington Parking Authority* and *Jackson v. Metropolitan Edison Co.* Not
only did the Court reach divergent results in these cases, finding state action
in the former though not in the latter, but the mode of analysis in each
opinion is dissimilar. It is incumbent upon this Court to determine which,
if either, of these cases—*Burton* or *Jackson*—may control the present situation and, in so doing, whether *Jackson* has superseded *Burton* as the pre-
eminent declaration on state action with respect to circumstances such as
we have here.

In *Burton*, the Court held that a private restaurant owner who refused
service to a customer because of his race, violated the Fourteenth Amendment where the restaurant was located in a building owned by a state-created
parking authority and leased from that authority. After a thorough review
of the relationship between the restaurant and the authority, the Supreme
Court concluded that the state had "so far insinuated itself into a position of
interdependence with [the restaurant] that it must be recognized as a joint
participant in the challenged activity, which, on that account, cannot be
considered to have been so 'purely private' as to fall without the scope of
the Fourteenth Amendment." It is thus apparent that the dispositive factor
in *Burton*, with respect to the state action issue, was the extent and nature
of the overall relationship between the state agency and the private enterprise.

Decided thirteen years after *Burton, Jackson* concerned a different type
of nongovernmental entity, namely, a privately owned and operated utility
corporation. The utility was, however, subject to extensive state regulation
in many particulars of its business. When the utility company terminated
the electric service of a customer without notice, without a hearing, or without an opportunity to pay any amounts due, the customer charged that she
had been denied due process. The Supreme Court rejected the due process
claim on the ground that, since state action was not present, the utility was
exempt from constitutional commands. It held that the Commonwealth of
Pennsylvania was not sufficiently connected with the challenged termination
to make the conduct of the private utility corporation attributable to the
state for purposes of the Fourteenth Amendment.

Important to the inquiry here is the analytical formula set forth in
Jackson respecting state action. For the Supreme Court stated there that,
when considering the vexing state action issue, the "inquiry must be whether
there is a sufficiently close nexus between the state and the challenged
action of the regulated entity so that the action of the latter may be fairly
treated as that of the State itself."

Appellants maintain that this "close nexus" test, rather than the "relationship" approach of *Burton,* should be applied in the case at bar. They contend that, for state action to exist, the Commonwealth must be closely involved with the challenged employment practices of the University. In so arguing, appellants imply that the vitality of *Burton* has been severely undermined by *Jackson,* and that the existence of a pervasive relationship between the Commonwealth and the University is not, standing alone, sufficient to undergird a ruling of state action. While *Jackson* may invite some concern as to the present status of *Burton,* we do not find appellants' reading of these cases to be convincing. To the contrary, in our view, *Burton* retains viability, and so its teachings may well bear on the present inquiry. . . .

It may be that only in the absence of an inextricably-linked relationship between the state and a private entity does the "close nexus" test of *Jackson* come into play. Where a private enterprise stands, in its operations, as a veritable partner with the state, then it seems proper to hold such enterprise subject to the same constitutional requirements to which the state is accountable. But the situation may be otherwise where no pervasive state-private relationship exists. For without such an arrangement, there would appear to be no basis for holding a private entity to constitutional strictures, unless the state is closely involved in the very activity challenged by a litigant. Thus, as we understand it, *Burton* and *Jackson* stand as two models of state-action analysis that have been designed by the Supreme Court to date, with the applicability of either approach resting on the type of setting which may be present.

C.

Having concluded that *Burton* retains vitality, we must examine the available materials concerning the nature and extent of the connection between the University of Pittsburgh and the Commonwealth. We do so to resolve whether the principles of *Burton* may control this appeal as well as to ascertain whether the district court's conclusion as to state action should be upheld. Such determinations often depend largely on the factual matrix that obtains. Indeed, the Supreme Court declared in *Burton* that "only by sifting facts and weighing circumstances . . ." can matters turning on state action be resolved. And such emphasis on the factual elements was echoed in *Jackson* as well.

Pursuant to instructions rendered by this Court during the previous appeal, the district judge conducted an extensive evidentiary investigation respecting the factual facets of the state action question. As the trial court set forth its findings in an exhaustive fashion, it is not necessary to restate them at length. Rather, we shall highlight only those facts that are critical to the issue whether this action should have been dismissed.

With respect to the overall relationship between the University and the Commonwealth, a most telling factor is the University of Pittsburgh-Commonwealth Act and the manner in which that legislation has been implemented. Such evidence would appear to indicate that the state is deeply enmeshed in operations of the University, including but not limited to its financing and its basic decision-making processes. Indeed, in light of the Act and the history of its effectuation, it is highly questionable whether the University may be described as a "purely private" institution, a characterization that would substantially immunize it from the dictates of the Constitution and the statutory progeny of that document.

Prior to the passage of the Act, Pitt was a private educational institution in dire financial straits. At the initiative of the University, overtures were made to the State Board of Education in an effort to ameliorate Pitt's monetary troubles. While agreeing to afford the requested aid, the Commonwealth was not content merely to inject public funds into the ailing institution. Instead, as will become evident, it conditioned a massive infusion of moneys on a comprehensive restructuring of the University to reflect the needs of the Commonwealth.

In connection with the pre-enactment consideration of the legislation, the State Board of Education adopted a resolution in March, 1966 which called for increased enrollment of and reduced tuition for Pennsylvania students at Pitt. The resolution also stated that "the University's program must be responsive to the educational needs of the Commonwealth. . . ." Similarly, in testimony before the district court regarding the statutes, a former Pitt Chancellor expressed the opinion that the Act represented a "commitment that the University has made to perform certain services for the state." Such comments in the legislative history and elsewhere demonstrate that the relationship between the University and the Commonwealth was intended to be a close one.

That the University of Pittsburgh-Commonwealth Act is especially damaging to the appellants' contention that state action is lacking becomes immediately clear. The Pennsylvania legislature in its statutory program boldly announces:

[I]t is hereby declared to be the purpose of this act to extend Commonwealth opportunities for higher education by establishing University of Pittsburgh as an *instrumentality* of the Commonwealth to serve as a *State-related* institution in the Commonwealth system of higher education.

And the body of the Act discloses that the proclamation of legislative policy, making the University a state "instrumentality" as well as a "state-related institution," is not empty verbiage. We are inclined to take the Commonwealth at its word, and, indeed, may well be obligated to do so at this point in the proceedings.

Examination of the Act, as adopted and implemented, suggests that the line of demarcation between the University and the Commonwealth was blurred, if not obliterated. Significantly, the legislation changed the name of the University to the "University of Pittsburgh—Of the Commonwealth System of Higher Education." Pitt's charter also was amended so that trustees appointed by the Governor of Pennsylvania, by the President Pro Tempore of the Senate and by the Speaker of the House constitute one-third of the voting members of the Board of Trustees. In addition, the Act names several state officials as *ex officio* trustees, including the Governor, the State Secretary of Education, and the Mayor of Pittsburgh, thus seeming to ensure that governmental representation on the Board is rather substantial.

The statutory program is not limited to a modification of the University's name or the composition of its Board of Trustees. It promises that there will be annual appropriations for Pitt. And since the passage of the legislation, public funds have poured into the coffers of the University, averaging more than one-third of its total operating budget. In fiscal year 1973-74, for example, the state appropriated roughly $48 million for Pitt, an amount representing over thirty-five per cent of the school's budget. And the generosity of the Commonwealth has increased with each passing year.

Under the University of Pittsburgh-Commonwealth Act, the state does not appear to provide annual appropriations with only minimal requirements respecting their use. Rather, Pitt may have surrendered much of its fiscal autonomy to the state, with the Commonwealth holding both the purse-strings as well as extensive financial control over the University.

In exchange for public funds, Pitt agreed to submit to stringent regulations of its fiscal and other affairs. Under the Act, then, the Commonwealth has reserved the right to specify the purposes for or areas in which public funds may be spent. Substantial powers are vested in the Auditor General as well. Not only may that official audit the use of state funds and disallow any expenditures therefrom which he deems improper, but he retains the right to review the University's expenditures of non-state moneys. Moreover, so as to ensure "proper accountability" on the part of Pitt, a comprehensive report detailing the amounts and purposes of *all* expenditures, from both state and private funds, must be filed with the Commonwealth. Consultations between the University and the state also are to be held respecting the *entire* budget.

In addition to the above features, the Act directs the Chancellor to submit an annual report to the Commonwealth regarding all University activities—instructional, administrative and financial. Furthermore, a 1972 amendment to the statutory arrangement requires detailed reports concerning, *inter alia*, the numbers of faculty and students as well as faculty teaching loads and salaries. The information required under this addendum to the Act must be provided by each school and each department within the University.

Finally, the University of Pittsburgh-Commonwealth Act pledges capital development assistance to Pitt. In essence, the benefits that state and authority programs for capital development bestow on wholly-owned state colleges are to be accorded the University as well. The state is authorized to acquire lands, construct facilities and lease or loan them to Pitt, and it has in fact done so. Through its General State Authority, the Commonwealth has provided about one-third of the University's buildings.

Between 1966 and 1974, the cost of the construction for such building projects has totaled approximately $94 million. In addition, the Pennsylvania Higher Education Facilities Authority has financed various capital improvements for Pitt, including one project costing $6.5 million and another, roughly $600,000.

All in all, the comprehensive statutory arrangement, carefully interweaving the functions of the University of Pittsburgh and the Commonwealth, and the manner in which it has been effectuated hardly suggests that state action does not exist. If anything, there would appear to be adequate grounds for believing that Pitt is vested with a status more closely akin to that of a state college rather than that of a private institution of higher education.

As we see it, there is an ample basis for concluding, at least at this time, that the relationship between Pitt and the Commonwealth may be "symbiotic" in a manner similar to that present in *Burton*. For the two entities, once denizens of separate societal realms, apparently are now dependent upon one another.

As discussed above, prior to adoption of the Act, the University desperately needed a source of funds to maintain its operations. The situation was described by Pitt officials and trustees as grave. At the same time, the Commonwealth desired to satisfy the needs of the populace for expanded facilities for higher education. As the existing state educational institutions were insufficient to satisfy the public demand, and because the creation of new state universities would have been extremely expensive, the decision was made to incorporate established, but financially ailing private institutions into the Commonwealth system of higher education. The state thus was able to satisfy the educational needs of its citizens at a cost considerably lower than would have been entailed by the creation of wholly *new* institutions. Concomitantly, Pitt was able to survive as an institution of higher education, even though it may have been forced to relinquish its traditional autonomy as a private facility.

Since the facts adduced thus far indicate that the relationship between the University of Pittsburgh and the Commonwealth is symbiotic in nature, or at least pervasive, we believe that the precepts of *Burton* may be applicable to the present appeal. Not only does it appear that the state in this situation, as in *Burton*, has "insinuated itself into a position of interdependence" with Pitt, but it seems to be a "joint participant" in the educational enterprise as well.

Moreover, the restaurant involved in *Burton* was situated in a public building, and the private entity leased its premises from the state. In *Jackson*, the Supreme Court suggested that the "actual holding" of *Burton* might be limited to lessees of public property. Even so, as previously indicated, many of the buildings within the Pitt complex were built by the state or its agencies with public funds and are leased to the University, including the very building within which Dr. Braden worked. It follows that even if *Burton* and its "relationship" theory of state action should be limited to a "lease" situation, the present appeal still may be governed by the teachings of that landmark decision. Consequently, the district court did not commit error when it declined to dismiss the complaint for a purported absence of state action.

D.

Although the factual matrix as presented here, considered against the backdrop of *Burton*, supports the district court's refusal to dismiss the complaint, it still is appropriate to consider the pronouncements of the small number of courts which have confronted situations similar to the one at hand. Two such opinions fortify the decision that we reach today.

Of these cases, the more pertinent is *Isaacs v. Board of Trustees of Temple University*, a case which also concerned sex discrimination claims. In denying a motion for summary judgment raised by Temple University, Judge Higginbotham indicated that the activities of that educational institution constituted state action. He did so on facts which closely parallel those in the present appeal.

The *Isaacs* opinion places substantial weight on the Temple University-Commonwealth Act, an identical twin to the statutory program enacted on behalf of Pitt. Not only do the provisions of the Temple legislation virtually duplicate those of the Pittsburgh enactments, but both Acts were drafted with the same objectives in mind and at roughly the same time. Like the Pitt Act, the Temple legislation was promulgated so that Temple could transcend crushing financial woes, while obligating that university to operate as an instrumentality of the Commonwealth and to serve the citizenry at large. After carefully reviewing the Temple-Commonwealth Act and the degree of state participation in that university, as we have done in the case *sub judice,* the *Isaacs* court stated that the "Commonwealth of Pennsylvania has so significantly involved itself in the affairs of Temple University that the latter's activities [constitute] 'state action' and action 'under color of' state law . . . ." In our view such a conclusion may prove to be appropriate in the present appeal which closely tracks *Isaacs.*

It should be observed that *Jackson* was decided immediately after the opinion in *Isaacs* was rendered. Since *Isaacs* so heavily relies, quite properly, on *Burton*, the analysis presented by Judge Higginbotham remains valid only so long as *Jackson* is not construed to overrule or devitalize *Burton.* As we fail to so read *Jackson*, the principles espoused in *Isaacs* remain supportive of the conclusion reached by the trial judge that state action cannot be ruled out summarily in the case at bar.

Because Pennsylvania's system of state-related universities, which includes Pitt and Temple, seems to be relatively distinctive, it is not surprising that other legal precedents pertinent to the case at hand are lacking. However, one court of appeals has considered a situation which may be an analogue to the present one. In *Powe v. Miles,* the Second Circuit dealt with an appeal from a dismissal of a complaint. The *Powe* suit challenged the suspension of students by Alfred University, a private educational institution.

and by the New York State College of Ceramics, a school administered by
Alfred under a contract with the State of New York. Speaking for a unanimous panel, Judge Friendly declared that the university administration was
not acting under color of state law when it suspended students at Alfred
proper, but was acting under color of state law when it disciplined students
at the College of Ceramics.

    Powe bears on our inquiry here because of its factual features as well as
the method of analysis exhibited in that portion of the opinion focusing on
the claims of the ceramics students. In evaluating whether the activities of
the College of Ceramics could constitute state action, Judge Friendly relied
quite heavily on a statutory program which set forth the arrangement between Alfred University and the State of New York.

    The legislation deemed to be so crucial in *Powe* is, in several important
respects, markedly similar to the University of Pittsburgh-Commonwealth
Act. For example, under the New York enactments, the State is to provide
substantial funds as well as major buildings and facilities for the ceramics
school. Similarly, as in the case before us, the statutory scheme in *Powe* expressly denominates the College of Ceramics as a state institution. Finally,
the New York legislation declares that Alfred is to serve as "the representative of the state university trustees"—a statement quite parallel to its correlative in the Pitt statutes.

    In *Powe*, then, state legislation, and the manner in which it was imple-
mented, proved to be the critical factor in the disposition of the state action
issue regarding students at the College of Ceramics. We believe that *Powe*
supports our emphasis on the statutory arrangement between Pitt and the
Commonwealth. And it would appear that the result we reach today is
consonant with that obtained in the *Powe* case.

E.

    While there are many other cases which have raised the question of
state action with respect to institutions of higher education, none of them
contained a factual configuration similar to that here. Perhaps the most
important of these cases, and one which is illustrative of the group, is *Cohen
v. Illinois Institute of Technology*. In *Cohen*, Judge (now Justice) Stevens,
writing for a panel of the Seventh Circuit, sustained the dismissal of a complaint which tendered a § 1983 claim. Although the defendant university
used the name "Illinois" in its institutional title, received some financial and
other support from the state and was subject to certain regulations, the
Cohen court declined to rule that state action existed.

    Nevertheless, *Cohen* would appear to be distinguishable from the case
at hand—chiefly because there is no statutory program which inextricably
links I.I.T. to the State of Illinois. Contrary to the Pitt situation, the level of
financial support offered I.I.T. by the state is minimal. Judge Stevens expressly stated that "the funds contributed by the State represent only a
small fraction of the cost of educating the students . . . ." In addition, I.I.T.
selected its own institutional name, unlike the statutory designation of the

University of Pittsburgh as a Commonwealth school. Moreover, the regulations imposed by the state are far less extensive in *Cohen* than in the present case. Basically, the Illinois provisions speak to the issue of accreditation and little else, whereas the University of Pittsburgh-Commonwealth Act is far more sweeping in its scope.

Perhaps the most important basis for distinguishing *Cohen* from this case is the absence there of other indicia of a close relationship between the state and the university, including, *inter alia*, (1) governmental participation in determining the composition of the board of trustees, (2) the review of the expenditure of private funds by state officials, (3) onerous reporting requirements; (4) a legislative history which discloses that the state desired to utilize the educational facilities of an existing institution rather than create new ones itself; and especially (5) the statutory declaration that Pitt is an "instrumentality" of the Commonwealth. Indeed, the *Cohen* opinion vigorously emphasizes that there was no "evidence that [I.I.T.] is . . . a State instrumentality . . . ." Had there been such evidence in *Cohen*, the Seventh Circuit may well have reached an opposite result and found state action. By its own terms, then, *Cohen* constitutes a case considerably different from the one with which we are now concerned.

As a final point, we recognize that *Cohen* appears to have utilized the "close nexus" test of *Jackson*. The analysis of Judge Stevens turns, in part, on the absence of "some nexus between the State . . . and defendants' wrongful conduct. . . ." Yet, it is important to bear in mind that *Cohen* applied the "close nexus" approach only after a careful evaluation of the facts revealed the absence of a tight bond between the state and the university. Following such factual scrutiny, Judge Stevens expressly concluded: "It is plain that the school is not so heavily dependent on the State as to be considered the equivalent of a public university . . . ." By contrast, as discussed above, sufficient facts may have been produced here to undergird an eventual finding that there is a symbiotic relationship between the state and Pitt so as to bring the present case within the ambit of *Burton*, not *Jackson* or *Cohen*. *Cohen* thus would appear to lend limited support to the appellants' arguments that state action is lacking here.

F.

In sum, we believe the district court did not commit error in declining to dismiss the complaint for a purported want of state action. In our view, there were adequate grounds for refusing to rule that the relationship between the University of Pittsburgh and the Commonwealth of Pennsylvania is such as to forbid the application of the constitutional commands, and the statutory derivations therefrom, to the University.

Accordingly, the judgment of the district court will be affirmed and the case remanded for action consistent with this opinion.

NOTES

1. The doctrine of state action which evolved principally from the civil rights cases such as Burton v. Wilmington Parking Authority, 365 U.S. 715 (1961), has not been

construed liberally in college and university cases although it is pleaded in almost every
case filed.   Chartering, tax exemption and minimal financing are not enough to
transform private college actions into state actions: Powe v. Miles, 407 F.2d 73 (2d Cir.
1968); Blackburn v. Fisk, 443 F.2d 121 (6th Cir. 1971); Greenya v. George Washington
University, 512 F.2d 556 (D.C. Cir. 1975), *cert. denied*, 423 U.S. 995 (1975); nor does
state certification or accreditation: Cohen v. Illinois Institute of Technology, 524 F.2d
818 (7th Cir. 1975), *cert. denied*, 425 U.S. 943 (1976); Grafton v. Brooklyn Law School,
478 F.2d 1137 (2d Cir. 1973); or receipt of federal funds: Williams v. Howard University,
528 F.2d 658 (D.C. Cir. 1976). For a summary of the numerous cases which touch upon
this issue, see *Action of Private Institutions of Higher Education as Constituting State
Action or Action under Color of Law for Purposes of Fourteenth Amendment and 42
USCA Sec. 1983*, 37 ALR Fed. 601.
     2. A differing point of view may be found in O'Neil, *Private Universities and Public
Law*, 19 Buffalo L. Rev. 155 (1969), in which Professor O'Neil argues that the "state
action" concept is outmoded.

IV. Religious Institutions

ROEMER v. BOARD OF PUBLIC WORKS OF MARYLAND
United States Supreme Court
426 U.S. 736 (1976)

MR. JUSTICE BLACKMUN announced the judgment of the Court and
delivered an opinion in which THE CHIEF JUSTICE and MR. JUSTICE
POWELL joined.
     We are asked once again to police the constitutional boundary between
church and state. Maryland, this time, is the alleged trespasser. It has enacted
a statute which, as amended, provides for annual noncategorical grants to
private colleges, among them religiously affiliated institutions, subject only
to the restrictions that the funds not be used for "sectarian purposes." A
three-judge District Court, by a divided vote, refused to enjoin the operation
of the statute, 387 F. Supp. 1282 (Md. 1974), and a direct appeal has been
taken to this Court pursuant to 28 U. S. C. § 1253.

I.

The challenged grant program was instituted by Laws of 1971, c. 626,
and is now embodied in Md. Ann. Code, Art. 77A, § §65-69 (1975). It
provides funding for "any private institution of higher learning within the
State of Maryland," provided the institution is accredited by the State Department of Education, was established in Maryland prior to July 1, 1970,
maintains one or more "associate of arts or baccalaureate degree" programs,
and refrains from awarding "only seminarian or theological degrees." § § 65-
66. The aid is in the form of an annual fiscal year subsidy to qualifying
colleges and universities. . . .
     Primary responsibility for the program rests with the Council for
Higher Education, an appointed commission which antedates the aid program, which has numerous other responsibilities in the educational field, and
which has derived from these a "considerable expertise as to the character

and functions of the various private colleges and universities in the State."
387 F. Supp., at 1285.

The Council performs what the District Court described as a "two-step screening process" to insure compliance with the statutory restrictions on the grants. First, it determines whether an institution applying for aid is eligible at all, or is one "awarding primarily theological or seminary degrees." Several applicants have been disqualified at this stage of the process. *Id.*, at 1289, 1296. Second, the Council requires that those institutions that are eligible for funds not put them to any sectarian use. An application must be accompanied by an affidavit of the institution's chief executive officer stating that the funds will not be used for sectarian purposes, and by a description of the specific nonsectarian uses that are planned. These may be changed only after written notice to the Council. By the end of the fiscal year the institution must file a "Utilization of Funds Report" describing and itemizing the use of the funds. The chief executive officer must certify the report and also file his own "Post-expenditure Affidavit," stating that the funds have not been put to sectarian uses. The recipient institution is further required to segregate state funds in a "special revenue account" and to identify aided nonsectarian expenditures separately in its budget. It must retain "sufficient documentation of the State funds expended to permit verification by the Council that funds were not spent for sectarian purposes." Any question of sectarian use that may arise is to be resolved by the Council, if possible, on the basis of information submitted to it by the institution and without actual examination of its books. Failing that, a "verification or audit" may be undertaken. The District Court found that the audit would be "quick and non-judgmental," taking one day or less. *Id.*, at 1296. . . .

II.

A system of government that makes itself felt as pervasively as ours could hardly be expected never to cross paths with the church. In fact, our State and Federal Governments impose certain burdens upon, and impart certain benefits to, virtually all our activities, and religious activity is not an exception. The Court has enforced a scrupulous neutrality by the State, as among religions, and also as between religious and other activities, but a hermetic separation of the two is an impossibility it has never required. It long has been established, for example, that the State may send a cleric, indeed even a clerical order, to perform a wholly secular task. In *Bradfield* v. *Roberts,* 175 U. S. 291 (1899), the Court upheld the extension of public aid to a corporation which, although composed entirely of members of a Roman Catholic sisterhood acting "under the auspices of said church," *id.*, at 297, was limited by its corporate charter to the secular purpose of operating a charitable hospital.

And religious institutions need not be quarantined from public benefits that are neutrally available to all. The Court has permitted the State to supply transportation for children to and from church-related as well as public schools *Everson* v. *Board of Education*, 330 U. S. 1 (1947). It has done the same with respect to secular textbooks loaned by the State on equal terms to students attending both public and church-related elementary schools. *Board of Education* v. *Allen*, 392 U. S. 236 (1968). Since it had not been shown in *Allen* that the secular textbooks would be put to other than secular purposes, the Court concluded that, as in *Everson*, the State was merely "extending the benefits of state laws to all citizens." *Id.*, at 242. Just as *Bradfield* dispels any notion that a religious person can never be in the State's pay for a secular purpose, *Everson* and *Allen* put to rest any argument that the State may never act in such a way that has the incidental effect of facilitating religious activity. The Court has not been blind to the fact that in aiding a religious institution to perform a secular task, the State frees the institution's resources to be put to sectarian ends. If this were impermissible, however, a church could not be protected by the police and fire departments, or have its public sidewalk kept in repair. The Court never has held that religious activities must be discriminated against in this way.

Neutrality is what is required. The State must confine itself to secular objectives, and neither advance nor impede religious activity. Of course, that principle is more easily stated than applied. The Court has taken the view that a secular purpose and a facial neutrality may not be enough, if in fact the State is lending direct support to a religious activity. The State may not, for example, pay for what is actually a religious education, even though it purports to be paying for a secular one, and even though it makes its aid available to secular and religious institutions alike. The Court also has taken the view that the State's efforts to perform a secular task, and at the same time avoid aiding in the performance of a religious one, may not lead it into such an intimate relationship with religious authority that it appears either to be sponsoring or to be excessively interfering with that authority. In *Lemon I* as noted above, the Court distilled these concerns into a three-prong test, resting in part on prior case law, for the constitutionality of statutes affording state aid to church-related schools:

> "First, the statute must have a secular legislative purpose; second, its principal or primary effect must be one that neither advances nor inhibits religion . . . ; finally, the statute must not foster 'an excessive government entanglement with religion.' " 403 U. S., at 612–613.

At issue in *Lemon I* were two state-aid plans, a Rhode Island program to grant a 15% supplement to the salaries of private, church-related school teachers teaching secular courses, and a Pennsylvania program to reimburse private church-related schools for the entire cost of secular courses also offered in public schools. Both failed the third part of the test, that of "excessive government entanglement." This part the Court held in turn required a consideration of three factors: (1) the character and purposes of the benefited institutions, (2) the nature of the aid provided, and (3) the resulting relationship between the State and the religious authority. *Id.*, at 615. As to the first of these, in reviewing the Rhode Island program, the

Court found that the aided schools, elementary and secondary, were characterized by "substantial religious activity and purpose." *Id.*, at 616. The State's efforts to supervise and control the teaching of religion in supposedly secular classes would therefore inevitably entangle it excessively in religious affairs. The Pennsylvania program similarly foundered.

The Court also pointed to another kind of church-state entanglement threatened by the Rhode Island and Pennsylvania programs, namely, their "divisive political potential." *Id.*, at 622. They represented "successive and very likely permanent annual appropriations that benefit relatively few religious groups." *Id.*, at 623. Political factions, supporting and opposing the programs, were bound to divide along religious lines. This was "one of the principal evils against which the First Amendment was intended to protect." *Id.*, at 622. It was stressed that the political divisiveness of the programs was "aggravated . . . by the need for continuing annual appropriations." *Id.*, at 623.

In *Tilton* v. *Richardson,* 403 U.S. 672 (1971), a companion case to *Lemon I*, the Court reached the contrary result. The aid challenged in *Tilton* was in the form of federal grants for the construction of academic facilities at private colleges, some of them church related, with the restriction that the facilities not be used for any sectarian purpose. Applying *Lemon I*'s three-part test, the Court found the purpose of the federal aid program there under consideration to be secular. Its primary effect was not the advancement of religion, for sectarian use of the facilities was prohibited. Enforcement of this prohibition was made possible by the fact that religion did not so permeate the defendant colleges that their religious and secular functions were inseparable. On the contrary, there was no evidence that religious activities took place in the funded facilities. Courses at the colleges were "taught according to the academic requirements intrinsic to the subject matter," and "an atmosphere of academic freedom rather than religious indoctrination" was maintained. 403 U. S., at 680-682 (plurality opinion).

Turning to the problem of excessive entanglement, the Court first stressed the character of the aided institutions. It pointed to several general differences between college and precollege education: College students are less susceptible to religious indoctrination; college courses tend to entail an internal discipline that inherently limits the opportunities for sectarian influence; and a high degree of academic freedom tends to prevail at the college level. It found no evidence that the colleges in *Tilton* varied from this pattern. Though controlled and largely populated by Roman Catholics, the colleges were not restricted to adherents of that faith. No religious services were required to be attended. Theology courses were mandatory, but they were taught in an academic fashion, and with treatment of beliefs other than Roman Catholicism. There were no attempts to proselytize among students, and principles of academic freedom prevailed. With colleges of this character, there was little risk that religion would seep into the teaching of secular subjects, and the state surveillance necessary to separate the two, therefore, was diminished. The Court next looked to the type of aid provided, and found it to be neutral or nonideological in nature. Like

Like the textbooks and bus transportation in *Allen* and *Everson*, but unlike the teachers' services in *Lemon I*, physical facilities were capable of being restricted to secular purposes. Moreover, the construction grant was a one-shot affair, not involving annual audits and appropriations.

As for political divisiveness, no "continuing religious aggravation" over the program had been shown, and the Court reasoned that this might be because of the lack of continuity in the church-state relationship, the character and diversity of the colleges, and the fact that they served a dispersed student constituency rather than a local one. "[C]umulatively," all these considerations persuaded the Court that church-state entanglement was not excessive. 403 U. S., at 684-689.

In *Hunt* v. *McNair*, 413 U. S. 734 (1973), the challenged aid was also for the construction of secular college facilities, the state plan being one to finance the construction by revenue bonds issued through the medium of a state authority. In effect, the college serviced and repaid the bonds, but at the lower cost resulting from the tax-free status of the interest payments. The Court upheld the program on reasoning analogous to that in *Tilton*. In applying the second of the *Lemon I*'s three-part test, that concerning "primary effect," the following refinement was added:

> "Aid normally may be thought to have a primary effect of advancing religion when it flows to an institution in which religion is so pervasive that a substantial portion of its functions are subsumed in the religious mission or when it funds a specifically religious activity in an otherwise substantially secular setting." 413 U. S., at 743.

Although the college which *Hunt* concerned was subject to substantial control by its sponsoring Baptist Church, it was found to be similar to the colleges in *Tilton* and not "pervasively sectarian." As in *Tilton*, state aid went to secular facilities only, and thus not to any "specifically religious activity." 413 U. S., at 743-745.

Committee for Public Education v. *Nyquist*, 413 U. S. 756 (1973), followed in *Lemon I*'s wake much as *Hunt* followed in *Tilton*'s. The aid in *Nyquist* was to elementary and secondary schools which, the District Court found, generally conformed to a "profile" of a sectarian or substantially religious school. The state aid took three forms: direct subsidies for the maintenance and repair of buildings; reimbursement of parents for a percentage of tuition paid; and certain tax benefits for parents. All three forms of aid were found to have an impermissible primary effect. The maintenance and repair subsidies, being unrestricted, could be used for the upkeep of a chapel or classrooms used for religious instruction. The reimbursements and tax benefits to parents could likewise be used to support wholly religious activities.

In *Levitt* v. *Committee for Public Education*, 413 U. S. 472 (1973), the Court also invalidated a program for public aid to church-affiliated schools. The grants, which were to elementary and secondary schools in New York, were in the form of reimbursements for the schools' testing and recordkeeping expenses. The schools met the same sectarian profile as did those in *Nyquist*, at least in some cases. There was therefore "substantial risk" that the state-funded tests would be "drafted with an eye, unconsciously or otherwise, to inculcate students in the religious precepts of the sponsoring church." 413 U. S., at 480.

Last Term, in *Meek* v. *Pittenger*, 421 U. S. 349 (1975), the Court ruled yet again on a state-aid program for church-related elementary and secondary schools. On the authority of *Allen,* it upheld a Pennsylvania program for lending textbooks to private school students. It found, however, that *Lemon I* required the invalidation of two other forms of aid to the private schools. The first was the loan of instructional materials and equipment. Like the textbooks, these were secular and nonideological in nature. Unlike the textbooks, however, they were loaned directly to the schools. The schools, similar to those in *Lemon I*, were ones in which "the teaching process is, to a large extent, devoted to the inculcation of religious values and belief." 421 U. S., at 366. Aid flowing directly to such "religion-pervasive institutions," *ibid.,* had the primary effect of advancing religion. See *Hunt* v. *McNair, supra.* The other form of aid was the provision of "auxiliary" educational services: remedial instruction, counseling and testing, and speech and hearing therapy. These also were intended to be neutral and nonideological, and in fact were to be provided by public school teachers. Still, there was danger that the teachers, in such a sectarian setting, would allow religion to seep into their instruction. To attempt to prevent this from happening would excessively entangle the State in church affairs. The Court referred again to the danger of political divisiveness, heightened, as it had been in *Lemon I* and *Nyquist,* by the necessity of annual legislative reconsideration of the aid appropriation. 421 U. S., at 372.

So the slate we write on is anything but clean. Instead, there is little room for further refinement of the principles governing public aid to church-affiliated private schools. Our purpose is not to unsettle those principles, so recently reaffirmed, see *Meek* v. *Pittenger, supra,* or to expand upon them substantially, but merely to insure that they are faithfully applied in this case.

III

The first part of *Lemon I*'s three-part test is not in issue; appellants do not challenge the District Court's finding that the purpose of Maryland's aid program is the secular one of supporting private higher education generally, as an economic alternative to a wholly public system. The focus of the debate is on the second and third parts, those concerning the primary effect of advancing religion, and excessive church-state entanglement. We consider them in the same order.

A

While entanglement is essentially a procedural problem, the primary-effect question is the substantive one of what private educational activities, by whatever procedure, may be supported by state funds. *Hunt* requires (1) that no state aid at all go to institutions that are so "pervasively sectarian" that secular activities cannot be separated from sectarian ones, and (2) that if secular activities *can* be separated out, they alone may be funded.

(1) The District Court's finding in this case was that the appellee colleges are not "pervasively sectarian." 387 F. Supp., at 1293. This conclusion is supported with a number of subsidiary findings concerning the role of religion on these campuses:

(a) Despite their formal affiliation with the Roman Catholic Church, the colleges are "characterized by a high degree of institutional autonomy." *Id.*, at 1287 n. 7. None of the four receives funds from, or makes reports to, the Catholic Church. The Church is represented on their governing boards, but, as with Mount Saint Mary's, "no instance of entry of Church considerations into college decisions was shown." *Id*, at 1295.

(b) The colleges employ Roman Catholic chaplains and hold Roman Catholic religious exercises on campus. Attendance at such is not required; the encouragement of spiritual development is only "one secondary objective" of each college; and "at none of these institutions does this encouragement go beyond providing the opportunities or occasions for religious experience." *Ibid.* It was the District Court's general finding that "religious indoctrination is not a substantial purpose or activity of any of these defendants." *Id.*, at 1296.

(c) Mandatory religion or theology courses are taught at each of the colleges, primarily by Roman Catholic clerics, but these only supplement a curriculum covering "the spectrum of a liberal arts program." Nontheology courses are taught in an "atmosphere of intellectual freedom" and without "religious pressures." Each college subscribes to, and abides by, the 1940 Statement of Principles on Academic Freedom of the American Association of University Professors. *Id.*, at 1288, 1293, and n. 3, 1295.

(d) Some classes are begun with prayer. The percentage of classes in which this is done varies with the college, from a "minuscule" percentage at Loyola and Mount Saint Mary's, to a majority at Saint Joseph. *Id.*, at 1293. There is no "actual college policy" of encouraging the practice. "It is treated as a facet of the instructor's academic freedom." *Ibid.* Classroom prayers were therefore regarded by the District Court as "peripheral to the subject of religious permeation," as were the facts that some instructors wear clerical garb and some classrooms have religious symbols. *Ibid.* The court concluded:

> "None of these facts impairs the clear and convincing evidence that courses at each defendant are taught 'according to the academic requirements intrinsic to the subject matter and the individual teacher's concept of professional standards.' [citing *Tilton* v. *Richardson*, 403 U. S., at 681]." *Id.*, at 1293–1294.

In support of this finding the court relied on the fact that a Maryland education department group had monitored the teacher education program at Saint Joseph College, where classroom prayer is most prevalent, and had seen "no evidence of religion entering into any elements of that program." *Id.*, at 1293.

(e)   The District Court found that, apart from the theology departments, see n. 20, *supra*, faculty hiring decisions are not made on a religious basis. At two of the colleges, Notre Dame and Mount Saint Mary's, no inquiry at all is made into an applicant's religion. Religious preference is to be noted on Loyola's application form, but the purpose is to allow full appreciation of the applicant's background. Loyola also attempts to employ each year two members of a particular religious order which once staffed a college recently merged into Loyola. Budgetary considerations lead the colleges generally to favor members of religious orders, who often receive less than full salary. Still, the District Court found that "academic quality" was the principal hiring criterion, and that any "hiring bias," or "effort by any defendant to stack its faculty with members of a particular religious group," would have been noticed by other faculty members, who had never been heard to complain. *Id.*, at 1294.

(f)   The great majority of students at each of the colleges are Roman Catholic, but the District Court concluded from a "thorough analysis of the student admission and recruiting criteria" that the student bodies "are chosen without regard to religion." *Id.*, at 1295.

We cannot say that the foregoing findings as to the role of religion in particular aspects of the colleges are clearly erroneous. Appellants ask us to set those findings aside in certain respects. Not surprisingly, they have gleaned from this record of thousands of pages, compiled during several weeks of trial, occasional evidence of a more sectarian character than the District Court ascribes to the colleges. It is not our place, however, to reappraise the evidence, unless it plainly fails to support the findings of the trier of facts. That is certainly not the case here, and it would make no difference even if we were to second-guess the District Court in certain particulars. To answer the question whether an institution is so "pervasively sectarian" that it may receive no direct state aid of any kind, it is necessary to paint a general picture of the institution, composed of many elements. The general picture that the District Court has painted of the appellee institutions is similar in almost all respects to that of the church-affiliated colleges considered in *Tilton* and *Hunt*. We find no constitutionally significant distinction between them, at least for purposes of the "pervasive sectarianism" test.

(2)   Having found that the appellee institutions are not "so permeated by religion that the secular side cannot be separated from the sectarian," 387 F. Supp., at 1293, the District Court proceeded to the next question posed by *Hunt*: whether aid in fact was extended only to "the secular side." This requirement the court regarded as satisfied by the statutory prohibition against sectarian use, and by the administrative enforcement of that prohibition through the Council for Higher Education. We agree. *Hunt* requires only that state funds not be used to support "specifically religious activity." It is clear that fund uses exist that meet this requirement. See *Tilton* v. *Richardson, supra; Hunt* v. *McNair, supra.* We have no occasion to elaborate further

on what is and is not a "specifically religious activity," for no particular use of the state funds is set out in this statute. Funds are put to the use of the college's choice, provided it is not a sectarian use, of which the college must satisfy the Council. If the question is whether the statute sought to be enjoined authorizes state funds for "specifically religious activity," that question fairly answers itself. The statute in terms forbids the use of funds for "sectarian purposes," and this prohibition appears to be at least as broad as *Hunt*'s prohibition of the public funding of "specifically religious activity." We must assume that the colleges, and the Council, will exercise their delegated control over use of the funds in compliance with the statutory, and therefore the constitutional, mandate. It is to be expected that they will give a wide berth to "specifically religious activity," and thus minimize constitutional questions. Should such questions arise, the courts will consider them. It has not been the Court's practice, in considering facial challenges to statutes of this kind, to strike them down in anticipation that particular applications may result in unconstitutional use of funds. See, *e.g., Hunt* v. *McNair,* 413 U. S., at 744, *Tilton* v. *Richardson,* 403 U. S., at 682 (plurality opinion).

B

If the foregoing answer to the "primary effect" question seems easy, it serves to make the "excessive entanglement" problem more difficult. The statute itself clearly denies the use of public funds for "sectarian purposes." It seeks to avert such use, however, through a process of annual interchange—proposal and approval, expenditure and review—between the colleges and the Council. In answering the question whether this will be an "excessively entangling" relationship, we must consider the several relevant factors identified in prior decisions:

(1)   First is the character of the aided institutions. This has been fully described above. As the District Court found, the colleges perform "essentially secular educational functions," 387 F. Supp., at 1288, that are distinct and separable from religious activity. This finding, which is a prerequisite under the "pervasive sectarianism" test to any state aid at all, is also important for purposes of the entanglement test because it means that secular activities, for the most part, can be taken at face value. There is no danger, or at least only a substantially reduced danger, that an ostensibly secular activity—the study of biology, the learning of a foreign language, an athletic event—will actually be infused with religious content or significance. The need for close surveillance of purportedly secular activities is correspondingly reduced. Thus the District Court found that in this case "there is no necessity for state officials to investigate the conduct of particular classes of educational programs to determine whether a school is attempting to indoctrinate its students under the guise of secular education." *Id.,* at 1289. We cannot say the District Court erred in this judgment or gave it undue significance. The Court took precisely the same view with respect

to the aid extended to the very similar institutions in *Tilton.* 403 U. S., at 687 (plurality opinion). See also *Hunt* v. *McNair, supra,* at 746.

(2) As for the form of aid, we have already noted that no particular use of state funds is before us in this case. The *process* by which aid is disbursed, and a use for it chosen, is before us. We address this as a matter of the "resulting relationship" of secular and religious authority.

(3) As noted, the funding process is an annual one. The subsidies are paid out each year, and they can be put to annually varying uses. The colleges propose particular uses for the Council's approval, and, following expenditure, they report to the Council on the use to which the funds have been put.

The District Court's view was that in light of the character of the aided institutions, and the resulting absence of any need "to investigate the conduct of particular classes," 387 F. Supp., at 1289, the annual nature of the subsidy was not fatal. In fact, an annual, ongoing relationship had existed in *Tilton*, where the Government retained the right to inspect subsidized buildings for sectarian use, and the ongoing church-state involvement had been even greater in *Hunt*, where the State was actually the lessor of the subsidized facilities, retaining extensive powers to regulate their use. See 387 F. Supp., at 1290.

We agree with the District Court that "excessive entanglement" does not necessarily result from the fact that the subsidy is an annual one. It is true that the Court favored the "one-time, single-purpose" construction grants in *Tilton* because they entailed "no continuing financial relationships or dependencies, no annual audits, and no government analysis of an institution's expenditures." 403 U. S. at 688 (plurality opinion). The present aid program cannot claim these aspects. But if the question is whether this case is more like *Lemon I* or more like *Tilton*—and surely that is the fundamental question before us—the answer must be that it is more like *Tilton....*

(4) As for political divisiveness, the District Court recognized that the annual nature of the subsidy, along with its promise of an increasing demand for state funds as the colleges' dependency grew, aggravated the danger of "[p]olitical fragmentation . . . on religious lines." *Lemon I*, 403 U. S., at 623. Nonetheless, the District Court found that the program "does not create a substantial danger of political entanglement." 387 F. Supp., at 1291. Several reasons were given. As was stated in *Tilton*, the danger of political divisiveness is "substantially less" when the aided institution is not an elementary or secondary school, but a college, "whose student constituency is not local but diverse and widely dispersed." 403 U. S., at 688 689. Furthermore, political divisiveness is diminished by the fact that the aid is extended to private colleges generally, more than two-thirds of which have no religious affiliation; this is in sharp contrast to *Nyquist*, for example, where 95% of the aided schools were Roman Catholic parochial schools. Finally, the substantial autonomy of the colleges was thought to mitigate political divisiveness, in that controversies surrounding the aid program are not likely to involve the Catholic Church itself, or even the religious char-

acter of the schools, but only their "fiscal responsibility and educational requirements." 387 F. Supp., at 1290-1291.

The District Court's reasoning seems to us entirely sound. Once again, appellants urge that this case is controlled by previous cases in which the form of aid was similar (*Lemon I, Nyquist, Levitt*), rather than those in which the character of the aided institution was the same (*Tilton, Hunt*). We disagree. Though indisputably relevant, see *Lemon I*, 403 U. S., at 623-624, the annual nature of the aid cannot be dispositive. On the one hand, the Court has *struck down* a "permanent," nonannual tax exemption, reasoning that "the pressure for frequent enlargement of the relief is predictable," as it always is. *Committee for Public Education* v. *Nyquist*, 413 U. S., at 797. On the other hand, in *Tilton* it has *upheld* a program for "one-time, single-purpose" construction grants, despite the fact that such grants would, in fact, be "annual," at least insofar as new grants would be annually applied for. 403 U. S., at 688. See *Lemon I*, 403 U. S., at 669 (opinion of WHITE, J.). Our holdings are better reconciled in terms of the character of the aided institutions, found to be so dissimilar as between those considered in *Tilton* and *Hunt,* on the one hand, and those considered in *Lemon I, Nyquist,* and *Levitt,* on the other.

There is no exact science in gauging the entanglement of church and state. The wording of the test, which speaks of "*excessive* entanglement," itself makes that clear. The relevant factors we have identified are to be considered "cumulatively" in judging the degree of entanglement. *Tilton* v. *Richardson*, 403 U. S., at 688. They may cut different ways, as certainly they do here. In reaching the conclusion that it did, the District Court gave dominant importance to the character of the aided institutions and to its finding that they are capable of separating secular and religious functions. For the reasons stated above, we cannot say that the emphasis was misplaced or the finding erroneous.

The judgment of the District Court is affirmed.

It is so ordered.

NOTES

1. Although the U. S. Supreme Court has generally not found the grant of public funds to sectarian institutions of higher education to be in violation of the First Amendment, not all state supreme courts have been as generous as the Missouri Supreme Court in Americans United v. Rogers, 538 S.W.2d 711 (1976), *cert. denied*, 429 U. S. 1029 (1976), in the construction of their own constitutions. That decision upheld a state tuition grant program which included grants to students attending sectarian colleges, despite the court's acknowledgment that the constitution of Missouri is more restrictive than the First Amendment in prohibiting expenditures of public funds in a manner tending to erode an absolute separation of church and state. In State ex rel. Rogers v. Swanson, 219 N.W.2d 726 (Neb. 1974), the Nebraska Supreme Court struck down a student tuition aid plan which could be used at private colleges as violative of the state constitution, since the legislative debate showed a clear intent to benefit private colleges. See also Harkness v. Patterson, 179 S.E.2d 907 (S.C. 1971); Miller v. Ayers, 191 S.E.2d 261 (Va. 1972); and Weiss v. Bruno, 509 P.2d 973 (Wash. 1973). However a similar Tennessee plan was upheld by a federal court in Americans United for Separation of Church and State v. Blanton, 433 F. Supp. 97 (M.D. Tenn. 1977), *aff'd*, 434 U.S. 803 (1977), after

the statute was amended to take out the original provision for the state financial officer to make direct lump sum payments to the private colleges rather than the individuals, as was a later South Carolina plan in Durham v. McLeod, 192 S.E.2d 202 (S.C. 1972) involving guaranteed student loans. *Roemer* guidelines have also been cited to uphold scholarship and tuition grants in North Carolina, Smith v. Board of Governors of the Univ. of N.C., 429 F. Supp. 871 (W.D. N.C. 1977); and Arkansas, Lendall v. Cook, 432 F. Supp. 971 (E.D. Ark. 1977).

2. The federal courts have, by and large, been more liberal in allowing public funds to go to postsecondary institutions. Tilton v. Richardson (discussed in *Roemer*), which distinguished higher education from elementary and secondary schools for the purposes of receipt of federal funds, listed the following factors: students in higher education are better able to distinguish among competing theories; students choose colleges which they attend and are not compelled to attend postsecondary institutions; and, students are generally more mature. The Supreme Court has found it much easier also to separate the sectarian and secular functions of colleges than similar functions in the public schools.

3. Religious colleges and universities are presently poised on the horns of a dilemma in regard to their constitutional status. Like private schools, religious colleges and universities have sought to be classified as nonsectarian for purposes of receiving federal and state funds. If religious institutions secularize their boards, remove requirements for compulsory chapel and courses in religion in order to qualify for public funds, can they then still ask that they be exempted from government regulation on the basis of free exercise of religion? See Gellhorn and Greenwalt, The Sectarian College and the Public Purse; Fordham–A Case Study (Dobbs Ferry, N.Y.: Oceana Publications, 1970). *See also* Harry A. Blanton, *The Entanglement Theory: Its Development and Some Implications for Future Aid to Church-related Higher Education,* Journal of Law and Education, Vol. 7, No. 3, July 1978, p. 359.

4. The courts have refused to recognize private school autonomy in cases in which schools argued that their religion required racial segregation, because discrimination could not be proved to be a clear religious tenet. Brown v. Dade Christian Schools, Inc., 556 F.2d 310 (5th Cir. 1977), *cert. denied*, 434 U.S. 1063 (1978). *See also* Runyon v. McCrary, 427 U.S. 160 (1976). On the other hand, Brigham Young University has succeeded in avoiding a Justice Department suit seeking to sexually integrate off-campus housing, on the basis of the religious nature of the institution. (Letter of Agreement, Brigham Young University and U.S. Department of Justice, June 8, 1978.)

5. In the 95th Congress, both the House and the Senate passed bills granting tuition credits for college tuition (the Packwood-Moynihan Bill, S.B. 2142-HR 3946, HR 12050) but were unable to agree over the amount of credit and whether credit should be extended to grammar schools. 36 Cong. Q. 1379; 36 Cong. Q. 2205 (1978). In Committee for Public Education v. Nyquist, 413 U.S. 756 (1973), the Supreme Court struck down a New York law allowing a taxpayer supporting a dependent in a nonpublic school to claim tax relief graduated according to his income; the Third Circuit recently invalidated a slightly different New Jersey state tax credit plan in Public Funds for Public Schools v. Byrne ____ F.2d ____ (3 Cir. 1979); but lower courts decisions do include approval of some plans. Minnesota Civil Liberties Union v. Roemer, 452 F. Supp. 1316 (D. Minn. 1978). See also, Kosydar v. Wolman, 353 F. Supp. 744 (S.D. Ohio 1972), *aff'd mem. sub nom.* Grit v. Wolman, 413 U.S. 901 (1973); Minnesota Civil Liberties Union v. State, 302 Minn. 216 (1974) *cert. denied*, 421 U.S. 988 (1975). Recently the Harvard Law Review has taken the position that:

> In the face of the significant burden on individual and institutional religious choice in the education area, a national tuition tax credit plan should be held a permissible way to balance separation and neutrality values so as to promote the overall first amendment goal of religious liberty. Note, *Government Neutrality and Separation of Church and State: Tuition Tax Credits* 92 Harv. L. Rev. 606 (1979).

Question: In light of the above, would a national tuition tax credit plan survive a Constitutional challenge?

V.   Charitable Immunity

HEIMBUCH v. PRESIDENT AND DIRECTORS
OF GEORGETOWN COLLEGE
United States District Court,
District of Columbia
251 F. Supp. 614 (1966)

MATTHEWS, District Judge.

The sole question before the court is whether the corporate defendant as a charitable institution is immune from liability in a tort action brought by plaintiff, who was seriously injured in a hazing activity while a freshman at Georgetown University. The University is one of the charitable activities conducted by the corporation. The corporate defendant will be referred to herein as Georgetown. . . .

Georgetown asserts that it was operating the University in its capacity as an eleemosynary corporation; that plaintiff as a student enrolled at the University was a beneficiary of Georgetown, that therefore Georgetown "is exempt from any liability or legal responsibility to plaintiff." The defendant Byrne also relies on the defense of charitable immunity to such extent as plaintiff alleges that Byrne was acting as Georgetown's agent at the time plaintiff was injured. . . .

At the time of the occurrence complained of plaintiff was paying the usual charges made to freshman students for board, tuition and incidentals. With an additional charge for making payment in three installments per semester, these charges amounted to $1808 for the 1956-1957 academic year; and were increased from year to year during plaintiff's attendance as a student at Georgetown to $2015 for the 1959-1960 academic year. The Auditor for Georgetown and the certified public accountant who audited Georgetown's books and records testified that these charges did not fully compensate Georgetown for the expense of the facilities and services furnished by it to plaintiff as a student. Also, Georgetown put on proof of overall operating expenses and operating income, and showed that such expenses exceeded such income. This showing included a specific showing of the operating results of the College of Arts and Sciences, which plaintiff attended as a freshman at the time of the occurrence complained of herein. These figures show an "Operating Deficit" for each of the years in which plaintiff attended Georgetown, and that such deficit was substantially offset by gifts from alumni and others and earnings on endowment and general reserve funds. But the showing made by Georgetown did not include the "per student" cost or expense, nor the number of students attending the College of Arts and Sciences from which the per student cost or expense might be ascertained; and the showing made does not define what is included within the terms "Operating Income" and "Operating Expenses". The evidence indicates that fees to members of the clergy were waived and scholarships granted, without any indication as to how they might be reflected in operating expenses; and there was evidence that Georgetown owns and maintains property not presently utilized in its charitable activities, without any indication as to whether rents from, and repair and maintenance of, such properties are included within "operating" income and expenses. By reason of these uncertainties, the Court is not satisfied that Georgetown has shown that the sums paid by plaintiff did not adequately compensate Georgetown for the facilities and accommodations furnished to him. . . .

The leading case if not the pioneer case in the United States for the doctrine of charitable immunity is McDonald v. Massachusetts General Hospital, 120 Mass. 432, decided in 1876, hereinafter referred to as *McDonald*. In that case a corporation, established for the maintenance of a public charitable hospital, was sued by a workman—a charity patient who claimed that his fractured thigh bone was negligently and improperly set. The sole authority relied upon by the court for its decision that the plaintiff had no remedy against the corporation was the English case of Holliday v. St. Leonard, 11 C.B. (N.S.) 192, decided in 1861. When the court in *McDonald* judicially created or resurrected and imported into this country the charitable immunity doctrine the English case on which *McDonald* rested had been judicially repudiated for some years in England and had not been thereafter revived by judicial or legislative action. Tucker v. Mobile Infirmary Ass'n, 191 Ala. 572, 68 So. 4, L.R.A.1915D, 1167 (1915) and the English cases there cited. Friend v. Cove Methodist Church, Inc., 65 Wash.2d 155, 396 P.2d 546, 551 (1964). Nevertheless, according to legal authorities, *McDonald* was relied on in many subsequent cases for upholding the charitable immunity doctrine. Mississippi Baptist Hospital v. Holmes, 214 Miss. 906, 55 So.2d 142, 152, 56 So.2d 709 (1951). Annotation, 25 A.L.R.2d 29, 39. Avellone v. St. John's Hospital, 165 Ohio St. 467, 135 N.E.2d 410, 412 (1956). Parker v. Port Huron Hospital, 361 Mich. 1, 105 N.W.2d 1, 6 (1960). Kojis v. Doctors Hospital, 12 Wis.2d 367, 107 N.W.2d 131, 132 (1961). Flagiello v. Pennsylvania Hospital, 417 Pa. 486, 208 A.2d 193, 199 (1965).

Dean Prosser in his handbook on the law of torts states that prior to 1942 "only two or three courts had rejected the immunity of charities outright"; that in the year 1942 "a devastating opinion of Judge Rutledge in the Court of Appeals of the District of Columbia reviewed all the arguments in favor of the immunity and demolished them so completely as to change the course of the law"; that it "has been followed by a flood of recent decisions holding that a charity is liable for its torts to the same extent as any other defendant" (citing cases); and that the "immunity of charities is clearly in full retreat." Prosser, Law of Torts, 2d ed. 1955, pp. 787, 789.

The District of Columbia case to which Dean Prosser referred is President and Directors of Georgetown College v. Hughes, 76 U.S.App.D.C. 123, 130 F.2d 810, hereinafter referred to as *Hughes*. The plaintiff in that case was a special nurse employed by a paying patient at a hospital operated by a charitable corporation. She was seriously and permanently injured by the negligent act of an employee of the hospital. The trial court (reserving the question of liability of the charitable corporation to a beneficiary of the charity) held that the plaintiff was a stranger to the charity in a legal sense, submitted to the jury the issue of negligence, and the jury found for the plaintiff. On appeal the court unanimously affirmed the judgment of the trial court but equally divided on the theory of the charitable corporation's liability. Three judges—Chief Justice Groner, Justice Stephens and Justice Vinson—were of the opinion that plaintiff was a stranger to the charity and hence was entitled to recover for the negligent act of the hospital's employee. Three other judges—Justice (Justin) Miller, Justice Edgerton and Justice Rutledge—were of the opinion that whether the plaintiff was stranger or beneficiary charitable corporations are liable for negligence the same as other persons and corporations.

It is argued by the attorney for Georgetown that the *Hughes* ruling does not bar the charitable immunity defense in the instant case because the plaintiff here is the charity's beneficiary, that is, Georgetown's beneficiary, while in *Hughes* the plaintiff was a stranger to the charity. This argument, however, is not well founded. Georgetown was so substantially compensated by plaintiff that he may not be deemed a "beneficiary" of Georgetown's charity but must be regarded as a stranger thereto in a legal sense.

In 1956 a somewhat similar ruling was made by the Supreme Court of New Jersey in Lindroth v. Christ Hospital, 21 N.J. 588, 123 A.2d 10. There the plaintiff in a negligence action was a surgeon who had been injured in the fall of a hospital elevator. As a surgeon he had use of the hospital facilities but rendered administrative services to the hospital and donated surgical services to its needy patients. The surgeon's patients paid the hospital for their care. The charitable immunity doctrine being raised by the charitable corporation operating the hospital, the court denied its applicability, holding that the surgeon was not a beneficiary of the charity but a stranger thereto within the principle of immunity of charitable corporations to negligence claims of their beneficiaries.

Assuming *arguendo* in the instant case that the plaintiff was a beneficiary of Georgetown as Georgetown claims, nevertheless, in the opinion of the court he is entitled to maintain this action against Georgetown. In other words, the court agrees with the view expressed by Mr. Justice Rutledge in *Hughes* that it does not matter whether the plaintiff is stranger or beneficiary a charitable corporation should respond as do private individuals, business corporations and others, if it is negligent. 76 U.S.App.D.C. 123 at page 141, 130 F.2d 810.

The doctrine of charitable immunity from tort liability not being applicable in the District of Columbia, the actions instituted by the plaintiff should be tried by a jury on the issue of negligence. . . .

CHAPTER 3

THE CONSTITUTIONALLY AUTONOMOUS UNIVERSITY

One of the major ways to guarantee the autonomy of a public university is to grant that institution autonomy in the state constitution. While some may argue that a statutory university such as the University of Missouri may attain broad independent powers through judicial sanction of their customary exercise, (see State ex rel. Curators of Missouri v. McReynolds, 193 S.W.2d 611 (1946); State ex rel. Curators of the University of Missouri v. Neill, 397 S.W.2d 666 (1966) and cases cited therein), the clearest and strongest independent status comes from constitutional autonomy.

One of the earliest state universities to be granted autonomy was the University of Michigan. However, it would appear that even a very strong constitutional provision must be protected by continuous legal action.

STERLING v. REGENTS OF THE UNIVERSITY OF MICHIGAN
Supreme Court of Michigan
68 N.W. 253 (1896)

In 1895 the legislature passed Act No. 257, Laws 1895, the material part of which reads as follows: "That the board of regents of the University of Michigan are hereby authorized and directed to establish a homeopathic medical college as a branch or department of said university, which shall be located in the city of Detroit, and the said board of regents are hereby authorized and directed to discontinue the existing homeopathic college now maintained in the city of Ann Arbor as a branch of said university and to transfer the same to the city of Detroit." The title of the act is "An act to amend sec. one of an act entitled, 'An act for the establishment of a homeopathic medical department of the University of Michigan,' approved April 27, 1875, being sec. 4932 of How. Ann. St." The regents of the university declined to comply with said act. The relator thereupon presented this petition for the writ of mandamus to compel the regents to comply with the act. The ground for such refusal is (1) that it was not, in their judgment, for the best interests of the university; (2) that the legislature has no constitutional right to interfere with or dictate the management of the university.* * * The claim which is made under the application of the relator, that the provisions of Act No. 257 command the discontinuance and removal of the homeopathic medical department of the university by the regents, without any reference to their power of supervision of the university, suggests to the regents the question whether such provisions do not curtail and impair the power of supervision and control of the university which has been vested in the regents by the constitution of the state. It is the purpose, as well as the plain duty, of the regents, to exercise, according to their best judgment, the supervision and control of the university, which has been vested in them by the state constitution, to promote both the interests of the university and the interests of the people of the state, which are involved in the welfare of the university.* * *

The University of Michigan was founded under an act of congress making an appropriation of lands for the support of a university in this state, approved May 20, 1826.* * *

Under the constitution of 1835, the legislature had the entire control and management of the university and the university fund. They could appoint regents and professors and establish departments. The university was not a success under this supervision by the legislature, and, as some of the members of the constitutional convention of 1850 said in their debates, "some of the denominational colleges had more students than did the university." Such was the condition of affairs when that convention met. It is apparent to any reader of the debates in this convention in regard to the constitutional provision for the university that they had in mind the idea of permanency of location, to place it beyond mere political influence, and to intrust it to those who should be directly responsible and amenable to the people. * * * The public men of those times were greatly interested in the university. Methods for its management were discussed by governors in their messages, by reports of the board of regents to the legislature, and by committees of the legislature. The general consensus of the opinion was that it should be under the control and management of a permanent board, who should be responsible for its management. The regents, in March, 1840, in obedience to a joint resolution of the legislature, reported that "the first change in the organic law deemed essential is the proper restriction of responsibility to the board of regents. At present the responsibility is divided, and the board would be greatly facilitated in their action were such amendments made as would throw entire responsibility on them." In the same report they also urged that the trust and management of the funds of the university should be placed in the regents. A select committee was appointed by the legislature in 1840 to inquire into the condition of the university. No more forcible argument could well be made than is found in that report for placing the entire control of the university in the hands of a permanent board, and taking it away from the legislature. House Documents 1840, p. 470. I quote from that report as follows: "* * * The argument by which legislatures have hitherto convinced themselves that it was their duty to legislate universities to death is this: 'It is a state institution, and we are the direct representatives of the people, and therefore it is expected of us; it is our right. The people have an interest in this thing, and we must attend to it.' As if, because a university belongs to the people, that were reason why it should be dosed to death for fear it would be sick, if left to be nursed, like other institutions, by its immediate guardians. Thus has state after state, in this American Union, endowed universities, and then, by repeated contradictory and over legislation, torn them to pieces with the same facility as they do the statute book, and for the same reason, because they have the right." All these reports and discussions were undoubtedly known to the members of the convention, and their action should be construed in the light of such knowledge. I am unable to find a single utterance by any member of that convention from which it could be inferred that the members believed or supposed that they were leaving the control of that institution to the legislature. The result has proved their wisdom, for the university, which was before practically a failure, under the guidance of this constitutional body, known as the "Board of Regents," has grown to be one of the most successful, the most complete, and the best-known institutions of learning in the world. * * *

The provisions of the constitution of 1850 in regard to the university are these (article 13):

"Sec. 2. The proceeds from the sales of all lands that have been or hereafter may be granted by the United States to this state, for educational purposes, and the proceeds of all lands or other property given by individuals, or appropriated by the state for like purposes, shall be and remain a perpetual fund, the interest and income of which, together with the rents of all such lands as may remain unsold, shall be inviolably appropriated and annually applied to the specific objects of the original gift, grant or appropriation."

"Sec. 6. There shall be elected in the year 1863, at the time of the election of a justice of the supreme court, eight regents of the university, two of whom shall hold their office for two years, two for four years, two for six years and two for eight years. They shall enter upon the duties of their office on the first of January next succeeding their election. At every regular election of a justice of the supreme court thereafter, there shall be elected two regents, whose term of office shall be eight years. When a vacancy shall occur in the office of regent, it shall be filled by appointment of the governor. The regents thus elected shall constitute the board of regents of the University of Michigan.

"Sec. 7. The regents of the university, and their successors in office, shall continue to constitute the body corporate, known by the name and title of the 'Regents of the University of Michigan.'

"Sec. 8. The regents of the university shall, at their first annual meeting, or so soon thereafter as may be, elect a president of the university, who shall be ex officio a member of their board, with the privilege of speaking but not of voting. He shall preside at the meetings of the regents, and be the principal executive officer of the university. The board of regents shall have the general supervision of the university, and the direction and control of all expenditures from the university interest fund."

The board of regents, elected under the new constitution, immediately took control of the university, interpreted the constitution in accordance with its plain provisions, denied the power of the legislature to interfere with its management or control, and for 46 years have declined obedience to any and every act of the legislature which they, upon mature reflection and

consideration, have deemed against the best interests of the institution. * * *
It is obvious to every intelligent and reflecting mind that such an institution
would be safer and more certain of permanent success in the control of
such a body than in that of the legislature, composed of 132 members,
elected every two years, many of whom would, of necessity, know but little
of its needs, and would have little or no time to intelligently investigate and
determine the policy essential for the success of a great university.

Now, in the face of the facts that the regents have for 46 years exercised such control, and openly asserted its exclusive right to do so; that the
courts have refused to compel them to comply with the acts of the legislature; that this court held in Weinberg v. Regents, 97 Mich. 246, 56 N. W.
608, that they were a constitutional body, upon whom was conferred this
exclusive control; and in the face of this plain constitutional provision,—
this court is now asked to hold that the regents are mere ministerial officers,
endowed with the sole power to register the will of the legislature, and to
supervise such branches and departments as any legislature may see fit to
provide for. By the power claimed, the legislature may completely dis-
member the university, and remove every vestige of it from the city of Ann
Arbor. It is no argument to say that there is no danger of such a result. The
question is one of power, and who shall say that such a result may not follow? The legislature did once enact that there should be a branch of the university in every judicial circuit. If the regents comply with the present act,
the next legislature may repeal it, and restore that department to the university at Ann Arbor, or place it elsewhere. Some legislatures have attached
conditions, and they have the undoubted right to do so, to appropriations
for the support of the university, and a subsequent legislature has removed
the conditions. Some legislatures have attached to appropriations the condition for the establishment of a homeopathic professorship in the old medical
department. Other legislatures have refused to attach any such condition.
What permanency would there be in an institution thus subject to the
caprice and will of every legislature? Under this power, the legislature could
remove the law department from the university at Ann Arbor to Detroit,
and provide that the law library, to which one citizen of Michigan has
donated $20,000, could also be removed. * * * It appears to us impossible
that such a power was contemplated. Furthermore, it renders nugatory the
express provision of the constitution that "the regents shall have the direction and control of all expenditures from the university interest fund." It is
significant that, at the time of the adoption of the constitution, this fund
constituted the sole support of the university, aside from fees which might
be received from students. The state had made no appropriations for its
support, and there is nothing to indicate that any such appropriations were
contemplated. It is unnecessary to argue that the above provision means
what it says, and that it takes away from the legislature all control over the
income from that fund. The power therein conferred would be without
force or effect if the legislature could control these expenditures by dictating what departments of learning the regents shall establish, and in what

places they shall be located. Neither does it need any argument to show that the power contended for would take away from the regents the control and direction of the expenditures from the fund. The power to control these expenditures cannot be exercised directly or indirectly by the legislature. It is vested in the board of regents in absolute and unqualified terms. This act, in express terms, prohibits the regents from using any of this fund to support a homeopathic department at the university of Ann Arbor, since it prohibits them from maintaining such a department there. This power cannot be sustained without overruling the case of Weinberg v. Regents. The basis of the majority opinion in that case is that the board of regents is a constitutional body, charged by the constitution with the entire control of that institution. The result could not have been reached upon any other basis. It was held not to be a state institution under the control and management of the legislature, as were the other corporations enumerated in the statute then under discussion. We there said: "Under the constitution, the state cannot control the regents. It cannot add to or take away from its property without the consent of the regents." We might with propriety rest our decision upon that case, and should be disposed to do so were it not for the urgent contention of the counsel on the part of the relator that that case does not apply. We are therefore constrained to state some further reasons to show that the legislature has no control over the university or the board of regents.

The board of regents and the legislature derive their power from the same supreme authority, namely, the constitution. In so far as the powers of each are defined by that instrument, limitations are imposed, and a direct power conferred upon one necessarily excludes its existence in the other, in the absence of language showing the contrary intent. Neither the university nor the board of regents is mentioned in article 4, which defines the powers and duties of the legislature; nor in the article relating to the university and the board of regents is there any language which can be construed into conferring upon or reserving any control over that institution in the legislature. They are separate and distinct constitutional bodies, with the powers of the regents defined. By no rule of construction can it be held that either can encroach upon or exercise the powers conferred upon the other.

The board of regents is the only corporation provided for in the constitution whose powers are defined therein. In every other corporation provided for in the constitution it is expressly provided that its powers shall be such as the legislature shall give. * * *

Thus in every case except that of the regents the constitution carefully and expressly reposes in the legislature the power to legislate and to control and define the duties of those corporations and officers. Can it be held that the framers of the constitution, and the people, in adopting it, had no purpose in conferring this power, viz. the "general supervision," upon the regents in the one instance, and in restricting it in the others? No other conclusion, in my judgment, is possible than that the intention was to place this institution in the direct and exclusive control of the people themselves, through a constitutional body elected by them. As already shown, the maintenance of this power in the legislature would give to it the sole control and general supervision of the institution, and make the regents merely ministerial officers, with no other power than to carry into effect the general supervision which the legislature may see fit to exercise, or, in other words, to register its will. We do not think the constitution can bear that construction. The writ is denied.

REGENTS v. MICHIGAN
Michigan Court of Appeals
47 Mich. App. 23 (1973)

Before: McGREGOR, P. J., and BRONSON and TARGONSKI, JJ....

This appeal results from a three-way struggle on the part of several governmental titans—the major universities, the State Legislature, and the State Board of Education—for the power effectively to control and direct the future course of higher education within this state....

Having determined that this matter is ripe for judicial determination, the first substantive issue is whether the trial court erred in ruling that certain sections of 1971 PA 122 unconstitutionally impinged upon the authority granted to plaintiffs by Const 1963, art 8, §5....

Of particular relevance in this case is Const 1963, art 8, §4, which provides as follows:

"Sec. 4. The legislature shall appropriate moneys to maintain the University of Michigan, Michigan State University, Wayne State University, Eastern Michigan University, Michigan College of Science and Technology, Central Michigan University, Northern Michigan University, Western Michigan University, Ferris Institute, Grand Valley State College, by whatever names such institutions may hereafter be known, and other institutions of higher education established by law. The legislature shall be given an annual accounting of all income and expenditures by each of these educational institutions. Formal sessions of governing boards of such institutions shall be open to the public."

Also germane to the instant case is Const 1963, art 8, §5, which states in pertinent part:

"Sec. 5. The regents of the University of Michigan and their successors in office shall constitute a body corporate known as the Regents of the University of Michigan; the trustees of Michigan State University and their successors in office shall constitute a body corporate known as the Board of Trustees of Michigan State University; the governors of Wayne State University and their successors in office shall constitute a body corporate known as the Board of Governors of Wayne State University. *Each board shall have general supervision of its institution and the control and direction of all expenditures from the institution's funds.*" (Emphasis added.)

The emphasized portion of the last-quoted excerpt constitutes the crux of the present dispute, which in its simplest terms involves a struggle between plaintiffs and the Legislature, regarding the extent to which the Legislature may place controls upon the spending of its appropriations to plaintiffs.

The nature and extent of proper legislative conditions upon the spending of appropriations made to the governing boards of plaintiff universities has long been a delicate problem which has engendered a considerable amount of litigation over the years in this jurisdiction. At issue is, of course, nothing less than the reconciling of the Legislature's recognized general prerogative to raise and to spend tax monies, with the equally important prerogative of the governing boards of plaintiff universities to control and direct the expenditure of funds appropriated to them by the Legislature. The complex question of defining the proper limits of the Legislature's power to condition the spending by university governing entities of appropriations made to the universities by the Legislature has been well stated in 55 Mich L Rev 728, 729-730 (1957) as follows:

> "While it must be recognized that the legislature's power to make appropriations to a constitutional university does not include and is separate from the power to control the affairs of such a university, the legislature can within reason attach conditions to its university appropriations. If a constitutional university accepts such conditioned funds, it is then bound by the conditions. There are not many decisions in this area, however, so the line between conditions the legislature can validly attach and those it cannot has not been drawn in a distinct fashion. Conditions which require the university to follow prescribed business and accounting procedures have generally been found to be valid. The courts have also sustained conditions which require, on penalty of losing part of the appropriation, annual reports to the governor, and fair and equitable distribution of an appropriation among the departments of the university or maintenance of university departments. It has also been held that the legislature can properly make non-teaching employees subject to the state's workmen's compensation law, and can require loyalty oaths by the teachers. On the other side of the line, a condition that the university move a certain department of the school has been held to be invalidly attached, and an attempt to limit the amount of the funds that can be spent for a given department is likewise an invalid condition. It is clear that limits should be placed on the use of the conditioned appropriation, for without such limits the legislature could use the conditioned appropriation to strip the university of its constitutional authority.". . . .

These opinions of the Attorney General indicate that *Board of Agriculture, supra,* has been interpreted as greatly restricting the permissible scope of legislative conditions vis-a-vis university appropriations. . . .

It is with this background that we examine the various sections of 1971 PA 122 which were declared unconstitutional by the trial court:

A.   Sections 16, 18 and 20, all of which were ruled invalid by the court, provide as follows:

"Sec. 16. No part of any appropriation made by this act may be used for the payment of any salary or wages to any faculty member or other employee or for the education of students convicted of the offense of interference with normal operations of any public institution of higher education as described in Act No. 26 of the Public Acts of 1970, being sections 752.581 to 752.583 of the Compiled Laws of 1948.

"Sec. 18. It is a condition of this appropriation that the net general fund subsidy appropriated herein to each institution of higher education may not be used to pay the cost of instruction for any student who wilfully damages university property as determined either by university officials or by the courts.

"Sec. 20. It is a condition of this appropriation that none of the appropriations contained in this act shall be used for the construction of buildings or operation of institutions of higher education not expressly authorized in section 1. No contract shall be let for construction of any self-liquidating project at any of the state supported institutions of higher education without first submitting to the appropriate legislative committees, schedules for the liquidation of the debt for the construction and operation of such project. Funds appropriated herein to each institution of higher education may not be used to pay for the construction, maintenance or operation of any self-liquidating projects."

A careful reading of the above sections reveals that the Legislature is attempting to control the internal operations of universities by dictating how the funds appropriated may be spent by the board of regents, governors, or trustees, as the case may be. Such control is clearly beyond the power of the Legislature. Const. 1963, art 8, §5 clearly vests the power to control and direct the expenditure of their institutional funds.

"Each board shall have general supervision of its institution and the control and direction of all expenditures from the institution's funds."

In *Sterling v Regents of University of Michigan*, 110 Mich 369, 381 (1896), the Court stated that the Constitution gave the regents the power to direct and control all expenditures of university funds. They then held further:

"The power therein conferred would be without force or effect if the legislature could control these expenditures by dictating what departments of learning the regents shall establish, and in what places they shall be located. *Neither does it need any argu-*

ment to show that the power contended for would take away from the regents the control and direction of the expenditures from the fund. The power to control these expenditures cannot be exercised directly or indirectly by the legislature. It is vested in the board of regents in absolute and unqualified terms." (Emphasis added.) . . .

Again, in *State Board of Agriculture v Auditor General*, 226 Mich 417, 424 (1924), the Court emphatically held that

" * * * the Constitution gave the regents the *absolute management* of the University, and the *exclusive control* of all funds received for its use." (Emphasis added.)

The trial court was corrected in ruling that §§16, 18 and 20 are invalid.

Sections 13 and 19 of 1971 PA 122, both of which were ruled invalid by the trial court, provide as follows:

"Sec. 13. It is a condition of this appropriation that no college or university having an enrollment of out of state students in excess of 20% of their total enrollment shall increase their enrollment of out of state students in either actual number or percentage over the actual numbers and percentages that were enrolled in the 1970-71 school year.

"Further it is the intent of the legislature that an out of state student shall pay a student fee equal to approximately 75% of the cost of instruction at the respective institution of higher education."

"Sec. 19. It is a condition of appropriation that each full time faculty member who is paid wholly from the line item instruction will teach as a part of his regular load a minimum of not less than 12 credit hours or 360 student credit hours or a combination of 18 credit or laboratory contact hours at developing colleges and universities, regional colleges and universities, and an average of 10 credit hours or 300 student credit hours or a combination of 15 credit or laboratory contact hours at graduate institutions. The above calculations on a semester basis will apply to institutions on a quarter or trimester basis equivalently. Any such faculty member who is paid partly from state funds appropriated herein and partly from funds derived from other sources shall teach a number of classroom hours in proportion to the salary paid from state funds appropriated herein."

In discussing § 13, defendants readily admit that plaintiffs "possess the constitutional authority to determine both how many out-of-state students will be enrolled and the tuition or student fee rates for such students at their respective institutions."

In rejecting both §§13 and 19 as unconstitutional, the trial court stated:

"The right to determine the number of out-of-state student enrollments, to set the fees to be charged such students, and to prescribe the minimum number of classroom hours to be taught by the faculty are matters solely within the exclusive authority of the plaintiffs. It cannot seriously be contended that such matters do not relate to the general supervision of the internal operations of plaintiffs' respective institutions, and the state-defendant admits as much in its brief * * * . By attaching these conditions the legislature is requiring plaintiffs to abdicate their constitutional right and duty to supervise their respective institutions. This court, therefore, declares sections 13 and 19 of 1971 PA 122 to be unconstitutional under Const 1963, art 8, §5."

In *Board of Agriculture v Auditor General, supra*, p 425, the Court held:
" * * * in order to avail itself of the money appropriated,"
it is not necessary that the governing board of a university
" * * * turn over to the legislature management and control of the college, or of any of its activities".

The clear intent of §§13 and 19, 1971 PA 122 was to assert control over the internal management of the affairs of the university. As such, the trial court correctly held that those sections were invalid under Const 1963, art 8, §5.

Section 26, also invalidated by the trial court, reads as follows:
"Sec. 26. If revenue from tuition and student fees excluding self-liquidating or activity fees exceeds in the aggregate the amount reported by the institutions of higher education in their notification of April 15, 1971 for Michigan resident students as a result of an increase in student fees or tuition the general fund subsidy appropriated for the support of that branch or institution of higher education shall automatically be reduced by the amount by which such revenue exceeds the amount reported. Each institution of higher education shall certify to the legislature not later than April 15, 1972 the schedule of tuition and student fees applicable to Michigan resident students for the fiscal year 1972-73.

"In computing student fees the revenue figures were derived according to the following schedule:

Rate Per Semester Hour		Rate Per Quarter Hour		Institution
Under-Graduate	Graduate	Under-Graduate	Graduate	Graduate
$21.00	$28.00	$14.00	$18.66	Michigan State University University of Michigan Wayne State University"

The crucial problem which must be resolved in analyzing §26 is whether or not said section constitutes a de facto attempt by the Legislature to establish tuition rates at plaintiff universities. All parties to this action explicitly concede that the power to establish tuition rates reposes exclusively in plaintiffs and not in the Legislature. Defendants admit in their brief that "it must first be recognized that [plaintiffs] herein, not the Legislature, possess the constitutional authority to establish tuition rates."

The trial judge discussed paragraph 1 of § 26 as follows:

"Section 26 provides that the general appropriation will 'automatically be reduced' by an amount equal to any monies received by plaintiffs as a result of an increase in student fees or tuition above that reported on April 15, 1971. The effect of such a provision is to prohibit the plaintiffs from increasing their revenues by increasing tuition rates and student fees, because any increase by the plaintiffs will automatically result in an equal decrease in funds already appropriated."

The lower court then concluded:

"Since the legislature could not directly prohibit plaintiffs from increasing their tuition rates or student fees, it cannot do so indirectly by deducting any increases from the funds appropriated to the plaintiffs. Further, as was previously stated, once the legislature makes a general appropriation to plaintiffs it becomes the property of the plaintiffs and passes beyond the control of the legislature.

"The court, therefore, holds that portion of section 26 which automatically reduces the appropriations to be unconstitutional in violation of Const 1963, art 8, § 5."

Defendants point out that the monies appropriated by 1971 PA 122 are to be disbursed by warrants issued from the State Treasury in 12 monthly installments. Defendants then aver that since the appropriated funds are to be disbursed on the "installment plan" the power over said funds has not passed out of the control of the Legislature prior to the time that the monies are actually distributed by the State Treasurer; hence, according to defendants, the appropriated funds are validly subject to legislative diminution via paragraph 1 of § 26, should plaintiffs subsequently increase their student fees or tuition rates.

However, defendants' contention is without merit. The appropriation vests in the recipient when made and thus precludes subsequent diminution by the Legislature. *Weinberg v Regents of the Univ of Mich, supra*, p 254.

Quite aside from the question as to when an appropriation vests in its recipient, paragraph 1 of § 26 appears to be so inextricably bound up with the second paragraph of § 26 and thus so contributes to the de facto legislative establishment of tuition fees at plaintiff universities that it seems invalid on this basis alone. The net effect of § 26 cannot be properly understood apart from an understanding of the interplay between paragraphs 1 and 2 of said section. As previously stated, paragraph 1 establishes an effective maximum tuition rate by providing that any tuition increase subsequent to the date of the appropriation simply decreases said appropriation by an amount equivalent to the net revenue resulting from the tuition increase. Paragraph 2 on the other hand, establishes an effective minimum tuition rate of $21.00 per undergraduate semester hour at plaintiff universities. The operation of paragraph 2 was lucidly explained by the trial judge in his written opinion as follows:

"Section 26 further establishes a schedule of student fees which was utilized by the legislature for the fiscal year 1971-72 in deriving the revenue figures of plaintiffs' institutions. The plaintiffs contend that this provision requires the universities to establish student fees in accordance with the amounts shown in the schedule. The State-defendant, upon the affidavit of the Director of the Bureau of Programs and Budget, contends that the section does not purport to establish the student fee rates to be actually charged by the plaintiffs, but only prescribe the rates to be included in the plaintiffs' budget requests.

"The section itself states only that 'In computing student fees the revenue figures were derived according to the following schedule.' It does not expressly require the plaintiffs to charge the fees listed, nor does it expressly provide for any reduction in appropriations if the plaintiffs charge greater or lesser fees. However, by using such a schedule to compute the revenue figures of the plaintiffs' institutions, the legislature is, in effect, prescribing a minimum student fee to be charged by each institution. For example, for each of the plaintiffs' institutions the legislature has established an undergraduate student fee of $21.00 per semester hour. By multiplying the number of undergraduates by $21.00 per each semester hour taken, the legislature derives the total undergraduate student fees received by the institution. This figure is then subtracted, along with any other income received by the institution, from the institution's gross operating expenses in order to arrive at the net general fund to be appropriated to maintain the institution.

"Thus, it can be seen that the fee schedule is more than a mere accounting procedure. If the university is actually charging a student fee of $20.00 per semester hour the legislature will still compute its revenue on the basis of $21.00 per semester hour. The legislature will be crediting the university with more income than it is actually receiving, and the net effect will be a reduction in state appropriations. The fee schedule, therefore, establishes a minimum rate to be charged by the plaintiffs, for if the plaintiffs charge their students less, they will automatically be reducing their net state appropriations. Further, if the plaintiffs charged a greater fee than that listed in the schedule the first provision of section 26 would automatically reduce the appropriations already made by the amount of the increase. Thus, by establishing both the maximum and minimum student fee the legislature has directly prescribed the exact student fee to be charged by the plaintiffs."

Since under §26 plaintiffs can in no way increase their revenues by raising the tuition rate subsequent to the legislative appropriation, and since plaintiffs in effect cannot decrease their tuition rate below the figure utilized by the Legislature in computing the appropriation, §26 comprises an ingenious method by which the Legislature seeks to regulate university tuition rates and thus attempts to indirectly what it admittedly cannot do directly. Thus, the trial court correctly declared §26 to be an unconstitutional infringement of plaintiffs' exclusive authority to establish tuition rates.

Lastly, we examine the claim made by the Michigan State Board of Education, that they have authority over the governing boards of the state universities.

The State Board of Education was established as a constitutional body corporate by Article VIII, §3, of the Michigan Constitution of 1963, which provides in part:

"Leadership and general supervision over all public education, including adult education and instructional programs in state institutions, except as to institutions of higher education granting baccalaureate degrees, is vested in a state board of education. It shall serve as the general planning and coordinating body for all public education, including higher education, and shall advise the legislature as to the financial requirements in connection therewith."

Section 3, Article VIII, Constitution of 1963, after providing for the state board, the superintendent of public instruction, and the election of its members, concludes with the following clear and unambiguous language:

"The power of the boards of institutions of higher education provided in this constitution to supervise their respective institutions and control and direct the expenditure of the institutions' funds shall not be limited by this section." . . .

Here, the straightforward language of this sentence has a plain meaning, namely, that whatever may be the role of the board in serving as a general planning and coordinating body, that role was not to limit, interfere, or in any way diminish the "power" of the universities' boards of control "to supervise their respective institutions and control and direct the expenditure of the institutions' funds". The authority claimed by the State Board of Education is not granted them by the Constitution.

We further note that the limitation on the authority of the board with respect to the appellee institutions was explained by the Constitutional Convention in its "Address to the People" as follows:

"The concluding paragraph of [Article VIII, Section 3] preserves for boards of institutions of higher education the power to supervise their respective institutions and control and direct the expenditures of their funds *as at present.*" (Emphasis added.)

It is obvious that what the members of the Constitutional Convention must have had in mind was the long series of Supreme Court decisions and Attorney General opinions, discussed above, which established the independent authority of the universities to be free from legislative interference in the operation of their respective institutions.

Thus, it was never contemplated by the drafters of the Constitution of 1963 that the state board would have any authority over the constitutionally sanctioned governing boards of the universities.

The judgment of the trial court is affirmed. No costs, a public question is involved.

All concurred.

NOTE

The Appeals Court decision in Regents of the University of Michigan v. State was affirmed at 235 N.W.2d 1 (1975), with the modification that the universities must submit debt liquidation schedules for self-liquidating debts to the legislature because a mere reporting measure does not violate the constitution, and that universities must submit proposed programs and financial requirements to the State Board of Education so the Board may better carry out its advisory duties. In a case decided in 1973, the Supreme Court of Michigan, following Branum v. State of Michigan and Board of Regents of the University of Michigan, 145 N.W.2d 860 (1966), held that the Board of Regents was subject to the Public Employers Relations Act although the scope of bargaining was deemed to be limited by the unique nature of the University. Regents of the University of Michigan v. Michigan Employment Relations Commission, 204 N.W.2d 218 (1973).

For a discussion of the uses of constitutional autonomy in relation to state governing boards of higher education, see Beckham, *Reasonable Independence for Public Higher Education: Legal Implications of Constitutionally Autonomous Status*, 7 Journal of Law and Education 177 (1978). *See also* Horowitz, *The Autonomy of the University of California Under the State Constitution*, 25 U.C.L.A. L. Rev. 23 (1977).

UNIVERSITY OF UTAH v. BOARD OF EXAMINERS OF STATE OF UTAH

Supreme Court of Utah

295 P.2d 348 (1956)

WORTHEN, Justice.

This is an appeal from a declaratory judgment holding that Article X, Section 4 of the Utah Constitution establishes the University as a constitutional corporation free from the control of the Legislature, administrative bodies, commissions and agencies and officers of the State.

The action was instituted by the University of Utah, acting through its Board of Regents, against the named defendants alleging that said defendants, pursuant to claimed legislative and constitutional mandate, asserted the legal right to exercise control over and management of the University in derogation of the claimed rights of the University and its Board of Regents granted by Article X, Section 4 of the Constitution of Utah.
* * *

The questions raised as to control and supervision of certain funds and as to the claimed curtailment of powers of the University will be resolved by our construction of Article X, Section 4 of the Constitution of Utah which provides:

> "The location and establishment by existing laws of the University of Utah, and the Agricultural College are hereby confirmed, and all the rights, immunities, franchises and endowments heretofore granted or conferred, are hereby perpetuated unto said University and Agricultural College respectively." . . . .

The defendants pray that a declaratory judgment be entered declaring that the University is a state institution subject to and bound by the laws of Utah from time to time enacted.

The issues were submitted to the court upon stipulations of fact, and the trial court decreed that the University is a constitutionally confirmed body corporate, perpetually vested with all the rights, immunities, franchises and endowments of the territorial institution, beyond the power of the Legislature, all administrative bodies, commissions, agencies, and officers of the State of Utah to infringe upon, curtail, abrogate, interfere with or obstruct the enjoyment of the same, or otherwise, or at all, assume, or exercise any jurisdiction over the affairs of the University of Utah, and the powers of its Board of Regents, except for the general control and supervision conceded by the University to the State Board of Education.

The trial court declared unconstitutional certain statutes which treated the University as other state institutions, requiring preaudit of bills, submission of work programs and deposit of funds into the State Treasury, including University funds from appropriations and dedicated credits.

What is the effect of the quoted section on the power of the Legislature to act respecting the University?

We must determine what rights, immunities, franchises and endowments are perpetuated unto the University by Article X, Section 4 of the Constitution. In order to answer this question, resort must be made to territorial laws fixing the rights and status of the University at the time the Constitution was adopted.

That the issues and questions presented may be understood, it is deemed advisable to set out the history of the plaintiff University in full detail.

1. The University of the State of Deseret was instituted and incorporated by an ordinance of the State of Deseret approved February 28, 1850, reading as follows:

> "Sec. 1. Be it ordained by the General Assembly of the State of Deseret: That a University is hereby instituted and incorporated, located at Great Salt Lake City, by the name and title of the University of the State of Deseret. * * *

2. The University was constituted a corporation de jure by the joint resolution legalizing the laws of the Provisional Government of the State of Deseret approved October 4, 1851, by the Legislative Assembly of the Territory of Utah as follows:

"*Resolved, by the Legislative Assembly of the Territory of Utah,* That the laws heretofore passed by the provisional government of the State of Deseret, and which do not *conflict with the "Organic Act,'* of said Territory, be, and the same are hereby declared to be legal, and in full force and virtue, and shall so remain until *superseded by the action of the Legislative Assembly of the Territory of Utah.*

"Approved October 4, 1851." (Emphasis added.)

3.   Its name was changed to the University of Utah by Ch. IX, Laws of Utah 1892, an act of the territorial legislature, approved February 17, 1892, as follows: * * *

"Section 1. The name of the University organized under an act approved February 28th 1850, and laws amendatory of and supplementary to said act, shall hereafter be 'University of Utah,' and with and by said name it is constituted and continued a body corporate, with perpetual succession, and it may have and use a corporate seal, and by said name sue and be sued, and contract and be contracted with. It is vested with all the *property*, credits, effects and franchises, and is subject to all the contracts, obligations and liabilities of the existing corporation.

"It may take and hold to its use by purchase, gift, devise or bequest, real and personal property and moneys, credits and effects, and by sale or exchange receive and use the proceeds of property not applicable to its uses in specie. It shall *be deemed a public corporation and be subject to the laws of Utah, from time to time enacted*, relating to its purposes and government, and its property, credits and effects shall be exempt from all taxes and assessments. * * *

Respondent contends that the language constituting the University a body corporate with perpetual succession, and declaring that it should be deemed a public corporation, were rights perpetuated by the Constitution, but that the words: *"and be subject to the laws of Utah, from time to time enacted, relating to its purposes and government"* were not a part of any right, immunity, franchise or endowment and were not perpetuated by the Constitution.

Appellants contend that the language: *"and be subject to the laws of Utah,* from time to time enacted, relating to its purposes and government," conditions every right, immunity, franchise and endowment mentioned in Chapter IX, Laws of 1892, and that the words are part and parcel of the rights.

Respondent urges that the words: "and be subject to the laws of Utah, from time to time enacted, relating to its purposes and government," are of no significance since the Legislative Assembly had the right to amend or repeal the *corporate* privileges and other rights granted without an express reservation of that right. The question then arises, why did the 1892 Legislative Assembly use the quoted language if it was unnecessary? We must assume that the Assembly knew that it was empowered to amend or repeal the act upon which respondent relies for its rights. We believe that the language declaring that the University should be subject to the laws of Utah from time to time enacted was used in Section 1 for the purpose of doing what appears to have been intended, to-wit: To make the University subject to the laws of Utah from time to time enacted. * * *

The following statement appears in respondent's brief: "The following institutions are constitutional corporations: University of Michigan; Michigan State College of Agriculture and Applied Science; University of Minnesota; University of Colorado; University of Idaho; Oklahoma Agricultural and Mechanical College; University of California; University of Georgia; and University of Utah."

The constitutions of the states wherein said institutions are located, respecting said universities and colleges, are different in form and substance from Article X, Section 4, Utah Constitution, and each carries specific provisions granting control and management of the university to the regents or vesting the lands granted by Congress or the proceeds thereof and other donations in the university.

Michigan Constitution 1850, Article 13, Section 8, provides: "The board of regents shall have the general supervision of the university, and the direction and control of all expenditures from the university interest fund."

Michigan Constitution of 1908, Article 11, Section 8—"The board shall have the general supervision of the college, and the direction and control of all agricultural college funds; and shall perform such other duties as may be prescribed by law."

Minnesota Constitution, Article VIII, Section 4, provides: "and all lands which may be granted hereafter by Congress, or other donations for said university purposes, shall vest in the institution referred to in this section."

Colorado Constitution, Article IX, Section 14, provides: "The board of regents shall have the general supervision of the university, and the exclusive control and direction of all funds of, and appropriations to, the university."

Idaho Constitution, Article IX, Section 10—(Regents were given "custody of the books, records, buildings and other property" and control over tax funds "subject to the orders of the Board of Regents.")

Oklahoma Constitution 1907, Article 6, Section 31—"A Board of Agriculture is hereby created to be composed of eleven members, all of whom shall be farmers * * * . Said Board shall be maintained as a part of the State government, and shall have jurisdiction over all matters affecting animal industry and animal quarantine regulations, and shall be the Board of Regents of all State Agricultural and Mechanical Colleges, and shall discharge such other duties and receive such compensation as may be provided by law."

California Constitution 1879, Article IX, Section 9—"The University of California shall constitute a public trust, to be administered by the existing corporation known as 'the Regents of the University of California,' *with full powers of organization and government*, subject only to such legislative control as may be necessary to insure compliance with the terms of the endowments of the university and the security of its funds. * * * *Said corporation shall be vested with the legal title and the management and disposition of the property* of the university and of property held for its benefit * * *." (As amended November 5, 1918.) (Emphasis added.)

Georgia Constitution, Article VIII, Section 4, Par. 1—"There shall be a Board of Regents of the University System of Georgia, and the government, control, and management of the University System of Georgia and all of its institutions in said system shall be vested in said Board of Regents of the University System of Georgia. * * *"

It should be further observed that the Michigan Constitution of 1850, Article 13, Section 6, provided for the election of the Regents of the University of Michigan; and that the Michigan Constitution of 1908, Article 11, Section 7, provided for the election of the State Board of Agriculture; and the Constitution of Colorado, Article IX, Section 12, provides for the election of the Regents of the University of Colorado, thus further distinguishing those institutions from the University of Utah, whose Regents are appointed by the Governor.

We are constrained to the view that the University of Utah is not brought into the group of constitutional corporations mentioned by respondent when there exists such differences between the Utah Constitution and the constitutional provisions affecting the other universities mentioned.

If the framers of the Utah Constitution had intended to create the University of Utah a constitutional corporation, completely autonomous and free from legislative control, it is difficult to understand why language such as was used in the constitutions of Michigan, Minnesota and the other constitutions referred to was not used.

Had the framers of the Utah Constitution added after "respectively" in Article X, Section 4: The Board of Regents of the University of Utah shall have general supervision of the University and the direction and control of all expenditures from the University Interest Fund, or All lands which may be granted hereafter by Congress, or other donations for said University purposes, shall vest in the University of Utah, we would be presented with language supporting respondent's argument.

That the framers of the Utah Constitution did not adopt language similar to the constitutions of Minnesota and Idaho, even though the Convention had before it the constitutions of those states is evidence that a different result was intended. Respondent relies heavily on the University of Michigan as supporting the argument for like result in the instant case. The framers of the Utah Constitution did not adopt language similar to that found in the Michigan Constitution, even though that language had been held by the Michigan court in 1893 to constitute the University of Michigan a constitutional corporation free from legislative control.

We are, therefore, of the opinion that the language used in Article X, Section 4, Constitution of Utah, is not so clear that it can be said that it created the University a constitutional corporation completely freed from legislative control. Rather, we are inclined to the view that the language failed to create the University a constitutional corporation free from legislative control. But if we accept the view that there is present some ambiguity and some justification for diverse opinions, we may look to other sources of interpretation to clarify the instrument. . . .

There is abundant contemporaneous construction of Article X, Section 4, inconsistent with or in direct contradiction of the position of the University. In fact, as heretofore observed, action was brought to have the court declare that substantial legislation enacted since statehood and to which there has been no objection by the University, be declared beyond the power of the Legislature to enact, notwithstanding the University has acquiesced for over 50 years with certain legislation now most criticized and objected to. * * *

For over 50 years the University has never raised the point of independent control, but during the period has accepted the declaration contained in Section 1, Chapter 83, Laws of 1896, that it "should be subject to the laws of this State" and has acquiesced in and complied with the legislative enactments relating to its purposes and government. * * *

Many statutes have been passed since statehood restricting the giving of certain courses of study and mandating the giving of others. By Chapter 133, Laws of 1905, the University was prohibited from including in its courses agriculture, horticulture, animal industry, veterinary science, domestic science and art (except in connection with the normal course). In 1921 c. 116, the University was prohibited from awarding degrees in domestic science or art. In 1923, c. 4, the University was required to give instruction in the Constitution of the United States. * * *

Chapter 65, Laws of Utah 1897 at page 248 provides for appropriations for University as follows:

"Appropriations

"To the University of Utah:

"For general maintenance for the two academic years ending June 30, 1899, or so much thereof as may be necessary $73,000.00

"*Provided,* that no officer or member of the faculty of said University, for all service *rendered to the State* during the term herein named shall be paid any salary in excess of $2,500.00 per annum." * * *

The Regents accepted the appropriation and, we may assume, expended it without protest. No objection was made that the Legislature *was powerless* to tell the Regents what salaries might be paid. * * *

The Regents, officials and personnel of the University in the early years after statehood were indeed grateful for the beneficence of those early legislatures, during which time appropriations for buildings, new schools and enlarged teaching staffs were made, without which the University would have failed to attain the eminence it now enjoys. The University enjoyed and thrived on its dependence on the Legislature, but lately it seeks a change. It chooses to declare that independence, which the institution never has had, and which has never, prior to the bringing of this action, been asserted. After these 50 years of acquiescence it is difficult to understand this sudden quest for independent control.

The people of Utah are proud of the great progress made by the University; its history and attainment are a glowing tribute to the Regents, the Presidents and the Faculties that have guided it along its glorious course as well as to its donors and the 30 legislatures that have furnished the funds to assure its growth. Nor is there anything made to appear which should cause alarm or concern to any. It must be conceded that had its Regents in those early years asserted its independence from the Legislature, it is doubtful that it would have attained a stature which would induce it to declare its independence. * * *

Let us consider the result were we to accept respondent's contention. The University contends and the trial court held that the State of Utah, including the Legislature, Board of Examiners, Finance Department and the other named defendants have no control, check or audit of the money used by the University, whether appropriated funds or dedicated funds; that the University is entitled to keep the same in its own bank and expend it free from any review or control, except post audit (but post audits are valuable only as a matter of history); that the Regents of the University may authorize out of state travel for University employees and pay the same without previous approval therefor by the Board of Examiners (yet the Governor, Secretary of State, Attorney General and all other state officers must obtain such previous approval); that the University is not subject to laws enacted by the Legislature, and the statutes so declaring are unconstitutional; that the University is authorized to draw from the Treasurer of the State of Utah quarter yearly in advance its biennial legislative appropriations for maintenance, whereas, all other legislative appropriations may be procured only after pre-audit and approval of some or all of the defendants; that the University may retain all unexpended surpluses from all funds, and that the Legislature has no power to order such surpluses closed out, and that any condition attached to appropriations to the University restricting the powers of the Board of Regents are unconstitutional and void; that the University is empowered to carry out its own building and expansion program without any control or supervision on the part of the State Building Board. In short, the University and its Board of Regents contend that they have been given a blank check enabling them to expend all funds without any semblance of supervision or control.

Article X, Section 1 of our Constitution provides:

"The Legislature shall provide for the establishment and *maintenance* of a uniform system of public schools, which shall be open to all children of the State, and be free from sectarian control." (Emphasis added.)

Article X, Section 2 of our Constitution declares:

"The public school system shall include kindergarten schools; common schools, consisting of primary and grammar grades; high schools, an agricultural college; a university, and such other schools as the Legislature may establish. The common schools shall be free. The other departments of the system shall be supported as provided by law. * * *"

Would it be contended by the University that under Article X, Section 1 it might compel the Legislature to appropriate money the University considers essential? Is it contended that the demands of the University are not subject to constitutional debt limits? If so, respondent would have the power to destroy the solvency of the State and all other institutions by demands beyond the power of the State to meet.

Article X, Section 5 provides:

"The proceeds of the sale of lands reserved by an Act of Congress, approved February 21st, 1855, for the establishment of the University of Utah, and of all the lands granted by an Act of Congress, approved July 16th, 1894, shall constitute permanent funds, to be safely invested and held by the State; and the income thereof shall be used exclusively for the support and maintenance of the different institutions and colleges, respectively, in accordance with the requirements and conditions of said acts of Congress."

Article X, Section 7 of our Constitution declares:

"All public School Funds shall be guaranteed by the State against loss or diversion."

It is inconceivable that the framers of the Constitution in light of the provisions of Sections 1, 5 and 7 of Article X, and the provision as to debt limitations, intended to place the University above the only controls available for the people of this State as to the property, management and government of the University. We are unable to reconcile respondent's position that the University has a blank check as to all its funds with no pre-audit and no restraint under the provisions of the Constitution requiring the State to safely invest and hold the dedicated funds and making the State guarantor of the public school funds against loss or diversion. To hold that respondent has free and uncontrolled custody and use of its property and funds, while making the State guarantee said funds against loss or diversion is inconceivable. We believe that the framers of the Constitution intended no such result.

Appellants and respondent agree that the interpretation which we put on Article X, Section 4 will determine the other questions presented. It has not been urged by respondent that if the University is subject to legislative control that any of the enactments complained of are invalid. Respondent's objection is that the Legislature had no power to confer on the Boards, Commissions and Officers the authority to supervise and control the University. Since no complaint is made against the defendants named, except that the duties being performed by them are in violation of respondent's constitutional rights because the Legislature could not legally invest said defendant with authority to infringe upon the rights secured by the Constitution, it must follow that the objections of respondent as to the acts complained of must fall by reason of the conclusion reached herein; that the University is a public corporation not above the power of the Legislature to control, and is subject to the laws of this State from time to time enacted relating to its purposes and government.

The judgment is reversed and remanded with directions to set aside the judgment entered and to enter a declaratory judgment in favor of the defendants in accordance with the opinions herein expressed, the respective parties to bear their own costs.

NOTES

1. Using a similar rationale, the Utah Supreme Court later ruled that the Utah legislature could create a State Board of Higher Education, even though the Utah Constitution "vested" supervisory control in the existing State Board of Education. State Board of Education v. State Board of Higher Education, 29 Utah 2d 110, 505 P.2d 1193 (1973).

2. The Supreme Court of Louisiana, however, has given strong independent status to Louisiana State University in Roy v. Edwards, 294 So.2d 507 (La. 1974), in which the creation of a state-wide board was declared unconstitutional.

3. A flurry of activity over constitutional autonomy seems to have emerged in the great plains states in recent years. In 1972 the state of Montana, in a move apparently contradicting the national trend toward more accountability, decided to amend its state constitution to give its state university constitutional autonomy. (Art. X, §9), See Waldoch, Constitutional Control of the Montana University System: A Proposed Revision, 33 Mont. L. Rev. 76 (1971) and Schaefer, The Legal Status of the Montana University System under the New Montana Constitution, 35 Mont. L. Rev. 189 (1974). In the opposite direction, the Nebraska legislature is presently considering two bills which would extend unprecedented legislative control over academic program decisions in its public institutions of higher education as well as create a centralized state data bank (see Jacobson, Takeover in Nebraska? The Chronicle of Higher Education, April 10, 1978 at p. 3). If these bills pass they will undoubtedly be subject to constitutional challenge since the Nebraska Supreme Court handed down an opinion in 1977 strongly affirming the constitutional autonomy of the University of Nebraska. The Court said:

> The Legislature cannot use an appropriation bill to usurp the powers or duties of the Board of Regents and to give directions to the employees of the University. The general government of the University must remain vested in the Board of Regents. [Board of Regents of Univ. of Neb. v. Exon, 256 N.W. 2d 330 (Neb. 1977)]

4. Finally, in North Dakota the state supreme court faced the ultimate question of constitutional autonomy in Walker v. Link, 232 N.W.2d 823 (1975), and ruled that: "... [n]either the Legislature nor the people can, without a constitutional amendment, refuse to fund a constitutionally mandated function" in a suit challenging an attempted

suspension of the university's appropriation. Thus, even though constitutionally autonomous universities must continuously ask legislatures for appropriations, under *Walker v. Link*, a legislature may not refuse to appropriate funds for such an institution. If a legislature refused to appropriate funds, and was successfully challenged in court by the university, could the court establish the amount of the appropriation? How would the court determine such a figure?

5. Provisions in the new Alaska and Hawaii Constitutions also appear to create constitutional autonomy for the University of Hawaii and the University of Alaska. (Hawaii Const. Art. IX, Secs. 4, 5; Alaska Const. Art. VII, Sec. 3.) *See further* Op. Att'y Gen. Hawaii, 61-84, University of Alaska v. National Aircraft Leasing Ltd., 536 P.2d 121 (1975). Evidently other states are considering the idea as well. *See* Beckham, *Constitutionally Autonomous Higher Education Governance: A Proposed Amendment to the Florida Constitution*, 30 U. Florida L. Rev. 543 (1978).

Question: Should a state university desiring more autonomy attempt to gain it through amendment of its state constitution?

CHAPTER 4

PUBLIC UNIVERSITIES WITHOUT CONSTITUTIONAL STATUS

I. The University as a Public Corporation

A. *Introduction*

Although colleges formed in the early days of the republic were of a mixed nature, they generally evolved into private universities. After the Dartmouth College decision in 1819 it became harder to claim private status. Noting that *Dartmouth* established the binding and immutable nature of private college charters, legislatures began to retain the right to modify subsequently granted charters. Colleges so chartered then became public rather than private corporations, unless funding was clearly from private sources. *See* Lewis v. Whittle, 77 Va. 415 (1883).

A contemporary issue concerns the legal nature and powers of the originally private university which has been forced to turn to direct public funding and hence public control as in Trustees of Rutgers College in New Jersey v. Richman, 125 A.2d 10 (1956), discussed *infra* in Chapter 13. Often the modern transition from private to public university is no more clear than was the original evolution of private status for the colonial colleges. And a change in status often becomes apparent in a lawsuit. *Braden v. University of Pittsburgh*, in Chapter 2 and *Briscoe v. Rutgers* in this chapter illustrate this problem.

This chapter deals with the majority of public universities and colleges which do not have constitutional status. As each institution has a unique mission and sense of institutional personality, so each institution tends to have unique legal characteristics. For example, the University of Maryland, while not constitutionally autonomous, has statutory autonomy. *See* Chapter 14, Laws of Maryland, 1952; 41 Opinions of the Atty. General 250 (1956); Opinion of the Attorney General, October 26, 1978. The practical application of this autonomy has been primarily in the employment area.

Public post-secondary institutions may range from public corporations with substantial degrees of autonomy, to institutions which are merely one state agency among many, to locally controlled junior colleges which are essentially part of the public school system. Whether a public university is fiscally controlled in the same manner and degree as the state highway department may have a substantial impact on that institution's academic freedom. Most public universities are not regarded as synonomous with state administrative agencies, but the degree of control or autonomy varies and is manifested in different ways, all of which directly affect the institution's ability to make independent educational decisions.

B.   The Land Grant Universities

UNIVERSITY OF ILLINOIS v. BARRETT

Supreme Court of Illinois

382 ILL. 321 (1943)

MR. JUSTICE SMITH delivered the opinion of the court:

This is an original petition for *mandamus.* . . .

The decisive question is whether the Attorney General is, by virtue of his office, and in his official capacity, the sole legal advisor, counsel and attorney for the university and its Board of Trustees. The solution of this question involves a determination of the status of the university as a corporate entity and its relation to the State government, as well as the powers vested in the Attorney General by the constitution and laws of this State.

By an act of July 2, 1862, (12 Stat. 503; 7 U. S. C. A. sec. 301 *et seq.*) the Congress of the United States made certain land grants to the several States for the endowment, support and maintenance of at least one college in each State, where the leading object should be to teach such branches of learning as are related to agriculture and the mechanic arts. . . .

That it was the purpose and intention of the Congress that the title to the land granted should vest in the several States for the maintenance of such colleges is clear from the language used in section I of the act, which reads: "There is granted to the several States, for the purposes hereinafter mentioned in sections 302 and 308, inclusive, of this chapter, an amount of public land, to be apportioned to each State a quantity equal to thirty thousand acres for each Senator and Representative in Congress to which the States are respectively entitled by the apportionment under the census of 1860." . . . .

By subsequent legislation, Congress has made substantial annual appropriations for the more complete endowment and maintenance of colleges for the benefit of agriculture and the mechanic arts, established in accordance with the provisions of the act of July 2, 1862. These appropriations are also made to the State. 7 U. S. C. A. 322.

In compliance with these conditions the legislature on February 28, 1867, passed an act creating a corporation to be styled "The Board of Trustees of the Illinois Industrial University." Laws of 1867, p. 123; Ill. Rev. Stat. 1941, chap. 144, par. 22.

By section I of this act, a corporate entity was created and its powers defined, as follows: "That it shall be the duty of the Governor of this State within ten days from the passage of this act, to appoint five trustees, resident in each of the judicial grand divisions of this state, who, together with one additional trustee, resident in each of the congressional districts of this state, to be appointed in like manner, with their associates and successors, shall be a body corporate and politic to be styled 'The Board of Trustees of the Illinois Industrial University, and by that name and style shall have perpetual succession, have power to contract and be contracted with, to sue and be sued, to plead and be impleaded, to acquire, hold, and convey real and personal property; to have and use a common seal, and to alter the same at pleasure; to make and establish by-laws, and to alter or repeal the same as they shall deem necessary, for the management or government, in all its various departments and relations, of the Illinois Industrial University, for the organization and endowment of which provision is made by this act. . . .

By section 7 of the act, the powers of the trustees were set out in the following language: "The trustees shall have power to provide the requisite buildings, apparatus, and conveniences; to fix the rates for tuition; to appoint such professors and instructors, and to establish and provide for the management of such model farms, model art, and other departments and professorships, as may be required to teach, in the most thorough manner, such branches of learning as are related to agriculture and the mechanic arts, and military tactics, without excluding other scientific and classical studies. They may accept the endowments of voluntary professorships or departments in the University, from any person or persons or corporations who may proffer the same, and, at any regular meeting of the board, may prescribe rules and regulations in relation to such endowments and declare on what general principles they may be admitted." Ill. Rev. Stat. 1941, chap. 144, par. 28. . . .

By an act of June 19, 1885, the name of the corporation was changed to "University of Illinois." (Ill. Rev. Stat. 1941, chap. 144, par. 48.) By an act of June 15, 1887, it was provided that the trustees shall be elected from the State at large at regular general elections, instead of being appointed by the Governor, as provided in section I of the original act. Ill. Rev. Stat. 1941, chap. 144, par. 41.

Relators contend that the university is a legal entity separate and distinct from the State; that it is not an agency, a board, commission or department of the State government; that it is a creature of the legislature having a legal personality all its own, that it has the power to employ its own counsel as a necessary incident to its corporate life, implied in the power to sue and be sued, and to plead and be impleaded.

On the other hand, respondents contend that the university is an agency or instrumentality of the State; that its trustees are State officers; that its funds and property belong to the State; that the Attorney General is the sole legal representative of the State, its agents and instrumentalities, and that it can only be lawfully represented by the Attorney General, who is the chief law officer of the State and all its departments. . . .

In the briefs on both sides and in the arguments at the bar, extensive theories have been classically expounded, analytical of the character and corporate powers of the Universities of Oxford and Cambridge. Comparisons of the charters of these universities with the charter powers of the University of Illinois, are made and relied upon by both sides. These great institutions trace their origin back to mediaeval times. The genesis of most of their powers antedate their charters. They were acquired by prescription before their charters were granted. Both before and after their charters were issued they exercised sovereign powers, even as against the Crown.

The traditions of Oxford extend back to the dynasty of King John. It was not actually chartered as a corporate entity, however, until during the reign of Elizabeth in 1570. The University of Cambridge is also of ancient origin. It was the outgrowth of certain public schools established by the Monks in the vicinity of Cambridge in the 12th century. It was not chartered as a corporate entity until many years later. Each of these colleges passed its own laws, enacted its own statutes and elected its own executive and legislative departments. They also maintained their own courts. Their statutes were confirmed by Royal decree. Each was authorized to, and did, elect two members of the British Parliament. In certain fields within their territorial and ecclesiastical jurisdiction they administered both the civil and criminal laws. They possessed liberties *de Academia*. Lord Mansfield in *Rex v. Vice Chancellor*, 3 Burr. 1647, said: "But there is a vast deal of difference between a new charter granted to a new corporation, (who must take it as it is given,) and a new charter given to a corporation already in being, and acting either under a former charter or under prescriptive usage. The latter, a corporation already existing, are not obliged to accept the new charter *in toto*, and to receive either all or none of it: they may act partly under it, and partly under their old charter or prescription. Whatever might be the notion in former times, it is most certain now, 'That the corporations of the universities are lay-corporations: and that the Crown cannot take away from them any rights that have been formerly subsisting in them under old charters or prescriptive usage.' The validity of these new charters must turn upon the acceptance of the university. When Queen Elizabeth gave these statutes, the University of Cambridge was of ancient establishment, and had many prescriptive rights, as well as former charters of very old date. And there was no intention to alter and overturn their ancient constitution. These statutes undoubtedly meant to leave a vast deal upon the ancient constitution of the university; without repealing or abrogating their old established customs, rights, and privileges; nor could the university mean to accept them upon any such terms. Therefore I am clear, that the Statutes of Queen Elizabeth cannot be set up, to invalidate establishments subsisting long before she was born." See also Holdsworth, A History of English Law, vol. I, p. 165, and Willard's, The Royal Authority and the Early English Universities, p. 1.

In its corporate status and in its powers and privileges the University of Illinois is in no sense comparable to the Universities of Oxford and Cambridge. The issues here involved must be solved by an examination of the statute creating the University of Illinois, and the applicable decisions of this court. Authorities from other jurisdictions, many of which have been cited and carefully examined, are of little aid. The controlling principles are found in our own decisions. The principles announced in these decisions are firmly established. They can neither be obscured by precatory admonitions nor brushed aside by skeptical prophecies.

Under the decisions of this court, there is little room for speculation or disagreement as to the character of the University of Illinois as a corporate entity. In the case of *Spalding* v. *People*, 172 Ill. 40, where the question was directly involved, it was definitely held that while the university is not strictly a municipal corporation, it is nevertheless, a public corporation. It was organized for the sole purpose of conducting and operating the university, as a State institution. It is not a private corporation. In *Thomas* v. *Board of Trustees of Industrial University*, 71 Ill. 310, the question of its corporate status was directly passed upon. It was there said: "There is nothing in the act from which it can be inferred that this institution was, in any respect, to be a private corporation, either in whole or in part. It was founded on donations from the general government, the county of Champaign, the Central railroad, and, it may be, from private individuals. These donations consisted of land scrip from the general government, lands and bonds given by Champaign county, freights by the railroad company, the title to which was transferred to the State, and became the property of the State, to hold in trust for the purposes of the university, and these trustees and officers were appointed by the authority of the State for its government and control. Private individuals have no interest in or control over it, but it is, in every sense of the term, a State institution. It, with its property, management and control, is entirely under the power of the General Assembly, and this has been recognized by the General Assembly by making subsequent appropriations for the erection of buildings, and to defray expenses, and by expressly prohibiting the board of trustees from obligating the State for the payment of any sum of money in excess of the appropriations thus made. (Sec. 3, acts 1871-2, p. 143.) The officers of the incorporation are paid, either directly or indirectly, from funds belonging to the State. All of the interest derived from the funds invested, from rents from real estate, and for tuition paid by pupils, or otherwise, belongs to the State, and hence there can be no pretense that the institution is private, or is to be governed by laws relating to private persons or corporations."

In *Board of Trustees of Industrial University* v. *Champaign County*, 76 Ill. 184, this court said: "It is true, that the General Assembly have created a body corporate, as the most convenient mode of controlling the institution, its property and affairs; but it will be observed that the State retains the power of appointing its trustees, and, no doubt, has power, through agents other than the trustees, to sell and dispose of the property of the institution, or they may, at pleasure, amend or even repeal the charter, as public policy or the interest of the university may require." In *Elliott* v. *University of Illinois*, 365 Ill. 338, the same principle was announced. . . .

It has no employees. Its employees are employees of the State. (*People ex rel. Redman* v. *Board of Trustees*, 283 Ill. 494.) Their selection and employment, however, are powers committed solely to the corporation. While it is true that the legislature has created a separate corporate entity, its powers are limited by the act of its creating. Such powers are limited to the purposes for which it was created. By creating the corporation and conferring upon it the powers delegated by the act of its creation, the State has committed to it the operation, administration and management of the University of Illinois. While the legislature has the power at any time to modify or change, or even may take away entirely the powers thus conferred on the corporation, it can only do so by legislation. As long as the present statute is in force, the State has committed to the corporate entity the absolute power to do everything necessary in the management, operation and administration of the university. . . .

Within the limitations imposed, it has power to contract, to sue and be sued, and to plead and be impleaded concerning any matters arising out of the operation of the university. Such powers can be taken from it only by an amendment or repeal of the statute, by which such powers are conferred. The only power the State can exercise with reference to the administration and operation of the university is by limiting or withholding appropriations, or by changing the statute.

It is a public corporation, created for the specific purpose of the operation and administration of the university. As such, it may exercise all corporate powers necessary to perform the functions for which it was created. It is vested with exclusive power to conduct and manage the business affairs of the university. It may employ professors, teachers and other employees, over whose employment, services or activities, the State has no control. The State may, and does, biennially, in its appropriations for expenses to be incurred, designate the number, classification and rate of compensation of employees to be paid from funds belonging to the State. In its internal corporate affairs the State has no voice except indirectly by curtailing its appropriations or restricting the classification of employees and the purposes for which appropriations may be used. . . .

While it is a public corporation, it was organized and exists for one specific purpose. It is unique in that it has and can own no property in its own right. Whatever property or interest in property it acquires belongs to the State, and is held by it as trustee for the use of the State. It has no taxing powers and no means of raising money or acquiring property, except through the operation of the university. Its power to borrow money and to issue bonds is granted and limited by the act of June 4, 1941. (Ill. Rev. Stat. 1941, chap. 144, par. 71 *et seq.*) True, it may receive donations and gifts, but whatever it may receive as such, like all other property which it acquires, it holds only as trustee for the State, the beneficial owner. It has no power to select its own trustees or managers. This power is reserved to the State. It functions solely as an agency of the State for the purpose of the operation and administration of the university, for the State. In doing this, it functions as a corporation, separate and distinct from the State and as a public corporate entity with all the powers enumerated in the applicable statutes, or necessarily incident thereto. It has and can exercise no sovereign powers. It is no part of the State or State government. As definitely held by this court in *Spalding* v. *People, supra,* by establishing the university the State created an agency of its own through which it proposed to accomplish certain educational objects, and the corporate entity created for that purpose is a public corporation belonging to the class of corporations enumerated in section 80 of division I of the Criminal Code. (Ill. Rev. Stat. 1941, chap. 38, par. 214.) Its contractual powers are so restricted by statute that it can create no liability or indebtedness against the State and no liability or indebtedness against itself as a corporate entity in excess of the funds in the hands of the treasurer of the university at the time of creating such liability or indebtedness and which may be specially and properly applied to the payment of the same. (Ill. Rev. Stat. 1941, chap. 144, par. 28.) No suit can be maintained against it which would adversely affect the rights of the State. *Schwing* v. *Miles*, 367 Ill. 436.

At such corporation it may formulate and carry out any educational program it may deem proper with complete authority over its faculty, employees and students, as well as all questions of policy. Incident to its corporate existence and the exercise of its corporate powers, it has the undoubted right to employ its own counsel or engage the services of any other employees it may deem necessary or proper, by contract or otherwise. This power is, however, always subject to the restriction that when such faculty members or other employees are to be paid from State funds, they must be within the classifications for which funds have been appropriated and are available.

In *Fergus* v. *Russel, supra*, we held that while the constitution prescribed no express powers or duties of the Attorney General, he was a common-law officer and possessed all the powers and duties of the attorney general at common law, as the chief law officer of the Crown. Under our form of government, all the prerogatives which pertained to the Crown in England under the common law are vested in the people. In this State the Attorney General was vested, by the constitution, with all of the common-law powers of that officer. The common law is as much a part of the law of this State, where it has not been expressly abrogated by statute, as the statutes themselves. By creating the office of Attorney General, under its well-known common-law designation, the constitution conferred upon it all the powers and duties of the attorney general under the common law and gave to the General Assembly the authority to confer and impose upon the incumbent of that office such additional powers and duties as it should see fit.

The same principles were announced in *Dahnke* v. *People*, 168 Ill. 102, *People ex rel. Gullett* v. *McCullough*, 254 id. 9, and *Chicago Mutual Life Indemnity Ass'n* v. *Hunt*, 127 id. 257. Neither the constitution nor the statutes, however, have conferred upon the Attorney General the power, or imposed upon him the duty, to represent public corporations, their managing trustees or other officers. No such powers or duties existed at the common law.

In the sense that it is a department or branch of the State government, the University of Illinois is not an agency or instrumentality of the State. It is a separate corporate entity, which functions as a public corporation. It is not the duty of the Attorney General to represent either the corporation or the trustees, by virtue of his office, as chief law officer of State. He has no right to do so. Both the university as a public corporation and its trustees are entitled to select their own legal counsel and advisor and to be represented in all suits brought by or against them by counsel of their own choice. As the managing or governing body of the university and all its property, clearly it would be the duty of the Attorney General to institute all appropriate proceedings against the corporation, and its officers and trustees, to either prevent or redress any breach of the trust. He would do this as the representative of the State and not as the representative of the corporation or its trustees. Ill. Rev. Stat. 1941, chap. 14, par. 4; *People ex rel. Barrett* v. *Finnegan*, 378 Ill. 387; *Saxby* v. *Sonnemann*, 318 id. 600; *Hunt* v. *Chicago Horse and Dummy Railway Co.* 121 id. 638. . . .

C.   *Implied Powers*

TURKOVICH v. BOARD OF TRUSTEES OF
THE UNIVERSITY OF ILLINOIS
Supreme Court of Illinois
143 N.E.2d 229 (1957)

MR. JUSTICE HOUSE delivered the opinion of the court:

This is a taxpayers' suit by Stephen and Betty Turkovich and Dahlen's Drug Stores, Inc., to enjoin the Board of Trustees of the University of Illinois from spending State funds for the construction, equipment and operation of a television station. The Auditor of Public Accounts and State Treasurer are joined as defendants, and plaintiffs seek to restrain them from paying out funds from the State Treasury for such purposes. Plaintiffs appeal from the decree of the circuit court of Sangamon County dismissing the complaint for want of equity. This court has jurisdiction since the constitutionality of a statute is involved and the case relates to the public revenue.

Plaintiffs contend that there is no valid appropriation for the purpose of constructing and operating a television station and that disbursement of funds under the appropriation acts involved is in violation of section 17, article IV, of the Illinois constitution. They further assert that if such acts be construed to permit such expenditure, then their failure to specify the purposes for which the appropriations were made violates section 16, article V, and section I, article IV. of said constitution. . . .

In the trial court plaintiffs contended that, wholly apart from the reach and validity of the appropriation acts in question, the University is without legal power and authority to maintain and operate an educational television station. . . .

The Board of Trustees was empowered to administer the University of Illinois by an act of the General Assembly passed in 1867. (Ill. Rev. Stat. 1953, chap. 144, pars. 22 *et seq.*) By section 7 thereof it was authorized to provide requisite buildings, apparatus and conveniences, to appoint professors and instructors and to teach in the most thorough manner such branches of learning as are related to agriculture and the mechanical arts, without excluding other scientific studies.

The Board of Trustees has, within such authorization, greatly expanded the facilities of the University. It has constructed and maintains the requisite buildings, apparatus and conveniences for and gives instruction in more than 2600 courses taught in 15 colleges, 5 schools, 2 divisions, 3 institutes and 2 Reserve Officers Training Corps, on three campuses. In addition, it maintains libraries, museums, hospitals, clinics, institutes, research programs, extension services, recreational facilities and a radio station.

A School of Journalism and Communications was established in 1927, pursuant to an act of the General Assembly. Three major curricula are offered by this school: journalism, advertising, and radio-television. Approximately one third of the student body in that school is enrolled in the latter curriculum.

The Board of Trustees in 1953 obtained a permit from the Federal Communications Commission to construct and operate a noncommercial television station. With the aid of gifts, including a transmitter, a television station was constructed which consisted of the erection of an antenna, the partitioning into rooms of space in the west hall of Memorial Stadium and the installation therein of the transmitting equipment. The station went on the air August 1, 1955, and has continually operated since. The Trustees allocated $24,000 for original construction and maintenance.

Professor Schooley, who is director in charge of radio and television broadcasting for the University, testified that the station was an experiment to see what could be done in program operations for a year or two. He indicated the desirability of expansion and relocation after the experimentation was completed.

According to the record the purposes of the University's television station are to train students to enter the field of communication and broadcasting; to give instruction for University credit; to carry on research in mass communication; to disseminate the results of research in all fields of learning at the University; to experiment in program planning and technique and to employ the medium for the education of the public at all levels.

There is nothing unusual in the University's power, in the objectives to be obtained, or the cost thereof, in the construction and operation of a television station. We take judicial notice of the fact that our great universities, through experimentation and research in many scientific fields totally beyond the comprehension of normal man, are the prime source of discoveries for the betterment of mankind. How then can we say that the University of Illinois should be restricted to specific authorizations in its proposed research and experimentation such as this?

The Board of Trustees has, by the statute creating the University, the power and authority to do everything necessary in the management, operating and administration of the University, including any necessary or incidental powers in the furtherance of the corporate purposes. *People ex rel. Board of Trustees* v. *Barrett,* 382 Ill. 321.

We are of the opinion that, aside from the question of the proper appropriation and use of State funds for the purpose, the construction and maintenance of a television station is well within the powers of the University without any additional statutory enactment upon the subject.

We now turn to the contention that there was no valid appropriation of State funds for the construction and operation of a television station. It is argued that the act making appropriations to the Board of Trustees to meet the ordinary and contingent expenses of the University of Illinois is not broad enough to permit the expenditure complained of. Apparently, it is plaintiffs' theory that activities of the University such as this must be particularized in the appropriation act or by separate enabling legislation. . . .

Similar appropriation acts for the University and many other branches and agencies of the State have been used continuously since the enactment of the Civil Administrative Code of 1917, (Ill. Rev. Stat. 1955, chap. 127, pars. 1 *et seq.*,) and the State Finance Act of 1919 (Ill. Rev. Stat. 1955, chap. 127, pars. 137 *et seq.*) It cannot reasonably be said that expenditures for purposes such as those complained of here would not have come to the attention of, and been curbed by, the legislature over the years if the funds appropriated were used for purposes not contemplated by that body. The General Assembly cannot be expected to allocate funds to each of the myriad activities of the University and thereby practically substitute itself for the Board of Trustees in the management thereof.

We have heretofore held that the construction and operation of a television station is within the powers delegated to the Board of Trustees. It follows that the several appropriation acts included funds for the construction, maintenance and operation of the television station as a part of the ordinary and contingent expenses of the University, and the Trustees had the authority to pay the cost thereof from such appropriations.

The final question is whether the Appropriation Act is violative of section 16 of article V of the constitution by failing to specify the object or purpose for which the appropriations were made, and an unlawful delegation of legislative power in violation of section I of article IV of the constitution.

Plaintiffs make the point that the Board of Trustees in its internal budget makes a separate allocation for television, but that it is not carried over into the Appropriation Act. A review of budgeting and appropriating procedure, under the Civil Administrative Code and State Finance Act, indicates that such a statement is misleading.

The various departments, divisions and colleges submit their estimated needs to the University Budget Committee. The estimates are then correlated and a report made to the President of the University who, in turn, makes his budget recommendation to the Board of Trustees. The Board then submits the University's budget, as approved by it, to the State Director of Finance, accompanied by a written statement explaining each item of appropriation requested. The University's internal budget is published as "The University Bulletin" and for the year 1954-1955, consisted of 272 pages. After hearings and revisions the Governor submits the budget to the General Assembly as a division of his biennial executive budget recommendations. An appropriation act, in the form outlined above, is then passed.

The several line items in the Appropriation Act are the totals of the needs in each category of the various departments, divisions and colleges. For example, the salaries of the professors in the College of Law and those in the College of Engineering are paid out of the line item for "Personal Services," and the equipment needed by both colleges is purchased out of the line item for "Equipment." This practice has been followed by the General Assembly for many years.

The impracticability of detailing funds for the many activities and functions of the University in the Appropriation Act is readily apparent. If, as plaintiffs' counsel argues, a $24,000 annual expenditure out of a biennial appropriation in excess of $82,000,000 is required, then practically every proposed expenditure would have to be itemized. Television cannot be singled out for special treatment merely because it is relatively new. It is one of the many activities incident to the management and operation of the University included in the single objective of maintaining an institution of higher learning.

We have been called upon to test various appropriation statutes with regard to the itemization requirements of section 16 of article V of the constitution. . . . The rationale of the foregoing cases is that the statutes appropriating funds in a lump sum for a single general purpose and without further itemization do not contravene the itemization provisions of said section 16 merely because the single general purpose may be subdivided into various details of the object and purpose, where it appears the various details are embraced within and reasonably related to the general purpose. . . .

In our opinion no constitutional provisions have been violated in the constitution and operation of the University television station, nor is the appropriation and expenditure of funds therefor. The decree of the circuit court of Sangamon County is correct, and it is hereby affirmed.

CURATORS OF THE UNIVERSITY OF MISSOURI v. NEILL
Supreme Court of Missouri
397 S.W.2d 666 (1966)

STORCKMAN, Chief Justice.

This is an original proceedings for a writ of mandamus brought by the Curators of the University of Missouri to require Robert Neill, the president of the Board of Curators, to execute revenue bonds which the Board proposes to issue for the construction of parking facilities for motor vehicles on the campus of the University of Missouri at Columbia, which bonds are to be paid, both principal and interest, solely from revenues derived from the operation of the parking facilities. . . .

The primary questions involved are whether the Curators have authority under the Constitution and statutes to construct the parking facility in question and, if such power exists, whether the Curators can borrow money and issue revenue bonds for that purpose. The Curators contend that they have constitutional power supplemented by statutes to perform both of these functions. The constitutional provision, § 9(a) of Art. IX of the 1945 Constitution, V.A.M.S., provides that: "The government of the state university shall be vested in a board of curators consisting of nine members appointed by the governor, * * *." The following section, 9(b), provides that: "The general assembly shall adequately maintain the state university and such other educational institutions as it may deem necessary."

The general assembly, in recognition of the broad grant of constitutional power, has also provided in § 172.010, RSMo 1959, V.A.M.S., that "the government" of the University shall be vested in the Board of Curators. Section 172.020 incorporates and creates the University as "a body politic" under the name, "The Curators of the University of Missouri", and, among other things, grants this public corporation the power to purchase and sell lands and chattels, and to condemn property for its public purposes.

Section 172.260 provides that: "It shall be the duty of the curators to provide for the protection and improvement of the site of the university of the state of Missouri, as selected and established by law; to erect and continue thereon all edifices designed for the use and accommodation of the officers and students of the university, and to furnish and adapt the same to the uses of the several departments of instruction." Thus, "the government" of the University is committed to the Curators both by the Constitution and the statutes and it is the Curators' duty "to provide for the protection and improvement of the site of the university" and "to meet and continue thereon all edifices" for the use of the officers and students of the University. . . .

The Curators are more than a mere regulatory agency. It is the clear intent of the Constitution and statutes to confer on the Curators the authority to select sites on which to carry out the functions of the University and to acquire real estate for such purposes by purchase or condemnation. It is also clear that the Curators are authorized to construct improvements on the real estate constituting the site of a University function. In fact such authority is spelled out as a *duty* of the Curators by § 172.260. For the possible origin of this grant of power and imposition of duty, see Constitution of Missouri 1820, Art. VI, § 2, V.A.M.S., Vol. 1, p. 91, Laws 1889, p. 265, and Laws 1909, p. 889. . . .

Our next inquiry concerns the power of the Curators to issue revenue bonds for the money necessary to defray the cost of constructing the parking facility. The respondent contends that the Curators have no express or implied power to issue revenue bonds for this purpose. This contention must be denied on the authority of State ex. rel. Curators of University of Missouri v. McReynolds, 354 Mo. 1199, 193 S.W.2d 611, a decision of this court en banc, which held that the Curators had implied power to issue revenue bonds for money borrowed to build dormitories and dining room facilities to take care of increased enrollment at the University. Regarding this aspect of the case, the McReynolds opinion states:

"* * * while the curators may have no general implied power to borrow money and issue securities, still it may be fairly implied from their express powers that under the particular circumstances they have the power presently to capitalize such future accumulation of fees even though they must borrow to do so. By borrowing by the method contemplated the curators do not create a general obligation, only a limited one. The only funds pledged are those to be realized from the operation of the particular properties to be built out of the proceeds of the bonds. There is no pledge of funds to be ultimately realized from tax revenues.

"* * * The broad powers historically exercised by the curators without specific legislative authority or appropriations present a different situation from an ordinary municipal corporation depending entirely upon taxation for its support and with powers rigidly limited by statute or charter.

"* * * By issuing the Dormitory Revenue Bonds the curators are merely adopting a modern device to implement the powers they have long and properly exercised." 193 S.W.2d at 613. . . .

We have considered all questions presented and decided them adversely to the respondent. Accordingly it is ordered that the peremptory writ of mandamus be issued.

All concur except FINCH, J., not participating.

NOTE

There have been several cases recently dealing with the power of a university to regulate campus parking and levy connected fines. Courts have held that it is not within general statutory powers to deduct parking fines from salary checks, Marquart v. Maucker, 215 N.W.2d 278 (Iowa 1974), Donow v. Board of Trustees of Southern Illinois University, 314 N.E.2d 704 (Ill. 1974). However, the Wisconsin Supreme Court has held that the towing and impounding of parked cars is within the powers granted to the Regents of the University of Wisconsin, Henkel v. Phillips, 260 N.W.2d 653 (Wis. 1978), and the Supreme Court of Montana has allowed regulation and fining as within constitutional delegations of powers in Montana State University v. Ransier, 536 P.2d 187 (Mont. 1975).

II.   The Transition from Private to Public University

FRANK BRISCOE CO. v. RUTGERS
Superior Court of New Jersey
130 N.J.S. 493 (1974)

Prior to the 1956 act, Rutgers was an incorporated college which had express power to sue and be sued.

The charter granted by Governor William Franklin on March 20, 1770 supplemented that granted by George III of England in 1766, and each in relevant part provides:

> * * * And we further of our special grace, certain knowledge,
> and mere motion, for us, our heirs, and successors, will, give,
> grant, and appoint, that the said trustees and their successors shall
> for ever hereafter, be in deed, fact, and name, a body corporate,

and politick, and that they the said body corporate and politick, shall be known as distinguished in all deeds, grants, bargains, sales, writings, evidences, moniments, or otherwise however, and in all courts for ever hereafter, shall and may sue, and be sued, plead, and be impleaded, by the name of the Trustees of Queen's-College in New Jersey; * * *.

Prior to 1956 Rutgers sued from time to time as its needs required. *Trustees of Rutgers College v. Morgan, Comptroller*, 70 *N. J. L.* 460 (Sup. Ct. 1904), aff'd 71 *N. J. L.* 663 (E. & A. 1905) (suit to collect money from the State of New Jersey for tuition for students admitted on state scholarships).

With this background is there any evidence that the Legislature intended to repeal the power to sue and be sued, and that the trustees consented to a loss of that power in the 1956 act? The courts have recited the care with which the 1956 Act was prepared. *Rutgers v. Kugler, supra.* ...

In 1956 the Legislature was not creating a new college. In creating a new college the Legislature may withhold the power "to sue and be sued." See *Oklahoma Agricultural & Mechanical College v. Willis, supra.* Compare the powers of the New Jersey College of Medicine and Dentistry, *N. J. S. A.* 18A:64C-8 (power to sue and be sued), with those of the College of Medicine and Dentistry of New Jersey, *N. J. S. A.* 18A:64G-6 (no power to sue or be sued).

In 1956 the Legislature was dealing with an existing incorporated college and could not without the trustee's consent take that power away. Prior to the development of the provision of our own national Constitution recognized in *Dartmouth College v. Woodward*, 4 *Wheat.* (U. S.) 518, 4 L. Ed. 629 (1819), the English courts held that new statutes imposing new conditions on the charter of an existing incorporated college were not applicable to such a college unless the trustees consented. *Rex v. Vice Chancellor of Cambridge University*, 3 *Burr.* 1647, 97 *Eng. Rep.* 1027 (K.B. 1765). The law of this State is the same. *Trustees of Rutgers College in N. J. v. Richman, supra.*

The relinquishment of such a power as that "to sue and be sued" is not to be assumed in the absence of convincing evidence to the contrary.

The Legislature provided in *N. J. S. A.* 18A:65-8 that

> No provision in this chapter contained shall be deemed or construed to create or constitute a debt, liability, or a loan or pledge of the credit, of the state of New Jersey.

Undoubtedly, this was intended to protect the State's treasury from debts created by Rutgers. There is no evidence that Rutgers ever referred anyone to the Legislature's committee on claims when suit was threatened. There is no evidence that in the 18 years since the 1956 act was passed the Legislature ever contended that Rutgers should refuse to pay disputed claims and send the matter to the Legislature. Until the enactment of the Medical and Dental Education Act of 1970 and the subsequent agreement, there is every indication that the State intended Rutgers to dispose of the claims in this action based on the contracts.

The court is aware that in deciding questions about the meaning of the 1956 act and the relation of Rutgers to the State caution is indicated. *Richardson Engineering Co. v. Rutgers, et al, supra* 51 *N. J.* at 215. Even though the State is present here, Rutgers and the State in the context of this case are not the true adversaries—plaintiff contractor and the State are.

Plaintiffs have a direct interest in the question of the power to sue because if Rutgers has that power, then under the exception clause in *N. J. S. A.* 59:13-1 Rutgers is not subject to that act. The decision of this question will avoid the alternative suggestion of Rutgers that it is not subject to the act because it is not one of the entities described in said act but an "autonomous public university." See *Rutgers v. Piluso*, 60 *N. J.* 142 (1972):

> The overall result of the legislature contract therefore is an autonomous public university—not merely a contractual relationship or an institution both public and private at the same time. This conclusion is further buttressed by several additional expressions in the act. The institution is specifically designated as "the instrumentality of the state for the purpose of operating the state university," *N. J. S. A.* 18A:65-2. The public policy of the state is expressly declared to be, indicative of an intent to create a full-fledged state agency, that:
>
> a. The corporation and the university shall be and continue to be given a high degree of self-government and that the government and conduct of the corporation and the university shall be free of partisanship; and
>
> b. resources be and continue to be provided and funds be and continue to be appropriated by the state adequate for the conduct of a state university with high educational standards and to meet the cost of increasing enrollment and the need for proper facilities. (*N. J. S. A.* 18A:65-27(I)).
>
> Most significantly for present purposes, these governmentally autonomous powers are directed to be exercised "without recourse or reference to any department or agency of the state, except as otherwise *expressly* provided by this chapter or other applicable statutes." (Emphasis added) *N. J. S. A.* 18A:65-28. And finally, it is provided that the act,
>
> * * * being deemed and hereby declared necessary for the welfare of the state and the people of New Jersey to provide for the development of public higher education in the state and thereby to increase the efficiency of the public school system of the state, shall be liberally construed to effectuate the purposes and intent thereof. (*N. J. S. A.* 18A:65-9. [at 157-158, footnote omitted]

Based on the provision of its charter authorizing Rutgers to sue and be sued, the absence of any affirmative evidence of an intent to repeal the right, the confirmation of existing charter power in the 1956 act, and on the history of Rutgers exercise of the power to sue and be sued in the courts after 1956, this court concludes Rutgers had the power to sue and be sued at the time the Contractual Liability Act was enacted and is not subject to said act. . . .

Motion denied.

III. Problems of Fiscal Control

BOARD OF REGENTS OF UNIVERSITY AND STATE COLLEGES v. FROHMILLER
Supreme Court of Arizona
208 P.2d 833 (1949)

Upon petition of the Board of Regents of the University and State Colleges of Arizona, an alternative writ of mandamus was issued by this court directed to Anna Frohmiller as State auditor, commanding her to issue warrants in payment of seventeen claims which petitioner had caused to be filed with respondent. Thirteen of the claims were against funds of the University, and four were against funds of the Arizona State College at Tempe. Claim No. 1 was for the cost of advertising for bids for construction of dormitories authorized by Chapter 65, Arizona Session Laws of 1945, which bids were rejected. Claims Nos. 2 and 3 were for bronze tablets permanently affixed to dormitories stating the name of the building, date of construction, members of the board, the architect, etc. Claims 4 to 13, inclusive, were for expenses incurred in the inauguration of a new president at the university; specifically, they were for rental of caps and gowns (bachelor's, master's, doctor's) for delegates, luncheon and reception, pictures of the inauguration and the new president, programs, direction signs for guidance of visitors, announcements, invitations, information folders, and public address system. The four claims against the funds of the Arizona State College at Tempe were in payment of chinaware, crystal, silverware, dining room suite, china cabinet, and dining room rug, to be used in connection with the Home Economics Department of the College, where students are given practice instruction in home management. All of the claims were presented and rejected twice. After the second rejection they were all presented to the governor, who rejected the first claim against the university funds (to pay for advertising for bids for construction); approved the second and third claims against the University funds (for bronze tablets to be affixed to buildings); rejected all the other claims (inauguration expenses against the University funds); and approved all the claims against the State College funds. . . .

The issuing of the warrants was not discretionary with the auditor. If all the necessary fact predicates existed for the issuance of the warrants, including a "public purpose," then the warrants must issue as a matter of right. In Proctor v. Hunt, 43 Ariz. 198, 29 P.2d 1058, 1060, we stated that if a claim is "on its face, *for a public purpose* and is properly itemized and accompanied by vouchers, and an appropriation has been made by law for that purpose, it is the mandatory duty of the auditor to approve said claim and to issue a warrant therefor; *no discretion being given, if the matters recited beforehand appear in the claim as presented.*" (Emphasis supplied.) It was the auditor's right to determine whether the expenditures presented by the claims were for a public purpose. In making this determination she exercised her judgment. But in so doing she exercised no discretion in the sense in which that word is used when coercive action by mandamus is resisted. She had no discretion to exercise in determining what were the facts, because the facts were not in dispute. If the facts showed a legal right to the warrants, discretion on the part of the auditor ceased to exist and the duty was enjoined. To successfully resist the writ, her determination must have been correct. If she was honestly of the opinion that the expenditures represented by the claims were for an illegal purpose she rightfully refused to issue the warrants and in so doing is not subject to criticism for being cautious. . . .

For similar reason respondent claims that she was and is without authority to issue warrants for the claims representing expenditures of the inauguration, and for the additional reason that these claims show on their face that such expenses were not for a public purpose.

At the outset we feel that it is advisable to decide whether the expenditures in connection with the inauguration ceremony were for a public purpose. What is "a public purpose" depends in part upon the time (age), place, objects to be obtained, modus operandi, economics involved, and countless other attendant circumstances. The phrase is incapable of fixed definition; examples bring more elucidation. See City of Tombstone v. Macia, 30 Ariz. 218, 219, 245 P. 677, 46 A.L.R. 828; Frohmiller v. Board of Regents, 1946, 64 Ariz. 362, 171 P.2d 356; City of Glendale v. White, 1948, 67 Ariz. 231, 194 P.2d 435. One of the attendant circumstances referred to has its seat in the human equation—the eyes, conscience, and philosophy of those called upon to judge. With these thoughts in mind we are moved to observe that in determining whether expenses incurred as an incident to the inauguration of a new president of the University are of a kind authorized by law it should be considered what the event is of inducting into office a new president, the purpose to be served by such a ceremony, and the practice observed by similar institutions with regard to a like event. The custom in other seats of learning need not at all set the pattern for ours, nor should we justify a formal and ceremonious inauguration of a president of the University upon the ground that this is what is done at Harvard or at Yale; but any general acceptance of the custom, country-wide in extent, must indicate some useful, and not merely an idle, purpose. By common knowledge the custom is generally followed, and in Arizona in the few inductions of a president of the University before the inauguration of Dr. Byron McCormick ceremonies of the same general nature were held, with incident expenses, and with no official objection that a public purpose was not served.

Ceremony, it is true, is not a necessity; a new president could be seated with no more ceremony than attends the swearing in of a constable, but this overlooks the nature of an institution of higher learning, the character and needs of a large body of undergraduates and their professors, the loyalties inspired in them by their university; the value of ritual and symbolism in developing those loyalties in formative minds; the calling of attention to the unity of all the colleges and schools of the University and the centering of control of a vast educational plant with its multitude of diverse interests and aspirations in the president. The dignity of the office is enhanced by such ceremonies. A failure to avail the University of the opportunity to signalize the importance of this event in its life when the reins of control are transferred to a new president might more readily subject the board to a charge of laxity and indifference to the psychological values inherent in the occasion than with extravagance for providing for a ceremonious celebration of so important an event. We have no hesitancy in holding that reasonable expenditures for the purposes exhibited by these claims fall in the category of expenditures for a "public purpose." No claim of unreasonableness has been made. The expenses were in the field of discretion vested in the board.

On this matter of discretion petitioner asserts that no discretion is vested in the state auditor over the expediency or legality of any expenditures made by the board of regents from funds under its supervision, and hence the auditor should not have questioned the expenses incident to the inauguration and should have promptly issued the warrants. This position cannot be maintained. . . .

The necessity, expediency, advisability, or policy actuating the creation of the debt is no official concern of the auditor. (Cases supra) It would seem that the desire of the board of regents to be an autonomous body, freed of all shackles, was given impetus by our recent decision in Hernandez v. Frohmiller, 1949, 68 Ariz. 242, 204 P.2d 854, 860, wherein the constitutionality of the state civil service law was under consideration. In passing the court made the observation that since the University and State Colleges were under the supervision of the board of regents by constitutional grant "to permit legislation to throw the employment and supervision of all personnel under the civil service law, except the teaching staff, would necessarily deprive the board of regents of a large portion of its constitutional supervisory power. We have no hesitation in holding that such legislation runs counter to said article 11, section 2, Arizona Constitution."

The board argues that legislation permitting the auditor to question claims arising out of its contractual authority is contrary to constitutional provisions vesting in the board the general conduct and supervision of the University and State Colleges, citing Arizona Constitution, article 11, sections 1, 2, 3, 4, and 5. We do not believe it is or was intended that this grant of power carried with it the power, authority, or privilege to spend the state's monies at will and with no review.

"* * * The fact that the university is incorporated does not make it any the less an arm, branch or agency of the state for educational purposes, and affects in no particular the power of the legislature over it.

*   *   *

"The fact that 'within the scope of its duties' the board of regents 'is supreme,' Fairfield v. J. W. Corbett Hardware Co., supra, does not, as appellee argues, relieve the auditor from the duty of approving the claims of university employees for wages or the governor from countersigning the warrants in payment thereof, any more than it relieves these officers from performing this same duty when the claims and warrants of other state employees are involved. It is the duty of the auditor before issuing a warrant in payment of a claim, including those approved by university authorities, to know that the claim is for services falling within the purpose of the appropriation against which the warrant is to be charged, and if it is not, disapprove it." State v. Miser, 50 Ariz. 244, 72 P.2d 408, 412.

It might have been added that not only is it the duty of the auditor to know that the claim falls within the purpose of the appropriation against which the warrant is to be charged, but also that the declared legislative purpose of the appropriation is actually for a "public purpose," and if the claim is not for a public purpose to disapprove it regardless of the fact that it is within the declared legislative purpose. Paramount to the right of review vested in the auditor is the ultimate right of the Supreme Court of Arizona to decide whether any claim is for a public purpose. . . .

NOTE

For a notable series of disputes over a state auditor's fiscal control over state college and university spending see Glover v. Sims, 3 S.E.2d 612 (W. Va. 1939); Board of Governors of W. Virginia University v. Sims, 59 S.E.2d 705 (1950); Board of Governors of W. Virginia University v. Sims, 68 S.E.2d 489 (1952); West Virginia Board of Education v. Sims, 81 S.E.2d 665 (1954); Board of Governors of W. Virginia University v. Sims, 82 S.E.2d 321 (1954); West Virginia Board of Education v. Sims, 101 S.E.2d 190 (1957). Final score: Colleges 6, Sims 0.

SEGO v. KIRKPATRICK
Supreme Court of New Mexico
524 P.2d 975 (1974)

We are here concerned with vetoes and attempted vetoes of certain language contained in the General Appropriations Act. . . .

The final veto which has been challenged and with which we are here concerned was the striking by the Governor of the following language from the category of Higher Education. . . .

The Governor gave as his reason for striking this language:

"Article XI, Section 13 of the New Mexico Constitution provides that the legislature shall provide for the control and management of each of the State's educational institutions by a board of regents. The effect of [the vetoed language] would be to cause confusion and to severely limit the flexibility of the boards of regents in the control and management of the institutions. * * *"

The University of New Mexico, New Mexico State University, New Mexico Highlands University, Eastern New Mexico University and New Mexico Institute of Mining and Technology have appeared through their respective regents as amici curiae and, in support of respondents, urge the validity of this veto by the Governor. These institutions also persuasively argue that the Legislature lacks authority to appropriate Federal funds, scholarships, gifts, donations, private endowments or other gratuities granted or given to or otherwise received by these institutions from sources other than the State of New Mexico, and lacked authority to provide that "the department of finance and administration may approve the temporary use of balances which shall be restored to the original amount prior to the close of the 63rd fiscal year."

Contrary to what petitioner says, these institutions do not contend that the Legislature may not even consider the availability of non-state funds in detailing the amount of general fund appropriations to be made to them. Their contention is that the Legislature may not validly assume to appropriate and consequently control the expenditure of these funds.

We fully appreciate that this cause arose out of challenges to vetoes and purported vetoes by the Governor under his partial veto powers. However, we have elected to confer standing on petitioner to raise issues touching on the validity or invalidity of these vetoes and purported vetoes because of the great public importance of the issues involved. We are of the opinion that the public interest in and importance of the issues involved are not limited solely to the question of the Governor's authority to strike certain language from House Bill 300. The question of the validity of the Legislature's inclusion of some of this language in its bill is also of great public interest and importance. The question of the authority of the Legislature to appropriate and control non-state funds available to these educational institutions has been raised and argued by the parties, and we shall decide this question as well as the question of the validity of the Governor's action in disapproving this language relating to the purported appropriations of non-state funds.

As to the authority of the Governor to veto this language under his partial veto power, we are of the opinion that this was a proper exercise of his power. This item or part of House Bill 300 related solely to Higher Education and to an attempt on the part of the Legislature to authorize additional appropriations to or expenditures by the agencies in this category of actual revenues, in the event these revenues should exceed the amounts appropriated from the six numbered and named funds and the Department of Finance and Administration should approve. However, these additional appropriations or expenditures were conditioned upon or limited by the provisions that "the department of finance and administration may approve the temporary use of balances which shall be restored to the original amount prior to the close of the 63rd fiscal year." . . . .

As to the authority of the Legislature to appropriate non-state funds available to the institutions of higher learning, we are of the opinion that the Legislature lacks authority to appropriate these funds or to control the use thereof through the power of appropriation.

The powers of control and management of each of these institutions is vested in a Board of Regents. Article XII, § 13, Constitution of New Mexico; § § 73-22-4; 73-25-3; 73-26-3 and 73-27-4, N.M.S.A. 1953 (Repl. Vol. 11, pt. 1, 1968). The Legislature has expressly recognized the authority of these institutions to receive benefits and donations from the United States and from private individuals and corporations; to buy, sell, lease or mortgage real estate; and to do all things, which in the opinions of the respective Boards of Regents, will be for the best interests of the institutions in the accomplishment of their purposes or objects. Section 73-30-15, N.M.S.A. 1953 (Repl. Vol. 11, pt. 1, 1968).

In Mac Manus v. Love, Colo., 499 P.2d 609 (1972), the Supreme Court of Colorado was faced with the question of whether the Colorado Legislature had the power to appropriate Federal funds. Article III of the Colorado Constitution contains language concerning separation of the powers vested in the three departments of government, which is identical with the language of Art. III, § 1 of the New Mexico Constitution. In construing and applying this language and some of its prior decisions, the Colorado court held "that federal contributions are not the subject of the appropriative power of the legislature" and the Legislature's attempt to do so was "[constitutionally] void as an infringement upon the executive function of administration." We agree.

As already stated, our Legislature clearly has the power, and perhaps the duty, in appropriating State monies to consider the availability of Federal funds for certain purposes, but it has no power to appropriate and thereby endeavor to control the manner and extent of the use or expenditure of Federal funds made available to our institutions of higher learning. Control over the expenditure of these funds rests with the Federal government and the Boards of Regents of the respective institutions. Likewise, funds in the form of scholarships, gifts, donations, private endowments or other gratuities granted or given to the institutions, or otherwise received by them from sources other than the State of New Mexico, are not subject to appropriation by the Legislature. These funds belong to the institutions, and these institutions must make full and complete reports thereof to the Governor, who in turn must transmit these reports to the Legislature. Article V, § 9, Constitution of New Mexico. However, the fact, that these reports and the information contained therein are made available to the Legislature for its information and use in the performance of its proper legislative functions, does not confer on the Legislature the power to appropriate and thereby limit or control the use or disbursement of these funds. The matter of expenditure or disbursement of these funds rests with the Boards of Regents, subject to applicable law. . . .

The preemptory writ of mandamus heretofore issued is affirmed.

It is so ordered.

IV. Powers of State-Wide Governing Boards

MOORE v. BOARD OF REGENTS OF UNIVERSITY
Court of Appeals of New York
407 N.Y.S.2d 452 (1978)

JASEN, Judge.

Presented for our review on this appeal is the issue whether the Board of Regents, through the Commissioner of Education, has the power to deny registration of doctoral degree programs offered by the State University of New York on the ground that they do not satisfy academic standards prescribed by the commissioner. . . .

We hold that the Education Law does empower the Board of Regents, acting through the Commissioner of Education, to require registration of doctoral degree programs offered by the State University and to deny registration to those programs it determines to be academically deficient.

To place the current dispute between the Regents and the State University in proper perspective, a brief review of the historical evolution of these bodies is appropriate. When first created by the Legislature, the Regents of the University of the State of New York succeeded to the powers of the governors of Kings College, which was then renamed Columbia College. (L.1784, ch. 51.) This grant of power endowed the Regents with full authority to govern and manage any college established in New York, all such institutions to be deemed part of the University of New York. (*Id.*) Subsequently, however, the Legislature altered the role of the Regents by granting to a board of trustees of Columbia College autonomous control over the operation of the college. (L.1787, ch. 82.) Concomitantly, this act endowed all colleges established in New York with the same rights and privileges vested in the trustees of Columbia College. (*Id.*) As a result, the Regents underwent a metamorphosis, the effect of which was to clothe it with a broad policy-making function over higher education in New York, leaving the day-to-day operation of the colleges to their own governing bodies. (See Carmichael, New York Establishes a State University 2 [1955].)

With the advent of the State University of New York (L.1948, ch. 695 [Education Law, §352]), however, the Regents became enmeshed in the day-to-day operation of this semi-independent educational corporation. To alter this governing structure, the Legislature subsequently vested in the Board of Trustees of the State University the same power to administer the day-to-day operations of the State University as trustees of private institutions of higher education had been granted. (L.1961, ch. 388.) Viewed in this historical perspective, the issue in the instant case can be framed as whether the Regents, as a policy-making body, possesses the power to require registration of doctoral degree programs or whether control over the offering of such programs lies within the ambit of the Trustees of the State University.

At the outset, we note that a critical function of the Regents is its preparation, once every four years, of a master plan "for the development and expansion of higher education" in New York. (Education Law, § 237, subd. 1.) This plan includes public as well as private institutions. The 1972 master plan, prepared by the Regents, and approved by the Governor, recognized the need for strengthening graduate programs and recommended that "institutions should withdraw those programs which, upon evaluation, prove to be (a) inactive or underenrolled, (b) of marginal quality and which cannot be strengthened by sharing resources with other institutions, and (c) below the minimum standards set by Commissioner's Regulations." Separate and apart from the policy recommendations concerning graduate programs contained in the 1972 master plan, section 210 of the Education Law specifically gives the Regents the power to "register domestic and foreign institutions in terms of New York standards". . . .

We see no reason why sections 210 and 215 should not be read together as the statutory authority for the power of the Regents to require registration of doctoral degree programs offered by institutions of higher education in New York. If the Regents, in the first instance, has the power to register institutions "in terms of New York standards" (Education Law, § 210), and the power to suspend the rights and privileges of an institution violating "any rule or law of the university" (Education Law, § 215), it would not appear unreasonable to conclude that the Regents also possesses the power to deny the registration of doctoral degree programs which it believes do not conform with standards set for institutions of higher education. Of course, the standards for registration set by the Regents must not be arbitrary or capricious, either in the abstract or in application to specific programs. To hold that the Regents is empowered to require registration of doctoral degree programs is not to insulate such administrative action from judicial scrutiny.

Of critical importance to the effectuation of the Regents' powers is the legislative function with which it has been endowed: that is, to determine the educational policies of the State and to "establish rules for carrying into effect the laws and policies of the state, relating to education, and the functions, powers, duties and trusts conferred or charged upon the university and the education department." (Education Law, § 207.) Implementing this power, the Regents, based upon the policy recommendations made in the 1972 master plan, established a rule providing the Commissioner of Education with authority to promulgate regulations governing the registration of courses of study in colleges, as well as in professional, technical and other schools. (8 NYCRR 13.1[a].) Acting upon this mandate, the commissioner promulgated a regulation requiring the registration of "[e]very curriculum creditable toward a degree offered by institutions of higher education" (8 NYCRR 52.1[a][1]).

To effectuate this registration requirement, the commissioner also promulgated a regulation setting forth standards to be employed in the determination whether to grant or deny the registration of degree programs offered by all institutions of higher education, both private and public. (8 NYCRR 52.2.) This regulation provided, *inter alia*, that "[e]ach member of the academic staff shall have demonstrated by his training, earned degrees, scholarship, experience, and by classroom performance or other evidence of teaching potential, his competence to offer the courses and discharge the other academic responsibilities which are assigned to him." (8 NYCRR 52.2[c].)

In reviewing the qualifications of the faculty of the English and History Departments at the State University of New York at Albany to offer doctoral programs, the commissioner, based upon reports submitted by the site visitation team and program evaluation committee, as well as upon the recommendation of the doctoral council, determined that the faculty in these departments were not sufficiently productive or prominent to support a doctoral program and, therefore, declined to register the programs. Indicia of faculty productivity or prominence relied upon by the commissioner focused upon the extent of research and publications credited to members of the faculty of the doctoral programs evaluated. Concerning the history program, the report of the visitation team concluded that the department was not widely known and that "[w]ith one outstanding exception * * * the members of the department, individually and collectively [did] not represent the kind of prominent scholars to whom one refers undergraduates in all parts of the country for graduate training." Similarly, the report of the visitation team evaluating the English program concluded "that in general the members of the department are not recognized nationally by appointment to national honorary bodies, MLA committees, or editorial boards."

In concluding that the Commissioner of Education did not act in excess of his powers in denying registration of these programs based upon this criteria, we reject, at the outset, appellant's contention that the power of the Regents is limited pursuant to chapter 388 of the Laws of 1961 to supervision and approval of the State University Trustees' master plan. The purpose of that legislation was not to exempt the State University from the authority of the Regents. On the contrary, the Legislature sought merely to place the State University on the same footing as private institutions of higher education in New York: that is to grant the trustees of the State University the same power to govern the day-to-day operations of the State University as trustees of private institutions possessed. It was intended to have, and in fact had, no effect on the broad policy-making function exercised by the Regents over both private and public institutions of higher education in New York.

In exercising this function, the Regents recommended in its 1972 master plan the withdrawal of academically deficient programs. Moreover, as previously discussed, sections 210 and 215 of the Education Law must be interpreted to empower the Regents to register degree programs as well as the institutions themselves in terms of New York standards. These standards, promulgated as regulations by the Commissioner of Education (8 NYCRR 52.2), provide the necessary authority for the commissioner's determination to deny the registration of the English and history doctoral programs offered by the State University of New York at Albany. . . .

As a word of caution we add that the power of the Regents is not unbridled. Its function is one of an overseer: a body possessed of broad policy-making attributes. In its broadest sense, the purpose of the Regents is "to encourage and promote education" (Education Law, § 201), a purpose which must be realized only through the powers granted to the Regents by the Legislature. (N.Y.Const., art. XI, § 2) In the absence of a specific grant of power by the Legislature (see, e.g., Education Law, § 210 [to register domestic and foreign institutions]; § 215 [to examine, inspect and visit institutions and to require their submission of reports]), the Regents cannot transform section 207 of the Education Law, the fountainhead of the Regents' rule-making power, into an all-encompassing power permitting the Regents' intervention in the day-to-day operations of the institutions of higher education in New York. Were this provision interpreted otherwise, it would run afoul of the constitutional prohibition (N.Y.Const., art. III, § 1), against the Legislature's delegation of lawmaking power to other bodies. (See *Matter of Levine v. Whalen,* 39 N.Y.2d 510, 515, 384 N.Y.S.2d 721, 723, 349 N.E.2d 820, 822; *Matter of Mooney v. Cohen,* 272 N.Y. 33, 37, 4 N.E.2d 73.) In view, however, of the specific powers granted by the Legislature to the Regents previously discussed, we believe that in the present case, section 207 operates as a means for the effectuation of independent powers, rather than as their source.

Accordingly, the order of the Appellate Division should be affirmed, without costs.

NOTE

See also State Board of Education v. State Board of Higher Education, 29 Utah 2d 110, 505 P.2d 1193 (1973) noted in Chapter 3, and Board of Regents of University of Oklahoma v. Childers, 170 P.2d 1018 (Okla. 1946). In Nord v. Guy, 141 N.W.2d 395 (S.D. 1966), the state supreme court found an unconstitutional delegation of legislative authority to the State Board of Higher Education in a law purporting to authorize the Board to determine which facilities would be constructed at different institutions, and at what cost.

V.   Governmental Immunity from Suit

A.   The Basic Concept

HOPKINS v. CLEMSON AGRICULTURAL COLLEGE OF SOUTH CAROLINA
United States Supreme Court
221 U.S. 636 (1911)

MR. JUSTICE LAMAR, . . . delivered the opinion of the court.

The plaintiff sued the Clemson Agricultural College of South Carolina, for damages to his farm, resulting from the College having built a dyke which forced the waters of the Seneca River across his land, whereby the soil had been washed away and the land ruined for agricultural purposes. . . .

That ruling and the assignments of error thereon raise the question as to whether a public corporation can avail itself of the State's immunity from suit, in a proceeding against it for so managing the land of the State as to damage or take private property without due process of law.

With the exception named in the Constitution, every State has absolute immunity from suit. Without its consent it cannot be sued in any court, by any person, for any cause of action whatever. And, looking through form to substance, the Eleventh Amendment has been held to apply, not only where the State is actually named as a party defendant on the record, but where the proceeding, though nominally against an officer, is really against the State, or is one to which it is an indispensable party. No suit, therefore, can be maintained against a public officer which seeks to compel him to exercise the State's power of taxation; or to pay out its money in his possession on the State's obligations; or to execute a contract, or to do any affirmative act which affects the State's political or property rights. . . .

But immunity from suit is a high attribute of sovereignty—a prerogative of the State itself—which cannot be availed of by public agents when sued for their own torts. The Eleventh Amendment was not intended to afford them freedom from liability in any case where, under color of their office, they have injured one of the State's citizens. To grant them such immunity would be to create a privileged class free from liability for wrongs inflicted or injuries threatened. Public agents must be liable to the law, unless they are to be put above the law. For how "can the principles of individual liberty and right be maintained if, when violated, the judicial tribunals are forbidden to visit penalties upon individual defendants . . . whenever they interpose the shield of the State. . . . The whole frame and scheme of the political institutions of this country, state and Federal, protest" against extending to any agent the sovereign's exemption from legal process. *Poindexter* v. *Greenhow*, 114 U. S. 270, 291. . . .

In this case there is no question of corporate existence and no claim that building the dyke was *ultra vires*. Plaintiff was denied a hearing not on the ground that his complaint did not set out a cause of action, but solely for the reason that even if the College did destroy his farm, the court had no jurisdiction over a public agent.

If the State had in so many words granted the College authority to take or damage the plaintiff's property for its corporate advantage without compensation, the Constitution would have substituted liability for the attempted exemption. But the State of South Carolina passed no such act and attempted to grant no such immunity from suit as is claimed by the College. On the contrary, the statute created an entity, a corporation, a juristic person, whose right to hold and use property was coupled with the provision that it might sue and be sued, plead and be impleaded, in its corporate name.

Reference is made, however, to *Kansas ex rel. Little* v. *University of Kansas*, and the note to 29 L. R. A. 378, where state colleges, prison boards, lunatic asylums and other public institutions have been held to be agents of the State not liable to suit unless expressly made so by statute. . . .

That general rule is of force in South Carolina, as appears from *Gibbs* v. *Beaufort*, 20 S.Car. 213, 218, cited in the opinion of the court below, where it was said that "a municipal corporation, instituted for the purpose of assisting a State in the conduct of local self government, is not liable to be sued in an action of tort for nonfeasance or misfeasance of its officers in regard to their public duties, unless expressly made so by statute." But the plaintiff is not seeking here to hold the College liable for the nonfeasance or misfeasance either of its own officers or officers of the public. This is a suit against the College itself for its own corporate act in building a dyke, whereby the channel had been narrowed, the swift current had been diverted from the usual course across the plaintiff's farm, and, as it is alleged, destroying the banks, washing away the soil and for all practical purposes as effectually depriving him of his property as if there had been a physical taking. . . .

For protecting the bottom land the College, for its own corporate purposes and advantage, constructed the dyke. In so doing it was not acting in any governmental capacity. The embankment was in law similar to one which might have been built for private purposes by the plaintiff on the other side of the river. If he had there constructed a dyke to protect his farm, and in so doing had taken or damaged the land of the College, he could have been sued and held liable. In the same way, and on similar principles of justice and legal liability, the College is responsible to him if, for its own benefit and for protecting land which it held and used, it built a dyke which resulted in taking or damaging the plaintiff's farm. 2 Dillon M. Corp. (4th ed.), § 966, p. 1180. . . .

Reversed.

MR. JUSTICE HARLAN dissents.

NOTES

1. The plaintiff in *Hopkins v. Clemson* sued for damages for a classic common law tort based on negligence in a non-governmental function of a public institution. Colleges and universities are sued primarily in two areas of tort: negligence and defamation. Negligence suits may cover slip and fall cases, injuries to students on a field trip or going to an athletic event, or even, possibly, educational malpractice. Most tort cases against colleges or universities are not different from the general run of tort cases, a subject too broad to be encompassed here. (*See generally* Prosser, Handbook of the Law of Torts.) The only distinctive aspect of negligence cases brought against educational institutions is found in those cases alleging breach of the duty to adequately supervise students, although even this distinctive educational tort is better developed in primary and secondary school cases. *See* Seitz, *Tort Liability of Teachers and Administrators for Negligent Conduct Towards Pupils*, 20 Cleveland State L. Rev. 551 (1971). In higher education it is found primarily in special situations deemed to be especially hazardous such as in athletic facilities or chemistry laboratories. *See* Parker, *The Authority of a College Coach: A Legal Analysis*, 49 Oregon L. Rev. 442 (1970). A related duty which arises in higher education is the duty to counsel students without negligence. The concept of counsellor liability has been raised in three major cases: Bogust v. Iverson, 102 N.W. 2d 228 (Wis. 1960); Morris v. Rousos, 397 S.W. 2d 504 (Texas 1965); and most recently, in Tarasoff v. Regents of the University of California, 551 P.2d 334 (1976). While the courts in the first two cases found for the defendant counsellors, these and other cases indicate a trend toward holding counsellors responsible for their professional activities. In *Tarasoff* the California Supreme Court held that a therapist at the University hospital had an affirmative duty to warn a potential victim, stating that, "the public policy favoring protection of the confidential character of patient-psychotherapist communications must yield to

the extent to which disclosure is essential to avert danger to others." (The patient did in fact kill the victim he had identified to the therapist.)

2. The other common law tort which arises in the context of higher education is defamation. The great fear of faculty and administrators was that the passage of the Buckley Amendment would expose to public, or more precisely, student, view letters of evaluation or recommendation which would form the basis for libel suits. However, early experience with student records law shows little activity of this type, perhaps due to the amendment which exempted records and letters written before and immediately after passage of the Act. Although there have been a few reports of such cases filed, there has been no major court opinion to date. *See* Chap. 21, *infra.*

3. The other area of defamation which crops up in colleges, and in which there has been more activity, concerns statements made in the evaluation of faculty and other employees. Generally, a so-called qualified immunity based on fair comment exists which protects most college officials from suits based on remarks made during faculty meetings or in tenure evaluations. For an excellent and extensive summary of tort problems in higher education, *see* Aiken, Adams and Hare, *Legal Liabilities in Higher Education: Their Scope and Management*, 3 J. of Coll. and Univ. Law 120 (1976).

4. More complex problems have arisen when Eleventh Amendment immunity comes in conflict with the Fourteenth Amendment and related civil rights statutes, which create the so-called "constitutional torts." Although the Supreme Court has clarified this area somewhat recently, in the *Monell* case, *infra*, it is still extraordinarily complex. It is important to note that while the Fourteenth Amendment gave Congress power to pass laws which allowed citizens to sue state governments and state officials in civil rights cases, it is still possible to argue that cases brought directly under the Fourteenth Amendment against states for monetary damages are subject to an Eleventh Amendment defense. *See Jagnandan, infra.*

5. Many of the legal issues discussed in cases involving civil rights legislation are based on elaborate theories developed to deal with the paradoxical relationship between the Eleventh and Fourteenth Amendments. Such theories often refer to the liability of a public official acting in his official capacity. Current issues include the definition of a "person" who can be sued under section 1983; the determination of the necessary mental state for individual liability; and the creation of limits on the availability of effective relief. These issues are discussed and defined in *Developments in the Law—Section 1983 and Federalism*, 90 Harv. L. Rev. 1133 (1977).

6. The Eleventh Amendment is an important concept to the public university. But what the Constitution giveth by way of Fourteenth Amendment causes of action cannot be taken away by Eleventh Amendment immunity. A qualified good faith immunity may still exist for officials in public institutions, but any state institution's argument for complete immunity under the Eleventh Amendment has been substantially weakened by *Monell.*

7. In *Developments in the Law—Section 1983 and Federalism*, 90 Harvard Law Rev. 1133, 1195-1197 (1977), the following observations are made about Eleventh Amendment immunity:

> [T]he eleventh amendment has been interpreted to operate as an independent bar to suit for either damages or equitable relief directly against states and their component agencies—but not their political subdivisions—under section 1983. Eleventh amendment jurisprudence has been marked by a consistent tension between the policies of sovereign immunity which the amendment reflects and the command of the federal system that the states conform their conduct to the mandates of the Constitution. In order to protect individual rights against unconstitutional state action, the Court has permitted aggrieved citizens to circumvent the eleventh amendment bar by permitting suits against state officials for equitable relief to restrain unconstitutional conduct, although such relief may often have a substantial, direct impact on the state treasury. However, relief which resembles a damage

recovery by providing retroactive compensation for an aggrieved citizen from state funds may not be ordered. The citizen subject to a constitutional deprivation may proceed against the state official personally for damages under the section 1983 cause of action only so long as the judgment will not operate on its face to force a recovery directly from the state treasury.

Even this eleventh amendment barrier to damage-like recoveries from the state treasury may apparently be overridden. The fourteenth amendment, which by its own terms imposes direct limits on the permissible scope of state action, sanctions "intrusions by Congress . . . into the judicial, executive, and legislative spheres of autonomy previously reserved to the States" by granting Congress the power to enforce its commands "by appropriate legislation." Under this power, Congress may provide for private suits against states or state officials which would otherwise be impermissible under the eleventh amendment.

B.   Fourteenth Amendment Actions

JAGNANDAN v. GILES
Fifth Circuit Court of Appeals
538 F.2d 1166 (1976)

RONEY, Circuit Judge:

Plaintiff Reverend W. L. Jagnandan, on behalf of himself and his two sons, brought a class action to challenge the constitutionality of a Mississippi statute which classified all alien students, even Mississippi residents, as nonresidents for tuition and fee purposes at state institutions of higher learning. A three-judge district court denied the class action request, declared the statute unconstitutional as being in contravention of the equal protection and due process clauses of the Fourteenth Amendment and granted injunctive relief. The court refused, however, to award plaintiffs reimbursement for the $3,495.00 in tuition and fees they had paid in excess of the amounts required of resident students, holding that such relief is barred by the Eleventh Amendment, as interpreted by the Supreme Court in *Edelman v. Jordan,* 415 U.S. 651, 94 S.Ct. 1347, 39 L.Ed.2d 662 (1974). *Jagnandan v. Giles,* 379 F.Supp. 1178 (N.D.Miss.1974). Plaintiffs appeal the denial of reimbursement for the excess tuition and fees paid pursuant to the unconstitutional statute. . . .

On the merits, we hold that the Eleventh Amendment bars suits in federal court to recover excess tuition paid pursuant to an unconstitutional statute, and affirm the three-judge district court.

The Jagnandans were citizens of the Republic of Guyana (formerly British Guiana in South America) lawfully admitted into this country as aliens with permanent resident classifications. Since September 1969 they have lived in West Point, Mississippi, where Reverend Jagnandan is a minister of a local church. Reverend Jagnandan pays Mississippi income taxes and owns an automobile registered in Mississippi. All three plaintiffs hold Mississippi driver's licenses. Each testified without reservation or qualification that he had no present intention of leaving the state, his purpose being to reside indefinitely in Mississippi. . . .

ELEVENTH AMENDMENT

The Mississippi statute requiring resident aliens residing in Mississippi to pay out-of-state tuition was ruled unconstitutional by the three-judge district court. *Jagnandan v. Giles,* 379 F.Supp. 1178 (N.D.Miss.1974). No appeal was taken from that holding. The court held, however, that the Eleventh Amendment bars plaintiffs' recovery of excess tuition payments made under the unconstitutional statute. In denying reimbursement the court relied on *Edelman v. Jordan,* supra, 415 U.S. 651, 94 S.Ct. 1347, 39 L.Ed.2d 662 (1974), and on *Edelman's* precursor, *Ford Motor Co. v. Department of Treasury,* 323 U.S. 459, 65 S.Ct. 347, 89 L.Ed. 389 (1945). This denial of relief is challenged on appeal.

In presenting their case for reversal plaintiffs assert five arguments: (1) defendants are personally liable for the excess tuition payments; (2) the State of Mississippi is not a party to this suit for Eleventh Amendment purposes; (3) Mississippi waived its immunity; (4) *Edelman v. Jordan* does not preclude the type of relief here sought; and (5) the Eleventh Amendment cannot be used to protect Fourteenth Amendment violations. Answering these points *seriatim* in the negative, we affirm the district court's denial of tuition refunds.

During the ratification process of the United States Constitution, and subsequent thereto, the sovereign states of this fledgling nation were concerned with the prospect that federal constitutional authority might be construed to allow suits against the states in federal courts when brought by a citizen of another state or foreign country. These fears were soon realized in *Chisholm v. Georgia,* 2 U.S. (2 Dall.) 419, 1 L.Ed. 440 (1793). *Chisholm* held that under the language of the Constitution and of the Judiciary Act of 1789 a state could be sued by a citizen of another state or foreign country. Reaction was swift and immediate. Barely five years later, in 1798, the Eleventh Amendment was ratified by the states. Unaltered since its ratification, the amendment provides simply:

> The judicial power of the United States shall not be construed
> to extend to any suit in law or equity, commenced or prosecuted
> against one of the United States by Citizens of another State, or
> by Citizens or Subjects of any Foreign State.

U.S.Const. Amend. XI.

The amendment has been judicially construed to bar federal jurisdiction over suits brought against a state by its own citizens, despite the absence of language to that effect. It also has been construed to encompass a suit brought by a foreign state. This bar, however, does not preclude a suit against the state when brought by the United States. Thus, when speaking of the Eleventh Amendment, the Court really talks in terms of the jurisdiction of federal courts to entertain suits and to grant relief against a state.

Personal Liability

At the outset we hold that the defendant University officials are not personally liable for the excess tuition payments tendered by plaintiffs. Thus, if plaintiffs are to recover, payment must come from defendants in their official capacity.

There is nothing in the record to indicate that defendants acted unreasonably or in a manner outside of their official capacity. Defendants were merely complying with the clear state mandate in collecting out-of-state tuition from these resident aliens. Defendants were not on notice of the statute's unconstitutionality prior to payment and acceptance of the money. They were acting in complete good faith.

Suit Against the State?

Plaintiffs next urge that for Eleventh Amendment purposes the defendants are not state entities and therefore the Eleventh Amendment is inapplicable. The initial defendants were the President of Mississippi State University and the Assistance to the Vice President for Business Affairs at the University. The district court, on its own motion, joined the Board of Trustees as a party defendant. 379 F.Supp. at 1180. *See* Fed.R.Civ.P. 19(a). We cannot agree with plaintiff's contention, because on our reading of the case law we are convinced that, effectively, the state is the true defendant to this suit.

By its own language the Eleventh Amendment indicates that a state must be sued before the bar to suit in federal court applies. The state must be a real or, at least, a nominal defendant. It is not necessary for the state to be actually named in the suit. It is enough that, in effect, the suit is against the state and any recovery will come from the state.

To make this determination, the Court must decide whether the suit is for all practical purposes against the state. In *Hander v. San Jacinto Jr. College,* 519 F.2d 273 (5th Cir.), *reh. denied,* 522 F.2d 204 (5th Cir. 1975), this Court affirmed the district court's award of back pay for a wrongfully discharged teacher. The Court recognized that a back pay award was the type of retroactive relief prohibited by *Edelman v. Jordan, supra,* 415 U.S. 651, 94 S.Ct. 1347, 39 L.Ed.2d 662 (1974). Nonetheless, an Eleventh Amendment challenge was bypassed in the suit against the governing junior college districts on the ground that under the peculiar Texas statutory and decisional law, the suit was not against the state. The junior college districts in *San Jacinto* were "primarily local institutions, created by local authority and supported largely by local revenues." 519 F.2d at 278. Thus, under the established law that local governmental institutions may not stand in the same light as the state for Eleventh Amendment purposes, there was no bar to the suit. What preserved jurisdiction in *San Jacinto* will not, however, assist the plaintiffs here. Under the instant facts, it is clear from statutory and decisional law that the State of Mississippi is the real party defendant. The district court implicitly recognized this when it stated,

Nor is there any question but that the refunds, if ordered, would not be paid by the defendants from personal funds, but would necessarily be a charge upon the state treasury, or at least that portion of the fisc dedicated to higher education.

379 F.Supp. at 1188.

The genesis of Mississippi State University (M.S.U.) is found in Chapter XIX of the Laws of the State of Mississippi, approved February 28, 1878. The school was first known as the Agricultural and Mechanical College of the State of Mississippi, Laws of Mississippi, ch. XIX, §2. Overseeing the school was a Board of Trustees appointed by the Governor with the advice and consent of the state senate. *Id.* §3. The Board was declared to be a body politic and corporate, capable of suing and being sued. *Id.* §5. The Governor was the *ex officio* president. *Id.* §6. The State Treasurer was the *ex officio* treasurer, empowered to keep and disburse all moneys of the school according to the orders of the Board. *Id.* §8. Later, Mississippi's universities were placed under the control of the Board of Trustees of state institutions of higher learning. The Agricultural and Mechanical College of Mississippi logo was changed to Mississippi State University by statute, although the school retained "all its property and the franchises, rights, powers, and privileges heretofore conferred on it by law [1878 Act]. . . ." Miss.Code Ann. §37-113-3 (1972).

Under state law Mississippi is inextricably involved in all facets of the Board's operation of the University, as well as the operation of other schools comprising the state's higher institutions of education. *See* Miss.Code Ann. §37-101-1 (1972). The Board's structure is detailed in the Mississippi Constitution. In part, the provision provides:

> Such Board shall have the power and authority to elect the heads of the various institutions of higher learning, and contract with all deans, professors and other members of the teaching staff, and all administrative employees of said institutions for a term not exceeding four years; but said Board shall have the power and authority to terminate any such contract at any time for malfeasance, inefficiency or contumacious conduct, but never for political reasons.
>
> Nothing herein contained shall in any way limit or take away the power of [sic] the Legislature had and possessed, if any, at the time of the adoption of this amendment, to consolidate or abolish any of the above named institutions. . . .

The Eleventh Amendment was fashioned to protect against federal judgments requiring payment of money that would interfere with the state's fiscal autonomy and thus its political sovereignty. Retroactive monetary relief for the constitutional violations here would have just that effect. Mississippi has devised a complex statutory design which governs the state's schools of higher education and their control by the Board of Trustees. The Board is required to submit budgetary proposals for legislative acceptance.

To require refund payments from the Board for overpayment of tuition fees would be the kind of tampering the Eleventh Amendment sought to avoid.

These fees appear to have been commingled with all moneys held by the University. Moreover, these types of fees were factored into the preparation of the annual budget for M.S.U. and were relied upon by the state legislature in determining the maximum amount of expenditures allowed. To compel payment would be to add an expenditure not figured in the budget. The fact that the sum is small, $3,495.00, compared to the overall University budget does not affect the determination. The Eleventh Amendment bar is not contingent on the magnitude of the monetary award sought against the state.

Waiver of Immunity

On oral argument plaintiffs urged that this case is indistinguishable from *Soni v. Board of Trustees of the Univ. of Tenn.,* 513 F.2d 347 (6th Cir. 1975); *cert. denied,* ___U.S.___, 96 S.Ct. 2623, 49 L.Ed.2d 372 (1976). In *Soni,* the Sixth Circuit awarded back pay to a university professor in the face of Eleventh Amendment contentions. Although the *Soni* record was incomplete on the issue of the University's identity as a state instrumentality, the court assumed without deciding that a suit against the University was a suit against the State of Tennessee. The court went on to hold, however, that there had been a waiver of federal court immunity based upon the University's charter, which read:

> The said trustees and their successors by the name aforesaid, may sue and be sued, plead and be impleaded, in any court of law or equity *in this State or elsewhere.* (emphasis added).

513 F.2d at 351. The *Soni* court found this to be a clear waiver of Tennessee's right not to be sued in federal court.

The principles guiding our determination on this issue are well settled. Waiver of the state's constitutional immunity must appear clearly and will not be easily implied. An immunity waived for state suit purposes does not necessarily waive immunity for federal courts.

There is nothing in the present record to indicate that Mississippi clearly intended to waive its Eleventh Amendment immunity. The sweeping state statutory language of waiver which controlled *Soni* is not equalled in this case. Section 5, chapter XIX of the 1878 Act simply provided that the Board could sue and be sued. No reference was made to any specific court. Section 5 provided:

> That each of the board of trustees herein provided for, and their successors in office, be and the same are hereby declared to be a body politic and corporate by their respective names and styles, and shall have a common seal, and each in its own name; *shall sue and be sued,* contract and be contracted with, and may own, purchase, sell and convey property, both real, personal and mixed (emphasis added).

The "sue and be sued" terminology has not, however, been carried into the present statutes. There is no equivalent of section 5 in the new statutes. No mention is made of the power to sue or to be sued either in the organizational statutes or in the general powers and duties of the Board. Under specific circumstances the Board is allowed to sue or be sued. In these instances, however, the waiver is limited to a narrowly defined activity. The consent to be sued is not given with such clarity as to amount to a waiver of Eleventh Amendment protection. As the Supreme Court stated in *Petty v. Tennessee-Missouri Bridge Comm'n,* 359 U.S. 275, 79 S.Ct. 785, 3 L. Ed.2d 804 (1959):

> [W]here a public instrumentality is created with the right "to sue and be sued" that waiver of immunity in the particular setting may be restricted to suits or proceedings of a special character in the state, not the federal, courts.

Id. at 277, 79 S.Ct. at 787.

In the statutes concerning Mississippi State University, there is no provision comparable to section 5 of the 1878 Act. Only §37-113-3 could be construed as referring back to any form of consent that may have been present in prior acts. In referring to the 1878 Act, this section states in part:

> [Mississippi State University] shall continue to exist as a body-politic and corporate, . . . with all its property and the franchises, rights, powers, and privileges heretofore conferred on it by law, or properly incident to such a body and necessary to accomplish the purpose of its creation[.]

This provision likewise lacks the clarity needed in order to infer the state's consent to be sued. . . .

Edelman v. Jordan

Plaintiffs contend that the refunding of previous excess tuition payments is not proscribed by the Supreme Court analysis of the Eleventh Amendment in *Edelman v. Jordan, supra,* 415 U.S. 651, 94 S.Ct. 1347, 39 L.Ed.2d 662 (1974). They further argue that this type of refund is more in the nature of equitable restitution and therefore different from the retroactive welfare benefits denied in *Edelman.* We disagree.

The United States Supreme Court has never specifically addressed the problem of refunded excess tuition payments *vis-a-vis* the Eleventh Amendment. The pre-*Edelman* case of *Vlandis v. Kline,* 412 U.S. 441, 93 S.Ct. 2230, 37 L.Ed.2d 63 (1973), *aff'g,* 346 F.Supp. 526 (D.Conn.1972), does not support plaintiffs' effort to bypass the Eleventh Amendment. It is true that *Vlandis* affirmed the refunding of excess out-of-state tuition fees paid by students who were in fact Connecticut residents. The primary issue in *Vlandis* concerned state statutes creating irrebuttable presumptions of non-residency. The Court found these to be violative of due process.

In *Vlandis,* however, the Eleventh Amendment issue was never briefed nor argued to the Court and was not discussed in the Court's opinion. The

Court in *Edelman* disavowed prior cases which had granted monetary relief against the state without consideration of Eleventh Amendment ramifications. Although *Vlandis* was not specifically named by the Court as being among this group, we do not read the omission as indicating the Court's approval of refunding tuition fees in the face of Eleventh Amendment contentions. Since *Edelman,* and not *Vlandis,* fully explored the Eleventh Amendment area, it is *Edelman* which must necessarily control our decision in the case before us. The status of *Vlandis* is thus similar to that of *Shapiro v. Thompson,* 394 U.S. 618, 89 S.Ct. 1322, 22 L.Ed.2d 600 (1969). There the Supreme Court affirmed the granting of retroactive welfare benefits without mention of the Eleventh Amendment. The Court in *Edelman* explicitly disapproved *Shapiro* to the extent it conflicted with *Edelman's* Eleventh Amendment holding. . . .

Plaintiffs additionally argue that this is really a suit for equitable restitution and is therefore not barred by the Eleventh Amendment. Plaintiffs reason that, unlike the welfare benefit cases, repayment of these tuition fees is not akin to a damage claim but merely prevents unjust enrichment of the University. The excess fees would never have been collected but for the unconstitutional statute. *Edelman's* reliance on *Ford Motor Co. v. Department of Treasury, supra,* 323 U.S. 459, 65 S.Ct. 347, 89 L.Ed. 389 (1945), forecloses acceptance of plaintiffs' argument. . . .

The Third Circuit has recently decided a case that on its face appears directly contrary to the Eleventh Amendment result reached on this appeal. *Samuel v. University of Pittsburgh,* 538 F.2d 991 (3rd Cir. 1976). Investigation below the surface of *Samuel* indicates that the case is inapposite to the appeal *sub judice.* The court in *Samuel* affirmed the granting of injunctive relief against defendant universities and state officials preventing the enforcement of a statewide residency rule on grounds of its unconstitutionality. That rule, for tuition purposes, required that the domicile of the wife is considered that of her husband's. The court also affirmed the district court's holding the universities liable for equitable restitution for the difference between the higher out-of-state tuition fees paid by married women residents because of the unconstitutional residency rule and the lesser in-state tuition charges.

A review of the district court's decision explains the apparent inconsistency between *Samuel* and the instant case. *Samuel v. University of Pittsburgh,* 375 F.Supp. 1119 (W.D.Pa.1974). Three universities involved in the suit included the University of Pittsburgh, Temple University and Penn State University. The district court at length explored the relationship between the three universities and the Commonwealth of Pennsylvania. This argument was rejected. The district court found the universities not to be state instrumentalities. As was documented in the *Suit Against the State?* section of this opinion, unlike the universities involved in *Samuel,* M.S.U. is one and the same with the State of Mississippi. Therefore the cosmetic similarity between these two cases does not withstand analysis. In the notation of issues involved in the *Samuel* appeal the court made no mention of a challenge to the district court's findings as to the universities' private status. The Third Circuit found the universities to be liable for restitution:

> The [district court] found that the Universities were unjustly enriched in that they wrongfully secured a benefit which it would be unconscionable for them to retain. We agree with this conclusion.

538 F.2d at 994. In light of the district court's extensive discussion of the essentially private nature of the universities, and the Third Circuit allowing restitution from those universities, it cannot be said that *Samuel* contravenes those principles relied on in the instant case. . . .

Effect of Fourteenth Amendment
Violation on Eleventh Amendment
Immunity

In their final argument plaintiffs contend that the Eleventh Amendment does not bar recovery for this Fourteenth Amendment violation. Plaintiffs argue that the earlier enacted Eleventh Amendment (adopted 1798) must give way to the Fourteenth Amendment (adopted 1868) which protects individuals against state encroachment upon their rights to due process and equal protection of the laws. The major portion of plaintiffs' brief deals with this argument.

The three-judge court rejected this argument and held that the Eleventh Amendment barred recovery of excess tuition payments. In reaching this conclusion the court relied upon *Edelman v. Jordan*, 415 U.S. 651, 94 S.Ct. 1347, 39 L.Ed.2d 662 (1974). It recognized that although *Edelman* did not rest upon Fourteenth Amendment grounds,

> the sweep of the majority opinion [in *Edelman*] apparently leaves no room for distinguishing money demands made against a state because of Fourteenth Amendment transgressions, at least in such areas, as here, where Congress had not passed enforcement legislation specifically directed against a state or states pursuant to Section 5 of the Amendment.

379 F.Supp. at 1189. Accordingly, the court held that

> [w]ithout specific guidance from the Supreme Court, we hold that the issue of ordering refunds to plaintiffs is foreclosed and no longer an open question, despite the footnote observation in Justice Marshall's dissent.

Id. at 1189.

Of course, *Edelman* does not hold that the Eleventh Amendment absolutely proscribes all monetary relief against a state in a federal court, even in Fourteenth Amendment cases. Insofar as one Amendment may override the other, the question was left open in *Edelman*, as Justice Marshall recognized in his dissent. *Edelman* is not, however, eliminated as an instructional device in attempting to come to grips with the sensitive constitutional issue raised by plaintiffs' arguments. The *Edelman* Court expressly overruled, as being inconsistent with the Eleventh Amendment, a series of Fourteenth Amendment cases allowing assessment of damages against the state. . . .

NOTES

1. In Edelman v. Jordan, 415 U.S. 651 (1974), the majority maintained that the Eleventh Amendment bars federal court actions by private parties seeking funds in the state treasury, even when the state has violated valid federal regulations under a federal spending program. In that case, beneficiaries under a federal-state program of Aid to the Aged, Blind, and Disabled sought retroactive payments wrongfully withheld by state officials. Justice Rehnquist's majority opinion explained that, though prospective injunctive relief against state officials acting unlawfully is available (under Ex parte Young, 209 U.S. 123, 1908), a decree ordering retroactive payments is impermissible under the Eleventh Amendment, since the funds, "must inevitably come from the general revenues" of the state. Justices Douglas, Brennan, Marshall and Blackmun dissented. Justices Douglas and Marshall argued that the state had waived its constitutional immunity by consenting to participate in a program partly supported by federal funds. A second Supreme Court opinion in this case, Quern v. Jordan, _____ U. S. _____ (1979) ruled that a state is *not* a person for purposes of § 1983, but that sending notices of possible claims does not violate Eleventh Amendment immunity.

2. As this case also indicates, it is possible to find that a state has waived its Eleventh Amendment immunity in particular circumstances, but the existence of waiver is difficult to establish.

3. In Fitzpatrick v. Bitzer, 427 U.S. 445 (1976), a Title VII case, the Supreme Court held that the Eleventh Amendment did not foreclose Congress' power to authorize the federal courts to enter an award against a state as a means of enforcing the substantive guarantees of the Fourteenth Amendment. The Court said:

> But we think that the Eleventh Amendment, and the principle of state sovereignty which it embodies, see *Hans* v. *Louisiana*, 134 U.S. 1 (1890), are necessarily limited by the enforcement provisions of §5 of the Fourteenth Amendment. In that section Congress is expressly granted authority to enforce "by appropriate legislation" the substantive provisions of the Fourteenth Amendment, which themselves embody significant limitations on state authority. When Congress acts pursuant to §5, not only is it exercising legislative authority that is plenary within the terms of the constitutional grant, it is exercising that authority under one section of a constitutional Amendment whose other sections by their own terms embody limitations on state authority. We think that Congress may, in determining what is "appropriate legislation" for the purpose of enforcing the provisions of the Fourteenth Amendment, provide for private suits against States or state officials which are constitutionally impermissible in other contexts. See *Edelman v. Jordan*, 415 U.S. 651 (1974); *Ford Motor Co. v. Department of Treasury*, 323 U.S. 459 (1945).

4. In order to apply Eleventh Amendment immunity, the court in *Jagnandan* found that Mississippi State University was an "arm of the state," a state agency indistinguishable from the state itself. What effect does this finding have on the academic autonomy of MSU?

5. As discussed earlier, tort actions brought against institutions of higher education may be divided into constitutional torts based on civil rights acts, which authorize suits against the government, and common-law torts. Is *Jagnandan* an example of a constitutional tort case?

6. Would the University of Illinois be entitled to Eleventh Amendment immunity from suit in a case like that brought by the Jagnandans? (*See University of Illinois v. Barrett, supra.*)

7. In *Jagnandan*, the court refers to *Vlandis v. Kline, infra*, Chapter 10, in which the Supreme Court assumed without discussing the issue that no Eleventh Amendment immunity existed in a case brought against the University of Connecticut by students

asking for a refund of out-state tuition. Compare the Supreme Court's discussion of a similar assumption in § 1983 cases against school boards in *Monell, infra.* Do *Monell* and *Vlandis v. Kline,* read together, indicate that absolute Eleventh Amendment immunity no longer exists for state universities? Does it matter that *Jagnandan* was brought directly under the Fourteenth Amendment?

C.   Section 1983 Actions

WOOD v. STRICKLAND
United States Supreme Court
420 U.S. 308 (1975)

MR. JUSTICE WHITE delivered the opinion of the Court.

Respondents Peggy Strickland and Virginia Crain brought this lawsuit against petitioners, who were members of the school board at the time in question, two school administrators, and the Special School District of Mena, Ark., purporting to assert a cause of action under 42 U.S.C. § 1983, and claiming that their federal constitutional rights to due process were infringed under color of state law by their expulsion from the Mena Public High School on the grounds of their violation of a school regulation prohibiting the use or possession of intoxicating beverages at school or school activities. The complaint as amended prayed for compensatory and punitive damages against all petitioners, injunctive relief allowing respondents to resume attendance, preventing petitioners from imposing any sanctions as a result of the expulsion, and restraining enforcement of the challenged regulation, declaratory relief as to the constitutional invalidity of the regulation, and expunction of any record of their expulsion. After the declaration of a mistrial arising from the jury's failure to reach a verdict, the District Court directed verdicts in favor of petitioners on the ground that petitioners were immune from damages suits absent proof of malice in the sense of ill will toward respondents. 348 F. Supp. 244 (WD Ark. 1972). The Court of Appeals, finding that the facts showed a violation of respondents' rights to "substantive due process," reversed and remanded for appropriate injunctive relief and a new trial on the question of damages. 485 F.2d 186 (CA8 1973). A petition for rehearing en banc was denied, with three judges dissenting. See *id.*, at 191. Certiorari was granted to consider whether this application of due process by the Court of Appeals was warranted and whether that court's expression of a standard governing immunity for school board members from liability for compensatory damages under 42 U.S.C. § 1983 was the correct one. 416 U.S. 935 (1974).

The violation of the school regulation prohibiting the use or possession of intoxicating beverages at school or school activities with which respondents were charged concerned their "spiking" of the punch served at a meeting of an extracurricular school organization attended by parents and students. At the time in question, respondents were 16 years old and were in the 10th grade. The relevant facts begin with their discovery that the punch had not been prepared for the meeting as previously planned. The girls then agreed to "spike" it. Since the county in which the school is located is "dry," respondents and a third girl drove across the state border into Oklahoma and purchased two 12-ounce bottles of "Right Time," a malt liquor. They then bought six 10-ounce bottles of a soft drink, and, after having mixed the contents of the eight bottles in an empty milk carton, returned to school. Prior to the meeting the girls experienced second thoughts about the wisdom of their prank, but by then they were caught up in the force of events and the intervention of other girls prevented them from disposing of the illicit punch. The punch was served at the meeting, without apparent effect.

Ten days later, the teacher in charge of the extracurricular group and meeting, Mrs. Curtis Powell, having heard something about the "spiking," questioned the girls about it. Although first denying any knowledge, the girls admitted their involvement after the teacher said that she would handle the punishment herself. The next day, however, she told the girls that the incident was becoming increasingly the subject of talk in the school and that the principal, P. T. Waller, would probably hear about it. She told them that her job was in jeopardy but that she would not force them to admit to Waller what they had done. If they did not go to him then, however, she would not be able to help them if the incident became "distorted." The three girls then went to Waller and admitted their role in the affair. He suspended them from school for a maximum two-week period, subject to the decision of the school board. Waller also told them that the board would meet that night, that the girls could tell their parents about the meeting, but that the parents should not contact any members of the board. . . .

The board subsequently agreed to hold another meeting on the matter, and one was held approximately two weeks after the first meeting. The girls, their parents and their counsel attended this session. The board began with a reading of a written statement of facts as it had found them. The girls admitted mixing the malt liquor into the punch with the intent of "spiking" it, but asked the board to forgo its rule punishing such violations by such substantial suspensions. Neither Mrs. Powell nor Waller was present at this meeting. The board voted not to change its policy and, as before, to expel the girls for the remainder of the semester.

The District Court instructed the jury that a decision for respondents had to be premised upon a finding that petitioners acted with malice in expelling them and defined "malice" as meaning "ill will against a person— a wrongful act done intentionally without just cause or excuse." 348 F.Supp. at 248. In ruling for petitioners after the jury had been unable to agree, the District Court found "as a matter of law" that there was no evidence from which malice could be inferred. *Id.*, at 253.

The Court of Appeals, however, viewed both the instruction and the decision of the District Court as being erroneous. Specific intent to harm wrongfully, it held, was not a requirement for the recovery of damages. Instead, "[i]t need only be established that the defendants did not, in the light of all the circumstances, act in good faith. The test is an objective, rather than a subjective one." 485 F.2d, at 191 (footnote omitted).

Petitioners as members of the school board assert here, as they did below, an absolute immunity from liability under § 1983 and at the very least seek to reinstate the judgment of the District Court. If they are correct and the District Court's dismissal should be sustained, we need go no further in this case. Moreover, the immunity question involves the construction of a federal statute, and our practice is to deal with possibly dispositive statutory issues before reaching questions turning on the construction of the Constitution. Cf. *Hagans* v. *Lavine,* 415 U.S. 528, 549 (1974). We essentially sustain the position of the Court of Appeals with respect to the immunity issue.

The nature of the immunity from awards of damages under § 1983 available to school administrators and school board members is not a question which the lower federal courts have answered with a single voice. There is general agreement on the existence of a "good faith" immunity, but the courts have either emphasized different factors as elements of good faith or have not given specific content to the good-faith standard.

This Court has decided three cases dealing with the scope of the immunity protecting various types of governmental officials from liability for damages under § 1983. In *Tenney* v. *Brandhove,* 341 U.S. 367 (1951), the question was found to be one essentially of statutory construction. Noting that the language of § 1983 is silent with respect to immunities, the Court concluded that there was no basis for believing that Congress intended to eliminate the traditional immunity of legislators from civil liability for acts done within their sphere of legislative action. That immunity, "so well grounded in history and reason. . . ," 341 U.S., at 376, was absolute and consequently did not depend upon the motivations of the legislators. In *Pierson* v. *Ray,* 386 U.S. 547, 554 (1967), finding that "[t]he legislative record gives no clear indication that Congress meant to abolish wholesale all common-law immunities" in enacting § 1983, we concluded that the common-law doctrine of absolute judicial immunity survived. Similarly, § 1983 did not preclude application of the traditional rule that a policeman, making an arrest in good faith and with probable cause, is not liable for damages, although the person arrested proves innocent. Consequently the Court said: "Although the matter is not entirely free from doubt, the same consideration would seem to require excusing him from liability for acting under a statute that he reasonably believed to be valid but that was later held unconstitutional, on its face or as applied." 386 U.S., at 555 (footnote omitted). Finally, last Term we held that the chief executive officer of a State, the senior and subordinate officers of the State's National Guard, and the president of a state-controlled university were not absolutely immune from liability under § 1983, but instead were entitled to immunity, under prior precedent and in light of the obvious need to avoid discouraging effective official action by public officers charged with a considerable range of responsibility and discretion, only if they acted in good faith as defined by the Court.

"[I]n varying scope, a qualified immunity is available to officers
of the executive branch of government, the variation being dependent upon the scope of discretion and responsibilities of the
office and all the circumstances as they reasonably appeared at
the time of the action on which liability is sought to be based. It
is the existence of reasonable grounds for the belief formed at
the time and in light of all the circumstances, coupled with good-
faith belief, that affords a basis for qualified immunity of executive officers for acts performed in the course of official conduct."
Scheuer v. *Rhodes,* 416 U.S. 232, 247-248 (1974).

Common-law tradition, recognized in our prior decisions, and strong
public-policy reasons also lead to a construction of § 1983 extending a
qualified good-faith immunity to school board members from liability for
damages under that section. Although there have been differing emphases
and formulations of the common-law immunity of public school officials
in cases of student expulsion or suspension, state courts have generally
recognized that such officers should be protected from tort liability under
state law for all good-faith, nonmalicious action taken to fulfill their official
duties.

As the facts of this case reveal, school board members function at
different times in the nature of legislators and adjudicators in the school
disciplinary process. Each of these functions necessarily involves the exercise of discretion, the weighing of many factors, and the formulation of
long-term policy. "Like legislators and judges, these officers are entitled to
rely on traditional sources for the factual information on which they decide
and act." *Scheuer* v. *Rhodes, supra,* at 246 (footnote omitted). As with
executive officers faced with instances of civil disorder, school officials,
confronted with student behavior causing or threatening disruption, also
have an "obvious need for prompt action, and decisions must be made in
reliance on factual information supplied by others." *Ibid.*

Liability for damages for every action which is found subsequently
to have been violative of a student's constitutional rights and to have caused
compensable injury would unfairly impose upon the school decisionmaker
the burden of mistakes made in good faith in the course of exercising his
discretion within the scope of his official duties. School board members,
among other duties, must judge whether there have been violations of
school regulations and, if so, the appropriate sanctions for the violations.
Denying any measure of immunity in these circumstances "would contribute
not to principled and fearless decision-making but to intimidation." *Pierson*
v. *Ray, supra,* at 554. The imposition of monetary costs for mistakes which
were not unreasonable in the light of all the circumstances would undoubtedly deter even the most conscientious school decisionmaker from exercising
his judgment independently, forcefully, and in a manner best serving the
long-term interest of the school and the students. The most capable candidates for school board positions might be deterred from seeking office if

heavy burdens upon their private resources from monetary liability were a likely prospect during their tenure.

These considerations have undoubtedly played a prime role in the development by state courts of a qualified immunity protecting school officials from liability for damages in lawsuits claiming improper suspensions or expulsions. But at the same time, the judgment implicit in this common-law development is that absolute immunity would not be justified since it would not sufficiently increase the ability of school officials to exercise their discretion in a forthright manner to warrant the absence of a remedy for students subjected to intentional or otherwise inexcusable deprivations.

Tenney v. *Brandhove, Pierson* v. *Ray,* and *Scheuer* v. *Rhodes* drew upon a very similar background and were animated by a very similar judgment in construing § 1983. Absent legislative guidance, we now rely on those same sources in determining whether and to what extent school officials are immune from damage suits under § 1983. We think there must be a degree of immunity if the work of the schools is to go forward; and, however worded, the immunity must be such that public school officials understand that action taken in the good-faith fulfillment of their responsibilities and within the bounds of reason under all the circumstances will not be punished and that they need not exercise their discretion with undue timidity.

> "Public officials, whether governors, mayors or police, legislators or judges, who fail to make decisions when they are needed or who do not act to implement decisions when they are made do not fully and faithfully perform the duties of their offices. Implicit in the idea that officials have some immunity—absolute or qualified—for their acts, is a recognition that they may err. The concept of immunity assumes this and goes on to assume that it is better to risk some error and possible injury from such error than not to decide or act at all." *Scheuer* v. *Rhodes,* 416 U.S., at 241-242 (footnote omitted).

The disagreement between the Court of Appeals and the District Court over the immunity standard in this case has been put in terms of an "objective" versus a "subjective" test of good faith. As we see it, the appropriate standard necessarily contains elements of both. The official himself must be acting sincerely and with a belief that he is doing right, but an act violating a student's constitutional rights can be no more justified by ignorance or disregard of settled, indisputable law on the part of one entrusted with supervision of students' daily lives than by the presence of actual malice. To be entitled to a special exemption from the categorical remedial language of § 1983 in a case in which his action violated a student's constitutional rights, a school board member, who has voluntarily undertaken the task of supervising the operation of the school and the activities of the students, must be held to a standard of conduct based not only on permissible intentions, but also on knowledge of the basic, unquestioned constitutional rights of his charges. Such a standard imposes neither an unfair burden upon a person assuming a responsible public office requiring a high degree of intelligence and judgment for the proper fulfillment of its duties, nor an unwarranted burden in light of the value which civil rights have in our legal system. Any lesser standard would deny much of the promise of § 1983. Therefore, in the specific context of school discipline, we hold that a school board member is not immune from liability for damages under § 1983 if he knew or reasonably should have known that the action he took within his sphere of official responsibility would violate the constitutional rights of the student affected, or if he took the action with the malicious intention to cause a deprivation of constitutional rights or other injury to the student. That is not to say that school board members are "charged with predicting the future course of constitutional law." *Pierson* v. *Ray,* 386 U.S., at 557. A compensatory award will be appropriate only if the school board member has acted with such an impermissible motivation or with such disregard of the student's clearly established constitutional rights that his action cannot reasonably be characterized as being in good faith. . . .

Respondents' complaint alleged that their procedural due process rights were violated by the action taken by petitioners. App. 9. The District Court did not discuss this claim in its final opinion, but the Court of Appeals viewed it as presenting a substantial question. It concluded that the girls were denied procedural due process at the first school board meeting, but also intimated that the second meeting may have cured the initial procedural deficiencies. Having found a substantive due process violation, however, the court did not reach a conclusion on this procedural issue. 485 F.2d, at 190.

Respondents have argued here that there was a procedural due process violation which also supports the result reached by the Court of Appeals. Brief for Respondents 27-28, 36. But because the District Court did not discuss it, and the Court of Appeals did not decide it, it would be preferable to have the Court of Appeals consider the issue in the first instance.

The judgment of the Court of Appeals is vacated and the case remanded for further proceedings consistent with this opinion.

So ordered.

MR. JUSTICE POWELL, with whom THE CHIEF JUSTICE, MR. JUSTICE BLACKMUN, and MR. JUSTICE REHNQUIST join, concurring in part and dissenting in part. . . .

Less than a year ago, in *Scheuer* v. *Rhodes,* 416 U.S. 232 (1974), and in an opinion joined by all participating members of the Court, a considerably less demanding standard of liability was approved with respect to two of the highest officers of the State, the Governor and Adjutant General. In that case, the estates of students killed at Kent State University sued these officials under § 1983. After weighing the competing claims, the Court concluded:

"These considerations suggest that, in varying scope, a qualified immunity is available to officers of the executive branch of government, the variation being dependent upon the scope of discretion and responsibilities of the office and all the circumstances as they reasonably appeared at the time of the action on which liability is sought to be based. *It is the existence of reasonable grounds for the belief formed at the time and in light of all the circumstances, coupled with good-faith belief, that affords a basis for qualified immunity of executive officers for acts performed in the course of official conduct.*" 416 U.S., at 247-248. (Emphasis added.)

The italicized sentence from *Scheuer* states, as I view it, the correct standard for qualified immunity of a government official; whether in light of the discretion and responsibilities of his office, and under all of the circumstances as they appeared at the time, the officer acted reasonably and in good faith. This was the standard applied to the Governor of a State charged with maliciously calling out National Guardsmen who killed and wounded Kent State students. Today's opinion offers no reason for imposing a more severe standard on school board members charged only with wrongfully expelling three teenage pupils. . . .

In view of today's decision significantly enhancing the possibility of personal liability, one must wonder whether qualified persons will continue in the desired numbers to volunteer for service in public education.

NOTE

The following discussion of the *Scheuer* and *Wood* decisions appeared in *Developments in the Law—Section 1983 and Federalism*, 90 Harvard L. Rev. 1133, 1211-17 (1977):*

The class of state executive officers to whom the Supreme Court was willing to extend this qualified immunity was broadened in the cases of *Scheuer v. Rhodes* and *Wood v. Strickland*, opinions which also served to define in some measure the nature of the good faith defense. In *Scheuer*, personal representatives of students killed during the disorders at Kent State University brought suit under section 1983 against the Governor of Ohio, officials of the national guard, and the president of Kent State. The district court dismissed the suit as barred by the eleventh amendment and on the ground that "executive immunity" shielded the defendants; the court of appeals agreed, finding that the defendants occupied positions requiring wide discretion, and that "since the courts have granted to themselves absolute immunity, it would seem incongruous for them not to extend the same privilege to the Executive."

Recognizing the difficulties necessarily entailed by any attempt to hold the highest executive officer of a state liable for his discretionary decisions, the Supreme Court nonetheless declined to find the governor absolutely immune. The section 1983 action was designed to "enforce provisions of the Fourteenth Amendment against those who carry a badge of authority of a State"; indeed, the danger from which it shields the citizen is the "misuse of power . . . made possible only because the wrongdoer is clothed with the authority of state law. . . ." Hence, the acts of a governor could not be treated as a "supreme and unchangeable edict, overriding all conflicting rights"; rather, the imperatives of the section 1983 action in combination with the necessities of discretionary executive conduct suggest that, in varying scope, a qualified immunity is available to officers of the executive branch of government, the variation being dependent upon the scope of discretion and responsibilities of the office and all the circumstances as they reasonably appeared at the time of the action on which liability is . . . based. It is the existence of reasonable grounds for the belief formed at the time and in light of all the circumstances coupled with good-faith belief, that affords a basis for qualified immunity.

Scheuer left open a number of questions about the scope of the good faith defense. In particular, the term "good faith" itself assumed a more objective or subjective meaning, depending on which court was interpreting it. This problem reached the Supreme Court in *Wood v. Strickland*, a suit in which the trial court had applied a subjective meaning of "good faith" and the court of appeals an objective one. Not surprisingly, the Supreme Court held that the good faith standard encompasses *both* a subjective and an objective element. Clearly, the defendant official must not have acted out of malice; moreover, "an act violating . . . constitutional rights can be no more justified by ignorance or disregard of settled, indisputable law . . . than by the presence of actual malice."

Wood and *Scheuer* taken together make it clear that the "immunity" extended to state executive officials is in fact a defense—a defense on the merits, involving proof of both state of mind and reasonableness of conduct. The first part of the defense has not caused many problems for courts; when there are conflicting allegations as to whether or not the defendant acted out of malice, the issue can readily be decided by the jury. What has proved more difficult has been to define the independent content of the reasonableness standard.

The contours of this standard are defined most broadly in *Scheuer*, which held that the showing required to satisfy it depends "upon the scope of discretion and responsibilities of the office and all the circumstances as they reasonably appeared. . . ." In part, this approximates the "reasonable man" test of negligence law; but it includes the additional element of the defendant official's range of discretion and the need to prevent undue inhibition of its exercise.

The Supreme Court's opinion in *Wood* can best be read as broadening the potential section 1983 damage liability of state executive officials by adding to the reasonableness test of *Scheuer* a provision for imputing malice where the official acts so as to violate clearly settled constitutional rights. But paradoxically, the opinion is also subject to an interpretation which would significantly reduce the possibility of damage liability: the only test actually articulated is whether the official acted maliciously, or in violation of rights he knew or reasonably should have known existed, with the category of rights encompassed under the latter test seemingly limited to those clearly established, since the official cannot be "charged with predicting the future course of constitutional law." Under the narrowing interpretation, the *Scheuer* reasonableness test would have no independent content, since in the absence of malice, unless rights of the clearly settled category were violated, no liability could be found.

But given the Court's citation of *Scheuer* and its apparent readiness to impute malice—leading to the possibility of an award of punitive damages—where the official ignores clearly settled constitutional rights, it is arguable that the Court intended to retain the *Scheuer* reasonableness test for damage liability. Indeed, many lower courts have taken this view, considering a wide variety of factors to determine whether the official action was reasonable. Under this view, the "clearly settled rights" prong of the liability test should be utilized sparingly, as it has in fact been used by lower courts since *Wood*, to find liability, apart from other factors indicative of reasonableness of official action, where the character of the right violated is so clearly settled that ignorance of it simply cannot be excused.

Absent violation of such a right—as when the right is newly articulated in the course of the damage action, involved in controversy in the lower courts, or extended to a new and different factual context—the jury should be permitted to inquire into the reasonableness of the official conduct under the *Scheuer* standard. Otherwise, the 1983 damage action will be deprived of much of its remaining vitality; officials will be able to escape liability for unreasonable acts, violative of constitutional rights, by showing that they did not act maliciously and by resort to formalistic arguments that the right violated was not of sufficiently settled legal status to warrant an imputation of malice. They may do so regardless of the circumstances surrounding the actions in question, the alternative courses of action open, or even the presence of an opportunity, upon reasonable inquiry, to have discovered that the questioned action would more likely than not be declared violative of the Constitution. . . .

MONELL v. DEPARTMENT OF SOCIAL SERVICES
United States Supreme Court
98 S.Ct. 2018 (1978)

Mr. Justice BRENNAN delivered the opinion of the Court.

Petitioners, a class of female employees of the Department of Social Services and the Board of Education of the City of New York, commenced this action under 42 U.S.C. § 1983 in July 1971. The gravamen of the complaint was that the Board and the Department had as a matter of official policy compelled pregnant employees to take unpaid leaves of absence before such leaves were required for medical reasons. Cf, *Cleveland Board of Education v. LaFleur*, 414 U.S. 632, 94 S.Ct. 791, 39 L.Ed.2d 52 (1974). The suit sought injunctive relief and back pay for periods of unlawful forced leave. Named as defendants in the action were the Department and its Commissioner, the Board and its Chancellor, and the city of New York and its Mayor. In each case, the individual defendants were sued solely in their official capacities.

On cross-motions for summary judgment, the District Court for the Southern District of New York held moot petitioners' claims for injunctive and declaratory relief since the City of New York and the Board, after the filing of the complaint, had changed their policies relating to maternity leaves so that no pregnant employee would have to take leave unless she was medically unable to continue to perform her job. 394 F.Supp. 853, 855. No one now challenges this conclusion. The court did conclude, however, that the acts complained of were unconstitutional under *LaFleur, supra.* 394 F.Supp., at 855. Nonetheless plaintiff's prayers for back pay were denied because any such damages would come ultimately from the City of New York and, therefore, to hold otherwise would be to "circumvent" the immunity conferred on municipalities by *Monroe v. Pape*, 365 U.S. 167, 81 S.Ct. 473, 5 L.Ed.2d 492 (1961). See 394 F.Supp., at 855.

On appeal, petitioners renewed their arguments that the Board of Education was not a "municipality" within the meaning of *Monroe v. Pape, supra,* and that, in any event, the District Court had erred in barring a damage award against the individual defendants. The Court of Appeals for the Second Circuit rejected both contentions. The court first held that the Board of Education was not a person under § 1983 because "it performs a vital governmental function . . . , and, significantly, while it has the right to determine how the funds appropriated to it shall be spent . . . , it has no final say in deciding what its appropriations shall be." 532 F.2d 259, 263 (1976) (citation omitted). The individual defendants, however, were "persons" under § 1983, even when sued solely in their official capacities. *Id.,* at 264. Yet, because a damage award would "have to be paid by a city that was held not to be amenable to such an action in *Monroe v. Pape,*" a damage action against officials sued in their official capacities could not proceed. *Id.,* at 265.

We granted certiorari in this case, 429 U.S. 1071, 97 S.Ct. 807, 50 L.Ed.2d 789, to consider

"Whether local governmental officials and/or local independent school boards are 'persons' within the meaning of 42 U.S.C. § 1983 when equitable relief in the nature of back pay is sought against them in their official capacities?" Pet. for Cert. 8.

Although, after pleanry consideration, we have decided the merits of over a score of cases brought under § 1983 in which the principal defendant was a school board—and, indeed, in some of which § 1983 and its jurisdictional counterpart, 28 U.S.C. § 1343, provided the only basis for jurisdiction—we indicated in *Mt. Healthy City Board of Ed. v. Doyle,* 429 U.S. 274, 279, 97 S.Ct. 568, 573, 50 L.Ed.2d 471 (1977), last Term that the question presented here was open and would be decided "another day." That other day has come and we now overrule *Monroe v. Pape, supra,* insofar as it holds that local governments are wholly immune from suit under § 1983.

I

In *Monroe v. Pape,* we held that "Congress did not undertake to bring municipal corporations within the ambit of [§ 1983]." 365 U.S., at 187, 81 S.Ct. at 484. The sole basis for this conclusion was an inference drawn from Congress' rejection of the "Sherman amendment" to the bill which became Civil Rights Act of 1871, 17 Stat. 13—the precursor of § 1983— which would have held a municipal corporation liable for damage done to the person or property of its inhabitants by *private* persons "riotously and tumultuously assembled." Cong. Globe, 42d Cong., 1st Sess, 749 (1871) (hereinafter "Globe"). Although the Sherman amendment did not seek to amend § 1 of the Act, which is now § 1983, and although the nature of the obligation created by that amendment was vastly different from that created by § 1, the Court nonetheless concluded in *Monroe* that Congress must have meant to exclude municipal corporations from the coverage of § 1 because "'the House [in voting against the Sherman amendment] had solemnly decided that in their judgment Congress had no constitutional power to impose any *obligation* upon county and town organizations, the mere instrumentality for the administration of state law.'" 365 U.S., at 190, 81 S. Ct. at 485 (emphasis added), quoting Globe, at 804 (Rep. Poland). This statement, we thought, showed that Congress doubted its "constitutional power . . . to impose *civil liability* on municipalities." 365 U.S., at 190, 81 S.Ct. at 486 (emphasis added), and that such doubt would have extended to any type of civil liability.

A fresh analysis of debate on the Civil Rights Act of 1871, and particularly of the case law which each side mustered in its support, shows, however, that *Monroe* incorrectly equated the "obligation" of which Representative Poland spoke with "civil liability." . . .

In addition, by 1871, it was well understood that corporations should be treated as natural persons for virtually all purposes of constitutional and statutory analysis. This had not always been so. When this Court first considered the question of the status of corporations, Chief Justice Marshall, writing for the Court, denied that corporations "as such" were persons as that term was used in Art. III and the Judiciary Act of 1789. See *Bank of the United States v. Deveaux*, 5 Cranch 61, 86, 3 L.Ed. 38 (1809). By 1844, however, the *Deveaux* doctrine was unhesitatingly abandoned:

> "[A] corporation created by and doing business in a particular state, is to be deemed *to all intents and purposes as a person*, although an artificial person, . . . capable of being treated as a citizen of that state, as much as a natural person." *Louisville R. Co. v. Letson*, 2 How. 497, 558, 11 L.Ed. 353 (1844) (emphasis added), discussed in Globe, at 752.

And only two years before the debates on the Civil Rights Act, in *Cowles v. Mercer County*, 7 Wall. 118, 121, 19 L.Ed. 86 (1869), the *Letson* principle was automatically and without discussion extended to municipal corporations. Under this doctrine, municipal corporations were routinely sued in the federal courts and this fact was well known to Members of Congress.

That the "usual" meaning of the word person would extend to municipal corporations is also evidenced by an Act of Congress which had been passed only months before the Civil Rights Act was passed. This Act provided that

> "in all acts hereafter passed . . . the word 'person' may extend and be applied to bodies politic and corporate . . . unless the context shows that such words were intended to be used in a more limited sense[.]" Act of Feb. 25, 1871, ch. 71, §2, 16 Stat. 431.

Municipal corporations in 1871 were included within the phrase "bodies politic and corporate" and, accordingly, the "plain meaning" of §1 is that local government bodies were to be included within the ambit of the persons who could be sued under §1 of the Civil Rights Act. Indeed, a Circuit Judge, writing in 1873 in what is apparently the first reported case under §1, read the Dictionary Act in precisely this way in a case involving a corporate plaintiff and a municipal defendant. See *Northwestern Fertilizing Co. v. Hyde Park*, 18 F.Cas. 393, 394 (CCND Ill.1873) (No. 10,336).

II

Our analysis of the legislative history of the Civil Rights Act of 1871 compels the conclusion that Congress *did* intend municipalities and other local government units to be included among those persons to whom § 1983 applies. Local governing bodies, therefore, can be sued directly under § 1983 for monetary, declaratory, or injunctive relief where, as here, the action that is alleged to be unconstitutional implements or executes a policy statement, ordinance, regulation, or decision officially adopted and promulgated by that body's officers. Moreover, although the touchstone of the § 1983 action against a government body is an allegation that official policy is responsible for a deprivation of rights protected by the Constitution, local governments, like every other § 1983 "person," by the very terms of the statute, may be sued for constitutional deprivations visited pursuant to governmental "custom" even though such a custom has not received formal approval through the body's official decisionmaking channels. As Mr. Justice Harlan, writing for the Court, said in *Adickes v. S. H. Kress & Co.*, 398 U.S. 144, 167-168, 90 S.Ct. 1598, 1613, 26 L.Ed.2d 142 (1970): "Congress included customs and usages [in § 1983] because of the persistent and widespread discriminatory practices of state officials. . . . Although not authorized by written law, such practices of state officials could well be so permanent and well settled as to constitute a 'custom or usage' with the force of law."

On the other hand, the language of § 1983, read against the background of the same legislative history, compels the conclusion that Congress did not intend municipalities to be held liable unless action pursuant to official municipal policy of some nature caused a constitutional tort. In particular, we conclude that a municipality cannot be held liable *solely* because it employs a tortfeasor—or, in other words, a municipality cannot be held liable under § 1983 on a *respondeat superior* theory. . . .

III

Although we have stated that *stare decisis* has more force in statutory analysis than in constitutional adjudication because, in the former situation, Congress can correct our mistakes through legislation, see, *e.g., Edelman v. Jordan*, 415 U.S. 651, 671, and n. 14, 94 S.Ct. 1347, 1365, 39 L.Ed.2d 662 (1974), we have never applied *stare decisis* mechanically to prohibit overruling our earlier decisions determining the meaning of statutes. See, *e.g., Continental T.V., Inc. v. GTE Sylvania, Inc.*, 433 U.S. 36, 47-49, 97 S.Ct 2549, 2559, 53 L.Ed.2d 568 (1977); *Burnet v. Coronado Oil & Gas Co.*, 285 U.S. 393, 406 n. 1, 52 S.Ct. 443, 454, 76 L.Ed. 815 (1932) (Brandeis, J., dissenting) (collecting cases). Nor is this a case where we should "place on the shoulders of Congress the burden of the Court's own error." *Girouard v. United States*, 328 U.S. 61, 70, 66 S.Ct. 826, 830; 90 L.Ed. 1084 (1946).

First, *Monroe v. Pape, supra,* insofar as it completely immunizes municipalities from suit under § 1983, was a departure from prior practice. See,
*e.g., Northwestern Fertilizing Co. v. Hyde Park, supra, City of Manchester v.
Leiby,* 117 F.2d 661 (CA1 1941); *Hannan v. City of Haverhill,* 120 F.2d
87 (CA1 1941); *Douglas v. City of Jeannette,* 319 U.S. 157, 63 S.Ct. 877, 87
L.Ed. 1324 (1943); *Holmes v. City of Atlanta,* 350 U.S. 879, 76 S.Ct.
141, 100 L.Ed. 776 (1955), in each of which municipalities were defendants
in § 1983 suits. Moreover, the constitutional defect that led to the rejection
of the Sherman amendment would not have distinguished between municipalities and school boards, each of which is an instrumentality of state administration. See pp. 2027-2031, *supra.* For this reason, our cases–decided
both before and after *Monroe,* see n. 5, *supra*–holding school boards liable
in § 1983 actions are inconsistent with *Monroe,* especially as *Monroe's* immunizing principle was extended to suits for injunctive relief in *City of
Kenosha v. Bruno,* 412 U.S. 507, 93 S.Ct. 2222, 37 L.Ed.2d 109 (1973).
And although in many of these cases jurisdiction was not questioned, we
ought not "disregard the implications of an exercise of judicial authority
assumed to be proper for [100] years." *Brown Shoe Co. v. United States,*
370 U.S. 294, 307, 82 S.Ct. 1502, 1514, 8 L.Ed.2d 510 (1962); see *Bank
of the United States v. Deveaux, supra,* at 88 (Marshall, C. J.) ("Those
decisions are not cited as authority . . . but they have much weight as they
show that this point neither occurred to the bar or the bench"). Thus,
while we have reaffirmed *Monroe* without further examination on three
occasions, it can scarcely be said that *Monroe* is so consistent with the warp
and woof of civil rights law as to be beyond question.

Second, the principle of blanket immunity established in *Monroe*
cannot be cabined short of school boards. Yet such an extension would
itself be inconsistent with recent expressions of congressional intent. In the
wake of our decisions, Congress not only has shown no hostility to federal
court decisions against school boards, but it has indeed rejected efforts to
strip the federal courts of jurisdiction over school boards. Moreover, recognizing that school boards are often defendants in school desegregation suits,
which have almost without exception been § 1983 suits, Congress has twice
passed legislation authorizing grants to school boards to assist them in
complying with federal court decrees. Finally, in the Civil Rights Attorneys'
Fees Award Act of 1976, 90 Stat. 2641, which allows prevailing parties (in
the discretion of the court) in § 1983 suits to obtain attorneys fees from
the losing party, the Senate stated:

> "[D]efendants in these cases are often State or local *bodies* or
> State or local officials. In such cases it is intended that the at-
> torneys' fees, like other items of costs, will be collected either
> directly from the official, *in his official capacity,* from funds of
> his agency or under his control, or *from the State or local govern-
> ment (whether or not the agency or government is a named
> party)."* S. Rep. No.94-1011, at 5; U.S.Code Cong. & Admin.News
> 1976, pp. 5908, 5913 (emphasis added; footnotes omitted).

Far from showing that Congress has relied on *Monroe*, therefore, events since 1961 show that Congress has refused to extend the benefits of *Monroe* to school boards and has attempted to allow awards of attorneys' fees against local governments even though *Monroe, City of Kenosha v. Bruno, supra,* and *Aldinger v. Howard,* 427 U.S. 1, 96 S.Ct. 2413, 49 L.Ed.2d 276 (1976), have made the joinder of such governments impossible.

Third, municipalities can assert no reliance claim which can support an absolute immunity. As Mr. Justice Frankfurter said in *Monroe*, "[t]his is not an area of commercial law in which, presumably, individuals may have arranged their affairs in reliance on the expected stability of decision." 365 U.S., at 221-222, 81 S.Ct., at 503 (dissent). Indeed, municipalities simply cannot "arrange their affairs" on an assumption that they can violate constitutional rights indefinitely since injunctive suits against local officials under § 1983 would prohibit any such arrangement. And it scarcely need be mentioned that nothing in *Monroe* encourages municipalities to violate constitutional rights or even suggests that such violations are anything other than completely wrong.

Finally, even under the most stringent test for the propriety of overruling a statutory decision proposed by Mr. Justice Harlan in *Monroe*—"that it [must] appear beyond doubt from the legislative history of the 1871 statute that [*Monroe*] misapprehended the meaning of the [section]," *Monroe v. Pape, supra,* 365 U.S. at 192, 81 S.Ct. at 487 (concurring opinion)—the overruling of *Monroe* insofar as it holds that local governments are not "persons" who may be defendants in § 1983 suits is clearly proper. It is simply beyond doubt that, under the 1871 Congress' view of the law, were § 1983 liability unconstitutional as to local governments, it would have been equally unconstitutional as to state officers. Yet everyone—proponents and opponents alike—knew § 1983 would be applied to state officers and nonetheless stated that § 1983 was constitutional. See p. 2031, *supra.* And, moreover, there can be no doubt that § 1 of the Civil Rights Act was intended to provide a remedy, to be broadly construed, against all forms of official violation of federally protected rights. Therefore, absent a clear statement in the legislative history supporting the conclusion that § 1 was not to apply to the official acts of a municipal corporation—which simply is not present—there is no justification for excluding municipalities from the "persons" covered by § 1.

For reasons stated above, therefore, we hold that *stare decisis* does not bar our overruling of *Monroe* insofar as it is inconsistent with Parts I and II of this opinion.

IV

Since the question whether local government bodies should be afforded some form of official immunity was not presented as a question to be decided on this petition and was not briefed by the parties nor addressed by the courts below, we express no views on the scope of any municipal immunity beyond holding that municipal bodies sued under § 1983 cannot be entitled to an absolute immunity, lest our decision that such bodies are subject to suit under § 1983 "be drained of meaning," *Scheuer v. Rhodes,* 416 U.S. 232, 248, 94 S.Ct. 1683, 40 L.Ed.2d 90 (1974). Cf. *Bivens v. Six Unknown Federal Narcotics Agents,* 403 U.S. 388, 397-398, 91 S.Ct. 1999, 29 L.Ed.2d 619 (1971).

V

For the reasons stated above, the judgment of the Court of Appeals is *Reversed.*

NOTES

1. If *Monell* does not automatically remove Eleventh Amendment immunity from all public colleges and universities, what factors might determine whether a given suit against a public institution would prevail?

2. In Aldridge v. Turlington, _____ F. Supp. _____ (N.D. Fla. 1978), a § 1983 case decided after *Monell,* it was argued that state governments stand on a different footing in relation to the federal government than do municipalities, since they are protected by the Tenth and Eleventh Amendments; and that therefore, a congressional intent to impose liability directly on states should not be inferred. The court held, however, that *Monell* stands for the conclusion that Congress intended no difference between states and municipalities, *Fitzpatrick v. Bitzer* having already established that Section 5 of the Fourteenth Amendment allows suits against states, when authorized by Congress.

3. In Bertot v. School District No. 1, Albany County, Wyoming, ___ F.2d ___ (10 Cir. 1978), the Tenth Circuit construed *Monell* and *Scheuer v. Rhodes* together to find that a qualified good faith immunity still existed for individual school board members and the school district itself in a suit for monetary damages for failure to rehire a teacher.

4. Shortly after the *Monell* decision Justice Brennan argued that *Monell* meant that states could be included as defendants in civil rights actions, Hutto v. Finney, 98 S.Ct. 2565 (1978). Justice Powell argued to the contrary in a concurring opinion at 2581. Later in the Term, in a per curiam opinion, the Court dismissed the state of Alabama from a § 1983 suit on Eleventh Amendment grounds. Alabama v. Pugh, 98 S.Ct. 3057 (1978). Thus, while some Eleventh Amendment immunity still exists, the law is at best unclear. *See, The Supreme Court, 1977 Term,* 92 Harvard L. Rev. 1, 323-326 (1978).

5. On March 5, 1979 the Supreme Court handed down three opinions dealing with Eleventh Amendment immunity. A history of the concept of sovereign immunity is set out in Nevada v. Hall _____ U.S. _____ (1979), in which the Court decided that the state of Nevada is not immune to suit in the courts of California. The inter-relation between the Eleventh Amendment and § 1983 of the Civil Rights Act of 1871 is considered in Quern v. Jordan _____ U.S. _____ (1979), a continuation of Edelman v. Jordan, 415 U.S. 651 (1974). Justice Rehnquist, in a ruling characterized as *dicta* by Justice Brennan in his dissent, ruled that § 1983 does not abrogate the Eleventh Amendment immunity of the states; a state is not a "person" for the purposes of § 1983. But, in Lake County Estates, Inc. v. Tahoe Regional Planning Agency _____ U.S. _____ (1979) the Court ruled that Eleventh Amendment state immunity did not extend to a bi-state regional planning agency which is a political subdivision rather than "an arm of the states." Thus it would appear that the concept of governmental immunity is an issue of interest and controversy before the present Court. A final definition, particularly for institutions of higher education, must depend on future decisions, but it would appear that derivative organizations and institutions have less guarantee of governmental immunity.

CHAPTER 5

MISCELLANEOUS ISSUES

I. **Taxation**

   A. *Introduction*

A GUIDE TO TAX POLICY
AND HIGHER EDUCATION*

SPECTRUM OF TAX ISSUES

The list of tax issues affecting higher education is practically inexhaustible. Federal, state and local governments constantly scrutinize their tax laws to determine whether these are serving broad, publicly accepted purposes, and whether these could be made to produce greater revenues.

At the federal level, pressures have mounted over the last two decades for a comprehensive revision of federal tax policy and practice. Both the federal individual income tax and estate tax are being studied to determine if they are consistent with tax theory and if they serve efficiently and fairly the public purposes for which they were enacted.

Two provisions of extraordinary interest to higher education that have drawn considerable attention from tax experts in government, universities, research centers, the press, the legal community, and organized citizens groups are the individual income tax charitable deduction and the estate tax charitable deduction. The individual income tax basically allows a taxpayer who itemizes personal deductions to take a deduction for his gifts to public charities. He is, however, limited overall in any year to a deduction equal to 50 percent of his adjusted gross income, and is further limited to a deduction of 30 percent of adjusted gross income for gifts of property whose market value has increased over its value at the time of acquisition by the taxpayer, and which would produce capital gains income if sold (appreciated property). There are many technical rules, definitions and interrelationships that complicate this seemingly simple basic description. It is enough to point out that this basic provision, with all its complex detail, has been the subject of much controversy and criticism over the past decade.

---

*Reference service published by the National Institute of Independent Colleges and Universities, February, 1978. Reprinted by permission of the National Institute of Independent Colleges and Universities. All rights reserved.

Professor Stanley S. Surrey of Harvard Law School, who served as Assistant Secretary of the Treasury for Tax Policy under Presidents Kennedy and Johnson, published two seminal law review articles in 1970.[1] They were based in part on a comprehensive study of the federal tax laws he had authored while at the Treasury. They raised serious questions about the charitable deduction and other exclusions, exemptions and deductions in the Internal Revenue Code. While others had previously made similar points about individual parts of the personal income tax,[2] Professor Surrey's articles provided a sophisticated conceptual framework for examining all of its provisions and evaluating them by common standards.

The key elements of this framework were the concepts of "tax expenditures" and the "Tax Expenditure Budget".[3] They were first introduced by him in a speech in late 1967 discussing the budgetary dilemmas confronting the Johnson Administration.[4] He noted that Congress and the Administration were only examining the federal programs financed directly by Congressionally authorized expenditures, but not those financed, indirectly in his view, through Congressionally enacted provisions in the federal individual income tax system. To remedy this, he recommended categorizing the latter kind of "spending" programs, "tax expenditures", and creating an annual "Tax Expenditure Budget" to show the impact of these on public policy. The first was published by the Department of the Treasury in January, 1968.

Oversimplifying, the tax expenditure concept is developed as follows. The ability to pay is deemed to be the proper basis for personal taxation. Net income is the best approximate measure of ability to pay according to the dominant theory of individual income taxation.[5] Certain deductions from gross income are essential to the calculation of net income. They are called income-defining deductions. Such deductions are considered to be an inherent part of the structure of an ideal income tax system. In general, under this theory, expenditures necessary for the earning or production of income are the only income-defining deductions. Any other deductions are

---

1. Surrey, "Tax Incentives as a Device for Implementing Government Policy: A Comparison with Direct Government Expenditures," 83 *Harvard Law Review* 705 (1070); and Surrey, "Federal Income Tax Reforms: The Varied Approaches Necessary to Replace Tax Expenditures with Direct Government Assistance," 84 *Harvard Law Review* 352 (1970). For earlier discussions, of the "comprehensive income tax base" and "tax expenditure budget" concepts see generally: Bittker, Galven, Musgrave and Pechman, *A Comprehensive Income Tax Base? A Debate* (1968); Aaron, "What is a Comprehensive Tax Base Anyway?," 22 *National Tax Journal* 543 (1969); Bittker, "Accounting for Federal 'Tax Subsidies' in the National Budget," 22 *National Tax Journal* 224 (1969); Surrey and Hellmuth, "The Tax Expenditure Budget—Response to Professor Bittker," 22 *National Tax Journal* 528 (1969); Bittker, "The Tax Expenditure Budget— A Reply to Professors Surrey and Hellmuth," 22 *National Tax Journal* 538 (1969).
2. See partial listing in note 1, supra. See also, for a popularization of many of the points made in these and other studies, Stern, *The Great Treasury Raid* (1965); and Stern, "Uncle Sam's Welfare Program—for the Rich," *New York Times*, April 16, 1972, (Magazine) at 28.
3. For a more detailed discussion of these concepts, see Surrey, *Pathways to Tax Reform* (1973); and the references in n. 1, supra.
4. Surrey, ibid., pp. vii, 3-4.
5. See H. Simons, *Personal Income Taxation* (1938), for the initial elaboration of the theory of personal income taxation upon which the concept of "tax expenditures" is based.

non-income-defining and represent a departure from the ideal standard. They must be justified, if at all, by some other rationale than that of tax theory.[6] According to Professor Surrey and other tax theorists generally in agreement with him, the non-defining deductions are classified as "tax expenditures". Because of each of these, the federal government collects less revenue than it would if the tax system allowed only theoretically essential deductions (or other adjustments to income). This lost or foregone revenue is, according to this concept, in effect "spent" through the tax system to accomplish certain public objectives, such as home ownership (home mortgage interest and real estate tax deduction), capital investment (accelerated depreciation and capital gains), and philanthropy (charitable deduction). He concluded that this tax "spending" should be periodically evaluated just as are, allegedly, those governmental programs for which Congress directly authorizes expenditures. Those "nonessential" tax deductions that prove to be effective, efficient and fair in accomplishing public objectives, compared to direct spending alternatives, might be retained in the tax law, but he doubted that many would upon analysis prove to be so justified. Otherwise, he argued that they should be repealed.

Of course, there are several major assumptions underlying these concepts, and there is disagreement over both the scope and validity of this conceptualization of the federal individual income tax system.[7] But, for the moment, as reference points to public policy, these disagreements are almost

6.   This is indeed greatly oversimplified. As Surry explains in *Pathways*, op. cit. at 17:

      The building of an income tax requires two types of provisions that collectively perform the following two functions. First, they provide the answers to those aspects of (questions about a normative model for an income tax structure) that would essentially be treated in much the same way by any group of tax experts building the structure of an income tax and being governed in that task by all the requirements implicit in such a tax because it is an *income tax*. These answers then become the structural provisions which shape a normative income tax. As an illustration, in this first category fall matters relating to the measurement of net income and the time periods for inclusion of that income.

      In every particular personal income tax law, there are also some adjustments to income (deductions, exclusions, exemptions) that are not truly part of a normative income tax, but which, although not theoretically "income-defining," do become structural parts of an income tax—and essential to the operation of that tax—and therefore are not tax expenditures. For example, as Treasury analysis indicates, the treatment of the family e.g., the tax burden on married couples in relation to single persons—is not part of a normative income tax. There is no preordained method of treatment that follows from the decision to adopt an income tax. Countries properly differ in the treatment depending on their attitudes toward marriage or women in the labor force and other such social and economic questions. The levels of personal exemptions and tax rates, and the degree of rate progressivity, are other examples mentioned in the treasury analysis that would fall in this second category. The treatment of the corporation—as a separate entity or its income integrated with that of the shareholders in some fashion—is still another example. The provisions incorporating the decisions in these areas are not tax expenditures. But the decisions have to be made before the structure of the income tax is complete and the tax is ready to be applied. As a consequence, this set of provisions, while necessary to the construction of an income tax is shaped by processes different in character from the processes determining the provisions in the first category, also relating to the inherent structure of an income tax. The tax expenditure provisions are, then, the provisions that may be found in an income tax law but that do not serve the two functions set forth above. (Surrey, *Pathways*, at 17-18).

7.   See generally Bittker, Galvin, Musgrave and Pechman, *A Comprehensive Income Tax Base? A Debate* (1968); and the other readings listed in n. 1., supra. . . .

purely academic. The tax expenditure concept has, at least for now, center stage and defines the terms of the debate.

These concepts were first used effectively in the debates leading to passage of the 1969 Tax Reform Act, which placed some significant limitations upon the charitable deduction. Since then, they have been firmly institutionalized into the federal governmental budget and tax processes by the enactment of the Congressional Budget and Impoundment Control Act of 1974,[8] by the annual publication of a "Tax Expenditure Budget" by the Treasury Department, and by their general use in public discussions of issues in federal income taxation. In reality, Professor Surrey and other proponents of these concepts[9] have set the agenda and provided the vocabulary for the debate on federal tax policy that has been underway since 1969. And, on that agenda, the charitable deduction is listed as an exception to or departure from the "normal" or ideal structure of the tax law.[10]

The scholarship of Professor Surrey and others was not the only factor directing public attention to the myriad provisions in the income tax. There was also a dramatic political factor. In January, 1969, just before leaving office, Secretary of the Treasury, Joseph W. Barr, announced that several hundred taxpayers with incomes in excess of $100,000 per year were paying no or almost no taxes. He attributed this fact to their widespread use of various legitimate deductions, exemptions, exclusions, and reduced rates in the tax law such as special treatment of capital gains income, home mortgage and other interest expense deductions, medical expense deductions, and the charitable deduction. This, too, had a major impact on the debate over the 1969 tax reform legislation. Each year since 1969, a similar announcement[11] has been published by the Treasury Department, keeping public attention drawn to the detailed provisions of the tax code.

---

8.   P.L. 93-344, July 12, 1974, 88 Stat. 278ff. For a discussion of the current effect of the "tax expenditure" concept in the Congressional budget process, especially Senator Kennedy's proposal to require review of each newly proposed "tax expenditure" by the authorization and appropriation committees responsible for its direct budgetary equivalents or counterparts prior to its consideration by the Senate Finance Committee or the House Committee on Ways and Means, see 50 *National Journal* 1908 (December 10, 1977).

9.   Professor Surrey is publicly the most well-known but not the only proponent of this "tax expenditure" concept. See, for example, articles in Pechman (editor), *Comprehensive Income Taxation* (1977); McDaniel, "Federal Matching Grants for Charitable Contributions: A Substitute for the Income Tax Deduction," 27 *Tax Law Review* 377 (1972); and Davies, "The Charitable Contributions Credit: A Proposal to Replace Section 501 (c) (3) Tax Exemption Organizations," 58 *Cornell Law Review 304* (1973).

10.   See, for example, *Special Analyses, Budget of the United States Government*, Fiscal Year 1978, pp. 128-30; Congressional Budget Office, *Five Year Projections, Fiscal Years 1978-1982: Supplemental Report on Tax Expenditures* (GPO, 1977). Note also, that this agenda, this listing of "tax expenditure", includes in addition to the charitable deduction such items of interest to higher education as the exclusion from income of scholarships and fellowships, and the dependency deduction for children over 18 pursuing higher educational courses of study.

11.   During consideration of the 1976 Tax Reform Act, this annual announcement played a major role. Many of these high income taxpayers were able to escape heavy taxation first, by making several adjustments to gross income (exclusion of one-half of long-term capital gains, for instance), to reduce their adjusted gross incomes, and second, by then adding up large amounts

These two factors, one conceptual and one political, continue to dominate discussion of the income tax system. The charitable deduction is a conspicuous item on that comprehensive tax agenda. The 1969 Tax Reform Act placed some significant limitations on certain kinds of charitable giving. During the Congressional consideration of that bill, the charitable community barely defeated proposals of even greater consequence for private philanthropy. Since then, no truly direct attack on the deduction has succeeded.

But it is not only the direct challenges to the charitable deduction that can affect seriously charitable giving. Even where the focus is on other parts of the tax code seemingly unrelated to the charitable deduction, there can be harmful consequences for philanthropy. For example, last summer, the Secretary of the Treasury included in a late draft of tax proposals for possible consideration by the President recommendations for sweeping changes in the laws governing the sale or exchange of so-called long term capital gains property. Had such changes been proposed, depending on the exact language of the legislation, they could have posed a severe threat to charitable giving. According to one econometric analysis of such a proposal, based on 1970 data, the potential cost in donations to all of education would have been eight percent of annual giving. [12]

An even more dramatic example is found in the so-called standard deduction. [13] This is the provision in tax law that allows a taxpayer to deduct a flat dollar amount rather than itemizing personal deductions such as home mortgage interest payments, property, sales and gasoline tax expenses, casualty losses, medical expenses and charitable gifts. In 1970, despite the burdensome calculations and record-keeping, 50 percent of all taxpayers itemized

---

of itemized personal deductions (interest expenses, medical expenses, property taxes, casualty losses, charitable contributions, etc.) and subtracting these from adjusted gross income to reduce their taxable incomes to very low levels. To some extent, the 1969 Tax Reform Act tried to adjust for the effect of the first type of adjustments by enacting the minimum tax on tax preference income, an additional, now 15 percent, tax on certain items of income excluded from regular taxation. For reasons largely having to do with allowable deductions from the minimum tax base, however, the minimum tax was still not reaching every high income taxpayer previously able to pay no taxes at all. Thus, in 1976, the Congress created a new item of tax preference income—itemized deductions in excess of 60 percent of adjusted gross income. The purpose was to ensure that every high income taxpayer would pay at least some minimum level of taxes.

12.   Feldstein, Martin S. and Amy Taylor, "The Income Tax and Charitable Contributions: Estimates and Simulations with the Treasury Tax Files," 3 *Research Papers Sponsored by The Commission on Private Philanthropy and Public Needs*, pp. 1419, 1436 and Table 6 at 1435.

13.   Technically, the standard deduction no longer exists in tax law. As of January 1, 1977, it has been replaced with a flat amount adjustment the law calls "zero bracket amount." This amount depends on the taxpayer's filing status. There are three different categories of filing status, and the zero bracket amounts corresponding to them are $1600, $2200, and $3200. These no longer involve separate deductions as such; instead the equivalent amount is built into the tax tables and tax rate schedules. Since these amounts are built into the tables and rate schedules, taxpayers itemizing deductions will have to make an adjustment in their calculations so as not to receive the benefit of both the "zero bracket amount" and their "itemized personal deductions." Obviously, however, any future increase in the "zero tax bracket" amounts will have the same effects on charitable giving as have had increases in the standard deduction. See Department of the Treasury, Internal Revenue Service, 1977 Instructions for form 1040, at p. 3.

their deductions rather than taking the standard deduction because this choice meant lower taxes for them. Since 1970, there have been five increases in the standard deduction. As a result, only 25 percent of all taxpayers today itemize their deductions. For the other 75 percent, taking the standard deduction means lower taxes than is possible by itemizing. Under President Carter's recent tax proposals, only 16 percent of all taxpayers would have any incentive to itemize deductions; 84 percent would take the standard deduction.[14]

What does this have to do with the charitable deduction? Quite simply, taxpayers who use the standard deduction cannot take the charitable deduction. They have, therefore, less incentive to make charitable contributions. There is no longer for them any public recognition given to the truly public character of their voluntary private gifts to institutions which serve the common goals of the community. As a result, they give less than they would have had they itemized their deductions.

This indirect effect on charitable giving of the increasing proportion of taxpayers taking the standard deduction has been measured; its magnitude is extraordinary. Recent studies[15] have estimated that charities have lost about $5 billion in gifts from 1970-1976 because of increased use of the standard deduction. These same studies estimate that this factor will have caused an additional loss of another $1.357 billion in annual charitable giving in 1977.

These immediate losses in annual giving, however, are the least of the harmful consequences of this trend. Over the longer run, younger alumni and alumnae, who will increasingly tend to use the standard deduction, will be less likely to develop early the habit of annual giving. The effect of this on annual giving will not be noticeable for a decade or more; by then, it will be too late. Of equal concern, as ever smaller numbers of taxpayers itemize, the universal character of charitable giving will be lost and the deduction will become politically vulnerable. As only the very well-to-do continue to itemize, the charitable deduction will appear to lose its unique status as the one deduction in the code that is given not for spending income on oneself, but for sharing it with the whole community. While leaders of higher education cannot and should not oppose increases in the standard deduction, they should be searching for and advocating ways to offset the negative effects these increases have on charitable giving.[16]

Similar criticisms and problems arise in connection with the estate tax charitable deduction. Basically, in determining the value of the estate that

---

14.   President's Tax Message to the Congress, January 20, 1978.

15.   Smith, Hayden, Council for Aid to Education, New York, New York (Unpublished Analysis).

16.   For example, philanthropic leaders might argue that every taxpayer should be able to take a deduction for charitable giving, whether or not he files the short form (1040A) or the long form (1040), and whether or not he itemizes personal deductions. This is often commonly referred to as "moving the deduction above the line," meaning making the charitable deduction a deduction from gross income, not from adjusted gross income, adjusted gross income being the "line." The result would be partially to protect the charitable deduction from future increases in the "zero bracket amount" (formerly, the standard deduction).

will be subject to taxation, the law allows an unlimited deduction for bequests to charity. While, as in the case of the individual income tax charitable deduction, there are complicating details, this basic characteristic of the estate tax is central. . . . The critics of the estate tax charitable deduction often focus on its unlimited character, especially in contrast to its income tax counterpart, as well as on its alleged interference with the estate tax' revenue potential and that tax' purpose to discourage intergenerational transfers within the same family of the control over the ownership or use of property.

In addition to such direct questions about this deduction, indirect problems also arise at the boundary between income taxation and estate taxation. This is especially so with respect to periodic proposals for the taxation of the appreciation (basically, the difference between current market value and the value at the time the property was acquired by the taxpayer) in property in the estate at the time of death, either through the income tax or through an added provision in the estate tax.

While the estate tax charitable deduction has not been as publicly a target of the "tax expenditure" school of tax theory as has the income tax provision, it has, nonetheless, been a target of critics of the estate tax system. The importance of this deduction to higher education, however, cannot be overstated. One estimate is that placing a 50 percent limit on the deductibility of charitable bequests would cost charities $4.40 in gifts for every $1.00 in added revenue for the government.

INITIAL FOCUS

It is obvious that higher education has a crucial interest in the debate over the federal tax system. But the direct and indirect threats to charitable giving are not the only federal tax issues that will affect higher education. Among others are:

(a)   the exemption of charities from income taxation;
(b)   the integration of the corporate and individual income taxes;
(c)   the withholding of taxes against dividend income;
(d)   the unrelated business income tax;
(e)   the social security and other payroll taxes;
(f)   the exclusion from taxation of scholarships, fellowships and related awards; and
(g)   the dependency deduction for children over age 18 attending colleges or universities.

Finally, there are serious tax issues affecting higher education at the state and local levels. Such issues as exemptions from state income and sales taxes and from local property taxes are on the agendas of many state and local governments. . . .

---

17.   Boskin, Michael J., "Estate Taxation and Charitable Bequests," 3 *Research Papers Sponsored by the Commission on Private Philanthropy and Public Needs* [The Filer Commission], pp. 1453, 1477 (1975).

SELECTED READINGS IN
TAXATION AND HIGHER EDUCATION

American Association of Fund Raising Counsel, Inc., *GIVING USA*, 1977 Annual Report. New York: 1977.

Andrews, William D., "A Consumption-Type or Cash Flow Personal Income Tax," 87 *Harvard Law Review* 1113 (1974).

Andrews, William D., "Personal Deductions in an Ideal Income Tax," 86 *Harvard Law Review* 309 (1972).

Association of American Universities, *Tax Reform and the Crisis of Financing Higher Education*. Washington: Association of American Universities, 1973.

Association of the Bar of the City of New York, "Proposal for Limitation on the Use of Tax Incentives," A Report by the Committee on Taxation. New York: 1976.

Bittker, Boris I. and C. Galvin, R. Musgrave and J. Pechman, *A Comprehensive Income Tax Base? A Debate.* (1968).

Bittker, Boris I., "Charitable Contributions: Tax Deductions or Matching Grants," 28 *Tax Law Review* 37 (1972).

Break, George F. and Pechman, Joseph A., *Federal Tax Reform: The Impossible Dream?* Washington: The Brookings Institution, 1975.

Coalition for the Public Good, *The Charitable Deduction: Its Role in Preserving a Viable Public-Private Relationship.* Alexandria, Virginia: 1975.

Commission on Private Philanthropy and Public Needs (The Filer Commission), *Giving in America: Toward a Stronger Voluntary Sector.* Washington: Department of the Treasury, 1975.

Commission on Private Philanthropy and Public Needs (The Filer Commission) *Research Papers Sponsored by the Commission on Private Philanthropy and Public Needs* (Five Volumes), Washington: Department of the Treasury, 1977. (Hereinafter, abbreviated *Filer*)

> Michael J. Boskin and Martin S. Feldstein, "Effects of the Charitable Deduction on Contributions by Low-Income and Middle-Income Households: Evidence from the National Survey of Philanthropy," 3 *Filer* 1441, (1975).

> Michael J. Boskin, "Estate Taxation and Charitable Bequests," 3 *Filer* 1453, (1975).

> Cheit, Earl and Theodore Lobman III, "Private Philanthropy and Higher Education: History, Current Impact and Public Policy Considerations," 2 *Filer* 453, (1975).

> Commentary on Commission Recommendations; Donee Group Report. 1 *Filer* 3.

Martin S. Feldstein, "Charitable Bequests, Estate Taxation, and Inter-generational Wealth Transfers," 3 *Filer* 1485, (1975).

Martin S. Feldstein and Charles Clotfelter, "Tax Incentives and Charitable Contributions in the United States: A Micro-economic Analysis," 3 *Filer* 1393, (1975).

Martin S. Feldstein and Amy Taylor, "The Income Tax and Charitable Contributions: Estimates and Simulations with the Treasury Tax Files," 3 *Filer* 1419, (1975).

Jenny, Haus H. and Mary Allen, "Philanthropy in Higher Education: Its Magnitude, Its Nature and Its Influence on College University Finance," 2 *Filer* 515, (1975).

Mansfield, Harry K. and Ronald Groves, "Legal Aspects of Charitable Contributions of Appreciated Property to Public Charities," 4 *Filer* 2251, (1975).

Myers, John Holt, "Estate Tax Deduction for Charitable Benefits: Proposed Limitations," 4 *Filer* 2299, (1975).

Council for Financial Aid to Education, *Voluntarism, Tax Reform, and Higher Education.* New York: Council for Financial Aid to Education, 1975.

Council for Financial Aid to Education, *Voluntary Support of Education,* 1975-76. New York: 1977.

Covey, Richard B., "Possible Changes in the Basic Rule for Property Transferred by Gift or a Death," *Taxes—The Tax Magazine* 831 (1972).

Davies, John H., "The Charitable Contributions Credit: A Proposal to Replace Section 501 (c) (3) Tax-Exempt Organizations," 58 *Cornell Law Review* 304 (1973).

Department of the Treasury, *Blueprints for Basic Tax Reform.* Washington: 1977.

Goode, Richard, *The Individual Income Tax.* Revised Edition. Washington: The Brookings Institution, 1976.

Kennedy, Senator Edward M., "Compendium of Papers on Federal Tax Reform," *Congressional Record* S-11591 (daily ed. July 2, 1976).

Levi, Julian H., "Financing Education and the Effect of the Tax Laws," in *Law and Contemporary Problems: Federal Taxation and Charitable Organizations,* Vol. XXXIX, No. 4, Durham, North Carolina: Duke University Press, Autumn 1975.

Levi, Julian H. and Sheldon Steinbach, *Patterns of Giving to Higher Education III: An Analysis of Voluntary Support of American Colleges and Universities 1972-74.* Washington, D.C.: American Council on Education, 1975.

McDaniel, Paul, "Alternatives to Utilization of the Federal Income Tax System to Meet Social Problems, 11 *Boston College Industrial and Commercial Law Review* 867 (1970).

McLure, Charles E. Jr., "Integration of the Personal and Corporate Income Taxes: The Missing Element in Recent Tax Reform Proposals," 88 *Harvard Law Review* 532 (1975).

Pechman, Joseph A. (ed.), *Comprehensive Income Taxation.* Washington: The Brookings Institution, 1977.

Peterson, George E. (ed.), *Property Tax Reform.* Washington: John C. Lincoln Institute and Urban Institute, 1973.

Staff of the House Committee on Ways and Means, 94th Congress, 2nd Session, "Background Materials on Federal Estate and Gift Taxation." Washington: 1976.

Stern, Emil, Jr., "Federal and State Tax Policies," in *Public Policies and Private Higher Education,* edited by David M. Breneman and Chester Finn, Jr., Washington, D. C.: The Brookings Institution, to be released in April 1978.

Surrey, Stanley S., "Federal Income Tax Reforms: The Varied Approaches Necessary to Replace Tax Expenditures with Direct Government Assistance," 84 *Harvard Law Review* 352 (1970).

Surrey, Stanley, "Tax Incentives as a Device for Implementing Government Policy: A Comparison with Direct Government Expenditures," 83 *Harvard Law Review* 705 (1970).

Surrey, Stanley, *Pathways to Tax Reform.* Cambridge, Massachusetts: Harvard University Press, 1973.

Surrey, Stanley, "The Federal Tax Legislative Process," 31 *Record of the Association of the Bar of the City of New York* 509 (1976).

B.   *"Feeder" Organizations*

UNIVERSITY HILL FOUNDATION v. C.I.R.
Ninth Circuit Court of Appeals
446 F.2d 701 (1971),
cert. denied, 405 U. S. 965 (1972)

DUNIWAY, Circuit Judge:

This case involves disputed income and excess-profits taxes in the aggregate amount of $10,070,677.25, for the period beginning with the fiscal year ended April 30, 1952, and ending with fiscal year ended April 30, 1965. The Commissioner of Internal Revenue appeals from a decision of the Tax Court finding the University Hill Foundation free from liability for the disputed taxes. We reverse. . . .

The Commissioner, on June 15, 1945, ruled on a temporary basis that the Foundation was tax exempt under Section 101(6) of the Internal Revenue Code of 1939. That subsection exempted from taxation

"(6) Corporations, and any community chest, fund, or foundation, organized and operated exclusively for religious, charitable,

scientific, literary, or educational purposes, or for the prevention of cruelty to children or animals, no part of the net earnings
of which inures to the benefit of any private shareholder or
individual, and no substantial part of the activities of which is
carrying on propaganda or otherwise attempting, to influence
legislation." . . . .

On April 4, 1956, the Commissioner revoked the exemption ruling.
The only ground for the revocation now pertinent is that the Foundation
was not "organized and operated exclusively for" exempt purposes under
section 101(6) or 501(c)(3). The revocation ruling was made effective beginning with the fiscal year ended April 30, 1952, i.e., the first fiscal year
beginning after December 31, 1950. The question is whether this ruling is
correct. We hold that it is.

1.   *The charitable exemption.*

Sections 101(6) (1939) and 501(c)(3) (1954) require that, to qualify
for the exemption, an organization such as the Foundation must be both
organized exclusively for and *operated* exclusively for religious, charitable,
or educational purposes. Commissioner of Internal Revenue v. John Danz
Charitable Trust, 9 Cir., 1960, 284 F.2d 726, 730, citing Universal Oil
Products Co. v. Campbell, 7 Cir., 1950, 181 F.2d 451, cert. den. 1950,
340 U.S. 850, 71 S.Ct. 78, 95 L.Ed. 623. The Tax Court properly determined that the organization requirement was satisfied in this case. 51 T.C. at
566. The only question under sections 101(6) and 501(c)(3), therefore, is
whether the Foundation was *operated* exclusively for exempt purposes.

Organizations directly engaged in concededly religious, charitable, or
educational activities are of course tax exempt; thus, in this case Loyola
University, the beneficiary of the Foundation's activities, is tax exempt.
The Foundation, however, is directly engaged not in educational activities,
but rather in commercial ventures, the profits from which are paid over to
Loyola University. The immediate question is whether that activity allows
us to characterize the Foundation as operated exclusively for exempt purposes. The question is one of first impression in this court.

a.   *Section 101(6) before 1951.*

Before 1951, when the Revenue Act of 1950 took effect, the courts
took two approaches in determining whether organizations such as the
Foundation were tax exempt under section 101(6). The first approach applied the so-called "destination of income" test, according to which an
organization was exempt under the section if all of its income was distributed exclusively for charitable purposes, even though the organization's
primary or sole activity consisted of carrying on active business operations. . . . The rationale underlying this test is that "the benefit from revenue is outweighed by the benefit to the general public welfare gained
through the encouragement of charity." C. F. Mueller Co. v. Commissioner

of Internal Revenue, *supra*, 190 F.2d at 122. The Tax Court applied the destination-of-income test in the instant case, concluding that under pre-1951 law the Foundation would be entitled to a section 101(6) exemption. 51 T.C. at 562, 567.

The second pre-1951 approach to section 101(6) focussed on the nature of the organization's activities and the source of the income, and expressly rejected the destination-of-income test as applied to organizations (like the Foundation) not directly engaged in exempt activity. This court has consistently adhered to this second, source-of-income approach. . . .

We think it clear that, under our construction of the pre-1951 section 101(6) exemption, the University Hill Foundation was *not* "operated exclusively for religious, charitable, or * * * educational purposes." The businesses involved in the 21 Cote-formula transactions were a diverse lot, including *inter alia* a hotel, three sand, gravel and concrete companies, three dairies, a foundry, and eight manufacturing concerns making and selling a wide variety of products. It is arguable that the Foundation was engaged in the respective trade or business of each of the companies whose assets it had bought and then leased. We need not decide this question, however, and we may assume that the Tax Court was correct in finding that the form of the transactions successfully shielded the Foundation from any direct involvement in the operating companies' businesses. 51 T.C. at 568-569. For, in any case, the Foundation was beyond any doubt engaged in a business of its own—the acquiring of business corporations and the selling of some and leasing of others of their assets to operating companies. The Foundation was, to coin a phrase, a used-business dealer. Its transactions "were not occasional or isolated ventures," Randall Foundation v. Riddell, *supra*, 244 F.2d at 807, and we do not intimate the result had that been the case. Here, the Foundation systematically participated, over a 9-year period, in 21 Cote transactions involving the purchase of 25 businesses and the sale of some and the lease of the rest of their assets. (See the table at 51 T.C. 556.) Here, as in the *Randall Foundation* case, the transactions "constituted almost the only activity of [the] Foundation during these years. 244 F.2d at 807. Moreover, the Foundation was a very special type of used-business dealer. It could engage successfully in its business only if it was tax exempt; its business was the buying of businesses and leasing them by the use of its tax exemption. As the Tax Court points out in its opinion, page 560,

> "The economic effect of these devices was to divide the net profits of each business; 20 percent to the operators, 8 percent to petitioner, and 72 percent to the sellers, with the operators claiming a deduction for the rentals as business expenses, the sellers reporting their profit on the sale as capital gains, and the petitioner claiming exemptions from tax as a charitable organization on the amounts received by it."

The deals would have been financially impossible if the Foundation had to pay tax on the "rents" that it received. Thus the Foundation was in the business of using its claimed tax exemption to buy used businesses.

As a direct consequence of those transactions, the Foundation gave to Loyola University during the years in question a total of $1,984,044.20, and it has accumulated since 1956 an additional $4 million or more which it intends to distribute to Loyola if this dispute is resolved favorably to the Foundation. These benefactions were the proceeds of activities whose primary purpose was to turn a profit; profit was essential, else nothing could have been donated to Loyola. And unlike the corporation in Squire v. Students Book Corp., 9 Cir., 1951, 191 F.2d 1018, "the business enterprise in which [the Foundation] is engaged" does not bear "a close and intimate relationship to the functioning of the College itself." *Id.* at 1020.

Nor is it an answer to say that since 1954 the Foundation has stopped *buying* businesses. This was done in response to Revenue Ruling 54-420, 1954-2 Cum. Bull. 128, which denies exemption to Cote-type transactions. The Foundation continued thereafter to be in the business-*leasing* business and in the business-lease-*selling* business, as it was before, and that business was still a profit-making enterprise, bearing no relationship to the functioning of Loyola University.

We conclude, therefore, that throughout the years in question the Foundation was engaged in commercial business for profit. That was what it was operated for. Even though the profits were ultimately distributable to an exempt institution, the Foundation was not "operated exclusively for" exempt purposes. Under our pre-1951 approach to section 101(6) the Foundation is not entitled to an income tax exemption.

b.   *Section 101(6) as amended in 1951.*

As we have seen, the Revenue Act of 1950 amended section 101 of the 1939 Code by adding to it the feeder organization paragraph that we have previously quoted. The purpose of the paragraph certainly was not to enlarge or broaden the section 101(6) exemption; quite the contrary. Several courts of appeals, including this court, have considered section 101(6) as thus amended in the light of its legislative history. Without exception, they concluded that in amending section 101 the Congress intended to require courts to adopt the source-of-income test previously followed by this circuit, rather than the destination-of-income test that had been followed in other circuits. . . .

As a result of the feeder organization amendment, application of this circuit's pre-1951 approach to the facts of the case before us leads indisputably to the proper analysis and conclusion, since the taxable years here in dispute all post-date 1951: The University Hill Foundation has not been operated exclusively for exempt purposes, and is not, in the absence of other considerations, entitled to an income tax exemption for the taxable years 1952-1965.

2.   *The real property leasing proviso of the feeder organization amendment.*

The primary purpose and effect of Congress' enacting the amendment was to exclude "feeder organizations" from the section 101(6) exemption.

The amendment defines a feeder organization as "[a]n organization operated for the primary purpose of carrying on a trade or business for profit * * * all of [whose] profits are payable to one or more organizations exempt * * * from taxation." We have determined that the Foundation is such an organization. The Foundation argues, and the Tax Court found, that the Foundation is nonetheless exempt because it falls within the proviso to the amendment. The proviso states:

"For purposes of this paragraph the term 'trade or business' shall not include the rental by an organization of its real property (including personal property leased with the real property)."

The Foundation's argument, accepted by the Tax Court and repeated before us, is that almost every one of the Cote transactions involved the lease of a business' assets some part of which consisted of real property, that a part of the rent paid by the operating company was therefore for that real property, and that the remainder of the assets leased constituted "personal property leased with real property." See 51 T.C. at 570-572. These views, we think, stand the feeder organization amendment on its head. They turn an amendment that was clearly intended to give effect to a narrow interpretation of section 101(6) into an amendment granting, as to the type of transaction here, an exemption broader than that which previously existed. We cannot believe that such was the intention of the proviso, and we decline to give it such a construction.

In so holding, however, we need not and do not accept the Commissioner's construction of the proviso. The Commissioner argues that the plain meaning of the proviso is that it applies only to leases consisting predominantly of real property and only incidentally of personal property, and that the leases here are not of that kind. In addition the Commissioner invokes the legislative history of the feeder organization amendment, asserting that that history clearly reveals Congress' intent *not* to grant tax exemptions to organizations doing precisely what the Foundation has done here. We think the opposing constructions given by the parties to the language of the proviso lead to inconclusive results, for on its face, the proviso neither indicates nor even hints what relative proportions of real versus personal property are required to render a lease transaction exempt. Accordingly, the application of the proviso to the case before us cannot be properly determined without an inquiry into the legislative history of the feeder organization amendment.

The legislative history of the Revenue Act of 1950 shows that Congress did not intend any feeder organization to be automatically exempt from taxation merely because its income derived from rental of property some part of which was real property. Certainly Congress drew a distinction between the rental of real property and the rental of personal property. Over and above that distinction, however, Congress was concerned with the nature of the transactions through which a feeder organization leased its real property. Thus, the House Report on the Revenue Act of 1950 stated:

"The tax applied to unrelated business income does not apply to * * * rents (other than certain rents on property acquired with

borrowed funds), and gains from sales of leased property. Your
committee believes that such 'passive' income should not be taxed
where it is used for exempt purposes because investments producing incomes of these types have long been recognized as proper for
educational and charitable organizations."

H.Rep. No. 2319, *supra*, in 1950-2 Cum. Bull. 409. During the House debate
Representative Lynch, speaking on behalf of the revenue bill, stated:

"The receipt of interest, dividends, and royalties does not constitute carrying on of an active business. In general, the receipt of rent
is also considered a proper activity for these organizations and is
not taxed. Historically, the colleges and other exempt organizations have often invested their endowments in rental property—and
the bill does not tax this.

"* * *

*   *   *

"* * * *However, it does tax a university which borrows on its
exemption to buy property in an attempt to receive tax-free
rents."*

96 Cong.Rec. 9366-67 (1950) (emphasis added). In particular the 1950
amendments were aimed at the abusive practices of tax-exempt organizations engaged in purchase and lease-back arrangements with private businesses. In such arrangements,

"huge rental payments are taken out of the scope of the income
tax in lease-back deals which are so favorable to the private businesses involved that no private investor could hope to offer the
same terms. Since all the tax-exempt institution need supply in
one of these transactions is its tax-exempt privileges, it is apparent that these are examples of tax-exempt organizations going
into the business world and selling their tax exemption to the
highest bidder. * * * *The committee feels that the tax-avoidance
racket involved in the sale or lease-back of the tax-exempt status
of these institutions must stop."*

Id. at 9366 (emphasis added). The House Report points out that these same
considerations apply both in strict lease-back cases, "where the vendor and
the lessee are the same person," and in cases, like the Cote transactions here,
where they are not. II.Rep. No. 2319, *supra*, in 1950-2 Cum.Bull. 411.

Thus, in enacting the feeder organization amendment, Congress expressed its intention to plug a much-abused tax loophole by refusing exemptions to feeder organizations in the business of acquiring property, including
real property, by trading on their exemption, and then leasing that property
as part of the tansaction by which they obtained it. The proviso of the
feeder organization amendment is intended only to protect feeder organizations whose income derives from real-estate investments of the "passive"
nature traditional among exempt institutions.

There is no question that the University Hill Foundation was in the
business of trading on its tax exemption in precisely the way Congress disap-

proved. We have recognized this on a previous occasion. A transaction essentially similar to the Foundation's Cote transactions was involved in Commissioner of Internal Revenue v. Brown, 9 Cir., 1963, 325 F.2d 313, aff'd 1965, 380 U.S. 563, 85 S.Ct. 1162, 14 L.Ed.2d 75. There we stated that "[t]here is no question that this transaction took the form that it did because the Institute is a tax-exempt corporation and that the price to be paid was probably greater for that reason." *Id*. at 316. Justice Harlan, concurring in Commissioner of Internal Revenue v. Brown, stated even more bluntly that "[o]bviously the Institute traded on its tax exemption," and suggested that "one may ask why, if the Government does not like the tax consequences of such sales, the proper course is not to attack the exemption." 380 U.S. at 580, 85 S.Ct. at 1171. That is what the Commissioner is doing here. Numerous commentators also share the view that in transactions like these Cote transactions the exempt organization is trading on its exemption, thereby obtaining considerable financial benefit for itself and for its partners in the transaction. See, *e.g.*, Note, Tax Problems of Bootstrap Sales to Exempt Foundations: A Comprehensive Approach, 18 Stan.L.Rev. 1148, 1150 (1966); Note, Bootstrap Acquisitions: The Next Battle, 51 Iowa L.Rev. 992-95 (1966); Lanning, Tax Erosion and the "Bootstrap Sale" of a Business—I, 108 U.Pa.L.Rev. 623, 637-38, 682-83 (1960). We conclude, therefore, that the Cote transactions undertaken by the University Hill Foundation do not fall within the proviso of the feeder organization amendment, now section 502 of the 1954 Code. Congress intended to deny tax exemption to organizations engaged in just such a business, and we must accordingly find the Foundation to be non-exempt.

In so holding, we neither approve nor disapprove the Commissioner's argument that the proviso refers only to the rental of property consisting predominantly of real property. Consequently, we need not and do not base our holding in any way on Congress' amendment of the proviso in the Tax Reform Act of 1969, Title I, § § 121(b)(2)(A), 121(b)(7), 83 Stat. 487, 538-539, 542, which allows an exemption only if "the rents attributable to such personal property are an incidental amount of the total rents received or accrued under the lease." We intimate no opinion whether, in passing the Revenue Act of 1950, Congress had intended this "incidental" limitation to be understood in the proviso or whether Congress was, in 1969, merely clarifying existing law. We hold, rather, that in 1950 Congress clearly intended to halt certain abusive tax-avoidance practices which can be identified without reference to the ratio of real to personal property, and that such a practice is clearly involved in this case. We are not purporting to reverse the Tax Court merely because the arrangements here in question are "undesirable from a tax standpoint," Brown v. Commissioner of Internal Revenue, *supra*, 325 F.2d at 316. We repeat what we said there: "If * * * the present situation * * * is undesirable from a tax standpoint, it is still possible for Congress to provide a remedy." We think that, insofar as tax exemption is concerned, Congress in 1950 did just that.

Reversed and remanded.

NOTE

For further study see Moran, Private Colleges: The Federal Tax System and Its Impact (Toledo: Center for the Study of Higher Education, The University of Toledo, 1977).

II.   Accreditation

MARLBORO CORP. v. ASS'N OF INDEPENDENT COLLEGES
First Circuit Court of Appeals
556 F.2d 78 (1977)

COFFIN, Chief Judge. . . .

Appellant Marlboro Corporation operates the Emery School, a private proprietary institution that offers a two-year non-degree program of training for court and conference stenotype reporters. The Accrediting Commission of appellee, the Association of Independent Colleges and Schools (AICS), is the only agency recognized by the United States Commissioner of Education to accredit business schools like Emery. Without accreditation from A.I.C.S., Emery is ineligible to participate in various federal student aid programs.

In December of 1975, the Commission voted to deny Emery's application for a new grant of accreditation, and shortly thereafter Emery was declared ineligible to participate in federal aid programs. Emery brought suit in state court, and AICS removed the case to federal district court. As amended in the district court, Emery's complaint alleges that the denial of accreditation deprived it of "rights protected by the due process and equal protection clauses of the Constitution of the United States, the rules and regulations of the United States Commissioner of Education, and the internal procedures of the defendant." Emery sought preliminary and permanent injunctions directing AICS to extend a grant of accreditation and to inform the federal Office of Education that accreditation had been granted, and other appropriate relief. . . .

Whether the Commission's procedures are, as the district court held, immune from constitutional scrutiny is a close question. While it is true that there is no governmental participation in AICS, *compare Burton v. Wilmington Parking Authority, supra; Parish v. National Collegiate Athletic Association*, 506 F.2d 1028, 1032 (5th Cir. 1975), the Commission has actively sought and received the federal recognition that makes its grant of accreditation a prerequisite to federal program eligibility. It appears that if AICS or an agency like it did not perform the accreditation function, "government would soon step in to fill the void." *Id.* at 1033. However, we find it unnecessary to decide whether this nexus renders the denial of accreditation government action since, even assuming that constitutional due process applies, the present record does not persuade us that any of Emery's procedural rights have been violated. We shall first summarize the proceedings and then discuss Emery's specific objections.

In August, 1974, the Commission ruled that Emery must undergo a complete reapplication and inspection for accreditation which would be considered at the April, 1975, meeting. Pursuant to the Commission's procedures for accreditation and reaccreditation, Emery submitted self-evaluation materials and was visited by an on-site inspection team which filed a substantially negative report. Emery then filed a written response to the visitation team's report, which took issue with most of the team's findings.

In April, 1975, the Commission extended Emery's accreditation through December 31, 1975, but deferred consideration of the application for a new grant of accreditation pending receipt of evidence of compliance with AICS criteria in twelve identified areas of weakness. Among the information requested were "an audited financial statement evidencing financial stability and certified by an independent certified public accountant", "[e]vidence of adequate library holdings to serve the educational program", and a "catalogue meeting all AICS criteria." The Commission's resolution directed Emery to file the requested information prior to June 30, 1975 so that the application could be considered at the August, 1975, meeting, and indicated that failure to file the items listed would be "sufficient grounds to deny the application for a new grant of accreditation."

In June Emery submitted a lengthy progress report which, adopting an approach very different from its initial response to the visitation team's report, expressed appreciation for the "candor and general objectivity" of the team's report, conceded that there were "deficiencies and shortcomings in The Emery School's curricular programs, administrative and supervisory practices, and physical facilities", and indicated its plans to remedy these deficiencies. At the August meeting, however, the Commission voted to deny Emery's application on the ground that the deficiencies noted in the April resolution had not been corrected. It referred by paragraph number to the items listed in the previous resolution, but again mentioned specifically the lack of a certified audited financial statement and an adequate catalogue, and gave as an additional reason for denial Emery's delinquent account with the Commission in the amount of $529.61. The resolution informed Emery of its right to appeal the denial at a hearing before the next meeting of the Commissioners.

Emery thereupon notified the Commission that it wished to appeal, and was advised to submit "information concerning the alleged deficiencies and any other materials which might assist the Commission in its determinations". In correspondence with the Commission staff Emery indicated that it was unable to file an audited and certified financial statement for the period required, but proposed to file instead an audited but uncertified statement covering the preceding eight months and a projected income statement for the following year. The staff responded that only the Commission could determine whether Emery's submission was acceptable. Emery also filed a report purporting to indicate that "we have corrected the deficiencies noted by the Commission", which described actions taken in response to each criticism; and tendered payment of the amount referred to in the August resolution.

On December 2, 1975 Edward Charles, President of the Emery School, accompanied by the school's attorney, appeared before the Commission. The institution was given thirty minutes to present its case and respond to questions from the Commissioners. Mr. Charles summarized the school's efforts to correct specific programmatic deficiencies and submitted as exhibits an on-site inspection report prepared by the private education consultant Emery had hired to assist its effort, and a proposal from another consulting firm the school intended to hire to upgrade its library holdings.

The Commissioner's questions focused on Emery's financial statements. Mr. Charles was unable to respond to questions about the method of accounting for undistributed federal grant and matching funds; whether "unallocated but drawn down" federal student aid money was used to cover the school's operating expenses; and the status of an outstanding loan to Mr. Charles himself, in a substantial amount, which was listed as an asset of the school. As the session was ending, the Chairman advised Mr. Charles that according to the Commission's records Emery still owed it $200.12, which bill was two years overdue and had been referred to an attorney for collection. Mr. Charles responded that he believed Emery had settled its account, but that he was prepared to pay immediately any amount still due.

On December 16 Emery was notified that the denial of accreditation was reaffirmed and that the institution's current grant of accreditation through December 31, 1975 would "expire with the passage of time". The resolution gave as grounds for denial the school's failure to submit an audited, certified financial statement evidencing financial stability; failure to demonstrate adequate library holdings to serve the educational program; and failure to pay a past due amount of $200.12.

We have recounted the proceedings at some length because we think that the extended process of consultation, communication, and reconsideration that the record reflects is significant in evaluating Emery's objections to specific alleged procedural flaws. Whether the process is measured against constitutional or common law standards, current doctrine teaches that procedural fairness is a flexible concept, in which the nature of the controversy and the competing interests of the parties are considered on a case-by-case basis. *Mathews v. Eldridge*, 424 U.S. 319, 334-35, 96 S.Ct. 893, 47 L.Ed.2d 18 (1976).

We have no doubt that due process did not, as Emery contends, require a full-blown adversary hearing in this context. The inquiry was broadly evaluative in nature, not, as might be the case in a withdrawal of accreditation for cause, *see* Operating Criteria § § 2-5-104, 2-5-105, accusatory. Emery was given ample opportunity to present its position by written submission and to argue it orally; if it did not make the best use of those opportunities (as by failing to bring its accountant to the hearing), the blame cannot be placed on the Commission. And, even if Emery was able to point to issues in this particular case on which confrontation and examination of witnesses might have been helpful, which it has not, any possible benefit to the institution is far outweighed by the burden that formalized proceedings would impose on the Commission. *See Mathews v. Eldridge, supra; Downing v. LeBritton*, 550 F.2d 689 at 692-693 (1st Cir. 1977). The Commission's procedures treat applicants for accreditation like capable professionals seeking the evaluation and recognition of their peers: we do not think that due process requires any more.

Emery next alleges that the President of a school in direct competition with Emery, which would "fall heir to" Emery's business if accreditation were denied, *see Gibson v. Berryhill*, 411 U.S. 564, 571, 93 S.Ct. 1689, 36 L.Ed.2d 488 (1973), improperly participated in the proceedings. The Commission asserts that this individual, though a member, and in fact Chairman of the Accrediting Commission, took no part in the discussion or vote on Emery's application. Emery disputes whether he in fact abstained from the closed discussion and voting but all that clearly appears from the record before us is that he was present at, but did not chair or participate in Emery's December hearing.

Decision by an impartial tribunal is an element of due process under any standard, *see generally* K. Davis, *Administrative Law Treatise* § 12.03, but here too the particular facts and "local realities" of any given case must determine whether there is an actual or apparent impropriety that amounts to a denial of due process. *See Gibson v. Berryhill, supra*, 411 U.S. at 579, 93 S.Ct. 1689. Emery points only to the presence of one individual at the final step in a prolonged process of evaluation and review as evidence of bias. It makes no showing that the decision was in fact tainted by bias. Indeed, the number of people who participated in the decision at various stages renders the risk of actual prejudice quite remote. Thus, Emery's real objection is to an appearance of impropriety resulting from the presence of a competitor at the final decision on Emery's accreditation. *See American Cyanimid Co. v. FTC,* 363 F.2d 757 (6th Cir. 1966). Emery asserts that the Chairman's competitive position "in no way became a part of the record of the proceedings in this case", but it seems apparent that the identity and presence of this close competitor were not hidden or unknown to Emery, *compare Commonwealth Coatings Corp. v. Continental Casualty Co.*, 393 U.S. 145, 89 S.Ct. 337, 21 L.Ed.2d 301 (1968). We think that Emery's sensibilities would be entitled to little consideration if it did not explain why it was unable to raise its objection to the apparent impropriety at the meeting. Nor do we think that the Commission's general practice of allowing interested commissioners to remain present without participating while their competitors are considered is necessarily objectionable: since many institutions are discussed at each semi-annual meeting of the Commission, and hearings are apparently quite tightly scheduled, the Commission asserts that it would be impractical to have interested Commissioners actually withdraw during discussions on competitors. *Cf. Davis, supra,* § 12.04 ("rule of necessity"). The question is troublesome, but on the present record we do not think that Emery has shown sufficient actual or apparent impropriety to render denial of preliminary relief an abuse of discretion.

Emery's remaining claims are less substantial. The charge that the Commission decision was "arbitrary and capricious" because based on insubstantial grounds is utterly frivolous. While it appears that Emery acted in good faith with respect to payment of its debts to the Commission, we doubt that the outstanding debt was determinative, and we agree with the district court that the irregularities in Emery's financial statement alone would have justified the Commission's decision. Finally, we also agree that the federal Office of Education's criteria for accrediting agencies, 45 C.F.R. § 149.6(b)(3), even assuming they are privately enforceable, do not require an appeal before a separate appeal body.

Affirmed.

NOTES

1. In Marjorie Webster Jr. College v. Middle States Ass'n of Colleges & Secondary Schools, Inc., 432 F.2d 650 (D.C. Cir. 1970), a proprietary junior college argued that Middle States' refusal to consider any applications for accreditation from proprietary institutions was a violation of the anti-trust provisions of the Sherman Act (15 U.S.C.A. § 3). The District Court sustained this argument but was overruled by the Court of Appeals which also declined to find a common law basis for interference in the accreditation process, stating:

> The increasing importance of private associations in the affairs of individuals and organizations has led to substantial expansion of judicial control over "The Internal Affairs of Associations not for Profit." Where membership in, or certification by, such an association is a virtual prerequisite to the practice of a given profession, courts have scrutinized the standards and procedures employed by the association notwithstanding their recognition of the fact that professional societies possess a specialized competence in evaluating the qualifications of an individual to engage in professional activities. The standards set must be reasonable, applied with an even hand, and not in conflict with the public policy of the jurisdiction. Even where less than complete exclusion from practice is involved, deprivation of substantial economic or professional advantages will often be sufficient to warrant judicial action.
>
> The extent of judicial power to regulate the standards set by private professional associations, however, must be related to the necessity for intervention. Particularly when, as here, judicial action is predicated not upon a legislative text but upon the developing doctrines of the common law, general propositions must not be allowed to obscure the specific relevant facts of each individual case. In particular, the extent to which deference is due to the professional judgment of the association will vary both with the subject matter at issue and with the degree of harm resulting from the association's action.
>
> With these factors in mind, we turn to consider the harm appellee will suffer by virtue of the challenged exclusion. We note in this regard that denial of accreditation by Middle States is not tantamount to exclusion of appellee from operating successfully as a junior college.... We do not believe, therefore, that the record supports the conclusion that appellee will be unable to operate successfully as a junior college unless it is considered for accreditation by appellant.
>
> Accordingly, we believe that judicial review of appellant's standards should accord substantial deference to appellant's judgment regarding the ends that it serves and the means most appropriate to those ends. Accreditation, as carried out by appellant, is as involved with educational philosophy as with yardsticks to measure the "quality" of education provided....

2. In Parsons College v. North Central Association of Colleges and Secondary Schools, 271 F.Supp. 65 (N.D. Ill. E.D. 1967), the college challenged its disaccreditation on due process grounds. The District Court found the college to be bound by the Association's

rules, and found no violation of those rules. The Court also made an extensive analysis based on common law "rudimentary due process" requirements, finding that Parsons failed to establish any violation of rudimentary due process requirements.

For further study *see*, Finkin, *Federal Reliance on Voluntary Accreditation: The Power to Recognize as the Power to Regulate*, 2 J. L. & Educ. 339 (1973); Kaplin and Hunter, *The Legal Status of the Educational Accrediting Agency: Problems in Judicial Supervision and Government Regulation*, 52 Cornell L.Q. 104 (1966).

III. State Sunshine Laws

ASSOCIATED STUDENTS OF U. OF COLO. v. REGENTS OF UNIV.
Supreme Court of Colorado
543 P.2d 59 (1975)

DAY, Justice.

This appeal involves a determination of the applicability of the Open Meetings Law of the Colorado Sunshine Act of 1972 to the Board of Regents of the University of Colorado. . . .

The Regents comprise the governing board of the University of Colorado (hereinafter "the university"), they are a constitutional body corporate, created by *Colo.Const.* Art. IX, Sec. 12. Prior to the 1972 Constitutional amendments to *Colo.Const.* Arts. VIII and IX, Art. IX, Sec. 14 provided as follows:

"Control of *University.* The board of regents shall have the general supervision of the university, and the exclusive control and direction of all funds of, and appropriations to, the university.

Employing the exact wording contained in that Article but adding "unless otherwise provided by law," Art. VIII, Sec. 5(2) was amended in November 1972 to grant to all governing boards of state educational institutions (including the Regents) ". . . the general supervision of their respective institutions and the exclusive control and direction of all funds . . . unless otherwise provided by law." Such language of control grants broad discretion to the Regents as a governing board. (*See Burnside v. Regents*, 100 Colo. 33, 64 P.2d 1271 (1937) re right to operate buses exempt from general Public Utilities law.) . . .

These are special provisions, conferring upon the Regents specific and particular powers. As the trial court correctly concluded, the Sunshine Act is a general law. General legislation does not repeal conflicting special statutory or constitutional provisions unless the intent to do so is clear and unmistakable. *People v. Burke*, 185 Colo. 19, 521 P.2d 783 (1974); *Denver v. Rinker.* 148 Colo. 441, 366 P.2d 548 (1961).

The students and faculty, as appellees, contend that under the ". . . unless otherwise provided by law" language in Sec. 5(2), any law, whether general or specific, is applicable to and effective against the Regents. We disagree. This phrase operates so that any qualification of the constitutional grant is to be construed as divesting the supervision and control granted only when a legislative enactment *expressly* so provides. Implied repeals are thereby intended to be guarded against. . . .

The trial court issued conflicting rulings in this case. One ruling properly, we perceive, was that the Sunshine Act cannot and does not repeal by implication the statute concerning the attorney-client evidentiary privilege. C.R.S.1963, 154-1-7(3) (now section 13-90-107(1)(b), C.R.S. 1973). Thus the provision concerning executive sessions involving "attorney-client communications" in the Laws of the Regents was upheld.

The court, however, erroneously failed to extend this same principle to the balance or to give effect to the special constitutional and statutory authority by which the Regents are empowered to supervise the University. The trial court limited its application of this principle after reaching the conclusion, which we find wholly untenable, that the Sunshine Act ". . . does not limit or infringe on the constitutional and statutory provisions governing the Board of Regents."

The court's interpretation of the applicability of the Sunshine Act if upheld would invalidate a law which the Regents are duly authorized to enact; and clearly this does, indeed, both limit and infringe upon the Regents' authority to govern the university. In order to reach such a result, the Sunshine Act would have to repeal both Art. VIII, Sec. 5(2) and section 124-2-11. As we noted above, such a repeal would have to be express; and the Act contains no such language.

In summary, we hold the specially granted authority of the Regents to govern the university and enact laws pursuant to that end can only be nullified by a legislative enactment (or constitutional amendment) expressly aimed at doing so.

Accordingly, the judgment of the trial court is reversed.

McLARTY v. BOARD OF REGENTS OF THE UNIVERSITY SYSTEM OF GEORGIA
Supreme Court of Georgia
200 S.E.2d 117 (1973)

UNDERCOFLER, Justice.

This litigation involves Georgia's "Government in Sunshine Law." Insofar as material here, that statute provides, "All meetings of any State department, agency, board, bureau, commission or political subdivision and the governing authority of any department, agency, board, bureau, commission or political subdivision of any county, municipal corporation, board of education or other political subdivision at which official actions are to be taken are hereby declared to be public meetings and shall be open to the public at all times." Ga.L.1972, p. 575 (Code Ann. §40-3301).

The issue here is whether a committee composed of faculty members and students of the University of Georgia which was organized by the Dean of Student Affairs primarily for the purpose of reviewing the Student Senate's recommended allocation of Student Activity Funds comes within the "Sunshine Law." The committee's meetings are not open to the public.

Student Activity Funds are derived from a mandatory fee of $4.00 per quarter paid by each student. It amounts to approximately $500,000 per year. The funds are allocated to support various recognized student organizations. At the University of Georgia it is the President's responsibility to submit a recommended allocation of such funds to the Chancellor of the University System for his approval. In carrying out this responsibility the President requested recommendations from the Dean of Student Affairs. The Dean of Student Affairs, for assistance in making such recommendations, in turn appointed the committee which is under attack here for holding private meetings.

The trial court held that the Student Activity Fund Committee did not come within the purview of the "Sunshine Law." We agree.

That part of the "Sunshine Law" which is pertinent here provides, "All meetings of any state department, agency, board, bureau, commission . . . at which official actions are to be taken . . ." are to be public. This language is clear. It applies to the meetings of the variously described bodies which are empowered to act officially for the State and at which such official action is taken. Official action is action which is taken by virtue of power granted by law, or by virtue of the office held, to act for and in behalf of the State. The "Sunshine Law" does not encompass the innumerable groups which are organized and meet for the purpose of collecting information, making recommendations, and rendering advice but which have no authority to make governmental decisions and act for the State. What the law seeks to eliminate are closed meetings which engender in the people a distrust of its officials who are clothed with the power to act in their name. It declares that the people, who possess ultimate sovereignty under our form of government, are entitled to observe the actions of those described bodies when exercising the power delegated to them to act on behalf of the people in the name of the State. There is no such compelling reason to require public meetings of advisory groups. They can take no official action. Generally their reports are submitted in writing and are available to the public well in advance of any official action and are considered by the official body in public meeting.

Accordingly the Student Activity Fund Committee, having no authority to take official action, is not a body which comes within the purview of the "Sunshine Law" and it is not required to hold its meetings in public. Under this holding we do not reach the question of what constitutes official action of those bodies which are subject to that law.

Judgment affirmed.

NOTES

1. In Cathcart v. Andersen, 517 P.2d 980 (1974), law students at the University of Washington sued to open the law school faculty meetings on the grounds that the law faculty was a decision-making body. The faculty demurred on the grounds, among others, that

the Board of Regents was the ultimate decision-making body for the university. The Washington Court of Appeals agreed with the students stating:

> The next question is whether the dean and faculty of the law school compose its governing body. The argument is made that they cannot be because the ultimate responsibility and authority for the government of the university is charged by statute to the Board of Regents. RCW 28B.20.100. Of course, the Board of Regents cannot delegate responsibilities charged to it as the governing body of the university. However, the board does have full authority to delegate its powers and duties. . . .

That the dean and faculty do exercise delegated power, is forcibly brought home in the opinion of the Washington State Supreme Court in DeFunis v. Odegaard, 82 Wash.2d 11, 507 P.2d 1169 (1973). In that case, the admission practices of the university as applied by the law school are brought into question by a rejected applicant, who commenced action against the Board of Regents, president, law dean and some of the law faculty, charging them with discrimination and seeking a court order directing his admission to the law school, or $50,000 in damages. . . .

The role of the dean and faculty in controlling admission to the law school is reported in *DeFunis* at 14 as follows:

> The dean and faculty of the law school, pursuant to the authority delegated to them by the Board of Regents and the president of the university, have established a committee on admissions and readmissions to determine who shall be admitted to the law school.

See Morris, Equal Protection, Affirmative Action and Racial Preferences in Law Admissions, DeFunis v. Odegaard, 49 Wash.L.Rev. 1 (1973). From a reading of the *DeFunis* case and the record before us, the conclusion is inescapable that the law dean and faculty do govern the law school. . . .

2. The Supreme Court of North Carolina, however, ruled that meetings of the University of North Carolina law school faculty were not subject to the open meeting law in that state because the law faculty was not a subsidiary governing body, but merely a group of employees. Student Bar Ass'n v. Byrd, 239 S.E.2d 415 (1977), A Tennessee Court reached the same result by holding that law school committees were creatures of the Dean, and "The Dean is not a public body. . . ." Fain v. Faculty of the College of Law of the Univ. of Tenn., 552 S.W.2d 752, 754 (1977), *cert. denied.___Tenn.___(1977).

3. An excellent analysis of the many facets of the various state laws, and a comprehensive collection of references and authorities may be found in Simon, *The Application of State Sunshine Laws to Institutions of Higher Education*, 4 J. of College and Univ. Law 83 (1977).

IV. Free Exercise of Religion

KEEGAN v. UNIVERSITY OF DELAWARE
Supreme Court of Delaware
349 A.2d 14 (1975)

McNEILLY, Justice:

This is an appeal from a decision of the Court of Chancery granting plaintiff, University of Delaware, summary judgment and a permanent injunction against defendants, priests and intervening University students, prohibiting religious worship services in a commons room of the dormitory in which the students live. The pertinent facts and history of this case are succinctly stated in the Court's opinion, 318 A.2d 135 (1974). We emphasize, however, that we are dealing with a very particular factual situation involving a University campus dormitory.

The University contends that the Establishment Clause of the First Amendment, made applicable to the States by the Fourteenth Amendment, supports and requires the ban of all religious worship services from campus facilities. The priests and students contend that the strict enforcement of the University's policy is an infringement upon the Free Exercise Clause of the First Amendment.

The Vice-Chancellor reasoned that although allowance of services in the University dormitory need not offend the Establishment Clause, the University's policy did not demonstrate a substantial infringement upon the priests and students' right to the free exercise of religion.

As we see the case, there are three issues. First, would the abolition of the present University policy prohibiting religious worship in the campus dormitory run afoul of the prescribed tests for violation of the Establishment Clause of the Federal Constitution? Second, does the University policy constitute a legally recognizable burden on the students' Constitutional right to freely exercise their religion? Third, if the students' right to freely exercise their religion is legally burdened, is such burden justified by a compelling State interest? . . .

We concur with the Vice-Chancellor's rationale in concluding that abolition of present University policy towards religious worship in the commons room of the dormitory need not run afoul of the prescribed tests for establishment violations, i.e., would not have an effect that primarily advances religion, would not reflect a sectarian legislative purpose, and would not foster excessive government entanglement with religion. See *Lemon v. Kurtzman,* 403 U.S. 602, 91 S.Ct. 2105, 29 L.Ed.2d 745 (1971); *Committee for Public Education v. Nyquist,* 413 U.S. 756, 93 S.Ct. 2955, 37 L.Ed.2d 948 (1973). To allow religious worship groups the same rights and privileges attendant with the use of the commons room of the dormitory as are accorded other group activities could reflect a lawful accommodation. *Zorach v. Clauson,* 343 U.S. 306, 72 S.Ct. 679, 96 L.Ed.2d 954 (1952); *Abington School District v. Schempp,* 374 U.S. 203, 83 S.Ct. 1560, 10 L.Ed.2d 844 (1953).

Thus, we hold that the University cannot support its absolute ban of all religious worship on the theory that, without such a ban, University policy allowing all student groups, including religious groups, free access to dormitory common areas would necessarily violate the Establishment Clause. The Establishment cases decided by the United States Supreme Court indicate that neutrality is the safe harbor in which to avoid First Amendment violations: neutral "accommodation" of religion is permitted, *Everson v. Board of Education,* 330 U.S. 1, 67 S.Ct. 504, 91 L.Ed. 711 (1947); *Zorach v. Clauson, supra,* while "promotion" and "advancement" of religion are not. *McCollum v. Board of Education,* 333 U.S. 203, 68 S.Ct. 461, 92 L.Ed. 649 (1948); *Abington School District v. Schempp, supra.* University policy without the worship ban could be neutral towards religion and could have the primary effect of advancing education by allowing students to meet together in the commons room of their dormitory to exchange ideas and share mutual interests. If any religious group or religion is accommodated or benefited thereby, such accommodation or benefit is purely incidental, and would not, in our judgment, violate the Establishment Clause. *Tilton v. Richardson*, 403 U.S. 672, 91 S.Ct. 2091, 29 L.Ed.2d 790 (1971). The commons room is already provided for the benefit of students. It is not a dedication of the space to promote religious interests. Therefore, in regard to the Establishment Clause, we agree with the view taken by the Court of Chancery.

The second issue presents us with more difficulty largely due to the words of degree frequently, and perhaps necessarily, employed by the United States Supreme Court. But it appears to us that the Vice-Chancellor applied the wrong test in the portion of his opinion on the Free Exercise Clause. While it is true that the opinion of the Court in *Sherbert v. Verner*, 374 U.S. 398, 406, 83 S.Ct. 1790, 1795, 10 L.Ed.2d 965 (1963) noted a "substantial infringement of appellant's First Amendment right", it did not indicate that this finding constituted the legal standard for the appellant's burden. Quite to the contrary, the Court, citing *Braunfeld v. Brown*, 366 U.S. 599, 607, 81 S.Ct. 1144, 6 L.Ed.2d 563 (1961), quoted the following language at 374 U.S. 404, at 83 S.Ct. 1794:

> "If the purpose or effect of a law is to impede the observance of one or all religions or is to discriminate invidiously between religions, that law is constitutionally invalid even though the burden may be characterized as being only indirect."

Similarly, the opinion of the court in *Sherbert,* at 374 U.S. 403, at 83 S.Ct. 1793, said that, if the State action is to be upheld:

> "it must be either because [it] represents no infringement by the State of [appellant's] constitutional rights of free exercise, or because any incidental burden on the free exercise of appellant's religion may be justified by a 'compelling state interest in the regulation of a subject within the State's constitutional power to regulate . . .' *NAACP v. Button*, 371 U.S. 415, 438, 83 S.Ct. 328, 341, 9 L.Ed.2d 405, 421."

Thus, it seems to us that, while the Court in *Sherbert* thought the situation there demonstrated a "substantial infringement" of religious freedom, even an "incidental burden" on the free exercise of religion must be justified by a "compelling state interest". Once the individual demonstrates some Constitutional burden, whether substantial or incidental, direct or indirect, upon his free exercise of religion, the State must show a "substantial interest" sufficient to sustain its acts. *Johnson v. Robison*, 415 U.S. 361, 384-386, 94 S.Ct. 1160, 39 L.Ed.2d 389 (1974); *Wisconsin v. Yoder,* 406 U.S. 205, 92 S.Ct. 1526, 32 L.Ed.2d 15 (1972); *Gillette v. United States,* 401 U.S. 437, 462, 91 S.Ct. 828, 28 L.Ed.2d 168 (1971); *Sherbert v. Verner, supra; Braunfeld v. Brown, supra.*

We recognize, as the University has argued on reargument, that there is nothing fixed or permanent about catch phrases in the judicial opinions cited above and that such words as "indirect" and "incidental" can refer to the relationship between the state action and its effect on the individual as well as to the severity of the burden on the individual. It is of course necessary to examine each factual situation.

But, if the burden is examined on the facts in this case, one must conclude it rises to a legally recognizable interest on the part of the students. The only activity proscribed by the regulation is worship regardless of whether one considers the proscription a direct or indirect burden on student activity. The commons area is already provided for student use and there is no request here that separate religious facilities be established. The area in question is a residence hall where students naturally assemble with their friends for many purposes. Religion, at least in part, is historically a communal exercise.

It may be that every class division involving religion would not constitute a burden in the Constitutional sense on the free exercise of religion. *Johnson v. Robison, supra.* It may be that this case can be viewed as the mere denial of an economic benefit. Indeed, it can be argued, as it has been, that the question is whether the University must permit the students to worship on University property. But, in terms of religious liberty, the question is better put, in our judgment, from the perspective of the individual student. Can the University prohibit student worship in a common area of a University dormitory which is provided for student use and in which the University permits every other student activity? It is apparent to us that such a regulation impedes the observance of religion in the sense of the *Sherbert* case.

Even in *Johnson v. Robison, supra*, where the impact of the statute, denial of veteran education benefits to alternative civilian service conscientious objectors, was less direct on religious exercise than the impact of the regulation here, the Court took care to find the Government's "substantial interest" was sufficient to sustain the challenged legislation. Thus, even there, the Court, for its decision, reached what we have designated the third issue in this case.

Counsel have agreed that this case is unique and precise precedents have not been supplied. While we recognize that different considerations may be involved under various Constitutional provisions, the varying nature of the legal proceedings, and varying factual situations, we nonetheless find some support for our views in two cases noted in the briefing and orally argued at re-argument by counsel for amicus curiae. In *Tucker v. Texas*, 326 U.S. 517, 66 S.Ct. 274, 90 L.Ed. 274 (1946), a freedom of press and religion case, the Supreme Court upheld the right of an ordained minister of Jehovah's Witnesses to distribute religious literature in a village owned by the United States, notwithstanding a request to leave by the manager of the village pursuant to his purported authority by federal regulation and Texas criminal law. The Court noted the village "had the characteristics of a typical American town." The case thus has similarities to the University owned dormitory situation here. Similarly, in *Healy v. James,* 408 U.S. 169, 92 S.Ct. 2338, 33 L.Ed.2d 266 (1972), it was held that a state supported college could not deny official recognition to student groups without justification, for such a denial would abridge the First Amendment rights of individuals to free expression and free association. At the outset, the opinion noted that "state colleges and universities are not enclaves immune from the sweep of the First Amendment." 408 U.S. at 180, 92 S.Ct. at 2345.

We also note the following language from *Wisconsin v. Yoder, supra*, 406 U.S. at 220-221, 92 S.Ct. at 1536.

> "The Court must not ignore the danger that an exception from a general obligation of citizenship on religious grounds may run afoul of the Establishment Clause, but that danger cannot be allowed to prevent any exception no matter how vital it may be to the protection of values promoted by the right of free exercise."

We think these conclusions in *Yoder* in regard to right of free exercise are worthy of weight here.

Finally, on the second issue, we do not think the cases of *Stein v. Oshinsky*, 348 F.2d 999 (2d Cir. 1965) and *Hunt v. The Board of Education*, 321 F.Supp. 1263 (S.D.W.Va.1971) dictate a different result than the conclusion we reach here. The Vice-Chancellor was careful to distinguish these cases, and we think he did so correctly. The *Stein* case upheld the prohibition of a voluntary prayer by kindergarten children in a classroom setting. The situation there approached a state sanctioned prayer imposed on children of an impressionable age supported by teacher supervisors. The *Hunt* case, while lacking the coercive situation found in *Stein*, still involved commuting high school students meeting voluntarily in classrooms or other premises of a high school. Neither case involved activity by adult residents of a living complex in common areas generally set aside for the benefit of such residents.

We conclude that the regulation involved here has, in this factual context, both the purpose and the effect of impeding the observance of religion and thus constitutes a legal burden on the students' Constitutional right to freely exercise their religion.

Since the state policy here impedes the observance of religion and acts as a prior restraint upon all religious worship, as opposed to all other activities, and thus constitutes legal burden upon the students' Constitutional rights, it requires a showing of a compelling state interest for justification. *Sherbert v. Verner, supra.* We therefore reach the third issue in the case. The State was not called upon to offer justification nor was any shown. The Vice-Chancellor erred in holding that the students had not shown the requisite infringement on their free exercise rights and in not demanding an evidentiary hearing on the issue of justification.

Reversed and remanded for further proceedings consistent with this opinion.

PART TWO

FACULTY RIGHTS

CHAPTER 6

ACADEMIC FREEDOM AND RELATED
SUBSTANTIVE CONSTITUTIONAL RIGHTS

I. The Concept of Academic Freedom

A. *Introduction*

Throughout the history of higher education there have been constant attempts by universities to keep their learning, teaching and research functions free from political interference by the state. At the same time, the funding agencies of higher education have consistently sought some measure of control over the expenditure of funds, evidenced currently by the concern over accountability.

The university position has been expressed in the traditions of institutional autonomy and academic freedom. A strong articulation of faculty academic freedom can be found in the late 19th century German movement under the leadership of Baron von Humbolt.[1] The translation of academic freedom into American colleges and universities was based more on tradition and customary practice than the law, until comparatively recent times. This tradition was supported strongly by the First Amendment which extended to all citizens broad rights of freedom of speech, freedom of press and freedom of association. In fact there is still debate over whether these First Amendment rights adequately protect the academic community, or whether it is an additional right, unique to academics, which needs further specific legal protection.

The move toward legal protection of academic freedom began in the 1930s with a concern over tenure as a means to protect professors' rights to speak and teach freely. In 1937, the Yale Law Journal, concerned over the dismissal of a Yale professor and the removal of the president of the University of Wisconsin, both reputedly for political purposes, published a note advocating tenure as a means of effecting academic freedom.[2] The effect of this article and others, and the supportive activities of the AAUP, was sufficient to establish tenure rights as a protection against arbitrary dismissal for political reasons. But this protection came largely through professional suasion rather than legislation or court decision. The real test of academic freedom as a legal concept came during the McCarthy era in the so-called "Red Menace" cases. In those cases the courts operated to protect faculty members from unwarranted interference by legislative investigations. The courts also struck down repressive state legislation and overly broad loyalty

---

1. See Ringer, The Decline of the German Mandarins (Cambridge: Harvard Univ. Press, 1955).
2. Comment, *Academic Freedom and the Law*, 46 Yale Law Journal 670 (1937).

oaths which could be used as a basis for political repression. However, a close reading of the Supreme Court cases decided during this period shows no clear definition of academic freedom as a separate legal right nor even any strong reliance on such a doctrine as a basis for court decisions. Perhaps the clearest indication of a protected legal right came later in Griswold v. Connecticut, 381 U.S. 479 (1965), the Connecticut birth control case, in which Justice Douglas wrote that the specific guarantees in the Bill of Rights have "penumbras formed by emanations from those guarantees that help give them life and substance." Justice Douglas's concept was that the right to academic freedom is within the "penumbra" of the First Amendment rights to free speech, free press and free association. He wrote:

> In other words, the State may not, consistently with the spirit of the First Amendment, contract the spectrum of available knowledge. The right of freedom of speech and press includes not only the right to utter or to print, but the right to distribute, the right to receive, the right to read . . . and freedom of inquiry, freedom of thought, and freedom to teach . . . indeed the freedom of the entire university community. . . . Without those peripheral rights the specific rights would be less secure. . . .

One of the more difficult questions posed by the study of a legal concept of academic freedom is the exact definition of the right to be maintained. William Van Alstyne argues persuasively, in *The Specific Theory of Academic Freedom and the General Issue of Civil Liberties*, 140 Annals of the American Academy 404 (1973), that the failure of the academic profession to clearly limit the definition of academic freedom has led to less legal protection than might otherwise have been proffered. In fact, the exact and distinct nature of a right to academic freedom which is entitled to legal protection is probably yet to be defined. Nevertheless, the establishment of academic freedom as a protectable interest is extremely important, particularly in a time of increasing encroachment by creeping regulatory efforts on local, state and national levels. In the United States today, no one would think of launching an explicit theoretical attack upon academic freedom, even if he intended to limit or undermine that liberty in practice. Yet freedom of expression in general has been so highly valued in the United States that there is some danger that the specific freedom of academe is less well protected legally than other more general freedoms. In order to analyze existing legal protection, it is necessary to come to some conclusions regarding the proper definition of academic freedom, and to see clearly what protection, if any, presently exists.

B.   Defining Academic Freedom

In 1940, the AAUP revised its earlier 1915 statement and promulgated the following statement on academic freedom:[3]

---

3.   *See* Joughin, ed., Academic Freedom and Tenure (Madison: Univ. of Wisconsin Press, 1969), pp. 33-36.

1940 Statement of Principles on Academic Freedom and Tenure

In 1915, at the time of the founding of the Association, a committee on academic freedom and tenure formulated a statement entitled a "Declaration of Principles." This statement set forth the concern of the Association for academic freedom and tenure, for proper procedures, and for professional responsibility. The Declaration was endorsed by the American Association of University Professors at its Second Annual Meeting, held December 31, 1915, and January 1, 1916.

In 1925, the American Council on Education called a conference of representatives of a number of its constituent members, among them the American Association of University Professors, for the purpose of preparing a statement in this area. There emerged the 1925 "Conference Statement on Academic Freedom and Tenure," which was endorsed in 1925 by the Association of American Colleges and in 1926 by the American Association of University Professors.

In 1940, following upon a series of conferences which began in 1934, representatives of the Association of American Colleges and the American Association of University Professors agreed upon a "Statement of Principles on Academic Freedom and Tenure," and upon three attached "Interpretations." The 1940 Statement, and its Interpretations, were endorsed by the two associations in 1941. In subsequent years endorsement has been officially voted by numerous other organizations.

*   *   *

The purpose of this statement is to promote public understanding and support of academic freedom and tenure and agreement upon procedures to assure them in colleges and universities. Institutions of higher education are conducted for the common good and not to further the interest of either the individual teacher or the institution as a whole. The common good depends upon the free search for truth and its free exposition.

Academic freedom is essential to these purposes and applies to both teaching and research. Freedom in research is fundamental to the advancement of truth. Academic freedom in its teaching aspect is fundamental for the protection of the rights of the teacher in teaching and of the student to freedom in learning. It carries with it duties correlative with rights.

Tenure is a means to certain ends; specifically: (1) Freedom of teaching and research and of extramural activities and (2) sufficient economic security to make the profession attractive to men and women of ability. Freedom and economic security, hence, tenure, are indispensable to the success of an institution in fulfilling its obligations to its students and to society.

Academic freedom

(a) The teacher is entitled to full freedom in research and in the publication of the results, subject to the adequate performance of his other academic duties; but research for pecuniary return should be based upon an understanding with the authorities of the institution.

(b) The teacher is entitled to freedom in the classroom in discussing his subject, but he should be careful not to introduce into his teaching controversial matter which has no relation to his subject. Limitations of academic freedom because of religious or other aims of the institution should be clearly stated in writing at the time of the appointment.

(c) The college or university teacher is a citizen, a member of a learned profession, and an officer of an educational institution. When he speaks or writes as a citizen, he should be free from institutional censorship or discipline, but his special position in the community imposes special obligations. As a man of learning and an educational officer, he should remember that the public may judge his profession and his institution by his utterances. Hence he should at all times be accurate, should exercise appropriate restraint, should show respect for the opinions of others, and should make every effort to indicate that he is not an institutional spokesman.

In 1969, Professor Fritz Machlup, in *On Some Misconceptions Concerning Academic Freedom*, in Joughin, ed., Academic Freedom and Tenure (Madison: Univ. of Wisconsin Press)*, p. 178, attempted a conceptual definition of academic freedom that was particularly relevant to higher education in the United States:

Academic freedom consists in the absence of, or protection from, such restraints or pressures—chiefly in the form of sanctions threatened by state or church authorities or by the authorities, faculties, or students of colleges and universities, but occasionally also by other power groups in society—as are designed to create in the minds of academic scholars (teachers, research workers, and students in colleges and universities) fears and anxieties that may inhibit them from freely studying and investigating whatever they are interested in, and from freely discussing, teaching, or publishing whatever opinions they have reached. . . .

Faithful to the original meaning of academic freedom, this definition comprises the freedom to learn as well as the freedom to teach. There have been countries and times in which the students' freedoms were more debated than the professors'. Where all institutions of higher learning are operated by the state and a student

---

* Machlup, Fritz, *On Some Misconceptions Concerning Academic Freedom*, in Joughin, ed., Academic Freedom and Tenure (Madison: The University of Wisconsin Press; © 1969 by the American Association of University Professors), p. 178. Reprinted by permission.

has no alternative place to study, the problem of his freedom is indeed of prime importance. In the present-day United States, the only important issue regarding the freedom to learn is linked with possible restrictions on the freedom to teach: the opportunities to learn are restricted if certain subjects or ideas are excluded from the curriculum or if teachers of certain persuasions are excluded from the faculty. In this country, freedom to teach has always been the more important problem, so much so that the American dictionary definitions of academic freedom confine themselves to the professors' side of it. . . .

Efforts to cast a better definition or to formulate more ringing pronouncements of the principles of academic freedom are unlikely to produce the clarifications that are needed at the present time. Since the positive meaning of a proposition is not clear as long as doubt is left concerning what it negates, attempts at clarification should critically analyse the logical status of supposed corollaries which may actually contradict the proposition if correctly understood. In this sense, a critical or negative statement will serve the purpose better than a reiteration of positive contentions. . . .

In 1968, the Harvard Law Review published a significant note outlining the evolution of the concept of academic freedom. The note also included an attempt at definition:

NOTE, DEVELOPMENTS IN THE LAW
—ACADEMIC FREEDOM*
81 Harv. L. Rev. 1045 (1968)

Academic freedom is that aspect of intellectual liberty concerned with the peculiar institutional needs of the academic community. The claim that scholars are entitled to particular immunity from ideological coercion is premised on a conception of the university as a community of scholars engaged in the pursuit of knowledge, collectively and individually, both within the classroom and without, and on the pragmatic conviction that the invaluable service rendered by the university to society can be performed only in an atmosphere entirely free from administrative, political, or ecclesiastical constraints on thought and expression. The modern American concept of *Lehrfreiheit*—freedom to teach—that characterized the nineteenth-century German university. In the German university the professor was free not only in his scholarly research, but also in his choice of what to discuss in the classroom. Although American educational theorists assimilated the notion of freedom of academic inquiry without modification, they subjected the notion of freedom in the classroom to the limitation that the university may prescribe in general terms the subject matter to be discussed by the professor. The modern American understanding of academic freedom also differs from the German concept of *Lehrfreiheit* in its concern for the professor's extramural freedom. In the European societies in which academic freedom developed the professional liberty of the university professor protected him only in the classroom, and not against the more repressive conditions that prevailed outside the university walls. But in this country, with its tradition of general freedom of expression, academic freedom has customarily encompassed the right of the professor to speak freely in his private capacity without fear of administrative or legal reprisal. According to this precept of academic freedom the professor is entitled to the same freedom to advocate ideas and join causes enjoyed by his fellow citizens; indeed, because of his position as intellectual leader, the scholar is especially encouraged to participate in the public forum.

The American concept of academic freedom is reflected not only in the recognition of substantive areas of intellectual liberty, but also in certain institutional arrangements designed to protect that freedom. The principal device of this sort is the system of tenure. Once a professor has successfully demonstrated his competence during a probationary period, the system of tenure protects him against arbitrary dismissal by forbidding dismissals without specified cause and by guaranteeing the individual an opportunity to be heard in his defense and, often, the right to be tried by a tribunal composed at least in part of his colleagues. In this way tenure promotes academic freedom by protecting the individual professor against dismissal for undisclosed or disguised ideologically repressive motives and, more generally, by providing for the entire faculty the economic security thought necessary to the realization of complete intellectual freedom. A second institutional arrangement relied upon with increasing frequency to protect academic freedom is participation by faculty members in academic government. By obtaining a voice in decisions of academic policy, faculty members are able to secure an area in which scholarship can thrive free from administrative restraint.

Throughout the history of academic freedom the position of the university student has differed rather markedly from that of the professor. In nineteenth-century Germany the university student enjoyed a unique range of educational liberty subsumed under the label *Lernfreiheit,* or freedom to learn. The student was free to wander from university to university, attending classes and pursuing a course of study entirely of his own choosing. The student at the American university has never enjoyed this "absence of administrative coercion in the learning situation" characteristic of German higher education. Indeed for a long period of time the American university was thought to be free to dictate the terms of the student's educational experience; only by virtue of the independence accorded to his professors did the student enjoy a degree of free inquiry in the classroom. But a growing recognition of the necessity for intellectual freedom in the learning process, as well as the social value of student extracurricular expression, has led to a revival of interest in student academic freedom. Recent comprehensive formulations of student academic freedom thus evince a range of concerns that parallel those expressed by proponents of teacher freedom: freedom of inquiry and expression in curricular activities, in extracurricular student affairs, and off campus; procedural fairness in disciplinary proceedings; and participation in the governance of the institution. . . .

The courts have only very recently begun to emerge as an instrument for the protection of academic freedom. At the present time, however, the scope of protection afforded by the law falls far short of the normative conception of academic freedom for several reasons. In the first place, there has never developed a unified legal theory of academic rights and duties derived from an assessment of the unique institutional demands, social policies, and personal interests involved in the educational situation. Rather, problems encountered under the nonlegal rubric of "academic freedom" have been assimilated to other established legal categories, such as contract or due process, and resolved subject to their limitations. Second, the courts have traditionally been reluctant to intrude upon the domain of educational affairs, not only in recognition of their lack of institutional competence in such matters, but also out of respect for the autonomy of educational institutions. Furthermore, since courts must accommodate with the scholar's demand for freedom the competing demands of the institution and the state for restriction, they are unlikely to furnish the full range of protection sought by members of the academic community alone.

As a consequence, the legal protection of academic freedom is limited in terms of the institutions to which it applies, the remedies that it accords, and the substantive rights to which it extends. The most important proposition about the judicial doctrine of academic freedom is that it currently applies almost exclusively to public education. Teachers and students at private institutions have been unable to secure the legal protections accorded to their counterparts at public schools and universities primarily because the provisions of the fourteenth amendment as yet have not been applied generally to private education. In addition, the contract theory has not proved to be a very appropriate tool for fashioning a law of academic freedom for private institutions. A second central proposition is that when issues of academic freedom have been presented, the courts have tended to emphasize procedural regularity rather than review the substantive basis for educational decisions. Similarly, the scope of substantive legal protection of academic freedom has been confined largely to extracurricular speech and association; the courts have almost never been asked, and have even less frequently been willing, to intrude into the classroom, the library, or the laboratory in order to protect intellectual liberty.

Although the legal protection currently afforded to academic freedom is thus quite limited, the doctrines inhibiting a more expansive judicial role are being gradually eroded as the courts are invoked more frequently by aggrieved students and teachers. For example, the commands of the fourteenth amendment could be interpreted to apply to private educational institutions, either selectively or comprehensively. Alternatively, the courts could attempt to fashion a special body of law explicitly defining the professional rights and obligations of members of the academic community—either within such traditional legal categories as contract or tort, or by the formulation of a branch of the law of private associations. Yet even if either of these developments occurred, legal protection would continue to be severely limited. Ordinarily only extreme cases reach the courts—those involving a serious individual injury or a compelling claim for judicial relief. The courts have at best only a limited competence in matters of academic policy such as curriculum, and they are generally unable to remedy ideological coercion through informal pressures and threats or to secure for the teacher or student an effective voice in the policy decisions that affect him. Consequently, teachers, and to a larger extent students, will probably continue to rely primarily on such alternative methods as private persuasion and collective bargaining for the securing of their demands.

NOTE

For further study of the American concept of academic freedom *see*: Hofstader and Metzger, The Development of Academic Freedom in the United States (New York City: Columbia University Press, 1955); Joughin, ed., Academic Freedom and Tenure (Madison: Univ. of Wisconsin Press, 1969); Emerson, The System of Freedom of Expression (New York City:Vintage Books, 1970); Van Alstyne, *The Constitutional Rights of Teachers and Professors*, 1970 Duke L.J. 841 (1970); Fellman, *Academic Freedom in American Law*, 1961 Wis. L. Rev. 3 (1961); Cowan, *Interference with Academic Freedom: The Pre-natal History of a Tort*, 4 Wayne L. Rev. 205 (1958); Murphy, *Academic Freedom— An Emerging Constitutional Right*, 28 Law & Contemp. Prob. 447 (1963); O'Neil, *Libraries, Liberties and the First Amendment*, 42 Cinn. L. Rev. 209 (1973); Wright, *The Constitution on Campus*, 22 Vand. L. Rev. 1027 (1969); Van Alstyne, *The Specific Theory of Academic Freedom and the General Issue of Civil Liberties*, 140 Annals of American Academy of Political and Social Science 404 (1972); Nahmod, *First Amendment Protection for Learning and Teaching: The Scope of Judicial Review*, 18 Wayne L. Rev. 1479 (1972); and Goldstein, *The Asserted Constitutional Right of Public School Teachers to Determine What They Teach*, 124 U. of Penn. L. Rev. 1293 (1976).

II.   Freedom to Teach and to Publish

A.   Freedom of Thought in Lecturing and Writing

One of the keystone cases defining academic freedom in the United States concerned Paul Sweezy, a former professor of economics at Harvard, who was invited to the University of New Hampshire where he gave several lectures expressing his views. (Sweezy, who described himself as a "classical Marxist" and "Socialist," had written books and articles on the general theme of the inevitable collapse of capitalism and rise of socialism.) Thereupon, Sweezy was subpoened by the New Hampshire Attorney General for extensive questioning pursuant to a joint resolution of the New Hampshire legislature authorizing an investigation of subversive activities. Sweezy answered most questions and stated clearly that he was not a Communist and did not advocate violent overthrow of the government. He refused to answer questions concerning 1) a lecture given by him at the University of New Hampshire; 2) his, or his wife's, political activities in the Progressive Party; and 3) his "opinions and beliefs." The New Hampshire Superior Court ordered Sweezy to answer, and when he did not, found him to be in contempt. This holding was affirmed by the New Hampshire Supreme Court and appealed to the U. S. Supreme Court.

SWEEZY v. NEW HAMPSHIRE
United States Supreme Court
354 U. S. 234 (1957)

Mr. Chief Justice WARREN announced the judgment of the Court, and delivered an opinion in which Mr. Justices BLACK, DOUGLAS and BRENNAN joined.

... The State Supreme Court thus conceded without extended discussion that petitioner's right to lecture and his right to associate with others were constitutionally protected freedoms which had been abridged through this investigation. These conclusions could not be seriously debated. Merely to summon a witness and compel him, against his will, to disclose the nature of his past expressions and associations is a measure of governmental interference in these matters. These are rights which are safeguarded by the Bill of Rights and the Fourteenth Amendment. We believe that there unquestionably was an invasion of petitioner's liberties in the areas of academic freedom and political expression—areas in which government should be extremely reticent to tread.

The essentiality of freedom in the community of American universities is almost self-evident. No one should underestimate the vital role in a democracy that is played by those who guide and train our youth. To impose any strait jacket upon the intellectual leaders in our colleges and universities would imperil the future of our Nation. No field of education is so thoroughly comprehended by man that new discoveries cannot yet be made. Particularly is that true in the social sciences, where few, if any, principles are accepted as absolutes. Scholarship cannot flourish in an atmosphere of suspicion and distrust. Teachers and students must always remain free to inquire, to study and to evaluate, to gain new maturity and understanding; otherwise our civilization will stagnate and die.

Equally manifest as a fundamental principle of a democratic society is political freedom of the individual. Our form of government is built on the premise that every citizen shall have the right to engage in political expression and association. This right was enshrined in the First Amendment of the Bill of Rights. Exercise of these basic freedoms in America has traditionally been through the media of political associations. Any interference with the freedom of a party is simultaneously an interference with the freedom of its adherents. All political ideas cannot and should not be channeled into the programs of our two major parties. History has amply proved the virtue of political activity by minority, dissident groups, who innumerable times

have been in the vanguard of democratic thought and whose programs were
ultimately accepted. Mere unorthodoxy or dissent from the prevailing mores
is not to be condemned. The absence of such voices would be a symptom of
grave illness in our society.

Notwithstanding the undeniable importance of freedom in the areas,
the Supreme Court of New Hampshire did not consider that the abridgment of petitioner's rights under the Constitution vitiated the investigation. In view of that court, "the answer lies in a determination of whether
the object of the legislative investigation under consideration is such as to
justify the restriction thereby imposed upon the defendant's liberties."
100 N.H., at 113-114, 121 A.2d at 791-792. It found such justification in
the legislature's judgment, expressed by its authorizing resolution, that there
exists a potential menace from those who would overthrow the government
by force and violence. That court concluded that the need for the legislature
to be informed on so elemental a subject as the self-preservation of government outweighed the deprivation of constitutional rights that occurred in
the process.

We do not now conceive of any circumstance wherein a state interest
would justify infringement of rights in these fields. But we do not need to
reach such fundamental questions of state power to decide this case. The
State Supreme Court itself recognized that there was a weakness in its conclusion that the menace of forcible overthrow of the government justified
sacrificing constitutional rights. There was a missing link in the chain of
reasoning. The syllogism was not complete. There was nothing to connect
the questioning of petitioner with this fundamental interest of the State. . . .

The respective roles of the legislature and the investigator thus revealed are of considerable significance to the issue before us. It is eminently
clear that the basic discretion of determining the direction of the legislative
inquiry has been turned over to the investigative agency. . . .

Instead of making known the nature of the data it desired, the legislature has insulated itself from those witnesses whose rights may be vitally
affected by the investigation. Incorporating by reference provisions from its
subversive activities act, it has told the Attorney General, in effect to screen
the citizenry of New Hampshire to bring to light anyone who fits into the
expansive definitions.

Within the very broad area thus committed to the discretion of the
Attorney General there may be many facts which the legislature might
find useful. There would also be a great deal of data which that assembly
would not want or need. In the classes of information that the legislature
might deem it desirable to have, there will be some which it could not validly
acquire because of the effect upon the constitutional rights of individual
citizens. Separating the wheat from the chaff, from the standpoint of the
legislature's object, is the legislature's responsibility because it alone can
make that judgment. In this case, the New Hampshire legislature has delegated that task to the Attorney General.

As a result, neither we nor the state courts have any assurance that the questions petitioner refused to answer fall into a category of matters upon which the legislature wanted to be informed when it initiated this inquiry. The judiciary are thus placed in an untenable position. Lacking even the elementary fact that the legislature wants certain questions answered and recognizing that petitioner's constitutional rights are in jeopardy, we are asked to approve or disapprove his incarceration for contempt.

In our view, the answer is clear. No one would deny that the infringement of constitutional rights of individuals would violate the guarantee of due process where no state interest underlies the state action. Thus, if the Attorney General's interrogation of petitioner were in fact wholly unrelated to the object of the legislature in authorizing the inquiry, the Due Process Clause would preclude the endangering of constitutional liberties. We believe that an equivalent situation is presented in this case. The lack of any indications that the legislature wanted the information the Attorney General attempted to elicit from petitioner must be treated as the absence of authority. It follows that the use of the contempt power, notwithstanding the interference with constitutional rights, was not in accordance with the due process requirements of the Fourteenth Amendment. . . .

The judgment of the Supreme Court of New Hampshire is
Reversed.

Mr. Justice FRANKFURTER, whom Mr. Justice HARLAN joins, concurring in the result.

. . . When weighed against the grave harm resulting from governmental intrusion into the intellectual life of a university, such justification for compelling a witness to discuss the contents of his lecture appears grossly inadequate. Particularly is this so where the witness has sworn that neither in the lecture nor at any other time did he ever advocate overthrowing the Government by force and violence.

Progress in the natural sciences is not remotely confined to findings made in the laboratory. Insights into the mysteries of nature are born of hypothesis and speculation. The more so is this true in the pursuit of understanding in the groping endeavors of what are called the social sciences, the concern of which is man and society. The problems are that the respective preoccupations and anthropology, economics, law, psychology, sociology and related areas of scholarship are merely departmentalized dealing, by way of manageable division of analysis, with interpenetrating aspects of holistic perplexities. For society's good—if understanding be an essential need of society—inquiries into these problems, speculations about them, stimulation in others of reflection upon them, must be left as unfettered as possible. Political power must abstain from intrusion into this activity of freedom, pursued in the interest of wise government and the people's well-being, except for reasons that are exigent and obviously compelling.

These pages need not be burdened with proof, based on the testimony of a cloud of impressive witnesses, of the dependence of a free society on free universities. This means the exclusion of governmental intervention in the intellectual life of a university. It matters little whether such intervention occurs avowedly or through action that inevitably tends to check the ardor and fearlessness of scholars, qualities at once so fragile and so indispensable for fruitful academic labor. One need only refer to the address of T. H. Huxley at the opening of Johns Hopkins University, the Annual Reports of President A. Lawrence Lowell of Harvard, the Reports of the University Grants Committee in Great Britain, as illustrative items in a vast body of literature. Suffice it to quote the latest expression on this subject. It is also perhaps the most poignant because its plea on behalf of continuing the free spirit of the open universities of South Africa has gone unheeded.

"In a university knowledge is its own end, not merely a means to an end. A university ccases to be true to its own nature if it becomes the tool of Church or State or any sectional interest. A university is characterized by the spirit of free inquiry, its ideal being the ideal of Socrates—'to follow the argument where it leads.' This implies the right to examine, question, modify or reject traditional ideas and beliefs. Dogma and hypothesis are incompatible, and the concept of an immutable doctrine is repugnant to the spirit of a university. The concern of its scholars is not merely to add and revise facts in relation to an accepted framework, but to be ever examining and modifying the framework itself.

.   .   .   .   .

"Freedom to reason and freedom for disputation on the basis of observation and experiment are the necessary conditions for the advancement of scientific knowledge. A sense of freedom is also necessary for creative work in the arts which, equally with scientific research, is the concern of the university.

.   .   .   .   .

". . . It is the business of a university to provide that atmosphere which is most conducive to speculation, experiment and creation. It is an atmosphere in which there prevail 'the four essential freedoms' of a university—to determine for itself on academic grounds who may teach, what may be taught, how it shall be taught, and who may be admitted to study." The Open Universities in South Africa 10-12. (A statement of a conference of senior scholars from the University of Cape Town and the University of the Witwatersrand, including A. v. d. S. Centlivres and Richard Feetham, as Chancellors of the respective universities.)

I do not suggest that what New Hampshire has here sanctioned bears any resemblance to the policy against which this South African remonstrance was directed. I do say that in these matters of the spirit inroads on legitimacy must be resisted at their incipiency. This kind of evil grows by what it is allowed to feed on. The admonition of this Court in another context is applicable here. "It may be that it is the obnoxious thing in its mildest and least repulsive form; but illegitimate and unconstitutional practices get their first footing in that way, namely, by silent approaches and slight deviations from legal modes of procedure." *Boyd v. United States*, 116 U.S. 616, 635.

NOTES

1. Does *Sweezy* protect faculty members from *any* necessity to testify before legislative committees? How could the "balance" be swung in the government's favor? In 1959, the Supreme Court decided Barenblatt v. U.S., 360 U.S. 109 (1959), a case concerning an instructor at the University of Michigan. In that case, the Court employed the "balancing test" to uphold Barenblatt's conviction for contempt of Congress based on his refusal to answer questions on his political and religious beliefs or on any other "personal and private affairs" or "associational activities." The Court balanced the Congressional power of self-preservation, "the ultimate value of any society," against Barenblatt's First Amendment rights, ruling that "investigatory power in this domain is not to be denied Congress solely because the field of education is involved. Nothing in the prevailing opinions in *Sweezy v. New Hampshire, supra,* stands for a contrary view."

2. What is the actual holding of the Court in *Sweezy*? What legal definition of academic freedom may be derived from *Sweezy*?

3. In *Barenblatt*, the Court contrasted Barenblatt's rights under the First Amendment with the rights of a witness under the Fifth Amendment. How do these rights differ?

4. In Shelton v. Tucker, 364 U.S. 479 (1960), Arkansas teachers and professors challenged a state statute requiring each instructor to file annually an affidavit listing without limitation every organization to which he had belonged or regularly contributed within the preceding five years. How would the Supreme Court decide, in light of *Sweezy* and *Barenblatt?*

B. Freedom of Thought and Personal Action

KAY v. BOARD OF HIGHER EDUCATION OF CITY OF NEW YORK
Supreme Court, New York County
18 N.Y.S. 2d 821 (1940)

McGEEHAN, Justice. . . .

The petitioner contends that the appointment of Bertrand Russell has violated the public policy of the state and of the nation because of the notorious immoral and salacious teachings of Bertrand Russell and because the petitioner contends he is a man not of good moral character.

It has been argued that the private life and writings of Mr. Russell have nothing whatsoever to do with his appointment as a teacher of philosophy. It has also been argued that he is going to teach mathematics. His appointment, however, is to the department of philosophy in City College.

In this consideration I am completely dismissing any question of Mr. Russell's attacks upon religion, but there are certain basic principles upon which this government is founded. If a teacher, who is a person not of good moral character, is appointed by any authority the appointment violates these essential prerequisites. One of the prerequisites of a teacher is good moral character. In fact, this is a prerequisite for appointment in civil service in the city and state, or political subdivisions, or in the United States. It needs no argument here to defend this statement. It need not be found in the Education Law. It is found in the nature of the teaching profession. Teachers are supposed not only to impart instruction in the class-room but by their example to teach students. The taxpayers of the City of New York spend millions to maintain the colleges of the City of New York. They are not spending that money nor was the money appropriated for the purpose of employing teachers who are not of good moral character. However, there is ample authority in the Education Law to support this contention.

Section 556 in the same general article, Article 20, entitled "Teachers and Pupils," reads as follows: "A school commissioner shall examine any charge affecting the moral character of any teacher within his district, first giving such teacher reasonable notice of the charge, and an opportunity to defend himself therefrom; and if he find the charge sustained, he shall annul the teacher's certificate, by whomsoever granted, and declare him unfit to teach; and if the teacher holds a certificate of the commissioner of education or of a former superintendent of public instruction or a diploma of a state normal school, he shall notify the commissioner of education forthwith of such annulment and declaration." . . .

The contention of the petitioner that Mr. Russell has taught in his books immoral and salacious doctrines, is amply sustained by the books conceded to be the writings of Bertrand Russell, which were offered in evidence. It is not necessary to detail here the filth which is contained in the books. It is sufficient to record the following: from "Education and the Modern World," pages 119 and 120: "I am sure that university life would be better, both intellectually and morally, if most university students had temporary childless marriages. This would afford a solution of the sexual urge neither restless nor surreptitious, neither mercenary nor casual, and of such a nature that it need not take up time which ought to be given to work." From "Marriage and Morals," pages 165 and 166: "For my part, while I am quite convinced that companionate marriage would be a step in the right direction, and would do a great deal of good, I do not think that it goes far enough. I think that all sex relations which do not involve children should be regarded as a purely private affair, and that if a man and a woman choose to live together without having children, that should be no one's business but their own. I should not hold it desirable that either a man or a woman should enter upon the serious business of a marriage intended to lead to children without having had previous sexual experience." ("The peculiar importance attached, at the present, to adultery, is quite irrational." From "What I Believe," page 50.)

The Penal Law of the State of New York is a most important factor in the lives of our people. As citizens and residents of our city we come within its protective scope. In dealing with human behavior the provisions of the Penal Law and such conduct as therein condemned must not be lightly treated or completely ignored. Even assuming that the Board of Higher Education possesses the maximum power which the Legislature could possibly confer upon it in the appointment of its teachers, it must act so as not to violate the Penal Law or to encourage the violation of it. Where it so acts as to sponsor or encourage violations of the Penal Law, and its actions adversely affect the public health, safety and morals, its acts are void and of no legal effect. A court of equity, with the powers inherent in that court, has ample jurisdiction to protect the taxpayers of the City of New York from such acts as this of the Board of Higher Education. . . .

When we consider the vast amount of money that the taxpayers are assessed each year to enforce these provisions of the law, how repugnant to the common welfare must be any expenditure that seeks to encourage the violation of the provisions of the Penal Law. Conceding arguendo that the Board of Higher Education has sole and exclusive power to select the faculty of City College and that its discretion cannot be reviewed or curtailed by this court or any other agency, nevertheless, such sole and exclusive power may not be used to aid, abet or encourage any course of conduct tending to a violation of the Penal Law. Assuming that Mr. Russell could teach for two years in City College without promulgating the doctrines which he seems to find necessary to spread on the printed pages at frequent intervals, his appointment violates a perfectly obvious canon of pedagogy, namely, that the personality of the teacher has more to do with forming a student's opinion than many syllogisms. A person we despise and who is lacking in ability cannot argue us into imitating him. A person whom we like and who is of outstanding ability, does not have to try. It is contended that Bertrand Russell is extraordinary. That makes him the more dangerous. The philosophy of Mr. Russell and his conduct in the past is in direct conflict and in violation of the Penal Law of the State of New York. When we consider how susceptible the human mind is to the ideas and philosophy of teaching professors, it is apparent that the Board of Higher Education either disregarded the probable consequences of their acts or were more concerned with advocating a cause that appeared to them to present a challenge to so-called "academic freedom" without according suitable consideration of the other aspects of the problem before them. While this court would not interfere with any action of the board in so far as a pure question of "valid" academic freedom is concerned, it will not tolerate academic freedom being used as a cloak to promote the popularization in the minds of adolescents of acts forbidden by the Penal Law. This appointment affects the public health, safety and morals of the community and it is the duty of the court to act. Academic freedom does not mean academic license. It is the freedom to do good and not to teach evil. Academic freedom cannot authorize a teacher to teach that murder or treason are good. Nor can it permit a teacher to teach directly or indirectly that sexual intercourse between students, where the female is under the age of eighteen years, is proper. This court can take judicial notice of the fact that students in the colleges of the City of New York are under the age of eighteen years, although some of them may be older.

Academic freedom cannot teach that abduction is lawful nor that adultery is attractive and good for the community. There are norms and criteria of truth which have been recognized by the founding fathers. We find a recognition of them in the opening words of the Declaration of Independence, where they refer to the laws of nature and of Nature's God. The doctrines therein set forth, which have been held sacred by all Americans from that day to this, preserved by the Constitution of the United States and of the several states and defended by the blood of its citizens, recognizing the inalienable rights with which men are endowed by their Creator must be preserved, and a man whose life and teachings run counter to these doctrines, who teaches and practices immorality and who encourages and avows violations of the Penal Law of the State of New York, is not fit to teach in any of the schools of this land. The judicial branch of our government under our democratic institutions, has not been so emasculated by the opponents of our institutions to an extent to render it impotent to act to protect the rights of the people. Where public health, safety and morals are so directly involved, no board, administrative or otherwise, may act in a absolute immunity from judicial review. The Board of Higher Education of the City of New York has deliberately and completely disregarded the essential principles upon which the selection of any teacher must rest. The contention that Mr. Russell will teach mathematics and not his philosophy does not in any way detract from the fact that his very presence as a teacher will cause the students to look up to him, seek to know more about him, and the more he is able to charm them and impress them with his personal presence, the more potent will grow his influence in all spheres of their lives, causing the students in many instances to strive to emulate him in every respect. . . .

Considering Dr. Russell's principles, with reference to the Penal Law of the State of New York, it appears that not only would the morals of the students be undermined, but his doctrines would tend to bring them, and in some cases their parents and guardians, in conflict with the Penal Law, and accordingly this court intervenes.

The appointment of Dr. Russell is an insult to the people of the City of New York and to the thousands of teachers who were obligated upon their appointment to establish good moral character and to maintain it in order to keep their positions. Considering the instances in which immorality alone has been held to be sufficient basis for removal of a teacher and mindful of the aphorism "As a man thinketh in his heart, so he is," the court holds that the acts of the Board of Higher Education of the City of New York in appointing Dr. Russell to the Department of Philosophy of the City College of the City of New York, to be paid by public funds, is in effect establishing a chair of indecency and in doing so has acted arbitrarily, capriciously and in direct violation of the public health, safety and morals of the people and of the petitioner's rights herein, and the petitioner is entitled to an order revoking the appointment of the said Bertrand Russell and discharging him from his said position, and denying to him the rights and privileges and the powers appertaining to his appointment. Settle final order accordingly.

NOTE

Do you think that *Kay* would survive constitutional challenge today? Is *Kay* significantly distinguishable from *Starsky v. Williams, infra?*

C.   Loyalty Oaths

WIEMAN v. UPDEGRAFF
United States Supreme Court
344 U. S. 183 (1952)

MR. JUSTICE CLARK delivered the opinion of the Court.

This is an appeal from a decision of the Supreme Court of Oklahoma upholding the validity of a loyalty oath prescribed by Oklahoma statute for all state officers and employees. . . . Appellants, employed by the State as members of the faculty and staff of Oklahoma Agricultural and Mechanical College, failed, within the thirty days permitted, to take the oath required by the Act. Appellee Updegraff, as a citizen and taxpayer, thereupon brought this suit in the District Court of Oklahoma County to enjoin the necessary state officials from paying further compensation to employees who had not subscribed to the oath. . . . [The appellants] sought a mandatory injunction directing the state officers to pay their salaries regardless of their failure to take the oath. Their objections centered largely on the following clauses of the oath:

". . . That I am not affiliated directly or indirectly . . . with any foreign political agency, party, organization or Government, or with any agency, party, organization, association, or group whatever which has been officially determined by the United States Attorney General or other authorized agency of the United States to be a communist front or subversive organization; . . . that I will take up arms in the defense of the United States in time of War, or National Emergency, if necessary; that within the five (5) years immediately preceding the taking of this oath (or affirmation) I have not been a member of . . . any agency, party, organization, association, or group whatever which has been officially determined by the United States Attorney General or other authorized public agency of the United States to be a communist front or subversive organization. . . ."

. . . .

The purpose of the Act, we are told, "was to make loyalty a qualification to hold public office or be employed by the State." . . . During periods of international stress, the extent of legislation with such objectives accentuates our traditional concern about the relation of government to the individual in a free society. The perennial problem of defining that relationship becomes acute when disloyalty is screened by ideological patterns and techniques of disguise that make it difficult to identify. Democratic government is not powerless to meet this threat, but it must do so without infringing the freedoms that are the ultimate values of all democratic living. In the adoption of such means as it believes effective, the legislature is therefore confronted with the problem of balancing its interest in national security with the often conflicting constitutional rights of the individual. . . . We are thus brought to the question touched on in *Garner, Adler,* and *Gerende:* whether the Due Process Clause permits a state, in attempting to bar disloyal

individuals from its employ, to exclude persons solely on the basis of organizational membership, regardless of their knowledge concerning the organizations to which they had belonged. For, under the statute before us, the fact
of membership alone disqualifies. If the rule be expressed as a presumption
of disloyalty, it is a conclusive one.

But membership may be innocent. A state servant may have joined a
proscribed organization unaware of its activities and purposes. In recent
years, many completely loyal persons have severed organizational ties after
learning for the first time of the character of groups to which they had belonged. "They had joined, [but] did not know what it was, they were good,
fine young men and women, loyal Americans, but they had been trapped
into it—because one of the great weaknesses of all Americans, whether
adult or youth, is to join something." At the time of affiliation, a group
itself may be innocent, only later coming under the influence of those who
would turn it toward illegitimate ends. Conversely, an organization formerly
subversive and therefore designated as such may have subsequently freed
itself from the influences which originally led to its listing.

There can be no dispute about the consequences visited upon a person
excluded from public employment on disloyalty grounds. In the view of the
community, the stain is a deep one; indeed, it has become a badge of infamy.
Especially is this so in time of cold war and hot emotions when "each man
begins to eye his neighbor as a possible enemy." Yet under the Oklahoma
Act, the fact of association alone determines disloyalty and disqualification;
it matters not whether association existed innocently or knowingly. To thus
inhibit individual freedom of movement is to stifle the flow of democratic
expression and controversy at one of its chief sources. We hold that the
distinction observed between the case at bar and *Garner, Adler* and *Gerende*
is decisive. Indiscriminate classification of innocent with knowing activity
must fall as an assertion of arbitrary power. The oath offends due process. . . .
We need not pause to consider whether an abstract right to public employment exists. It is sufficient to say that constitutional protection does extend
to the public servant whose exclusion pursuant to a statute is patently arbitrary or discriminatory. . . .

Reversed.

MR. JUSTICE FRANKFURTER, whom MR. JUSTICE DOUGLAS
joins, concurring.

The times being what they are, it is appropriate to add a word by way
of emphasis to the Court's opinion, which I join.

The case concerns the power of a State to exact from teachers in one
of its colleges an oath that they are not, and for the five years immediately
preceding the taking of the oath have not been, members of any organization listed by the Attorney General of the United States, prior to the passage of the statute, as "subversive" or "Communist-front." Since the affiliation which must thus be forsworn may well have been for reasons or for

purposes as innocent as membership in a club of one of the established political parties, to require such an oath, on pain of a teacher's loss of his position in case of refusal to take the oath, penalizes a teacher for exercising a right of association peculiarly characteristic of our people. See Arthur M. Schlesinger, Sr., Biography of a Nation of Joiners, 50 Am. Hist. Rev. 1 (1944), reprinted in Schlesinger, Paths To The Present, 23. Such joining is an exercise of the rights of free speech and free inquiry. By limiting the power of the States to interfere with freedom of speech and freedom of inquiry and freedom of association, the Fourteenth Amendment protects all persons, no matter what their calling. But, in view of the nature of the teacher's relation to the effective exercise of the rights which are safeguarded by the Bill of Rights and by the Fourteenth Amendment, inhibition of freedom of thought, and of action upon thought, in the case of teachers brings the safeguards of those amendments vividly into operation. Such unwarranted inhibition upon the free spirit of teachers affects not only those who, like the appellants, are immediately before the Court. It has an unmistakable tendency to chill that free play of the spirit which all teachers ought especially to cultivate and practice; it makes for caution and timidity in their associations by potential teachers.

The Constitution of the United States does not render the United States or the States impotent to guard their governments against destruction by enemies from within. It does not preclude measures of self-protection against anticipated overt acts of violence. Solid threats to our kind of government—manifestations of purposes that reject argument and the free ballot as the means for bringing about changes and promoting progress—may be met by preventive measures before such threats reach fruition. However, in considering the constitutionality of legislation like the statute before us it is necessary to keep steadfastly in mind what it is that is to be secured. Only thus will it be evident why the Court has found that the Oklahoma law violates those fundamental principles of liberty "which lie at the base of all our civil and political institutions" and as such are imbedded in the due process of law which no State may offend. *Hebert* v. *Louisiana*, 272 U.S. 312, 316.

That our democracy ultimately rests on public opinion is a platitude of speech but not a commonplace in action. Public opinion is the ultimate reliance of our society only if it be disciplined and responsible. It can be disciplined and responsible only if habits of open-mindedness and of critical inquiry are acquired in the formative years of our citizens. The process of education has naturally enough been the basis of hope for the perdurance of our democracy on the part of all our great leaders, from Thomas Jefferson onwards.

To regard teachers—in our entire educational system, from the primary grades to the university—as the priests of our democracy is therefore not to indulge in hyperbole. It is the special task of teachers to foster those habits of open-mindedness and critical inquiry which alone make for responsible citizens, who, in turn, make possible an enlightened and effective public opinion. Teachers must fulfill their function by precept and practice, by the very atmosphere which they generate; they must be exemplars of open-mindedness and free inquiry. They cannot carry out their noble task if the conditions for the practice of a responsible and critical mind are denied to them. They must have the freedom of responsible inquiry, by thought and action, into the meaning of social and economic ideas, into the checkered history of social and economic dogma. They must be free to sift evanescent doctrine, qualified by time and circumstance, from that restless, enduring process of extending the bounds of understanding and wisdom, to assure which the freedoms of thought, of speech, of inquiry, of worship are guaranteed by the Constitution of the United States against infraction by National or State government.

The functions of educational institutions in our national life and the conditions under which alone they can adequately perform them are at the basis of these limitations upon State and National power. These functions and the essential conditions for their effective discharge have been well described by a leading educator:

"Now, a university is a place that is established and will function for the benefit of society, provided it is a center of independent thought. It is a center of independent thought and criticism that is created in the interest of the progress of society, and the one reason that we know that every totalitarian government must fail is that no totalitarian government is prepared to face the consequences of creating free universities.

"It is important for this purpose to attract into the institution men of the greatest capacity, and to encourage them to exercise their independent judgment.

"Education is a kind of continuing dialogue, and a dialogue assumes, in the nature of the case, different points of view.

"The civilization which I work and which I am sure, every American is working toward, could be called a civilization of the dialogue, where instead of shooting one another when you differ, you reason things out together.

"In this dialogue, then, you cannot assume that you are going to have everybody thinking the same way or feeling the same way. It would be unprogressive if that happened. The hope of eventual development would be gone. More than that, of course, it would be very boring.

"A university, then, is a kind of continuing Socratic conversation on the highest level for the very best people you can think of, you can bring together, about the most important questions, and the thing that you must do to the uttermost possible limits is to guarantee those men the freedom to think and to express themselves.

"Now, the limits on this freedom, the limits on this freedom, cannot be merely prejudice, because although our prejudices might be perfectly satisfactory, the prejudices of our successors or of those who are in a position to bring pressure to bear on the institution, might be subversive in the real sense, subverting the American doctrine of free thought and free speech." Testimony of Robert M. Hutchins, Associate Director of the Ford Foundation, November 25, 1952, in Hearings before the House Select Committee to Investigate Tax-Exempt Foundations and Comparable Organizations, pursuant to H. Res. 561, 82d Cong., 2d Sess.

KEYISHIAN v. BOARD OF REGENTS
OF THE UNIVERSITY OF THE STATE OF NEW YORK
United States Supreme Court
385 U. S. 589 (1967)

MR. JUSTICE BRENNAN delivered the opinion of the Court.

Appellants were members of the faculty of the privately owned and operated University of Buffalo, and became state employees when the University was merged in 1962 into the State University of New York, an institution of higher education owned and operated by the State of New York. As faculty members of the State University their continued employment was conditioned upon their compliance with a New York plan, formulated partly in statutes and partly in administrative regulations, which the State utilizes to prevent the appointment or retention of "subversive" persons in state employment.

Appellants Hochfield and Maud were Assistant Professors of English, appellant Keyishian an instructor in English, and appellant Garver, a lecturer in philosophy. Each of them refused to sign, as regulations then in effect required, a certificate that he was not a Communist, and that if he had ever been a Communist, he had communicated that fact to the President of the State University of New York. Each was notified that his failure to sign the certificate would require his dismissal. Keyishian's one-year-term contract was not renewed because of his failure to sign the certificate. . . .

The Feinberg Law charged the State Board of Regents with the duty of promulgating rules and regulations providing procedures for the disqualification or removal of persons in the public school system who violate the 1917 law or who are ineligible for appointment to or retention in the public school system under the 1939 law. The Board of Regents was further directed to make a list, after notice and hearing, of "subversive" organizations, defined as organizations which advocate the doctrine of overthrow of government by force, violence, or any unlawful means. Finally, the Board was directed to provide in its rules and regulations that membership in any listed organization should constitute prima facie evidence of disqualification for appointment to or retention in any office or position in the public schools of the State.

The Board of Regents thereupon promulgated rules and regulations containing procedures to be followed by appointing authorities to discover persons ineligible for appointment or retention under the 1939 law, or because of violation of the 1917 law. The Board also announced its intention to list "subversive" organizations after requisite notice and hearing, and provided that membership in a listed organization after the date of its listing should be regarded as constituting prima facie evidence of disqualification, and that membership prior to listing should be presumptive evidence that membership has continued, in the absence of a showing that such membership was terminated in good faith. Under the regulations, an appointing official is forbidden to make an appointment until after he has first inquired of an applicant's former employers and other persons to ascertain whether the applicant is disqualified or ineligible for appointment. In addition, an annual inquiry must be made to determine whether an appointed employee has ceased to be qualified for retention, and a report of findings must be filed....

Section 3021 requires removal for "treasonable or seditious" utterances or acts....

We cannot gainsay the potential effect of this obscure wording on "those with a conscientious and scrupulous regard for such undertakings." *Baggett* v. *Bullitt*, 377 U. S. 360, 374. Even were it certain that the definition referred to in § 105 was solely Penal Law § 160, the scope of § 105 still remains indefinite. The teacher cannot know the extent, if any, to which a "seditious" utterance must transcend mere statement about abstract doctrine, the extent to which it must be intended to and tend to indoctrinate or incite to action in furtherance of the defined doctrine. The crucial consideration is that no teacher can know just where the line is drawn between "seditious" and nonseditious utterances and acts.

Other provisions of § 105 also have the same defect of vagueness. Subdivision 1 (a) of § 105 bars employment of any person who "by word of mouth or writing wilfully and deliberately advocates, advises or teaches the doctrine" of forceful overthrow of government. This provision is plainly susceptible of sweeping and improper application. It may well prohibit the employment of one who merely advocates the doctrine in the abstract without any attempt to indoctrinate others, or incite others to action in furtherance of unlawful aims. See *Herndon* v. *Lowry*, 301 U. S. 242; *Yates* v. *United States*, 354 U. S. 298; *Noto* v. *United States*, 367 U. S. 290; *Scales* v. *United States*, 367 U. S. 203. And in prohibiting "advising" the "doctrine" of unlawful overthrow does the statute prohibit mere "advising" of the existence of the doctrine, or advising another to support the doctrine? Since "advocacy" of the doctrine of forceful overthrow is separately prohibited, need the person "teaching" or "advising" this doctrine himself "advocate" it? Does the teacher who informs his class about the precepts of Marxism or the Declaration of Independence violate this prohibition?

Similar uncertainty arises as to the application of subdivision 1 (b) of § 105. That subsection requires the disqualification of an employee involved with the distribution of written material "containing or advocating, advising or teaching the doctrine" of forceful overthrow, and who himself "advocates, advises, teaches, or embraces the duty, necessity or propriety of adopting the doctrine contained therein." Here again, mere advocacy of abstract doctrine is apparently included. And does the prohibition of distribution of matter "containing" the doctrine bar histories of the evolution of Marxist doctrine or tracing the background of the French, American, or Russian revolutions? The additional requirement, that the person participating in distribution of the material be one who "advocates, advises, teaches, or embraces the duty, necessity or propriety of adopting the doctrine" of forceful overthrow, does not alleviate the uncertainty in the scope of the section, but exacerbates it. Like the language of § 105, subd. 1 (a), this language may reasonably be construed to cover mere expression of belief. For example, does the university librarian who recommends the reading of such materials thereby "advocate . . . the . . . propriety of adopting the doctrine contained therein"?

We do not have the benefit of a judicial gloss by the New York courts enlightening us as to the scope of this complicated plan. In light of the intricate administrative machinery for its enforcement, this is not surprising. The very intricacy of the plan and the uncertainty as to the scope of its proscriptions make it a highly efficient *in terrorem* mechanism. It would be a bold teacher who would not stay as far as possible from utterances or acts which might jeopardize his living by enmeshing him in this intricate machinery. The uncertainty as to the utterances and acts proscribed increases that caution in "those who believe the written law means what it says," *Baggett* v. *Bullitt, supra,* at 374. The result must be to stifle "that free play of the spirit which all teachers ought especially to cultivate and practice. . . ." That probability is enhanced by the provisions requiring an annual review of every teacher to determine whether any utterance or act of his, inside the classroom or out, came within the sanctions of the laws. . . .

There can be no doubt of the legitimacy of New York's interest in protecting its education system from subversion. But "even though the governmental purpose be legitimate and substantial, that purpose cannot be pursued by means that broadly stifle fundamental personal liberties when the end can be more narrowly achieved." *Shelton* v. *Tucker*, 364 U. S. 479, 488. The principle is not inapplicable because the legislation is aimed at keeping subversives out of the teaching ranks. . . .

Our Nation is deeply committed to safeguarding academic freedom, which is of transcendent value to all of us and not merely to the teachers concerned. That freedom is therefore a special concern of the First Amendment, which does not tolerate laws that cast a pall of orthodoxy over the classroom. "The vigilant protection of constitutional freedoms is nowhere more vital than in the community of American schools." *Shelton* v. *Tucker, supra,* at 487. The classroom is peculiarly the "marketplace of ideas." The Nation's future depends upon leaders trained through wide exposure to that robust exchange of ideas which discovers truth "out of a multitude of tongues, [rather] than through any kind of authoritative selection." . . .

The regulatory maze created by New York is wholly lacking in "terms susceptible of objective measurement." *Cramp* v. *Board of Public Information, supra*, at 286. It has the quality of "extraordinary ambiguity" found to be fatal to the oaths considered in *Cramp* and *Baggett* v. *Bullitt.* "[M]en of common intelligence must necessarily guess at its meaning and differ as to its application. . . ." *Baggett* v. *Bullitt, supra,* at 367. Vagueness of wording is aggravated by prolixity and profusion of statutes, regulations, and administrative machinery, and by manifold cross-references to interrelated enactments and rules.

We therefore hold that §3021 of the Education Law and subdivisions 1 (a), 1 (b) and 3 of § 105 of the Civil Service Law as implemented by the machinery created pursuant to § 3022 of the Education Law are unconstitutional.

NOTES

1. Is Justice Frankfurter, in his concurring opinion in *Wieman v. Updegraff,* attempting to define a right possessed by teachers which is different from that held by the ordinary citizen? Is the right superior? Does he succeed?

2. Is academic freedom for the protection of professors or for the protection of society?

3. In 1968 in Knight v. Board of Regents of University of State of New York, 390 U.S. 36 (1968), the Supreme Court affirmed without opinion a district court opinion upholding the following faculty loyalty oath:

> Oath to support federal and state constitutions. It shall be unlawful for any citizen of the United States to serve as teacher, instructor or professor in any school or institution in the public school system of the state or in any school, college, university or other educational institution in this state, whose real property, in whole or in part, is exempt from taxation under section four of the tax law unless and until he or she shall have taken and subscribed the following oath or affirmation: "I do solemnly swear (or affirm) that I will support the constitution of the United States of America and the constitution of the State of New York, and that I will faithfully discharge, according to the best of my ability, the duties of the position of * * * (title of position and name or designation of school, college, university or institution to be here inserted), to which I am now assigned."

What distinguishes the *Knight* oath from the Oklahoma oath declared invalid in *Wieman v. Updegraff?* See also Cramp v. Board of Public Instruction, 368 U. S. 278 (1961), in which a Florida loyalty oath statute was found unconstitutionally vague, and Baggett v. Bullitt, 377 U.S. 360 (1964), in which the Court invalidated a Washington loyalty oath statute on the grounds of vagueness, uncertainty and overbreadth.

4. Loyalty oaths are still required in many universities. For an interesting account of a contemporary experience with the California requirement, *see* Mitford, *My Short and Happy Life As A Distinguished Professor,* 234 Atlantic Monthly 90 (1974).

D.   *The Chilling Effect of Criminal Investigation*

SLOCHOWER v. BOARD OF HIGHER EDUCATION
OF NEW YORK CITY
United States Supreme Court
350 U. S. 551 (1956)

MR. JUSTICE CLARK delivered the opinion of the Court.

This appeal brings into question the constitutionality of §903 of the Charter of the City of New York. That section provides that whenever an employee of the City utilizes the privilege against self-incrimination to avoid answering a question relating to his official conduct, "his term or tenure of office or employment shall terminate and such office or employment shall be vacant, and he shall not be eligible to election or appointment to any office or employment under the city or any agency." Appellant Slochower invoked the privilege against self-incrimination under the Fifth Amendment before an investigating committee of the United States Senate, and was summarily discharged from his position as associate professor at Brooklyn College, an institution maintained by the City of New York. He now claims that the charter provision, as applied to him, violates both the Due Process and Privileges and Immunities Clauses of the Fourteenth Amendment.

On September 24, 1952, the Internal Security Subcommittee of the Committee on the Judiciary of the United States Senate held open hearings in New York City. The investigation, conducted on a national scale, related to subversive influences in the American educational system. At the beginning of the hearings the Chairman stated that education was primarily a state and local function, and therefore the inquiry would be limited to "considerations affecting national security, which are directly within the purview and authority of the subcommittee." Hearings Before the Subcommittee to Investigate the Administration of the Internal Security Act and Other Internal Security Laws of Senate Committee on the Judiciary, 82d Cong., 2d Sess. 1. Professor Slochower, when called to testify, stated that he was not a member of the Communist Party, and indicated complete willingness to answer all questions about his associations or political beliefs since 1941. But he refused to answer questions concerning his membership during 1940 and 1941 on the ground that his answers might tend to incriminate him. The Chairman of the Senate Subcommittee accepted Slochower's claim as a valid assertion of an admitted constitutional right.

*   *   *

Slochower had 27 years' experience as a college teacher and was entitled to tenure under state law. McKinney's New York Laws, Education Law, §6206(2). Under this statute, appellant may be discharged only for cause, and after notice, hearing, and appeal. §6206(10). The Court of Appeals of New York, however, has authoritatively interpreted §903 to mean that "the assertion of the privilege against self incrimination is equivalent to a resignation." *Daniman* v. *Board of Education*, 306 N. Y. 532, 538, 119 N. E. 2d 373, 377. Dismissal under this provision is therefore automatic and there is no right to charges, notice, hearing, or opportunity to explain.

*   *   *

The problem of balancing the State's interest in the loyalty of those in its service with the traditional safeguards of individual rights is a continuing one. To state that a person does not have a constitutional right to government employment is only to say that he must comply with reasonable, lawful, and nondiscriminatory terms laid down by the proper authorities.

*   *   *

But in each of these cases it was emphasized that the State must conform to the requirements of due process. In *Wieman* v. *Updegraff,* 344 U. S. 183, we struck down a so-called "loyalty oath" because it based employability solely on the fact of membership in certain organizations. We pointed out that membership itself may be innocent and held that the classification of innocent and guilty together was arbitrary. This case rests squarely on the proposition that "constitutional protection does extend to the public servant whose exclusion pursuant to a statute is patently arbitrary or discriminatory." 344 U. S., at 192.

*   *   *

At the outset we must condemn the practice of imputing a sinister meaning to the exercise of a person's constitutional right under the Fifth Amendment. The right of an accused person to refuse to testify, which had been in England merely a rule of evidence, was so important to our forefathers that they raised it to the dignity of a constitutional enactment, and it has been recognized as "one of the most valuable prerogatives of the citizen." *Brown* v. *Walker,* 161 U.S. 591, 610. We have reaffirmed our faith in this principle recently in *Quinn* v. *United States,* 349 U.S. 155. In *Ullmann* v. *United States,* 350 U. S. 422, decided last month, we scored the assumption that those who claim this privilege are either criminals or perjurers. The privilege against self-incrimination would be reduced to a hollow mockery if its exercise could be taken as equivalent either to a confession of guilt or a conclusive presumption of perjury. As we pointed out in *Ullmann*, a witness may have a reasonable fear of prosecution and yet be innocent of any wrongdoing. The privilege serves to protect the innocent who otherwise might be ensnared by ambiguous circumstances. See Griswold, The Fifth Amendment Today (1955).

With this in mind, we consider the application of §903. As interpreted and applied by the state courts, it operates to discharge every city employee who invokes the Fifth Amendment. In practical effect the questions asked are taken as confessed and made the basis of the discharge. No consideration is given to such factors as the subject matter of the questions, remoteness of the period to which they are directed, or justification for exercise of the privilege. It matters not whether the plea resulted from mistake, inadvertence or legal advice conscientiously given, whether wisely or unwisely. The heavy hand of the statute falls alike on all who exercise their constitutional privilege, the full enjoyment of which every person is entitled to receive. Such action falls squarely within the prohibition of *Wieman* v. *Updegraff, supra.*

*   *   *

Without attacking Professor Slochower's qualification for his position in any manner, and apparently with full knowledge of the testimony he had given some 12 years before at the state committee hearing, the Board seized upon his claim of privilege before the federal committee and converted it through the use of §903 into a conclusive presumption of guilt. Since no inference of guilt was possible from the claim before the federal committee, the discharge falls of its own weight as wholly without support. There has not been the "protection of the individual against arbitrary action" which Mr. Justice Cardozo characterized as the very essence of due process. *Ohio Bell Telephone Co.* v. *Commission,* 301 U. S. 292, 302.

This is not to say that Slochower has a constitutional right to be an associate professor of German at Brooklyn College. The State has broad powers in the selection and discharge of its employees, and it may be that proper inquiry would show Slochower's continued employment to be inconsistent with a real interest of the State. But there has been no such inquiry here. We hold that the summary dismissal of appellant violates due process of law.

The judgment is reversed and the cause is remanded for further proceedings not inconsistent with this opinion.

Reversed and remanded.

HAMMOND v. BROWN
United States District Court
323 F.Supp. 326 (N. D. Ohio, E. D., 1971)

WILLIAM K. THOMAS, District Judge. . . .

The indictments grow out of events of May 1 through May 4, 1970, that took place on and off the campus of Kent State University in Kent, Ohio. Dealing with those events on October 4, 1970, the President's Commission on Campus Unrest issued a "Special Report—The Kent State Tragedy." The Special Grand Jury Report, the validity of which is an issue in this case, attempts to chronicle the same events. The issues in these cases, as this court sees them, neither require nor permit a general factual inquiry, and this court makes no independent findings as to what transpired during those four days in May in the Kent community.

*   *   *

The claimed violation of First Amendment rights violative of Due Process presents a different matter. Let us assume a member of the Kent State faculty reads the Grand Jury's criticism of "over-emphasis on dissent * * * in the classrooms of some members of the University faculty" and the Report's comment that this dissent "becomes the order of the day to the exclusion of all normal behavior and expression." He may reasonably believe that people in the Kent community (university and city) who have read Parts VIII and IX of the Report, may well think the Report may refer to him. People in the community may well believe that a particular faculty member is one of the "small minority of the total faculty" who depart from "all normal behavior and expression."

A Report of the Special Grand Jury, an official accusatory body of the community, that criticizes faculty members for "over-emphasis on dissent," thus seeking to impose norms of "behavior and expression," restricts and interferes with the faculty members' exercise of protected expression. The record reveals that this is happening.

Impairment of First Amendment freedom of expression is directly resulting from the Special Grand Jury Report. This is disclosed by candid and credited testimony of members of the faculty who appeared as witnesses. Because of the Report instructors have altered or dropped course materials for fear of classroom controversy. For example, an assistant professor of English, after reading the Report, "scratched three poems" from her outline in her Introduction to Poetry course. The poems are "Politics" by William Butler Yeats, "Prometheus" by Lord Byron, and "Dover Beach" by Matthew Arnold.

In "Politics," Yeats writes "And maybe what they say is true/of war and war's alarms."

A university professor may add or subtract course content for different reasons. But when a university professor is fearful that "war's alarm," a poet's concern, may produce "inflammatory discussion" in a poetry class, it is evident that the Report's riptide is washing away protected expression on the Kent campus.

Other evidence cumulatively shows that this teacher's reaction was not isolated. The Report is dulling classroom discussion and is upsetting the teaching atmosphere. This effect was described by other faculty witnesses. When thought is controlled, or appears to be controlled, when pedagogues and pupils shrink from free inquiry at a state university because of a report of a resident Grand Jury, then academic freedom of expression is impermissibly impaired. This will curb conditions essential to fulfillment of the university's learning purposes.

Issued by a Grand Jury purporting to act under the color of state law, the Report is not protected by the First Amendment as suggested by Attorney General Brown. "The freedom of speech and of the press * * * is * * * secured to all *persons* by the Fourteenth against abridgment by a state." (Emphasis added) Schneider v. State, 308 U.S. 147, 160, 60 S.Ct. 146, 150, 84 L.Ed. 155 (1939). Freedom of speech is a personal liberty that cannot be abridged by any arm of the state. An arm of the state, in this instance a grand jury, cannot corporately assert the freedom of speech that each of its members personally may exercise. Such a doctrine would permit any arm of the state to neutralize and cancel out protected personal freedoms and liberties.

Part IX of the Report, exemplified by the quoted excerpts, abridges the exercise of protected expression by the plaintiffs who are members of the Kent State University faculty and other persons of the same class on whose behalf the *Adamek* plaintiffs bring their action. Imposed under the color of state law, Part IX of the Report is determined and declared to deprive these parties of rights guaranteed under the Constitution in violation of 42 U.S.C. § 1983 (1964).

Part IX of the Report also renders the Report illegal under the pendent state law claim. The Report unlawfully trespasses upon the doctrine of separation of powers, as that doctrine relates to the executive branch of government of which Kent State University is a part. Typical of its trespasses is attributing to those "charged with the administration of the University," the

> major responsibility for the incidents occurring on the Kent State University campus on May 2nd, 3rd, and 4th * * *.

The doctrine of separation of powers is further violated when the Grand Jury, sitting as a self-appointed, albeit conscientious, board of regents, amplifies its previous judgment of blame. Part IX adds a number of the Jury's moral and social judgments, including the following:

> The administration at Kent State University has fostered an attitude of laxity, over-indulgence, and permissiveness with its students and faculty to the extent that it can no longer regulate the activities of either and is particularly vulnerable to any pressure applied from radical elements within the student body or faculty.

In King v. Jones, 319 F.Supp. 653 (N.D.Ohio, November 3, 1970), Judge Ben C. Green lifted the Portage County Common Pleas Court ban on statements by Grand Jury witnesses. Afterwards, President Robert I. White of Kent State University issued a statement on the Special Grand Jury Report. In his conclusion he notes the "difficult" role of Grand Jurors and their effort to "honestly report their findings." Thus, President White accepted the mistaken assumption of the Special Grand Jury that its role included the right to make findings. He then adds:

> At the same time, we must recognize that their general report reflects a frightening misunderstanding of the role and mission of higher education.

At the trial he harked back to the Grand Jury's criticism of the administration's "permissiveness." He testified:

> I'm resisting—I would be resisting the implication that permissiveness, insofar as it related to relaxed views toward who could speak, who could assemble, who could print, what could be taught in related matters, I would have to resist any challenge to those. If that were being permissive to have such a relaxed attitude, then I shall have to continue to be permissive, and I think every university in the nation needs to be.

This reveals the restraining influence of a Grand Jury when, acting in excess of its authority as a criminal accusatory body, it makes and reports its official criticisms and judgments on the conduct of the administration of a state university that is located within the county. . . .

NOTES

1. What actual protection was extended to Professor Slochower by the Supreme Court? Can this case be characterized as a protection of academic freedom? See also Barenblatt v. U.S., 360 U. S. 109 (1959) where First and Fifth Amendment rights are contrasted. In Beilan v. Board of Public Education, 357 U.S. 399 (1956), the Court

upheld the dismissal of a public school teacher who pleaded the Fifth Amendment and was dismissed for "incompetency."

2. Was the Kent State professor who dropped three poems from her curriculum over-reacting to the Grand Jury Report? To what does the Court in *Hammond v. Brown* refer when it states that "academic freedom of expression" has been curtailed? Where does the Court find legal protection for that freedom?

3. *Hammond v. Brown* was affirmed by the Sixth Circuit at 450 F.2d 480 (1971). Additional facts and analysis may be found in O'Neil, No Heroes, No Villains (San Francisco: Jossey-Bass, 1973).

III.   Free Speech in the Academic Context

The First Amendment Freedom which most closely approaches academic freedom is Free Speech. The question then arises over the exact balancing of the teacher's right to free speech and the state's right as an employer to regulate the conduct of its employees.

PICKERING v. BOARD OF EDUCATION
Supreme Court of the United States
591 U.S. 563, 88 S.Ct. 1731, 20 L.Ed.2d 811 (1968)

MR. JUSTICE MARSHALL delivered the opinion of the Court.

Appellant Marvin L. Pickering, a teacher in Township High School District 205, Will County, Illinois, was dismissed from his position by the appellee Board of Education for sending a letter to a local newspaper in connection with a recently proposed tax increase that was critical of the way in which the Board and the district superintendent of schools had handled past proposals to raise new revenue for the schools. Appellant's dismissal resulted from a determination by the Board, after a full hearing, that the publication of the letter was "detrimental to the efficient operation and administration of the schools of the district" and hence, under the relevant Illinois statute, Ill. Rev. Stat., c. 122, §10-22.4 (1963), that "interests of the school require[d] [his dismissal]." . . .

At the hearing the Board charged that numerous statements in the letter were false and that the publication of the statements unjustifiably impunged the "motives, honesty, integrity, truthfulness, responsibility and competence" of both the Board and the school administration. The Board also charged that the false statements damaged the professional reputations of its members and of the school administrators, would be disruptive of faculty discipline, and would tend to foment "controversy, conflict and dissension" among teachers, administrators, the Board of Education, and the residents of the district. . . .

The Illinois courts reviewed the proceedings solely to determine whether the Board's findings were supported by substantial evidence and whether, on the facts as found, the Board could reasonably conclude that appellant's publication of the letter was "detrimental to the best interests of the schools." Pickering's claim that his letter was protected by the First Amendment was rejected on the ground that his acceptance of a teaching position in the public schools obliged him to refrain from making statements about the operation of the schools "which in the absence of such position he would have an undoubted right to engage in." . . .

To the extent that the Illinois Supreme Court's opinion may be read to suggest that teachers may constitutionally be compelled to relinquish the First Amendment rights they would otherwise enjoy as citizens to comment on matters of public interest in connection with the operation of the public schools in which they work, it proceeds on a premise that has been unequivocally rejected in numerous prior decisions of this Court. . . . At the same time it cannot be gainsaid that the State has interests as an employer in regulating the speech of its employees that differ significantly from those it possesses in connection with regulation of the speech of the citizenry in general. The problem in any case is to arrive at a balance between the interests of the teacher, as a citizen, in commenting upon matters of public concern and the interest of the State, as an employer, in promoting the efficiency of the public services it performs through its employees. . . .

Because of the enormous variety of fact situations in which critical statements by teachers and other public employees may be thought by their superiors, against whom the statements are directed, to furnish grounds for dismissal, we do not deem it either appropriate or feasible to attempt to lay down a general standard against which all such statements may be judged. However, in the course of evaluating the conflicting claims of First Amendment protection and the need for orderly school administration in the context of this case, we shall indicate some of the general lines along which an analysis of the controlling interests should run.

An examination of the statements in appellant's letter objected to by the Board reveals that they, like the letter as a whole, consist essentially of criticism of the Board's allocation of school funds between educational and athletic programs, and of both the Board's and the superintendent's methods of informing, or preventing the informing of, the district's taxpayers of the real reasons why additional tax revenues were being sought for the schools. The statements are in no way directed towards any person with whom appellant would normally be in contact in the course of his daily work as a teacher. Thus no question of maintaining either discipline by immediate superiors or harmony among coworkers is presented here. Appellant's employment relationships with the Board and, to a somewhat lesser extent, with the superintendent are not the kind of close working relationships for which it can persuasively be claimed that personal loyalty and confidence are necessary to their proper functioning. Accordingly, to the extent that the Board's position here can be taken to suggest that even comments on matters of public concern that are substantially correct . . . may furnish grounds for dismissal if they are sufficiently critical in tone, we unequivocally reject it.

We next consider the statements in appellant's letter which we agree to be false. The Board's original charges included allegations that the publication of the letter damaged the professional reputations of the Board and the superintendent and would foment controversy and conflict among the Board, teachers, administrators, and the residents of the district. However, no evidence to support these allegations was introduced at the hearing. So far as the record reveals, Pickering's letter was greeted by everyone but its main target, the Board, with massive apathy and total disbelief. The Board must, therefore, have decided, perhaps by analogy with the law of libel, that the statements were *per se* harmful to the operation of the schools.

However, the only way in which the Board could conclude, absent any evidence of the actual effect of the letter, that the statements contained therein were *per se* detrimental to the interest of the schools was to equate the Board members' own interests with that of the schools. Certainly an accusation that too much money is being spent on athletics by the administrators of the school system . . . cannot reasonably be regarded as *per se* detrimental to the district's schools. Such an accusation reflects rather a difference of opinion between Pickering and the Board as to the preferable manner of operating the school system, a difference of opinion that clearly concerns an issue of general public interest. . . .

More importantly, the question whether a school system requires additional funds is a matter of legitimate public concern on which the judgment of the school administration, including the School Board, cannot, in a society that leaves such questions to popular vote, be taken as conclusive. On such a question free and open debate is vital to informed decision-making by the electorate. Teachers are, as a class, the members of a community most likely to have informed and definite opinions as to how funds allotted to the operation of the schools should be spent. Accordingly, it is essential that they be able to speak out freely on such questions without fear of retaliatory dismissal.

In addition, the amounts expended on athletics which Pickering reported erroneously were matters of public record on which his position as a teacher in the district did not qualify him to speak with any greater authority than any other taxpayer. The Board could easily have rebutted appellant's errors by publishing the accurate figures itself, either via a letter to the same newspaper or otherwise. We are thus not presented with a situation in which a teacher has carelessly made false statements about matters so closely related to the day-to-day operations of the schools that any harmful impact on the public would be difficult to counter because of the teacher's presumed greater access to the real facts. Accordingly, we have no occasion to consider at this time whether under such circumstances a school board could reasonably require that a teacher make substantial efforts to verify the accuracy of his charges before publishing them.

What we do have before us is a case in which a teacher has made erroneous public statements upon issues then currently the subject of public attention, which are critical of his ultimate employer but which are neither shown nor can be presumed to have in any way either impeded the teacher's proper performance of his daily duties in the classroom or to have interfered with the regular operation of the schools generally. In these circumstances we conclude that the interest of the school administration in limiting teachers' opportunities to contribute to public debate is not significantly greater than its interest in limiting a similar contribution by any member of the general public.

The public interest in having free and unhindered debate on matters of public importance—the core value of the Free Speech Clause of the First Amendment—is so great that it has been held that a State cannot authorize the recovery of damages by a public official for defamatory statements directed at him except when such statements are shown to have been made either with knowledge of their falsity or with reckless disregard for their truth or falsity. New York Times Co. v. Sullivan, 376 U.S. 254 (1964); St. Amant v. Thompson, 390 U.S. 727 (1968). Compare Linn v. United Plant Guard Workers, 383 U.S. 53 (1966). The same test has been applied to suits for invasion of privacy based on false statements where a "matter of public interest" is involved. Time, Inc. v. Hill, 385 U. S. 374 (1967). It is therefore perfectly clear that, were appellant a member of the general public, the State's power to afford the appellee Board of Education or its members any legal right to sue him for writing the letter at issue here would be limited by the requirement that the letter be judged by the standard laid down in *New York Times.*

This Court has also indicated, in more general terms, that statements by public officials on matters of public concern must be accorded First Amendment protection despite the fact that the statements are directed at their nominal superiors. Garrison v. Louisiana, 379 U.S. 64 (1964); Wood v. Georgia, 370 U.S. 375 (1962). In *Garrison*, the *New York Times* test was specifically applied to a case involving a criminal defamation conviction stemming from statements made by a district attorney about the judges before whom he regularly appeared.

While criminal sanctions and damage awards have a somewhat different impact on the exercise of the right to freedom of speech from dismissal from employment, it is apparent that the threat of dismissal from public employment is nonetheless a potent means of inhibiting speech. We have already noted our disinclination to make an across-the-board equation of dismissal from public employment for remarks critical of superiors with awarding damages in a libel suit by a public official for similar criticism. However, in a case such as the present one, in which the fact of employment is only tangentially and insubstantially involved in the subject matter of the public communication made by a teacher, we conclude that it is necessary to regard the teacher as the member of the general public he seeks to be.

In sum, we hold that, in a case such as this, absent proof of false statements knowingly or recklessly made by him, a teacher's exercise of his right to speak on issues of public importance may not furnish the basis for his dismissal from public employment. Since no such showing has been made in this case regarding appellant's letter . . . his dismissal for writing it cannot be upheld and the judgment of the Illinois Supreme Court must, accordingly, be reversed and the case remanded for further proceedings not inconsistent with this opinion.

It is so ordered.

GIVHAN v. WESTERN LINE CONSOLIDATED SCHOOL DISTRICT
United States Supreme Court
99 S.Ct. 693 (1979)

Mr. Justice REHNQUIST delivered the opinion of the court.

Petitioner Bessie Givhan was dismissed from her employment as a junior high English teacher at the end of the 1970-1971 school year.[1] At the time of petitioner's termination, respondent Western Line Consolidated School District was the subject of a desegregation order entered by the United States District Court for the Northern District of Mississippi. Petitioner filed a complaint in intervention in the desegregation action, seeking reinstatement on the dual grounds that nonrenewal of her contract violated the rule laid down by the Court of Appeals for the Fifth Circuit in *Singleton v. Jackson Municipal Separate School District*, 419 F.2d 1211 (C.A.5 1969), rev'd and remanded *sub nom. Carter v. West Feliciana Parish School Board*, 396 U.S. 290, 90 S.Ct. 608, 24 L.Ed.2d 477 (1970), on remand, 425 F.2d 1211 (C.A.5 1970), and infringed her right of free speech secured by the First and Fourteenth Amendments of the United States Constitution. In an effort to show that its decision was justified, respondent school district introduced evidence of, among other things,[2] a series of private encounters between petitioner and the school principal in which petitioner allegedly made "petty and unreasonable demands" in a manner variously described by the principal as "insulting," "hostile," "loud," and "arrogant." After a two-day bench trial, the District Court held that petitioner's termination had violated the First Amendment. Finding that petitioner had made "demands" on but two occasions and that those demands "were neither 'petty' nor 'un-

---

[1.]   In a letter to petitioner dated July 23, 1971, District Superintendent C. L. Morris gave the following reasons for the decision not to renew her contract:
"(1) [A] flat refusal to administer standardized National tests to the pupils in your charge; (2) an announced intention not to cooperate with the administration of the Glen Allan Attendance Center; (3) and an antagonistic and hostile attitude to the administration of the Glen Allan Attendance Center demonstrated throughout the school year."

[2.]   In addition to the reasons set out in the District Superintendent's termination letter to petitioner, n. 1, *ante*, the school district advanced several other justifications for its decision not to rehire petitioner. The Court of Appeals dealt with these allegations in a footnote:
"Appellants also sought to establish these other bases for the decision not to rehire: (1) that Givhan 'downgraded' the papers of white students; (2) that she was one of a number of teachers who walked out of a meeting about desegregation in the fall of 1969 and attempted to disrupt it by blowing automobile horns outside the gymnasium; (3) that the school district had received a threat by Givhan and other teachers not to return to work when schools reopened on a unitary basis in February, 1970; and (4) that Givhan had protected a student during a weapons shakedown at Riverside in March, 1970, by concealing a student's knife until completion of a search. The evidence on the first three of these points was inconclusive and the district judge did not clearly err in rejecting or ignoring it. Givhan admitted the fourth incident, but the district judge properly rejected that as a justification for her not being rehired, as there was no evidence that [the principal] relied on it in making his recommendation." 555 F.2d, at 1313 n. 7.

reasonable,' insomuch as all of the complaints in question involved employment policies and practices at [the] school which [petitioner] conceived to
be racially discriminatory in purpose or effect," the District Court concluded
that "the primary reason for the school district's failure to renew [petition-
er's] contract was her criticism of the policies and practices of the school
district, especially the school to which she was assigned to teach." Pet. for
Cert. 35A. Accordingly, the District Court held that the dismissal violated
petitioner's First Amendment rights, as enunciated in *Perry v. Sindermann*,
408 U.S. 593, 92 S.Ct. 2694, 33 L.Ed.2d 570 (1972), and *Pickering v.
Board of Education*, 391 U.S. 563, 88 S.Ct. 1731, 20 L.Ed.2d 811 (1968),
and ordered her reinstatement.

The Court of Appeals for the Fifth Circuit reversed. Although it found
the District Court's findings not clearly erroneous, the Court of Appeals concluded that because petitioner had privately expressed her complaints and
opinions to the principal, her expression was not protected under the First
Amendment. Support for this proposition was thought to be derived from
Pickering, supra, Perry, supra, and *Mt. Healthy City School District v. Doyle*,
429 U.S. 274, 97 S.Ct. 568, 50 L.Ed.2d 471 (1977), which were found to
contain "[t]he strong implication . . . that private expression by a public
employee is not constitutionally protected." 555 F.2d 1309, 1318 (C.A.5
1977). The Court of Appeals also concluded that there is no constitutional
right to "press even 'good' ideas on an unwilling recipient," saying that to
afford public employees the right to such private expression "would in effect force school principals to be ombudsmen, for damnable as well as laudable expressions." *Id.*, at 1319. We are unable to agree that private expression
of one's views is beyond constitutional protection, and therefore reverse the
Court of Appeals' judgment and remand the case so that it may consider the
contentions of the parties freed from this erroneous view of the First
Amendment.

This Court's decisions in *Pickering, Perry,* and *Mt. Healthy* do not support the conclusion that a public employee forfeits his protection against
governmental abridgment of freedom of speech if he decides to express his
views privately rather than publicly. While those cases each arose in the context of a public employee's public expression, the rule to be derived from
them is not dependent on that largely coincidental fact.

In *Pickering* a teacher was discharged for publicly criticizing, in a letter
published in a local newspaper, the school board's handling of prior bond
issue proposals and its subsequent allocation of financial resources between
the schools' educational and athletic programs. Noting that the free speech
rights of public employees are not absolute, the Court held that in determining whether a government employee's speech is constitutionally protected, "the interests of the [employee], as a citizen, in commenting upon
matters of public concern" must be balanced against "the interest of the
State, as an employer, in promoting the efficiency of the public services
it performs through its employees." *Pickering v. Board of Education, supra,*
391 U.S., at 568, 88 S.Ct., at 1734. The Court concluded that under the

circumstances of that case "the interest of the school administration in limiting teachers' opportunities to contribute to public debate [was] not significantly greater than its interest in limiting a similar contribution by any member of the general public." *Id.*, at 573, 88 S.Ct., at 1737. Here the opinion of the Court of Appeals may be read to turn in part on its view that the working relationship between principal and teacher is significantly different from the relationship between the parties in *Pickering*, as is evidenced by its reference to its own opinion in *Abbott v. Thetford*, 534 F.2d 1101 (C.A. 5 1976) (en banc), cert. denied, 430 U.S. 954, 97 S.Ct. 1598, 51 L.Ed.2d 804 (1977). But we do not feel confident that the Court of Appeals' decision would have been placed on that ground notwithstanding its view that the First Amendment does not require the same sort of *Pickering* balancing for the private expression of a public employee as it does for public expression[4]

Perry and *Mt. Healthy* arose out of similar disputes between teachers and their public employers. As we have noted, however, the fact that each of these cases involved public expression by the employee was not critical to the decision. Nor is the Court of Appeals' view supported by the "captive audience" rationale. Having opened his office door to petitioner, the principal was hardly in a position to argue that he was the "*unwilling* recipient" of her views.

The First Amendment forbids abridgment of the "freedom of speech." Neither the Amendment itself nor our decisions indicate that this freedom is lost to the public employee who arranges to communicate privately with his employer rather than to spread his views before the public. We decline to adopt such a view of the First Amendment. . . .

The Court of Appeals in the instant case rejected respondents' *Mt. Healthy* claim that the decision to terminate petitioner would have been made even if her encounters with the principal had never occurred:

> "The [trial] court did not make an express finding as to whether the same decision would have been made, but on this record the [respondents] do not, and seriously cannot, argue that the same decision would have been made without regard to the 'demands.' Appellants seem to argue that the preponderance of the evidence shows that the same decision would have been justified, but that is not the same as proving that the same decision would have been made. . . . Therefore [respondents] failed to make a successful 'same decision anyway' defense." 555 F.2d, at 1315.

[4.]   Although the First Amendment's protection of government employees extends to private as well as public expression, striking the *Pickering* balance in each context may involve different considerations. When a teacher speaks publicly, it is generally the *content* of his statements that must be assessed to determine whether they "in any way either impeded the teacher's proper performance of his daily duties in the classroom or . . . interfered with the regular operation of the schools generally." *Pickering v. Board of Education, supra,* 391 U.S., at 572-573, 88 S.Ct., at 1737. Private expression, however, may in some situations bring additional factors to the *Pickering* calculus. When a government employee personally confronts his immediate superior, the employing agency's institutional efficiency may be threatened not only by the content of the employee's message, but also by the manner, time, and place in which it is delivered.

Since this case was tried before *Mt. Healthy* was decided, it is not surprising that respondents did not attempt to prove in the District Court that the decision not to rehire petitioner would have been made even absent consideration of her "demands." Thus, the case came to the Court of Appeals in very much the same posture as *Mt. Healthy* was presented in this Court. And while the District Court found that petitioner's "criticism" was the "primary" reason for the school district's failure to rehire her, it did not find that she would have been rehired *but for* her criticism. Respondents' *Mt. Healthy* claim called for a factual determination which could not, on this record, be resolved by the Court of Appeals.[5]

Accordingly, the judgment of the Court of Appeals is vacated and the case remanded for further proceedings consistent with this opinion.

So ordered.

NOTE

In Roseman v. Indiana U. of Penn., at Indiana, 520 F.2d 1364 (3rd Cir. 1975), a faculty member argued that *Pickering* should be extended to protect remarks made by a faculty member in a faculty meeting. The Third Circuit disagreed making the following distinctions:

> The communications made by the plaintiff in the case before us differ from Pickering's in two crucial respects. In the first place, Roseman's expressions were essentially private communications in which only members of the Foreign Languages Department and the Dean of the College of Arts and Sciences were shown by the plaintiff to have had any interest. Pickering's letter to the editor, urging the electorate with respect to a pending tax proposal, was, by contrast, a classic example of public communication on an issue of public interest. In *Pickering*, as in other cases, the Supreme Court inquired into the public nature of a communication in determining the degree of First Amendment protection. As Roseman's communications were made in forums not open to the general public and concerned an issue of less public interest than Pickering's, the First Amendment interest in their protection is correspondingly reduced.

> The second respect in which Roseman's communications differ from Pickering's is in their potentially disruptive impact on the functioning of the Department. Pickering's attacks were on a remote superintendent and school board; in contrast, Roseman's called into question the integrity of the person immediately in charge of running a department which, it is fair to assume, was more intimate than a school district. The district court found that "plaintiff's attacks upon Faust's integrity in a faculty meeting would undoubtedly have the effect of interfering with harmonious relationships with plaintiff's superiors and coworkers." 382 F.Supp. at 1339. In making this finding, the district court reflected a similar concern expressed by the Supreme Court, which noted that Pickering's statements were "in no way directed towards any person with whom [Pickering] would normally be in contact in the course of his daily work as a teacher." *Pickering, supra,* 391 U.S. at 569-70,

---

[5.]   We cannot agree with the Court of Appeals that the record in this case does not admit of the argument that petitioner would have been terminated regardless of her "demands." Even absent consideration of petitioner's private encounters with the principal, a decision to terminate based on the reasons detailed at nn. 1 and 2, *ante,* would hardly strike us as surprising. Additionally, in his letter to petitioner setting forth the reasons for her termination, District Superintendent Morris makes no mention of petitioner's "demands" and "criticism." See n. 1, *ante.*

88 S.Ct. at 1735. Because of this, Pickering's case raised "no question of maintaining either discipline by immediate superiors or harmony among co-workers."

Would *Roseman* be decided differently in light of the Supreme Court's opinion in *Givhan?*

STARSKY v. WILLIAMS
United States District Court, D. Arizona
353 F.Supp. 900 (1972)

MUECKE, District Judge.

Plaintiff has filed this action under the Civil Rights Act, 42 U.S.C. 1981-1985, alleging that his termination as an assistant professor at Arizona State University violates his federal First and Fourteenth Amendment rights. . . .

Plaintiff admits that not every act he is accused of is constitutionally protected, but he argues that his discharge is principally based on an impermissibly restrictive view of his First Amendment rights. Defendants argue that the Board of Regents acted within its lawful discretion in dismissing plaintiff for a series of unprofessional acts, and for speech which loses constitutional protection in that it amounts to a verbal act, or lacks professional restraint and accuracy. . . .

The record shows that on January 14, 1970, Professor Starsky absented himself from a regularly scheduled class at Arizona State University and attended a rally in front of the Administration Building at the University of Arizona, where he was one of eight or ten speakers protesting the arrest of certain students of the University of Arizona. The entire incident attracted a considerable amount of public attention, (Tr. Peek, 820 In. 19-821 In. 2) and undoubtedly was the incident which caused disciplinary actions to be initiated against the plaintiff.

The January 31, 1970 minutes of the Board of Regents show the following resolution:

The Arizona Board of Regents recognizes and supports the principle that when a faculty member speaks or writes as a private citizen, he should be free from institutional censorship or discipline. The Board is also mindful, however, that a faculty member's special position in the community imposes upon him the particular obligations and serious responsibilities of conducting his behavior and activities in the best interests of the university and his profession.

The Board instructs the President of Arizona State University to institute proceedings in accordance with due process and university procedures to recommend what appropriate disciplinary action, if any, should be taken in regard to Assistant Professor Morris J. Starsky including whether his appointment be renewed or terminated.

An Ad Hoc Committee was appointed consisting of Arizona State University professors. This Committee met, deliberated, and prepared a report.

On February 21, 1970, portions of the report of the Ad Hoc Committee were read at a meeting of the Board of Regents. The report recommended against instituting proceedings for dismissal as it "... does not have sufficient evidence to warrant formal proceedings concerning dismissal." The report included a letter from the local chapter of the American Association of University Professors, including the following statement:

Failure to meet a class even for an illegitimate reason is not in and of itself sufficient reason to recommend formal proceedings. . . .

The charges against plaintiff are set forth in the transcript of the Committee's hearing. There is a "summary charge" stating in part that as measured by the American Association of University Professors (hereinafter called A.A.U.P.) 1940 Statement of Principles on Academic Freedom and Tenure, plaintiff has "failed to act responsibly as a member of the teaching profession, has willfully violated Regents' policies and University regulations, has not exercised appropriate restraint as becomes a university professor in his public activities. . . ."

The A.A.U.P.'s principles by which the charges were to be judged are set forth as approved by the Board in its June 10, 1970 meeting:

The college or university teacher is a citizen, a member of a learned profession, and an officer of an educational institution. When he speaks or writes as a citizen, he should be free from institutional censorship or discipline, but his special position in the community imposes special obligations. As a man of learning and an educational officer, he should remember that the public may judge his profession and his institution by his utterances. Hence he should at all times be accurate, should exercise appropriate restraint, should show respect for the opinions of others, and should make every effort to indicate that he is not an institutional spokesman. . . .

The Committee found that plaintiff's failures were "not sufficiently grave to warrant a finding that his services . . . have been unsatisfactory." The Committee concluded:

. . . we now find on the basis of the present record inadequate grounds for dismissal. . . .

Arizona State University President H. K. Newburn then wrote a letter to the Board of Regents recommending some sanctions less than dismissal.

The minutes of the Board's meeting on June 10, 1970 show that the members read the transcript and exhibits and the Committee recommendations. No discussion of the evidence or recommendations is shown. The Board concluded:

This Board finds and concludes that Dr. Starsky did indeed do substantially all the acts and deeds with which he is charged (except as to three specified activities as to which no evidence was offered and except that instead of initiating, urging and encouraging the incident of November 20, 1968, Dr. Starsky supported and

participated in such incident in violation of the Regent's ordinance).

In addition, the Board specifically finds that Dr. Starsky, by his
own testimony, would not consider himself bound in the future
to obey or enforce the rules and regulations of the University and
this Board.

Accordingly, this Board further finds and concludes from the
evidence and from the aggregate thereof, that Dr. Starsky has
been guilty of substantial, wrongful, and prejudicial acts of professional misconduct, of substantial violations of the principles
above quoted, intemperate and unrestrained behavior, inaccurate
and misleading statements, and general unfitness for a position
with the faculty at Arizona State University, which is the core of
the separate specifications with which he was charged.

It is therefore the judgment of the Board that the interests of
education in the State of Arizona require that Dr. Starsky no
longer be permitted to teach on the campuses under the jurisdiction of the Board. . . .

The Board gave no indication of the reasons or the evidence it relied on
in its disagreement with the Committee. Thus, this Court is in the unusual
position of having on the one hand what amounts to detailed findings of
fact and conclusions of law from a faculty committee which conducted the
actual hearings and found that infractions were not sufficiently serious to
find plaintiff unfit, or to warrant his discharge; and having on the other hand,
only a bald statement of conclusions by the Board of Regents to support its
determination of "unfitness." Comity commands us to support the Board's
conclusions if they are supportable by any reasonable inference from the
evidence. The summary nature of the Board's conclusions handicaps us, however, in discovering the basis for the Board's rationale. Both the Committee
and the Board based its conclusion upon the same evidence which this Court
now has before it. Since out of the eight specific charges on which evidence
was received, seven are based in whole or in part upon the spoken or written
word outside of the classroom, it now becomes our duty to make the independent factual findings necessary in this kind of constitutional case. To do
this, we must examine the evidence in some detail. . . .

A claim of "free speech" should not excuse actions by a teacher that would
normally evoke the kind of discipline applied in this case. Conversely, the
employer should not selectively enforce rules, or use minor infractions as
an ostensible reason for discipline or discharge in a case where the unprotected conduct complained of would normally evoke only mild disciplinary
action or perhaps no discipline at all but for the protected conduct or speech.

However, if judged by constitutional standards, there are valid as well
as invalid reasons for the discipline or discharge of a teacher, such discipline
or discharge will not be set aside by the federal court so long as the invalid
reasons are not the primary reasons or motivation for the discharge. . . .

As to the seven charges involving words, we must ask two questions: First, are the words subject to federal constitutional guaranty? Second, as to those charges involving speech as a citizen, are the words protected by the Board's own standards proclaiming that when a faculty member speaks as a citizen, exercising his constitutional right of free speech, he should be free of institutional discipline? The second question may be raised to constitutional significance, since plaintiff was given notice and repeated assurance throughout these proceedings that the charges against him would be governed by certain A.A.U.P. principles which appear in the bylaws of the faculty constitution. If the Board used standards substantially more restrictive than its avowed principles a serious due process question would be raised.

In determining whether the words involved are protected, we shall attempt to balance two basic interests. The United States Supreme Court has repeatedly emphasized that "The vigilant protection of constitutional freedom is nowhere more vital than in the community of American schools." Keyishian v. Board of Regents of U. of St. of N. Y., 385 U. S. 589, 603, 87 S.Ct. 675, 683, 17 L.Ed.2d 629 (1967). On the other hand, the courts have recognized that academic freedom may have to be balanced against school administrators' right to forbid conduct which would "materially and substantially interfere with the requirements of appropriate discipline in the operation of the school." Tinker v. Des Moines Independent Com. Sch. Dist., 393 U. S. 503, 509, 89 S.Ct. 733, 738, 21 L.Ed.2d 731 (1969).

This balancing test is quite easy in the two incidents involving charges of personally insulting speech delivered on the campus within students' hearing. Although the language used in the Sumner incident may be subject to sufficient First Amendment protection to defeat a tort or a criminal action, there are important considerations of school discipline here. The content of the speech in calling Mr. Sumner a "bastard," etc., adds very little to the world of ideas. It communicates only vituperation, bad temper, and a kind of loss of personal dignity on the part of a faculty member that may be the exact kind of conduct meant to be avoided by the A.A.U.P. standard of "appropriate" restraint. The school's interest in discipline in demanding some minimum of courtesy in a faculty member's on-campus relationships with school officials outweighs the free speech interests here.

The question asked by plaintiff as to whether he could make a citizen's arrest of a member of the faculty of the Engineering College does not involve the same kind of undignified conduct. The speech consists of an honest, if misguided, inquiry as to whether plaintiff could legally take a certain course of action. The evidence shows that plaintiff honestly believed that Dean Welch was performing an illegal act in refusing to permit the posting of an anti-war handbill, and that this belief was shared by other professors. It is significant that John Duffy, Director of Security, did not know the answer to the question, and that none of the Administration witnesses found the question abusive. The question was promptly dropped and there was no evidence as to any action. We find no issue of "verbal act." The interests of honest inquiry here outweigh the interests of discipline. We find this is protected speech.

The Administration Building incident is somewhat more complicated. The Board found culpability in an event covering a two-day period during which plaintiff was found to have supported and participated with students in the occupation of certain offices in violation of regulations concerning student-faculty relationships. We agree with the Committee that the evidence does not support the charge, and like the Committee, we find aspects of plaintiff's conduct as a peacemaker most commendable. Plaintiff raises a further issue that the outcry, "Cady is copping (or selling) out," is protected speech. Defendants argue that this outcry under these circumstances was calculated to arouse a violent response and is therefore a "verbal act" within the meaning of Siegel v. Regents of U. of Cal., 308 F.Supp. 832 (D.C.1970). . . .

The verbal act in *Siegel* is a deliberate incitement to seize fenced private property in a tense situation.

At the Administration Building, there was no question of "seizing" private property. . . .

It is difficult to view Professor Starsky's outcry apart from the Administration's testimony of his "influence" over students, from all of the evidence of his interest and concern with the students, and from the evidence of three separate acts of persuading students not to take extreme action, once at the Engineering Building and twice during the Administrative Building event. The many acts illustrate the kind of rapport that Professor Starsky had with students, and his ability in his own words to "use that influence to try to keep people (from) engaging in lunatic fringe sorts of activity." Common sense tells us that this kind of "influence" can only be maintained by complete frankness with students. Although we may wish that Professor Starsky had found a more polite form of communication, his frankness with the students in giving them information of interest to them at the instant he heard it, is certainly part of the picture of his own relationships with students, and the credibility he had with them, and part of the reason he was successful on at least three occasions that we know of in controlling potentially extreme student action.

In weighing Professor Starsky's interest in imparting information which would help maintain his rapport with the students against the fears of the Administration, we are mindful of the test laid out in Tinker v. Des Moines:

> . . . in our system, undifferentiated fear or apprehension of disturbance is not enough to overcome the right to freedom of expression. Any departure from absolute regimentation may cause trouble. Any variation from the majority's opinion may inspire fear. Any word spoken, in class, in the lunchroom, or on the campus, that deviates from the views of another person may start an argument or cause a disturbance. But our Constitution says we must take this risk. . . .

Supra, at 508 of 393 U.S., 737 of 89 S.Ct. . . .

The copies of a letter distributed only to faculty at the entrance of a faculty meeting is "pure" speech. Our discussion of the facts basically is dispositive of the constitutional issue, since we found that the objections to the letter derived entirely from its wording, that nothing in the letter called for immediate action at Arizona State University, and that the purpose of the letter was informational, i.e., to acquaint the faculty with the causes of unrest at Columbia University. The crux of the criticism of the letter is its disrespect for authority. The kind of "disrespect" is based on mere quotation of a dialogue involving in part advocacy of a complete change in the nature of authority. In the absence of any incitement to direct violent action, this kind of abstract revolutionary philosophy is protected. Thus in Keyishian v. Board of Regents of U. of St. of N. Y., 385 U.S. 589, 598, 87 S.Ct. 675, 682, 17 L.Ed.2d 629 (1967), a regulation barring employment of a teacher who "by word of mouth or writing willfully and deliberately advocates, advises or teaches the doctrine of forceful overthrow of government" was found unconstitutionally vague since "It may well ... prohibit the employment of one who merely advocates the doctrine in the abstract. . . ."

There is a serious constitutional question as to whether speech can be stifled because the ideas or wording expressed upset the "austere" faculty atmosphere; certainly the Board has no legitimate interest in keeping a university in some kind of intellectual austerity by an absence of shocking ideas. Insofar as the plaintiff's words upset the Legislature or faculty because of the contents of his views, and particularly the depth of his social criticism, this is not the kind of detriment for which plaintiff can constitutionally be penalized. The United States Supreme Court has emphasized that:

> The vigilant protection of constitutional freedoms is nowhere more vital than in the community of American schools. (citation). The classroom is peculiarly the "marketplace of ideas." The Nation's future depends upon leaders trained through wide exposure to that *robust exchange of ideas* which discovers truth "out of a multitude of tongues, [rather] than through any kind of authoritative selection." (Emphasis supplied).

. . . .

Although this balancing test is technically the same for on-campus speech and speech as a citizen, as a practical matter it may be easier for the school to show a counterbalancing interest where the speech is closely connected with the speaker's on-campus duties. Thus, there may be circumstances in which school discipline requires that a professor acting within his capacity as a teacher, or in his personal relationship on campus, may be held to professional standards of appropriate restraint or greater personal courtesy than that which may be demanded of other citizens, and when a teacher speaks within his own expertise, the school may have a substantial interest in holding him to higher standards of accuracy than if he were an ordinary citizen. However, these narrower standards may not be applied to a faculty member when he speaks publicly as a citizen, in the absence of a showing of an employer's interest sufficient to counterbalance the citizen's interest in his constitutional rights.

The very nature of the charges and the Board's findings against Professor Starsky insofar as they relate to his public speech as a citizen show that the Board failed to recognize its own avowed standards of freedom from discipline when a faculty member "speaks or writes as a citizen."

Thus, the Board in finding plaintiff guilty of the summary charge ". . . has not exercised appropriate restraint as becomes a university professor in his public activities. . .", applied a narrow professional standard to Professor Starsky's speech as a citizen.

Throughout the statement of charges and the findings the Board fails to distinguish those circumstances in which Professor Starsky spoke as a professional, under circumstances where the interests of the school balanced First Amendment interest sufficiently to warrant a narrower professional standard of speech, from those circumstances in which Professor Starsky spoke publicly as a citizen and had the right to the same broad constitutional protection afforded every citizen. . . .

In each of the utterances by the plaintiff, certain aspects of the administration of a university are attacked, and there is a call for basic change; but in each case, the attack is on the basis of the power structure, the ideology, the political philosophy of the administration, and never on the basis of individual personality. In none of the speeches is there a call for disobedience or disrespect or disruption in the sense that the audience is told to specifically disobey the Administration's rulings. Professor Starsky's attack is a more profound and philosophical one; he calls for a complete social revolution, and he defends himself from actions by the Board.

This Court finds that the Board, in discharging Professor Starsky on the basis of narrow professional standards of accuracy, respect and restraint applied to public statements made as a citizen, has violated its own A.A.U.P. standards not to discipline a teacher when he "speaks or writes as a citizen," and has violated Professor Starsky's rights to freedom of speech by applying constitutionally impermissible standards to speech made as a citizen. . . .

We can conclude from this that the evidence fails to show the plaintiff is unfit for his position. The Board's finding of unfitness is primarily or substantially motivated by those charges which impermissibly restrict plaintiff's First Amendment rights.

Yet, something more seems to need to be said here. The finding of fitness or unfitness in this case involves something more than addition of charges. During the course of the thirteen hearings involved in this case, everyone seemed to agree that you could not get a picture of the man's six years of service (or disservice) to the University by merely looking at each incident involved in the charges. The prosecutor spoke of these incidents as building blocks, with the whole picture adding up to a lack of professionalism, that may not be apparent in any one incident alone. . . .

We find that Professor Starsky's expressions tend to be an abstract kind of marxist, socialist, trotskyist social revolution that calls for social revolution at some future time, but that nowhere calls for the kind of immediate, violent action that might constitute a direct threat to the school's disciplinary interest. . . .

The record as a whole supports a picture of Professor Starsky as a person who used his own influence to control the lunatic fringes, who counseled order and non-violence, and who, although he called for profound social change and was willing to go along on peaceful demonstrations, consistently acted to prevent heads from being bashed in. . . .

Looking at the evidence as a whole insofar as it reflects the sum and substance of six years as a member of the faculty, an acknowledged and respected teacher and scholar, and a man with national visibility; and after carefully studying all the evidence which the Board of Regents had before it as a basis for its action, the isolated incidents that could reasonably lead to some disciplinary action were of such a minor nature or long ago, and the major emphasis in the charges is so clearly based upon protected ideology, that this Court must conclude that the primary reason for the discipline of Professor Starsky is grounded in his exercise of his First Amendment rights in expressing unpopular views.

We therefore grant plaintiff's motion for summary judgment on the issue of liability and declare that plaintiff's termination violates his right to free speech and involves a violation of federal due process insofar as the discharge was based on standards of academic freedom narrower than the standards noticed in the charges.

NOTES

1. The Court in *Starsky* states that "comity commands us to support the Board's conclusions." What is comity? Is it a correct basis for upholding decisions by the Board of Regents? What standard of review should courts use in reviewing regental personnel decisions?

2. The Court states that the standard of protected speech is *narrower* when Professor Starsky spoke professionally than when he spoke as a citizen. What is the basis for this difference? What does it say about academic freedom?

3. The substantive findings of *Starsky v. Williams* were affirmed by the Ninth Circuit at 512 F.2d 109 (1975), but the case was remanded to determine whether Starsky had waived his rights by signing a contract for a final sabbatical year. The full story of the events in the *Starsky* case are reported in Hoult, The March to the Right: A Case Study in Political Repression (Cambridge, Mass.: Schenkman Publ. Co. 1972).

4. The following discussion of Peacock v. Bd. of Regents of the University and State Colleges of Arizona, 510 F.2d 1324 (9th Cir. 1975), is taken from Virginia Davis Nordin, *The Legal Protection of Academic Freedom*, in The Courts and Education, Seventy-seventh Yearbook of the National Society for the Study of Education, Part I, ed. Clifford P. Hooker (Chicago: University of Chicago Press, 1978), at pp. 329-31 (footnotes omitted):

> *Departmental autonomy: the freedom to act on ideas held.* The threat to academic freedom from institutional management was defined differently in the more unusual *Peacock* case, also from Arizona. The circumstances described as an academic power struggle were not so unusual. It was unusual, however, that the losing party sought to enforce his rights in the federal courts, thereby further testing whether our present constitutional provisions

do indeed protect academic freedom in some of its nether reaches. Yet the legal definition of the protection afforded against political-governmental regulation, both external and internal, is important to those considering the potential for death by nibbling, particularly in view of what would appear to be the inevitable decline in the influence of the AAUP and other professional organizations.

In this case, a department chairman was summarily dismissed from his administrative duties as department head by the University of Arizona. During the subsequent strife he was further summarily dismissed from his tenured faculty position, without a prior hearing, although he was offered a postsuspension hearing. He brought suit for damages and equitable relief to redress the denial of his due process right to a hearing prior to his dismissal. It was essentially an internal due process case, testing what procedures, if any, the (public) university must grant an academic before relieving him of administrative duties. It is a case important to academic freedom because it has to do with departmental autonomy, the theoretical power base of faculty freedom.

It is interesting to note that the court recognized that the university never questioned Professor Peacock's professional competence but sought to remove him solely because of his lack of cooperation stemming from *differences of opinion about how to run a medical school* and did not intimate that Peacock refused to perform tasks assigned by the administration or that his lack of cooperation ever damaged the medical school or the hospital. Nevertheless, the court never raised or discussed the concept of academic freedom but instead took a *Roth-Sindermann-Arnett* approach, which analyzed Peacock's personal liberty and property interests in the department chairmanship. Perhaps there is no legally recognized interest other than one personal to Peacock, and perhaps his personal interest does not encompass departmental autonomy, a term not synonymous with, but related to, academic freedom. Nonetheless, the court did see fit to cite "the common law of the campus" to establish that heads of departments are appointed by and serve at the sufferance of the university president, that they can attain no tenure in the position, that they are subject to the unfettered discretion of the president who can dismiss them at any time for any reason, and, above all, that the position of department chairman is "quasi-administrative." The court found that this "common law" overcomes a written contract with clear provisions. The court might also have ventured into the murky waters of the importance of departmental autonomy to academic freedom in a public university, at least to the extent of granting a predismissal hearing in this case.

Thus we come to the question of whether academic freedom, like religious freedom, includes the freedom to act on ideas held. A finding that the concept of academic freedom includes not only the right to research and to disseminate conclusions through publications or speaking, but also the right to organize curriculum and take *academic* action based on those conclusions, does not necessarily mean automatic anarchy any more than the constitutional protection of the free exercise of religion has allowed any and all religious practices to prevail in our society (for example, polygamy or snake-handling). In this case, for example, the plaintiff, on appeal, was asking only for a right to a predismissal hearing—a hearing which might have brought out whether or not a serious deprivation of constitutional freedom was the basis for the action. The Ninth Circuit Court of Appeals, using a strictly employment approach, found that postsuspension hearing satisfied the requirements of due process, since loyalty and cooperation are imperative. "We conclude that the potential threat to the administration of the medical school, and the incidental threat of disruption at the University Hospital outweighs his interest in a presuspension hearing."

IV. The Freedom to Learn

A.   Foreign Scholars

KLEINDIENST v. MANDEL
United States Supreme Court
408 U. S. 753 (1972)

MR. JUSTICE BLACKMUN delivered the opinion of the Court.

The appellees have framed the issue here as follows:

"Does appellants' action in refusing to allow an alien scholar to enter the country to attend academic meetings violate the First Amendment rights of American scholars and students who had invited him?" . . . .

Ernest E. Mandel resides in Brussels, Belgium, and is a Belgian citizen. He is a professional journalist and is editor-in-chief of the Belgian Left Socialist weekly La Gauche. He is author of a two-volume work entitled Marxist Economic Theory published in 1969. He asserted in his visa applications that he is not a member of the Communist Party. He has described himself, however, as "a revolutionary Marxist." He does not dispute, see 325 F. Supp. 620, 624, that he advocates the economic, governmental, and international doctrines of world communism.

Mandel was admitted to the United States temporarily in 1962 and again in 1968. On the first visit he came as a working journalist. On the second he accepted invitations to speak at a number of universities and colleges. On each occasion, although apparently he was not then aware of it, his admission followed a finding of ineligibility under § 212(a)(28), and the Attorney General's exercise of discretion to admit him temporarily, on recommendation of the Secretary of State, as § 212(d)(3)(A) permits.

On September 8, 1969, Mandel applied to the American Consul in Brussels for a nonimmigrant visa to enter the United States in October for a six-day period, during which he would participate in a conference on Technology and the Third World at Stanford University. He had been invited to Stanford by the Graduate Student Association there. The invitation stated that John Kenneth Galbraith would present the keynote address and that Mandel would be expected to participate in an ensuing panel discussion and to give a major address the following day. The University, through the office of its president, "heartily endorse[d]" the invitation. When Mandel's intended visit became known, additional invitations for lectures and conference participations came to him from members of the faculties at Princeton, Amherst, Columbia, and Vassar, from groups in Cambridge, Massachusetts, and New York City, and from others. One conference, to be in New York City, was sponsored jointly by the Bertrand Russell Peace Foundation and the Socialist Scholars Conference; Mandel's assigned subject there was "Revolutionary Strategy in Imperialist Countries." Mandel then filed a second visa application proposing a more extensive itinerary and a stay of greater duration. . . .

The Department of State in fact had recommended to the Attorney General that Mandel's ineligibility be waived with respect to his October visa application. The Immigration and Naturalization Service, however, acting on behalf of the Attorney General, see 28 U. S. C. §510, in a letter dated February 13, 1970, to New York counsel stated that it had determined that Mandel's 1968 activities while in the United States "went far beyond the stated purposes of his trip, on the basis of which his admission had been authorized and represented a flagrant abuse of the opportunities afforded him to express his views in this country." The letter concluded that favorable exercise of discretion, provided for under the Act, was not warranted and that Mandel's temporary admission was not authorized.

Mandel's address to the New York meeting was then delivered by transatlantic telephone.

In March Mandel and six of the other appellees instituted the present action against the Attorney General and the Secretary of State. The two remaining appellees soon came into the lawsuit by an amendment to the complaint. All the appellees who joined Mandel in this action are United States citizens and are university professors in various fields of the social sciences. They are persons who invited Mandel to speak at universities and other forums in the United States or who expected to participate in colloquia with him so that, as the complaint alleged, "they may hear his views and engage him in a free and open academic exchange.". . . .

In a variety of contexts this Court has referred to a First Amendment right to "receive information and ideas":

"It is now well established that the Constitution protects the right to receive information and ideas. 'This freedom [of speech and press] . . . necessarily protects the right to receive . . . .' *Martin* v. *City of Struthers*, 319 U. S. 141, 143 (1943). . . ." *Stanley* v. *Georgia*, 394 U. S. 557, 564 (1969). . . .

In the present case, the District Court majority held:

"The concern of the First Amendment is not with a non-resident alien's individual and personal interest in entering and being heard, but with the rights of the citizens of the country to have the alien enter and to hear him explain and seek to defend his views; that, as *Garrison* [v. *Louisiana*, 379 U. S. 64 (1964)] and *Red Lion* observe, is of the essence of self-government." 325 F. Supp., at 631.

The Government disputes this conclusion on two grounds. First, it argues that exclusion of Mandel involves no restriction on First Amendment rights at all since what is restricted is "only action—the action of the alien in coming into this country.". . . . In light of the Court's previous decisions concerning the "right to receive information," we cannot realistically say that the problem facing us disappears entirely or is nonexistent because the mode of regulation bears directly on physical movement. . . .

The Government also suggests that the First Amendment is inapplicable because appellees have free access to Mandel's ideas through his books and

speeches, and because "technological developments," such as tapes or telephone hook-ups, readily supplant his physical presence. This argument
overlooks what may be particular qualities inherent in sustained, face-to-
face debate, discussion and questioning. While alternative means of access
to Mandel's ideas might be a relevant factor were we called upon to balance First Amendment rights against governmental regulatory interests—a
balance we find unnecessary here in light of the discussion that follows in
Part V—we are loath to hold on this record that existence of other alternatives extinguishes altogether any constitutional interest on the part of the
appellees in this particular form of access.

Recognition that First Amendment rights are implicated, however, is
not dispositive of our inquiry here. In accord with ancient principles of the
international law of nation-states, the Court in *The Chinese Exclusion Case*,
130 U. S. 581, 609 (1889), and in *Fong Yue Ting* v. *United States*, 149 U. S.
698 (1893), held broadly, as the Government describes it, Brief for Appellants 20, that the power to exclude aliens is "inherent in sovereignty, necessary for maintaining normal international relations and defending the country against foreign encroachments and dangers—a power to be exercised
exclusively by the political branches of government. . . ." Since that time,
the Court's general reaffirmations of this principle have been legion. The
Court without exception has sustained Congress' "plenary power to make
rules for the admission of aliens and to exclude those who possess those
characteristics which Congress has forbidden." *Boutilier* v. *Immigration and
Naturalization Service*, 387 U. S. 118, 123 (1967). "[O]ver no conceivable
subject is the legislative power of Congress more complete than it is over"
the admission of aliens. *Oceanic Navigation Co.* v. *Stranahan*, 214 U. S. 320,
339 (1909). In *Lem Moon Sing* v. *United States*, 158 U. S. 538, 547 (1895),
the first Mr. Justice Harlan said:

> "The power of Congress to exclude aliens altogether from the
> United States, or to prescribe the terms and conditions upon
> which they may come to this country, and to have its declared
> policy in that regard enforced exclusively through executive offi-
> cers, without judicial intervention, is settled by our previous
> adjudications."

We are not inclined in the present context to reconsider this line of
cases. Indeed, the appellees, in contrast to the *amicus*, do not ask that we
do so. . . . They argue that the Executive's implementation of this congressional mandate through decision whether to grant a waiver in each individual
case must be limited by the First Amendment rights of persons like appellees.
Specifically, their position is that the First Amendment rights must prevail,
at least where the Government advances no justification for failing to grant
a waiver. They point to the fact that waivers have been granted in the vast
majority of cases.

Appellee's First Amendment argument would prove too much. In almost every instance of an alien excludable under § 212(a)(28), there are
probably those who would wish to meet and speak with him. The ideas of

most such aliens might not be so influential as those of Mandel, nor his American audience so numerous, nor the planned discussion forums so impressive. But the First Amendment does not protect only the articulate, the well known, and the popular. Were we to endorse the proposition that governmental power to withhold a waiver must yield whenever a bona fide claim is made that American citizens wish to meet and talk with an alien excludable under § 212(a)(28), one of two unsatisfactory results would necessarily ensue. Either every claim would prevail, in which case the plenary discretionary authority Congress granted the Executive becomes a nullity, or courts in each case would be required to weigh the strength of the audience's interest against that of the Government in refusing a waiver to the particular alien applicant, according to some as yet undetermined standard. The dangers and the undesirability of making that determination on the basis of factors such as the size of the audience or the probity of the speaker's ideas are obvious. Indeed, it is for precisely this reason that the waiver decision has, properly, been placed in the hands of the Executive. . . .

In summary, plenary congressional power to make policies and rules for exclusion of aliens has long been firmly established. In the case of an alien excludable under § 212(a)(28), Congress has delegated conditional exercise of this power to the Executive. We hold that when the Executive exercises this power negatively on the basis of a facially legitimate and bona fide reason, the courts will neither look behind the exercise of that discretion, nor test it by balancing its justification against the First Amendment interests of those who seek personal communication with the applicant. What First Amendment or other grounds may be available for attacking exercise of discretion for which no justification whatsoever is advanced is a question we neither address nor decide in this case.

Reversed.

MR. JUSTICE DOUGLAS, dissenting. . . .

The Attorney General stands astride our international terminals that bring people here to bar those whose ideas are not acceptable to him. Even assuming, *arguendo*, that those on the outside seeking admission have no standing to complain, those who hope to benefit from the traveler's lectures do.

Thought control is not within the competence of any branch of government. Those who live here may need exposure to the ideas of people of many faiths and many creeds to further their education. We should construe the Act generously by that First Amendment standard, saying that once the State Department has concluded that our foreign relations permit or require the admission of a foreign traveler, the Attorney General is left only problems of national security, importation of heroin, or other like matters within his competence.

We should assume that where propagation of ideas is permissible as being within our constitutional framework, the Congress did not undertake to make the Attorney General a censor. For as stated by Justice Jackson in *Thomas* v. *Collins.* 323 U. S. 516, 545 (concurring), "[t]he very purpose of the First Amendment is to foreclose public authority from assuming a guardianship of the public mind through regulating the press, speech, and religion. In this field every person must be his own watchman for truth, because the forefathers did not trust any government to separate the true from the false for us." . . .

B.   Unpopular Expression on Campus

BROOKS v. AUBURN UNIVERSITY
5th Circuit Court of Appeals
412 F.2d 1171 (1969)

BELL, Circuit Judge:

This appeal involves a decree of the district court restraining the president of Auburn University, Dr. Harry M. Philpott, from barring the scheduled appearance and speech on the Auburn campus of the Reverend William Sloan Coffin. The decree also required the payment to Reverend Coffin of an agreed honorarium and travel expenses. We agree with the result reached by the district court and therefore affirm.

The decree, entered on the complaint of plaintiffs who were students and members of the faculty at Auburn, rested on the premise that Dr. Philpott was denying them their First Amendment right to hear the speaker. The First Amendment, applicable to a state university through the Fourteenth Amendment, embraces the right to hear. Cf. Martin v. City of Struthers, 1943, 319 U.S. 141, 63 S.Ct. 862, 87 L.Ed. 1313; Lamont v. Postmaster General, 1965, 381 U.S. 301, 85 S.Ct. 1493, 14 L.Ed.2d 398. . . .

The record demonstrates that Auburn had no rules or regulations governing speaker eligibility. The practice was for the Public Affairs Seminar Board, an officially chartered student-faculty board, to pass on requests from student groups to invite speakers. Funds were allocated to the Board by the university from student fees for use in obtaining speakers. The Human Affairs Forum wrote the Board under date of November 13, 1968 requesting $650.00 needed for honorarium and expense purposes in bringing Reverend Coffin, Chaplain at Yale University, to Auburn for a speaking engagement on February 7, 1969. The Board, at a formal meeting on November 20, 1968, approved the request. The approval was communicated in writing to the chairman of the Human Affairs Forum by letter dated November 21, 1968.

Dr. Philpott then notified the Public Affairs Seminar Board that the Reverend Coffin would not be allowed to speak on the Auburn University campus because he was a convicted felon and because he might advocate breaking the law. These reasons had not previously been invoked at Auburn to bar a speaker. . . .

Attributing the highest good faith to Dr. Philpott in his action, it nevertheless is clear under the prior restraint doctrine that the right of the faculty and students to hear a speaker, selected as was the speaker here, cannot be left to the discretion of the university president on a pick and choose basis.

As stated, Auburn had no rules or regulations as to who might or might not speak and thus no question of a compliance with or a departure from such rules or regulations is presented. This left the matter as a pure First Amendment question; hence the basis for prior restraint. Such a situation of no rules or regulations may be equated with a licensing system to speak or hear and this has been long prohibited. Cantwell v. Connecticut, 1940, 310 U. S. 296, 60 S.Ct. 900, 84 L.Ed. 1213.

It is strenuously urged on behalf of Auburn that the president was authorized in any event to bar a convicted felon or one advocating lawlessness from the campus. This again depends upon the right of the faculty and students to hear. We do not hold that Dr. Philpott could not bar a speaker under any circumstances. Here there was no claim that the Reverend Coffin's appearance would lead to violence or disorder or that the university would be otherwise disrupted. There is no claim that Dr. Philpott could not regulate the time or place of the speech or the manner in which it was to be delivered. . . .

The responsibilities on courts and university presidents in the area of First Amendment rights is heavy indeed. Judge Godbold, in a special concurring opinion in Ferrell v. Dallas Independent School District, 5 Cir., 1968, 392 F.2d 697, 704, put it well when he said:

"A school may not stifle dissent because the subject matter is out of favor. Free expression is itself a vital part of the educational process. But in measuring the appropriateness and reasonableness of school regulations against the constitutional protections of the First and Fourteenth Amendments the courts must give full credence to the role and purposes of the schools and of the tools with which it is expected that they deal with their problems, and careful recognition to the differences between what are reasonable restraints in the classroom and what are reasonable restraints on the street corner." . . .

We find no departure from these teachings in the decree which forms the subject matter of this appeal.

Affirmed.

FURUMOTO v. LYMAN

United States District Court, N. D. California
362 F.Supp. 1267 (1973)

On January 18, 1972, shortly after 11:00 A.M., approximately fifteen people, including plaintiffs, entered Room 127, McCullough Building, on the Stanford University campus, where a scheduled quiz in a course on electrical engineering was being given under the supervision of Professor William Shockley. The racial or ethnic composition of the group was mostly non-Caucasian. Although plaintiffs were registered Stanford students it is not clear that all members of the group were Stanford students. The group's sole purpose was to condemn Shockley's view of genetics while demanding that he debate one Cedric Clark publicly. The intrusion was a planned event, with the members of the group acting in concert. . . .

Plaintiffs' First Amendment Rights

Although it is not entirely clear from plaintiffs' complaint, one element of their claim seems to be that defendants punished them for their expression of opposition to racism, thus denying them their rights under the First Amendment.

That the plaintiffs as students retained their First Amendment rights upon entering the University is clear beyond question. Tinker v. Des Moines School Dist., 393 U.S. 503, 506 89 S.Ct. 733, 21 L.Ed.2d 731 (1969); Healy v. James, 408 U.S. 169, 180, 92 S.Ct. 2338, 33 L.Ed.2d 266 (1972). But those rights do not include an absolute right to determine how, where, and when such protected expression will take place:

"* * * conduct by the student, in class or out of it, which for any reason—whether it stems from time, place, or type of behavior—materially disrupts classwork or involves substantial disorder or invasion of the rights of others is, of course, not immunized by the constitutional guarantee of freedom of speech." 393 U.S. at 513, 89 S.Ct. at 740.

. . . .

That the Stanford regulations are consistent with these authorities is clear from a consideration of the history of the problem which led to their adoption and the very nature of a university environment. Although American campus life has become quiescent in the past few months, the history of university upheavals and turmoil is too recent to require any detailed statement. In the words of the Report of the President's Commission on Campus Unrest, p. 1/5 (1970), "* * * the last decade clearly shows a gradual movement toward more disruptive, violent, and even terrorist tactics in campus protest, and a steady and significant growth in the number of radical students and tactical extremists." After studying the history of the campus disturbances, the Commission found that:

"Universities have not adequately prepared themselves to respond to disruption. They have been without suitable plans, rules, or sanctions. Some administrators and faculty members have responded irresolutely. Frequently, announced sanctions have not been applied. Even more frequently, the lack of appropriate organization within the university has rendered its response ineffective. The university's own house must be placed in order." (p. R-2).

It is to this deficiency which Stanford was plainly responding with its Policy on Campus Disruption. That Policy was not an unreasonable response considering the fragility of a university, the inherent inconsistency of authoritarianism with intellectual freedom, and the need for order:

"An institution committed to intellectual freedom, to individuality, and to the toleration of eccentricity, is bound to be loosely

organized at best, and its internal processes of governance and law
are bound to be somewhat uncertain." (p. 4/10).

Stanford's Policy on Campus Disruption is limited to the most egregious
interferences with campus order and the rights of others. It does not approach being prior restraint, as in Hammond v. South Carolina State College,
272 F. Supp. 947, 949-950 (D.S.C.1967). Nor does it interfere with the
right of free association. See Healy v. James, 408 U. S. 169, 181-184, 92
S.Ct. 2338, 33 L.Ed.2d 266 (1972). There is no evidence that Stanford officials used the regulations to intimidate plaintiffs or any other members of
the academic community.

In this case plaintiffs and other members of the disrupting group had
other means available for challenging Professor Shockley to a debate. Even
if, as plaintiffs have indicated elsewhere, there was need to have black people
confront Shockley, there was no reason given why they could not have
waited until after class to present, briefly but completely, their challenge.
Even here, they did not, of course, have a right to infringe his personal
liberty.

At the oral argument on this motion, counsel for plaintiffs put forward
the position that in academic life a professor must debate his views publicly
if challenged. While this Court would agree that this may be desirable as a
part of intellectual responsibility to consider opposing views and respond to
them, that responsibility cannot extend to mandate public debating. Such a
requirement would in itself be a potential inhibitor of academic freedom,
since many individuals simply do not have the personality or talents to perform comfortably and adequately in oral debating. Such a requirement, if
widely adopted, could drive otherwise qualified and valuable scholars from
academic life. Professor Shockley thus had a First Amendment right to
choose the medium for his response to his challengers or indeed even
whether to respond at all. Plaintiffs cannot justify their actions by claiming
that Professor Shockley would otherwise have been able to avoid a public
debate.

Plaintiffs' counsel also advanced the position that each member of the
academic community has the right to respond to activities which he finds
morally offensive, determined by his personal standards, in ways that he
feels are necessary. While this Court admires the forthrightness of counsel
and his belief in the integrity of individual judgment, it views such a principle as ultimately destructive of the university and of free social life in general
in that it would likely lead either to anarchy or to the rule of the mob. *Cf.*
Furutani v. Ewigleben, 297 F.Supp. 1163, 1165 (N.D.Cal.1969).

For these reasons, this Court holds that the defendants did not deny
nor interfere with plaintiffs' First Amendment rights. . . .

CONCLUSION

This case and this opinion have necessarily involved a review of society's
legal response to the campus unrest of the past decade. Plaintiffs' substantive claims have been found to be opposed by an overwhelming legal con-

sensus. That consensus is not necessarily the idealistic view expressed by Mill of the power of freedom of speech to lead to the "truth;" but the principle is established that a university cannot survive if it becomes a political arena in which direct action is justifiable in terms of personal moral codes. The President's Commission on Campus Unrest has expressed this idea:

> "Academic institutions must be free—free from outside interference, and free from internal intimidation. Far too many people who should know better—both within university communities and outside them—have forgotten this first principle of academic freedom. The pursuit of knowledge cannot continue without the free exchange of ideas." Report of the President's Commission on Campus Unrest, p. R-11.

Plaintiffs' action against the Stanford Trustees and Professor Shockley is dismissed for failure to state a claim upon which relief can be granted. As to the remaining defendants their motion for summary judgment is granted.

NOTE

1. In Pickings v. Bruce, 430 F.2d 595 (8th Cir. 1970), students and faculty members at Southern State College, in Arkansas, were sanctioned for writing a letter to an off-campus church questioning its policies on integration, and for refusing to accede to a request of the college administrators to cancel a speaking invitation to off-campus speakers. The Eighth Circuit, citing Tinker v. Des Moines School Dist., 393 U. S. 503 (1969), held against the administration on both issues, since there was a failure to prove any substantial threat of campus disruption. *See* further, Van Alstyne, *Political Speakers at State Universities: Some Constitutional Considerations*, 111 U. Pa. L. Rev. 328 (1963); Wright, *The Constitution on the Campus*, 22 Vand. L. Rev. 1027 (1969); and *Report of the President's Commission on Campus Unrest*, Washington, D.C. Government Printing Office (1970).

CHAPTER 7

FACULTY TENURE

I. Introduction

   A. Definition of Tenure–A Historical Perspective

The definition of tenure which is most prevalent in American Higher Education is found in the 1940 *Statement of Principles,* promulgated by the American Association of University Professors (AAUP) and the American Association of Colleges. It provides:

> The purpose of this statement is to promote public understanding and support of academic freedom and tenure and agreement upon procedures to assure them in colleges and universities. Institutions of higher education are conducted for the common good and not to further the interest of either the individual teacher or the institution as a whole. The common good depends upon the free search for truth and its free exposition.
>
> Academic freedom is essential to these purposes and applies to both teaching and research. Freedom in research is fundamental to the advancement of truth. Academic freedom in its teaching aspect is fundamental for the protection of the rights of the teacher in teaching and of the student to freedom in learning. It carries with it duties correlative with rights.
>
> Tenure is a means to certain ends; specifically: (1) Freedom of teaching and research and of extra-mural activities, and (2) A sufficient degree of economic security to make the profession attractive to men and women of ability. Freedom and economic security, hence tenure, are indispensable to the success of an institution in fulfilling its obligations to its students and to society. . . .

Academic Tenure

(*a*) After the expiration of a probationary period teachers or investigators should have permanent or continuous tenure, and their services should be terminated only for adequate cause, except in the case of retirement for age, or under extraordinary circumstances because of financial exigencies.

In the interpretation of this principle it is understood that the following represents acceptable academic practice:

(1) The precise terms and conditions of every appointment should be stated in writing and be in the possession of both institution and teacher before the appointment is consummated.

218

(2) Beginning with appointment to the rank of full-time instructor or a higher rank, the probationary period should not exceed seven years, including within this period full-time service in all institutions of higher education; but subject to the proviso that when, after a term of probationary service of more than three years in one or more institutions, a teacher is called to another institution it may be agreed in writing that his new appointment is for a probationary period of not more than four years, even though thereby the person's total probationary period in the academic profession is extended beyond the normal maximum of seven years. Notice should be given at least one year prior to the expiration of the probationary period, if the teacher is not to be continued in service after the expiration of that period.

(3) During the probationary period a teacher should have the academic freedom that all other members of the faculty have.

(4) Termination for cause of a continuous appointment, or the dismissal for cause of a teacher previous to the expiration of a term appointment, should, if possible, be considered by both a faculty committee and the governing board of the institution. In all cases where the facts are in dispute, the accused teacher should be informed before the hearing in writing of the charges against him and should have the opportunity to be heard in his own defense by all bodies that pass judgment upon his case. He should be permitted to have with him an adviser of his own choosing who may act as counsel. There should be a full stenographic record of the hearing available to the parties concerned. In the hearing of charges of incompetence the testimony should include that of teachers and other scholars, either from his own or from other institutions. Teachers on continuous appointment who are dismissed for reasons not involving moral turpitude should receive their salaries for at least a year from the date of notification of dismissal whether or not they are continued in their duties at the institution.

(5) Termination of a continuous appointment because of financial exigency should be demonstrably bona fide.

One of the best and most thorough scholarly works detailing the historical development of tenure is Professor Walter P. Metzger's, *Academic Tenure in America: A Historical Essay,* which appears as a long chapter in Faculty Tenure: A Report and Recommendations by the Commission on Academic Tenure in Higher Education (1973). In his work, Professor Metzger traces tenure "from the time it emerged in the high middle ages" to the present. The excerpt that follows is Professor Metzger's analysis of the development of the AAUP statement on tenure.

W. P. METZGER, ACADEMIC TENURE IN AMERICA:
A HISTORICAL ESSAY, in FACULTY TENURE: A
REPORT AND RECOMMENDATIONS BY THE COMMISSION
ON ACADEMIC TENURE IN HIGHER EDUCATION*
93, 148, 152-155 (1973)

To what precise institutional innovations did the AAUP commit itself? When one reviews the decretals of the association, one finds that it did not hold consistently to one position but adopted as many as four, more or less sequentially, as it gathered experience from its investigations, rode the tide of such events as depression and war, negotiated agreements with administrators, and changed the character of its leadership (lost some philosophers and gained more lawyers). Giving each of these positions a rough descriptive tag and placing them in chronological order, one might say that the 1915 General Report on Academic Freedom and Academic Tenure (the philosophical birth cry of the Association) adopted the model of the guild; that the 1925 Conference Statement (the first joint effort of the AAUP and the Association of American Colleges, an administrative organization) adopted the model of the expert counsel; that the 1940 and 1958 Statements (also interorganizational agreements) adopted the model of the Civil Service and the model of the criminal court. The last two schemes have taken over and now dominate academic thinking on this subject. . . .

The records show that it was the representatives of the AAC who insisted on unlimited probationary periods, the financial exigency exception, and the inclusion of that world war relic, "treason," among the grounds that would justify removal. But the representatives of the AAUP were not tough bargainers on these or other questions. Their mood of conservatism and conciliation reflected the changes that had occurred within a decade: the decline of progressive fervor, the extinction of syndicalist ideas, the fatigue that often follows a rousing organizational birth. Whatever else may have been the cause, it is clear that the effect of the 1925 agreement was to give the profession rather limp defenses against the economic havoc that would soon descend.

In 1940, the two associations, after several years of negotiation, agreed to a new Statement of Principles, one that was destined to become the most widely endorsed and most influential of all such formularies. This statement embodied two important rationales, neither of which had heretofore been prominent. One of these absorbed the emphasis on the routinization of job security that might have been picked up from Civil Service situations. For example, this statement was the first to use the term *probationary* to describe the pretenure stint, thus making it clear that it *was* a pretenure stint and not a collection point for a supply of cheap, submissive, and unhopeful labor. This statement was the first to dissociate tenure from rank and tie it exclusively to years of service; moreover, so that all need not start afresh in each new employment, it was the first to include in the reckoning all the years spent in the profession (though by written agreement only a three-year portion of

---

* W. P. Metzger, *Academic Tenure in America: A Historical Essay,* in Faculty Tenure: A Report and Recommendations by the Commission on Academic Tenure in Higher Education (San Francisco: Jossey-Bass, © 1973). Reprinted by permission.

outside service might be allowed to count). As a result, it became possible for the first time to advance the notion of *de facto* tenure—tenure that would accrue to the faculty member not by institutional say-so but by many turns of the working clock. Also featured in the 1940 Statement were several efforts to plug the holes left in the dikes of tenure by the 1925 agreement. Except in the case of financial exigency, all dismissals were to be for cause and all were to be judicially determined. Except for the statement that faculty hearings were to be provided if possible (the qualification was inserted to cover the very small institution, where colleagues might be too close to colleagues to wish to serve), everything in this document suggested that the faculty had to judge to make the action truly judicial. And—without ceremony—the frightful and frightening word *treason* was dropped.

Not everything in the 1940 Statement went to shoring up security. Considerable attention was paid to competing values—institutional flexibility, quality control. Thus, it reaffirmed the proposition that tenure alone conferred judicial citizenship and that probationers could be let go at the expiration of a term appointment, provided due notice had been sent. It dropped all reference to faculty review of such nonrenewals; it did not revive the notion of determinative faculty verdicts when issues of freedom were involved. It set the maximum period of probation at seven years, which was shorter than the AAUP founders had suggested but longer than the fledgling unions then proposed. Moreover, by setting up a purely temporal yardstick, it made the institution reach the in or out question without delay or equivocation, after the requisite interval had elapsed. Even so, this statement was of all the most security minded. It went further than any other in broadening tenure coverage, making it accessible to the still-youthful mass where once it had been reserved for the titled few. And it made tenure not just codable, but enforceable.

In the previous statements, very little had been said about how predismissal hearings should be conducted. As far as faculty hearings were concerned, this omission may have reflected self-romanticization: the AAUP founders in particular seemed to believe that academics were equipped by career-long training to deal with knotty human questions, that all that was needed to deliver justice was to ensure that they would have the right to judge. To some extent, too, this omission may have reflected the lack of legal talent at the drafting table, a lack that Ralph Himstead, the first lawyer to serve as general secretary of the association, would repair in the later round. In any event, the 1940 Statement was the first to make a serious effort to approximate what may be called the trial hearing, in contradistinction to the looser, less regulated, and more extemporaneous scholarly research type. It reverted to the demand for written charges; it added the right of the accused to an adviser who might act as counsel; it provided for a full and accessible stenographic record of the proceedings. Its sequel, the 1958 Statement on Procedural Standards in Faculty Dismissal Hearings, went much further in this direction, providing for preliminary hearings, prespecification of procedural standards, limited cross-examination, explicit findings on every charge, and a method of articulating the faculty's proximate judgment with the trustees' review and final vote. These efforts to judicialize the dismissal process by adding to it the techniques worked out in the courts may be said to have had rather mixed effects. Insofar as they have served to remind the faculty and the governing boards that they trade in reputations and must carefully test their wares, these efforts may have been on the whole quite salutary. But insofar as they suggest that academic trials and criminal trials are more than cousins and might be twins, insofar as they threaten to increase the due process pollution of the environment, they have the capacity to be pernicious. There is much to praise in a lawyerly approach, but there is much to deplore in the signs of creeping legalism.

NOTES

1. Other significant works dealing with the development of academic tenure are: Byse & Joughin, Tenure in American Higher Education (1959); Fuchs, *Academic Freedom—Its Basic Philosophy, Functions, and History*, 28 Law and Contemp. Prob. 431 (1963); Hofstadter & Metzger, The Development of Academic Freedom In The United States (1955); Jones, *The American Concept of Academic Freedom*, in Academic Freedom and Tenure (Joughin, ed., 1967); Note, *Academic Freedom and the Law*, 46 Yale L. J. 670 (1937); Note, *Developments in the Law—Academic Freedom*, 81 Harv. L. Rev. 1045 (1968); Shaw, Academic Tenure in American Higher Education (1971); B. Smith, The Tenure Debate (1973).

2. The 1940 AAUP statement on tenure is found in 27 AAUP Bull. 40 (1941). The genesis of the 1940 statement is the 1915 General Declaration of Principles, 1 AAUP Bull. 20 (1915). As noted in the Metzger article, subsequent development occurred with the adoption of the 1925 "Conference Statement" on academic freedom and tenure; this statement is reported in 27 AAUP Bull. 43 (1941). Additional AAUP statements supplementing the 1940 statement may be found in Statement on Procedural Standards In Faculty Dismissal Proceedings, 54 AAUP Bull. 439 (1968); Statement on Procedural Standards in the Renewal or Nonrenewal of Faculty Appointments, 57 AAUP Bull. 206 (1971); Terminations of Faculty Appointments Because of Financial Exigency, Discontinuance of a Program or Department, or Medical Reasons, 62 AAUP Bull. 17 (1976). Interpretations of the AAUP statements may be found in Academic Freedom and Tenure: 1940 Statements of Principles and Interpretive Comments, 60 AAUP Bull. 269 (1974). The last cited publication also lists eighty-eight professional associations that have endorsed the AAUP principles.

3. A good recent article on the AAUP tenure statements is Brown and Finkin, *The Usefulness of AAUP Policy Statements,* 64 AAUP Bull. 5 (March 1978).

B.   Academic Tenure in the United States—A Brief Look at the Current Picture

In his essay in Faculty Tenure, Professor Metzger observes that:

The story of judicial tenure after 1940 is the story of an idea that gains in favor, even in regions that were once inhospitable to it. With variations, the basic protocol came to be enacted in all but two categories of institution—those that were so dominated by administrations that faculty initiatives of any kind were objectionable and those that were so protected by genteel custom that faculty dismissals by any ceremony were unthinkable. To account for the success of this idea, one might cite a number of promoting agencies. Among the important abetting factors was the work of the AAUP—its case reports and public censures that named and shamed transgressors into correction; its control of the 1940 Statement, which it could apply with scriptural fidelity or interpret with Talmudic ingenuity. [Faculty Tenure, p. 155]

Although opposition to tenure has appeared to increase somewhat during the 1970s, largely in response to problems associated with financial exigency, tenure is nevertheless still very much a fact of life in the higher education community in the United States. A survey conducted in 1972 for the Commission on Academic Tenure In Higher Education revealed that tenure plans of one sort or another were in force in all public and private universities and all four-year public colleges. The survey also indicated that tenure plans were operative in 94% of the private colleges and in over two-thirds of the two-year colleges in the United States. In Faculty Tenure and Contract Systems—Current Practice (ACE Special Report 1972), W. T. Furniss estimated that 94% of all faculty members in colleges and universities in the United States were employed by institutions that conferred tenure.

While it is true that tenure is widespread, it is likewise true that there is no uniformity with respect to the application of tenure in American colleges and universities. The 1940 AAUP statement on tenure has, for years, been viewed as a model definition of tenure; however, the AAUP definition has never gained universal acceptance. This point was emphasized in Byse and Joughin, Tenure In American Higher Education 133 (1959), where the authors noted that:

> Tenure is embodied in a bewildering variety of policies, plans and practices; the range reveals extraordinary differences in generosity, explicitness, and intelligibility. Large or small, public or private, nonsectarian or religiously affiliated, there is no consensus concerning either the criteria or the procedures for acquiring and terminating tenure.

It is also important to recall that tenure is not an inviolate right. It is merely an arrangement (developed pursuant to contract, statute, rule or practice) that may be modified from time to time and may include numerous exceptions. In Tenure: A Summary, Explanation and "Defense," 57 AAUP Bull. 328 (1971), Professor William Van Alstyne aptly observed that:

> Tenure, accurately and unequivocally defined, lays no claim whatever to a guarantee of lifetime employment. Rather, tenure provides only that no person continuously retained as a full-time faculty member beyond a specified lengthy period of probationary service may thereafter be dismissed without adequate cause. Moreover, the particular standards of "adequate cause" to which the tenured faculty is accountable are themselves wholly within the prerogative of each university to determine through its own published rules, save only that those rules not be applied in a manner which violates the academic freedom or the ordinary

personal civil liberties of the individual. An institution may provide for dismissal for "adequate cause" arising from failure to
meet a specified norm of performance or productivity, as well as
from specified acts of affirmative misconduct. In short, there is not
now and never has been a claim that tenure insulates any faculty
member from a fair accounting of his professional responsibilities
within the institution which counts upon his service.

In a practical sense, tenure is translatable principally as a statement of formal assurance that thereafter the individual's professional security and academic freedom will not be placed in question
without the observance of full academic due process.

The pro and con debate over tenure has lasted almost since the inception of the concept and it will probably continue without end. Proponents
of tenure argue that it is an essential ingredient of academic freedom; it encourages faculty members to give long-term commitments to the institution;
it helps to attract high quality professional talent; it assures that professional criteria, and not personal favor, will be used to measure competence;
it forces institutions to weed out faculty persons who show no potential for
outstanding scholarship; and it offers some economic value to offset the
generally lower financial rewards in higher education.

Opponents of tenure contend that academic freedom can be assured
without tenure. They argue further that tenure limits the ability of an institution to recruit younger faculty, especially in times of financial exigency;
imposes rigid financial burdens on the institution; forces the institution to
carry nonproductive faculty persons; results in reduced quality in teaching
versus research; allows for excessive "political" activity by faculty members
under the guise of academic freedom; and encourages the perpetuation of
existing departments and programs without regard to current need.

Whatever else may be said about tenure, it must be recognized that it
has continued to exist in the United States in large measure because it is
still seen as a legitimate means of promoting and protecting independent
thought in teaching, research and scholarship. As noted by Professors Byse
and Joughin:

Academic freedom and tenure do not exist because of a peculiar
solicitude for the human beings who staff our academic institutions. They exist, instead in order that society may have the
benefit of honest judgment and independent criticism which
otherwise might be withheld because of fear of offending a dominant social group or transient social attitude.

NOTES

1. For a fuller discussion of the pro and con arguments over tenure, and for a discus-
sion of some alternatives to tenure, see pages 11-20 in Faculty Tenure: A Report and
Recommendations By The Commission on Academic Tenure in Higher Education (1973).
See also B. Smith, The Tenure Debate (1973).

2. For some relatively recent articles dealing with tenure systems in the United States, see R. Brown, *Tenure Rights in Contractual and Constitutional Context,* 6 Journ. of Law & Ed. 279 (July 1977); Matheson, *Judicial Enforcement of Academic Tenure: An Examination,* 50 Wash. L. Rev. 597 (1975); Furniss, Faculty Tenure and Contract Systems— Current Practice (American Council on Education Special Report 1972).

3. As noted in P. Hollander, Legal Handbook For Educators, 132 (Westview Press 1978), "generally, the concept of tenure or continuing appointment has not been deemed appropriate as a protection for higher education administrators, and has seldom been found." Thus, absent an employment contract which affords some job protection, a university or college administrator will typically serve at the pleasure of the institution.

II.   Acquisition of Tenure

A.   *Introduction*

COMMISSION ON ACADEMIC TENURE IN HIGHER EDUCATION, FACULTY TENURE*
2-4 (1973)

On every aspect of tenure, institutional policies and practices vary: definition of tenure; its legal basis; criteria for appointment, reappointment, and award of tenure; length of probationary period; categories of personnel eligible for tenure; relationship between tenure and rank; procedures for recommending appointments and awarding tenure; procedures for appeal from adverse decisions; procedures to be followed in dismissal cases; role of faculty, administration, students, and governing board in personnel actions; methods of evaluating teaching, scholarship, and public service; and retirement arrangements. In all these and many more, the range of variation among the 2600 institutions of higher education (and sometimes even within institutions—from division to division or even from department to department) is enormous.

Some institutions have formal tenure policies and procedures; many do not. Some institutions provide explicit statements concerning qualifications and criteria for reappointment and award of tenure; many, perhaps most, do not.

In some institutions personnel policies are communicated clearly and authoritatively to the faculty; in others there is widespread ignorance, confusion, or difference in interpretation, not only among the younger faculty but often among the senior faculty and administrators responsible for personnel actions.

In some institutions an effort is made to assist the young faculty member to develop as a teacher and scholar; in many, the young teacher is given virtually no assistance or information about his strengths or shortcomings until the time of final decision on reappointment.

A few institutions exercise close control over the proportion of tenured faculty; most, at least until recently, have not had policies governing the relative size of the tenured and nontenured groups.

In some institutions personnel actions originate with and generally follow the recommendations of departmental personnel committees or other faculty groups; in others the chairman or dean makes the effective recom-

---

*   Faculty Tenure: A Report and Recommendations by the Commission on Academic Tenure in Higher Education (San Francisco: Jossey-Bass, © 1973). Reprinted by permission.

mendation, with or without formal consultation with the faculty; in still others the president or other principal administrative officer plays the central role.

In some institutions methods have been established for obtaining student evaluations of faculty performance—sometimes formally, sometimes informally; sometimes in a uniform manner, sometimes with wide variation from department to department or even from one individual to another. In other institutions there is no serious attempt to reflect student opinion in personnel decisions.

As noted above, the 1940 AAUP statement on tenure is probably the most widely accepted plan for tenure acquisition in the United States. However, there are numerous variations on the basic AAUP theme. For example, the tenure acquisition plan at the University of Tennessee, cited in Soni v. Board of Trustees, 513 F.2d 347 (1975), reads as follows:

> After the expiration of a probationary period, teachers or investigators should have permanent or continuous tenure, and their services should be terminated only for adequate cause, except in the case of retirement for age, or under extraordinary circumstances because of bona fide financial necessities of the University. The precise terms and conditions of every appointment should be stated in writing and be in the possession of both institution and teacher before the appointment is consummated.
>
> Beginning with appointment to the rank of full-time Instructor or a higher rank, the probationary period should not exceed seven years, including within this period full-time service in all institutions of higher education; but subject to the proviso that when, after a term of probationary service of more than three years in one or more institutions, a teacher is called to this institution it may be agreed in writing that his new appointment is for a probationary period of not more than four years, even though thereby the person's total probationary period in the academic profession is extended beyond the normal maximum of seven years. Notice should be given at least one year prior to the expiration of the probationary period if the teacher is not to be continued in service after the expiration of that period. During the probationary period a teacher should have the freedom and responsibility that all other members of the faculty have. . . .
>
> 1. All initial appointments shall be without *tenure* unless the letter of appointment states otherwise. Ordinarily, tenure will be considered after completion of a probationary period of not more than three years for a person in the rank of Assistant Professor, and may be considered after one year for persons in the ranks of Associate Professor or Professor. (A full-time Instructor may be placed on tenure upon the recommendation of the department head and dean of the college and when approved in writing

by the Academic Vice Chancellor. Instructors usually serve a probationary period without tenure not to exceed seven years.)

2. Proposals to bestow tenure, either at the time of a first appointment or subsequently, shall be the responsibility of those
who initiate recommendations for academic promotions.

Generally, as with the Tennessee plan, a faculty member obtains tenure
after a probationary period and pursuant to some prescribed institutional
standards. A few states have statutes governing the award of tenure in public
colleges and universities. However, the more common situation in public
higher education is that the responsibility for employing faculty has been
delegated to an administrative body such as a Board of Regents. In private
educational institutions, the tenure granting body is usually a Board of
Trustees, Overseers, or the like.

Normally the grant of faculty tenure follows the recommendation of the
faculty and the positive affirmative action by the institution. The criteria
used to determine whether tenure should be granted to a particular faculty
candidate vary widely among institutions of higher education. A tenure
criteria statement used at the University of Michigan College of Literature,
Science and the Arts is a good sample of what may be required for a tenured appointment; the statement reads as follows:

Appointment or promotion to the assistant professorship in
the College carries no presumption of promotion to tenure.
Tenure is earned by excellent teaching, outstanding research and
writing, and substantial additional service, each of which must be
relevant to the goals and needs of the University, College, and the
Department. It is based upon the achievement of distinction in an
area of learning, and the prediction of continued eminence throughout the individual's professional career. Less than outstanding
performance in the three areas should not be construed as an adequate basis for promotion.

Some colleges and universities will weigh teaching more heavily than
research, or vice versa, in the tenure review process. Some schools may also
take into account budgetary considerations or academic program needs in
deciding whether to grant tenure.

NOTES

1. For examples of court review of tenure acquisition procedures, *see* Sheppard v.
West Virginia Bd. of Regents, 378 F.Supp. 4 (1974) (the grant of tenure requires positive and affirmative action by the Board of Regents); Cusumano v. Ratchford, 507 F.
2nd 980 (8th Cir. 1974) (faculty members who received notice during last probationary
year that they would be reappointed to a terminal one-year term and not rehired thereafter did not acquire tenure, de facto or otherwise, and thus had no constitutional right
to statement of reasons for nonreappointment or a hearing thereon).

2. For a review of tenure acquisition plans in the United States, *see* Byse and Joughin,
Tenure in American Higher Education: Plans, Practices and the Law (Ithaca, N.Y.:
Cornell University Press, 1959); Dressel, *A Review of the Tenure Policies of Thirty-One
Major Universities*, Educational Record, 1963, 44, 248-253; Shaw, Academic Tenure in
American Higher Education (Chicago: Adams, 1971); Brown, *Tenure Rights In Con-
tractual and Constitutional Context*, 6 J. of Law & Ed. 279 (July 1977).

B.   Tenure by Default

BRUNO v. DETROIT INSTITUTE OF TECHNOLOGY
Court of Appeals of Michigan
51 Mich.App. 593, 215 N.W.2d 745 (1974)

Valkenburg, Judge. * * *

The principle question involved in this appeal is whether or not the plaintiff had acquired tenure in his teaching position while employed by defendant. The answer to the question depends entirely upon the construction given to the language of paragraph III(1) of defendant's tenure policy as it existed in 1963, which provided:

"Any faculty member on full-time * * * contract * * * staff appointment * * * who, in the opinion of the President and the Academic Deans has acceptably performed his duties for a period of at least three consecutive years at the Institute, has been assigned the rank of Associate or Full Professor, and has been tendered his fourth or succeeding annual contract and has accepted same, shall be considered to hold tenure."

Defendant first argues that tenure is not automatically bestowed upon those persons who have fulfilled the conditions set forth in paragraph III(1). Defendant would have this Court construe the phrase "shall be considered to hold tenure" to mean that the question of an otherwise qualified person's tenure would be taken under consideration but that the person would not become a tenured professor until some affirmative action is taken on the part of defendant with respect to granting tenure. While granting that the verb "shall be considered" could, in some contexts, be construed to mean that the matter "shall be given thought and reflection", such a construction here seems strained. Used in this context, the phrase is more properly construed to mean shall be "deemed" or "adjudged". See 8A, Words and Phrases, p. 230. At best the meaning of the phrase is ambiguous, and therefore would be construed against the party who drafted it. Elby v. Livernois Engineering Co., 37 Mich.App. 252, 194 N.W.2d 429 (1971). Accordingly, we construe the phrase "shall be considered to hold tenure" to mean that all persons who have fulfilled the enumerated qualifications were deemed to be tenured professors without any further action on the part of defendant. . . .

The question thus becomes whether plaintiff was a qualified person within the meaning of paragraph III(1). . . .

One of the qualifications to obtain tenure is that the person "in the opinion of the President and the Academic Deans has acceptably performed his duties for a period of at least three consecutive years at the Institute". Defendant urges this Court to construe that language to mean that there must be some affirmative determination by the president and deans that plaintiff has indeed performed in an acceptable manner and that such a determination must be conveyed to plaintiff before he would be eligible to attain tenured status.

Clearly the language does not require that the president and deans formally pass upon whether plaintiff has acceptably performed his duties and certainly the language cannot be read so broadly as to require that a formal notice of such a determination be conveyed to plaintiff before he would gain tenure. The language used requires only that the president and deans be of the opinion that plaintiff has acceptably performed his duties for the requisite period. The word "acceptable" is defined as "barely satisfactory or adequate". Webster's Third New International Dictionary (1970 ed), p 11. "Acceptably performed his duties" would therefore mean that the duties were performed in a fashion that was at least satisfactory or adequate. It follows then that if the duties were not "acceptably performed" the quality of the person's performance would not reach the level considered to be barely satisfactory or adequate. Because the lack of any criticism by defendant with respect to plaintiff's work at any time prior to August 1966, coupled with defendant's yearly renewal of plaintiff's contract and appointment in 1964 as an associate professor, is inconsistent with any present assertion plaintiff had not "acceptably performed his duties", defendant will not now be heard to deny that it was of the opinion that plaintiff's duties had been acceptably discharged. The language being ambiguous as to how the opinion with respect to the acceptability of plaintiff's performance is to be expressed, we hold that defendant's action in continuing plaintiff's employment and in remaining silent as to any inadequacy is a sufficient overt expression that plaintiff's performance was deemed acceptable.

As to the assertion that to qualify for tenure plaintiff must have held the rank of associate or full professor for three consecutive years, we will only say that any reasonable reading of the language of paragraph III(1) will not support such a conclusion. Paragraph III(1) requires only that the person (1) have acceptably performed his duties for three consecutive years, (2) have obtained an associate or full professorship, and (3) have been presented with and accepted a fourth or succeeding annual contract. As of the date of the entry into the contract for 1965-1966 plaintiff had fulfilled each of these qualifications; therefore, plaintiff had tenure with defendant as of that date. Accordingly, the decision of the trial court is reversed. . . .

Damages for the years from the 1966-1967 academic year to the present should be easily ascertained upon proof by plaintiff of the average salary of similarly situated associate professors employed by defendant. . . .

It would further appear that plaintiff is entitled to future damages. . . .

The proper method of computing these future damages is: (1) On the basis of past experience, project the anticipated level of compensation for similarly situated associate professors at defendant institution for each of the years until the date at which plaintiff would have retired had he been allowed to continue his employment relationship at defendant institution; (2) On the basis of past experience, project the anticipated earnings of plaintiff premised upon good-faith attempts on plaintiff's part to secure employment in his chosen profession; (3) Subtract the anticipated earnings of plaintiff for each of the years from the anticipated salary he would have received at defendant institution in the corresponding year; (4) Reduce the difference for each year to its worth as of the date of the filing of the complaint; and (5) Take the sum of these properly mitigated and reduced figures.

NOTES

1. Normally, a probationary faculty member acquires tenure through satisfactory compliance with the prescribed institutional standards, and upon the recommendation of the faculty and the positive action of the institution's governing body. However, as seen in *Bruno,* and in Chung v. Park, 369 F.Supp. 959 (M.D.Pa. 1974), a faculty member may acquire tenure by default where the institution fails to give a timely notice of non-renewal prior to the expiration of the probationary period. Is it a good policy to have a tenure plan that specifically provides that retention of a faculty member beyond a stated probationary term confers tenure? How should this matter be handled?

2. Suppose that the tenure policy in *Bruno* had also provided:

> Tenure is not granted automatically but is the result of action by the Board of Regents upon the recommendation of the college.

Would the result have been different?

In Sheppard v. West Virginia Board of Regents, 378 F.Supp. 4 (1974), the court held that similar language in the Faculty Handbook required an affirmative act by the Board in order for the faculty member to acquire tenure. Similarly, the court in Cusumano v. Ratchford, 507 F.2d 980 (8th Cir. 1974) noted that:

> It cannot serve the public welfare or promote the best interests of either the university or its professional staff to have a body of teachers, whatever their number, the permanent tenures of whom rest upon administrative neglect or oversight as to notice of termination.

3. In LaTemple v. Wamsley, 549 F.2d 185 (10th Cir. 1977), a faculty member was awarded one year of damages when school officials failed to give timely notice of dismissal on a year-to-year contract.

C.   University and College Practices and Regulations: The Effect of Disclaimers

GREENE v. HOWARD UNIVERSITY
District of Columbia Circuit Court of Appeals
412 F.2d 1128 (1969)

McGOWAN, Circuit Judge:

This appeal is from the denial by the District Court of motions for a preliminary injunction. 271 F.Supp. 609 (1967). One group of appellants consists of four persons who were students at Howard University in the spring of 1967 when serious disturbances occurred on the campus. The second is made up of five faculty members holding non-tenured positions at that time. After making an investigation which purported to find both groups actively involved in the disorders, the University, without according them a hearing of any kind although one was requested, terminated the connection of both student and faculty appellants with the school as of the close of the academic year on June 30. . . .

III

The teacher appellants had not achieved a tenure status and thus, in the familiar academic tradition, the renewal of their appointments was at the University's pleasure. They do not now challenge the general applicability of this principle. Instead, they assert that the University failed in its obligation, incident to their contracts, to give the appropriate advance notice of non-renewal. They point out that, far from having given such notice, the University explicitly refrained from doing so under circumstances which warranted appellants in entertaining and acting upon the clear expectations that their reappointments would be forthcoming. In these conditions, say appellants, irrespective of the generally unqualified nature of the University's power to determine whether non-tenure teachers shall continue beyond their appointed terms, the University was required, if it gave a last-minute notice of non-renewal because of alleged campus misconduct, to allow appellants to be heard on those charges before making them the occasion of non-renewal.

It is helpful in this regard to examine the relevant sections of the Faculty Handbook, a manual which governs the relationship between faculty members and the University. Section VIII states the normal University practice with respect to dismissals:

A. The Board of Trustees reserves the right of dismissal, regardless of tenure, in cases of moral delinquency, or other personal conduct incompatible with the welfare of the University. In such cases, the President of the University reserves the right of immediate suspension, regardless of tenure. The person concerned, upon written request, shall be given a hearing before a committee of the Board of Trustees, prior to the meeting of the Board of Trustees at which final action on the case is taken under procedures to be established by the Board of Trustees.

B. The Board of Trustees reserves the right of dismissal, regardless of tenure, for professional conduct incompatible with the best interests of the University. The person will be given reasonable notice and an opportunity to be heard by a committee of his peers with the right to a hearing by a committee of the Board of Trustees, prior to the meeting of the Board of Trustees at which final action on the case is taken under procedures to be established by the Board of Trustees.

Section IX states its position as to notice of Non-reappointment and Reappointment:

Notice of Non-reappointment and Reappointment: It will be the practice of the University, without contractual obligation to do so, to give written notice at the following times to officers of instruction whose services are no longer required: A) Deans will give notice each year to those whose terms expire and whom they do not propose to recommend for reappointment, not later than December 15 of that year; B) The Board of Trustees will give notice to those teachers whose terms expire and whose services are no longer required, directly following its meeting in January of each year.

EXCEPTIONS: An exception to this practice will obtain in the case of teachers on one-year appointments to whom the Board of Trustees will give notice immediately following its meeting in April; the Dean will give notice to such persons not later than March 15. Teachers not to be continued as regular appointees at the conclusion of seven years of service will be notified one year prior to the expiration of the seventh year.

A member of the faculty who wishes to resign from an appointment at the end of a given year is expected to notify his dean or the proper administrative official in writing not later than April 15th of that year."

It is clear from a close examination of these sections, buttressed by affidavits and depositions admitted in the District Court, that the usual practice of the University was to inform non-tenured faculty members by January or April, depending on the length of their appointments, whether they would be reappointed for the next school year.[4] This gave them the opportunity to seek employment elsewhere in the event they were not rehired. And it is significant to note in Section IX a corresponding obligation of the faculty member to inform the University if he intends not to return the next year, a provision presumably added to the Handbook in order to insure that the University would not be obligated to search for a replacement at a time after the market has become foreshortened.[5]

It is instructive against this background to look at those facts which are undisputed in the case of Dr. Andress Taylor, a teacher appellant whose situation is not untypical of that of the other such appellants. On March 15, 1967, Dr. Taylor's name was among those recommended by his Dean to be continued as an Assistant Professor of English for a term of two years to run from July 1, 1967 to June 30, 1969. On or about April 1, 1967, Dr. Taylor requested from his department head a leave of absence for the next academic year in order that he might take a position with the Southern Teaching Program. The chairman, however, ruled that Dr. Taylor's services were required at Howard in that period; and Dr. Taylor, in reliance upon this opinion, rejected the offer.

On May 5, 1967, Dr. Taylor received a "good" rating from his department chairman. On May 22, 1967, the chairman assigned him a course for the fall semester and requested that he produce a reading list. On June 2, 1967, the Director of the Summer School wrote to Dr. Taylor that he had

---

[4.] This usual practice, of course, can be raised to the level of a contractual obligation. *See* note 3, *supra.*

[5.] Appellants' reliance upon the University's intention to reemploy them was obvious. This provision buttresses that reliance by imposing an obligation on faculty members upon which the University might rely.

been recommended for an appointment to the staff of the 1967 summer session at Howard.

However, on June 20, 1967 Dr. Taylor received a letter, dated June 19, 1967, but apparently postmarked June 20, 1967, from the Dean of his school informing him that, after the automatic termination of his contract on June 30, 1967, he was not to be "reappointed by the University."

It must be clear that, for all practical intents and purposes, Dr. Taylor had been rehired to teach at Howard for a further period. The record here indicates that the University abruptly changed its mind about this reappointment because its unilateral investigation of the campus disturbances implicated Dr. Taylor. But the record also discloses that Dr. Taylor received no opportunity to be heard on the existence or extent of his involvement in the turmoil, either before or after the non-reappointment letter was sent.

It should be pointed out, moreover, that Dr. Taylor and his fellow appellants were relying not only on personal assurances from University officials and on their recognition of the common practice of the University, but also on the written statements of University policy contained in the Faculty Handbook under whose terms they were employed. [7] The Handbook makes clear, in writing, what the appellants knew to be true in practice: a faculty member, if not finally informed by April 15 (with preliminary notice by March 15) that his contract was not to be renewed, had legitimate reason to believe that he could rely on returning to Howard the following semester.

In the District Court, as here, the University does not deny the force of its regulations and practices in respect of appearing to elevate timely notice of non-reappointment to a contractual status. It argues only that what it gave with one hand it took away simultaneously with the other. It takes its stand, as did the District Court, upon the inclusion in Section IX of the Handbook of the words "without contractual obligation to do so" in the affirmative statement of its purpose to give such notice by certain fixed dates. This qualifying clause, so it is said, relieves the University of any and all obligations of any kind with respect to the observance of its regulations, and vests in the University an unfettered discretion to deny reappointment at any time up to midnight of June 30 whether or not earlier notice has been given.

Thus, as noted above, when notice of non-reappointment is withheld beyond the required date, we think some qualifications come into being— qualifications, moreover, which are not to be automatically considered as negated by the disclaimer invoked here, nor which, indeed, are necessarily at odds with it as a matter of rational interpretation of the bargain the

---

[7.] In this regard, the court may take judicial notice of the fact that, in its Handbook, the University purports to accept as guiding principles the policy of the American Association of University Professors in matters of academic tenure. . . .

parties may be taken to have struck.[10] Contracts are written, and are to be read, by reference to the norms of conduct and expectations founded upon them. This is especially true of contracts in and among a community of scholars, which is what a university is. The readings of the market place are not invariably apt in this non-commercial context.

The employment contracts of appellants here comprehend as essential parts of themselves the hiring policies and practices of the University as embodied in its employment regulations and customs. The very phrase relied upon by the District Court is in a Faculty Handbook which is replete with other provisions in conflict with the spirit of the use of that phrase now sought to be made. Those provisions seem to us to contemplate a hearing before separating from the academic community for alleged misconduct one who, although a non-tenured employee, has acquired a different dimension of relationship because of the expectations inherent in the University's failure to give notice as contemplated by its own regulations.

That new relationship does not at all mean that the University must invariably reappoint whenever it fails to give notice at the specified time. Of course there may be happenings after that time which bear upon the fitness of a particular person to continue as a member of an academic community. But, in the circumstances which are undisputedly shown by this record, and as we construe the contractual undertakings between the University and these appellants, we hold that appellants should have been afforded an opportunity to give their version of the events which led to their non-reappointment because of misconduct. . . .

We think the record as it stands adequately supports our conclusion that the University acted in contravention of its contractual undertakings *vis-a-vis* the teacher appellants, and we see no necessity for further litigation of this issue in the District Court. What remains is the question of what pecuniary damage, if any, the individual teacher appellants have suffered by reason of the University's failure to effect nonreappointment in a manner compatible with its contractual obligations. The legal injury done by that failure could not now be repaired by affording appellants the hearing which they sought and were denied at the time their reappointments were withheld. The breach of contract resides in the failure to give the hearing then, and does not turn upon what the outcome of such a hearing might be now.

Although the denial of injunctive relief presently appealed from is left undisturbed, we remand the case to the District Court for the purpose of permitting any of the faculty appellants to pursue, if he so chooses, a claim for the monetary damage, if any, attributable to the non-reappointment. The District Court will permit such amendment of the complaints as may be sought to this end, and it will otherwise proceed further in a manner consistent herewith.

[10.] The disclaimer may well have been included in the manual out of an abundance of caution, only for the purpose of guaranteeing that the other sections of the manual could be applied in the case of a non-tenured faculty member who had not received notice of termination before April 15, but as to whom the University had newly-discovered cause not to reappoint in the period between April 15 and the beginning of the next academic year.

NOTES

1. Is the proposed remedy in *Greene* adequate to address the wrong suffered by the plaintiffs? Should the court have compelled the university to reinstate the plaintiffs? Suppose the plaintiffs had been given a "hearing" before dismissal; would the court then review the judgment of the university to determine whether a legitimate basis for dismissal existed to support plaintiffs' nonrenewal?

2. As in *Greene*, the courts have not hesitated to find that documents such as an institution's constitution, charter, bylaws, regulations or Faculty Handbook have been either expressly or impliedly incorporated into the employment agreement. *See, e.g.,* Collins v. Parsons College, 203 N.W. 2d 594 (Ia. 1973); Adamian v. Jacobsen, 523 F. 2d 929 (9th Cir. 1975); Browzin v. Catholic Univ. of America, 527 F.2d 843 (D.C. Cir. 1975); Rehor v. Case Western Reserve, 43 Ohio 2d 224, 331 N.E. 2d 416 (1975); and Hillis v. Meister, 82 N.M. 474, 483 P.2d 1314 (1971).

3. Following the judgment of the Supreme Court in Perry v. Sindermann, 408 U.S. 593 (1972), much has been made of *"de facto* tenure" as a means of tenure acquisition. In *Perry,* the Court noted that:

A teacher. . .who has held his position for a number of years, might be able to show from the circumstances of his service—and from other relevant facts—that he has a legitimate claim of entitlement to job tenure. . . . [T] here may be an unwritten "common law" in a particular university that certain employees shall have the equivalent of tenure.

Perry involved a claim for "procedural due process" and the Court ruled that if a person was found to have *de facto* tenure this would be enough to ensure procedural due process before dismissal. However, it is not at all clear that *de facto* tenure (as distinguished from "tenure by default") exists as a viable concept in cases other than those involving claims for procedural due process. In other words, a faculty member may be found to have *de facto* tenure which will ensure a hearing before dismissal but this same *de facto* tenure may not be enough to guarantee job entitlement. *See, e.g.,* Bignall v. North Idaho College, 538 F.2d 243 (9th Cir. 1976) and Soni v. Bd. of Trustees, Univ. of Tennessee, 376 F.Supp. 289 (E.D. Tenn. 1974), *aff'd,* 513 F.2d 347 (6th Cir. 1975). In Willins v. Univ. of Massachusetts, 570 F.2d 403 (1st Cir. 1978), the court held that the evidence sustained a determination that the university had no *de facto* tenure system so that the discharge of plaintiff did not violate such a system; and that neither the denial itself nor the fact that the denial was based upon a lack of scholarly publications of the teacher in eleven years since she received her master's degree infringed any liberty interest of the teacher.

In University of Texas v. Assaf, 46 U.S.L.W. 3659 (1978), the District Court had ruled that, where university rules provided that nontenured faculty members will be notified by a certain date that they will or will not be reappointed and where the university failed to comply with that rule of notification, the notice failure gave rise to a justified expectation of reappointment, and a property right, entitling the faculty member to a due process hearing prior to termination. The Court of Appeals judgment reversing the District Court was vacated by the Supreme Court.

The matter of *de facto* tenure will be covered further in section V., *infra.*

4. Absent some clear showing of proscribed discrimination or violation of constitutional right, the courts have generally been reluctant to overturn faculty judgments on tenure. *See* generally Green v. Bd. of Regents of Texas Tech. Univ., 335 F.Supp. 249 (N.D. Tex. 1971), *aff'd,* 474 F.2d 594 (5th Cir. 1973); Faro v. New York Univ., 502 F.2d 1229 (2d Cir. 1974); Jones v. Hopper, 410 F.2d 1323 (10th Cir. 1969); and Johnson v. Univ. of Pittsburgh, 435 F.Supp. 1328 (W.D. Pa. 1977). State courts have been equally reluctant to review decisions not to grant tenure. Generally, state court inquiries have been limited to whether the institution has complied with the terms of the parties' contract and applicable regulations in arriving at the decision not to renew the faculty member. See Raney v. Bd. of Trustees, Coalinga Jr. Col. Dist., 239 Cal. App. 256, 48 Cal.

Rptr. 555 (Dist. Ct. App. 1966); Bd. of Trustees v. Sherman, 373 A.2d 626 (Md. Ct. App. 1977); and Rhine v. Int'l Y.M.C.A. College, 339 Mass. 610, 162 N.E. 2d 56 (1959). In New York Inst. of Technology v. State Division of Human Rights, 353 N.E. 2d 598 (N.Y. Ct. of Appeals 1976), the highest court in New York ruled that the State Division of Human Rights could confer tenure as a remedy for a victim of unlawful employment discrimination, but "only under the gravest of circumstances, where all other conceivable remedies have proved ineffective." The court held that tenure could not be imposed in a case where the plaintiff had been denied a fair opportunity to apply for tenure.

III. Enforcement of Tenure

A.   General Principles

WORZELLA v. BOARD OF REGENTS
Supreme Court of South Dakota
93 N.W. 2d 411 (1958)

HANSON, Judge.

The petitioner, Dr. W. W. Worzella, seeks a writ of mandamus compelling the State Board of Regents to reinstate him as professor of agronomy or as head of the agronomy department at South Dakota State College. The circuit court refused relief and he appeals.

Dr. Worzella was first employed as a professor of agronomy at State College on October 1, 1943. Thereafter he served continuously on that faculty until discharged by the Board of Regents on January 11, 1958. He was dismissed after an extensive investigation into the personnel and administrative affairs of State College by the Board. After the investigation the Board prepared a written report. With reference to Dr. Worzella the Board found he "* * * wittingly or unwittingly, permitted himself and his name to become involved in serious personal disputes and activities in the many years above referred to, and has * * * been guilty of insubordination; that by virtue of the controversial character he has become, it would not be to the best interests of South Dakota State College for him to be retained." The Board concluded "the retention of Dr. W. W. Worzella as head of the Department of Agronomy is incompatible to the best interest and welfare of State College, its students, and the State of South Dakota as a whole, and that he should be summarily dismissed and relieved from all further duties under his current contract; his compensation, however, to continue as therein provided during the remainder of this fiscal year." His summary dismissal followed.

Dr. Worzella contends he has permanent tenure under a tenure policy approved by the Board of Regents and could be dismissed only in compliance with its substantive and procedural provisions. It is conceded that no complaint was filed, notice given, or hearing held pursuant thereto. However, the Board maintains the tenure policy did not, and could not, abrogate its constitutional and statutory power to dismiss all officers, instructors, and employees under its control. . . .

The exact meaning and intent of this so-called tenure policy eludes us. Its vaporous objectives, purposes, and procedures are lost in a fog of nebulous verbiage. We gather from it, in general, that a faculty member who is retained on the staff at State College for over three years gains permanent tenure. He cannot thereafter be divested of tenure unless a complaint against him is filed by the president of the college. He is then entitled to have notice of hearing, and a hearing before a Tenure Committee consisting of seven faculty members. It further provides that "since the final decision must be made by the President" it is desirable that he sit with the Tenure Committee during the formal hearing as an auditor. At the conclusion of the hearing the committee makes its recommendations to the president. The president must then decide whether to recommend the dismissal of the accused faculty member to the Board of Regents. The faculty member whose dismissal is recommended may appeal for a hearing before the Board. The concluding paragraph states that the tenure policy is based "upon good faith between the college administration and the individual faculty member".

The policy statement is silent as to the Board of Regents' authority. By inference we may assume the Board would have power to discharge a faculty member having tenure when recommended by the Tenure Committee and President. Otherwise the Board would have no authority to act. Apparently the Board could not discharge or remove a faculty member with tenure for any reason if the President failed or refused to file a complaint, or if the Tenure Committee and President failed or refused to recommend dismissal. We believe this to be an unlawful abdication of the Board's exclusive prerogative and power.

The Board of Regents is a constitutionally created administrative body charged with the control of all institutions of higher learning "under such rules and restrictions as the legislature shall provide". § 3, art. XIV. . . .

[statutory provisions omitted]

The above statutory provisions merely confirm and clarify the Board of Regents' constitutional power to employ and dismiss all officers, instructors, and employees at all institutions under its control. These provisions become a part of every contract of employment entered into by the Board. Gillan v. Board of Regents of Normal Schools, 88 Wis. 7, 58 N.W. 1042, 24 L.R.A. 336. It cannot be restricted, surrendered, or delegated away. Our constitution prescribes that our state university and colleges "shall be under the control" of the Board of Regents. Without the right to employ, and the power to discharge, its employees the Board loses its constitutional right of control. The same result was reached in a recent comparable case in North Dakota involving similar constitutional and statutory provisions. See Posin v. State Board of Higher Education, N.D., 86 N.W.2d 31.

Under SDC 15.0714 the Board of Regents "may delegate provisionally to the president, dean, principal, or faculty of any school under its control, so much of the authority conferred by this section as in its judgment seems proper * * *." This is a limited power. It does not empower the Board to delegate away all of its powers or its constitutional duty of control. Under its provisions the Board may only delegate the limited authority conferred on it by the same section. . . .

In South Dakota, under the present tenure policy at State College, the Board of Regents cannot remove a faculty member for any reason or cause on its own volition. Without the prior action and approval of the President and Tenure Committee the Board is powerless to act. The President and Tenure Committee do not serve in an advisory capacity only. Their action and approval are conditions precedent to any dismissal of college personnel by the Board. Such delegation of authority to subordinates is an unlawful encroachment upon the Board of Regents' constitutional and statutory power of control over such college. A writ of mandamus was, therefore, properly denied by the trial court.

Affirmed.

All the Judges concur.

NOTES

1. A judgment similar to the one rendered in *Worzella* was issued in Posin v. State Board of Higher Education, 86 N.W. 2d 31 (N.D. 1957). However, in *Posin*, the terminated teacher at least received the appropriate hearing and other rights accorded him by the tenure plan.

2. Is the court in *Worzella* accurate when it states that "the merits of academic tenure are not involved" in this decision? How does the constitutional provision, which places the state university and the colleges under the control of the Board of Regents, prevent the Board from delegating some of its power to the president and the faculty? If in fact control of the college was in the Board, could it not act through its chief executive officer, the president? If the tenure plan required the president to submit his recommendations to the Board for its action, rather than allowing for executive discretion, could *Worzella* be decided as it was? Would Dr. Worzella have fared better if he proceeded on a breach of contract theory? For a critical comment on these and other questions, see Byse, *Academic Freedom, Tenure, and the Law: A Comment On Worzella v. Board of Regents*, 73 Harv. L. Rev. 304 (1959).

3. Tenure plans have met a similar fate at institutions which were authorized to terminate employees "at will." To some courts, such provisions "deprived the governing board of power to make a contract with a teacher for any definite term. . .and that attempts by it to do so were wholly nugatory in a legal sense." Cobb v. Howard Univ., 106 F.2d 860, 864 (D.C. Cir. 1939). *See also,* State ex rel. Hunsicker v. Board of Regents, 209 Wis. 83, 244 N.W. 618 (1932). Other courts have achieved a more moderate result by reasoning that the authority to terminate "at will" did not deprive the Board of the power to make reasonable contracts. *See e.g.,* Board of Regents v. Mudge, 21 Kan. 233 (1878). *See also* Byse & Joughin, Tenure In American Education 79-82 (1959).

4. A wide range of contract defenses have been asserted to prevent enforcement of tenure agreements. For example *see* State ex rel. Keeney v. Ayers, 108 Mont. 547, 92 P.2d 306 (1939) (lack of mutuality); Collins v. Parsons, 203 N.W. 2d 594 (Ia. 1973) (insufficient consideration and waiver); and Brookfield v. Drury, 139 Mo. 399, 123 S.W. 86 (1909) (statute of frauds). As in *Greene,* some institutions have attempted to avoid contractual liability through the use of disclaimers. See Hillis v. Meister, 82 N.M. 474, 483 P.2d 1314 (1971). However, there has been little recent success with any of these efforts. See generally, Brown, *Tenure Rights in Contractual and Constitutional Context,* 6 J. of L. and Educ. 279, 288-94 (1977) and Byse & Joughin, Tenure in American Education 82-94 (1959).

B.   *Modifications to Existing Tenure Plans*

REHOR v. CASE WESTERN RESERVE UNIV.
Supreme Court of Ohio
331 N.E. 2d 416 (1975)

Plaintiff, Charles F. Rehor, was a tenured professor of English at Case Western Reserve University in Cleveland, which institution of higher learning is the defendant in this lawsuit.

Plaintiff commenced employment at Cleveland College in 1929, teaching primarily in the fields of English and Journalism. Cleveland College became a part of Western Reserve University in 1942. From 1942 through June 30, 1967, plaintiff was employed under contract as a professor at Western Reserve University. Plaintiff was granted tenure by Western Reserve University prior to 1948. At all times during which plaintiff was a faculty member there the retirement age was 70 years.

In July 1967, a federation of Case Institute of Technology and Western Reserve University took place and was organized under the laws of Ohio as a corporation not for profit, known as Case Western Reserve University. Plaintiff continued under contract as a professor at defendant university from July 1, 1967, to his retirement on June 30, 1973.

Defendant assumed the employment contracts between former Western Reserve University and its faculty members, including plaintiff. After the federation, defendant began a review of the separate policies, rules and regulations of the two former institutions and the adoption of uniform policies, rules and regulations for defendant, its faculty, students and administration.

On April 16, 1969, defendant's Board of Trustees, duly acting through its executive committee, adopted a resolution amending defendant's faculty retirement policy, specifically as outlined and recommended by the *as hoc* University Committee on Faculty Retirement in a memorandum to President Robert W. Morse, dated January 15, 1968.

The amended retirement policy provided that retirement of all faculty members was to be at age 65, subject to the following conditions: (a) Contributions by the university to its retirement pension program would cease at age 65; (b) upon reaching the designated age of 65, the faculty member would have the option of continued employment either full time or part time to age 68; (c) between the ages of 68 and 70 the faculty member could petition to be reappointed on a part-time or full-time basis, and, upon recommendation of the appropriate university committees, could be reappointed for a one-year or two-year period; and (d) reappointments on an annual basis only could be continued beyond age 70, these to be initiated only by the university committees.

This amended retirement policy was communicated to all faculty members, including the plaintiff, in writing on April 6, 1970. Plaintiff was specifically advised in writing by defendant on June 2, 1970, that the date of his retirement would be June 30, 1973. . . .

Plaintiff was 68 years of age on September 5, 1972, and was retired as of June 30, 1973, in accordance with defendant's amended retirement policy. Pursuant to the terms of the amended retirement policy, plaintiff petitioned the appropriate faculty committee for a recommendation that he be reappointed beyond age 68. After committee consideration, no action was taken on that petition. Plaintiff also petitioned the president of defendant university by letter, dated July 19, 1971, for reappointment beyond age 68; this request was refused by the president in writing on September 22, 1971.

On April 27, 1973, plaintiff filed a complaint in the Court of Common Pleas of Cuyahoga County, praying for a judgment, declaring that he is entitled to remain in the employ of defendant until the age of 70, unless discharged for cause, for injunctive relief, for compensatory damages in the amount of $50,000, and for exemplary damages in the amount of $100,000, together with reasonable attorney fees. . . . The trial court found in favor of defendant and entered judgment for the university and against plaintiff. The trial court made separate findings of fact and conclusions of law at plaintiff's request.

Upon appeal, the Court of Appeals reversed the judgment of the Court of Common Pleas, entered final judgment for plaintiff, and remanded the cause to the Court of Common Pleas for further proceedings on the computation of damages.

J. J. P. CORRIGAN, Justice.

Fundamentally, this is an employment contract case. It is concerned with the period of employee's term of employment.

However, the lawsuit more importantly involves an interpretation of "tenure," as that term is used in employment contracts of professors with colleges and universities. But, with more particularity, the cause also involves the retirement of a tenured professor because of age. . . .

Defendant contends that, where a university faculty member is employed, using standard annual reappointment forms which do not set forth in full the terms and conditions of employment, the university's employment policies, rules and regulations become part of the employment contract between the university and the faculty member.

Plaintiff admits in his brief that; "There has been universal acceptance of this proposition by both the parties and the courts below insofar as it holds that the full contract between the plaintiff and defendant contains the various rules and regulations and policies of the university* * *." Plaintiff, later in his brief, states: "As far as defendant's Proposition of Law No. 1 is concerned, the plaintiff simply restates that he agrees with it as long as it is deemed to include the possibility of such a contract conferring vested rights to future benefits upon the parties to it."

The latter qualification of plaintiff brings to the front and center paragraph one of the syllabus of the Court of Appeals decision, which reads as follows:

"An award of academic tenure vests a university faculty member with the right to continued reappointment to the faculty unless sufficient cause is shown for his termination."

We do not agree with that conclusion of the Court of Appeals.

Academic tenure does not, in the manner expressed, vest a faculty member with the right to continued reappointment to the faculty, and we so hold. A vested right is a right fixed, settled, absolute, and not contingent upon anything. Such is not the case here.

The only signed documents evidencing the employment agreement between Professor Rehor and Case Western Reserve University are the annual reappointment forms, which appear as exhibits in the record. There are also 12 annual reappointment contracts in the record between Professor Rehor and former Western Reserve University. The annual reappointment forms do not state the components of tenure or of retirement. Likewise, they do not state faculty fringe benefits, perquisites of faculty appointment, or faculty standards. All of these matters are established by various policies, rules and regulations adopted by defendant and promulgated to its faculty.

It is agreed by plaintiff and defendant that a university's policies, rules and regulations relating to faculty members become a part of the employment contract as a matter of law. . . .

Accordingly, we agree with defendant's first proposition of law and hold that the retirement policy of defendant established in its policies, rules and regulations—which includes the amended retirement policy adopted April 16, 1969—was part of the annual employment agreements between plaintiff and defendant after July 1, 1967.

II.

Defendant urges, as its second proposition of law, that a university's grant of tenure to a faculty member does not preclude the university from thereafter changing the retirement age for all faculty members including the tenured faculty member, provided the change is reasonable and uniformly applicable.

Here, it is stipulated that Professor Rehor had academic tenure. The purpose of academic tenure, as used in the academic community, is the preservation of academic freedom and the correlative protection of economic security for teachers. It insures that a professor will not lose his job for exercising academic freedom, namely, his rights to teach, to think and to speak in accordance with his conscience in the traditions of the academic community. In the establishment of tenure, the former Western Reserve University provided, in its 1964 Faculty Handbook:

"A faculty member shall have academic freedom and tenure in accordance with the current statement of principles as approved jointly by the American Association of University Professors and the Association of American Colleges."

In a supplemental statement to its 1940 Statement of Principles on Academic Freedom and Tenure, the American Association of University Professors, in 1950, issued its "Statement of Principles on Academic Retirement and Insurance Plans," which was reaffirmed in 1969. Paragraph 9 of that statement reads:

"When a new retirement policy or annuity plan is initiated or an old one changed, reasonable transition provisions, either by special financial arrangements or by the gradual inauguration of the new plan, should be made for those who would otherwise be adversely affected."

And, paragraph 1d. of that same statement recommends that the retirement policy of a university should:

"Be reviewed periodically by faculty and administration of the institution, with appropriate recommendations to the institution's governing board, to assure that the plans continue to meet the needs, resources, and objectives of the institution and the faculty."

So, paragraph 9 of the policy statement on retirement demonstrates the understanding of the academic community that the retirement policy of a university can be changed, and paragraph 1d. points out that a retirement policy should be changed if needed. . . .

We approve defendant's proposition of law No. 2, and reject the conclusion of law reached by the Court of Appeals, as stated in paragraph three of its syllabus, that:

"Where a faculty member is awarded tenure by a university and the faculty bylaws of the university at that time state that the mandatory retirement age for faculty is 70 years, such provision in the faculty bylaws becomes a binding term of the faculty member's employment contract with the university, the faculty member has a vested right to be reappointed to the faculty to age 70, and the university cannot thereafter lower the faculty member's mandatory retirement age without abridging the employment contract."

III.

Defendant, in his proposition of law No. 3, asserts that a university's bylaw, stating that the board of trustees shall from time to time adopt such rules and regulations governing the appointment and tenure of the members of the faculty as the board of trustees deems necessary, includes a reservation of the right to change the retirement age of the faculty.

The right of defendant to change its retirement policy appears in Article VI of the bylaws of Western Reserve University's Board of Trustees, which provides:

"The Board of Trustees shall from time to time adopt such rules and regulations governing the appointment and tenure of members of the several faculties as said board deems necessary."

The Court of Appeals allowed that Article VI was a reservation of right, but considered it as a power over appointment and tenure generally and viewed the statement of retirement policy set forth in the 1964 Faculty Handbook as an express provision. Then, citing *Freeland v. Freeland* (C.A. 6, 1940), 110 F.2d 966, the Court of Appeals held that the express provision of the contract controlled the general provision so that defendant's reserved right in Article VI did not apply to the retirement policy set out in the 1964 Faculty Handbook.

As we view these two clauses, we are of the opinion that each is an express clause and the reserved right to change applies to all aspects of tenure, including retirement.

Either the retirement policy set forth in Section IV of the university's Statement of Principles for Appointment, Tenure and Separation for the Guidance of Faculties is part of and protected by tenure, or it is not; and, if the retirement policy is a part of tenure, and we hold that it is, then the reserved right to change rules of tenure includes the right to change the retirement policy.

We accept and approve defendant's third proposition of law.

IV.

The fourth proposition of law advanced by defendant is to the effect that an employment contract between a university and a tenured faculty member may be amended by the parties in writing when supported by adequate consideration.

Defendant amended its retirement policy in 1969. This changed plaintiff's retirement age from 70 to 68 years with a right in plaintiff to be appointed beyond age 68 upon recommendation of a faculty committee. On July 6, 1970, after having been advised of the amended retirement policy and its specific application to him, plaintiff signed his 1970-1971 annual reappointment form which gave him a $500 salary increase. On May 6, 1971, plaintiff signed his 1971-1972 reappointment form, which also specified a $500 salary increase. Then, on May 17, 1972, plaintiff executed a 1972-1973 reappointment form which provided that it was a "[t]erminal appointment, with retirement on June 30, 1973," and it carried another $500 salary increase.

Thus, there was demonstrated adequate consideration for the amendment of the employment contract by the change in the retirement policy of the university.

CONCLUSION.

The trial court correctly concluded that the contract between the parties permitted defendant to change its retirement policy; further, that plaintiff had consented to that change and that there was not a breach of contract.

For the reasons stated above, the judgment of the Court of Appeals is reversed, and the judgment of the Court of Common Pleas is reinstated.

Judgment reversed.

*   *   *

CELEBREZZE, Justice (dissenting).

While I can accept many of the general statements of the majority as correct statements of legal theory, when that theory is brought into contact with the specific facts of *this* case, I am unable to concur in the result. . . .

I find no evidence in the record that Professor Rehor accepted the modification in the term of his employment in return for the three $500 increments. Of course, the mere fact that the University offered the salary increments does not show that they were offered explicitly for that reason. Without an agreement supported by sufficient consideration there can be no effective modification. This is not to say that the University could not change the retirement age; only that those adversely affected must be compensated. Here there is no showing of an agreement, and the adequacy of the consideration is certainly in doubt. . . .

NOTES

1. Would the judgment of the court in *Rehor* permit the Board of Trustees to change the retirement age to 39? According to the majority's view, the reserved right to change applied to all aspects of tenure. Would that permit the abolition of tenure?

2. Committee A of the AAUP has proposed that where the mandatory retirement age is reduced, "the higher age should still apply in the case of faculty members who are within twenty years of that age at the time of the change." 61 AAUP Bull. 16 (1975).

3. *See* also, M. Finkin, *Contract, Tenure and Retirement: A Comment on Rehor v. Case Western Reserve University,* 4 Human Rights 343 (1975).

DRANS v. PROVIDENCE COLLEGE

Supreme Court of Rhode Island
383 A.2d 1033 (1978)

KELLEHER, Justice.

This is a declaratory judgment action in which the plaintiff, a former professor at Providence College, asked the Superior Court to rule that he was not subject to the mandatory retirement age of 65 established by the college in 1969 because he had secured academic tenure prior to that time. After a hearing, the trial justice ruled that the plaintiff was subject to the college's mandatory retirement policy, and judgment to this effect was entered in the Superior Court. . . .

In May of 1955, Professor Drans accepted a promotion and a 5-year contract as an Associate Professor. In 1960 he was made a full professor and offered a new contract that contained no termination date. The plaintiff testified that he asked the then President of the college about his open-ended contract and was assured that it meant he (Professor Drans) could teach at Providence College as long as he was able and willing to do so.

In 1966 the college for the first time articulated an official policy regarding tenure. Its pertinent portions, which were set forth in the Faculty Manual, read as follows:

> 3. A member of the faculty who has been granted tenure at Providence College may not be dismissed, except as provided in the following statement on tenure formulated by a joint conference of committees from the Association of American Universities and the American Association of University Professors:

"The termination for cause of a continuous appointment, or the dismissal for cause of a teacher previous to the expiration of term appointment, should, if possible, be considered by both a faculty committee and the governing board of the institution. In all cases where the facts are in dispute, the accused teacher should be informed in writing of the charges against him and should have the opportunity to be heard in his own defense by all bodies that pass judgment on his case. He should be permitted to have an advisor of his own choosing who may act as counsel. There should be a full stenographic record of the hearing available to the parties concerned. In the hearing of the charges of incompetence, the testimony should include that of teachers and other scholars, either from his own or from other institutions.

*   *   *

"Providence College accepts this statement as its basic policy governing dismissal under tenure."

It should be noted that this policy made no mention of retirement for age as a possible ground for the termination of tenured professors.

The policy statement set out in the Faculty Manual was taken from the *1940 Statement of Principles on Academic Freedom and Tenure* (1940 Statement of Principles) published by a Joint Conference of the American Association of University Professors (AAUP) and the Association of American Colleges (AAC). In April 1966 plaintiff was sent a letter formally notifying him that he had been granted tenure.

In 1967 a completely revised Faculty Manual was published, which incorporated in more elaborate detail the tenure provisions of the 1940 Statement of Principles.

"C. *Tenured Faculty*

"Tenure at Providence College signifies that those who have been granted tenured status on the faculty will not have this status terminated or their teaching services discontinued, except for the following causes:

"i.   Retirement because of age;

"ii. Extraordinary and unavoidable circumstances of financial exigency;

"iii. Grave cause, e.g., proven professional incompetence, physical or mental disability, scandalous conduct, neglect of duty, criminal acts."

The 1967 manual was the first indication that tenured rights might be limited by retirement because of age. The 1940 Statement of Principles, which the manual referred to, provided as follows:

"After the expiration of a probationary period, teachers or investigators should have permanent or continuous tenure, and their service should be terminated only for adequate cause, except in the

case of retirement for age, or under extraordinary circumstances
because of financial exigencies."

In 1968 the college amended the 1967 Faculty Manual by expressly endors-
ing the 1940 Statement of Principles and incorporating the above language
into the manual.

The college initially adopted a mandatory retirement age in 1969, and
the Faculty Manual was amended to read as follows:

"In accordance with the action of the Faculty Senate (11/13/68)
and of the Corporation of Providence College (2/28/69) the retirement age for members of the faculty is set at 65 years, as of July 1,
the beginning of the fiscal year, except that after that age they
may apply to the President for yearly appointments and be so appointed at his discretion."

Professor Drans testified that he first became aware of this mandatory
retirement policy in January or February of 1970, when he returned to the
college from a leave of absence in Mexico. His complaint to the Faculty
Senate that the college retirement plan could not apply to him fell upon
deaf ears.

In 1971 the college notified the lay faculty that the college would now
make all future contributions to the TIAA fund on their behalf. The plaintiff then consented to his inclusion in the TIAA pension plan by filling out
an application form. He selected age 65 as his retirement age in the application, a figure he could change at any time.

Each year plaintiff was with the college he was sent a "Notice of Contract for Teaching Services." Each notice stated his rank, department, status,
and salary for the ensuing year. These one-page forms did not set forth any
other terms and conditions of plaintiff's employment (i.e. courseload, vacations, retirement, dismissal, etc.). Each year plaintiff's salary was increased, and each year he signed and returned the form. After 1972, however,
Professor Drans refused to sign the contracts tendered to him although he
continued to teach at the college until he reached the age of 65 in 1976.

The single issue presented in this controversy is whether plaintiff's
tenurial rights limited the right of the college to initiate a mandatory retirement policy that would affect the faculty members who were enjoying the
benefits of tenure. The trial justice found that plaintiff had acquired tenure
in 1960 because the tenure policy had been impliedly incorporated within
the contract he had signed that year. The court then held that the subsequently enacted mandatory retirement provisions of the Faculty Manual
necessarily became incorporated into his succeeding contracts. Specifically,
the trial justice ruled that Professor Drans, by his April 1970 signing of a
form which indicated the salary that was to be paid to him during the
1970-71 academic year, had agreed to be bound by the college's mandatory
retirement policy. . . .

We cannot subscribe to the views expressed by the trial justice when
he ruled that, although the college could not have forced the professor to
retire at 65, the professor had agreed to be bound by the college's retire-

ment plan when in April 1970 he signed a notice which notified him that his $13,910 annual salary for the academic (and fiscal) year 1970-71 would be payable in 12 installments. Initially, we will consider the question of consent and then discuss faculty tenure and how it relates to a college's retirement policies.

Consent

First of all, nothing on the face of the renewal contract notified the professor that, by accepting the contract, he was embracing and approving the college's new mandatory retirement policy. . . .

Tenure vis-a-vis Compulsory Retirement

Since the professor did not agree to be bound by the mandatory retirement policy, two questions remain. First, did the grant of tenure to the professor at a time when the college had no retirement policy limit the authority of the college from subsequently adopting a retirement policy? Second, even if the college had the authority to institute or change its retirement policy, can that new policy be validly applied to the professor? . . .

Tenure in the academic community commonly refers to a status granted, usually after a probationary period, which protects a teacher from dismissal except for serious misconduct or incompetence. *Collins v. Parsons College,* 203 N.W.2d at 597; *American Association of University Professors v. Bloomfield College,* 129 N.J.Super. 249, 322 A.2d 846, 853 (1974); *Rehor v. Case Western Reserve University; Developments in the Law—Academic Freedom,* 81 Harv.L.Rev. 1045, 1049 (1968). The primary function of tenure is the perservation of academic freedom. The 1940 Statement of Principles provides:

"Tenure is a means to certain ends; specifically: (1) Freedom of
teaching and research and of extramural activities and (2) a sufficient degree of economic security to make the profession attractive
to men and women of ability. Freedom and economic security,
hence, tenure, are indispensable to the success of an institution
in fulfilling its obligations to its students and to society."

The job security which tenure provides is thought to benefit society by encouraging a scholar to vigorously pursue and disseminate his research without fear of reprisal or rebuke from those who support the conventional wisdom. Van Alstyne, *Tenure: A Summary, Explanation, and "Defense,"* 57 AAUP Bull. 328, 330.

With these principles in mind, we find it difficult indeed to hold that tenure precludes the imposition of a mandatory retirement policy under all circumstances. If the scope of tenurial protection is no broader than necessary to protect academic freedom and to provide enough job security to make the profession attractive to young men and women, then an academic institution should have the authority to institute a mandatory retirement program. As long as the retirement plan is adopted in good faith, the age chosen is reasonable, and the policy is uniformly applied to all faculty members, the essential functions of tenure will not be compromised. *Rehor v. Case Western Reserve University.*

So far as we have been able to discover, *Rehor* is the only case in the country which has directly decided this issue. . . . The Supreme Court of Ohio upheld the power of the university to make reasonable, uniform changes in its retirement policies and further held that the plaintiff had consented to this contractual change. We believe that the holdings present an inconsistency which undermines the rationale upon which the court in *Rehor* reached its ultimate conclusion. If, as the court said, a university's personnel policies are impliedly incorporated into a professorial contract, then the college's unilateral right to make reasonable alterations thereof must be denied. On the other hand, if the college has the inherent or reserved authority to make changes unilaterally, it is idle to speak of retirement as a contractual term to which pedagogical consent is a sine qua non.

We believe the proper balancing of the prerogatives of the university and the rights of individual faculty members should be gleaned from the contract of the parties and from their reasonable expectations regarding university-wide regulations, rules, and policies. Many courts have implied some or all of the rules, regulations, bylaws, and policies of a university into faculty employment contracts. . . .

[Citations omitted]

. . . With the exception of *Rehor*, these cases concerned faculty members who were dismissed or not reinstated in a manner which, they claimed, was contrary to certain university-wide policies or procedures. *Rehor* interpreted this line of authority, incorrectly in our view, as holding that *all* of a university's rules, regulations, etc., are impliedly incorporated into faculty employment contracts. As we review the broad range of topics encompassed in the Providence College Faculty Manual (use of audiovisual aids, purchase requests, parking privileges, traffic regulations, etc.), we cannot subscribe to this all-inclusive incorporation. The effective management of our academic institutions would be seriously compromised if the contractual assent of every single faculty member was required before the college could, say, rewrite the procedures for borrowing a book from the library or change the discount rate being offered the faculty at the campus book store.

Having in mind the purpose of tenure and the reasonable expectations of those who wish to pursue a professional teaching career at an institution of higher learning, we must reject Professor Drans' claim that his 1960 acquisition of tenure exempted him from the compulsory retirement program instituted by the college in 1969. He should have been aware that sometime during his teaching career his employer might see fit to install a retirement plan which would include some type of mandatory provision whereby a teacher would be required to forego any further classroom activities. The 1940 Statement of Principles recognized the need for institutional flexibility when it expressly provided for retirement for age as a permissible ground for the termination of tenured professors. The importance of this statement cannot be underestimated. Promulgated by a joint committee of the American Association of University Professors and the Association of American Colleges, the 1940 Statement, as with their other joint statements, was widely circulated and widely accepted in the academic community and, indeed, by Providence College. *Browzin v. Catholic University of America,* 174 U.S.App.D.C. 60, 64 n.8, 527 F.2d 843, 847 n.8 (1975). . . .

. . . Therefore, we conclude that the college had the power and authority, consistent with its outstanding tenurial obligations to unilaterally institute a reasonable, uniformly applicable, mandatory retirement policy.

Special Treatment

Having decided that the college could institute its compulsory retirement program, we must now decide whether it should be applied to Professor Drans, who was 58 at the time the policy first became effective. Amicus AAUP contends that the college should be compelled to make some type of adjustment that will cushion the financial and emotional shock suffered by the professor's departure from academia's front lines. Support for this belief can be found in another joint study by the AAUP–AAC, which resulted in the *1950 Statement on Retirement.*

"When a new retirement policy or annuity plan is initiated or an old one changed, reasonable provision either by special financial arrangements or by the gradual inauguration of the new plan should be made for those adversely affected." *Academic Retirement and Related Subjects,* 36 AAUP Bull. 97, 116 (1950).

In its accompanying report, the joint committee explained the necessity for the requirement as follows:

"The Committee would particularly emphasize the necessity of making equitable provisions for any staff member who may be adversely affected by a change in the retirement policy or plans of the institution with which he is associated. When long inattention is suddenly changed into action, long-time policies are sometimes initiated without reasonable provisions for those adversely affected. If, for instance, it has been customary to allow faculty members to teach until well after 70, and a fixed retirement age of, say, 68 is suddenly established, all of those past or nearing that age have their expectations suddenly changed unless special financial provisions are made for them or the plan is initiated gradually." *Academic Retirement and Related Subjects,* 36 AAUP Bull. 97, 110 (1950).

Amicus Boston University refers to a report by a subcommittee of the Association of American Law Schools (AALS), which concluded that a compulsory retirement policy may be changed in good faith and made applicable to all, including those with tenure, "if it does not defeat reasonable expectations." *Proceedings of the Association of American Law Schools,* 1969, Part II, at 178-81.

Obviously, as we examine the AAUP's advocacy of the "adversely affected" approach and study the AALS's "reasonable expectations" theory, we see that both the professoriate and the administration recognize that there may be times when the college administration, because of its desire to maintain institutional flexibility, must make some type of an accommodation so that the economic security expectations of the tenured may be preserved. Equally clear is the fact that no fixed formula exists by which a determination can be made as to which tenured retiree is entitled to receive special consideration. However, there are several factors which merit consideration, including: (1) the length of time remaining between the announcement of the retirement plan or its modification and its actual application to the faculty member; (2) the age of the professor; (3) the professor's ability and willingness to teach beyond the retirement date; (4) the extent to which the unexpected retirement may be financially burdensome; (5) the prior notice, if any, the professor had that retirement was in the offing; (6) the type of pension plan, if any, available at the institution; and (7) whether the retirement plan contains a provision whereby the responsible authority is given discretion to make annual appointments of faculty members that extend beyond the retirement date.

Having suggested some of the criteria that might be considered as we deal with the special treatment phase of this controversy, we can do no more because we believe that the professor's eligibility for "a reasonable transition provision" is best resolved, at least initially, in the Superior Court. Since we have stressed throughout this opinion that disputes involving tenure and retirement should be resolved by referring to the reasonable expectations within the academic community, after remand, evidence can be adduced in the Superior Court on the question as to what has been done, if anything, for those teachers who have found themselves in the same position as was Professor Drans when he learned that compulsory retirement was to be a way of academic life at Providence College. In remanding the case to the Superior Court, we would emphasize that we have ruled that the college had the authority to institute a retirement policy for all its faculty members, including those with tenure, but that this power is limited by an implied obligation to make reasonable transition provisions when the common practice within the academic community would dictate such a course of action.

The plaintiff's appeal is sustained, the judgment appealed from is vacated, and the case is remanded to the Superior Court for further proceedings.

NOTES

1. Would the result in *Rehor* have been any different if the Ohio Supreme Court had followed the principles set forth in *Drans*?

2. Where did the court in *Drans* get the authority to establish "criteria that might be considered . . . to deal with the special treatment phase" of the case? Are these criteria contractually based? Or do they arise pursuant to college policy? Or are they mandated by some external law? Are the criteria mandatory and exclusive? Can the criteria be changed in the future? If so, by whom?

3. How are *Drans* and *Rehor* affected by the Age Discrimination in Employment Act, discussed *infra* in Chapter 18? Can a university or college create a tenure plan giving tenure to faculty members only until they reach age 65, with reappointment on an annual basis until age 70? How about a tenure plan limited to a maximum of 20 years for all new hires, with year-to-year appointments thereafter?

IV. Termination of Tenure

A. Termination for Cause

A tenured faculty member's right to continuous employment can be terminated for adequate cause. However, the definition of "cause" remains a difficult and unsettled problem in the academic community. In Faculty Tenure, at p. 73, it was noted that:

The difficulty is understandable. A definition of "cause" clear enough to provide a basis for fair proceedings and yet capable of commanding the broad assent of the academic community both in what it includes and what it excludes, is inherently difficult to construct. Given the great diversity of views about the nature of higher education, and the role of faculty, general agreement may indeed be impossible to secure. And given the traditional diversity of institutional objectives and commitments—adversity that should be encouraged rather than reduced—individual institutions obviously should have the major responsibility formulating their own definition of adequate cause for dismissal.

To avoid problems associated with judicial and legislative meddling in academic affairs, the Commission on Academic Tenure in Higher Education recommended:

. . . that "adequate cause" in faculty dismissal proceedings should be restricted to a) demonstrated incompetence or dishonesty in teaching or research, b) substantial and manifest neglect of duty, and c) personal conduct which substantially impairs the individual fulfillment of his institutional responsibilities. The burden of proof in establishing the cause for dismissal rests upon the institution. [Faculty Tenure, at 75.]

B. N. Shaw, in Academic Tenure In American Higher Education 62-65 (1971), reported that, in state universities and land-grant colleges, only about half of the eighty institutions surveyed provided specific criteria for the interpretation of "cause." In addition, he found that twenty-five distinct criteria for measuring cause were employed by the institutions which had adopted some standards.

BOARD OF TRUSTEES OF COMPTON
COLLEGE v. STUBBLEFIELD
Court of Appeals of California
16 Cal. App. 3d 820, 94 Cal. Rptr. 318 (1971)

COMPTON, Associate Justice.

On March 4, 1969, the Board of Trustees of the Compton Junior College District (hereinafter referred to as the Board) pursuant to Education Code sections 13403, 13404 and 13408, suspended defendant, a certified teacher, from his employment with the Compton Junior College District and notified him of the Board's intention to dismiss him after 30 days. The suspension and dismissal were based upon charges of immoral conduct and evident unfitness for service as provided by section 13403 of the Education Code. . . .

The evidence of defendant's conduct which the trial court found to be true, a finding which is not assailed by defendant on appeal, can be briefly summarized as follows.

After teaching a class on the night of January 28, 1969, defendant drove a female student, and member of that class, in his car to a location on a side street near Compton College and parked. The location is in an area of industrial construction and was not lighted.

At some time after defendant parked, a Los Angeles County Deputy Sheriff spotted defendant's car. The car appeared to the deputy to be abandoned and he went to investigate. When the deputy illuminated defendant's car with his headlights and searchlight, defendant then sat up. When the deputy approached defendant's car, illuminating the interior with his flashlight, he observed that defendant's pants were unzipped and lowered from the waist, exposing his penis. The student was nude from the waist up, and her capri pants were unzipped and open at the waist.

The deputy orally identified himself as a police officer. In addition, he was wearing a yellow raincoat with a badge on the chest and a helmet bearing a sheriff's emblem. Defendant recognizing that the deputy was a police officer, threw open the left car door, nearly striking the deputy, and shouted, "Get the hell away from me, you dirty cop."

As the deputy was standing behind the still open left door, defendant shifted the car into reverse, accelerated rapidly backward, knocking the deputy to the pavement and causing minor injuries to the deputy and damage to his clothing.

Defendant then drove away. The deputy pursued defendant in his patrol car with his red lights flashing, and his siren and searchlight on; during the chase defendant drove at speeds between 80 and 100 miles per hour and refused to yield until the student, by persuasion and by attempting to force the steering wheel to the right, caused defendant to stop. . . .

It would seem that, as a minimum, responsible conduct upon the part of a teacher, even at the college level, excludes meretricious relationships with his students and physical and verbal assaults on duly constituted authorities in the presence of his students.

Defendant quickly calls to our attention the recent pronouncement of our Supreme Court in Morrison v. State Board of Education, 1 Cal.3d 214, at p. 217, 82 Cal.Rptr. 175, at p. 177, 461 P.2d 375, at p. 377.

In that case the court held that the revocation of a teaching credential upon grounds of "immoral and unprofessional conduct and acts involving moral turpitude" could not be supported by evidence limited to a showing that on one occasion three years in the past, while under severe stress, the teacher had engaged in an undescribed but noncriminal private act "of a homosexual nature" with a consenting adult. The court concluded that, "* * * the State Board of Education can revoke a life diploma or other document of certification and thus prohibit local school officials from hiring a particular teacher only if that individual has in some manner indicated that he is unfit to teach."

Defendant contends that *Morrison* prohibits his discharge because the evidence adduced against him concerned only his conduct and did not expressly demonstrate how that conduct rendered him unfit to teach. We do not agree with defendant's broad interpretation of that case.

Substantial factual distinctions exist between *Morrison* and the instant case in terms of the lapse of time between the conduct and the discharge, the locales where the conduct occurred and the status of the parties involved.

Another substantial difference is that between the *revocation of a teacher's certificate* and dismissal from employment in a single school district. Thus the court stressed that a teacher "is entitled to a careful and reasoned inquiry into his fitness to teach by the Board of Education *before he is deprived of his right to pursue his profession."* (Emphasis added.) *(Morrison, supra,* 1 Cal.3d at pp. 238-239, 82 Cal.Rptr. at p. 194, 461 P.2d at p. 394.)

The clear import of that decision, then, is that a teacher may be discharged or have his certificate revoked on evidence that either his conduct indicates a potential for misconduct with a student or that his conduct while not necessarily indicating such a potential, has gained sufficient notoriety so as to impair his on-campus relationships.

There is no requirement that both the potential and the notoriety be present in each case.

While in this case no evidence was offered which directly dealt with notoriety, the very fact that a police officer, in the course of his official duties, easily discovered defendant and his companion, demonstrates the tenuous security from public attention provided by the front seat of defendant's automobile. Moreover, upon detection, defendant chose to assault the police officer and attempt an escape through dark city streets at high speeds thereby ultimately insuring further public attention.

The integrity of the educational system under which teachers wield considerable power in the grading of students and the granting or withholding of certificates and diplomas is clearly threatened when teachers become involved in relationships with students such as is indicated by the conduct here. The findings and conclusions of the trial court are amply supported by the record. . . . [T]he conduct of the defendant in this case constitutes immoral conduct which indicates unfitness to teach. . . .

NOTES

1. Are all nonmarital, sexual relationships between faculty and students grounds for termination for cause? Should factors such as whether the person is an undergraduate, graduate, or post-graduate student or whether the student is enrolled in the faculty member's class, department or school bear on the issue? If Stubblefield had been with his wife or another woman, not a student, could he have been terminated for cause?

2. Immorality is the most prevalent ground for termination of a tenured professor for cause. Of course, "immorality" is capable of broad definition. See Koch v. Board of Trustees of University of Illinois, 39 Ill. App. 2d 51, 187 N.E. 2d 340 (1963), *cert. den.*, 375 U.S. 989 (1964), where a faculty member was terminated for publishing in a university newspaper a letter, which among other things, asserted that premarital intercourse among college students is not in and of itself improper. Could the decision in *Koch* withstand an attack on the basis of a denial of free speech?

3. Other common grounds which have been held to justify dismissal for cause are "incompetence," Chung v. Park, 514 F.2d 382 (3rd Cir. 1975) (inability to communicate effectively with students, unwillingness to cooperate with department in identification and solution of problems, and inability to accept a full share of the teaching responsibility); "neglect of duty," Shaw v. Board of Trustees of Frederick Community College, 549 F.2d 929 (4th Cir. 1976) (failure to attend a required faculty workshop and to participate in commencement exercises following an expressed directive to do so); and "insubordination," State ex rel. Richardson v. Board of Regents of Univ. of Nevada, 70 Nev. 347, 269 P.2d 265 (1954) (dismissal for distribution of an article which was critical of the university president was not justified because it did not constitute "a willful disregard of express or implied direction or such defiant attitude as to be the equivalent thereto").

4. In Atkinson v. Bd. of Trustees of Univ. of Arkansas, 559 S.W. 2d 473 (Arkansas Sup. Ct. 1977), a rule prohibiting certain law faculty members from assisting in the handling of any lawsuit was held to be an unconstitutional violation of equal protection because the prohibition applied to only three of six types of law school faculty positions and applied to only one of two law schools funded by the state.

B.   Termination Due to Financial Exigency

Financial exigency is another form of adequate cause for termination of the tenured faculty member. Terminations on that basis were first recognized in the 1925 Conference Statement of the AAUP, which required that it be done as a "last resort." The 1940 Statement has now become the standard for many tenure plans. It provides in part:

a) After the expiration of a probationary period, teachers and investigators should have permanent or continuous tenure and their service should be terminated only for adequate cause, except in the case of retirement for age or under extraordinary circumstances because of financial exigencies. . . .

5) Termination of a continuous appointment because of financial exigency should be demonstrably bona fide.

To help understand the concept of financial exigency, the AAUP has promulgated recommended institutional regulations. See, *Termination of Faculty Appointments Because of Financial Exigency, Discontinuance of a Program or Department, or Medical Reasons.* 62 AAUP Bull. 17 (1976). While the term "financial exigency" has been used for a long time, it was never defined prior to adoption of these regulations. Regulation 4(c)(1) defines a demonstrably bona fide financial exigency as an "imminent financial crisis which threatens the survival of the institution as a whole and which cannot be alleviated by less drastic means." The American Council on Education has refused to endorse this definition because it seemingly requires that the institution be on the brink of bankruptcy and thus is an unrealistically narrow limitation on the power to terminate. *See,* W. Todd Furniss, *The 1976 AAUP Retrenchment Policy,* 57 Educ. Rec. 133 (1977).

AAUP v. BLOOMFIELD COLLEGE
Superior Court of New Jersey
Chancery Division
129 N.J. Super. 249, 322 A.2d 846 (1974)

ANTELL, J.S.C.

This is an action for declaratory relief and specific performance with respect to the academic tenure of faculty members at Bloomfield College, a private institution of higher education licensed under the laws of the State of New Jersey. Plaintiff American Association of University Professors, Bloomfield College Chapter (hereinafter AAUP), is a labor organization within the meaning of the National Labor Relations Act, 29 U.S.C.A., § 152, and for the purposes of Article I, paragraph 19 of the 1947 New Jersey Constitution, which has been certified and recognized by the National Labor Relations Board as the exclusive representative for collective bargaining on behalf of the college faculty. The individual plaintiffs include faculty members who seek clarification of their claimed tenured status and those whose service has been terminated and seek reinstatement to their former positions. Their periods of accumulated service range from 8 to 22 years. In addition to Bloomfield College, also named as defendants are Merle F. Allshouse, president of the college, and the individual members of the college board of trustees.

The legal basis of plaintiffs' claim of tenure is to be found in the *Faculty Handbook* of the college under the heading of "Bloomfield College Policies on Employment and Tenure" (hereinafter "Policies"). This document forms an essential part of the contractual terms governing the relationship between the college and the faculty. . . .

Under paragraph C thereof Bloomfield College recognizes that tenure is a means to certain ends, specifically: (1) freedom of teaching and research and of extramural activities, and (2) a sufficient degree of economic security to make the profession attractive to men and women of ability. Freedom and security, hence tenure, are indispensable to the success of an institution in fulfilling its obligations to its students and to society.

Following a probationary period of seven years, which has been completed by all the individual plaintiffs, subparagraph C(3) provides:

* * * a teacher will have tenure and his services may be terminated only for adequate cause, except in case of retirement for age, or under extraordinary circumstances because of financial exigency of the institution.

Pertinent also is subparagraph C(6) of the "Policies" which provides:

Termination of continuous appointment because of financial exigency of the institution must be demonstrably *bona fide*. A situation which makes drastic retrenchment of this sort necessary precludes expansion of the staff at other points at the same time, except in extraordinary circumstances.

On June 21, 1973 the board of trustees adopted Resolution R-58 which in material part resolved:

* * * [U]pon the recommendation of the Executive Committee, the President, the Dean of the College, and with the advice of the special Evaluation Committee for the reduction of faculty size due to financial exigency, and in accordance with the action of the Board on March 1 and the recommendation of the Academic Affairs Committee that thirteen faculty members be terminated in the reduction of faculty size due to financial exigency, the following persons be informed that they will be terminated as of June 30, 1974, and their duties for the 1973-74 academic year be defined to include no teaching, participation in College governance, or voting privileges. * * *

*   *   *

That every faculty member be informed on or before June 30, 1973 that all 1973-74 contracts are one-year terminal contracts. The Board of Trustees through its Academic Affairs Committee will call together from among the remaining 54 members of the faculty an evaluation committee to determine what faculty members will remain at the College beyond June 30, 1974. This Committee to Define and Evaluate Personnel Needs will define personnel needs for the new academic program priorities which are set and the curricular revisions which are made, and will evaluate existing faculty members to determine their qualifications for meeting these needs. Their recommendations are to be made no later than November 30, 1973. All faculty members will be notified by December 15, 1973, as to their contract status for the 1974-75 academic year.

Acting thereunder, defendant Allshouse under date of June 29, 1973 notified 13 members of the faculty that it was his "unpleasant duty to inform you that the Board of Directors, at its meeting on June 21, 1973, took action to terminate your services as part of the reduction of the faculty size due to financial exigency." They were further advised:

Following the Board's action and in accordance with our prior oral conversation, this will serve to advise you formally that you have been relieved of all duties as a Bloomfield College faculty member; and, therefore, you will not be obliged to and will not perform any services for the College or participate in College governance after June 30, 1973.

The letter expresses the hope that the recipient

* * * understand the need for the College to take stern measures in a time of financial exigency despite the personal disappointment and anguish which are inevitably part of such a decision. You have made an invaluable contribution to the College, and I deeply regret that our present situation makes this action necessary.

On the same date all the remaining members of the faculty, tenured and nontenured, were notified by letter memorandum that at the June 21 meeting the board of trustees "took action to the effect that every faculty member should be informed that all 1973-74 contracts are one-year terminal contracts." The letter continues:

The notice of termination does not necessarily imply that you will be terminated at the end of the 1973-74 academic year, but it provides a base from which each faculty member can negotiate a learning contract which meets both personal professional interests and College needs.

During the period between June 21, 1973 and the commencement of the school year in September 1973 the College engaged the services of 12 new and untenured teachers to serve on its faculty. Defendants assert that these were hired to replace others who were lost to the school over a period of time as the result of "normal attrition," not those who were terminated under Resolution R-58.

Among the roster of plaintiffs are included (1) those faculty members who received termination notices and seek reinstatement to their former positions, and (2) those whose employment was continued, but subject to one-year terminal contracts. The latter ask declaratory judgment that their tenured status is unaffected by the action of the board of trustees in adopting Resolution R-58. As is clearly implied by the excerpted documents, defendants justify the resolution on the basis of "financial exigency." The issue projected is whether the action accomplished by Resolution R-58 in abrogating tenure and terminating the employment of tenured faculty members at Bloomfield College was "demonstrably bona fide" as having been taken "under extraordinary circumstances because of the financial exigency of the institution." Complementary thereto is the question as to whether the circumstances were further "extraordinary" so as to allow at the same time for the hiring of 12 new teachers.

Bloomfield College is a small commuter-type institution tracing its origins to an academy founded in 1807 by the Presbyterian Church. It was established as the German Theological School in 1868 and is affiliated with the New Jersey Synod of the United Presbyterian Church. It serves a student body which has been described as ethnically mixed, presenting a low academic profile and embracing a large minority group representation. Students are drawn mainly from the lower middle and upper middle and upper lower economic strata and for the most part are enrolled in the school's business and nursing departments.

Present annual tuition is $2,000, up from $1,330 in 1969. Enrollment for the present year, 1973-74, is 867, down from 1,069 in 1972. The portent of these figures lies in the fact that three-fourths of the school's financial support is derived from enrollment income.

Enrollment projections testimonially offered by college officials for 1974-75 range between 450 and 638. Those were given without factual foundation and are said to have been based upon unspecified "demographic studies." They are in curious contrast to the projected enrollment of 905 for the same period, gradually increasing to 1,030 during the school year 1978-79, which appears at page 17 of the Bloomfield College President's Report dated March 1974. The discrepancy is rationalized by President Allshouse's explanation in part that to publish the bleak truth in his report would have disserved the interest of public relations and been damaging to college morale. Although in final form, it has been decided to withhold the report from public distribution for reasons of economy, not because of any errors in its content.

Although the decreased enrollment for the 1973-74 year was accurately forecast in the spring of 1973, the previous year's projection fell short of the actual enrollment by 131 students. This miscalculation was never explained, and is noted with interest for the reason that the faculty reduction from 76 to 54 was deliberately brought about to achieve, supposedly, a 17 to 1 student-faculty ratio based upon anticipated enrollment for the 1973-74 school year. That this decision rested upon data of demonstrated unreliability is pertinent to a determination as to the college's good faith.

The reduction referred to was the combined result of discharging the 13 teachers, "normal attrition" to the extent of 21 teachers who left for various reasons between June 30, 1972 and August 31, 1973, and addition of the 12 newcomers between June 21 and September 30, 1973. Consideration was given to retaining the discharged faculty members instead of hiring new ones, but this alternative was rejected upon the belief, it is said, that the former would not fit in with proposed program innovations which were envisioned by the college as part of its overall rehabilitation. The changes were described in the evidence as "new directions," and were planned to set the college on a unique academic course. Their design was to reduce the number of majors and departments by bringing them all into 12 broad interdisciplinary areas in order to improve administration and curricular planning. The ultimate objective, so it was said, was to turn around the enrollment projections by (1) offering career oriented prospective students a firm liberal arts foundation, (2) enhancing the distinctiveness of attending Bloomfield for what it could offer as a small college, and (3) responding "very seriously" to the personal needs of the students.

Apart from the installation of a special freshman seminar and advisory program and greater emphasis on the development of evening and part-time enrollment of mature women and special groups, and possibly the improvement of administrative controls, the practical changes to be accomplished by the new directions were never clearly stated. Despite the references to interdisciplinary approaches, the basic disciplines still prevail, and whatever revisions may have been made are minor in nature. Notable also on the question of bona fides is the fact that the decision to install the new directions was not made until the fall of 1973, some months after the adoption of Resolution R-58 and after the institution of plaintiffs' suit. In any event, the results assertedly anticipated by the new programs are not now seen as attainable. Present projections forecast continued reductions in enrollment.

Turning to a consideration of the college's assets and liabilities, we note first that its budget for the 1972-73 school year was $3,652,000. For the year 1973-74 it is $3,397,000. The planned cash deficit for 1972 was $123,000 and for 1973 $191,000, with estimates that it will probably rise to $231,000 for the year. Between June 30, 1973 and March 31, 1974 it reached $145,000. By cash deficit is meant the amount by which the accounts payable and direct loans exceed available cash. In June 1973 its operating deficit, i. e., the amount by which current liabilities exceed current assets, was $368,000. In 1973 the college endowment fund was $945,000, reflecting a 21% decline from the previous year, of which 17.19% occurred between January 1 and March 31, 1973. Cash flow problems intensified around June 1973, with accounts payable accumulating to the point where some went back to February 1973, and were compounded by financing difficulties. Interest on loans rose from 8% to 11%, higher borrowing costs resulted from the college's loss of status as a prime lending risk some years ago, and the declining value of the endowment portfolio further restricted borrowing capacity. As the result of conferences—which were, coincidentally, carried on during the hearings and of which the court was kept aware—its bank will now determine its lending status on a week-to-week basis and will advance no funds other than those necessary to meet payrolls. Under these circumstances a freeze has been placed upon all expenses other than payroll.

It is recognized by the administration that existing mortgages could be recast in order to ease the cash situation, but this decision has been deferred for the reason that the ultimate costs would eventually increase the financial burden. The prospect of rising fixed costs, the built-in limitation on tuitions resulting from the economic character of the student body, and reductions of federal aid with no corresponding increases in state aid programs are additional negative factors. Lack of available scholarship aid is another deterrent to the college's financial reanimation. At present it can only put 4% of its budget into scholarships, a figure which should be as high as 15% to 17%. Help is needed from federal or other outside sources, and without such assistance the school is burdened by a "tuition-subsidy gap." It is believed that enrollment and tuition income will continue to decline for the following three reasons: (1) the pool from which the college has historically drawn in terms of age and economic background is itself being diminished, a widespread phenomenon; (2) inability to develop a sufficiently attractive academic program, and (3) costs. In addition, it is believed that the present location of the college in Essex County is not conducive to further growth for the reason that the area is already overburdened with educational facilities in terms of existing need.

The remaining significant asset of the college in addition to its tuition income, the college property and its endowment fund, is the Knoll Golf Club. The Knoll is a property of 322 acres, having two golf courses, two clubhouses, a swimming pool and a few residences. It was purchased by the college around the end of 1966 or early 1967 with the intention of using it for the establishment of an educational plant. The purchase price was $3,325,000, and was paid for by $900,000 cash, a bank loan of $300,000 and a mortgage of $2,125,000. The $900,000 was provided as a gift to the college by the Presbyterian Church out of monies raised as part of its Fifty Million Dollar Fund, a fund-raising project conducted by the church. These monies are dedicated to purposes of educational capital development and cannot be used for any other purpose.

Conservative estimates as to the market value of The Knoll in its present condition lie between $5,000,000 and $7,000,000. The net yield to the college out of a $5,000,000 sale, after taxes and the liquidation of secured debts, would be around $1,536,000. At $7,000,000 the sale would yield $2,366,000. In addition, there would also be realized some $795,000 owing to the college's current operating fund as well as approximately $727,000, being the present value of the gift from the Fifty Million Dollar Fund, subject, of course to the terms and restrictions of that benefaction.

Although the college does not carry The Knoll as a liability, the income received therefrom does not exceed what is necessary to meet carrying charges. It is required, however, to make substantial cash advances during the year to sustain the operation, and these, of course, are additional burdens upon its already strained cash position. At year's end 1972 and 1973 these advances totaled $263,000 and $269,000, respectively.

The salient economic features of this property in its present posture, therefore, are that it is altogether lacking in income-producing characteristics, that it compels some degree of cash diversion from the operating needs of the college, and that its sale would release sufficient cash to meet the college's immediate and reasonably foreseeable financial requirements.

Present plans for the future of The Knoll are uncertain. The one being most seriously entertained is the installation of a large development which would occupy 202.5 acres of land. Site plans and proposals show an 84-month building plan projecting 61 units of low-density housing, 240 units of luxury housing, 2 medium-rise buildings having 340 units, as well as medium-density townhouses and condominiums. Negotiations preliminary to necessary zoning applications are taking place, but even assuming zoning approval is obtained (a prospect which is by no means assured), a lead time of at least two years must precede actual construction. Needless to say, the successful completion of such a program would greatly enhance the value of The Knoll to the college as a sustaining asset, but it is obvious that retention of the property for long-term appreciation necessarily requires that the college forego the benefit of the improved cash position which would be realized from a near term sale.

Without question, the economic health of the college is poor. A more definitive diagnosis is that the problem is chiefly one of liquidity, a difficulty with which the college has been coping for many years. Although a recent audit shows $56,000 in cash as against accounts payable of $301,000, previous years' figures show that in 1968 there was only $808 against $985,000 in accounts payable, in 1971 $6,000 available against $1,247,000 in accounts payable, in 1972 $6,000 available as against $777,000, and as of June 30, 1973 $12,302 available as against $1,018,000. The college's dilemma is real, but not unique. Although financially beleaguered, as Mr. Ritterskamp, who testified on behalf of the college as an expert in the financing of higher education, said, "all private education is in financial trouble today."

Notwithstanding the problem of cash flow, Bloomfield College is a very substantial educational institution with a net worth of $6,600,000, reflecting assets of $12,600,000 and liabilities of $6,000,000, based upon book values which show The Knoll as an asset worth only $3,370,000. The college is by no means insolvent, even though it is difficult for it to meet obligations as they mature. Although its preference is to exploit The Knoll's long-term possibilities, its choices are by no means restricted to this course of action. The option of selling the property now is perhaps more realistic as a survival measure since it would supply immediate liquidity. Near-term infusion of needed cash could start an economic recovery leading the college at some future time to a firmer financial base from which to move into more speculative, more rewarding ventures of the kind now under consideration. While the program of development being investigated might eventually provide vast financial resources, they would not begin to benefit the college for many years during which it would presumably continue its penurious standards to the detriment of its standing as an educational institution.

Regardless, however, of what the future may offer, the sale of The Knoll as an available alternative to the abrogation of tenure is a viable one and fairly to be considered on the meritorious issues.

Also to be noted are the facts concerning the accreditation of the college by the Middle States Association of Colleges and Secondary Schools, the regional accrediting body for educational institutions in New Jersey. In March 1970 the college was examined by the Association and only temporary accreditation granted for a two-year period to allow the Association to resolve its doubts concerning the college's finances and long-term prospects. During this interval the college filed annual plans, and full accreditation was finally granted through 1975 when it is expected that a regular visit will be made and every aspect of the college reviewed. Until then its accreditation will remain intact and the college will have at least that much time to correct those factors which adversely affect its financial base. . . .

As recited in the Bloomfield College "Policies" and in the 1940 "Statement of Principles," "Tenure is a means to certain ends; specifically: (1) Freedom of teaching and research and of extra mural activities, and (2) A sufficient degree of economic security to make the profession attractive to men and women of ability."

. . . Although academic tenure does not constitute a guarantee of life employment, *i.e.*, tenured teachers may be released for "cause" or for reasons of the kind here involved, it denotes clearly defined limitations upon the institution's power to terminate the teacher's services. . . .

A resolution of this controversy is not referable merely to the criterion of "financial exigency.". . .

Its applicable register of meaning is to be found somewhere between the understanding offered by the chairman of the college's board of trustees as "an urgent financial situation about which something had to be done in order to stay in business," and that propounded by the Princeton professor of economics who advocated that financial exigency exists "when, taking into account all assets, potential assets, sources of funding, income and all alternative courses of action, the continued viability of the institution becomes impossible without abrogating tenure."

Conceding that the college is under financial stress, and that "something had to be done," it does not follow that the college's freedom of response extends to the unilateral revocation of a contractually protected employment status and the discharge of tenured teachers as a matter of unbridled discretion. Similarly, although it may be appropriate to inspect the available resources and alternatives open to the college, this does not imply authority on the part of the court to substitute its judgment for that of the trustees, to weigh the wisdom of their action, to modify wayward or imprudent judgments in their formulation of educational or financial policy, or to decide whether the survival of the institution remains "possible" by the choice of other courses of action. The trustees, after all, have the best insight into the college's problems and will have the continuing duty of determining and providing for its future priorities. Their considered judgment in matters of policy is not lightly to be displaced. Interests must be balanced, and while the court must refrain from interfering with the policy-making and administrative processes of the college, still, it is called upon to protect important contractual rights against excesses in the mobilization of administrative and policy-making powers. . . .

The test best suited to effectuate the intent of the parties on judicial review of the college's action . . . is whether the action taken followed from the board's demonstrably bona fide belief, under honestly formulated standards, in the existence of a financial exigency and extraordinary attendant circumstances, and in the necessity for terminating tenured faculty members as a means of relieving the exigent condition. Interrelated therewith is the question of whether sufficient credible evidence of "exigency" and "extraordinary circumstances" exists as to provide a basis for the conclusions reached in the exercise of a reasonable and prudent judgment.

Except for policy differences touching upon the presumption of correctness and burden of proof, the test proposed is materially comparable to that used on judicial review of actions by governmental administrative agencies and in cases involving the discharge of tenured teachers for cause. . . .

The court concludes that the actions of Bloomfield College with respect to the tenured status of its faculty members in terminating the services of some and placing others on one-year employment contracts under the circumstances presented overflowed the limits of its authority as defined by its own Policies, and therefore failed to constitute a legally valid interruption in the individual plaintiffs' continuity of service. Whatever other motivations defendants might have had, they have failed to demonstrate by a preponderance of the evidence that their purported action was in good faith related to a condition of financial exigency within the institution. These conclusions are compelled by the following enumerated considerations:

(1) Although some financial relief might have been realized by discontinuing the services of the 13 faculty members, it has not been suggested how the college could possibly have been similarly benefited by placing the entire remaining faculty, including tenured personnel, on one-year terminal contracts. This startling action could have produced no immediate financial benefit, could not have been inspired by financial exigency, and can only be interpreted as a calculated repudiation of a contractual duty without any semblance of legal justification. It was a gratuitous challenge to the principle of academic tenure. Its clear implication of ulterior design and lack of sensitivity to the question of moral correctness reflect adversely upon the claimed bona fides of discharging the 13 faculty members for the same given reason.

(2) The hiring of 12 new faculty members between June 21 and September 30, 1973 (the period during which the action complained of took place) has not been justified by a showing of "extraordinary circumstances" as required by subparagraph C(6) of the Bloomfield College "Policies." The record is lacking, in fact, any evidence from which it can be determined what the financial consequences of these hirings were, whether they resulted in a savings to the college, and if so in what amount. The explanation that the newcomers were brought in to meet the demands of a modified curriculum is totally unacceptable. Although the testimony is richly festooned with references to "teaching-learning contracts," "interdisciplinary programs," "steady state," "new directions," and "career tracks," the phrases lack content of any value in understanding what the new program was all about. . . .

The court had the benefit of the testimony of Dr. William Keast. Dr. Keast is a Professor of English at the University of Texas and serves as chair-

man of the Commission on Academic Tenure of the American Council on
Education.

    . . . Based on the testimony of this witness the court is of the view that
termination of tenure based on changes in academic programs can be justified
only after a faculty evaluation of the problem. The "standard practice" is to
involve the maximum amount of faculty participation to insure sound professional judgment that the long-term purposes of the college will be fulfilled, to insure that the new programs are clearly desirable educationally,
that the financial considerations are demonstrably bona fide, and that the
best professional judgment is made as to those places in the faculty where
reductions should be made in order to achieve the long-term purposes of
the college.

    (3) The financial problem is one of liquidity, which, as the evidence
demonstrates, has plagued the college for many years. The board chairman
himself testified that he cannot "remember when financing was ever easy."
Unless we are prepared to say that financial exigency is chronic at Bloomfield College, it is difficult to say how, by any reasonable definition, the
circumstances can now be pronounced exigent.

    Recognizing the right of the board of trustees to make its own business
judgments as to how to improve cash flow, still, the yield from a sale of The
Knoll has been conservatively estimated at between 1½ and 4 million dollars.
Apart from the discontinuation of cash advances to the golf club, the immediate benefits which the college would realize from such a cash infusion has
been described. What effect this would have on the school's long-term
future is, of course, uncertain. However, it clearly enhances the probability
that it will be able to continue as a college for the foreseeable future. This
much certainly cannot be said of the expansive development program now
being explored. By so commenting, we do not suggest that one or the other
of the courses is to be preferred, but that the college's claim of financial
exigency can be validated only in its role as an educational institution, not as
the aspiring proprietor of high rise apartments, condominiums and luxury
dwellings. Its desire to retain this investment for long-term appreciation is
not a factor which the court may weigh in passing upon the existence of a
financial exigency. Its immediate duty is to maintain its educational programs and refrain from acts of faithlessness toward the faculty members by
whom it has been competently served. In this light the facts surrounding its
economic existence cannot reasonably support its claim of demonstrably
bona fide financial exigency.

    (4) Internal memoranda transmitted within the college itself during
the critical period of time are themselves revealing as to the real objectives
to be achieved by the adoption of Resolution R-58. For example, in his
memorandum to the faculty dated April 12, 1973 President Allshouse advised the faculty of his opposition to the "faculty substitute plan." Reason
3, upon which he places reliance, reads:

        The document explicitly placed adherence to the 1940 and
    1958 AAUP Statements on academic freedom, tenure, and due

process as the primary criterion for staff reductions rather than academic planning for the *long term viability of the College.* [Emphasis supplied].

It would appear that Dr. Allshouse's real concern is more fully addressed to balancing problems of long-term concern against basic contractual obligations, whereas the position relied on herein is a claim of financial exigency, an immediate, compelling crisis. His hostility to the basic concept of tenure is further elaborated in his report to the board of trustees dated June 21, 1973 wherein, under paragraph B, he analyzes at great length the faculty's "substitute plan" and in so doing engages almost entirely in partisan polemics having to do with the *pros* and *cons* of tenure unrelated to any question of financial crisis.

(5) Revealing also is the first paragraph in the report to the board of trustees from the college's Commission to Review Tenure and Retirement Policy dated June 21, 1973 in which it clearly focuses upon the issue of the "tenure system," not with a bona fide attempt to reconcile the fact of tenure with the reality of a true financial exigency. . . .

(6) Further confirming the impression that the defendants' primary objective was the abolition of tenure at Bloomfield College, not the alleviation of financial stringency, is their careful eschewal of other obvious remedial measures such as across-the-board salary reductions for all faculty members and reduction of faculty size by nonrenewal of contracts with teachers on probationary status, rather than termination of those who had earned tenured status by years of competent service.

The conclusions herein reached are not in their nature unique. Courts have not hesitated to invalidate the dismissal of tenured personnel where the reasons of economy given for their dismissal were shown to have been used as a subterfuge. . . .

Defendant's resistance to the remedy of specific performance rests upon that line of authority denying such relief in the case of contracts for personal services on the ground that equity will not compel the continuation of an obnoxious personal relationship. . . . The rationale of these authorities within the context of a teaching contract case is well expressed in Greene v. Howard University, 271 F.Supp. 609 (D.C.D.C.1967), rem. on other grounds 134 U.S.App.D.C. 81, 412 F.2d 1128 (1969). After stating that such a contract may not be enforced by specific performance, the court observed:

> It would be intolerable for the courts to interject themselves and to require an educational institution to hire or to maintain on its staff a professor or instructor whom it deemed undesirable and did not wish to employ. For the courts to impose such a requirement would be an interference with the operation of institutions of higher learning contrary to established principles of law and to the best tradition of education. [271 F.Supp. at 615].

But the conditions upon which this reasoning rests do not prevail in the case presented. . . .

This is not a case in which termination was based on any dissatisfaction with the services rendered, but ostensibly only by reason of financial exigency. It was an action taken with deep regret and with recognition of the "invaluable contribution to the College" made by the terminated faculty members. . . .

For the reasons given it is concluded that the individual plaintiffs who were terminated from their positions as faculty members of Bloomfield College are entitled to reinstatement under the terms and conditions of the "Bloomfield College Policies on Employment and Tenure." By way of declaratory relief it will further be adjudged that all plaintiffs serving as tenured faculty members of Bloomfield College prior to June 21, 1973 are now, and shall continue, on tenured status within the terms of the "Bloomfield College Policies on Employment and Tenure," and that the provisions of Resolution R-58 to the contrary, adopted on June 21, 1973 by the Bloomfield College Board of Trustees, as well as all administrative actions taken thereunder by defendants, are in all respects inefficacious.

AAUP v. BLOOMFIELD COLLEGE
Superior Court of New Jersey
Appellate Division
136 N.J. Super. 442, 346 A.2d 615 (1975)

LARNER, J.A.D.

Defendants appeal from a judgment entered in favor of plaintiffs reinstating the individual plaintiffs to the Bloomfield College faculty and declaring invalid those portions of a resolution of the Board of Trustees of Bloomfield College dated June 21, 1973 terminating the tenure of plaintiffs and other remaining faculty members.

*   *   *

Giving due deference to the fact-finding function of the trial judge, we nevertheless conclude that there is insufficient credible evidence to contradict the existence of "extraordinary circumstances because of financial exigency" in view of the admitted absence of liquidity and cash flow.[1]

In our opinion, the mere fact that this financial strain existed for some period of time does not negate the reality that a "financial exigency" was a fact of life for the college administration within the meaning of the underlying contract. The interpretation of "exigency" as attributed by the trial court is too narrow a concept of the term in relation to the subject matter involved. A more reasonable construction might be encompassed within the phrase "state of urgency." In this context, the evidence was plentiful as to the proof of the existence of the criterion of the financial exigency required by the contract.

[1.]   Subsequent to the decision below the college filed a Chapter XI petition in the Federal Bankruptcy Court.

In this vein it was improper for the judge to rest his conclusion in whole or in part upon the failure of the college to sell the Knoll property which had been acquired several years before in anticipation of the creation of a new campus at a different locale. The trial judge recognized that the exercise of the business judgment whether to retain or sell this valuable capital asset was exclusively for the board of trustees of the college and not for the substituted judgment of the court. Despite this, he engaged in an extensive analysis to demonstrate the potential ability of the institution to emerge from its dilemma by disposing of the Knoll property, thereby realizing substantial cash assets and relieving itself of the recurring financial loss involved in maintaining the same. Whether such a plan of action to secure financial stability on a short-term basis is preferable to the long-term planning of the college administration is a policy decision for the institution. Its choice of alternative is beyond the scope of judicial oversight in the context of this litigation. . . .

Does the foregoing view by the court lead to the conclusion that the ultimate finding in favor of plaintiffs is erroneous? The answer is no.

The existence of the "financial exigency" *per se* does not necessarily mean that the termination of tenure was proper. The key factual issue before the court was whether that financial exigency was the *bona fide* cause for the decision to terminate the services of 13 members of the faculty and to eliminate the tenure of remaining members of the faculty. Under subparagraph C(6) of the contract not only must the financial exigency be demonstrably *bona fide* but the termination *because* of that exigency must also be *bona fide*. Causation and motivation therefore emerged as the prime factual issue for determination by the trial judge. Was the financial exigency the true *bona fide* reason for adoption of the termination resolution? Or was the resolution dictated by other motivations, with reliance upon the existing financial picture a mere subterfuge? The answers to these queries were essential in order to determine whether the action under attack complied with the contractual obligation of the college to demonstrate that its interference with tenure was a *bona fide* result of its financial status.

The trial judge made full factual findings on this issue of *bona fide* causation and arrived at the conclusion that defendants failed to establish "by a preponderance of the evidence that their purported action was in good faith related to a condition of financial exigency within the institution." This finding is supported by the subordinate findings and analysis contained in his opinion. . . .

In view of the uncertainty in admeasuring damages because of the indefinite duration of the contract and the importance of the status of plaintiffs in the milieu of the college teaching profession, it is evident that the remedy of damages at law would not be complete or adequate. . . .

The relief granted herein is appropriate to achieve equity and justice.

Judgment is affirmed.

NOTES

1. What is the definition of "financial exigency" adopted by the Appellate Division in *Bloomfield*? How does this definition differ from the one adopted by the lower court? Is either definition consistent with the AAUP position on this matter?

2. The Keast Commission suggested that problems of the sort seen in *Bloomfield* "can be handled equitably and in the best interests of the institution as a whole only if faculty play a key role in decisions about the institution's response to fiscal crisis. . .." [Faculty Tenure, at p. 87]. Do you agree with this suggestion? What "key roles" should have been assigned to the members of the faculty at Bloomfield College?

3. Is there any way that officials at Bloomfield College could have achieved the desired cutback without being overturned by the courts? Is *Bloomfield* really a case about "financial exigency" or does it simply involve an unsuccessful attempt to eliminate tenure? Is there any way that the officials at Bloomfield College could have eliminated tenure? Does the decision in *Rehor, supra* help?

4. Another definition of "financial exigency" was adopted in Lumpert v. Univ. of Dubuque, 255 N.W. 2d 168 (Iowa Ct. of Appeals 1977) (unpublished opinion). The plaintiff in *Lumpert,* a tenured faculty member, contested his termination on account of financial exigency. Defendant University's Faculty Manual, which was part of plaintiff's contract, provided:

> After the expiration of the probationary period, continuous appointment shall be established and services are to be terminated only for adequate cause.
>
> It is understood that continuous appointment is based upon need for services of the appointee and the financial ability of the institution to continue the appointment.

The University's defense was that plaintiff's termination was for reasons of financial exigency and that his continuous appointment was dependent upon the financial ability of the University to continue it. The Court of Appeals, in upholding a lower court judgment in favor of defendant, ruled as follows:

> On the issue of financial exigency, evidence was presented by the University of deficits for a four-year period prior to plaintiff's termination of employment. The undisputed evidence on this issue shows that the University had the following yearly deficits; 1. Fiscal 1970, $62,676; Fiscal 1971, $147,093; Fiscal 1972, $121,464; Fiscal 1973, $235,898. In addition, the University owed approximately $200,000 to the federal government for construction of buildings. Because of the poor financial situation of the University, the federal government allowed the University in 1972 and 1973 to waive payments of $180,000 to an escrow account. This amount is not reflected in the aforesaid deficits. In order to meet these deficits, the University used money from unrestricted endowments from the period June 1970 to June 1973. In 1970 this endowment fund amounted to $170,000. By June 1973, it was down to $114. None of these figures was challenged by plaintiff for accuracy. Plaintiff claimed that the deficit was primarily chargeable to the seminary part of the University rather than to the college. Although this was undoubtedly true, the evidence also showed deficits in college financing.
>
> The termination of Lumpert's employment was part of the administration's attempt to remedy its consistent deficit financial situation. Lumpert was one of two professors of foreign language whose contracts were terminated. Other foreign language professors had been terminated in earlier years. The entire department of foreign languages was discontinued. The administration pointed out that it was a member of a tri-college agreement with Loras College and Clarke College where language departments were available. Under this arrangement, a student from one of the colleges could take courses at the other two. Thus, no student at the University of Dubuque would be deprived of the opportunity to take foreign languages. The administration had

also made considerable reduction in staff in the seminary for financial reasons. . . .

The question whether a financial exigency existed is primarily a matter of subjective judgment to be exercised by the University officials charged with the responsibility of operating the University. We do not believe it is a question of fact to be determined by a jury. Moreover, we do not believe it is a matter for the substitution of the court's judgment or the juror's judgment for that of the administrative body. . . .

There is no evidence of bad faith or of reasons other than financial exigency for plaintiff's termination to create a jury question in the case at bar.

We hold that the defense of financial exigency was proved as a matter of law and that the trial court's judgment for defendant n.o.v. on that ground is substantiated by the record. Judge affirmed.

The decision in *Lumpert* was affirmed by the Iowa Supreme Court. Although the decision was rendered on a "no precedent" basis, it nevertheless raises some important questions about the meaning of "financial exigency." For example, the dissenting judge in *Lumpert* argued that tenured faculty members should not be let go pursuant to "financial exigency" until "other available alternatives [are] fully and fairly considered. . . ."

In its instructions to the jury, the trial court in *Lumpert* distinguished between "financial ability" and "financial exigency," as follows:

1. Financial ability is defined as the quality or state of being able to provide the necessary funds in order to achieve the desired ends of the educational institution by rearranging the expenditure and income of funds in the institution in such a way as to provide necessary funds to meet the annual expenditures, with sufficient revenue to prevent the loss of funds. Financial ability is not synonymous with financial exigency since the need for rearrangement of funds does not have to be urgent, critical or pressing under the concept of financial ability.

2. Financial exigency is defined as the critical, pressing or urgent need on the part of the educational institution to reorder its monetary expenditures within the institution in such a way as to remedy and relieve the state or urgency within said institution created by the inability of the institution to meet its annual monetary expenditures with sufficient revenue to prevent a sustained loss of funds.

What are the main differences between the tests of "financial exigency" seen in *Lumpert* and *Bloomfield?* Will the tests produce significantly different results in most cases?

In Brown, *Financial Exigency,* 62 AAUP Bull. 5 (1976), the author suggests that the decision in *Lumpert* is a disaster. Do you agree?

5. Traditionally, wrongfully terminated plaintiffs have been denied reinstatement and limited to money damages because of the court's aversion to the imposition of an undesirable personal relationship upon the defendant. Other courts have viewed reinstatement as an extraordinary equitable remedy and limited its application to situations involving either racial discrimination or where the termination was in reprisal for the exercise of constitutionally protected rights. *See* Decker v. No. Idaho Col., 552 F.2d 872 (9th Cir. 1977). In the public sector, courts have been more willing to grant reinstatement, with relief being obtained through the use of prerogative writs. *See, e.g.,* State ex rel. Keeney v. Ayers, 108 Mont. 547, 92 P.2d 306 (1939); State ex rel. Richardson v. Bd. of Regents of Univ. of Nevada, 70 Nev. 347, 269 P.2d 265 (1954). These actions are based on the theory that the wrongful termination was in violation of the state law and it is therefore proper for the courts to compel the public officials to act within the law. See also Davis, *Enforcing Academic Tenure: Reflections and Suggestions,* 161 Wisc. L. Rev. 200.

6. In Hartman v. Merged Area VI Community College, 270 N.W.2d 822 (1978), the Iowa Supreme Court ruled that declining enrollment was not "good cause" under a state

law to justify the dismissal of a teacher during the term of a contract of employment.

7. In Krotkoff v. Goucher College, 585 F.2d 675 (4th Cir. 1978), the court upheld the dismissal of a tenured professor on the basis of "evidence [that] overwhelmingly demonstrate[d] that the college was confronted by pressing financial need." The court ruled that the plaintiff's contractual relationship with Goucher College did not exempt her from dismissal due to financial exigency. The court also observed that "tenure is not generally understood to preclude demonstrably bona fide dismissal for financial exigency," that even when a tenure contract or university bylaws do not specifically mention financial exigency. "the courts [have] construed tenure as implicitly granting colleges the right to make bona fide dismissals for financial reasons;" and that "the existence of financial exigency should be determined by the adequacy of a college's operating funds rather than its capital assets."

C.   Termination Due to Program Discontinuance

BROWZIN v. CATHOLIC UNIV. OF AMERICA
United States Court of Appeals
District of Columbia Circuit
527 F.2d 843 (D.C. Cir. 1975)

J. SKELLY WRIGHT, Circuit Judge:

Dr. Boris Browzin, the plaintiff and appellant, was hired by Catholic University in September 1962 as a professor in the School of Engineering and Architecture. In 1962 and succeeding years he taught a full load of courses, concentrating primarily in the field of Structures and the field of Soil Mechanics. In late 1969 the School of Engineering and Architecture was faced with a severe budget reduction, and the administration, in conjunction with the faculty, began considering retrenchment and reorganization of the school. The administration also took steps to cut back on the faculty, releasing some faculty members who were nontenured, and a few, including Browzin, who had achieved tenure. The Dean informed Browzin of this decision in a letter dated November 11, 1969. In it he stated that after a "detailed review of all of our current programs," he had identified certain areas in which the University had no great strength and could not hope to achieve strength under the new budgetary limitations. Two of those areas were Soil Mechanics and Hydrology, which were Browzin's particular responsibility. Consequently, those courses would no longer be offered after the 1969-70 academic year, and Browzin's appointment was to be terminated as of January 31, 1971—a date some 14 months after the letter giving notice of termination. The Dean emphasized that he was motivated by financial considerations alone in making the difficult termination decision. . . .

Browzin sued, charging that this termination breached his contract with Catholic University. Before trial the parties stipulated that Dr. Browzin was a highly qualified professor in the field of civil engineering, that he was a tenured professor, and that Catholic University was faced with a *bona fide* financial exigency at the time the termination occurred. They also stipulated that the standards which were to govern the case were to be found in the 1968 Recommended Institutional Regulations on Academic Freedom and Tenure, propounded by the American Association of University Professors (AAUP). Tr. at 6. It was, in effect, a stipulation that the 1968 Regulations had been adopted as part of the contract between Browzin and the University, an adoption entirely consistent with the Statutes of the University and the University's previous responses to AAUP actions.

Of particular relevance is Regulation 4(c), which provides in pertinent part:

> Where termination of appointment is based upon financial exigency, or bona fide discontinuance of a program or department of instruction, Regulation 5 [dealing with dismissals for cause] will not apply * * *. In every case of financial exigency or discontinuance of a program or department of instruction, the faculty member concerned will be given notice as soon as possible, and never less than 12 months' notice, or in lieu thereof he will be given severance salary for 12 months. Before terminating an appointment because of the abandonment of a program or department of instruction, the institution will make every effort to place affected faculty members in other suitable positions. If an appointment is terminated before the end of the period of appointment, because of financial exigency, or because of the discontinuance of a program of instruction, the released faculty member's place will not be filled by a replacement within a period of two years, unless the released faculty member has been offered reappointment and a reasonable time within which to accept or decline it.

54 AAUP Bulletin 448, 449 (1968). . . .

I

The major issue on this appeal centers upon the trial court's interpretation of the third sentence of Regulation 4(c): "Before terminating an appointment because of the abandonment of a program or department of instruction, the institution will make every effort to place affected faculty members in other suitable positions." Unlike the other three sentences of the Regulation, this sentence does not in terms speak to terminations based upon financial exigency; it speaks only of discontinuances of programs or departments of instruction. The District Court found this to be a crucial distinction, and held that the "suitable position" requirement does not apply to terminations resulting in any way from financial exigency. Since Browzin's termination did stem from the University's *bona fide* financial difficulties, the court ruled that the University had no obligation to seek another suitable position within the institution for him.

The *amicus* charges that this interpretation was erroneous. Drawing extensively on the history of the AAUP's efforts which culminated in the 1968 Regulations, it makes an impressive showing that the "suitable position" requirement was meant to apply even in terminations based strictly on financial exigency.

To understand this contention, Regulation 4(c) must be placed in context. It deals with terminations based on financial exigency or discontinuation of programs of instruction. But such terminations are not the central concern of the tenure system, nor of the 1968 Regulations. The real concern is with arbitrary or retaliatory dismissals based on an administrator's or a trustee's distaste for the content of a professor's teaching or research, or even for positions taken completely outside the campus setting. If a professor had no protection against such actions, he might well be deterred from pursuing his studies or his teaching in the paths that seem to him to be best. The tenure system, as embodied in the 1968 Regulations and in previous efforts by the AAUP and others, is designed to eliminate the chilling effect which the threat of discretionary dismissal casts over academic pursuits. It is designed to foster our society's interest in the unfettered progress of research and learning by protecting the profession's freedom of inquiry and instruction. *See generally 1940 Statement of Principles on Academic Freedom and Tenure,* reprinted in 60 AAUP Bulletin 269, 270 (1974); *Developments in the Law—Academic Freedom,* 81 Harv.L.Rev. 1045, 1085 (1968). Under the Regulations a professor achieves "tenure," a permanent status within the university, after completing a probationary period, usually seven years. Thereafter, as provided in Regulation 5, he can only be dismissed for adequate cause "related, directly and substantially, to the fitness of the faculty member in his professional capacity as a teacher or researcher." In such cases he has extensive procedural rights, including the right to a detailed notice of the reasons why the administration seeks dismissal, the right to a hearing before a university body wherein those seeking dismissal bear the burden of proof, and the right to representation by counsel.

Regulation 5, however, does not cover all possible cases of termination. A university must have some flexibility to respond to drastic reductions in funds or to the need for a change in curriculum—and it is this sort of issue which faces us here. Because of the need for flexibility, Regulation 4(c) provides an exception to the "for cause" termination procedures required by Regulation 5 in the case of financial exigency or program discontinuance. In those situations the same elaborate procedural safeguards do not apply because they are not entirely suitable to the issues arising when the university changes its curriculum or reacts to reduced funding. . . .

In sum, we are left with conflicting indications as to the meaning of the third sentence of Regulation 4(c). . . .

Fortunately, we are not required to resolve this apparent conflict between purpose and history on the one hand and the language of the Regulation on the other because there are other reasons which compel us to hold, regardless of the resolution of that conflict, that the "suitable position" requirement applied to the termination of Browzin's appointment. Financial exigency is in the case, but so is *abandonment of a program of instruction*—a matter expressly covered by the third sentence of Regulation 4(c). . . .

The third sentence of Regulation 4(c) must be read to apply here. It makes no difference that financial exigency loomed in the background. The University did discontinue Browzin's program of instruction. It was therefore under an obligation to make every effort to find him another suitable position in the institution.

II

The District Court's erroneous ruling that the third sentence was inapplicable does not necessitate reversal, however, for the court made an alternative finding. It ruled that even if the "suitable position" requirement applied, "the plaintiff's own evidence failed to prove a prima facie case that the University failed to make every effort to place him in another suitable position, or that such a suitable position existed * * * ." Findings at 5-6. We are unable to conclude that this finding was clearly erroneous. *See* Rule 52(a), Fed.R.Civ.P. Although Browzin testified that the school had held no meetings with him before the notice of termination in an effort to find a suitable alternative position, this testimony does not by any means preclude the possibility that the University engaged in such efforts. . . . Moreover, appellant chose to try the case on the theory that there *was* a suitable position available within the Department of Civil Engineering. Tr. at 14, 228-230. His counsel stressed again and again that Browzin was not limited to Soil Mechanics and Hydrology, the terminated courses, but that he was equipped to teach in the continuing area of Structural Design. However, Browzin's own witness indicated that the Structural Design courses could be taught by several members of the faculty and were in fact being given at the time by another tenured professor two years Browzin's senior, a point finally conceded by appellant's counsel. Tr. at 230. Teaching Structural Design might have been a suitable position for Browzin, but it was by no means available at the time of his termination.

Amicus AAUP suggests that this finding by the District Court should be reversed because the court erroneously placed the burden of proof on Browzin to demonstrate that the University had failed to make every effort to place him in another suitable position. In the usual case the burden of course rests on the plaintiff as to all elements of his action for breach of contract. Nonetheless, there is some merit to the position of *amicus.* Ordinarily a litigant does not have the burden of establishing facts peculiarly within the knowledge of the opposing party. The University here was plainly in a far better position to know what efforts were or were not undertaken to find for Browzin another post within the University. This principle, however, cannot help appellant on this appeal. . . .

If there was error in the court's handling of the burden of proof issue below, it was precisely the kind of error that could have been corrected if properly called to the judge's attention. After appellant rested his case, perhaps the District Court would have gone on to hear the University's witnesses. Very likely we would not then be faced with a suggestion that we remand for such a course now, nearly two years after the trial and six years after the events in question. Appellant's failure to object, although he had ample opportunity to do so, precludes his raising the burden of proof issue here.

The only other substantial issue on this appeal stems from the fourth sentence of Regulation 4(c). It provides that "the released faculty member's place will not be filled by a replacement within a period of two years," unless the displaced member has an opportunity to accept the post himself. There is no question but that Browzin was never offered the opportunity to return to his former place at Catholic University. Another professor did, however, join the Department approximately a year and a half after Browzin left, hired to teach Water Resources. The evidence showed that Browzin had competence in two of the branches of Water Resources, namely Hydrology and Hydraulics, which relate specifically to design of structures meant to control the flow or retention of water. He did not, however, have any particular background in the third branch, Planning. Tr. at 88. The University wished to emphasize the Planning branch of the subject, focusing more on the question whether a certain structure should be built rather than how to build structures already decided upon. The University reasoned that it could attract more students this way, since the growing interest in protection of the environment was making the Planning emphasis especially attractive. It also believed that it had a greater chance of obtaining grants for studies with such an emphasis than for studies of the more traditional type. And there was some indication that an outside committee reviewing the school's accreditation in mid-1971 had been the impetus for creating the new post. . . .

The District Court found as a fact that the other professor had not been hired to fill Browzin's place. We are unable to conclude that that finding was clearly erroneous. . . .

IV

Amicus asserts that Browzin's 14-month notice was insufficient, contending that the 12-month requirement announced in the Regulations should be considered to run from the conclusion of an academic year, rather than simply from the date of notification. Appellant, however, never breathed a hint of this contention in the District Court, and we do not consider it open to him on appeal.

SCHEUER v. CREIGHTON UNIV.
Supreme Court of Nebraska
260 N.W. 2d 595 (1977)

SPENCER, Justice. . . .

Edwin G. Scheuer, Jr., was a tenured assistant professor at the School of Pharmacy of Creighton University, Omaha, Nebraska. Creighton University is a private institution of higher education with its principal place of business in Omaha, Douglas County, Nebraska. Scheuer had been granted the status of a tenured member of the faculty of Creighton University in 1971.

The School of Pharmacy is one of four schools making up the Health Sciences Division of the University, the others being Medicine, Dentistry, and Nursing. Each of the four schools has its own Dean, with the Vice President for the Health Services being responsible for the entire Health Sciences Division.

Creighton University operates on a June 1 to May 31 fiscal year. The budget for each school year is prepared in the fall of the preceding year. The School of Pharmacy has three sources of income: Tuition and fees; income generated from clinical services; and federal funds. A large part of the federal funds received were "capitation funds," which represent a certain amount of federal funds given to health science schools for each student educated. These funds were contingent upon the school agreeing to a specified enrollment increase. Additionally, in the School of Pharmacy, the funds were further conditioned on the school expanding its clinical pharmacy program.

In the fiscal year 1975-1976, the School of Pharmacy received approximately $160,000 in federal "capitation funds." For this same fiscal year, the School of Pharmacy's entire budget was between $600,000 and $700,000. In spite of federal aid, the School of Pharmacy had operated at a deficit since 1971. These deficits and the federal funding have been as follows:

Fiscal Year	Deficit	Federal Funding
1971-72	$11,407	$ 76,580
1972-73	68,311	70,199
1973-74	40,353	83,615
1974-75	56,656	142,733
1975-76	56,000	159,782

In June of 1975, the Vice President for the Health Sciences Division learned the Division was facing a $900,000 deficit for the fiscal year 1975-1976, which had just begun. The School of Pharmacy was responsible for approximately $50,000 of that deficit. Later that same summer, he learned the entire Health Sciences Division was facing a reduction of funds for the year 1976-1977, in the amount of $2,000,000, and this sum was on top of the already expected loss of $900,000. Of the $2,000,000 loss in funds for the Division, approximately $160,000 of that loss was attributable to the School of Pharmacy as a result of the loss of "capitation funds."

Adding to the problems of the School of Pharmacy was the fact that it was moving into a new building in the spring of 1976. This move created $100,000 in additional expenses for the School of Pharmacy. . . .

The record indicates steps were taken to cut costs without impairing the essential goal of maintaining the integrity of the program in the School of Pharmacy. Cuts were made first in the area of nonsalary costs, such as equipment, traveling, and office supplies. A freeze was placed on faculty salaries. Steps were taken to terminate certain nonfaculty positions. These steps were not sufficient, so it then became necessary to reduce the faculty. After a review of the various positions and their relation to the program, it was found necessary to terminate four faculty members. One of them was the plaintiff. Plaintiff was chosen because the only course he taught was medicinal chemistry which could also be taught by a tenured faculty member who had seniority over him and who also could teach biochemistry which plaintiff had stated he could not teach. . . .

Both parties agree that termination procedures are governed by the Creighton University faculty handbook. The handbook provides: "The right of tenure may not be revoked except for cause. In general we understand by 'cause', professional incompetence; medical-physical incapacity; substantial and manifest neglect of duty; grave misconduct (including inciting the immediate impairment of the institution's functions, or personally and physically causing such impairment); personal conduct substantially impairing the individual's performance of his appropriate functions within the University community; *and financial exigency on the part of the institution.* The burden of showing cause and of substantiating such a showing with a preponderance of the evidence is upon the institution.* * *

"Where termination of appointment is based upon financial exigency, which may be considered to include bona fide discontinuance of a program or department of instruction or the reduction in size thereof, faculty members affected may have the issued (sic) reviewed by the Academic Senate or Academic Council, or by the Faculty Grievance Committee, with ultimate review of controverted issues by the Board of Directors. In cases of financial exigency, including discontinuance or reduction of a program or department of instruction, the faculty member concerned is to be given notice as soon as possible but never less than 12 months before termination; or, in lieu thereof, he may be given severance salary for 12 months. . . .

It is undisputed that Creighton University as a whole was not in a real state of financial exigency. However, as set out hereafter, the testimony of its Treasurer might suggest otherwise. The trial judge found plaintiff's appointment could be terminated upon a showing of financial exigency in the School of Pharmacy. We approach the case on that premise. . . .

The termination procedures contained in the faculty handbook closely parallel those proposed by the American Association of University Professors in its *1968 Recommended Institutional Regulations on Academic Freedom and Tenure.* The brief of amicus curiae suggests that the American Association of University Professors, hereinafter called AAUP, has since adopted its *1976 Recommended Institutional Regulations on Academic Freedom and Tenure.* This for the first time defines "financial exigency" as "an imminent financial crisis which threatens the survival of the institution as a whole and which cannot be alleviated by less drastic means." . . .

So far as we have been able to ascertain, there is not a single case in any jurisdiction which sustains the plaintiff's position. The only case on point cited by the plaintiff, *Browzin v. Catholic University of America,* 174 U.S.

App.D.C. 60, 527 F.2d 843 (1975), would appear to support the defendant's contention rather than that of the plaintiff. . . .

If we read that case correctly, the financial exigency existed in the School of Engineering and Architecture. It was in that school the contract terms were applied after two courses of study were eliminated. We read the case to suggest a financial exigency in the School of Engineering and Architecture was sufficient cause to terminate Browzin's employment. The Dean emphasized he was motivated solely by financial considerations in making the difficult termination decision. At the close of plaintiff's case the trial court sustained defendant's motion to dismiss. The Court of Appeals affirmed. . . .

The *Browzin* court determined the cancellation of courses taught by the plaintiff was a discontinuance of a program of instruction. It therefore concluded the regulation based upon termination of appointment for financial exigency or bona fide discontinuance of a program was applicable. As heretofore suggested, *Browzin* is supportive of defendant's position. The Creighton faculty handbook provides for termination of an appointment based upon "financial exigency, which may be considered to include bona fide discontinuance of a program or department of instruction or the reduction in size thereof." The curtailing of the medicinal chemistry course in the School of Pharmacy is within the ambit of this provision.

The evidence supports a finding that plaintiff's termination was based upon a bona fide reduction in size of a program of instruction. For accreditation purposes and in order to obtain federal funding, the School of Pharmacy was required to emphasize its clinical pharmacy program. Medicinal chemistry, which plaintiff taught, was reduced to a 1 semester, 3 hour, course for freshman students. Another tenured faculty member, who had both rank and seniority over plaintiff, was qualified to teach medicinal chemistry as well as biochemistry. He assumed both these duties and plaintiff, who could teach only medicinal chemistry, was released. The record fully supports a finding the process used to select plaintiff for termination was not only fair and reasonable but tended to maintain the most viable and best overall program for the School of Pharmacy within the financial limits of that college.

We do not accept the 1976 recommendation of the American Association of University Professors defining "financial exigency" so as to limit that term to an imminent crisis which threatens the survival of the institution as a whole. This definition was adopted several years subsequent to the execution of the contract being interpreted herein. It has no probative value as to the meaning of the term at the time of the contract.

Plaintiff's interpretation of the language "financial exigency on the part of the institution" entirely ignores the other provisions of the contract. To accept plaintiff's definition would require Creighton to continue programs running up large deficits so long as the institution as a whole had financial resources available to it. The inevitable result of this type operation would be to spread the financial exigency in one school or department to the entire University. This could likely result in the closing of the entire institution. . . .

If we read the record correctly, Creighton as an institution has less than $2,000,000 of unrestricted general funds available every year. Common sense dictates that plaintiff's contention is untenable. To sustain it, we must hold no tenured employee in any college may be released until the institution exhausts its total assets or at the very least reaches the point where its very survival as an institution is in jeopardy.

We specifically hold the term "financial exigency" as used in the contract of employment herein may be limited to a financial exigency in a department or college. It is not restricted to one existing in the institution as a whole.

The evidence is fairly conclusive the School of Pharmacy was faced with a financial exigency for the fiscal year 1976-1977. It had been operating with a deficit for the past 5 years. The deficit for 1974-1975 and 1975-1976 had reached $56,000 for each year. The deficit faced for 1976-1977 was in excess of $200,000. This deficit would be more than three times greater than any previous deficit.

The Vice President for Financial Affairs, who was Treasurer of Creighton University, testified the University generally subsidized each college in the amount of 6 to 7½ percent of the budget for that college. This subsidy came from the University general fund, which is made up of endowment earnings, Jesuit net contributed income, and gift income from the public. These sources total approximately $1,750,000 a year.

To continue the existing pharmacy program, the University would have been required to more than double the subsidy for that college, to the detriment of its other schools. The Treasurer further testified Creighton University as a whole was in a delicate financial position. While stating the University was not then in a state of financial exigency, he did state it was on the edge of financial exigency. It was his further testimony that Creighton's endowment is only 1/10th of what it should have for a private university of its size.

For the reasons discussed above, the judgment of the District Court is correct and should be affirmed.

NOTES

1. Is the court in *Scheuer* correct in its interpretation of the holding in *Browzin*? What would the court in *Browzin* have done if the parties had not stipulated to the fact of a financial exigency?

2. Why does the court in *Scheuer* fail to distinguish between dismissals attributable to financial exigency versus program reductions or discontinuances? Certainly, financial exigency can result in or require program discontinuance, but it is also a separate basis for terminating tenured faculty. The AAUP has recognized this distinction in the 1976 RIR, 62 AAUP Bull. 19 (1976), which reads as follows:

   Discontinuance of Program or Department Not Mandated by Financial
   Exigency. . . .

(d) Termination of an appointment with continuous tenure, or of a probationary or specified appointment before the end of the specified term, may
occur as a result of bona fide formal discontinuance of a program or department of instruction. The following standards and procedures will apply.

> (1) The decision to discontinue formally a program or depart-
> ment of instruction will be based essentially upon educational
> considerations as determined primarily by the faculty as a whole
> or an appropriate committee thereof. (Note: "Educational con-
> siderations" do not include cyclical or temporary variation in
> enrollment. They must reflect long range judgments that the edu-
> cational mission of the institution as a whole will be enhanced by
> the discontinuance.)

While the AAUP RIR is limited to program discontinuance, the underlying policies
should arguably also be applicable to a reduction in the size or scope of a program.

One problem with the *Scheuer* definition of financial exigency, at least from the
perspective of the faculty member, is that it seemingly gives the university a free hand
to release tenured faculty. This is so because most university programs run at a deficit
and if a deficit is all that is required, tenured faculty will have very little protection. In
addition, by using strictly financial exigency, rather than program discontinuance, as a
basis for dismissal, the administration is able to avoid the AAUP suggestion that "the
decision to discontinue formally a program or department of instruction [should] be
based essentially upon educational considerations as determined primarily by the
faculty. . . ." The court in *Scheuer* seemingly ignores the fact that many factors other than
economics bear on the issue of whether a program should be continued. Is there any
justification for the approach followed by the court in *Scheuer*?

3. What would the court in *Scheuer* have done if the plaintiff had been dismissed
pursuant to a program discontinuance or reduction *unrelated to any financial exigency*?

4. An institution has in its language department a French professor, a Russian professor and a Spanish professor, all of whom have tenure. None of the professors is competent in another foreign language. The institution has an opportunity to hire a bright,
young professor who could proficiently teach all three languages. May the institution
hire the young professor and terminate the tenured professors? Is the result changed
if the language department is at two-thirds or one-half capacity because of declining
enrollments? If the institution is facing financial exigency?

5. Once an institution has established that a financial exigency exists, should it also
be required to show that plaintiff's termination was in fact a good faith effort to alleviate
the crisis, or should the faculty member be required to prove that the institution has
acted in an arbitrary or capricious manner in violation of its obligation of good faith?
Should the answer differ depending upon whether the plaintiff is alleging a deprivation of
procedural due process rights or breach of contract? *See* Note: *The Dismissal of Tenured
Faculty for Reasons of Financial Exigency,* 51 Ind. L. J. 417, 429-31 (1976), and Note,
*Financial Exigency as Cause for Termination of Tenured Faculty Members in Private
Post Secondary Educational Institutions,* 62 Ia. L. Rev. 481, 516-519 (1976).

V. Overriding Constitutional Considerations: The Requirement of Pro-
cedural Due Process in Public Institutions

BOARD OF REGENTS v. ROTH
Supreme Court of the United States
408 U.S. 564, 92 S.Ct. 2701, 33 L. Ed. 2d 548 (1972)

MR. JUSTICE STEWART delivered the opinion of the Court.

In 1968 the respondent, David Roth was hired for his first teaching job
as assistant professor of political science at Wisconsin State University-

Oshkosh. He was hired for a fixed term of one academic year. The notice of his faculty appointment specified that his employment would begin on September 1, 1968, and would end on June 30, 1969. The respondent completed that term. But he was informed that he would not be rehired for the next academic year.

The respondent had no tenure rights to continued employment. Under Wisconsin statutory law a state university teacher can acquire tenure as a "permanent" employee only after four years of year-to-year employment. Having acquired tenure, a teacher is entitled to continued employment "during efficiency and good behavior." A relatively new teacher without tenure, however, is under Wisconsin law entitled to nothing beyond his one-year appointment. There are no statutory or administrative standards defining eligibility for re-employment. State law thus clearly leaves the decision whether to rehire a nontenured teacher for another year to the unfettered discretion of University officials. . . . Rules promulgated by the Board of Regents provide that a nontenured teacher "dismissed" before the end of the year may have some opportunity for review of the "dismissal." But the Rules provide no real protection for a nontenured teacher who simply is not re-employed for the next year. He must be informed by February first "concerning retention or non-retention for the ensuing year." But "no reason for non-retention need be given. No review or appeal is provided in such case."

In conformance with these Rules, the President of Wisconsin State University-Oshkosh informed the respondent before February 1, 1969, that he would not be rehired for the 1969-1970 academic year. He gave the respondent no reason for the decision and no opportunity to challenge it at any sort of hearing.

The respondent then brought this action in a federal district court alleging that the decision not to rehire him for the next year infringed his Fourteenth Amendment rights. He attacked the decision both in substance and procedure. First, he alleged that the true reason for the decision was to punish him for certain statements critical of the University administration, and that it therefore violated his right to freedom of speech. [5] Second, he alleged that the failure of University officials to give him notice of any reason for nonretention and an opportunity for a hearing violated his right to procedural due process of law.

The District Court granted summary judgment for the respondent on the procedural issue, ordering the University officials to provide him with reasons and a hearing. 310 F. Supp. 972. The Court of Appeals, with one judge dissenting, affirmed this partial summary judgment. 446 F.2d 806. We granted certiorari. 404 U.S. 909, 92 S. Ct. 227, 30 L. Ed. 2d 181. The only

---

[5.] While the respondent alleged that he was not rehired because of his exercise of free speech, the petitioners insisted that the non-retention decision was based on other, constitutionally valid grounds. The District Court came to no conclusion whatever regarding the true reason for the University President's decision. . . .

question presented to us at this stage in the case is whether the respondent had a constitutional right to a statement of reasons and a hearing on the University's decision not to rehire him for another year. [6] We hold that he did not.

The requirements of procedural due process apply only to the deprivation of interests encompassed within the Fourteenth Amendment's protection of liberty and property. When protected interests are implicated the right to some kind of prior hearing is paramount. [7] But the range of interests protected by procedural due process is not infinite. . . .

Undeniably, the respondent's re-employment prospects were of major concern to him—concern that we surely cannot say was insignificant. And a weighing process has long been a part of any determination of the *form* of hearing required in particular situations by procedural due process. But, to determine whether due process requirements apply in the first place, we must look not to the "weight" but to the *nature* of the interest at stake. See Morrissey v. Brewer, 405 U.S.___,___, 92 S. Ct. 2593, 32 L. Ed. 2d___. We must look to see if the interest is within the Fourteenth Amendment's protection of liberty and property.

"Liberty" and "property" are broad and majestic terms. They are among the "[g]reat [constitutional] concepts . . . purposely left to gather meaning from experience. . . . [T]hey relate to the whole domain of social and economic fact, and the statesmen who founded this Nation knew too well that only a stagnant society remains unchanged." National Mutual Ins. Co. v. Tidewater Transfer Co., 337 U.S. 582, 646, 69 S. Ct. 1173, 1195, 93 L. Ed. 1556 (Frankfurter, J., dissenting). For that reason the Court has fully and finally rejected the wooden distinction between "rights" and "privileges" that once seemed to govern the applicability of procedural due process rights. [9] The Court has also made clear that the property interests protected by procedural due process extend well beyond actual ownership

---

[6.] The courts that have had to decide whether a nontenured public employee has a right to a statement of reasons or a hearing upon nonrenewal of his contract have come to varying conclusions. Some have held that neither procedural safeguard is required. *E.g.*, Orr v. Trinter, 444 F.2d 128 (CA6); Jones v. Hopper, 410 F.2d 1323 (CA10); Freeman v. Gould Special School District, 405 F.2d 1153 (CA8). At least one court has held that there is a right to a statement of reasons but not a hearing. Drown v. Portsmouth School District, 435 F.2d 1182 (CA1). And another has held that both requirements depend on whether the employee has an "expectancy" of continued employment. Ferguson v. Thomas, 430 F.2d 852, 856 (CA5).

[7.] Before a person is deprived of a protected interest, he must be afforded opportunity for some kind of a hearing, "except for extraordinary situations where some valid governmental interest is at stake that justifies postponing the hearing until after the event." . . .

[9.] In a leading case decided many years ago, the Court of Appeals for the District of Columbia Circuit held that public employment in general was a "privilege," not a "right," and that procedural due process guarantees therefore were inapplicable. Bailey v. Richardson, 86 U.S. App. D.C. 248, 182 F.2d 46, aff'd by an equally divided Court, 341 U.S. 918, 71 S. Ct. 669, 95 L. Ed. 1352. The basis of this holding has been thoroughly undermined in the ensuing years. For, as Mr. Justice Blackmun wrote for the Court only last year, "this Court now has rejected the concept that constitutional rights turn upon whether a governmental benefit is characterized as a 'right' or as a 'privilege.'" Graham v. Richardson, 403 U.S. 365, 374, 91 S. Ct. 1848, 1853, 29 L. Ed. 2d 534.

of real estate, chattels, or money.[10] By the same token, the Court has required due process protection for deprivations of liberty beyond the sort
of formal constraints imposed by the criminal process.

Yet, while the Court has eschewed rigid or formalistic limitations on the
protection of procedural due process, it has at the same time observed certain
boundaries. For the words "liberty" and "property" in the Due Process
Clause of the Fourteenth Amendment must be given some meaning. . . .

The State, in declining to rehire the respondent, did not make any
charge against him that might seriously damage his standing and associations
in his community. It did not base the nonrenewal of his contract on a charge,
for example, that he had been guilty of dishonesty, or immorality. Had it
done so, this would be a different case. For "[w]here a person's good name,
reputation, honor, or integrity is at stake because of what the government is
doing to him, notice and an opportunity to be heard are essential.". . .

In such a case, due process would accord an opportunity to refute the
charge before University officials. In the present case, however, there is no
suggestion whatever that the respondent's interest in his "good name, reputation, honor or integrity" is at stake.

Similarly, there is no suggestion that the State, in declining to re-employ
the respondent, imposed on him a stigma or other disability that foreclosed
his freedom to take advantage of other employment opportunities. The
State, for example, did not involve any regulations to bar the respondent
from all other public employment in State universities. Had it done so, this,
again, would be a different case. . . .

To be sure, the respondent has alleged that the nonrenewal of his
contract was based on his exercise of his right to freedom of speech. But
this allegation is not now before us. The District Court stated proceedings
on this issue, and the respondent has yet to prove that the decision not to
rehire him was, in fact, based on his free speech activities.[14]

Hence, on the record before us, all that clearly appears is that the
respondent was not rehired for one year at one University. It stretches the

---

[10.] See, *e.g.*, Connell v. Higginbotham, 403 U.S. 207, 208, 91 S. Ct. 1772, 1773, 29 L. Ed. 2d
418; Bell v. Burson, 402 U.S. 535, 91 S. Ct. 1586, 29 L. Ed. 2d 90; Goldberg v. Kelly, 397
U.S. 254, 90 S. Ct. 1011, 25 L. Ed. 2d 287.

[14.] See n. 5, *infra*. The Court of Appeals, nonetheless, argued that opportunity for a hearing and a
statement of reasons were required here "as a *prophylactic* against non-retention decisions improperly motivated by exercise of protected rights." 446 F.2d, at 810 (emphasis supplied).
While the Court of Appeals recognized the lack of a finding that the respondent's nonretention
was based on exercise of the right of free speech, it felt that the respondent's interest in liberty
was sufficiently implicated here because the decision not to rehire him was made "with a background of controversy and unwelcome expressions of opinion." *Ibid.*

When a State would directly impinge upon interests in free speech or free press, this Court has
on occasion held that opportunity for a fair adversary hearing must precede the action, whether
or not the speech or press interest is clearly protected under substantive First Amendment
standards. . . .

In the respondent's case, however, the State has not directly impinged upon interests in free
speech or free press in any way comparable to a seizure of books or an injunction against meetings. Whatever may be a teacher's rights of free speech, the interest in holding a teaching job at
a state university, *simpliciter,* is not itself a free speech interest.

concept too far to suggest that a person is deprived of "liberty" when he simply is not rehired in one job but remains as free as before to seek another. Cafeteria Workers v. McElroy, 367 U.S. at 895-896, 81 S. Ct. at 1748-1749, 6 L. Ed. 2d 1230.

The Fourteenth Amendment's procedural protection of property is a safeguard of the security of interests that a person has already acquired in specific benefits. These interests—property interests—may take many forms.

Thus the Court has held that a person receiving welfare benefits under statutory and administrative standards defining eligibility for them has an interest in continued receipt of those benefits that is safeguarded by procedural due process. Goldberg v. Kelly, 397 U.S. 254, 90 S. Ct. 1011, 25 L. Ed. 2d 287. Similarly, in the area of public employment, the Court has held that a public college professor dismissed from an office held under tenure provisions, Slochower v. Board of Education, 350 U.S. 551, 76 S. Ct. 637, 100 L. Ed. 692, and college professors and staff members dismissed during the terms of their contracts, Wieman v. Updegraff, 344 U.S. 183, 73 S. Ct. 215, 97 L. Ed. 216, have interests in continued employment that are safeguarded by due process. Only last year, the Court held that this principle "proscribing summary dismissal from public employment without hearing or inquiry required by due process" also applied to a teacher recently hired without tenure or a formal contract, but nonetheless with a clearly implied promise of continued employment. Connell v. Higginbotham, 403 U.S. 207, 208, 91 S. Ct. 1772, 1773, 29 L. Ed. 2d 418.

Certain attributes of "property" interests protected by procedural due process emerge from these decisions. To have a property interest in a benefit, a person clearly must have more than an abstract need or desire for it. He must have more than a unilateral expectation of it. He must, instead, have a legitimate claim of entitlement to it. It is a purpose of the ancient institution of property to protect those claims upon which people rely in their daily lives, reliance that must not be arbitrarily undermined. It is a purpose of the constitutional right to a hearing to provide an opportunity for a person to vindicate those claims.

Property interests, of course, are not created by the Constitution. Rather they are created and their dimensions are defined by existing rules or understandings that stem from an independent source such as state law— rules or understandings that secure certain benefits and that support claims of entitlement to those benefits. Thus the welfare recipients in Goldberg v. Kelly, *supra,* had a claim of entitlement to welfare payments that was grounded in the statute defining eligibility for them. The recipients had not yet shown that they were, in fact, within the statutory terms of eligibility. But we held that they had a right to a hearing at which they might attempt to do so.

Just as the welfare recipients' "property" interest in welfare payments was created and defined by statutory terms, so the respondent's "property" interest in employment at the Wisconsin State University-Oshkosh was created and defined by the terms of his appointment. Those terms secured his interest in employment up to June 30, 1969. But the important fact in this case is that they specifically provided that the respondent's employment was to terminate on June 30. They did not provide for contract renewal absent "sufficient cause." Indeed, they made no provision for renewal whatsoever.

Thus the terms of the respondent's appointment secured absolutely no interest in re-employment for the next year. They supported absolutely no possible claim of entitlement to re-employment. Nor, significantly, was there any state statute or University rule or policy that secured his interest in re-employment or that created any legitimate claim to it.[16] In these circumstances, the respondent surely had an abstract concern in being rehired, but he did not have a *property* interest sufficient to require the University authorities to give him a hearing when they declined to renew his contract of employment. . . .

We must conclude that the summary judgment for the respondent should not have been granted, since the respondent has not shown that he was deprived of liberty or property protected by the Fourteenth Amendment. The judgment of the Court of Appeals, accordingly, is reversed and the case is remanded for further proceedings consistent with this opinion. It is so ordered. Reversed and remanded.

PERRY v. SINDERMANN
Supreme Court of the United States
408 U.S. 593, 92 S. Ct. 2694, 33 L. Ed. 2d 570 (1972)

MR. JUSTICE STEWART delivered the opinion of the Court.

From 1959 to 1969 the respondent, Robert Sindermann, was a teacher in the state college system of the State of Texas. After teaching for two years at the University of Texas and for four years at San Antonio Junior College, he became a professor of Government and Social Science at Odessa Junior College in 1965. He was employed at the college for four successive years, under a series of one-year contracts. He was successful enough to be appointed, for a time, the cochairman of his department.

During the 1968-1969 academic year, however, controversy arose between the respondent and the college administration. The respondent was elected president of the Texas Junior College Teachers Association. In this capacity, he left his teaching duties on several occasions to testify before committees of the Texas Legislature, and he became involved in public disagreements with the policies of the college's Board of Regents. In particular, he aligned himself with a group advocating the elevation of the

---

[16.] To be sure, the respondent does suggest that most teachers hired on a year-to-year basis by the Wisconsin State University-Oshkosh are, in fact, rehired. But the District Court has not found that there is anything approaching a "common law" of re-employment, see Perry v. Sindermann, 405 U.S. — at —, 92 S. Ct. 2694, at —, 32 L. Ed. 2d —, so strong as to require University officials to give the respondent a statement of reasons and a hearing on their decision not to rehire him.

college to four-year status—a change opposed by the Regents. And, on one occasion, a newspaper advertisement appeared over his name that was highly critical of the Regents. Finally, in May 1969, the respondent's one-year employment contract terminated and the Board of Regents voted not to offer him a new contract for the next academic year. The Regents issued a press release setting forth allegations of the respondent's insubordination. [1]   But they provided him no official statement of the reasons for the nonrenewal of his contract. And they allowed him no opportunity for a hearing to challenge the basis of the nonrenewal. . . .

The Court of Appeals reversed the judgment of the District Court. Sindermann v. Perry, 430 F.2d 939. First, it held that, despite the respondent's lack of tenure, the nonrenewal of his contract would violate the Fourteenth Amendment if it in fact was based on his protected free speech. Since the actual reason for the Regents' decision was "in total dispute" in the pleadings, the court remanded the case for a full hearing on this contested issue of fact. *Id.* at 942-943. Second, the Court of Appeals held that, despite the respondent's lack of tenure, the failure to allow him an opportunity for a hearing would violate the constitutional guarantee of procedural due process if the respondent could show that he had an "expectancy" of re-employment. It, therefore, ordered that this issue of fact also be aired upon remand. . . .

The first question presented is whether the respondent's lack of a contractual or tenure right to re-employment, taken alone, defeats his claim that the nonrenewal of his contract violated First and Fourteenth Amendments. We hold that it does not.

For at least a quarter century, this Court has made clear that even though a person has no "right" to a valuable governmental benefit and even though the government may deny him the benefit for any number of reasons, there are some reasons upon which the government may not act. It may not deny a benefit to a person on a basis that infringes his constitutionally protected interests—especially, his interest in freedom of speech. For if the government could deny a benefit to a person because of his constitutionally protected speech or associations, his exercise of those freedoms would in effect be penalized and inhibited. This would allow the government to "produce a result which [it] could not command directly." Speiser v. Randall, 357 U.S. 513, 526, 78 S. Ct. 1332, 1342, 2 L. Ed. 2d 1460. Such interference with constitutional rights is impermissible. . . . We have applied the principle regardless of the public employee's contractual or other claim to a job. Compare Pickering v. Board of Education, *supra,* with Shelton v. Tucker, *supra.*

Thus the respondent's lack of a contractual or tenure "right" to re-employment for the 1969-1970 academic year is immaterial to his free

---

[1.]   The press release stated, for example, that the respondent had defied his superiors by attending legislative committee meetings when college officials had specifically refused to permit him to leave his classes for that purpose.

speech claim. Indeed, twice before, this Court has specifically held that the nonrenewal of a nontenured public school teacher's one-year contract may not be predicated on his exercise of First and Fourteenth Amendment rights. Shelton v. Tucker, *supra;* Keyishian v. Board of Regents, *supra.* We affirm these holdings here.

In this case, of course, the respondent has yet to show that the decision not to renew his contract, was, in fact, made in retaliation for his exercise of the constitutional right of free speech. The District Court foreclosed any opportunity to make this showing when it granted summary judgment. Hence, we cannot now hold that the Board of Regents' action was invalid.

But we agree with the Court of Appeals that there is a genuine dispute as to "whether the college refused to renew the teaching contract on an impermissible basis—as a reprisal for the exercise of constitutionally protected rights." 430 F.2d, at 943. The respondent has alleged that his nonretention was based on his testimony before legislative committees and his other public statements critical of the Regents' policies. And he has alleged that this public criticism was within the First and Fourteenth Amendment's protection of freedom of speech. Plainly, these allegations present a *bona fide* constitutional claim. For this Court has held that a teacher's public criticism of his superiors on matters of public concern may be constitutionally protected and may, therefore, be an impermissible basis for termination of his employment. Pickering v. Board of Education, *supra.*

For this reason we hold that the grant of summary judgment against the respondent, without full exploration of this issue, was improper.

The respondent's lack of formal contractual or tenure security in continued employment at Odessa Junior College, though irrelevant to his free speech claim, is highly relevant to his procedural due process claim. But it may not be entirely dispositive.

We have held today in Board of Regents v. Roth, *supra,* that the Constitution does not require opportunity for a hearing before the nonrenewal of a nontenured teacher's contract, unless he can show that the decision not to rehire him somehow deprived him of an interest in "liberty" or that he had a "property" interest in continued employment, despite the lack of tenure or a formal contract. In *Roth* the teacher had not made a showing on either point to justify summary judgment in his favor.

Similarly, the respondent here has yet to show that he has been deprived of an interest that could invoke procedural due process protection. As in *Roth,* the mere showing that he was not rehired in one particular job, without more, did not amount to a showing of a loss of liberty. [5] Nor did it amount to a showing of a loss of property.

But the respondent's allegations—which we must construe most favorably to the respondent at this stage of the litigation—do raise a genuine issue

---

[5.]   The Court of Appeals suggested that the respondent might have a due process right to some kind of hearing simply if he *asserts* to college officials that their decision was based on his constitutionally protected conduct. 430 F.2d at 944. We have rejected this approach in Board of Regents v. Roth, *supra,* 408 U.S. at — n.14, 92 S. Ct., at 2708 n.14.

as to his interest in continued employment at Odessa Junior College. He alleged that this interest, though not secured by a formal contractual tenure provision, was secured by a no less binding understanding fostered by the college administration. In particular, the respondent alleged that the college had a *de facto* tenure program, and that he had tenure under that program. He claimed that he and others legitimately relied upon an unusual provision that had been in the college's official Faculty Guide for many years:

"*Teacher Tenure*: Odessa College has no tenure system. The Administration of the College wishes the faculty member to feel that he has a permanent tenure as long as his teaching services are satisfactory and as long as he displays a cooperative attitude toward his co-workers and his superiors, and as long as he is happy in his work."

Moreover, the respondent claimed legitimate reliance upon guidelines promulgated by the Coordinating Board of the Texas College and University System that provided that a person, like himself, who had been employed as a teacher in the state college and university system for seven years or more has some form of job tenure. Thus the respondent offered to prove that a teacher, with his long period of service, at this particular State College had no less a "property" interest in continued employment than a formally tenured teacher at other colleges, and had no less a procedural due process right to a statement of reasons and a hearing before college officials upon their decision not to retain him.

We have made clear in *Roth* . . . that "property" interests subject to procedural due process protection are not limited by a few rigid, technical forms. Rather, "property" denotes a broad range of interests that are secured by "existing rules or understandings." . . . A person's interest in a benefit is a "property" interest for due process purposes if there are such rules or mutually explicit understandings that support his claim of entitlement to the benefit and that he may invoke at a hearing.

A written contract with an explicit tenure provision clearly is evidence of a formal understanding that supports a teacher's claim of entitlement to continued employment unless sufficient "cause" is shown. Yet absence of such explicit contractual provision may not always foreclose the possibility that a teacher has a "property" interest in re-employment. For example, the law of contracts in most, if not all, jurisdictions long has employed a process by which agreements, though not formalized in writing, may be "implied." 3 Corbin on Contracts, § § 561-672A. Explicit contractual provisions may be supplemented by other agreements implied from "the promisor's words and conduct in the light of the surrounding circumstances." *Id.*, at § 562. And, "[t]he meaning of [the promisor's] words and acts is found by relating them to the usage of the past." *Ibid.*

A teacher, like the respondent, who has held his position for a number of years, might be able to show from the circumstances of this service—and from other relevant facts—that he has a legitimate claim of entitlement to job tenure. Just as this Court has found there to be a "common law of a particular industry or of a particular plant" that may supplement a collective-bargaining agreement, United Steelworkers v. Warrior & Gulf Nav. Co., 363 U.S. 574, 579, 80 S. Ct. 1347, 1351, 4 L. Ed. 2d 1409, so there may be an unwritten "common law" in a particular university that certain employees shall have the equivalent of tenure. This is particularly likely in a college or university, like Odessa Junior College, that has no explicit tenure system even for senior members of its faculty, but that nonetheless may have created such a system in practice. See Byse & Joughin, Tenure in American Higher Education 17-28.

In this case, the respondent has alleged the existence of rules and understandings, promulgated and fostered by state officials, that may justify his legitimate claim of entitlement to continued employment absent "sufficient cause." We disagree with the Court of Appeals insofar as it held that a mere subjective "expectancy" is protected by procedural due process, but we agree that the respondent must be given an opportunity to prove the legitimacy of his claim of such entitlement in light of "the policies and practices of the institution." 430 F.2d, at 943. Proof of such a property interest would not, of course, entitle him to reinstatement. But such proof would obligate college officials to grant a hearing at his request, where he could be informed of the grounds for his nonretention and challenge their sufficiency.

Therefore, while we do not wholly agree with the opinion of the Court of Appeals, its judgment remanding this case to the District Court is affirmed.

Affirmed.

NOTES

1. The Fourteenth Amendment provides that a person shall not be deprived of life, liberty or property without due process of law. As noted in Johnson v. Bd. of Regents, 377 F.Supp. 227 (W.D. Wis. 1974), due process is a flexible concept and the scope and depth of the due process protection may vary with the nature of the interest involved. For example, where a faculty member is being terminated for cause, the possible substantial negative implications of such an action compelled the court in Ferguson v. Thomas, 430 F.2d 852, 856 (5th Cir. 1970), to hold that minimum procedural due process required that:

(a) he be advised of the cause or causes for his termination in sufficient detail to fairly enable him to show any error that may exist,

(b) he be advised of the names and the nature of the testimony of witnesses against him,

(c) at a reasonable time after such advice he must be accorded a meaningful opportunity to be heard in his own defense,

(d) that hearing should be before a tribunal that both possesses some academic expertise and has an apparent impartiality toward the charges.

Other cases which have required similar standards are: Kaprelian v. Texas Woman's Univ., 509 F.2d 133 (5th Cir. 1975); Grimes v. Nottoway Co. Sch. Bd., 462 F.2d 650 (4th Cir. 1972), cert. den., 409 U.S. 1008 (1972); Hostrop v. Bd. of Jr. Col. Dist., 471 F.2d 488 (7th Cir. 1972), cert. den., 411 U.S. 967 (1973); and Chung v. Park, 514 F.2d 382 (3rd Cir. 1975). However, in Downing v. LeBritton, 550 F.2d 689 (1st Cir. 1977), the court ruled that in a post-termination procedure, a regulation preventing a discharged employee from having a representative who was not an employee of the university did not violate due process.

2. Since termination for financial exigency did not raise negative implications about the faculty members involved in *Johnson, supra*, the court held that due process required far less by way of procedural protections. (See discussion *infra* at Note 9.)

3. Codd v. Velger, 429 U.S. 624 (1977), presents another variation of the adjustable nature of the procedural due process concept. In *Codd,* when plaintiff, a probationary, public employee, was dismissed without a hearing, he alleged that defendant employer's placement of certain derogatory information in his personnel file stigmatized him and that he was therefore entitled to a hearing. The Supreme Court, in a per curiam decision, rejected his claim because plaintiff did not allege or prove that the stigmatizing information was substantially false. The Court reasoned that since plaintiff was not challenging the truth of the information, there was no reason for the hearing because,

> The hearing required where a nontenured employee has been stigmatized in the course of a decision to terminate his employment is solely to provide the person an opportunity to clear his name.

4. Two noteworthy Ninth Circuit cases, Bignall v. No. Idaho College, 538 F.2d 243 (9th Cir. 1976) and Decker v. No. Idaho College, 552 F.2d 872 (9th Cir. 1977), raise questions about the scope of the protection afforded by the procedural due process requirement. *Bignall* was an action by a faculty member with *"de facto* tenure" challenging a decision to terminate her appointment because of financial exigency. Although Mrs. Bignall eventually received the full range of procedural due process protections and the court upheld her termination, the court (in a footnote) raised an important question about the nature of *"de facto"* tenure, as follows:

> The finding that Mrs. Bignall had *de facto* tenure does not automatically lead to the conclusion that she had rights identical to those granted tenure under the college tenure program. The granting of tenure is a complex ramified process. A holding that one has an expectancy of continuous employment on the other hand is a rather gross conclusion that may merely signify that the holder of the expectancy cannot be summarily dismissed. [538 F.2d 248-249]

Decker, like Mrs. Bignall, was a faculty member with *de facto* tenure who had not been given a hearing prior to his termination. When the trial court concluded that he was entitled to a hearing, the court, with the consent of the parties, conducted it. The court then concluded that since Decker had been deprived of his right to a hearing, he was entitled to one year of back pay. However, since the court found that Decker had been dismissed for cause, reinstatement was denied.

5. The finding of the court in *Decker*, that the plaintiff was dismissed for "cause," is given as if to suggest that cause is necessary to justify dismissal. However, it is not entirely clear why the standard of "cause" was selected by the court as the substantive protection under the *de facto* tenure system found to exist in *Decker*. In addition, it is not at all clear what the court would have done if it had found that the plaintiff in *Decker* was dismissed following an adequate hearing but without just cause. Since the so-called *de facto* tenure system existed without any substantive design, plaintiff may have been limited to a claim that his dismissal was "arbitrary and capricious" and thus his dismissal violated substantive due process. However, as recently noted by the Court in Kelley v. Johnson, 96 S.Ct. 1440 (1976), the standard of review under substantive due process is very narrow indeed, and certainly significantly less than a "cause" standard of review.

Furthermore, it should be recalled that in Codd v. Velger, 429 U.S. 624 (1977), the Court in dicta suggested that procedural due process does not require a "determination . . . of whether or not . . . the employee was properly refused reemployment." Therefore, in *Decker,* it can be argued that absence of "cause" was irrelevant and that the only thing that the court really had to worry about was whether or not the plaintiff had adequate procedural due process.

6. In both *Bignall* and *Decker,* the terminated faculty member was deprived of a hearing by the employer and had to resort to the district court to obtain procedural due

process. If the institutions had provided satisfactory hearings, then a question arises as to what, if any, review would have been available to plaintiffs in court. Plaintiffs will always be able to pursue any legitimate claims arising pursuant to substantive constitutional protections, such as Free Speech or Equal Protection. In addition, certain rights afforded by statute, such as those arising under Title VII of the Civil Rights Act of 1964, may normally be pursued in court after administrative action. Otherwise, the dicta in *Codd* suggests that procedural due process does not afford substantive protection and, therefore, no review may be possible to challenge the judgment rendered after procedural due process has been given.

On this same point, it is noteworthy that the Supreme Court in *Perry v. Sindermann, supra,* stated that Sindermann

> must be given an opportunity to prove the legitimacy of his claim of such entitlement in light of the policies and practices of the institution. . . . [But] proof of such a property interest would not of course entitle him to reinstatement.

If *de facto* tenure is not equivalent to regular tenure, as tenure is understood in the academic community, what is it? Can *de facto* tenure be acquired where an institution has adopted a formal tenure policy? *See* Soni v. Bd. of Trustees of Univ. of Tennessee, 376 F.Supp. 289 (E.D. Tenn. 1974), *aff'd,* 513 F.2d 347 (6th Cir. 1975).

7. The decision in Mt. Healthy v. Doyle, 429 U.S. 274 (1977), presents another limitation on the individual's protection from impermissible conduct by a public employer. In *Mt. Healthy,* the plaintiff, a nontenured teacher, established that a substantial factor in the employer's decision not to rehire him was his conduct, which was constitutionally protected by the free speech provision of the First Amendment. The lower court concluded that, "if the nonpermissible reason, *e.g.* the exercise of First Amendment rights, played a substantial part in the decision not to renew,—even in the face of other permissible grounds, the decision may not stand." Recognizing the serious consequences of reinstatement, the Supreme Court held that the school district should have been afforded the opportunity to show, by the preponderance of the evidence, that it would have reached the same decision as to respondent's reemployment even in the absence of the protected conduct. Thus, under *Mt. Healthy,* it appears that a nontenured faculty member could be non-renewed for constitutionally impermissible reasons, provided that there are also other reasons which furnish an adequate basis for dismissal or non-renewal. Since a nontenured faculty member could be non-renewed for no reason at all, is there any reason, other than fairness, to give the non-renewed person any indication of the basis for the decision? Should the *Mt. Healthy* test apply in a case involving claims of race or sex discrimination?

8. Two other important cases dealing with procedural due process issues are: Bishop v. Wood, 96 S.Ct. 2074 (1976) (dismissal of employee for failure to follow orders, causing low morale and unsuitable conduct did not interfere with any "liberty" interest in reputation since the grounds for dismissal had not been publicly disclosed to anyone but plaintiff); and Arnett v. Kennedy, 94 S.Ct. 1633 (1974) (*post*-dismissal hearing may be sufficient to protect an employee's constitutional right to procedural due process).

9. As noted earlier, a number of courts have held that "adversary proceedings" are not required by procedural due process in cases involving faculty cutbacks due to financial exigency. In Johnson v. Bd. of Regents, 377 F.Supp. 227 (W.D. Wis. 1974), *aff'd,* 510 F.2d 975 (9th Cir. 1975), the court defined due process to mean:

> furnishing each plaintiff with a reasonably adequate written statement of the basis for the initial decision to lay-off;
> furnishing each plaintiff with a reasonably adequate description of the manner in which the initial decision had been arrived at;
> making a reasonably adequate disclosure to each plaintiff of the information and data upon which the decision-makers had relied; and
> providing each plaintiff the opportunity to respond.

See also Levitt v. Bd. of Trustees of Nebraska State Colleges, 376 F.Supp. 945 (D. Neb. 1974), where it was held that:

[W] here lack of funds necessitated releasing a sizeable number of the faculty, certainly it was peculiarly within the province of the school administration to determine which teachers should be released, and which retained.

Where there is a showing that the administrative body, in exercising its judgment, acts from honest convictions, based upon facts which it believes for the best interest of the school, and there is no showing that the acts were arbitrary or generated by ill will, fraud, collusion or other such motives it is not the province of a court to interfere and substitute its judgment for that of the administrative body. [376 F.Supp. at 950]

Accord: Klein v. Bd. of Higher Education of City of New York, 434 F.Supp. 1113 (S.D.N.Y. 1977).

CHAPTER 8

UNIONIZATION AND COLLECTIVE BARGAINING

=====================

I.   Introduction

Collective bargaining has arrived on campus; however, this arrival has not been without controversy. The appearance of collective bargaining at the City University of New York in 1969 represented a break from the long-standing tradition that unions had no place in the world of academics. The tradition was founded on the belief that the goals, interests and professional status of academic employees were incompatible with the collective bargaining system used in the industrial sector. Thus, even in the early 1960s the likelihood of finding academic employees participating in collective bargaining was remote. But by the 1970s collective bargaining had not only arrived on campus, it has assumed a significant role in academic life on a number of campuses.

A major force opposing collective bargaining in higher education was removed in 1973 when the American Association of University Professors issued the following statement on collective bargaining:

> As large segments of the American faculty community manifest an interest in collective bargaining, there is a pressing need to develop a specialized model of collective bargaining in keeping with the standards of higher education. From its vantage point as the paramount national organization in formulating and implementing the principles that govern relationships of academic life, the Association has the unique potential, indeed the responsibility, to achieve through its chapters a mode of collective bargaining consistent with the best features of higher education. To leave the shaping of collective bargaining to organizations lacking the established dedication to principles developed by the Association and widely accepted by the academic community endangers those principles. To the extent that the Association is influential in the shaping of collective bargaining, the principles of academic freedom and tenure and the primary responsibility of a faculty for determining academic policy will be secured. . . . The implementation of Association-supported principles, reliant upon professional traditions and upon moral suasion, can be effectively supplemented by a collective bargaining agreement and given the force of law. [*AAUP Statement on Collective Bargaining*, AAUP Bulletin (Summer 1973).]

With this policy swing, the AAUP joined the American Federation of Teachers (AFT) and National Education Association (NEA) as one of the three leading national "union" organizers of academic employees. Created in 1915, the AAUP had resisted the union movement on campus until 1972. However, when the successes of the NEA and AFT began to multiply, the AAUP changed its position and entered the competition to organize academic employees in higher education. By late 1976 the AAUP had organized 42 four-year institutions and 3 two-year institutions.

Organized in 1916 as part of the American Federation of Labor, the AFT is generally considered to be more "union-like" and "militant" than either AAUP or NEA. Until the 1960s the AFT had few associations in higher education; however, AFT's successful efforts with collective bargaining (and strikes) at the elementary and secondary school levels in the 1960s and 1970s made it an attractive organization to many faculties plagued by the deteriorating economy in the 1970s. By 1976, AFT had secured bargaining rights at 185 institutions of higher education, including 86 four-year institutions.

The oldest of the three organizations, NEA was formed in 1857 and created a division for higher education in 1870. Believing that the division was ineffective the NEA eliminated it in 1920, but brought it back into existence in 1943. The focus of the NEA was originally on the quality of education and not the conditions of employment for teachers. However, by the turn of the twentieth century, the NEA had initiated a movement to upgrade salaries and working conditions of public school teachers. This movement eventually carried the NEA into community colleges and four-year state schools which were linked to public education. During the 1960s the Association's authorization of "refusals to work" and actual strikes suggested that the focus of NEA had again shifted. As the acceptance of collective bargaining in academia increased, the organizing activity of the NEA broadened and in 1973 it joined the Coalition of American Public Employees (CAPE) for joint organizing, collective bargaining, and political action. By the end of 1976 the NEA had been selected as the bargaining agent for academic employees on 192 college and university campuses.

NOTES

1. A good study of union organization of academic employees can be found in Means and Semas, Faculty Collective Bargaining: A Chronicle of Higher Education Handbook (Washington D.C.: Editorial Projects for Education, 1976). Another interesting study on faculty organization is Ladd and Lipset, Professors, Unions, and American Higher Education (Berkeley, Cal.: The Carnegie Foundation, 1973), where the authors report that:

The AAUP has had its greatest relative membership strength in universities, whereas prior to the collective bargaining elections and organization drives of the early seventies, the heartland of NEA faculty membership was the four-year colleges, particularly those that were once primarily for teacher training; and AFT had its main base at community colleges. Differentiating by quality strata reveals the AAUP with its highest proportional membership in middle-tier schools, whereas NEA, AFT, and local faculty association membership rises steadily with movement from the highest to the lowest stratum. At elite colleges and universities, places where faculty members generally have the most individual prestige and bargaining power, and where fears over such issues as academic freedom are low because threats are minimal, a large majority of professors (60 percent) are not members of any of the unions or associations. At institutions of the lowest stratum, in contrast, association membership is very high, with only a small minority (18 percent) unaffiliated. About three-fourths of major college faculty who belong to one of the associations are in the AAUP, as compared to only 35 percent of all association members at institutions of the lowest rank. [*Id*. at 41-42]

2. The traditional role of faculty senates at many institutions of higher education has caused some authorities to suggest that faculty senates might serve as bargaining agents for academic employees. See Brown, *Collective Bargaining in Higher Education*, 67 Mich. L. Rev. 1067 (1969). However, this idea has not as yet proven to be a viable alternative to traditional union organization. One problem with the use of a faculty senate as a bargaining agent is that a senate group which includes university administrators as voting members and receives university support in the form of office space and clerical staff might be unlawfully "assisted" or "dominated" by the university employer under Section 8(a)(2) of the NLRA. With respect to the faculty senate question, the National Labor Relations Board has observed, in Adelphi University, 79 LRRM 1545, at 1556, note 31 (1972), that:

> The delegation by the University to such elected groups of a combination of functions, some of which are, in the typical industrial situation, normally more clearly separated as managerial on the one hand and as representative of employee interests on the other, could raise questions both as to the validity and continued viability of such structures under our Act, particularly if an exclusive bargaining agent is designated.

See also Northeastern University, 89 LRRM 1862 (1975); Kahn, *Current and Emerging Labor Relations Issues in Higher Education*, 2 J. Coll. & U. L. 123 (Winter 1974-75); and Finkin, *The NLRB in Higher Education*, 5 U. Tol. L. Rev. 608 (1973).

3. Some of the better writings dealing with collective bargaining in higher education are: Gee, *Organizing the Halls of Ivy: Developing a Framework for Viable Alternatives in Higher Education Employment*, 1973 Utah L. Rev. 233 (1973); Feller & Finkin, *Legislative Issues in Faculty Collective Bargaining*, Faculty Bargaining in Public Higher Education: A Report and Two Essays (San Francisco: Jossey-Bass Publishers, 1977); Finkin, *The NLRB in Higher Education*, 5 U. Tol. Rev. 608 (1973); Garbarino, *State Experience in Collective Bargaining*, Faculty Bargaining in Public Higher Education: A Report and Two Essays 30 (San Francisco: Jossey-Bass Publishers, 1977); Kahn, *The NLRB and Higher Education: The Failure of Policymaking Through Adjudication*, 21 UCLA L. Rev. 63 (1973); Ladd and Lipset, Professors, Unions and American Higher Education (Berkeley, Cal.: The Carnegie Commission on Higher Education, 1973); Means and Semas, *Faculty Collective Bargaining*, A Chronicle of Higher Education Handbook (Washington, D.C.: Editorial Projects for Education, Inc., 1976); Menard and DiGiovanni, *NLRB Jurisdiction Over Colleges and Universities: A Plea for Rulemaking*, 16 Wm. & Mary L. Rev. 599 (1975); Mintz, *Faculty Collective Bargaining in Higher Education: A Management Perspective*, 3 J. Law & Educ. 413 (1974); Tice, ed., Faculty Bargaining in the Seventies (Ann Arbor, Mich.: Inst. of Continuing Legal Education, 1973); Tice, ed., Faculty Power: Collective Bargaining on Campus (Ann Arbor, Mich.: Inst. of Continuing Legal Education, 1972); Weisberger, *Faculty Grievance Arbitration in Higher Education: Living with Collective Bargaining*, (Ithaca, N.Y.: Inst. of Public Employment, Monograph No. 5, 1976); Wollett, *Faculty Collective Bargaining in Higher Education: An Organization Perspective*, 3 J. Law & Educ. 425 (1974); *Collective Negotiations in Higher Education: A Symposium*, 1971 Wis. L. Rev. 1 (1971); *Is Public Sector Grievance Arbitration Different From the Private Sector*, 7 J. Law & Educ. 539 (1978); and *Reasons Why Faculty Members Accept or Reject Unions in Higher Education*, 7 J. Law & Educ. 51 (1978).

4. Since collective bargaining involves an enormous body of law and practice, which itself could fill a complete book, no attempt will be made here to give exhaustive treatment to this subject. Rather, this chapter is designed to give the reader an overview of

some of the most significant issues concerning labor relations law as it affects higher education. A reader desiring more complete information with respect to legal questions in this area should consult any of the following texts: Gorman, Labor Law—Basic Text (St. Paul: West, 1976); Edwards, Clark & Craver, Labor Relations Law in the Public Sector, 2d ed. (Charlottesville, Va.: Bobbs-Merrill/Michie, 1979); Smith, Merrifield & St. Antoine, Labor Relations Law, 5th ed. (Indianapolis: Bobbs-Merrill, 1974); Meltzer, Labor Law, 2d. ed. (Boston: Little, Brown & Co., 1977); Cox, Bok & Gorman, Cases on Labor Law, 8th ed. (Mineola, N.Y.: Foundation Press, 1977); Morris, The Developing Labor Law (Chicago: ABA, 1971) (plus annual Supplements); Oberer, Hanslowe & Andersen, Labor Law, 2d ed. (St. Paul: West, 1979); and Leslie, Cases and Materials on Labor Law: Process and Policy (Boston: Little, Brown & Co., 1979).

II.   The General Legal Framework for Collective Bargaining

A.   The Public-Private Dichotomy

The legal controls of collective bargaining are dictated in significant measure by the public-private dichotomy of institutions in higher education. Once the status of an institution is established as public or private, the determination of the applicable law is relatively simple. Private institutions, which meet the jurisdictional requirements established by the National Labor Relations Board (NLRB) are subject to federal regulation under the National Labor Relations Act (NLRA), 49 Stat. 449 (1935), as amended by 61 Stat. 136 (1947), 65 Stat. 601 (1951), 72 Stat. 945 (1958), 73 Stat. 541 (1959); 29 U.S.C. § § 151-169 (1974). Public institutions are excluded from the jurisdiction of the NLRB and subject only to state regulation, where it exists.

The caveat is that the distinction between public and private institutions is not always a simple one to draw. A category of quasi-public institutions has resulted from increased government funding and regulation of private institutions and changes in the governance of both public and private institutions. To further complicate the distinction, the definition of public and private has been made dependent upon the purpose for which an institution is being categorized. Thus, for the purpose of collective bargaining, an institution's status as public or private will be determined according to the NLRA or state labor legislation. Section 2(2) of the NLRA, which exempts any state or its political subdivision thereof, has been interpreted to preclude NLRB jurisdiction over institutions which are either "(1) created directly by the State, so as to constitute a department or administrative arm of the government, or (2) administered by individuals who are responsible to public officials or to the general public." Minneapolis Society of Fine Arts, 78 LRRM 1609, at 1610 (1971). Guidelines which have been developed by the NLRB to examine the status of an institution include whether or not the institution was privately chartered, the amount of financial support received by the institution, and/or the extent of government control over internal management of the institution. Yet the determination of an institution's status may still be difficult as is evidenced in a review of previous NLRB decisions.

The decision in Temple University, 79 LRRM 1196 (1972), highlights the problem of the quasi-public institution. In Temple, it was held that, although the University was in form a private, nonprofit institution, the Board would not assert its jurisdiction. The Board found that under a 1965 state statute Temple, which had been a private institution since 1888, had been made an instrumentality of the state. Furthermore, it was found that the University had become a quasi-public institution due to extensive and direct state control of university activities and substantial state involvement in university financial affairs. The NLRB did not find that the quasi-public institution was exempt as a political subdivision of the state, but, rather, that jurisdiction should be declined because of the "unique" nexus between the university and state. No explanation was provided as to the relationship between the political subdivision exemption and the quasi-public exclusion.

In Howard University, 86 LRRM 1389 (1974), a private institution was found to have a "unique relationship with the federal government" due to its establishment under a federal charter and receipt of federal funds allocated from the HEW budget. Because of this unique relationship effective collective bargaining could only be carried on with the participation of many federal agencies, over which the Board had no jurisdiction. Consequently, the NLRB found it necessary to decline jurisdiction. But upon reconsideration, a newly composed Board decided that Howard University was not a public university nor an instrumentality of the federal government. The factors upon which the Board relied to reverse its prior decision included: a lack of government control over appointments to the Board of Trustees, total university control over its own construction contracts, no governmental involvement in the university's allocation and spending of private funds, and university freedom to act with respect to personnel and labor relations matters. Howard University, 92 LRRM 1249 (1976).

In 1976, an institution was found to be private for the purpose of collective bargaining, notwithstanding the fact that the university received 25% of its gross annual revenue from the state. University of Vermont and State Agricultural College, 91 LRRM 1570 (1976). The receipt of state financial assistance was insufficient to eliminate NLRB jurisdiction over the university which was privately chartered and substantially independent in its internal operations. See Chronicle of Higher Education, April 12, 1976.

NOTE

The following is a brief description of the National Labor Relations Board:

I. STATUTORY AUTHORITY

The National Labor Relations Board was created by the National Labor Relations (Wagner) Act of July 5, 1935, 49 Stat. 449, as amended by the Labor-Management Relations (Taft-Hartley) Act of 1947, 61 Stat. 136, and the Labor-Management Reporting and Disclosure (Landrum-Griffin) Act of 1959, 73 Stat. 519, 29 U. S. C. 151 et seq.

II. JURISDICTION

The NLRB administers the National Labor Relations Act, as amended. Under the National Labor Relations Act employees are guaranteed the right to organize unions, to bargain collectively, and to engage in concerted activities for their mutual aid and protection, as well as the right to refrain from such activities. The Act also prohibits or restricts certain union conduct such as secondary boycotts and specified kinds of organizational or recognition picketing.

The two principal functions of the Board are (1) resolving questions "affecting commerce" concerning the representation of employees, and (2) preventing employers or unions from engaging in unfair labor practices "affecting commerce," as specified in section 8 of the Act. Although its statutory jurisdiction is generally coextensive with congressional authority under the commerce clause, the NLRB will not exercise jurisdiction unless the employer involved meets certain jurisdictional standards which the Board has established. . . .

III. DESCRIPTION OF ORGANIZATION

The NLRB is composed of five Board members and an independent General Counsel. Subject to Senate approval, the President appoints Board members for five-year terms and the General Counsel for a four-year term. All are eligible for reappointment. Three members of the Board ordinarily constitute a quorum.

The Board has final authority over all phases of representation proceedings. The General Counsel, however, has sole authority to investigate charges that an unfair labor practice has been committed in violation of section 8 of the Act, to decide whether to issue a formal complaint under section 10, and to prosecute such complaints when issued. Final authority to determine whether there has been an unfair labor practice rests with the Board. The Trial Examiners' Division, as a part of the Board's staff, is responsible for conducting hearings and issuing trial examiners' decisions in unfair labor practice cases.

The General Counsel also exercises general supervision over all attorneys employed by the Board (other than trial examiners and legal assistants to Board members) and over the personnel in the regional offices. . . .

IV. SOME ILLUSTRATIVE PROCEDURES

A. Questions of Representation

Section 9 of the Act provides that the representative selected by the majority of the employees in an appropriate bargaining unit shall be the exclusive bargaining representative for all the employees in the unit. An employer may recognize a union without formal procedures if satisfied that it represents a majority of his employees. Otherwise, questions of representation may be resolved by the Board in a section 9 election proceeding ("R" case).

An election proceeding is initiated by the filing of a petition for certification by employees or a union ("RC" petition) or by an employer who has been presented with a demand for recognition ("RM" petition). A petition for decertification may be filed by employees or a union asserting that a certified or currently recognized bargaining agent no longer represents a majority of the employees ("RD" petition). Only one valid election will be conducted in a bargaining unit during any twelve-month period. Furthermore, a lawful contract between an employer and a union will bar an election for its full term, but not exceeding three years.

Certification or decertification petitions must be filed with the regional office in the area where the bargaining unit is located. An agent of the regional office then investigates whether there exist such requirements for a Board election as jurisdiction, an appropriate unit, and an adequate showing of interest on the part of a petitioning union (i.e., designation of the union by 30% of the employees). If the regional director concludes that the conditions for an election have not been met, the petitioner must withdraw his petition or the regional director will dismiss it. Ten days are allowed to request the Board in Washington to review a dismissal.

When it appears that a question of representation affecting commerce exists, the regional agent will attempt to get the parties to agree to either of two types of consent election procedures. One (the "consent election agreement") provides that any disputes in connection with the election will be determined by the regional director, and the other (the "stipulation for certification") provides that such disputes will be determined by the Board. If no agreement can be reached, the regional director issues a formal notice of hearing. A hearing is then conducted by a hearing officer. All parties are entitled to be represented by counsel, to submit evidence, cross-examine witnesses, make objections, and present oral argument. Traditional rules of evidence are not controlling.

Following the close of the hearing each party may file a brief with the regional director. Exercising authority delegated by the Board, the regional director then directs an election, dismisses the petition, or otherwise disposes of the issues raised. Within ten days after service of the regional director's order or direction, a party may file a request for review with the Board in Washington. Filing such a request does not stay the regional director's action, but no election is conducted until the Board has ruled on the request. Review by the Board is granted only for compelling reasons. Briefs may be filed with the Board if review is granted, but oral argument is rarely allowed in representation cases.

An election is conducted under the supervision of the regional director in whose region the case is pending. All elections are by secret ballot. Any party may be represented by observers, and any party or Board agent may challenge voters, whose ballots are then impounded. To gain certification, or to avoid decertification, a union must receive a majority of the valid votes cast.

After the tally of the ballots has been furnished, each party has five working days to file objections to the conduct of the election or to conduct affecting the results of the election. If there are timely objections or if the challenged ballots are sufficient in number to affect the results of the election, the regional director makes an investigation. Then he issues a report on objections or an order resolving the issues himself. Where a report has been issued, parties may file exceptions with the Board, which may decide the matter upon the record or order a hearing if significant factual issues are raised by the exceptions. Where the regional director has issued an order, parties are limited to requesting the Board for review. In cases of consent elections, either the regional director or the Board has sole authority to resolve disputed questions, depending on what procedure the parties have chosen. Runoff elections are required when at least three choices appear on the ballot, i.e., two unions and "neither," and no choice receives a majority of the valid ballots cast.

A certification by the Board in itself carries no sanctions. A refusal to bargain after a valid certification, however, constitutes an unfair labor practice.

Ordinarily the Board will not proceed with an election petition if unfair labor practice charges involving the same employees are also pending. This rule applies without exception when the charge alleges employer domination or support of a union, or a refusal to bargain by a union or employer. A party charging another type of violation may request the Board to continue processing the representation case. On the other hand, if the pending charge alleges that a union is engaging in certain prohibited organizational or recognition picketing, section 8(b)(7)(C) of the Act provides for a special "expedited election." A quick vote is obtained by eliminating the hearing that normally precedes a direction of election, reducing the time allowed for appeals, and eliminating the use of briefs. Unless the union wins the election, it cannot continue its picketing.

B. Union Shop Referendum

An employer and a union representing a majority of the employees in a bargaining unit may enter into a union shop agreement requiring all employees in the unit to join the union within 30 days, or after seven days in the construction industry. This authority may be rescinded for a period of one year, however, by a majority of all the employees in a unit who are eligible to vote (not just a majority of those casting valid ballots). The Board will conduct a "deauthorization" election upon the filing of a petition ("JD" petition) on behalf of 30% of the employees in the unit. This type of petition is processed in the same general way as representation petitions, except that a deauthorization election is not barred by an outstanding valid contract.

C. Unfair Labor Practice Cases

An unfair labor practice proceeding ("C" case) can be initiated by any individual or organization, as long as a charge is filed within six months of the alleged offense. The charge may allege that an employer has violated section 8(a) of the Act ("CA" case) by coercing or discriminating against employees because of union membership or non-membership, or by dominating or assisting a particular union, or by refusing to bargain with a union representing a majority of his employees. The charge may allege that a union has violated section 8(b) of the Act by coercing employees, causing an employer to discriminate against employees, or refusing to bargain in good faith with an employer ("CB" case); by engaging in a secondary boycott or similar activity ("CC" case); by engaging in a jurisdictional strike ("CD" case); or by carrying on proscribed organizational or recognition picketing ("CP" case). Or the charge may allege that either a union or employer has violated section 8(e) by entering into a forbidden "hot cargo" agreement ("CE" case). All charges are normally filed in the regional office for the region where the unfair labor practices allegedly occurred. The charging party is responsible for effecting service.

A regional agent investigates the charges. If insufficient grounds for formal proceedings are disclosed, the charging party has to withdraw his charge or the regional director will dismiss it. The charging party has ten days to appeal a dismissal to the General Counsel in Washington, whose decision is final. At all stages of the proceedings Board agents will encourage voluntary settlements. These may be (1) informal adjustments between the parties, (2) informal settlements requiring the party charged to post notices of the terms of the settlement, or (3) formal settlements which include the issuance of a cease and desist order by the Board.

Formal proceedings begin when the regional director issues a complaint in the name of the Board. The complaint will describe the unfair labor practices alleged and will contain a notice of hearing before a trial examiner, not less than ten days after service and usually longer. The respondent has ten days after service to file an answer. If the charges are not denied or explained, all allegations are deemed admitted.

Counsel for the General Counsel is responsible for preparing a case to support the allegations of the complaint. However, all parties, including the charging party, are entitled to appear at the hearing and participate either personally or through counsel. They may call witnesses and submit evidence, cross-examine witnesses, make motions and objections, and present oral argument. So far as practicable, hearings are conducted in accordance with the rules of evidence applicable in federal district courts.

Upon request, any party to the proceeding may submit a brief or proposed findings of fact and conclusions of law to the trial examiner. The trial examiner then prepares his decision, setting forth his findings and conclusions together with recommendations for disposition of the case. The trial examiner's decision is filed with the Board in Washington and copies are served on all parties. The case is thereafter transferred to the Board.

Within twenty days after transfer of the case to the Board any party may file exceptions to the trial examiner's decision, along with a supporting brief. Within ten days after the due date for exceptions, any other party may file an answering brief or cross-exceptions together with a supporting brief. Oral argument may be requested at the time exceptions or cross-exceptions are filed, but this is granted only in important cases. Special leave is required for the filing of reply briefs. Matters not included in the exceptions normally may not thereafter be urged either before the Board or reviewing courts. If no exceptions are filed, the recommendations of the trial examiner are adopted by the Board. Where there are exceptions, the Board may decide the matter on the record, after oral argument, or after reopening the record and receiving further evidence.

The decision and order issued by the Board may adopt, modify, or reject the findings and recommendations of the trial examiner. Where violations of the Act are found, the Board customarily orders the respondent to cease and desist from his unlawful conduct and to take such affirmative action, e.g., providing back pay to employees discriminated against, as may be necessary to remedy the violation. Affirmative action always includes the posting of notices describing the respondent's obligations.

Until the transcript of the record has been filed in a reviewing court, the Board retains the power to modify or set aside its findings, conclusions, or order. In "extraordinary circumstances" a party may move for reconsideration, rehearing, or reopening of the record after the Board decision or order.

D. Injunctions against Unfair Labor Practices

Section 10(j) of the Act gives the Board the discretionary power, which is seldom used, to apply to a federal district court for a temporary injunction whenever a complaint has been issued alleging the commission of any unfair labor practice. Far more significant is the "mandatory injunction" provision, section 10(l), which requires the Board to seek temporary injunction whenever a charge has been made, and it appears to be true, that a union is engaging in a secondary boycott or similar activity or is carrying on forbidden organizational or recognition picketing, or that a union or employer has entered into a prohibited "hot cargo" agreement. When issued, such injunctions remain in effect while the unfair labor practices proceeding is pending.

E. Jurisdictional Disputes

Section 10(k) provides for special procedures to be followed when it is charged that a union is engaging in a jurisdictional strike. The parties are given ten days after they receive notice that such charges have been filed to submit evidence that they have agreed upon a method for voluntary adjustment of the dispute, such as use of the Joint Board for the Settlement of Jurisdictional Disputes in the construction industry. If they fail to agree, the regional director will issue a notice of a hearing before a hearing officer at which all the parties and any affected employers may appear and submit evidence regarding the dispute. Following the hearing the Board itself, upon the written record or after oral argument or the submission of briefs, determines the dispute by making an affirmative award of the work in question to one of the competing groups of employees. If there is a voluntary adjustment or compliance with the Board's decision, the original charge is dismissed. Otherwise, a formal complaint may be issued and the case handled like other unfair labor practice proceedings.

V. JUDICIAL REVIEW

Any party aggrieved by a final Board order in an unfair labor practice case may obtain review in an appropriate federal court of appeals. The Board itself through its General Counsel may petition an appropriate court of appeals for enforcement of a Board order. There are no time limitations on seeking either review or enforcement.

In the absence of extraordinary circumstances no objection will be considered by a court unless it was urged before the Board. Findings of the Board with respect to questions of fact, "if supported by substantial evidence on the record considered as a whole," are conclusive. Failure to comply with a court decree enforcing a Board order may result in a civil or criminal contempt proceeding initiated by the Board. The judgment and decree of a court of appeals is subject to further review by the Supreme Court on certiorari.

Board certifications in representation cases are not regarded as final orders and are not directly reviewable by the courts. But certifications may be tested in an unfair labor practice proceeding if the employer refuses to bargain. In addition, an injunction may be obtained against the Board if it violates constitutional standards or statutory prohibitions in a representation proceeding. Also not subject to judicial review are dismissals of unfair labor practice charges by the Board's General Counsel.

B.   *The NLRA and Private Institutions*

    1.   NLRB Jurisdictional Standards for Nonprofit Educational Institutions

CORNELL UNIVERSITY & ASSOCIATION
OF CORNELL EMPLOYERS – LIBRARIES
National Labor Relations Board
74 LRRM 1269 (1970)

Cornell University and Syracuse University, the employers herein, have filed representation petitions seeking elections to determine the bargaining representatives of certain of their non-academic employees. Association of Cornell Employees–Libraries (herein called ACE) has also filed a petition seeking to represent a group of library employees.

The threshhold question is whether the Board has or should assert jurisdiction over nonprofit colleges and universities in view of the 1951 decision in the Columbia University case. In that case, the Board decided that it would not effectuate the policies of the Act 'to assert its jurisdiction over a nonprofit, educational institution where the activities involved are noncommercial in nature and intimately connected with charitable and educational activities of the institution.'

All the petitioners urge the Board to overrule the Columbia University case. Syracuse and Cornell argue that the operations and activities of educational institutions as a class, and of Cornell and Syracuse in particular, have an overwhelming impact and effect on interstate commerce, that the operations of universities and colleges have increasingly become matters of Federal interest, and that this interest coupled with the failure of the States adequately to recognize and legislate for labor relations affecting these institutions and their employees now justifies the Board in asserting jurisdiction. In support of their contention as to the impact of the operations of Syracuse and Cornell, as well as of educational institutions as a class, upon interstate commerce, the Employers have presented extensive documentation of financial activities which are set forth hereinafter. . . .

Discussion

Section 2(2) of the Act defines an "employer" as follows:

'. . . any persons acting as an agent of an employer, directly or indirectly, but shall not include the United States or any wholly owned Government corporation, or any Federal Reserve Bank, or any State or political subdivision thereof, or any corporation or association operating a hospital, if no part of the net earnings inures to the benefit of any private shareholder or individual. . . .'

Although Section 2(2) specifically excludes nonprofit hospitals from the Act's coverage, it contains no such exclusion of private, nonprofit educational institutions. In the Columbia University case, the Board reviewed the then recently enacted Taft-Hartley amendments to the National Labor Relations Act and concluded that

'. . . the activities of Columbia University affect commerce sufficiently to satisfy the requirements of the statute and the standards established by the Board for the normal exercise of its jurisdiction. . . .'

However, the Board, as a discretionary matter, declined to assert such jurisdiction because of statements in the House Conference Report which seemed to indicate approval of what the Report believed to have been the Board's pre-1947 practice of declining in the exercise of its discretion to assert jurisdiction over certain nonprofit organizations. . . .

In the intervening two decades since Columbia University was decided, the Board has declined to assert jurisdiction over nonprofit universities if the activity involved was noncommercial and intimately connected with the school's educational purpose. However, an analysis of the cases reveals that the dividing line separating purely commercial from noncommercial activity has not been easily defined. . . .

No claim is made that education is not still the primary goal of such institutions. Indeed, more than two million students are enrolled in colleges today, almost double the number attending in 1951. Yet to carry out its educative functions, the university has become involved in a host of activities which are commercial in character.

Thus, the approximately 1,450 private four- and two-year colleges and universities in the United States have on their payrolls some 247,000 full-time professionals and 263,000 full- and part-time nonprofessional employees. Operating budgets of private educational facilities were an estimated $6 billion in 1969, an increase of $300 million over the previous fiscal year. Income is derived not only from the traditional sources such as tuition and gifts, but from the purely commercial avenues of securities investments and real estate holdings. Revenues of private institutions of higher education for fiscal year 1966-67 totaled over 6 billion. More than $1.5 billion of that sum came from Government appropriations. Private colleges and universities also realized a commercial profit of $70, 678,000 from furnishing housing and food services.

Expenditures to operate and maintain these academic communities necessarily include purchases of food, furniture, office equipment, supplies, utilities, and the like, much of which is obtained through the channels of interstate commerce. Merely to house its students the average private college budgeted $323,000 for fiscal 1969, and allotted another $360,000 for food services. Further, the expanding nature of higher education is reflected in the amount of new construction being planned. In 1969, over 1,000 institutions planned some 3,000 separate building projects with a total estimated value of $4.35 billion, one-half billion dollars more than was appropriated the preceding year.

Another phenomenon clearly distinguishing the current situation from the one which existed in 1951 is the expanded role of the Federal Government in higher education. In the last 12 years alone, three legislative acts have been passed which authorize allocations of millions of dollars of Federal aid for education. Total Federal funds for private and public education in

1969 amounted to $5 billion. This figure, moreover, does not include moneys expended for student loans, sponsored research, or Government-approved construction. . . .

However, those who oppose Board jurisdiction contend that many private colleges, unlike Cornell and Syracuse, have remained relatively small and local in character and labor disputes involving their employees do not burden interstate commerce. They also allege that private colleges represent a declining proportion of higher educational institutions in the United States. Therefore, if the National Labor Relations Board were to take jurisdiction, it would be over only a fractional segment of the field. A more logical approach, they submit, is to have all such institutions subject to State control, thereby avoiding the conflict and instability that allegedly would result were both Federal and local agencies to function within a single State. We find no merit in these arguments.

It may be true that Cornell and Syracuse count among the largest of the private universities in the country. Nevertheless, within this class of employers, there are a number which, although smaller than these two universities, are sufficiently large so that their activities have a substantial impact on commerce. . . .

The evidence clearly establishes that universities are enlarging both their facilities and their economic activities to meet the needs of mounting numbers of students. Greatly increased expenditures by the Federal Government also testify to an expanding national interest in higher education. Keeping pace with these developments is the surge of organizational activity taking place among employees on college campuses. With or without Federal regulation, union organization is already a *fait accompli* at many universities. Indeed, labor disputes have already erupted at a number of universities. As advancing waves of organization swell among both nonprofessional and academic employees, it is unreasonable to assume that such disputes will not continue to occur in the future.

As noted previously, Section 14(c) was enacted primarily to provide forums to resolve labor disputes for those employers and employees who were denied Federal relief. Congress was aware that by 1959 only 12 States had any labor relations law. Presumably, Congress then expected that the other States would establish agencies to fill the void. If so, these expectations have been disappointed. To date, a total of 15 States have enacted labor-management legislation. In only eight of these States has the legislation been written or interpreted so as to expressly cover employees of private educational institutions. Moreover, even in those eight, the laws may be inadequate. For example, New York for years has had an equivalent of the Wagner Act, yet it contains no remedies for unfair labor practices which may be committed by unions. To put it another way, there are 35 states without labor codes under which matters such as union organization, collective bargaining, and labor disputes may be determined.

Consequently, we are convinced that assertion of jurisdiction is required over those private colleges and universities whose operations have a substantial effect on commerce to insure the orderly, effective and uniform application of the national labor policy.

In view of all the foregoing considerations, we can no longer adhere to the position set forth in the Columbia University decision. Accordingly, that case is overruled. Charged with providing peaceful and orderly procedures to resolve labor controversy, we conclude that we can best effectuate the policies of the Act by asserting jurisdiction over nonprofit, private educational institutions where we find it to be appropriate.

At this time, the Board is not prepared to establish jurisdictional standards for nonprofit colleges and universities as a class for the instant proceedings do not give us a sufficient basis for selecting an appropriate measure by which to determine whether the policies of the Act will be effectuated by the exercise of jurisdiction in a particular case. Therefore, we leave the development of an appropriate jurisdictional standard for subsequent adjudication.

Whatever dollar-volume standard we ultimately adopt for asserting jurisdiction over educational institutions can best be left to determination in future situations involving institutions which are far nearer the appropriate dividing line. In view of the foregoing facts disclosing the substantial involvement in operations in commerce and affecting commerce by Cornell and Syracuse Universities, there is no question that Cornell and Syracuse are engaged in commerce within the meaning of the Act. Accordingly, we find that it will effectuate the policies of the Act to assert jurisdiction herein. * * *

2.   NLRB Jurisdiction Over Academic Employees

The NLRB extended its jurisdiction over academic employees in C. W. Post Center of Long Island University, 77 LRRM 1001 (1971), where it was held that:

> As the individuals involved herein have the usual incidents of the employer-employee relationship and are employees within the meaning of the Act, they are entitled to its benefits. . . .
> [We are] of the view that the policy-making and quasi-supervisory authority which adheres to full-time faculty status but is exercised by them only as a group does not make them supervisors within the meaning of Section 2(11) of the Act, or managerial employees who must be separately represented. Accordingly, . . . full-time university faculty members qualify in every respect as professional employees under Section 2(12) of the Act, and are therefore entitled to all benefits of collective bargaining if they so desire.

NLRB jurisdiction over educational institutions was approved by the First Circuit Court of Appeals in NLRB v. Wentworth Institute, 515 F.2d 550 (1st Cir. 1975). The case came before the Court when the NLRB sought enforcement of an order directing Wentworth to bargain with the certified representative of the faculty. Wentworth opposed the refusal to bargain charge on the grounds that the legislative history of the NLRA and earlier Board policy implied that educational institutions were excluded from NLRB jurisdiction. The First Circuit rejected Wentworth's implied exclusion argument by stating that the Act was clear on its face and could not be understood to preclude jurisdiction. In response to the employer's claim that the Board's belated assertion of jurisdiction over colleges and universities was contrary to Congressional intent and existing precedent, the Court noted that:

> [T]he Board never ruled that it lacked jurisdiction—only that the Conference Report language was a "guide", presumably to the exercise of its discretion. Congressional silence after that qualified pronouncement casts little light on the subject of jurisdictional outer limits. . . . With respect to the Board's own precedents, it is not an abuse of discretion for the Board to reappraise its position in light of developments in society, as long as its new construction is consistent with the language and tenor of the Act.

The decision in *Wentworth* should be contrasted with a decision by the Second Circuit in NLRB v. Yeshiva, 582 F.2d 686 (1978), where it was held that full-time university faculty had "managerial status" and thus were exempt from coverage under the NLRA. The *Yeshiva* decision appears *infra*.

NOTES

1. The *Cornell University* decision reversed the long-standing position of the Board not to assert jurisdiction over private, nonprofit colleges and universities. See Trustees of Columbia University, 29 LRRM 1098 (1951), for the Board's decision not to assert jurisdiction. The basis for that decision was the Board's finding that the policies of the NLRA would not be effected if the Board asserted jurisdiction over nonprofit educational institutions "where the activities involved [were] noncommercial in nature and intimately connected with the charitable purposes and educational activities of the institution." *Trustees of Columbia University, supra,* at 1099. When denying jurisdiction, the Board recognized that the activities of Columbia University were sufficient to satisfy the requirements and standards used by the Board for the normal exercise of jurisdiction.

What factors might have influenced the Board's decision to make a major policy shift in the *Cornell University* case? Why is the impact of educational institutions on interstate commerce so much greater in 1970 than it was in 1951? How would you respond to the suggestion that the Board had merely shifted its emphasis from the educational activities of an institution to its financial structure?

2. Shortly after the *Cornell University* decision, the Board established a fixed formula for the determination of jurisdiction over nonprofit educational institutions. Under the Board standard, institutions with a minimum gross revenue of not less than $1 million annually are subject to NLRB jurisdiction. 29 C.F.R. § 103.1.

3. A major criticism of the *Cornell University* case was the failure of any party to consider the impact on faculty members if the Board should assume jurisdiction over private, nonprofit educational institutions. See Kahn, *The NLRB and Higher Education: The Failure of Policymaking Through Adjudication,* 21 UCLA L. Rev. 63 (1973).

4. In *NLRB v. Catholic Bishop of Chicago,* the Supreme Court ruled that the NLRA did not give the NLRB jurisdiction over teachers in church-operated schools that teach both religious and secular subjects. 47 U.S.L.W. 4283 (1979).

C.   *Public Institutions*

1.   The Constitutional Right to Join and Form Unions

**UNIVERSITY OF NEW HAMPSHIRE CHAPTER OF THE AMERICAN
ASSOCIATION OF UNIVERSITY PROFESSORS v. HASELTON**
United States District Court
397 F.Supp. 107 (D. N.H. 1975)

BOWNES, *District Judge.*

This is an action brought pursuant to U.S.C. §2281 and §2284, Plaintiffs requested that a Three-Judge Court be convened to declare unconstitutional and permanently enjoin the operation of N.H. RSA 98 C as it applies to them. N.H. RSA 98 C is a public employment relations statute which confers upon state employees the right to engage in collective bargaining. The statute defines employees as:

classified employees of the state, and non-academic employees (exclusive of department heads and executive officers) of the University of New Hampshire including Keene State College and Plymouth State College as defined by the board of trustees of the university . . . . N.H. RSA 98 C: 1

The net effect of the statutory classification is to confer collective bargaining rights upon state employees in general, while specifically denying these rights to the academic employees of the State University System. Academic employees of the New Hampshire Vocational-Technical Colleges are not specifically excluded by the statutory terms and these persons have the right to engage in collective bargaining. . . .

There are two issues before the court:

(1) Whether the State's refusal to confer collective bargaining rights upon academic employees is an abridgment of their First Amendment rights; and

(2) Whether the statutory classification created by N.H. RSA 98 C violates the equal protection clause of the Fourteenth Amendment.

RULINGS OF LAW

First Amendment

The First Amendment rights of association, assembly, and freedom of speech guarantee to public employees the right to organize collectively and select representatives to engage in collective bargaining. *McLaughlin* v. *Tilendis,* 398 F.2d 287 (7th Cir. 1968); *Police Officers' Guild, Nat. U. of Pol. Of.* v. *Washington,* 369 F.Supp. 543 (D.D.C.1973); *United Federation of Postal Clerks* v. *Blount,* 325 F.Supp. 879 (D.D.C.1971); *National Association of Letter Carriers* v. *Blount,* 305 F.Supp. 546 (D.C.C.1969); The Supreme Court has characterized "the right to organize and select representatives for lawful purposes of collective bargaining . . . as a 'fundamental right' . . . ." *Auto. Workers* v. *Wis. Board,* 336 U. S. 245, 259, 69 S.Ct. 516, 524, 93 L.Ed. 651 (1948).

Plaintiffs do not allege nor has there been any showing that their First Amendment rights are impinged by the operation of N.H. RSA 98 C. As far as plaintiffs are concerned, the statute maintains the status quo; they are free to unionize in order to advance their ideas and interests. The State, however, does not have a constitutional obligation to respond to plaintiffs' demands or to enter into a contract with them. There is no

constitutional right . . . to make collective bargaining mandatory. As a matter of Constitutional law, this Court agrees with the other courts which have held that no such right exists. See Lontine v. Van Cleave, 483 F.2d 966, 968 (10th Cir. 1973); Newport News Fire Fighters Ass'n Local 794 v. City of Newport News. 339 F.Supp. 13, 17 (E.D.Va. 1972); Atkins v. City of Charlotte, 296 F.Supp. 1068, 1077 (W.D.N.C. 1969); Cook County Police Ass'n v. City of Harvey, 8 Ill.App.3d 147, 289 N.E.2d 226 (1972). As was stated in *Atkins, supra* 296 F.Supp. at 1077: "There is nothing in the United States Constitution which entitles one to have a contract with another who does not want it. It is but a step further to hold that the state may lawfully forbid such contracts with its instrumentalities. The solution, if there be one, from the viewpoint of the firemen, is that labor unions may someday persuade state government of the asserted value of collective bargaining agreements, but this is a political matter and does not yield to judicial solution." [The right to a collective bargaining agreement, so firmly entrenched in American labor-management relations, rests upon national legislation and not upon the federal Constitution.] *Confederation of Police* v. *City of Chicago,* 382 F.Supp. 624, 628-629 (N.D.Ill.1974).

Traditionally, the right to be recognized in the collective bargaining process has been hammered out either through the legislative process or by the economic forge of the strike, and not by judicial decrees. *Cf. Timberlane Reg. Sch. Dist.* v. *Timberlane Reg. Ed. Ass'n,* 317 A.2d 555 (N.H.1974). The operation of N.H. RSA 98 C does not impede the plaintiffs' rights to collectively organize or participate in an economic strike. Plaintiffs' First Amendment rights remain untarnished and unaffected.

EQUAL PROTECTION CLAIM

. . . .

Collective bargaining is a recent phenomenon in higher education.[6] The university community remained the last bastion against the spread of collec-

---

[6.]   "As of June 1, 1973, eighteen states have enacted public employment relation statutes applicable to academic employees in all state or local institutions of higher learning. Due to the rapidly expanding concept of bargaining in the public sector, there exist great difficulties at any point in time in determining exactly which states allow collective negotiations among their academic personnel." Gee, Organizing the Halls of Ivy: Developing a Framework for Viable Alternatives in Higher Education Employment, 1973 Utah L.Rev. 233, n. 2. *See generally,* Wollett, The Status and Trends of Collective Negotiations for Faculty in Higher Education, 1971 Wis.L.Rev. 2.

tive bargaining for two essential reasons: first, most universities have internal governance procedures; and, second, many academics believed that their professional status and independence would be tarnished by the collective bargaining process.

Ideally, the governance of a university is based upon the concept of "shared authority." Central to the concept is the tenet that academics are given extensive authority to participate in university governance. The theory is that the university setting, unlike the industrial world, is a single community comprised of an amalgamation of components which, in a joint effort, create an atmosphere of mutuality and cooperation. *Cf. N.L.R.B.* v. *Wentworth Institute*, 515 F.2d 550 at 556 (1st Cir. 1975).

In order to effectuate the goals of shared authority, most higher institutions have established university senates. A properly balanced senate, which evenly disperses power and control, enabling the faculty to have an active participation in university governance, negates the need for collective bargaining.[9] The need to collectively bargain arises only when academics believe that they are not effectively represented in the process of institutional decision-making.

An examination of the governance system at the Durham campus indicates that academic authority is more elusive than shared. In 1969 the governing structure of the University was changed so that, for the first time in any university, undergraduates were given parity with the faculty in a single unicameral body. The traditional academic senate was abolished. At present, the University Senate serves as an advisory body to the Board of Trustees. The entire University community is represented in the Senate: students, hourly employees, and professional and technical employees. The faculty has only minority representation.

The major administrative officers of the University are appointed without either the advice or consent of the faculty. The faculty has no voice in matters of tenure, salary or faculty appointments. These decisions are made solely by the administration with only minimal faculty advisement.

But the structure of the University's governance can change again, as it did in 1969. The New Hampshire University Senate was the subject of a recent study which suggested numerous changes in the Senate's structure so as to make it a more effective mechanism for faculty participation. (Azzi Commission on University Governance). At present, the proposal has not been initiated.

Despite the fact that the academic employees at the Durham campus do not effectively partake in the University's governance, as they do in many other universities, we find that a rational basis does exist for the legislature's refusal to extend collective bargaining to university academic employees.

Although collective bargaining in educational circles has gained increasing acceptance, its critics have pointed out that it injects into university

---

[9.]   Brown, Professors and Unions: The Faculty Senate: An Effective Alternative to Collective Bargaining in Higher Education? 12 W. & M. L. Rev. 252 (1970).

decision-making an adversarial process resting on the influence of the bargaining unit. The dynamics of this process, it is argued, is egalitarian and majoritarian, and, the process of making trade-offs to reach a settlement, may result in a failure to recognize the interests inherent in a wide diversity of disciplines,[12] with consequent adverse effect on some professors.[13]

Fearing the effect of these forces on an institution of higher learning, a Task Force of the American Association of Higher Education recommended, in 1966, that, in order to promote the spirit of cooperation, a university should use internal governance mechanisms rather than resorting to external bargaining techniques.[14] While controversy continues, the commentators seem to agree on one point—that the employment conditions in higher education are unique and deserve special statutory consideration. We cannot fail to observe also that where collective bargaining for academics has been introduced into public universities, it has been accomplished mainly by statute. *See* note 6, *supra.* And the Court of Appeals for this Circuit has implicitly recognized the propriety of legislative judgment in this area.

We recite these observations not to take sides on an issue of great complexity, but to indicate that the New Hampshire legislature in excluding the Durham faculty from the collective bargaining statute was not lacking in a rational basis for its decision. Specifically, it could conclude that a faculty bargaining unit, particularly if it sought to bargain broadly on curriculum, admissions, degree requirements, and other educational policy matters, would undermine and disrupt its present effort at university-wide governance. No similar internal governance experiment is being undertaken at the vocational schools. The legislature could also conclude that the disparate interests of various academic departments in the University would not be as well served by collective treatment as the more unified interests of the vocational schools. We think there is sufficient dissimilarity between the vocational colleges and the University to support a legislative distinction. We note finally that the legislature may be given some latitude for experimentation in

---

[12.] "Collective negotiations in universities and colleges places all academic disciplines at the same bargaining table. . . . In some areas involving items such as curriculum, academic programs, admission requirements, and other similar variables, the diversity of disciplines could create significant problems of reconciliation for negotiations and their constituents.

"Collective bargaining involves tradeoffs in order to reach a mutual settlement. In the heat of negotiations, especially as a strike deadline looms over the proceedings, there is a strong temptation to trade items rather than settle on the true merits of each. This, of course, is characteristic of any bargaining situation, but 'horse-trading' of issues without careful consideration of the long-run impact could be exceedingly disastrous in such a highly-complex and diversified field as higher education." Allen, Organizing the Eggheads: Professors and Collective Bargaining, 23 Lab.L.J. 606, 614 (1972).

[13.] "Collective bargaining inherently subjects many policy determinations to the rule of the organizational majority, and majority rule often reflects deep suspicion of individual initiative or advantage. Thus, collective negotiations could have an adverse effect on teachers with special ability." Wollett, The Coming Revolution in Public School Management, 67 Mich.L. Rev. 1017, 1029 (1969). By the same token, we recognize that in the absence of collective bargaining many other junior faculty members of a faculty may feel equally adversely affected.

[14.] American Association of Higher Education Task Force Report, Faculty Participation in Academic Government cited in Brown, *supra* note 9, at 284.

attempting to resolve the problems of internal relationships in the academic setting. *See Williamson* v. *Lee Optical Co.,* 348 U.S. 483, 75 S.Ct. 461, 99 L.Ed. 563 (1955).

NOTES

1. As noted in *Haselton,* most courts considering the issue have ruled that while public employees may have a constitutional right to form and join unions, there is no constitutional right to engage in collective bargaining.

2. Do you agree with the judgment in *Haselton* that there was a "rational basis" for denying bargaining rights to the Durham faculty?

2.   Collective Bargaining Rights Granted by State Statutes

REGENTS OF THE UNIVERSITY OF MICHIGAN v. MERC
Supreme Court of Michigan
389 Mich. 96 (1973)

SWAINSON, Justice.

In 1966, a group of interns, residents and post-doctoral fellows connected with the University of Michigan Hospital and its affiliates organized the University of Michigan Interns-Residents Association (hereinafter referred to as the Association). The Association attempted to bargain with the University Hospital Administrators concerning the compensation of interns and residents. The University asserted its right to unilaterally determine such compensation. On March 19, 1970 the Association filed a written request that the Regents of the University of Michigan recognize it as the bargaining representative of the interns, residents and post-doctoral fellows serving at the University Hospital and its affiliates. The Regents denied this request on or about March 31, 1970.

The Association then filed a petition for representation with the Michigan Employment Relations Commission (hereinafter referred to as MERC) on April 19, 1970. . . .

On March 16, 1971 a majority of the members of the commission issued a decision holding:

1. That the Association is a labor organization within the meaning of the Michigan Public Employees Relations Act (hereinafter referred to as PERA).

2. That the University of Michigan is a public employer subject to the provisions of PERA and thus the commission has jurisdiction of the matter.

3. That the members of the Association are public employees under the provisions of PERA.

4. The employment relationship between the parties is not a casual one as that term is used to designate exclusions from a bargaining unit. . . .

On January 21, 1972 the majority of the Court of Appeals reversed the findings of the MERC and held as a matter of law that interns, residents, and post-doctoral fellows cannot be characterized as employees. . . .

Both petitioners cite numerous cases holding that our Court should not substitute its own judgment for that of an administrative agency. We agree with that principle of law but such agreement merely assumes that we are dealing with a purely factual question. In this case, the Court is of the opinion that it is also dealing with questions of law, particularly since respondent contends that it would violate Article VIII, section 5 of the 1963 Constitution[2] to apply the provisions of the PERA to members of the Association. . . .

The threshold issue is whether the application of the provisions of PERA to the members of the Association would violate Article VIII, section 5 of the 1963 Constitution by infringing upon the autonomy of the Regents in the operation of the educational sphere of the University of Michigan. It should be noted that both the MERC and the Court of Appeals found that the University of Michigan is a public employer within the meaning of the PERA. The Regents have not appealed this issue. We believe that both the MERC and the Court of Appeals were correct in holding that the University of Michigan is a public employer within the meaning of the PERA.

In Regents of the University of Michigan v. Labor Mediation Board, 18 Mich. App. 485, 171 N.W.2d 477 (1969), the Regents filed a complaint for declaratory judgment contending they were not a public employer within the meaning of the PERA. The complaint was filed after the Labor Mediation Board had ruled that the University of Michigan was subject to the provisions of the PERA. Both the trial court and the Court of Appeals ruled against the Regents. The Court of Appeals stated (p. 490, 171 N.W.2d p. 479). . . .

"We conclude on the basis of the foregoing that the plaintiff is a public body corporate deriving its being from the people, and is supported by the people, and the regents, who are State officers, are elected by the people. Thus, the plaintiff is a public employer."

In a companion case, Board of Control of Eastern Michigan University v. Labor Mediation Board, 18 Mich.App. 435, 171 N.W.2d 471 (1969) the Court of Appeals held that Eastern Michigan University was a public employer. Our Court granted leave to appeal and affirmed the judgment of the Court of Appeals. 384 Mich. 561, 184 N.W.2d 921 (1971). The Court stated (pp. 565-567, 184 N.W.2d p. 922):

[2.]   Const. 1963, art. 8, §5 reads as follows:

"The regents of the University of Michigan and their successors in office shall constitute a body corporate known as the Regents of the University of Michigan; the trustees of Michigan State University and their successors in office shall constitute a body corporate known as the Board of Trustees of Michigan State University; the governors of Wayne State University and their successors in office shall constitute a body corporate known as the Board of Governors of Wayne State University. Each board shall have general supervision of its institution and the control and direction of all expenditures from the institution's funds. Each board shall, as often as necessary, elect a president of the institution under its supervision. He shall be the principal executive officer of the institution, be ex-officio a member of the board without the right to vote and preside at meetings of the board. The board of each institution shall consist of eight members who shall hold office for terms of eight years and who shall be elected as provided by law. The governor shall fill board vacancies by appointment. Each appointee shall hold office until a successor has been nominated and elected as provided by law."

"The powers and prerogatives of Michigan universities have been jealously guarded not only by the boards of those universities but by this Court in a series of opinions running as far back as 1856. See, The People ex rel. Drake v. The Regents of the University of Michigan (1856), 4 Mich. 98; The People v. The Regents of the University (1869), 18 Mich. 469; * * *."

"The above cases reflect the holdings of this Court that a constitutional corporation, such as plaintiff, has 'the entire control and management of its [the University's] affairs and property.' Weinberg v. The Regents of the University of Michigan, *supra*, 97 Mich. 246, 56 N.W. 605. In the main, they deal with situations where the legislature attempted to impose its will upon the internal operations of a university.

*   *   *

"Here we find no plenary grant of powers which, by any stretch of the imagination, would take plaintiff's operations outside of the area of public employment. 'Public employment' is clearly intended to apply to employment or service in all governmental activity, whether carried on by the state or by townships, cities, counties, commissions, boards or other governmental instrumentalities. It is the entire public sector of employment as distinguished from private employment. The public policy of this State as to labor relations in public employment is for legislative determination. The sole exception to the exercise of legislative power is the State classified civil service, the scheme for which is spelled out in detail in Article 11 of the Constitution of 1963. We conclude that the autonomy sought by plaintiff in the area of labor relations is unnecessary for it to maintain 'the entire control and management of its affairs and property.'"

Thus, it is clear that the rationale of the *Eastern Michigan* case is applicable to the University of Michigan at least insofar as the issue of the University being a public employer is concerned. Article VIII, section 6 of the 1963 Constitution provides in part:

"Other institutions of higher education established by law having authority to grant baccalaureate degrees shall each be governed by a board of control which shall be a body corporate. The board shall have general supervision of the institution and the control and direction of all expenditures from the institution's funds."

The Convention comment to this section states:

"This is a new section relating to governing bodies of other state supported institutions of higher learning which have authority to grant baccalaureate degrees.

"The provisions relative to their boards of control are similar to those for the institutions named in Sec. 5 of this Article."

Since the Eastern Michigan University Board is now on a comparable level with the Regents of the University of Michigan, and since Eastern Michigan University is a public employer within the meaning of the PERA, then the University of Michigan is also a public employer within the meaning of the PERA.

The key contention of the respondent, concurred in by a majority of the Court of Appeals, that to hold the members of the Association are employees would contravene Article VIII, section 5 of the 1963 Constitution. This constitutional provision has its roots in Article XIII, sections 6-8 of the 1850 Constitution. The desires of the framers of the 1850 and subsequent constitutions to provide autonomy to the Board of Regents in the educational sphere have been protected by our Court for over a century. This concern for the educational process to be controlled by the Regents does not and cannot mean that they are exempt from all the laws of the state. When the University of Michigan was founded in the 19th Century it was comparatively easy to isolate the University and keep it free from outside interference. The complexities of modern times makes this impossible. Problems concerning the disputes between employees and public employers were not given full constitutional recognition until the 1963 Constitution. The people, through the passage of Article IV, section 48 of the 1963 Constitution have deemed the resolution of public employee disputes a matter of public policy. This Court must attempt to harmonize the various constitutional provisions and give meaning to all of them. . . .

[W]e believe that the two sections of the 1963 Constitution can be harmonized. We hold that interns, residents and post-doctoral fellows may be employees and have rights to organize under the provisions of PERA without infringing on the constitutional autonomy of the Board of Regents. . . .

Because of the unique nature of the University of Michigan, above referred to, the scope of bargaining by the Association may be limited if the subject matter falls clearly within the educational sphere. Some conditions of employment may not be subject to collective bargaining because those particular facets of employment would interfere with the autonomy of the Regents. For example, the Association clearly can bargain with the Regents on the salary that their members receive since it is not within the educational sphere. While normally the employees can bargain to discontinue a certain aspect of a particular job, the Association does not have the same latitude as other public employees. For example, interns could not negotiate working in the pathology department because they found such work distasteful. If the administrators of medical schools felt that a certain number of hours devoted to pathology was necessary to the education of the intern, our Court would not interfere since this does fall within the autonomy of the Regents under Article VIII, section 5. Numerous other issues may arise which fall between these two extremes and they will have to be decided on a case by case basis. Our Court will not, as it has not in the past, shirk its duty to protect the autonomy of the Regents in the educational sphere. Thus, we hold that it does not violate Article VIII, section 5 of the 1963 Constitution if the members of the Association are held to be public employees. . . .

Finally, we must determine whether the findings by the Michigan Employment Relations Commission that members of the Association are employees is supported by competent, material and substantial evidence on the record. We hold that it is.

There is ample evidence to support the findings of the Commission that the members of the Association are employees. . . .

The fact that they are continually acquiring new skills does not detract from the findings of the MERC that they may organize as employees under the provisions of PERA. Members of all professions continue their learning throughout their careers. For example, fledgling lawyers employed by a law firm spend a great deal of time acquiring new skills, yet no one would contend that they are not employees of the law firm. . . .

The judgment of the Court of Appeals is reversed and the decision of the MERC is affirmed. No costs, a public question being involved.

NOTES

1. In Board of Regents v. Carter, 89 LRRM 2216 (1975), the South Dakota Supreme Court held that the state public employment statute was not an infringement on the constitutional authority vested in the Board of Regents. The Court found that the Board of Regents' control over educational institutions was subject to certain rules and restrictions enacted by the state legislature. The Court noted that the state statute did not require the parties to a collective bargaining relationship to agree or make concessions and, therefore, the law left intact the authority of the Board to act unilaterally with respect to specific subjects. The Court thus concluded that the "Board's basic right to control is left untouched" and the public employment statute was a permissible restriction on the exercise of that control.

2. At its best, the legal framework for collective bargaining in the public sector could be described as a mixed pattern of legislation. This is in part due to the various approaches taken by state legislatures when determining the public employee's right to bargain collectively. The possible alternatives range from simply no legislation, to legislation absolutely prohibiting collective bargaining, to multi-provision legislation covering specific areas of public employment. Another cause of the mixed pattern is the extensive number of topics which collective bargaining statutes may include or exclude, such as: union recognition and elections, bargaining units, bargaining duty, bargaining subjects, mediation and arbitration, fact-finding, contract clauses, working conditions, union security, unfair labor practices, strikes and picketing, and enforcement. As a consequence it would be impossible to present even an overview of all of the labor law legislation in the public sector in this one chapter. Probably the best single source dealing with collective bargaining in the public sector is Edwards, Clark and Craver, Labor Relations Law in the Public Sector, 2d ed., (Charlottesville, Va.: Bobbs-Merrill/Michie, 1979).

3. Among states without public employment legislation, the majority rule is that public employers may consent to participate in collective bargaining and make an agreement with employee representatives even though collective bargaining is not mandated by statute. See, e.g., Dayton Classroom Teachers Ass'n v. Dayton Bd. of Educ., 323 N.E. 2d 714 (Ohio S.Ct., 1975). However, the majority rule is not without opposition. In Commonwealth of Virginia v. County Board of Arlington County, 232 S.E.2d 30 (1977), the Virginia Supreme Court held that county board and school board policies permitting collective bargaining with a labor organization were invalid absent express statutory

authority. The court found that the policies and agreements executed by the boards "not only have seriously restricted the rights of individual employees to be heard but also have granted to labor unions a substantial voice in the boards' ultimate right of decision in important matters affecting both the public employee-employer relationship and the public duties imposed by law upon the boards."

4. Even where it is established that a public employer may enter into a collective bargaining relationship, the employees may nevertheless find that certain portions of their agreement with the employer are unenforceable. Collective bargaining agreements in the public sector may be attacked as an unlawful delegation of legislative authority. In states with legislation authorizing collective bargaining, the unlawful delegation doctrine has been used to challenge the permissible scope of bargaining or to question the enforceability of an arbitrator's award. *See, e.g.,* Great Neck Bd. Educ. v. Areman, 41 N.Y.2d 527, 362 N.E.2d 943 (1977). *See generally,* Toole, *Judicial Activism in Public Sector Grievance Arbitration*, 33 The Arbitration Journal 6 (Sept. 1978).

However, in considering such challenges, many public sector jurisdictions have followed the lead of the New York Court of Appeals in Bd. of Educ. of Union Free School Dist. No. 3 v. Associated Teachers of Huntington, Inc., 30 N.Y.2d 122, 282 N.E.2d 109 (1972). In *Huntington* a school board and a teachers' union entered into a collective bargaining agreement and thereafter the school board brought suit questioning the legality of five provisions in the agreement. Four of the provisions related "to the payment of economic benefits in the form of either salary increases or reimbursement for certain expenses incurred, and the fifth provide[d] for arbitration in cases in which tenure[d] teachers have been disciplined." The school board contended that "absent a statutory provision *expressly* authorizing a school board to provide for a particular term or condition of employment, it [was] legally prohibited from doing so." The court held that the proper test was whether there was "some other applicable statutory provision explicitly and definitively prohibit[ing] the public employer from making an agreement as to a particular term or condition of employment." The court further stated that if an employer "asserts a lack of power to agree to any particular term or condition of employment, it has the burden of demonstrating the existence of a specific statutory provision which circumscribes the exercise of such power." Finding that the school board had not met this burden, the court sustained the legality of each of the five questioned contract clauses. *See generally* Clark, *The Scope of the Duty to Bargain in Public Employment*, in Labor Relations Law in the Public Sector 81 (Chicago: ABA Section of Labor Relations Law, 1977).

5. Some states, particularly those without a statute authorizing public sector bargaining, have adopted a different test to determine whether a disputed provision in a public sector contract is legally enforceable. For example, in Wesclin Educ. Ass'n v. Bd. of Education, 30 Ill.App.3d 67, 331 N.E.2d 335 (1975), a school board entered into a collective bargaining agreement which contained an elaborate evaluation procedure that was to be utilized prior to the dismissal of non-tenured teachers. The issue, as phrased by the court, was "whether a school board can impose upon itself conditions precedent to the dismissal of a non-tenured teacher, which are in excess of the conditions imposed by the School Code." After noting that "[s]tatutes conferring powers on a school board must be strictly construed and should be construed not only as a grant of power but also as a limitation thereof," the court held that the school board had no authority to agree to the evaluation procedure on the ground that the school board could not agree to "conditions precedent to the dismissal of non-tenured teachers which are in excess of the conditions imposed by the School Code." *See also* Bd. of Trustees v. Cook County College Teachers Union, Local 1600, 343 N.E.2d 473 (Ill. S.Ct. 1976).

III.   Collegiality: The Unique Characteristic

NATIONAL LABOR RELATIONS BOARD c. YESHIVA UNIVERSITY
Second Circuit Court of Appeals
582 F.2d 686 (1978)

MULLIGAN, C. J.: The National Labor Relations Board (the Board) has applied for enforcement of its order of August 24, 1977, reported at 231 NLRB No. 98, requiring respondent Yeshiva University (Yeshiva) to recognize the Yeshiva University Faculty Association (the Union) as the exclusive bargaining agent of a unit of Yeshiva's full-time faculty members. The petition for enforcement of the Board's order is denied. . . .

On this appeal, Yeshiva argues principally, as it did before the Board, that the full-time faculty of the University are managerial and/or supervisory employees within the meaning of the Act and are therefore excluded from the Act's coverage. Yeshiva also urges that two assistant deans and faculty who are departmental or divisional chairmen, or who are members of certain committees on University affairs, exercise additional authority which mandates their classification as supervisors and/or managers. Before examining these contentions it is necessary to review the structure of *Yeshiva* and the role played by the faculty in the operation and governance of the University.

II

Yeshiva University is a private institution of higher education chartered under the laws of the State of New York. Its offices and educational facilities are located on four widely separated campuses in New York City. We are here concerned with Yeshiva's six undergraduate colleges and programs, and four graduate schools. Approximately 2,500 full and part-time students are enrolled at Yeshiva. The University is staffed by 209 full-time and 150 part-time faculty members.

Yeshiva has a self-perpetuating Board of Trustees with no administrative position at the school apart from their membership on the Board. The University's chief executive officer is the President. There are, in addition, three vice-presidents at Yeshiva (for student affairs, business affairs, academic affairs) as well as a Bursar, Registrar, Director of Admissions and several University deans. An Executive Council of deans and administrators makes recommendations to the President with respect to various matters. Two other committees, the Council of Graduate Schools and the Council of Undergraduate Schools advise the President and Board regarding interdivisional programs designed to increase coordination and cooperation among the schools and divisions of the University. These councils consist of elected student and faculty representatives from each school or division, the dean or director of each academic unit and members of the University administration, including the President. A Faculty Handbook sets forth University policies regarding faculty appointments, promotion, tenure, termination and sabbaticals.

Each of the schools or divisions is headed by a dean or director. Most of the schools have a faculty assembly or student-faculty senate as well as a committee structure, including, *inter alia*, a curriculum committee, a standards committee, and a welfare committee. The faculty of each school meet periodically and at Stern College, Yeshiva College, and the Belfer and Ferkauf Graduate Schools the faculties meet and conduct their affairs according to written by-laws and/or constitutions which have been approved by the President. Only two of the schools, Yeshiva College and the Belfer Graduate School, have assistant deans. These two assistant deans are teaching faculty members.

Each school, college and program at Yeshiva enjoys great autonomy in determining its own curriculum, grading system, and academic standards as well as in a wide variety of other matters. . . .

Two other important organs of University-wide faculty governance should be mentioned. The Faculty Review Committee is composed of eight tenured faculty members who are elected from the various schools of the University. The Committee has jurisdiction to review faculty grievances, particularly those concerning promotion and tenure. If the grievance is not satisfactorily resolved after the Committee has notified the Dean of the interested school, the Committee is authorized to recommend action to the President. Faculty members, along with students and administrators, also sit on a recently formed Committee on Academic Priorities and Resource Allocation. The purpose of this Committee is to provide a long-range scale of academic and fiscal priorities at Yeshiva. . . .

The major issue raised in this case is whether the full-time faculty of Yeshiva are supervisors within section 2(11) of the Act, 29 U.S.C. § 152(11), and/or managerial personnel within the Board's own definition as adopted by the courts, and therefore whether these faculty members are improperly included as employees in the bargaining unit.

Section 2(11) defines a supervisor as follows:

The term "supervisor" means any individual having authority, in the interest of the employer, to hire, transfer, suspend, lay off, recall, promote, discharge, assign, reward or discipline other employees, or responsibility to direct them, or to adjust their grievances, or to effectively recommend such action, if in connection with the foregoing the exercise of such authority is not of a merely routine or clerical nature, but requires the use of independent judgment.

It is well settled in the industrial context that possession of any one of the enumerated powers in section 2(11) or the power to effectively recommend with respect to any one of them is sufficient to satisfy the statutory definition of a supervisor. . . .

The record, which has been set forth in some detail in Part II and which is not controverted by the Board, strongly supports the contention of Yeshiva that its full-time faculty, acting at times through committees or department chairmen, and at other times as a body, exercises supervisory and managerial functions as defined by section 2(11) of the Act and within the Board's prior holdings as discussed in *NLRB v. Bell Aerospace Co., Division of Textron, Inc.* We stress that our function is not to examine *in vacuo* the governance procedures of all four-year private institutions of learning described in the briefs of the *amici* universities as "mature" institutions of higher education. Many such institutions have apparently adopted a collegial decision making process in which the faculty plays a decisive role in the development of institutional policy. Given the great diversity in governance structure and allocation of power at such universities it is appropriate to address ourselves solely to the situation at the institution involved in this proceeding. *NLRB v. Wentworth Institute*, 515 F.2d 550, 556 (1st Cir. 1975). The record here discloses that in many instances the full-time faculty of the schools of Yeshiva without question effectively recommend the hiring, promotion, salary and tenure of the faculty of the University in a manner which can hardly be described as routine or clerical. They further perform managerial functions not only by their personnel decisions but by adopting the standards of admission, the curriculum, the grading system and the graduation require- ·ments of their school. Moreover, in particular cases the hiring of deans, the physical location of a school, teaching loads, and even the tuition to be charged were controlled by the full-time faculty. Indeed, the ability of the full-time faculty effectively to recommend or even to exercise many of the enumerated powers of section 2(11) and to formulate and effectuate University policy is not really disputed here. The Board's decision of December 5, 1975 treated the issue summarily. . . .

Thus, without any analysis the Board found that Yeshiva's full-time faculty were neither supervisors nor managerial personnel simply by stating that the substantial authority of the faculty was wielded in their capacity as professionals and by invoking three doctrines promulgated in earlier Board rulings. Since we are unpersuaded that these four justifications for the Board's decision on this point withstand careful scrutiny, we will analyze them, *seriatim*, below.

A. The Full-Time Faculty Are Professional Employees.

Under section 2(12) of the Act, 29 U. S. C. § 152(12), a professional employee is specifically included within the Act's coverage despite the fact that in the performance of his work he must exercise consistent discretion and judgment. Yeshiva does not argue that its full-time faculty members are not professional within the statutory definition of that term. They are obviously engaged in work which is "predominately intellectual," requiring advanced knowledge in a field of learning, and they do not perform work which is "routine mental, manual, mechanical, or physical" in nature. However, the fact that employees are professional does not preclude them from also being categorized as supervisory or managerial employees ineligible for inclusion in a bargaining unit. . . .

Whether, as a matter of policy, faculty members of institutions of higher learning are advantaged or disadvantaged by collective bargaining is an issue which has understandably created divergent views.[13] But the Board, like the court, is bound both by the Act and by prior judicial interpretations of it. Unquestionably, a university full-time faculty member has the authority to determine the content of his course, the method he employs in teaching it, and the evaluation of his students' academic performance. *New York University, supra,* at 5. These factors place such faculty members squarely within the language of section 2(12) and these attributes of professionalism should not characterize them as managerial or supervisory.

However, the issue as we perceive it in this case involves not simply the professor's exercise of discretion in conducting the courses he is employed to teach. Rather, the issue here is the extensive control of Yeshiva's faculty over what courses are taught in the institution, who teaches them, the number of teaching hours required of the faculty, and the rank, salary, and tenure status of other faculty members. We are further concerned by the crucial role of the full-time faculty in determining other central policies of the institution including, *inter alia*, the curriculum, admissions and graduation requirements, tuition, and in one instance, even the situs of a school. When faculty members have such power—as the record indicates they do at Yeshiva—they no longer are simply exercising individual professional expertise. They are, in effect, substantially and pervasively operating the enterprise. . . .

B.   The Full-Time Faculty Acts Collectively.

The Board here adheres to the view it first expressed in *C. W. Post Center of Long Island University,* 189 NLRB 904 [1971]), and has reiterated in *Northeastern University,* 218 NLRB 247 (1975); *University of Miami,* 213 NLRB 634 (1974); *Adelphi University supra, and Fordham University, supra.* The Board's position is that since the faculty's supervisory and managerial functions are exercised "on a collective basis" rather than by individual faculty members, they must be denied status as supervisory or managerial personnel. The Board's rationale is not adequately explained in this or in its prior opinions. Section 2(11) does, however, state that it is applicable to "an individual" who possesses the enumerated indicia of supervision. Since the control here in issue is not that of

---

[13.]   *Compare*, e.g., Kahn, The NLRB and Higher Education: The Failure of Policymaking. Through Adjudication, 21 U. C. L. A. L. Rev. 63, 79-83 (1973) (hereinafter cited as Kahn); Kadish, The Theory of the Profession and its Predicament, 58 A. A. U. P. Bull. 120, 122 (1972); and Brown, Collective Bargaining in Higher Education, 67 Mich. L. Rev. 1067, 1072 (1969), *with* The Carnegie Commission on Higher Education, Governance of Higher Education, A Report and Recommendation (1973); and Bloustein, A Chamber of Horrors?, in The Effects of Faculty Collective Bargaining on Higher Education 110 (R. Hewitt ed. 1973).

    The Board acknowledges in its brief that the activities of the full-time faculty at Yeshiva might suggest managerial or supervisory status in other contexts, but not in the case of an institution of higher learning. The legal justification for a different standard for university faculty is not made clear. The Board does comment, however, that labor organizations currently administer collective bargaining agreements for faculty at over 500 colleges and universities across the country, and, therefore, the Board's position comports with "widely shared recognition of the organizational rights of faculty."

individual faculty member over nonprofessionals, but the collective control exercised by the faculty either in concert, through department chairman, or through faculty dominated committees, it must be conceded that if read literally the statutory definition can be construed not to cover the full-time faculty. Since students are not employees the individual faculty supervision over students does not fit within the statutory definition, which requires that the supervisory power be directed to employees. There is the further logical difficulty of holding that the supervisory employees supervise other supervisory employees, cf. *General Dynamics Corp., supra,* at 859; *Post-Newsweek Stations, Capital Area, Inc.,* [1973 CCH NLRB ¶25,344] 203 NLRB 522 (1973), although this is somewhat defused when we consider that in many of Yeshiva's schools the full-time faculty also supervise collectively the activities of the part-time faculty.

Certainly, however, this Board interpretation is not the only reasonable reading of the language of section 2(11). In view of the statute's ambiguity we are disturbed by other holdings of the Board in which the collective exercise of supervisory authority was *not* grounds for exclusion from that status. Thus in *Florida Southern College,* 196 NLRB 888, 889 (1972), a case decided after the Board's rulings in *C. W. Post, supra, Fordham University, supra,* and *Adelphi University, supra,* the Board excluded a teaching dean from the faculty bargaining unit because he sat on a *committee* which made effective recommendations regarding the hiring and firing of faculty members. See also *Western Saw Manufacturers, Inc.,* 155 NLRB 1323, 1329 n. 11 (1965) (foreman held a supervisor in part due to service on a board which determined employee termination). The inconsistent interpretation of this provision by the Board is also troublesome in that the Board refers this court to no legislative history of the section—and our own review has uncovered none—which clearly supports the "collective authority" doctrine which the Board urges upon us. Rather, the history of section 2(11) indicates that such collective supervision simply was not actively considered by Congress at that time. . . .

Logically, we see no reason that the fact that the policies of a company are created by a group (as indeed they usually are by the Board of Directors) rather than by an individual should be of significance in determining whether an individual has managerial status, and the Board has advanced no satisfactory rationale for the weight it has given this factor.

C.   *The Faculty Acts on Their Own Behalf and Not in the Interest of the Employer.*

As it has done consistently in the past, the Board here denied managerial or supervisory status to the full-time faculty on the additional ground that the faculty is alleged to be acting on its own behalf and not on behalf of Yeshiva, its employer. The record in no way supports this proposition and in its argument the Board simply advances the conclusory statement that collegial action by peers is inherently action in the interest of the faculty themselves, not in the interest of the University *qua* employer. . . .

Aside from the record, there is nothing in the Board's reasoning which would support the proposition that the full-time faculty is somehow acting on its own behalf and not that of the University. In fact, a realistic assessment of the way in which a university such as Yeshiva functions demonstrates the inapplicability of the "interest of the faculty" analysis in such a context:

> The faculty, by the very nature of the educational process in institutions of higher education, participates in decision making which in private industry would normally be regarded as a management prerogative. The faculty at most four-year colleges and universities has a voice in determining standards for admissions, curriculum, degree requirements, faculty hiring and promotion, and even tuition rates. Such a state of independence is entirely unknown among the professionals in private industry. Furthermore, in higher education there is no sharp dividing line between the employer and the employees. The university is, ideally, a professional community in which common educational interests supersede all potential divisions between the faculty and the administration. The university's unique set of goals (education, research, and service) is achieved only by a series of specialist communities working together through their common concern for enlarging and applying their own spheres of knowledge. Thus, there is no sharp dividing line between the community of administrators and the community of faculty, for both have the common goal of striving to further the institution as a house of learning.

Kahn, supra, at 68 (citation omitted).

This concept of "shared authority" in the university and private four year college has its origins in the Middle Ages when teachers united "into a corporate body enjoying more or less autonomy" over the operation of the institution. McHugh, Collective Bargaining With Professionals in Higher Education: Problems in Unit Determinations, 1971 Wis. L. Rev. 55, 65 (hereinafter cited as McHugh). In 1966, a Statement on Government of Colleges and Universities, 52 A. A. U. P. Bull. 375 (1966) (hereinafter cited as Statement), which was jointly formulated and approved by the American Association of University Professors, the American Council of Education, and the Association of Governing Boards of Universities and Colleges, applauded the principle of shared authority among the Board of Trustees, the administration, and the faculty. The statement recognized that

> [t]hese three components have the joint authority and responsibility for governing the institution, and the essential and overriding idea is that the enterprise is joint and that there must be "adequate communication among these components, and full opportunity for appropriate joint planning and effort."

Kahn, supra, at 71.

Whatever the situation may be in other institutions, the record here establishes no significant divergence between the interests of the faculty and those of the administration or the Board of Trustees. On the contrary, the faculty has initiated, and the administration has repeatedly accepted, major policy determinations which constitute the essence of the University's educational venture. We cannot conclude that the full-time faculty here has acted in its own interest. . . .

D.   *The Faculty is Not Managerial or Supervisory Because it is Subject to the Ultimate Authority of the Board of Trustees.*

Although none of the criteria applied by the Board which we have so far discussed has any particular appeal, the concept that the faculty has neither managerial nor supervisory status because it is subject to the ultimate authority of the Board of Trustees is particularly unconvincing. Normally, every corporation is ultimately operated by its Board of Directors, W. Cary, Corporations 153 (4th ed. 1969), and yet that fact obviously has never precluded a finding that there are managerial or supervisory employees in the corporation. Certainly the President and Vice-Presidents of Yeshiva as well as its Deans are subject to the ultimate authority of the Board of Trustees and yet this does not preclude them from holding managerial or supervisory status. . . .

Private universities are usually created by charter under the corporation law of the state where they are located. Kahn, *supra*, at 124; see e.g., N. Y. N. F. P. Corp. Law § 701 (McKinney's Supp. 1976). Hence, invariably there will be ultimate authority existing in a Board of Trustees or Directors. II. Oleck, Non-Profit Corporations, Organizations and Associations 300, 622 (1965). If this factor alone is to preclude full-time faculty members from assuming managerial or supervisory status, no matter what their actual involvement in the governance of an educational institution, then it is difficult to contemplate *any situation* where the statutory and Board-created exemptions can be applied. . . .

Oddly, the Board also found that department chairmen and faculty who serve on the Committee on Academic Priorities and Resource Allocation and on the University Faculty Review Committee were neither supervisors nor managers because they serve "primarily as instruments of the faculty" in these matters. If we accept the Board's argument that these chairmen and faculty committee members are simply instruments of the faculty, the Board is in the inconsistent position of finding that the full-time faculty at Yeshiva manages or supervises effectively by its collective or collegial action although this is the very process the Board utilizes to disqualify them as supervisors or managers. Another apparent contradiction is the Board's recognition of the ultimate authority of the Board of Trustees of Yeshiva although this body only acts collectively. Indeed, on the record here the "ultimate authority" of the trustees has little, if any, practical effect since, as at most universities, *McHugh, supra*, at 68; Statement, *supra*, at 376-77, the trustees' authority has been delegated to the faculty and administration.

It is clear that the Congress, when it amended the Act in 1947, had no contemplation that it would be applied to professional faculties in private institutions of higher learning. Their governance is unique and has no counterpart in the commercial business models the Act was designed to regulate. Absent a legislative amendment, it would seem that an appropriate method to explore fully the special problems created by the Board's assumption of jurisdiction here would be by rule-making. . . .

NOTES

1. In reaching the conclusion that the faculty was not acting in its own behalf but in the interest of the university, the Second Circuit opinion embraced the concept of "shared authority." Is the shared authority principle as applicable today as it was 15 years ago? 10 years ago? Can a distinction be made between the exercise of authority and the power to influence? How "accountable" are faculty members to the administration when they exercise their authority? Could a finding of managerial status be precluded if faculty members are not held accountable when exercising their authority? See Finkin, *The NLRB in Higher Education*, 5 U. Tol. L. Rev. 608, at 617-18 (1973).

2. Consider the decision in *University of New Hampshire Chapter of AAUP v. Haselton, supra,* where the Federal District Court found that governance by shared authority was more an illusion than a reality, yet held that collective bargaining by academic employees could be properly prohibited by statute.

Taking the facts from *Haselton, supra,* how would the Second Circuit decide the case if it had involved an otherwise appropriate assertion of jurisdiction by the NLRB? Would the Court follow *Yeshiva* (and exclude full-time faculty) or would it reach a different result because of the illusory nature of faculty authority found in *Haselton?*

IV. The Appropriate Bargaining Unit

A. Institutions Covered by the NLRA

N.Y.U. & N.Y.U. CHAPTER OF A.A.U.P.
& N.Y.U. FACULTY OF LAW ASSOCIATION
National Labor Relations Board
83 LRRM 1549 (1973)

The Petitioner in Case 2–RC–15719, New York University Chapter, American Association of University Professors, seeks a unit comprising all full-time faculty of New York University and half-time faculty in the school of dentistry, including professional librarians, but excluding all other employees, subject to the stipulations entered into by the parties. Intervenor, United Federation of College Teachers, Local 1460, AFT, AFL-CIO, seeks essentially the same unit as the AAUP but would include regular part-time faculty as well. The Petitioner in Case 2–RC–15757, NYU Faculty of Law Association, seeks a unit of all full-time faculty members of the law school, excluding the dean, associate deans, assistants to the dean, law librarian, guards and supervisors as defined in the Act and all other employees. The Faculty of Law Association would not include part-time faculty and has disclaimed any interest in a unit broader than the law school. . . .

The law school is located in Vanderbilt Hall at the University's Washington Square Center. The Hall is owned by the Law Center Foundation and occupied only by the law school, with the exception of the fourth floor, which is leased to the University and occupied by the central administration. The foundation is a separate not-for-profit corporation with assets of $15 million and is the administrator for application of the earnings of the C. F. Mueller Company to the law school. Legally, though not necessarily as a matter of practice, this relationship among the foundation, law school, and University appears to be unique and without exact parallel at the University.

The University's vice chancellor testified that the law school had a "greater measure of identifiable proprietary right or interest in its building." The rank distribution, while more concentrated at the upper level than in the University as a whole, is comparable to that at certain other schools or institutes of the University. The grant of tenure is determined in the same manner as it is at the rest of the University. Although the decision may, as a matter of practice, be arrived at more quickly, there apparently is no minimum period of service necessary to qualify the members of any of the university faculties for tenure consideration. Fringe benefits are the same throughout the University, no salary imbalance is demonstrated in the record, the law faculty is proportionately represented in the university senate and the faculty council, and has access to universitywide grievance machinery. There is some faculty overlap with other schools, and the law school participates with other schools in certain institutes and programs. The law school is accredited by the Association of American Law Schools and the American Bar Association; as one might expect, a unique distinction, if only in the identity of the accrediting bodies. Similarly, educational supervision is exercised by the Court of Appeals of the State of New York.

Based on the foregoing we conclude that a separate law school unit would be appropriate, but that an overall unit would also be appropriate. In such circumstances the desires of the law faculty are critical, and, therefore, we shall not make a final unit determination at this time. Instead we shall direct an election among the law school faculty to determine whether they wish to be merged into a universitywide unit. As in our recent decision in Syracuse, we find that the law faculty's special interests and allegiance differ in kind from those of the bulk of the faculty. Accordingly, the law faculty will choose between representation and nonrepresentation both as part of an overall unit and as a separate unit.[8]

With the exception of the Intervenor, United Federation of College Teachers, which requests it, the parties oppose including regular part-time faculty (save for half-time faculty in the school of dentistry, whom the AAUP would include) in any unit found appropriate. This issue has been raised before and it has consistently been resolved in favor of inclusion.

[8.]   For the reasons set forth in their dissent in Syracuse, supra, Members Fanning and Panello would direct a normal "Globe" election to allow the law faculty to vote on whether they desire separate representation. However, in their view, here, as in Syracuse, there is no reason to adopt a special voting procedure which would permit separate nonrepresentation.

However, after careful reflection, we have reached the conclusion that part-time faculty do not share a community of interest with full-time faculty, and therefore, should not be included in the same bargaining unit. In Fordham University, 193 NLRB 134, 78 LRRM 1464, the Board honored an agreement to exclude part-time faculty from the bargaining unit, citing University of New Haven, Inc., 190 NLRB No. 102, 77 LRRM 1273, which held that regular part-time faculty must be included in the same unit as full-time faculty, absent agreement of the parties to exclude them. We are now convinced that the differences between the full-time and part-time faculty are so substantial in most colleges and universities that we should not adhere to the principle announced in the New Haven case. We shall *exclude* all adjunct professors and part-time faculty members who are not employed in "tenure track" positions.

The Board has long recognized "that mutuality of interest in wages, hours, and working conditions is the prime determinant of whether a given group of employees constitutes an appropriate unit." The record in this case convinces us that there is no real mutuality of interest between the part-time and full-time faculty at New York University because of the difference with respect to (1) compensation, (2) participation in University government, (3) eligibility for tenure, and (4) working conditions.

There is a marked difference in the compensation paid the part-time faculty and the full-time faculty. The record reveals that a substantial percentage of the part-time faculty receives a modest sum which corresponds to a respectable honorarium. Generally an adjunct's primary work interest is elsewhere and his primary income is received from sources other than the University. Fringe benefits (including medical, hospital, and life insurance, as well as retirement pension) are available to all full-time faculty. They are not available to part-time faculty members.

The part-time faculty members do not participate in the governance of the University. . . .

We must always be mindful that a unit determination should be appropriate for bargaining purposes. We are persuaded that there exists such a dissimilarity of interest in the wages and working conditions of part-time and full-time faculty that we should not include them in a single unit. We should not endanger the potential contribution which collective bargaining may provide in coping with the serious problems confronting our colleges and universities by improper unit determinations. In our judgment, the grouping of the part-time and full-time faculty into a single bargaining structure will impede effective collective bargaining. . . .

The Employer would exclude, while the AAUP and the UFCT would include, professional librarians. The Employer's position is based on its contention that librarians lack a community of interest with the faculty and that they exercise sufficient supervisory authority to compel their exclusion.

Professional librarians are titled curator, associate curator, assistant curator, or library associate in descending order of rank. Unlike faculty, the function of a librarian may change with title, and promotion may depend on the existence of a vacancy. Further distinguishing librarians from faculty are their regular workweek; retirement age; tenure requirements; separate grievance procedure; lack of proportional representation in the university senate (though the dean of libraries, like other deans, is a member); and, perhaps more basically, the fact that they are not considered faculty. On the other hand, they are a professional group, charged with the responsibility for accumulating appropriate materials and serving the other members of the university community in that respect, and most fringe benefits are available to them. We conclude that they possess a sufficient community of interest to be included in the unit, as a closely allied professional group whose ultimate function, aiding and furthering the educational and scholarly goals of the University, converges with that of the faculty, though pursued through different means and in a different manner.

Their interest in the unit does not, however, put an end to the matter, as the Employer also argues for their exclusion in whole or in part, as supervisors. Initially, we reject the Employer's contention that all professional librarians possess supervisory authority over nonunit employees to a degree requiring their exclusion. The Employer's brief concedes that eight librarians do not perform supervisory duties as part of their everyday work. Additionally, however, as we noted in Adelphi, supra, the supervisory exclusion is primarily aimed at situations where this authority is regularly exercised over employees whose inclusion in the unit is sought by the union. Where professional employees have spent less than 50 percent of their time supervising nonunit employees, they have been included in the unit. . . .

Applying this standard we shall exclude as supervisors only those professional librarians who supervise other employees in the unit or who spend more than 50 percent of their time supervising nonunit employees. . . .

Though the issue is not advanced by the parties in this precise context, faculty who exercise authority over student employees whose employment is dependent upon, and related to, their student status, where the relationship is basically that of student and teacher, as appears to be the case with respect to those students whose exclusion has been stipulated, are not supervisors within the meaning of the Act and will be included in the unit. Fordham University, supra. Additionally, the 50-percent rule for determining exclusion on the basis of a supervisory relationship with nonunit employees, as set forth above in connection with professional librarians, appears to be applicable and to yield the same result.

As noted earlier, the Employer also contends that faculty who are principal investigators are supervisors. A principal investigator is a faculty member who has originated a proposal acceptable to an outside agency for contract research and is responsible for its conduct. In this capacity he may hire and supervise other persons, including faculty. As we held in Fordham, supra, since such employees are not employees of this Employer, the relationship does not make the principal investigator a supervisor for the purposes of this proceeding.

The status of faculty on terminal contracts is also disputed. The Employer argues that they should be excluded from the unit as lacking a community of interest in the long-range responsibilities and relationships which unite the remainder of the faculty. However, faculty may be on terminal contract for a period as long as a year, during which period they may participate fully in all university activities. It cannot be gainsaid that they continue to have a substantial interest in the employment relationship. As in Manhattan College, 195 NLRB No. 23, 79 LRRM 1253, there is no evidence in the record that terminal-contract faculty were not hired as permanent employees subject to termination on the same bases as other employees in the unit. They will be included since, while their employment continues, they have a substantial community of interest with their colleagues.

In virtually every case since we asserted jurisdiction over universities the status of department chairmen, or heads, has been in issue. That is true here as well. Attempting to identify and resolve the complex threads, and even the nuances, of the relationship among the faculty, administration, and department chairmen is not an easy task, nor one usually susceptible to a completely satisfactory conclusion. Though chairmen have a certain formal responsibility with respect to decisions on the appointment, salary, promotion, and tenure of full-time faculty, it appears that they act primarily as instruments of the faculty in these matters. The chairmen, in these respects, therefore stand on the same footing as the faculty, whence their authority flows. The University's vice chancellor testified that the central issue in all personnel matters is the judgment of one's peers and that chairmen are more nearly aligned with the faculty than with the administration. The Employer, the only party contesting the inclusion of chairmen in the unit, does not argue to the contrary. Instead, it relies on the authority of chairmen with respect to part-time faculty.

However, as we have already concluded that part-time faculty must be excluded from the unit, and since there is no indication in the record that their supervisory responsibilities with respect to part-time faculty even approach consuming 50 percent of their time, we conclude that chairmen are not supervisors for the purposes of this proceeding and shall include them in the unit.

The Intervenor and the Employer would treat directors of graduate and undergraduate programs in the same manner as chairmen while the AAUP, which favors inclusion, would consider them on their own merits. Program directors are appointed in large departments which, because of their size, require a further breakdown. Directors have much the same duties and function as chairmen and frequently act in consultation with the department chairman. We have already concluded that chairmen are not supervisors for the purposes of this proceeding; the argument for the exclusion of directors rests on the same basis. Therefore, and since the only party which would treat directors on their own merits urges inclusion, we conclude that directors are not supervisors and shall include them in the unit.

NOTES

1. What type of factors was the Board considering when deciding whether a group of employees had a sufficient community of interests with the other employees in the unit? *See* Catholic University of America, 83 LRRM 1548 (1973) for an application of the community of interest standard set forth in *New York University*. *See also*, Goddard College, 88 LRRM 1228 (1975).

2. The Board decision to exclude all part-time faculty from the bargaining unit in the *New York University* case represented a major policy change. The Board's original position had been to include regular part-time faculty in units with full-time faculty. *See* C. W. Post, 77 LRRM 1001 (1971). *See also* Fordham University, 78 LRRM 1177 (1971), where the Board allowed for the exclusion of part-time faculty pursuant to an agreement by the parties.

The First Circuit has approved the *New York University* decision excluding part-time faculty because of the lack of a mutuality of interest. Trustees of Boston University v. NLRB, 575 F.2d 301 (1st Cir. 1978). Under what circumstances could the argument be made that the part-time faculty have a sufficient community of interest to be included in the unit? Do you agree with the Board's position that all part-time faculty should be excluded? *Consider* Kendall College v. NLRB, 570 F.2d 216 (7th Cir. 1978), where pro-rated part-time faculty were included in the bargaining unit because of their substantial ties to the college.

3. In Kendall College v. NLRB, 570 F.2d 216 (7th Cir. 1978), the Seventh Circuit denied a petition for review of the Board's determination of an appropriate bargaining unit. The Board had excluded part-time faculty employed on the basis of a per-course contract because the interests of those part-time employees were sufficiently different from the interests of the full-time and pro-rated part-time faculty. When declining review of this decision, the Seventh Circuit stated that appropriate unit determinations are primarily the responsibility of the Board and that such determinations include discretionary judgments by the Board which will rarely be disturbed. The Seventh Circuit found no merit in the argument that the Board's decision in *Kendall College* was an unprecedented exception to the general practice of including part-time employees in bargaining units. The Court criticized the argument for assuming "that the Board is obsequiously bound to apply its general principles to all unit determinations without recognizing the special circumstances and conditions of a particular segment of industrial life, and further assumes that in this case the Board could not evaluate and reconsider [previously announced principles] in light of its experience in making unit determinations."

4. If part-time faculty members are to be excluded from the faculty bargaining unit should they be allowed to form their own bargaining unit? In Stoddard College, 88 LRRM 1228 (1975), the American Federation of Teachers sought to represent part-time faculty if they were excluded from the bargaining unit because of their part-time status. The Board refused the request of the AFT, finding that the facts did not establish a community interest sufficient to warrant a bargaining unit.

Viewing the part-time faculty as a heterogeneous group, the Board held that any common identification with the employer was insufficient to overcome the differences in wages, hours, responsibilities, locations, and conditions of employment. Has this decision created a form of "no-man's land" for part-time faculty?

5. For a Board decision on the status of academic advisors and career counselors, *see* Mount Vernon College, 95 LRRM 1349 (1977). In that case the academic advisor-career counselor was excluded from the faculty bargaining unit even though she was a member of the faculty, voted at faculty meetings, served on a faculty subcommittee, and reported directly to the dean of academic affairs. The exclusion was partly justified on the ground that an academic advisor-career counselor was not a professional employee as defined in the NLRA. What arguments might be made to convince the Board that an academic advisor-career counselor is a professional employee? See Northeastern University, 89 LRRM 1862 (1975).

6. Numerous decisions have considered the status of department chairmen. For cases excluding department chairmen from the faculty unit see C. W. Post, 77 LRRM 1001 (1971) (department chairmen had some responsibility for hiring of faculty members and thus were supervisors); Adelphi University, 79 LRRM 1545 (1972) (department chairman's authority to recommend personnel decisions for part-time faculty and allocate merit increases without approval by the faculty was sufficient to show supervisory status of chairmen); New York University, 91 LRRM 1165 (1975) (the Board found that the authority of department chairmen to effectively recommend personnel decisions, evaluate faculty performance, and assign class schedules placed them in a supervisory role). When department chairmen have been included in a faculty unit it has generally been found that the chairmen shared their authority with the department's faculty. *See, e.g.,* Fordham University, 78 LRRM 1177 (1971) (department chairmen did not direct the work of the faculty, nor make personnel recommendations on their own); University of Detroit, 78 LRRM 1273 (1971) (recommendation made by a department chairman was just one of several made to the university official or body which had the authority to make a final decision); Fordham University, 87 LRRM 1643 (1974) (duties of department chairmen were executed in an atmosphere of collegiality where decisions were made by the faculty as a group subject to review by administrative officials); Northeastern University, 89 LRRM 1862 (1975) (powers of the department chairmen had been diffused among other department faculty).

7. For a good discussion of the Board "50% rule" (outlined in *New York University, supra*), *see* Finkin, *The Supervisory Status of Professional Employees*, 45 Fordham L. Rev. 805 (1977).

8. The Board has been criticized for its policy of excluding law faculties from campus-wide faculty groups as was done in *New York University. See* Finkin, *The NLRB in Higher Education*, 5 U. Tol. L. Rev. 608 (1973). It has been argued that the rationale to justify the law school exclusion in *New York University* could be applied to justify separate units for most academic disciplines. Do you agree?

In University of Miami, 87 LRRM 1634 (1974), the Board approved the separation of the Marine and Atmospheric Science School and the Medical School from a unit consisting of university faculty members. The Board relied on the separate location of the schools, sources of income from outside the university, significantly lower student-teacher ratios, and substantial differences in salaries and contracts.

However, in University of Vermont, 91 LRRM 1570 (1976), the Board decided that the faculty of the School of Allied Health Services shared a close community of interest with other faculty members and should therefore be included in the overall faculty unit. In the same opinion the Board found that the Medical School faculty should be excluded from the overall unit since it lacked a community of interests with other faculty members.

At least one circuit court has held that, although some factors used to justify exclusion of law and medical school faculties might be seen to be applicable to other professional school faculties, there are special factors which significantly distinguish law and medical schools from other professional school situations. Trustees of Boston University v. NLRB, 575 F.2d 301 (1st Cir. 1978).

9. Multi-campus units have been found appropriate where the campus facilities are integrated and centralized, the working conditions and terms of employment are identical, and the university senate consisted of representatives from all campuses. Fairleigh Dickinson University, 84 LRRM 1033 (1973).

10. For other decisions concerning the exclusion or inclusion of other employee groups *see*: C. W. Post, 77 LRRM 1001 (1971) (excluding research associates and assistants from the faculty unit); Rensselaer Polytechnic Institute, 89 LRRM 1844 (1975) (research associates and assistants share a sufficient community of interest to be included in the faculty unit); Adelphi University, 79 LRRM 1545 (1972) (graduate students lack the sufficient community of interest to be included in the faculty unit as they were primarily students working toward a degree); University of Miami, 87 LRRM 1634 (1974)

(coaches were excluded from faculty bargaining unit where their sole function was to coach intercollegiate sports); Rensselaer Polytechnic Institute, 89 LRRM 1844 (1975) (members of the physical education staff had qualifications and responsibilities similar to other faculty members and thus were included in the faculty unit); Goddard College, 88 LRRM 1228 (1975) (visiting faculty members were excluded from the faculty unit since they had no expectation of permanent employment at the institution which they were visiting).

11. For some good cases involving unit determination questions affecting non-academic employees, *see* Stanford University, 79 LRRM 1356 (1972); California Institute of Technology, 77 LRRM 1849 (1971); Tuskegee Institute, 86 LRRM 1082 (1974); Tulane University, 79 LRRM 1366 (1972); and Duke University, 78 LRRM 1547 (1971).

12. Do student employees share a sufficient community of interest to be included in a non-academic bargaining unit? See Barnard College, 83 LRRM 1483 (1973).

13. In 1974, voluntary, non-profit hospitals were brought under the jurisdiction of the NLRB by a Congressional amendment of the NLRA. For a discussion of the special interests involved in hospital cases see Baylor University Medical Center v. NLRB, 578 F.2d 351 (D. C. Cir. 1978).

B.   Unit Determinations in the Public Sector

The bargaining units found to be appropriate in public institutions have often paralleled those in private institutions under the NLRB's jurisdiction. This is attributable to the emulation of the NLRA by state public employment statutes and the reliance on NLRB case precedent by state public employment boards. Yet, there have been some notable differences in the public sector. For instance, there are states which prescribe the appropriate unit by statute or require that the "most," rather than "an," appropriate bargaining unit be selected. Also, a number of states have a policy against undue fragmentization which may dictate in favor of district or statewide units.

In Minnesota State College Board v. PERB, 228 N.W.2d 551 (1975), the court reversed the Public Employee Relations Board and ruled that the appropriate unit for state college faculty members was a statewide unit. In reaching this conclusion, the court noted that:

(1) The legislature has moved to coordinate the entire statewide college system under the auspices of the State College Board and has therefore indicated an intent that uniformity be established.

(2) The SCB has implemented this intention and has promulgated rules which govern each institution on a state-wide, rather than individual, basis.

(3) The system-wide unit, in all aspects, has proved to be a more efficient and economical method of administering the state college system.

(4) Competition between college units, both in the physical plants and in employer-employee benefits is reduced upon utilization of the state-wide system, because it reduces the possibility of varying benefits.

(5) Past utilization of the state-wide approach indicates that it has not stifled individualized interests at each of the colleges; that distances and locations have not prevented effective coordination between the faculty and the SCB; that a substantial majority of the state college system faculty favors a state-wide unit; and that a state-wide unit has been established for the 18 junior colleges incorporating a master contract with flexible provisions for each campus.

Similar factors were discussed by the Nebraska Supreme Court in University Professors v. University of Nebraska, 95 LRRM 2122 (1977); yet, the Court found that an individual campus unit was appropriate. Although the University of Nebraska system is organized under a single Board of Regents and Central Administration, the Court of Industrial Relations found that decisions were made at the local and departmental level with little integration of operations. The three major administrative units in the system could be distinguished by the programs they offered and the type of degree they awarded. Eleven factors were deemed relevant to the court's determination of the appropriate bargaining unit: (1) prior bargaining history; (2) centralization of management and labor policy; (3) extent of faculty interchange between campuses; (4) degree of interdependence of autonomy of the campuses; (5) differences or similarities in skills or functions of the employees; (6) geographical location of the campuses in relation to each other; (7) uniformity of wages, benefits, and conditions of employment; (8) current means of governing the university; (9) established policies of the employer; (10) community of interest of employees; and (11) possibility of over-fragmentation of bargaining units. Following an analysis of these eleven factors, the Court held that individual campus units were warranted by a sufficient difference in the community of interest at the three major institutions. The following considerations were given to support the court's decision:

Employee bodies which represented faculty concerns, such as the faculty senate or committee on academic freedom and tenure, exist on a campus level, and not at the systems level. There is no significant faculty interchange between campuses. UN-L and UN-O function largely independent of each other so far as the faculty on each campus is concerned. Although the general skills of the University faculty are similar, the different missions and roles of each campus affect faculty interests and conditions of employment on each campus. The geographic location of the two campuses contributes to the lack of community of interest between the faculty on each campus. Although the Board has ultimate power to make decisions affecting the faculty on both campuses, this power in fact is diffused throughout the system, and administrators on each campus play a critical role in regard to employee matters. Faculty of UN-L perceive themselves as having a community of interest different from, and often in contrast with, the community of interest at UN-O. Finally, due to the unique situation presented, the likelihood of undue fragmentations appears to be minimal under the evidence adduced.

V.   The Legal Duty to Bargain

Although the following case involves a dispute arising in the public sector, the decision provides a good discussion of some of the applicable caselaw governing the duty to bargaining in both the public and private sectors.

CENTRAL MICHIGAN UNIVERSITY FACULTY ASSOCIATION
v. CENTRAL MICHIGAN UNIVERSITY
Supreme Court of Michigan
(1978)

BLAIR MOODY, JR., J.

On April 30, 1973, the academic senate of Central Michigan University passed a resolution adopting a teaching effectiveness program which provided that students, as well as department faculty, evaluate the faculty members. Although the form of and weight to be given the student evaluations in department recommendations were not specified, the program did provide that "[d]epartmental recommendations for reappointment, promotion and tenure should be accompanied by evidence of teaching effectiveness".

On January 28, 1974, the Central Michigan University Faculty Association charged the university with an unfair labor practice. The faculty association claimed that Section I of the teaching effectiveness program was a mandatory subject of collective bargaining and, therefore, it was impermissible for the university to unilaterally adopt the program.

Administrative Law Judge Shlomo Sperka upheld the faculty association's unfair labor practice charge, finding that the university had violated § 10 of the Public Employment Relations Act (hereinafter PERA) by unilaterally adopting and implementing the teaching effectiveness program without bargaining with the exclusive, certified collective bargaining agent of its faculty.

The university appealed to the Michigan Employment Relations Commission (hereinafter MERC). In a split decision, the 2-member majority reversed Judge Sperka's decision and dismissed the unfair labor practice charge. After discussing the difference between institutions of higher learning and other public employers as related to the scope of bargaining, the MERC majority found the program in question to be predominantly a matter of educational policy and not mandatorily negotiable. . . .

The Court of Appeals, over the dissent of the Honorable Michael F. Cavanagh, upheld the MERC decision. 75 Mich App 101. 254 NW2d 802 (1977). We granted leave to appeal. 401 Mich 831 (1977).

I

The issue on this appeal is whether the elements, procedures and criteria involving evaluations for purposes of reappointment, retention and promotion are "other terms and conditions of employment" within the meaning of the PERA. The crux of this issue is the question whether the nature of the public employment alters the scope of mandatory bargaining. . . .

The duty of a public employer to bargain collectively with the employees' representative is set forth in §15 of the PERA, patterned after §8(d) of the National Labor Relations Act (hereinafter NLRA). Section 15 provides, in relevant part:

"A public employer shall bargain collectively with the representatives of its employees as defined in section 11 and is authorized to make and enter into collective bargaining agreements with such representatives. For the purposes of this section, to bargain collectively is the performance of the mutual obligation of the employer and the representative of the employees to meet at reasonable times and confer in good faith with respect to wages, hours, and other terms and conditions of employment." MCL 423.215; MSA 17.455(15).

In both the PERA and the NLRA, the collective bargaining obligation is defined as the mutual duty of labor and management to bargain in good faith with respect to "wages, hours, and other terms and conditions of employment". The subjects included within the phrase "wages, hours, and other terms and conditions of employment" are referred to as "mandatory subjects" of bargaining. Once a specific subject has been classified as a mandatory subject of bargaining, the parties are required to bargain concerning the subject, and neither party may take unilateral action on the subject absent an impasse in negotiations. See generally Morris, ed, The Developing Labor Law, (Washington, D C: Bureau of National Affairs, Inc, 1971) chs 14-16; *National Labor Relations Board* v *Wooster Division of Borg-Warner Corp,* 356 US 342; 78 S Ct 718; 2 L Ed2d 823 (1958), *Fibreboard Paper Products Corp* v *National Labor Relations Board,* 379 US 203; 85 S Ct 398; 13 L Ed 2d 233; 6 ALR3d 1130 (1964).

The United States Supreme Court has concluded that one of the primary purposes of the NLRA is labor relations peace and that this objective can best be achieved by adopting a liberal approach to what constitutes a mandatory subject of bargaining. . . .

In *Detroit Police Officers Ass'n* v *Detroit*, 391 Mich 44, 55, 214 NW2d 803 (1974), this Court looked to the private sector for examples of mandatory subjects of collective bargaining and found:

"[S]uch subjects as hourly rates of pay, overtime pay, shift differentials, holiday pay, pensions, no-strike clauses, profit sharing plans, rental of company houses, grievance procedures, sick leave, work-rules, *seniority and promotion*, compulsory retirement age, and management rights clauses, *are* examples of *mandatory subjects of bargaining.* " (Emphasis added.). . . .

In the instant case we are asked whether the elements, procedures and criteria involving evaluations for purposes of reappointment, retention and promotion are "other terms and conditions of employment". MCL 423.215; MSA 17.455(15). We conclude that reappointment, retention and promotion criteria are "other terms and conditions of employment" and are a mandatory subject of collective bargaining.

II

Having reached this conclusion, we must now address the critical question whether the nature of the public employment alters the scope of the collective bargaining obligation of particular public employers. The university makes essentially a two-fold argument for excluding the procedures and criteria for reappointment, retention and promotion from the mandatory subject category to which they would otherwise belong. First, the university maintains that the unique status accorded the state universities by constitutional and statutory authority justifies excluding the subject of promotion and retention evaluation criteria from the scope of the mandatory bargaining obligation. . . . In decreeing that "wages, hours and other terms and conditions of employment" are mandatory subjects of collective bargaining, the Legislature focused on the effect a particular aspect of the employment relationship has on the *employees' status*, not the effect is has on the "business", *i.e.*, the effect on educational policies. The statutory test of the PERA is whether the particular aspect of the employment relationship is a "term or condition of employment". Under the act, a particular aspect of the employment relationship is a mandatory subject of collective bargaining, even if it may be said to be only minimally a condition of employment. . . .

[W]e find the unique status accorded state universities by constitutional and statutory authority does not alter the scope of their collective bargaining obligation under the PERA. If university professors are truly unique and thus different from other public employees, the Legislature must carve out an exception to the PERA. This Court cannot.

III

Alternatively, the university contends that the incorporation of student evaluations into the criteria for faculty promotion and retention is predominantly a matter of education policy and, therefore, outside the arena of mandatory collective bargaining. We are urged that the case of *Regents of the University of Michigan* v *Employment Relations Comm*, 389 Mich 96; 204 NW2d 218 (1973), supports this position. . . .

[However, under *Regents*] the scope of collective bargaining is limited only if the subject matter "falls clearly within the educational sphere". In the instant case, the procedures and criteria adopted affect the retention, tenure and promotion of faculty members. These are clearly matters within the employment sphere, crucial to the employer-employee relationship. They are not matters within the educational sphere as that phrase was used in *Regents, supra*.

We agree with the analysis of Court of Appeals dissenter Judge Michael Cavanagh:

"I cannot agree * * * that evaluative criteria for purposes of tenure and promotion are strictly 'educational policy'. This matter bears directly on the means by which the administration will determine whether or not untenured faculty members will continue their positions. Surely the criteria for that decision are important to the members of the bargaining unit. While evaluation of teaching effectiveness is not a trivial element of the university's education program, I cannot perceive the method of that evaluation to be integral to the university's mission: to educate. *I would strike the balance in favor of the limited obligation to bargain before unilateral imposition of new criteria. This would not block the ultimate adoption of student evaluations as part of the criteria of teaching effectiveness; it would merely impose the reasonable burden upon the university to consult the association and discuss the program before its implementation.*" (Emphasis added.) *Central Michigan University Faculty Ass'n, supra,* 114.

Consequently, we reverse the MERC and Court of Appeals majority opinions and reinstate the decision and recommended order of the Administrative Law Judge.

M.S. COLEMAN, dissenting.

. . . .

We are asked to decide whether Part I of the teaching effectiveness program is a mandatory subject of collective bargaining, as distinct from a permissive or illegal subject. The Court has recently defined these terms as having the same meaning under PERA as under the NLRA:

"Mandatory subjects of collective bargaining are those within the scope of 'wages, hours, and other terms and conditions of employment'. [MCL 423.215; MSA 17.455(15).] If either party proposes a mandatory subject, both parties are obligated to bargain about it in good faith.

"Permissive subjects of collective bargaining are those which fall outside the scope of 'wages, hours, and other terms and conditions of employment', and may be negotiated only if both parties agree.

"Illegal subjects are those which even if negotiated will not be enforced because adoption would be violative of the law or of the NLRA." *Pontiac Police Officers Ass'n* v *Pontiac,* 397 Mich 674, 679; 246 NW2d 831 (1976), *Detroit Police Officers Ass'n* v *Detroit,* 391 Mich 44, 54; 214 NW2d 803 (1974). See generally *Fibreboard Paper Products Corp* v *NLRB,* 379 US 203; 85 S Ct 398; 13 L Ed 2d 233 (1964), *NLRB* v *Borg-Warner Corp,* 356 US 342; 78 S Ct 718; 2 L Ed 2d 823 (1958).

Therefore, the issue is whether Part I of the program encompasses mandatory or permissive subjects of bargaining. To sharpen the issue further, we accept MERC's statement that:

"The scope of bargaining issues in educational institutions has been presented in terms of whether an employer's action or activity is educational policy or a condition of employment. The PERA bargaining obligation, under this theory, applies only to the latter. Under this theory, the issue may be framed in the alternative. If the portion of the 'Teaching Effectiveness—Implementing Recommendations' document to which objection is made by the Association is educational policy, the University Board of Trustees had power to adopt and implement it. If, on the other hand, Item I of the 'Teaching Effectiveness—Implementing Recommendations' document is a condition of employment, PERA requires collective bargaining before adoption by the Board of Trustees."

The evaluative criteria and procedures, as an element of the teaching effectiveness program—but also bearing upon faculty reappointment, tenure, and promotion—fall into that area of overlap and conflict between the uncontroverted extremes of "educational policy" and "employment conditions". The growth of litigation testing the scope of the bargaining obligation in the public sector of higher education suggests that the majority of disputed items fall into this zone of overlap.

We note that the governing system employed at the University places members of the faculty on both sides of the bargaining table. They make many management decisions within the Academic Senate structure and yet are represented by the Association which challenges these same decisions. The teaching effectiveness program was originated and developed within the Senate structure but is challenged as a creature of the University.

As noted above, many courts recently have been asked to decide issues concerning the scope of mandatory bargaining in the public sector. Two basic approaches for resolving the problem have evolved.

Some courts have required bargaining whenever employer actions "significantly relate to", "concern" or "materially affect" conditions of employment.[6]   Because this type of test for determining the scope of the bargaining obligation is inherently biased toward mandatory negotiability, it has been observed that:

"This standard ['significant relation' standard] is inadequate because it does not properly recognize the competing interests at stake where there is an overlap between conditions of employment on the one hand and management prerogatives on the other. By

---

[6.]   *E.G., Clark County School Dist v Local Government Employee-Management Relations Board*, 90 Nev 442; 530 P2d 114 (1974), *Aberdeen Education Ass'n v Aberdeen Board of Education*, 88 SD 127; 215 NW2d 837 (1974), *Allied Chemical & Alkali Workers v Pittsburgh Plate Glass Co*, 404 US 157, 178-179; 92 S Ct 383; 30 L Ed 2d 341 (1971) (private sector). See also, *Los Angeles Employees Ass'n, Local 660 v Los Angeles County*, 33 Cal App 3d 1; 108 Cal Rptr 625 (1973).

focusing on only one-half of the overlap problem, this standard gives undue weight to conditions of employment." Clark, *The Scope of the Duty to Bargain in Public Employment*, Labor Relations Law in the Public Sector (A. Knapp, Ed, 1977), p 92.

Other courts have adopted a test which attempts to weigh the effects on both management and union prerogatives—the balancing test. The Oregon Court of Appeals recently stated that:

"[T]he appropriate test to be applied in determining whether a proposed subject is a 'condition of employment' and therefore a mandatory subject of bargaining is to balance the element of educational policy involved against the effect that the subject has on a teacher's employment." *Sutherlin Education Ass'n v Sutherlin School District No 130*, 25 Or App 85; 548 P2d 204, 205 (1976).

Courts in Kansas, Pennsylvania and Alaska have also found the balancing standard to be appropriate.[7] We further note that MERC has previously recognized the advantages of the balancing test. In *Westwood Education Ass'n v Westwood Community Schools,* 7 MERC Lab Op 313,320 (1972), the majority stated that "[a] balancing approach to bargaining may be more suited to the realities of the public sector than the dichotomized scheme—mandatory and non-mandatory—used in the private sector".

We find that the balancing approach is an even-handed method for resolving scope questions. It "acknowledges that both parties have significant interests at stake" and "is well suited to a case by case determination of negotiability because it does not begin with a bias". Clark, *supra,* pp 94-95. Such an approach is particularly appropriate to public sector decision-making in institutions of higher education because of variables not present in the private sector. Therefore, we determine that issues of the scope of mandatory collective bargaining in higher education under PERA shall be resolved by weighing the effects of a given subject upon educational policies against the effects upon the faculty member's interest in "wages, hours, and other terms and conditions of employment". . . .

At the University, the objectives and methods of enhancing the excellence of higher education and assisting the faculty toward effective teaching are within the ambit of educational policy.

We find, therefore, that Part I of the teaching effectiveness program impacts heavily upon matters of educational policy and only peripherally upon conditions of employment. Consequently, it is not a subject of mandatory collective bargaining.

[7.]   *National Education Ass'n of Shawnee Mission, Inc v Board of Education of Shawnee Mission,* 212 Kan 741, 753; 512 P 2d 426, 435 (1973), *Pennsylvania Labor Relations Board v State College Area School District,* 461 Pa Supreme Ct 494, 507; 337 A2d 262 (1975), *Kenai Peninsula Borough School District v Kenai Peninsula Education Ass'n,* 572 P 2d 416, 422-423 (Alaska 1977). (Although the Alaska court did not expressly adopt the balancing test, it is clear that the court approved of and used the test.)

Our holding is in accord with decisions in other jurisdictions. In *Association of College Faculties v Dungan*, 64 NJ 338; 316 A2d 425 (1974), the New Jersey Supreme Court held that a unilateral implementation of a program for granting tenure and evaluating tenured faculty, including student input, was a matter of major educational policy. The New Jersey version of PERA also requires bargaining over "terms and conditions of employment". 34 NJ Stat Ann 13A-5.3. The Court suggested, however, that it would have been better labor relations policy to have discussed the program with the faculty prior to implementation. We note that the Central Michigan University program was developed exclusively by the Academic Senate itself over a three year period.

An analogous issue was decided by the New York Public Employee Relations Board in *In the Matter of Board of Higher Education of City of New York*, 7 PERB ¶7-3028, p 3042 (1974). After consultations with the faculty union, the Faculty Senate and the Student Senate, the Board implemented student participation on the Personnel and Budget Committees of City University of New York. These committees recommended faculty reappointment, tenure and promotion. During subsequent contract negotiations, the faculty union demanded that the students be barred from the committees. The PERB held that student representation was not a subject of mandatory bargaining and noted:

"There is a difference between the role of college teachers as employees and their policy-making function which goes by the name of collegiality. Unlike most employees, college teachers function as both employees and as participants in the making of policy. Because of this dual role, it has been argued elsewhere that they are not entitled to representation in collective bargaining. In *Matter of Fordham University*, [193 NLRB 134, 78 LRRM 1177 (1971)], the National Labor Relations Board dismissed this challenge to the right of college teachers to representation and pointed out that the two types of interests of college teachers are compatible because they are addressed in different institutional structures. The NLRB specifically noted that the policymaking responsibilities of college teachers are exercised through academic committees and faculty senates, while they remain employees for the purpose of determining their terms and conditions of employment under the National Labor Relations Act.

"We, too, distinguish between the role of faculty as employees and its role as a participant in the governance of its colleges. * * * The right of the faculty to negotiate over terms and conditions of employment does not enlarge or contract the traditional prerogatives of collegiality; neither does it subsume them. These prerogatives may continue to be exercised through the traditional channels of academic committees and faculty senates * * *. We note with approval the observation that, 'faculty must continue to manage, even if that is an anomaly. They will, in a sense, be on both sides of the bargaining table'. We would qualify this observation, however; faculty may be on both sides of the table, but not their union."

The present trend of student and faculty involvement in university governance is a fact in our time of rapid change which must be squarely faced. The New York PERB in *Board of Higher Education, supra,* directs attention to the fact that student participation in faculty evaluation recognizes the interests of those other than employer and employee:

"It would be a perversion of collective negotiations to impose it [mandatory bargaining] as a technique for resolving such disputes and thus disenfranchising other interested groups."

Although there is logic in some of the arguments that collective bargaining in an institution of higher education will eventually eliminate collegiality and block out social and educational interests of any but the employer and employee,[8] we believe it possible to have an external bargaining agent without atrophy of academic agencies such as the Senate.

The balancing test assures, so far as possible, a fair resolution of competing statutory, constitutional and policy considerations. It is an appropriate instrument for piercing the veil of the "gray area" of overlapping responsibilities, objectives and interests.

In the balancing, we can afford some weight to the role of students whose interest as ultimate beneficiaries of University education is real. The prerogatives and autonomy of the Board, as appointed *public* officials, are also given equal consideration with the interests of the faculty. This result

---

[8.]   If a faculty union could require bargaining over any subject which *affected* employment conditions, the role of a faculty legislative body would disappear over time. Professor Brown has described the problem as follows:

"Some statutes contain limitations on the scope of bargainable issues, but neither the limitations nor the generalization meets the special problem of a university faculty. That problem, stripped to its essentials, is to prevent the pervasive and traditional areas of faculty academic authority from being absorbed into the newly created collective bargaining process. Once a bargaining agent has the weight of statutory certification behind it, a familiar process comes into play. First, the matter of salaries is linked to the matter of workload; workload is then related directly to class size, class size to range of offerings, and range of offerings to curricular policy. Dispute over class size may also lead to bargaining over admissions policies. This transmutation of academic policy into employment terms is not inevitable, but it is quite likely to occur. Thus, an expert task force of the American Asssociation for Higher Education, in a calm appraisal of the pros and cons of industrial-style collective bargaining for higher education, concluded that an academic agency such as a faculty senate would probably 'atrophy' in the shadow of an external bargaining agent. If the faculty considers such an outcome undesirable, it is possible to argue that the bargaining agent, whether external or internal, is after all under the faculty's control—a majority can in due course repudiate it and choose a new one. But this may be easier prescribed than accomplished." Brown, *Collective Bargaining in Higher Education*, 67 Mich L Rev 1067, 1075-1076 (1969). (Footnotes omitted.)

is of particular importance given the inherent political nature of collective bargaining in the public sector.[9]

With the Alaska Supreme Court, we are persuaded that it is in the public interest to guard against a shift in the control of educational policy from the boards to the unions through successive rounds of bargaining. That Court said:

> "Such a result could threaten the ability of elective government officials and appointive officers subject to their authority * * * to perform their functions in the broad public interest." *Kenai Peninsula Borough School District v Kenai Peninsula Education Association*, 572 P2d 416, 419 (Alaska 1977).

NOTES

1. The material that follows was excerpted from Edwards, *The Emerging Duty to Bargain in the Public Sector*, 71 Mich. L. Rev. 885 (1973) (footnotes omitted). Although what appears here is not an exhaustive treatment of the subject, it will at least give the reader a better understanding of some of the significant differences between the public and private sectors with respect to the duty to bargain:

In private sector labor relations, the duty to bargain is defined by section 8(d) of the NLRA as

> the mutual obligation of the employer and the representative of the employees to meet at reasonable times and confer in good faith with respect to wages, hours, and other terms and conditions of employment, . . . but such obligation does not compel either party to agree to a proposal or require the making of a concession. . . .

The obligation to negotiate in good faith has been interpreted by the courts as requiring a duty to participate actively in deliberations with a sincere desire and intention to reach an agreement. Normally, this would encompass give and take on both sides until some agreement is reached, but there is no legal duty to agree. Furthermore, the NLRA does not preclude an employer from bargaining in good faith for unilateral control over a matter covered by the duty to bargain. Similarly, the failure to make a counter-proposal is not a per se violation of the NLRA; however, such a failure, in the context of the totality of a party's conduct at the bargaining table, may lead to the inference of bad faith bargaining. In essence, the requirement of good faith bargaining in the private sector is simply that both parties manifest a type of attitude and conduct which will be conducive to the reaching of an agreement. . . .

Statutes concerned with public sector bargaining may be divided into two categories: those providing for "collective negotiations" and the so-called "meet and confer" statutes. In states, such as Michigan, which have adopted the collective-negotiations approach, the statutory definition of the duty to bargain is often identical or very similar to that found in the NLRA. It is probably safe to assume that these statutes were intentionally designed to incorporate by reference private sector precedents. . . .

Before attempting an appraisal of legislation based on the meet-and-confer model, it may be helpful to contrast it with the collective-negotiations approach presently recognized in the private sector. "Meet-and-confer negotiations" can be defined as the

> process of negotiating terms and conditions of employment intended to emphasize the differences between public and private employment conditions. Negotiations under "meet and confer" laws usually imply discussions leading to unilateral adoption of policy by legislative body rather than written con-

---

[9.]   See, *e.g.*, Summers, *Public Employee Bargaining: A Political Perspective*, 83 Yale L J 1156 (1974), Project, *Collective Bargaining and Politics in Public Employment*, 19 UCLA L Rev 887 (1972).

tract, and take place with multiple employee representatives rather than an
exclusive bargaining agent.

This decision fairly describes what was originally intended by the meet-and-confer standard of bargaining. Implicit in the *pure* meet-and-confer approach is the assumption that
the private sector bargaining model would be overly permissive if applied without qualification to the public sector. In other words, it is argued that public employers should
retain broad managerial discretion in the operation of a governmental agency, subject
only to the recall of the electorate. Thus, under the pure meet-and-confer bargaining
model, the outcome of any public employer-employee discussions will depend more on
management's determinations than on bilateral decisions by "equals" at the bargaining
table. In contrast, the parties in the private sector meet as equals and are free to negotiate
to a point of impasse all "mandatory" subjects of bargaining—matters concerning wages,
hours, and conditions of employment. . . .

Most critics of meet-and-confer have argued that any bargaining structure which rele-
gates the employees' representative to the status of a "conferee" or "discussant," rather
than a negotiator, is patently deficient. But this criticism rests on the assumption that the
bargaining process is in fact different under a meet-and-confer, as opposed to a collective-
negotiations, model. However, the recent history of collective bargaining in the public
sector suggests that there is relatively little difference in bargaining tactics or techniques
under these two models. Unions in the public sector have pressed for the same type of
demands and with the same vigor under both models. Moreover, many of the states
which have passed meet-and-confer statutes have so distorted the pure meet-and-confer
bargaining model that it is no longer accurate to say that the parties governed by these
statutes do not meet as "equals." . . . .

While it is plain that in some states, the parties do not meet as equals at the bargaining table, there are other meet-and-confer jurisdictions in which the matter has not been
so neatly resolved. In Kansas, for example, the duty to meet and confer encompasses
more than a mere exhortation to the public employer to "consider" employees' proposals; it is a mutual obligation to "meet and confer in order . . . *to endeavor to reach
agreement* on conditions of employment." Other meet-and-confer statutes state even
more explicitly that the employer's duty goes beyond listening to its employees' suggestions. For example, the Montana statute makes it an unfair labor practice for a government employer to refuse to "meet, confer, or negotiate *in good faith*." . . . .

In the preceding discussion of how the bargaining process varies from state to state,
it has been assumed that each state has adopted the same bargaining procedures for all
public employees. Actually, some state legislatures have grouped public employees into
several classes for the purposes of defining bargaining rights, and each class tends to be
burdened with its own restrictions. . . .

The class of public employees most often differentiated from the others is teachers.
As noted hereafter, some state statutes reflect the view that certain professional employees—administrators, technicians, and scientists, but primarily teachers—are valuable
resource personnel and that they should therefore be available for consultation on policy
matters, in a nonadversary situation, lest their expertise be lost to the public employer.
As a consequence, some statutes not only seek to protect the right of these employees to
bargain with respect to what are traditionally viewed as mandatory subjects of bargaining, but also preserve for these employees the right to *discuss* other matters which, absent
statutory provisions, would be either wholly within the discretion of the public employer
or not a mandatory subject of bargaining. Under the new Minnesota public employee relations statute, for example, all public employees have the right to "meet-and-negotiate" with
respect to terms and conditions of employment, while "professional employees" have the
additional right to "meet and confer". . . over items not defined as "terms and conditions of employment." Minnesota is unique in its bifurcation of the duty to bargain in
a single statute. Several other states have separate statutes designed to *narrow* the scope
of bargaining for professionals so as to avoid adversary confrontations on policy issues.

The type of bargaining authorized for teachers is often given the name "professional
negotiations." However, the use of this term may be meaningless as a practical matter.

For example, in the Kansas statute applying to teachers, "professional negotiations" has virtually the same meaning as does the modified meet-and-confer obligation, discussed above, which covers other public employees. Similarly, in Vermont, "professional negotiations" is defined to mean "meeting, conferring, consulting, discussing *and negotiating*." Thus the term may merely reflect the attempts by some state legislatures to avoid traditional collective bargaining in situations involving professional employees. . . .

If, as hereinabove suggested, there is no real difference in the technique of bargaining under most meet-and-confer and collective-negotiations laws, then the crucial inquiry must involve the scope of bargaining under either approach. And even if the process of bargaining differs between meet-and-confer and collective-negotiations states (because the parties negotiate as "equals" only under the latter approach), we are still not told much about the effective scope of bargaining in the states which have opted for the collective-negotiations approach. A state statutory requirement that the parties negotiate as "equals" will be insignificant if the statute also narrowly limits the scope of bargaining. . . .

In the private sector, the scope of bargaining is derived from the words "wages, hours, and other terms and conditions of employment," found in section 8(d) of the NLRA. Subjects covered by this phrase are deemed to be mandatory, and the employer must bargain with respect to them. Other matters are either permissive or illegal subjects of bargaining. Bargaining with respect to permissive subjects is discretionary for both parties, and neither is required to bargain in good faith to the point at which agreement or impasse is reached. The parties are not explicitly forbidden from discussing matters which are illegal subjects of bargaining, but a contract provision embodying an illegal subject is, of course, unenforceable.

In the public sector, the NLRA language is frequently incorporated in state statutes to establish the broad outlines of the scope of bargaining. State courts and public employment relations boards have likewise frequently relied upon the mandatory-permissive-illegal distinction, although the distinction probably has little relevance in the *pure* meet-and-confer states, where the employer's duty to consider *any* proposal is not very great. The public sector differs greatly from the private sector, however, in the *method* by which this distinction is delineated. In the private sector, the line between mandatory and permissive subjects of bargaining is drawn on an ad hoc basis, as the NLRB and the courts subject the distinction to constant redefinition and refinement. In the public sector, there is an attempt to accomplish much more by statute, generally in the form of specific restrictions on the subject matter of bargaining. In some cases, state statutes exclude specific matters from the category of mandatory subjects of bargaining; presumably, however, these matters are still bargainable on a permissive basis. In other cases, public employers are forbidden altogether from bargaining about certain listed subjects. . . .

Another source of restrictions on the scope of bargaining is narrow judicial interpretation of statutory language. Just as courts have been hesitant to impose a duty to bargain on the public employer, so have they been reluctant to give expansive interpretations to the language governing the scope of bargaining. The desire to avoid illegal delegations of power, as well as the reluctance to permit employee groups to encroach upon areas entrusted to the discretion of a political agency are unquestionably valid, if often overstated, concerns of the court. These concerns are reinforced by legislative policy statements which virtually mandate a conservative approach to statutory interpretation. . . .

Delineating the scope of bargaining is even more difficult where statutory management-rights clauses and other statutory exclusions are involved. While the whole thrust of private sector case law is to define what is bargainable by constant refinement of the term "wages, hours and conditions of employment," statutory exclusions are attempts to define bargainability in terms of what is *not* bargainable. Furthermore, while deviations from NLRA language leave the scope of bargaining unclear, statutory exclusions create even more confusion. Some state statutes, for instance, provide that the public employer has the unfettered right to "maintain the efficiency of government operations." Others declare that the employer has no duty to bargain with respect to the mission of the agency or matters of inherent managerial policy. It surely is not clear what these terms mean. . . .

Once it has been established that a subject is a mandatory or permissive subject of bargaining, the next issue is: When may an employer refuse to bargain further and take unilateral action instead?

In the private sector, an employer cannot take unilateral action with regard to a mandatory subject where there has been no bargaining. However, following negotiations to a point of impasse on a mandatory subject, the employer can take unilateral action, so long as it does not exceed the terms of his final offer to the union.

In the private sector, it has also generally been held that an employer may take unilateral action at any time with respect to a permissive subject. These rules would seem applicable in those states where the pure collective-negotiations model regulates the public sector. In *pure* meet-and-confer states, a public employer presumably is free to implement unilaterally any proposals once the statutory obligation to discuss them with the union has been satisfied. In the *modified* meet-and-confer states, there is simply no precedent to aid in the determination of how long an employer must confer with the union in order to satisfy the obligation to "meet and confer in good faith." It may be assumed that the obligation is satisfied once it can truly be said that the employer has seriously considered all of the union's proposals that are properly the subject of bargaining. But whether there is an obligation to meet and confer to a point of impasse may depend upon the terms of the governing statute.

Most public employers in jurisdictions which require collective negotiations must bargain at least to impasse. However, the duration of the duty to bargain in the public sector may extend beyond impasse because most states and the federal government prescribe elaborate impasse resolution mechanisms, including mediation, fact-finding, legislative hearings, and compulsory arbitration, which may be invoked following impasse. Both the public employer and union are required to participate in the impasse procedures, once invoked, in a further effort to reach a mutually satisfactory settlement. Impasse procedures thus clearly contemplate further "negotiations" by the parties even where both sides have declared an impasse. As a result, a public employer may not be able to take unilateral action with regard to a mandatory subject, if at all, until after all impasse procedures have been exhausted. . . .

Most collective-negotiations states and some modified meet-and-confer states now provide for the enforcement of the duty to bargain by codes of unfair labor practices, which are often patterned after section 8 of the NLRA and administered by state labor relations boards. In Minnesota the remedy for unfair labor practices is an action in district court. In Oregon, a refusal to bargain in good faith is not specifically made an unfair labor practice but is subject to fact-finding hearings by the Oregon PERB. In a number of other states, however, no unfair labor practices are stipulated; presumably, the aggrieved party in these cases should seek equitable relief in court, provided that the statute otherwise requires good faith bargaining.

Whatever the bargaining obligation placed upon public employers and employees, it must be made inescapable. Strict enforcement is particularly important in view of the fact that strikes—even those provoked by a public employer's unfair labor practice—are ordinarily prohibited in absolute terms. But effective enforcement is difficult where legislatures and courts are inclined to stress the differences between public and private sectors to the end of limiting the effectiveness of the bargaining process in the public sector. For example, good faith bargaining cannot thrive when public employers are led to believe that they may escape the consequences of a bad bargain by a postnegotiations court challenge on the ground that the disputed contract was ultra vires. In such an atmosphere, the employer may be tempted to choose the easy path of agreeing to contract provisions with which it cannot comply and which it has no intention of honoring. Precedents such as *Huntington Teachers*, in which the New York court of appeals flatly rejected the board of education's contention that it lacked authority to agree to the challenged provisions can only enhance effective collective bargaining. The public employer must be convinced that it will be required to live with whatever agreement is executed.

The need to appropriate public money to pay for negotiated increases in wages and benefits is another characteristic unique to the public sector that creates enforcement problems. It may be conceded that, without its consent, a state legislature may not be compelled to make appropriations; however, a public employer should not be able to use a failure to appropriate as an excuse for either a refusal to bargain or the total repudiation of an existing agreement. Rather, both parties should be expected to make whatever adjustments are necessary to accommodate the financial limitations of the employer. In other words, the requirement of good faith bargaining should not terminate in the face of fiscal obstacles.

An example of the type of adjustment that parties can make to deal with financial limitations was seen in the Massachusetts decision, *Norton Teachers' Association v. Town of Norton.* In that case, the teachers were paid below the negotiated salary rate during the first year of the contract because of an insufficient legislative appropriation. As a consequence, the agreement was amended to make an appropriate increase in the salaries for the subsequent year. The Massachusetts supreme court upheld the authority of the school committee to agree to the amended contract on the basis of its authority to manage the public schools. The court prohibited the town from withholding the necessary appropriation, which was otherwise available, to cover the salary increases; the wage obligations were seen as being no different from any other public debt.

Where public employers have attempted to use financial considerations as excuses for refusing to bargain or for repudiating an agreement, courts and labor boards have recently exhibited a willingness to intervene. In a recent Michigan case, *City of Flint*, the city refused to bargain with the general employees of the municipality pending arbitration of a dispute involving the city firemen and possible arbitration with police. The city claimed that it could not make a wage offer since it would not know how much money was available until after the arbitration. The Michigan Employment Relations Commission, however, determined that the city could not refuse to bargain with one group of employees because of the financial uncertainty resulting from a dispute with another group. The New York PERB reached an analogous result in *City of Albany*.

The lesson of the Michigan and New York cases is clear: financial uncertainty is no justification for a total refusal to bargain. It is just as clear, however, that such uncertainty can be a basis for a hard-line position in negotiations. Hard bargaining is not in itself an unfair labor practice, even in the private sector. The public employer can take appropriations cutbacks into consideration in bargaining, just as a private employer can take a sales decrease or a decline in profits into account. Similarly, the public employer can take into consideration the impact of bargaining on other units, as in cases where pattern settlements are the rule or wage-parity agreements are in effect. But there is a line between hard bargaining and no bargaining, and vigorous enforcement of the duty to bargain can help to clarify the contours of that line.

It is increasingly apparent in the developing case law that once a contract has been signed, the public employer must, in effect, "adopt" the contract and do everything reasonably within its power to see that it is carried out. One way to "adopt" is for the public employer to make economic benefits under the contract a priority item in its budget. Illustratively, in *Board of Education of the City of Buffalo*, the New York PERB held that the board of education did not have complete discretion to rearrange school programs following the legislature's grant of a smaller appropriation than had been requested. Mandatory subjects covered in the contract with the union were held to take precedence over nonmandated programs in the allocation of money under a less-than-fully-funded budget. . . .

2. Other readings to consider dealing with the process and scope of the duty to bargain are: Gross, Cullen & Hanslowe, *Good Faith in Labor Negotiations: Tests and Remedies*, 53 Cornell L. Rev. 1009 (1968); Smith, *The Evolution of the "Duty to Bargain" Concept in American Law*, 39 Mich. L. Rev. 1065 (1941); Cox, *The Duty to*

Bargain in Good Faith, 71 Harv. L. Rev. 1401 (1958), Gorman, Labor Law—Basic Text (St. Paul, Minn.: West Publishing Co., 1976); Morris, The Developing Labor Law (Chicago: ABA, 1971), Clark, *The Scope of the Duty to Bargain in Public Employment*, in Labor Relations Law in the Public Sector A. Knapp, ed. (Chicago: ABA, 1977).

3. The twin issues of strikes and impasse procedures raise special problems in both the private and public sectors. Although employees in the private sector do have the right to engage in economic action in support of collective bargaining, there is no unlimited right to strike in the private sector. There are numerous instances where strikes are either unprotected or legally forbidden:

(a) Use of violence—*see* NLRB v. Fansteel Metallurgical Corp., 306 U.S. 240, 59 S. Ct. 490, 83 L. Ed. 627 (1939); NLRB v. Thayer Co., 213 F.2d 748 (1st Cir. 1954), *cert. denied*, 348 U.S. 883 (1954).

(b) Unlawful means—*see* NLRB v. Fansteel Metallurgical Corp., 306 U.S. 240, 59 S. Ct. 490, 83 L. Ed. 627 (1939) and Apex Hosiery Co. v. Leader, 310 U.S. 469, 60 S. Ct. 982, 84 L. Ed. 1311 (1940) (sit-down strikes); C.G. Conn Ltd. v. NLRB, 108 F.2d 390 (7th Cir. 1939); Valley City Furniture Co., 110 N.L.R.B. 1589, *enf'd*, 230 F.2d 947 (6th Cir. 1956) (partial strike or slowdown); Allen Bradley Co. v. IBEW Local 3, 325 U.S. 797, 65 S. Ct. 1533, 89 L. Ed. 1939 (1945); United Mine Workers v. Pennington, 381 U.S. 657, 85 S. Ct. 1585, 14 L. Ed. 2d 626 (1965) (combination with business to violate antitrust laws); Carnegie-Illinois Steel Co. v. United Steelworkers, 353 Pa. 420, 45 A.2d 857 (1946) (mass picketing).

(c) Strikes in pursuit of unlawful objectives—*see, e.g.,* NLRB v. IBEW Local 1212, 364 U.S. 573, 81 S. Ct. 330, 5 L. Ed. 2d 302 (1961) ("jurisdictional strike" in violation of Section 8(b)(4)(D) of the NLRA); Brooks v. NLRB, 348 U.S. 96, 75 S. Ct. 176, 99 L. Ed. 125 (1954) (strike by uncertified union to gain recognition during period when another union has been certified).

4. In the private sector, strikes in violation of a contractual no-strike commitment constitute unprotected activity. *See, e.g.,* NLRB v. Sands Mfg. Co., 306 U.S. 332, 59 S.Ct. 508, 83 L.Ed. 682 (1939). A union breach of a contractual no-strike pledge may be remedied by a damage action under Section 301 of the Labor Management Relations Act. *See* Atkinson v. Sinclair Ref. Co., 370 U.S. 238, 82 S.Ct. 1318, 8 L.Ed.2d 462 (1962). Furthermore, in the private sector it is now clear that a federal or state court may issue an injunction to halt a strike over a grievable or arbitrable matter where "a collective bargaining contract contains a mandatory grievance adjustment or arbitration procedure." Boys Markets, Inc. v. Retail Clerks Local 770, 398 U.S. 235, 90 S.Ct. 1583, 26 L.Ed.2d 199 (1970). *But cf.* Buffalo Forge Co. v. Steelworkers, 428 U.S. 397, 96 S.Ct. 3141, 49 L.Ed.2d 1022 (1976), where the Court held that the Norris-LaGuardia Act precludes a federal court from enjoining a sympathy strike supporting a work dispute involving a different bargaining unit.

5. Peaceful picketing in furtherance of a labor objective may raise special constitutional questions. In Thornhill v. Alabama, 310 U.S. 88, 60 S.Ct. 296, 84 L.Ed. 460 (1940), the Supreme Court equated peaceful picketing with freedom of speech and accorded it protection against abridgement under the First and Fourteenth Amendments, subject to the same legislative restrictions as other forms of speech. However, the expansive pronouncements of *Thornhill* were modified and limited by a later series of cases in which the Court held that picketing, because it involved not only communication of ideas but also elements of patrolling and signaling, was not immune from all state regulation. Since union picketers are not only exercising their right of speech, but also are engaging in an exercise of economic power, the Court held that when such activity is "counter to valid state policy in a domain open to state regulation," it can be restricted, even though it arises in the course of a labor controversy. *See, e.g.,* Teamsters v. Vogt, Inc., 354 U.S. 284, 77 S.Ct. 1166, 1 L.Ed.2d 1347 (1957); Giboney v. Empire Storage Co., 336 U.S. 490, 69 S.Ct. 684, 93 L.Ed. 834 (1949).

6. In Hudgens v. NLRB, 424 U.S. 507, 96 S.Ct. 1029, 47 L.Ed.2d 128 (1976), the Supreme Court held that even though private shopping centers are open to the general public and frequently perform functions similar to traditional community business blocks, persons desiring to engage in peaceful labor picketing on the private premises do not enjoy constitutional protection vis-a-vis the owners of such plazas. However, if such individuals have no alternative communication channels available through which they can reach their intended audience, they may receive protection from employer interference under the NLRA. *See* NLRB v. Babcock & Wilcox Co., 351 U.S. 105, 76 S.Ct. 679, 100 L.Ed. 975 (1956). *But cf.* Sears, Roebuck and Co. v. San Diego Dist. Council of Carpenters, 98 S.Ct. 1745, 56 L.Ed.2d 209 (1978), where the Court recognized the general authority of states to apply their trespass laws to peaceful labor pickets who trespass upon private retail premises.

7. Neither an economic striker nor an unfair labor practice striker may be discharged under the NLRA. *See, e.g.,* NLRB v. International Van Lines, 409 U.S. 48 (1972). However, "economic strikers" may be *permanently* replaced by the employer. In NLRB v. Mackay Radio & Tel. Co., 304 U.S. 333 (1938), the Supreme Court ruled that the employer "has [not] lost the right to protect and continue his business by supplying places left vacant by strikers. And he is not bound to discharge those hired to fill the places of strikers, upon the election of the latter to resume their employment" *See generally,* Gorman, Labor Law—Basic Text, pp. 326-355 (St. Paul: West 1976).

8. In the public sector strikes are often forbidden by state statute or common law doctrine. However, in recent years, a number of state legislatures have given public sector employees a limited right to strike after the bargaining parties have used certain prescribed impasse procedures. In most states, however, strikes by public employees are still seen to be unlawful; in place of strikes, most state statutes have set forth impasse resolution procedures, which may include mediation, factfinding, and/or binding arbitration. *See generally*, Chapters 6 and 7 in Edwards, Clark & Craver, Labor Relations Law in the Public Sector, 2d ed. (Charlottesville, Va.: Bobbs-Merrill/Michie, 1979); Newman, *Interest Arbitration—Practice and Procedures,* in Labor Relations Law in the Public Sector (Chicago: ABA, 1977).

PART THREE

STUDENT RIGHTS

CHAPTER 9

SUBSTANTIVE CONSTITUTIONAL RIGHTS OF STUDENTS

I. Introduction

Student riots have a long history. St. Augustine complained of students "disgracefully out of control." Several of Yale's early presidents resigned due to student protest. An account of a mid-nineteenth century riot in the Harvard Yard has a strongly contemporary flavor. Morison reports that, after the students had broken windows and destroyed furniture, President Quincy decided to bring in the civil authorities, as well as dismissing the students for a year. He continues:

> Then, hell broke loose! Quincy had violated one of the oldest academic traditions: that the public authorities have no concern with what goes on inside a university, so long as the rights of outsiders are not infringed. . . . Furniture and glass in the recitation rooms of the University were smashed, and the fragments hurled out of the windows. . . . A terrific explosion took place in chapel; . . . Quincy never recovered his popularity. [Morison, Three Centuries of Harvard, 1636-1936 (Cambridge, Mass.: Harvard Univ. Press, 1936), at 252-53.]

According to Ross, in the very earliest days of the development of their autonomous natures, medieval universities sought to establish exclusive jurisdiction over the members of their communities in order to protect fractious students, in particular from prosecution by civil authorities:

> The university was largely an autonomous corporation whose members were free from most, if not all, of the usual civil regulations and laws. . . . As a result, public misconduct of students or masters was not tried in civic courts but was referred to university authorities for consideration and/or discipline. . . . This idea that students were less subject to civil law than nonstudents and responsible only to university authority—which emerged in this time and persisted to a degree until 1960, was decisive in defining the student's role in the university. By accepting the authority of the university. . . , the student accepted a position in which obedience to the university hierarchy was required. It was a position of advantage, for generally discipline in the university was less harsh than in the larger community. . . .
>
> It established also in the university a specific attitude to students, for whom it was responsible in every respect. [Ross, The University: The Anatomy of Academe (New York: McGraw-Hill, 1976) at 69-70.]

While there have been occasional aberrations, institution and student alike have adhered to that understanding for centuries. The student riots of the 1960s changed those basic assumptions and thereby changed drastically and perhaps irrevocably the autonomous posture of the university in the larger community. Administrators who turned to public police force to quell riots in order to protect property and lives may have had no alternative, but in so doing they modified centuries-old social and legal assumptions about the university. Once students became subject to prosecution in the courts, it is not surprising that they returned to the courts to establish individual rights for themselves as students under a new system of governance. The increased intrusion of the courts into university affairs undoubtedly began with this era.

Although the history of higher education contains reports of student protests from the earliest days, for a long time students had no legally articulated rights against the interests of church and state embodied in institutions of higher education. Early analyses of students' rights in higher education in this country were often couched in terms of the nature of the student-university relationship. One of the oldest theories rested on the *in loco parentis* doctrine as described in Gott v. Berea College, 161 S.W. 204, 206 (1913):

> College authorities stand in loco parentis concerning the physical and moral welfare and mental training of the pupils, and we are unable to see why, to that end, they may not make any rule or regulation for the government or betterment of their pupils that a parent could for the same purpose.

In colonial times, students often did arrive at "college" at the age of fourteen or fifteen, and administrators did act as surrogate parents. However, today's students are often well over twenty-one, let alone the new eighteen-year-old age of majority, and different rules apply.

Other theoretical descriptions of student status held that a student had a privilege, but not a right to attend college. Board of Trustees v. Waugh, 105 Mass. 623, 62 So. 827 (1913), *aff'd*, 237 U.S. 589 (1915). *But see* Knight v. State Board of Education, 200 F.Supp. 174 (M.D. Tenn. 1961). Or that the university administration held the educational institution in trust for the student. People ex rel Tinkoff v. Northwestern University, 33 Ill. App. 244, 77 N.E.2d 345 (1947), *cert. den.*, 335 U.S. 829 (1948); Anthony v. Syracuse Univ., 231 N.Y.S. 435 (1928). *See also* Goldman, *The University and the Liberty of Its Students—A Fiduciary Theory*, 54 Ky. L. J. 643 (1966) for a more recent, related theory. However, all of these theories have been discounted by more recent court decisions. Court cases tend to use either a contract or constitutional rights analysis, with the death knell of *in loco parentis* sounding in Dixon v. Alabama, 294 F.2d 150 (5th Cir. 1961), *cert. den.*, 368 U.S. 930 (1961) which established due process rights for students on campus. *Dixon* relied heavily on Warren Seavey's seminal article, *Dismissal of Students: "Due Process"*, 70 Harv. L. Rev. 1406 (1957), in which Seavey observed:

It is shocking that the officials of a state educational institution, which can function properly only if our freedoms are preserved, should not understand the elementary principles of fair play. It is equally shocking to find that a court supports them in denying to a student the protection given to a pickpocket. . . . [*Id.* at 1407]

The contract theory holds that there is a mutual agreement, a contract or quasi-contract, between the student and the school to which both parties must adhere. The university is to be bound by statements made in the college catalogue and elsewhere as contract "terms," and the student to a promise to obey college rules. The constitutional theory extends primarily to public universities, except where private universities can be said to be taking state action for the purposes of the Fourteenth Amendment. "Contracts," on the other hand, have been more often found between students and private universities. Early cases used a contract theory to enforce college disciplinary theories against students but currently the obverse is the rule as students, and parents, seek to enforce consumer rights against colleges.

Another mode of analysis is to consider the legal sources for student rights. Beyond the Constitution, and institutional "contracts" the list can be expanded to include state statutes which recently have begun to include students' rights in codes covering university governance, collective bargaining agreements, federal statutes, such as the Family Rights and Privacy of Records Act (The Buckley Amendment), and informal sources such as the "Joint Statement on Rights and Freedoms of Students" presently in use on many campuses.

In studying students' rights cases it is important to keep in mind that the courts have made a clear distinction between cases dealing with academic questions and those relating to social infractions. In the former situation, academic abstention almost always operates to leave university procedures and decisions undisturbed on contract and constitutional grounds. See Lyons v. Salve Regina College, 565 F.2d 200 (1st Cir. 1977); Johnson v. Sullivan, 571 P.2d 798 (Mont. 1977). *But see* Ross v. Pennsylvania State University, 445 F. Supp. 147 (M.D. Penn. 1978). The *Horowitz* case *infra* adheres to this approach. Compare also Stephen Goldstein's analysis of the "host function" and the "educational function" of the public schools in *The Scope and Sources of School Board Authority to Regulate Student Conduct and Status: A Non-Constitutional Analysis,* 117 U.Pa. L. Rev. 373, 387 (1969).

The student-as-consumer movement apparently has caused some courts to become involved in what are primarily academic decisions under the guise of "contract interpretation." In 1977 a Tennessee trial court awarded almost $50,000 in damages to students for the failure of an academic program at Vanderbilt University (see *Note,* Chap. 11). Even this case, however, did not include a court evaluation of students' academic performance. In another theoretical approach, a federal district court found that a graduate student had a property interest in a degree which he was not awarded for academic reasons, and was therefore entitled to a due process hearing since there was an element of discretion in the award. Interestingly, the court found that the student did *not* have a property interest in his graduate assistantship. Ross v. Pennsylvania State Univ., 445 F. Supp. 147 (M.D. Penn. 1978). For the most part, however, even courts seeking to protect student civil rights in the 1960s also recognized the need to interfere as little as possible with the academic community. For example, in 1968 the U.S. District Court for the Western District of Missouri, sitting en banc, issued a *General Order on Judicial Standards of Procedure and Substance in Review of Student Discipline in Tax Supported Institutions of Higher Education* (45 F.R.D. 133) as an appendix to its decision in which it wrote:

> Education is the living and growing source of our progressive civilization, of our open repository of increasing knowledge, culture and our salutary democratic traditions. As such, education deserves the highest respect and the fullest protection of the courts in the performance of its lawful missions. . . . Only where erroneous and unwise actions in the field of education deprive students of federally protected rights or privileges does a federal court have power to intervene in the educational process.

As a conclusion to its section entitled "Lawful Missions of Tax Supported Higher Education," the Missouri court added:

> If it is true, as it well may be, that man is in a race between education and catastrophe, it is imperative that educational institutions not be limited in the performance of their lawful missions by unwarranted judicial interference.

Nevertheless, courts are suddenly less reluctant to involve themselves in academic disputes, particularly if student discipline for social action is involved. As a result of the new involvement of courts a number of student and administrative organizations sought to codify the emerging legal issues and collaborated in making "A Joint Statement on Rights and Freedoms of Students" now in use on many campuses. The preamble to that "Statement" reads:

> In June, 1967, a joint committee, comprised of representatives from the American Association of University Professors, U.S. National Student Association, Association of American Colleges, National Association of Student Personnel Administrators, and National Association of Women Deans and Counselors, met in Washington, D.C., and drafted the Joint Statement on Rights and Freedoms of Students published below.
>
> The multilateral approach which produced this document was also applied to the complicated matter of interpretation, implementation, and enforcement, with the drafting committee recommending (a) joint efforts to promote acceptance of the new standards on the institutional level, (b) the establishment of machinery to facilitate continuing joint interpretation, (c) joint consultation before setting up any machinery for mediating dis-

putes or investigating complaints, and (d) joint approaches to regional accrediting agencies to seek embodiment of the new principles in standards for accreditation.

However neither the Missouri Order or the Joint Statement has emerged as a strong code of student behavior. Students' legal rights are continuing to develop issue by issue, case by case, in the traditional common law manner.

II.   Freedom of Association and Expression

In Tinker v. Des Moines Independent School District, 393 U.S. 503, 506 (1969), Justice Fortas wrote that schoolchildren do not "shed their constitutional rights to freedom of speech or expression at the schoolhouse gate," thereby extending at least a limited form of constitutional protection to all minors. With the age of majority now lowered to 18, there is no question that college students can use the United States Constitution to assert certain rights against state institutions or private institutions acting pursuant to "state action."

A.   Student Associations

HEALY v. JAMES
United States Supreme Court
408 U.S. 169 (1972)

MR. JUSTICE POWELL delivered the opinion of the Court.

This case, arising out of a denial by a state college of official recognition to a group of students who desired to form a local chapter of Students for a Democratic Society (SDS), presents this Court with questions requiring the application of well-established First Amendment principles. While the factual background of this particular case raises these constitutional issues in a manner not heretofore passed on by the Court, and only infrequently presented to lower federal courts, our decision today is governed by existing precedent.

As the case involves delicate issues concerning the academic community, we approach our task with special caution, recognizing the mutual interest of students, faculty members, and administrators in an environment free from disruptive interference with the educational process. We also are mindful of the equally significant interest in the widest latitude for free expression and debate consonant with the maintenance of order. Where these interests appear to compete the First Amendment, made binding on the States by the Fourteenth Amendment, strikes the required balance.

I

We mention briefly at the outset the setting in 1969-1970. A climate of unrest prevailed on many college campuses in this country. There had been widespread civil disobedience on some campuses, accompanied by the seizure of buildings, vandalism, and arson. Some colleges had been shut down altogether, while at others files were looted and manuscripts destroyed. SDS chapters on some of those campuses had been a catalytic force during this period. Although the causes of campus disruption were many and complex, one of the prime consequences of such activities was the denial of the lawful exercise of First Amendment rights to the majority of students by the few. Indeed, many of the most cherished characteristics long associated with institutions of higher learning appeared to be endangered. Fortunately, with the passage of time, a calmer atmosphere and greater maturity now pervade our campuses. Yet, it was in this climate of earlier unrest that this case arose.

Petitioners are students attending Central Connecticut State College (CCSC), a state-supported institution of higher learning. In September 1969 they undertook to organize what they then referred to as a "local chapter" of SDS. Pursuant to procedures established by the College, petitioners filed a request for official recognition as a campus organization with the Student Affairs Committee, a committee composed of four students, three faculty members, and the Dean of Student Affairs. The request specified three purposes for the proposed organization's existence. It would provide "a forum of discussion and self-education for students developing an analysis of American society"; it would serve as "an agency for integrating thought with action so as to bring about constructive changes"; and it would endeavor to provide "a coordinating body for relating the problems of leftist students" with other interested groups on campus and in the community. The Committee, while satisfied that the statement of purposes was clear and unobjectionable on its face, exhibited concern over the relationship between the proposed local group and the National SDS organization. In response to inquiries, representatives of the proposed organization stated that they would not affiliate with any national organization and that their group would remain "completely independent."

In response to other questions asked by Committee members concerning SDS' reputation for campus disruption, the applicants made the following statements, which proved significant during the later stages of these proceedings:

"Q. How would you respond to issues of violence as other S. D. S. chapters have?

"A. Our action would have to be dependent upon each issue.

"Q. Would you use any means possible?

"A. No I can't say that; would not know until we know what the issues are.

"Q. Could you envision the S. D. S. interrupting a class?

"A. Impossible for me to say."

With this information before it, the Committee requested an additional filing by the applicants, including a formal statement regarding affiliations. The amended application filed in response stated flatly that "CCSC Students for a Democratic Society are not under the dictates of any National organization." At a second hearing before the Student Affairs Committee, the question of relationship with the National organization was raised again. One of the organizers explained that the National SDS was divided into several "factional groups," that the national-local relationship was a loose one, and that the local organization accepted only "certain ideas" but not all of the National organization's aims and philosophies.

By a vote of six to two the Committee ultimately approved the application and recommended to the President of the College, Dr. James, that the organization be accorded official recognition. In approving the application, the majority indicated that its decision was premised on the belief that varying viewpoints should be represented on campus and that since the Young Americans for Freedom, the Young Democrats, the Young Republicans, and the Liberal Party all enjoyed recognized status, a group should be available with which "left wing" students might identify. The majority also noted and relied on the organization's claim of independence. Finally, it admonished the organization that immediate suspension would be considered if the group's activities proved incompatible with the school's policies against interference with the privacy of other students or destruction of property. The two dissenting members based their reservation primarily on the lack of clarity regarding the organization's independence.

Several days later, the President rejected the Committee's recommendation, and issued a statement indicating that petitioners' organization was not to be accorded the benefits of official campus recognition. His accompanying remarks . . . indicate several reasons for his action. He found that the organization's philosophy was antithetical to the school's policies, and that the group's independence was doubtful. He concluded that approval should not be granted to any group that "openly repudiates" the College's dedication to academic freedom.

Denial of official recognition posed serious problems for the organization's existence and growth. Its members were deprived of the opportunity to place announcements regarding meetings, rallies, or other activities in the student newspaper; they were precluded from using various campus bulletin boards; and—most importantly—nonrecognition barred them from using campus facilities for holding meetings. This latter disability was brought home to petitioners shortly after the President's announcement. Petitioners circulated a notice calling a meeting to discuss what further action should be taken in light of the group's official rejection. The members met at the coffee shop in the Student Center ("Devils' Den") but were disbanded on the President's order since nonrecognized groups were not entitled to use such facilities.

Their efforts to gain recognition having proved ultimately unsuccessful, and having been made to feel the burden of nonrecognition, petitioners resorted to the courts. They filed a suit in the United States District Court for the District of Connecticut, seeking declaratory and injunctive relief against the President of the College, other administrators, and the State Board of Trustees. Petitioners' primary complaint centered on the denial of First Amendment rights of expression and association arising from denial of campus recognition. The cause was submitted initially on stipulated facts, and, after a short hearing, the judge ruled that petitioners had been denied procedural due process because the President had based his decision on conclusions regarding the applicant's affiliation which were outside the record before him. The court concluded that if the President wished to act on the basis of material outside the application he must at least provide petitioners a hearing and opportunity to introduce evidence as to their affiliations. 311 F. Supp. 1275, 1279, 1281. While retaining jurisdiction over the case, the District Court ordered respondents to hold a hearing in order to clarify the several ambiguities surrounding the President's decision. One of the matters to be explored was whether the local organization, true to its repeated affirmations, was in fact independent of the National SDS. *Id.*, at 1282. And if the hearing demonstrated that the two were not separable, the respondents were instructed that they might then review the "aims and philosophy" of the National organizations. *Ibid.*

Pursuant to the court's order, the President designated Dean Judd, the Dean of Student Affairs, to serve as hearing officer and a hearing was scheduled. The hearing, which spanned two dates and lasted approximately two hours, added little in terms of objective substantive evidence to the record in this case. Petitioners introduced a statement offering to change the organization's name from "CCSC local chapter of SDS" to "Students for a Democratic Society of Central Connecticut State College." They further reaffirmed that they would "have no connection whatsoever to the structure of an existing national organization." Petitioners also introduced the testimony of their faculty adviser to the effect that some local SDS organizations elsewhere were unaffiliated with any national organization. The hearing officer, in addition to introducing the minutes from the two pertinent Student Affairs Committee meetings, also introduced, *sua sponte*, portions of a transcript of hearings before the United States House of Representatives Internal Security Committee investigating the activities of SDS. Excerpts were offered both to prove that violent and disruptive activities had been attributed to SDS elsewhere and to demonstrate that there existed a national organization that recognized and cooperated with regional and local college campus affiliates. Petitioners did not challenge the asserted existence of a National SDS, nor did they question that it did have a system of affiliations of some sort. Their contention was simply that their organization would not associate with that network. Throughout the hearing the parties were acting at cross purposes. What seemed relevant to one appeared completely immaterial to the other. This failure of the hearing to advance the litigation was, at bottom, the consequence of a more basic failure to join issue on the considerations that should control the President's ultimate decision, a problem to which we will return in the ensuing section.

Upon reviewing the hearing transcript and exhibits, the President reaffirmed his prior decision to deny petitioners recognition as a campus organization. The reasons stated, closely paralleling his initial reasons, were that the group would be a "disruptive influence" at CCSC and that recognition would be "contrary to the orderly process of change" on the campus. . . .

II

At the outset we note that state colleges and universities are not enclaves immune from the sweep of the First Amendment. "It can hardly be argued that either students or teachers shed their constitutional rights to freedom of speech or expression at the schoolhouse gate." *Tucker* v. *Des Moines Independent School District*, 393 U. S. 502, 506 (1969). Of course, as Mr. Justice Fortas made clear in *Tinker*, First Amendment rights must always be applied "in light of the special characteristics of the . . . environment" in the particular case. *Ibid.* And, where state-operated educational institutions are involved, this Court has long recognized "the need for affirming the comprehensive authority of the States and of school officials, consistent with fundamental constitutional safeguards, to prescribe and control conduct in the schools." *Id.*, at 507. Yet, the precedents of this Court leave no room for the view that, because of the acknowledged need for order, First Amendment protections should apply with less force on college campuses than in the community at large. Quite to the contrary, "[t]he vigilant protection of constitutional freedoms is nowhere more vital than in the community of American schools." *Shelton* v. *Tucker*, 364 U. S. 479, 487 (1960). The college classroom with its surrounding environs is peculiarly the "'marketplace of ideas,'" and we break no new constitutional ground in raffirming this Nation's dedication to safeguarding academic freedom. *Keyishian* v. *Board of Regents*, 385 U. S. 589, 603 (1967); *Sweezy* v. *New Hampshire*, 354 U. S. 234, 249-250 (1957) (plurality opinion of Mr. Chief Justice Warren), 262 (Frankfurter, J., concurring in result).

Among the rights protected by the First Amendment is the right of individuals to associate to further their personal beliefs. While the freedom of association is not explicitly set out in the Amendment, it has long been held to be implicit in the freedoms of speech, assembly, and petition. See, *e.g., Baird* v. *State Bar of Arizona*, 401 U. S. 1, 6 (1971); *NAACP* v. *Button*, 371 U. S. 415, 430 (1963); *Louisiana ex rel. Gremillion* v. *NAACP*, 366 U. S. 293, 296 (1961); *NAACP* v. *Alabama ex rel. Patterson*, 357 U. S. 449 (1958) (Harlan, J., for a unanimous Court). There can be no doubt that denial of official recognition, without justification, to college organizations burdens or abridges that associational right. The primary impediment to free association flowing from nonrecognition is the denial of use of campus facilities for meetings and other appropriate purposes. The practical effect of nonrecognition was demonstrated in this case when, several days after the President's decision was announced, petitioners were not allowed to hold a meeting in the campus coffee shop because they were not an approved group.

Petitioners' associational interests also were circumscribed by the denial of the use of campus bulletin boards and the school newspaper. If an organization is to remain a viable entity in a campus community in which new students enter on a regular basis, it must possess the means of communicating with these students. Moreover, the organization's ability to participate in the intellectual give and take of campus debate, and to pursue its stated purposes, is limited by denial of access to the customary media for communicating with the administration, faculty members, and other students. Such impediments cannot be viewed as insubstantial. . . .

We do not agree with the characterization by the courts below of the consequences of nonrecognition. We may concede, as did Mr. Justice Harlan in his unanimous opinion of the Court in *NAACP* v. *Alabama ex rel. Patterson,* 357 U. S., at 461, that the administration "has taken no direct action . . . to restrict the rights of petitioner's members to associate freely." But the Constitution's protection is not limited to direct interference with fundamental rights. The requirement in *Patterson* that the NAACP disclose its membership lists was found to be an impermissible, though indirect, infringement of the members' associational rights. Likewise, in this case, the group's possible ability to exist outside the campus community does not ameliorate significantly the disabilities imposed by the President's action. We are not free to disregard the practical realities. MR. JUSTICE STEWART has made the salient point: "Freedoms such as these are protected not only against heavy-handed frontal attack, but also from being stifled by more subtle governmental interference." *Bates* v. *City of Little Rock,* 361 U. S. 516, 523 (1960). See also *Sweezy* v. *New Hampshire,* 354 U. S., at 263 (Frankfurter, J., concurring in result); *Watkins* v. *United States,* 354 U.S. 178, 197 (1957).

The opinions below also assumed that petitioners had the burden of showing entitlement to recognition by the College. While petitioners have not challenged the procedural requirement that they file an application in conformity with the rules of the College, they do question the view of the courts below that final rejection could rest on their failure to convince the administration that their organization was unaffiliated with the National SDS. For reasons to be stated later in this opinion, we do not consider the issue of affiliation to be a controlling one. But, apart from any particular issue, once petitioners had filed an application in conformity with the requirements the burden was upon the College administration to justify its decision of rejection. See, *e.g., Law Students Civil Rights Research Council* v. *Wadmond,* 401 U. S. 154, 162-163 (1971); *United States* v. *O'Brien,* 391 U. S. 367, 376-377 (1968); *Speiser* v. *Randall,* 357 U. S. 513 (1958). It is to be remembered that the effect of the College's denial of recognition was a form of prior restraint, denying to petitioners' organization the range of associational activities described above. While a college has a legitimate interest in preventing disruption on the campus, which under circumstances requiring the safeguarding of that interest may justify such restraint, a "heavy burden" rests on the college to demonstrate the appropriateness of that action. See *Near* v. *Minnesota,* 283 U. S. 697, 713-716 (1931); *Organization for a Better Austin* v. *Keefe,* 402 U. S. 415, 418 (1971); *Freedman* v. *Maryland,* 380 U. S. 51, 57 (1965).

III

These fundamental errors—discounting the existence of a cognizable First Amendment interest and misplacing the burden of proof—require that the judgments below be reversed. But we are unable to conclude that no basis exists upon which nonrecognition might be appropriate. Indeed, based on a reasonable reading of the ambiguous facts of this case, there appears to be at least one potentially acceptable ground for a denial of recognition. Because of this ambiguous state of the record we conclude that the case should be remanded, and, in an effort to provide guidance to the lower courts upon reconsideration, it is appropriate to discuss the several bases of President James' decision. Four possible justifications for nonrecognition, all closely related, might be derived from the record and his statements. Three of those grounds are inadequate to substantiate his decision: a fourth, however, has merit.

A

From the outset the controversy in this case has centered in large measure around the relationship, if any, between petitioners' group and the National SDS. The Student Affairs Committee meetings, as reflected in its minutes, focused considerable attention on this issue; the court-ordered hearing also was directed primarily to this question. Despite assurances from petitioners and their counsel that the local group was in fact independent of the National organization, it is evident that President James was significantly influenced by his apprehension that there was a connection. Aware of the fact that some SDS chapters had been associated with disruptive and violent campus activity, he apparently considered that affiliation itself was sufficient justification for denying recognition.

Although this precise issue has not come before the Court heretofore, the Court has consistently disapproved governmental action imposing criminal sanctions or denying rights and privileges solely because of a citizen's association with an unpopular organization. See, *e.g.*, *United States* v. *Robel*, 389 U. S. 258 (1967); *Keyishian* v. *Board of Regents*, 385 U. S. at 605-610; *Elfbrandt* v. *Russell*, 384 U. S. 11 (1966); *Scales* v. *United States*, 367 U. S. 203 (1961). In these cases it has been established that "guilt by association alone, without [establishing] that an individual's association poses the threat feared by the Government," is an impermissible basis upon which to deny First Amendment rights. *United States* v. *Robel, supra*, at 265. The government has the burden of establishing a knowing affiliation with an organization possessing unlawful aims and goals, and a specific intent to further those illegal aims.

Students for a Democratic Society, as conceded by the College and the lower courts, is loosely organized, having various factions and promoting a number of diverse social and political views, only some of which call for unlawful action. Not only did petitioners proclaim their complete independence from this organization, but they also indicated that they shared only some of the beliefs its leaders have expressed. On this record it is clear that the relationship was not an adequate ground for the denial of recognition.

B

Having concluded that petitioners were affiliated with, or at least retained an affinity for, National SDS, President James attributed what he believed to be the philosophy of that organization to the local group. He characterized the petitioning group as adhering to "some of the major tenets of the national organization," including a philosophy of violence and disruption. Understandably, he found that philosophy abhorrent. In an article signed by President James in an alumni periodical, and made a part of the record below, he announced his unwillingness to "sanction an organization that openly advocates the destruction of the very ideals and freedoms upon which the academic life is founded." He further emphasized that the petitioners' "philosophies" were "counter to the official policy of the college."

The mere disagreement of the President with the group's philosophy affords no reason to deny it recognition. As repugnant as these views may have been, especially to one with President James' responsibility, the mere expression of them would not justify the denial of First Amendment rights. Whether petitioners did in fact advocate a philosophy of "destruction" thus becomes immaterial. The College, acting here as the instrumentality of the State, may not restrict speech or association simply because it finds the views expressed by any group to be abhorrent. As Mr. Justice Black put it most simply and clearly:

> "I do not believe that it can be too often repeated that the free-doms of speech, press, petition and assembly guaranteed by the First Amendment must be accorded to the ideas we hate or sooner or later they will be denied to the ideas we cherish." *Communist Party* v. *SACB*, 367 U. S. 1, 137 (dissenting opinion) (1961).

C

As the litigation progressed in the District Court, a third rationale for President James' decision—beyond the questions of affiliation and philosophy—began to emerge. His second statement, issued after the court-ordered hearing, indicates that he based rejection on a conclusion that this particular group would be a "disruptive influence at CCSC." This language was under-scored in the second District Court opinion. In fact, the Court concluded that the President had determined that CCSC-SDS' "prospective campus activities were likely to cause a disruptive influence at CCSC." 319 F. Supp., at 116.

If this reason, directed at the organization's activities rather than its philosophy, were factually supported by the record, this Court's prior decisions would provide a basis for considering the propriety of nonrecognition. The critical line heretofore drawn for determining the permissibility of regulation is the line between mere advocacy and advocacy "directed to inciting or producing imminent lawless action and . . . likely to incite or produce such action." *Brandenburg* v.*Ohio*, 395 U. S. 444, 447 (1969) (unanimous *per curiam* opinion). See also *Scales* v. *United States*, 367 U. S. at 230-232, *Noto* v. *United States*, 367 U. S. 290, 298 (1961); *Yates* v. *United States*, 354 U. S. 298 (1957). In the context of the "special characteristics of the school environment," the power of the government to prohibit "lawless action" is not limited to acts of a criminal nature. Also prohibitable are actions which "materially and substantially disrupt the work and discipline of the school." *Tinker* v. *Des Moines Independent School District*, 393 U. S., at 513. Associational activities need not be tolerated where they infringe reasonable campus rules, interrupt classes, or substantially interfere with the opportunity of other students to obtain an education.

The "Student Bill of Rights" at CCSC, upon which great emphasis was placed by the President, draws precisely this distinction between advocacy and action. It purports to impose no limitations on the right of college student organizations "to examine and discuss *all* questions of interest to them." (Emphasis supplied.) But it also states that students have no right (1) "to deprive others of the opportunity to speak or be heard," (2) "to invade the privacy of others," (3) "to damage the property of others," (4) "to disrupt the regular and essential operation of the college," or (5) "to interfere with the rights of others." The line between permissible speech and impermissible conduct tracks the constitutional requirement, and if there were an evidential basis to support the conclusion that CCSC-SDS posed a substantial threat of material disruption in violation of that command the President's decision should be affirmed.

The record, however, offers no substantial basis for that conclusion. The only support for the view expressed by the President, other than the reputed affiliation with National SDS, is to be found in the ambivalent responses offered by the group's representatives at the Student Affairs Committee hearing, during which they stated that they did not know whether they might respond to "issues of violence" in the same manner that other SDS chapters had on other campuses. Nor would they state unequivocally that they could never "envision . . . interrupting a class." Whatever force these statements might be thought to have is largely dissipated by the following exchange between petitioners' counsel and the Dean of Student Affairs during the court-ordered hearing:

> Counsel: ". . . I just read the document that you're offering [minutes from Student Affairs Committee meeting] and I can't see that there's anything in it that intimates that these students contemplate any illegal or disruptive practice."
> Dean: "No. There's no question raised to that, counselor. . . ."
> App. 73-74.

Dean Judd's remark reaffirms, in accord with the full record, that there was no substantial evidence that these particular individuals acting together would constitute a disruptive force on campus. Therefore, insofar as non-recognition flowed from such fears, it constituted little more than the sort of "undifferentiated fear or apprehension of disturbance [which] is not enough to overcome the right to freedom of expression." *Tinker* v. *Des Moines Independent School District*, 393 U. S., at 508.

D

These same references in the record to the group's equivocation regarding how it might respond to "issues of violence" and whether it could ever "envision . . . interrupting a class," suggest a fourth possible reason why recognition might have been denied to these petitioners. These remarks might well have been read as announcing petitioners' unwillingness to be bound by reasonable school rules governing conduct. The College's Statement of Rights, Freedoms, and Responsibilities of Students contains, as we have seen, an explicit statement with respect to campus disruption. The regulation, carefully differentiating between advocacy and action, is a reasonable one, and petitioners have not questioned it directly. Yet their statements raise considerable question whether they intend to abide by the prohibitions contained therein.

As we have already stated in Parts B and C, the critical line for First Amendment purposes must be drawn between advocacy, which is entitled to full protection, and action, which is not. Petitioners may, if they so choose, preach the propriety of amending or even doing away with any or all campus regulations. They may not, however, undertake to flout these rules. MR. JUSTICE BLACKMUN, at the time he was a circuit judge on the Eighth Circuit, stated:

> "We . . . hold that a college has the inherent power to promulgate rules and regulations; that is has the inherent power properly to discipline; that it has power appropriately to protect itself and its property; that it may expect that its students adhere to generally accepted standards of conduct." *Esteban* v. *Central Missouri State College*, 415 F.2d 1077, 1089 (CA8 1969), cert. denied, 398 U. S. 965 (1970).

Just as in the community at large, reasonable regulations with respect to the time, the place, and the manner in which student groups conduct their speech-related activities must be respected. A college administration may impose a requirement, such as may have been imposed in this case, that a group seeking official recognition affirm in advance its willingness to adhere to reasonable campus law. Such a requirement does not impose an impermissible condition on the students' associational rights. Their freedom to speak out, to assemble, or to petition for changes in school rules is in no sense infringed. It merely constitutes an agreement to conform with reasonable standards respecting conduct. This is a minimal requirement, in the interest of the entire academic community, of any group seeking the privilege of official recognition.

Petitioners have not challenged in this litigation the procedural or substantive aspects of the College's requirements governing applications for official recognition. Although the record is unclear on this point, CCSC may have, among its requirements for recognition, a rule that prospective groups affirm that they intend to comply with reasonable campus regulations. Upon remand it should first be determined whether the College recognition procedures contemplate any such requirement. If so, it should then be ascertained whether petitioners intend to comply. Since we do not have the terms of a specific prior affirmation rule before us, we are not called on to decide whether any particular formulation would or would not prove constitutionally acceptable. Assuming the existence of a valid rule, however, we do conclude that the benefits of participation in the internal life of the college community may be denied to any group that reserves the right to violate any valid campus rules with which it disagrees.

IV

We think the above discussion establishes the appropriate framework for consideration of petitioners' request for campus recognition. Because respondents failed to accord due recognition to First Amendment principles, the judgments below approving respondents' denial of recognition must be reversed. Since we cannot conclude from this record that petitioners were willing to abide by reasonable campus rules and regulations, we order the case remanded for reconsideration. We note, in so holding, that the wide latitude accorded by the Constitution to the freedoms of expression and association is not without its costs in terms of the risk to the maintenance of civility and an ordered society. Indeed, this latitude often has resulted, on the campus and elsewhere, in the infringement of the rights of others. Though we deplore the tendency of some to abuse the very constitutional privileges they invoke, and although the infringement of rights of others certainly should not be tolerated, we reaffirm this Court's dedication to the principles of the Bill of Rights upon which our vigorous and free society is founded.

Reversed and remanded.

MR. CHIEF JUSTICE BURGER, concurring.

I am in agreement with what is said in the Court's opinion and I join in it. I do so because I read the basis of the remand as recognizing that student organizations seeking the privilege of official campus recognition must be willing to abide by valid rules of the institution applicable to all such organizations. This is a reasonable condition insofar as it calls for the disavowal of resort to force, disruption, and interference with the rights of others.

The District Judge was troubled by the lack of a comprehensive procedural scheme that would inform students of the steps to be taken to secure recognized standing, and by the lack of articulated criteria to be used in evaluating eligibility for recognition. It was for this reason, as I read the record, that he remanded the matter to the college for a factual inquiry and for a more orderly processing in a *de novo* hearing within the college administrative structure. It is within that structure and within the academic community that problems such as these should be resolved. The courts, state or federal, should be a last resort. Part of the educational experience of every college student should be an experience in responsible self-government and this must be a joint enterprise of students and faculty. It should not be imposed unilaterally from above, nor can the terms of the relationship be dictated by students. Here, in spite of the wisdom of the District Court in sending the case back to the college, the issue identified by the Court's opinion today was not adequately addressed in the hearing.

The relatively placid life of the college campus of the past has not prepared either administrators or students for their respective responsibilities in maintaining an atmosphere in which divergent views can be asserted vigorously, but civilly, to the end that those who seek to be heard accord the same right to all others. The "Statement of Rights, Freedoms, and Responsibilities of Students," sometimes called the "College Bill of Rights," in effect on this campus, and not questioned by petitioners, reflected a rational adjustment of the competing interests. But it is impossible to know from the record in this case whether the student group was willing to acknowledge an obligation to abide by that "Bill of Rights."

Against this background, the action of the Court in remanding this issue is appropriate.

MR. JUSTICE DOUGLAS.

While I join the opinion of the Court, I add a few words. . . .

The present case is minuscule in the events of the 60's and 70's. But the fact that it has to come here for ultimate resolution indicates the sickness of our academic world, measured by First Amendment standards. Students as well as faculty are entitled to credentials in their search for truth. If we are to become an integrated, adult society, rather than a stubborn status quo opposed to change, students and faculties should have communal interests in which each age learns from the other. Without ferment of one kind or another, a college or university (like a federal agency or other human institution) becomes a useless appendage to a society which traditionally has reflected the spirit of rebellion. . . .

MR. JUSTICE REHNQUIST, concurring in the result.

While I do not subscribe to some of the language in the Court's opinion, I concur in the result that it reaches. As I understand the Court's holding, the case is sent back for reconsideration because respondents may not have made it sufficiently clear to petitioners that the decision as to recognition would be critically influenced by petitioners' willingness to agree in advance to abide by reasonable regulations promulgated by the College.

I find the implication clear from the Court's opinion that the constitutional limitations on the government's acting as administrator of a college differ from the limitations on the government's acting as sovereign to enforce its criminal laws. The Court's quotations from *Tinker* v. *Des Moines Independent School District*, 393 U. S. 503, 506 (1969), to the effect that First Amendment rights must always be applied "in light of the special characteristics of the . . . environment," and from *Esteban* v. *Central Missouri State College*, 415 F.2d 1077, 1089 (CA8 1969), to the effect that a college "may expect that its students adhere to generally accepted standards of conduct," emphasize this fact.

Cases such as *United Public Workers* v. *Mitchell*, 330 U. S.75 (1947), and *Pickering* v. *Board of Education*, 391 U. S. 563 (1968), make it equally clear that the government in its capacity as employer also differs constitutionally from the government in its capacity as the sovereign executing criminal laws. The Court in *Pickering* said:

"The problem in any case is to arrive at a balance between the interests of the teacher, as a citizen, in commenting upon matters of public concern and the interest of the State, as an employer, in promoting the efficiency of the public services it performs through its employees." 391 U. S., at 568.

Because of these acknowledged distinctions of constitutional dimension based upon the role of the government, I have serious doubt as to whether cases dealing with the imposition of criminal sanctions, such as *Brandenburg* v. *Ohio*, 395 U. S. 444 (1969), *Scales* v. *United States*, 367 U. S. 203 (1961), and *Yates* v. *United States*, 354 U. S. 298 (1957), are properly applicable to this case dealing with the government as college administrator. I also doubt whether cases dealing with the prior restraint imposed by injunctive process of a court, such as *Near* v. *Minnesota*, 283 U. S. 697 (1931), are precisely comparable to this case, in which a typical sanction imposed was the requirement that the group abandon its plan to meet in the college coffee shop.

Prior cases dealing with First Amendment rights are not fungible goods, and I think the doctrine of these cases suggests two important distinctions. The government as employer or school administrator may impose upon employees and students reasonable regulations that would be impermissible if imposed by the government upon all citizens. And there can be a constitutional distinction between the infliction of criminal punishment, on the one hand, and the imposition of milder administrative or disciplinary sanctions, on the other, even though the same First Amendment interest is implicated by each.

Because some of the language used by the Court tends to obscure these distinctions, which I believe to be important, I concur only in the result.

GAY ALLIANCE OF STUDENTS v. MATTHEWS
Fourth Circuit Court of Appeals
544 F.2d 162 (1976)

WINTER, Circuit Judge:

*   *   *

GAS is an association of students, organized September 1, 1974, the stated purposes of which are (a) to develop a supportive community among individuals who believe in the right of self-determination with regard to sexual orientation, (b) to convene educational situations for members of GAS and for members of the university community regarding homosexual life, and (c) to advocate "gay" rights in concert with the civil liberties of all people. GAS disavows any purpose to provide professional counseling or therapy for persons having emotional or psychological problems arising out of or exhibited by specific sexual proclivities or patterns of sexual behavior. While the majority of its members are bisexual or homosexual in orientation, there is no membership requirement of a particular sexual orientation. Together with providing educational activities and discussion opportunities, GAS conducts social activities, including dances.

After GAS was formed, its members submitted to the VCU Office of the Dean of Student Affairs an application for registration as a student organization. The application, with revisions suggested by VCU's administration, was filed at the beginning of the fall term of 1974 in accordance with VCU's rules and regulations governing the registration of student organizations. Registration, if granted, carries with it these rights and privileges:

(a) Inclusion in a directory, furnished to each student, setting forth the names and activities of student organizations which a student may join;

(b) the furnishing of VCU consultation services on financial management, budget preparation and financial records;

(c) the use of VCU buildings for meetings and activities:

(d) the use of the campus newspaper, the campus radio station, and the VCU bulletin boards to advertise the time and place of meetings and activities; and

(e) eligibility to seek and obtain VCU funding for carrying on activities.

The application was not processed in the usual manner. It was referred to the Vice President for Student Affairs who forwarded it to VCU's governing body, The Board of Visitors, for ultimate decision. That body, by a split vote, rejected it without assigning reasons for its action. . . .

At the outset, we state what this case is not. There is neither claim nor evidence that GAS as such engages in unlawful activities. So far as this record establishes, it is, at most, a "pro-homosexual" political organization advocating a liberalization of legal restrictions against the practice of homosexuality and one seeking, by the educational and informational process, to generate understanding and acceptance of individuals whose sexual orientation is wholly or partly homosexual.

GAS correctly posits its claim to registration upon the first amendment associational rights of its members. *Healy v. James*, 408 U.S. 169, 183, 92 S.Ct. 2338, 2347, 33 L.Ed.2d 266 (1972), makes clear that, in the context of the scope of protection which the first amendment affords to associational rights on a state-supported college campus, "the Constitution's protection is not limited to direct interference with fundamental rights." Quoting from *Bates* v. *City of Little Rock*, 361 U.S. 516, 523, 80 S.Ct. 412, 416, 4 L.Ed.2d 480 (1960), the Court added: "[f]reedoms such as these are protected not only against heavy-handed frontal attack, but also from being stifled by more subtle governmental interference."

Consistent with *Healy* and *Bates*, we thus reject VCU's argument that the members of GAS have suffered no infringement of their associational rights because all that has been withheld is VCU's official seal of approval. Absent registration, there are admittedly no direct barriers to the members of GAS continuing to meet, to discuss the problems which homosexuals face, and to take lawful action to ameliorate some of these problems. But VCU concedes that a lack of recognition will hinder its recruitment efforts as well as to deny it VCU's services which are afforded to other registered student organizations. These denials are within the scope of *Healy,* and therefore we conclude that there has been a denial of first amendment rights unless there is justification for the refusal of registration.

We turn therefore to VCU's purported justification for denying registration and the sequelae of registration.

One of the VCU's reasons for denying the application was that granting recognition to GAS would increase the number of students who would join the organization. The premise of the argument is that registration of GAS would indicate VCU approval of GAS's aims and objectives and thus serve as an encouragement to students to join who might otherwise be disinterested in becoming members. Factually and legally, we disagree that registration would connote VCU approval of GAS's aims and objectives. First, VCU's registration of the large variety of other political, social and cultural organizations carries with it no approval by VCU of their aims and objectives. Indeed, an administrator of VCU testified flatly that "the registration and recognition of an organization does not, in any sense, carry with it approval or endorsement of the organization's aims." Second, we held in *National Socialist White People's Party v. Ringers*, 473 F.2d 1010, 1015 (4 Cir. 1973) (in banc), that when, under the compulsion of the first amendment, the state provides state-supported facilities to groups having discriminatory membership policies, state approval or support of those policies is not thereby forthcoming. We think that principle applicable here.

To the extent that registration would serve to encourage membership in GAS, aside from any implied approval by VCU, the result would accord with the purposes of the first amendment. "Among the rights protected by the First Amendment is the right of individuals to associate to further their personal beliefs." *Healy v. James,* 408 U.S. at 181, 92 S.Ct. at 2346. If it is the right of an individual to associate with others in furtherance of their mutual beliefs, that right is furthered if those who may wish to join GAS are encouraged by the fact of registration to take that step.

Another reason assigned by VCU for denying registration is that some students would suffer detriment thereby. As expressed in VCU's brief, "affiliation of individuals with homosexual activist organizations may have adverse consequences to some individuals involved." We are not impressed by this purported reason. The very essence of the first amendment is that each individual makes his own decision as to whether joining an organization would be harmful to him, and whether any countervailing benefits outweigh the potential harm. We are aware that in recent years colleges and universities increasingly are voluntarily surrendering the role of *parens patriae* of their students which they formerly occupied. But even if not surrendered voluntarily, the state and its agents are forbidden from usurping the students' right to choose. In this respect, the governing bodies of schools have no greater authority than do other state officials. *Healy v. James,* 408 U.S. at 180, 92 S.Ct. 2338; *Tinker v. Des Moines Indep. Community School Dist.,* 393 U.S. 503, 89 S.Ct. 733, 21 L.Ed.2d 731 (1969). As the Supreme Court noted in *Healy,* a state college or university "may not restrict speech or association simply because it finds the views expressed by any group to be abhorrent." 408 U.S. at 187-88, 92 S.Ct. at 2349. Similarly, VCU may not hinder the exercise of first amendment rights simply because it feels that exposure to a given group's ideas may be somehow harmful to certain students.

VCU also relies on the proposition that "[a]s a matter of logic, the existence of GAS as a recognized campus organization would increase the opportunity for homosexual contacts" as a justification for denying recognition.

The meaning of the phrase "increase the opportunity for homosexual contacts" is not entirely clear. If the University is attempting to prevent homosexuals from meeting one another to discuss their common problems and possible solutions to those problems, then its purpose is clearly inimical to basic first amendment values. Individuals of whatever sexual persuasion have the fundamental right to meet, discuss current problems, and to advocate changes in the *status quo,* so long as there is no "incitement to imminent lawless action." *E. g., Brandenburg v. Ohio*, 395 U.S. 444, 89 S.Ct. 1827, 23 L.Ed.2d 430 (1969).

If, on the other hand, VCU's concern is with a possible rise in the incidence of actual homosexual conduct between students, then a different problem is presented. We have little doubt that the University could constitutionally regulate such conduct. . . .

"[T]he critical line for First Amendment purposes must be drawn between advocacy, which is entitled to full protection, and action, which is not." *Healy v. James,* 408 U.S. at 192, 92 S.Ct. at 2851. There is no evidence that GAS is an organization devoted to carrying out illegal, specifically proscribed sexual practices. While Virginia law proscribes the practice of certain forms of homosexuality, Va.Code § 18.2-361, Virginia law does not make it a crime to *be* a homosexual. Indeed, a statute criminalizing such status and prescribing punishment therefor would be invalid. *See Robinson v. California*, 370 U.S. 660, 82 S.Ct. 1417, 8 L.Ed.2d 758 (1962).

It follows that even if affording GAS registration does increase the opportunity for homosexual contacts, that fact is insufficient to overcome the associational rights of members of GAS. . . .

Finally, VCU argues that its refusal to recognize GAS is justified because recognition of GAS would tend to attract other homosexuals to the University. For the reasons we discussed in regard to the claim of allegedly increased opportunities for homosexual contacts, we hold that this justification is prohibited overbreadth and therefore is legally insufficient to allow VCU to withhold recognition from GAS. . . .

For the foregoing reasons, we conclude that so long as VCU maintains a program of registration of student organizations, its refusal to register GAS on the same terms and conditions as those applied to other student organizations violated the first and fourteenth amendments. . . .

NOTES

1. In *Gay Alliance of Students v. Matthews* the court also held that the withholding of recognition denied GAS Fourteenth Amendment equal protection since no substantial government interest justified the university's denial of recognition. In Gay Lib v. University of Missouri, 558 F.2d 848 (8th Cir. 1977), in which similar issues were raised, the district court found that the withholding of recognition was justified, because recognition would probably result in felonious acts of sodomy in violation of state law. For related reasons the district court saw no denial of equal protection. The Court of Appeals reversed the decision below citing *Gay Alliance of Students v. Matthews*. The court ruled that the university had not presented adequate evidence (through its expert witnesses) of the likelihood of imminent lawless action. Nor did the recorded aims and purposes of the organization evidence an intent to violate state law or university regulations. *See also*, Gay Students Organization of the University of New Hampshire v. Bonner, 509 F.2d 652 (1st Cir. 1974); Mississippi Gay Alliance v. Goudelock, 536 F.2d 1073 (5th Cir. 1976).

2. In Futrell v. Ahrens, 88 N.M. 284, (1975), students sought to use Justice Douglas' concurring opinion in U.S. Department of Agriculture v. Moreno, 413 U.S. 528 (1973) to establish a constitutional right of association which would invalidate a New Mexico State University regulation prohibiting visitation by persons of the opposite sex in dormitory rooms. The Supreme Court of New Mexico ruled that even if a personal right of association existed,

> We are unwilling to hold that the Regents, who have the power and the duty to enact and enforce reasonable rules and regulations for the conduct of the University, have infringed upon the plaintiffs' constitutionally protected rights by its regulation against intervisitation of men and women in a dormitory room. . . . The regulation is reasonable, serves legitimate educational purposes, and promotes the welfare of the students at the University.

B.   Freedom Not to Associate

GOOD v. ASSOCIATED STUDENTS OF UNIV. OF WASHINGTON
Supreme Court of Washington,
En Banc.
542 P.2d 762 (1975)

BRACHTENBACH, Associate Justice.

This is an action by three University of Washington students, individually and as representatives of a class, against the University of Washington (U of W), its regents, the Associated Students of the University of Washington (ASUW) and others. The controversy stems from required student membership in the ASUW, the activities of that organization and the financial support thereof by the university through a mandatory services and activities fee, a portion of which is allocated to the ASUW. . . .

Plaintiffs raise two primary issues: (1) Does the university have the authority to allocate funds to the ASUW? (2) Are students' First Amendment rights violated by (a) the requirement that they be members of the ASUW; (b) that they are charged a fee to support the ASUW?

With respect to the issue of the university's authority to fund the ASUW, plaintiffs first argue that the board of regents has no statutory authority to make such an allocation of student fees. We disagree. . . .

We believe that the range of powers given to the board is sufficiently wide to encompass their decision to provide student activities and services through a separate nonprofit corporation, so long as that entity is in essence an agency of the university and subject to ultimate control by the board. This view is buttressed by the fact that the legislature is well aware of the corporate nature of the ASUW. . . .

Plaintiffs counter with the argument that the university, in fact, has never initiated, altered or terminated any ASUW activity, program or position and, therefore, it is not an arm and agency of the university, but an independent entity. Failure to exercise a power which is statutorily vested in a body such as the regents does not mean that the power does not exist. The statutes grant the regents ultimate control over student services and activities programs. The regents have acknowledged and asserted that power in their policy statements. The ASUW bylaws recognize where final authority is vested. Use of that power and authority lies within the judgment of the regents.

The legislature has generally directed the purposes for which these fees may be expended:

Services and activities fees shall be used as otherwise provided by law or by rule or regulation of the board of trustees or regents of each of the state's colleges or universities for the express purpose of funding student activities and programs of their particular institution.

RCW 28B.15.041. Whether the ASUW has exceeded these statutory purposes is a factual matter not determined by the record in its present state. Additional evidence will be necessary for the trial court to resolve this issue. Later herein we will address the appropriate relief to be granted if it is found that expenditures have been made for purposes beyond those authorized by statute. Our holding necessarily causes to fail plaintiffs' contentions that there is a gift of public money or a prohibited state interest in a corporation.

However, there remains plaintiffs' assertion that their First Amendment rights have been violated by the requirement of mandatory membership in the ASUW and financial support thereof. The main thrust of plaintiff's position is that they have a constitutionally protected right to *not* associate with any group, just as they enjoy a concomitant right to associate with any group of their choice. We agree. . . .

Freedom to associate carries with it a corresponding right to not associate. We have not been cited, nor have we discovered, a case which squarely holds that the right of non-association is as much protected as the right of association. Various writers assert the proposition, apparently deeming it to be self-evident. C. Rice, *Freedom of Association,* xviii and 88 (1962); 21 U. Miami L.Rev. 791, 808 (1967); 56 Nw.U.L.Rev. 777, 778 (1962).

There are judicial expressions, in dicta and dissents, which recognize the freedom from forced association. For example, in *Ex parte Smith*, 135 Mo. 223, 227, 36 S.W. 628, 629 (1896), it was said: "We deny the power of any legislative body in this country to choose for our citizens whom their associates shall be."

In apparent dictum, the United States Supreme Court in *Gilmore v. Montgomery*, 417 U.S. 556, 94 S.Ct. 2416, 2427, 41 L.Ed.2d 304 (1974), quoted from an earlier dissent by Justice Douglas as follows: "Government may not tell a man or woman who his or her associates must be. The individual can be as selective as he desires." In dissenting in *International Ass'n of Machinists v. Street*, 367 U.S. 740, 81 S.Ct. 1784, 6 L.Ed.2d 1141 (1961), Justice Black said at 791, 81 S.Ct. at 1811:

> Our Government has no more power to compel individuals to support union programs or union publications than it has to compel the support of political programs, employer programs or church programs. And the First Amendment, fairly construed, deprives the Government of all power to make any person pay out one single penny against his will to be used in any way to advocate doctrines or views he is against, whether economic, scientific, political, religious or any other.

Again in dissent, Justice Douglas said in *Lathrop v. Donohue*, 367 U.S. 820, 881, 81 S.Ct. 1826, 1858, 6 L.Ed.2d 1191 (1961):

> The right of association is an important incident of First Amendment rights. The right to belong—or not to belong—is deep in the American tradition.

The Supreme Court has struggled with this concept in a series of cases involving mandatory union membership and, in one instance, an integrated bar association, but has not met the issue head on. . . .

Notwithstanding the convolutions of the above opinions of the United States Supreme Court, we have no hesitancy in holding that the state, through the university, may not compel membership in an association, such as the ASUW, which purports to represent *all* the students at the university, including these plaintiffs. That association expends funds for political and economic causes to which the dissenters object and promotes and espouses political, social and economic philosophies which the dissenters find repugnant to their own views. There is no room in the First Amendment for such absolute compulsory support, advocation and representation. We recognize that First Amendment rights are not absolute, but the university presents no arguments or facts to justify any exception, narrow as it would have to be, which might exist if a compelling state interest were presented.

Thus we hold that the university may not mandate membership of a student in the ASUW.

It does not follow, however, that plaintiffs cannot be required to pay a mandatory services and activities fee. The legislature has directed the regents to charge such fee, RCW 28B.15.100, and in so doing the legislature acted within its authority. *Litchman v. Shannon*, 90 Wash. 186, 155 P.783 (1916).

Remaining is the issue whether these fees may be used for purposes to which plaintiffs object.

At this point we must balance the plaintiffs' First Amendment rights against the traditional need and desirability of the university to provide an atmosphere of learning, debate, dissent and controversy. Neither is absolute. If we allow mandatory financial support to be unchecked, the plaintiffs' rights may be meaningless. On the other hand if we allow dissenters to withhold the minimal financial contributions required we would permit a possible minority view to destroy or cripple a valuable learning adjunct of university life. With these balancing principles in mind, we proceed.

When a student enrolls at a university he or she enters an academic community—a world which allows the teaching, advocacy and dissemination of an infinite range of ideas, theories and beliefs. They may be controversial or traditional, radical or conformist. But the university is the arena in which accepted, discounted—even repugnant—beliefs, opinions and ideas challenge each other. In this tradition, the regents have decided to grant the ASUW a high degree of initiative and responsibility in conducting its affairs.

Dissenting students should not have the right to veto every event, speech or program with which they disagree. On the other hand, the ASUW is not totally unchecked in its use of these fees mandatorily extracted from students. First, it must not exceed the statutory purposes discussed above. Second, it cannot become the vehicle for the promotion of one particular viewpoint, political, social, economic or religious.

The cases which the university relies upon to sustain mandatory student fees recognize the delicate balance between the rights of the dissenters who must finance controversial programs and the desirability of the university providing a forum for wide-ranging ideas. Yet these cases are premised on the proposition that there must be in fact a spectrum presented, not a single track philosophy. In *Veed v. Schwartzkopf*, 353 F.Supp. 149 at 152 (D.C. Neb.1973), affirmed without opinion, 478 F.2d 1407 (8 Cir. 1973), *cert. denied* 414 U.S. 1135, 94 S.Ct. 878, 38 L.Ed.2d 760 (1974), the court said:

> Whether such activities in fact are educational in nature is for the Board of Regents to determine, subject only to the limitations that the determination be not arbitrary or capricious and that it not have the effect of imposing upon the student the acceptance or practice of religious, political or personal views repugnant to him or chilling his exercise of his constitutional rights.

Likewise in *Larson v. Board of Regents*, 189 Neb. 688, 690, 204 N.W.2d 568, 570 (1973), the court held:

> [T]he fact that the plaintiffs may disagree with the views expressed by some of the speakers brought to the campus is not controlling. If such views are expressed only as a part of the exchange

of ideas and there is no limitation or control imposed so that only one point of view is expressed through the program, there is no violation of the constitutional rights of the plaintiffs. Within reasonable limits, it is appropriate that many different points of view be presented to the students. . . . The plaintiffs' evidence does not support their assertion that the entire activity has been directed toward a particular point of view.

.   .   .   .

Where a university newspaper is supported by mandatory student fees, or by other university funds, reasonable supervision is required by the university authorities with a view to promoting and permitting the reflection of a broad spectrum of university life and reasonable representation of the various aspects of student thought and action.

As indicated above there is a factual issue as to whether the ASUW has exceeded the statutory purposes contained in RCW 28B.15.041. The other material issue of fact is whether the Board of Regents, acting through its appropriate personnel, has failed to enforce its "guidelines relating to the expenditure of public funds and the use of university facilities by the ASUW and other affected organizations," which guidelines are dated March 23, 1971. . . .

Until these factual matters are resolved by the trial court we cannot decree the full extent of relief to be granted. We have pointed out that it would be inappropriate to totally enjoin the collection of fees or their allocation to the ASUW. Whether the defendants should be required to establish a fund from which each plaintiff, including the class, would be reimbursed for present and past fees unlawfully or wrongfully collected cannot be answered at this stage. We point out that the status of this case as a class action is not before this court. There is only passing reference in the record to the determination and establishment of a class, as required by the rules, and we are unable to pass upon that issue. . . .

This case is remanded to the superior court for further proceedings consistent with this opinion.

NOTES

1. Freedom of association, along with freedom of press, speech, and religion, has been used, with little success, in several additional cases challenging mandatory student fees: Veed v. Schwartzkopf, 353 F.Supp. 149 (D. Neb. 1973); Lace v. University of Vermont, 303 A.2d 475 (Vt. 1973); Uzzell v. Friday, 547 F.2d 801 (4th Cir. 1977). In Arrington v. Taylor, 380 F.Supp. 1348 (M.D.N.C. 1974) students challenged the use of student fees to support a student newspaper on the grounds that the paper supported political views with which they did not agree. The federal district court found no constitutional violation in such use of mandatory student fees, noting that the newspaper had never been used for the furtherance of a particular position, but was an open forum for ideas. *Accord*, Hickman v. Board of Regents of Univ. Tex., 552 S.W. 2d 616 (1977), Larson v. Board of Regents of University of Nebraska, 204 N.W. 2d 568 (Neb. 1973).

2. *See also* Abood v. Detroit Board of Education, 431 U.S. 209 (1977), in which the U.S. Supreme Court ruled that teachers could not be forced to make union "fair share" payments which went for political activities, and Fishbein, *Legal Aspects of Student Activities Fees,* 1 J. of Coll. and Univ. Law 190 (1974).

3. In Mississippi Gay Alliance v. Goudelock, 536 F.2d 1073 (5th Cir. 1976), the Fifth Circuit ruled that a student newspaper could not be forced to take advertising from an off-campus group. Because of the independence of the newspaper from faculty and administrative control, no "state action" was involved.

C.   Political Activities

PICKINGS v. BRUCE
Eighth Circuit Court of Appeals
430 F.2d 595 (1970)

HEANEY, Circuit Judge.

This appeal concerns the right of college administrators to sanction a student organization, its officers and faculty advisors, for writing a letter to an off-campus church questioning its policies on integration and for refusing to accede to a request of the college administrators to cancel a speaking invitation extended by the organization. . . .

President Bruce investigated the matter, criticized those involved in the incident, asked the student who authored the letter to resign from his elected position with SURE, and asked SURE's two faculty advisors, both of whom had approved the letter, to resign from their advisory positions. The student and advisors resigned as requested but retained their membership in the organization. Subsequently, one of the two resigned faculty advisors was directed by President Bruce to limit his activities at the College to teaching, to restrict his advising to teaching situations, and to refrain from sponsoring any college organization or program. SURE was placed on probation for the remainder of the academic year because of its involvement in the church incident, the implied terms of probation being that SURE would confine its activities to the campus. . . .

The primary question raised here is whether the defendants interfered with the plaintiffs' constitutional rights by restricting the plaintiffs for their parts in writing the letter to the church and in extending the speaker invitation to the Neals. For reasons stated below, we hold that the plaintiffs' First Amendment rights of free expression and association were violated.

THE LETTER TO THE CHURCH

Students and teachers retain their rights to freedom of speech, expression and association while attending or teaching at a college or university. Tinker v. Des Moines Community School Dist., 393 U.S. 503, 506, 89 S.Ct. 733, 21 L.Ed.2d 731 (1969). They have a right to express their views individually or collectively with respect to matters of concern to a college or to a larger community. They are neither required to limit their expression of views to the campus or to confine their opinions to matters that affect the academic community only. Pickering v. Board of Education, 391 U.S. 563,

88 S.Ct. 1731, 20 L.Ed.2d 811 (1968); Dickey v. Alabama State Board of Education, 273 F.Supp. 613 (M.D. Ala.1967), appeal dismissed 394 F.2d 490 (5th Cir. 1968). It follows that here the administrators had no right to prohibit SURE from expressing its views on integration to the College View Baptist Church or to impose sanctions on its members or advisors for expressing these views. Such statements may well increase the tensions within the College and between the College and the community, but this fact cannot serve to restrict freedom of expression. Tinker v. Des Moines Community School Dist., supra, 393 U.S. at 508-509, 89 S.Ct. 733.

THE SPEAKING INVITATION TO
THE NEALS

Recent case law indicates that student organizations have a broad right to sponsor controversial speakers on-campus. We have been unable to find a single case decided in the 1960's in which a speaker ban has been upheld by a federal court. One limitation would appear to be that the administrators could enforce a ban, if they could reasonably forecast that the Neals' presence on-campus would substantially interfere with the work of school, the rights of students and the maintenance of appropriate discipline.

The District Court adopted the *Tinker* test and justified its conclusion that substantial interference could be forecast upon three findings. First, SURE was on probation at the time it issued the invitation. This fact, however, cannot serve as a basis for the administration's action since the imposition of probation was, of itself, a violation of the plaintiffs' constitutional rights. Furthermore, the defendants emphasized in their testimony that the probation was not intended to restrict the plaintiffs in any way in their on-campus activities.

Second. the District Court concluded that "disruptive activities" were underway on-campus at the time that the invitation was extended. There is no evidence in the record, however, to support the court's finding. SURE had been chartered as an organization for six months prior to this incident. It had conducted its activities in a mature, responsible manner during that entire period. The campus had been completely peaceful during the entire period. Not only had it been free of incidents involving interference with the rights of students or faculty during the period, but no demonstrations of any kind had taken place. It is clear from the evidence that the students and faculty were anxious about the war, the draft and racial injustice. It is also clear that these anxieties were sharpened by unrest on other college campuses and by the controversy arising from the letter to the church. But there is no showing that these tensions could reasonably have been expected to explode into aggressive, disruptive action or even group demonstrations simply because of the Neals' appearance on-campus for the purpose of showing a film.

Third, the court found that the Neals had a record and reputation for causing disturbances and had caused a disturbance at Henderson State College in Arkadelphia, Arkansas. There is no support in the record for the first conclusion, and only slight support for the second. The evidence shows only that the Neals were arrested on the Henderson campus for trespassing. There is no evidence in the record that the Neals had urged the students to violate any law or college regulation or that their appearance on-campus had resulted in any substantial interference with the rights of other students or with the work of school. The record shows only that the faculty had some difficulty in getting the students to return to their dormitories by the appointed hour after the Neals' arrest.

Upon a reading of the entire record, we are convinced that the administrators could reasonably have concluded no more than: that the Neals' appearance would expose the students and faculty to the militant views of a couple that was seeking substantial change in race relations; that these views would be apt to exacerbate the tensions between the College and the community; and that these views would be apt to provoke discussions between students and encourage them to action. These conclusions, however, cannot justify an infringement of First Amendment rights:

"* * * [I]n our system, undifferentiated fear or apprehension of disturbance is not enough to overcome the right to freedom of expression. Any departure from absolute regimentation may cause trouble. Any variation from the majority's opinion may inspire fear. Any word spoken, in class, in the lunchroom, or on the campus, that deviates from the views of another person may start an argument or cause a disturbance. But our Constitution says we must take this risk, * * * and our history says that it is this sort of hazardous freedom—this kind of openness—that is the basis of our national strength and of the independence and vigor of Americans who grow up and live in this relatively permissive, often disputatious society." Tinker v. Des Moines Community School Dist., *supra*, 393 U.S. at 508-509, 89 S.Ct. at 737-738.

We hold that under the circumstances of this case, the defendants had no right to demand that the speaking invitation to the Neals be withdrawn nor to impose sanctions for the refusal to withdraw it. . . .

*   *   *

NOTE

In Siegel v. Regents of the University of California, 308 F. Supp. 832 (N.D. Calif. 1970), the court held that the First Amendment protection of free speech did not prevent the expulsion of a student whose public speech in a park resulted in a student riot. Similarly, the same district court ruled that neither the First Amendment, nor the Fourteenth Amendment, nor the Civil Rights Act of 1871 protected students who disrupted an engineering class of Professor William Schockley's to demand that he publicly debate his views on racial genetics. Furumoto v. Lyman, 362 F. Supp. 1267 (N.D. Calif. 1973).

III. Freedom of the Press

PAPISH v. BOARD OF CURATORS OF THE UNIVERSITY OF MISSOURI
United States Supreme Court
410 U.S. 667 (1973)

Per Curiam.

Petitioner, a graduate student in the University of Missouri School of Journalism, was expelled for distributing on campus a newspaper "containing forms of indecent speech" in violation of a bylaw of the Board of Curators. The newspaper, the Free Press Underground, had been sold on this state university campus for more than four years pursuant to an authorization obtained from the University Business Office. The particular newspaper issue in question was found to be unacceptable for two reasons. First, on the front cover the publishers had reproduced a political cartoon previously printed in another newspaper depicting policemen raping the Statue of Liberty and the Goddess of Justice. The caption under the cartoon read: ". . . With Liberty and Justice for All." Secondly, the issue contained an article entitled "M----f--- Acquitted," which discussed the trial and acquittal on an assault charge of a New York City youth who was a member of an organization known as "Up Against the Wall, M----f---."

Following a hearing, the Student Conduct Committee found that petitioner had violated Par. B of Art. V of the General Standards of Student Conduct which requires students "to observe generally accepted standards of conduct" and specifically prohibits "indecent conduct or speech." Her expulsion, after affirmance first by the Chancellor of the University and then by its Board of Curators, was made effective in the middle of the spring semester. Although she was then permitted to remain on campus until the end of the semester, she was not given credit for the one course in which she made a passing grade. . . .

The District Court's opinion rests, in part, on the conclusion that the banned issue of the newspaper was obscene. The Court of Appeals found it unnecessary to decide that question. Instead, assuming that the newspaper was not obscene and that its distribution in the community at large would be protected by the First Amendment, the court held that on a university campus "freedom of expression" could properly be "subordinated to other interests such as, for example, the conventions of decency in the use and display of language and pictures." *Id.*, at 145. The court concluded that "[t]he Constitution does not compel the University . . . [to allow] such publications as the one in litigation to be publicly sold or distributed on its open campus." *Ibid.*

This case was decided several days before we handed down *Healy* v. *James,* 408 U. S. 169 (1972), in which, while recognizing a state university's undoubted prerogative to enforce reasonable rules governing student conduct, we reaffirmed that "state colleges and universities are not enclaves immune from the sweep of the First Amendment." *Id.*, at 180. See *Tinker* v. *Des Moines Independent School District*, 393 U. S. 503 (1969). We think

Healy makes it clear that the mere dissemination of ideas–no matter how offensive to good taste–on a state university campus may not be shut off in the name alone of "conventions of decency." Other recent precedents of this Court make it equally clear that neither the political cartoon nor the headline story involved in this case can be labeled as constitutionally obscene or otherwise unprotected. *E. g., Kois* v. *Wisconsin*, 408 U. S. 229 (1972); *Gooding* v. *Wilson*, 405 U. S. 518 (1972); *Cohen* v. *California*, 403 U.S. 15 (1971). There is language in the opinions below which suggests that the University's action here could be viewed as an exercise of its legitimate authority to enforce reasonable regulations as to the time, place, and manner of speech and its dissemination. While we have repeatedly approved such regulatory authority, *e.g., Healy* v. *James*, 408 U.S., at 192-193, the facts set forth in the opinions below show clearly that petitioner was expelled because of the disapproved *content* of the newspaper rather than the time, place, or manner of its distribution.

Since the First Amendment leaves no room for the operation of a dual standard in the academic community with respect to the content of speech, and because the state University's action here cannot be justified as a non-discriminatory application of reasonable rules governing conduct, the judgments of the courts below must be reversed. Accordingly the petition for a writ of certiorari is granted, the case is remanded to the District Court, and that court is instructed to order the University to restore to petitioner any course credits she earned for the semester in question and, unless she is barred from reinstatement for valid academic reasons, to reinstate her as a student in the graduate program.

Reversed and remanded.

JOYNER v. WHITING
Fourth Circuit Court of Appeals
477 F.2d 456 (1973)

BUTZNER, Circuit Judge:

Johnnie Edward Joyner, editor of the *Campus Echo*, the official student newspaper of North Carolina Central University, and Harvey Lee White, president of the university's student government association, appeal from an order of the district court, which (a) denied their application for declaratory and injunctive relief to secure reinstatement of financial support for the *Echo*, and (b) permanently enjoined Albert N. Whiting, president of the university, and his successors in office, from granting future financial support to any campus newspaper. Joyner v. Whiting, 341 F.Supp. 1244 M.D.N.C.1972). Joyner and White assert that the decree violates the First and Fourteenth Amendments. President Whiting urges affirmance on the ground that the paper's segregationist editorial policy and racially discriminatory practices violate the Fourteenth Amendment and the Civil Rights Act of 1964. We reverse because the president's irrevocable withdrawal of financial support from the *Echo* and the court's decree reinforcing this action abridge the freedom of the press in violation of the First Amendment. . . .

Fortunately, we travel through well charted waters to determine whether the permanent denial of financial support to the newspaper because of its editorial policy abridged the freedom of the press. The First Amendment is fully applicable to the states, Gitlow v. New York, 268 U.S. 652, 666, 45 S.Ct. 625, 69 L.Ed. 1138 (1925); Stromberg v. California, 283 U.S. 359, 368, 51 S.Ct. 532, 75 L.Ed. 1117 (1931), and precedent establishes "that state colleges and universities are not enclaves immune from [its] sweep." A college, acting "as the instrumentality of the State, may not restrict speech . . . simply because it finds the views expressed by any group to be abhorrent.
Healy v. James, 408 U.S. 169, 180, 187, 92 S.Ct. 2338, 2345, 2349, 33 L.Ed.2d 266 (1972); *see* Wright, The Constitution on the Campus, 22 Vand. L. Rev. 1027, 1037 (1969). It may well be that a college need not establish a campus newspaper, or, if a paper has been established, the college may permanently discontinue publication for reasons wholly unrelated to the First Amendment. But if a college has a student newspaper, its publication cannot be suppressed because college officials dislike its editorial comment. Panarella v. Birenbaum, 37 A.D.2d 987, 327 N.Y.S.2d 755, 757 (1971); *cf.* Danskin v. San Diego Unified School Dist., 28 Cal.2d 536, 171 P.2d 885, 892 (1946). This rule is but a simple extension of the precept that freedom of expression may not be infringed by denying a privilege. Sherbert v. Verner, 374 U.S. 398, 404, 83 S.Ct. 1790, 10 L.Ed.2d 965 (1963).

The principles reaffirmed in *Healy* have been extensively applied to strike down every form of censorship of student publications at state-supported institutions. Censorship of constitutionally protected expression cannot be imposed by suspending the editors, suppressing circulation, requiring imprimatur of controversial articles, excising repugnant material, withdrawing financial support, or asserting any other form of censorial oversight based on the institution's power of the purse.

But the freedom of the press enjoyed by students is not absolute or unfettered. Students, like all other citizens, are forbidden advocacy which "is directed to inciting or producing imminent lawless action and is likely to incite or produce such action." *See* Brandenburg v. Ohio, 395 U.S. 444, 447, 89 S. Ct. 1827, 1829, 23 L.Ed.2d 430 (1969). Tinker v. Des Moines Ind. Community School Dist., 393 U.S. 503, 513, 89 S.Ct. 733, 740, 21 L.Ed.2d 731 (1969), expressly limits the free and unrestricted expression of opinion in schools to instances where it does not "materially and substantially interfere with the requirements of appropriate discipline in the operation of the school." . . .

A college newspaper's freedom from censorship does not necessarily imply that its facilities are the editor's private domain. When a college paper receives a subsidy from the state, there are strong arguments for insisting that its columns be open to the expression of contrary views and that its publication enhance, not inhibit, free speech. *Cf.* Red Lion Broadcasting Co., Inc. v. FCC, 395 U.S. 367, 390, 89 S.Ct. 1794, 23 L.Ed.2d 371 (1969).

However, this case provides no occasion for formulating a principle akin to the fairness doctrine for the college press. The record does not disclose that Joyner rejected any articles that were opposed to his editorial policy, and President Whiting does not claim the paper refused to publish his pro-integration plea.

The president, emphasizing that the students are still free to publish and circulate a newspaper on the campus without university support, protests that the denial of financial support cannot be considered censorship because it is permanent. Permanency, he suggests, does not link the ebb and flow of funds with disapproval or approval of editorial policy. Absent this correlation, he claims, there is no censorship. But this argument overlooks the fact that one of the reasons for the president's withdrawal of funds was his displeasure with the paper's editorial policy. The abridgement of freedom of the press is nonetheless real because it is permanent. Freedom of the press cannot be preserved, as Mr. Justice Frankfurter noted, by prohibitions calculated "to burn the house to roast the pig." Butler v. Michigan, 352 U.S. 380, 383, 77 S.Ct. 524, 526, 1 L.Ed.2d 412 (1957). The president has failed to carry the "heavy burden of showing justification for the imposition of" a prior restraint on expression. Organization for a Better Austin v. Keefe, 402 U.S. 415, 419, 91 S.Ct. 1575, 29 L.Ed.2d 1 (1971). He has proved only that he considers the paper's editorial comment to be abhorrent, contrary to the university's policy, and inconsistent with constitutional and statutory guarantees of equality. This is plainly insufficient. Healy v. James, 408 U.S. 169, 187, 92 S.Ct. 2338, 33 L.Ed.2d 266 (1972); *cf.* Brandenburg v. Ohio, 395 U.S. 444, 449, 89 S.Ct. 1827, 23 L.Ed.2d 430 (1969).

Similarly, the district court's permanent injunction against the university's funding of the paper cannot stand. The court's grant of the injunction was intended to protect the student press by eliminating the inducement of future financial support "as a possible method for censorship." But the proper remedy against censorship is restraint of the censor, not suppression of the press. A court, no less than the executive and the legislature, must defer to the First Amendment. Twice in the history of the nation the Supreme Court has reviewed injunctions that imposed prior restraints on the publication of newspapers, and twice the Court has held the restraints to be unconstitutional. New York Times Co. v. United States, 403 U.S. 713, 91 S.Ct. 2140, 29 L.Ed.2d 822 (1971); Near v. Minnesota, 283 U.S. 697, 51 S.Ct. 625, 75 L.Ed. 1357 (1931). In both instances the proof was insufficient to overcome the presumption of unconstitutionality under which prior restraint of expression labors. Because this case is marked by the same defect, the injunction must be dissolved. . . .

NOTES

1. In a second issue in *Joyner* the court ruled that the president was justified in prohibiting racial discrimination in staffing the newspaper and accepting advertising, because under *Healy v. James, supra,* campus organizations claiming First Amendment rights must comply with valid campus regulations. The valid remedy, however, would be an injunction by the district court, not a withdrawal of funds.

2. For additonal cases on censorship or support of student publications at state-financed institutions *see:* Channing Club v. Board of Regents of Texas Tech University, 317 F.Supp. 688 (N.D. Tex. 1970); Quarterman v. Byrd, 453 F.2d 54 (4th Cir. 1971); Eisner v. Stamford Board of Education, 440 F.2d 803 (2nd Cir. 1971); Trujillo v. Love, 322 F.Supp. 1266 (D. Colo. 1971); Korn v. Elkins, 317 F.Supp. 138 (D. Md. 1970); Antonelli v. Hammond, 308 F.Supp. 1329 (D. Mass. 1970); Dickey v. Alabama State Board of Education, 273 F.Supp. 613 (M.D. Ala. 1967); Panarella v. Birenbaum, 327 N.Y.S. 2d 755 (1971); Schiff v. Williams, 519 F.2d 257 (5th Cir. 1975); Bazaar v. Fortune, 476 F.2d 570, reh. 489 F.2d 225 (5th Cir. 1973), *See generally: Developments in the Law–Academic Freedom*, 81 Harv. L. Rev. 1045, 1130 (1968).

IV. Freedom to Petition for Redress of Grievances

MARYLAND PUBLIC INTEREST RESEARCH GROUP v. ELKINS
Fourth Circuit Court of Appeals
565 F.2d 864 (1977)

ALBERT V. BRYAN, Senior Circuit Judge:

This First Amendment case questions the right of the Board of Regents, the governing body of the University of Maryland, College Park Campus, to forbid a recognized student organization to use its share of the institution's required student-activities-fees for purposes of litigation.

The organization, styled the Maryland Public Interest Research Group (Mary-PIRG), was accorded official standing at the University "to advocate the public interest in areas of concern to students enrolled in the College Park Campus". Sponsored projects are those designed to enhance the educational experience of its volunteers through participation in investigation, study and exposition of current social problems among the student body as well as the people generally. Among others, these comprehended unjust apartment rents, discriminatory employment practices, secrecy of Government papers, public health research and official misconduct of public and University officials. It is staffed not only by students but also with attorneys who provide the counselling where legal matters are implicated. In its areas, MaryPIRG pleads, it needs resort to the courts for substantive relief advancing its goals, particularly in seeking information from Governmental agencies.

The group received the approval of the Student Government Association (SGA), the agency responsible for advising the University on allocations of the student-activities-fees. SGA receives a budget from each student activity detailing the funds desired for pursuit of its enterprises. This submission, after evaluation by SGA, is passed on to the Regents for approval, modification or rejection.

Beginning in the 1974-75 academic year, MaryPIRG asked for an allowance by SGA to include moneys for "project expenses" consisting of litigation costs. The request was granted in a reduced sum. Thereafter the Regents approved the SGA recommendation, "on the condition that [Mary-PIRG] not use any of the funds so appropriated to pay litigation expenses". This limitation has continued in subsequent years, although larger amounts have been allocated to MaryPIRG for its general aims. . . .

Freedom to sue has not been denied MaryPIRG by the Board's resolve. Only the direction of State funds to that end has been withdrawn; otherwise it may go to court unreservedly. Moneys received as gifts, contributions or from other sources, such as "several Maryland campuses", may be devoted to such ends as MaryPIRG may wish. Actually the restriction is not a bar practically, for the record reveals that there are in truth such outside funds available and reasonably to be anticipated. . . .

These figures destroy the slightest hint of discrimination. Other proofs evincing fair treatment of MaryPIRG are these: its participants are credited on their academic records for their work; office space is provided on campus; and procurement of furniture is assisted. In 1974 it was the beneficiary of the next to largest share of student-activity-fees among the 40 campus groups, and in 1975-76 the largest, $38,619.00, was accorded the plaintiff. Even after the litigation embargo was actuated MaryPIRG was granted the equivalent of its previous year's allowance.

There is no affirmative commandment upon the University to activate MaryPIRG's exercise of First Amendment guarantees; the only commandment is not to infringe their enjoyment. . . . In reality, the plaintiff is asking the Board to finance the plaintiff's assertion of the Amendment. In this it cannot succeed. . . .

The thesis for the decision on review, thoughtfully expounded by the District Judge, is that the Board of Regents could not constitutionally prevent the use of student-activities-fees for litigation by MaryPIRG—a form of prior restraint—without advancing a compelling State interest sufficient to justify an exception to the First Amendment's preclusion. The burden of this showing, he believed, was upon the Regents. *Cf. Healy v. James*, 408 U.S. 169, 184, 92 S.Ct. 2338, 33 L.Ed.2d 266 (1972). But even accepting this premise *arguendo,* it cannot be doubted that the facts here demonstrated a State interest so compelling as to remove its action from the play of the Amendment.

To begin with, in the circumstances the employment of the mandatory fees is primarily a determination for the Board. *Ex facie* it is a concern within its governmental province—a matter *intra vires* the Board. Further, we cannot see the limitation as an ill-advised policy or abused discretion. On the contrary, its soundness is testified to by the well recognized considerations now to be mentioned. The group is already provided the counsel of lawyers. As its members are not law students, litigation would not be a form of education for them. Throughout pendency, from commencement to judgment, suits and actions would assume in the public mind the stature of declarations of University thought as well as that of its entire student body, while in truth it could well be neither.

In this vein, it is important to know that MaryPIRG and its operation find many students in disagreement with its creed. Hence, without the restriction the Regents could find themselves devoting moneys, in part forcibly demanded of the dissidents, to causes distasteful to them. A further understandable motivation of the Board was the apprehension that litigation by

MaryPIRG could result in assessment of costs, or judgments for other liabilities, against it, in the event of unsuccess at trials. The Board prefers that the University stand neutral, both actually and apparently. Other instances are not hard to conceive, justifying the wisdom of a prohibition of the outlay of fees to finance litigation.

The facts alone in this case create compelling grounds for letting the Board's restriction survive the exactions of the First Amendment.

The decree and orders on appeal must be set aside.

Vacated.

V.   Freedom from Unwarranted Search and Seizure

SMYTH v. LUBBERS
United States District Court for the
Western District of Michigan
398 F. Supp. 777 (1975)

FOX, Chief Judge.

The five original plaintiffs in this case were students at Grand Valley State Colleges in Allendale, Michigan [hereafter referred to as the College], during the 1973-74 academic year. All resided in dormitory rooms on campus. On January 30, 1974, College officials acting under color or authority of College regulations, searched each of the plaintiffs' rooms without warrants, and discovered substances alleged to be marijuana. . . .

No consent was given to the searches, and the searches were conducted without a warrant. Evidence was seized in both searches. Stip. Ex. Nos. 5, 6; Stipulation Nos. 7, 12, 17.

After the search, the plaintiffs were charged with "disorderly conduct and possession of narcotic drugs in violation of both State of Michigan laws and/or Grand Valley State Colleges regulations." Stip. Ex. Nos. 8, 9.

The plaintiffs chose to be tried by the All College Judiciary. . . .

Both plaintiffs challenged the admissibility of the evidence seized as a result of the January 30 search of their rooms. . . .

Notwithstanding the suppression of the alleged marijuana in his case, the Judiciary found Smyth guilty of possession of marijuana on the basis of testimonial evidence and he was suspended from the College for a period of two years. He likewise was acquitted of the charge of disorderly conduct.

No criminal proceedings have been instituted by the College or civil authorities against the plaintiffs.

Grand Valley State Colleges is a publicly created and publicly financed institution of higher education under the general supervision of a Board of Control. M.C.L.A. Sec. 390.841 (Supp. 1975-1976). The defendants are executive officers and employees of the institution, and are being sued in their representative and individual capacities. . . .

It is elementary that a party stating a claim under the Fourteenth Amendment and its implementing statutes, including 42 U.S.C. Sec. 1983, must allege official or state action, as distinguished from purely private action. Here, the plaintiffs complain of actions taken by the College officers and employees under color of law in their representative capacities. Such allegations are necessary to, and do, state a claim upon which relief can be granted under Sec. 1983. . . .

The Fourth Amendment provides, "The right of the people to be secure in their persons, houses, papers, and effects, against unreasonable searches and seizures, shall not be violated, and no Warrants shall issue, but upon probable cause, supported by Oath or affirmation, and particularly describing the place to be searched, and the persons or things to be seized." The resolution of Stipulated Issues 3 and 5 requires the essential Fourth Amendment inquiry into the "reasonableness" of the search and seizure in question, and the way in which that "reasonableness" derives content and meaning through reference to the warrant clause. See United States v. United States District Court, 407 U.S. 297, 309-310, 92 S.Ct. 2125, 32 L.Ed.2d 752 (1972); Coolidge v. New Hampshire, 403 U.S. 443, 473-484, 91 S.Ct. 2022, 29 L.Ed.2d 564 (1971). This in turn requires a careful identification and weighing of the respective interests of the plaintiff and the College in light of the Fourth Amendment, since the specific content and incidents of the Fourth Amendment right of privacy are shaped by the context in which the right is asserted. Terry v. Ohio, 392 U.S. 1, 9, 88 S.Ct. 1868, 20 L.Ed.2d 889 (1968).

The focus of the initial inquiry is whether the plaintiff Smith had a "reasonable expectation of freedom from governmental intrusion," Mancusi v. DeForte, 392 U.S. 364, 368, 88 S.Ct. 2120, 2124, 20 L.Ed.2d 1154 (1968). Smith was an adult at the time of the search in question, and thus was in general entitled to the same rights of privacy as any other adult in our society. In this, Smith was no different from the vast majority of Michigan college students. These students are in a different position from most elementary and secondary school students who are minors and are presumptively subject to a greater degree of supervision.

The place which was searched was Smith's college dormitory room. Smith had signed a Residence Hall Contract for the 1973-74 academic year. Presumably, Smith, as other students, resided in his room full time during the school, except for short vacations. His room is deemed his residence by the State of Michigan for voting purposes. Mich.Const. of 1963, Art. II, Sec. 1; Wilkins v. Bentley, 385 Mich. 670, 189 N.W.2d 423 (1971); M.C. L.A. Sec. 168.11(a). The plaintiff's dormitory room is his house and home for all practical purposes, and he has the same interest in the privacy of his room as any adult has in the privacy of his home, dwelling, or lodging. Because of the material and psychological importance of a man's home, the college dormitory room is not in the least like a licensed business establishment. Cf., United States v. Biswell, 406 U.S. 311, 92 S.Ct. 1593, 32 L.Ed.2d 87 (1972).

The Fourth Amendment by its terms protects "houses". The "physical entry of the home is the chief evil against which the wording of the Fourth Amendment is directed," United States District Court, supra, 407 U.S. at 313, 92 S.Ct. at 2134, and it is established that the privacy protected by the

Fourth Amendment is a fundamental constitutional right. Wolf v. Colorado, 338 U.S. 25, 69 S.Ct. 1359, 93 L.Ed. 1782 (1949). The plaintiff's interest in the privacy of his room is not at the "outer limits" as the College argues, but on the contrary is at the very core of the Fourth Amendment's protections.

In assessing the existence and scope of the right to privacy in any particular case, the nature of the governmental intrusion is a factor to be weighed. Because the Fourth Amendment, unlike, for example, the Sixth, is not limited to criminal prosecutions, it applies to "all alike, whether accused of crime or not." . . .

This case clearly involves a full search which focused upon the room of a specific individual who was suspected of criminal activity, and which aimed at discovering specific evidence. The search was not "administrative" in the sense of a generalized or routine inspection for violations of housing, health, or other regulatory code. See People v. Dajnowicz, 43 Mich.App. 465, 204 N.W. 2d. 281 (1972).

Since the College authorities were looking for marijuana in Smith's room, the search was specifically for instrumentalities of crime, defining "instrumentalities" here as contraband. It is a misdemeanor to possess marijuana under federal law, 21 U.S.C. Secs. 812(c), 844(a) and Michigan law, M.C.L.A. Secs. 335.305(3), 335.314(c), 335.341(4). The College regulation against possession of marijuana merely tracks federal and state law. The College regulation under which the search was conducted makes no distinction based on the source of law, but says that College may conduct a warrantless search on reasonable cause to believe that there are continuing violations of "federal, state *or* local *or* College regulations." (Emphasis added.). . .

Moreover, contrary to the defendants' implicit assumption, the College's resort to its own internal proceedings will not insulate either the College from the intrusion of civil authorities into its affairs or Smith from the institution of formal criminal proceedings against him. The matter is entirely outside the control of the College, and the search and seizure in question puts Smith in severe jeopardy. The Michigan Controlled Substances Act provides that marijuana "shall be seized and summarily forfeited to the state." M.C.L.A. Secs. 335.355(1)(a), 335.355(6). The Attorney General may bring an action against the College for the recovery of the marijuana. M.C.L.A. Sec. 600.4541. The marijuana may, perhaps, be used against Smith in a formal criminal proceeding, either to prove guilt directly, or to impeach his testimony even if it cannot be used to prove guilt. Walder v. United States, 347 U.S. 62, 74 S.Ct. 354, 98 L.Ed. 503 (1954); Harris v. New York, 401 U.S. 222, 91 S.Ct. 643, 28 L.Ed.2d 1 (1971). In any event, the seized marijuana can be the basis of state or federal grand jury questions directed to Smith (or any College official). United States v. Calandra, 414 U.S. 338, 94 S.Ct. 613, 38 L.Ed.2d 561 (1974).

Smith's suspension from school for one term is a harsher punishment than he was likely to receive from either a state court for conviction on or after April 9, 1974, or a federal court, for a first-time offense of simple possession of marijuana. Under federal provisions, 21 U.S.C. Sec. 844(b)(1), and state provisions which became effective on April 9, 1974, M.C.L.A. Sec. 335.347 (Supp. 1975-1976), the sentencing court has broad discretion to place such a first-time offender on probation for one year and, if the terms of the probation are not violated, to discharge the person and dismiss the charges without adjudication of guilt. The policy of the United States and the State of Michigan is that, except in extraordinary circumstances, simple possession of marijuana as a first offense is not so serious an offense as to warrant severe punishment, but is best treated by leaving the offender in society without serious social disability other than close supervision. In suspending Smith, the College forecloses further progress toward a degree at its institution for a substantial period, evicts him from his lodgings, exiles him to the streets in a time of substantial unemployment, and otherwise separates him from his normal society. . . .

On the whole, the court finds that on January 30, 1974, the plaintiff Smith was in the same position as a person suspected of a criminal offense, and that the search and seizure in question were as hostile and intrusive as the typical policeman's search for a seizure of the instrumentalities of crime in a person's home. The court finds no factors which would render this a less hostile or more benign "administrative" search.

Referring to Stipulated Issue No. 5, the College contends that, assuming the College's room search regulation was constitutional and reasonable, Smith, in living in a campus dormitory room which he rented from the College, waived objections to any reasonable searches of his room conducted pursuant to the College search regulation. The Residence Hall Contract which Smith signed provided that residence in the dormitory was subject to all the College regulations. . . .

The court assumes the College is contending that by signing the contract Smith waived objections, or consented, to any search conducted in accordance with the College regulation, even if the search did not otherwise comply with the Fourth Amendment. Smith had knowledge of the College regulation, and if the only issue was Smith's subjective expectation of privacy, then the regulation and the contract would foreclose his objections here. However, the test is a "reasonable" expectation of privacy, which necessarily adds an objective element. A person's expectation of privacy might be objectively too low if, for example, he had no expectation of privacy at all because of the authorities' announced intention to ignore the Fourth Amendment.

This problem really belongs to the law of unconstitutional conditions. The state cannot condition attendance at Grand Valley State Colleges on a waiver of constitutional rights. Robinson v. Board of Regents of Eastern Kentucky University, 475 F.2d 707 (6th Cir. 1973). It follows that the College cannot suspend a student for a term on the basis of the fruits of a search conducted pursuant to just such a required waiver. Furthermore, a blanket authorization in an adhesion contract that the College may search the room for violation of whatever substantive regulations the College chooses to adopt and pursuant to whatever search regulation the College chooses to adopt is not the type of focused, deliberate, and immediate consent contemplated by the Constitution. Accordingly, the court finds that the plaintiff Smith has not waived his Fourth Amendment right of privacy or his right to object to the violation thereof. The regulation and search in question must stand or fall apart from the residency contract. Cf., Piazzola v. Watkins, 442 F.2d 284 (5th Cir. 1971); Commonwealth v. McCloskey, 217 Pa.Super. 432, 272 A.2d 271 (1970).

The College contends it is an institution having "special characteristics" which justify the regulation and search in question. Healy, supra, 408 U.S. at 180, 92 S.Ct. 2338. The College advances a general proposition that regulations which are essential to the maintenance of order and discipline on school property are constitutionally reasonable even though such regulations infringe on outer limits of constitutional rights, citing Burnside v. Byars, 363 F.2d 744, 748 (5th Cir., 1966); Moore, supra, 284 F.Supp. at 730. The College argues that the search regulation is essential to the maintenance of order and discipline on the campus, and that the search conducted pursuant to that regulation was accordingly reasonable within the meaning of the Fourth Amendment. The theory is that the special characteristics of the College defeat or seriously qualify whatever expectation of privacy the student might have in other contexts or vis-a-vis other social institutions.

This court rejects the theory that College officials acting pursuant to regulations may infringe on the outer limits of an adult's constitutional rights. Burnside and Moore, upon which the College relies, were decided before Tinker, supra, which rejected the proposition that students "shed their constitutional rights . . . at the schoolhouse gate." 393 U.S. at 506, 89 S.Ct. at 736. The Fourth Amendment is flexible enough to meet a variety of public needs, but it will not admit of slight infringements. Boyd, supra, 116 U.S. at 635, 6 S.Ct. 524. Nor does the Civil Rights Act of 1871, 42 U.S.C. Sec. 1983, under which the plaintiffs sue here, permit slight infringements. As the United States Court of Appeals for the Fourth Circuit recently stated, "There is no warrant for any separation of constitutional rights into redressable rights and non-redressable rights, of major and minor unconstitutional deprivations, and Section 1983 makes no such distinction and authorizes no such separation." Pritchard v. Perry, 508 F.2d 423, 425 (4 Cir. 1975). Finally, as noted above, Smith's interest in the privacy of his room is not at the "outer limits" but at the core of the Fourth Amendment.

The basic question is the extent of the College's supervisory power in relation to the Fourth Amendment. Conclusory statements about the College's need for order and discipline are not enough. There is no challenge to the substantive drug regulation; the issue is the means of enforcement. There are a variety of means, but each actually used must be consistent with constitutional limitations. "In our system, state-operated schools may not be enclaves of totalitarianism. School officials do not possess absolute authority over their students." Tinker, supra, 393 U.S. at 511, 89 S.Ct. at 739.

The College is unjustifiably claiming extraordinary powers. The College drug regulations track federal and state laws, yet the College contends that its interests are so important that it may use means of enforcement—warrantless police searches on less than probable cause—which are not available to either the federal or state governments. Indeed, the College is claiming that its drug regulations are more important than the domestic security of the United States, which will not justify such action as the College took here. Cf., United States v. United States District Court, supra. Since nearly all college students in Michigan are adults, the College cannot have such a high interest in maintaining strict discipline as elementary and secondary schools. The College is also unlike military or quasi-military organizations, where the need for discipline is more acute than in civilian society. See Parker v. Levy, 417 U.S. 733, 94 S.Ct. 2547, 41 L.Ed.2d 439 (1974).

The College has not established that the search regulation is essential to the enforcement of the drug laws and regulations on campus. There are other ways of enforcing the regulations than with midnight warrantless police searches. Where persons are using or selling marijuana openly so as to provoke complaints from dormitory residents, the alleged offender may be charged and the complaining witnesses may testify against him or her. Indeed, that is what happened in the case of the plaintiff Smyth. Another alternative is for the College to secure a search warrant, as set forth below.

Similarly, the College has not established that obedience to the drug laws and regulations is so crucial to the performance of its educational function that extraordinary means of enforcement must be allowed. Possession and use of alcohol are certainly no less foreign to education than possession and use of marijuana. Yet the possession and use of alcohol in the dormitories are permitted by the College. Student Handbook at 14-15. Mr. Douglas Ballard, Resident Advisor of Smith's dormitory and the College official in the best position to know the practical effects of failure to comply with the College drug regulations, agreed that he was not concerned with any student conduct which did not in fact bother him or other students in the dormitory. College Hearing, Tr., at 233. If anyone is the victim of purely private possession and use of marijuana, it is not the College, the other students, or the educational function.

While the College has an important interest in enforcing drug laws and regulations, and a duty to do so, it does not have such special characteristics or such a compelling interest as to justify setting aside the usual rights of privacy enjoyed by adults.

On the basis of the foregoing, the Court concludes that the plaintiff Smith had a reasonable expectation of freedom from official intrusion into his dormitory room and that therefore the Fourth Amendment applies to this case. It remains to determine more precisely what the Amendment requires.

The College regulation in question allows a search of dormitory rooms when "College officials have *reasonable cause* to believe that students are continuing to violate federal, state or local laws or College regulations. . . ."

(Emphasis added.) Following Moore, supra, the College defines "reasonable cause" as more than mere suspicion but less than probable cause. Apart from the Warrant Clause, the issue is whether "reasonable cause" is a constitutionally adequate standard. Limited warrantless searches on less than probable cause are allowed under certain circumstances. Terry, supra. But the type of chance street encounter and limited search at issue in Terry has little in common with the police search of a dormitory room at 12:45 A.M. according to a plan drawn in advance. Although "school regulations are not to be measured by the standards which prevail for the criminal law and for criminal procedure," Esteban, supra, 415 F.2d at 1090, people enjoy Fourth Amendment rights of privacy whether a formal criminal prosecution is brought or not. Nor can it be argued that the standard of "probable cause" is too technical for the College to administer. The standard of "reasonable cause" is no less technical than that of "probable cause." But the "probable cause" standard is not too technical in any event. As the Supreme Court has said, the probabilities with which we deal in the area of probable cause "are not technical; they are the factual and practical considerations of everyday life on which reasonable and prudent men, not legal technicians, act." Brinegar v. United States, 338 U.S. 160, 175, 69 S.Ct. 1302, 1310, 93 L.Ed. 1879 (1949). College administrators, faculty, and advanced students have more formal education than many law enforcement officials who routinely operate successfully under the "probable cause" standard.

The only possible justification for requiring less than probable cause for a search of an adult student's lodging, whether with or without a warrant, is that the student's interest in privacy is somehow less than that of other adults; or that the College's interest in enforcing laws and regulations is somehow greater than that of the community. But these contentions have already been rejected.

The court concludes that the failure of the College regulation to require that there is "probable cause" to justify a room search renders the regulation constitutionally invalid.

The search in question was conducted by campus police officers who were also Ottawa County deputy sheriffs and by school officials without a warrant. The plaintiff contends that a warrant was required. The College contends that the search warrant procedure is "out of place" on the college campus, and contains seriously objectionable features in the college setting. The College assumes that a requirement of a search warrant would necessarily mean that the school authorities would have to call the off-campus police in order to obtain a search warrant, and that students would be prosecuted in the formal criminal process. . . .

The defendants in this case have consistently emphasized the extent to which they have the duty to enforce College regulations. They are plainly executive officers charged with investigation and prosecution, and certainly used constitutionally sensitive means in this case—*a warrantless police search of an adult's room on less than probable cause*— to accomplish their purpose.

They are thus not "neutral and detached magistrates" who may authorize searches within the contemplation of the Fourth Amendment. . . .

The College insists that in order to obtain a search warrant, it must invoke the formal criminal process, including the outside police. In the absence of constitutionally adequate procedures for securing a proper warrant, the College cannot search an adult's room for contraband, but must take its evidence to the off-campus police and leave the matter in their hands. However, there are possible alternative procedures which may be constitutionally adequate and which the College perhaps ought to explore. . . .

Whether or not the College officials and campus police are eligible to apply for search warrants under existing Michigan statutes, the College may consider requesting the legislature for a special statute explicitly entitling them to secure a search warrant from a civil magistrate. . . .

The College might also explore the possibility of a warrant procedure internal to the institution. The Constitution requires that a search warrant be issued by a magistrate who is neutral and detached. If the All College Judiciary is competent to try violations of College regulations, it may be competent to issue search warrants which are sufficient for College purposes alone, although the court does not decide this point here.

Securing a warrant to search a student's room, whether from a civil magistrate or from the College judiciary, means some inconvenience to the College officials. However, this is not an inconvenience to be weighed against the claims of administrative efficiency, Coolidge, supra, 403 U.S. at 481, 91 S.Ct. 2022; United States District Court, supra, 407 U.S. at 315, 92 S.Ct. 2125, and is an inconvenience justified in a free society to protect the constitutional value of privacy, United States District Court, 407 U.S. at 321, 92 S.Ct. 2125, which adults who happen to be students share in equally with other citizens.

Securing a search warrant in advance is not without important collateral benefits. The record of the College hearing in this case, which was directed only toward the question of whether or not the College complied with its own regulations, demonstrates the difficulty of establishing "reasonable cause" for a search by after the fact testimony alone. A prior affidavit and warrant build a record, establish the presumptive validity of the search, and minimize the burden of justification in post-search hearings. A proper warrant minimizes the possibility or scope of collateral attacks on constitutional grounds in federal or state courts. . . .

The court concludes that under the circumstances presented here, the defendants were constitutionally required to get a search warrant from a neutral and detached magistrate before searching Smith's room, and the failure of the defendants to secure such a warrant renders the search and seizure unreasonable and constitutionally invalid. The failure of the College regulation to require a warrant in the absence of exigent circumstances renders the regulation constitutionally invalid.

The final problem is whether an exclusionary rule applies in this case. The parties have not briefed this question separately, but much that they say goes to this issue. The court might hold that the evidence seized from Smith's room by the College authorities, although seized in violation of his constitutional right of privacy, was admissible in the College disciplinary hearing whether or not it would be admissible in a formal criminal proceeding. . . .

If there were no exclusionary rule in this case, the College authorities would have no incentive to respect the privacy of its students. Students do not normally have the means to maintain a protracted damage action. In addition, those whose rights are violated cannot recover damages except from those who acted in bad faith. See Wood v. Strickland, 420 U.S. 308, 95 S.Ct. 992, 43 L.Ed.2d 214 (1975). Where, as here, the authorities who violated the Constitution were not demonstrably guilty of bad faith, the exclusionary rule remains the only possible deterrent, the only effective way to positively encourage respect for the constitutional guarantee. This conclusion is consistent with, and perhaps required by, Calandra, supra, which was premised upon the availability of an exclusionary rule applicable to the authorities' case in chief, as well as the genuine possibility of recovery in a damage action.

In addition, the College hearing officer suppressed the evidence against Smyth because the College did not comply with its regulations. It would be anomolous too to hold that an exclusionary rule does not apply when the College fails to comply with the Constitution of the United States, but does apply when the College fails to comply with its own regulations. The Constitution is of higher dignity than a College regulation, and ought to provide at least equal protection. . . .

The court concludes that the evidence seized in the illegal search of Smith's room could not be used against him in the College disciplinary proceedings. Accordingly, the College must retry him, without the evidence, or dismiss the charges. . . .

Because the convictions of both Smyth and Smith by the All College Judiciary were based upon constitutionally inadequate standards of proof, the suspensions in accordance with these convictions cannot be enforced. . . .

NOTES

1. In Piazzola v. Watkins 442 F.2d 284 (5 Cir. 1971), cited in *Smyth*, the court ruled that college officials could not delegate to law enforcement officials their right to search a room without a warrant. The court said:

By a similar process of reasoning, we must conclude that a student who occupies a college dormitory room enjoys the protection of the Fourth Amendment. True the University retains broad supervisory powers which permit it to adopt the regulation heretofore quoted, provided that regulation is reasonably construed and is limited in its application to further the University's function as an educational institution. The regulation cannot be construed or applied so as to give consent to a search for evidence for the primary purpose of a criminal prosecution. Otherwise, the regulation itself would constitute an unconstitutional attempt to require a student to waive his protection from unreasonable searches and seizures as a condition to his occupancy of a college dormitory room. [*Id.* at 289]

2. The Supreme Court of Ohio has also ruled that a police officer may not enter a dormitory room through an open door and conduct a search without a warrant. *City of Athens v. Wolf*, 313 N.E.2d 405 (Ohio 1974). However, other lower court decisions have ruled that search of a room by college authorities without a warrant does not violate the Fourth Amendment, particularly if some threat to campus discipline can be proved. *Moore v. Student Affairs Committee of Troy State University*, 284 F. Supp. 725 (M.D. Ala. 1968); *U.S. v. Coles*, 302 F. Supp. 99 (D. Me. 1969); *Keene v. Rodgers*, 316 F. Supp. 217 (D. Me. 1970). *See also*: *People v. Lanthier*, 97 Cal. Rptr. 297 (1971). In this last case the California Supreme Court validated a search of a university library carrel without a warrant by college officials based on a "compelling urgency" (there were complaints of a noxious odor) and allowed use of the evidence so obtained. *See also*: Hillman, *Admissibility of Evidence Seized by University Officials in Violation of Fourth Amendment Standards*, 56 Cornell L. Rev. 509 (1971).

CHAPTER 10

PROCEDURAL DUE PROCESS FOR STUDENTS

I. Due Process in Disciplinary Cases

DIXON v. ALABAMA STATE BOARD OF EDUCATION
Fifth Circuit Court of Appeals
294 F.2d 150 (1961)

RIVES, Circuit Judge.

The question presented by the pleadings and evidence, and decisive of this appeal, is whether due process requires notice and some opportunity for hearing before students at a tax-supported college are expelled for misconduct. We answer that question in the affirmative.

The misconduct for which the students were expelled has never been definitely specified. . . .

The evidence clearly shows that the question for decision does not concern the sufficiency of the notice or the adequacy of the hearing, but is whether the students had a right to any notice or hearing whatever before being expelled. After careful study and consideration, we find ourselves unable to agree with the conclusion of the district court that no notice or opportunity for any kind of hearing was required before these students were expelled.

Whenever a governmental body acts so as to injure an individual, the Constitution requires that the act be consonant with due process of law. The minimum procedural requirements necessary to satisfy due process depend upon the circumstances and the interests of the parties involved. As stated by Mr. Justice Frankfurter concurring in Joint Anti-Fascist Refugee Committee v. McGrath, 1951, 341, U.S. 123, 163, 71 S.Ct. 624, 644, 95 L.Ed. 817:

> "Whether the *ex parte* procedure to which the petitioners were subjected duly observed 'the rudiments of fair play', * * * cannot * * * be tested by mere generalities or sentiments abstractly appealing. The precise nature of the interest that has been adversely affected, the manner in which this was done, the reasons for doing it, the available alternatives to the procedure that was followed, the protection implicit in the office of the functionary whose conduct is challenged, the balance of hurt complained of and good accomplished—these are some of the considerations that must enter into the judicial judgment." . . .

The appellees urge upon us that under a provision of the Board of Education's regulations the appellants waived any right to notice and a hearing before being expelled for misconduct.

"Attendance at any college is on the basis of a mutual decision
of the student's parents and of the college. Attendance at a particular college is voluntary and is different from attendance at a public
school where the pupil may be required to attend a particular
school which is located in the neighborhood or district in which
the pupil's family may live. Just as a student may choose to withdraw from a particular college at any time for any personally-
determined reason, the college may also at any time decline to
continue to accept responsibility for the supervision and service
to any student with whom the relationship becomes unpleasant
and difficult."

We do not read this provision to clearly indicate an intent on the part of the
student to waive notice and a hearing before expulsion. If, however, we
should so assume, it nonetheless remains true that the State cannot condition the granting of even a privilege upon the renunciation of the constitutional right to procedural due process. See Slochower v. Board of Education, 1956, 350 U.S. 551. . . .

The precise nature of the private interest involved in this case is the
right to remain at a public institution of higher learning in which the plaintiffs were students in good standing. . . .

Surely no one can question that the right to remain at the college in
which the plaintiffs were students in good standing is an interest of extremely great value.

Turning then to the nature of the governmental power to expel the
plaintiffs, it must be conceded, as was held by the district court, that that
power is not unlimited and cannot be arbitrarily exercised. Admittedly,
there must be some reasonable and constitutional ground for expulsion or
the courts would have a duty to require reinstatement. The possibility of
arbitrary action is not excluded by the existence of reasonable regulations.
There may be arbitrary application of the rule to the facts of a particular
case. Indeed, that result is well nigh inevitable when the Board hears only
one side of the issue. In the disciplining of college students there are no
considerations of immediate danger to the public, or of peril to the national security, which should prevent the Board from exercising at least
the fundamental principles of fairness by giving the accused students notice
of the charges and an opportunity to be heard in their own defense. Indeed,
the example set by the Board in failing so to do, if not corrected by the
courts, can well break the spirits of the expelled students and of others
familiar with the injustice, and do inestimable harm to their education.

The district court, however, felt that it was governed by precedent,
and stated that, "the courts have consistently upheld the validity of regulations that have the effect of reserving to the college the right to dismiss
students at any time for any reason without divulging its reason other than
its being for the general benefit of the institution." [186 F.Supp. 951.] With
deference, we must hold that the district court has simply misinterpreted the
precedents.

The language above quoted from the district court is based upon language found in 14 C.J.S. Colleges and Universities § 26, p. 1360, which in turn, is paraphrased from Anthony v. Syracuse University, 224 App.Div. 487, 231 N.Y.S. 435, reversing 130 Misc.2d 249, 223 N.Y.S. 796, 797. (14 C.J.S. Colleges and Universities § 26, pp. 1360, 1363 note 70.) This case, however, concerns a private university and follows the well-settled rule that the relations between a student and a private university are a matter of contract. The Anthony case held that the plaintiffs had specifically waived their rights to notice and hearing. See also Barker v. Bryn Mawr, 1923, 278 Pa. 121, 122 A. 220. The precedents for public colleges are collected in a recent annotation cited by the district court. 58 A.L.R.2d 903-920. . . .

It was not a case denying any hearing whatsoever but one passing upon the adequacy of the hearing, which provoked from Professor Warren A. Seavey of Harvard the eloquent comment:

"At this time when many are worried about dismissal from public service, when only because of the overriding need to protect the public safety is the identity of informers kept secret, when we proudly contrast the full hearings before our courts with those in the benighted countries which have no due process protection, when many of our courts are so careful in the protection of those charged with crimes that they will not permit the use of evidence illegally obtained, our sense of justice should be outraged by denial to students of the normal safeguards. It is shocking that the officials of a state educational institution, which can function properly only if our freedoms are preserved, should not understand the elementary principles of fair play. It is equally shocking to find that a court supports them in denying to a student the protection given to a pickpocket."

Dismissal of Students: "Due Process," Warren A. Seavey, 70 Harvard Law Review 1406, 1407. We are confident that precedent as well as a most fundamental constitutional principle support our holding that due process requires notice and some opportunity for hearing before a student at a tax-supported college is expelled for misconduct.

For the guidance of the parties in the event of further proceedings, we state our views on the nature of the notice and hearing required by due process prior to expulsion from a state college or university. They should, we think, comply with the following standards. The notice should contain a statement of the specific charges and grounds which, if proven, would justify expulsion under the regulations of the Board of Education. The nature of the hearing should vary depending upon the circumstances of the particular case. The case before us requires something more than an informal interview with an administrative authority of the college. By its nature, a charge of misconduct, as opposed to a failure to meet the scholastic standards of the college, depends upon a collection of the facts concerning the charged misconduct, easily colored by the point of view of the witnesses. In such circumstances, a hearing which gives the Board or the administrative authorities of the college an opportunity to hear both sides in considerable detail is best suited to protect the rights of all involved. This is not to imply that a full-dress judicial hearing, with the right to cross-examine witnesses, is required. Such a hearing, with the attending publicity and disturbance of college activities, might be detrimental to the college's educational atmosphere and impractical to carry out. Nevertheless, the rudiments of an adversary proceeding may be preserved without encroaching upon the interests of the college. In the instant case, the student should be given the names of the witnesses against him and an oral or written report on the facts to which each witness testifies. He should also be given the opportunity to present to the Board, or at least to an administrative official of the college, his own defense against the charges and to produce either oral testimony or written affidavits of witnesses in his behalf. If the hearing is not before the Board directly, the results and findings of the hearing should be presented in a report open to the student's inspection. If these rudimentary elements of fair play are followed in a case of misconduct of this particular type, we feel that the requirements of due process of law will have been fulfilled.

The judgment of the district court is reversed and the cause is remanded for further proceedings consistent with this opinion.

Reversed and remanded.

[Dissent omitted]

NOTES

1. The Fourteenth Amendment provides in part that "No state shall make or enforce any law which shall abridge the privileges or immunities of citizens of the United States; nor shall any state deprive any person of life, liberty, or property, without due process of law." These few words have occasioned hundreds of court opinions and a library of comment. To what extent due process requirements can and should be extended to educational institutions is still under debate. Two recent and contrasting views on the purpose and meaning of the Fourteenth Amendment in relation to education may be found in Richard Kluger's Simple Justice (New York: Vintage Books/Random House, 1977) and Raoul Berger, Government by Judiciary (Cambridge, Mass.: Harvard University Press, 1977).

2. As a result of the cases generated by the student protest movement of the 1960s it is now completely clear that at least in the area of social infraction, due process does belong on campus. The questions remain, how much due process, and for which purposes? None of the college student disciplinary cases arising from actual disruption ever reached the Supreme Court, although a secondary school case, Goss v. Lopez, 419 U.S. 565 (1975), did. In Goss, the Supreme Court ruled that before suspending a student the administration must grant him "oral or written notice of the charges against him and if he denies them an explanation of the evidence the authorities have an opportunity to present his side of the story." Since the Supreme Court based its decision in part on the fact the secondary students are required to attend school, the application to post-secondary institutions has been unclear. However, in Horowitz, infra, the Court seems to apply Goss to institutions of higher education by contrasting student rights to due process in a Goss disciplinary situation, with the lack of student rights to due process where an academic deficiency or infraction is involved.

3. The circuit courts which have considered student disciplinary cases, with the notable exception of the Seventh Circuit in Soglin v. Kauffman, 418 F.2d 163 (7th Cir. 1969), have tended to uphold institutional rules against students' due process challenges.

However, even those cases which disallow due process claims give some recognition to due process requirements. In Esteban v. Central Missouri State College, 415 F.2d 1077 (8th Cir. 1969), *cert. den.* 398 U.S. 965 (1970), for example, Judge Blackmun wrote:

> Let there be no misunderstanding as to our precise holding. We do not hold that any college regulation, however loosely framed, is necessarily valid. We do not hold that a school has the authority to require a student to discard any constitutional right when he matriculates. We do hold that a college has the inherent power to promulgate rules and regulations; that it has the inherent power properly to discipline; that it has power appropriately to protect itself and its property; that it may expect that its students adhere to generally accepted standards of conduct; that, as to these, flexibility and elbow room are to be preferred over specificity; that procedural due process must be afforded. . . . (as Judge Hunter by his first opinion here specifically required) by way of adequate notice, definite charge, and a hearing with opportunity to present one's own side of the case and with all necessary protective measures; that school regulations are not to be measured by the standards which prevail for the criminal law and for criminal procedure; and that the courts should interfere only where there is a clear case of constitutional infringement.

4. Language in some cases allows the inference that courts were deciding against antisocial behavior rather than against due process. In Blanton v. State University of New York, 489 F.2d 377 (2d Cir. 1973), the Second Circuit looked to the reasonableness of the overall fact situation to determine that students had not been deprived of the process by a failure to accord them rights to notice, cross-examination and an impartial hearing board. Judge Friendly wrote:

> In the path-breaking decision recognizing the due process rights of students at state universities, Dixon v. Alabama State Board of Education, 294 F.2d 150, 158-159 (5 Cir. 1961), Judge Rives outlined a number of procedural standards for school disciplinary actions, but then added: "This is not to imply that a full-dress judicial hearing, with the right to cross-examine witnesses, is required." . . . [N]ote our statement in Winnick v. Manning, *supra*, 460 F.2d 545 at 550, that if a case of a substantial suspension of a state university student has resolved itself into a problem of credibility, "cross-examination of witnesses might [be] essential to a fair hearing." . . . .
>
> If the three students had considered that the Committee's recommendations for their suspension had been based on an incorrect version of the facts, it was open to them to raise the point before President MacVittie. We are left with the firm impression that the students made no real attempt to convince anyone that Dean Stahl had not done what she and Dean Keller said she had done and that the claim about cross-examination is an afterthought of resourceful counsel.
>
> Less stressed is plaintiff Blanton's contention that the committee's inquiry went beyond the questions stated in Vice President Young's letter. Apparently her complaint is that her interview included some reference to the kicking incident on December 5. However, the transcript of the hearing reveals that it was Miss Blanton who first mentioned the incident in answer to the question, "Do you feel you were doing harm to anyone else?" Moreover, the incident was so much a part of the background for Dean Salters' action on Sunday morning that its introduction could hardly have come as a surprise. While "[n]o court since *Dixon* has denied that the student must be given prior notice of the grounds on which the charge is based," it is also true that a notice "need not be drawn with the precision of a criminal indictment." C. Wright, *supra*, 22 Vand.L.Rev. at 1072.

Plaintiffs' final due process point is that Dean Salters attended the meeting of the Discipline Hearing Committee—apparently as "a non-voting coordinator" representing the Vice President for Student Affairs, see n. 4 *supra*. They claim that since he participated in the Sunday morning incident, his presence "divested the Discipline Hearing Committee of its impartiality."

In Wasson v. Trowbridge, 382 F.2d 807, 813 (2 Cir. 1967), we dealt with a related problem. We there held that in the administration of student discipline, there was no absolute bar to inclusion even on the hearing panel of persons having had some previous contact with the incident, but that in such event the student should be given an opportunity "to show that members of the panel had had such prior contact with his case that they could be presumed to have been biased." It would follow *a fortiori* that Dean Salters' mere presence at the hearing would not invalidate the decision, especially since there was no factual controversy concerning his directions to the students on Sunday morning. In any event the students were given a full opportunity to present their case to a decision maker with no previous involvement in the incident, President MacVittie. He was in no way bound by the Committee's recommendation, but was free to make his own determination of the facts and his own decision of the proper punishment. If a state university supplies such a decision maker before the process is ended, a previous flaw, if any, becomes immaterial.

See also Jenkins v. Louisiana State Board of Education, 506 F.2d 992 (5th Cir. 1975).

5. In what is perhaps a backward glance at academic abstention, the court in Yench v. Stockmar, 483 F.2d 820 (10th Cir. 1973), refused to find a procedural defect in the expulsion of a student editor who wore a Mickey Mouse hat instead of a mortarboard to his graduation exercises. Noting that "[e]very disciplinary event cannot give rise to a constitutional question and a right to have the federal courts intervene" (823) the court ruled that while the Colorado School of Mines had failed to follow its own disciplinary procedures, the fault lay with the student who had waived his rights by failing to object. The court, however, remanded the case for a determination of "whether or not the wearing of the Mickey Mouse hat at graduation was the exercise of a right of constitutional dimensions," 824. While such an issue may appear to verge on the ridiculous much of the early comment on student disciplinary cases viewed the conflict as one between student academic freedom and university control necessary for a more institutional form of academic freedom. (*See*, for example, Henry Steele Commager's article, *The University and Freedom: Lehrfreiheit and Lehrnfreheit*, 34 J. Higher Education 361 (1963).)

6. In Soglin v. Kauffman, 418 F.2d 163 (7th Cir. 1969), the leading case upholding due process for students by establishing the necessity for preexisting, written standards of conduct, the court said:

No one disputes the power of the University to protect itself by means of disciplinary action against disruptive students. Power to punish and the rules defining the exercise of that power are not, however, identical. Power alone does not supply the standards needed to determine its application to types of behavior or specific instances of "misconduct." As Professor Fuller has observed: "The first desideratum of a system for subjecting human conduct to the governance of rules is an obvious one: there must be rules." Fuller, Law and Morality, p. 46 (2d printing, 1965). The proposition that government officers, including school administrators, must act in accord with rules in meting out discipline is so fundamental that its validity tends to be assumed by courts engaged in assessing the propriety of specific regulations. See Tinker v. Des Moines School District, 393 U.S. 503, 513-514, 89 S.Ct. 733, 21 L.Ed.2d 731. The doctrines of vagueness and overbreadth, already applied in academic contexts, presuppose the existence of rules whose coherence and boundaries may be questioned. *Cf.* Keyishian v. Board of Regents, 385 U.S. 589, 87 S.Ct. 675, 17 L.Ed.2d 629; Snyder v. Board of

Trustees, University of Illinois, 286 F.Supp. 927 (N.D.Ill.1968; 3-judge court); Buttny v. Smiley, 281 F.Supp. 280 (D.Colo.1968). These same considerations also dictate that the rules embodying standards of discipline be contained in properly promulgated regulations. University administrators are not immune from these requirements of due process in imposing sanctions. Consequently, in the present case, the disciplinary proceedings must fail to the extent that the defendant officials of the University of Wisconsin did not base those proceedings on the students' disregard of university standards of conduct expressed in reasonably clear and narrow rules.

7. The issue of whether procedural due process requirements apply equally to private institutions has been approached in a novel way by the Tenth Circuit. In Slaughter v. Brigham Young University, 514 F.2d 622 (10th Cir. 1975), the court held that the proceeding prior to Slaughter's expulsion for violation of the Student Code of Conduct "met the requirements of the constitutional procedural due process doctrine as it is presently applied to public universities." "It is not necessary under these circumstances," the court added, "to draw any distinction, if there be any, between the requirements in this regard for private and for public institutions." The court essentially used the adherence to due process to give weight to the reasonableness of the college administration's conclusions stating:

> When the courts lay down requirements for procedural due process in these situations as required by the Constitution, and when the school administrators follow such requirements (and other basic conditions are met), some weight must then be given to their determination of the facts when there is substantial evidence to support it. Thus if the regulations concerned are reasonable; if they are known to the student or should have been; if the proceedings are before the appropriate persons with authority to act, to find facts, or to make recommendations; and if procedural due process was accorded the student, then the findings when supported by substantial evidence must be accorded some presumption of correctness. The adequacy of the procedure plus the substantial evidence element constitute the basis and the record to test whether the action was arbitrary. The fact-finding procedures were adequate.

8. For additional study in this area see Wright, *The Constitution on the Campus*, 22 Vand. L. Rev. 1027 (1969); Smart, *The Fourteenth Amendment and University Disciplinary Procedure*, 34 Mo. L. Rev. 236 (1969); Symposium, *Legal Aspects of Student Institutional Relationships*, 45 Denver L.J. Vol. 497 (1968); Blasi, *Prior Restraints on Demonstrations*, 68 Mich. L. Rev. 1482 (1970); Beaney & Cox, *Fairness in University Disciplinary Proceedings*, 22 Case-Western L. Rev. 390 (1971); Cozier, *Student Discipline Systems in Higher Education*, ERIC Higher Education Research Report No. 7 (1973).

II.   The Impermissible Irrebuttable Presumption

VLANDIS v. KLINE
United States Supreme Court
412 U.S. 441 (1973)

MR. JUSTICE STEWART delivered the opinion of the Court.

Like many other States, Connecticut requires nonresidents of the State who are enrolled in the state university system to pay tuition and other fees at higher rates than residents of the State who are so enrolled. ... What is at issue here is Connecticut's statutory definition of residents and nonresidents for purposes of the above provision.

Section 126(a)(2) of Public Act No. 5, amending § 10-329(b), provides that an unmarried student shall be classified as a nonresident, or "out of state," student if his "legal address for any part of the one-year period immediately prior to his application for admission at a constituent unit of the state system of higher education was outside of Connecticut." With respect to married students, § 126(a)(3) of the Act provides that such a student, if living with his spouse, shall be classified as "out of state" if his "legal address at the time of his application for admission to such a unit was outside of Connecticut." These classifications are permanent and irrebuttable for the whole time that the student remains at the university since § 126(a)(5) of the Act commands that: "The status of a student, as established at the time of his application for admission at a constituent unit of the state system of higher education under the provisions of this section, shall be his status for the entire period of his attendance at such constituent unit." The present case concerns the constitutional validity of this conclusive and unchangeable presumption of nonresident status from the fact that, at the time of application for admission, the student, if married, was then living outside of Connecticut, or, if single, had lived outside the State at some point during the preceding year. . . .

The appellees do not challenge, nor did the District Court invalidate, the option of the State to classify students as resident and nonresident students, thereby obligating nonresident students to pay higher tuition and fees than do bona fide residents. The State's right to make such a classification is unquestioned here. Rather, the appellees attack Connecticut's irreversible and irrebuttable statutory presumption that because a student's legal address was outside the State at the time of his application for admission or at some point during the preceding year, he remains a nonresident for as long as he is a student here. This conclusive presumption, they say, is invalid in that it allows the State to classify as "out-of-state students" those who are, in fact, bona fide residents of the State. The appellees claim that they have a constitutional right to controvert that presumption of nonresidence by presenting evidence that they are bona fide residents of Connecticut. The District Court agreed: "Assuming that it is permissible for the state to impose a heavier burden of tuition and fees on non-resident than on resident students, the state may not classify as 'out of state students' those who do not belong in that class." 346 F.Supp., at 528. We affirm the judgment of the District Court.

Statutes creating permanent irrebuttable presumptions have long been disfavored under the Due Process Clauses of the Fifth and Fourteenth Amendments. In *Heiner* v. *Donnan*, 285 U.S. 312 (1932), the Court was faced with a constitutional challenge to a federal statute that created a conclusive presumption that gifts made within two years prior to the donor's death were made in contemplation of death, thus requiring payment by his estate of a higher tax. In holding that this irrefutable assumption was so arbitrary and unreasonable as to deprive the taxpayer of his property without due process of law, the Court stated that it had "held more than once that a statute creating a presumption which operates to deny a fair opportunity to rebut it violates the due process clause of the Fourteenth Amendment." . . . .

The same considerations obtain here. It may be that most applicants to Connecticut's university system who apply from outside the State or within a year of living out of State have no real intention of becoming Connecticut residents and will never do so. But it is clear that not all of the applicants from out of State inevitably fall in this category. Indeed, in the present case, both appellees possess many of the indicia of Connecticut residency, such as year-round Connecticut homes, Connecticut drivers' licenses, car registrations, voter registrations, etc.; and both were found by the District Court to have become bona fide residents of Connecticut before the 1972 spring semester. Yet, under the State's statutory scheme, neither was permitted any opportunity to demonstrate the bona fides of her Connecticut residency for tuition purposes, and neither will ever have such an opportunity in the future so long as she remains a student.

The State proffers three reasons to justify that permanent irrebuttable presumption. The first is that the State has a valid interest in equalizing the cost of public higher education between Connecticut residents and non-residents, and that by freezing a student's residential status as of the time he applies, the State ensures that its bona fide in-state students will receive their full subsidy. The State's objective of cost equalization between bona fide residents and nonresidents may well be legitimate, but basing the bona fides of residency solely on where a student lived when he applied for admission to the University is using a criterion wholly unrelated to that objective. As is evident from the situation of the appellees, a student may be a bona fide resident of Connecticut even though he applied to the University from out of State. Thus, Connecticut's conclusive presumption of nonresidence, instead of ensuring that only its bona fide residents receive their full subsidy, ensures that certain of its bona fide residents, such as the appellees, do *not* receive their full subsidy, and can never do so while they remain students.

Second, the State argues that even if a student who applied to the University from out of State may at some point become a bona fide resident of Connecticut, the State can nonetheless reasonably decide to favor with the lower rates only its established residents, whose past tax contributions to the State have been higher. According to the State, the fact that established residents or their parents have supported the State in the past justifies the conclusion that applicants from out of State—who are presumed not to be such established residents—may be denied the lower rates, even if they have become bona fide residents.

Connecticut's statutory scheme, however, makes no distinction on its face between established residents and new residents. Rather, through § 122, the State purports to distinguish, for tuition purposes, between residents and nonresidents by granting the lower rates to the former and denying them to the latter. In these circumstances, the State cannot now seek to justify its classification of certain bona fide residents as nonresidents, on the basis that their Connecticut residency is "new."

Moreover, § 126 would not always operate to effectuate the State's asserted interest. For it is not at all clear that the conclusive presumption required by that section prevents only "new" residents, rather than "established" residents, from obtaining the lower tuition rates. For example, a student whose parents were lifelong residents of Connecticut, but who went to college at Harvard, established a legal address there, and applied to the University of Connecticut's graduate school during his senior year, would be permanently classified as an "out of state student," despite his family's status as "established" residents of Connecticut. Similarly, the appellee Kline may herself be a "new" resident of Connecticut; but her husband is an established, lifelong resident, whose past tax contribution to the State, under the State's theory, should entitle his family to the lower rates. Conversely, the State makes no attempt to ensure that those students to whom it does grant in-state status are "established" residents of Connecticut. Any married person, for instance, who moves to Connecticut before applying to the University would be considered a Connecticut resident, even if he has lived there only one day. Thus, even in terms of the State's own asserted interest in favoring established residents over new residents, the provisions of § 126 are so arbitrary as to constitute a denial of due process of law.

The third ground advanced to justify § 126 is that it provides a degree of administrative certainty. The State points to its interest in preventing out-of-state students from coming to Connecticut solely to obtain an education and then claiming Connecticut residence in order to secure the lower tuition and fees. The irrebuttable presumption, the State contends, makes it easier to separate out students who come to the State solely for its educational facilities from true Connecticut residents, by eliminating the need for an individual determination of the bona fides of a person who lived out of State at the time of his application. Such an individual determination, it is said, would not only be an expensive administrative burden, but would also be very difficult to make, since it is hard to evaluate when bona fide residency exists. Without the conclusive presumption, the State argues, it would be almost impossible to prevent out-of-state students from claiming a Connecticut residence merely to obtain the lower rates.

In *Stanley* v. *Illinois, supra,* however, the Court stated that "the Constitution recognizes higher values than speed and efficiency." 405 U.S., at 656. The State's interest in administrative ease and certainty cannot, in and of itself, save the conclusive presumption from invalidity under the Due Process Clause where there are other reasonable and practicable means of establishing the pertinent facts on which the State's objective is premised. In the situation before us, reasonable alternative means for determining bona fide residence are available. Indeed, one such method has already been adopted by Connecticut; after § 126 was invalidated by the District Court, the State established reasonable criteria for evaluating bona fide residence for purposes of tuition and fees at its university system. These criteria, while perhaps more burdensome to apply than an irrebuttable presumption, are certainly sufficient to prevent abuse of the lower, in-state rates by students who come to Connecticut solely to obtain an education.

In sum, since Connecticut purports to be concerned with residency in allocating the rates for tuition and fees in its university system, it is forbidden by the Due Process Clause to deny an individual the resident rates on the basis of a permanent and irrebuttable presumption of nonresidence, when that presumption is not necessarily or universally true in fact and when the State has reasonable alternative means of making the crucial determination. Rather, standards of due process require that the State allow such an individual the opportunity to present evidence showing that he is a bona fide resident entitled to the in-state rates. Since § 126 precluded the appellees from ever rebutting the presumption that they were nonresidents of Connecticut, that statute operated to deprive them of a significant amount of their money without due process of law.

We are aware, of course, of the special problems involved in determining the bona fide residence of college students who come from out of State to attend that State's public university. Our holding today should in no wise be taken to mean that Connecticut must classify the students in its university system as residents, for purposes of tuition and fees, just because they go to school there. Nor should our decision be construed to deny a State the right to impose on a student, as one element in demonstrating bona fide residence, a reasonable durational residency requirement, which can be met while in student status. We fully recognize that a State has a legitimate interest in protecting and preserving the quality of its colleges and universities and the right of its own bona fide residents to attend such institutions on a preferential tuition basis.

We hold only that a permanent irrebuttable presumption of nonresidence—the means adopted by Connecticut to preserve that legitimate interest—is violative of the Due Process Clause, because it provides no opportunity for students who applied from out of State to demonstrate that they have become bona fide Connecticut residents. The State can establish such reasonable criteria for in-state status as to make virtually certain that students who are not, in fact, bona fide residents of the State, but who have come there solely for educational purposes, cannot take advantage of the in-state rates. Indeed, as stated above, such criteria exist; and since § 126 was invalidated, Connecticut, through an official opinion of its Attorney General, has adopted one such reasonable standard for determining the residential status of a student. The Attorney General's opinion states:

> "In reviewing a claim of in-state status, the issue becomes essentially one of domicile. In general, the domicile of an individual is his true, fixed and permanent home and place of habitation. It is the place to which, whenever he is absent, he has the intention of returning. This general statement, however, is difficult of application. Each individual case must be decided on its own

particular facts. In reviewing a claim, relevant criteria include year-round residence, voter registration, place of filing tax returns, property ownership, driver's license, car registration, marital status, vacation employment, etc." . . . .

MR. JUSTICE WHITE, concurring in the judgment.

In *Starns* v. *Malkerson*, 401 U.S. 985 (1971), a regulation issued by the Board of Regents provided that no student could qualify for the lower, in-state tuition to the University of Minnesota until he had been a bona fide domiciliary of the State for one year. The District Court upheld the law, 326 F. Supp. 234 (Minn. 1970), and we affirmed summarily, although the effect of the Regents' regulation was to prevent an admitted Minnesota domiciliary from being treated as such for a period of one year. I thought the case warranted plenary treatment, but I did not then, nor do I now, disagree with the judgment. Because I have difficulty distinguishing, on due process grounds, whether deemed procedural or substantive or whether put in terms of conclusive presumptions, between the Minnesota one-year re-quirement and the Connecticut law that, for tuition purposes, does not permit Connecticut residence to be acquired while attending Connecticut schools, I cannot join the Court's opinion.

I concur in the judgment, however, because Connecticut, although it may legally discriminate between its residents and nonresidents for purposes of tuition, here invidiously discriminates among at least three classes of bona fide Connecticut residents. First, there are those unmarried students who have resided in Connecticut one year prior to application or who later reside in Connecticut for a year without going to school. They pay the substan-tially lower in-state tuition. Second, there are the married students who have a legal address in Connecticut at the time of application. They also pay the lower tuition, whether or not they have resided in Connecticut for a year prior to application. Third, there are the unmarried students whose legal address has been outside Connecticut at some time during the year prior to application but who later become legal residents of Connecticut, before or after application or before or after matriculation, and remain such for at least one year. These students, although year-long residents, must continue to pay out-of-state tuition for as long as they are in school. . . .

[I] t is clear that we employ not just one, or two, but, as my Brother MARSHALL has so ably demonstrated, a "spectrum of standards in review-ing discrimination allegedly violative of the Equal Protection Clause." . . . I am uncomfortable with the dichotomy, for it must now be obvious, or has been all along, that, as the Court's assessment of the weight and value of the individual interest escalates, the less likely it is that mere administrative convenience and avoidance of hearings or investigations will be sufficient to justify what otherwise would appear to be irrational discriminations.

Here, it is enough for me that the interest involved is that of obtaining a higher education, that the difference between in-state and out-of-state tuition is substantial and that the State, without sufficient justification, imposes a one-year residency requirement on some students but not on others, and also refuses, no matter what the circumstances, to permit the requirement to be satisfied through bona fide residence while in school. It is plain enough that the State has only the most attenuated interest in terms of administrative convenience in maintaining this bizarre pattern of discrimination among those who must or must not pay a substantial tuition to the University. The discrimination imposed by the State is invidious and violates the Equal Protection Clause.

MR. JUSTICE MARSHALL, with whom MR. JUSTICE BRENNAN joins, concurring.

...Because the Court finds sufficient basis in the Due Process Clause of the Fourteenth Amendment to dispose of the constitutionality of the Connecticut statute here at issue, it has no occasion to address the serious equal protection questions raised by this and other tuition residency laws. In the absence of full consideration of those equal protection questions, I would leave the validity of a one-year residence requirement for a future case in which the issue is squarely presented.

In addition, I cannot agree with my Brother REHNQUIST's assertion in dissent that the Court's opinion today represents a return to the doctrine of substantive due process. This case involves only the validity of the conclusive presumption of nonresidency erected by the State, and, as such, concerns nothing more than the procedures by which the State determines whether or not a person is a resident for tuition purposes.

NOTES

1. In his dissent, Mr. Justice Rehnquist states that what the Supreme Court's opinion in *Vlandis* concedes to the states by way of distinguishing between residents and non-residents is, "all but useless in making students who come from out of State pay even a portion of their fair share of the cost of the education that they seek to receive." Has Justice Rehnquist's fear been realized? Why or why not?

2. The current Supreme Court has decided several significant cases on the irrebuttable presumption theory, and it is likely that the theory will become active in the lower courts as well. In Samuel v. University of Pittsburgh, 375 F.Supp. 1119 (W.D.Pa. 1974), married female students filed a successful class action attacking a state statute which provided that for tuition purposes the domicile of the wife is always that of the husband. And, in Krasnow v. Virginia Polytechnic Institute, 551 F.2d 591 (4th Cir. 1977), a student argued that being subjected to campus discipline based on conviction for possession of drugs off campus created an unconstitutional irrebuttable presumption that drug possession detrimentally affected the university. The Fourth Circuit disagreed stating that the presumption was within the prerogative of the university and that hearings were available to students so sanctioned.

3. For a discussion of the Supreme Court's use of the irrebuttable presumption, with particular reference to *Vlandis v. Kline*, see Dixon, *The Supreme Court and Equality: Legislative Classifications, Desegregation, and Reverse Discrimination*, 62 Cornell L. Rev. 494, 514 (1977), and authorities cited therein.

III.   Due Process in Academic Decision-Making

BOARD OF CURATORS OF THE
UNIVERSITY OF MISSOURI v. HOROWITZ
United States Supreme Court
98 S.Ct. 948 (1978)

MR. JUSTICE REHNQUIST delivered the opinion of the Court.

Respondent, a student at the University of Missouri-Kansas City Medical School, was dismissed by petitioner officials of the School during her final year of study for failure to meet academic standards. . . . We granted certiorari, 430 U.S. 964, 97 S.Ct. 1642, 52 L.Ed.2d 355, to consider what procedures must be accorded to a student at a state educational institution whose dismissal may constitute a deprivation of "liberty" or "property" within the meaning of the Fourteenth Amendment. We reverse the judgment of the Court of Appeals.

I

Respondent was admitted with advanced standing to the Medical School in the fall of 1971. During the final years of a student's education at the School, the student is required to pursue in "rotational units" academic and clinical studies pertaining to various medical disciplines such as Obstetrics-Gynecology, Pediatrics, and Surgery. Each student's academic performance at the School is evaluated on a periodic basis by the Council on Evaluation, a body composed of both faculty and students, which can recommend various actions including probation and dismissal. The recommendations of the Council are reviewed by the Coordinating Committee, a body composed solely of faculty members, and must ultimately be approved by the Dean. Students are not typically allowed to appear before either the Council or the Coordinating Committee on the occasion of their review of the student's academic performance.

In the spring of respondent's first year of study, several faculty members expressed dissatisfaction with her clinical performance during a pediatrics rotation. The faculty members noted that respondent's "performance was below that of her peers in all clinical patient-oriented settings," that she was erratic in her attendance at clinical sessions, and that she lacked a critical concern for personal hygiene. Upon the recommendation of the Council on Evaluation, respondent was advanced to her second and final year on a probationary basis.

Faculty dissatisfaction with respondent's clinical performance continued during the following year. For example, respondent's docent, or faculty advisor, rated her clinical skills as "unsatisfactory." In the middle of the year, the Council again reviewed respondent's academic progress and concluded that respondent should not be considered for graduation in June of that year; furthermore, the Council recommended that, absent "radical improvement," respondent be dropped from the School.

Respondent was permitted to take a set of oral and practical examinations as an "appeal" of the decision not to permit her to graduate. Pursuant to this "appeal," respondent spent a substantial portion of time with seven practicing physicians in the area who enjoyed a good reputation among their peers. The physicians were asked to recommend whether respondent should be allowed to graduate on schedule and, if not, whether she should be dropped immediately or allowed to remain on probation. Only two of the doctors recommended that respondent be graduated on schedule. Of the other five, two recommended that she be immediately dropped from school. The remaining three recommended that she not be allowed to graduate in May and be continued on probation pending further reports on her clinical progress. Upon receipt of these recommendations, the Council on Evaluation reaffirmed its prior position.

The Council met again in mid-May to consider whether respondent should be allowed to remain in school beyond June of that year. Noting that the report on respondent's recent surgery rotation rated her performance as "low-satisfactory," the Council unanimously recommended that "barring receipt of any reports that Miss Horowitz has improved radically, [she] not be allowed to re-enroll in the . . . School of Medicine." The Council delayed making its recommendation official until receiving reports on other rotations; when a report on respondent's emergency rotation also turned out to be negative, the Council unanimously reaffirmed its recommendation that respondent be dropped from the School. The Coordinating Committee and the Dean approved the recommendation and notified respondent, who appealed the decision in writing to the University's Provost for Health Sciences. The Provost sustained the School's actions after reviewing the record compiled during the earlier proceedings.

II

A

To be entitled to the procedural protections of the Fourteenth Amendment, respondent must in a case such as this demonstrate that her dismissal from the School deprived her of either a "liberty" or a "property" interest. Respondent has never alleged that she was deprived of a property interest. Because property interests are creatures of state law, *Perry v. Sindermann*, 408 U.S. 593, 599-603, 92 S.Ct. 2694, 2698-2700, 33 L.Ed.2d 570 (1972), respondent would have been required to show at trial that her seat at the Medical School was a "property" interest recognized by Missouri state law. Instead, respondent argued that her dismissal deprived her of "liberty" by substantially impairing her opportunities to continue her medical education or to return to employment in a medically related field.

The Court of Appeals agreed, citing this Court's opinion in *Board of Regents v. Roth*, 408 U.S. 564, 92 S.Ct. 2701, 33 L.Ed.2d 548 (1972). In that case, we held that the State had not deprived a teacher of any liberty or property interest in dismissing the teacher from a nontenured position. . . .

We have recently had an opportunity to elaborate upon the circumstances under which an employment termination might infringe a protected liberty interest. In *Bishop v. Wood*, 426 U.S. 341, 96 S.Ct. 2074, 48 L.Ed.2d 684, we upheld the dismissal of a policeman without a hearing; we rejected the theory that the mere fact of dismissal, absent some publicization of the reasons for the action, could amount to a stigma infringing one's liberty. . . .

B

We need not decide, however, whether respondent's dismissal deprived her of a liberty interest in pursuing a medical career. Nor need we decide whether respondent's dismissal infringed any other interest constitutionally protected against deprivation without procedural due process. Assuming the existence of a liberty or property interest, respondent has been awarded at least as much due process as the Fourteenth Amendment requires. The School fully informed respondent of the faculty's dissatisfaction with her clinical progress and the danger that this posed to timely graduation and continued enrollment. The ultimate decision to dismiss respondent was careful and deliberate. These procedures were sufficient under the Due Process Clause of the Fourteenth Amendment. We agree with the District Court that respondent

> "was afforded full procedural due process by the [school]. In fact, the Court is of the opinion, and so finds, that the school went beyond [constitutionally required] procedural due process by affording [respondent] the opportunity to be examined by seven independent physicians in order to be absolutely certain that their grading of the [respondent] in her medical skills was correct."

In *Goss v. Lopez*, 419 U.S. 565, 95 S.Ct. 729, 42 L.Ed.2d 725 (1975), we held that due process requires, in connection with the suspension of a student from public school for disciplinary reasons, "that the student be given oral or written notice of the charges against him and, if he denies them, an explanation of the evidence the authorities have and an opportunity to present his side of the story." *Id.*, at 581, 95 S.Ct., at 740. The Court of Appeals apparently read *Goss* as requiring some type of formal hearing at which respondent could defend her academic ability and performance. All that *Goss* required was an "informal give-and-take" between the student and the administrative body dismissing him that would, at least, give the student "the opportunity to characterize his conduct and put it in what he deems the proper context." *Id.*, at 584, 95 S.Ct., at 741. But we have frequently emphasized that "[t]he very nature of due process negates any concept of inflexible procedures universally applicable to every imaginable situation." *Cafeteria Workers v. McElroy*, 367 U.S. 886, 895, 81 S.Ct. 1743, 1748, 6 L.Ed.2d 1230 (1961). The need for flexibility is well illustrated by the significant difference between the failure of a student to meet academic standards and the violation by a student of valid rules of conduct.

This difference calls for far less stringent procedural requirements in the case of an academic dismissal.

Since the issue first arose 50 years ago, state and lower federal courts have recognized that there are distinct differences between decisions to suspend or dismiss a student for disciplinary purposes and similar actions taken for academic reasons which may call for hearings in connection with the former but not the latter. Thus, in *Barnard v. Inhabitants of Shelburne*, 216 Mass. 19, 102 N.E. 1095 (1913), the Supreme Judicial Court of Massachusetts rejected an argument, based on several earlier decisions requiring a hearing in disciplinary contexts, that school officials must also grant a hearing before excluding a student on academic grounds. According to the court, disciplinary cases have

> "no application. . . . Misconduct is a very different matter from failure to attain a standard of excellence in studies. A determination as to the fact involves investigation of a quite different kind. A public hearing may be regarded as helpful to the ascertainment of misconduct and useless or harmful in finding out the truth as to scholarship." *Id.*, at 22, 102 N.E., at 1097. . . .

Reason, furthermore, clearly supports the perception of these decisions. A school is an academic institution, not a courtroom or administrative hearing room. In *Goss,* this Court felt that suspensions of students for disciplinary reasons have a sufficient resemblance to traditional judicial and administrative factfinding to call for a "hearing" before the relevant school authority. While recognizing that school authorities must be afforded the necessary tools to maintain discipline, the Court concluded that

> "it would be a strange disciplinary system in an educational institution if no communication was sought by the disciplinarian with the student in an effort to inform him of his dereliction and to let him tell his side of the story in order to make sure that an injustice is not done. . . . [R]equiring effective notice and informal hearing permitting the student to give his version of the events will provide a meaningful hedge against erroneous action. At least the disciplinarian will be alerted to the existence of disputes about facts and arguments about cause and effect." 419 U.S. 565, 580, 583-584, 95 S.Ct. 729, 739, 741, 42 L.Ed.2d 725.

Even in the context of a school disciplinary proceeding, however, the Court stopped short of requiring a *formal* hearing since "further formalizing the suspension process and escalating its formality and adversary nature may not only make it too costly as a regular disciplinary tool but also destroy its effectiveness as a part of the teaching process." *Id.*, at 583, 95 S.Ct., at 741.

Academic evaluations of a student, in contrast to disciplinary determinations, bear little resemblance to the judicial and administrative factfinding proceedings to which we have traditionally attached a full hearing requirement. In *Goss*, the school's decision to suspend the students rested on factual conclusions that the individual students had participated in demonstrations that had disrupted classes, attacked a police officer, or caused physical damage to school property. The requirement of a hearing, where the student could present his side of the factual issue, could under such circumstances "provide a meaningful hedge against erroneous action." *Ibid.* The decision to dismiss respondent, by comparison, rested on the academic judgment of school officials that she did not have the necessary clinical ability to perform adequately as a medical doctor and was making insufficient progress toward that goal. Such a judgment is by its nature more subjective and evaluative than the typical factual questions presented in the average disciplinary decision. Like the decision of an individual professor as to the proper grade for a student in his course, the determination whether to dismiss a student for academic reasons requires an expert evaluation of cumulative information and is not readily adapted to the procedural tools of judicial or administrative decisionmaking.

Under such circumstances, we decline to ignore the historic judgment of educators and thereby formalize the academic dismissal process by requiring a hearing. The educational process is not by nature adversarial; instead it centers around a continuing relationship between faculty and students, "one in which the teacher must occupy many roles—educator, adviser, friend, and, at times, parent-substitute." *Goss v. Lopez,* 419 U.S. 565, 594, 95 S.Ct. 729, 746, 42 L.Ed.2d 725 (1975) (Powell, J., dissenting). This is especially true as one advances through the varying regimes of the educational system, and the instruction becomes both more individualized and more specialized. In *Goss,* this Court concluded that the value of some form of hearing in a disciplinary context outweighs any resulting harm to the academic environment. Influencing this conclusion was clearly the belief that disciplinary proceedings, in which the teacher must decide whether to punish a student for disruptive or insubordinate behavior, may automatically bring an adversarial flavor to the normal student-teacher relationship. The same conclusion does not follow in the academic context. We decline to further enlarge the judicial presence in the academic community and thereby risk deterioration of many beneficial aspects of the faculty-student relationship. We recognize, as did the Massachusetts Supreme Judicial Court over 60 years ago, that a hearing may be "useless or even harmful in finding out the truth as to scholarship." *Barnard v. Inhabitants of Shelburne, supra.*

"Judicial interposition in the operation of the public school system of the Nation raises problems requiring care and restraint. . . . By and large, public education in our Nation is committed to the control of state and local authorities." *Epperson v. Arkansas,* 393 U.S. 97, 104, 89 S.Ct. 266, 270, 21 L.Ed.2d 228 (1968). We see no reason to intrude on that historic control in this case.

III

In reversing the District Court on procedural due process grounds, the Court of Appeals expressly failed to "reach the substantive due process ground advanced by Horowitz." 528 F.2d 1317, 1321 n. 5. Respondent urges that we remand the cause to the Court of Appeals for consideration of this additional claim. In this regard, a number of lower courts have implied in dictum that academic dismissals from state institutions can be enjoined if "shown to be clearly arbitrary or capricious." *Mahavongsanan v. Hall, supra,* 529 F.2d, at 449. See *Gaspar v. Bruton, supra,* 513 F.2d, at 850, and citations therein. Even assuming that the courts can review under such a standard an academic decision of a public educational institution, we agree with the District Court that no showing of arbitrariness or capriciousness has been made in this case. Courts are particularly ill-equipped to evaluate academic performance. The factors discussed in Part II with respect to procedural due process speak a *fortiori* here and warn against any such judicial intrusion into academic decisionmaking. . . .

Mr. Justice MARSHALL, concurring in part and dissenting in part.

I agree with the Court that, "[a]ssuming the existence of a liberty or property interest, respondent has been awarded at least as much due process as the Fourteenth Amendment requires." *Ante,* at 952. I cannot join the Court's opinion, however, because it contains dictum suggesting that respondent was entitled to even less procedural protection than she received. I also differ from the Court in its assumption that characterization of the reasons for a dismissal as "academic" or "disciplinary" is relevant to resolution of the question of what procedures are required by the Due Process Clause. Finally, I disagree with the Court's decision not to remand to the Court of Appeals for consideration of respondent's substantive due process claim.

I

We held in *Goss v. Lopez,* 419 U.S. 565, 95 S.Ct. 729, 42 L.Ed.2d 725 (1975), that

"due process requires, in connection with a suspension of 10 days or less, that the student be given oral or written notice of the charges against him and, if he denies them, an explanation of the evidence the authorities have and an opportunity to present his side of the story." *Id.,* at 581, 95 S.Ct., at 740.

There is no question that respondent received these protections, and more....

These meetings and letters plainly gave respondent all that *Goss* requires: several notices and explanations, and at least three opportunities "to present [her] side of the story." 419 U.S., at 581, 95 S.Ct., at 740. I do not read the Court's opinion to disagree with this conclusion. Hence I do not understand why the Court indicates that even the "informal give-and-take" mandated by *Goss, id.,* at 584, 95 S.Ct., at 741, need not have been provided here. See *ante,* at 952-953, 955. This case simply provides no legitimate opportunity to consider whether "far less stringent procedural requirements," *id.,* at 953, than those required in *Goss* are appropriate in other school contexts. While I disagree with the Court's conclusion that "far less" is adequate, as discussed *infra*, it is equally disturbing that the Court decides an issue not presented by the case before us. As Mr. Justice Brandeis warned over 40 years ago, the "'great gravity and delicacy'" of our task in constitutional cases should cause us to "'shrink'" from "'anticipat-[ing] a question of constitutional law in advance of the necessity of deciding it,'" and from "'formulat[ing] a rule of constitutional law broader than is required by the precise facts to which it is to be applied.'" *Ashwander v. TVA*, 297 U.S. 288, 345-347, 56 S.Ct. 466, 483, 80 L.Ed. 688 (1936) (concurring opinion).

II

In view of the Court's dictum to the effect that even the minimum procedures required in *Goss* need not have been provided to respondent, I feel compelled to comment on the extent of procedural protection mandated here. I do so within a framework largely ignored by the Court, a framework derived from our traditional approach to these problems. According to our prior decisions as summarized in *Mathews v. Eldridge*, 424 U.S. 319, 96 S. Ct. 893, 47 L.Ed.2d 18 (1976), three factors are of principal relevance in determining what process is due:

> "First, the private interest that will be affected by the official action; second, the risk of an erroneous deprivation of such interest through the procedures used, and the probable value, if any, of additional or substitute procedural safeguards; and finally, the Government's interest, including the function involved and the fiscal and administrative burdens that the additional or substitute procedural requirement would entail." *Id.*, at 335, 96 S.Ct., at 903.

As the Court recognizes, the "private interest" involved here is a weighty one: "the deprivation to which respondent was subjected—dismissal from a graduate medical school—was more severe than the 10-day suspension to which the high school students were subjected in *Goss*." *Ante*, at 953 n. 3. One example of the loss suffered by respondent is contained in the stipulation of facts: respondent had a job offer from the psychiatry department of another university to begin work in September 1973; the offer was contingent on her receiving the M.D. degree. In summary, as the Court of Appeals noted:

> "The unrefuted evidence here establishes that Horowitz has been stigmatized by her dismissal in such a way that she will be unable to continue her medical education, and her chances of returning to employment in a medically related field are severely damaged." 528 F.2d 1317, 1321 (CA8 1976).

As Judge Friendly has written in a related context, when the State seeks "to deprive a person of a way of life to which [s]he has devoted years of preparation and on which [s]he . . . ha[s] come to rely," it should be required first to provide a "high-level of procedural protection."

Neither of the other two factors mentioned in *Mathews* justifies moving from a high level to the lower level of protection involved in *Goss*. There was at least some risk of error inherent in the evidence on which the dean relied in his meetings with and letters to respondent; faculty evaluations of such matters as personal hygiene and patient and peer rapport are neither as "sharply focused" nor as "easily documented" as was, *e.g.,* the disability determination involved in *Mathews,* 424 U.S., at 343, 96 S.Ct., at 907. See *Goss v. Lopez, supra,* 419 U.S., at 580, 95 S.Ct., at 739 (when decision-maker "act[s] on the reports and advice of others . . . [t]he risk of error is not at all trivial").

Nor can it be said that the university had any greater interest in summary proceedings here than did the school in *Goss*. Certainly the allegedly disruptive and disobedient students involved there, see *id.,* at 569-571, 95 S.Ct., at 733-734, posed more of an immediate threat to orderly school administration than did respondent. As we noted in *Goss,* moreover, "it disserves . . . the interest of the State if [the student's] suspension is in fact unwarranted." *Id.,* at 579, 95 S.Ct., at 739. Under these circumstances —with respondent having much more at stake than did the students in *Goss,* the administration at best having no more at stake, and the meetings between respondent and the dean leaving some possibility of erroneous dismissal—I believe that respondent was entitled to more procedural protection than is provided by "informal give-and-take" before the school could dismiss her.

The contours of the additional procedural protection to which respondent was entitled need not be defined in terms of the traditional adversarial system so familiar to lawyers and judges. See *Mathews v. Eldridge, supra,* 424 U.S., at 348, 96 S.Ct., at 909. We have emphasized many times that "[t]he very nature of due process negates any concept of inflexible procedures universally applicable to every imaginable situation." *Cafeteria Workers v. McElroy,* 367 U.S. 886, 895, 81 S.Ct. 1743, 1748, 6 L.Ed.2d 1230 (1961). . . .

In the instant factual context the "appeal" provided to respondent, see *ante,* at 950, served the same purposes as, and in some respects may have been better than, a formal hearing. In establishing the procedure under which respondent was evaluated separately by seven physicians who had had little or no previous contact with her, it appears that the medical school placed emphasis on obtaining "a fair and neutral and impartial assessment." In order to evaluate respondent, each of the seven physicians spent approximately one half-day observing her as she performed various clinical duties and then submitted a report on her performance to the dean. It is difficult to imagine a better procedure for determining whether the school's allegations against respondent had any substance to them. Cf. *Mathews v. Eldridge, supra,* 424 U.S., at 337-338, 344, 96 S.Ct., at 904, 907 (use of independent physician to examine disability applicant and report to decisionmaker). I therefore believe that the appeal procedure utilized by respondent, together with her earlier notices from and meetings with the dean, provided respon-

dent with as much procedural protection as the Due Process Clause requires.

III

The analysis in Parts I and II of this opinion illustrates that resolution
of this case under our traditional approach does not turn on whether the
dismissal of respondent is characterized as one for "academic" or "disciplinary" reasons. In my view, the effort to apply such labels does little to
advance the due process inquiry, as is indicated by examination of the
facts of this case.

The minutes of the meeting at which it was first decided that respondent should not graduate contain the following:

> "This issue is *not one of academic achievement*, but of perform-
> ance, relationship to people and ability to communicate." App.
> 218 (emphasis added).

By the customary measures of academic progress, moreover, no deficiency
was apparent at the time that the authorities decided respondent could not
graduate; prior to this time, according to the stipulation of facts, respondent
had received "credit" and "satisfactory grades" in all of her courses, including clinical courses.

It may nevertheless be true, as the Court implies, *ante*, at 955 n. 6,
that the school decided that respondent's inadequacies in such areas as personal hygiene, peer and patient relations, and timeliness would impair her
ability to be "a good medical doctor." Whether these inadequacies can be
termed "pure academic reasons," as the Court calls them, *ibid*., is ultimately
an irrelevant question, and one placing an undue emphasis on words rather
than functional considerations. The relevant point is that respondent was
dismissed largely because of her conduct, just as the students in *Goss* were
suspended because of their conduct.

The Court makes much of decisions from state and lower federal courts
to support its point that "dismissals for academic . . . cause do not necessitate a hearing." *Ante*, at 954. The decisions on which the Court relies, however, plainly use the term "academic" in a much narrower sense than does
the Court, distinguishing "academic" dismissals from ones based on "misconduct" and holding that, when a student is dismissed for failing grades, a
hearing would serve no purpose. These cases may be viewed as consistent
with our statement in *Mathews v. Eldridge* that "the probable value . . . of
additional . . . procedural safeguards" is a factor relevant to the due process
inquiry. 424 U.S., at 335, 96 S.Ct., at 903, quoted at p. 960, *supra*; see 424
U.S., at 343-347, 96 S.Ct., at 907-909. But they provide little assistance in
resolving cases like the present one, where the dismissal is based not on
failing grades but on conduct-related considerations.

In such cases a talismanic reliance on labels should not be a substitute
for sensitive consideration of the procedures required by due process. When
the facts disputed are of a type susceptible to determination by third parties,
as the allegations about respondent plainly were, see *ante*, at 955-956 n. 6,

there is no more reason to deny all procedural protection to one who will suffer a serious loss than there was in *Goss v. Lopez*, and indeed there may be good reason to provide even more protection, as discussed in Part II, *supra.* A court's characterization of the reasons for a student's dismissal adds nothing to the effort to find procedures that are fair to the student and the school, and that promote the elusive goal of determining the truth in a manner consistent with both individual dignity and society's limited resources.

IV

While I agree with the Court that respondent received adequate procedural due process, I cannot join the Court's judgment because it is based on resolution of an issue never reached by the Court of Appeals. That court, taking a properly limited view of its role in constitutional cases, refused to offer dictum on respondent's substantive due process claim when it decided the case on procedural due process grounds. . . .

I would reverse the judgment of the Court of Appeals and remand for further proceedings.

CHAPTER 11

THE CONTRACT THEORY: THE STUDENT AS CONSUMER

I. The Contract Theory Applied to Private Universities

A. *Express Contract*

STEINBERG v. CHICAGO MEDICAL SCHOOL
Appellate Court of Illinois
354 N.E.2d 586 (1976)

DEMPSEY, Justice:

In December 1973 the plaintiff, Robert Steinberg, applied for admission to the defendant, the Chicago Medical School, as a first-year student for the academic year 1974-75 and paid an application fee of $15. The Chicago Medical School is a private, not-for-profit educational institution, incorporated in the State of Illinois. His application for admission was rejected and Steinberg filed a class action against the school, claiming that it had failed to evaluate his application and those of other applicants according to the academic entrance criteria printed in the school's bulletin. Specifically, his complaint alleged that the school's decision to accept or reject a particular applicant for the first-year class was primarily based on such nonacademic considerations as the prospective student's familial relationship to members of the school's faculty and to members of its board of trustees, and the ability of the applicant or his family to pledge or make payment of large sums of money to the school. The complaint further alleged that by using such unpublished criteria to evaluate applicants the school had breached the contract, which Steinberg contended was created when the school accepted his application fee. . . .

The defendant filed a motion to dismiss, arguing that the complaint failed to state a cause of action because no contract came into existence during its transaction with Steinberg inasmuch as the school's informational publication did not constitute a valid offer. The trial court sustained the motion to dismiss and Steinberg appeals from this order.

The 1974-75 bulletin of the school, which was distributed to prospective students, represented that the following criteria would be used by the school in determining whether applicants would be accepted as first-year medical students:

"Students are selected on the basis of scholarship, character, and motivation without regard to race, creed, or sex. The student's potential for the study and practice of medicine will be evaluated on the basis of academic achievement, Medical College Admission Test results, personal appraisals by a pre-professional advisory committee or individual instructors, and the personal interview, if requested by the Committee on Admissions." . . .

A contract is an agreement between competent parties, based upon a consideration sufficient in law, to do or not do a particular thing. It is a promise or a set of promises for the breach of which the law gives a remedy, or the performance of which the law in some way recognizes as a duty. *Rynearson v. Odin-Svenson Development Corp.* (1969), 108 Ill.App.2d 125, 246 N.E.2d 823. A contract's essential requirements are: competent parties, valid subject matter, legal consideration, mutuality of obligation and mutuality of agreement. Generally, parties may contract in any situation where there is no legal prohibition, since the law acts by restraint and not by conferring rights. *Berry v. DeBruyn* (1898), 77 Ill.App. 359. However, it is basic contract law that in order for a contract to be binding the terms of the contract must be reasonably certain and definite. *Kraftco Corp. v. Koblus* (1971), 1 Ill.App.3d 635, 274 N.E.2d 153.

A contract in order to be legally binding must be based on consideration. *Wickstrom v. Vern E. Alden Co.* (1968), 99 Ill.App.2d 254, 240 N.E.2d 401. Consideration has been defined to consist of some right, interest, profit or benefit accruing to one party or some forbearance, disadvantage, detriment, loss or responsibility given, suffered or undertaken by the other. *Riddle v. La Salle National Bank* (1962), 34 Ill.App.2d 116, 180 N.E.2d 719. Money is a valuable consideration and its transfer or payment or promises to pay it or the benefit from the right to its use, will support a contract.

In forming a contract, it is required that both parties assent to the same thing in the same sense (*La Salle National Bank v. International Limited* (1970), 129 Ill.App.2d 381, 263 N.E.2d 506) and that their minds meet on the essential terms and conditions. *Richton v. Farina* (1973), 14 Ill.App.3d 697, 303 N.E.2d 218. Furthermore, the mutual consent essential to the formation of a contract, must be gathered from the language employed by the parties or manifested by their words or acts. The intention of the parties gives character to the transaction and if either party contracts in good faith he is entitled to the benefit of his contract no matter what may have been the secret purpose or intention of the other party. *Kelly v. Williams* (1911), 162 Il.App. 571.

Steinberg contends that the Chicago Medical School's informational brochure constituted an invitation to make an offer; that his subsequent application and the submission of his $15 fee to the school amounted to an offer; that the school's voluntary reception of his fee constituted an acceptance and because of these events a contract was created between the school and himself. He contends that the school was duty bound under the terms of the contract to evaluate his application according to its stated standards and that the deviation from these standards not only breached the contract, but amounted to an arbitrary selection which constituted a violation of due process and equal protection. . . .

The school counters that no contract came into being because informational brochures, such as its bulletin, do not constitute offers, but are construed by the courts to be general proposals to consider, examine and negotiate. The school points out that this doctrine has been specifically applied in Illinois to university informational publications. *People ex rel. Tinkoff v. Northwestern University* (1947), 333 Ill.App. 224, 77 N.E.2d 345. In *Tinkoff*, a rejected applicant sued to force Northwestern to admit him, claiming that the university had violated the contract that arose when he demonstrated that he had met the school's academic entrance requirements and had submitted his application and fee. His primary contention was that the school's brochure was an offer and that his completion of the acts, required by the bulletin for application, constituted his acceptance.

In rejecting this argument, the court stated:

"Plaintiffs complain Tinkoff, Jr. was denied the right to contract as guaranteed by the Illinois and United States constitutions. We need only say that he had no right to contract with the University. His right to contract for and pursue an education is limited by the right which the University has under its charter. We see no merit to plaintiff's contention that the rules and regulations were an offer of contract and his compliance therewith and acceptance giving rise to a binding contract. The wording of the bulletin required further action by the University in admitting Tinkhoff, Jr. before a contract between them would arise."

The court based its holding on the fact that Northwestern, as a private educational institution, had reserved in its State charter the right to reject any application for any reason it deemed adequate.

Although the facts of the *Tinkoff* case are similar to the present situation, we believe that the defendant's reliance upon it is misplaced. First, Steinberg is not claiming that his submission of the application and the $15 constituted an acceptance by him; he is merely maintaining that it was an offer, which required the subsequent acceptance of the school to create a contract. Also, it is obvious that his assertion that the bulletin of the school only amounted to an invitation to make an offer, is consistent with the prevailing law and the school's own position.

More importantly, Steinberg is not requesting that the school be ordered to admit him as a student, pursuant to the contract, but only that the school be prohibited from misleading prospective students by stating in its informational literature, evaluation standards that are not subsequently used in the selection of students. Furthermore, the school does not allege, nor did it demonstrate by way of its bulletin or its charter that it had reserved the right to reject any applicant for any reason. It only stated certain narrow standards by which each and every applicant was to be evaluated.

In relation to the preceding argument, the school also maintains that the $15 application fee did not amount to a legal consideration, but only constituted a pre-contracting expense. Consequently, the school argues that as a matter of law the $15 is not recoverable as damage even if a contract was eventually entered into and breached. *Chicago Coliseum Club v. Dempsey* (1932), 265 Ill.App. 542. . . .

We agree with Steinberg's position. We believe that he and the school entered into an enforceable contract; that the school's obligation under the contract was stated in the school's bulletin in a definitive manner and that by accepting his application fee—a valuable consideration—the school bound itself to fulfill its promises. Steinberg accepted the school's promises in good faith and he was entitled to have his application judged according to the school's stated criteria.

The school argues that he should not be allowed to recover because his complaint did not state a causal connection between the rejection of his application and the school's alleged use of unpublished evaluation criteria. It points out that there is an equal probability that his application was rejected for failing to meet the stated standards, and since the cause of his damages is left to conjecture they may be attributed as easily to a condition for which there is no liability as to one for which there is.

This argument focuses on the wrong point. Once again, Steinberg did not allege that he was damaged when the school rejected his application. He alleged that he was damaged when the school used evaluation criteria other than those published in the school's bulletin. This ultimate, well-pleaded allegation was admitted by the school's motion to dismiss. *Logan v. Presbyterian-St. Luke's Hospital* (1968), 92 Ill.App.2d 68, 235 N.E.2d 851. . . .

Alternatively, the school asserts that if Steinberg is entitled to recover, the recovery should be limited to $15 because he is not a proper representative of the class of applicants that was supposed to be damaged by the school's use of unpublished entrance standards. Fundamentally, it argues that it had no contract with Steinberg and since he does not have a cause of action, he cannot represent a class of people who may have similar claims. We have found, however, that he does have a cause of action. . . .

Steinberg alleged that in applying for admission to the school, each member of the class assumed that the school would use the selection factors set out in its 1974-75 bulletin, and that admission fees were paid and contracts created, but that each contract was breached in the same manner as his. This allegation established a community of interest between him and the other members of the class in terms of subject matter and remedy, and since he has a valid cause of action against the school, the class has also. He is a proper representative of the class and his suit is a proper vehicle to resolve the common factual and legal issues involved even though the members of the class suffered damage in separate transactions.

However, the class action cannot be as extensive as Steinberg's complaint requested. Recovery cannot be had by everyone who applied to the medical school during the ten years prior to the filing of his complaint. His action was predicated on standards described in the school's 1974-75 brochure; therefore, the class to be represented is restricted to those applicants who sought admission in reliance on the standards in that brochure.

We agree with the school's contention that a State through its courts does not have the authority to interfere with the power of the trustees of a private medical school to make rules concerning the admission of students. The requirement in the case of public schools, applicable because they belong to the public, that admission regulations must be reasonable is not pertinent in the case of a private school or university. 33 I.L.P. Schools, §312. We also agree that using unpublished entrance requirements would not violate an applicant's right to due process and equal protection of law. The provisions of the due process clause of the Federal constitution are inhibitions upon the power of government and not upon the freedom of action of private individuals. 16 Am.Jur.2d, Constitutional Law, sec. 557. The equal protection clause of the 14th Amendment does not prohibit the individual invasion of individual rights. *Gilmore v. City of Montgomery* (1974), 417 U.S. 556, 94 S.Ct. 2416, 41 L.Ed.2d 304. . . .

NOTES

1. The decision in *Steinberg* is unusual in that the court finds a clear contract situation. More often the relationship is said to be a quasi-contract or contractual in nature, as in Zumbrun v. University of Southern California, 101 Cal. Rptr. 499 (Ct. App. 1972), where the court stated, "The basic legal relationship between a student and a private university or college is contactual *in nature*" emphasis added), citing numerous authorities (at p. 504). This view is elaborated in University of Miami v. Militana, 184 So.2d 701, 704 (1966), where the court said:

> The operation of a private college or university is touched with eleemosynary characteristics. Even though the public has a great interest in seeing these institutions encouraged and supported, they are operated as a private business. This being true, the college may set forth the terms under which it will admit and subsequently graduate students who subject themselves to the rules, regulations and regimen of the college. It is generally accepted that the terms and conditions for graduation are those offered by the publications of the college at the time of enrollment. As such, they have some of the characteristics of a contract between the parties, and are sometimes subject to civil remedies in courts of law. . . .

See also: Militana v. University of Miami, 236 So.2d 162 (1970).

2. While some courts as in *Basch* and *Giles* in this chapter have assumed the existence of some form of contract and made decisions on questions of interpretation of contract terms, others, as in *Slaughter v. Brigham Young University, infra,* have stressed the importance of the difference between a clear commercial contract and a quasi-contractual relationship.

3. Corbin, in his treatise on contracts, states that

> The term *quasi* is introduced as a weasel word, that sucks all the meaning of the word that follows it; . . .   •

> A quasi contractual obligation is one that is created by the law for reasons of justice, without any expression of assent and sometimes even against a clear expression of dissent. . . .

> It must be admitted, or indeed asserted, that considerations of equity and morality play a large part in the process of finding a promise by inference of fact as well as in constructing a quasi contract without any such inference at all. The exact terms of the promise that is "implied" must frequently be

determined by what equity and morality appear to require after the parties have come into conflict. Corbin on Contracts (St. Paul: West Publ. Co., 1951), at 27-28.

4. The courts in *Slaughter* and other quasi-contract cases use contract law as an analogy to define and describe university-student relations. This approach allows a court to pick and choose those aspects of contract law which it feels can be applied with validity to the student-university relation, without adhering rigidly to ramifications of contract law and theory, and this would appear to be the better approach.

5. Some courts will undoubtedly still take a more direct contract approach to student cases, particularly where there is a written document such as a residency contract, or where a limited aspect of the overall student-institution relationship is involved. While no contract theory has yet alleged an obligation to teach "wisdom" as in Trustees of Columbia University v. Jacobsen, 148 A.2d 63, *appeal dismissed* in 156 A.2d 251 (1959), it is undeniable that the student consumer movement is growing. The original use of the contract theory to enforce student disciplinary rules, as in Anthony v. Syracuse University, 231 N.Y.S. 435 (1928); Carr v. St. John's University, N.Y., 187 N.E.2d 18 (Ct. App. N.Y. 1962); and Dehaan v. Brandeis University, 150 F.Supp. 626 (D. Mass. 1957) has given way to cases brought to enforce students' rights against universities. The contract theory has been the most successful legal approach by the student consumer movement which has also used theories of fraud, misrepresentation and negligence. Some of these theories may be found in Comment, *Consumer Protection and Higher Education— Student Suits Against Schools*, 37 Ohio State L.J. 608 (1976).

6. For a more general description of the issues in the student consumer movement *see* Stark & Associates, The Many Faces of Educational Consumerism (Lexington, Mass.: D.C. Heath, Inc., 1977); and for a discussion of the student as consumer in collective bargaining *see* Kahn, *The NLRB and Higher Education: The Failure of Policymaking Through Adjudication*, 21 U.C.L.A. L. Rev. 63, 74 (1973). *See also* Comment, *Educational Malpractice*, 124 U. Pa. L. Rev. 755 (1976).

B.   Quasi-Contract

SLAUGHTER v. BRIGHAM YOUNG UNIVERSITY
United States Court of Appeals
514 F.2d 622 (10th Cir. 1975)

SETH, Circuit Judge.

Brigham Young University appeals from judgment upon jury verdict awarding Hayes Slaughter $88,283.00 in damages in a diversity action based on his expulsion by the University from its graduate school. . . .

The operative facts will be described as the several issues on appeal are considered. The complaint is upon contract theory alone. The University is not a tax-supported school, but instead is owned, supported, and operated by the Church of Jesus Christ of Latter-day Saints.

Plaintiff's status as a graduate student working toward a doctorate required that he meet the academic requirements of the University, and that he abide by its rules of conduct or ethical standards. He had been in attendance for several years, and without question he was familiar with both sets of standards. The committee supervising his work and the administrative officials here concerned had the authority to determine whether plaintiff was meeting both requirements.

The incident which precipitated the review of plaintiff's performance by the University authorities was one on the conduct or ethical side rather than an academic deficiency. It arose from the assertion that plaintiff had used the name of Professor Thorne, one of his advisors, as a coauthor with plaintiff of two articles submitted to a technical journal for publication. The articles were so published without the knowledge in advance of Dr. Thorne, without his review of them nor participation in any way as an author. It was apparent that this was done by the plaintiff to improve his chances to have the articles published. Prior efforts to have the articles published in plaintiff's name alone had not been successful. The work on the material published for the most part, was done by plaintiff before coming to the University.

The question raised was whether these acts were a violation of the University rules as to conduct. The Code of Student Conduct in part required that students observe ". . . high principles of honor, integrity and morality," also that they: "Be honest in all behavior. This includes not cheating, plagiarizing, or knowingly giving false information." These regulations were reasonable, were clear, and as definite as possible in view of the subject treated. There are no First Amendment issues. . . .

The complaint was based on a contract theory and that alone, but neither the conclusory allegations of the complaint showed, nor did the proof submitted by the plaintiff establish, a contract between plaintiff and the University in the disciplinary context. The Graduate School Catalogue and the conduct-honor codes were the only evidence as to the "contract." The trial court's rigid application of commercial contract doctrine advanced by plaintiff was in error, and the submission on that theory alone was error.

It is apparent that *some* elements of the law of contracts are used and should be used in the analysis of the relationship between plaintiff and the University to provide some framework into which to put the problem of expulsion for disciplinary reasons. This does not mean that "contract law" must be rigidly applied in all its aspects, nor is it so applied even when the contract analogy is extensively adopted. There are other areas of the law which are also used by courts and writers to provide elements of such a framework. These included in times past *parens patriae*, and now include private associations such as church membership, union membership, professional societies; elements drawn from "status" theory, and others. Many sources have been used in this process, and combinations thereof, and in none is it assumed or required that all the elements of a particular doctrine be applied. The student-university relationship is unique, and it should not be and cannot be stuffed into one doctrinal category. It may also be different at different schools. There has been much published by legal writers advocating the adoption of various categories to be applied to the relationship. *See* 72 Yale L.J. 1387; 48 Indiana L.J. 253; 26 Stanford L.Rev. 95; 38 Notre Dame Lawyer 174. There are also many cases which refer to a contractual relationship existing between the student and the university, especially private schools. *See* Carr v. St. John's University, 17 A.D.2d 632, 231 N.Y.S.2d 410; University of Miami v. Militana, 184 So.2d 701 (Fla. App.); Zumbrun v. University of Southern California, 25 Cal.App.3d 1, 101 Cal.Rptr. 499; Drucker v. New York University, 59 Misc.2d 789, 300 N.Y.S. 2d 749. But again, these cases do not adopt *all* commercial contract law by their use of certain elements.

In contrast, the complete adoption of commercial contract doctrine by the trial court as to this disciplinary matter resulted in its conclusion that since the University had breached the "contract" by its dismissal of plaintiff, he was entitled to damages based on what he would have earned had he received his doctorate. This was some sort of substantial performance remedy. It assumed that plaintiff was excused from, or would have completed, his academic requirements. This was an unwarranted assumption by the court under the facts, but was necessary to support the damage theory it had adopted. The court thus erroneously instructed the jury:

"The court has also determined as a matter of law, and charges that you are obliged to follow the court's view on this matter, that by virtue of his expulsion plaintiff was excused from submission of a dissertation, from the final oral examination and from any other performance of his contractual obligations after March 14, 1972, which is the date he was expelled."

In its strict contract application, the trial court also instructed that only "substantial" compliance by plaintiff with the Student Code was required. By this "substantial" compliance standard, the jury was in effect instructed that a little dishonesty would not matter. This cannot be the measure and the court cannot so modify the Student Code. Again the blanket application of commercial contract doctrines led to such a result.

Ordinarily the remedy available in these circumstances would be reinstatement rather than damages. It is, however, apparent that damages arising from a wrongful dismissal could in the proper case be alleged and be shown without an assumption that the academic requirements were met, but these elements would be quite different from the ones here asserted, and would look more like those applied in tort actions. Under plaintiff's proof and theory, no damages could be recovered, and it was error to submit the issues to the jury.

There was no contract established at trial as alleged in his complaint, and no breach of contract by the University. There was, in short, a failure to prove the cause of action. The motion of the University for a directed verdict should have been granted.

The judgment is set aside, and the case is reversed with instructions to enter judgment for the defendant.

C.   Construction of Contract Terms

BASCH v. GEORGE WASHINGTON UNIVERSITY
District of Columbia Court of Appeals
370 A.2d 1364 (1977)

PER CURIAM:

Appellants, all students at the George Washington University School of Medicine and Health Sciences, brought this action for breach of contract individually as well as on behalf of a class of similarly affected students. Appellee moved, under Super.Ct.Civ.R. 12(b)(6), to dismiss the suit for failure to state a claim upon which relief could be granted. In an order dated November 11, 1975, the trial court treated that motion as one for summary judgment, and granted such judgment in favor of the appellee, George Washington University. This appeal followed. . . .

The dispositive facts in the case are not in dispute. Appellants represent a class of approximately 500 students attending the medical school in all four current classes. Prior to their acceptance of the University's offer to attend the medical school, each of these students received a copy of *The George Washington University Bulletin: School of Medicine and Health Sciences*. While the language of the bulletins received by each class varied somewhat, all of the parties agreed that those differences were insignificant, and that only the language in the 1974-75 bulletin need be considered for purposes of this action. That bulletin specifically set the tuition rate for the 1974-75 academic year at $3,200, but went on to state that:

> Academic year tuition increases have been estimated as follows: 1975-76, $200; 1976-77, $200, 1977-78, $200; 1978-79, $200.... Every effort will be made to keep tuition increases within these limits. However, it is not possible to project future economic data with certainty, and circumstances may require an adjustment in this estimate.

Appellants aver that their decision to attend the medical school was based, in part, in reliance on these estimates. Subsequently, on January 17, 1975, the University issued a "Statement on Tuition Rates" which provided:

> The Board of Trustees of The George Washington University has approved a tuition of $5000 per year (two semesters) for the fiscal year 1975-76 for all candidates for the degree of Doctor of Medicine in the School of Medicine and Health Sciences. This increase in tuition rate was necessitated by the anticipated impact of inflation and on the projection of a recently (mid-December) proposed decrease in the funding support provided by the District of Columbia Medical and Dental Manpower Act, a Federal Government program. The combination of the projected increase in expenses due to inflation and decrease in income totals approximately $900,000 and the increase of $1600 per student above the original approved $3400 per student will yield an amount

approximately equal to the projected gap. The operations of the School of Medicine and Health Sciences are planned to proceed on a no-growth basis; that is, there will be no increase in staffing or in other aspects of the programs of the School.

In addition, the Board of Trustees also approved a *maximum* tuition rate for the academic year 1976-1977 of $12,500 for each candidate for the degree of Doctor of Medicine. The exact amount, which will be set by the President of the University under authority granted him by the Trustees will be determined when the extent of the impact of cost increases and the antici- pated loss of funding support from such federal programs as the Medical and Dental Manpower Act and the Health Professions Capitation Grant Program are determined. Continuation of cur- rent rates of inflation combined with *total* loss of funding support from federal programs would necessitate the maximum $12,500 tuition rate for 1976-77. Both local and national efforts to pro- vide financial support to students continue; and should efforts to secure funding support to the School prove fruitful, tuition will be set at the lowest feasible figure. [Emphasis in original.]

On August 7, 1975, appellants initiated this action, arguing below that the new tuition rates were instituted in breach of their contracts with the University as evidenced by the projected increases in the University's bulletin. They are renewing this contention on appeal. . . .

Appellants' first contention on appeal is that the tuition estimates in the bulletin contractually bound the University to tuition increases of only $200 per year unless it could prove that "future economic data" warranted an adjustment in that estimate. They aver that no adequate explanation was given for the $1,800 increase they were actually charged, and urge therefore that the University breached a contractual obligation it owed to them. In light of the language of the bulletin, we find this contention to be without merit.

All of the parties in the instant case admit what is a general rule—that the relationship between a university and its students is contractual in nature. It is also accepted that the terms set down in a university's bulletin become a part of that contract. *See Zumbrun v. University of Southern California,* 25 Cal.App.3d 1, 10, 101 Cal.Rptr. 499, 504 (1972); *University of Miami v. Militana,* 184 So.2d 701, 704 (Fla. Dist.Ct.App.1966); *Auser v. Cornell University,* 71 Misc.2d 1084, 1088, 337 N.Y.S.2d 878, 882 (Sup.Ct.1972). However, the mere fact that the bulletin contained language regarding projected tuition increases is not enough to support a finding that the language amounted to a contractual obligation. University bulletins customarily contain a great deal of information concerning what the pro- spective student may expect when he or she enters the university community. Whether a given section of the bulletin also becomes part of the contractual obligations between the students and the university, then, must depend upon general principles of contract construction.

In construing the terms of a contract, the document itself must be viewed as a whole. It has been noted that:

> In ascertaining intent, we consider not only the language used in the contract but also the circumstances surrounding the making of the contract, the motives of the parties and the purposes which they sought to accomplish. . . . [*Connecticut Co. v. Division 425, Amalgamated Street, Electric Ry. & Motor Coach Employees*, 147 Conn. 608, 616, 164 A.2d 413, 417 (1960).]

See also Gellatly Construction Co. v. City of Bridgeport, 149 Conn. 588, 593, 182 A.2d 625, 627-28 (1962). Furthermore, the terms of the document are to be given their common meaning. *National Symphony Orchestra Ass'n v. Konevsky*, D.C.Mun.App., 44 A.2d 694, 695 (1945); *see Mascaro v. Snelling & Snelling of Baltimore, Inc.*, 250 Md. 215, 229, 243 A.2d 1, 9, *cert. denied*, 393 U.S. 981, 89 S.Ct. 451, 21 L.Ed.2d 442 (1968); *J. E. Hathman, Inc. v. Sigma Alpha Epsilon Club*, 491 S.W.2d 261, 264 (Mo.1973) (en banc). In arriving at that meaning, the court should view the language of the document as would a reasonable person in the position of the parties. . . .

Appellants contend in their brief that, taken individually, the words "estimated," "approximate," and "projected," found in the tuition paragraph in the bulletin, do not render the paragraph too illusory to be construed as laying down a contractual obligation on the part of the University. We do not find this approach to be persuasive. While it is true that any of those words, standing alone and in a different context, might not make a statement too indefinite to be enforced as a contractual obligation, it has been well noted that:

> Words . . . do not always have the same import, and frequently nuances of meaning are sharply revealed by their association with other words, for . . . they are known by the company they keep.
> . . . [*Smedley Co. v. Employers Mutual Liability Insurance Co.*, 143 Conn. 510, 515, 123 A.2d 755, 758 (1956).]

See also Gellatly Construction Co. v. City of Bridgeport, supra; Bertrand v. Jones, 58 N.J.Super. 273, 283, 156 A.2d 161, 167 (1959); *Northway Village No. 3, Inc. v. Northway Properties, Inc.*, 430 Pa. 499, 505-06, 244 A.2d 47, 50 (1968). Viewing the pertinent language as a whole, in the context of a university bulletin, we cannot conclude that a reasonable person would have assumed that the University intended to bind itself by the construction appellants urge on us. The Restatement of Contracts §32 (1932), provides:

> An offer must be so definite in its terms, or require such definite terms in the acceptance, that the promises and performances to be rendered by each party are reasonably certain.

Rather than being definite, the pertinent words from the bulletin, particularly when viewed in combination with each other, are the types of words that preclude accuracy by their very nature. *White v. United States*, 38 App.D.C. 131, 137 (1912); *see Indiana Gas & Water Co. v. Williams*, 132

Ind.App. 8, 175 N.E.2d 31, 33 (1961); *J. E. Hathman, Inc., v. Sigma Alpha Epsilon Club, supra* at 266. At best, these words expressed an expectancy by the University regarding future increases. This is not a promise susceptible of enforcement.

> It is well established that mere expectancy of a continued course of conduct is not enough, even in situations where the disappointment of expectations results in a heavy financial loss. . . . [*Tauber v. Jacobson*, D.C.App., 293 A.2d 861, 867 (1972).]

Our finding of no contractual obligation is supported by holdings in other cases that have dealt with the construction of broad language in university bulletins. In *Mahavongsanan v. Hall*, 529 F.2d 448 (5th Cir. 1976), *reversing* 401 F.Supp. 381 (N.D.Ga. 1975), the circuit court found that Georgia State University had not contractually bound itself to maintain the same graduation requirements set out in its bulletin. The district court had observed that:

> The only requirement for plaintiff's degree in effect at the time that plaintiff enrolled was the completion of a prescribed course of study of not less than 60 graduate hours . . . with at least a "B" average. . . . [401 F.Supp. at 382.]

The bulletin there also provided that "[a]dditional regulations pertaining to standards of performance may be prescribed by the respective schools." *Id.* at 383. The circuit court, in reversing the district court's holding that the university was precluded from instituting an additional requirement of comprehensive examinations, stated:

> The appellee's claim of a binding, absolute unchangeable contract is particularly anomalous in the context of . . . post graduate level work. [529 F.2d at 450.]

See also Greene v. Howard University, 271 F.Supp. 609 (D.D.C.1967); *University of Miami v. Militana, supra; Southern Methodist University v. Evans*, 131 Tex. 333, 115 S.W.2d 622 (Tex.Comm'n of App.1938). While none of these cases deal with tuition increases, they are still analogous to the instant case. To require appellee by law to operate at a financial loss would, given the finite nature of budgeting, have a direct effect on the quality of education the University could provide to the appellants. It has been noted that while

> [t]he operation of a private college or university is touched with eleemosynary characteristics . . . they are [still] operated as a private business. [*University of Miami v. Militana, supra* at 704.] . . .

GILES v. HOWARD UNIVERSITY
United States District Court, District of Columbia
428 F.Supp. 603 (1977)

JOHN H. PRATT, District Judge. . . .
The undisputed facts are as follows:
During the 1973-1974 and 1974-1975 academic years, the Howard University College of Medicine had in effect a "Student Promotions Policy" which provided, *inter alia:*

II. No student having a failure or incomplete grade in any fresh-man . . . course will be promoted to the next class.

III. A student who fails in an anatomy, biochemistry, micro-biology, pharmacology and/or physiology course will be given a passing grade if he obtains a standard score of 380 or more in that subject in a "special" National Board Examination or regu-lar National Board Examination.

IV. A student who has failing grades in one or two courses which terminate at the end of the first semester will be given an oppor-tunity to participate fully in second semester work and to attend the Directed Study Program. Such student, however, should understand the implications of failing any additional course. . . .

.   .   .   .   .

VIII. If the student fails to remove the one deficiency or two deficiencies at the end of the Directed Study Program he will be dropped from the College of Medicine or may be allowed to re-peat the year (as determined by the Promotions Committee). . . .
If allowed to repeat the year, the Promotions Committee may also require such student to audit any course, including a course already passed to enable him to maintain his fund of basic science knowledge.

Plaintiff enrolled in the Howard University College of Medicine in August 1973. He passed all his first semester classes except biochemistry, which he failed. The College permitted him to participate fully in the second semester program, however, provided he agreed to retake biochemistry in the Directed Study Program during the summer of 1974. He passed all his second semester courses but failed biochemistry in the Directed Study Pro-gram during the summer. Plaintiff then received a letter from the Dean of the Medical College, Marion Mann, M.D., informing him that he would be allowed to continue as a medical student if he repeated biochemistry and retook and obtained satisfactory grades in the other courses in his curri-culum that he had already passed. Dean Mann's letter also stated:

Section IV of the Student Promotions Policy is applicable only to students who begin the academic year in good academic stand-ing. The Committee hereby informs you that you are not in good academic standing but are on probation; and that if you fail *any* course during the first semester, you will be dropped from the College of Medicine.

Plaintiff repeated the courses and passed biochemistry, but failed anatomy. On March 7, 1975, he was dropped from the College of Medicine. He there-upon requested readmission. By letter of July 7, 1975, Dean Mann informed the plaintiff that his request for readmission had been considered and that the committee considering the request would be reconvened if the plaintiff passed special National Board Examinations in anatomy, biochemistry, micro-biology, and physiology. The plaintiff took these examinations and failed all four. No further action was taken on his request for readmission. . . .

With respect to his breach of contract claim, the plaintiff alleges that the Medical College's "Student Promotions Policy" constitutes a contract between him and the University which the University breached. Specifically, he alleges that the University breached the contract by imposing conditions upon him that were not provided for in the Student Promotions Policy after he had twice failed biochemistry. The promotions policy makes it clear that the University had the option of dismissing plaintiff at this juncture. It is also clear that the University could have required the plaintiff to repeat his first year and to audit any course. The policy is silent as to what other options the University may have had.

Assuming the Student Promotions Policy constituted a contract between plaintiff and the University, the task before the Court is to interpret the contract to determine the intent of the parties. Contract interpretation is a function of the court where, as here, no extrinsic evidence is necessary to determine an agreement's meaning and/or the meaning is so clear that reasonable men could reach only one conclusion. J. Calamari & J. Perillo, Contracts §49 (1970). Since it is apparent that this is not an integrated agreement, the standard is that of reasonable expectation—what meaning the party making the manifestation, the University, should reasonably expect the other party to give it. Id. §47, at 90.

Under the contract, the University reserved to itself the right to dismiss a student who failed a class and did not succeed in removing the deficiency through the Directed Study Program. It seems apparent, therefore, that it also reserved the right to require such a student to comply with any reasonable condition to retain his student status. Plaintiff would have us apply the canon "expressio unius est exclusio alterius" to the agreement and hold that by stating it could require a retained student to audit any course, the University thereby relinquished its right to impose any other condition upon continued enrollment. This result is patently unreasonable. It would tie the hands of University officials trying to assist marginal students and maintain academic standards.

After reading the Student Promotions Policy, the reasonable expectation of any student is that if he fails a course and does not make up the deficiency in the Directed Study Program, he can be dismissed or can be retained upon compliance with any reasonable condition. This is the interpretation the Court gives the Student Promotions Policy. It does not render meaningless the "audit any course" language. That language applies to both freshman and sophomore students. When read in light of the Court's interpretation, it means that when allowed to repeat a year a sophomore may be required to audit freshman classes or a freshman may be required to audit other classes.

Under this interpretation, the plaintiff has failed to adduce any evidence of a violated contract right. He has also failed to present any facts to show improper motivation or irrational action on the part of the University or any of its officials. On the contrary, all the evidence indicates the University went out of its way to help the plaintiff remain in medical school without compromising its academic standards. It gave him at least three "second chances." Under these circumstances, the facts necessary to sustain an actionable claim have not been shown. *Williams v. Howard Univ.*, 174 U.S.App.D.C. 85, 528 F.2d 658, *cert. denied*, 429 U.S. 850, 97 S.Ct. 138, 50 L.Ed.2d 123 (1976). The defendants' motion for summary judgment on the common law claim will therefore be granted.

   An Order consistent with this Memorandum Opinion has been entered today.

NOTES

   The Chancery Court of Nashville, Tennessee, recently handed down a decision awarding damages to doctoral students in a graduate management program at Vanderbilt University, because the Ph.D. program had disintegrated to the point where the university was not fulfilling its obligations to the students. Lowenthal v. Vanderbilt, Chancery Court, Davidson County, Tennessee, No. A8525, August 15, 1977. Although the opinion is unreported, and was not appealed, it contains several rulings which are of general interest as indicative of future directions of the application of contract theory, especially in the student as consumer movement:

   1. *The nature of the student-university relationship.* Several different theories have been posited to describe the legal nature of the relationship between the student and the university. Most of the "student-consumer" cases adopt a contractual approach, using the college catalogue as the basic contract document. The Vanderbilt case continues this approach, adding the following refinements: The Court finds that the basic relationship is contractual, or in the nature of a contract, and finds that the court has the duty, power and responsibility to enforce such contracts. This finding by the court allows the court to delve into academic standards, at least as regards students, in some detail. Thus, even though the court recognizes and follows the doctrine of academic abstention, whereby the courts abstain from interference in internal university affairs, the enforcement of a contract concept leads to anything but abstention in this case.

   a. What constitutes the contract? If the court finds a contractual relationship between university and student, it is important to determine which documents or oral representation constitute the "contract" in order to determine which terms will be enforced. In other words, how does a court determine which documents or other promises constitute the terms of the university's obligation to students? In *Vanderbilt*, the court refers to (1) the school's catalogue, (2) the guidelines for doctoral study and (3) oral representation by the faculty, and finds that "Even the written documents which helped compose the contract were not followed by the GSM faculty". (Slip op. at 17).

   b. The terms of the contract. In *Vanderbilt*, the court, after finding a "contractual relationship," goes on to discuss the relative power of the university as contrasted with the student and concludes that the university has "an enormous responsibility and corresponding duty . . . to exercise the power fairly, consistently, and without arbitrariness and prejudice." In determining Vanderbilt's responsibilities to the students in this particular situation, the court states that, once it has made a promise to do so, a university has a duty (1) to provide a high quality of academic training, (2) leading to an academically respectable doctoral degree, (3) which may be earned by the satisfaction of reasonable and consistent standards and procedures, and must (4) provide the faculty and financial resources necessary to accomplish this end. . . .

2. *Responsibility of the administration.* In the Vanderbilt case the court mentioned two activities of the administration which caused the university to be legally responsible for the failure of the graduate management program. (As in many opinions, the court never clearly defines what "the university" is for the purposes of the court's decision. Here it probably refers to the central, campus-wide administrative officers, but that is not entirely clear. One of the questions left open by this case is, which administrative officers act on behalf of the university in the sense that they obligate the university when they receive information.)

a. Initial funding. The court, in passing, stated that one of the reasons for the failure of the graduate management program at Vanderbilt was the failure of the administration to give adequate initial funding to the program to allow it to succeed. If this standard is adopted more widely, administrators authorizing new programs may have to evaluate carefully the resources available and the chances of success of the program, particularly where, as in the Vanderbilt case, the program is new, innovative and flexible in its design. A failure to make available adequate funds at the beginning may mean an ultimate responsibility if the program falters and the students enrolled in it fail.

b. Actual knowledge of the disintegration of the program. The court put particular emphasis and discussion on the fact that the central administration knew that the doctoral program in the school of graduate management was faltering. The court implies, without discussing in detail, that the central administration had the responsibility and the capacity to ameliorate the situation more quickly than it did. The court points to the fact that the Executive Vice President of the university was on the business school faculty and attended at least two meetings at which the state of the doctoral program was made clear. Therefore, the court concludes, the administration had actual knowledge of the situation and consequently an immediate duty to take steps, which it failed to do. The court also criticizes the administration's "positive statement" response to the trouble when it finally reached the Presidential level, stating that "Had decisive action been taken when the administration first learned of the GSM chaos, surely the doctoral program could have been saved." (Slip op. at 36).

In *Vanderbilt*, the administration intervened to determine whether the program faculty had improperly changed the program requirements in the middle of the program. It was the conclusion of the graduate school dean who investigated that generally graduate students could rely on program requirements at the time they enrolled and it was considered bad practice to change the requirements substantially after enrollment. This conclusion evidently was based on an assessment of custom and practice in higher education, but runs contrary to the Fifth Circuit's Conclusions in Mahavongsanan v. Hall, 529 F.2d 448, *reh den.* 531 F.2d 575 (1976). While the court felt that this was an important point, the finding of liability is based on the disintegration of the program of which the change in requirements was partial evidence, not on the change in requirements itself.

3. *Interference in academic decision-making.* While the court in *Vanderbilt* takes notice of the doctrine of academic abstention and adheres to it, it must be strongly pointed out that the court does in fact delve deeply into the details of the academic program, its management and the requirements for progress and completion. All of this is by way of interpreting whether the university had violated its "contractual" obligation. *Vanderbilt* makes it clear that the courts can use the contractual theory to make a detailed, and in this case embarrassingly candid, analysis of faculty behavior, and university administration. In this case, the reluctance of the courts to interfere in academic decision-making was not even limited to non-interference in academic assessment of students. In *Vanderbilt*, the court assessed the initial requirements for the doctoral program, the background and work done by each student, the advising relationship, the methodology for revising the program, the number of pages of written work done by each graduate student, the propriety or impropriety of the faculty meetings and their effectiveness in

the graduate school of management as far as this particular program went and many other matters which ordinarily might be considered to be outside the competence of the courts to assess. Thus, it is important to keep in mind the contractual theory in regard to relations between the university and its students. The court recognized that, "There is an important distinction between suits which seek review of university determinations of academic qualifications and suits which charge that the institution had breached its contract with students. The distinction is crucial. . . ." (Slip op. at 13). The "distinction" appears to mean that a contract theory can justify judicial evaluation of academic qualifications of students and the conduct of professors in some circumstances.

4. *Measure of damages.* After finding the university liable, the court considered the following measures of damage:

a. Tuition. Students who paid their own tuition (some were on foundation funds) were entitled to a full refund together with any interest they had paid on loans to finance their stay.

b. Books. No recovery since books are still of value to the students.

c. Duplicating and clerical costs. Recovery allowed where specific evidence presented (about $2,100 for all students).

d. Travel expenses. No recovery.

e. Loss of earnings. Although the court notes that there may be future such awards in university breach of contract cases as the courts recognize the income value of education, no losses of earnings were proved in this case.

The court's concluding paragraphs are instructive:

> Vanderbilt University enjoys a tradition and reputation for excellence and quality in higher education. In a sharp departure from that tradition, Vanderbilt hastily embarked upon a vague and ill-defined doctoral studies program when it knew or should have known that it did not have the resources to operate the program. Vanderbilt received something of value from these plaintiffs and gave little or nothing in return. The university must bear the responsibility for its conduct.
>
> Vanderbilt has argued that a finding that it breached its contract with the students will have dire consequences for it and higher education generally. To the contrary, should this court ignore the obvious failure of Vanderbilt to live up to its contractual obligations to these students, it would be a signal to Vanderbilt and other institutions that they are immune from the same legal principles which govern other relationships in our society. While the university-student relationship is indeed unique, it does not vest a university with unlimited power to do or not to do as it pleases without facing the consequences. *Lowenthal v. Vanderbilt,* Chancery Court, Davidson County, Tennessee, No. A-8525, August 15, 1977.

II.   The Contract Theory Applied to Public Universities

A.   No Unchangeable Contract

MAHAVONGSANAN v. HALL
Fifth Circuit Court of Appeals
529 F.2d 448 (1976)

DYER, Circuit Judge:

Srisuda Mahavongsanan sued the Dean of the School of Education of Georgia State University, various professors, and the University's Board of Regents, asserting a deprivation of her civil rights for their arbitrary and capricious refusal to award her a master's degree in education. She claimed denial of procedural and substantive due process, and breach of contract.

The district court permanently enjoined the defendants from withholding the degree plaintiff sought. We reverse. . . .

Subsequent to the judgment of the lower court, appellants awarded appellee the degree for which she had matriculated, notwithstanding their academic determination that appellant had not met the university's qualifications for the degree. Appellees now point to this *fait accompli* in light of *Defunis v. Odegaard*, 1974, 416 U.S. 312, 94 S.Ct. 1704, 40 L.Ed.2d 164, as compelling dismissal of the instant case as moot. Appellants respond that unlike *Defunis,* their academic integrity continues to be jeopardized in the existence of the court-ordered grant of a diploma because the diploma constitutes public endorsement of competence and achievement which was unmerited.

We agree with appellants that this case is not moot. . . . Appellants have made clear that, if granted relief, they will revoke the degree unwillingly awarded appellee. Moreover, the appellants have a further interest, to eliminate an ongoing stigma of erosion of their academic certification process. The case is not moot. . . .

Appellee finally contends that the university breached its contract with her. We find this to be without merit because of the wide latitude and discretion afforded by the courts to educational institutions in framing their academic degree requirements. *Militana, supra.* Implicit in the student's contract with the university upon matriculation is the student's agreement to comply with the university's rules and regulations, which the university clearly is entitled to modify so as to properly exercise its educational responsibility. *See, Foley v. Benedict,* 1932, 122 Tex. 193, 55 S.W. 2d 805, 810. The appellee's claim of a binding, absolute unchangeable contract is particularly anomalous in the context of training professional teachers in post graduate level work.

Reversed.

NOTE

In Healy v. Larsson, 323 N.Y.S.2d 625, *aff'd* 348 N.Y.S.2d 971, *aff'd* 318 N.E.2d 608 (1974), a New York Court noted that "there is no reason why . . . the *Carr* (contract) principle should not apply to a public university or community college" and awarded a degree to a community college student who claimed that a guidance counselor had misled him as to degree requirements. The granting of a degree (M.D.) was also mandated by the court in DeMarco v. University of Health Sciences, 352 N.E.2d 356 (Ill. App. 1976) where the court found that the catalogue constituted a contract between the students and the institution. *See* further Elaine H. El-Khawas, John C. Hoy, Alfred L. Moye, *The Student Consumer Movement,* 58 Education Record 169 (1977).

B.   Implied Promise by University

BEHREND v. STATE
Court of Appeals of Ohio
379 N.E.2d 617 (1978)

HOLMES, Judge.

This matter involves the appeal of a judgment of the Court of Claims of Ohio. The facts which gave rise to this action, and to this appeal, are as follows:

The appellants in this case are former students of the Ohio University School of Architecture in Athens, Ohio, who attended the university for the purpose of receiving an accredited degree in architecture. However, in April of 1969, the School of Architecture lost its accreditation. Subsequent action was taken to get the school reaccredited, which included hiring a new director, improving the physical plant, and increasing the size of the faculty.

The appellants were repeatedly assured by members of the university's faculty and administrative personnel that if they attended the school and worked extremely hard they could obtain an accredited degree in architecture. According to the evidence, it would appear that on the strength of these assurances, the appellants attended and worked diligently, not only on their own projects, but in rehabilitating the physical plant.

In October of 1973, an accrediting committee of the National Architectural Accrediting Board (NAAB), known as the "Botsai Committee," visited Ohio University for the purpose of evaluating the School of Architecture for possible reaccreditation. At that time, the president of the university and members of the faculty made commitments to the "Botsai Committee" that the School of Architecture would continue to work toward accreditation, and would meet all of the prerequisites to receiving accreditation for the School of Architecture. Thereafter, the "Botsai Committee" informed the university that they would recommend a two-year accreditation to the NAAB board of directors. The evidence tends to show that it was the general feeling of all concerned that once the committee made a recommendation of this nature, it was virtually assured of being accepted by the full board, and accreditation granted.

Later, however, based on a significant decrease in student enrollment and rather severe budget constraints, a review of the budget for the College of Fine Arts and how such funds were to be allocated among the various schools within the college, including the School of Architecture, was made by the dean of the college and the budget and curriculum committees of the college. The fine arts and curriculum committees voted in 1974 to phase out the School of Architecture. The president of the university approved the recommendation to phase out the School of Architecture.

The "Botsai Committee," upon learning of the university's plans to abolish the school, withdrew its initial recommendation to accredit *in toto*. The board of trustees of the university met in May of 1974, and voted unanimously to phase out the School of Architecture. After this resolution by the trustees, the school continued to function until all presently enrolled students could graduate if they so desired.

The determination of the major issues presented in this case as set forth in assignment of error number two is, in the main, based upon the relationship which existed between Ohio University and these students. Generally it may be stated that when a student enrolls in a college or university, pays his or her tuition and fees, and attends such school, the resulting relationship may reasonably be construed as being contractual in nature.

The specific nature of the contractual relationship may well vary with the specific situation presented. However, it may be said that where one enrolls in a college or university in order to obtain instruction in a given professional discipline, he or she does so with the reasonable thought that such college or university has been accredited by the appropriate accrediting agency.

It is not unreasonable for one matriculating to an institution of higher learning, which offers course materials and degrees in a certain professional field, to assume that the credits for courses taken at such institution, and any degree thereafter that might be granted, would qualify the student or the graduate for the appropriate professional examination.

Such is the situation presented here where Ohio University offered courses in architecture which looked to a degree in such professional discipline. Although the college had lost its accreditation in 1969, the staff of the college, as well as the dean, continued to convey the thought to these student plaintiffs that every effort would be made to again be accredited. In fact, the record will show that repeated statements were made by the staff and administration of the School of Architecture that there was no great problem in again being accredited.

Our holding that there was an implied contract by Ohio University with these student plaintiffs that the latter be provided accredited academic training is not saying that the board of trustees was powerless to discontinue certain educational school and departments pursuant to the determination of the board. The board of trustees has the jurisdiction to make the policy determination of the continued existence of the various departments within the university.

However, where a determination is made affecting those with whom the university had contracted, unless there is shown to be an impossibility of performance, the contract must be fulfilled, or damages awarded. Here, instead of showing an impossibility of performance, Ohio University proved that the College of Fine Arts, and then the board of trustees of the university, made a selection of academic goals and that the other departments in the College of Fine Arts were chosen to continue rather than the School of Architecture.

The holding here goes to the issue of whether a student may claim damages when the course materials he or she has taken, and hours of credit toward a degree, either are not acceptable to another school upon transfer, because of the lack of accreditation, or when the student has graduated but may not take the professional exam without further work and delay, or when the student has been delayed in the process of his transferring to another college or university offering an accredited course in architecture.

The damages to these students will necessarily vary dependent upon whether or not they were able to transfer credits and, if not, the additional time and expense of taking other courses. Also, there will have to be proof of any pecuniary loss due to delay of those in transferring to other schools, and proof of loss of delay in being able to take the appropriate state professional exams. All of such must be proven by the individual claimant based upon the facts of his or her given case. . . .

Based on all of the foregoing, the judgment of the Court of Claims is hereby reversed, and this matter is remanded to such court for further proceedings according to this decision and pursuant to law.

Judgment reversed.

WHITESIDE and REILLY, J. J., concur.

CHAPTER 12

MISCELLANEOUS ISSUES CONCERNING STUDENT RIGHTS

I. Domicile of Married Women

SAMUEL v. UNIVERSITY OF PITTSBURGH
United States District Court W.D. Pennsylvania
375 F.Supp. 1119 (1974)

TEITELBAUM, District Judge.

This is a class action brought by the named plaintiffs against the University of Pittsburgh, Pennsylvania State University and Temple University (hereinafter referred to as Pitt, Penn State and Temple, respectively), certain named officers of those universities, and the Governor, Attorney General and Auditor General of the Commonwealth of Pennsylvania. By Opinion and Order of this Court dated August 21, 1972 (56 F.R.D. 435), the plaintiffs were determined to represent all married female students who since 1967 have attended any of the three defendant universities and who were classified as out-of-state students for tuition purposes on the basis of Rule B(2) of the Auditor General of Pennsylvania. The plaintiffs seek to have this Court declare Rule B(2) unconstitutional and to enjoin the defendants from administering any residency policy based upon Rule B(2) or its equivalent. In addition, the plaintiffs claim that they are entitled to restitution for those amounts paid in excess of the in-state tuition rate. . . .

Since the determination of a student's domicile necessarily involves a factual determination of the student's intent to remain in a given place for an indefinite period, difficult problems are presented for the university. Since a person's future plans are often uncertain during the time he is attending college, and since at the same time, the student is often well-aware of the financial benefit he gains by giving information weighted to his advantage, the university is faced with serious administrative difficulties in making thousands of residency determinations in a given school year. Certainly, a state should not be discouraged from seeking excellence in its educational facilities or sustain injury from approaching it.

Rule B(2), in effect from June 1967 until February 1972, provided that the domicile of a wife *was* that of her husband. Rule B-3, in effect from July 1972 until April 1973, provided that a married woman's residence *was prima facie* that of her husband. Rule A(3), in effect from April 1973 until the present, states that a married woman *is presumed* to have the domicile of her husband and sets out the nine factors which will be considered in rebuttal of that presumption: (1) a lease or evidence of permanent residence, and/or (2) payment of state and local taxes, and/or (3) transfer of bank accounts, stock registration, etc. to Pennsylvania and/or

(4) an agreement for full-time, post-graduation employment in Pennsylvania, and/or (5) a Pennsylvania driver's license, and/or (6) membership in Pennsylvania social, athletic, civic, political or religious organizations, and/or (7) registration to vote in Pennsylvania, and/or (8) a statement of intention to reside indefinitely in Pennsylvania, and/or (9) considerations of demeanor. No single factor of the nine is conclusive in making the determination of residency and that is as it should be, for, as noted above, the task of making residency determinations is an especially difficult one which is properly left in the discretion of the appropriate university officials.

But, the singularly striking aspect of the application of residency rules at the defendant universities is the fact that no rule, rebuttable or irrebuttable, has ever existed to tie the residency classification of any group other than married women to the classification of someone else. Married men, single men and single women must indeed submit residency classification information to the registrars of their respective universities, but in their case no formal or informal rule has ever existed to tie their classification to that of another group, be it wives, parents, roommates or whomever. During the period in question, the policy of the three defendant universities, following the guidelines of the defendant state officials, has been to presume that a woman married to an out-of-state resident is herself an out-of-state resident, while a man married to an out-of-state resident was not presumed to be an out-of-state resident.

Defendants propose three justifications for imposing the presumptions outlined above upon married female students:

(1) Defendants' interest in preserving their fiscal integrity by providing a state-subsidized education only to residents of the Commonwealth.

(2) The validity in actual fact of the common law presumption that a woman has the domicile of her husband.

(3) The administrative convenience of operating under such a presumption.

The defendants' justifications stand essentially unchallenged. As to (1), Vlandis v. Kline, *supra*, has conclusively established that a non-private university has the qualified right to differentiate between resident and non-resident students for tuition purposes. As to (2), statistical summaries presented in evidence before this Court indicate that in 1972, 96.5% of all married women in the United States lived with their husbands. The third justification, that of administrative convenience, is of course not to be denigrated, but like the other two it is clearly superseded in importance by the constitutional right of all individuals to equal treatment before the law.

In Shapiro v. Thompson, 394 U.S. 618, 89 S.Ct. 1322, 22 L.Ed.2d 600 (1969), the states of Pennsylvania and Connecticut sought to justify their denial of welfare payments to persons with less than one year's state residency on grounds of administrative convenience, buttressed by appeals to the importance of protecting state fiscal integrity from welfare cheats and transient indigents. The justifications in *Shapiro,* though found to be valid, did not withstand constitutional scrutiny. The welfare residency restrictions were struck down as violative of equal protection.

The traditional scholarly analysis of the equal protection decisions of the Supreme Court dictates a three-tier approach to the problem. Where a legislative classification entails only economic or financial repercussions, as in a statutory differentiation between similar businesses for purposes of regulation, the lenient "rational relationship" test is imposed. E. g., Morey v. Doud, 354 U.S. 457, 77 S.Ct. 1344, 1 L.Ed.2d 1485 (1957). For the classification to pass constitutional muster, it need only be demonstrated there exists a rational relationship between the means used and the end sought to be fostered. But where "fundamental rights" are involved or where "suspect criteria" are utilized in making the classification, more stringent standards are applied and accordingly it becomes more likely that the differentiation under examination will be found to be violative of equal protection guarantees.

Where a "fundamental right" is involved, the state must demonstrate a "compelling governmental interest" to justify making the differentiation, or the differentiation will fall. Shapiro v. Thompson, *supra*, wherein the right to interstate travel was deemed to be "fundamental", was the last case in which the Supreme Court expressly applied the compelling governmental interest test. Previously, the Court had held the right to procreation (Skinner v. Oklahoma, 316 U.S. 535, 62 S.Ct. 1110, 86 L.Ed. 1655, 1942), the right to bail (Stack v. Boyle, 342 U.S. 1, 72 S.Ct. 1, 96 L.Ed. 3, 1951), and the right to vote (Williams v. Rhodes, 393 U.S. 23, 89 S.Ct. 5, 21 L. Ed.2d 24, 1968) to be "fundamental rights".

Where a "suspect criterion" is involved, the legislative differentiation is constitutionally permissible only if it can pass the test of "rigid judicial scrutiny". Needless to say, few if any classifications involving suspect criteria have been found to be constitutionally permissible. As of yet, only race (McLaughlin v. Florida, 379 U.S. 184, 85 S.Ct. 283, 13 L.Ed.2d 222 1964) and national origin (Korematsu v. United States, 323 U.S. 214, 65 S.Ct. 193, 89 L.Ed. 194, 1944) may unequivocally be said to be suspect criteria.

Plaintiffs in this case urge the Court to hold that sex is a suspect criterion and cite Frontiero v. Richardson, 411 U.S. 677, 93 S.Ct. 1764, 36 L.Ed.2d 583 (1973) as support for the proposition that sex is, or should be, termed a suspect criterion by this Court. In *Frontiero*, the Supreme Court reversed a lower court decision which had upheld a federal statute mandating different treatment for female armed forces members than was accorded to males. Four justices based their decision on an express finding that sex is a suspect classification. But three other justices, while concurring in the result reached, refused to so hold. A fourth concurred on the basis of the due process clause of the Fifth Amendment. There was no majority opinion holding sex to be a suspect criterion.

Since the three-tier approach to equal protection questions outlined above is, or should be, merely an analytical device designed to simplify complex equal protection questions into their basic elements, it is not mandatory for a district court to apply its terminology. I will not do so here and I will not hold sex to be a suspect criterion. It must be recognized that judicial adherence to the semantic framework of the three-tier approach inevitably entails far-reaching consequences. Once a "fundamental right" has been designated as such, or a "suspect criterion" judicially established, then, in the minds of the legal community, the burden of justification has irrevocably shifted to the defense in any circumstance, no matter how benign, wherein the "suspect" group or the "fundamental right" is affected in an allegedly discriminatory manner. The policy implications, to thoughtful practitioners and commentators, of the simple act of labeling sex as a suspect classification are profound.

Perhaps in an attempt to avoid the disproportionately significant impact of using the old semantic framework, at least one commentator has discerned a shift among Supreme Court justices away from the traditional three-tiered approach and toward a unitary equal protection standard. In Gunther, The Supreme Court—Foreword, 86 Harv. L. Rev. 1, 18-20 (1972), it is noted that:

> "[T]he Court has apparently narrowed the linguistic gap between the two standards; it has avoided the terminology of the two-tiered review in some cases by posing instead certain fundamental inquiries applicable to 'all' equal protection claims. Thus, in Weber v. Aetna Casualty & Surety Co., 406 U.S. 164 [92 S.Ct. 1400, 31 L.Ed.2d 768] (1972), . . . the Court stated, 406 U.S. at 173 [92 S.Ct.1400], that the 'essential' inquiry in all equal protection cases is inevitably a dual one. What legitimate state interest does the classification promote? What fundamental personal rights might the classification endanger?"

It is this unitary approach to equal protection questions extracted from Supreme Court decisions which the Court will follow in this case. This approach might well be termed a rigorous rational basis test, so as to distinguish it from the traditional rational basis test, whose application invariably ended with the classification being found non-violative of equal protection. See, e.g., Morey v. Doud, *supra.*

This Court's inquiry in this case has been whether there is a rational governmental interest furthered by the residency rules of the defendants. This Court finds that there is—the dual interest of administrative convenience and preservation of fiscal integrity. But the inquiry does not end with an answer to the first question. It has then been asked whether certain fundamental personal rights, in the non-conclusory sense that that phrase is used in Weber v. Aetna Casualty and Surety Co., have been infringed. Operating upon a special sensitivity to sex as a classifying factor, this Court finds that the residency rules promulgated and administered by the defendants in this case have resulted in the denial of equal protection to plaintiff class members. . . .

II.   Dormitory Residency

PROSTROLLO v. UNIVERSITY OF SOUTH DAKOTA
Eighth Circuit Court of Appeals
507 F.2d 775 (1974)
cert. denied, 95 S.Ct. 1687 (1975)

LAY, Circuit Judge. . . .

The named plaintiffs, Gail Prostrollo and Lynn Severson, are students at the University of South Dakota. They brought this suit on behalf of themselves and other students similarly situated to challenge a regulation which requires all single freshman and sophomore students to live in University residence halls. They contend that enforcement of this rule encroaches upon their right of privacy and denies them equal protection of the laws. The district court found that the *primary* purpose of the regulation was to ensure housing income sufficient to pay off the revenue bonds which had been issued to finance the construction of the dormitories. It concluded that the regulation was unconstitutional, since it established an arbitrary and unreasonable classification which had no rational relationship to this purpose and therefore denied petitioners equal protection of the laws. Prostrollo v. University of South Dakota, 369 F.Supp. 778 (D.S.D.1974). We find the regulation constitutional and reverse and remand the case with directions to enter judgment for the defendants.

The challenged regulation provides:

All single freshman and sophomore students are required to live in university residence halls. Exceptions to this policy must be approved by the Director of Resident Services prior to the beginning of the semester.

School officials offered several justifications for this parietal rule. Dr. Richard L. Bowen, the University president, said that the rule had at least two purposes. First, he stated, it was intended to provide a standard level of occupancy to ensure repayment of the government bonds which provided capital for the dormitory construction. Second, he said, it was meant to ensure that younger students who must of necessity live away from home while attending the University would avail themselves of the learning experience in self-government, group discipline, and community living that dorm life provides, as well as the increased opportunity for enriching relationships with the staff and other students. Aaron Schnell, Director of Resident Services, emphasized the educational benefits of living on campus, such as the availability of films and discussion forums. Dr. Richard Gibb, the Commissioner of Higher Education for the South Dakota Board of Regents, freely admitted the financial reasons for the rule, but throughout his testimony, he also emphasized the various educational advantages of dormitory living. Michael Easton, the Director of Student Services, observed:

[T]he facilities for studying are more accessible to those people who live on campus. It's easier for them to get to the library, for example; the atmosphere on campus is more conducive to study.

It's encouraged. . . . There are control factors which eliminate the amount of confusion and noise. The emphasis on campus is academic . . . where off campus it's frequently not.

The overall evidence demonstrates that these University officials believe that dormitory living provides an educational atmosphere which assists *younger* students, as underclassmen, in adjusting to college life. [4] The testimony reflects a belief that students who become "established" and well-oriented in their early years are more prone to develop those good study habits which will assist them in their years as upperclassmen. Despite this testimony, the district court in its original opinion, as well as in a supplemental opinion filed under a Rule 60(b) proceeding, emphasized its factual conclusion that the *primary* purpose of the parietal rule was to defray the costs of the revenue bonds. It found the reasons relating to educational values expressed by school officials to be "unconvincing and unsupported by the evidence." It was on the basis of the finding of this primary purpose that the court concluded that the classification had no rational connection to the purpose of the regulation and therefore denied plaintiffs

---

[4.]   The defendants have adopted answers to interrogatories from another pending case in the federal district court in the Southern District of Iowa. Iowa university officials were asked to list the advantages and disadvantages of dormitory living. They listed them as follows:

ADVANTAGES	DISADVANTAGES
1) meals prepared	1) too restrictive
2) maid service	2) isolation from the opposite sex
3) meet more people	3) student not responsible for self
4) group activities, movies	4) can't study
5) ideal location	5) too noisy
6) laundry service	6) too expensive
7) activities	7) no liquor
8) communication	8) rooms too crowded
9) more a part of campus life	9) parking
10) experiencing different life styles	10) standing in line
11) supervision for young and immature	11) poor quality of food
12) equipment available	12) lack of privacy
13) develop feeling of belonging	13) no choice of roommates
14) educational environment	14) having roommates
15) counselors available	15) not sufficient study lounges
16) advisors spot problems early	16) prolongs adolescence
17) feel a part of group	17) too social
18) Reserve Library	18) maybe escape
19) forced to meet people and get along	
20) more recreational opportunities	
21) vending machines	
22) stores in dorms	
23) refrigerators	
24) freedom from household duties	
25) learn to be more tolerant of others	
26) easier to keep up with current activities	
27) help one another with homework	
28) easier to meet people	

equal protection of the law. *Cf.* Mollere v. Southeastern Louisiana College, 304 F.Supp. 826 (E.D.La.1969).

We need not decide whether the court's finding regarding the primary purpose of the rule is clearly erroneous. The district court's error, we believe, was in deciding the reasonableness of the classification on the basis of a single "primary" purpose in the face of evidence revealing multiple purposes. . . .

The district court concluded that the challenged classification (freshmen and sophomores) had no rational connection to the purpose of paying off the bonds. We would agree. However, there is no evidence on the record that the classification in question was ever intended to have any connection with that purpose. In *Molerre, supra,* relied upon by the district court, where a similar regulation was struck down, the *only* reason women under the age of 21 and freshman men were required to live in the dormitories was because as a group they approximated the number needed to fill the dormitory vacancies. 304 F.Supp. at 827. To the contrary in the present case the only evidence of why the classification was created was the testimony of University officials that they felt that freshman and sophomore students benefited more directly from the educational values of dormitory living. . . .

We find there exists a rational connection between one of the permissible purposes for the regulation and the classification made.

Right of Privacy

Although the district court did not pass on the plaintiffs' other contention, *i.e.,* that the regulation violates their right of privacy, this claim is argued on appeal and we must decide it. Aside from equal protection arguments, any law may, of course, be invalid if it clearly violates a fundamental constitutional right. Plaintiffs urge, however, that it is now recognized that when a legislative classification appears to have been made on a suspect basis or encroaches upon a fundamental right, the state has the burden of demonstrating a "compelling interest" which required it. We agree that when those circumstances exist closer judicial scrutiny is required under an equal protection challenge. . . . That is not the case here, however.

First, we think it obvious that the classification involved was not made on a "suspect" basis. *See* Johnson v. Robinson, 415 U.S. 361, 375 n. 14, 94 S.Ct. 1160, 39 L.Ed.2d 389 (1974). The class within the regulation is created on the basis of educational attainment. This classification has never been recognized as an inherently irrational basis for differentiating between persons otherwise equal. . . .

We move then to the consideration of whether the right involved is "explicitly or implicitly protected by the Constitution." *See* San Antonio School District v. Rodriguez, 411 U.S. 1, 93 S.Ct. 1278, 1281, 36 L.Ed.2d 16 (1973).

The basic challenge asserted by plaintiffs is that the parietal rule affects (a) their right of privacy and (b) their freedom of association. Plaintiffs rely on Shapiro v. Thompson, 394 U.S. 618, 89 S.Ct. 1322, 22 L.Ed.2d 600

1969), which requires the demonstration of a "compelling state interest" before a fundamental right may be encroached upon. However, before applying the compelling interest rule it is basic that both the nature and importance of the rights affected and the extent or nature of the encroachment must first be weighed to determine if the challenged rule constitutes a serious abridgement of a basic interest. *Cf.* Memorial Hospital v. Maricopa County, 415 U.S. 250, 94 S.Ct. 1076, 39 L.Ed.2d 306 (1974); Cole v. Housing Authority, 435 F.2d 807 (1st Cir. 1970).

Plaintiffs urge that inherent within the right of privacy is the right to choose one's home and to live with whomever one chooses. As much as we may strive to protect these goals, we cannot agree that the right to choose one's place of residence is necessarily a fundamental right. Cases too numerous to mention have upheld restrictions on this interest. *See, e.g.*, Village of Belle Terre v. Boraas, 416 U.S. 1, 94 S.Ct. 1536, 39 L.Ed.2d 797 (1974) (zoning ordinance). This "right" is akin to the interest in education, which the Supreme Court recently held not to be the kind of interest which will invoke the compelling interest test. *See* San Antonio School District v. Rodriguez, 411 U.S. 1, 35, 93 . . . The interest in living precisely where one chooses is not fundamental within our constitutional scheme.

Freedom of association has been recognized as a fundamental right, NAACP v. Alabama, 357 U.S. 449, 78 S.Ct. 1163, 2 L.Ed.2d 1488 (1958), but even fundamental rights are not so absolute as to be protected from all incidental effects of otherwise legitimate legislation. . . .

Fundamental to our reasoning is the fact that we are dealing with education, an area in which "[s]chool authorities are traditionally charged with broad power to formulate and implement educational policy. . . ." Swann v. Board of Education, 402 U.S. 1, 16, 91 S.Ct. 1267, 1276, 28 L.Ed.2d 554 (1971). We are also cognizant of the wisdom of Mr. Justice Holmes' statement in Missouri, Kansas & Texas Ry. Co. v. May, 194 U.S. 267, 24 S.Ct. 638, 48 L.Ed. 971 (1904), where he observed:

> When a state legislature has declared that, in its opinion, policy requires a certain measure, its action should not be disturbed by the courts under the 14th Amendment, unless they can see clearly that there is no fair reason for the law that would not require with equal force its extension to others whom it leaves untouched.

Id. at 269, 24 S.Ct. at 639.

This parietal rule and its challenged classification are directed toward a permissible objective. The classification is not based on any patently invidious basis. We conclude that the rule is reasonable and not arbitrary and that it "bears a rational relationship to a permissible state objective." . . . We find this test to be met here. *Accord*. Pratz v. Louisiana Polytechnic Institute, 316 F.Supp. 872 (W.D.La.1970), appeal dismissed, 401 U.S. 951, 91 S.Ct. 1186, 28 L.Ed.2d 234, aff'd, 401 U.S. 1004, 91 S.Ct. 1252, 28 L.Ed. 2d 541 (1971); Poynter v. Drevdahl, 359 F.Supp. 1137 (W.D.Mich.1972).

NOTE

1. The proper approach to Fourteenth Amendment classifications is also discussed in Bynes v. Toll, 512 F.2d 252 (2d Cir. 1975) which considered a university rule prohibiting children of students from living on campus. The court used the rational basis test to rule that, in view of the broad discretion vested in the university to fashion educational policy and to regulate the conduct of its students, it was rational for the university to be concerned for the safety of children living on campus. (The axiom "Mother knows best" was specifically held to be irrelevant). A similar result was reached by the Texas Supreme Court in Texas Woman's University v. Chayklintaste, 530 S.W.2d 927 (Tex. 1975), although an earlier decision in the same case invalidated a classification by sex, 521 S.W. 2d 949 (Tex.Civ.App. 1975).

2. In Cooper v. Nix 496 F.2d 1285 (5 Cir. 1974), a case stemming from the same fact situation as Pratz v. Louisiana Polytechnic Institute cited in *Prostrollo*, the court upheld a student objection to the implementation of a residency exemption by which the college automatically exempted students over 23, although the exemption was broadly worded to cover those who could demonstrate a need for exemption. Interestingly the suit was brought only on behalf of the college's 21- and 22-year-olds, reflecting, perhaps, the then applicable age of majority. For an excellent discussion of the implications of the new age of majority see D. J. Hanson, *The Lowered Age of Majority: Its Impact on Higher Education,* Assoc. of American Colleges, 1975.

III. Representation on the Board of Trustees

BENNER v. OSWALD
United States Third Circuit Court of Appeals
592 F.2d 174 (1979)

ALDISERT, *Circuit Judge.*

The question is whether the equal protection clause of the fourteenth amendment requires undergraduate student participation in the election of certain members of the Pennsylvania State University (Penn State) board of trustees. The district court ruled that the students had no such right. They have appealed. Finding no error, we affirm.

All material facts are set forth in stipulated findings contained in the district court opinion, *Benner v. Oswald*, 444 F.Supp. 545 (M.D. Pa. 1978). The board of trustees is composed of 32 members. Five serve as ex officio members including the president of the University, the state governor and three members of his cabinet. Six other trustees are appointed by the governor with the consent of the senate. The student appellants do not challenge the method by which these eleven trustees are selected, but they do challenge the selection of the remaining 21 trustees. Of this latter group, 9 trustees are elected by the alumni association and 12 are elected by the members of county agricultural and industrial societies of Pennsylvania. Students *qua* students, therefore, do not participate in the election process. They complain that the refusal to allow them to participate in the selection process of these 21 trustees denies them rights guaranteed by the equal protection clause. . . .

Alumni trustees are chosen for staggered three-year terms and are elected in a process that begins early in each year when nomination ballots

are mailed by the University to alumni who have been active members of the
alumni association or who have contributed to the University within the
past two years or who specifically request a nomination ballot. Approximately 50,000 nomination ballots are mailed. All nominees receiving 50 or
more votes are eligible for the election if they consent. Normally between 8
and 12 nominees vie for the three positions. Election ballots are then mailed
to the alumni and approximately 14,000 alumni cast their ballots each year.

Agricultural and industrial trustees, also chosen for staggered three-
year terms, are elected by specially chosen delegates during the annual commencement week. The agricultural trustee selection process begins around
January when the University sends to all county agricultural extension
directors the list of agricultural societies which were eligible to send delegates during the previous year. Each county agricultural extension director
determines whether the agricultural societies for his county remain eligible
and whether there are new societies to be added to the eligibility list. At the
time of the district court hearing there were 397 agricultural societies
eligible to send delegates. The industrial trustee selection process is similar.
The University determines which industrial societies and associations were
eligible to send delegates the previous year. The list is sent to five officials
who are responsible for updating the list. At the time of the district court
hearing, 160 mining, manufacturing and engineering societies were eligible
to send delegates. Approximately 450 delegates participate annually. In
1977, there were 207 delegates representing agricultural societies, and 198
delegates representing industrial societies. . . .

Appellees would have us affirm the judgment of the district court
without addressing the merits of the constitutional issues. They would have
us do this, albeit for reasoning inconsistent with that of the trial court,
Rhoads v. Ford Motor Co., 514 F.2d 931, 934 (3d Cir. 1975), by holding
that the actions and selection of the board of trustees do not amount to
state action for purposes of the equal protection clause. They contend that
although Pennsylvania supplies funds for the operation of the University,
no members of either the executive or the legislative branches of the commonwealth participate officially in the selection process of the board. They
argue that other than the ex officio trustees and the trustees appointed by
the governor, no state officers participate in formulating essential University
policy. Accordingly, they urge us to conclude that the requisite connection
between the commonwealth and the University is not present. We disagree
and determine that there is sufficient state involvement to constitute state
action within the meaning of 42 U.S.C. § 1983. . . .

In *Chalfant v. Wilmington Institute,* 574 F.2d 739, 744 (3d Cir. 1978)
(in banc), we dispelled any possible uncertainties in this respect and put to
rest the very argument relied upon by the appellees in these proceedings:

> In *Braden v. University of Pittsburgh*, 552 F.2d 948, 957 (3d Cir.
> 1977) (en banc), we reiterated the *Hollenbaugh* holding that
> *Jackson* had not substituted a single nexus test for an ad hoc
> analysis of the facts and circumstances of each case as it arises.

Braden also recognized explicitly that *Jackson* did not overrule *Burton v. Wilmington Parking Authority,* 365 U.S. 715, 81 S.Ct. 856, 6 L.Ed.2d 45 (1961). In dealing with *Burton*, Judge Adams, writing for this court in *Braden* observed:

> Speaking for a unanimous panel [in *Hollenbaugh v. Carnegie Free Library*], Judge Aldisert declared: "The state's extensive participation in the comprehensive program may obviate a need to show involvement in the specific activity challenged [as] is illustrated by *Burton. . . .*"

552 F.2d at 958 n.45. Thus, the law in this circuit is clear. The *Jackson* nexus test, whatever it means in the context of the activities of what the Supreme Court considers to be private enterprises, cannot be applied mechanically in other contexts. We have expressly rejected the application of the *Jackson* test, which was enunciated within the context of a private enterprise electric utility, to the analysis of state action in a public library, a university, or any other public educational institution. *Hollenbaugh* and *Braden* hold that the status of the individual actor is irrelevant if the institution on whose behalf he acted is found, upon an examination of all the relevant factors, to be an instrumentality of a state or local government.

574 F.2d at 744-75 (footnotes omitted).

We therefore conclude that the district court properly analyzed and applied the teachings of this court by determining that state action could be found, either (1) when the state and the entity whose activities were challenged are joint participants in a symbiotic relationship or (2) where the entity is pervasively regulated by the state and a sufficient nexus exists between the state and the challenged activity. . . .

We turn now to the constitutional arguments advanced by the student appellants. At the beginning of the 1960's judicial intervention under the banner of equal protection was virtually unknown outside racial discrimination cases. In recent years the concept has been given broad judicial expansion in matters affecting criminal trials, interstate travel, alienage, and a host of other social, economic and political interests including voting. In all equal protection cases some classification has occurred, but the standard of judicial scrutiny is usually dependent upon the subject matter of the classification. In some cases the classification itself is deemed suspect. In others, while the classification is not suspect, the individual right affected is denominated as fundamental. For example, voting in a governmental election is considered a fundamental right. *Dunn v. Blumstein,* 405 U.S. 330 (1972); *Bullock v. Carter,* 405 U.S. 134 (1972); *Hadley v. Junior College District,* 397 U.S. 50 (1970); *Kramer v. Union Free School District,* 395 U.S. 621 (1969). *See also Roe v. Wade,* 410 U.S. 113 (1973) (right of a uniquely private nature); *Shapiro v. Thompson,* 394 U.S. 618 (1969) (right of interstate travel); *Williams v. Rhodes,* 393 U.S. 23 (1968) (rights guaranteed by the first amendment); *Skinner v. Oklahoma ex rel. Williamson,* 316 U.S. 535

(1942) (right to procreate). If the case involves a fundamental right or a suspect classification, the state activity will be subject to strict judicial scrutiny and will prevail only if the state shows that such action is justified by a "compelling state interest." *American Party of Texas v. White,* 415 U.S. 767, 780 (1974).

On the other hand, state regulations bearing upon rights and classifications not so denominated are subject to a relatively relaxed standard of judicial scrutiny, and will pass muster if the purpose of the classification bears some rational relationship to a legitimate state purpose. *San Antonio School District v. Rodriguez,* 411 U.S. 1 (1973). As the Supreme Court has recently stated: "'The Fourteenth Amendment does not prohibit legislation merely because it is special, or limited in its application to a particular geographical or political subdivision of the state.' . . . Rather, the Equal Protection Clause is offended only if the statute's classification 'rests on grounds wholly irrelevant to the achievement of the State's objective.' . . . ." *Holt Civic Club v. Tuscaloosa,* ___ U.S. ___, 47 U.S.L.W. 4008, 4011 (November 28, 1978) (citations omitted). The rational basis standard presumes such legislative action to be valid. It reflects the courts' awareness that the drawing of lines which create distinct classifications is peculiarly a legislative task and an unavoidable one. *Massachusetts Board of Retirement v. Murgia,* 427 U.S. 307, 314 (1976).

The student appellants advance two arguments in their constitutional attack on the trustee selection process. Primarily, they contend they are being denied a fundamental right to vote and the selection process must therefore be scrutinized under the compelling state interest test. In this regard, the students assert that the teachings of *Kramer v. Union School District,* 395 U.S. 621 (1969), and similar cases should control the disposition of this case. Alternatively they urge that even if we examine the selection process under the less stringent rational basis test we should find it constitutionally defective.

We must first determine which test to employ in our analysis. The students assert that a right to vote for trustees of a university is equivalent to a right to vote for elected members of local, state and federal government. They suggest that their individual interest denied by the University's method of selecting trustees is equivalent to the denial of an individual's right to vote in public elections.

In *Kramer, supra,* at issue was a New York statute that limited the right to vote in local school board elections to persons, otherwise eligible to vote in general elections, who owned or leased taxable real property in the school district or who had children enrolled in public school in the particular district. The Court held that in an election of general interest, voting restrictions other than those pertaining to residence, age and citizenship must promote a compelling state interest in order to be constitutional. Because the New York statute in question did not accomplish the articulated state goal with sufficient precision, it was struck down as a denial of equal protection. 395 U.S. at 632.

Likewise, in *Hadley v. Junior College District of Kansas City,* 397 U.S. 50 (1970), certain residents and taxpayers of the Kansas City school district, one of eight school districts which made up the junior college district of metropolitan Kansas City, mounted a constitutional assault on the Missouri statute that apportioned their right to vote for the trustees who conducted and managed the affairs of the junior college district. The statute provided for the election of six trustees and for the apportionment to be made on the basis of the number of school age children who reside in each district. The Kansas City school district contained approximately 60% of the total number of school age children in the junior college district but was apportioned only 50% of the total number of trustees. In holding that the right to vote for trustees had been unconstitutionally diluted, the Court determined that "as a general rule, whenever a state or local government decides to select persons by popular election to perform governmental functions, the Equal Protection Clause of the Fourteenth Amendment requires each qualified voter must be given an equal opportunity to participate in that election. . . ." *Id.* at 56.

Examining these teachings we note that the cases involve general government elections. Such elections are seen as directly relating to the Constitution: "statutes distributing the franchise constitute the foundation of our representative society." *Kramer, supra,* 395 U.S. at 626. "The right to vote freely for the candidate of one's choice is of the essence of a democratic society, and any restrictions on that right strike at the heart of representative government. And the right of suffrage can be denied by a debasement or dilution of the weight of a citizen's vote just as effectively as by wholly prohibiting the free exercise of the franchise." *Reynolds v. Sims,* 377 U.S. 553 at 555 (1964) (footnote omitted). "Like *Skinner v. Oklahoma,* . . . such a case 'touches a sensitive and important area of human rights,' and 'involves one of the basic civil rights of man,' . . . . Undoubtedly, the right of suffrage is a fundamental matter in a free and democratic society. Especially since the right to exercise one's vote in an unimpaired manner is preservative of other basic civil and political rights, any alleged infringement of the right of citizens to vote must be carefully and meticulously scrutinized. Almost a century ago, in *Yick Wo. v. Hopkins,* 118 U.S. 356, the Court referred to 'the political franchise of voting' as 'a fundamental political right, because preservative of all rights.' 118 U.S., at 370." *Id.,* 377 U.S. at 561-62.

But we refuse to accept the formulation of the student appellants that the right to vote for a university trustee is equivalent to a right to vote in a participatory democracy. We will not conclude that the University trustee selection process is a general public election, or that the trustees perform general governmental functions. The University's board of trustees controls no viable political sub-division and has less power than a local school district. It cannot acquire property by condemnation, levy or collect taxes, or pass on petitions to annex school districts. It simply does not possess the minimum governmental powers associated with municipal, school district, county, state, or federal offices. At most, the board has the authority to approve a budget and set a level of tuition. And even in the setting of tuition, they do not have a free hand. The parties have stipulated that "[t]he level of tuition is based upon estimates of expense and of income from other sources, including the estimated amount of the state appropriation, endowment income, recovery of indirect costs on government contracts and other miscellaneous sources." 444 F.Supp. at 555.

With regard to the students' contention, we are mindful of Justice Holmes' observation in *Hudson County Water Co. v. McCarter,* 209 U.S. 349, 355 (1908):

> All rights tend to declare themselves absolute to their logical extreme. Yet all in fact are limited by the neighborhood of principles of policy which are other than those on which the particular right is founded, and which become strong enough to hold their own when a certain point is reached. . . . The boundary at which the conflicting interests balance cannot be determined by any general formula in advance, but points in the line, or helping to establish it, are fixed by decisions that this or that concrete case falls on the nearer or farther side.

Paraphrasing the Supreme Court's latest decision in this field which made a reference to Holmes's statement, "The line heretofore marked by [the Supreme] Court's voting qualifications decisions coincides with the [public and political nature] of the governmental unit at issue, and we hold that appellants' case . . . falls on the farther side." *Holt Civic Club Inc. v. Tuscaloosa, supra,* 47 U.S.L.W. at 4011.

We therefore conclude that the duties of the trustees are not commensurate with the duties of elected public officials; that these duties do not involve the responsibilities going to "the essence of a democratic society," and do not implicate decisions that are "preservative of all rights." Because the trustees' duties do not approach the quantum of responsibilities of officials selected in a political democracy, we conclude that any individual interests affected by the selection process classifications are not fundamental rights so as to require recourse to the strict judicial scrutiny standard.

Our remaining task is to decide whether any rational basis exists to support the distinction which limits participation in the trustee selection process to members of local agricultural and industrial societies and alumni.

The University originated as the Farmer's High School of Pennsylvania and under the federal statute providing the donation of public lands, it became a land grant college committed to the teaching of agriculture and the mechanic arts. We agree with Judge Muir's determination:

> Penn State argues that because of its historic commitment to both agriculture and industrial goals, it is entitled to give members of agricultural and industrial societies a voice in the operation of the university to the exclusion of other interested groups. The Court cannot say as a matter of law that the distinction made between agricultural and industrial societies and other interested groups,

including undergraduate students, is wholly unrelated to the achievement of Penn State's underlying objective which is the governance of the affairs of the University. Therefore, the charter provisions which give local agricultural and industrial societies a voice in selecting members of Penn State's board of trustees but which deny it to undergraduate students do not violate the equal protection clause.

414 F.Supp. at 561-62.

Allowing alumni to participate in the selection process is justified by the premise that those alumni who cast ballots are graduates of the University who have a continuing interest in its affairs. Alumni support of their *alma mater* is a universal phenomenon in the United States and alumni provide an important source of political, social, and financial sustenance. The record here reveals that for the period 1953 through 1977 alumni have contributed the sum of $11,247,076 through lifetime gifts or testamentary bequests. An alumni association has been active at Penn State for over 100 years, and the record demonstrates significant participation in University activities.

Applying the rational basis test, we cannot conclude that the trustee selection process which limits participation to alumni and agricultural and industrial groups is irrational. "A statutory discrimination will not be set aside if any state of facts reasonably may be conceived to justify it." *McGowan v. Maryland*, 366 U.S. 420, 426 (1961). . . .

The judgment of the district court will be affirmed.

IV. Scholarships for Resident Aliens

NYQUIST v. MAUCLET
United States Supreme Court
432 U.S. 1 (1977)

MR. JUSTICE BLACKMUN delivered the opinion of the Court.

New York, by statute, bars certain *resident* aliens from state financial assistance for higher education. N. Y. Educ. Law §661(3) (McKinney Supp. 1976). This litigation presents a constitutional challenge to that statute.

I

New York provides assistance, primarily in three forms, to students pursuing higher education. The first type is the Regents college scholarship. These are awarded to high school graduates on the basis of performance in a competitive examination. §§605(1) and 670. Currently, in the usual case, a recipient is entitled to $250 annually for four years of study without regard to need. §§670(2) and (3)(b). The second and chief form of aid is the tuition assistance award. These are noncompetitive; they are available to both graduate and undergraduate students "enrolled in approved programs and who demonstrate the ability to complete such courses." §§604(1) and 667(1). The amount of the award depends on both tuition and income. The ceiling on assistance was $600, although it has been increased for under-graduates to $1,500. §§667(3) and (4). The third form of assistance is the student loan. §§680-684. The loan is guaranteed by the State; a borrower meeting certain income restrictions is entitled to favorable interest rates and generally to an interest-free grace period of at least nine months after he completes or terminates his course of study. . . .

The statute obviously serves to bar from the assistance programs the participation of all aliens who do not satisfy its terms. Since many aliens, such as those here on student visas, may be precluded by federal law from establishing a permanent residence in this country, see, *e. g.,* 8 U.S.C. § 1101(a)(15)(F)(i); 22 CFR § 41.45 (1976), the bar of § 661(3) is of prac-tical significance only to resident aliens. The Court has observed of this affected group: "Resident aliens, like citizens, pay taxes, support the econ-omy, serve in the Armed Forces, and contribute in myriad other ways to our society." *In re Griffiths*, 413 U.S. 717, 722 (1973).

II

Appellee Jean-Marie Mauclet is a citizen of France and has lived in New York since April 1969. He has been a permanent resident of the United States since November of that year. He is married to a United States citizen and has a child by that marriage. The child is also a United States citizen. App. 49. Mauclet by affidavit stated: "Although I am presently qualified to apply for citizenship and intend to reside permanently in the United States, I do not wish to relinquish my French citizenship at this time." . . . He ap-plied for a tuition assistance award to aid in meeting the expenses of his graduate studies at the State University of New York at Buffalo. Because of his refusal to apply for United States citizenship, his application was not processed. *Id.*, at 49-50.

Appellee Alan Rabinovitch is a citizen of Canada. He was admitted to this country in 1964 at the age of nine as a permanent resident alien. He is unmarried and, since his admission, has lived in New York with his parents and a younger sister, all of whom are Canadian citizens. He registered with Selective Service on his 18th birthday. He graduated in 1973 from the New York public school system. . . . As a result of a commendable performance on the competitive Regents Qualifying Examinations, Rabinovitch was in-formed that he was qualified for, and entitled to, a Regents college scholar-ship and tuition assistance. He later was advised, however, that the offer of the scholarship was withdrawn since he intended to retain his Canadian citizenship. *Id.*, at 69, 25. Rabinovitch entered Brooklyn College without financial aid from the State. He states that he "does not intend to become a naturalized American, but . . . does intend to continue to reside in New York." . . .

III

The Court has ruled that classifications by a State that are based on alienage are "inherently suspect and subject to close judicial scrutiny."

Graham v. *Richardson*, 403 U.S. 365, 372 (1971). See *Examining Board* v. *Flores de Otero*, 426 U.S. 572, 601-602 (1976); *In re Griffiths*, 413 U.S., at 721; *Sugarman* v. *Dougall*, 413 U.S. 634, 642 (1973). In undertaking this scrutiny, "the governmental interest claimed to justify the discrimination is to be carefully examined in order to determine whether that interest is legitimate and substantial, and inquiry must be made whether the means adopted to achieve the goal are necessary and precisely drawn." *Examining Board* v. *Flores de Otero*, 426 U.S., at 605. See *In re Griffiths*, 413 U.S., at 721-722. Alienage classifications by a State that do not withstand this stringent examination cannot stand.

Appellants claim that §661(3) should not be subjected to such strict scrutiny because it does not impose a classification based on alienage. Aliens who have applied for citizenship, or, if not qualified for it, who have filed a statement of intent to apply as soon as they are eligible, are allowed to participate in the assistance programs. Hence, it is said, the statute distinguishes "only within the 'heterogeneous' class of aliens" and "does not distinguish between citizens and aliens *vel non*." Brief for Appellants 20. Only statutory classifications of the latter type, appellants assert, warrant strict scrutiny.

Appellants also assert that there are adequate justifications for §661-(3). First, the section is said to offer an incentive for aliens to become naturalized. Second, the restriction on assistance to only those who are or will become eligible to vote is tailored to the purpose of the assistance program, namely, the enhancement of the educational level of the electorate. Brief for Appellants 22-25. Both justifications are claimed to be related to New York's interest in the preservation of its "political community." See *Sugarman* v. *Dougall*, 413 U.S., at 642-643, 647-649; *Dunn* v. *Blumstein*, 405 U.S. 330, 344 (1972).

The first purpose offered by the appellants, directed to what they describe as some "degree of national affinity," Brief for Appellants 18, however, is not a permissible one for a State. Control over immigration and naturalization is entrusted exclusively to the Federal Government, and a State has no power to interfere. U. S. Const., Art. 1, § 8, cl. 4. See *Mathews* v. *Diaz*, 426 U.S. 67, 84-85 (1976); *Graham* v. *Richardson*, 403 U.S., at 376-380; *Takahashi* v. *Fish & Game Comm'n*, 334 U.S. 410, 419 (1948). But even if we accept, *arguendo*, the validity of the proferred justifications, we find them inadequate to support the ban. . . .

Nor does the claimed interest in educating the electorate provide a justification; although such education is a laudable objective, it hardly would be frustrated by including resident aliens, as well as citizens, in the State's assistance programs.

Resident aliens are obligated to pay their full share of the taxes that support the assistance programs. There thus is no real unfairness in allowing resident aliens an equal right to participate in programs to which they contribute on an equal basis. And although an alien may be barred from full involvement in the political arena, he may play a role—perhaps even a leadership role—in other areas of import to the community. The State surely is not harmed by providing resident aliens the same educational opportunity it offers to others.

Since we hold that the challenged statute violates the Fourteenth Amendment's equal protection guarantee, we need not reach appellees' claim that it also intrudes upon Congress' comprehensive authority over immigration and naturalization. See *Graham* v. *Richardson*, 403 U.S., at 378; *Truax* v. *Raich*, 239 U.S. 33, 42 (1915).

The judgments of the District Court are affirmed.

V. State Governance Statutes

STUDENT ASSOCIATION OF THE UNIVERSITY OF WISCONSIN-MILWAUKEE v. BAUM
Supreme Court of Wisconsin
74 Wis.2d 283 (1976)

BEILFUSS, Chief Justice. . . .

In July of 1974 the legislature merged all of the state universities into one university system with one board of regents, with the chancellor of each of the several campuses responsible to the board of regents.

One of the sections of the statutes enacted to effectuate the merger is sec. 36.09(5). It is as follows:

"(5) *Students.* The students of each institution or campus subject to the responsibilities and powers of the board, the president, the chancellor and the faculty shall be active participants in the immediate governance of and policy development for such institutions. As such, students shall have primary responsibility for the formulation and review of policies concerning student life, services and interests. Students in consultation with the chancellor and subject to the final confirmation of the board shall have the responsibility for the disposition of those student fees which constitute substantial support for campus student activities. The students of each institution or campus shall have the right to organize themselves in a manner they determine and to select their representatives to participate in institutional governance."

In April of 1974 the constitution of the plaintiff-student association was certified by the election commission. It provides that all students currently enrolled at the University of Wisconsin-Milwaukee are members of SA (student association); that all legislative power is vested in a student senate to be elected at large by the members; and that the president and the vice-president are to be elected at large. The powers and duties of the senate, the president, and various other officers are also set forth and power of recall is retained by the members.

The student senate is the legislative body. It delegated to the president, Michael J. DeLonay, the power to appoint student members to university committees in September of 1974. . . .

The plaintiffs argue that the final sentence of sec. 36.09(5), Stats., is plain and unambiguous upon its face and that no construction of the statute to determine legislative intent is necessary or permissible.

The sentence in question is as follows: "The students of each institution or campus shall have the right to organize themselves in a manner they determine and to select their representatives to participate in institutional governance."

If this sentence could be considered without regard to the rest of the section and balance of ch. 36, Stats., and if there is in fact no ambiguity in it, their position would be correct. However, we conclude the sentence cannot be construed without reference to the balance of the section and the entire chapter because the whole chapter deals with the governance of the university system. We further conclude the sentence is not unambiguous. Therefore the rule does not apply and the court must construe the statute.

The first sentence of sec. 36.09(5), Stats., is as follows: "The students of each institution or campus subject to the responsibilities and powers of the board, the president, the chancellor and the faculty shall be active participants in the immediate governance of and policy development for such institutions." The rights of the student are therefore subject to some qualifications.

The student rights are subject to the responsibilities of the board of regents. The primary responsibility for governance of the system, as outlined in sec. 36.09(1)(a), Stats., is vested in the board. To do this the board is mandated to enact policies and rules for governing the system. The chancellor is vested with the responsibility of administering board policies. In September of 1974, the board established interim guidelines for implementation of sec. 36.09(5). The guidelines provide that "[w]here student membership on a given policy development agency is authorized . . . , procedures for establishing such membership should also be defined." The guidelines went on to note that these procedures should be in the spirit of sec. 36.09(5). Student membership would be required by sec. 36.09(5) on any committee which deals with the immediate governance of and policy development for the university.

The establishment of the various university committees, the composition of the committees as to administration, faculty and students, and the scope of the activities and authority of the committees are matters clearly within the authority of the board of regents and administered by the chancellor.

We now turn to a consideration of the three committees in question and a construction of sec. 36.09(5), Stats., in relation to them.

As set forth above, the students were allotted two members of the Physical Environment Committee. In July of 1974, sec. 36.09(5), Stats., became effective and gave the students the right to select their representatives. DeLonay, as president of the student association, appointed the allotted two members in August of 1974. However, his authority to appoint them at that time is open to challenge. The senate of the student association did not authorize him to make committee appointments until September of 1974. The chancellor refused to recognize DeLonay's appointments and personally appointed two of his own choice in September, 1974. It was his opinion, until interim guidelines were established that the *UW Law and Regulations of 1969,* as promulgated by the regents, controlled the appointment of student representatives.

We conclude that when sec. 36.09(5), Stats., became effective in July, 1974, the chancellor lost his authority to make these appointments. The statute gave this authority to the students as of that time. It is well settled that if a rule or directive of an administrative body or officer is in conflict with a newly enacted statute, the statute must take precedence. The students had the right to select their representatives on the Physical Environment Committee.

For the same reasons the student appointments to the Interim Guidelines Committee by the assistant chancellor were invalid. However, the question is now moot because the committee was only advisory on an ad hoc basis and is now disbanded.

A more difficult question arises in determining whether the method used for the selection of the student members of the Segregated Fee Advisory Committee was in compliance with the statute. Sec. 36.09(5) emphasizes the student right in this area. It provides: "Students in consultation with the chancellor and subject to the final confirmation of the board shall have the responsibility for the disposition of those student fees which constitute substantial support for campus student activities."

The chancellor, for reasonable and laudable reasons, concluded that the eleven student members of this committee should be in fact representative of the organizations and interests of the variety of campus activities that were eligible for an allocation of the segregated funds.

There is no question but that the students had "the right to organize themselves in a manner they determine." The student association is a student organization. All students are members of the association, all have a right to vote for the president, vice-president and the members of the legislative body, the student senate. Upon their face the election procedures appearing in the student association constitution are fair and complete. There is no substantial challenge to the assertion that the student association is the only campus organization that represents all of the students. If we were confronted with competing organizations or all students were not eligible for membership in this organization, the board, the chancellor, and this court would be faced with a different problem. The facts as revealed by the record are that there are no competing campus-wide organizations and all students are members. The student association, under these facts, must be recognized as the organized representative of the students.

The question still remains whether the student association, through its elected representatives, can select student committee members by appointment or whether the chancellor could require a general student election with specific qualifications for candidates for nomination and election.

We again set forth the statutory sentence: "The students of each institution or campus shall have the right to organize themselves in a manner they determine and to select their representatives to participate in institutional governance." Is the students' right to select their representatives an integral part of their right to organize in a manner they determine or is it two separate rights—one to organize and the other to select representatives?

There are two accepted methods for interpretation of statutes. The first, determining legislative intent, looks to extrinsic factors for construction of the statute. The second, determining what the statute means, looks to intrinsic factors such as punctuation or common meaning of words for construction of the statute. 2A Sutherland, *Statutory Construction* (4th ed. 1973), secs. 45.05, 45.07 and 45.14. Whichever of these methods is used, the cardinal rule in interpreting statutes is that the purpose of the whole act is to be sought and is favored over a construction which will defeat the manifest object of the act. *Statutory Construction, supra,* at pp. 56-57, sec. 46.05.

While a general student election to select student representatives to the various university committees does not offend the statute, was it the intention of the legislature to require it?

The legislative intent of this section was to give students the statutory right to organize themselves as they determined and through the organization select their representatives to participate in institutional governance. If the right to organize and to select representatives is seen as two distinct rights without an integral relationship to each other, the possible effect could be the negation of one of these rights. For example, if a chancellor retains the right to dictate students shall be selected by election with two from this organization and one or two from other organizations, or persons with special interests, as was done here, the right to organize becomes meaningless. While students retain their right to organize, the administration can thwart the authority of the organization and deal with other students more to its liking. It can deal with two students from the dorms, two from publications, and others. This may be much easier. While these motives are not present in this case, an interpretation which does not recognize the right to organize and select representatives as integrally related could result in such a situation in the future. In addition, if the chancellor retains the power to direct students shall be elected from some organization or another, does he not also have the power to say a particular committee requires that students be in the upper ten percent of their academic class. And if this power is present, the students' right to select their representatives could be only an illusion. If the students' right to organize themselves and select their representatives is viewed as two different rights, the purpose of the statute may not be carried out. In order to give effect to the legislative intent of this section, the right to organize and select representatives must be seen as one right, which must be free of administrative interference if it is, in reality, to be a right.

In construing this section we should also look to the grammatical construction of the statute. Our reading of this sentence indicates that there are two entirely different meanings which could be found in these words which are both grammatically correct. The first is that the statute should be read as follows: The students of each institution or campus shall have the right to organize themselves in a manner they determine and [the right] to select their representatives to participate in institutional governance. This reading supplies the second use of the words "the right" and one could argue that these words are understood or implicit in the sentence as it now reads. The second is to omit insertion of the second use of the words "the right." Without inserting these words the students have one right rather than two. This right is the right to organize themselves in a manner they determine and to select their representatives to institutional governance. Both interpretations are grammatically correct but we believe the second interpretation is a better reflection of what the legislature intended. The statute does not say "the students shall have the rights." If it did, this would suggest two rights rather than one, or if the sentence contained the word "right" immediately before "to select their representatives," it would be clear that the students have two rights. This is not the case. The statute only says the students have the "right." One right. The right to organize and to select. Because these two interpretations are possible, we must ask which conforms more closely to the intent of the legislature. We believe it is the second. This construction will give students the right without interference from the administration. Interpreting this final sentence in this way does not create a conflict with the preamble of this section. This first sentence merely says that students' rights to participate are subject to the responsibilities and powers of the board, president, chancellor and faculty. Where there is a specific and general provision in the same statute, the specific provision must control.

We conclude that the student association had the statutory authority to select the student members of the Segregated Fee Allocations Committee and that the chancellor exceeded his authority under the facts of this action.

Judgment reversed.

ABRAHAMSON, Justice (concurring).

The court today holds that the Chancellor could not directly appoint students of his choosing to the Physical Environment Committee and that the Chancellor could not unilaterally determine the structure and mode of selection of student representation on the Segregated Fee Advisory Committee. I concur in these results. Sec. 36.09(5), Stats., grants to the students, not the administration, the right to select student representatives in institutional governance and thus precludes unilateral determination by the Chancellor of the manner in which the students' right of selection is to be exercised. However, I write this concurring opinion lest the majority opinion be misunderstood and be thought to endorse—which it does not—the Student Association's complete power to appoint students to committees.

The last sentence of sec. 36.09(5), Stats., provides:

". . . The students of each institution or campus shall have the right to organize themselves in a manner they determine and to select their representatives to participate in institutional governance."

I cannot agree with the reasoning of the majority that this sentence creates a single right, which it characterizes as the students' "right to organize themselves as they determined and through the organization select their representatives to participate in institutional governance." The plain meaning of the sentence is that two rights are conferred and that both are conferred upon the students:

1. The *students* . . . shall have the right to organize themselves in a manner they determine, and

2. The *students* . . . shall have the right to . . . select their representatives to participate in institutional governance.

There is no ambiguity here. The briefs of the Student Association concede that there are two student rights and both are given to the students not to student organizations. The legislature could easily have provided for the result reached by the majority, but it did not do so. The rights of selection of representatives and of organization are no doubt interrelated. However, two rights are created in the students, and both must be protected. . . .

PART FOUR

FEDERAL REGULATION
OF HIGHER EDUCATION

CHAPTER 13

THE IMPACT OF FEDERAL REGULATION ON HIGHER EDUCATION

INTRODUCTION: SOME HISTORICAL PERSPECTIVES

For years institutions of higher education, especially in the private sector, operated relatively free from direct regulation by the federal government; during the nineteenth century, private colleges subsisted mostly on private donations. The traditional legal view in the nineteenth century was that society was served not merely by the continued existence of private colleges but by their continued *independent* existence. This view, which was best articulated by Justice Marshall in the now-famous *Dartmouth College* case (referred to in Part One), rejected the notion that private colleges were required to function pursuant to a "public trust" merely because the education of the young was of great benefit to society. Justice Marshall thus questioned:

> That education is an object of national concern and a proper subject of legislation, all admit. . . . But is education altogether in the hands of government? Does every teacher of youth become a public officer, and do donations for the purpose of education necessarily become public property so far that the will of the legislature not the will of the donor, becomes the law of the donation? These questions are of serious moment to society, and deserve to be well considered.[1]

There is good evidence to at least suggest that the decision in *Dartmouth* mirrored prevailing political science viewpoints concerning the proper relationship between government and institutions of higher education in the late eighteenth and early nineteenth centuries.[2] Although several "state universities" had been established by the turn of the nineteenth century, notably in Georgia, North Carolina, South Carolina, Tennessee and Virginia, private universities were allowed to exist mostly free from state control. Thus, *Dartmouth* seemingly endorsed a dominant societal view that supported "the right of initiating groups to control what they had created, to gain from the state equal privileges with all other groups and to retain them even against the state itself." [3]

Trustees of Rutgers College in New Jersey v. Richman, 125 A2d 10 (1956), decided nearly 150 years after Justice Marshall had rendered his

---

1. Trustees of Dartmouth College v. Woodward, 4 Wheat. 518 (1819).
2. *See, e.g.,* B. Bailyn, Education in the Forming of American Society (Vintage Books, 1960), pp. 41-47; H. J. Perkinson, Two Hundred Years of American Educational Thought (David McKay Co., 1976), pp. 41-48.
3. B. Bailyn, Education In The Forming of American Society, p. 47.

opinion in Dartmouth, provides an interesting contrast. Rutgers, a private college administered by a self-perpetuating board of trustees, had, for 30 years prior to the time of litigation, been receiving increasing amounts of money from the New Jersey treasury. In the mid-fifties the state legislature passed a charter amendment bill, very much like the one at issue in *Dartmouth*, transferring almost all meaningful control of the college to a board dominated by public appointees. Two important factors serve to distinguish *Rutgers* from *Dartmouth:* first, Rutgers could not survive financially without a continued and, in fact, dramatically increased infusion of public funds; second, the Rutgers College board of trustees had consented to the proposed takeover by the state. The *Rutgers* opinion accepts as given the financial dependence of Rutgers on public funding and concludes that through this relationship the college had evolved from a private institution, whose trustees were fiduciaries carrying out a private charter and the wishes of its donors, to an "instrumentality of the state whose property and educational facilities are impressed with a public trust for higher education of the people of the state." 125 A2d at 17.

It is hardly surprising that the state saw fit to take over Rutgers in the circumstances there presented. What is most interesting about the *Rutgers* case, however, is the rationale offered to support the result achieved. When one reads *Rutgers,* it appears that the Chancellor's opinion leaps from an assertion that (1) private funding is a characteristic of a private institution, to a conclusion that (2) no institution can remain "private" and receive public funds. This second proposition surely is not self-evident, nor does it follow from the first.

The problem Rutgers faced is a problem faced today to a greater or lesser degree by many institutions of higher learning: the exercise of broad governmental power that may attend government largesse. The notion that Rutgers, a private institution, should lose *some* autonomy when it chose to accept state money seems, on balance, quite proper; public funds, after all, must serve some "public purpose." What seems problematic, however, is the assumption advanced in *Rutgers* that the basic educational "purpose" being served will remain uncompromised by drastic changes in academic management and control.

The theoretical and philosophical questions raised by *Dartmouth* and *Rutgers* are questions which must be addressed in dealing with the impact of federal regulation on higher education. One question is whether public money imposes a "public trust." If it does, who decides whether that trust is being furthered or breached and by what standard? Does the standard change with the proportion or amount of public funds? Second, does the infusion of public money bring not only increased public oversight but also an erosion of the special nature of the institution itself? That is, assuming that it is possible in 1979 to distinguish between "public" and "private" colleges and universities, is this distinction meaningful?

The issue might be better framed by addressing the differences between educational and noneducational institutions. Perhaps the mission of institutions of higher education cannot be performed in an environment regulated to a degree appropriate for a steel mill. If this is so, attention should focus not on the public-private dichotomy but on the important differences between the "community of scholars" and other potential subjects of government regulation.

However, claims of institutional "specialness" will be given short shrift by those who follow the *Rutgers* line of reasoning. Education serves a public purpose; it is a public good. Therefore, the public will inevitably contribute money and demand some degree of public input and control. On this view, *Rutgers* was rightly decided. Perhaps the Chancellor there was merely recognizing fiscal reality and social need; "ivory tower" and "community of scholars" arguments may represent pedagogical concepts which are luxuries society can no longer afford to support with public money.

On the other hand, it is clear that focusing on the public purpose of education yields no ultimate answers. If education is a public good, society's responsibility is to provide it in the most effective way. The central question remains: is education best provided by educational institutions which are highly regulated or relatively autonomous? If the former, the *Rutgers* approach may be correct; if the latter, the proper view may be that public money ought to be given to institutions of higher education, *whether public or private*, in line with a policy that emphasizes the value of academic freedom.

Another issue which goes to the heart of the problem is that of when "regulation" becomes "control." There is no real debate that at bottom line universities are subject to minimal standards of regulation. For example, in the area of equal employment opportunity they clearly are not and should not be entitled to discriminate against Blacks because they are Black. But it is equally clear that direct governmental control over hiring, promotion or tenure will be seen by universities as intolerable intrusions. The gray-area cases necessarily provide the most argument: an institution will fight for "autonomy" in "academic" matters and "authority" to administer its "internal affairs." The waffle words are obvious: on the one hand, they reflect important and abiding policy choices and issues; on the other hand, "regulation," "control" and others, as applied, may be no more than labels used to express the institutional interests of the speaker.

THE CURRENT SITUATION IN FOCUS

A study of "law and higher education" will of necessity focus in large measure on relationships between the federal government and institutions of higher learning. One sort of federal "law" of importance to educators is judge-made law, the paradigmatic example being a Supreme Court decision construing the United States Constitution. Such a decision may alter or redefine the "law" in areas such as due process, equal protection or freedom of expression.

The so-called "Warren Court" of the nineteen-sixties handed down a number of landmark decisions in the areas of school integration, student conduct, political and civil rights, and due process that had a significant impact on educational opportunity and educational institutions. However, the "Burger Court" of the nineteen-seventies has been a less activist court, especially in the enforcement of individual rights, and it appears instead to have embraced a philosophy of judicial abstention. As a consequence, it is unlikely that the current Court will be the source of new "law," except that which seeks to restrict or overturn the constitutional doctrines of the more activist Warren Court.

In contrast to the somewhat diminishing importance of judge-made law, at least on the federal level, is an impressive and significant increase in the impact of federal legislative and administrative control on higher education. During the last twenty years, the nature of federal involvement with four-year colleges and universities has changed in a dramatic fashion. In the fifties the federal government saw these institutions as important to scientific and medical research and as the provider of specialized education to a younger generation whose size and aspirations had grown enormously since the Second World War. Congress responded to these needs with appropriations to finance the construction of new facilities and to provide scholarships and low-cost loans to students themselves.

By the nineteen-sixties government support had increased to the point where government aid in many cases was likely to exceed a quarter or even a half of a given university's budget. Increasing dependence on Washington was a fact of life but one viewed by many as a necessary cost of the support and maintenance of first-rate graduate departments and research facilities. However, as the character of the link between Washington and academe evolved from one of financial dependence to one of financial dependence-coupled-with-regulation it began to be called into question.

In his report to the Board of Overseers for the year 1974-75, President Derek Bok of Harvard University argued that:

> The government has begun to exert its influence in new ways to encourage colleges and universities to conform to a variety of public policies. Some of these efforts have merely taken the form of extending familiar pieces of social legislation. . .to cover higher education. But the government has recently acted in ways that strike more directly at the central academic functions of colleges and universities.
>> —Rules have been issued to regulate the internal operations of educational institutions by requiring them to grant equal admissions to women and minority groups, to institute grievance procedures in cases of alleged discrimination, and to open confidential files for student inspection. . . .
>> —The work of scientific investigators has been regulated by restrictions affecting fetal research and experimentation on human subjects.

—Rather than simply increase federal aid to universities,
Congress has cut certain programs and expanded others
in ways that dramatize the power of the purse to alter
the shape and priorities of the university. . . .

In retrospect, it is not surprising that government chose to play
a stronger hand in influencing higher education. If universities accepted huge sums in federal aid for research and training, public officials could not fail to pay attention to the way in which the tax dollars were spent. . . .

Nevertheless, the rising tide of government intervention has begun to provoke serious concern from many colleges and universities. Kingman Brewster has pointed to "a growing tendency for the central government to use the spending power to prescribe education policies." In his colorful phrase, the government has adopted a philosophy best described as "now that I have bought the button, I have a right to design the coat." Other critics have complained of the mounting costs of complying with federal regulations, especially at a time when all educational institutions are hard pressed for funds to maintain essential academic programs.

Government officials have also had some sharp comments to make about the attitudes of college and university spokesmen toward Washington. Congressman John Brademas expressed these criticisms well by calling for "a little more information and a little less admonition from the higher education community." Beneath these complaints lies a deeper concern. The quality of government regulation does not depend simply on the intelligence and judgment of public officials but on the adequacy of the information and advice that these officials receive to assist them in their work. . . .

It is important to examine these complaints and consider how public officials should employ their powers over our colleges and universities. Federal support has played an indispensable role in strengthening higher education. Having given its aid, the government is bound to continue exercising supervision if only because higher education has become so large and the functions it performs so critical to the society.   Yet precisely because these functions are so important, it is vital that the government use its powers wisely to protect the public interest without weakening the institutions it seeks to regulate.

A university administrator is presented with a scheme characterized by excessive bureaucratization, expense and competing institutional values, often in situations in which priorities have not been established or stand in conflict. Faced with this picture, the university administrator must develop a model for analyzing the "cost" of regulation and compliance and standards for assessment of the positive and negative results achieved by the enforcement of and compliance with various schemes of federal regulation.

I.   Three Models of Federal Regulation

When one considers how federal regulation impacts on the human and financial resources of four-year universities and colleges, it is helpful to distinguish the various types of regulation.

One category of regulation includes laws designed to affect relationships between institutions of higher education and individuals. In many such cases, enforcement may contemplate a *total* termination of federal funds in the event of noncompliance. (Under this form of regulation the government may also retain the power to cut off funds in categories two and three noted hereinbelow.)

A second category of regulation includes direct "grant fund" programs, *with strings attached.* Noncompliance with the "strings attached" forms of regulation may result in either the loss of the specific grant funds or the total termination of all federal monies given to the institution for any purpose.

A third category of regulation includes programs providing for an infusion of government money to satisfy more general educational and training needs of society and to enrich institutions of higher education (*e.g.*, Comprehensive Health Manpower Training Act of 1971, 42 U.S.C. § 292b). Money in this third category may be given with no strings attached, except, of course, that the money must be used for the appropriated purpose.

II.   Recent Legislative Developments

During the past 15 years there has been a massive increase in federal regulation whether by Presidential Executive Order or Congressional acts passed pursuant to the Spending Power and the Commerce Clause under Article I Section 8 or pursuant to Section 5 of the 14th Amendment. Some examples are:

1. *Executive Order 11246 (as amended)*—Prohibits discrimination in employment on the basis of race, color, religion, sex and national origin by all federal government contractors. Subject to specified limitations and regulations established by the Office of Federal Contract Compliance, contractors (including universities) are required to establish and maintain affirmative action programs to eliminate and prevent discrimination.

2. *Title VI of the Civil Rights Act of 1964 (42 U.S.C. § 2000d)*— Prohibition against exclusion from, participation in, denial of benefits and discrimination under federally assisted programs on the basis of race, color or national origin.

3. *Title IX of the Education Amendments of 1972 (20 U.S.C. § 1681)*—Prohibits educational institutions that receive federal funds from discrimination on the basis of sex.

4. *Title VII of the Civil Rights Act of 1964 (42 U.S.C. § 2000e)*— *Equal Employment Opportunity Act*—Prohibits (with minor exceptions) employment discrimination on the basis of race, color, religion, sex or national origin. The Act creates the Equal

Employment Opportunity Commission (EEOC) and empowers it to prevent acts defined by Title VII as unlawful by investigating charges of discrimination, effecting conciliation when appropriate, and bringing a civil action when conciliation fails. In addition Title VII creates a private right of action in certain circumstances.

5. *Buckley Amendment (Family Educational Rights and Privacy Act 20 U.S.C. § 1232g (1974))*—Regulates and limits the use to be made of information in student files.

6. *Rehabilitation Act of 1973 (29 U.S.C. § 794)*—Section 504 provides that "no otherwise qualified handicapped individual . . . shall solely by reason of his handicap, be excluded from the participation in, denied the benefits of, or be subject to discrimination under any program or activity receiving Federal financial assistance."

7. *The Health Professions Educational Assistance Act of 1976, Pub. L. No. 94-484*—Expresses a Congressional determination that overspecialization in the medical profession has resulted in an inadequate number of primary-care physicians. Since persons in the health professions are viewed as a national health resource and the federal government shares the responsibility of assuring that they are available to meet the health needs of the American people, the act states that "it is therefore appropriate to provide support for [their] education and training . . . in a manner which will assure the availability of health professions personnel to all of the American people."

III. Is Compliance Practicable?

Institutions of higher education face increasingly complex bureaucracies administering extensive, overlapping and sometimes inconsistent regulations. For example, in the area of equal employment opportunity, employment practices of higher education institutions are regulated and administered by:
1. Equal Employment Opportunity Commission
2. Department of Labor
3. Department of Justice
4. Various state agencies

These agencies (along with private party litigants in certain cases) enforce:
1. Title VII and Title IX of the Civil Rights Act of 1964
2. § § 1981 and 1983 of the Civil Rights Acts of 1866 and 1871 (42 U.S.C.)
3. Executive Order 11246
4. Rehabilitation Act of 1973
5. State laws

Or, looked at in the context of a more narrowly drawn problem, a university or college dealing with the problem of sex discrimination in the area of faculty hiring and promotion must consider the application of at least five pieces of federal and state regulation:

1. Title VII of the Civil Rights Act of 1964 (as amended by the Equal Employment Opportunity Act of 1972)
2. The Equal Pay Act of 1963 (29 U.S.C. § 206) (amended by the Education Amendments of 1972)
3. Title IX of the Education Amendments of 1972
4. Executive Order 11246 (as amended by E.O. 11375)
5. State Fair Employment Practices acts

This proliferation of regulation has resulted in protest or at least expressions of serious concern from university administrators and federal regulators alike. The administrative agencies are being whipsawed by the conflicting demands of their two constituencies: the regulated institutions pressuring them for practicable solutions; the public and especially designated beneficiaries of regulation seeking "full compliance."

IV. The Buckley Amendment: A Paradigm

How does a representative piece of federal regulation impact on the human and financial resources of an institution? A useful answer must involve an applied as well as a theoretical analysis.

For example, the Buckley Amendment, which reaches far into the affairs of institutions of higher education, was passed without benefit of full public hearings on or committee consideration of the abuses at which it was directed or the costs it would impose. One cost to be measured is financial and administrative. Thus, for instance, the "cost" of compliance to a small, financially strapped college may be measurable not only in dollars but in academic programs unfunded.

In addition to paper work and bureaucratization, the Buckley Amendment has also imposed "costs" in terms of academic discretion which may negatively affect other federal policies. Admissions officers may claim that recommendations in student files have become blander and less informative; hence admissions decisions must often be made on the basis of grades and scores on standardized tests not geared to producing an optimally diverse or unbiased pattern of acceptances.

Yet another problem which has received some attention is the implications of the Buckley Amendment for educational researchers; some have contended that the "privacy aspects" of the law may in some instances render the university unable to evaluate its own performance because of lack of access to its own information.

V. Some Perspectives on the Regulation Issue

In a more general vein, there are a number of important policy questions that must be answered in any examination of the impact of federal regulation on higher education. Some of these questions are outlined hereinbelow:

1. Individual Versus Institutional Rights

Although protection of the rights of groups and institutions under the rubric of freedom of association has certain intellectual appeal, how do we deal with our suspicions about the motives of those who protest that their group will be injured or destroyed if exposed to external regulation? The problem becomes more complex when the form of regulation at issue is one designed not to serve general governmental aims but to protect the rights of individuals. Essentially the problem posed is one of perspective. When regulation is imposed on a small institution by the federal or state government, the institution looks small and helpless. But if looked at from the perspective of an individual whose rights are being protected from intrusion or denial by the institution, the problem looks quite different.

2. Perceived Versus Actual Impact

Granting the need for and appropriateness of certain forms of federal regulation, how do we measure impact on an educational institution? Can we meaningfully distinguish and compare *perceived* impact and *actual* impact? This impact may be measured in terms of its cost, whether to the institution or to government, or in terms of its resultant measurable social change. For example, in the case of HEW-mandated hiring of women faculty under E.O. 11246 we might ask:

a. How many women would not have been hired by institution X but for federal policy, federal intervention or threat of sanction? Did these people fill existing positions?

b. How do these women compare to other faculty in terms of performance, retention, promotion and tenure?

c. At what cost to the institution was this progress achieved? We might inquire as to *subjective costs:* Was financial or other discretion eliminated? Was institutional dignity somehow violated? We would also wish to measure *actual cost in dollars:* How much has been spent on hiring and salaries? How much has been spent on public relations and "compliance" paperwork?

d. At what cost to government was this progress achieved? Can we determine the cost of obtaining compliance at this institution? Can we estimate total program cost and divide by the number of jobs procured? Can we measure the extent of the litigation in which HEW is involved on this issue? In relation to good results? In relation to the number of cases settled informally by other procedures?

3. The Concept of Regulatory Maturity

The way in which an academic institution copes with a given regulatory scheme may be related to the "maturity" of the legislation itself or the institution's relationship with the relevant administrative body. One thesis might be that new, and hence as a practical matter unknown, legislation will create a level of institutional uncertainty which is bound to engender a storm of protest addressed more to the uncertainty itself than to the merits or demerits of a new program. On this theory, any start-up cost is *perceived* as extremely high and as requiring protest purely as a matter of principle. On the other hand, difficulties reported in dealing with mature schemes of regulation would tend to focus more on details and problems of actual implementation and to reflect on on-going relationships between the institution, government agency and a relevant public.

Another theory would be that institutions find it less burdensome to comply with new regulations when standards are somewhat amorphous and enforcement lax, and more difficult to comply with exacting standards later on. If a pattern were to emerge, it would be possible to derive a compliance model based on statute maturity that would be capable of generalization and refinement.

4.   The Concept of Regulatory Process

Does the form of regulation matter? If what we are talking about is the preservation of both educational institutions and legislatively expressed substantive moral values, are there patterns of regulation or enforcement more likely than others to serve these competing ends? Could a partial answer be found in political process? For example, before issuing proposed regulations under § 504, the Department of Health, Education and Welfare held ten meetings across the country to which interested parties were invited to offer their comments and recommendations concerning implementation. Former HEW Secretary Mathews expressed satisfaction with the results of this "early and more meaningful" public involvement in the regulatory process. Discussion in the proposed rules (45 CFR Part 84) highlights modifications made in response to public comment. Mathews' expressed goal was to make HEW more "legislative;" under his leadership HEW actively sought public input in order to make more "representative" decisions. The agency's orientation was to negotiation and conciliation rather than enforcement. Policy choices in favor of public input are intuitively satisfying, but we must attend to substance as well as form: Do they result in regulations better suited to the legislative purpose? Do they result in regulations more likely to engender compliance? Do they result in regulations better only for the vocal interest groups involved whose motives or needs may be in conflict with those of the "public" generally?

5.   Who is the Proper Decision Maker?

This suggests the question of where policy judgments should be made and that of where in fact they are made. Is a particular question properly one for Congress, for an administrative agency, or for the university itself? Assuming a principled basis on which to decide such theoretical questions, it remains a matter of practical interest to learn what really happens and at what level. Whether Congress, HEW or the university, is it a general or a foot soldier who is likely to make the critical choices?

6.   Talk May be Cheaper than Compliance

Policy choices can be made through appropriations without any ostensible change in the substantive declarations of existing statutes. How does an educational institution deal with regulations when, due to inadequate manpower or funds or changes in the political climate, the enforcement effort is seriously diminished? How does nonenforcement affect short-run decisions such as whether to hire individual A or B? How does it affect long-run decisions and planning, such as whether to invest thought and effort in developing a full-scale affirmative action plan? Further, should we be concerned about keeping regulations on the books which invite random and discriminatory enforcement?

7.   What Protection Does the Community of Scholars Need?
What Protection Can Society Afford to Render?

There seems to be a generally accepted belief that institutions of higher education are "special" and deserving of special treatment; if educators hope to advocate this view to inform national policy, it must be defined and limited. If some freedoms are essential to the "community of scholars," we need to know what they are and what values they promote.

Assuming that we can identify qualities essential to the existence of the community of scholars, we must consider in any given case whether academic integrity should be permitted to override competing values. More specifically:

a.   In some cases will academic needs outbalance federal goals altogether? This question asks whether the essential nature of the university qua university can withstand certain forms of intrusion.

b.   In other cases, e.g., equality of educational opportunity, federal regulation is clearly appropriate. Should the special nature of educational institutions mandate particular methods of federal treatment and proscribe others?

The aim of these questions is to isolate and identify some of the considerations relevant to an analysis of the relationship between legislative or administrative "law" and higher education. Clearly the same or similar issues will arise in the context of judge-made law as well. It is hoped that these questions will provide the reader with some stimulus for reflection as he or she encounters the materials that follow.

NOTE

For some useful discussions on the subject of the impact of regulation on higher education, see A 1976 Declaration of Independence, The Chronicle of Higher Education, April 19, 1976, p. 5; Bok, The President's Report, 1974-75 (Cambridge: Harvard University, 1975); Brewster, The Report of the President, Yale University: 1974-75 (New Haven: Yale University, 1975); Carnegie Commission on Higher Education, Institutional

Aid: Federal Support to Colleges and Universities (1972); Moynihan, *The Politics of Higher Education,* in Vol. II of "American Higher Education: Toward an Uncertain Future," Daedalus (Winter 1975), pp. 128-147; *Nature and Needs of Higher Education: The Report of the Commission on Financing Higher Education* (New York: Columbia Univ. Press, 1952); Oaks, *A Private University Looks At Government Regulation,* 4 Journ. of College and Univ. Law 1-12 (Fall 1976); Saunders, *Easing the Burden of Federal Regulation: The Next Move Is Ours,* 57, Educational Record, No. 4; C. Van Alstyne & S. Coldren, The Costs of Implementing Federally Mandated Social Programs at Colleges and Universities (Washington: American Council on Education, 1976).

CHAPTER 14

EQUAL EDUCATIONAL OPPORTUNITY
AND RACIAL DESEGREGATION

I.   The Constitutional Mandate

A.   Introduction

Equal educational opportunity is a critical, but as yet unobtained goal. It is an elusive standard that has gone through major metamorphoses in the last quarter of a century. In 1896, the Supreme Court announced that racially segregated, but tangibly equal facilities satisfied the equal protection burden of the Fourteenth Amendment. The Court found it unthinkable that "in the nature of things," the drafters of the Fourteenth Amendment "could . . . have . . . intended to abolish distinctions based upon color, or to enforce social, as distinguished from political equality, or a commingling of the two races upon terms unsatisfactory to either." Plessy v. Ferguson, 163 U.S. 537, 544 (1896). In 1978, Justice Powell, in The Board of Regents of the University of California v. Bakke, 98 S.Ct. 2733 (1978), found not only that racial diversity, the unthinkable of the *Plessy* Court, was a protected value of the First Amendment, but that it served as a permissible justification for certain voluntary affirmative action admissions programs.

The materials in this portion of the chapter explore the breadth of the 14th Amendment guarantee of equal opportunity in the context of higher education. The first part focuses on the scope of the duty imposed on the state to remedy the continuing effects of de jure segregation. The second part focuses on voluntary affirmative action admissions programs. It explores the outer limits of a state's constitutional authority to take steps to remedy the effects of generalized societal discrimination.

BROWN v. BOARD OF EDUCATION
Supreme Court of the United States
347 U.S. 483 (1954)

MR. CHIEF JUSTICE WARREN delivered the opinion of the Court.

These cases come to us from the States of Kansas, South Carolina, Virginia, and Delaware. . . .

In each of the cases, minors of the Negro race . . . seek the aid of the courts in obtaining admission to the public schools of their community on a nonsegregated basis. In each instance, they had been denied admission to schools attended by white children under laws requiring or permitting segregation according to race. This segregation was alleged to deprive the plaintiffs of the equal protection of the laws under the Fourteenth Amendment. In each of the cases other than the Delaware case, a three-judge federal district court denied relief to the plaintiffs on the so-called "separate but equal" doctrine announced by this Court in *Plessy* v. *Ferguson*, 163 U.S. 537. Under that doctrine, equality of treatment is accorded when the races are provided substantially equal facilities, even though these facilities be separate. In the Delaware case, the Supreme Court of Delaware adhered to that doctrine, but ordered that the plaintiffs be admitted to the white schools because of their superiority to the Negro schools. . . .

In the first cases in this Court construing the Fourteenth Amendment, decided shortly after its adoption, the Court interpreted it as proscribing all state-imposed discriminations against the Negro race. The doctrine of "separate but equal" did not make its appearance in this Court until 1896 in the case of *Plessy* v. *Ferguson, supra*, involving not education but transportation. . . . In this Court, there have been six cases involving the "separate but equal" doctrine in the field of public education. . . .

In . . . recent cases, all on the graduate school level, inequality was found in that specific benefits enjoyed by white students were denied to Negro students of the same educational qualifications. *Missouri ex rel. Gaines* v. *Canada*, 305 U.S. 337; *Sipuel* v. *Oklahoma*, 332 U.S. 631; *Sweatt* v. *Painter*, 339 U.S. 629; *McLaurin* v. *Oklahoma State Regents*, 339 U.S. 637. In none of these cases was it necessary to re-examine the doctrine to grant relief to the Negro plaintiff. And in *Sweatt* v. *Painter, supra*, the Court expressly reserved decision on the question whether *Plessy* v. *Ferguson* should be held inapplicable to public education.

In the instant cases, that question is directly presented. Here, unlike *Sweatt* v. *Painter,* there are findings below that the Negro and white schools involved have been equalized, or are being equalized, with respect to buildings, curricula, qualifications and salaries of teachers, and other "tangible" factors. Our decision, therefore, cannot turn on merely a comparison of these tangible factors in the Negro and white schools involved in each of the cases. We must look instead to the effect of segregation itself on public education.

In approaching this problem, we cannot turn the clock back to 1868 when the Amendment was adopted, or even to 1896 when *Plessy* v. *Ferguson* was written. . . .

Today, education is perhaps the most important function of state and local governments. Compulsory school attendance laws and the great expenditures for education both demonstrate our recognition of the importance of education to our democratic society. It is required in the performance of our most basic public responsibilities, even service in the armed forces. It is the very foundation of good citizenship. Today it is a principal instrument in awakening the child to cultural values, in preparing him for later professional training, and in helping him to adjust normally to his environment. In these days, it is doubtful that any child may reasonably be expected to succeed in life if he is denied the opportunity of an education.

Such an opportunity, where the state has undertaken to provide it, is a right which must be made available to all on equal terms.

We come then to the question presented: Does segregation of children in public schools solely on the basis of race, even though the physical facilities and other "tangible" factors may be equal, deprive the children of the minority group of equal educational opportunities? We believe that it does.

In *Sweatt* v. *Painter, supra,* in finding that a segregated law school for Negroes could not provide them equal educational opportunities, this Court relied in large part on "those qualities which are incapable of objective measurement but which make for greatness in a law school." In *McLaurin* v. *Oklahoma State Regents, supra,* the Court, in requiring that a Negro admitted to a white graduate school be treated like all other students, again resorted to intangible considerations: ". . . his ability to study, to engage in discussions and exchange views with other students, and, in general, to learn his profession." Such considerations apply with added force to children in grade and high schools. To separate them from others of similar age and qualifications solely because of their race generates a feeling of inferiority as to their status in the community that may affect their hearts and minds in a way unlikely ever to be undone. . . . Whatever may have been the extent of psychological knowledge at the time of *Plessy* v. *Ferguson*, this finding is amply supported by modern authority. Any language in *Plessy* v. *Ferguson* contrary to this finding is rejected.

We conclude that in the field of public education the doctrine of "separate but equal" has no place. Separate educational facilities are inherently unequal. Therefore, we hold that the plaintiffs and others similarly situated for whom the actions have been brought are, by reason of the segregation complained of, deprived of the equal protection of the laws guaranteed by the Fourteenth Amendment. This disposition makes unnecessary any discussion whether such segregation also violates the Due Process Clause of the Fourteenth Amendment. . . .

NOTES

1. In Bolling v. Sharpe, 347 U.S. 497 (1954), the Supreme Court extended the holding of *Brown* to the Due Process Clause of the Fifth Amendment. The Court held that segregation of the District of Columbia public school system constituted an arbitrary deprivation of liberty. The Court stated that: "In view of our decision [in *Brown*] that the constitution prohibits the states from maintaining racially segregated public schools, it would be unthinkable that the same constitution would impose a lesser duty on the Federal Government." 347 U.S. at 500.

2. The groundwork for *Brown* was laid by a series of cases in which the Supreme Court ordered the admission of black students to white-only graduate schools. The Court adhered to the *Plessy* format by finding intangible inequalities between the facilities offered to blacks and whites. In Missouri ex rel. Gaines v. Canada, 305 U.S. 337 (1938), the Court invalidated Missouri's refusal to admit blacks to the only publicly supported law school in the state, holding that the state's offer to pay out-of-state tuition for black law school applicants pending establishment of a state law school for blacks, did not satisfy the state's obligation to provide equal facilities within its own jurisdiction. Also, in Sipuel v. Board of Regents of University of Oklahoma, 332 U.S. 631 (1948), the Court

ordered the admission of a black female applicant to the University of Oklahoma Law School since the state had not yet established a separate law school for blacks.

Sweatt v. Painter, 339 U.S. 629 (1950), went a step further than *Gaines*, and required the admission of blacks to the University of Texas Law School, despite the fact that a state law school for blacks had recently been established. The Court held:

> "[W]e cannot find substantial equality in the educational opportunities offered white and Negro law students by the State. . . . What is more important, the University of Texas Law School possesses to a far greater degree those qualities which are incapable of objective measurement but which make for greatness in a law school. Such qualities, to name but a few, include reputation of the faculty, experience of the administration, position and influence of the alumni, standing in the community, traditions and prestige. . . . The law school to which Texas is willing to admit petitioner excludes from its student body members of the racial groups which number 85% of the population of the State and include most of the lawyers, witnesses, jurors, judges and other officials with whom petitioner will inevitably be dealing when he becomes a member of the Texas Bar." *Id.*, at 633-34.

Finally, in McLaurin v. Oklahoma State Regents, 339 U.S. 637 (1950), the Supreme Court held that the segregation of black graduate students within the classrooms, libraries and cafeteria facilities of the University violated the 14th Amendment. The Court concluded that such intra-school segregation impaired petitioner's ability to study, to exchange views with other students, and to learn his profession.

B.   The Scope of the Duty of Desegregate

The Supreme Court rendered a decision on the appropriate remedy for school segregation in Brown v. Board of Education, 349 U.S. 294 (1955), "*Brown II*." The decision established flexible guidelines for the desegregation process. Local school authorities were entrusted with the primary responsibility for planning and implementing desegregation programs. School districts were held to a standard of "good faith implementation" of programs designed to achieve desegregation "as soon as practicable."

The commands of *Brown II* gained clarity through numerous court challenges. In Green v. County School Board of New Kent County, 391 U.S. 430 (1968), the Court held that the Fourteenth Amendment imposed an affirmative duty on school authorities not only to dismantle the duality of a formerly segregated school system, but to create a "unitary system in which racial discrimination would be eliminated root and branch." 391 U.S. at 437-38. The New Kent County School Board had adopted a "freedom-of-choice" desegregation plan. The plan allowed children to choose between two schools, one predominantly white, the other all-black.

The Court found that in the three years of the plan's operation, not a single white child had chosen to attend the all-black school, and only 115 black children, or 15% of those living in the district, had chosen to attend the white school. This left 85% of the County's pupils attending a single-race school. The segregation continued despite the racially intermingled housing pattern which existed in the rural county. In fact, the record indicated that the County's school buses traveled overlapping routes to transport children to and from the two schools. The Court concluded that the school board's "freedom-of-choice" plan failed to "'effectuate a transition' to a unitary system," and was thereby constitutionally defective. 391 U.S. at 441. The Court ordered the school board to come forward with an affirmative plan "to convert promptly to a system without a 'white' school and a 'Negro' school, but just schools." 391 U.S. at 442.

Institutions of higher education have never been held fully subject to the duties imposed by *Green.* While it is uniformly agreed that public colleges and universities must dismantle dual systems, few federal courts would impose the same scope of duty on institutions of higher education that are imposed on elementary and secondary schools.[1] The courts point to differences in the nature of the institutions, and in the role a court ought to play in overseeing them. In Alabama State Teachers Ass'n v. Alabama Public School and College Authority, 289 F.Supp. 784 (M.D. Ala. 1968), *aff'd per curiam*, 393 U.S. 400 (1969), the court noted:

"Plaintiffs fail to take account of some significant differences between the elementary and secondary public schools and institutions of higher education and of some related differences concerning the role the courts should play in dismantling the dual systems. . . . Higher education is neither free nor compulsory. Students choose which, if any, institution they will attend. In making that choice they face the full range of diversity in goals, facilities, equipment, course offerings, teacher training and salaries, and living arrangements, perhaps only to mention a few. From where legislators sit, of course, the system must be viewed on a statewide basis. In deciding to open a new institution or . . . where to locate it, the legislature must consider a very complicated pattern of demand for and availability of the above-listed variables, including, also, impact on the dual system. We conclude that in reviewing such a decision to determine whether it maximized desegregation we would necessarily be involved, consciously or by default, in a wide range of educational policy decisions in which courts should not become involved." 289 F.Supp. at 787-88.

The three-judge district court deciding the case, held that racially neutral admissions coupled with minority faculty recruitment, satisfy the duty imposed by the Fourteenth Amendment, even though vestiges of duality still exist. 289 F.Supp. at 789.

Alabama State Teachers involved a suit brought by black college and school instructors to enjoin the state of Alabama from upgrading an extension center of the predominantly white Auburn University, located in the City of Montgomery, into a new four-year college. The City already contained Alabama State University, a historically black four-year school. It was claimed that the duplication of Alabama State's facilities at the site of the already-existing extension center of the Auburn University extension would merely serve to perpetuate the dual system of higher education in

---

1.   *See* Florida ex rel. Hawkins v. Board of Control, 350 U.S. 413 (1956).

Alabama.[2] The court rejected plaintiff's arguments, and refused to enjoin construction of the new college. Noting that Auburn University was already under a court order to admit all qualified blacks, the court concluded that the branch would be a new institution, not necessarily white or black, "but just a school." 289 F.Supp. at 789.

In reaching its decision the court ruled that the standards of *Green, supra,* did not control in the sphere of higher education. The court acknowledged the analogy between the "freedom-of-choice" plan rejected by *Green,* and the racially neutral admissions program proposed in the present case, but declared the analogy to be inapposite. 289 F.Supp. at 790. The court concluded that the Fourteenth Amendment did not require state institutions of higher education to "take whatever steps might be necessary to create a unitary system." To the contrary, the court was satisfied that mere abstention from active discrimination fulfilled the State's constitutional burden.

Norris v. State Council of Higher Education for Virginia, 327 F.Supp. 1368 (E.D. Va. 1971), *aff'd sub nom.,* Board of Visitors of the College of William and Mary in Virginia, 404 U.S. 907 (1971), involving another three-judge district court, came out with the opposite result. Under a similar fact situation, the court refused to follow *Alabama State Teachers Ass'n, supra,* and granted an injunction to prevent the escalation of a two-year branch of the College of William and Mary, which was predominantly white, into a four-year institution. The court found that the escalation would seriously impede the efforts of Virginia State University, a neighboring black four-year college, to desegregate. *Alabama State Teachers* was distinguished on the grounds that the Auburn campus would be an entirely new institution without a history of racial identification. In the present case, the new school would be formed from an already-existing school which for the previous ten years had possessed an all-white faculty and a virtually all-white student body.[3]

The Court held the university to the standard set down by *Green.* It concluded that the constitution requires more than "good faith admission and employment policies." *Norris, supra,* at 1372. The Court stated:

"In *Green,* though the Court was dealing with discrimination affecting public school pupils, it defined a constitutional duty owed as well to college students. The means of eliminating discrimination in public schools necessarily differ from its elimination in colleges, but the state's duty is as exacting." *Id.,* at 1373.

The *Norris* Court would therefore require states to attempt to maximize opportunities for integration in their planning and policy decisions.

In a third case, Sanders v. Ellington, 288 F.Supp. 937 (M.D. Tenn. 1968), the court applied the *Green* standard, but nonetheless refused to bar

---

2.   *See* Swann v. Charlotte-Mecklenburg Board of Education, 402 U.S. 1 (1971), which held, with respect to elementary and secondary schools, that decisions concerning future school construction and abandonment cannot be used, and must not serve, to perpetuate or reestablish a dual system.

3.   Note that both *Alabama State Teachers* and *Norris* were summarily affirmed by the Supreme Court.

construction of a new educational facility on the campus of the predominantly white University of Tennessee-Nashville. The Court found that Tennessee Agricultural and Industrial State University, a nearby black institution, would not be adversely affected by the new construction since the programs offered at the two schools did not significantly overlap. However, the court did require the state to submit a statewide plan to eliminate all evidence of duality remaining in the higher education system, with particular emphasis on the problems in Nashville. (In April of 1979, the Sixth Circuit Court of Appeals, by a 2-1 vote, upheld the District Court's ruling ordering the merger of Tennessee State and the University of Tennessee as a means of desegregating the state's system of higher education.)

The *Sanders* court reviewed Tennessee's desegregation efforts on two different occasions. In Geier v. Dunn, 337 F.Supp. 573 (M.D. Tenn. 1972), the court found that little progress had been made towards the desegregation of Tennessee A & I (now Tennessee State University). The court concluded that the "open-door" policy adopted at Tennessee State was ineffective. The court therefore required promulgation of a more specific desegregation program. Five years later, discouraged by the lack of progress in Nashville, the *Sanders* court ordered the merger of the University of Tennessee-Nashville with Tennessee State University under the governance of the State University's Board of Regents. [4] Geier v. Blanton, 427 F.Supp. 644 (M.D. Tenn. 1977). The court concluded that a gradual merger of the white institution into the black was the most practicable and effective solution. This order is now on appeal and a decision is pending.

The courts in *Alabama State Teachers, Norris* and *Sanders,* agree that the Fourteenth Amendment commands the dismantling of dual systems of higher education. Each court, however, varied in the scope of duty it was willing to impose on the universities. A neutral admissions policy was found satisfactory in *Alabama State Teachers,* even though the vestiges of a dual system remained intact, while *Norris* required the creation of a completely unitary system in which discrimination would be eliminated "root and branch." The *Sanders* court rejected "open-door" admissions as inadequate, yet refused to enjoin the construction of a new facility at a competing predominantly white school.

At a minimum then, it appears that the Equal Protection Clause requires the creation of a unitary system of public higher education. However, the degree of affirmative obligation to be imposed, and speed with which this goal must be attained is still the subject of broad dispute. Because litigation under the Fourteenth Amendment has provided inconsistent remedies to the problems of de jure segregation in higher education, and no remedy for de facto segregation in higher education, focus has shifted away from

---

4.   As an example of an alternative remedy, a federal court in Alabama, in a case involving segregated public trade schools and junior colleges, ordered the State to eliminate duplicate programs between the all-black and the all-white trade schools, and to implement geographic school attendance zones. The 5th Circuit affirmed the order although it was 'reluctant' to require school attendance zones for college-age level institutions. *See* Lee v. Macon County Board of Education, 453 F.2d 524 (5th Cir. 1971).

the Fourteenth Amendment to statutory enforcement (Title VI of the Civil Rights Act of 1964, 42 U.S.C. § 2000d, discussed in the final part of the chapter) and voluntary remedies. Affirmative action admissions programs have been responsible for most of the progress made in recent years.

NOTES

1. To what extent can private universities be held subject to the duty to integrate? Does the receipt of state financial aid constitute enough governmental involvement to bring an institution under the purview of the 14th Amendment? In Braden v. The University of Pittsburgh, 552 F.2d 948 (3rd Cir. 1977), the Third Circuit held that state appropriations plus public regulation amounted to state action. With lesser degrees of state involvement, most courts have rejected claims alleging state action on the part of private colleges and universities. *See, e.g.,* Lamb v. Rantoul, 561 F.2d 409, 410-11 (1st Cir. 1977); Cohen v. Illinois Inst. of Technology, 524 F.2d 818, 827 (7th Cir. 1975), *cert. denied,* 425 U.S. 943 (1976); Greenya v. George Washington University, 512 F.2d 556, 561-62 (D.C. Cir. 1975), *cert. denied,* 423 U.S. 995 (1976). For further discussion of these questions see: Comment, *Constitutional Law—State Action—Hiring and Promotion Practices of Private University Receiving Public Funds Held State Action—Braden v. University of Pittsburgh,* 52 N.Y.U. L. Rev. 1401 (1977); and Note, *State Action: Theories for Applying Constitutional Restrictions to Private Activity,* 74 Colum. L. Rev. 654 (1974).

The Civil Rights Act of 1866, 42 U.S.C. § 1981, (which guarantees the equal right to make and enforce contracts), does not contain a state action requirement, and in Runyon v. McCrary, 427 U.S. 160 (1976), the Supreme Court held that a private, commercially operated school could not refuse to admit black students. § 1981 has also been held to prohibit a private sectarian school from operating on a racially segregated basis, when the school's policy of excluding blacks was not in the exercise of religion. Brown v. Dade Christian Schools, Inc., 556 F.2d 310 (5th Cir. 1977). *See also:* Comment, *Racial Exclusion by Religious Schools: Brown v. Dade Christian Schools, Inc.,* 91 Harv. L. Rev. 879 (Feb. 1978); and Note, *Racial Discrimination in Church Schools,* 38 La. L. Rev. 874 (Sept. 1978).

2. Are sex-segregated educational facilities permissible under the 14th Amendment? The Third Circuit, in Vorchheimer v. School District of Philadelphia, 532 F.2d 880 (3d Cir. 1976), *aff'd per curiam* (by an equally divided court), 430 U.S. 703 (1977), confirmed the "lingering validity" of *Plessy's* "separate but equal" formulation for gender-based classifications. The court held that segregation of the schools did not violate the 14th Amendment because attendance at the schools was voluntary and the educational opportunities offered were essentially equal. The court stated:

> Race is a suspect classification under the Constitution, but the Supreme Court has declined to so characterize gender. We are committed to the concept that there is no fundamental difference between races and therefore, in justice, there can be no dissimilar treatment. But there are differences between the sexes which may, in limited circumstances, justify disparity in law. 532 F.2d at 886.

(The court also rejected plaintiff's claim that the single-sex schools violated the Equal Educational Opportunities Act of 1974, § 202 et seq., 20 U.S.C. § 1701 et seq. For a case holding that the EEOA does prohibit sex-segregation, even though the 14th Amendment may not, *see* U.S. v. Hinds County School Board, 560 F.2d 619 (5th Cir. 1977).)

In Kirstein v. The Rector and Visitors of the University of Virginia, 309 F.Supp. 184 (E.D. Va. 1970), a 'male-only' admissions policy in effect at the University of Virginia at Charlottesville was struck down because the educational opportunities of the Charlottesville campus were not 'afforded' by other state-operated institutions. The court noted that along with the differences in curriculum, "there exists at Charlottesville a 'prestige' factor that is not available at other Virginia educational institutions."

309 F.Supp. at 187. The court did not reach the question of whether "the now discountenanced principle of 'separate but equal' may have lingering validity in another area—for the facilities elsewhere are not equal with respect to these plaintiffs." *Id.*, at f.n. 1. *See also*, Waldie v. Schlesinger, 509 F.2d 508 (D.C. Cir. 1974), *reh. denied* (1975), reversing the grant of a summary judgment for the government in a suit challenging the "men only" admissions policies of the U.S. Air Force and Naval Academies.

For further material on this topic *see*: Note, *Single-Sex Public Schools: The Last Bastion of "Separate but Equal"?* 1977 Duke L.J. 259 (March, 1977); and Comment, *Plessy Revived: The Separate But Equal Doctrine and Sex-Segregated Education*, 12 Harv. Civ. Rts. Civ. Lib. L. Rev. 585 (1977).

3. Does *Brown* require all formerly segregated universities to become "racially balanced," *e.g.* predominantly white? Should this include black colleges that possess a special ability to aid disadvantaged black students? It is coming to be recognized that the traditional black colleges in the South serve a unique and necessary function. Yet, many of these institutions have become the focal point of desegregation orders issued by H.E.W. and the courts. *See, e.g.*, Hunnicutt v. Burge, 356 F.Supp. 1227 (M.D. Ga. 1973). Can an argument be constructed which would allow the identity of such colleges to be preserved? For further discussion of this topic *see:* Chronicle of Higher Education, *The Effects of School Desegregation: The Debate Goes On*, Vol. XVII, Nov. 6, 1978, p. 1; *Ibid., Challenges for a Proud Black University*, Vol. XVII, Nov. 27, 1978, pp. 8-9; *Ibid., Predominantly Black Grambling is Likely to Stay That Way*, Vol. XVII, Oct. 30, 1978, pp. 7-8; Washington Post, *Black Colleges: The Right to Segregate*, Jan. 1, 1979, at A-15; and Gallagher, *Higher Education and the Black Student: Retrospect and Prospect*, 19 How. L.J. 29 (1975).

4. Some general articles on the subject matter of this section include: Comment, *Racially Identifiable Dual Systems of Higher Education: The 1971 Affirmative Duty to Desegregate*, 18 Wayne L. Rev. 1069 (1972); Note, *Integrating in Higher Education: Defining the Scope of the Affirmative Duty to Integrate*, 57 Iowa L. Rev. 898 (1972); and Wilkinson, *The Supreme Court and Southern School Desegregation, 1955-1970: A History and Analysis,* 64 Va. L. Rev. 485 (May, 1978).

C. The Outer Limit: Voluntary Preferential Admissions Programs

REGENTS OF THE UNIVERSITY OF CALIFORNIA v. BAKKE
United States Supreme Court
98 S.Ct. 2733 (1978)

MR. JUSTICE POWELL announced the judgment of the Court.

This case presents a challenge to the special admissions program of the petitioner, the Medical School of the University of California at Davis, which is designed to assure the admission of a specified number of students from certain minority groups. The Superior Court of California sustained respondent's challenge, holding that petitioner's program violated the California Constitution, Title VI of the Civil Rights Act of 1964, 42 U.S.C. §2000d, and the Equal Protection Clause of the Fourteenth Amendment. The court enjoined petitioner from considering respondent's race or the race of any other applicant in making admissions decisions. It refused, however, to order respondent's admission to the Medical School, holding that he had not carried his burden of proving that he would have been admitted but for the constitutional and statutory violations. The Supreme Court of California affirmed those portions of the trial court's judgment declaring the special admissions program unlawful and enjoining petitioner from considering the race of any applicant. It modified that portion of the judgment denying respondent's requested injunction and directed the trial court to order his admission.

For the reasons stated in the following opinion, I believe that so much of the judgment of the California court as holds petitioner's special admissions program unlawful and directs that respondent be admitted to the Medical School must be affirmed. For the reasons expressed in a separate opinion, my Brothers THE CHIEF JUSTICE, MR. JUSTICE STEWART, MR. JUSTICE REHNQUIST, and MR. JUSTICE STEVENS concur in this judgment.

I also conclude for the reasons stated in the following opinion that the portion of the court's judgment enjoining petitioner from according any consideration to race in its admissions process must be reversed. For reasons expressed in separate opinions, my Brothers MR. JUSTICE BRENNAN, MR. JUSTICE WHITE, MR. JUSTICE MARSHALL, and MR. JUSTICE BLACKMUN concur in this judgment.

Affirmed in part and reversed in part.

I

The Medical School of the University of California at Davis opened in 1968 with an entering class of 50 students. In 1971, the size of the entering class was increased to 100 students, a level at which it remains. No admissions program for disadvantaged or minority students existed when the school opened, and the first class contained three Asians but no blacks, no Mexican-Americans, and no American Indians. Over the next two years, the faculty devised a special admissions program to increase the representation of "disadvantaged" students in each medical school class. The special program consisted of a separate admissions system operating in coordination with the regular admissions process.

Under the regular admissions procedure, a candidate could submit his application to the medical school beginning in July of the year preceding the academic year for which admission was sought. Record 149. Because of the large number of applications, the admissions committee screened each one to select candidates for further consideration. Candidates whose overall undergraduate grade point averages fell below 2.5 on a scale of 4.0 were summarily rejected. *Id.*, at 63. About one out of six applicants was invited for a personal interview. *Ibid.* Following the interviews, each candidate was rated on a scale of 1 to 100 by his interviewers and four other members of the admissions committee. The rating embraced the interviewers' summaries, the candidate's overall grade point average, grade point average in science courses, and scores on the Medical College Admissions Test (MCAT), letters of recommendation, extracurricular activities, and other biographical data. *Id.*, at 62. The ratings were added together to arrive at each candidate's "benchmark" score. Since five committee members rated each candidate in 1973, a perfect score was 500; in 1974, six members rated each candidate, so that a perfect score was 600. The full committee then reviewed the file and scores of each applicant and made offers of admission on a "rolling" basis. The chairman was responsible for placing names on the waiting list. They were not placed in strict numerical order; instead, the chairman had discretion to include persons with "special skills." *Ibid.*

The special admissions program operated with a separate committee, a majority of whom were members of minority groups. *Id.*, at 163. On the 1973 application form, candidates were asked to indicate whether they wished to be considered as "economically and/or educationally disadvantaged" applicants; on the 1974 form the question was whether they wished to be considered as members of a "minority group," which the medical school apparently viewed as "Blacks," "Chicanos," "Asians," and "American Indians." *Id.*, at 65-66, 146, 197, 203-205, 216-218. If these questions were answered affirmatively, the application was forwarded to the special admissions committee. No formal definition of "disadvantage" was ever produced, *id.*, at 163-164, but the chairman of the special committee screened each application to see whether it reflected economic or educational deprivation. Having passed this initial hurdle, the applications then were rated by the special committee in a fashion similar to that used by the general admissions committee, except that special candidates did not have to meet the 2.5 grade point average cut-off applied to regular applicants. About one-fifth of the total number of special applicants were invited for interviews in 1973 and 1974. Following each interview, the special committee assigned each special applicant a benchmark score. The special committee then presented its top choices to the general admissions committee. The latter did not rate or compare the special candidates against the general applicants, *id.*, at 388, but could reject recommended special candidates for failure to meet course requirements or other specific deficiencies. *Id.*, at 171-172. The special committee continued to recommend special applicants until a number prescribed by faculty vote were admitted. While the overall class size was still 50, the prescribed number was eight; in 1973 and 1974, when the class size had doubled to 100, the prescribed number of special admissions also doubled, to 16. *Id.*, at 164, 166.

From the year of the increase in class size—1971—through 1974, the special program resulted in the admission of 21 black students, 30 Mexican-Americans, and 12 Asians, for a total of 63 minority students. Over the same period, the regular admissions program produced one black, six Mexican-Americans, and 37 Asians, for a total of 44 minority students. Although disadvantaged whites applied to the special program in large numbers, see n. 5, *supra*, none received an offer of admission through that process. Indeed, in 1974, at least, the special committee explicitly considered only "disadvantaged" special applicants who were members of one of the designated minority groups. Record 171.

Allan Bakke is a white male who applied to the Davis Medical School in both 1973 and 1974. In both years Bakke's application was considered by the general admissions program, and he received an interview. His 1973 interview was with Dr. Theodore H. West, who considered Bakke "a very desirable applicant to [the] medical school." *Id.*, at 225. Despite a strong benchmark score of 468 out of 500, Bakke was rejected. His application had come late in the year, and no applicants in the general admissions process with scores below 470 were accepted after Bakke's application was completed. *Id.*, at 69. There were four special admissions slots unfilled at that time, however, for which Bakke was not considered. *Id.*, at 70. After his 1973 rejection, Bakke wrote to Dr. George H. Lowrey, Associate Dean and Chairman of the Admissions Committee, protesting that the special admissions program operated as a racial and ethnic quota. *Id.*, at 259.

Bakke's 1974 application was completed early in the year. *Id.*, at 70. His student interviewer gave him an overall rating of 94, finding him "friendly, well tempered, conscientious and delightful to speak with," *Id.*, at 229. His faculty interviewer was, by coincidence, the same Dr. Lowrey to whom he had written in protest of the special admissions program. Dr. Lowrey found Bakke "rather limited in his approach" to the problems of the medical profession and found disturbing Bakke's "very definite opinions which were based more on his personal viewpoints than upon a study of the total problem." *Id.*, at 226. Dr. Lowrey gave Bakke the lowest of his six ratings, an 86; his total was 549 out of 600. *Id.*, at 230. Again, Bakke's application was rejected. In neither year did the chairman of the admissions committee, Dr. Lowrey, exercise his discretion to place Bakke on the waiting list. *Id.*, at 64. In both years, applicants were admitted under the special program with grade point averages, MCAT scores, and bench mark scores significantly lower than Bakke's.[7]

[7.]   The following table compares Bakke's science grade point average, overall grade point average, and MCAT Scores with the average scores of regular admittees and of special admittees in both 1973 and 1974. Record, 210, 223, 231, 234:

Class Entering in 1973

	SGPA	OGPA	Verbal	MCAT (Percentiles) Quantitative	Science	Gen. Infor.
Bakke.	3.44	3.51	96	94	97	72
Average of Regular Admittees	3.51	3.49	81	76	83	69
Average of Special Admittees.	2.62	2.88	46	24	35	33

Class Entering in 1974

	SGPA	OGPA	Verbal	MCAT (Percentiles) Quantitative	Science	Gen. Infor.
Bakke.	3.44	3.51	96	94	97	72
Average of Regular Admittees	3.36	3.29	69	67	82	72
Average of Special Admittees.	2.42	2.62	34	30	37	18

Applicants admitted under the special program also had benchmark scores significantly lower than many students, including Bakke, rejected under the general admissions program, even though the special rating system apparently gave credit for overcoming "disadvantage." Record 181, 388.

After the second rejection, Bakke filed the instant suit in the Superior Court of California.[8] . . .

. . . The trial court found that the special program operated as a racial quota, because minority applicants in the special program were rated only against one another, Record 388, and 16 places in the class of 100 were reserved for them. *Id.*, at 295-296. Declaring that the University could not take race into account in making admissions decisions, the trial court held the challenged program violative of the Federal Constitution, the state constitution and Title VI. The court refused to order Bakke's admission, however, holding that he had failed to carry his burden of proving that he would have been admitted but for the existence of the special program.

Bakke appealed from the portion of the trial court judgment denying him admission, and the University appealed from the decision that its special admissions program was unlawful and the order enjoining it from considering race in the processing of applications. The Supreme Court of California . . . held that the Equal Protection Clause of the Fourteenth Amendment required that "no applicant may be rejected because of his race, in favor of another who is less qualified, as measured by standards applied without regard to race." *Id.*, at 55, 553 P.2d, at 1166.

Turning to Bakke's appeal, the court ruled that since Bakke had established that the University had discriminated against him on the basis of his race, the burden of proof shifted to the University to demonstrate that he would not have been admitted even in the absence of the special admissions program. . . . In its petition for rehearing below, however, the University conceded its inability to carry that burden. Appendix B to Application for Stay, at 19-20. The California court thereupon amended its opinion to direct that the trial court enter judgment ordering Bakke's admission to the medical school. 18 Cal. 3d, at 64, 553 P.2d, at 1172. That order was stayed pending review in this Court. 429 U.S. 953 (1976). We granted certiorari to consider the important constitutional issue. 429 U.S. 1090 (1977).

II.

*   *   *

A

At the outset we face the question whether a right of action for private parties exists under Title VI. Respondent argues that there is a private right of action, invoking the test set forth in *Cort* v. *Ash*, 422 U.S. 66, 78 (1975). He contends that the statute creates a federal right in his favor, that legis-

---

[8.]   Prior to the actual filing of the suit, Bakke discussed his intentions with Peter C. Storandt, Assistant to the Dean of Admissions at the Davis Medical School. Record 259-269. Storandt expressed sympathy for Bakke's position and offered advice on litigation strategy. Several *amici* imply that these discussions render Bakke's suit "collusive." There is no indication, however, that Storandt's views were those of the medical school or that anyone else at the school even was aware of Storandt's correspondence and conversations with Bakke. Storandt is no longer with the University.

lative history reveals an intent to permit private actions, that such actions would further the remedial purposes of the statute, and that enforcement of federal rights under the Civil Rights Act generally is not relegated to the States. . . .

Petitioner denies the existence of a private right of action, arguing that the sole function of §601, see n. 11, *supra*, was to establish a predicate for administrative action under §602, 42 U.S.C. §2000d-1. In its view, administrative curtailment of federal funds under that section was the only sanction to be imposed upon recipients that violated §601. . . .

We find it unnecessary to resolve this question in the instant case. The question of respondent's right to bring an action under Title VI was neither argued nor decided in either of the courts below, and this Court has been hesitant to review questions not addressed below. . . . We therefore do not address this difficult issue. Similarly, we need not pass upon petitioner's claim that private plaintiffs under Title VI must exhaust administrative remedies. We assume only for the purposes of this case that respondent has a right of action under Title VI. . . .

B

The language of §601, like that of the Equal Protection Clause, is majestic in its sweep:

"No person in the United States shall, on the ground of race, color, or national origin, be excluded from participation in, be denied the benefits of, or be subjected to discrimination under any program or activity receiving Federal financial assistance."

The concept of "discrimination," like the phrase "equal protection of the laws," is susceptible to varying interpretations, for as Mr. Justice Holmes declared, "[a] word is not a crystal, transparent and unchanged, it is the skin of a living thought and may vary greatly in color and content according to the circumstances and the time in which it is used." *Towne* v. *Eisner*, 245 U.S. 418, 425 (1918). We must, therefore, seek whatever aid is available in determining the precise meaning of the statute before us. . . . Examination of the voluminous legislative history of Title VI reveals a congressional intent to halt federal funding of entities that violate a prohibition of racial discrimination similar to that of the Constitution. Although isolated statements of various legislators, taken out of context, can be marshalled in support of the proposition that §601 enacted a purely color-blind scheme, without regard to the reach of the Equal Protection Clause, these comments must be read against the background of both the problem that Congress was addressing and the broader view of the statute that emerges from a full examination of the legislative debates.

The problem confronting Congress was discrimination against Negro citizens at the hands of recipients of federal moneys. Indeed, the color-blindness pronouncements cited in the margin at n. 19, generally occur in the midst of extended remarks dealing with the evils of segregation in federally funded programs. Over and over again, proponents of the bill detailed the plight of Negroes seeking equal treatment in such programs. There simply was no reason for Congress to consider the validity of hypothetical preferences that might be accorded minority citizens; the legislators were dealing with the real and pressing problem of how to guarantee those citizens equal treatment.

In addressing that problem, supporters of Title VI repeatedly declared that the bill enacted constitutional principles.

*   *   *

In the Senate, Senator Humphrey declared that the purpose of Title VI was "to insure that Federal funds are spent in accordance with the Constitution and the moral sense of the Nation." *Id.*, at 6544. Senator Ribicoff agreed that Title VI embraced the constitutional standard: "Basically, there is a constitutional restriction against discrimination in the use of federal funds; and title VI simply spells out the procedure to be used in enforcing that restriction." *Id.*, at 13333. Other Senators expressed similar views.

Further evidence of the incorporation of a constitutional standard into Title VI appears in the repeated refusals of the legislation's supporters precisely to define the term "discrimination." Opponents sharply criticized this failure, but proponents of the bill merely replied that the meaning of "discrimination" would be made clear by reference to the Constitution or other existing law. . . .

In view of the clear legislative intent, Title VI must be held to proscribe only those racial classifications that would violate the Equal Protection Clause or the Fifth Amendment.

III.

A

. . . The parties disagree as to the level of judicial scrutiny to be applied to the special admissions program. Petitioner argues that the court below erred in applying strict scrutiny, as this inexact term has been applied in our cases. That level of review, petitioner asserts, should be reserved for classifications that disadvantage "discrete and insular minorities." See *United States* v. *Carolene Products Co.*, 304 U.S. 144, 152 n. 4 (1938). Respondent, on the other hand, contends that the California court correctly rejected the notion that the degree of judicial scrutiny accorded a particular racial or ethnic classification hinges upon membership in a discrete and insular minority and duly recognized that the "rights established [by the Fourteenth Amendment] are personal rights." *Shelley* v. *Kraemer,* 334 U.S. 1, 22 (1948).

En route to this crucial battle over the scope of judicial review, the parties fight a sharp preliminary action over the proper characterization of the special admissions program. Petitioner prefers to view it as establishing a "goal" of minority representation in the medical school. Respondent, echoing the courts below, labels it a racial quota. [26]

This semantic distinction is beside the point: the special admissions program is undeniably a classification based on race and ethnic background. To the extent that there existed a pool of at least minimally qualified minority applicants to fill the 16 special admissions seats, white applicants could compete only for 84 seats in the entering class, rather than the 100 open to minority applicants. Whether this limitation is described as a quota or a goal, it is a line drawn on the basis of race and ethnic status.

The guarantees of the Fourteenth Amendment extend to persons. Its language is explicit: "No state shall . . . deny to any person within its jurisdiction the equal protection of the laws." It is settled beyond question that the "rights created by the first section of the Fourteenth Amendment are, by its terms, guaranteed to the individual. They are personal rights," *Shelley* v. *Kraemer, supra*, at 22. Accord, *Missouri ex rel. Gaines* v. *Canada, supra*, at 351; *McCabe* v. *Atchison, T. & S. F. R. Co.*, 235 U.S. 151, 161-162 (1914). The guarantee of equal protection cannot mean one thing when applied to one individual and something else when applied to a person of another color. If both are not accorded the same protection, then it is not equal.

Nevertheless, petitioner argues that the court below erred in applying strict scrutiny to the special admissions programs because white males, such as respondent, are not a "discrete and insular minority" requiring extraordinary protection from the majoritarian political process. *Carolene Products Co., supra*, at 152-153, n. 4. This rationale, however has never been invoked in our decisions as a prerequisite to subjecting racial or ethnic distinctions to strict scrutiny. Nor has this Court held that discreteness and insularity constitute necessary preconditions to a holding that a particular classification is invidious. . . . These characteristics may be relevant in deciding whether or not to add new types of classifications to the list of "suspect" categories or whether a particular classification survives close examination. . . . Racial and ethnic classifications, however, are subject to stringent examination without regard to these additional characteristics. . . .

Racial and ethnic distinctions of any sort are inherently suspect and thus call for the most exacting judicial examination.

[26.]   Petitioner defines "quota" as a requirement which must be met but can never be exceeded, regardless of the quality of the minority applicants. Petitioner declares that there is no "floor" under the total number of minority students admitted; completely unqualified students will not be admitted simply to meet a "quota." Neither is there a "ceiling," since an unlimited number could be admitted through the general admissions process. On this basis the special admissions program does not meet petitioner's definition of a quota.

    The court below found—and petitioner does not deny—that white applicants could not compete for the 16 places reserved solely for the special admissions program. 18 Cal. 3d, at 44, 553 P. 2d, at 1159. Both courts below characterized this as a "quota" system.

B

This perception of racial and ethnic distinctions is rooted in our Nation's constitutional and demographic history. The Court's initial view of the Fourteenth Amendment was that its "one pervading purpose" was "the freedom of the slave race, the security and firm establishment of that freedom, and the protection of the newly-made freeman and citizen from the oppressions of those who had formerly exercised dominion over him." *Slaughter-House Cases*, 16 Wall. 36, 71 (1873). The Equal Protection Clause, however, was "[v]irtually strangled in its infancy by post-civil-war judicial reactionism." It was relegated to decades of relative desuetude while the Due Process Clause of the Fourteenth Amendment, after a short germinal period, flourished as a cornerstone in the Court's defense of property and liberty of contract. . . .

By that time it was no longer possible to peg the guarantees of the Fourteenth Amendment to the struggle for equality of one racial minority. During the dormancy of the Equal Protection Clause, the United States had become a nation of minorities. Each had to struggle—and to some extent struggles still to overcome the prejudices not of a monolithic majority, but of a "majority" composed of various minority groups of whom it was said— perhaps unfairly in many cases—that a shared characteristic was a willingness to disadvantage other groups. As the Nation filled with the stock of many lands, the reach of the Clause was gradually extended to all ethnic groups seeking protection from official discrimination. . . .

Although many of the Framers of the Fourteenth Amendment conceived of its primary function as bridging the vast distance between members of the Negro race and the white "majority," *Slaughter-House Cases, supra*, the Amendment itself was framed in universal terms, without reference to color, ethnic origin, or condition of prior servitude. As this Court recently remarked in interpreting the 1866 Civil Rights Act to extend to claims of racial discrimination against white persons, "the 39th Congress was intent upon establishing in federal law a broader principle than would have been necessary to meet the particular and immediate plight of the newly freed Negro slaves." *McDonald* v. *Santa Fe Trail Transp. Co.*, 427 U.S. 273, 296 (1976). And that legislation was specifically broadened in 1870 to ensure that "all persons," not merely "citizens," would enjoy equal rights under the law. . . .

*   *   *

Petitioner urges us to adopt for the first time a more restrictive view of the Equal Protection Clause and hold that discrimination against members of the white "majority" cannot be suspect if its purpose can be characterized as "benign."[34] The clock of our liberties, however, cannot be turned back to

---

[34.]   In the view of MR. JUSTICE BRENNAN, MR. JUSTICE WHITE, MR. JUSTICE MARSHALL, and MR. JUSTICE BLACKMUN, the pliable notion of "stigma" is the crucial element in analyzing racial classifications. See, *e.g., post*, at 38, The Equal Protection Clause is not framed in terms of "stigma." Certainly the word has no clearly defined constitutional meaning. It reflects a subjective judgment that is standardless. *All* state-imposed classifications that rearrange

1868, *Brown* v. *Board of Education, supra*, at 492; accord, *Loving* v. *Virginia, supra*, at 9. It is far too late to argue that the guarantee of equal protection to *all* persons permits the recognition of special wards entitled to a degree of protection greater than that accorded others. "The Fourteenth Amendment is not directed solely against discrimination due to a 'two-class theory'—that is, based upon differences between 'white' and Negro." *Hernandez, supra*, at 478.

Once the artificial line of a "two-class theory" of the Fourteenth Amendment is put aside, the difficulties entailed in varying the level of judicial review according to a perceived "preferred" status of a particular racial or ethnic minority are intractable. The concepts of "majority" and "minority" necessarily reflect temporary arrangements and political judgments. As observed above, the white "majority" itself is composed of various minority groups, most of which can lay claim to a history of prior discrimination at the hands of the state and private individuals. Not all of these groups can receive preferential treatment and corresponding judicial tolerance of distinctions drawn in terms of race and nationality, for then the only "majority" left would be a new minority of White Anglo-Saxon Protestants. There is no principled basis for deciding which groups would merit "heightened judicial solicitude" and which would not. [36] . . .

---

burdens and benefits on the basis of race are likely to be viewed with deep resentment by the individuals burdened. The denial to innocent persons of equal rights and opportunities may outrage those so deprived and therefore may be perceived as invidious. These individuals are likely to find little comfort in the notion that the deprivation they are asked to endure is merely the price of membership in the dominant majority and that its imposition is inspired by the supposedly benign purpose of aiding others. One should not lightly dismiss the inherent unfairness of, and the perception of mistreatment that accompanies, a system of allocating benefits and privileges on the basis of skin color and ethnic origin. Moreover, MR. JUSTICE BRENNAN, MR. JUSTICE WHITE, MR. JUSTICE MARSHALL, and MR. JUSTICE BLACKMUN offer no principle for deciding whether preferential classifications reflect a benign remedial purpose or a malevolent stigmatic classification, since they are willing in this case to accept mere *post hoc* declarations by an isolated state entity—a medical school faculty—unadorned by particularized findings of past discrimination, to establish such a remedial purpose.

[36.]   As I am in agreement with the view that race may be taken into account as a factor in an admissions program, I agree with my Brothers BRENNAN, WHITE, MARSHALL, and BLACKMUN that the portion of the judgment that would proscribe all consideration of race must be reversed. See Part V, *infra*. But I disagree with much that is said in their opinion.

They would require as a justification for a program such as petitioner's, only two findings: (i) that there has been some form of discrimination against the preferred minority groups "by society at large," *post*, at 45 (it being conceded that petitioner had no history of discrimination), and (ii) that "there is reason to believe" that the disparate impact sought to be rectified by the program is the "product" of such discrimination. . . .

The breadth of this hypothesis is unprecedented in our constitutional system. The first step is easily taken. No one denies the regrettable fact that there has been societal discrimination in this country against various racial and ethnic groups. The second step, however, involves a speculative leap: but for this discrimination by society at large, Bakke "would have failed to qualify for admission" because Negro applicants—nothing is said about Asians, cf., *e.g., post.* at 50 n. 57—would have made better scores. Not one word in the record supports this conclusion, and the plurality offers no standard for courts to use in applying such a presumption of causation to other racial or ethnic classifications. This failure is a grave one, since if it may be concluded *on this record* that each of the minority groups preferred by the petitioner's special program is entitled to the benefit of the presumption, it would seem difficult to determine that any of the dozens of minority groups that have suffered "societal discrimination" cannot also claim it, in any area of social intercourse. See Part IV-B, *infra*.

Moreover, there are serious problems of justice connected with the idea of preference itself. First, it may not always be clear that a so-called preference is in fact benign. Courts may be asked to validate burdens imposed upon individual members of particular groups in order to advance the group's general interest. . . . Second, preferential programs may only reinforce common stereotypes holding that certain groups are unable to achieve success without special protection based on a factor having no relationship to individual worth. See *DeFunis* v. *Odegaard*, 416 U.S. 312, 343 (Douglas, J., dissenting). Third, there is a measure of inequity in forcing innocent persons in respondent's position to bear the burdens of redressing grievances not of their making.

By hitching the meaning of the Equal Protection Clause to these transitory considerations, we would be holding, as a constitutional principle, that judicial scrutiny of classifications touching on racial and ethnic background may vary with the ebb and flow of political forces. Disparate constitutional tolerance of such classifications well may serve to exacerbate racial and ethnic antagonisms rather than alleviate them. . . .

If it is the individual who is entitled to judicial protection against classifications based upon his racial or ethnic background because such distinctions impinge upon personal rights, rather than the individual only because of his membership in a particular group, then constitutional standards may be applied consistently. Political judgments regarding the necessity for the particular classification may be weighed in the constitutional balance. *Korematsu* v. *United States*, 323 U.S. 214 (1944), but the standard of justification will remain constant. This is as it should be, since those political judgments are the product of rough compromise struck by contending groups within the democratic process. When they touch upon an individual's race or ethnic background, he is entitled to a judicial determination that the burden he is asked to bear on that basis is precisely tailored to serve a compelling governmental interest. The Constitution guarantees that right to every person regardless of his background. . . .

C

Petitioner contends that on several occasions this Court has approved preferential classifications without applying the most exacting scrutiny. Most of the cases upon which petitioner relies are drawn from three areas: school desegregation, employment discrimination, and sex discrimination. Each of the cases cited presented a situation materially different from the facts of this case.

The school desegregation cases are inapposite. Each involved remedies for clearly determined constitutional violations. *E. g., Swann* v. *Charlotte-Mecklenburg Board of Education*, 402 U.S. 1 (1971); *McDaniel* v. *Barresi*, 402 U.S. 39 (1971); *Green* v. *County School Board*, 391 U.S. 430 (1968). Racial classifications thus were designed as remedies for the vindication of constitutional entitlement. Moreover, the scope of the remedies were not permitted to exceed the extent of the violations. *E. g., Dayton Board of*

Education v. *Brinkman,* 433 U.S. 406 (1977); *Milliken* v. *Bradley,* 418 U.S. 717 (1974); see *Pasadena City Board of Education* v. *Spangler,* 427 U.S. 424 (1976). See also *Austin Indep. School Dist.* v. *United States,* 429 U.S. 990, 991-995 (1976) (POWELL, J., concurring). Here, there was no judicial determination of constitutional violation as a predicate for the formulation of remedial classification.

The employment discrimination cases also do not advance petitioner's cause. For example, in *Franks* v. *Bowman Transportation Co.,* 424 U.S. 747 (1975), we approved a retroactive award of seniority to a class of Negro truck drivers who had been the victims of discrimination—not just by society at large, but by the respondent in that case. While this relief imposed some burdens on other employees, it was held necessary " 'to make [the victims] whole for injuries suffered on account of unlawful employment discrimination.' " *Id.,* at 771, quoting *Albemarle Paper Co.* v. *Moody,* 422 U.S. 405, 418 (1975). The courts of appeals have fashioned various types of racial preferences as remedies for constitutional or statutory violations resulting in identified, race-based injuries to individuals held entitled to the preference. *E. g., Bridgeport Guardians, Inc.* v. *Civil Service Commission,* 482 F.2d 1333 (CA2 1973); *Carter* v. *Gallagher,* 452 F.2d 315, modified on rehearing en banc, 452 F.2d 327 (CA8 1972). Such preferences have also been upheld where a legislative or administrative body charged with the responsibility made determinations of past discrimination by the industries affected, and fashioned remedies deemed appropriate to rectify the discrimination. *E. g., Contractors Association of Eastern Pennsylvania* v. *Secretary of Labor,* 442 F.2d 159 (CA3), cert. denied, 404 U.S. 954 (1971; [40] *Associated General Contractors of Massachusetts, Inc.* v. *Altschuler,* 490 F.2d 9 (CA1 1973), cert. denied, 416 U.S. 957 (1974); cf. *Katzenbach* v. *Morgan,* 384 U.S. 641 (1966). But we have never approved preferential classifications in the absence of proven constitutional or statutory violations. [41]

[40.] Every decision upholding the requirement of preferential hiring under the authority of Executive Order 11246 has emphasized the existence of previous discrimination as a predicate for the imposition of a preferential remedy. *Contractors Association, supra; Southern Illinois Builders Assn.* v. *Ogilvie,* 471 F.2d 680 (CA7 1972); *Joyce* v. *McCrane,* 320 F.Supp. 1284 (N.J. 1970); *Weiner* v. *Cuyahoga Community College District,* 19 Ohio 2d 35, 249 N. E. 907, cert. denied, 396 U. S. 1004 (1970). See also *Rosetti Contr. Co.* v. *Brennan,* 408 F. 2d 1039, 1041 (CA7 (1975); *Associated General Contractors of Massachusetts, Inc.* v. *Altschuler,* 490 F. 2d 9 (CA1 1973), cert. denied, 416 U. S. 957 (1974); *Northeast Const. Co.* v. *Romney,* 157 U.S. App. D. C. 381, 485 F.2d 752, 754, 761 (1973).

[41.] This case does not call into question congressionally authorized administrative actions, such as consent decrees under Title VII or approval of reapportionment plans under §5 of the Voting Rights Act of 1965, 42 U.S.C. §1973c. In such cases, there has been detailed legislative consideration of the various indicia of previous constitutional or statutory violations, *e. g., South Carolina* v. *Katzenbach,* 383 U.S. 301, 308-310 (1966) (§5), and particular administrative bodies have been charged with monitoring various activities in order to detect such violations and formulate appropriate remedies. See *Hampton* v. *Mow Sun Wong,* 426 U.S. 88, 103 (1976).

Furthermore, we are not here presented with an occasion to review legislation by Congress pursuant to its powers under §2 of the Thirteenth Amendment and §5 of the Fourteenth Amendment to remedy the effects of prior discrimination. *Katzenbach* v. *Morgan,* 384 U.S. 641 (1966); *Jones* v. *Alfred H. Mayer Co.,* 392 U.S. 409 (1968). We have previously recognized the special competence of Congress to make findings with respect to the effects of

Nor is petitioner's view as to the applicable standard supported by the fact that gender-based classifications are not subjected to this level of scrutiny. *E. g., Califano* v. *Webster*, 430 U.S. 313, 316-317 (1977); *e.g., Craig* v. *Boren*, 429 U. S. 190, 211 n.* (1976) (POWELL, J., concurring). Gender-based distinctions are less likely to create the analytical and practical problems present in preferential programs premised on racial or ethnic criteria. With respect to gender there are only two possible classifications. The incidence of the burdens imposed by preferential classifications is clear. There are no rival groups who can claim that they, too, are entitled to preferential treatment. Classwide questions as to the group suffering previous injury and groups which fairly can be burdened are relatively manageable for reviewing courts. See, *e. g., Califano* v. *Goldfarb*, 430 U. S. 199, 212-217 (1977); *Weinberger* v. *Wiesenfeld*, 420 U. S. 636, 645 (1975). The resolution of these same questions in the context of racial and ethnic preferences presents far more complex and intractable problems than gender-based classifications. More importantly, the perception of racial classifications as inherently odious stems from a lengthy and tragic history that gender-based classifications do not share. In sum, the Court has never viewed such classifications as inherently suspect or as comparable to racial or ethnic classifications for the purpose of equal-protection analysis. . . .

[P]etitioner contends that our recent decision in *United Jewish Organizations* v. *Carey*, 430 U. S. 144 (1977), indicates a willingness to approve racial classifications designed to benefit certain minorities, without denominating the classifications as "suspect." The State of New York had redrawn its reapportionment plan to meet objections of the Department of Justice under §5 of the Voting Rights Act of 1965, 42 U.S.C. §1973c. Specifically, voting districts were redrawn to enhance the electoral power of certain "nonwhite" voters found to have been the victims of unlawful "dilution" under the original reapportionment plan. *United Jewish Organizations* . . . properly is viewed as a case in which the remedy for an administrative finding of discrimination encompassed measures to improve the previously disadvantaged group's ability to participate, without excluding individuals belonging to any other group from enjoyment of the relevant opportunity —meaningful participation in the electoral process.

In this case, . . . there has been no determination by the legislature or a responsible administrative agency that the University engaged in a discriminatory practice requiring remedial efforts. Moreover, the operation of petitioner's special admissions program is quite different from the remedial measures approved in those cases. It prefers the designated minority groups at the expense of other individuals who are totally foreclosed from competition for the 16 special admissions seats in every medical school class. Because of that foreclosure, some individuals are excluded from enjoyment of a state-provided benefit—admission to the medical school—they otherwise would receive. When a classification denies an individual opportunities

---

identified past discrimination and its discretionary authority to take appropriate remedial measures.

or benefits enjoyed by others solely because of his race or ethnic background, it must be regarded as suspect. . . .

IV

We have held that in "order to justify the use of a suspect classification, a State must show that its purpose or interest is both constitutionally permissible and substantial, and that its use of the classification is 'necessary . . . to the accomplishment' of its purpose or the safeguarding of its interest." . . .

A

If petitioner's purpose is to assure within its student body some specified percentage of a particular group merely because of its race or ethnic origin, such a preferential purpose must be rejected not as insubstantial but as facially invalid. Preferring members of any one group for no reason other than race or ethnic origin is discrimination for its own sake. This the Constitution forbids. E. g., Loving v. Virginia, supra, at 11; McLaughlin v. Florida, supra, at 196; Brown v. Board of Education, 347 U.S. 483 (1954).

B

The State certainly has a legitimate and substantial interest in ameliorating, or eliminating where feasible, the disabling effects of identified discrimination. The line of school desegregation cases, commencing with Brown, attests to the importance of this state goal and the commitment of the judiciary to affirm all lawful means towards its attainment. In the school cases, the States were required by court order to redress the wrongs worked by specific instances of racial discrimination. That goal was far more focused than the remedying of the effects of "societal discrimination," an amorphous concept of injury that may be ageless in its reach into the past.

We have never approved a classification that aids persons perceived as members of relatively victimized groups at the expense of other innocent individuals in the absence of judicial, legislative, or administrative findings of constitutional or statutory violations. . . .

. . . After such findings have been made, the governmental interest in preferring members of the injured groups at the expense of others is substantial, since the legal rights of the victims must be vindicated. In such a case, the extent of the injury and the consequent remedy will have been judicially, legislatively, or administratively defined. Also, the remedial action usually remains subject to continuing oversight to assure that it will work the least harm possible to other innocent persons competing for the benefit. Without such findings of constitutional or statutory violations, [44] it cannot be said that the government has any greater interest in helping one individual

---

[44.]   MR. JUSTICE BRENNAN, MR. JUSTICE WHITE, MR. JUSTICE MARSHALL, and MR. JUSTICE BLACKMUN misconceive the scope of this Court's holdings under Title VII when they suggest that "disparate impact" alone is sufficient to establish a violation of that statute and, by analogy, other civil rights measures. See post, at 39-45, and n. 42. That this was not

than in refraining from harming another. Thus, the government has no compelling justification for inflicting such harm.

Petitioner does not purport to have made, and is in no position to make, such findings. Its broad mission is education, not the formulation of any legislative policy or the adjudication of particular claims of illegality. For reasons similar to those stated in Part III of this opinion, isolated segments of our vast governmental structures are not competent to make those decisions, at least in the absence of legislative mandates and legislatively determined criteria.[45] . . .

. . . Before relying upon those sorts of findings in establishing a racial classification, a governmental body must have the authority and capability to establish, in the record, that the classification is responsive to identified discrimination. See, *e.g., Califano* v. *Webster*, 430 U. S. 313, 316-321 (1977); *Califano* v. *Goldfarb*, 430 U. S. 199, 212-217 (1977). Lacking this capability, petitioner has not carried its burden of justification on this issue.

Hence, the purpose of helping certain groups whom the faculty of the Davis Medical School perceived as victims of "societal discrimination" does not justify a classification that imposes disadvantages upon persons like respondent, who bear no responsibility for whatever harm the beneficiaries of the special admissions program are thought to have suffered. To hold otherwise would be to convert a remedy heretofore reserved for violations of legal rights into a privilege that all institutions throughout the Nation could grant at their pleasure to whatever groups are perceived as victims of societal discrimination. That is a step we have never approved. Cf. *Pasadena City Board of Education* v. *Spangler*, 427 U. S. 424 (1976).

---

the meaning of Title VII was made quite clear in the seminal decision in this area, *Griggs* v. *Duke Power Co.*, 401 U.S. 424 (1971):

"*Discriminatory preference* for any group, minority or majority, is precisely and only what Congress has proscribed. What is required by Congress is the removal of *artificial, arbitrary, and unnecessary barriers* to employment when the barriers operate invidiously to discriminate on the basis of racial or other impermissible classification." *Id.*, at 431 (emphasis added).

Thus, disparate impact is a basis for relief under Title VII only if the practice in question is not founded on "business necessity," *ibid.*, or lacks "a manifest relationship to the employment in question," *id.*, at 432. See also *McDonnell Douglas Corp.* v. *Green*, 411 U. S. 792, 802-803, 805-806 (1973). Nothing in *this record*—as opposed to some of the general literature cited by MR. JUSTICE BRENNAN, MR. JUSTICE WHITE, MR. JUSTICE MARSHALL, and MR. JUSTICE BLACKMUN—even remotely suggests that the disparate impact of the general admissions program at Davis Medical School, resulting primarily from the sort of disparate test scores and grades set forth in footnote 7, *supra*, is without educational justification.

Moreover, the presumption in *Griggs*—that disparate impact without any showing of business justification established the existence of discrimination in violation of the statute—was based on legislative determinations, wholly absent here, that past discrimination had handicapped various minority groups to such an extent that disparate impact could be traced to identifiable instances of past discrimination. . . .

[45.] For example, the University is unable to explain its selection of only the three favored groups —Negroes, Mexican-Americans, and Asians—for preferential treatment. The inclusion of the last group is especially curious in light of the substantial numbers of Asians admitted through the regular admissions process. See also n. 37, *supra*.

C

Petitioner identifies, as another purpose of this program, improving the delivery of health care services to communities currently underserved. It may be assumed that in some situations a State's interest in facilitating the health care of its citizens is sufficiently compelling to support the use of a suspect classification. But there is virtually no evidence in the record indicating that petitioner's special admissions program is either needed or geared to promote that goal. . . .

*   *   *

D

The fourth goal asserted by petitioner is the attainment of a diverse student body. This clearly is a constitutionally permissible goal for an institution of higher education. Academic freedom, though not a specifically enumerated constitutional right, long has been viewed as a special concern of the First Amendment. The freedom of a university to make its own judgments as to education includes the selection of its student body. . . .

*   *   *

The atmosphere of "speculation, experiment and creation"—so essential to the quality of higher education—is widely believed to be promoted by a diverse student body. As the Court noted in *Keyishian,* it is not too much to say that the "nation's future depends upon leaders trained through wide exposure" to the ideas and mores of students as diverse as this Nation of many peoples.

Thus, in arguing that its universities must be accorded the right to select those students who will contribute the most to the "robust exchange of ideas," petitioner invokes a countervailing constitutional interest, that of the First Amendment. In this light, petitioner must be viewed as seeking to achieve a goal that is of paramount importance in the fulfillment of its mission.

It may be argued that there is greater force to these views at the undergraduate level than in a medical school where the training is centered primarily on professional competency. But even at the graduate level, our tradition and experience lend support to the view that the contribution of diversity is substantial. . . .

Ethnic diversity, however, is only one element in a range of factors a university properly may consider in attaining the goal of a heterogeneous student body. Although a university must have wide discretion in making the sensitive judgments as to who should be admitted, constitutional limitations protecting individual rights may not be disregarded. Respondent urges—and the courts below have held—that petitioner's dual admissions program is a racial classification that impermissibly infringes his rights under the Fourteenth Amendment. As the interest of diversity is compelling in the context of a university's admissions program, the question remains whether the program's racial classification is necessary to promote this interest. *In re Griffiths,* 413 U. S. 717, at 721-722 (1973).

V

A

It may be assumed that the reservation of a specified number of seats in each class for individuals from the preferred ethnic groups would contribute to the attainment of considerable ethnic diversity in the student body. But petitioner's argument that this is the only effective means of serving the interest of diversity is seriously flawed. In a most fundamental sense the argument misconceives the nature of the state interest that would justify consideration of race or ethnic background. It is not an interest in simple ethnic diversity, in which a specified percentage of the student body is in effect guaranteed to be members of selected ethnic groups, with the remaining percentage an undifferentiated aggregation of students. The diversity that furthers a compelling state interest encompasses a far broader array of qualifications and characteristics of which racial or ethnic origin is but a single though important element. Petitioner's special admissions program, focused *solely* on ethnic diversity, would hinder rather than further attainment of genuine diversity.

*   *   *

The experience of other university admissions programs, which take race into account in achieving the educational diversity valued by the First Amendment, demonstrates that the assignment of a fixed number of places to a minority group is not a necessary means toward that end. An illuminating example is found in the Harvard College program:

"In recent years Harvard College has expanded the concept of diversity to include students from disadvantaged economic, racial and ethnic groups. Harvard College now recruits not only Californians or Louisianans but also blacks and Chicanos and other minority students.

.   .   .   .   .

"In practice, this new definition of diversity has meant that race has been a factor in some admission decisions. When the Committee on Admissions reviews the large middle group of applicants who are 'admissible' and deemed capable of doing good work in their courses, the race of an applicant may tip the balance in his favor just as geographic origin or a life spent on a farm may tip the balance in other candidates' cases. A farm boy from Idaho can bring something to Harvard College that a Bostonian cannot offer. Similarly, a black student can usually bring something that a white person cannot offer." See Appendix hereto.

.   .   .   .   .

"In Harvard college admissions the Committee has not set target-quotas for the number of blacks, or of musicians, football players, physicists or Californians to be admitted in a given years. . . . But that awareness [of the necessity of including more than a token number of black students] does not mean that the Committee sets the minimum number of blacks or of people from west of the Mississippi who are to be admitted. It means only that in choosing among thousands of applicants who are not only 'admissible' academically but have other strong qualities, the Committee, with a number of criteria in mind, pays some attention to distribution among many types and categories of students." Brief for Columbia University, Harvard University, Stanford University, and the University of Pennsylvania, as *Amici Curiae,* App. 2, 3.

In such an admissions program, race or ethnic background may be deemed a "plus" in a particular applicant's file, yet it does not insulate the individual from comparison with all other candidates for the available seats. The file of a particular black applicant may be examined for his potential contribution to diversity without the factor of race being decisive when compared, for example, with that of an applicant identified as an Italian-American if the latter is thought to exhibit qualities more likely to promote beneficial educational pluralism. Such qualities could include exceptional personal talents, unique work or service experience, leadership potential, maturity, demonstrated compassion, a history of overcoming disadvantage, ability to communicate with the poor, or other qualifications deemed important. In short, an admissions program operated in this way is flexible enough to consider all pertinent elements of diversity in light of the particular qualifications of each applicant, and to place them on the same footing for consideration, although not necessarily according them the same weight. Indeed, the weight attributed to a particular quality may vary from year to year depending upon the "mix" both of the student body and the applicants for the incoming class.

This kind of program treats each applicant as an individual in the admissions process. The applicant who loses out on the last available seat to another candidate receiving a "plus" on the basis of ethnic background will not have been foreclosed from all consideration for that seat simply because he was not the right color or had the wrong surname. It would mean only that his combined qualifications, which may have included similar nonobjective factors, did not outweigh those of the other applicant. His qualifications would have been weighed fairly and competitively, and he would have no basis to complain of unequal treatment under the Fourteenth Amendment. [52]

It has been suggested that an admissions program which considers race only as one factor is simply a subtle and more sophisticated—but no less effective—means of according racial preference than the Davis program. A facial intent to discriminate, however, is evident in petitioner's preference program and not denied in this case. No such facial infirmity exists in an

---

[52.]　The denial to respondent of this right to individualized consideration without regard to his race is the principal evil of petitioner's special admissions program. Nowhere in the opinion of MR. JUSTICE BRENNAN, MR. JUSTICE WHITE, MR. JUSTICE MARSHALL, and MR. JUSTICE BLACKMUN is this denial even addressed.

admissions program where race or ethnic background is simply one element—to be weighed fairly against other elements—in the selection process.
"A boundary line," as Mr. Justice Frankfurter remarked in another connection, "is none the worse for being narrow." *McLeod* v. *Dilworth*, 322
U. S. 327, 329 (1944). And a Court would not assume that a university,
professing to employ a facially nondiscriminatory admissions policy, would
operate it as a cover for the functional equivalent of a quota system. In
short, good faith would be presumed in the absence of a showing to the
contrary in the manner permitted by our cases. See, *e.g., Arlington Heights*
v. *Metropolitan Housing Development Corp.*, 429 U. S. 252 (1977); *Washington* v. *Davis*, 426 U. S. 229 (1976); *Swain* v. *Alabama*, 380 U. S. 202
(1965).[53]

B

. . . When a State's distribution of benefits or imposition of burdens
hinges on the color of a person's skin or ancestry, that individual is entitled
to a demonstration that the challenged classification is necessary to promote
a substantial state interest. Petitioner has failed to carry this burden. For
this reason, that portion of the California court's judgment holding petitioner's special admissions program invalid under the Fourteenth Amendment must be affirmed.

C

In enjoining petitioner from ever considering the race of any applicant,
however, the courts below failed to recognize that the State has a substantial
interest that legitimately may be served by a properly devised admissions
program involving the competitive consideration of race and ethnic origin.
For this reason, so much of the California court's judgment as enjoins
petitioner from any consideration of the race of any applicant must be
reversed.

VI

With respect to respondent's entitlement to an injunction directing his
admission to the Medical School, petitioner has conceded that it could not
carry its burden of proving that, but for the existence of its unlawful special
admissions program, respondent still would not have been admitted. Hence,
respondent is entitled to the injunction, and that portion of the judgment
must be affirmed.

[53.]   Universities, like the prosecutor in *Swain*, may make individualized decisions, in which ethnic
background plays a part, under a presumption of legality and legitimate educational purpose.
So long as the university proceeds on an individualized, case-by-case basis, there is no warrant
for judicial interference in the academic process. If an applicant can establish that the institution does not adhere to a policy of individual comparisons, or can show that a systematic
exclusion of certain groups results, the presumption of legality might be overcome, creating
the necessity of proving legitimate educational purpose.

APPENDIX

Harvard College Admissions Program

For the past 30 years Harvard College has received each year applications for admission that greatly exceed the number of places in the freshman class. The number of applicants who are deemed to be not "qualified" is comparatively small. The vast majority of applicants demonstrate through test scores, high school records and teachers' recommendations that they have the academic ability to do adequate work at Harvard, and perhaps to do it with distinction. Faced with the dilemma of choosing among a large number of "qualified" candidates, the Committee on Admissions could use the single criterion of scholarly excellence and attempt to determine who among the candidates were likely to perform best academically. But for the past 30 years the Committee on Admissions has never adopted this approach. The belief has been that if scholarly excellence were the sole or even predominant criterion, Harvard College would lose a great deal of its vitality and intellectual excellence and that the quality of the educational experience offered to all students would suffer. . . .

The belief that diversity adds an essential ingredient to the educational process has long been a tenet of Harvard College admissions. Fifteen or twenty years ago, however, diversity meant students from California, New York, and Massachusetts; city dwellers and farm boys; violinists, painters and football players; biologists, historians and classicists; potential stockbrokers, academics and politicians. The result was that very few ethnic or racial minorities attended Harvard College. In recent years Harvard College has expanded the concept of diversity to include students from disadvantaged economic, racial and ethnic groups. . . .

In practice, this new definition of diversity has meant that race has been a factor in some admission decisions. When the Committee on Admissions reviews the large middle group of applicants who are "admissible" and deemed capable of doing good work in their courses, the race of an applicant may tip the balance in his favor just as geographic origin or a life spent on a farm may tip the balance in other candidates' cases. A farm boy from Idaho can bring something to Harvard College that a Bostonian cannot offer. Similarly, a black student can usually bring something that a white person cannot offer. The quality of the educational experience of all the students in Harvard College depends in part on these differences in the background and outlook that students bring with them.

In Harvard College admissions the Committee has not set target-quotas for the number of blacks, or of musicians, football players, physicists or Californians to be admitted in a given year. At the same time the Committee is aware that if Harvard College is to provide a truly heterogeneous environment that reflects the rich diversity of the United States, it cannot be provided without some attention to numbers. It would not make sense, for example, to have 10 or 20 students out of 1,100 whose homes are west of the Mississippi. Comparably, 10 or 20 black students could not begin to bring to their classmates and to each other the variety of points of view, backgrounds and experiences of blacks in the United States. Their small numbers might also create a sense of isolation among the black students themselves and thus make it more difficult for them to develop and achieve their potential. Consequently, when making its decisions, the Committee on Admissions is aware that there is some relationship between numbers and achieving the benefits to be derived from a diverse student body, and between numbers and providing a reasonable environment for those students admitted. But that awareness does not mean that the Committee sets a minimum number of blacks or of people from west of the Mississippi who are to be admitted. It means only that in choosing among thousands of applicants who are not only "admissible" academically but have other strong qualities, the Committee, with a number of criteria in mind, pays some attention to distribution among many types and categories of students.

The further refinements sometimes required help to illustrate the kind of significance attached to race. The Admissions Committee, with only a few places left to fill, might find itself forced to choose between A, the child of a successful black physician in an academic community with promise of superior academic performance, and B, a black who grew up in an inner-city ghetto of semi-literate parents whose academic achievement was lower but who had demonstrated energy and leadership as well as an apparently-abiding interest in black power. If a good number of black students much like A but few like B had already been admitted, the Committee might prefer B; and vice versa. If C, a white student with extraordinary artistic talent, were also seeking one of the remaining places, his unique quality might give him an edge over both A and B. Thus, the critical criteria are often individual qualities or experience not dependent upon race but sometimes associated with it.

* * *

Opinion of MR. JUSTICE BRENNAN, MR. JUSTICE WHITE, MR. JUSTICE MARSHALL, and MR. JUSTICE BLACKMUN, concurring in the judgment in part and dissenting.

. . . The difficulty of the issue presented—whether Government may use race-conscious programs to redress the continuing effects of past discrimination—and the mature consideration which each of our Brethren has brought to it have resulted in many opinions, no single one speaking for the Court. But this should not and must not mask the central meaning of today's opinions: Government may take race into account when it acts not to demean or insult any racial group, but to remedy disadvantages cast on minorities by past racial prejudice, at least when appropriate findings have been made by judicial, legislative, or administrative bodies with competence to act in this area.

* * *

We agree with MR. JUSTICE POWELL that, as applied to the case before us, Title VI goes no further in prohibiting the use of race than the Equal Protection Clause of the Fourteenth Amendment itself. We also agree that the effect of the California Supreme Court's affirmance of the judgment of the Superior Court of California would be to prohibit the University from establishing in the future affirmative action programs that take race into account. See *ante*, at 1 n.*. Since we conclude that the affirmative admissions program at the Davis Medical School is constitutional, we would reverse the judgment below in all respects. MR. JUSTICE POWELL agrees that some uses of race in university admissions are permissible and, therefore, he joins with us to make five votes reversing the judgment below insofar as it prohibits the University from establishing race-conscious programs in the future.[1]

I

*   *   *

The Fourteenth Amendment, the embodiment in the Constitution of our abiding belief in human equality, has been the law of our land for only slightly more than half its 200 years. And for half of that half, the Equal Protection Clause of the Amendment was largely moribund so that, as late as 1927, Mr. Justice Holmes could sum up the importance of that Clause by remarking that it was "the last resort of constitutional arguments." *Buck* v. *Bell*, 274 U. S. 200, 208 (1927). Worse than desuetude, the Clause was early turned against those whom it was intended to set free, condemning them to a "separate but equal" status before the law, a status always separate but seldom equal. Not until 1954—only 24 years ago—was this odious doctrine interred by our decision in *Brown* v. *Board of Education*, 347 U. S. 483 (1954) (*Brown I*), and its progeny, which proclaimed that separate schools and public facilities of all sorts were inherently unequal and forbidden under our Constitution. Even then inequality was not eliminated with "all deliberate speed." . . .

Against this background, claims that law must be "color-blind" or that the datum of race is no longer relevant to public policy must be seen as aspiration rather than as description of reality. This is not to denigrate aspiration; for reality rebukes us that race has too often been used by those who would stigmatize and oppress minorities. . . .

II

. . . We join Parts I and V-C of our Brother POWELL's opinion and three of us agree with his conclusion in Part II that this case does not require us to resolve the question whether there is a private right of action under Title VI.

In our view, Title VI prohibits only those uses of racial criteria that would violate the Fourteenth Amendment if employed by a State or its agencies; it does not bar the preferential treatment of racial minorities as a means of remedying past societal discrimination to the extent that such action is consistent with the Fourteenth Amendment. . . .

[1.]   We also agree with MR. JUSTICE POWELL that a plan like the "Harvard" plan, see *ante*, at 43-47, is constitutional under our approach, at least so long as the use of race to achieve an integrated student body is necessitated by the lingering effects of past discrimination.

III

A

*   *   *

Our cases have always implied that an "overriding statutory purpose," *McLaughlin* v. *Florida*, 379 U. S. 184, 192 (1964), could be found that would justify racial classifications. See, *e. g., ibid.; Loving* v. *Virginia*, 388 U. S. 1, 11 (1967); *Korematsu* v. *United States*, 323 U. S. 214, 216 (1944); *Hirabayashi* v. *United States*, 320 U. S. 81, 100-101 (1943). . . .

We conclude, therefore, that racial classifications are not *per se* invalid under the Fourteenth Amendment. Accordingly, we turn to the problem of articulating what our role should be in reviewing state action that expressly classifies by race.

B

Respondent argues that racial classifications are always suspect and, consequently, that this Court should weigh the importance of the objectives served by Davis' special admissions program to see if they are compelling. . . .

Unquestionably we have held that a government practice or statute which restricts "fundamental rights" or which contains "suspect classifications" is to be subjected to "strict scrutiny" and can be justified only if it furthers a compelling government purpose and, even then, only if no less restrictive alternative is available. See, *e. g., San Antonio Indep. School Dist.* v. *Rodriquez*, 411 U. S. 1, 16-17 (1973); *Dunn* v. *Blumstein*, 405 U. S. 330 (1972). But no fundamental right is involved here. See *San Antonio, supra,* at 29-36. Nor do whites as a class have any of the "traditional indicia of suspectness: the class is not saddled with such disabilities, or subjected to such a history of purposeful unequal treatment, or relegated to such a position of political powerlessness as to command extraordinary protection from the majoritarian political process."

Moreover, if the University's representations are credited, this is not a case where racial classifications are "irrelevant and therefore prohibited." *Hirabayashi*, 320 U. S., at 100. Nor has anyone suggested that the University's purposes contravene the cardinal principle that racial classifications that stigmatize—because they are drawn on the presumption that one race is inferior to another or because they put the weight of government behind racial hatred and separatism—are invalid without more. . . .

On the other hand, the fact that this case does not fit neatly into our prior analytic framework for race cases does not mean that it should be analyzed by applying the very loose rational-basis standard of review that is the very least that is always applied in equal protection cases. "'[T]he mere recitation of a benign, compensatory purpose is not an automatic shield which protects against any inquiry into the actual purposes underlying a statutory scheme.'" *Califano* v. *Webster*, 430 U. S. 313, 317 (1977), quoting *Weinberger* v. *Weisenfeld*, 420 U. S. 636, 648 (1975). Instead, a number of considerations—developed in gender discrimination cases but which carry even more force when applied to racial classifications—lead us to conclude that racial classifications designed to further remedial purposes "'must serve important governmental objectives and must be substantially related to achievement of those objectives.'" *Califano* v. *Webster, supra*, at 316, quoting *Craig* v. *Boren*, 429 U. S. 190, 197 (1976). [35]

First, race, like "gender-based classifications too often [has] been inexcusably utilized to stereotype and stigmatize politically powerless segments of society." *Kahn* v. *Shevin*, 416 U. S. 351, 357 (1974) (dissenting opinion). . . .

Second, race, like gender and illegitimacy, see *Weber* v. *Aetna Cas. & Surety Co.*, 406 U. S. 164 (1972), is an immutable characteristic which its possessors are powerless to escape, or set aside. . . .

In sum, because of the significant risk that racial classifications established for ostensibly benign purposes can be misused, causing effects not unlike those created by invidious classifications, it is inappropriate to inquire only whether there is any conceivable basis that might sustain such a classification. Instead, to justify such a classification an important and articulated purpose for its use must be shown. In addition, any statute must be stricken that stigmatizes any group or that singles out those least well represented in the political process to bear the brunt of a benign program. Thus our review under the Fourteenth Amendment should be strict—not "'strict' in theory and fatal in fact," because it is stigma that causes fatality—but strict and searching nonetheless.

IV

Davis' articulated purpose of remedying the effects of past societal discrimination is, under our cases, sufficiently important to justify the use of race-conscious admissions programs where there is a sound basis for conclud-

---

[35.]   We disagree with our Brother POWELL's suggestion, *ante*, at 31, that the presence of "rival groups who can claim that they, too, are entitled to preferential treatment," *ibid.*, distinguishes the gender cases or is relevant to the question of scope of judicial review of race classifications. We are not asked to determine whether groups other than those favored by the Davis program should similarly be favored. All we are asked to do is to pronounce the constitutionality of what Davis has done.

But, were we asked to decide whether any given rival group—German-Americans, for example—must constitutionally be accorded preferential treatment, we do have a "principled basis," *ante*, at 25, for deciding this question, one that is well-established in our cases: The Davis program expressly sets out four classes which receive preferred status. *Ante*, at 4. The program clearly distinguishes whites, but one cannot reason from this to a conclusion that German-Americans, as a national group, are singled out for invidious treatment. And even if the Davis program had a differential impact on German-Americans, they would have no constitutional claim unless they could prove that Davis intended invidiously to discriminate against German-Americans. See *Village of Arlington Heights* v. *Metropolitan Housing Corp.*, 429 U. S. 252, 264-265 (1977); *Washington* v. *Davis*, 426 U. S. 229, 238-241 (1976). If this could not be shown, then "the principle that calls for the closest scrutiny of distinctions in laws denying fundamental rights . . . is inapplicable," *Katzenbach* v. *Morgan*, 384 U. S. 641, 657 (1967), and the only question is whether it was rational for Davis to conclude that the groups it preferred had a greater claim to compensation than the groups it excluded. See *ibid.; San Antonio Indep. School Dist.* v. *Rodriguez*, 411 U. S. 1, 18-39 (1973) (applying *Katzenbach* test to state action intended to remove discrimination in educational opportunity). Thus, claims of rival groups, although they may create thorny political problems, create relatively simple problems for the courts.

ing that minority underrepresentation is substantial and chronic, and that the handicap of past discrimination is impeding access of minorities to the medical school.

A

*   *   *

[T]he conclusion that state educational institutions may constitutionally adopt admissions programs designed to avoid exclusion of historically disadvantaged minorities, even when such programs explicitly take race into account, finds direct support in our cases construing congressional legislation designed to overcome the present effects of past discrimination. Congress can and has outlawed actions which have a disproportionately adverse and unjustified impact upon members of racial minorities and has required or authorized race-conscious action to put individuals disadvantaged by such impact in the position they otherwise might have enjoyed. See *Franks* v. *Bowman, supra; International Brotherhood of Teamsters* v. *United States*, 431 U. S. 324 (1977). Such relief does not require as a predicate proof that recipients of preferential advancement have been individually discriminated against; it is enough that each recipient is within a general class of persons likely to have been the victims of discrimination. See *id.*, at 357-362. Nor is it an objection to such relief that preference for minorities will upset the settled expectations of nonminorities. See *Franks, supra.* . . .

These cases cannot be distinguished simply by the presence of judicial findings of discrimination, for race-conscious remedies have been approved where such findings have not been made. . . . Indeed, the requirement of a judicial determination of a constitutional or statutory violation as a predicate for race-conscious remedial actions would be self-defeating. Such a requirement would severely undermine efforts to achieve voluntary compliance with the requirements of law. . . .

. . . Moreover, the presence or absence of past discrimination by universities or employers is largely irrelevant to resolving respondent's constitutional claims. The claims of those burdened by the race-conscious actions of a university or employer who has never been adjudged in violation of an antidiscrimination law are not any more or less entitled to deference than the claims of the burdened nonminority workers in *Franks* v. *Bowman*, 424 U. S. 747 (1976), in which the employer had violated Title VII, for in each case the employees are innocent of past discrimination. And, although it might be argued that, where an employer has violated an antidiscrimination law, the expectations of nonminority workers are themselves products of discrimination and hence "tainted," see *Franks, supra*, at 776, and therefore more easily upset, the same argument can be made with respect to respondent. If it was reasonable to conclude—as we hold that it was—that the failure of minorities to qualify for admission at Davis under regular procedures was due principally to the effects of past discrimination, then there is a reasonable likelihood that, but for pervasive racial discrimination, respondent would have failed to qualify for admission even in the absence of Davis' special admissions program. [41]

Thus, our cases under Title VII of the Civil Rights Act have held that, in order to achieve minority participation in previously segregated areas of public life, Congress may require or authorize preferential treatment for those likely disadvantaged by societal racial discrimination. Such legislation has been sustained even without a requirement of findings of intentional racial discrimination by those required or authorized to accord preferential treatment, or a case-by-case determination that those to be benefited suffered from racial discrimination. These decisions compel the conclusion that States also may adopt race-conscious programs designed to overcome substantial, chronic minority underrepresentation where there is reason to believe that the evil addressed is a product of past racial discrimination. [42]

. . . Nothing whatever in the legislative history of either the Fourteenth Amendment or the Civil Rights Acts even remotely suggests that the States are foreclosed from furthering the fundamental purpose of equal opportunity to which the Amendment and those Acts are addressed. Indeed, voluntary initiatives by the States to achieve the national goal of equal opportunity have been recognized to be essential to its attainment. "To use

---

[41.]   Our cases cannot be distinguished by suggesting, as our Brother POWELL does, that in none of them was anyone deprived of "the relevant benefit." *Ante*, at 32; *id*., at 33. Our school cases have deprived whites of the neighborhood school of their choice; our Title VII cases have deprived nondiscriminating employees of their settled seniority expectations; and *UJO* deprived the Hassidim of bloc voting strength. Each of these injuries was constitutionally cognizable as is respondent's here.

[42.]   We do not understand MR. JUSTICE POWELL to disagree that providing a remedy for past racial prejudice can constitute a compelling purpose sufficient to meet strict scrutiny. See *ante*, at 35-36. Yet, because petitioner is a university, he would not allow it to exercise such power in the absence of "judicial, legislative, or administrative findings of constitutional or statutory violations. *Ibid*. While we agree that reversal in this case would follow *a fortiori* had Davis been guilty of invidious racial discrimination or if a federal statute mandated that universities refrain from applying any admissions policy that had a disparate and unjustified racial impact, see, *e. g., McDaniel* v. *Barresi*, 402 U. S. 39 (1971); *Franks* v. *Bowman Transp. Co.*, 424 U. S. 747 (1976), we do not think it of constitutional significance that Davis has not been so adjudged.

Generally, the manner in which a State chooses to delegate governmental functions is for it to decide. Cf. *Sweezy* v. *New Hampshire*, 354 U. S. 234, 256 (1957) (Frankfurter, J., concurring). California, by constitutional provision, has chosen to place authority over the operation of the University of California in the Board of Regents. See Cal. Const. Art. IX, §9(a) (1978). Control over the University is to be found not in the legislature, but rather in the Regents who have been vested with full legislative (including policymaking), administrative, and adjudicative powers by the citizens of California. . . . We, unlike our Brother POWELL, find nothing in the Equal Protection Clause that requires us to depart from established principle by limiting the scope of power the Regents may exercise more narrowly than the powers that may constitutionally be wielded by the Assembly.

Because the Regents can exercise plenary legislative and administrative power, it elevates form over substance to insist that Davis could not use race-conscious remedial programs until it had been adjudged in violation of the Constitution or an antidiscrimination statute. For, if the Equal Protection Clause required such a violation as a predicate, the Regents could simply have promulgated a regulation prohibiting disparate treatment not justified by the need to admit only qualified students, and could have declared Davis to have been in violation of such a regulation on the basis of the exclusionary effect of the admissions policy applied during the first two years of its operation. See *infra*, at 46.

the Fourteenth Amendment as a sword against such state power would stultify that Amendment." *Railway Mail Assn.* v. *Corsi*, 326 U. S. 88, 98 (Frankfurter, J., concurring). We therefore conclude that Davis' goal of admitting minority students disadvantaged by the effects of past discrimination is sufficiently important to justify use of race-conscious admissions criteria.

B

*   *   *

Certainly, on the basis of the undisputed factual submissions before this Court, Davis had a sound basis for believing that the problem of under-representation of minorities was substantial and chronic and that the problem was attributable to handicaps imposed on minority applicants by past and present racial discrimination. . . .

*   *   *

Moreover, we need not rest solely on our own conclusion that Davis had sound reason to believe that the effects of past discrimination were handicapping minority applicants to the Medical School, because the Department of Health, Education, and Welfare, the expert agency charged by Congress with promulgating regulations enforcing Title VI of the Civil Rights Act of 1964, see *supra*, pp. 18-19, has also reached the conclusion that race may be taken into account in situations where a failure to do so would limit participation by minorities in federally funded programs, and regulations promulgated by the Department expressly contemplate that appropriate race-conscious programs may be adopted by universities to remedy unequal access to university programs caused by their own or by past societal discrimination. See *supra*, p. 21, discussing 45 CFR § § 80.3-(b)(6)(ii) and 80.5(j). It cannot be questioned that, in the absence of the special admissions program, access of minority students to the Medical School would be severely limited and, accordingly, race-conscious admissions would be deemed an appropriate response under these federal regulations. . . .

. . . In these circumstances, the conclusion implicit in the regulations—that the lingering effects of past discrimination continue to make race-conscious remedial programs appropriate means for ensuring equal educational opportunity in universities—deserves considerable judicial deference. . . .

C

The second prong of our test—whether the Davis program stigmatizes any discrete group or individual and whether race is reasonably used in light of the program's objective—is clearly satisfied by the Davis program.

It is not even claimed that Davis' program in any way operates to stigmatize or single out any discrete and insular, or even any identifiable, nonminority group. Nor will harm comparable to that imposed upon racial minorities by exclusion or separation on grounds of race be the likely result of the program. It does not, for example, establish an exclusive preserve for minority students apart from and exclusive of whites. Rather, its purpose is to overcome the effects of segregation by bringing the races together. True, whites are excluded from participation in the special admissions program, but this fact only operates to reduce the number of whites to be admitted in the regular admissions program in order to permit admission of a reasonable percentage—less than their proportion of the California population—of otherwise underrepresented qualified minority applicants.

. . . Unlike discrimination against racial minorities, the use of racial preferences for remedial purposes does not inflict a pervasive injury upon individual whites in the sense that wherever they go or whatever they do there is a significant likelihood that they will be treated as second-class citizens because of their color. This distinction does not mean that the exclusion of a white resulting from the preferential use of race is not sufficiently serious to require justification; but it does mean that the injury inflicted by such a policy is not distinguishable from disadvantages caused by a wide range of government actions, none of which has ever been thought impermissible for that reason alone.

In addition, there is simply no evidence that the Davis program discriminates intentionally or unintentionally against any minority group which it purports to benefit. The program does not establish a quota in the invidious sense of a ceiling on the number of minority applicants to be admitted. Nor can the program reasonably be regarded as stigmatizing the program's beneficiaries or their race as inferior. The Davis program does not simply advance less qualified applicants; rather, it compensates applicants, whom it is uncontested are fully qualified to study medicine, for educational disadvantage which it was reasonable to conclude was a product of state-fostered discrimination. Once admitted, these students must satisfy the same degree requirements as regularly admitted students; they are taught by the same faculty in the same classes, and their performance is evaluated by the same standards by which regularly admitted students are judged. Under these circumstances their performance and degrees must be regarded equally with the regularly admitted students with whom they compete for standing. . . .

D

We disagree with the lower courts' conclusion that the Davis program's use of race was unreasonable in light of its objectives. First, as petitioner argues, there are no practical means by which it could achieve its ends in the foreseeable future without the use of race-conscious measures. . . .

Second, the Davis admissions program does not simply equate minority status with disadvantage. Rather, Davis considers on an individual basis each applicant's personal history to determine whether he or she has likely been disadvantaged by racial discrimination. The record makes clear that only minority applicants likely to have been isolated from the mainstream of American life are considered in the special program; other minority applicants are eligible only through the regular admissions program. . . .

E

Finally, Davis' special admissions program cannot be said to violate the Constitution simply because it has set aside a predetermined number of places for qualified minority applicants rather than using minority status as a positive factor to be considered in evaluating the applications of disadvantaged minority applicants. For purposes of constitutional adjudication, there is no difference between the two approaches. In any admissions program which accords special consideration to disadvantaged racial minorities, a determination of the degree of preference to be given is unavoidable, and any given preference that results in the exclusion of a white candidate is no more or less constitutionally acceptable than a program such as that at Davis. Furthermore, the extent of the preference inevitably depends on how many minority applicants the particular school is seeking to admit in any particular year so long as the number of qualified minority applicants exceeds that number. There is no sensible, and certainly no constitutional, distinction between, for example, adding a set number of points to the admissions rating of disadvantaged minority applicants as an expression of the preference with the expectation that this will result in the admission of an approximately determined number of qualified minority applicants and setting a fixed number of places for such applicants as was done here.

The "Harvard" program, see *ante*, at 43-47, as those employing it readily concede, openly and successfully employs a racial criterion for the purpose of ensuring that some of the scarce places in institutions of higher education are allocated to disadvantaged minority students. That the Harvard approach does not also make public the extent of the preference and the precise workings of the system while the Davis program employs a specific, openly stated number, does not condemn the latter plan for purposes of Fourteenth Amendment adjudication. It may be that the Harvard plan is more acceptable to the public than is the Davis "quota." If it is, any State, including California, is free to adopt it in preference to a less acceptable alternative, just as it is generally free, as far as the Constitution is concerned, to abjure granting any racial preferences in its admissions program. But there is no basis for preferring a particular preference program simply because in achieving the same goals that the Davis Medical School is pursuing, it proceeds in a manner that is not immediately apparent to the public.

IV

Accordingly, we would reverse the judgment of the Supreme Court of California holding the Medical School's special admissions program unconstitutional and directing respondent's admission, as well as that portion of the judgment enjoining the Medical School from according any consideration to race in the admissions process.

*   *   *

MR. JUSTICE STEVENS, with whom THE CHIEF JUSTICE, MR. JUSTICE STEWART, and MR. JUSTICE REHNQUIST join, concurring in the judgment in part and dissenting in part.

It is always important at the outset to focus precisely on the controversy before the Court. It is particularly important to do so in this case because correct identification of the issues will determine whether it is necessary or appropriate to express any opinion about the legal status of any admissions program other than petitioner's.

I

This is not a class action. The controversy is between two specific litigants. Allan Bakke challenged petitioner's special admissions program, claiming that it denied him a place in medical school because of his race in violation of the Federal and California Constitutions and of Title VI of the Civil Rights Act of 1964, 42 U.S.C. § 2000d *et seq.* . . .

Section 601 of the Civil Rights Act of 1964 provides:
> "No person in the United States shall, on the ground of race, color, or national origin, be excluded from participation in, be denied the benefits of, or be subjected to discrimination under any program or activity receiving Federal financial assistance."

The University, through its special admissions policy, excluded Bakke from participation in its program of medical education because of his race. The University also acknowledges that it was, and still is, receiving federal financial assistance. The plain language of the statute therefore requires affirmance of the judgment below. A different result cannot be justified unless that language misstates the actual intent of the Congress that enacted the statute or the statute is not enforceable in a private action. Neither conclusion is warranted. . . .

The University's special admissions program violated Title VI of the Civil Rights Act of 1964 by excluding Bakke from the medical school because of his race. It is therefore our duty to affirm the judgment ordering Bakke admitted to the University.

Accordingly, I concur in the Court's judgment insofar as it affirms the judgment of the Supreme Court of California. To the extent that it purports to do anything else, I respectfully dissent.

*   *   *

MR. JUSTICE MARSHALL.

I agree with the judgment of the Court only insofar as it permits a university to consider the race of an applicant in making admissions decisions. I do not agree that petitioner's admissions program violates the Constitution. For it must be remembered that, during most of the past 200 years, the Constitution as interpreted by this Court did not prohibit the most ingenious and pervasive forms of discrimination against the Negro. Now, when a State acts to remedy the effects of that legacy of discrimination, I cannot believe that this same Constitution stands as a barrier.

*   *   *

The position of the Negro today in America is the tragic but inevitable consequence of centuries of unequal treatment. Measured by any benchmark of comfort or achievement, meaningful equality remains a distant dream for the Negro.

A Negro child today has a life expectancy which is shorter by more than five years than that of a white child. The Negro child's mother is over three times more likely to die of complications in childbirth, and the infant mortality rate for Negroes is nearly twice that for whites. The median income of the Negro family is only 60% that of the median of a white family, and the percentage of Negroes who live in families with incomes below the poverty line is nearly four times greater than that of whites.

When the Negro child reaches working age, he finds that America offers him significantly less than it offers his white counterpart. For Negro adults, the unemployment rate is twice that of whites, and the unemployment rate for Negro teenagers is nearly three times that of white teenagers. A Negro male who completes four years of college can expect a median annual income of merely $110 more than a white male who has only a high school diploma. Although Negroes represent 11.5% of the population, they are only 1.2% of the lawyers and judges, 2% of the physicians, 2.3% of the dentists, 1.1% of the engineers and 2.6% of the college and university professors.

The relationship between those figures and the history of unequal treatment afforded to the Negro cannot be denied. At every point from birth to death the impact of the past is reflected in the still disfavored position of the Negro.

In light of the sorry history of discrimination and its devastating impact on the lives of Negroes, bringing the Negro into the mainstream of American life should be a state interest of the highest order. To fail to do so is to ensure that America will forever remain a divided society.

I do not believe that the Fourteenth Amendment requires us to accept that fate. Neither its history nor our past cases lend any support to the conclusion that a University may not remedy the cumulative effects of society's discrimination by giving consideration to race in an effort to increase the number and percentage of Negro doctors.

*   *   *

As has been demonstrated in our joint opinion, this Court's past cases establish the constitutionality of race-conscious remedial measures. . . .

Nothing in those cases suggests that a university cannot similarly act to remedy past discrimination. [12] It is true that in both *UJO* and *Webster* the use of the disfavored classification was predicated on legislative or admin-

---

[12.] Indeed, the action of the University finds support in the regulations promulgated under Title VI by the Department of Health, Education, and Welfare and approved by the President, which authorize a federally funded institution to take affirmative steps to overcome past discrimination against groups even where the institution was not guilty of prior discrimination. 45 CFR §80.3(b)(6)(ii).

istrative action, but in neither case had those bodies made findings that there had been constitutional violations or that the specific individuals to be benefited had actually been the victims of discrimination. Rather, the classification in each of those cases was based on a determination that the group was in need of the remedy because of some type of past discrimination. There is thus ample support for the conclusion that a university can employ race-conscious measures to remedy past societal discrimination, without the need for a finding that those benefited were actually victims of that discrimination.

While I applaud the judgment of the Court that a university may consider race in its admissions process, it is more than a little ironic that, after several hundred years of class-based discrimination against Negroes, the Court is unwilling to hold that a class-based remedy for that discrimination is permissible. In declining to so hold, today's judgment ignores the fact that for several hundred years Negroes have been discriminated against, not as individuals, but rather solely because of the color of their skins. It is unnecessary in 20th century America to have individual Negroes demonstrate that they have been victims of racial discrimination; the racism of our society has been so pervasive that none, regardless of wealth or position, has managed to escape its impact. The experience of Negroes in America has been different in kind, not just in degree, from that of other ethnic groups. It is not merely the history of slavery alone but also that a whole people were marked as inferior by the law. And that mark has endured. The dream of America as the great melting pot has not been realized for the Negro; because of his skin color he never even made it into the pot.

*   *   *

I fear that we have come full circle. After the Civil War our government started several "affirmative action" programs. This Court in the *Civil Rights Cases* and *Plessy* v. *Ferguson* destroyed the movement toward complete equality. For almost a century no action was taken, and this nonaction was with the tacit approval of the courts. Then we had *Brown* v. *Board of Education* and the Civil Rights Acts of Congress, followed by numerous affirmative action programs. *Now,* we have this Court again stepping in, this time to stop affirmative action programs of the type used by the University of California. . . .

NOTES

1. What is the real difference between the Davis program and the Harvard program (set out in the appendix to Powell's opinion)? Why does Powell approve of one and not the other? Should all distinctions based on race be subject to the strictest level of judicial scrutiny, even though their purpose is to benefit the group being distinguished? Do all racial classifications have a "stigmatizing" effect? How is Powell able to distinguish race-based remedies from the Davis preferential admissions program? Why are the school desegregation cases "inapposite"?

2. How far would the Brennan group opinion allow a school to go in its attempts to remedy societal discrimination? Assume that a predominantly black southern state university could prove that it is extremely successful in helping disadvantaged students from the black community and is specially geared for this end. Could an argument be con-

structed from the Brennan group opinion which could save the autonomy of the school from a court-ordered integration plan?

3. Powell states that Davis-type programs would be valid if they were based on proper administrative or legislative findings of past discrimination. What type of body would be competent to make such findings? Would it have made a difference if the Board of Regents of the University of California was authorized by a state statute to formulate regulations for all state employees working at one of the University of California campuses? What if the Board of Regents had a specific delegation of power from the state to make "findings" of discrimination, and to implement any type of admissions program they felt was necessary to remedy this discrimination? *See, e.g.*, Weber v. Kaiser Aluminum & Chemical Corp., 563 F.2d 216 (5th Cir. 1977), *reversed*, June 27, 1979; Detroit Police Officers Ass'n v. Young, 446 F.Supp. 979 (E.D. Mich. 1978); and E.E.O.C. v. American Telephone & Telegraph, 14 FEP Cas. 1210 (3d Cir. 1977), *cert. denied*, 46 U.S.L.W. 3801 (1978).

4. Powell further states that the purpose of improving the delivery of health care services of communities currently underserved may "in some situations" be sufficiently compelling to support the use of a suspect classification. What types of situations would he find acceptable? *See, e.g.*, Morton v. Mancari, 417 U.S. 535 (1974) which held in part that an employment preference for Indians in the Bureau of Indian Affairs was not racial discrimination in violation of the 5th Amendment but was rather a mere "employment criterion reasonably designed to further the cause of Indian self-government and to make the BIA more responsive to the needs of its constituent groups." 417 U.S. at 554.

5. To comply with the *Bakke* decision, the Medical School of the University of California at Davis has adopted a computer-operated "point system" to screen applications. Any applicant who is either a member of a minority group or is "disadvantaged" will automatically receive five points (fifteen are needed to survive the initial screening). 100 applicants from the group eliminated by this screening will be selected for further consideration. The Chronicle of Higher Education, *Post-Bakke Admission Plan Adopted at Davis*, Vol. XVII, Oct. 30, 1978, p. 13.

6. An excellent discussion of *Bakke* is contained in McCormack, ed., *The Bakke Decision: Implications for Higher Education Admissions*, a Report of the ACE-AALS Committee on Bakke. For good discussions of the issues involved in the *Bakke* case, *see:* Ely, *The Constitutionality of Reverse Racial Discrimination*, 41 U. Chi. L. Rev. 723 (1974); Greenawalt, *Judicial Scrutiny of "Benign" Racial Preference in Law School Admissions*, 75 Colum. L. Rev. 559 (1975); Lavinsky, *DeFunis v. Odegaard: The "Non-Decision" with a Message*, 75 Colum. L. Rev. 521 (1975); O'Neil, *Racial Preference and Higher Education: The Larger Context*, 60 Va. L. Rev. 925 (1974); Posner, *The DeFunis Case and the Constitutionality of Preferential Treatment of Racial Minorities*, 1974 S.Ct. Rev. 1; and Sandalow, *Racial Preferences in Higher Education: Political Responsibility and the Judicial Role*, 42 U. Chi. L. Rev. 653 (1975).

II. Statutory Enforcement: Title VI of the Civil Rights Act of 1964

A. Introduction

In Title VI of the Civil Rights Act of 1964, 42 U.S.C. § 2000d, et seq., Congress proposed a federal solution to the problems of segregation and racial discrimination. Dissatisfied with the progress made through constitutional litigation in the courts,[5] Congress hoped to mobilize desegregation by providing a statutory remedy which could be administered through the

---

5.   For example, in North Carolina, at the time Title VI was enacted (ten years after the *Brown* decision), the traditionally white institutions of higher education in the public system had only gone from 100% white to 99% white, and the black institutions had gone from 100% to 99.9% black. Even as late as 1970, before any enforcement actions under Title VI had been taken,

regulatory process. The central provision of the Act declares:

No person in the United States shall, on the ground of race, color, or national origin, be excluded from participation in, be denied the benefits of, or be subjected to discrimination under any program or activity receiving Federal financial assistance. 42 U.S.C. § 2000d.

The ultimate sanction for violation of the Act is the termination of funds. By thus conditioning the extension of assistance, Congress sought to place the power of the federal fisc behind a national civil rights policy.

The Title VI mandate was expressed in the broadest terms, leaving the task of clarification to the individual agencies. Each agency is charged with the responsibility of defining and enforcing § 2000d in the context of the particular programs it administers.[6] The approval of the president must be obtained for all regulations promulgated under the Act. Voluntary compliance is the end goal of the scheme. The termination of funds is primarily a bargaining device to be imposed only when voluntary compliance cannot be secured. Further, the termination of funds must be limited to "the particular political entity, or part thereof, or other recipient as to whom . . . a finding [of noncompliance] has been made and, shall be limited in its effect to the particular program, or part thereof, in which such noncompliance has been so found." 42 U.S.C. § 2000d-1. A full report justifying each decision to terminate funds must be filed by the agency with the

---

the white institutions were 98.1% white and the black institutions were 98% black. *See* C. Lloyd, *Adams v. Califano: A Case Study in the Politics of Regulation*, (Jan. 1978), p. 39, (a Working Paper for the Sloan Commission on Government and Higher Education).

6.   The implementation section of the Act reads:

Each Federal department and agency which is empowered to extend Federal financial assistance to any program or activity, by way of grant, loan, or contract other than a contract of insurance or guaranty, is authorized and directed to effectuate the provisions of section 2000d of this title with respect to such program or activity by issuing rules, regulations, or orders of general applicability which shall be consistent with achievement of the objectives of the statute authorizing the financial assistance in connection with which the action is taken. No such rule, regulation, or order shall become effective unless and until approved by the President. Compliance with any requirement adopted pursuant to this section may be effected (1) by the termination of or refusal to grant or to continue assistance under such program or activity to any recipient as to whom there has been an express finding on the record, after opportunity for hearing, of a failure to comply with such requirement, but such termination or refusal shall be limited to the particular political entity, or part thereof, or other recipient as to whom such a finding has been made and, shall be limited in its effect to the particular program, or part thereof, in which such noncompliance has been so found, or (2) by any other means authorized by law: *Provided, however*, That no such action shall be taken until the department or agency concerned has advised the appropriate person or persons of the failure to comply with the requirement and has determined that compliance cannot be secured by voluntary means. In the case of any action terminating, or refusing to grant or continue, assistance because of failure to comply with a requirement imposed pursuant to this section, the head of the Federal department or agency shall file with the committees of the House and Senate having legislative jurisdiction over the program or activity involved a full written report of the circumstances and the grounds for such action. No such action shall become effective until thirty days have elapsed after the filing of such report. 42 U.S.C. § 2000d-1.

appropriate House and Senate Committees. In addition to terminating funds, the agencies are authorized to enforce compliance "by any other means authorized by law." *Id.*

Two limitations to the scope of the Act bear mention. The first of these exempts employment practices from coverage under the Title "except where a primary objective of the Federal financial assistance is to provide employment." [7] 42 U.S.C. § 2000d-3. The other excepts out programs "under which Federal financial assistance is extended by way of a contract of insurance or guaranty." 42 U.S.C. § 2000d-4.

B. Title VI in Higher Education

1. The Basic Scheme

The Department of Health, Education, and Welfare is the primary enforcement agency for Title VI in higher education. [8]   HEW has issued general regulations for the implementation of Title VI, which can be found at 45 C.F.R. § § 80.1-80.13. [9] The regulations are broadly applicable to "any program for which Federal financial assistance is authorized to be extended . . . under a law administered by the Department." *Id.*, § 80.2. The term "financial assistance" is defined to include any government agreement or contract "which has as one of its purposes, the provision of assistance." *Id.*, § 80.13(f). Thus, everything from low-interest student loans [10] to grants for construction improvements are subject to regulation under Title VI.

The regulations prohibit any practice which has either a disparate effect on, or results in the "different treatment" of, individuals of a particular race, color, or national origin. *Id.*, § 80.3. Intent is not prerequisite to a finding of discrimination under the Act. Recipients must consider the racial impact of the decisions they make on such things as resource and financial aid allocation, admissions requirements, and site selection for new programs and facilities. The regulations require affirmative action to be taken to overcome the continuing effects of past discriminatory practices. In the absence of prior discrimination, the regulations allow recipients to take steps to over-

---

7. The section provides in full: "Nothing contained in this subchapter shall be construed to authorize action under this subchapter by any department or agency with respect to any employment practice of any employer, employment agency, or labor organization except where a primary objective of the Federal financial assistance is to provide employment." 42 U.S.C. § 2000d-3.

8. In addition to HEW's responsibility for its own programs, fifteen agencies, ranging from NASA to the Department of Commerce, have delegated to HEW their enforcement responsibilities for the grants extended to them to insititutions of higher education. See 36 Geo. Wash. L. Rev. 824, at 870, f.n. 204 (1968).

9. To date, HEW has failed to promulgate specific guidelines for higher education, despite at least one court order requiring it to do so. See notes following *Adams v. Richardson* below.

10. In the student loan situation, the university is viewed as the "recipient" of low-interest loans paid to students, and is thereby subject to Title VI. The "ultimate beneficiary," the student, is exempted from regulation. *Id.*, § 80.2. See Bob Jones University v. Johnson, 396 F.Supp. 597 (D.S. Car. 1974); *aff'd* 529 F.2d 514 (4th Cir. 1975), which held that a private religious college was a "recipient" of the veterans' benefits awarded to its veteran-students, thereby justifying a cut-off of the benefits for the college's failure to comply with Title VI.

come "conditions which resulted in limiting participation by persons of a particular race, color, or national origin." *Id.*, §80.3(b)(6)(ii).[11]

As a condition to the receipt of Federal assistance, each applicant must submit to HEW an "assurance" of compliance, *Id.*, at §80.4. The assurance contractually obligates the recipient to comply, as to the program or facility receiving the federal funding, with all requirements imposed by the regulations. Institutions of higher education are required to include in their assurances the additional agreement that their admissions policies and "all other practices relating to the treatment of students" will also be in compliance, whether or not the program receiving assistance bears any relation to these practices. *Id.*, §80.4(d)(1). These additional promises are presumed to extend to the admissions and student treatment practices of the entire university or college, "unless the applicant establishes to the satisfaction of the responsible Department official, that the institution's practices in designated parts or programs of the institution will in no way affect its practices in the program for which federal financial assistance is sought, or the beneficiaries of or participants in such program." *Id.*, §80.4(d)(2).

2.   The Politics of Regulation

Despite the existence of this broad-reaching regulatory scheme, Title VI has never been fully implemented in the field of higher education. Desegregation in higher education involves a myriad of political and social concerns, ranging from academic freedom and autonomy, to the future of black colleges. Little consensus exists on these issues, even between the minority interest groups involved. It is therefore not surprising that HEW has attempted to avoid its enforcement responsibilities in the area. It has chosen instead to focus its energies on the elementary and secondary school level, where the desegregation remedies have already been worked out by the courts.

Between 1969 and 1970, HEW, in its first attempt to enforce Title VI in higher education, sent out letters of noncompliance to ten states that it had determined were operating racially segregated educational systems. The states were requested to submit to HEW a desegregation plan within 120 days. Five of the states totally ignored the request, and the other five submitted plans that were later found unacceptable. HEW, however, took no further actions against either group. In late 1970, Kenneth Adams and a coalition of black interest groups, led by the Legal Defense Fund of the N.A.A.C.P., brought suit against HEW claiming that the agency had "defaulted" in the administration of its responsibilities under Title VI. *See,* Adams v. Richardson, 351 F.Supp. 636, at 637 (D.C. 1972). The plaintiffs sought a court order requiring HEW to implement the provisions of the Act and to begin enforcement procedures against the ten states that had received noncompliance letters.

---

11.   The scope of voluntary affirmative action which will be permitted under Title VI before a reverse discrimination will be found is discussed at length in Regents of the University of California v. Bakke, 98 S. Ct. 2733 (1978).

ADAMS v. RICHARDSON
United States Court of Appeals
480 F.2d 1159 (D.C.Cir. 1973)

Before BAZELON, Chief Judge, and WRIGHT, McGOWAN, TAMM, LEVENTHAL, ROBINSON, MacKINNON, ROBB and WILKEY, Circuit Judges sitting en banc.

PER CURIAM:

This action was brought to secure declaratory and injunctive relief against the Secretary of Health, Education, and Welfare, and the Director of HEW's Office of Civil Rights. Appellees, certain black students, citizens, and taxpayers, allege in their complaint that applicants have been derelict in their duty to enforce Title VI of the Civil Rights Act of 1964 because they have not taken appropriate action to end segregation in public educational institutions receiving federal funds. [1] The matter was before the District Court on cross motions for summary judgment, on an extensive record consisting of depositions and documentary evidence.

The District Court found appellants' performance to fall below that required of them under Title VI, and ordered them to (1) institute compliance procedures against ten state-operated systems of higher education, (2) commence enforcement proceedings against seventy-four secondary and primary school districts found either to have reneged on previously approved desegregation plans or to be otherwise out of compliance with Title VI, (3) commence enforcement proceedings against forty-two districts previously deemed by HEW to be in presumptive violation of the Supreme Court's ruling in Swann v. Charlotte-Mecklenburg Board of Education, 402 U.S. 1, 91 S.Ct. 1267, 28 L.Ed.2d 554 (1971), (4) demand of eighty-five other secondary and primary districts an explanation of racial disproportion in apparent violation of *Swann*, (5) implement an enforcement program to secure Title VI compliance with respect to vocational and special schools, (6) monitor all school districts under court desegregation orders to the extent that HEW resources permit, and (7) make periodic reports to appellees on their activities in each of the above areas.

We modify the injunction concerning higher education and affirm the remainder of the order.

I

Appellants insist that the enforcement of Title VI is committed to agency discretion, and that review of such action is therefore not within the jurisdiction of the courts. But the agency discretion exception to the general rule that agency action is reviewable under the Administrative

---

[1.] . . . By regulation issued under the foregoing statutory authority, 45 C.F.R. 80.8 (1972), the procedure for effecting compliance is described as fund termination or "any other means authorized by law." The regulation goes on to say that such other means may include a reference to the Department of Justice with a recommendation that appropriate proceedings be brought by it. We are not asked to decide on this appeal whether reference of cases to the Justice Department will in all cases completely satisfy HEW's obligations under the statute.

Procedure Act, 5 U.S.C. § § 701-02, is a narrow one, and is only "applicable in those rare instances where 'statutes are drawn in such broad terms that in a given case there is no law to apply'. . . . The terms of Title VI are not so broad as to preclude judicial review. A substantial and authoritative body of case law provides the criteria by which noncompliance can be determined, and the statute indicates with precision the measures available to enforce the Act.

Appellants rely almost entirely on cases in which courts have declined to disturb the exercise of prosecutorial discretion by the Attorney General or by United States Attorneys. . . . Those cases do not support a claim to *absolute* discretion and are, in any event, distinguishable from the case at bar. Title VI not only requires the agency to enforce the Act, but also sets forth specific enforcement procedures. . . .

More significantly, this suit is not brought to challenge HEW's decisions with regard to a few school districts in the course of a generally effective enforcement program. To the contrary, appellants allege that HEW has consciously and expressly adopted a general policy which is in effect an abdication of its statutory duty. We are asked to interpret the statute and determine whether HEW has correctly construed its enforcement obligations.

A final important factor distinguishing this case from the prosecutorial discretion cases cited by HEW is the nature of the relationship between the agency and the institutions in question. HEW is actively supplying segregated institutions with federal funds, contrary to the expressed purposes of Congress. It is one thing to say the Justice Department lacks the resources necessary to locate and prosecute every civil rights violator; it is quite another to say HEW may affirmatively continue to channel federal funds to defaulting schools. The anomaly of this latter assertion fully supports the conclusion that Congress's clear statement of an affirmative enforcement duty should not be discounted.

Appellants attempt to avoid the force of this argument by saying that, although enforcement is required, the means of enforcement is a matter of absolute agency discretion, and that they have chosen to seek voluntary compliance in most cases. This position is untenable in light of the plain language of the statute. . . .

The Act sets forth two alternative courses of action by which enforcement may be effected. In order to avoid unnecessary invocation of formal enforcement procedures, it includes the proviso that the institution must first be notified and given a chance to comply voluntarily. Although the Act does not provide a specific limit to the time period within which voluntary compliance may be sought, it is clear that a request for voluntary compliance, if not followed by responsive action on the part of the institution within a reasonable time, does not relieve the agency of the responsibility to enforce Title VI by one of the two alternative means contemplated by the statute. A consistent failure to do so is a dereliction of duty reviewable in the courts. . . .

The injunction does not direct the termination of any funds, nor can any funds be terminated prior to a determination of noncompliance. In this suit against the agency, in contrast to actions brought against individual school systems, our purpose, and the purpose of the District Court order as we understand it, is not to resolve particular questions of compliance or non-compliance. It is rather, to assure that the agency properly construes its statutory obligations, and that the policies it adopts and implements are consistent with those duties and not a negation of them.

III

With this broad purpose in mind, we turn to the substance of the order. We have examined the record in relation to the findings of fact made by the District Court, and can only conclude that they are unassailable. Rule 52(a), Fed.R.Civ.P. Accordingly, with the exception of the higher education problem discussed below, the order must be, and is, affirmed.

In the field of higher education, the District Court found that between January, 1969, and February, 1970, HEW concluded that ten states[8] were operating segregated systems of higher education in violation of Title VI. HEW then directed each state to submit a desegregation plan within 120 days. Five ignored the request, and five submitted unacceptable plans, as to which HEW has not made any formal comments in the intervening years. Nevertheless, HEW has neither instituted any enforcement proceedings itself nor referred any of the cases to the Department of Justice. Although noting HEW's representations that negotiations with the 10 states are still pending, on the basis of these findings the district judge required institution of compliance proceedings within 120 days.

We agree with the District Court's conclusion that HEW may not neglect this area of its responsibility. However, we are also mindful that desegregation problems in colleges and universities differ widely from those in elementary and secondary schools, and that HEW admittedly lacks experience in dealing with them. It has not yet formulated guidelines for desegregating state-wide systems of higher learning,[9] nor has it commented formally upon the desegregation plans of the five states which have submitted them. As regrettable as these revelations are, the stark truth of the matter is that HEW must carefully assess the significance of the variety of new factors as it moves into an unaccustomed area. None of these factors justifies a failure to comply with a Congressional mandate; they may, however, warrant a more deliberate opportunity to identify and accommodate them.

The problem of integrating higher education must be dealt with on a state-wide rather than a school-by-school basis.[10] Perhaps the most serious

---

[8.] Louisiana, Mississippi, Oklahoma, North Carolina, Florida, Arkansas, Pennsylvania, Georgia, Maryland and Virginia are the states in question.

[9.] See 45 C.F.R. §80.6(a) (1972); Alabama NAACP State Conference of Branches v. Wallace, 269 F.Supp. 346, 351-352 (M.D.Ala.1967).

[10.] It is important to note that we are not here discussing discriminatory admissions policies of individual institutions. To the extent that such practices are discovered, immediate corrective action is required, but we do not understand HEW to dispute that point. This controversy concerns the more complex problem of system-wide racial imbalance.

problem in this area is the lack of state-wide planning to provide more and better trained minority group doctors, lawyers, engineers and other professionals. A predicate for minority access to quality post-graduate programs is a viable, coordinated state-wide higher education policy that takes into account the special problems of minority students and of Black colleges. As *amicus* points out, these Black institutions currently fulfill a crucial need and will continue to play an important role in Black higher education.[11]

Since some years have elapsed since the initial call was made by HEW for the submission of state higher education plans, we think such a cycle may best be begun by requiring HEW to call upon the states in question—those that have submitted plans earlier as well as those who have not—to submit plans within 120 days, and thereafter to be in active communication with those states whose plans are not acceptable. If an acceptable plan has not been arrived at within an additional period of 180 days, HEW must initiate compliance procedures. As judges well know, the setting down of a case for hearing does not automatically terminate voluntary negotiations nor eliminate the possibility of agreement. The need to prepare for actual hearing frequently causes litigants to focus on their weaknesses as well as their desires. . . .

The injunction issued by the District Court relating to state-operated systems of higher education is modified as set forth above. In all other respects, the judgment appealed from is

Affirmed.

NOTES

1. Events following the *Adams* decision:

(a) In June of 1974, HEW found acceptable the desegregation plans submitted by eight of the ten states involved in the *Adams* order. The two remaining states, Louisiana and Mississippi, were referred by HEW to the Department of Justice for the commencement of enforcement proceedings.

(b) In 1977, the *Adams* plaintiffs returned to court challenging HEW's acceptance of the eight desegregation plans. See Adams v. Califano, 430 F.Supp. 118 (D.C. 1977). The plaintiffs charged that the plans failed to meet the requirements HEW, itself, had earlier specified. In the *Califano* decision, the court found, based upon HEW's own admissions, that the plans accepted by HEW in 1974 were in fact inadequate.

The court ordered HEW to devise criteria specifying the elements of an acceptable statewide plan for the desegregation of higher education which would "take into account the unique importance of Black colleges." 430 F.Supp. at 120. The court gave HEW 90 days to develop the criteria. The states [12] were then to submit, within 60 days of receipt of the desegregation criteria, a revised desegregation plan. HEW was ordered to either accept or reject the revised plans within 120 days thereafter.

The criteria published in revised form at 43 F.R. 6658 (February 1978), apply only to states which formerly operated dual systems of public higher education. They provide in pertinent part:

[11.]   The brief is that filed by the National Association for Equal Opportunity in Higher Education, a voluntary association of the presidents of 110 predominantly Negro colleges and universities, both state-supported and private.

12.   Only six of the eight states were subject to the *Califano* order. Between the time the *Califano* suit was filed and the time it was decided, Pennsylvania had entered into independent negotiations with HEW and the *Adams* plaintiffs and Maryland had obtained a temporary injunction against further HEW enforcement. (See Note 3, below.)

ELEMENTS OF A PLAN
I. DISESTABLISHMENT OF THE STRUCTURE
OF THE DUAL SYSTEM

. . . .

To achieve the disestablishment of the structure of the dual system, each plan shall:

A. *Define the mission of each institution within the state system on a basis other than race. . . .*

B. *Specify steps to be taken to strengthen the role of traditionally black institutions in the state system. . . .*

C. *Commit the state to take specific steps to eliminate educationally unnecessary program duplication among traditionally black and traditionally white institutions in the same service area. . . .*

D. *Commit the state to give priority consideration to placing any new undergraduate, graduate, or professional degree programs, courses of study etc., which may be proposed, at traditionally black institutions, consistent with their missions.*

E. *Commit the state to withhold approval of any changes in the operation of the state system or of any institutions that may have the effect of thwarting the achievement of its desegregation goals.*

F. *Commit the State to advise OCR of proposed major changes in the mission or the character of any institution within the state system which may directly or indirectly affect the achievement of its desegregation goals prior to their formal adoption. . . .*

G. *Specify timetables for sequential implementation of the actions necessary to achieve these goals as soon as possible but no later than within five years (by the close of the fifth full academic year after the plan is accepted) unless compelling justification for a longer period for compliance is provided to and accepted by the Department. . . .*

H. *Commit the state and all its involved agencies and subdivisions to specific measures for achievement of the above objectives. . . .*

II. DESEGREGATION OF STUDENT
ENROLLMENT

. . . .

To achieve the desegregation of student enrollment, each plan shall:

A. *Adopt the goal that for two year and four year undergraduate public higher education institutions in the state system, taken as a whole, the proportion of black high school graduates throughout the state who enter such institutions shall be at least equal to the proportion of white high school graduates throughout the state who enter such institutions.*

B. (1) *Adopt the goal that there shall be an annual increase, to be specified by each state system, in the proportion of black students in the traditionally white four year undergraduate public higher education institutions in the state system taken as a whole and in each such institution; and*

(2) *Adopt the objective of reducing the disparity between the proportion of black high school graduates and the proportion of white high school graduates entering traditionally white four year and upper division undergraduate public higher education institutions in the state system; and adopt the goal of reducing the disparity by at least fifty per cent by the final academic year of the plan. However this shall not require any state to increase by that date black student admissions by more than 150% above the admissions for the academic year preceding the year in which the plan is requested by HEW.*

C. *Adopt the goal that the proportion of black state residents who graduate from undergraduate institutions in the state system and enter graduate study or professional schools in the state system shall be at least equal to the proportion of white state residents who graduate from undergraduate institutions in the state system and enter such schools. . . .*

D. *Adopt the goal of increasing the total proportion of white students attending traditionally black institutions. . . .*

E. *Commit the state to take all reasonable steps to reduce any disparity between the proportion of black and white students completing and graduating from the two year, four year and graduate public institutions of higher education, and establish interim goals, to be specified by the state system for achieving annual progress.*

F. *Commit the state to expand mobility between two year and four year institutions as a means of meeting the goals set forth in these criteria.*

G. *Specify numeric goals for II. A, B, and C, and timetables for sequential implementation of actions necessary to achieve these goals as soon as possible but not later than within five years unless another date is specified in this section.*

H. *Commit the state and all its involved agencies and subdivisions to specific measures to achieve these goals. . . .*

III. DESEGREGATION OF FACULTY, ADMINISTRATIVE STAFFS, NONACADEMIC PERSONNEL, AND GOVERNING BOARDS

. . . .

To achieve the desegregation of faculty, administrators, other personnel, and governing boards, each plan shall:

A. *Adopt the goal that the proportion of black faculty and of administrators at each institution and on the staffs of each governing board, or any other state higher education entity, in positions not requiring the doctoral degree, shall at least equal the proportion of black students graduating with masters degrees in the appropriate discipline from institutions within the state system, or the proportion of black individuals with the required credentials for such positions in the relevant labor market area, whichever is greater.*

B. *Adopt the goal that the proportion of black faculty and of administrators at each institution and on the staffs of each governing board or any other state higher education entity, in positions requiring the doctoral degree, shall at least equal the proportion of black individuals with the credentials required for such positions in the relevant labor market area.*

C. *Adopt the goal that the proportion of black non-academic personnel (by job category) at each institution and on the staffs of each governing board or any other state higher education entity, shall at least equal the proportion of black persons in the relevant labor market area.*

D. *Assure hereafter and until the foregoing goals are met that for the traditionally white institutions as a whole, the proportion of blacks hired to fill faculty and administrative vacancies shall not be less than the proportion of black individuals with the credentials required for such positions in the relevant labor market area.*

E. *Specify numeric goals and timetables for sequential implementation of the actions necessary to achieve these objectives including interim benchmarks from which progress toward the objectives may be measured. . . .*

F. *Commit the state system to take specific measures to achieve these objectives. . . .*

G. *Adopt the goal of increasing the numbers of black persons appointed to systemwide and institutional governing boards and agencies so that these boards and agencies may be more representative of the racial population of the state or of the area served. . . .*

43 F.R. 6658 (Feb. 15, 1978)

(c) On December 29, 1977, a settlement was reached between the *Adams* plaintiffs and HEW.[13]   The agreement provided the framework of a June 14, 1976 order of the *Adams* case, containing a set of timetables and deadlines, would be extended beyond the Southern states to cover all educational institutions receiving HEW funds. The settlement order further required HEW: (1) to eliminate any backlog of complaints by the end of fiscal year 1979; (2) to decide within 150 days of starting a compliance review whether or not the institution is in compliance with the law; and (3) to conduct a sufficient number of compliance reviews within specified time limits to insure adequate compliance with the relevant laws. 43 F.R. 7048 at 7049 (Feb. 1978).

2. In 1976, the Governor of Maryland, representing the state system of higher education, and the Mayor and City Council of Baltimore, representing the Baltimore school system, filed a suit against HEW seeking an injunction against further enforcement proceedings under Title VI. See Mandel v. U.S. Department of Health, Education and Welfare, 411 F.Supp. 542, (D. Md. 1976). The plaintiffs claimed that HEW had failed to seek, in good faith, compliance by voluntary means, as is required by § 2000d-1 of the Act. After reviewing HEW's enforcement record, the court concluded that HEW did not obey the Act with respect to either the City of Baltimore or the State of Maryland, "in that [it] arbitrarily and whimsically failed to attempt to work toward compliance by voluntary means" 411 F.Supp. at 563. The court pointed to HEW's persistent failure to offer guidance on how compliance could be achieved. The court therefore enjoined HEW from either going forward with the pending administrative enforcement proceedings against Baltimore and Maryland, or from deferring consideration of applications for future funding until HEW had: (1) adopted administrative regulations, setting forth specific standards for compliance with Title VI in the administration of programs of federal financial assistance to institutions of higher education; (2) made a separate and specific analysis of each statutory aid program to determine the existence of noncompliance in the administration of such program; and (3) specified the actions which, in HEW's view, are necessary to remedy the alleged noncompliance and specified standards by which the existence of noncompliance will be determined.

HEW appealed the district court decision in Mayor and City Council of Baltimore v. Mathews, 562 F.2d 914 (4th Cir. 1977). The Fourth Circuit, in a 4–3 decision, affirmed the district court order relating to higher education, but reversed the finding that HEW was in default with respect to the Baltimore school system. The court placed a 90-day time limit on HEW for the promulgation of guideline regulations.

In Mayor & City Council of Baltimore v. Mathews, 571 F.2d 1273 (4th Cir. 1978), the Court of Appeals vacated its earlier decision because one of the judges who had voted with the majority on the case, died before the dissenting opinion had been released. The court therefore decided to discount the judge's vote, withdrew the opinions that had been written, and affirmed the district court's order by an equally divided court. Circuit Judge Winter, who had written the earlier majority opinion, dissented, urging that a full rehearing should have been granted. A petition for certiorari was filed, but was denied. Lee v. HEW, 47 U.S.L.W. 3224 (1978). As of March 1979, HEW had still not promulgated the higher education regulations ordered by the district court. This was despite the fact that HEW's own regulations obligated it to supply specific guidelines. See 45 C.F.R. § 80.6(a). The criteria prepared by HEW is response to the *Adams v. Califano* order do not qualify as regulations since they were not formulated in accordance with the proper administrative procedure.

3. As to the current status of the six states involved in the *Adams v. Califano* order, HEW has accepted the final desegregation plans of Florida, Arkansas, Oklahoma, and

---

13.   In Adams v. Mathew, 536 F.2d 417 (D.C. Cir. 1976), the Women's Equity Action League was given leave to intervene in the *Adams* suit to bring claims under Title IX of the Education Amendments Act of 1972, 20 USC § 1681 et seq. The settlement of the *Adams* suit therefore involved the WEAL plaintiffs also.

Virginia. The two states still out of compliance are Georgia and North Carolina. The major area of dispute between the two states and HEW centers on Section I.C. of the *Adams* criteria, which requires the elimination of "educationally unnecessary program duplication among traditionally black and traditionally white institutions in the same service area." Section I.C., Revised Criteria, 43 F.R. 6658, at 6661. In Georgia, the conflict had narrowed to only one black college and its neighboring white institutions. North Carolina, however, informed HEW that, while they had identified over 100 duplicated programs, they did not intend to eliminate them because none of them were "educationally unnecessary." Lawyers for the N.A.A.C.P. Legal Defense Fund urged HEW to immediately move to cut off the state's higher education funds. HEW then gave North Carolina until March 11, 1979 to submit an acceptable plan. *See* The Chronicle of Higher Education, *Government Accepts Virginia's Plan for Desegregating Higher Education,* Vol. XVII, January 22, 1979, p. 17; *Ibid., HEW Pressured to Speed Desegregation,* Vol. XVII, November 20, 1978, p. 7; and *Ibid., U. of North Carolina Could Lose U.S. Funds,* Vol. XVI, March 27, 1978, p. 13.

4. In February 1978, HEW announced that it would review eight states' public systems of higher education to determine whether they are in conformity with the *Adams* criteria. All of them are southern or border states. *See,* The Chronicle of Higher Education, *U.S. Accepts 3 States' Plans for Desegregation, Rejects 3,* Vol. XV, February 13, 1978, p. 3. As of March 1979, HEW had never attempted to enforce Title VI against northern institutions of higher education.

5. Is the statewide approach, called for in the *Adams v. Richardson* opinion, limited to the context of public systems of higher education? Don't private colleges and universities have to be taken into account to have an effective desegregation plan? The *Adams* criteria are applicable only to the desegregation of public systems of higher education which were formerly segregated by law. What elements should a desegregation plan for a private institution contain? What should the criteria be for states that did not have de jure segregation?

6. In light of the *Adams* case, would it be a per se violation of Title VI for a state to close down one of its black colleges? What if the state only has one traditionally black institution, but the quality of the institution is clearly substandard? Is lack of quality a permissible justification for a state's decision to close down a black institution? *See,* The Chronicle of Higher Education, *Students Organize to Save Public Black Colleges,* Vol. XVI, May 1, 1978, p. 3.

What steps do the *Adams* criteria take to insure the "unique quality" of black colleges? In 1979, President Carter ordered the directors of all federal departments and agencies to take steps to strengthen traditionally black colleges by allowing them to take a larger part in government programs. Specifically, the President ordered his department heads to: (1) review federal grant and contract programs to insure that black colleges are being informed of, and have a "fair opportunity to participate" in the programs; (2) identify areas where aid to black colleges can be increased within current funding programs; (3) establish goals and timetables that would provide for increased government spending at black institutions; and (4) appoint a "high-level" liaison person to oversee these activities. *See* The Chronicle of Higher Education, *Carter Orders Greater Effort to Help Black Colleges,* Vol. XVII, January 22, 1979, p. 17.

7. The federal fund cut-off remedy of Title VI has been criticized as an unworkable sanction. Through 1978, it had never been applied against an academic institution for a substantive violation of the Act. There have been a few minor cases where funding has been terminated for failure to comply with procedural requirements. *See,* 36 Geo. Wash. L. Rev. 824, 918-19 (1968). Agencies are reluctant to enforce Title VI, because of the injustice worked on the innocent beneficiaries of federal aid when that aid is suddenly terminated.

8. For an excellent study on *Adams* and the politics of implementing Title VI, see C. Lloyd, *Adams v. Califano: A Case Study in the Politics of Regulation* (Jan. 1978) (a working paper for the Sloan Commission on Government and Higher Education). Other

sources on the subject include: Rentschler, *Courts and Politics: Integrating Higher Educa-tion in North Carolina,* 7 NOLPE Schl. L.J. 1, (1977); and Note, *Constitutional Law– Affirmative Duty to Desegregate State Systems of Higher Education without Eliminating Racially Identifiable Schools: Adams v. Richardson,* 5 N. Car. Cent. L.J. 365 (1974).

3.   Substantive Issues Under Title VI

a. The Existence of a Private Cause of Action

The question of whether a private cause of action exists under Title VI has not yet been answered. The latest word on the subject is contained in Regents of the University of California v. Bakke, 98 S.Ct. 2733, (1978). In the *Bakke* decision, four justices expressed the view that a private cause of action exists, four Justices assumed that one existed for the purposes of the case, and one Justice, Justice White, expressed the view that a private cause of action does not exist. In Lau v. Nichols, 414 U.S. 563 (1974), however, the Supreme Court upheld a private Title VI claim. Justice White, in his separate opinion in *Bakke*, distinguished *Lau* on the grounds that in *Lau*: (1) standing was not raised as an issue by the parties; (2) the standing alleged by the plaintiffs was that of third-party beneficiaries of the funding contract between HEW and the school district (this theory was not alleged in *Bakke*); and (3) the plaintiffs alleged jurisdiction under 42 U.S.C. § 1983, rather than directly under the provisions of Title VI, 98 S.Ct. at 2794, f.n. 1. Other Title VI cases which have allowed standing to private plaintiffs include: Flanagan v. President and Directors of Georgetown College, 417 F.Supp. 377 (D.C. 1976); Stewart v. New York University, 430 F.Supp. 1305 (S.D.N.Y. 1976); and Bossier Parish School Board v. Lemon, 370 F.2d 847 (5th Cir. 1967), *cert. denied,* 388 U.S. 911 (involving primary and secondary education).

b. The Scope of the Nondiscrimination Standard

FLANAGAN v. PRESIDENT & DIRECTORS OF GEORGETOWN COLLEGE
United States District Court, District of Columbia
417 F.Supp. 377 (1976)

GASCH, District Judge.

This is an action under Title VI, section 601 of the Civil Rights Act of 1964, 78 Stat. 241, 252, 42 U.S.C. § 2000d, alleging that defendants have discriminated against plaintiff on the basis of race in the allocation of finan-cial aid to students at the Georgetown University Law Center. . . . Plaintiff seeks a permanent injunction against these alleged discriminatory actions and $3,700 in damages, representing the amount of financial aid plaintiff alleges he would have been awarded had he not been the subject of this alleged discrimination. . . .

Upon consideration of the entire record herein and for the reasons to be detailed in this Memorandum, the Court concludes that plaintiff is en-titled to a partial summary judgment on the question of liability but the determination of damages (if any) must await further action by the parties.

I.

Plaintiff is a white (Caucasian) student, enrolled since September, 1973, at Georgetown University Law Center. . . .

Since 1967, the Law Center Committee on Admissions with the approval of the Law Center faculty has developed an Affirmative Action program in an effort to increase the enrollment at the Law Center of certain "minority" students. Efforts were made to recruit potential "minority" students, and to develop proposals for financial assistance to "minority" students. By 1972, however, these efforts had achieved relatively little success. The Law Center's Ad Hoc Committee on Minority Affairs attributed this to the lack of financial assistance opportunities available to potential "minority" students. This Ad Hoc Committee presented certain proposals to the Law Center faculty in February, 1972. On February 24, 1972, the faculty passed a resolution which defendants summarize as follows:

> the Law Center Admissions Committee would consist of five faculty members and three students representing student groups known as La Raza, BALSA and the Student Bar Association; the Committee would, *inter alia*, in reviewing and passing upon applications for admission, give renewed consideration to those "minority" or "disadvantaged" persons not clearly acceptable based upon traditional admissions indices; *sixty percent (60%) of available scholarship funds for the freshman class in 1972 would go to such persons*; and the program would continue for three years.

The scholarship funds that are made available 60% to "minority" students and 40% to "non-minority" students are funds that originate from Georgetown's own revenues, and are referred to as "Direct University Scholarships." The term "minority" student as used by the Law Center in implementing these policies includes not only persons in discernible ethnic and racial groups (Black Americans, Native Americans, Asian Americans, Spanish-speaking Americans), but also applicants with social, educational, cultural, and/or financial disadvantages. The defendants assert, "[u]nder this minority definition applied by the Office of Admissions, other ethnic or social groups, including whites or Caucasians, may qualify and have qualified for minority status." Defendants further indicated that in plaintiff's first year class of 623 students there were 68 "minority" students, or less than 11%.

Within the two groups of first year students, "minority" and "non-minority," the scholarship funds are distributed on the basis of demonstrated financial need, as reflected in the standardized, confidential Graduate and Professional School Financial Aid Service (GAPSFAS) form submitted by all applicants to the Educational Testing Service (ETS) in Princeton, New Jersey. . . .

In plaintiff's case he was not accepted for admission for the academic year 1973-74 until June, 1973, by which time all Direct University Scholarship funds available for "non-minority" applicants had been exhausted.

The Direct University Scholarship funds available for "minority" students, however, were not exhausted. During the second semester of the 1973-74 academic year, the Financial Aid Committee reviewed the financial aid applications of many students, including plaintiff, and awarded plaintiff a scholarship of $400 for the second semester of that academic year.

II.

. . . .

Plaintiff [has moved for summary judgment arguing] that by segregating first-year students into two classes on the basis of race and allocating scholarship funds so that 60% of the funds were made available to 11% of the first-year students and 40% to the remaining 89% of the first-year class, defendants violated . . . [Title VI] as well as the relevant regulations of the United States Department of Health, Education and Welfare (H.E.W.). These regulations are designed to implement Title VI as it relates to programs funded by H.E.W. The federal financial assistance plaintiff alleges defendants received includes federal grants, loans, and interest subsidies totalling over $7 million for the construction of the Law Center building under the Higher Education Facilities Act, Pub.L. 88-204, 77 Stat. 363 (repealed 1972), administered by H.E.W. Plaintiff alleges that defendants' actions are in violation of specific prohibitions in the H.E.W. regulations, as well as the general prohibition in the statute. Section 80.3(b)(1) of Title 45 C.F.R. provides:

A recipient under any program to which this part applies may not, directly or through contractual or other arrangements, on ground of race, color, or national origin:

.   .   .   .   .

(iii) Subject an individual to segregation or separate treatment in any matter related to his receipt of any service, financial aid or other benefit under the program;

.   .   .   .   .

(v) Treat an individual differently from others in determining whether he satisfies any admission, enrollment, quota, eligibility, membership or other requirement or condition which individuals must meet in order to be provided any service, financial aid, or other benefit provided under the program.

As direct evidence of the discriminatory effect of defendants' policies, plaintiff points to the documentary information supplied by defendants. . . [which] for example, indicates that plaintiff, with a financial need estimate of $2,700 received a $400 scholarship award, while three "minority" students with lesser financial need estimates of $2,550, $2,300 and $2,190, received respectively, $1,885, $1,825, and $1,895.

III.

Defendants' opposition to plaintiff's motion is in four parts. First, it is argued that plaintiff has failed to demonstrate that the classification of first year students as either "minority" or "non-minority" is discrimination on the basis of race as prohibited by Title VI. Second, defendants assert that plaintiff has failed to demonstrate that (or at least there is a material issue of fact as to whether) the Law Center has received "substantial" federal financial assistance so as to bring the actions of defendants within the purview of Title VI. Third, defendants assert that their financial aid policies are part of a bona fide affirmative action program to increase minority enrollment at the Law Center and are therefore not in violation of Title VI. . . .

A.   It is not disputed that the "minority" classification receiving 60% of the scholarship funds is the "favored" classification. Indeed the evidence . . . clearly indicates this. The issue on discrimination then comes down to what persons are afforded "minority" status.

In paragraph 11 of plaintiff's Statement of Material Facts Not in Issue he asserts:

> For purposes of the [1972] faculty resolution, "Minority Students" includes Native-Americans (American Indians), Spanish-speaking Americans (Chicanos and Puerto Ricans), Afro-Americans, and Asian Americans. White (Caucasian) American students are excluded from the classification.

It is this classification on a racial [and national origin] basis that plaintiff alleges is discriminatory, and in violation of Title VI. Defendants argue, however, that there is nothing in the record to support this definition and it is specifically disputed in the affidavit of defendant Wilmot:

> For purposes of the said faculty policy guideline and the allocation of Direct University Scholarships, "minority" status includes not only discernible ethnic and racial groups (Black Americans, Native Americans, Asian Americans, Spanish-speaking Americans), but also applicants with social, educational, cultural and/or financial disadvantages. Under this minority definition applied by the Office of Admissions, other ethnic or racial groups, including whites or Caucasians, may qualify and have qualified for minority status.

Unfortunately for defendants this definition of "minority" is equally susceptible to an allegation of improper discrimination. Certain ethnic and racial groups are automatically accorded "minority" status, while whites or Caucasians must make a particular showing in order to qualify. The fact that some whites or Caucasians have qualified for minority status does not lessen the discriminatory nature of the classification. Access to the "favored" category is made more difficult for one racial group than another. This in itself is discrimination as prohibited by Title VI as well as the Constitution. . . .

C.   Defendants argue that the 1972 faculty resolution on financial aid policy is part of a bona fide affirmative action program to increase "minority" representation at the Law Center. Defendants point to the H.E.W. Regulations for justification for such affirmative action. Thus, 45 C.F.R. §80.3(b)(6) provides:

(i) In administering a program regarding which the recipient has previously discriminated against persons on the ground of race, color or national origin, the recipient must take affirmative action to overcome the effects of prior discrimination.

(ii) Even in the absence of such prior discrimination, a recipient in administering a program may take affirmative action to overcome the effects of conditions which resulted in limiting participation by persons of a particular race, color, or national origin.

Defendants appear to be arguing that reasonable preferences in favor of "minority" persons in order to remedy past discriminatory practices are permissible.

As there has been no showing that defendants were guilty of past discrimination, 45 C.F.R. §80.3(b)(6)(i) is inapplicable. Thus defendants' entire legal defense is grounded on the concept of affirmative action embodied in 45 C.F.R. §80.3(b)(6)(ii). This regulation, however, does not define affirmative action. Defendants would have the Court conclude that affirmative action is any action which gives a preference to "minorities" regardless of its impact on "non-minorities." While there is authority for the proposition that any affirmative action granting preferences to one race or sex over another is constitutionally infirm. *Cramer v. Virginia Commonwealth University*, Civil Action No. 75-0271-R, 415 F.Supp. 673 (E.D. Va. 1976), this Court need not rely on such an extreme position. Affirmative action may be justified provided it does not violate the non-discrimination provisions of Title VI and is administered on a racially *neutral* basis. . . . Where an administrative procedure is permeated with social and cultural factors (as in a law school's *admission* process), separate treatment for "minorities" may be justified in order to insure that all persons are judged in a racially neutral fashion.

But in the instant case, we are concerned with the question of financial need, which, in the final analysis, cuts across racial, cultural, and social lines. There is no justification for saying that a "minority" student with a demonstrated financial need of $2,000 requires more scholarship aid than a "non-minority" student with a demonstrated financial need of $3,000. . . . While an affirmative action program may be appropriate to ensure that all persons are afforded the same opportunities or are considered for benefits on the same basis, it is not permissible when it allocates a scarce resource (be it jobs, housing, or financial aid) in favor of one race to the detriment of others. . . . Such is the situation in this case. Under no circumstances would the defendants' policy of awarding 60% of scholarship aid to the 11% of the students who are in the favored classification be justifiable under the banner of affirmative action. . . .

CONCLUSION

In light of the facts of this case and especially considering that the defendant Law School has accepted from the United States a substantial grant, for the construction of its Law Center, the defendant is obligated to its programs in a non-discriminatory manner. This includes the awarding of student aid in the form of scholarships. In this, as in other matters, a balancing test must be applied, for the statute and applicable regulations prohibit discrimination, but the regulations also make provision for affirmative action programs. The ultimate question is whether in order to carry out its affirmative action program the defendant may allocate 60% of its available scholarship funds to 11% of its entering students for the reason that they constitute a "minority." This in the Court's judgment is arbitrary, offends against the non-discrimination provisions of the Act, and is a violation of plaintiff's rights.

NOTES

1. Does Title VI merely incorporate the purposeful discrimination standard of the Constitution, or does it establish a more stringent standard, such as the "disparate effects" test of Title VII of the Civil Rights Act? HEW's regulations import an "effects" standard for the statute. Thus, practices having a disparate impact on individuals of a particular race, are treated as being discriminatory, even though an intent to discriminate is absent.

In Lau v. Nichols, 414 U.S. 563 (1974) (a case brought by a group of Chinese claiming that the failure to provide special language assistance for non-English speaking elementary and secondary school students constituted unlawful discrimination), the Supreme Court appeared to adopt HEW's "effects" standard. In holding the defendant school system in violation of Title VI, the Court stated:

> [HEW's regulations specify that] [d]iscrimination is barred which has that *effect* even though no purposeful design is present: a recipient "may not . . . utilize criteria or methods of administration which have the effect of subjecting individuals to discrimination" or have "the effect of defeating or substantially impairing accomplishment of the objectives of the program as respect individuals of a particular race, color, or national origin." [45 C.F.R.] §80.3(b)(2).
>
> It seems obvious that the Chinese-speaking minority receive fewer benefits than the English-speaking majority from respondents' school system which denies them a meaningful opportunity to participate in the educational program—all earmarks of the discrimination banned by [HEW's] regulations. 414 U.S. at 568 (emphasis in original).

2. For a discussion on the merits of the *Flanagan* case, see Joyner, *"Reverse" Discrimination in Student Financial Aid for Higher Education: The Flanagan Case in Perspective*, 6 J. of L. & Ed. 327 (1977).

c. The Program Specific Approach

The scope of HEW's jurisdiction over recipients of federal assistance is limited by §2000d-1 of the Act, which provides:

> . . . Compliance with any requirement adopted pursuant to this section may be effected (1) by the termination of . . . assistance . . . but such termination or refusal thall be limited to the particular political entity, or part thereof, or other recipient as to whom such a finding [of noncompliance] has been made and, *shall be limited in its effect to the particular program*, or part thereof, in which such non-compliance has been so found. . . . 42 U.S.C. §2000d-1 (emphasis added).

This provision was added to the Act to insure that fund cut-offs would be "pinpointed" specifically to those programs in which federal money was being used to perpetuate discriminatory practices.

The effectiveness of the limitation depends on the definition of what constitutes a "program." In the context of desegregation, an expansive definition was applied to institutions of higher education. In Adams v. Richardson, 480 F.2d 1159 (D.C. Cir. 1973), the court held that statewide systems of education constitute single "programs." By contrast, in cases involving primary and secondary education, a restrictive definition has been applied. For example, in Board of Public Instruction of Taylor County v. Finch, 414 F.2d 1068 (5th Cir. 1969), it was held that each grant made to a recipient constitutes a separate "program" for which independent findings of noncompliance must be made.[14]

Beyond the desegregation context, HEW's regulations assume broad agency jurisdiction over institutions of higher education. The regulations require higher education recipients to assure Title VI compliance not only with respect to practices in the program receiving federal assistance, but also with respect to admission and other practices relating to the treatment of students. 45 C.F.R. §80.4(d)(1). The regulations further create the presumption that the assurance, "insofar as [it] relates to the institution's practices with respect to admissions or other treatment of individuals as students," applies to the *entire* institution, not just the department receiving federal funds. *Id.*, at §80.4(d)(2). The presumption can be rebutted only by a showing, "to the satisfaction of the responsible Department official, that the institution's practices in designated parts or programs of the institution will in no way affect its practices in the program of the institution for which Federal financial assistance is sought." *Id.* Under this scheme, a graduate school research grant could be terminated upon a finding of discrimination in undergraduate admissions. (See the illustration at 45 C.F.R. §80.5(c)). Through this extended assurance requirement HEW, in effect, redefines "program" to include an entire university, thereby expanding the scope of Title VI coverage beyond just the federally funded activities. The legality of this regulation remains to be tested in court.

Another provision, relating to grants for facilities, extends the reach of Title VI even further. The section states that if a "facility" has been provided with the aid of federal money, all "service[s], financial aid, or other benefits provided *in or through*" *that facility* shall be treated as "programs" receiving federal assistance in and of themselves. *Id.*, at §80.3-(b)(4) (emphasis added). The illustration for this section provides:

> "In grants to assist in the construction of facilities for the provision of health, educational or welfare services, assurances will be required that services will be provided without discrimination, to

---

14.   The court in Mandel v. U.S. Dept. of Health, Educ. and Welfare, 411 F.Supp, 542 (D. Md. 1976), went one step further, and held that even pre-termination negotiations must be conducted on an individual grant-by-grant basis.

the same extent that discrimination would be prohibited as a condition of federal operating grants for the support of such services. . ." *Id.* at §80.5(e).

For example, in *Flanagan v. President and Directors of Georgetown College,* the court held that discriminatory practices in the distribution of student financial aid, none of which came from the federal government, violated Title VI because it was provided "through a *facility* provided with the aid of Federal financial assistance." *Id.,* at §80.3(b)(4). The court noted:

"Plaintiff has alleged that Georgetown received total federal benefits of over $7,000,000 for the construction of the Law Center building. . . . [The defendants] argue, however, that these funds are unrelated [because] the scholarship funds . . . come solely from Georgetown's own funds. Therefore, the argument continues, there has been no discrimination in the use of federal funds, so as to bring the discrimination in the scholarship program within the purview of Title VI. . . .

[However,] financial aid provided through the Law Center, which has been provided with Federal financial assistance, must be dispensed in accordance with Title VI and the HEW Regulations. . . .

It is the conclusion of the Court, . . . that by accepting federal financial assistance for the construction of the Law Center, Georgetown and the Law Center were required to refrain from discriminating on the basis of race in providing any service, financial aid or other benefit to its Law Center students. 417 F.Supp. at 382-84.

In Stewart v. New York University, 430 F.Supp. 1305 (S.D.N.Y. 1976), the opposite result was reached. The case involved a reverse discrimination challenge to a law school minority admissions program. The Court held that in order to state a cause of action under Title VI:

. . . plaintiff must show that the Federal financial assistance received by the Law School constitutes more than a *de minimus* portion of its annual revenues and that there is some material connection between said assistance and the minority admissions policy challenged therein. 430 F.Supp. at 1314.

To support jurisdiction under Title VI, the plaintiff had pointed to the law school's $625,000 indebtedness to HUD for the construction of a law school dormitory. The court nonetheless dismissed plaintiff's claim for failure to show an adequate connection between the assistance and the practices complained of. The Court held that the HUD indebtedness was insufficient to state a cause of action, because the discrimination alleged involved the minority admissions policy, not the dormitory.

NOTES

1. In U.S. v. El Camino Community College Distr., 454 F.Supp. 825 (C.D. Cal. 1978), the United States brought a declaratory judgment action to determine the scope of

HEW's authority to investigate compliance with Title VI. The defendant community college claimed that the "pinpoint" provision of §2000d-1 limited HEW's investigative authority to those programs actually receiving federal funds. The court held that the "pinpoint" section of 2000d-1 was inapplicable to the question of the scope of HEW's investigative authority, because it refers only to the power to *terminate* funds. The court concluded that the community college was "contractually bound [by their assurance of compliance] to permit [HEW] to conduct a Title VI investigation and [that] the scope of [HEW's] *investigative authority* is not confined to investigation of the federally assisted programs or activities." 454 F.Supp. at 830 (emphasis in original).

2. For a good discussion of the program specific issue, *see,* Note, *Administrative Cutoff of Federal Funding under Title VI: A Proposed Interpretation of "Program,"* 52 Ind. L.J. 651 (1977). For general discussions of the Title VI scheme, *see:* Slippen, *Administrative Enforcement of Civil Rights in Public Education: Title VI, HEW, and the Civil Rights Reviewing Authority,* 21 Wayne L. Rev. 931 (1975); and Comment, *Title VI of the Civil Rights Act of 1964—Implementation and Impact,* 36 Geo. Wash. L. Rev. 824-1006 (1968).

CHAPTER 15

TITLE IX OF THE EDUCATION AMENDMENTS OF 1972

I. Introduction

Title IX of the 1972 Education Amendments, 20 U.S.C. § 1681-86, prohibits discrimination on the basis of sex in any education program or activity which receives federal financial assistance. This statutory scheme is quite similar to Title VI of the 1964 Civil Rights Act, 42 U.S.C. § 2000d et. seq. (1970), which prohibits discrimination on the basis of race, color or national origin in any program receiving federal financial assistance. However, Title IX, unlike Title VI, is expressly limited only to educational programs and activities.

To implement the policies of Title IX, the Department of Health, Education and Welfare has, after extensive public comment, adopted regulations which can be found in 45 CFR § § 86.1-86.71. The regulations must be viewed along with the Statute to appreciate fully the scope of Title IX.

The central or core prohibition of Title IX is found in § 901(a) of the Act of § 1681(a) of the Statute. It provides in part that:

> . . . no person in the United States shall, on the basis of sex, be excluded from participation in, be denied the benefits of or be subjected to discrimination under any education program or activity receiving federal financial assistance. . . .

This broad statutory proscription is limited by a number of general exceptions. The statute does not apply to educational institutions controlled by religious organizations in situations where the statutory proscription would be inconsistent with the religious tenets of the institution. Nor does it apply to educational institutions whose primary purpose is the training of individuals for military service or the merchant marine. A third general exception, found in § 907 of the Act, states that Title IX does not prohibit an educational institution from maintaining separate living facilities for different sexes.

In addition to the general exceptions, there are also some specific exceptions in the area of admissions and membership practices. Regarding admissions, the Act applies only to vocational, professional, graduate higher education, and to most public undergraduate education. Those public undergraduate institutions with a tradition of admitting only students of one sex, which had been continually followed from the establishment of the institution, are also exempted from the application of Title IX to their admission process. The admission practices of private institutions of undergraduate higher education are also exempted. The membership practices of social fraternities, social sororities, and voluntary youth organizations, as well as the YMCA, YWCA, Girl Scouts, Boy Scouts, and Campfire Girls, have also been specifically exempted from the coverage of Title IX.

The enforcement provisions of Title IX in § 902 of the Act are virtually identical to those found in § 602 of Title VI of the Civil Rights Act of 1964, 42 U.S.C. § 2000d-1 (1970). All departments or agencies empowered to extend federal financial assistance to an education program or activity are directed to adopt rules or regulations to effectuate the provisions of Title IX. Compliance may be obtained through the termination of federal financial assistance or the refusal to grant future financial assistance only after it has been determined at a hearing that the recipient institution has failed to comply with the rules or regulations and that voluntary compliance cannot be obtained by any other means.

II.   Enforcement

A.   Private Suits

CANNON v. UNIV. OF CHICAGO
Seventh Circuit Court of Appeals
559 F.2d 1063 (1977)

BAUER, Circuit Judge.

Plaintiff Geraldine Cannon brought this civil rights suit against defendants, the University of Chicago, Northwestern University, and various individual officers of the schools, after she was rejected as an applicant for admission to the medical schools. She alleges that she was denied admission because of her age and sex. The trial court dismissed the suit for failure to state a claim upon which relief could be granted. We affirm.

Plaintiff at the time of application was 39 years old with a bachelor's degree from Trinity College of Deerfield, Illinois. Her medical college admission test scores placed her in the lower half of the applicant group. Her undergraduate grade point average in basic science was 3.17 on a 4.00 scale.

Although the plaintiff's academic credentials were good, statistics for the 1975 entering class at the University of Chicago Pritzker School of Medicine indicate the plaintiff faced overwhelming competition; 5,427 persons applied for the 104 positions available at the medical school. In sharp contrast to plaintiff's grades, the overall average of the entering class was 3.70. The Dean of the medical school stated in an affidavit that there were at least 2,000 unsuccessful applicants who had better academic qualifications than the plaintiff. . . .

Title IX of the Education Amendments of 1972, 20 U.S.C. § 1681, et seq., prohibits discrimination based on sex in most educational institutions receiving federal financial assistance. Title IX states:

"No person in the United States shall, on the basis of sex, be excluded from participation in, be denied the benefits of, or be subjected to discrimination under any education program or activity receiving Federal financial assistance."

Plaintiff maintains that Title IX provides an independent basis of federal jurisdiction for her action. On the other hand, the defendants claim that Title IX does not provide an independent cause of action in federal court, but rather, provides for mandatory administrative procedures followed only then by judicial review. . . .

Plaintiffs rely heavily upon previous decisions based upon Title VI of the Civil Rights Act of 1964, 42 U.S.C. § 2000d, *et seq.*, the language of which is identical to Title IX except that it bars racial discrimination. But our reading of the cases does not indicate that Title VI provides a private right of action for each individual discriminatee. Those cases involved an attempt by a large number of plaintiffs to enforce a national constitutional right. See *Lau v. Nichols*, 414 U.S. 563, 94 S.Ct. 786, 39 L.Ed.2d 1 (1974); *Bossier Parish School Board v. Lemon*, 370 F.2d 847 (5th Cir. 1967). . . .

In enacting Title IX Congress established a scheme through which its prohibition against sex discrimination would be enforced by HEW, the administrative agency empowered to extend the federal aid. The statute encourages voluntary compliance in the first instance, an opportunity for an administrative hearing on the issue of discrimination if necessary, and the withdrawal of federal funds as a last resort for a recalcitrant institution which has been found to discriminate in violation of the Act.[12] After department or agency action, there is a right to judicial review. [13]

It is clear that no individual right of action can be inferred from Title IX in the face of the carefully constructed scheme of administrative enforcement contained in the Act. . . .

[12.]　20 U.S.C. § 1682 states, inter alia:

"Each Federal department and agency which is empowered to extend Federal financial assistance to any education program or activity. . . is authorized and directed to effectuate the provisions of section 1681 of this title with respect to such program or activity by issuing rules, regulations, or orders . . . . Compliance . . . may be effected (1) by the termination of or refusal to grant or to continue assistance under such program or activity to any recipient as to whom there has been an express finding on the record, after opportunity for hearing, of a failure to comply with such requirement. . . . Provided, however, That no such action shall be taken until the department or agency concerned has advised the appropriate person or persons of the failure to comply with the requirement and has determined that compliance cannot be secured by voluntary means. . . ."

[13.]　20 U.S.C. § 1683 states:

"Any department or agency action taken pursuant to section 1682 of this title shall be subject to such judicial review as may otherwise be provided by law for similar action taken by such department or agency on other grounds. In the case of action, not otherwise subject to judicial review, terminating or refusing to grant or to continue financial assistance upon a finding of failure to comply with any requirement imposed pursuant to section 1682 of this title, any person aggrieved (including any State or political subdivision thereof and any agency of either) may obtain judicial review of such action in accordance with chapter 7 of Title 5, and such action shall not be deemed committed to unreviewable agency discretion within the meaning of section 701 of that title."

From a policy viewpoint we see little to be gained by involving the judiciary in every individual act of discrimination based upon sex. Perhaps our resources would be better spent in litigation challenging wholesale sexual discrimination against a large number of men or women by a particular educational institution. [16] Title VI has been effectively employed in this fashion, and we see no reason why Title IX would not provide a similar jurisdictional base for those cases where the administrative abilities of HEW would be inundated or inadequate. However, for the day-to-day problems, stemming from the long overdue social revolution in equality of the sexes, we think the HEW administrative procedure is best. Although some commentators[18] have taken the view that working through HEW is painstakingly slow and ineffective, we fail to see how a private lawsuit by individual parties would facilitate an end to sex discrimination. To allow a private right of action would be engaging in judicial legislation. Considering our already overburdened system we fail to see why we should stretch a statute by judicial interpretation to the point where it would allow additional litigation which we may not be able to properly accommodate. . . .

Accordingly, the decision of the district court in dismissing the complaint is hereby affirmed.

AFFIRMED.

On Rehearing

After issuing our opinion in this case, we granted plaintiff's petition for rehearing of the issue of whether a private right of action lies under Title IX of Public Law 92-318 in the circumstances of this case. We took this step principally to give the parties an opportunity to develop the question of whether the inclusion of Title IX within the provisions of the Civil Rights Attorney's Fees Award Act of 1976, Pub.L. No. 94-559 § 2, 90 Stat. 2641, requires a different resolution of the Title IX issue presented to us. Also, we were concerned that we had misconstrued the import of *Lau v. Nichols*, 414 U.S. 563, 94 S.Ct. 786, 39 L.Ed.2d 1 (1974), in resolving the Title IX issue against the plaintiff. . . .

I.

Shortly after our decision of the case at bar, Congress enacted the Civil Rights Attorney's Fees Award Act of 1976, Pub.L. No. 94-559, § 2, 90 Stat. 2641 (codified at 42 U.S.C.A. § 1988 (1977 Supp.)). The statute provides in relevant part:

"In any action or proceeding to enforce a provision of . . . title IX of Public Law 92-318, . . . the court, in its discretion, may allow the prevailing party, other than the United States, a reasonable attorney's fee as part of the costs.". . .

[16.]   We note, but do not decide, that a suit brought by a large group to enforce the national interest against sexual discrimination may be possible under Title IX. Certainly it was permitted by the Supreme Court under Title VI in *Lau v. Nichols, supra.*

[18.]   See Shelton & Berndt, "Sex Discrimination in Vocational Education: Title IX and Other Remedies," 62 *Calif.L.Rev.* 1121, 1153-54 (1974); Comment, 53 *Tex.L.Rev.* 103, 120 (1974).

Notwithstanding plaintiff's strained efforts to rewrite the legislative history of Title IX, we find nothing in the legislative history of the Attorney's Fees Award Act that gives us cause to reconsider our holding that no private right of action exists under Title IX. As defendants argue, the legislative history indicates that Congress included Title IX within the Act only to provide for the possibility that the statute might be construed in the future as authorizing judicial implication of a private right of action. This seems clear from a colloquy among Representatives Quie, Anderson, Drinan, Bauman and Railsback, in which Representatives Quie and Bauman expressed concern that the Attorney's Fee Award Act might be construed as impliedly authorizing private individuals to bring suit under Title IX. 122 Cong. Rec. H. 12152-53 (daily ed. Oct. 1, 1976). Representatives Anderson, Drinan and Railsback, all supporters of the bill, denied that it would effect any change in pre-existing law concerning an individual's right to sue under Title IX. . . .

II.

Although our principal motivation in granting rehearing was to obtain the parties' views on the potential impact of the Attorney's Fees Award Act of 1976 on our resolution of the Title IX issue, we were also curious as to why the Department of Health, Education and Welfare, which had consistently supported its codefendants' position that no private cause of action lies under Title IX, did an about face on the merits of that issue in its answer to plaintiff's petition for rehearing. . . .

Whatever the reason for the Department's change of heart, it has now adopted the position that implication of a private cause of action under Title IX is justified under the criteria set out in *Cort v. Ash*, 422 U.S. 66, 95 S.Ct. 2080, 45 L.Ed.2d 26 (1975):

"In determining whether a private remedy is implicit in a statute not expressly providing one, several factors are relevant. First, is the plaintiff 'one of the class for whose *especial* benefit the statute was enacted.'—that is, does the statute create a federal right in favor of the plaintiff? Second, is there any indication of legislative intent, explicit or implicit, either to create such a remedy or to deny one? Third, is it consistent with the underlying purposes of the legislative scheme to imply such a remedy for the plaintiff? And finally, is the cause of action one traditionally relegated to state law, in an area basically the concern of the States, so that it would be inappropriate to infer a cause of action based solely on federal law?" *Id.* at 78, 95 S.Ct. at 2088 (emphasis in original) (citations omitted.) . . .

We are told that because federal court decisions implying a private right of action under Title VI of the Civil Rights Act of 1964 existed at the time Title IX was adopted, we may infer that Congress intended that a private judicial remedy be made available under Title IX in view of Congress's explicit intent to pattern the remedial provisions of Title IX after those of

Title VI. First of all, we do not read those decisions as affirmatively establishing the existence of an implied private right of action under Title VI at the time Title IX was enacted. More important, there is nothing in the legislative history of Title IX itself indicating that Congress was even aware of those decisions, let alone intended to adopt their construction of Title VI.

Given the lack of any explicit or implicit intent to create a private judicial remedy in the legislative history of Title IX itself, we remain of the view that Congress's express provision of a sophisticated scheme of administrative enforcement should be construed as an indication of an implicit legislative intent to exclude any private judicial remedies for violations of Title IX other than the judicial review mechanism Congress made available to private parties in the statute. . . .

We recognize, of course, that *Cort v. Ash, supra* at 82, states that it is not necessary for the legislative history of a statute to show an explicit intent to create a private right of action for us to imply one for violations of a federally created right. It does not follow, however, that we *must* imply a private right of action simply because the legislative history shows no explicit intent to deny one. Were we confronted with an alleged violation of a fundamental federal constitutional or statutory right for which Congress has provided no remedy at all, or for which the remedies available have proven to be wholly inadequate to the task of protecting those rights, we might take a different view of the matter. . . .

We adhere to our previous holding that no private right of action lies under Title IX in the circumstances of this case.

NOTES

1. On May 14, 1979, the Supreme Court reversed the opinion of the Seventh Circuit in *Cannon v. University of Chicago*, 47 USLW 4549, and ruled that petitioner could maintain her lawsuit despite the absence of any express authorization for it in Title IX. To reach this result, Justice Stevens, writing for the majority, relied strictly on the factors enunciated in *Cort v. Ash*, 422 U.S. 66 (1975). The Court first found that since Title IX explicitly confers a benefit on persons discriminated against on the basis of sex, petitioner was clearly a member of the class for whose special benefit the statute was enacted. It further found that the legislative history of Title IX indicates that Congress intended to create a private cause of action because Title IX was patterned after Title VI of the Civil Rights Act of 1964. The Court also observed that:

> Title IX, like its model Title VI, sought to accomplish two related, but nevertheless somewhat different, objectives. First, Congress wanted to avoid the use of federal resources to support discriminatory practices; second, it wanted to provide individual citizens effective protection against those practices. Both of these purposes were repeatedly identified in the debates on the two statutes.
>
> The first purpose is generally served by the statutory procedure for the termination of federal financial support for institutions engaged in discriminatory practices. That remedy is, however, severe and often may not provide an appropriate means of accomplishing the second purpose if merely an isolated violation has occurred. In that situation, the violation might be remedied more efficiently by an order requiring an institution to accept an applicant who had been improperly excluded. Moreover, in that kind of situation it makes little sense to impose on an individual, whose only interest is in obtain-

ing a benefit for herself, or on HEW, the burden of demonstrating that an institution's practices are so pervasively discriminatory that a complete cutoff of federal funding is appropriate. The award of individual relief to a private litigant who has prosecuted her own suit is not only sensible but is fully consistent with—and in some cases even necessary to—the orderly enforcement of the statute.

In response to the University's claim that litigation under Title IX would prove to be burdensome and that it might have an adverse effect on academic autonomy, Justice Stevens wrote:

> This argument is not original to this litigation. It was forcefully advanced in both 1964 and 1972 by the congressional opponents of Title VI and Title IX, and squarely rejected by the congressional majorities that passed the two statutes. In short, respondents' principal contention is not a legal argument at all; it addresses a policy issue that Congress has already resolved.
>
> History has borne out the judgment of Congress. Although victims of discrimination on the basis of race, religion, or national origin have had private Title VI remedies available at least since 1965 . . . respondents have not come forward with any demonstration that Title VI litigation has been so costly or voluminous that either the academic community or the courts have been unduly burdened. Nothing but speculation supports the argument that university administrators will be so concerned about the risk of litigation that they will fail to discharge their important responsibilities in an independent and professional manner.

Justices Powell, Blackmun and White dissented. Justice Rehnquist, with whom Justice Stewart concurred, joined the Stevens' opinion because "Congress, at least during the period of the enactment of the several titles of the Civil Rights Act, tended to rely to a large extent on the courts to *decide* whether there should be a private right of action. . . ." However, Justice Rehnquist observed that the "Court in the future should be extremely reluctant to imply a cause of action absent . . . specificity on the part of the Legislative Branch."

2. In January 1978, the Departments of Labor and HEW negotiated settlements of several time-worn lawsuits. The suits, *Adams v. Califano, Brown v. Califano* and *Women's Equity Action League v. Califano*, charged HEW and the HEW Office of Civil Rights with inadequate enforcement laws prohibiting race and sex bias in higher education. A report of the settlement appeared in the March 1978 edition of *On Campus With Women*, published by the Association of American College's Project on the Status and Education of Women, as follows:

> The recent settlement of three major civil rights lawsuits filed against the Department of Health, Education and Welfare (HEW) will affect millions of women on college campuses across the country. The federal government is now under a court order to initiate a substantial enforcement effort to end sex discrimination in all levels of education. Attorneys representing the groups that brought the suits—Women's Equity Action League (WEAL), National Association for the Advancement of Colored People (NAACP) Defense and Education Fund, Mexican-American Legal Defense and Education Fund, and the National Federation for the Blind—have hailed the settlement as "a landmark and a great step forward for civil rights." Marcia Greenberger of the Center for Law and Social Policy which represented WEAL and other women's organizations stated, "It requires HEW to become serious about sex discrimination."
>
> The suits, the oldest of which was filed in 1970, accused HEW of doing little or nothing to end discrimination on the basis of race, sex, and physical handicap. WEAL, in conjunction with the National Organization for Women, Association for Women in Science, Federation of Organizations for Professional Women, National Education Association, and National Student Associ-

ation, charged HEW with lack of enforcement of Title IX, which prohibits discrimination in federally assisted education programs, and of Executive Order 11246, which prohibits employment discrimination by federal contractors.

A key part of the order requires HEW to establish a series of deadlines for handling individual complaints, HEW will have to eliminate its backlog by September 30, 1979. The backlog of nearly 3,000 complaints dates back to the early 1970's. HEW must comply with the court order or else risk being held in contempt of court.

Under the settlement, HEW is also committed to ask Congress for funds for an additional 898 staffers who will not only investigate individual cases of discrimination, but who will also initiate general compliance reviews of universities and school districts. The new staff will double the number of employees at HEW's Office for Civil Rights (OCR). Required procedures include notification of complaints to affected institutions as well as the complainant. Both parties must be informed of applicable timeframes and procedures [*WEAL et al. v. Califano et al.,* U.S. District Court (D.C.) No. 1720-74, January 9, 1978)].

B.   *"Program Specific" Regulations*

ROMEO COMMUNITY SCHOOLS v. U.S. DEPT. OF HEW
United States District Court
438 F.Supp. 1021, 1033 (E.D. Mich. 1977)

. . . There is a . . . limitation on HEW's enforcement powers under § 1682 which is relevant here. HEW's authority to terminate federal funds for non-compliance with § 1682 is "limited in its effect to the particular program, or part thereof, in which such non-compliance has been found." This limiting language makes the sanction provided by § 1682 "program specific." HEW is prohibited from terminating financial assistance to some programs in a school's curriculum simply because other programs are not in compliance with § 1681. Thus, HEW must determine the appropriateness of aid termination under § 1682 on a program-by-program basis.

This limitation on HEW's enforcement power is implicitly a limitation on HEW's authority to regulate as well. HEW cannot regulate the practices of an educational institution unless those practices result in sex discrimination against the beneficiaries of some federally assisted education program operated by the institution. The focus of § 1681—elimination of sex discrimination in federally funded education programs—must be the focus of HEW's regulations under § 1682 as well. To this extent, HEW's regulatory power is also "program specific."

Regulation of employment practices, however, is inherently non-"program specific." An educational institution's employment policies are general in nature, covering, by and large, all faculty employees involved in all of an institution's education programs, whether federally funded or not. Regulation of those policies by HEW will therefore necessarily entail the regulation of employment practices unrelated to the particular programs funded by the federal government and without regard to whether such practices result in sex discrimination against the beneficiaries of those programs. Compliance with HEW's regulations under Subpart E will inevitably require modifications of employment policies which apply generally to all faculty employees and education programs throughout the system. Yet the federal interest involved here, as defined by the scope of §§1681 and 1682, is much narrower and does not appear to justify this kind of regulatory leverage. In Romeo's case, for example, only one out of every ten education programs receives federal financial assistance; less than 5% of Romeo's faculty employees are involved in any federally financed programs. . . . HEW could not enforce its regulations as to employment practices in Romeo's non-federally funded education programs except by terminating aid to those programs which are federally funded, and this would constitute a clear violation of the programmatically specific limitation on HEW's enforcement powers contained in §1682. [18]

NOTES

1. In Seattle Univ. v. HEW, 16 FEP Cas. 719 (W.D. Wash. 1978), the court ruled that:
    . . . [T]he only direct sanction provided by §1682 for use by Federal agencies
    is a "program specific" one. HEW is prohibited from terminating the financial
    assistance to some programs in an educational institution's curriculum simply
    because another program is not in compliance with §1681.
See also Bd. of Public Instruction of Taylor v. Finch, 414 F.2d 1068, 1077 (5th Cir. 1969) (requiring that the cut-off of federal funds under Title VI be limited " 'to the particular program or part thereof' not found in compliance with the act").

2. Section 1681(a) in Title IX prohibits sex discrimination "under any educational program or activity receiving Federal financial assistance, . . ." This is the basis for the finding in Romeo Community Schools that Title IX is designed to be "program specific," i.e. to eliminate sex discrimination only in federally funded programs.

This view is buttressed by the language of Section 1682 in Title IX, which states, in part, that:
    compliance with any requirement adopted pursuant to this section may be
    effected (1) by the termination or refusal to grant or to continue assistance
    under such program or activity to any recipient as to whom there has been
    an express finding on the record, after opportunity for hearing, of a failure to
    comply with such requirement, but such termination or refusal shall be
    limited to the particular political entity, or part thereof, or other recipient
    as to whom such a funding has been made, and shall be limited in its effect
    to the particular program or part thereof in which such noncompliance has
    been so found.

3. While the particular program limitation on the termination power may be consistent with the position that the purpose of the Act is to obtain compliance and not to punish violators, it is not the only enforcement provision available. Section 1682 of the Act also provides that compliance may be effected "by any other means authorized by

---

[18.]   HEW contends that the term "program or activity" as used in §1681 refers to the entire operation of the recipient educational institution. Brief in Support of Defendant's Motion to Dismiss or, In the Alternative, For Summary Judgment, p. 23. Hence, HEW argues that it may regulate employment practices through a school district's entire system. This novel and protean interpretation of a well-established statutory term was thoroughly refuted in Board of Public Instruction of Taylor Co. v. Finch, 414 F.2d 1068, 1077 (5th Cir. 1969).

law." Thus, it is conceivable that injunctive relief or other equitable remedies may be available to a party alleging a violation of this Act. However, the court in *Seattle University, supra*, specifically rejected the suggestion that the "by any other means authorized by law" clause could be read expansively to allow HEW to regulate programs other than those receiving federal financial assistance.

4. It is clear that, to date, HEW is unwilling to go along with the "program specific" limitation in enforcement of Title IX. In a *HEW General Counsel Opinion*, dated April 18, 1978, and reported at 46 U.S.L.W. 2587 (May 9, 1978), the General Counsel expressed the view that Title IX covered revenue producing intercollegiate activity even though such activity did not always benefit from direct federal assistance:

The question is whether an institution of higher education that is receiving federal financial assistance must comply with the prohibition against sex discrimination imposed by Title IX in the administration of its revenue producing intercollegiate athletic activities. In the General Counsel's opinion, a revenue producing intercollegiate athletic program is an education program or activity within the meaning of Title IX and an integral part of the general undergraduate education program of the institution of higher education. Thus, an institution of higher education must comply with the prohibition against sex discrimination imposed by Title IX in the administration of any revenue producing intercollegiate athletic activity if either the activity or the general education program of which the activity is a part is receiving federal financial assistance.

While there is no reference anywhere in Title IX to revenue producing athletics, there is some indication that the term "education program or activity" is to have an expansive meaning. Section 901(a) provides a series of exemptions from the general prohibition. Among them are exemptions for the Boy Scouts, Girl Scouts, and social fraternities and sororities. Absent these exemptions, it can be assumed that each of these groups would be subject to the prohibition against sex discrimination as an education program or activity. A definition of "education program or activity" that encompasses social fraternities and sororities also encompasses intercollegiate athletics, including revenue producing athletics.

The legislative history of Title IX tends to support a broad view of what is an education program or activity, but is less clear with respect to whether athletics are included in the term. However, any ambiguity as to whether revenue producing intercollegiate athletics are an education program or activity was eliminated by the enactment of Section 844 of the Education Amendments of 1974. The language and history of that section make it clear that Congress intended that revenue producing intercollegiate athletics be included within the definition of that term.

There are some revenue producing intercollegiate athletic activities that clearly receive direct federal financial assistance. Such direct assistance, however, is not common. Other kinds of assistance that bear a less direct relationship to revenue producing intercollegiate athletics, particularly student financial assistance, such as guaranteed student loans and grants provided by the federal Government, is federal financial assistance to the institution. Historically, intercollegiate athletics have been described as an integral part of the general undergraduate education. Therefore, student financial assistance is federal financial assistance to the revenue producing athletic programs of the student's institution of higher education.

It is well settled that, with respect to discrimination prohibited by Title VI of the 1964 Civil Rights Act, federal financial assistance may not be provided to any program or activity that is either administered in a discriminatory manner or "infected by a discriminatory environment." Under this "infection" doctrine, a federal grantee is required to comply with Title VI in the administration of an activity that does not receive federal assistance if that activity is so closely related to, and such an integral part of, a program that does receive federal assistance that discrimination in the administration of the former would infect the latter. This infection doctrine is also applicable to Title IX of the 1972 Education Amendments. Revenue producing intercollegiate athletics are so integral to the general undergraduate education program of an institution of higher education that sex discrimination in the administration of a revenue producing athletic activity would necessarily infect the general undergraduate education program of the institution. Thus, an institution receiving federal financial assistance for its general undergraduate education program must comply with the prohibitions against sex discrimination imposed by Title IX in the administration of its revenue producing intercollegiate athletic activities regardless of whether those activities are themselves receiving federal financial assistance.

In addition, HEW's proposed Policy Interpretation issued in December, 1978 for comment applies the provisions and regulations of Title IX to revenue producing sports, 43 Fed. Reg. 58070-76 (December 11, 1978).

It is noteworthy that HEW's "infection theory" has been held to be inapplicable in the context of Title IX enforcement. *See*: Seattle Univ. v. HEW, 16 FEP Cas. 719 (W.D. Wash. 1978); Romeo Community Schools v. U.S. Dept. of HEW, 438 F.Supp. 1021 (E.D. Mich. 1977).

III.   Substantive Coverage of Title IX

A.   Employment Discrimination Cases

ROMEO COMMUNITY SCHOOLS v. U.S. DEPT. OF HEW
United States District Court
438 F.Supp. 1021 (E.D. Mich. 1977)

FEIKENS, District Judge.

This is an action for declaratory judgment and permanent injunction, brought under 28 U.S.C. §2201 and the Administrative Procedures Act, 5 U.S.C. §701, *et seq.*, by plaintiff Romeo Community Schools (Romeo) against defendant Department of Health, Education, and Welfare (HEW). Plaintiff challenges the authority of defendant to promulgate certain administrative regulations under Title IX of the Education Amendments of 1972, 20 U.S.C. §1681, *et seq.*, governing sex discrimination in federally funded education programs. Specifically, plaintiff challenges the legality of the regulations contained in 45 C.F.R. Part 86, Subpart E, §86.51, *et seq.*, which purport to regulate sex discrimination in the employment relationship between federally funded public schools and their teacher employees. The case is before the court on cross-motions for summary judgment. . . .

The issue of HEW's authority to promulgate regulations governing employment relations under Title IX is essentially one of statutory construction. Title IX was patterned after Title VI of the Civil Rights Act of 1964, 42 U.S.C. §§2000d–d-5, which prohibits race discrimination in all federally funded programs. Most of the provisions of Title IX are virtual carbon copies of parallel provisions in Title VI; indeed, Title IX was originally contemplated as a simple amendment to Title VI adding sex discrimination in federally assisted education programs to the general prohibitory language of § 2000d. Both Title IX and Title VI contain similar provisions regarding investigation and enforcement, the imposition of sanctions, the promulgation of regulations by HEW, and judicial review.

There is, however, one important difference between these two statutes: Title VI contains a provision specifically excluding discrimination in employment from its coverage:

§ 2000d-3

Nothing contained in this subchapter shall be construed to authorize action under this subchapter by any department or agency with respect to any employment practice of any employer, employment agency, or labor organization except where a primary objective of the Federal financial assistance is to provide employment.

Title IX contains no parallel provision.

This fact, in defendant's view, is clear proof that Congress did not mean to limit the scope of Title IX to exclude coverage of sex discrimination in employment. Defendant argues that a "commonsense" reading of § 1681, standing alone, shows that teachers fall within the class of individuals protected by this provision, since the statute provides that "no person" shall be subjected to discrimination, and the term "person" includes both students and teachers. Thus, HEW construes its legislative mandate as authorizing direct regulation of sex discrimination in employment by federally funded schools; it is HEW's position that such discrimination is itself grounds for terminating a school's federal aid, without regard to whether students are affected by the school's employment policies.

Defendant also relies on the legislative history of Title IX to show a congressional intent to regulate employment practices under § 1681. Senator Birch Bayh, the Senate sponsor of Title IX, made these remarks during introduction of the bill:

Amendment 874 is broad, but basically it closes loopholes in existing legislation relating to general education programs and *employment* resulting from those programs. . . . More specifically, the heart of this amendment is a provision banning sex discrimination in educational programs receiving Federal funds. The amendment would cover such crucial aspects as admission procedures, scholarships, and *faculty employment*, with limited exceptions.

[118 Cong.Rec. ¶ 2745 (daily ed., February 28, 1972) emphasis supplied]
Moreover, Congress reviewed the Title IX regulations in July, 1975, under 20 U.S.C. § 1232(d), and declined to disapprove them. From the hearings held regarding these regulations, it is clear that HEW's authority to regulate employment practices under Title IX was specifically discussed and considered. Again, Senator Bayh:

[T]he heart of these guidelines is the prohibition of the thwarting of equal opportunity for female students and teachers at any educational level.

These views were shared by Representative Patsy Mink:

[T]he legislative history of Title IX indicates that employment was indeed covered by the broad mandate of the law for nondiscrimination on the basis of sex. The original House bill included an exemption for employment patterned after the exemption in Title VI of the Civil Rights Act. The Senate version contained no such exemption, indicating that employment was covered. In conference, the language of the Senate version was adopted.

Hearings, *supra*, p. 164.

The Secretary further argues that his own interpretation of Title IX's scope is entitled to great weight as an official and contemporaneous interpretation by the enforcing agency. . . .

The absence of an explicit provision in Title IX, similar to §604 of Title VI, 42 U.S.C. §2000d-3, excluding employment discrimination from its coverage does not show a congressional intent to make Title IX broader than Title VI in this respect. Rather, this discrepancy must be traced to the fact that Title IX was enacted as part of a larger legislative program which also included an amendment to Title VII of the Civil Rights Act of 1964, 42 U.S.C. §2000e, *et seq.*, enlarging the scope of *that* provision to include sex discrimination in employment, as well as an amendment to the Equal Pay Act, giving the Secretary of Labor authority to regulate sex discrimination in educational employee compensation. 29 U.S.C. §206(d). A provision similar to §604 was left out of this package in order to avoid the inherent contradiction between such a provision and these amendments.

HEW's arguments based on the legislative history of Title IX are not compelling. Senator Bayh's quoted assertion of employment discrimination coverage by Title IX in his remarks during introduction of this bill was made in reference to the entire Title IX legislative package, including the Title VII and Equal Pay Act amendments. The legislative history of the regulations themselves is entitled to little if any weight in determining the scope of §1681. These regulations were reviewed some three years after the enactment of Title IX and by a different Congress. Nor is the congressional failure to disapprove the regulations any indication of their validity. 20 U.S.C. §1232 expressly provides that the failure of Congress to disapprove regulations promulgated by HEW is not evidence of approval and creates no presumption of validity.

Plaintiff has mustered its own presentation of Title IX's legislative history to support an alternative construction of its coverage. . . . The court, however, will not pursue plaintiff's analysis of the legislative history of this Act further, for there is a much more obvious and relevant source for determining the scope of Title IX and that is Title IX itself. . . . Though cast in broad terms, §1681 nevertheless addresses itself only to sex discrimination against the participants in and the beneficiaries of federally assisted education programs. Section 1681 must therefore be read to protect from sex discrimination only those persons for whom the federally assisted education programs are established, and this can only mean the school children in those programs. As a reference to faculty employees, the language of §1681 is indirect, if not obscure. Teachers participate in these programs only to the extent that they may teach and help administer some of them; teachers benefit from these programs only to the extent that the funds for them may be used to pay their salaries; teachers are "subjected to discrimination *under*" these programs, (emphasis added), only to the extent that the programs themselves may be established and operated in an employment-related discriminatory way. Teachers, in short, are hard pressed to fit themselves within the plain meaning of §1681's prohibitory language, general as it may appear on its face. When Congress means to statutorily regulate employment discrimination, it uniformly does so in more explicit terms than this.

HEW's "commonsense" interpretation of §1681 notwithstanding, the court is constrained to read this language as a prohibition on sex discrimination against students and only students. . . .

This construction of §1681 is further supported by an analysis of §1682, which defines HEW's enforcement power under the Act. As noted previously, the only sanction permitted under §1682 is termination of federal funds to the noncomplying institution. This aid termination provision, quite obviously, is of limited enforcement value. Imposition of this sanction will not necessarily compel a delinquent school system to modify or eliminate its discriminatory practices, but will necessarily penalize the students involved or enrolled in the affected programs. In a situation where the students themselves are the victims of sex discrimination, it is reasonable to assume that Congress balanced the costs and benefits involved and determined that any benefit which students might derive from the education programs financed by HEW was more than outweighed by the sex discrimination in those programs. A termination of federal aid under these circumstances has obvious justification.

However, in a situation where a federally assisted school system discriminates against its teacher employees, the §1682 sanction has very limited justification. Termination of federal aid will have no more enforcement value in such a case, and the students participating in affected programs will still be the ones to suffer from the aid termination sanction, even though the sanction will not be imposed for the purpose of enforcing their rights. The court doubts that Congress would resort to such an arbitrary enforcement measure where alternative methods of prohibiting employment discrimination, more effective and less costly than this, are readily available. . . .

An even more persuasive indication that Congress did not intend to regulate employment practices under §1681 is the fact that Congress specifically provided for such regulation under both Title VII and the Equal

Pay Act elsewhere in the very same legislation. . . . While Congress does, as defendant points out, tend to widely delegate regulatory authority in the field of civil rights, it is difficult to believe that Congress felt any real need under Title IX to delegate to HEW such marginal regulatory authority as an addition to that already clearly and adequately established in two other federal regulatory agencies.

For all of these reasons, the court holds that HEW's regulations purporting to govern employment discrimination in federally funded educational institutions are not in furtherance of the legislative purpose of § 1681, and are therefore not authorized by § 1682.

NOTES

1. In Seattle Univ. v. HEW, 16 FEP Cas. 719 (W.D. Wash. 1978), the court concurred with the judgment in *Romeo Community Schools* and ruled that:

> Since both §§ 1681 and 1682 are "program specific," HEW's regulation of *general employment* practices is inappropriate and unauthorized.

2. Other cases following *Romeo* are: McCarthy v. Burkholder, 448 F.Supp. 41 (D.C. Kansas 1978); Brunswick School Bd. v. Califano, 17 FEP Cas. 475 (D.C. Maine 1978) (holding that HEW cannot enforce sanctions against a school board because the school board refused to treat pregnancy equally with other disabilities for all job related purposes).

B.   Sex-Segregated Programs

YELLOW SPRINGS EXEMPTED VILLAGE SCHOOL DISTRICT BD. OF ED. v. OHIO HIGH SCHOOL ATHLETIC ASSOCIATION
United States District Court
443 F.Supp. 753 (S.D. Ohio 1978)

ORDER

CARL B. RUBIN, District Judge. . . .

I

FACTS

1. Three groups of litigants are involved in this action: The Ohio High School Athletic Association (Association); Robert Holland, Assistant Director of Health, Physical Education and Recreation, Ohio Department of Education, Franklin B. Walter, Superintendent of Public Instruction, Ohio Department of Education, and the Ohio Board of Education (State Defendants); and The Yellow Springs Exempted School District Board of Education (Board).

2. The Association is a nonprofit organization which coordinates interscholastic athletic activity among secondary schools in Ohio. It is composed of approximately 830 secondary schools, most of which are public, and it is supported by gate receipts collected at sports tournaments that are held at public school facilities. Membership is voluntary and is available to any secondary school accredited by the Ohio Department of Education.

3. The Association administers interscholastic athletic programs through its scheduling and rule-making functions. The rules which it promulgates are binding upon its members and may not be waived. Members who disregard them are subject to suspension from the Association. Such suspension, in effect, eliminates a school from any interscholastic athletic competition since Association members are prohibited from competing against non-members. . . .

7. The activity which forged this dispute occurred in 1974. Two female students, who were enrolled in a school within the Board's jurisdiction, competed for and were awarded positions on the school's interscholastic basketball team. Because of their sex, the Board excluded them from the team and, instead, created a separate girls' basketball team on which they could participate.

By so doing, the Board complied with Association Rule 1, §6, which prohibits mixed gender interscholastic athletic competition in contact sports, such as basketball. A failure of such exclusion would place in jeopardy membership in the Association and would exclude the basketball team from interscholastic competition.

OPINION

These questions require determination:

A.   Are the State defendants proper parties?

B.   Is State action present?

C.   Have the State defendants and the Association violated the Fourteenth Amendment of the United States Constitution?. . .

[The court found that the State was a proper party to the lawsuit and that, since the State was "intimately involved in the administration of interscholastic athletics," there was "state action" present.]

C.   The Due Process Clause

The Association's exclusionary rule deprives school girls of liberty without due process of law. . . .

Two governmental objectives could be proffered to support the Association rule. First, the State arguably has an interest in preventing injury to public school children. Second, the State could contend that prohibiting girls from participating with boys in contact sports will maximize female athletic opportunities. Both are palpably legitimate goals. To achieve these goals, however, the State must assume without qualification that girls are uniformly physically inferior to boys. The exclusionary rule, as it relates to the objective of preventing injury, creates a conclusive presumption that girls are physically weaker than boys. The rule, as it relates to the objective of maximization of female opportunities, creates an equally conclusive presumption that girls are less proficient athletes than boys. However, these presumptions are in fact indistinguishable since both posit that girls are somehow athletically inferior to boys solely because of their gender.

A permanent presumption is unconstitutional in an area in which the presumption might be rebutted if individualized determinations were made. *Cleveland Bd. of Edu. v. LaFleur*, 414 U.S. 632, 94 S.Ct. 791, 39 L.Ed.2d 52 (1974); *Vlandis v. Kline*, 412 U.S. 441, 93 S.Ct. 2230, 37 L.Ed.2d 63 (1973); *Stanley v. Illinois*, 405 U.S. 645, 92 S.Ct. 1208, 31 L.Ed.2d 551 (1972). The athletic capabilities of females is such an area. Although some women are physically unfit to participate with boys in contact sports, it does not "necessarily and universally" follow that all women suffer similar disabilities. *Vlandis, supra,* at 452. Babe Didrikson could have made anybody's team. Accordingly, school girls who so desire, must be given the opportunity to demonstrate that the presumption created by the rule is invalid. They must be given the opportunity to compete with boys in interscholastic contact sports if they are physically qualified.

The consequences of this determination carry beyond the State level. For the federal regulations also are unconstitutional insofar as they suggest that mixed gender competition, creation of separate teams for girls and boys in each sport, or creation of an all male team in contact sports are independent and wholly satisfactory methods of compliance. Separate teams may, in fact, be satisfactory if they ensure due process. However, their existence cannot serve as an excuse to deprive qualified girls positions on formerly all boy teams, regardless of the sport. The Due Process Clause of the Fifth Amendment necessarily forbids that which its counterpart prohibits under the Fourteenth Amendment.

To the extent it authorizes recipients of federal aid to deny physically qualified girls the right to compete with boys in interscholastic contact sports, Subsection (b) of 45 CFR 86.41 [40] is violative of the Fifth Amendment and must be held to be unconstitutional.

In view of the foregoing, the Court considers it unnecessary to rule upon questions raised under either the Supremacy Clause or the Equal Protection Clause.

The foregoing is intended to set forth the precedential underpinnings of this Court's ruling. It is addressed to those who will scrutinize the legal reasoning of this opinion. However, it is not only legal scholars, commentators and appellate courts who might have occasion to review this matter. There are many who may also be affected who are not trained in the law and who likewise seek an explanation. For them, the following has been added.

[40.]   Title 45, Code of Federal Regulations, Part 86, Section 41 Subsection (b) provides that, despite the general admonition against sex discrimination in athletics announced in 45 CFR 86.41(a),

> . . . a recipient may operate or sponsor separate teams for members of each sex where selection for such teams is based upon competitive skill or the activity involved is a contact sport. However, where a recipient operates or sponsors a team in a particular sport for members of one sex but operates or sponsors no such team for members of the other sex, and athletic opportunities for members of that sex have previously been limited, members of the excluded sex must be allowed to try out for the team offered unless the sport involved is a contact sport. For the purposes of this part, contact sports include boxing, wrestling, rugby, ice hockey, football, basketball and other sports the purpose of major activity of which involves bodily contact.

It has always been traditional that "boys play football and girls are cheerleaders." Why so? Where is it written that girls may not, if suitably qualified, play football? There may be a multitude of reasons why a girl might elect not to do so. Reasons of stature or weight or reasons of temperament, motivation or interest. This is a matter of personal choice. But a prohibition without exception based upon sex is not. It is this that is both unfair and contrary to personal rights contemplated in the Fourteenth Amendment to the United States Constitution.

It may well be that there is a student today in an Ohio high school who lacks only the proper coaching and training to become the greatest quarterback in professional football history. Of course the odds are astronomical against her, but isn't she entitled to a fair chance to try?

CONCLUSIONS OF LAW

A.   This Court has jurisdiction under 28 U.S.C. §1343(3) and (4) and 28 U.S.C. §1331(a).

B.   State officials are proper parties to a suit alleging failure to end unconstitutional conduct of subordinates where such conduct was known to them and which they had a duty to prevent.

C.   Conduct of defendant Ohio High School Athletic Association constitutes State action where constitutional violations are charged.

D.   Association Rule 1 §6, insofar as it prohibits mixed gender competition in interscholastic contact sports, deprives physically qualified girls of liberty without due process of law and perforce also violates 42 U.S.C. §1983.

E.   Subsection (b) of 42 C.F.R. §86.41 deprives physically qualified girls of liberty without due process of law to the extent it authorizes recipients of federal aid to deny girls the right to compete with boys in interscholastic contact sports. . . .

F.   . . . . The defendants should be and are hereby permanently enjoined from continuing to enforce or to maintain Association Rule 1 §6, or from enforcing, promulgating, or maintaining any rule, regulation, directive, custom or usage which bars physically qualified girls from participating with boys in interscholastic contact sports. The defendants should be and are further enjoined from disciplining, imposing sanctions, or otherwise penalizing the Morgan Middle School, any official thereof, its basketball team, any member thereof, or its coach because of participation on said team by females.

NOTES

1. Is the *Yellow Springs* decision likely to advance or retard women's rights under Title IX? Does the court in *Yellow Springs* expressly outlaw all sex-segregated programs?

2. For another case reaching the same result on a somewhat different theory, see Leffel v. Wisconsin Interscholastic Athletic Ass'n., 444 F.Supp. 1117 (E.D. Wisc. 1978). The court in *Leffel* held that although a defendant athletic association was in compliance with Title IX, which permits the exclusion of female athletes from male teams in "contact" sports, defendant's failure to establish a separate girls' team in interscholastic competition constituted a denial of equal protection of the law.

IV. Comments on the HEW Regulations Implementing Title IX

There are six subparts to the regulations which the Secretary of Health, Education and Welfare has adopted to implement Title IX. They can be found in 45 C.F.R., Part 86, 40 Fed. Reg. 24128-54 (June 4, 1975). Subpart A deals with definitions, affirmative action and assurances, and the notification policy requirements. Subpart B describes the coverage and the exceptions in the Act. Subparts C, D and E set forth the rules regarding discrimination on the basis of sex in admissions and recruitment, in education programs and activities and in employment related programs and activities. Subpart F incorporates by reference the procedural provisions applicable to Title VI of the Civil Rights Act of 1964 found at 45 C.F.R. § § 80-6–80-11 and 45 C.F.R., Part 81.

A. Definitions

Some of the very broad definitions in Subpart A are good indicators of the wide range of the application of Title IX intended by the Secretary of HEW. For example, federal financial assistance is defined to include not only the grant, loan, sale or lease of funds, property or services to an institution, but also government scholarships or grants to students for payment to a given institution. Further, any contract, other than a contract of insurance or a guaranty, which has as a purpose the provision of assistance to any educational program or activity, is within the definition. Another example of the broad scope can be found in the definition of "institution of graduate higher education." An institution could qualify as an "institution of graduate higher education," even though it awards no degrees and offers no academic study, if it "operates ordinarily for the purpose of facilitating research by persons who have received the highest graduate degree in any field of study." Another important definition is that of an "administratively separate unit." That term means a school, department or college of an educational institution (other than a local educational agency) admission to which is independent of admission to any other component of such institution.

B. Affirmative Action

Subpart A also places some affirmative obligations upon the recipient of federal financial assistance. While there is no requirement for affirmative action, in the absence of explicit finding of discrimination, the regulations do require each institution to conduct a self-evaluation of current policies and practices relating to the admission of students and employment of both academic and non-academic personnel. Recipients of federal financial assistance are required to give assurances of compliance and commitments to take whatever action is necessary to remedy existing discrimination or the present effects of past discrimination. The regulations further require recipients of federal financial assistance to designate an employee to coordinate compliance efforts and to investigate complaints of alleged discrimination according to a grievance procedure which it has adopted. Lastly, the recipient is required to publish notice of that procedure and of the fact that it does not discriminate on the basis of sex.

C.   Religious Exemption

An important provision in Subpart B is the procedure for the procurement of religious exemption to the Act. The regulations require that if an educational institution wishes to claim this exemption, the highest ranking official of the institution has to identify in writing the particular provisions of the Act which conflict with a specific tenet of the religious organization which controls the institution.

D.   Student Admissions and Recruitment

Subpart C covers the area of student admissions and recruitment. There are several exceptions to the general prohibition of discrimination on the basis of sex. Specifically, the prohibition does not apply to private undergraduate institutions and those public undergraduate institutions with a continued tradition of single sex admissions. The use of ranking, quotas or other differential treatment by sex are explicitly prohibited. Rules or policies which discriminate on the basis of a student's actual or potential parental, family or marital status are also prohibited. The regulations do, however, permit the use of tests or other criteria for admission which have a disproportionate adverse affect on persons on the basis of sex if,

> . . . the use of such test or criteria is shown to predict validly success in the education program or activity in question and alternative tests or criteria which do not have such a disproportionately adverse affect are shown to be unavailable.

E.   Equal Treatment in Programs and Activities

Subpart D deals with the treatment which must be accorded individuals in education programs and activities. Included within the broad scope of educational programs and activities are housing, counseling services, health and insurance benefits, financial assistance as well as athletic and locker facilities. The general provision against discrimination on the basis of sex in any academic, extracurricular, research occupational training or other educational program or activity is followed by a number of specific prohibitions. Conditions for the receipt or denial of any aid, benefit or service cannot be different on the basis of sex. Since a person cannot be subjected to different rules of behavior or rules of appearance on the basis of sex, different curfew regulations or hair length requirements for men and women are not permitted. Similarly, different rules for residency or domicile for eligibility for in-state tuition and fees are specifically prohibited.

F.   Sex-Segregated Housing; Off-Campus Housing; External Programs

Housing, separated on the basis of sex, may be provided if it is done in proportion to the number of students of each sex applying for housing and it is comparable in quality and cost for each sex. Where an educational institution assists students by soliciting, listing or approving off-campus housing, it must take reasonable steps to assure itself that the housing is provided students in a nondiscriminatory fashion. A similar obligation is placed upon recipients of federal financial assistance which participate in programs such as educational consortia or student teaching assignments with institutions which might not be directly within the scope of Title IX. Regardless of whether Title IX applies to those programs, the recipient of federal financial assistance must assure itself that those programs also comply with the Act.

G.   Single Sex Scholarships

Educational institutions are permitted to participate in the administration of single sex scholarships or fellowships (e.g., the Rhodes Scholarship or the Clare Fellowship) established by will, trust, or other legal instrument, or the act of foreign governments, provided that similar opportunities are made available for the other sex. This is an exemption to the general provision that financial assistance both as to type and amount shall be awarded on a nondiscriminatory basis.

H.   Athletic Scholarships

Another exemption in the student financial assistance area is in athletic scholarships or awards. When each sex may participate in a specific athletic program, reasonable opportunities for each sex, in proportion to the number of participants, is required. However, separate scholarships or grants-in-aid are permitted where separate teams are permitted.

I.   "Separate but Equal" Rule for Athletics

While discrimination on the basis of sex in interscholastic, intercollegiate, club or intramural athletics is generally prohibited, separate teams for the members of each sex are permitted where selection for the teams is based on competitive skill or the activity involved is a "contact sport." Contact sports include boxing, wrestling, rugby, ice hockey, football and basketball. If a school offers only one team in non-contact sport, with the participants selected on the basis of competitive skill, and athletic opportunities for the excluded sex have been limited in the past, then members of the excluded sex must be allowed to try out for the team.

J.   Definition of Equal Athletic Opportunity

The regulations require the educational institution to provide equal athletic opportunity for members of both sex. Some of the factors to be considered in determining whether equal athletic opportunities exist are: the provision of equipment, supplies, medical and training facilities and services; the compensation of coaches; and the provision of locker rooms and practice and competitive facilities. The regulations specifically note that unequal aggregate expenditure does not constitute noncompliance.

Many questions have been raised about the Athletic Regulations. Because of the "program specific" limitation noted above, it has been asserted that the HEW regulations should not apply to most collegiate athletic programs because these programs do not receive direct federal financial assistance. However, in September 1975, in a memorandum entitled, "Elimination of Sex Discrimination in Athletic Programs," the Director of the Office of Civil Rights at HEW stated that the regulations:

apply to each segment of a federally assisted educational institution whether or not that segment is the subject of direct financial support through the Department. Thus, the fact that a particular segment of an athletic program is supported by funds received from various other sources (such as student fees, general revenues, gate receipts, alumni donations, booster clubs and non-profit foundations) does not remove it from the reach of the Statute and hence the regulatory requirements.

See reference in Dunkle and Sandler, *Sex Discrimination Against Students: Implications of Title IX of the Education Amendments of 1972*, 18 Inequality in Education 12 (Oct. 1974). The 1975 memorandum is plainly the forerunner to the April 18, 1978 *HEW General Counsel Opinion*, 46 U.S.L.W. 2587 (May 9, 1978), which appears herein in the "NOTES" at the end of Section II-B. *See also* Title IX of the Education Amendments of 1972; A Proposed Policy Interpretation, 43 Fed. Reg. 58070-76 (December 11, 1978).

K.   Exemption for Textbooks and Curricular Materials

Subpart D ends with a specific exemption from Title IX for textbooks and curricular materials. While it is clear that those materials can play a critical role in sex stereotyping, this exclusion prevailed on First Amendment considerations.

Subpart E of the regulations pertains to employment in educational programs and activities. Discrimination on the basis of sex is prohibited in many aspects of employment, including the use of tests and other criteria which have a disproportionately adverse effect, recruitment and advertising, compensation and job classification. While the regulations recognize that sex may be a bona fide occupational qualification, they specifically state that pregnancy and other related conditions are to be treated as a temporary disability for job related purposes. Regarding fringe benefits, the regulations allow either equal benefits or equal contributions.

V.   Proposed Policy Interpretation: More on Athletics

In December, 1978 HEW published for comment a proposed policy interpretation of Title IX requirements on intercollegiate athletics. The interpretation is applicable to club and intramural sports as well. It is designed to provide a framework within which complaints can be resolved, and to provide institutions of higher education with additional guidance on the requirements of the law. The interpretation bases compliance on participation rates, rather than enrollment, and while it requires procedures to increase opportunities for women in competitive athletics, it also recognizes that certain revenue producing sports, such as football and basketball, may require greater expenditures without having a discriminatory effect. The statement reads as follows:

Proposed Policy Interpretation

A college or university intercollegiate athletic program will be in compliance with Title IX if:

I. It has eliminated discrimination in financial support and other benefits and opportunities in its existing athletic program; and

II. It follows an institutional policy that includes procedures and standards for developing an athletic program that provides equal opportunities for men and women to accommodate their interests and abilities.

Part I is designed to eliminate discrimination in current athletic programs by requiring substantially equal per capita expenditures for men and women in financially measurable benefits and opportunities such as: scholarships, recruitment, equipment and supplies, living and travel expenses, and publicity. Differences in per capita expenditures controlled by the nature of the sport or the scope of the competition are allowed. With respect to benefits and opportunities that are not financially measurable, the policy requires comparability.

Part II is designed to eliminate the discriminatory effect of the historic emphasis on men's intercollegiate sports by requiring institutions to adopt procedures for the expansion of women's athletic programs.

The final policy interpretation is to take effect in the fall of 1979.

NOTES

1. Opposition to Title IX has been widespread, especially among private smaller colleges which receive little federal aid. In a scathing indictment of federal regulation of higher education, Dallin Oaks, President of Brigham Young University, has argued that:

If H.E.W. succeeds in this attempt [under Title IX] to extend its regulatory authority over every program or activity of all institutions that receive or benefit from any federal financial assistance in any individual program or activity, H.E.W. will have accomplished a direct bureaucratic repeal of the limiting language enacted by Congress. (An Address before the Opening General Session of the Pennsylvania Association of Colleges and Universities, Hershey, Pennsylvania, Sept. 25, 1978.)

Do you agree with this appraisal?

2. Some of the better notes and articles on Title IX are: Buek & Orleans, *Sex Discrimination: A Bar to a Democratic Education: Overview of Title IX of the Education Amendments of 1972*, 6 Conn. L. Rev. 1 (1973); Cox, *Intercollegiate Athletics and Title IX*, 46 Geo. Wash. L. Rev. 34 (1977); Dunkle & Sandler, *Sex Discrimination Against Students: Implications of Title IX of the Education Amendments of 1972*, 18 Inequality in Education 12 (1974); Kadzielski, *Title IX of the Education Amendments of 1972: Change or Continuity*, 6 J. of L. & Educ. 183 (1977); Note, *Implementing Title IX: The*

HEW Regulations, 124 U. Pa. L. Rev. 806 (1976); Note, *Title IX of the 1972 Education Amendments: Preventing Sex Discrimination in Public Schools*, 53 Tex. L. Rev. 103 (1974); Note, *Sex Discrimination and Intercollegiate Athletics*, 61 Ia. L. Rev. 420 (1975); Note, *HEW's Regulations Under Title IX of the Education Amendments of 1972: Ultra Vires Challenges*, 1976 BYU Law Review 133; Kuhn, *Title IX: Employment and Athletics Are Outside H.E.W.'s Jurisdiction*, 65 Georgetown L.J. 49 (1976).

CHAPTER 16

CONSTITUTIONAL AND STATUTORY PROTECTIONS AGAINST EMPLOYMENT DISCRIMINATION ON THE BASIS OF RACE, COLOR, SEX, RELIGION AND NATIONAL ORIGIN

I. Introduction

A. Employment Discrimination in the United States

Discrimination on the basis of race, color, sex, religion and national origin has always been pervasive in the United States. The early days of this country saw the introduction of slavery and the decimation of the Native American population. Colonists who came here to escape religious persecution in Europe persecuted others because of their differing religious views. Women were denied the right to vote and, if married, the right to dispose of their own property. Each successive immigrant group faced barriers such as the signs proclaiming that "No Irish Need Apply." During World War II, United States citizens of Japanese heritage were uprooted from their homes and businesses and held in government camps for the duration of the war. Today, thousands of blacks and Spanish-surnamed Americans remain crowded in ghettos, deprived of equal access to decent education, employment and housing. Many Native Americans still live in poverty on reservations and women still have not achieved equality under the law.

One of the most persistent problems of discrimination in the United States is the denial of equal employment opportunities because of some personal characteristic, usually unalterable, which is irrelevant to the performance of the job. Race, color, sex, national origin, religion, handicap or age are the most frequently encountered bases of discrimination in employment. Although discrimination can manifest itself in many ways, the courts have recognized certain definite patterns of discrimination as proscribed by existing legislation.

First, the most obvious, is the differential *treatment* of persons on the basis of their race, sex, age or other personal characteristics. Refusing to hire blacks for faculty positions and paying women lower salaries than men at each professional rank are examples of differential treatment in the higher education context. Differential treatment can originate from personal prejudices, institutional practices, or policies that are built on stereotypes with respect to the assumed capabilities of a given class of potential or current employees. The origins of differential treatment are unimportant in most circumstances. If the basis for the discrimination is prohibited, differential treatment is almost always unlawful.

A less obvious form of discrimination occurs when an employment practice is even-handed in its application, but has a disparate *effect* on a protected class of employees. For example, where an employer uses criteria for employment which are not shown to be necessary to the performance of a particular job, and which have the effect of excluding a protected class of people, the courts have held that unlawful discrimination exists. The fact that the employer does not intend to discriminate is irrelevant. Thus, if an employer requires a high school diploma for employment in a factory and significantly fewer blacks than whites in the relevant labor market area have high school diplomas, a disproportionate number of blacks would be excluded from jobs. In this situation, the employer would have the burden of showing that a high school diploma is in fact necessary to the performance of those jobs. It would not be enough to show that a certain level of intellectual capacity was required because a person might have the necessary intellectual skills without having a high school diploma.

Although the effects test is routinely followed in many employment discrimination cases, the courts have appeared to be less rigorous in applying the test when the setting changes from blue collar to academic work. For example, it is frequently assumed that a doctorate degree and written publications are valid prerequisites for employment, promotion and tenure in academia. However, colleges and universities are rarely required to prove the job relatedness of these credentials in employment discrimination cases.

Although legislation such as Title VII does not distinguish between institutions of higher education and other employers, the developing caselaw appears to allow for a modified definition of proscribed discrimination in cases involving academe. For instance, in Johnson v. University of Pittsburgh, 435 F. Supp. 1328 (W.D. Pa. 1977), the Court made the following observation:

> The court is thoroughly appreciative of the important and serious issues involved in this case. On the one hand we have the important problem as to whether sex discrimination is operating to the detriment of women in the halls of academia. If so Congress has mandated that it must be eradicated. Colleges and universities must understand this and guide themselves accordingly. On the other hand we also have the important question as to whether the federal courts are to take over the matter of promotion and tenure for college professors when experts in the academic field agree that such should not occur. In determining qualifications in such circumstances the court is way beyond its field of expertise and in the absence of a clear carrying of the burden of proof by the plaintiff, we must leave such decisions to the Ph.D.s in academia.

1.   Bona Fide Seniority Systems

As a general matter, there is one important exception to the prohibition against discrimination due to disparate effects. This exception arises if the disparate effect is a result of the application of a bona fide seniority system. The Supreme Court has held that "an otherwise neutral, legitimate seniority system does not become unlawful under Title VII simply because it may perpetuate pre-Act discrimination." Further, the Court held that "Section 703(h) [of Title VII] on its face immunizes all bona fide seniority systems, and does not distinguish between the perpetuation of pre- and post-Act discrimination." This holding, which was rendered in 1977, overruled a doctrine developed in the lower courts which found present discrimination where a seniority or transfer system effectively locked members of a protected class into less desirable jobs in which they had been placed as a result of pre-Act discrimination. Although the seniority question has been important in the industrial context, it is a matter of only limited significance in faculty employment discrimination cases.

2.   Tests of "Reasonable Accommodation"

An employer's failure to make reasonable accommodation to the requirements of an employee's religion or handicap also may result in a finding of discrimination, unless the employer can demonstrate that undue hardship would result. However, to avoid conflict with the Establishment Clause of the First Amendment, the Supreme Court has narrowly construed the Title VII requirement of reasonable accommodation to an employee's religious practices.

Under regulations promulgated pursuant to the Rehabilitation Act of 1973, all federal contractors covered by the Act have a duty to accommodate to an employee's physical or mental handicaps, "unless the contractor can demonstrate that such an accommodation would impose an undue hardship on the conduct of the contractor's business." Although this regulation was modelled after the section of Title VII requiring accommodation to religious practice, it presents no problem of constitutional conflict which would necessitate a narrow construction.

B.   The Effects of Employment Discrimination

The economic impact of employment discrimination against minority persons and women is profound. As the data below will indicate, minority persons and women in the United States have, for many years, continually suffered from limited job access, relatively low incomes and high unemployment.

In 1976, the median income for white workers was $12,098; however, the median income for black workers was $9,032, i.e., about 75% of the white workers' income level.

Although much has been said about the alleged improvement of the economic position of black families in recent years, the overall income gap between black and white families actually widened during the first half of the 1970s. In 1970, black family income was 61% of white family income; however, by 1976 this figure had decreased to 59%.

The problem of race discrimination is compounded by the fact of the continually high rate of unemployment among black workers. For example, the unemployment rate for all workers in August 1977 was 7.1%; however, for black workers the unemployment rate was 15.5%, the highest such rate since 1954.

The low income and high unemployment among black workers has resulted in a disproportionate number of black families falling below the poverty line. In 1976, 9.4% of all families had incomes below the poverty level, but 27.9% of all black families were living in poverty, compared to 7.1% of white families.

Employment opportunities for blacks have been further limited by the severe problem of teen-age unemployment. In an article appearing in the *New York Times Magazine*, October 23, 1977, it was reported that:

> In the ghettos, . . . minority youth have an official unemployment rate of 44%—and the Urban League suggests the real number is 60%. . . . Today . . . after twenty years of black economic progress and political gains, unemployment among black teen-agers is almost two and a half times that of white teen-agers, while their labor-force participation has sunk to only 75% of the white level. These figures mean that since the early 50's, black teenage unemployment has risen about three times faster annually than white unemployment.

The other side of the problem is sex discrimination. One of the worst effects of sex discrimination in employment is the reduced income of women workers. In 1974, about 70% of all women workers were either single, widowed, divorced, separated or married to men making less than $10,000 per year. Yet, in 1976, the median incomes for full-time workers by race and sex were: white males—$14,272; black males—$10,222; white females—$8,376; black females—$7,831. Thus, the incomes of white women were only about 59% of those of white men and 82% of those of black men. Black women, with a double burden of discrimination, had incomes of only about 55% of white men and 75% of black men. Women also have a higher unemployment rate than men. In August 1977, the unemployment rate was 8.3% for women and 6.3% for men.

The income disparities between men and women result, in part, from the segregation of jobs by race, sex or national origin. Women and minorities traditionally have been channeled into certain jobs both by employers and by societal expectations. Thus, for example, until recently, women have tended to be clerical workers, nurses, teachers and household workers. Black women have been even more restricted in job opportunities.

Employment discrimination within the academic community is also a grave problem. Even though it is often more difficult to measure and prove race or sex discrimination in the academic context, this should not be taken to suggest that no such discrimination exists. On this point, the report of the House Committee on Education and Labor, issued in connection with the adoption of the 1972 Amendments to Title VII, noted that:

Discrimination against minorities and women in the field of education is as pervasive as discrimination in any other area of employment. In the field of higher education, the fact that black scholars have been generally relegated to all-black institutions, or have been restricted to lesser academic positions when they have been permitted entry into white institutions is common knowledge. Similarly, in the area of sex discrimination, women have long been invited to participate as students in the academic process, but without the prospect of gaining employment as serious scholars.

The proportional underemployment of minority persons and women in academia is well recognized. For example, a 1977 survey report released by the College and University Personnel Association, entitled *Women and Minorities in Administration of Higher Education Institutions: Employment Patterns and Salary Comparisons,* indicated that white men held about 79% of the administrative positions at surveyed institutions, white women held 14%, minority men held 5% and minority women held under 2%.

In Vol. 63, No. 3 of the *AAUP Bulletin* (August 1977), it was reported that, in institutions employing both men and women, the percentages of faculty persons who were women in 1976-77 were:

Professor	8.4%
Associate Professor	16.7%
Assistant Professor	29.7%

The 29.7% figure at the "Assistant Professor" level looks encouraging if one assumes that persons in this category are recent hires on the way up in the tenure track. However, it is also noteworthy that the percentage of women at the full professor level dropped from 10.1% in 1974-75 to 8.4% in 1976-77.

Another example of the problem of proportional underrepresentation may be seen in the law school context. A 1976 American Bar Association survey indicated that there were approximately 3,700 full-time law professors and 485 deans and administrators who teach in law school in the United States. However, only 136 (or 3.6%) of the law teachers and only 29 (or 6%) of the administrator-teachers were black. More importantly, only 36 (less than 1%) of the black teachers were at the level of full professor. There were 335 women in the law professor group, but only a handful of these were black.

Once hired, women and minorities are not always assured of equal treatment. The AAUP survey indicated that in 1976-77, the average salary for women faculty members was $15,350, whereas the average salary for men in faculty ranks was $19,020. See 63 *AAUP Bulletin* 146 (1977). There are two apparent reasons for this gap. The first is the distribution of men and women at each rank of employment. Faculty positions in institutions of higher learning are arranged hierarchically with corresponding gradations of compensation. The AAUP study showed that, in the 1976-77 school year, full professors received an average salary of $23,930, associate professors received $18,100, assistant professors received $14,820 and instructors received $11,920. This data becomes significant in light of the relatively low percentage of women employed at the highest ranks. In 1976-77, only 7% of all full-time women faculty members were at the level of "professor," compared with 30% of all full-time men.

A second cause of the disparity between the average salaries of men and women is the pay differential *within* each rank. According to the AAUP study, women earned an average of 5.1% less than men in each position in 1976-77, as follows:

Academic Rank	Men	Women
Professor	$24,290	$22,220
Associate Professor	18,340	17,540
Assistant Professor	15,120	14,440
Instructor	12,300	11,630

Unfortunately, data on the economic position of minority faculty members has not been compiled in one useful source. Kent G. Mommsen's article, *Black Doctorates in American Higher Education: A Cohort Analysis,* in the Journal of Social and Behavioral Science (Spring 1974), indicates that the average yearly salary for black Ph.D.s was only slightly less—$62—than the average salary for all Ph.D.s when institutional salary alone was considered for the 1969-70 academic year. Thomas Sowell, using data from the American Council on Education for the year 1972-73, determined that full-time white faculty earned an average of $640 more than full-time black faculty. However, Sowell noted that:

...[W]hen degree level and degree quality are held constant, blacks earned more than whites with doctorates of whatever ranking, while whites had an edge of less than $100 per year among academics without a doctorate.... Blacks who had published at all had higher salaries than whites with the same number of publications. [Sowell, *Affirmative Action Reconsidered,* American Enterprise Institute, 1975, pp. 15-17]

Sowell concedes that there is a gross "underutilization" of minority persons in the academic world, but he argues that existing disparities between minority and white faculty persons and between men and women can be attributed to factors other than race or sex discrimination. Sowell contends that most of these differences can be explained by the fact that there are more white than black Ph.D.s; that large numbers of blacks are distributed in the lower paying fields of specialization; and that black faculty persons are primarily located in the south where salaries tend to be lower. In addition, Sowell asserts that academic women more frequently subordinate their careers to their spouses' careers, or to the general well-being of their families, than do academic men. He infers that women are voluntarily less likely to advance their careers than men.

Some of what Professor Sowell says is correct, especially if one assumes that the Ph.D. is a valid criterion for measuring job performance. However, Sowell may be somewhat shortsighted in suggesting that most of the cited disparities can be attributed to factors other than discrimination. It is true that black faculty have for years been largely confined to black institutions in the south, but this has resulted in significant measure from long-standing patterns of racial segregation in this country. It is likewise true that there are relatively few minority Ph.D.s in certain fields of specialization, thus limiting the pool of qualified applicants pursuant to traditional hiring standards; however, it must be recalled that one of the reasons for this dearth of Ph.D.s is that minority persons and women have for years been excluded from a number of significant Ph.D. programs.

Change is beginning to occur in academia, primarily because of "affirmative action" programs undertaken by colleges and universities during the 1970s. However,

> We now stand in a transition period between actual past deficiencies of major proportions and potential future achievements of true equality and opportunity. . . .
>
> There are at least two tragedies involved in this transition period:
>
> One, that it should be necessary at all . . . .
>
> Two, that it should take place in the 1970s and beyond. The 1960s saw a doubling of faculty members. The 1980s may even see a slight decline. The effort at redress of past errors comes 10 years too late to be easily effective. Now there are too few new appointments and too many candidates even from among the majority male group alone. The transition will take longer and will involve more individual disappointments than if it had taken place earlier. . . .
>
> Nevertheless, the transition must take place, and higher education will be better and stronger and more effective as a result of it, but there also will be costs. Transition periods are seldom easy, and this one is no exception. Report of The Carnegie Council on Policy Studies in Higher Education, Making Affirmative Action Work, (San Francisco: Jossey-Bass Publ., 1975)

NOTES

1. For further and more comprehensive data and discussion concerning the effects of employment discrimination in higher education, *see* generally, Astin & Bayer, *Sex Discrimination in Academe*, Educational Record 52 (Spring 1972); Bayer & Astin, *Sex Differences in Academic Rank and Salary Among Science Doctorates in Teaching*, 3 Journal of Human Resources 196 (1968); Bernard, Academic Women (University Park, Pa.: Pennsylvania State University Press, 1964); Caplow & McGee, The Academic Marketplace (1961); Divine, *Women in the Academy: Sex Discrimination in University Faculty Hiring and Promotion*, 5 Journal of Law and Education 429 (1976); Fulton, Rewards and Fairness: Academic Women in the United States, Centre for Research in the Educational Services, University of Edinburgh, Occasional Paper No. 15 (1973); Goldstein,

Affirmative Action: Equal Employment Rights for Women in Academia, 74 Teachers College Record 395 (1973); Gordon & Morton, *A Low Mobility of Wage Discrimination with Special Reference to Sex Differentials,* 7 Journal of Economic Theory 241 (1974); Johnson & Stafford, *The Earnings and Promotion of Women Faculty,* 64 American Economic Review 888 (1974); Johnson and Stafford, *Women and the Academic Labor Market,* in Sex Discrimination and the Division of Labor (C. Lloyd ed., New York: Columbia U. Press, 1975); Koch & Chizman, *Sex Discrimination and Affirmative Action in Faculty Salaries,* Economic Inquiry 16 (March, 1976); Lester, Antibias Regulation of Universities: Faculty Problems and Their Solutions (New York: McGraw-Hill, 1974); Lester, *The Equal Pay Boondoggle,* 7 Change 38 (1975); Lester, *Labor-Market Discrimination and Individualized Pay: The Complicated Case of University Faculty,* in Equal Rights and Industrial Relations 197 (IRRA, March, 1977); Mommsen, *Black Ph.D.s in the Academic Marketplace: Supply, Demand, and Price,* 45 Journal of Higher Education 253 (1974); Moore & Wagstaff, Black Educators in White Colleges (San Francisco: Jossey-Bass, 1970); *No Progress This Year: Report on the Economic Status of the Profession, 1976-77,* 63 AAUP Bulletin 146 (1977); Rafky, *The Black Academic in the Marketplace,* 3 Change 65 (1971); Sandler, *Backlash in Academe: A Critique of the Lester Report on Affirmative Action,* 76 Teachers College Record 401 (1975); Sowell, *Affirmative Action Reconsidered: Was it Necessary in Academia?,* American Enterprise Institute for Public Policy Research Evaluative Studies, No. 27 (1975); Vetter & Babco, Professional Women and Minorities (Washington, D.C.: Scientific Manpower Commission, 1978) 140-159; Winston, *Through the Back Door: Academic Racism and the Negro Scholar in Historical Perspective,* 100 Daedalus 695 (1971).

2. For additional information concerning the effects of employment discrimination in society at large, *see* EEOC, Equal Employment Opportunity Report–1974 (Research Report No. 50, 1976); U.S. Dept. of Commerce, The Social and Economic Status of the Black Population in the United States 1974 (Special Studies Series P-23, No. 54, July 1975); U.S. Dept. of Commerce, Characteristics of the Population Below the Poverty Level: 1975 (Series P-60, No. 106, June 1977); U.S. Dept. of Commerce, Money Income in 1975 of Families and Persons in the United States (Series P-60, No. 105, June 1977); U.S. Dept. of Labor Women's Bureau, Women in the Labor Force–Annual Averages 1976-1975 (Feb. 1977); U.S. Dept. of Labor, Labor Force Developments: Third Quarter 1977 (Bureau of Labor Statistics, Oct. 17, 1977); U.S. Dept. of Commerce, Money Income and the Poverty Status of Families and Persons in the United States: 1976 (Series P-60, No. 107, Sept. 1977); U.S. Dept. of Labor, Why Women Work (July 1976); U.S. Dept. of Labor Women's Bureau, The Earnings Gap Between Women and Men (Oct. 1976); U.S. Dept. of Labor Women's Bureau, Women in the Labor Force–July 1977-1976 (August 1977); U.S. Dept. of Labor Women's Bureau, Minority Women Workers: A Statistical Overview (1977); U.S. Dept. of Labor Women's Bureau, Women Workers Today (1976); U.S. Dept. of Labor Women's Bureau, Unemployment in Recessions: Women and Black Workers (April 1977); National Urban League, Black Families in the 1974-75 Depression (Research Dept., July 1975); Stafford and Duncan, The Use of Time and Technology by Households in the United States (Univ. of Michigan, Dept. of Economics, July 1977); Edwards, *Race Discrimination in Employment: What Price Equality?* in Civil Liberties and Civil Rights (Urbana: Univ. of Illinois Press, 1977) (see in particular the extensive bibliography and statistical charts on pp. 126-144); U.S. Commission on Civil Rights, *To Eliminate Employment Discrimination,* Vol. V in The Federal Civil Rights Enforcement Effort–1974 (July 1975); Becker, The Economics of Discrimination, 2nd ed. (Chicago: Univ. of Chicago Press, 1971); Oaxaca, *Theory and Measurement in the Economics of Discrimination,* and Butler & Heckman, *The Government's Impact on the Labor Market Status of Black Americans: A Critical Review,* in Equal Rights and Industrial Relations (IRRA, 1977), Thurow, *The Economic Progress of Minority Groups,* Challenge (March-April 1976), p. 20.

C.   Reorganization of Equal Employment Opportunity Programs

REORGANIZATION PLAN NO. 1 OF 1978

Prepared by the President and transmitted to the Senate and the House of Representatives in Congress assembled, February 23, 1978, pursuant to the provisions of Chapter 9 of Title 5 of the United States Code.

Equal Employment Opportunity

Section 1. *Transfer of Equal Pay Enforcement Functions.*

All functions related to enforcing or administering Section 6 (d) of the Fair Labor Standards Act, as amended, (29 U.S.C. 206 (d)) are hereby transferred to the Equal Employment Opportunity Commission. Such functions include, but shall not be limited to, the functions relating to equal pay administration and enforcement now vested in the Secretary of Labor, the Administrator of the Wage and Hour Division of the Department of Labor, and the Civil Service Commission pursuant to Sections 4 (d) (1); 4 (f); 9; 11 (a), (b) and (c); 16 (b) and (c) and 17 of the Fair Labor Standards Act, as amended, (29 U.S.C. 204 (d) (1); 204 (f); 209; 211 (a), (b) and (c); 216 (b) and (c) and 217) and Section 10 (b) (1) of the Portal-to-Portal Act of 1947, as amended, (29 U.S.C. 259).

Section 2. *Transfer of Age Discrimination Enforcement Functions.*

All functions vested in the Secretary of Labor or in the Civil Service Commission pursuant to Sections 2, 4, 7, 8, 9, 10, 11, 12, 13, 14, and 15 of the Age Discrimination in Employment Act of 1967, as amended, (29 U.S.C. 621), 623, 626, 627, 628, 629, 630, 631, 632, 633, and 633a) are hereby transferred to the Equal Employment Opportunity Commission. All functions related to age discrimination administration and enforcement pursuant to Sections 6 and 16 of the Age Discrimination in Employment Act of 1967, as amended, (29 U.S.C. 625 and 634) are hereby transferred to the Equal Employment Opportunity Commission.

Section 3. *Transfer of Equal Opportunity in Federal Employment Enforcement Functions.*

(a) All equal opportunity in Federal employment enforcement and related functions vested in the Civil Service Commission pursuant to Section 717 (b) and (c) of the Civil Rights Act of 1964, as amended, (42 U.S.C. 2000 e-16 (b) and (c)), are hereby transferred to the Equal Employment Opportunity Commission.

(b) The Equal Employment Opportunity Commission may delegate to the Civil Service Commission or its successor the function of making a preliminary determination on the issue of discrimination whenever, as a part of a complaint or appeal before the Civil Service Commission on other grounds, a Federal employee alleges a violation of Section 717 of the Civil Rights Act of 1964, as amended. (42 U.S.C. 2000e-16) provided that the Equal Employment Opportunity Commission retains the function of making the final determination concerning such issue of discrimination.

Section 4. *Transfer of Federal Employment of Handicapped Individuals Enforcement Functions.*

All Federal employment of handicapped individuals enforcement functions and related functions vested in the Civil Service Commission pursuant to Section 501 of the Rehabilitation Act of 1973 (29 U.S.C. 791) are hereby transferred to the Equal Employment Opportunity Commission. The function of being co-chairman of the Interagency Committee on Handicapped Employees now vested in the Chairman of the Civil Service Commission pursuant to Section 501 is hereby transferred to the Chairman of the Equal Employment Opportunity Commission.

Section 5. *Transfer of Public Sector 707 Functions.*

Any function of the Equal Employment Opportunity Commission concerning initiation of litigation with respect to State or local government, or political subdivisions under Section 707 of Title VII of the Civil Rights Act of 1964, as amended, (42 U.S.C. 2000 e-6) and all necessary functions related thereto, including investigation, findings, notice and an opportunity to resolve the matter without contested litigation, are hereby transferred to the Attorney General, to be exercised by him in accordance with procedures consistent with said Title VII. The Attorney General is authorized to delegate any function under Section 707 of said Title VII to any officer or employee of the Department of Justice.

Section 6. *Transfer of Functions and Abolition of the Equal Employment Opportunity Coordinating Council.*

All functions of the Equal Employment Opportunity Coordinating Council, which was established pursuant to Section 715 of the Civil Rights Act of 1964, as amended, (42 U.S.C. 2000 e-14), are hereby transferred to the Equal Employment Opportunity Commission. The Equal Employment Opportunity Coordinating Council is hereby abolished.

Section 7. *Savings Provision.*

Administrative proceedings including administrative appeals from the acts of an executive agency (as defined by Section 105 of Title 5 of the United States Code, commenced or being conducted by or against such executive agency will not abate by reason of the taking effect of this Plan. Consistent with the provisions of this Plan, all such proceedings shall continue before the Equal Employment Opportunity Commission otherwise unaffected by the transfers provided by this Plan. Consistent with the provisions of this Plan, the Equal Employment Opportunity Commission shall accept appeals from those executive agency actions which occurred prior to the effective date of this Plan in accordance with law and regulations in effect on such effective date. Nothing herein shall affect any right of any person to judicial review under applicable law.

COMPARISON OF CURRENT AND PROPOSED ALLOCATION
OF EQUAL EMPLOYMENT AUTHORITIES

CURRENT DISPERSED RESPONSIBILITY		EQUAL EMPLOYMENT AUTHORITIES		PROPOSED CONSOLIDATION	
AGENCY	PROGRAM	DISCRIMINATION COVERED	EMPLOYERS COVERED	AGENCY	TIMING
EEOC	TITLE VII	RACE, COLOR, RELIGION, SEX, NATIONAL ORIGIN	PRIVATE AND PUBLIC NON-FEDERAL EM-PLOYERS AND UNIONS	EEOC	
LABOR (Wage and Hour)	EQUAL PAY ACT, AGE DISCRIMINA-TION ACT	SEX, AGE	PRIVATE AND PUBLIC NON-FEDERAL EM-PLOYERS AND UNIONS	EEOC	JULY 1979 JULY 1979
CIVIL SERVICE COMMISSION	TITLE VII, EXE-CUTIVE ORDER 11478, EQUAL PAY ACT, AGE DISCRIMINATION ACT, REHABILI-TATION ACT	RACE, COLOR, RELIGION, SEX, NATIONAL ORIGIN, AGE, HANDICAPPED	FEDERAL GOVERNMENT	EEOC	OCTOBER 1978
EEOCC*	COORDINATION OF ALL FEDERAL EQUAL EMPLOY-MENT PROGRAMS	. . . .	. . . .	EEOC	JULY 1978
LABOR (OFCCP)	VIETNAM VETER-ANS READJUST-MENT ACT, RE-HABILITATION ACT	VETERANS HANDICAPPED	FEDERAL CONTRACTORS		
COMMERCE DEFENSE ENERGY EPA GSA HEW HUD INTERIOR SBA DOT TREASURY	EXECUTIVE ORDERS 11246, 11375	RACE, COLOR, RELIGION, SEX, NATIONAL ORIGIN	FEDERAL CONTRACTORS	LABOR (OFCCP)	OCTOBER 1978
JUSTICE	TITLE VII, EXECUTIVE OR-DER 11246, SELECTED FEDER-AL GRANT PRO-GRAMS	RACE, COLOR, RELIGION, SEX, NATIONAL ORIGIN VARIED	PUBLIC NON-FEDERAL EM-PLOYERS FEDERAL CONTRACTORS AND GRANTEES	JUSTICE	NO CHANGE

*A number of Federal grant statutes include a provision barring employment discrimination by recipients based on a variety of grounds including race, color, sex, and national origin. Under the reorganization plan, the activities of these agencies will be coordinated by the EEOC.

Section 8. *Incidental Transfers.*

So much of the personnel, property, records and unexpended balances of appropriations, allocations and other funds employed, used, held, available, or to be made available in connection with the functions transferred under this Plan, as the Director of the Office of Management and Budget shall determine, shall be transferred to the appropriate department, agency, or component at such time or times as the Director of the Office of Management and Budget shall provide, except that no such unexpended balances transferred shall be used for purposes other than those for which the appropriation was originally made. The Director of the Office of Management and Budget shall provide for terminating the affairs of the Council abolished herein and for such further measures and dispositions as such Director deems necessary to effectuate the purposes of this Reorganization Plan.

Section 9. *Effective Date.*

This Reorganization Plan shall become effective at such time or times, on or before October 1, 1979, as the President shall specify, but not sooner than the earliest time allowable under Section 906 of Title 5 of the United States Code.

II. Constitutional Protections

WASHINGTON v. DAVIS
United States Supreme Court
96 S. Ct. 2040 (1976)

MR. JUSTICE WHITE delivered the opinion of the Court.

This case involves the validity of a qualifying test administered to applicants for positions as police officers in the District of Columbia Metropolitan Police Department. The test was sustained by the District Court but invalidated by the Court of Appeals. We are in agreement with the District Court and hence reverse the judgment of the Court of Appeals.

I

This action began on April 10, 1970, when two Negro police officers filed suit against the then Commissioner of the District of Columbia, the Chief of the District's Metropolitan Police Department and the Commissioners of the United States Civil Service Commission. An amended complaint, filed December 10, alleged that the promotion policies of the Department were racially discriminatory and sought a declaratory judgment and an injunction. The respondents Harley and Sellers were permitted to intervene, their amended complaint asserting that their applications to become officers in the Department had been rejected, and that the Department's recruiting procedures discriminated on the basis of race against black applicants by a series of practices including. but not limited to, a written personnel test which excluded a disproportionately high number of Negro applicants. These practices were asserted to violate respondents' rights "under the due process clause of the Fifth Amendment to the United States Constitution, under 42 U.S.C. § 1981 and under D. C. Code § 1-320."

According to the findings and conclusions of the District Court, to be accepted by the Department and to enter an intensive 17-week training program, the police recruit was required to satisfy certain physical and character standards, to be a high school graduate or its equivalent and to receive a grade of at least 40 on "Test 21," which is "an examination that is used generally throughout the federal service," which "was developed by the Civil Service Commission not the Police Department" and which was "designed to test verbal ability, vocabulary, reading and comprehension." 348 F.Supp., at 16.

The validity of Test 21 was the sole issue before the court on the motions for summary judgment. The District Court noted that there was no claim of "an intentional discrimination or purposeful discriminatory actions" but only a claim that Test 21 bore no relationship to job performance and "has a highly discriminatory impact in screening out black candidates." 348 F.Supp., at 16. Petitioners' evidence, the District Court said, warranted three conclusions: "(a) The number of black police officers, while substantial, is not proportionate to the population mix of the city. (b) A higher percentage of blacks fail the Test than whites. (c) The Test has not been validated to establish its reliability for measuring subsequent job performance." *Ibid.* This showing was deemed sufficient to shift the burden of proof to the defendants in the action, petitioners here; but the court nevertheless concluded that on the undisputed facts, respondents were not entitled to relief. The District Court relied on several factors. Since August 1969, 44% of new police force recruits had been black; that figure also represented the proportion of blacks on the total force and was roughly equivalent to 20-29-year-old blacks in the 50-mile radius in which the recruiting efforts of the Police Department had been concentrated. It was undisputed that the Department had systematically and affirmatively sought to enroll black officers many of whom passed the test but failed to report for duty. The District Court rejected the assertion that Test 21 was culturally slanted to favor whites and was "satisfied that the undisputable facts prove the test to be reasonably and directly related to the requirements of the police recruit training program and that it is neither so designed nor operated to discriminate against otherwise qualified blacks.". . .

Having lost on both constitutional and statutory issues in the District Court, respondents brought the case to the Court of Appeals claiming that their summary judgment motion, which rested on purely constitutional grounds, should have been granted. The tendered constitutional issue was whether the use of Test 21 invidiously discriminated against Negroes and hence denied them due process of law contrary to the commands of the Fifth Amendment. The Court of Appeals, addressing that issue, announced that it would be guided by Griggs v. Duke Power Co., 401 U.S. 424 (1971), a case involving the interpretation and application of Title VII of the Civil

Rights Act of 1964, and held that the statutory standards elucidated in that case were to govern the due process question tendered in this one. 168 U. S. App. D. C. 42, 512 F. 2d 956 (1975). The court went on to declare that lack of discriminatory intent in designing and administering Test 21 was irrelevant; the critical fact was rather that a far greater proportion of blacks— four times as many—failed the test than did whites. This disproportionate impact, standing alone and without regard to whether it indicated a discriminatory purpose, was held sufficient to establish a constitutional violation, absent proof by petitioners that the test was an adequate measure of job performance in addition to being an indicator of probable success in the training program, a burden which the court ruled petitioners had failed to discharge. That the Department had made substantial efforts to recruit blacks was held beside the point and the fact that the racial distribution of recent hirings and of the Department itself might be roughly equivalent to the racial makeup of the surrounding community, broadly conceived, was put aside as a "comparison [not] material to this appeal." . . .

II

Because the Court of Appeals erroneously applied the legal standards applicable to Title VII cases in resolving the constitutional issue before it, we reverse its judgment in respondents' favor. Although the petition for certiorari did not present this ground for reversal, our Rule 40(1)(d)(2) provides that we "may notice a plain error not presented"; and this is an appropriate occasion to invoke the rule.

As the Court of Appeals understood Title VII,[10] employees or applicants proceeding under it need not concern themselves with the employer's possibly discriminatory purpose but instead may focus solely on the racially differential impact of the challenged hiring or promotion practices. This is not the constitutional rule. We have never held that the constitutional standard for adjudicating claims of invidious racial discrimination is identical to the standards applicable under Title VII, and we decline to do so today.

The central purpose of the Equal Protection Clause of the Fourteenth Amendment is the prevention of official conduct discriminating on the basis of race. It is also true that the Due Process Clause of the Fifth Amendment contains an equal protection component prohibiting the United States from invidiously discriminating between individuals or groups. Bolling v. Sharpe, 347 U.S. 497 (1954). But our cases have not embraced the proposition that a law or other official act, without regard to whether it reflects a racially discriminatory purpose, is unconstitutional solely because it has a racially disproportionate impact.

[10.] Although Title VII standards have dominated this case, the statute was not applicable to federal employees when the complaint was filed, and although the 1972 amendments extending the title to reach government employees were adopted prior to the District Court's judgment, the complaint was not amended to state a claim under that title, nor did the case thereafter proceed as a Title VII case. Respondents' motion for partial summary judgment, filed after the 1972 amendments, rested solely on constitutional grounds; and the Court of Appeals ruled that the motion should have been granted. . . .

.... Wright v. Rockefeller, 376 U.S. 52 (1964), upheld a New York congressional apportionment statute against claims that district lines had been racially gerrymandered. The challenged districts were made up predominantly of whites or of minority races, and their boundaries were irregularly drawn. The challengers did not prevail because they failed to prove that the New York legislature "was either motivated by racial considerations or in fact drew the districts on racial lines"; the plaintiffs had not shown that the statute "was the product of a state contrivance to segregate on the basis of race or place of origin." 376 U.S., at 56, 58. The dissenters were in agreement that the issue was whether the "boundaries . . . were purposefully drawn on the racial lines." 376 U.S., at 67.

The school desegregation cases have also adhered to the basic equal protection principle that the invidious quality of a law claimed to be racially discriminatory must ultimately be traced to a racially discriminatory purpose. That there are both predominantly black and predominantly white schools in a community is not alone violative of the Equal Protection Clause. The essential element of *de jure* segregation is "a current condition of segregation resulting from intentional state action . . . the differentiating factor between *de jure* segregation and so-called *de facto* segregation . . . is *purpose* or *intent* to segregate." Keyes v. School District No. 1, 413 U.S. 189, 205, 208, (1973). See also *id.*, at 199, 211, 213. The Court has also recently rejected allegations of racial discrimination based solely on the statistically disproportionate racial impact of various provisions of the Social Security Act because "the acceptance of appellant's constitutional theory would render suspect each difference in treatment among the grant classes, however lacking the racial motivation and however rational the treatment might be." Jefferson v. Hackney, 406 U.S. 535, 548 (1972).

This is not to say that the necessary discriminatory racial purpose must be express or appear on the face of the statute, or that a law's disproportionate impact is irrelevant in cases involving Constitution-based claims of racial discrimination. A statute, otherwise neutral on its face, must not be applied so as invidiously to discriminate on the basis of race. Yick Wo v. Hopkins, 118 U.S. 356 (1886). It is also clear from the cases dealing with racial discrimination in the selection of juries that the systematic exclusion of Negroes is itself such an "unequal application of the law . . . as to show intentional discrimination." *Akins* v. *Texas, supra*, at 404. Smith v. Texas, 311 U.S. 128 (1940); Pierre v. Louisiana, 306 U.S. 354 (1939); Neal v. Delaware, 103 U.S. 370 (1881). . . . With a prima facie case made out, "the burden of proof shifts to the State to rebut the presumption of unconstitutional action by showing that permissible racially neutral selection criteria and procedures have produced the monochromatic result." [citing cases.]

Necessarily, an invidious discriminatory purpose may often be inferred from the totality of the relevant facts, including the fact, if it is true, that the law bears more heavily on one race than another. It is also not infrequently true that the discriminatory impact—in the jury cases for example, the total or seriously disproportionate exclusion of Negroes from jury venires—

may for all practical purposes demonstrate unconstitutionality because in various circumstances the discrimination is very difficult to explain on non-racial grounds. Nevertheless, we have not held that a law, neutral on its face and serving ends otherwise within the power of government to pursue, is invalid under the Equal Protection Clause simply because it may affect a greater proportion of one race than of another. Disproportionate impact is not irrelevant, but it is not the sole touchstone of an invidious racial discrimination forbidden by the Constitution. Standing alone, it does not trigger the rule. McLaughlin v. Florida, 379 U.S. 184 (1964), that racial classifications are to be subjected to the strictest scrutiny and are justifiable only by the weightiest of considerations.

[Here follows a discussion of Palmer v. Thompson, 403 U.S. 217 (1971), and Wright v. Council of the City of Emporia, 407 U.S. 451 (1972), which indicate that in certain circumstances racial impact of a law, rather than discriminatory purpose, may be the critical factor invalidating the law.]

Both before and after *Palmer* v. *Thompson*, however, various Courts of Appeals have held in several contexts, including public employment, that the substantially disproportionate racial impact of a statute or official practice standing alone and without regard to discriminatory purpose, suffices to prove racial discrimination violating the Equal Protection Clause absent some justification going substantially beyond what would be necessary to validate most other legislative classifications. The cases impressively demonstrate that there is another side to the issue; but, with all due respect, to the extent that those cases rested on or expressed the view that proof of discriminatory racial purpose is unnecessary in making out an equal protection violation, we are in disagreement.

As an initial matter, we have difficulty understanding how a law establishing a racially neutral qualification for employment is nevertheless racially discriminatory and denies "any person equal protection of the laws" simply because a greater proportion of Negroes fail to qualify than members of other racial or ethnic groups. Had respondents, along with all others who had failed Test 21, whether white or black, brought an action claiming that the test denied each of them equal protection of the laws as compared with those who had passed with high enough scores to qualify them as police recruits, it is most unlikely that their challenge would have been sustained. Test 21, which is administered generally to prospective government employees, concededly seeks to ascertain whether those who take it have acquired a particular level of verbal skill; and it is untenable that the Constitution prevents the government from seeking modestly to upgrade the communicative abilities of its employees rather than to be satisfied with some lower level of competence, particularly where the job requires special ability to communicate orally and in writing. Respondents, as Negroes, could no more successfully claim that the test denied them equal protection than could white applicants who also failed. The conclusion would not be different in the face of proof that more Negroes than whites had been disqualified by Test 21. That other Negroes also failed to score well would, alone, not demonstrate that respondents individually were being denied equal protection of the laws by the application of an otherwise valid qualifying test being administered to prospective police recruits.

Nor on the facts of the case before us would the disproportionate impact of Test 21 warrant the conclusion that it is a purposeful device to discriminate against Negroes and hence an infringement of the constitutional rights of respondents as well as other black applicants. As we have said, the test is neutral on its face and rationally may be said to serve a purpose the government is constitutionally empowered to pursue. Even agreeing with the District Court that the differential racial effect of Test 21 called for further inquiry, we think the District Court correctly held that the affirmative efforts of the Metropolitan Police Department to recruit black officers, the changing racial composition of the recruit classes and of the force in general, and the relationship of the test to the training program negated any inference that the Department discriminated on the basis of race or that "a police officer qualifies on the color of his skin rather than ability." 348 F. Supp., at 18.

Under Title VII, Congress provided that when hiring and promotion practices disqualifying substantially disproportionate numbers of blacks are challenged, discriminatory purpose need not be proved, and that it is an insufficient response to demonstrate some rational basis for the challenged practices. It is necessary, in addition, that they be "validated" in terms of job performance in any one of several ways, perhaps by ascertaining the minimum skill, ability or potential necessary for the position at issue and determining whether the qualifying tests are appropriate for the selection of qualified applicants for the job in question. However this process proceeds, it involves a more probing judicial review of, and less deference to, the seemingly reasonable acts of administrators and executives than is appropriate under the Constitution where special racial impact, without discriminatory purpose, is claimed. We are not disposed to adopt this more rigorous standard for the purposes of applying the Fifth and the Fourteenth Amendments in cases such as this.

A rule that a statute designed to serve neutral ends is nevertheless invalid, absent compelling justification, if in practice it benefits or burdens one race more than another would be far reaching and would raise serious questions about, and perhaps invalidate, a whole range of tax, welfare, public service, regulatory, and licensing statutes that may be more burdensome to the poor and to the average black than to the more affluent white.

Given that rule, such consequences would perhaps be likely to follow. However, in our view, extension of the rule beyond those areas where it is already applicable by reason of statute, such as in the field of public employment, should await legislative prescription. . . .

III

We also hold that the Court of Appeals should have affirmed the judgment of the District Court granting the motions for summary judgment filed by petitioners and the federal parties. Respondents were entitled to relief on neither constitutional nor statutory grounds.

The District Court . . . assumed that Title VII standards were to control the case, identified the determinative issue as whether Test 21 was sufficiently job related and proceeded to uphold use of the test because it was "directly related to a determination of whether the applicant possesses sufficient skills requisite to the demands of the curriculum a recruit must master at the police academy." 348 F. Supp., at 17. The Court of Appeals reversed because the relationship between Test 21 and training school success, if demonstrated at all, did not satisfy what it deemed to be the crucial requirement of a direct relationship between the performance on Test 21 and performance on the policeman's job.

We agree with petitioners and the federal parties that this was error. The advisability of the police recruit training course informing the recruit about his upcoming job, acquainting him with its demands, and attempting to impart a modicum of required skills seems conceded. It is also apparent to us, as it was to the District Judge, that some minimum verbal and communicative skill would be very useful, if not essential, to satisfactory progress in the training regimen. Based on the evidence before him, the District Judge concluded that Test 21 was directly related to the requirements of the police training program and that a positive relationship between the test and training-course performance was sufficient to validate the former, wholly aside from its possible relationship to actual performance as a police officer. This conclusion of the District Judge that training-program validation may itself be sufficient is supported by regulations of the Civil Service Commission, by the opinion evidence placed before the District Judge, and by the current views of the Civil Service Commissioners who were parties to the case. Nor is the conclusion foreclosed by either *Griggs* or *Albemarle Paper Co.* v. *Moody*, 422 U.S. 405 (1975); and it seems to us the much more sensible construction of the job-relatedness requirement.

The District Court's accompanying conclusion that Test 21 was in fact directly related to the requirements of the police training program was supported by a validation study, as well as by other evidence of record; and we are not convinced that this conclusion was erroneous.

The federal parties, whose views have somewhat changed since the decision of the Court of Appeals and who still insist that training-program validation is sufficient, now urge a remand to the District Court for the purpose of further inquiry into whether the training-program test scores, which were found to correlate with Test 21 scores, are themselves an appropriate measure of the trainee's mastership of the material taught in the course and whether the training program itself is sufficiently related to actual performance of the police officer's task. We think a remand is inappropriate. The District Court's judgment was warranted by the record before it, and we perceive no good reason to reopen it, particularly since we were informed at oral argument that although Test 21 is still being administered, the training program itself has undergone substantial modification in the course of this litigation. If there are now deficiencies in the recruiting practices under prevailing Title VII standards, those deficiencies are to be directly addressed in accordance with the appropriate procedures mandated under that Title.

The judgment of the Court of Appeals accordingly is reversed.

NOTES

1. The Supreme Court's holding in *Washington v. Davis* was subsequently expanded upon in Village of Arlington Heights v. Metropolitan Housing Development Corp., 429 U.S. 252 (1977), where MHDC challenged a denial by the village, Arlington Heights, of a rezoning request to accommodate low and moderate income residences. One issue left unresolved by *Davis* was the nature and degree of discriminatory "purpose" necessary to show a violation of the Equal Protection Clause. In *Arlington Heights*, the Court found that:

> *Davis* does not require a plaintiff to prove that the challenged action rested solely on racially discriminatory purposes. Rarely can it be said that a legislature or administrative body operating under a broad mandate made a decision motivated solely by a single concern, or even that a particular purpose was the "dominant" or "primary" one. In fact, it is because legislators and administrators are properly concerned with balancing numerous competing considerations that courts refrain from reviewing the merits of their decisions, absent a showing of arbitrariness or irrationality. But racial discrimination is not just another competing consideration. When there is proof that a discriminatory purpose has been a motivating factor in the decision, this judicial deference is no longer justified. [429 U.S. at 265-66.]

How far is the Supreme Court likely to extend this theory? For example, suppose that a black faculty member is denied promotion on the recommendation of a faculty committee consisting of thirty members. Suppose further that the recommendation is made pursuant to a unanimous vote, but that five of the thirty members of the committee were motivated by racial animus. Would this satisfy the test of discriminatory purpose? What if the decision not to promote is 16-14 under the same circumstances? If the sixteen had ten reasons not to promote and only one of these was racism?

2. *Arlington Heights* also addressed the problem of proving a racially discriminatory motive, as follows: "The legislative or administrative history may be highly relevant, especially where there are contemporary statements by members of the decision-making body, minutes of its meetings, or reports. In some extraordinary instances the members might be called to the stand at trial to testify concerning the purpose of the official action, although even then such testimony frequently will be barred by privilege." 429 U.S. at 268. How realistic is it to expect that legislators and administrators will readily admit that they intended to discriminate against minorities? Perhaps the evidentiary difficulty of proceeding under the Constitution is one reason why academicians have chosen, instead, to pursue remedies under Title VII.

3. Although *Washington v. Davis* involved a claim under the Due Process Clause of the Fifth Amendment, which is directed at the federal government, many constitutional claims of employment discrimination have been brought against colleges and universities under the Civil Rights Act of 1871, 42 U.S.C. § 1983, which incorporates the Fourteenth Amendment Equal Protection Clause. Section 1983 reads as follows:

> Every person who, under color of any statute, ordinance, regulation, custom, or usage, of any State or Territory, subjects, or causes to be subjected, any citizen of the United States or other person within the jurisdiction thereof to the deprivation of any rights, privileges, or immunities secured by the Constitution and laws, shall be liable to the party injured in an action at law, suit in equity, or other proper proceeding for redress.

4. Section 1983 has been construed to require "state action" as a prerequisite to suit. Many institutions of higher learning are organized, owned and operated by the state and,

therefore, are clearly vulnerable to suit under this statute. However, in other cases, governmental involvement is less obvious. In such cases, the courts generally consider a number of factors to determine whether there is sufficient state action to warrant suit under § 1983. For example, in Braden v. University of Pittsburgh, 552 F.2d 948, the Third Circuit found the requisite close and symbiotic relationship between the state and the university by considering a number of factors, including:

> (1) governmental participation in determining the composition of the board of trustees; (2) the review of the expenditure of private funds by state officials; (3) onerous reporting requirements; (4) a legislative history [of a state statute] which discloses that the state desired to utilize the educational facilities of an existing institution rather than create new ones itself; and especially (5) the statutory declaration that Pitt is an "instrumentality" of the Commonwealth. [552 F.2d at 965]

See also Isaacs v. Board of Trustees of Temple University, 385 F.Supp. 473 (E.D. Pa. 1974), and Weise v. Syracuse Univ., 10 FEP Cas. 1331 (2d Cir. 1975). In Berrios v. Inter American University, 535 F.2d 1330 (1st Cir. 1976) the court decided that limited financial assistance (through tax exemptions and student aid) and government accreditation were not evidence of a sufficiently close relationship to invoke the Equal Protection Clause and § 1983. Generally, courts have been reluctant to find state action in arguably private institutions. *See, e.g.,* Greenya v. George Washington University, 512 F.2d 556 (D.C. Cir. 1975), *cert. denied,* 423 U.S. 995 (1976); Spark v. Catholic University, 510 F.2d 1277 (D.C. Cir. 1975); Blouin v. Loyola University, 506 F.2d 20 (5th Cir. 1975); Wahba v. New York University, 492 F.2d 96 (2d Cir.), *cert. denied,* 419 U.S. 874 (1974); Blackburn v. Fisk University, 443 F.2d 121 (6th Cir. 1971); Browns v. Mitchell, 409 F.2d 593 (10th Cir. 1969). This reflects an interest in preserving the "autonomy and diversity of private colleges and universities." Berrios v. Inter American University, 535 F.2d at 1333.

5. In Monell v. Dept. of Social Services, 98 S. Ct. 2018, 17 F.E.P. Cas. 873 (1978), the Supreme Court ruled that municipalities, school boards and other local government units are "persons" within the meaning of § 1983 and, thus, may be sued for monetary, declaratory or injunctive relief thereunder. The decision in *Monell* overturns the Court's 1961 decision to the contrary in Monroe v. Pape, 365 U.S. 167.

III.   Section 1981 of the Civil Rights Act of 1866

Section 1981 (42 U.S.C. § 1981) reads as follows:

All persons within the jurisdiction of the United States shall have the same right in every State and Territory to make and enforce contracts, to sue, be parties, give evidence, and to the full and equal benefit of all laws and proceedings for the security of persons and property as is enjoyed by white citizens, and shall be subject to like punishment, pains, penalties, taxes, licenses, and exactions of every kind, and to no other.

The Supreme Court, in the Civil Rights Cases, 109 U.S. 322, (1833), determined that the Civil Rights Act of 1866 was passed pursuant to the Thirteenth Amendment's prohibition of slavery and that Congress ". . . undertook to wipe out these burdens and disabilities, the necessary incidents of slavery, constituting every race and color, and without regard to previous servitude, those fundamental rights which are the essence of civil freedom. . . ." Since the Thirteenth Amendment had no state action requirement, the court suggested that under the amendment "legislation, so far as necessary and proper to eradicate all forms and incidents of slavery and involuntary servitude, may be direct and primary, operating upon the acts of individuals, whether sanctioned by State legislation or not. . . ." 109 U.S. at 22. In Jones v. Mayer Co., 392 U.S. 409, 422-37 (1968), the Supreme Court examined the legislative history of § 1981 and concluded that Congress had intended to reach purely private conduct.

The use of § 1981 in cases involving private employment discrimination was approved by the Supreme Court in Johnson v. Railway Express Agency, Inc., 421 U.S. 454, in 1975.

In general, § 1981 has been utilized extensively only in racial discrimination cases. The Supreme Court added a new dimension to the law in McDonald v. Santa Fe Trail Transportation Co., 427 U.S. 273 (1976), when it found that "§ 1981 is applicable to racial discrimination in private employment against white persons." 427 U.S. at 287. It deduced from the legislative history that the law was intended to protect "all persons" from racial discrimination in the making and enforcement of contracts.

Courts have also held that § 1981, unlike Title VII, prohibits discrimination based on alienage. See, e.g., Guerra v. Manchester Terminal Corp., 498 F.2d 641 (5th Cir. 1974) ("as the detailed study of the legislative history by the able district judge below demonstrates, subsequent congressional action explicitly broadened the language of the portion of the 1866 Act that has become § 1981 to include 'all persons' in order to bring aliens within its coverage." 498 F.2d at 653). Several courts have permitted an action to be brought under § 1981 on the basis of national origin where the plaintiff is Spanish-surnamed, but have usually barred such actions where other national origins are involved. See, e.g., Sabala v. Western Gillette, Inc., 516 F.2d 1251 (5th Cir. 1975) (protection extended to Mexican-Americans); Maldonado v. Broadcast Plaza, Inc., 10 FEP Cas. 839 (D. Conn. 1974) (protection extended to Puerto Ricans); Budinsky v. Corning Glass Works, 425 F.Supp. 786 (W. Pa. 1977) (protection denied to plaintiff of Slavic origin). Coverage of sex discrimination under § 1981 however, has been consistently rejected. See, e.g., League of Academic Women v. Regents of University of California, 343 F. Supp. 636 (N.D. Cal. 1972); Braden v. University of Pittsburgh 343 F.Supp. 836 (W.D. Pa. 1972), 477 F.2d 1 (3d Cir. 1973) (remanding on other grounds).

Because the Civil Rights Act of 1866 contains no federal statute of limitations, the Supreme Court has held that federal district courts should apply the most appropriate state statute, except in those cases where its application would be inconsistent with the federal policy underlying § 1981. Johnson v. Railway Express Agency, 421 U.S. 454, 463-65 (1975). For a method of determining which state statute is most appropriate, see Shaw v. Garrison, 545 F.2d 980 (5th Cir. 1977). Does the absence of uniformity by the application of state law encourage "forum shopping" by plaintiffs bringing § 1981 actions?

In Johnson v. Railway Express Agency, 421 U.S. at 459, the Supreme Court quoted a House Report on Title VII stating that "'the remedies available to the individual under Title VII are co-extensive with the indiv[i]dual's right to sue under the provisions of the Civil Rights Act of 1866. . . .', H.R. Rep. No. 92-238, p. 19 (1971);" and thus held that the actions are "separate, distinct, and independent." 421 U.S. at 461. Consequently, since 1972 it has been possible for plaintiffs in higher education cases to bring actions under both statutes. When the alleged discriminatory institution is public or quasi-public, a suit under the Constitution and 42 U.S.C. § 1983 may also be pursued.

There are advantages and disadvantages to each remedy. Sections 1981 and 1983 are attractive because they do not have the complicated procedural requirements of Title VII. These include the necessity for exhausting state remedies, see 42 U.S.C. 2000e-5(c), (d), the relatively brief statutory period of limitations and the requisite one hundred and eighty days of negotiation and conciliation.[1] Additionally, the coverage of § 1981 (and, in some instances, § 1983) is broader, i.e., it has no exemption, as does Title VII, for employers with fewer than fifteen employees and for employers in industries not affecting commerce. (Of course § 1983 is limited by its application to state action alone and § 1981 is limited in its protection of fewer groups.) In some cases, § § 1981 and 1983 will provide the only available relief for unlawful employment discrimination.

Nevertheless, there are incentives for pursuing remedies under Title VII. Conciliation agreements arrived at through EEOC negotiations are more economical means of securing redress than are judicial judgments. In some cases the EEOC will bring the action in court itself, thus relieving the complainant of all legal expenses. Another important feature of Title VII is its provision of attorney's fees, at the court's discretion, for the prevailing party. 42 U.S.C. § 2000e-5(k). In Alyeska Pipeline Service Co. v. Wilderness Society, 421 U.S. 240 (1975), the Court held that attorney's fees could not ordinarily be awarded absent specific statutory authorization. Since § § 1981 and 1983 do not so provide, aggrieved persons unable to afford attorney's fees are more likely to file charges pursuant to Title VII.

See Larson, The Development of Section 1981 as a Remedy for Racial Discrimination in Private Employment, 7 Harv. Civ. Rights–Civ. Liberties L. Rev. 56 (1972), for a more in-depth comparison of § 1981 and Title VII procedural matters.

Perhaps the greatest incentive for bringing an action under Title VII is the lesser burden of proof it imposes upon plaintiffs in establishing a prima facie case of discrimination. Before Washington v. Davis, many federal

---

1. Ordinarily aggrieved persons must file charges with the Equal Employment Opportunity Commission within 180 days after the alleged unlawful employment practice. If charges are first filed with a state or local agency, the complainant has 300 days after the alleged unlawful employment practice occurred or within 30 days after receiving notice that the agency has terminated its own proceedings, whichever is earlier, to file with the EEOC.

   If no conciliation agreement is reached within 30 days after the charge is filed, the EEOC may bring a civil action against a private respondent or may refer the case to the Attorney General if the respondent is a government or governmental agency. If neither the EEOC or the Attorney General file suit within 180 days after the filing of the charge, the person aggrieved is so notified and has 90 days to bring a civil action in a federal district court. 42 U.S.C. § 2000e-5(e).

courts applied Title VII standards and assumed that a showing of disparate effects was sufficient evidence of unlawful discrimination under the Constitution. *See, e.g.,* Davis v. Washington, 512 F.2d 956, 959 (D.C. Cir. 1975) ("Once it is shown that a particular selection procedure has an exclusionary effect on minority applicants, there is a heavy burden on the employer to show that the discriminatory procedure 'bear[s] a demonstrable relationship to successful performance of the jobs for which they were used,'" quoting Griggs v. Duke Power Co., 401 U.S. 424, 431 (1971), a Title VII case.) Since it is so difficult to prove discriminatory intent, it is possible that § 1983, and possibly even § 1981, is no longer a viable alternative for most complainants.

IV.   Title VII of the Civil Rights Act of 1964, as Amended in 1972

GRIGGS v. DUKE POWER CO.
Supreme Court of the United States
401 U.S. 424 (1971)

MR. CHIEF JUSTICE BURGER delivered the opinion of the Court.

We granted the writ in this case to resolve the question whether an employer is prohibited by the Civil Rights Act of 1964, Title VII, from requiring a high school education or passing of a standardized general intelligence test as a condition of employment in or transfer to jobs when (a) neither standard is shown to be significantly related to successful job performance, (b) both requirements operate to disqualify Negroes at a substantially higher rate than white applicants, and (c) the jobs in question formerly had been filled only by white employees as part of a longstanding practice of giving preference to whites.

Congress provided, in Title VII of the Civil Rights Act of 1964, for class actions for enforcement of provisions of the Act and this proceeding was brought by a group of incumbent Negro employees against Duke Power Company. All the petitioners are employed at the Company's Dan River Steam Station, a power generating facility located at Draper, North Carolina. At the time this action was instituted, the Company had 95 employees at the Dan River Station, 14 of whom were Negroes; 13 of these are petitioners here.

The District Court found that prior to July 2, 1965, the effective date of the Civil Rights Act of 1964, the Company openly discriminated on the basis of race in the hiring and assigning of employees at its Dan River plant. The plant was organized into five operating departments: (1) Labor, (2) Coal Handling, (3) Operations, (4) Maintenance, and (5) Laboratory and Test. Negroes were employed only in the Labor Department where the highest paying jobs paid less than the lowest paying jobs in the other four "operating" departments in which only whites were employed. Promotions were normally made within each department on the basis of job seniority. Transferees into a department usually began in the lowest position.

In 1955 the Company instituted a policy of requiring a high school education for initial assignment to any department except Labor, and for transfer from the Coal Handling to any "inside" department (Operations, Maintenance, or Laboratory). When the Company abandoned its policy of restricting Negroes to the Labor Department in 1965, completion of high school also was made a prerequisite to transfer from Labor to any other department. From the time the high school education requirement was instituted to the time of the trial, however, white employees hired before the time of the high school education requirement continued to perform satisfactorily and achieve promotions in the "operating" departments. Findings on this score are not challenged.

The Company added a further requirement for new employees on July 2, 1965, the date on which Title VII became effective. To qualify for placement in any but the Labor Department it became necessary to register satisfactory scores on two professionally prepared aptitude tests, as well as to have a high school education. Completion of high school alone continued to render employees eligible for transfer to the four desirable departments from which Negroes had been excluded if the incumbent had been employed prior to the time of the new requirement. In September 1965 the Company began to permit incumbent employees who lacked a high school education to qualify for transfer from Labor or Coal Handling to an "inside" job by passing two tests—the Wonderlic Personnel Test, which purports to measure general intelligence, and the Bennett Mechanical Comprehension Test. Neither was directed or intended to measure the ability to learn to perform a particular job or category of jobs. The requisite scores used for both initial hiring and transfer approximated the national median for high school graduates.

The District Court had found that while the Company previously followed a policy of overt racial discrimination in a period prior to the Act, such conduct had ceased. The District Court also concluded that Title VII was intended to be prospective only and, consequently, the impact of prior inequities was beyond the reach of corrective action authorized by the Act.

The Court of Appeals was confronted with a question of first impression, as are we, concerning the meaning of Title VII. After careful analysis a majority of that court concluded that a subjective test of the employer's intent should govern, particularly in a close case, and that in this case there was no showing of a discriminatory purpose in the adoption of the diploma and test requirements. On this basis, the Court of Appeals concluded there was no violation of the Act.

The Court of Appeals reversed the District Court in part, rejecting the holding that residual discrimination arising from prior employment practices was insulated from remedial action. The Court of Appeals noted, however, that the District Court was correct in its conclusion that there was no showing of a racial purpose or invidious intent in the adoption of the high school diploma requirement or general intelligence test and that these standards had been applied fairly to whites and Negroes alike. It held that, in the absence of a discriminatory purpose, use of such requirements was permitted by the Act. In so doing, the Court of Appeals rejected the claim that because these two requirements operated to render ineligible a markedly disproportionate number of Negroes, they were unlawful under Title VII unless shown to be job related. We granted the writ on these claims.

The objective of Congress in the enactment of Title VII is plain from the language of the statute. It was to achieve equality of employment opportunities and remove barriers that have operated in the past to favor an identifiable group of white employees over other employees. Under the Act, practices, procedures, or tests neutral on their face, and even neutral in terms of intent, cannot be maintained if they operate to "freeze" the status quo of prior discriminatory employment practices.

The Court of Appeals' opinion, and the partial dissent, agreed that, on the record in the present case, "whites register far better on the Company's alternative requirements" than Negroes.[6] 420 F.2d 1225, 1239 n. 6. This consequence would appear to be directly traceable to race. Basic intelligence must have the means of articulation to manifest itself fairly in a testing process. Because they are Negroes, petitioners have long received inferior education in segregated schools and this Court expressly recognized these differences in *Gaston County* v. *United States,* 395 U. S. 285 (1969). There, because of the inferior education received by Negroes in North Carolina, this Court barred the institution of a literacy test for voter registration on the ground that the test would abridge the right to vote indirectly on account of race. Congress did not intend by Title VII, however, to guarantee a job to every person regardless of qualifications. In short, the Act does not command that any person be hired simply because he was formerly the subject of discrimination, or because he is a member of a minority group. Discriminatory preference for any group, minority or majority, is precisely and only what Congress has proscribed. What is required by Congress is the removal of artificial, arbitrary, and unnecessary barriers to employment when the barriers operate invidiously to discriminate on the basis of racial or other impermissible classification.

Congress has now provided that tests or criteria for employment or promotion may not provide equality of opportunity merely in the sense of the fabled offer of milk to the stork and the fox. On the contrary, Congress has now required that the posture and condition of the job-seeker be taken into account. It has—to resort again to the fable—provided that the vessel in

---

[6.] In North Carolina, 1960 census statistics show that, while 34% of white males had completed high school, only 12% of Negro males had done so. U.S. Bureau of the Census, U.S. Census of Population: 1960, Vol. 1, Characteristics of the Population, pt. 35, Table 47.

Similarly, with respect to standardized tests, the EEOC in one case found that use of a battery of tests, including the Wonderlic and Bennett tests used by the Company in the instant case, resulted in 58% of whites passing the tests, as compared with only 6% of the blacks. Decision of EEOC, CCH Empl. Prac. Guide, ¶17,304.53 (Dec. 2, 1966). See also Decision of EEOC 70-552, CCH Empl. Prac. Guide, ¶6139 (Feb. 19, 1970).

which the milk is proffered be one all seekers can use. The Act proscribes not only overt discrimination but also practices that are fair in form, but discriminatory in operation. The touchstone is business necessity. If an employment practice which operates to exclude Negroes cannot be shown to be related to job performance, the practice is prohibited.

On the record before us, neither the high school completion requirement nor the general intelligence test is shown to bear a demonstrable relationship to successful performance of the jobs for which it was used. Both were adopted, as the Court of Appeals noted, without meaningful study of their relationship to job-performance ability. Rather, a vice president of the Company testified, the requirements were instituted on the Company's judgment that they generally would improve the overall quality of the work force.

The evidence, however, shows that employees who have not completed high school or taken the tests have continued to perform satisfactorily and make progress in departments for which the high school and test criteria are now used. The promotion record of present employees who would not be able to meet the new criteria thus suggests the possibility that the requirements may not be needed even for the limited purpose of preserving the avowed policy of advancement within the Company. In the context of this case, it is unnecessary to reach the question whether testing requirements that take into account capability for the next succeeding position or related future promotion might be utilized upon a showing that such long-range requirements fulfill a genuine business need. In the present case the Company has made no such showing.

The Court of Appeals held that the Company had adopted the diploma and test requirements without any "intention to discriminate against Negro employees." 420 F.2d, at 1232. We do not suggest that either the District Court or the Court of Appeals erred in examining the employer's intent; but good intent or absence of discriminatory intent does not redeem employment procedures or testing mechanisms that operate as "built-in headwinds" for minority groups and are unrelated to measuring job capability.

The Company's lack of discriminatory intent is suggested by special efforts to help the undereducated employees through Company financing of two-thirds the cost of tuition for high school training. But Congress directed the thrust of the Act to the *consequences* of employment practices, not simply the motivation. More than that, Congress has placed on the employer the burden of showing that any given requirement must have a manifest relationship to the employment in question.

The facts of this case demonstrate the inadequacy of broad and general testing devices as well as the infirmity of using diplomas or degrees as fixed measures of capability. History is filled with examples of men and women who rendered highly effective performance without the conventional badges of accomplishment in terms of certificates, diplomas, or degrees. Diplomas and tests are useful servants, but Congress has mandated the commonsense proposition that they are not to become masters of reality.

The Company contends that its general intelligence tests are specifically permitted by §703(h) of the Act. That section authorizes the use of "any professionally developed ability test" that is not "designed, intended *or used* to discriminate because of race. . . ." (Emphasis added.)

The Equal Employment Opportunity Commission, having enforcement responsibility, has issued guidelines interpreting §703(h) to permit only the use of job-related tests. The administrative interpretation of the Act by the enforcing agency is entitled to great deference. See, *e. g., United States* v. *City of Chicago,* 400 U.S. 8 (1970); *Udall* v. *Tallman,* 380 U.S. 1 (1965); *Power Reactor Co.* v. *Electricians,* 367 U.S. 396 (1961). Since the Act and its legislative history support the Commission's construction, this affords good reason to treat the guidelines as expressing the will of Congress.

Section 703(h) was not contained in the House version of the Civil Rights Act but was added in the Senate during extended debate. For a period, debate revolved around claims that the bill as proposed would prohibit all testing and force employers to hire unqualified persons simply because they were part of a group formerly subject to job discrimination. Proponents of Title VII sought throughout the debate to assure the critics that the Act would have no effect on job-related tests. Senators Case of New Jersey and Clark of Pennsylvania, comanagers of the bill on the Senate floor, issued a memorandum explaining that the proposed Title VII "expressly protects the employer's right to insist that any prospective applicant, Negro or white, *must meet the applicable job qualifications.* Indeed, the very purpose of Title VII is to promote hiring on the basis of job qualifications rather than on the basis of race or color." 110 Cong. Rec. 7247. (Emphasis added.) Despite these assurances, Senator Tower of Texas introduced an amendment authorizing "professionally developed ability tests." Proponents of Title VII opposed the amendment because, as written, it would permit an employer to give any test, "whether it was a good test or not, so long as it was professionally designed. Discrimination could actually exist under the guise of compliance with the statute." 110 Cong. Rec. 13504 (remarks of Sen. Case).

The amendment was defeated and two days later Senator Tower offered a substitute amendment which was adopted verbatim and is now the testing provision of §703(h). Speaking for the supporters of Title VII, Senator Humphrey, who had vigorously opposed the first amendment, endorsed the substitute amendment, stating: "Senators on both sides of the aisle who were deeply interested in Title VII have examined the text of this amendment and have found it to be in accord with the intent and purpose of that title." 110 Cong. Rec. 13724. The amendment was then adopted. From the sum of the legislative history relevant in this case, the conclusion is inescapable that the EEOC's construction of §703(h) to require that employment tests be job related comports with congressional intent.

Nothing in the Act precludes the use of testing or measuring procedures; obviously they are useful. What Congress has forbidden is giving these devices and mechanisms controlling force unless they are demonstrably a reasonable measure of job performance. Congress has not commanded that the less qualified be preferred over the better qualified simply because of minority origins. Far from disparaging job qualifications as such, Congress has made such qualifications the controlling factor, so that race, religion, nationality, and sex become irrelevant. What Congress has commanded is that any tests used must measure the person for the job and not the person in the abstract.

The judgment of the Court of Appeals is, as to that portion of the judgment appealed from, reversed.

MR. JUSTICE BRENNAN took no part in the consideration or decision of this case.

NOTES

1. When first enacted, Title VII did not cover educational institutions "with respect to the employment of individuals to perform work connected with the educational activities of such institution[s]." [42 U.S.C. § 2000e-1 (1970)] This exemption was eliminated with the passage of the Equal Employment Opportunities Act of 1972. *See* Pub. L. 92-261.

2. When there is a showing that a neutral employment practice has had an adverse disproportionate impact on a protected group, the employer has the burden of demonstrating the "business necessity" of that practice. Johnson v. Pike Corp. of America, 332 F.Supp. 490, 495 (C.D. Cal. 1971), in considering the legality of a dismissal of a black employee who had an excessive number of wage garnishments, stated:

> Where the discrimination shown results, not from disparate treatment, but from the foreseeable effect of a policy neutral on its face, *Griggs* indicates that under some circumstances the policy may be justified by a showing of "business necessity." Such a showing is an affirmative defense on which the defendant has the burden of proof. In the present case, defendant corporation has argued that Rule 6 is justified on a number of grounds. Specifically, the defendant has argued that the dismissal policy is justified because of the expense and time attendant to responding to attachments and garnishments by various sections of the company's management and clerical staffs, because of the annoyance and time involved in answering letters and telephone calls from its employees' creditors, and, finally, because garnishments result in a loss of efficiency on behalf of the employee whose wages have been garnisheed.

> The exact boundaries and contours of the phrase "business necessity" are still uncertain. The court, in Local 189, United Papermakers and Paperworkers v. United States, *supra*, stated that the policy or practice must be "essential to the safe and efficient operation" of the business. 416 F.2d at 989. In *Griggs*, the Court stated that a permissible practice must be one which can be shown to be "related to job performance" or "measuring job capability."

> If the defendant's justifications of Rule 6 are examined in the light of the Supreme Court's definition of business necessity, they are not sufficient. The sole permissible reason for discriminating against actual or prospective employees involves the individual's capability to perform the job effectively. This approach leaves no room for arguments regarding inconvenience, annoyance or even expense to the employer. While the argument that wage garnishment results in a loss of efficiency by the employee is entitled to consideration, the court cannot correlate wage garnishment with work efficiency. Certainly the argument that an employee whose wages are being partially withheld for the benefit of his creditors will apply himself less enthusiastically to his work is at best only speculative. If he is an unproductive worker, he may

be terminated because he is unproductive, but not for a supposedly casual relationship which has the effect of being racially discriminatory.

It might be argued that *Griggs* should not be followed since the question whether business necessity includes expense and inconvenience to the employer was not presented to the Supreme Court. While there may be in many situations a clear distinction between business necessity relating to job capability and business necessity relating to the employer's expense and inconvenience, it is submitted that the Court in *Griggs* intended the definition therein outlined to be exclusive. The Court liberally construed Title VII in order to implement the congressional directive that members of minority groups be insured equal opportunity in employment. All attempts to depart from this mandate must be carefully scrutinized. The Court has stated that the only permissible reason for tolerating discrimination is "business necessity" which is "related to job performance." The ability of the individual effectively and efficiently to carry out his assigned duties is, therefore, the only justification recognized by the law.

See also Wallace v. Debron Corp., 494 F.2d 674 (8th Cir. 1974), where it was held that the employer must at least prove that its garnishment policy fosters employee productivity and that there is no acceptable alternative that will accomplish that goal equally well with a lesser differential racial impact. [494 F.2d at 677]

3. Some scholars have criticized the application of this rigid business necessity test to cover "pure effects" discrimination cases. In Lopatka, *A 1977 Primer on the Federal Regulation of Employment Discrimination,* 1977 Ill. L.F. 69, 85-86, the author rejected the holdings of *Johnson v. Pike Corp. of America* and *Wallace v. Debron* (see note 2 *supra*) with the following comment:

The courts read the job-relatedness requirement of *Griggs*, which was enunciated as a touchstone for education requirements and employment tests, to mean that an employer may use an increase in efficiency to justify a practice only if the increase was related to the ability of an employee to carry out his assigned duties. Because the employer's administrative expense and inconvenience in responding to garnishments was unrelated to the garnisheed employees' job performance, the courts refused even to consider the employer's administrative expense and inconvenience. Thus, the only argument the courts would consider was that garnishments result in the loss of employee efficiency. One court dismissed this argument as speculative, but the other court remanded the case for a factual determination. The arbitrary refusal of these courts to consider an employee's total productivity, which includes not only his performance on the job but also other costs to his employer, is difficult to justify. If expanded, this approach, for example, might require an employer to subsidize travel costs of minority employees from their urban homes to the employer's suburban plant. . . .

Is this a valid criticism? Can we never ask employers to share some of the costs of securing equal employment opportunity in our society?

4. A widely followed test for determining "business necessity" was delineated by the Fourth Circuit in Robinson v. Lorillard Corp., 444 F.2d 791 (4th Cir. 1971). There it was held that:

The test is whether there exists an overriding legitimate business purpose such that the practice is necessary to the safe and efficient operation of the business. Thus, the business purpose must be sufficiently compelling to override any racial impact; the challenged practice must effectively carry out the business purpose it is alleged to serve; and there must be available no acceptable alternative policies or practices which would better accomplish the business purpose advanced, or accomplish it equally well with a lesser differential racial impact. . . .

5. *Problems.* In light of *Griggs* and the other cases discussed above, how would you answer the following questions?

(a) Can a university refuse to hire a black job applicant as an assistant professor of chemistry because he does not have a Ph.D. where a disproportionate number of blacks in this field do not hold Ph.D.s?

(b) Can a university refuse to hire a woman as an athletic director because it is well known that alumni who financially support the athletic program have a strong bias against women in sports?

(c) Can a university fire a woman athletic director because she is not an effective fund raiser due to the sex bias of the alumni?

6. In Scott v. University of Delaware, 17 FEP Cas. 1486 (1978), a federal district court in Delaware ruled that a university requirement of a Ph.D. degree or its equivalent as a prerequisite for appointment to a professorial position did not violate Title VII, despite the disparate impact of the requirements on blacks. The court indicated that the requirement was justified by the university's legitimate business interest in hiring persons who are most likely to be successful in adding to the fund of knowledge in their chosen disciplines and effective in the teaching of graduate students in those disciplines. The court also indicated that no alternative criterion had been suggested that would serve the business interest as well.

7. Although the *Griggs'* definition of discrimination has been followed in most contexts, the Supreme Court has rejected its application in the area of seniority rights. In Teamsters v. United States, 431 U.S. 324 (1977), the Court construed §703(h) of Title VII to mean that "an otherwise neutral, legitimate seniority system does not become unlawful under Title VII simply because it may perpetuate pre-Act discrimination." The Court found that the employer was guilty of "systematic and purposeful employment discrimination" by limiting blacks and Spanish-surnamed persons to less desirable jobs as "servicemen" or "local city drivers," while reserving most of the better "line driver" (over-the-road) truck driver jobs for whites. This discrimination was furthered by a seniority system which created separate lines of seniority for line drivers and city drivers and provided that any city driver who transferred to line driver had to forfeit all of his seniority credit and start at the bottom of the line driver seniority list.

The holding in *Teamsters* served to overturn an unbroken line of decisions in eight Courts of Appeal that had either held or approved the principle that §703(h) does not immunize seniority systems that perpetuate the effects of prior discrimination. The rationale for these cases was first expressed in Quarles v. Philip Morris, Inc., 279 F.Supp. 505 (E.D. Va. 1968), where it was held that "a departmental seniority system that has its genesis in racial discrimination is not a *bona fide* seniority system" under Title VII. Justice Stewart, writing for the majority in *Teamsters*, distinguished the lower court decisions by concluding that they "rest[ed] upon the proposition that a seniority system that perpetuates the effects of pre-Act discrimination cannot be bona fide *if an intent to discriminate entered into its very adoption."* (emphasis added)

In addition to immunizing seniority systems which perpetuate pre-Act discrimination, the Court also made it clear that:

. . . the operation of seniority system is not unlawful under Title VII even though it perpetuates post-Act discrimination that has not been the subject of a timely charge by the discriminatees. [97 S.Ct. 1843, 1861 n. 30]

The court took this holding directly from United Air Lines v. Evans, 431 U.S. 553 (1977), a case decided on the same day as *Teamsters*. In *Evans*, the plaintiff resigned from her position as flight attendant in 1968 because of the airline's rule against employing married women in her position. She did not file a timely charge with the EEOC and consequently her claim based upon the discriminatory employment policy was barred. When the no-marriage rule was eliminated, the plaintiff was rehired as a new employee, without any seniority credit. The court decided that:

The statute does not foreclose attacks on the current operation of seniority systems which are subject to challenge as discriminatory. But such a challenge to a neutral system may not be predicated on the mere fact that a past event which has no present legal significance has affected the calculation of seniority credit, even if the past event might at one time have justified a valid claim against the employer.

In *Teamsters,* the Court enlarged this holding by making the further observation that:

[In *Teamsters*] the Government has sued to remedy the post-Act discrimination directly, and there is no claim that any relief would be time barred. But this is simply an additional reason not to hold the seniority system unlawful, since such a holding would in no way enlarge the relief to be awarded. . . . Section 703(h) on its face immunizes all bona fide seniority systems, and does not distinguish between the perpetuation of pre- and post-Act discrimination. [431 U.S. at 348 n. 30]

Thus, in *Teamsters,* the Court held that since "the seniority system [at issue] did not have its genesis in racial discrimination, and [since] it was negotiated and . . . maintained free from any illegal purpose," it is protected under § 703(h) even though it perpetuated the effects of both pre-Act and post-Act unlawful discrimination. [431 U.S. at 356]

8. In Fitzpatrick v. Bitzer, 427 U.S. 445 (1976), the Court upheld the 1972 amendment extending coverage of Title VII to state employees (and, consequently, to academicians employed in public institutions of higher education). The Court ruled that Congress had properly acted to protect state government employees from employment discrimination pursuant to Section 5 of the Fourteenth Amendment. In addition, the Court held that the Eleventh Amendment did not bar an award of retroactive retirement benefits and attorneys' fees for individuals who proved that a state retirement system discriminated against them because of their sex. However, the Court noted in passing, that "apart from their claim that the Eleventh Amendment bars enforcement of the remedy established by Title VII . . . respondent state officials do not contend that the substantive provisions of Title VII as applied here are not a proper exercise of congressional authority under § 5 of the Fourteenth Amendment." 427 U.S. at 456 n. 11. It is not clear whether the Court meant to suggest that such an argument might be entertained in the future.

9. For detailed discussion of the procedural requirements of Title VII, *see* Belton, *Title VII of the Civil Rights Act of 1964: A Decade of Private Enforcement and Judicial Developments,* 20 St. Louis Univ. L.J. 225 (1976); and Schlei & Grossman, Employment Discrimination Law, 769-1082 (Washington, D.C.: BNA, Inc., 1976).

V.   Burden of Proof under Title VII

SWEENEY v. BD. OF TRUSTEES
OF KEENE STATE COLLEGE
First Circuit Court of Appeals
569 F.2d 169 (1978)

TUTTLE, Senior Circuit Judge: —

This appeal presents important issues relating to the existence of discrimination against women in the awarding of promotions and the fixing of salaries at Keene State College. Dr. Christine Sweeney, a faculty member in the Department of Education at Keene since 1969, failed twice in her efforts to achieve promotion to the rank of full professor before finally succeeding in 1976. Attributing her earlier failure to sexual bias, she seeks a backdating of her promotion to the date of her first attempt and an accompanying adjustment in her salary for the intervening years. In addition, the plaintiff alleges that sex discrimination accounts for the disparity between the average salaries of males and females on the Keene faculty and claims that she has been paid less than men who carry a substantially equal workload.

Dr. Sweeney has brought suit under Title VII of the 1964 Civil Rights Act, 42 U.S.C. §§2000e et seq. as amended by the Equal Employment Opportunity Act of 1972, Pub. L. No. 92-261, 86 Stat. 103; the Equal Pay Act of 1963, 29 U.S.C. §206(d), as amended by the Education Amendments of 1972, 29 U.S.C. §213(a), Pub. L. No. 92-318, 86 Stat. 235; Title IX of the Education Amendments of 1972, 20 U.S.C. §§1681 et seq.; 42 U.S.C. §1983, and the Fourteenth Amendment to the United States Constitution. Named as defendants are Keene State College, its Board of Trustees, its president, and two former deans.

Following a four-day trial, the United States District Court for the District of New Hampshire ruled against Dr. Sweeney on the Equal Pay, §1983, Fourteenth Amendment, and Title IX counts, but permitted her a partial recovery under Title VII. The district court found that Dr. Sweeney had been a victim of sex discrimination in her second effort to gain promotion and ordered her promotion backdated to 1975, with the appropriate back pay. The court also awarded the plaintiff attorneys' fees and costs of $17,766.56. Although the court specifically found a pattern of sex discrimination against females in hiring, promotion, and salaries, no injunction against further discrimination was issued.

In their appeal, the defendants seek to persuade this Court that the plaintiff's evidence was insufficient to prove a violation of Title VII. . . .

I.

Keene State College, a division of the University of New Hampshire, is a small liberal arts college located in Keene, New Hampshire. Originally dedicated to the training of teachers, it presently grants bachelor's degrees in a variety of other fields as well as a master's degree in education. Dr. Sweeney earned a bachelor of education degree from Keene in 1943, a master of arts from Catholic University in 1956, and a Ph.D. from Catholic University in 1962. She taught at the primary and secondary levels from 1943 until 1960 and served as a graduate assistant at Catholic University in the 1961-62 school year. Appointed an instructor at Catholic University in 1962, Dr. Sweeney remained there until 1966, when she joined the faculty at Emmanuel College as an assistant professor. She was promoted to the rank of associate professor at Emmanuel, effective in the fall of 1968, with an anticipated salary of $9,000, but left that school before the start of the 1968-1969 academic year. In January, 1969 Dr. Sweeney was appointed an associate professor of education at Keene and received $5,000 for the spring semester. Her initial position was supervisor of student teaching, but she has subsequently assumed various other teaching responsibilities in the department of education. In addition to her course load, Dr. Sweeney has served on numerous college and department committees and on the Professional Standards Board for the State Board of Education. This summary of her credentials is by no means exhaustive but suffices to demonstrate that Dr. Sweeney possessed the education and experience typical of college teachers.

From the record it appears that Dr. Sweeney's career at Keene went smoothly until 1971. In the spring of that year, she was selected by a committee within her department to accompany a group of students to England the following fall. The trip was part of a student exchange program developed by the Department of Education, and Dr. Sweeney had been quite active in the program. At the time of the plaintiff's selection a man was selected for a second fall trip and another woman was selected as an alternate. Final approval of the faculty advisors rested with Dean Clarence Davis, and he refused to permit Dr. Sweeney to make the trip, selecting the alternate instead. Although the dean refused to tell the plaintiff his reasons for this decision, he testified at trial that he had acted upon the recommendation of the coordinator of the program, a female, who had advised him that the alternate was better qualified.

Plaintiff attempted to convince the trial court that this decision resulted from sex discrimination by showing that no women have been selected for subsequent trips and that no men have been disapproved. However, the trial court specifically found that the dean's decision rested on factors other than sex discrimination. This fact finding is amply supported by the evidence, because a woman took Dr. Sweeney's slot and the unfavorable recommendation came from a woman. Nevertheless, the incident plays a role in later developments and is mentioned for that reason.

*   *   *

In spite of the England incident, Dr. Sweeney was granted tenure in 1972 with no apparent difficulty. In the 1972-73 academic year, she sought promotion to the rank of full professor, the highest rank in the academic setting.[2] Like many other colleges and universities, Keene employs a peer-review system for screening requests for tenure and promotion. These requests, initiated either by the faculty member or by the department chairman on behalf of the faculty member, are sent to the dean of the college, who, in turn, forwards the matter to the Faculty Evaluations Advisory Committee (FEAC), a five-member panel elected each year by the entire faculty from persons in the highest two academic ranks. The FEAC measures the record and qualifications of the applicant against the standards set forth in the faculty manual [3] and makes a recommendation to the dean either for or against promotion. . . .

If still unsuccessful, an appeal can be taken to the Faculty Appeals Committee (FAC), also composed of elected faculty members. This panel's authority is limited to determining whether due process has been accorded or whether new evidence has been presented. The FAC presents its findings

---

[2.]   The normal progression in academic rank is from instructor to assistant professor, associate professor, and, finally, full professor.

[3.]   The criteria specified in the faculty manual for promotion are teaching effectiveness, scholarly qualifications, service to the college, and community activities. The Faculty Senate has issued guidelines for interpreting these criteria. In addition, a teacher must normally spend a minimum number of years in one rank before ascending to the next level. For promotion to the rank of full professor, the faculty manual calls for four years as an associate professor.

to the college president, who in turn submits any favorable recommendations to the Board of Trustees. The president expressed a reluctance to overturn an FEAC decision unless the FAC found arbitrary or unfair action.

The plaintiff was recommended for promotion by her department and
its chairman, Dr. Paul Blacketor, during the 1972-73 school year. An all-
male FEAC voted unanimously against promotion and Dean Davis concurred.

*   *   *

The plaintiff appealed to the FAC in July 1973, citing the lack of reasons as evidence of unfairness. In a letter to President Leo Redfern eight
months later, the FAC stated that the FEAC had refused to explain its adverse decision and that Dean Davis had declined to discuss his disapproval of
Sweeney for the England trip. Therefore, the committee could not determine whether the trip incident had influenced the FEAC decision. Giving
Dr. Sweeney the benefit of the doubt on the question of unfairness, the FAC
strongly recommended that Dr. Sweeney be considered by the current
(1973-74) FEAC even though she herself had not initiated a new request for
promotion during that academic year because of her pending appeal. The
president declined to permit what he viewed as a short-circuiting of normal
procedures and notified the FAC in April of 1974 of his decision. Shortly
thereafter, Sweeney filed charges of sex discrimination with the New Hampshire Commission of Human Rights and the EEOC.

The plaintiff sought promotion again during the 1974-75 academic
year. A new FEAC, entirely male, voted against her promotion and the dean
once again concurred. This time, however, the dean informed the plaintiff by
letter that the decision was based on her failure to meet the qualifications
enunciated in the faculty manual and he quoted a portion of it to her. [5]

Alleging sex discrimination in her second appeal to the FAC, Dr.
Sweeney submitted additional information to that committee to counter
each of the objections cited by Dean Davis. After examining her case, the
FAC sent a lengthy letter to President Redfern decrying the unprofessional
treatment of the plaintiff and insisting that she be given more detailed reasons for the adverse decision.

As a result of this prodding by the FAC, President Redfern conferred
with Dean Davis and former FEAC members to ascertain the grounds for her
non-promotion. The list of criticisms which the president conveyed to Dr.
Sweeney included allegations that she had narrow, rigid, and old-fashioned
views, tended to personalize professional matters, kept minutes of the graduate faculty meetings which fell below a professional caliber, and emphasized
to her students the importance of maintaining an even height of window
shades in a classroom.

[5.] The dean's letter stated:
       This decision is based upon the evaluation of FEAC which indicates that you have not ful-
       filled the qualifications as stated in the Faculty Manual; namely, that your teaching and re-
       search has [sic] not been "marked by the perspective of maturity and experience, or by some
       creative attribute generally recognizable in the academic world as a special asset to a faculty."

Dr. Sweeney's third try for promotion, during the 1975-76 academic year, was successful. The FEAC, composed of four men and a woman, voted unanimously in her favor only a few months after the plaintiff's meeting with the president. Her promotion was effective July 1, 1976.

At trial, the plaintiff presented statistical evidence to substantiate her claim of sex discrimination. She and other witnesses testified about specific instances of allegedly sex-biased treatment. Experts in the areas of education and sex discrimination were also called to testify. In a lengthy opinion which contains a thorough review of the testimony and exhibits, the district court found that the evidence established a pattern of sex discrimination at Keene State College in hiring, promotion, and salaries. Applying the approach employed by the Supreme Court in McDonnell Douglas Corp. v. Green, 411 U.S. 792, 5 FEP Cases 965 (1973), the district court held that the plaintiff had established a prima facie case of sex discrimination in her second promotion effort in violation of Title VII and that the defendants had not rebutted her evidence. Based on the plaintiff's qualifications, length of time at Keene, and her rapport with her colleagues, the court believed that Dr. Sweeney would not have been promoted in her first try even if she had been a male.

*   *   *

II.

The defendants strenuously argue on appeal that Dr. Sweeney has provided insufficient proof of discriminatory motivation to support a finding of disparate treatment. We recognize that disparate treatment cases, such as this one, differ from disparate impact cases, such as Griggs v. Duke Power Co., 401 U.S. 424, 3 FEP Cases 175 (1971).[8] We also recognize that proof of discriminatory motive is critical in a disparate treatment case. International Brotherhood of Teamsters v. United States, 45 LW 4506, 14 FEP Cases 1514 (U.S. May 31, 1977); McDonnell Douglas Corp. v. Green, 411 U.S. 792, 5 FEP Cases 965 (1973). This is necessarily so because the gist of a disparate treatment claim is that an employee has been treated less favorably than others because of race, color, religion, sex, or national origin. What we

---

[8.]   The distinction between disparate treatment and disparate impact cases was explained by the Supreme Court in International Brotherhood of Teamsters v. United States:

"Disparate treatment" such as alleged in the present case is the most easily understood type of discrimination. The employer simply treats some people less favorably than others because of their race, color, religion, sex, or national origin. *Proof of discriminatory motive is critical, although it can in some situations be inferred from the mere fact of differences in treatment....* Undoubtedly disparate treatment was the most obvious evil Congress had in mind when it enacted Title VII....

Claims of disparate treatment may be distinguished from claims that stress "disparate impact." The latter involves employment practices that are facially neutral in their treatment of different groups but that in fact fall more harshly on one group than another and cannot be justified by business necessity.... Proof of discriminatory motive, we have held, is not required under a disparative impact theory. Compare, e.g., Griggs v. Duke Power Co., 401 U.S. 424, 430-432, 3 FEP Cases 175 with McDonnell Douglas Corp. v. Green, 411 U.S. 792, 802-806, 5 FEP Cases 965, 969-970. 45 LW 4506, 4509 n. 15, 14 FEP Cases 1514, 1519 (U.S. May 31, 1977) (citations omitted) (emphasis added).

reject is an effort by the defendants to elevate the quantum of proof to such a level that a litigant is necessarily doomed to failure.

The Supreme Court has never said that an individual plaintiff seeking to establish a claim of disparate treatment in violation of Title VII must present direct evidence of discriminatory intent. Even in Washington v. Davis, 426 U.S. 220, 12 FEP Cases 1415 (1976), which held that discriminatory intent is an essential element of a claim based upon the equal protection clause of the Fourteenth Amendment, the Supreme Court recognized that circumstantial evidence was one means of proving purposeful discrimination. . . .

Particularly in a college or university setting, where the level of sophistication is likely to be much higher than in other employment situations, direct evidence of sex discrimination will rarely be available. The Congress was no doubt aware of this fact when it extended Title VII to colleges and universities for the first time in 1972. The legislative history contains numerous indications of Congress' concern for the status of women in academia. Statistical evidence presented to the Congress at that time made glaringly clear that "[w]hen they have been hired into educational institutions, particularly in institutions of higher education, women have been relegated to positions of lesser standing than their male counterparts." . . .

Of course, legislative sympathy for the plight of female college teachers does not alleviate Dr. Sweeney's obligation to prove herself the victim of sex discrimination in order to recover under Title VII. In fact, the difficulty of her task is underlined by the lack of cases in which plaintiffs have succeeded in similar challenges to sex discrimination in academia. Admittedly, most if not all of these female plaintiffs have lost. Keyes v. Lenoir Rhyne College, 552 F.2d 579, 15 FEP Cases 925 (4th Cir.), cert. denied, 46 LW 3258, 16 FEP Cases 501 (U.S. Oct. 18, 1977); Faro v. New York University, 502 F.2d 1229, 8 FEP Cases 609 (2d Cir. 1974); Green v. Bd. of Regents of Texas Tech University, 474 F.2d 594, 5 FEP Cases 677 (5th Cir. 1973) (suit under § 1983); Johnson v. University of Pittsburgh, No. 73-120, 15 FEP Cases 1516 (W.D. Pa., dec. Aug. 1, 1977), dissolving preliminary injunction issued in 359 F.Supp. 1002, 5 FEP Cases 1182 (W.D. Pa. 1973); Peters v. Middlebury College, 409 F.Supp. 857, 12 FEP Cases 297 (D. Vt. 1976); Van deVate v. Boling, 379 F.Supp. 925, 12 FEP Cases 17 (E.D. Tenn. 1974). Whether the evidence presented in these cases fell significantly short of the evidence in this case we do not know. However, we voice misgivings over one theme recurrent in those opinions: the notion that courts should keep "hands off" the salary, promotion, and hiring decisions of colleges and universities. This reluctance no doubt arises from the courts' recognition that hiring, promotion, and tenure decisions require subjective evaluation most appropriately made by persons thoroughly familiar with the academic setting. Nevertheless, we caution against permitting judicial deference to result in judicial abdication of a responsibility entrusted to the courts by Congress. That responsibility is simply to provide a forum for the litigation of complaints of sex discrimination in institutions of higher learning as readily as for other Title VII suits.

A.

It is clear from McDonnell Douglas Corp. v. Green, 411 U.S. 792, 5 FEP Cases 965 (1973), and International Brotherhood of Teamsters v. United States, 45 LW 4506, 14 FEP Cases 2514 (U.S. May 31, 1977), that an individual plaintiff who alleges disparate treatment because of her sex must prove that her unfavorable treatment was sexually premised. Both of those cases explore the nature of proof and the allocation of the burden of proof in cases alleging disparate treatment. Neither requires *direct* proof of discriminatory motive. . . .

The quantum of proof sufficient to constitute a prima facie case cannot be expressed in any general rule. In McDonnell Douglas, where the plaintiff alleged that racial discrimination motivated his employer's refusal to rehire him after he had participated in an illegal stall-in, the Supreme Court found that a prima facie case had been made out by the plaintiff's showing that he belonged to a racial minority, that he was a qualified applicant for an existing job opening, that he was rejected despite his qualifications, and that the employer continued to seek applicants of his qualifications for the job opening after his rejection. 411 U.S. at 802, 5 FEP Cases at 969. These requirements do not impress us as imposing a very arduous burden upon a plaintiff. . . .

A combination of statistics and specific instances of discrimination provided sufficient evidence of discrimination in Teamsters. . . .

B.

Dr. Sweeney clearly showed that she was a member of a protected class within Title VII, that she was qualified for promotion,[18] that she was rejected, and that others of her qualifications were promoted. She went further and presented statistical evidence which supports an inference of sex bias in promotion decisions. Most persuasive of the statistics was the fact that only four women in the entire history of Keene State College have achieved the rank of full professor. There have never been more than two women professors in any given academic year and this has occurred in only two years since 1968. In all other years since 1968, only one woman occupied the top rank. In contrast, the number of male professors has gone from ten in 1969-70 to 23 in 1975-76. A similarly striking discrepancy exists in the rank of associate professor. There were only three female associates in 1969-70 and six in 1975-76, while the males in that rank numbered 17 in 1969-70 and 35 in 1975-76. While women represent approximately 20% of the faculty, a figure which compares fairly favorably with the percentage of

---

[18.] The very fact of Dr. Sweeney's ultimate promotion demonstrates that she was qualified for promotion. The record does not reveal any significant change in her credentials from 1973 to 1976, although she did become more active in Keene's reading program. Because the plaintiff carried this insignia of collegiate approval into her trial, the district court was not required to serve as super-FEAC in passing upon her qualifications. Furthermore, several witnesses testified that Dr. Sweeney was qualified for promotion as early as 1973.

women in the applicable labor pool, males held slightly more than 90% of
the full professor slots in 1969-70 and 92% in 1975-76. In fact, there have
been more male professors than male instructors every year since 1969-70,
despite the defendants' insistence that entry to the top rank is a significant
achievement reserved for the excellent few.

In spite of their overall percentage on the faculty, women presently
outnumber men in the instructor level. While many of the women in these
lower levels may be new faculty members, that still does not account for the
striking imbalance in the upper ranks. Moreover, the evidence showed that
while men had been appointed to the faculty as full professors on many occasions since 1969, no woman has ever been appointed initially above the
rank of associate professor. This fact supports the district court's finding of
a pattern of discriminatory hiring. Dr. Sweeney also showed that no female
has ever been promoted to the highest rank without a terminal degree, while
several male professors do not possess such a degree. This statistical evidence
supports the district court's finding that a double standard was applied in
promotion decisions. The evidence also showed that women were underrepresented in the English, Art, History, Biology, Psychology and Industrial
Education Departments.

The defendant attempted to rebut these statistics by pointing to highly
qualified men who remained in the lower ranks longer than Dr. Sweeney.
While this evidence is informative, the district court was not required to find
that it totally dispelled the inference of discrimination created by the other
statistics. Likewise, evidence of males who failed to be promoted on their
first try does not necessarily rebut the inference of the plaintiff's more
striking statistics. At best, these tales of individual males' struggles account
for the district court's conclusion that Dr. Sweeney would not have achieved
promotion in her first effort even if she had been a male. It is true that the
defendants were able to find instances where an individual male of superior
qualifications encountered difficulties in reaching the level of professor. But
these examples were countered by other situations where females fared
worse. In short, the plaintiff did not prove the existence of a completely
consistent pattern, but she offered sufficient evidence to sustain the district
court's findings. . . .

In addition to statistical evidence, Dr. Sweeney presented testimony
concerning other instances from which sex discrimination could be inferred.[20] An important part of her case centered around the ineffectiveness
of Keene's affirmative action effort. Although a faculty committee drafted
an affirmative action plan in 1973, no such plan was officially adopted until
1976. . . . Moreover, the testimony reveals that the person who nominally
served as affirmative action coordinator did virtually nothing to advance the

---

[20.] Some parts of this evidence were less persuasive than others. For example, the references to
women as "girls" in some personnel files and the existence of a distaff club open to faculty
wives and female faculty members may be indicative of outdated thinking but would hardly,
without more, prove a case.

rights of women on the Keene campus. He admitted as much in his own testimony.

Certainly the most striking evidence presented in this context concerned the affirmative action coordinator's response to Dr. Sweeney's filing of charges with the State Human Rights Commission. Not only did he attempt to get the plaintiff to answer the interrogatories sent to Keene by the Human Rights Commission, a measure which cannot be condoned, he also wrote to the president of Smith College for information on how that school had responded to a charge of sex discrimination because he was "concerned that that form of anarchy may creep north into our virgin territory.". . .

From our careful review of all the evidence we conclude that the trial court's finding that sex discrimination impeded the plaintiff's second promotion effort was not clearly erroneous.

With regard to the court's finding against the plaintiff on the issue of salary discrimination, we likewise hold that the fact-findings were not clearly erroneous.

BOARD OF TRUSTEES OF KEENE STATE COLLEGE v. SWEENEY
Supreme Court of the United States
47 U.S.L.W. 3330
18 FEP Cas. 520 (1978)

PER CURIAM:—The petition for a writ of certiorari is granted. In Furnco Construction Corp. v. Waters, 438 U.S.——, 17 FEP Cases 1062 (June 29, 1978), we stated that "[t]o dispel the adverse inference from a prima facie showing under McDonnell Douglas, the employer need only 'articulate some legitimate, nondiscriminatory reason for the employee's rejection.'" Id., at ——, 17 FEP Cases, at 1066 (slip op., at 10), quoting McDonnell Douglas Corp. v. Green, 411 U.S. 792, 802, 5 FEP Cases 965, 969 (1973). We stated in McDonnell Douglas, supra, that the plaintiff "must . . . be afforded a fair opportunity to show that [the employer's] stated reason for [the plaintiff's] rejection was in fact pretext." 411 U.S. at 804, 5 FEP Cases, at 970. The Court of Appeals in the present case, however, referring to McDonnell Douglas, supra, stated that "in requiring the defendant to *prove absence of discriminatory motive*, the Supreme Court placed the burden squarely on the party with the greater access to such evidence." Sweeney v. Board of Trustees of Keene State College, 569 F.2d 169, 177, 16 FEP Cases 378, 384 (CA1 1978) (emphasis added).[1]

[1.]   While the Court of Appeals did make the statement that the dissent quotes, post. at 2, 18 FEP Cases, at 522, it also made the statement quoted in the text above. These statements simply contradict one another. The statement quoted in the text above would make entirely superfluous the third step in the Furnco – McDonnell Douglas analysis, since it would place on the employer at the second stage the burden of showing that the reason for rejection was not a pretext, rather than requiring such proof from the employee as a part of the third step. We think our remand is warranted both because we are unable to determine which of the two conflicting standards the Court of Appeals applied in reviewing the decision of the District Court in this case, and because of the implication in its opinion that there is no difference between the two standards. We of course intimate no view as to the correct result if the proper test is applied in this case.

While words such as "articulate," "show," and "prove," may have more or less similar meanings depending upon the context in which they are used, we think that there is a significant distinction between merely "articulat[ing] some legitimate, nondiscriminatory reason" and "prov[ing] absence of discriminatory motive." By reaffirming and emphasizing the McDonnell Douglas analysis in Furnco Construction Corp. v. Waters, supra, we made it clear that the former will suffice to meet the employee's prima facie case of discrimination. Because the Court of Appeals appears to have imposed a heavier burden on the employer than Furnco warrants, its judgment is vacated and the case is remanded for reconsideration in the light of Furnco, supra, at —, 17 FEP Cases, at 1066 (slip. op., at 10).[2]

MR. JUSTICE STEVENS, with whom MR. JUSTICE BRENNAN, MR. JUSTICE STEWART, and MR. JUSTICE MARSHALL join, dissenting.

Whenever this Court grants certiorari and vacates a Court of Appeals judgment in order to allow that court to reconsider its decision in the light of an intervening decision of this Court, the Court is acting on the merits. Such action always imposes an additional burden on Circuit Judges who—more than any other segment of the Federal Judiciary—are struggling desperately to keep afloat in the flood of federal litigation. For that reason, such action should not be taken unless the intervening decision has shed new light on the law which, if it had been available at the time of the Court of Appeals' decision, might have led to a different result.

In this case, the Court's action implies that the recent opinion in Furnco Construction Corp. v. Waters, 438 U.S. ——, 17 FEP Cases 1062 (June 29, 1978), made some change in the law as explained in McDonnell Douglas Corp. v. Greene, 411 U.S. 792 5 FEP Cases 965. When I joined the Furnco opinion, I detected no such change and I am still unable to discern one. In both cases, the Court clearly stated that when the complainant in a Title VII trial establishes a prima facie case of discrimination, "the burden which shifts to the employer is merely that of proving that he based his employment decision on a legitimate consideration, and not an illegitimate one such as race." [1]

[2.] We quite agree with the dissent that under Furnco and McDonnell Douglas the employer's burden is satisfied if he simply "explains what he has done" or "produc[es] evidence of legitimate nondiscriminatory reasons." Post. at 4, 18 FEP Cases, at 522. But petitioners clearly did produce evidence to support their legitimate nondiscriminatory explanation for refusing to promote respondent during the years in question. See 569 F.2d 172-173, 178, 16 FEP Cases 380-381, 385; Pet. for Cert. B-2 to B-24. Nonetheless, the Court of Appeals held that petitioners had not met their burden because the proffered legitimate explanation did not "rebut" or "disprove" respondent's prima facie case or "prove absence of nondiscriminatory motive." 569 F.2d at 177-179, 16 FEP Cases, at 384-385; see Pet. for Cert. B-25. This holding by the Court of Appeals is further support for our belief that the court appears to have imposed a heavier burden on the employer than Furnco, and the dissent here, requires.

[1.] This language is quoted from the following paragraph in Furnco:
"When the prima facie case is understood in the light of the opinion in McDonnell Douglas, it is apparent that the burden which shifts to the employer is merely that of proving that he based his employment decision on a legitimate consideration, and not an illegitimate one such

The Court of Appeals' statement of the parties' respective burdens in this case is wholly faithful to this Court's teachings in McDonnell Douglas. The Court of Appeals here stated:
"As we understand those cases [McDonnell Douglas and International Brotherhood of Teamsters, 431 U.S. 324, 14 FEP Cases 1514), a plaintiff bears the initial burden of presenting evidence sufficient to establish a prima facie case of discrimination. *The burden then shifts to the defendant to rebut the prima facie case by showing that a legitimate, non-discriminatory reason accounted for its actions.* If the rebuttal is successful, the plaintiff must show that the stated reason was a mere pretext for discrimination. *The ultimate burden of persuasion on the issue of discrimination remains with the plaintiff who must convince the court by a preponderance of the evidence that he or she has been the victim of discrimination.*" Sweeney v. Board of Trustees of Keene State College, 569 F.2d 169, 177, 16 FEP Cases 378, 384 (CA1 1978) (emphasis added). This statement by the Court of Appeals virtually parrots this Court's statements in McDonnell Douglas and Furnco. Nonetheless this Court vacates the judgment on the ground that "the Court of Appeals appears to have imposed a heavier burden on the employer than Furnco warrants." Post, at 2, 18 FEP Cases, at 521. As its sole basis for this conclusion, this Court relies on a distinction drawn for the first time in this case "between merely 'articulat[ing] some legitimate, nondiscriminatory reason' and 'prov[ing] absence of discriminatory motive.'" Post, at 2, 18 FEP Cases, at 521. [2] This novel distinction has two parts, both of which are illusory and unequivocally rejected in Furnco itself.

---

as race. To prove that, he need not prove that he pursued the course which would both enable him to achieve his own business goal *and* allow him to consider the *most* employment applications. Title VII forbids him from having as a goal a work force selected by any proscribed discriminatory practice, but it does not impose a duty to adopt a hiring procedure that maximizes hiring of minority employees. To dispel the adverse inference from a prima facie showing under McDonnell Douglas, the employer need only articulate some legitimate nondiscriminatory reason for the employee's rejection." 438 U.S., at ——, 17 FEP Cases, at 1066 (emphasis in original).

The comparable passage in McDonnell Douglas reads as follows:

"The burden then must shift to the employer to articulate some legitimate, nondiscriminatory reason for the employee's rejection. We need not attempt in the instant case to detail every matter which fairly could be recognized as a reasonable basis for a refusal to hire. Here petitioner has assigned respondent's participation in unlawful conduct against it as the cause for his rejection. We think that this suffices to discharge petitioner's burden of proof at this stage and to meet respondent's prima facie case of discrimination." 411 U.S., at 802-803, 5 FEP Cases, at 969.

[2.]   The Court also suggests that "further support" for its decision is derived from the Court of Appeals' "holding" that "respondent had not met its burden because the proffered legitimate explanation did not 'rebut' or 'disprove' petitioners prima facie case . . . 569 F.2d, at 177-179, 16 FEP Cases, at 384, 385," Post, at 2 n. 2, 18 FEP Cases, at 521. The actual "holding" of the Court of Appeals was that "the trial court's finding that sex discrimination impeded the plaintiff's second promotion was not clearly erroneous." 569 F.2d, at 179. 16 FEP Cases, at 386. The Court of Appeals reached this conclusion by considering all of the evidence presented by both parties to determine whether the evidence of discrimination offered by the plaintiff was "sufficient to sustain the district court's finding" in light of the counter evidence offered by the employer. Ibid. Such factual determinations by two federal courts are entitled to a strong presumption of validity.

First is a purported difference between "articulating" and "proving" a legitimate motivation. Second is the difference between affirming a nondiscriminatory motive and negating a discriminatory motive.

With respect to the first point, it must be noted that it was this Court in Furnco, not the Court of Appeals in this case, that stated that the employer's burden was to "*prov[e]* that he based his employment decision on a legitimate consideration." [3] Indeed, in the paragraph of this Court's opinion in Furnco cited earlier, the words "prove" and "articulate" were used interchangeably, and properly so. For they were descriptive of the defendant's burden in a trial context. In litigation the only way a defendant can "articulate" the reason for his action is by adducing evidence that explains what he has done; when an executive takes the witness stand to "articulate" his reason, the litigant for whom he speaks is thereby proving those reasons. If the Court intends to authorize a method of articulating a factual defense without proof, surely the Court should explain what it is.

The second part of the Court's imaginative distinction is also rejected by Furnco. When an employer shows that a legitimate nondiscriminatory reason accounts for his action, he is simultaneously demonstrating that the action was not motivated by an illegitimate factor such as race. Furnco explicitly recognized this equivalence when it defined the burden on the employer as "that of proving that he based his employment decision on a legitimate consideration, and not an illegitimate one such as race." Whether the issue is phrased in the affirmative or in the negative, the ultimate question involves an identification of the real reason for the employment decision. On that question—as all of these cases make perfectly clear—it is only the burden of producing evidence of legitimate nondiscriminatory reasons which shifts to the employer; the burden of persuasion, as the Court of Appeals properly recognized, remains with the plaintiff.

In short, there is no legitimate basis for concluding that the Court of Appeals erred in this case—either with or without the benefit of Furnco. The Court's action today therefore needlessly imposes additional work on Circuit Judges who have already considered and correctly applied the rule the Court directs them to reconsider and reapply.

NOTES

1. How should *Sweeney* be decided on remand? Is the Supreme Court decision in *Sweeney* faithful to the Court's earlier decision in *Griggs* and *McDonnell Douglas*? (The Court's opinions in *McDonnell Douglas* and *Furnco Construction Co.* are discussed herein below in Note 3.)

2. *The Academic Abstention Doctrine.* Paaintiffs have rarely succeeded in persuading federal courts that they were discriminated against by institutions of higher education be-

---

[3.]   438 U.S., at ___ , 17 FEP Cases, at 1066 (emphasis added). Quoted in n. 1, supra. It should also be noted that the Court of Appeals did not state that the petitioner's burden here was to "prove" anything; rather, the burden which shifted to the defendants was to "show" a legitimate reason for its action.

cause of their sex, race, religion or national origin. This is partially a consequence of the judiciary's deferential attitude toward academic employment. In Faro v. New York University, 502 F.2d 1229, 1231-32 (2d Cir. 1974), the court stated:

> Of all fields, which the federal courts should hesitate to invade and take over, education and faculty appointments at a University level are probably the least suited for federal court supervision. Dr. Faro would remove any subjective judgments by her faculty colleagues in the decision-making process by having the courts examine "the university's recruitment, compensation, promotion and termination and by analyzing the way these procedures are applied to the claimant personally' (Applts' Br., p. 26). All this information she would obtain through extensive discovery, either by the EEOC or the litigant herself. This argument might well lend itself to a *reductio ad absurdum* rebuttal. Such a procedure, in effect, would require a faculty committee charged with recommending or withholding advancements or tenure appointments to subject itself to court inquiry at the behest of disgruntled candidates as to why the unsuccessful was not as well qualified as the successful. This decision would then be passed on by a Court of Appeals or even the Supreme Court.

In a subsequent opinion, in Powell v. Syracuse Univ., 47 U.S.L.W. 2094 (2d Cir. 1978), Judge Smith observed that:

> This anti-interventionist policy has rendered universities virtually immune to charges of employment bias, at least when that bias is not expressed overtly. The court fears, however, that the common-sense position taken in Faro, namely that courts must be ever-mindful of relative institutional competences, has been pressed beyond all reasonable limits, and may be employed to undercut the explicit legislative intent of Title VII.
>
> The Equal Employment Opportunity Act of 1972 amended Title VII to bring educational institutions within the Act's purview. The legislative history of the amendment clearly evidences Congress' particular concern for the problem of employment bias in an academic setting. It might be said that far from taking an anti-interventionist position, Congress has instructed courts to be particularly sensitive to evidence of academic bias. Accordingly, while the court remains mindful of the undesirability of judicial attempts to second-guess the professional judgments of faculty peers, it agrees with the First Circuit when it cautioned "against permitting judicial deference to result in judicial abdication of a responsibility entrusted to the courts by Congress.

However, in a separate concurring opinion, Judge Moore argued that:

> Any court reluctance to interfere with the decision-making process of universities does not come from an interest in promoting discrimination. Rather, such reluctance reflects the courts' inability to perform a discriminating analysis of the qualifications of each candidate for hiring or advancement, taking into consideration his or her educational experience, the specifications of the particular position, and the personality of the candidate. Courts have not abdicated their responsibility to uphold the Equal Employment Opportunity Act of 1972. Instead, they have indicated the difficulty faced by courts in attempting to evaluate the ability of a faculty member. This difficulty has done no more than create a justified reluctance among the courts to override the rational and well-considered judgment of those possessing expertise in the field. If this court took a "common sense position" in Faro— and there is no good reason here presented to abandon this approach—it appears to have the support of many other courts.

Which view is more sound?

The Court in Green v. Board of Regents, 335 F.Supp. 249 (N.D. Tex. 1971), *aff'd* 474 F.2d 594 (5th Cir. 1973), adopted a similar position when it asserted that the evaluation of professors for promotion is "necessarily judgmental" and refused to "substitute its judgment for the rational and well-considered judgment of those possessing expertise in the field."

3. The Supreme Court's decision in McDonnell Douglas Corp. v. Green, 411 U.S. 792 (1973), sets forth the basic tests with respect to the burden of proof in Title VII cases brought by individual complainants. The complainant in *McDonnell Douglas Corp.* was employed by the defendant as a mechanic and laboratory technician until he was laid off in the course of a reduction of the work force. Green protested that his discharge was racially motivated and participated in an action which resulted in the illegal blocking of access to the defendant's plant. When the corporation later advertised for mechanics, Green applied for a position but was rejected. Upon review of the case, the Supreme Court stated:

> In this case respondent, the complainant below, charges that he was denied employment "because of his involvement in civil rights activities" and "because of his race and color." Petitioner denied discrimination of any kind, asserting that its failure to re-employ respondent was based upon and justified by his participation in the unlawful conduct against it. Thus, the issue at the trial on remand is framed by those opposing factual contentions. The two opinions of the Court of Appeals and the several opinions of the three judges of the court attempted, with a notable lack of harmony, to state the applicable rules as to burden of proof and how this shifts upon the making of a prima facie case. We now address this problem.
>
> The complainant in a Title VII trial must carry the initial burden under the statute of establishing a prima facie case of racial discrimination. This may be done by showing (i) that he belongs to a racial minority; (ii) that he applied and was qualified for a job for which the employer was seeking applicants; (iii) that, despite his qualifications, he was rejected; and (iv) that, after his rejection, the position remained open and the employer continued to seek applicants from persons of complainant's qualifications. In the instant case, we agree with the Court of Appeals that respondent proved a prima facie case. . . . Petitioner sought mechanics, respondent's trade, and continued to do so after respondent's rejection. Petitioner, moreover, does not dispute respondent's qualifications and acknowledges that his past work performance in petitioner's employ was "satisfactory."
>
> The burden then must shift to the employer to articulate some legitimate, nondiscriminatory reason for respondent's rejection. We need not attempt in the instant case to detail every matter which fairly could be recognized as a reasonable basis for a refusal to hire. Here petitioner has assigned respondent's participation in unlawful conduct against it as the cause for his rejection. We think that this suffices to discharge petitioner's burden of proof at this stage and to meet respondent's prima facie case of discrimination. . . .
>
> Petitioner's reason for rejection thus suffices to meet the prima facie case, but the inquiry must not end here. While Title VII does not, without more, compel rehiring of respondent, neither does it permit petitioner to use respondent's conduct as a pretext for the sort of discrimination prohibited by § 703(a)(1). On remand, respondent must, as the Court of Appeals recognized, be afforded a fair opportunity to show that petitioner's stated reason for respondent's rejection was in fact pretextual. Especially relevant to such a showing would be evidence that white employees involved in acts against petitioner of comparable seriousness to the "stall-in" were nevertheless retained or rehired. Petitioner may justifiably refuse to rehire one who was engaged in unlawful, disruptive acts against it, but only if this criterion is applied alike to members of all races.

Other evidence that may be relevant to any showing of pretextuality includes facts as to the petitioner's treatment of respondent during his prior term of employment, petitioner's reaction, if any, to respondent's legitimate civil rights activities, and petitioner's general policy and practice with respect to minority employment. On the latter point, statistics as to petitioner's employment policy and practice may be helpful to a determination of whether petitioner's refusal to rehire respondent in this case conformed to a general pattern of discrimination against blacks. Jones v. Lee Way Motor Freight, Inc., 421 F.2d 245 (10th Cir. 1970); Blumrosen, Strangers in Paradise: Griggs v. Duke Power Co., and the Concept of Employment Discrimination, 71 Mich. L. Rev. 59, 91-94 (1972). In short, on the retrial respondent must be given a full and fair opportunity to demonstrate by competent evidence that the presumptively valid reasons for his rejection were in fact a coverup for a racially discriminatory decision.

As noted by the Supreme Court's decision in *Sweeney, supra*, the basic tests concerning the burden of proof in an employment discrimination case were further amplified in Furnco Construction Corp. v. Waters, 17 FEP Cas. 1062 (1978). In *Furnco*, the Court considered what evidence was necessary in order to establish unlawful discrimination under Title VII. In *Furnco*, the employers' superintendent, who had the responsibility for hiring bricklayers needed for a particular steel mill job, hired from a list of bricklayers known to him to be experienced and qualified and he also hired other experienced bricklayers recommended by Company officials and by a black employee. No hiring was done at the job site. Although the Court unanimously held that three plaintiffs who had unsuccessfully sought employment at the job site had made out a prima facie case of discrimination (due to proven disparate treatment), the question remained as to how the employer could overcome the inference of discrimination. On this latter point, the Court ruled that the employer should have at least been given an opportunity to show "some legitimate nondiscriminatory reason" for the rejection of the minority applicants. Most noteworthy was the Court's holding that Title VII does not impose any duty on an employer to adopt a hiring procedure that maximizes hiring of minority applicants. In commenting on *Furnco*, Professor Raymond Goetz, in *Labor Law Decisions of the Supreme Court, 1977-78 Term,* 98 L.R.R. 325 (BNA, Inc., August 21, 1978), observed that:

One of the things that made this case unusual was the existence of a voluntary affirmative action program that had resulted in hiring a number of blacks about triple their representation in the area labor force. Such a successful effort to hire qualified black bricklayers might be expected to overcome the presumption that the refusal to hire at the gate was racially motivated, a crucial factor in disparate treatment such as this. Though not conclusive, it is objective evidence to support the contention that the real motive for turning down applications at the gate was the business purpose of obtaining a highly-qualified work force as efficiently as possible. Yet, the net effect of the company's procedure was that while certain black bricklayers benefitted from it, others were disadvantaged. As Justice Rehnquist noted, Title VII is designed to provide an equal employment opportunity for *each* applicant without regard to whether members of the applicant's race are already proportionately represented in the work force.

4. In higher education discrimination cases, the issue of qualifications is the most troublesome. Unlike industrial employment, where requisite skills are often objectively measurable, academic employment usually depends upon vague and subjective standards. *See, e.g.,* Green v. Board of Regents, 335 F.Supp. 249, 250 (N.D. Tex. 1971), *aff'd* 474 F.2d 594 (5th Cir. 1973) ("(a) teaching ability, (b) publications and scholarly activity, and (c) service to the community and to the University"); E.E.O.C. v. Tufts Institution of Learning, 421 F.Supp. 152, 160 (D. Mass. 1975) ("quality of mind, intellectual force,

scholarship, teaching effectiveness, and contributions to departmental objectives and those of the whole University.") The court's response in *Tufts Institution of Learning* to the problem of assessing qualifications in academe represents the views of many judges:

> In applying the criteria for academic advancement, the weighing of the factors properly to be considered can seldom, if ever, be reduced to measurements by mechanical processes or standardized tests. In the absence of specific standards in the Act or under the regulations, the criteria and procedures established by a university . . . are controlling. Thus where the criteria are reasonably related to the professional duties of the academic position sought and to the personal qualifications of the applicant, and are applied through prescribed or settled procedures fairly and reasonably followed, the court should not substitute its judgment for that of the university authorities.

Does this "rational relationship" test follow *Griggs v. Duke Power Co.*?

5. Academic employment criteria are particularly susceptible to covert unlawful discrimination. In Mecklenburg v. Montana State Board of Regents of Higher Education, 13 EPD Par. 11,438, it was held that the defendant had violated Title VII in its treatment of women faculty members. An important element of the proof was that

> promotional decisions . . . reflect the defendant's implementation of a non-standardized merit system. There are a great number of variables which those in the promotion review process are allowed to consider. In addition, the various academic departments at the university may weigh these factors differently. Thus, those who play a role in the promotion process may apply a number of vague and subjective standards, and there are no safeguards in the procedures to avert sex discriminatory practices.

But see: Poddar v. Youngstown State Univ., 480 F.2d 192 (6th Cir. 1973); Van De Vate v. Boling, 379 F.Supp. 925 (E.D. Tenn. 1974).

VI. Use of Statistical Evidence as Proof of Discrimination

HAZELWOOD SCHOOL DISTRICT v. UNITED STATES
Supreme Court of the United States
97 S. Ct. 2736 (1977)

MR. JUSTICE STEWART delivered the opinion of the Court.

The petitioner Hazelwood School District covers 78 square miles in the northern part of St. Louis County, Mo. In 1973 the Attorney General brought this lawsuit against Hazelwood and various of its officials, alleging that they were engaged in a "pattern or practice" of employment discrimination in violation of Title VII of the Civil Rights Act of 1964, as amended, 42 U.S.C. § 2000e *et seq.* (1970 & Supp. V). The complaint asked for an injunction requiring Hazelwood to cease its discriminatory practices, to take affirmative steps to obtain qualified Negro faculty members, and to offer employment and give backpay to victims of past illegal discrimination.

Hazelwood was formed from 13 rural school districts between 1949 and 1951 by a process of annexation. By the 1967-1968 school year, 17,550 students were enrolled in the district, of whom only 59 were Negro; the number of Negro pupils increased to 576 of 25,166 in 1972-1973, a total of just over 2%.

From the beginning, Hazelwood followed relatively unstructured procedures in hiring its teachers. Every person requesting an application for a teaching position was sent one, and completed applications were submitted to a central personnel office, where they were kept on file. During the early 1960s the personnel office notified all applicants whenever a teaching position became available, but as the number of applications on file increased in the late 1960s and early 1970s, this practice was no longer considered feasible. The personnel office thus began the practice of selecting anywhere from three to 10 applicants for interviews at the school where the vacancy existed. The personnel office did not substantively screen the applicants in determining which of them to send for interviews, other than to ascertain that each applicant, if selected, would be eligible for state certification by the time he began the job. Generally, those who had most recently submitted applications were most likely to be chosen for interviews.

Interviews were conducted by a department chairman, program coordinator, or the principal at the school where the teaching vacancy existed. Although those conducting the interviews did fill out forms rating the applicants in a number of respects, it is undisputed that each school principal possessed virtually unlimited discretion in hiring teachers for his school. The only general guidance given to the principals was to hire the "most competent" person available, and such intangibles as "personality, disposition, appearance, poise, voice, articulation, and ability to deal with people" counted heavily. The principal's choice was routinely honored by Hazelwood's superintendent and Board of Education.

In the early 1960s Hazelwood found it necessary to recruit new teachers, and for that purpose members of its staff visited a number of colleges and universities in Missouri and bordering States. All the institutions visited were predominantly white, and Hazelwood did not seriously recruit at either of the two predominantly Negro four-year colleges in Missouri. As a buyer's market began to develop for public school teachers, Hazelwood curtailed its recruiting efforts. For the 1971-1972 school year, 3,127 persons applied for only 234 teaching vacancies; for the 1972-1973 school year, there were 2,373 applications for 282 vacancies. A number of the applicants who were not hired were Negroes.[5]

Hazelwood hired its first Negro teacher in 1969. The number of Negro faculty members gradually increased in successive years; six of 957 in the 1970 school year; 16 of 1,107 by the end of the 1972 school year; 22 of 1,231 in the 1973 school year. By comparison, according to 1970 census figures, of more than 19,000 teachers employed in that year in the St. Louis area, 15.4% were Negro. That percentage figure included the St. Louis City School District, which in recent years has followed a policy of attempting to maintain a 50% Negro teaching staff. Apart from that school district, 5.7% of the teachers in the county were Negro in 1970.

Drawing upon these historic facts, the Government mounted its "pattern or practice" attack in the District Court upon four different fronts. It adduced evidence of (1) a history of alleged racially discriminatory practices, (2) statistical disparities in hiring, (3) the standardless and largely subjective hiring procedures, and (4) specific instances of alleged discrimination against 55 unsuccessful Negro applicants for teaching jobs. Hazelwood offered

---

[5.]   The parties disagree whether it is possible to determine from the present record exactly how many of the job applicants in each of the school years were Negroes.

virtually no additional evidence in response, relying instead on evidence introduced by the Government, perceived deficiencies in the Government's case, and its own officially promulgated policy "to hire all teachers on the basis of training, preparation and recommendations, regardless of race, color or creed." [6]

The District Court ruled that the Government had failed to establish a pattern or practice of discrimination. The court was unpersuaded by the alleged history of discrimination, noting that no dual school system had ever existed in Hazelwood. The statistics showing that relatively small numbers of Negroes were employed as teachers were found nonprobative, on the ground that the percentage of Negro pupils in Hazelwood was similarly small. The court found nothing illegal or suspect in the teacher hiring procedures that Hazelwood had followed. Finally, the court reviewed the evidence in the 55 cases of alleged individual discrimination, and after stating that the burden of proving intentional discrimination was on the Government, it found that this burden had not been sustained in a single instance. Hence, the court entered judgment for the defendants. . . .

The Court of Appeals for the Eighth Circuit reversed. After suggesting that the District Court had assigned inadequate weight to evidence of discriminatory conduct on the part of Hazelwood before the effective date of Title VII, the Court of Appeals rejected the trial court's analysis of the statistical data as resting on an irrelevant comparison of Negro teachers to Negro pupils in Hazelwood. The proper comparison, in the appellate court's view, was one between Negro teachers in Hazelwood and Negro teachers in the relevant labor market area. Selecting St. Louis County and St. Louis City as the relevant area, the Court of Appeals compared the 1970 census figures, showing that 15.4% of teachers in that area were Negro, to the racial composition of Hazelwood's teaching staff. In the 1972-1973 and 1973-1974 school years, only 1.4% and 1.8%, respectively, of Hazelwood's teachers were Negroes. This statistical disparity, particularly when viewed against the background of the teacher hiring procedures that Hazelwood had followed, was held to constitute a prima facie case of a pattern or practice of racial discrimination.

In addition, the Court of Appeals reasoned that the trial court had erred in failing to measure the 55 instances in which Negro applicants were denied jobs against the four-part standard for establishing a prima facie case of individual discrimination set out in this Court's opinion in *McDonnell Douglas Corp. v. Green*, 411 U.S. 792, 802, 93 S.Ct. 1817, 1824, 36 L.Ed.2d 668. Applying that standard, the appellate court found 16 cases of individual discrimination, which "buttressed" the statistical proof. Because Hazelwood had not rebutted the Government's prima facie case of a pattern or practice

---

[6.] The defendants offered only one witness, who testified to the total number of teachers who had applied and were hired for jobs in the 1971-1972 and 1972-1973 school years. They introduced several exhibits consisting of a policy manual, policy book, staff handbook, and historical summary of Hazelwood's formation and relatively brief existence.

of racial discrimination, the Court of Appeals directed judgment for the Government and prescribed the remedial order to be entered.

The petitioners primarily attack the judgment of the Court of Appeals for its reliance on "undifferentiated work force statistics to find an unrebutted prima facie case of employment discrimination." [12] The question they raise, in short, is whether a basic component in the Court of Appeals' finding of a pattern or practice of discrimination—the comparatively small percentage of Negro employees in Hazelwood's teaching staff—was lacking in probative force.

This Court's recent consideration in *International Brotherhood of Teamsters v. United States,* —— U.S. ——, 97 S.Ct. 1843, 52 L.Ed.2d —— of the role of statistics in pattern or practice suits under Title VII provides substantial guidance in evaluating the arguments advanced by the petitioners. See also *Village of Arlington Heights v. Metropolitan Housing Development Corp.,* —— U.S. ——, at —— 97 S.Ct. 555, at 564, 50 L.Ed.2d 450; *Washington v. Davis,* 426 U.S. 229, 241-242, 96 S.Ct. 2040, 2048-2049, 48 L.Ed.2d 597. Where gross statistical disparities can be shown, they alone may in a proper case constitute prima facie proof of a pattern or practice of discrimination. *Teamsters, supra,* n.20 at ——, 97 S.Ct., at 1856.

There can be no doubt, in light of the *Teamsters* case, that the District Court's comparison of Hazelwood's teacher work force to its student population fundamentally misconceived the role of statistics in employment discrimination cases. The Court of Appeals was correct in the view that a proper comparison was between the racial composition of Hazelwood's teaching staff and the racial composition of the qualified public school teacher population in the relevant labor market. [13]

[12.]   In their petition for certiorari and brief on the merits, the petitioners have phrased the question as follows:

"Whether a court may disregard evidence that an employer has treated actual job applicants in a nondiscriminatory manner and rely on undifferentiated workforce statistics to find an unrebutted prima facie case of employment discrimination in violation of Title VII of the Civil Rights Act of 1964."

Their petition for certiorari and brief on the merits did raise a second question—"[w]hether Congress has authority under Section 5 of the Fourteenth Amendment to prohibit by Title VII of the Civil Rights Act of 1964 employment practices of an agency of a state government in the absence of proof that the agency purposefully discriminated against applicants on the basis of race." That issue, however, is not presented by the facts in this case. The Government's opening statement in the trial court explained that its evidence was designed to show that the scarcity of Negro teachers at Hazelwood "is the result of purpose" and is attributable to "deliberately continued employment policies." Thus here, as in *International Brotherhood of Teamsters v. United States,* —— U.S. ——, 97 S.Ct. 1843, 52 L.Ed.2d ——, "[t]he Government's theory of discrimination was simply that the [employer], in violation of §703(a) of Title VII, regularly and purposefully treated Negroes . . . less favorably than white persons." At —— – ——, 97 S.Ct. at 1854.

[13.]   In *Teamsters,* the comparison between the percentage of Negroes on the employer's work force and the percentage in the general areawide population was highly probative, because the job skill there involved—the ability to drive a truck—is one that many persons possess or can fairly readily acquire. When special qualifications are required to fill particular jobs, comparisons to the general population (rather than to the smaller group of individuals who possess the necessary qualifications) may have little probative value. The comparative statistics introduced by the Government in the District Court, however, were properly limited to public school teachers, and therefore this is not a case like *Mayor v. Educational Equality League,*

See *Teamsters, supra,* ____ U.S. ____, 97 S.Ct., at 1855, and n. 17. The percentage of Negroes on Hazelwood's teaching staff in 1972-1973 was 1.4% and in 1973-1974 it was 1.8%. By contrast, the percentage of qualified Negro teachers in the area was, according to the 1970 census, at least 5.7%. [14] Although these differences were on their face substantial, the Court of Appeals erred in substituting its judgment for that of the District Court and holding that the Government had conclusively proved its "pattern or practice" lawsuit.

The Court of Appeals totally disregarded the possibility that this prima facie statistical proof in the record might at the trial court level be rebutted by statistics dealing with Hazelwood's hiring after it became subject to Title VII. Racial discrimination by public employers was not made illegal under Title VII until March 24, 1972. A public employer who from that date forward made all its employment decisions in a wholly nondiscriminatory way would not violate Title VII even if it had formerly maintained an all-white work force by purposefully excluding Negroes.[15] For this reason, the Court cautioned in the *Teamsters* opinion that once a prima facie case has been established by statistical work force disparities, the employer must be given an opportunity to show "that the claimed discriminatory pattern is a product of pre-Act hiring rather than unlawful post-Act discrimination." *Id.,* at 97 S.Ct., at 1867.

---

415 U.S. 605, 94 S.Ct. 1323, 39 L.Ed.2d 630, in which the racial-composition comparisons failed to take into account special qualifications for the position in question. *Id.,* at 620-621, 94 S.Ct. at 1333-1334.

Although the petitioners concede as a general matter the probative force of the comparative work force statistics, they object to the Court of Appeals' heavy reliance on these data on the ground that applicant flow data, showing the actual percentage of white and Negro applicants for teaching positions at Hazelwood, would be firmer proof. As we have noted, see n. 5, *supra,* there was not clear evidence of such statistics. We leave it to the District Court on remand to determine whether competent proof of those data can be adduced. If so, it would, of course, be very relevant. Cf. *Dothard v. Rawlinson,* ____ U.S. ____, ____, 97 S.Ct. 2720, 2727, 52 L.Ed.2d ____.

[14.] As is discussed below, the Government contends that a comparative figure of 15.4% rather than 5.7%, is the appropriate one. ... But even assuming *arguendo* that the 5.7% figure urged by the petitioners is correct, the disparity between that figure and the percentage of Negroes on Hazelwood's teaching staff would be more than fourfold for the 1972-1973 school year, and threefold for the 1973-1974 school year. A precise method of measuring the significance of such statistical disparities was explained in *Castaneda v. Partida,* ____ U.S. ____, at ____, 97 S.Ct. 1272, at 1281, 51 L.Ed.2d 498, n. 17. It involves calculation of the "standard deviation" as a measure of predicted fluctuations from the expected value of a sample. Using the 5.7% figure as the basis for calculating the expected value, the expected number of Negroes on the Hazelwood teaching staff would be roughly 63 in 1972-1973 and 70 in 1973-1974. The observed number in those years was 16 and 22, respectively. The difference between the observed and expected values was more than six standard deviations in 1972-1973 and more than five standard deviations in 1973-1974. The Court in *Castaneda* noted that "[a]s a general rule for such large samples, if the difference between the expected value and the observed number is greater than two or three standard deviations," then the hypothesis that teachers were hired without regard to race would be suspect. *Ibid.*

[15.] This is not to say that evidence of pre-Act discrimination can never have any probative force. Proof that an employer engaged in racial discrimination prior to the effective date of Title VII might in some circumstances support the inference that such discrimination continued, particularly where relevant aspects of the decisionmaking process had undergone little change.

The record in this case showed that for the 1972-1973 school year, Hazelwood hired 282 new teachers, 10 of whom (3.5%) were Negroes; for the following school year it hired 123 new teachers, five of whom (4.1%) were Negroes. Over the two-year period, Negroes constituted a total of 15 of the 405 new teachers hired (3.7%). Although the Court of Appeals briefly mentioned these data in reciting the facts, it wholly ignored them in discussing whether the Government had shown a pattern or practice of discrimination. And it gave no consideration at all to the possibility that post-Act data as to the number of Negroes hired compared to the total number of Negro applicants might tell a totally different story.

What the hiring figures prove obviously depends upon the figures to which they are compared. The Court of Appeals accepted the Government's argument that the relevant comparison was to the labor market area of St. Louis County and St. Louis City, in which, according to the 1970 census, 15.4% of all teachers were Negro. The propriety of that comparison was vigorously disputed by the petitioners, who urged that because the City of St. Louis has made special attempts to maintain a 50% Negro teaching staff, inclusion of that school district in the relevant market area distorts the comparison. Were that argument accepted, the percentage of Negro teachers in the relevant labor market area (St. Louis County alone) as shown in the 1970 census would be 5.7% rather than 15.4%.

The difference between these figures may well be important; the disparity between 3.7% (the percentage of Negro teachers hired by Hazelwood in 1972-1973 and 1973-1974) and 5.7% may be sufficiently small to weaken the Government's other proof, while the disparity between 3.7% and 15.4% may be sufficiently large to reinforce it.[17] In determining which of the two figures—or very possibly, what intermediate figure—provides the most accu-

---

[17.]   Indeed, under the statistical methodology explained in *Castaneda v. Partida;* —— U.S. ——, at ——, 97 S.Ct. 1272, at 1281, 51 L.Ed.2d 498 n. 17, involving the calculation of the standard deviation as a measure of predicted fluctuations, the difference between using 15.4% and 5.7% as the areawide figure would be significant. If the 15.4% figure is taken as the basis for comparison, the expected number of Negro teachers hired by Hazelwood in 1972-1973 would be 43 (rather than the actual figure of 10) of a total of 282, a difference of more than five standard deviations; the expected number of 1973-1974 would be 19 (rather than the actual figure 5) of a total of 123, a difference of more than three standard deviations. For the two years combined, the difference between the observed number of 15 Negro teachers hired (of a total of 405) would vary from the expected number of 62 by more than six standard deviations. Because a fluctuation of more than two or three standard deviations would undercut the hypothesis that decisions were being made randomly with respect to race, *ibid.,* each of these statistical comparisons would reinforce rather than rebut the Government's other proof. If, however, the 5.7% areawide figure is used, the expected number of Negro teachers hired in 1972-1973 would be roughly 16, less than two standard deviations from the observed number of 10; for 1973-1974, the expected value would be roughly seven, less than one standard deviation from the observed value of 5; and for the two years combined, the expected value of 23 would be less than two standard deviations from the observed total of 15. A more precise method of analyzing these statistics confirms the results of the standard deviation analysis. See F. Mosteller, R. Rourke & C. Thomas, Probability with Statistical Applications 494 (2d ed. 1970).

These observations are not intended to suggest that precise calculations of statistical significance are necessary in employing statistical proof, but merely to highlight the importance of the choice of the relevant labor market area.

rate basis for comparison to the hiring figures at Hazelwood, it will be necessary to evaluate such considerations as (i) whether the racially based hiring policies of the St. Louis City School District were in effect as far back as 1970, the year in which the census figures were taken;[18] (ii) to what extent those policies have changed the racial composition of that district's teaching staff from what it would otherwise have been; (iii) to what extent St. Louis' recruitment policies have diverted to the city teachers who might otherwise have applied to Hazelwood;[19] (iv) to what extent Negro teachers employed by the city would prefer employment in other districts such as Hazelwood; and (v) what the experience in other school districts in St. Louis County indicates about the validity of excluding the City School District from the relevant labor market.

It is thus clear that a determination of the appropriate comparative figures in this case will depend upon further evaluation by the trial court. As this Court admonished in *Teamsters,* "statistics . . . come in infinite variety. . . . [T]heir usefulness depends on all of the surrounding facts and circumstances." At ——, 97 S.Ct., at 1856-1857. Only the trial court is in a position to make the appropriate determination after further findings. And only after such a determination is made can a foundation be established for deciding whether or not Hazelwood engaged in a pattern or practice of racial discrimination in its employment practices in violation of the law.[20]

We hold, therefore, that the Court of Appeals erred in disregarding the post-Act hiring statistics in the record, and that it should have remanded the case to the District Court for further findings as to the relevant labor market area and for an ultimate determination of whether Hazelwood engaged in a pattern or practice of employment discrimination after March 24, 1972.[21] Accordingly, the judgment is vacated, and the case is remanded to the District Court for further proceedings consistent with this opinion.

It is so ordered.

[18.] In 1970 Negroes constituted only 42% of the faculty in St. Louis city schools, which could indicate either that the city's goals were not yet in effect or simply that they had not yet been achieved.

[19.] The petitioners observe, for example, that Harris Teachers College in St. Louis, whose 1973 graduating class was 60% Negro, is operated by the city. It is the petitioners' contention that the city's public elementary and secondary schools occupy an advantageous position in the recruitment of Harris graduates.

[20.] Because the District Court focused on a comparison between the percentage of Negro teachers and Negro pupils in Hazelwood, it did not undertake an evaluation of the relevant labor market, and its casual dictum that the inclusion of the city of St. Louis "distorted" the labor market statistics was not based upon valid criteria. 392 F.Supp., at 1287.

[21.] It will also be open to the District Court on remand to determine whether sufficiently reliable applicant flow data are available to permit consideration of the petitioners' argument that those data may undercut a statistical analysis dependent upon hirings alone.

NOTES

1. *Hazelwood*, along with *Teamsters, supra,* were the first significant statements by the Supreme Court concerning the use of statistical evidence in Title VII cases. It is noteworthy that the Court, at footnote 14, in *Hazelwood* seems to adopt the "two or three standard deviations" rule from Castaneda v. Partida, 97 S.Ct. 1272 (1977). In *Casteneda* the Court found that a prima facie case of discrimination against Mexican-Americans in jury selection was established, in part because statistics for the pertinent period (1962-1972) showed that, although the county's population was 79.1% Mexican-American, only 39% of the persons summoned for grand jury service were in such class. The Court observed at footnote 17, that:

> If the jurors were drawn randomly from the general population, then the number of Mexican-Americans in the sample could be modeled by a binomial distribution. . . . Given that 79.1% of the population is Mexican-American, the expected number of Mexican-Americans among the 870 persons summoned to serve as grand jurors over the 11-year period is approximately 688. The observed number is 339. Of course, in any given drawing some fluctuation from the expected number is predicted. The important point, however, is that the statistical model shows that the results of a random drawing are likely to fall in the vicinity of the expected value. . . . The measure of the predicted fluctuations from the expected value is the standard deviation, defined for the binomial distribution as the square root of the product of the total number in the sample (here 870) times the probability of selecting a Mexican-American (0.791) times the probability of selecting a non-Mexican-American (0.209). . . . Thus, in this case the standard deviation is approximately 12. As a general rule for such large samples, if the difference between the expected value and the observed number is greater than two or three standard deviations, then the hypothesis that the jury drawing was random would be suspect to a social scientist. The 11-year data here reflect a difference between the expected and observed number of Mexican-Americans of approximately 29 standard deviations. A detailed calculation reveals that the likelihood that such a substantial departure from the expected value would occur by chance is less than 1 in 10.

In reaching this conclusion, the Court relied on Finkelstein, *The Application of Statistical Decision Theory to the Jury Discrimination Cases*, 80 Harv. L. Rev. 338 (1966); P. Hoel, Introduction to Mathematical Statistics (4th ed. 1971); F. Mosteller, R. Rourke & G. Thomas, Probability with Statistical Applications (2d ed. 1970).

2. *See generally* Gastwirth & Haber, *Defining the Labor Market for Equal Employment Standards,* 99 Monthly Lab. Rev. 32 (March 1976); Note, *Beyond the Prima Facie Case in Employment Discrimination Law: Statistical Proof and Rebuttal*, 89 Harv. L. Rev. 387 (1975); Note, *Employment Discrimination: Statistics and Preferences Under Title VII*, 59 Va. L. Rev. 463 (1973); Oaxaca, *Theory and Measurement in the Economics of Discrimination,* in Equal Rights and Industrial Relations 1 (IRRA 1977); Rosenblum, *The Use of Labor Statistics and Analysis in Title VII Cases: Rios, Chicago and Beyond,* 1 Ind. Rel. L. J. 685 (1977).

VII. Discriminatory Employment Tests
ALBEMARLE PAPER CO. v. MOODY
Supreme Court of the United States
422 U.S. 405, 95 S. Ct. 2362, 45 L. Ed. 2d 280 (1975)

MR. JUSTICE STEWART delivered the opinion of the Court.

These consolidated cases raise two important questions under Title VII of the Civil Rights Act of 1964, 78 Stat. 253, as amended by the Equal Employment Opportunity Act of 1972, 86 Stat. 103, 42 U. S. C. § § 2000(e): First: When employees or applicants for employment have lost the opportunity to earn wages because an employer has engaged in an unlawful discriminatory employment practice, what standards should a federal district court follow in deciding whether to award or deny backpay? Second: What must an employer show to establish that pre-employment tests racially discriminatory in effect, though not in intent, are sufficiently "job related" to survive challenge under Title VII?

I. The respondents—plaintiffs in the District Court—are a certified class of present and former Negro employees at a paper mill in Roanoke Rapids, North Carolina; the petitioners—defendants in the District Court—are the plant's owner, the Albemarle Paper Company, and the plant employees' labor union, Halifax Local No. 425. In August of 1966, after filing a complaint with the Equal Employment Opportunity Commission (EEOC), and receiving notice of their right to sue, the respondents brought a class action in the United States District Court for the Eastern District of North Carolina, asking permanent injunctive relief against "any policy, practice, custom, or usage" at the plant that violated Title VII. The respondents assured the court that the suit involved no claim for any monetary awards on a class basis, but in June of 1970, after several years of discovery, the respondents moved to add a class demand for backpay. The court ruled that this issue would be considered at trial.

At the trial, in July and August of 1971, the major issues were the plant's seniority system, its program of employment testing, and the question of backpay. In its opinion of November 9, 1971, the court found that the petitioners had "strictly segregated" the plant's departmental "lines of progression" prior to January 1, 1964, reserving the higher paying and more skilled lines for whites. . . . The "racial identifiability" of whole lines of progression persisted until 1968, when the lines were reorganized under a new collective-bargaining agreement. The court found, however, that this reorganization left Negro employees "locked in the lower paying job classifications." . . . The formerly "Negro" lines of progression had been merely tacked on to the bottom of the formerly "white" lines, and promotions, demotions, and layoffs continued to be governed—where skills were "relatively equal"—by a system of "job seniority." Because of the plant's previous history of overt segregation, only whites had seniority in the higher job categories. Accordingly, the court ordered the petitioners to implement a system of "plantwide" seniority.

The court refused, however, to award backpay to the plaintiff class for losses suffered under the "job seniority" program. . . .

The court also refused to enjoin or limit Albemarle's testing program. Albemarle had required applicants for employment in the skilled lines of progression to have a high school diploma and to pass two tests, the Revised Beta Examination, allegedly a measure of nonverbal intelligence, and the Wonderlic Test (available in alternate Forms A and B), allegedly a measure of verbal facility. After this Court's decision in Griggs v. Duke Power Company, 401 U. S. 424 (1971), and on the eve of trial, Albemarle engaged an industrial psychologist to study the "job relatedness" of its testing program. His study compared the test scores of current employees with supervisorial judgments of their competence in ten job groupings selected from the middle or top of the plant's skilled lines of progression. The study showed a statistically significant correlation with supervisorial ratings in three job groupings for the Beta test, in seven job groupings for either Form A or Form B of the Wonderlic Test, and in two job groupings for the required battery of both the Beta and the Wonderlic Test. . . .

We granted certiorari because of an evident circuit conflict as to the standards governing awards of backpay and as to the showing required to establish the "job relatedness" of pre-employment tests.

II. Whether a particular member of the plaintiff class should have been awarded any backpay and, if so, how much, are questions not involved in this review. The equities of individual cases were never reached. Though at least some of the members of the plaintiff class obviously suffered loss of wage opportunities on account of Albemarle's unlawfully discriminatory system of job seniority, the District Court decided that *no* backpay should be awarded to *anyone* in the class. The court declined to make such an award on two stated grounds: the lack of "evidence of bad faith non-compliance with the Act," and the fact that "the defendants would be substantially prejudiced" by an award of backpay that was demanded contrary to an earlier representation and late in the progress of the litigation. Relying directly on Newman v. Piggie Park Enterprises, 390 U.S. 400, the Court of Appeals reversed, holding that backpay could be denied only in "special circumstances." The petitioners argue that the Court of Appeals was in error—that a district court has virtually unfettered discretion to award or deny backpay, and that there was no abuse of that discretion in this case. [8]. . . .

The petitioners contend that the statutory scheme provides no guidance, beyond indicating that backpay awards are within the District Court's discretion. We disagree. It is true that backpay is not an automatic or mandatory remedy; like all other remedies under the Act, it is one which the courts

---

[8.]   The petitioners also contend that no backpay can be awarded to those unnamed parties in the plaintiff class who have not themselves filed charges with the EEOC. We reject this contention. The courts of appeals that have confronted the issue are unanimous in recognizing that backpay may be awarded on a class basis under Title VII without exhaustion of administrative procedures by the unnamed class members. . . . The Congress plainly ratified this construction of the Act in the course of enacting the Equal Employment Opportunity Act of 1972, Pub. L. 92-261, 86 Sat. 103. . . .

"may" invoke. The scheme implicitly recognizes that there may be cases calling for one remedy but not another, and—owing to the structure of the federal judiciary—these choices are of course left in the first instance to the district courts. But such discretionary choices are not left to a court's "inclination, but to its judgment; and its judgment is to be guided by sound legal principles." United States v. Burr, 25 Fed. Cas. 30, 35 (Marshall, C.J.). The power to award backpay was bestowed by Congress, as part of a complex legislative design directed at an historic evil of national proportions. A court must exercise this power "in light of the large objectives of the Act," Hecht Co. v. Bowles, 321 U. S. 321, 331. . . .

The District Court's decision must therefore be measured against the purposes which inform Title VII. As the Court observed in Griggs v. Duke Power Co., *supra,* 401 U. S. at 429-430, the primary objective was a prophylactic one. . . . Backpay has an obvious connection with this purpose. If employers faced only the prospect of an injunctive order, they would have little incentive to shun practices of dubious legality. It is the reasonably certain prospect of a backpay award that "provide[s] the spur or catalyst which causes employers and unions to self-examine and to self-evaluate their employment practices and to endeavor to eliminate, so far as possible, the last vestiges of an unfortunate and ignominious page in this country's history." United States v. N. L. Industries, 479 F.2d 354, 379.

It is also the purpose of Title VII to make persons whole for injuries suffered on account of unlawful employment discrimination. This is shown by the very fact that Congress took care to arm the courts with full equitable powers. . . . Where racial discrimination is concerned, "the [district] court has not merely the power but the duty to render a decree which will so far as possible eliminate the discriminatory effects of the past as well as bar like discrimination in the future." Louisiana v. United States, 380 U.S. 145, 154. And where a legal injury is of an economic character,

"[t]he general rule is, that when a wrong has been done, and the law gives a remedy, the compensation shall be equal to the injury. The latter is the standard by which the former is to be measured. The injured party is to be placed as near as may be, in the situation he would have occupied if the wrong had not been committed." Wicker v. Hoppock, 6 Wall. 94, at 99.

The "make whole" purpose of Title VII is made evident by the legislative history. The backpay provision was expressly modeled on the backpay provision of the National Labor Relations Act. . . .

It follows that, given a finding of unlawful discrimination, backpay should be denied only for reasons which, if applied generally, would not frustrate the central statutory purposes of eradicating discrimination throughout the economy and making persons whole for injuries suffered through past discrimination. The courts of appeals must maintain a consistent and principled application of the backpay provision, consonant with the twin statutory objectives, while at the same time recognizing that the trial court will often have the keener appreciation of those facts and circumstances peculiar to particular cases.

The District Court's stated grounds for denying backpay in this case must be tested against these standards. The first ground was that Albemarle's breach of Title VII had not been in "bad faith." This is not a sufficient reason for denying backpay. Where an employer *has* shown bad faith—by maintaining a practice which he knew to be illegal or of highly questionable legality—he can make no claims whatsoever on the Chancellor's conscience. But, under Title VII, the mere absence of bad faith simply opens the door to equity; it does not depress the scales in the employer's favor. If backpay were awardable only upon a showing of bad faith, the remedy would become a punishment for moral terpitude, rather than a compensation for workers' injuries. This would read the "make whole" purpose right out of Title VII, for a worker's injury is not less real simply because his employer did not inflict it in "bad faith." Title VII is not concerned with the employer's "good intent or absence of discriminatory intent" for Congress directed the thrust of the Act to the *consequences* of employment practices, not simply the motivation." Griggs v. Duke Power Co., *supra,* 401 U. S. at 432. . . . To condition the awarding of backpay on a showing of "bad faith" would be to open an enormous chasm between injunctive and backpay relief under Title VII. There is nothing on the face of the statute or in its legislative history that justifies the creation of drastic and categorical distinctions between those two remedies.

The District Court also grounded its denial of backpay on the fact that the respondents initially disclaimed any interest in backpay, first asserting their claim five years after the complaint was filed. . . .

To deny backpay because a *particular* cause has been prosecuted in an eccentric fashion, prejudicial to the other party, does not offend the broad purposes of Title VII. This is not to say, however, that the District Court's ruling was necessarily correct. Whether the petitioners were in fact prejudiced, and whether the respondents' trial conduct was excusable, are questions that will be open to review by the Court of Appeals, if the District Court, on remand, decides again to decline to make any award of backpay. . . .

III.   In Griggs v. Duke Power Co., 401 U.S. 424, this Court unanimously held that Title VII forbids the use of employment tests that are discriminatory in effect unless the employer meets "the burden of showing that any given requirement [has] . . . a manifest relation to the employment in question." *Id.* at 432. This burden arises, of course, only after the complaining party or class has made out a prima facie case of discrimination—has shown that the tests in question select applicants for hire or promotion in a racial pattern significantly different from that of the pool of applicants. See McDonnell Douglas Corp. v. Green, 411 U. S. 792, 802. If an employer does then meet the burden of proving that its tests are "job related," it remains open to the complaining party to show that other tests or selection devices, without a similarly undesirable racial effect, would also serve the employer's legitimate interest in "efficient and trustworthy workmanship." *Id.* at 801. Such a showing would be evidence that the employer was using its tests merely as a "pretext" for discrimination. *Id.* at 804-805. In the present case, however, we are concerned only with the question whether Albemarle has shown its tests to be job related. . . .

The EEOC has issued "Guidelines" for employers seeking to determine, through professional validation studies, whether their employment tests are job related. 29 CFR Part 1607 (1974). These Guidelines draw upon and make reference to professional standards of test validation established by the American Psychological Association. The EEOC Guidelines are not administrative "regulations" promulgated pursuant to formal procedures es-tablished by the Congress. But, as this Court has heretofore noted, they do constitute "[t]he administrative interpretation of the Act by the enforcing agency," and consequently they are "entitled to great deference." Griggs v. Duke Power Co., *supra,* 401 U.S. at 433-434. See also Espinoza v. Farah Mfg. Co., 414 U.S. 86, 94.

The message of these Guidelines is the same as that of the *Griggs* case—that discriminatory tests are impermissible unless shown, by profes-sionally acceptable methods, to be "predictive of or significantly correlated with important elements of work behavior which comprise or are relevant to the job or jobs for which candidates are being evaluated." 29 CFR § 1607.4(c).

Measured against the Guidelines, Albemarle's validation study is materi-ally defective in several respects:

(1) Even if it had been otherwise adequate, the study would not have "validated" the Beta and Wonderlic test battery for all of the skilled lines of progression for which the two tests are, apparently, now required. The study showed significant correlations for the Beta Exam in only three of the eight lines. Though the Wonderlic Test's Form A and Form B are in theory identi-cal and interchangeable measures of verbal facility, significant correlations for one Form but not for the other were obtained in four job groupings. In two job groupings neither Form showed a significant correlation. Within some of the lines of progression, one Form was found acceptable for some job groupings but not for others. Even if the study were otherwise reliable, this odd patchwork of results would not entitle Albemarle to impose its testing program under the Guidelines. A test may be used in jobs other than those for which it has been professionally validated only if there are "no significant differences" between the studied and unstudied jobs. 29 CFR § 1607.4(c)(2). The study in this case involved no analysis of the attributes of, or the particular skills needed in, the studied job groups. There is accord-ingly no basis for concluding that "no significant differences" exist among the lines of progression, or among distinct job groupings within the studied lines of progression. Indeed, the study's checkered results appear to compel the opposite conclusion.

(2) The study compared test scores with subjective supervisorial rank-ings. While they allow the use of supervisorial rankings in test validation,

the Guidelines quite plainly contemplate that the rankings will be elicited with far more care than was demonstrated here. Albemarle's supervisors were asked to rank employees by a "standard" that was extremely vague and fatally open to divergent interpretations. Each "job grouping" contained a number of different jobs, and the supervisors were asked, in each grouping, to

> "determine which ones [employees] they felt irrespective of the job that they were actually doing, but in their respective jobs, did a better job than the person they were rating against. . . ."

There is no way of knowing precisely what criteria of job performance the supervisors were considering, whether each of the supervisors was considering the same criteria—or whether, indeed, any of the supervisors actually applied a focused and stable body of criteria of any kind. There is, in short, simply no way to determine whether the criteria *actually* considered were sufficiently related to the Company's legitimate interest in job-specific ability to justify a testing system with a racially discriminatory impact.

(3)   The company's study focused, in most cases, on job groups near the top of the various lines of progression. In *Griggs v. Duke Power Co., supra,* the Court left open "the question whether testing requirements that take into account capability for the next succeeding position or related future promotion might be utilized upon a showing that such long-range requirements fulfill a genuine business need." 401 U.S. at 432. The Guidelines take a sensible approach to this issue, and we now endorse it:

> "If job progression structures and seniority provisions are so established that new employees will probably, within a reasonable period of time and in a great majority of cases, progress to a higher level, it may be considered that candidates are being evaluated for jobs at that higher level. However, where job progression is not so nearly automatic, or the time span is such that higher level jobs or employees' potential may be expected to change in significant ways, it shall be considered that candidates are being evaluated for a job at or near the entry level." 29 CFR § 1607.4(c)(1).

The fact that the best of those employees working near the top of a line of progression score well on a test does not necessarily mean that that test, or some particular cutoff score on the test, is a permissible measure of the minimal qualifications of new workers, entering lower level jobs. In drawing any such conclusion, detailed consideration must be given to the normal speed of promotion, to the efficacy of on-the-job training in the scheme of promotion, and to the possible use of testing as a promotion device, rather than as a screen for entry into low-level jobs. The District Court made no findings on these issues. The issues take on special importance in a case, such as this one, where incumbent employees are permitted to work at even high-level jobs without passing the company's test battery. See 29 CFR § 1607.11.

(4)   Albemarle's validation study dealt only with job-experienced, white workers; but the tests themselves are given to new job applicants,

who are younger, largely inexperienced, and in many instances nonwhite. The Standards of the American Psychological Association state that it is "essential" that

> "[t]he validity of a test should be determined on subjects who are
> at the age or in the same educational or vocational situation as the
> persons for whom the test is recommended in practice."

The EEOC Guidelines likewise provide that "[d]ata must be generated and results separately reported for minority or non-minority groups wherever technically feasible." 29 CFR § 1607.5(b)(5). In the present case, such "differential validation" as to racial groups was very likely not "feasible," because years of discrimination at the plant have insured that nearly all of the upper level employees are white. But there has been no clear showing that differential validation was not feasible for lower-level jobs. More importantly, the Guidelines provide:

> "If it is not technically feasible to include minority employees
> in validation studies conducted on the present work force, the
> conduct of a validation study without minority candidates does
> not relieve any person of his subsequent obligation for validation
> when inclusion of minority candidates becomes technically feas-
> ible." 29 CFR § 1607.5(b)(1). . . . "[E]vidence of satisfactory
> validity based on other groups will be regarded as only provisional
> compliance with the guidelines pending separate validation of the
> test for the minority groups in question." 29 CFR § 1607.5(b)(5).

For all these reasons, we agree with the Court of Appeals that the District Court erred in concluding that Albemarle had proved the job relatedness of its testing program and that the respondents were consequently not entitled to equitable relief. . . .

Accordingly, the judgment is vacated, and these cases are remanded to the District Court for proceedings consistent with this opinion.

It is so ordered.

NOTE

In light of some of the cases discussed under the heading of "Burden of Proof Under Title VII," is it likely that the courts will ever give full effect to the principles enunciated in *Albemarle* in cases involving claims of employment discrimination in higher education?

VIII. Sex Discrimination

DOTHARD v. RAWLINSON
Supreme Court of the United States
97 S. Ct. 2720 (1977)

MR. JUSTICE STEWART delivered the opinion of the Court.

The appellee, Dianne Rawlinson, sought employment with the Alabama Board of Corrections as a prison guard, called in Alabama a "correctional counselor." After her application was rejected, she brought this class suit under Title VII of the Civil Rights Act of 1964, 78 Stat. 253, as amended, 42 U.S.C. §2000e *et seq.* (1970 ed. and Supp. V), and under 42 U.S.C. §1983, alleging that she had been denied employment because of her sex in violation of federal law. A three-judge Federal District Court for the Middle District of Alabama decided in her favor. *Mieth v. Dothard*, 418 F.Supp. 1169. . . .

I

At the time she applied for a position as correctional counselor trainee, Rawlinson was a 22-year-old college graduate whose major course of study had been correctional psychology. She was refused employment because she failed to meet the minimum 120-pound weight requirement established by an Alabama statute. The statute also establishes a height minimum of 5 feet and 2 inches.

After her application was rejected because of her weight, Rawlinson filed a charge with the Equal Employment Opportunity Commission, and ultimately received a right to sue letter. She then filed a complaint in the District Court on behalf of herself and other similarly situated women, challenging the statutory height and weight minima as violative of Title VII and the Equal Protection Clause of the Fourteenth Amendment. A three-judge court was convened. While the suit was pending, the Alabama Board of Corrections adopted Administrative Regulation 204, establishing gender criteria for assigning correctional counselors to maximum security institutions for "contact positions," that is, positions requiring continual close physical proximity to inmates of the institution. Rawlinson amended her class-action complaint by adding a challenge to regulation 204 as also violative of Title VII and the Fourteenth Amendment.

Like most correctional facilities in the United States, Alabama's prisons are segregated on the basis of sex. Currently the Alabama Board of Corrections operates four major all-male penitentiaries—Holman Prison, Kilby Corrections Facility, G. K. Fountain Correction Center, and Draper Correctional Center. The Board also operates the Julia Tutwiler Prison for Women, the Frank Lee Youth Center, the #4 Honor Camp, the State Cattle Ranch, and nine Work Release Centers, one of which is for women. The Julia Tutwiler Prison for Women and the four male penitentiaries are maximum security institutions. Their inmate living quarters are for the most part large dormitories, with communal showers and toilets that are open to the dormitories and hallways. The Draper and Fountain penitentiaries carry on extensive farming operations, making necessary a large number of strip searches for contraband when prisoners re-enter the prison buildings.

A correctional counselor's primary duty within these institutions is to maintain security and control of the inmates by continually supervising and observing their activities.[8] To be eligible for consideration as a correc-

---

[8.] The official job description for a correctional counselor position emphasizes counseling as well as security duties; the District Court found that "correctional counselors are persons commonly referred to as prison guards. Their duties primarily involve security rather than counseling." 418 F.Supp. at 1175.

tional counselor, an applicant must possess a valid Alabama driver's license, have a high school education or its equivalent, be free from physical defects, be between the ages of 20½ years and 45 years at the time of appointment, and fall between the minimum height and weight requirements of five feet and two inches and 120 pounds, and the maximum of six feet and ten inches and 300 pounds. Appointment is by merit, with a grade assigned each applicant based on experience and education. No written examination is given.

At the time this litigation was in the District Court, the Board of Corrections employed a total of 435 people in various correctional counselor positions, 56 of whom were women. Of those 56 women, 21 were employed at the Julia Tutwiler Prison for Women, 13 were employed in noncontact positions at the four male maximum security institutions, and the remaining 22 were employed at the other institutions operated by the Alabama Board of Corrections. Because most of Alabama's prisoners are held at the four maximum security male penitentiaries, 336 of the 435 correctional counselor jobs were in those institutions, a majority of them concededly in the "contact" classification. Thus, even though meeting the statutory height and weight requirements, women applicants could under Regulation 204 compete equally with men for only about 25% of the correctional counselor jobs available in the Alabama prison system.

II

In enacting Title VII, Congress required "the removal of artificial, arbitrary, and unnecessary barriers to employment when the barriers operate invidiously to discriminate on the basis of racial or other impermissible classification." *Griggs v. Duke Power Co.,* 401 U.S. 424, 431, 91 S.Ct. 849, 853, 28 L.Ed.2d 158. The District Court found that the minimum statutory height and weight requirements that applicants for employment as correctional counselors must meet constitute the sort of arbitrary barrier to equal employment opportunity that Title VII forbids. The appellants assert that the District Court erred both in finding that the height and weight standards discriminate against women, and in its refusal to find that, even if they do, these standards are justified as "job related."

A

The gist of the claim that the statutory height and weight requirements discriminate against women does not involve an assertion of purposeful discriminatory motive. It is asserted, rather, that these facially neutral qualification standards work in fact disproportionately to exclude women from eligibility for employment by the Alabama Board of Corrections. We dealt in *Griggs v. Duke Power Co., supra* and *Albemarle Paper Co. v. Moody,* 422 U.S. 405, 95 S.Ct. 2362, 45 L.Ed.2d 280, with similar allegations that facially neutral employment standards disproportionately excluded Negroes from employment, and those cases guide our approach here.

Those cases make clear that to establish a prima facie case of discrimination, a plaintiff need only show that the facially neutral standards in question select applicants for hire in a significantly discriminatory pattern. Once it is thus shown that the employment standards are discriminatory in effect, the employer must meet "the burden of showing that any given requirement [has] . . . a manifest relation to the employment in question." *Griggs v. Duke Power Co.*, 401 U.S., at 432, 91 S.Ct., at 854. If the employer proves that the challenged requirements are job related, the plaintiff may then show that the other selection devices without a similar discriminatory effect would also "serve the employer's legitimate interest in 'efficient and trustworthy workmanship.'" *Albemarle Paper Co. v. Moody*, 422 U.S., at 425, 95 S.Ct., at 2375, quoting *McDonnell Douglas Corp. v. Green*, 411 U.S. 792, 801, 93 S.Ct. 1817, 1823, 36 L.Ed.2d 668.

Although women 14 years of age or older comprise 52.75% of the Alabama population and 36.89% of its total labor force, they hold only 12.9% of its correctional counselor positions. In considering the effect of the minimum height and weight standards on this disparity in rate of hiring between the sexes, the District Court found that the 5'2" requirement would operate to exclude 33.29% of the women in the United States between the ages of 18-79, while excluding only 1.28% of men between the same ages. The 120-pound weight restriction would exclude 22.29% of the women and 2.35% of the men in this age group. When the height and weight restrictions are combined, Alabama's statutory standards would exclude 41.13% of the female population while excluding less than one percent of the male population. [12] Accordingly, the District Court found that Rawlinson had made out a prima facie case of unlawful sex discrimination.

The appellants argue that a showing of disproportionate impact on women based on generalized national statistics should not suffice to establish a prima facie case. They point in particular to Rawlinson's failure to adduce comparative statistics concerning actual applicants for correctional counselor positions in Alabama. There is no requirement, however, that a statistical showing of disproportionate impact must always be based on analysis of the characteristics of actual applicants. See *Griggs v. Duke Power Co.*, 401 U.S., at 430, 91 S.Ct., at 853. The application process might itself not adequately reflect the actual potential applicant pool, since otherwise qualified people might be discouraged from applying because of a self-recognized inability to meet the very standards challenged as being discriminatory. See *International Brotherhood of Teamsters v. United States*, —— U.S.___, ____ __ ____, 97 S.Ct. 1843, 1869-1971, 51 L.Ed.2d _____. A

[12.]   Affirmatively stated, approximately 99.76% of the men and 58.87% of the women meet both these physical qualifications. From the separate statistics on height and weight of males it would appear that after adding the two together and allowing for some overlap the result would be to exclude between 2.35 and 3.63% of males from meeting Alabama's statutory height and weight minima. None of the parties has challenged the accuracy of the District Court's computations on this score, however, and the discrepancy is in any event insignificant in light of the gross disparity between the female and male exclusions. Even under revised computations the disparity would greatly exceed the 34% to 12% disparity that served to invalidate the high school diploma requirement in the *Griggs* case. *Griggs v. Duke Power Co.*, 401 U.S., at 430, 91 S.Ct. at 853.

potential applicant could easily measure her height and weight and conclude that to make an application would be futile. Moreover, reliance on general population demographic data was not misplaced where there was no reason to suppose that physical height and weight characteristics of Alabama men and women differ markedly from those of the national population.

For these reasons, we cannot say that the District Court was wrong in holding that the statutory height and weight standards had a discriminatory impact on women applicants. The plaintiffs in a case such as this are not required to exhaust every possible source of evidence, if the evidence actually presented on its face conspicuously demonstrates a job requirement's grossly discriminatory impact. If the employer discerns fallacies or deficiencies in the data offered by the plaintiff, he is free to adduce countervailing evidence of his own. In this case no such effort was made.

B

We turn, therefore, to the appellants' argument that they have rebutted the prima facie case of discrimination by showing that the height and weight requirements are job related. These requirements, they say, have a relationship to strength, a sufficient but unspecified amount of which is essential to effective job performance as a correctional counselor. In the District Court, however, the appellants produced no evidence correlating the height and weight requirements with the requisite amount of strength thought essential to good job performance. Indeed, they failed to offer evidence of any kind in specific justification of the statutory standards.[14]

If the job-related quality that the appellants identify is bona fide, their purpose could be achieved by adopting and validating a test for applicants that measures strength directly.[15]   Such a test, fairly administered, would fully satisfy the standards of Title VII because it would be one that "measure[s] the person for the job and not the person in the abstract." *Griggs v. Duke Power Co.,* 401 U.S., at 436, 91 S.Ct., at 856. But nothing in the present record even approaches such a measurement.

For the reasons we have discussed, the District Court was not in error in holding that Title VII of the Civil Rights Act of 1964, as amended,

---

[14.]   In what is perhaps a variation on their constitutional challenge to the validity of Title VII itself, see n. 1, *supra,* the appellants contend that the establishment of the minimum height and weight standards by statute requires that they be given greater deference than is typically given private employer-established job qualifications. The relevant legislative history of the 1972 amendments extending Title VII to the States as employers does not, however, support such a result. Instead, Congress expressly indicated the intent that the same Title VII principles be applied to governmental and private employers alike. See H.R.Rep. No. 92-238, 92d Cong., 1st Sess., p. 17 (1971); S.Rep.No. 92-415, 92d Cong., 1st Sess., p. 10 (1971); U.S. Code Cong. & Admin. News 1972, p. 2137. See also *Schaeffer v. San Diego Yellow Cabs,* 462 F.2d 1002 (CA9). Thus for both private and public employers, "The touchstone is business necessity," *Griggs,* 401 U.S., at 431, 91 S.Ct., at 853; a discriminatory employment practice must be shown to be necessary to safe and efficient job performance to survive a Title VII challenge.

[15.]   Cf. EEOC Guidelines on Employee Selection Procedures, 29 CFR § 1607. See also *Washington v. Davis,* 426 U.S. 229, 246-247, 96 S.Ct. 2040, 2050-2051, 48 L.Ed.2d 597; *Albemarle Paper Co. v. Moody,* 422 U.S. 405, 95 S.Ct. 2362, 45 L.Ed.2d 280; *Officers for Justice v. Civil Service Commission,* 395 F.Supp. 378 (ND Cal.).

prohibits application of the statutory height and weight requirements to Rawlinson and the class she represents.

III

Unlike the statutory height and weight requirements, Regulation 204 explicitly discriminates against women on the basis of their sex. In defense of this overt discrimination, the appellants rely on §703(e) of Title VII, which permits sex-based discrimination "in those certain instances where . . . sex . . . is a bona fide occupational qualification reasonably necessary to the normal operation of that particular business or enterprise."

The District Court rejected the bona fide occupational qualification (bfoq) defense, relying on the virtually uniform view of the federal courts that §703(e) provides only the narrowest of exceptions to the general rule requiring equality of employment opportunities. This view has been variously formulated. In *Diaz v. Pan American World Airways*, 442 F.2d 385, 388, the Court of Appeals for the Fifth Circuit held that "discrimination based on sex is valid only when the *essence* of the business operation would be undermined by not hiring members of one sex exclusively." (Emphasis in original.) In an earlier case, *Weeks v. Southern Bell Telephone and Telegraph Co.*, 5 Cir., 408 F. 228, 235, the same court said that an employer could rely on the bfoq exception only by proving "that he had reasonable cause to believe, that is, a factual basis for believing, that all or substantially all women would be unable to perform safely and efficiently the duties of the job involved." See also *Phillips v. Martin Marietta Corp.*, 400 U.S. 542, 91 S.Ct. 496, 27 L.Ed.2d 613. But whatever the verbal formulation, the federal courts have agreed that it is impermissible under Title VII to refuse to hire an individual woman or man on the basis of stereotyped characterizations of the sexes, and the District Court in the present case held in effect that Regulation 204 is based on just such stereotypical assumptions.

We are persuaded—by the restrictive language of §703(e), the relevant legislative history, and the consistent interpretation of the Equal Employment Opportunity Commission [19]—that the bfoq exception was in fact meant to be an extremely narrow exception to the general prohibition of discrimination on the basis of sex. [20] In the particular factual circumstances of this case, however, we conclude that the District Court erred in rejecting the State's contention that Regulation 204 falls within the narrow ambit of the bfoq exception.

[19.] The EEOC issued guidelines on sex discrimination in 1965 reflecting its position that "the bona fide occupational qualification as to sex should be interpreted narrowly." 29 CFR §1604.2(a). It has adhered to that principle consistently, and its construction of the statute can accordingly be given weight. See *Griggs v. Duke Power Co.*, 401 U.S., at 434, 91 S.Ct., at 855; *McDonald v. Santa Fe Trail Transportation Co.*, 427 U.S. 273, 279-280, 96 S.Ct. 2574, 2577-2578, 49 L.Ed.2d 493.

[20.] In the case of a state employer, the bfoq exception would have to be interpreted at the very least so as to conform to the Equal Protection Clause of the Fourteenth Amendment. The parties do not suggest, however, that the Equal Protection Clause requires more rigorous scrutiny of a State's sexually discriminatory employment policy than does Title VII. There is

The environment in Alabama's penitentiaries is a peculiarly inhospitable one for human beings of whatever sex. Indeed, a federal district court has held that the conditions of confinement in the prisons of the State, characterized by "rampant violence" and a "jungle atmosphere," are constitutionally intolerable. *James v. Wallace,* 406 F.Supp. 318, 325 (MD Ala.). The record in the present case shows that because of inadequate staff and facilities, no attempt is made in the four maximum security male penitentiaries to classify or segregate inmates according to their offense or level of dangerousness—a procedure that, according to expert testimony, is essential to effective penalogical administration. Consequently, the estimated 20% of the male prisoners who are sex offenders are scattered throughout the penitentiaries' dormitory facilities.

In this environment of violence and disorganization, it would be an oversimplification to characterize Regulation 204 as an exercise in "romantic paternalism." Cf. *Frontiero v. Richardson,* 411 U.S. 677, 684, 93 S.Ct. 1764, 1769, 36 L.Ed.2d 583. In the usual case, the argument that a particular job is too dangerous for women may appropriately be met by the rejoinder that it is the purpose of Title VII to allow the individual woman to make that choice for herself. More is at stake in this case, however, than an individual woman's decision to weigh and accept the risks of employment in a "contact" position in a maximum security male prison.

The essence of a correctional counselor's job is to maintain prison security. A woman's relative ability to maintain order in a male, maximum security, unclassified penitentiary of the type Alabama now runs could be directly reduced by her womanhood. There is a basis in fact for expecting that sex offenders who have criminally assaulted women in the past would be moved to do so again if access to women were established within the prison. There would also be a real risk that other inmates, deprived of a normal heterosexual environment, would assault women guards because they were women. [22] In a prison system where violence is the order of the day, where inmate access to guards is facilitated by dormitory living arrangements, where every institution is understaffed, and where a substantial portion of the inmate population is composed of sex offenders mixed at random with other prisoners, there are few visible deterrents to inmate assaults on women custodians.

The plaintiffs' own expert testified that dormitory housing for aggressive inmates poses a greater security problem than single-cell lockups, and further testified that it would be unwise to use women as guards in a prison where even 10% of the inmates had been convicted of sex crimes and were

---

thus no occasion to give independent consideration to the District Court's ruling that Regulation 204 violates the Fourteenth Amendment as well as Title VII.

[22.] The record contains evidence of an attack on a female clerical worker in an Alabama prison, and of an incident involving a woman student who was taken hostage during a visit to one of the maximum security institutions.

not segregated from the other prisoners. [23]   The likelihood that inmates would assault a woman because she was a woman would pose a real threat not only to the victim of the assault but also to the basic control of the penitentiary and protection of its inmates and the other security personnel. The employee's very womanhood would thus directly undermine her capacity to provide the security that is the essence of a correctional counselor's responsibility.

There was substantial testimony from experts on both sides of this litigation that the use of women as guards in "contact" positions under the existing conditions in Alabama maximum security male penitentiaries would pose a substantial security problem, directly linked to the sex of the prison guard. On the basis of that evidence, we conclude that the District Court was in error in ruling that being male is not a bona fide occupational qualification for the job of correctional counselor in a "contact" position in an Alabama male maximum security penitentiary.

The judgment is accordingly affirmed in part and reversed in part, and the case is remanded to the District Court for further proceedings consistent with this opinion.

It is so ordered.

MR. JUSTICE MARSHALL, with whom MR. JUSTICE BRENNAN joins, concurring in part and dissenting in part.

I agree entirely with the Court's analysis of Alabama's height and weight requirements for prison guards, and with its findings that these restrictions discriminate on the basis of sex in violation of Title VII. Accordingly, I join Parts I and II of the Court's opinion. I also agree with much of the Court's general discussion in Part III of the bona fide occupational qualification exception contained in § 703(e) of Title VII.

. . .I must, however, respectfully disagree with the Court's application of the bfoq exception in this case. . . .

Some women, like some men, undoubtedly are not qualified and do not wish to serve as prison guards, but that does not justify the exclusion of all women from this employment opportunity. . . .   [N]o governmental "business" may operate "normally" in violation of the Constitution. Every action of government is constrained by constitutional limitations. While those limits may be violated more frequently than we wish, no one disputes that the "normal operation" of all government functions takes place within them. A prison system operating in blatant violation of the Eighth Amendment is an exception that should be remedied with all possible speed, as Judge Johnson's comprehensive order in *James v. Wallace, supra,* is designed to do. In the meantime, the existence of such violations should not be legitimatized by calling them "normal." Nor should the Court accept them as justifying

---

[23.]   Alabama's penitentiaries are evidently not typical. The appellees' two experts testified that in a normal, relatively stable maximum security prison—characterized by control over the inmates, reasonable living conditions, and segregation of dangerous offenders—women guards could be used effectively and beneficially. Similarly, an *amicus* brief filed by the State of California attests to that State's success in using women guards in all-male penitentiaries.

conduct that would otherwise violate a statute intended to remedy age-old discrimination.

The Court's error in statutory construction is less objectionable, however, than the attitude it displays toward women. Though the Court recognizes that possible harm to women guards is an unacceptable reason for disqualifying women, it relies instead on an equally speculative threat to prison discipline supposedly generated by the sexuality of female guards. There is simply no evidence in the record to show that women guards would create any danger to security in Alabama prisons significantly greater than already exists. All of the dangers—with one exception discussed below—are inherent in a prison setting whatever the gender of the guards.

The Court first sees women guards as a threat to security because "there are few visible deterrents to inmate assaults on women custodians." *Ante,* at 2730. In fact, any prison guard is constantly subject to the threat of attack by inmates and "invisible" deterrents are the guard's only real protection. No prison guard relies primarily on his or her ability to ward off an inmate attack to maintain order. Guards are typically unarmed and sheer numbers of inmates could overcome the normal complement. Rather, like all other law enforcement officers, prison guards must rely primarily on the moral authority of their office and the threat of future punishment for miscreants. As one expert testified below, common sense, fairness, and mental and emotional stability are the qualities a guard needs to cope with the dangers of the job. App. 81. Well qualified and properly trained women, no less than men, have these psychological weapons at their disposal. . . .

It appears that the real disqualifying factor in the Court's view is "[t]he employee's very womanhood." *Ante,* at 2730. The Court refers to the large number of sex offenders in Alabama prisons, and to "the likelihood that inmates would assault a woman because she was a woman." *Ibid.* In short, the fundamental justification for the decision is that women as guards will generate sexual assaults. With all respect, this rationale regrettably perpetuates one of the most insidious of the old myths about women—that women, wittingly or not, are seductive sexual objects. The effect of the decision, made I am sure with the best of intentions, is to punish women because their very presence might provoke sexual assaults. It is women who are made to pay the price in lost job opportunities for the threat of depraved conduct by prison inmates. Once again, "[t]he pedestal upon which women have been placed has . . ., upon closer inspection, been revealed as a cage." *Sail'er Inn, Inc., v. Kirby,* 5 Cal.3d 1, 20, 95 Cal. Rptr. 329, 341, 485 P.2d 529, 541 (1971). It is particularly ironic that the cage is erected here in response to feared misbehavior by imprisoned criminals. . . . Presumably, one of the goals of the Alabama prison system is the eradication of inmates' antisocial behavior patterns so that prisoners will be able to live one day in free society. Sex offenders can begin this process by learning to relate to women guards in a socially acceptable manner. To deprive women of job opportunities because of the threatened behavior of convicted criminals is to turn our social priorities upside down.

Although I do not countenance the sex discrimination condoned by the majority, it is fortunate that the Court's decision is carefully limited to the facts before it. I trust the lower courts will recognize that the decision was impelled by the shockingly inhuman conditions in Alabama prisons, and thus that the "extremely narrow [bfoq] exception" recognized here, *ante,* at 2729, will not be allowed "to swallow the rule" against sex discrimination. See *Phillips v. Martin Marietta Corp., supra,* 400 U.S. at 545, 91 S.Ct. at 498. Expansion of today's decision beyond its narrow factual basis would erect a serious roadblock to economic equality for women.

NOTES

1. In General Electric Co. v. Gilbert, 429 U.S. 125 (1976), the Supreme Court ruled that employers who exclude pregnancy-related disabilities from coverage under otherwise comprehensive income protection plans do not discriminate on the basis of sex in violation of Title VII. Justice Rehnquist, writing for the majority in *Gilbert,* stated that the company's challenged disability benefits plan did not exclude anyone because of gender, "but merely removed one physical condition—pregnancy—from the list of compensable disabilities." In reaching this conclusion, the Court relied heavily on its 1974 decision in Geduldig v. Aiello, 417 U.S. 484, where it was held that disparity in treatment between pregnancy-related and other disabilities was not sex discrimination under the Equal Protection Clause of the Fourteenth Amendment.

On October 31, 1978, President Carter signed into law (P.L. 95-552) a pregnancy disability amendment to Title VII which was specifically designed to overturn the Supreme Court's judgment in *Gilbert.* The pregnancy disability amendment reads as follows:

> 701. (k) The terms "because of sex" or "on the basis of sex" include, but are not limited to, because of or on the basis of pregnancy, childbirth or related medical conditions; and women affected by pregnancy, childbirth, or related medical conditions shall be treated the same for all employment-related purposes, including receipt of benefits under fringe benefit programs, as other persons not so affected but similar in their ability or inability to work, and nothing in section 703(h) of this title shall be interpreted to permit otherwise. This subsection shall not require an employer to pay for health insurance benefits for abortion, except where the life of the mother would be endangered if the fetus were carried to term, or except where medical complications have arisen from an abortion: Provided, That nothing herein shall preclude an employer from providing abortion benefits or otherwise affect bargaining agreements in regard to abortion.

2. One year after the decision in *Gilbert,* the Court ruled in Nashville Gas Company v. Satty, 434 U.S. 136 (1977), that employers will be found to violate Title VII when they force women who are absent from work due to pregnancy to forfeit accumulated job seniority. The Court distinguished *Satty* from *Gilbert* on the ground that the employer in *Satty* had "not merely refused to extend to women a benefit that men cannot and do not receive, but had imposed on women a substantial burden that men need not suffer." Why did the Court in *Satty* grant any relief if, as stated in *Gilbert,* discrimination based on pregnancy is not sex discrimination under Title VII?

3. The courts have uniformly found that state protective laws which restrict the hours or conditions under which women may work are invalid under Title VII. *See, e.g.,* Rosenfeld v. Southern Pacific Co., 444 F.2d 1219 (9th Cir. 1971). Where a state law grants a benefit, such as minimum wages or rest periods, to women only, the courts are in conflict as to whether the law should be invalidated or extended to cover men also. *Compare* Hays v. Potlatch Forests, Inc., 465 F.2d 1081 (8th Cir. 1972), *with* Homemakers, Inc. v.

Division of Industrial Welfare, 509 F.2d 20 (9th Cir. 1974), *cert. denied*, 423 U.S. 1063 (1976). The EEOC Guidelines, 29 CFR § 1604.2(b)(3) (1975), provide that restrictive state protective laws do not come within the BFOQ provisions of Title VII and that benefits, where provided for women, must be extended to men.

4. In general, the courts have held that employers may not impose different standards on male and female employees. Thus, an employer may not exclude mothers, but not fathers, from employment. Phillips v. Martin Marietta Corp., 400 U.S. 542 (1971). Similarly, an employer may not terminate female flight attendants upon marriage if male flight attendants are retained. Sprogis v. United Air Lines, 444 F.2d 1194 (7th Cir. 1971), *cert. denied*, 404 U.S. 991 (1971). An employer's discharge of a pregnant unmarried employee was found to be in violation of Title VII in Jacobs v. Martin Sweets Co., 550 F.2d 364 (6th Cir. 1977). Further, the suspension of a newly married female employee for her refusal to change her name on personnel forms to that of her husband constituted a violation of Title VII. Allen v. Lovejoy, 553 F.2d 522 (6th Cir. 1977).

An exception to the requirement of equal standards for male and female employees has developed in the area of grooming standards. Where an employer imposes sex-differentiated hair regulations, most Circuit Courts have held that there is no Title VII violation because hair length is not an immutable characteristic nor is the right to wear it at a given length a fundamental right. *See, e.g.,* Fagan v. National Cash Register Co., 481 F.2d 1115 (D.C. Cir. 1973); Willingham v. Macon Telegraph Publishing Co., 507 F.2d 1084 (5th Cir. 1975) (*en banc*); Earwood v. Continental Southeastern Lines, 539 F.2d 1349 (4th Cir. 1976); Barker v. Taft Broadcasting Co., 549 F.2d 400 (6th Cir. 1977).

5. Two Circuit Courts have held that negative employment consequences resulting from a woman's refusal of her employer's sexual advances constitute a violation of Title VII. Barnes v. Costle, 561 F.2d 983 (D.C. Cir. 1977); Tomkins v. Public Service Electric and Gas Co., 16 FEP Cases 22 (3rd Cir. 1977).

6. Although the proscription against sex discrimination is now well-established under Title VII, especially since the Supreme Court's ruling in *Dothard v. Rawlinson, supra,* women have nevertheless had difficulty in prevailing in Title VII suits against colleges and universities. As noted above, women have had little success in overcoming the academic abstention doctrine and, thus, have failed in most legal challenges to sex discrimination in academia. *See, e.g.,* Keyes v. Lenoir Rhyne College, 552 F.2d 579 (4th Cir. 1977), *cert. denied*, 434 U.S. 904 (1977); Faro v. New York University, 502 F.2d 1229 (2d Cir. 1974); Green v. Bd. of Regents of Texas Tech. Univ., 474 F.2d 594 (5th Cir. 1973); Johnson v. Univ. of Pittsburgh, 15 FEP Cas. 1516 (W.D. Pa. 1977); Peters v. Middlebury College, 409 F.Supp. 857 (D. Vt. 1976); Van de Vate v. Boling, 379 F.Supp. 925 (E.D. Tenn. 1974).

CITY OF LOS ANGELES v. MANHART
Supreme Court of the United States
46 U.S.L.W. 41 (1978)

MR. JUSTICE STEVENS delivered the opinion of the Court.

As a class, women live longer than men. For this reason, the Los Angeles Department of Water and Power required its female employees to make larger contributions to its pension fund than its male employees. We granted certiorari to decide whether this practice discriminated against individual female employees because of their sex in violation of § 703(a)(1) of the Civil Rights Act of 1964, as amended.

For many years the Department has administered retirement, disability, and death benefit programs for its employees. Upon retirement each employee is eligible for a monthly retirement benefit computed as a fraction of his or her salary multiplied by years of service. The monthly benefits for men and women of the same age, seniority, and salary are equal. Benefits are funded entirely by contributions from the employees and the Department, augmented by the income earned on those contributions. No private insurance company is involved in the administration or payment of benefits.

Based on a study of mortality tables and its own experience, the Department determined that its 2,000 female employees on the average, will live a few years longer than its 10,000 male employees. The cost of a pension for the average retired female is greater than for the average male retiree because more monthly payments must be made to the average woman. The Department therefore required female employees to make monthly contributions to the fund which were 14.84% higher than the contributions required of comparable male employees. Because employee contributions were withheld from pay checks, a female employee took home less pay than a male employee earning the same salary. . . .

It is now well recognized that employment decisions cannot be predicated on mere "stereotyped" impressions about the characteristics of males or females. Myths and purely habitual assumptions about a woman's inability to perform certain kinds of work are no longer acceptable reasons for refusing to employ qualified individuals, or for paying them less. This case does not, however, involve a fictional difference between men and women. It involves a generalization that the parties accept as unquestionably true: women, as a class, do live longer than men. The Department treated its women employees differently from its men employees because the two classes are in fact different. It is equally true, however, that all individuals in the respective classes do not share the characteristic which differentiates the average class representatives. Many women do not live as long as the average man and many men outlive the average woman. The question, therefore, is whether the existence or nonexistence of "discrimination" is to be determined by comparison of class characteristics or individual characteristics. A "stereotyped" answer to that question may not be the same as the answer which the language and purpose of the statute command.

The statute makes it unlawful "to discriminate against any *individual* with respect to his compensation, terms, conditions or privileges of employment, because of such *individual's* race, color, religion, sex, or national origin." 42 U.S.C. § 2000e-2(a)(1) (emphasis added). The statute's focus on the individual is unambiguous. It precludes treatment of individuals as simply components of a racial, religious, sexual, or national class.

That proposition is of critical importance in this case because there is no assurance that any individual woman working for the Department will actually fit the generalization on which the Department's policy is based. Many of those individuals will not live as long as the average man. While they were working, those individuals received smaller paychecks because of their sex, but they will receive no compensating advantage when they retire. . . .

Even if the statutory language were less clear, the basic policy of the statute requires that we focus on fairness to individuals rather than fairness to classes. Practices which classify employers in terms of religion, race, or sex tend to preserve traditional assumptions about groups rather than thoughtful scrutiny of individuals. The generalization involved in this case illustrates the point. Separate mortality tables are easily interpreted as reflecting innate differences between the sexes; but a significant part of the longevity differential may be explained by the social fact that men are heavier smokers than women.

Finally, there is no reason to believe that Congress intended a special definition of discrimination in the context of employee group insurance coverage. It is true that insurance is concerned with events that are individually unpredictable, but that is characteristic of many employment decisions. Individual risks, like individual performance, may not be predicted by resort to classifications proscribed by Title VII. Indeed, the fact that this case involves a group insurance program highlights a basic flaw in the department's fairness argument. For when insurance risks are grouped, the better risks always subsidize the poorer risks. Healthy persons subsidize medical benefits for the less healthy; unmarried workers subsidize the pensions of married workers; persons who eat, drink, or smoke to excess may subsidize pension benefits for persons whose habits are more temperate. Treating different classes of risks as though they were the same for purposes of group insurance is a common practice which has never been considered inherently unfair. To insure the flabby and the fit as though they were equivalent risks may be more common than treating men and women alike; but nothing more than habit makes one "subsidy" seem less fair than the other.

An employment practice which requires 2,000 individuals to contribute more money into a fund than 10,000 other employees simply because each of them is a woman, rather than a man, is in direct conflict with both the language and the policy of the Act. Such a practice does not pass the simple test of whether the evidence shows "treatment of a person in a manner which but for the person's sex would be different." It constitutes discrimination and is unlawful unless exempted by the Equal Pay Act or some other affirmative justification.

II

Shortly before the enactment of Title VII in 1964, Senator Bennett proposed an amendment providing that a compensation differential based on sex would not be unlawful if it was authorized by the Equal Pay Act, which had been passed a year earlier. The Equal Pay Act requires employers to pay members of both sexes the same wages for equivalent work, except when the differential is pursuant to one of four specified exceptions. The Department contends that the fourth exception applies here. That exception authorizes a "differential based on any other factor other than sex."

The Department argues that the different contributions exacted from men and women were based on the factor of longevity rather than sex. It is plain, however, that any individual's life expectancy is based on a number of factors, of which sex is only one. The record contains no evidence that any factor other than the employee's sex was taken into account in calculating the 14.84% differential between the respective contributions by men and women. We agree with Judge Duniway's observation that one cannot "say that an actuarial distinction based entirely on sex is 'based on any other factor other than sex'. Sex is exactly what it is based on." 553 F.2d, at 588.

We are also unpersuaded by the Department's reliance on a colloquy between Senator Randolph and Senator Humphrey during the debate on the Civil Rights Act of 1964. Commenting on the Bennett Amendment, Senator Humphrey expressed his understanding that it would allow many differences in the treatment of men and women under industrial benefit plans, including earlier retirement options for women. Though he did not address differences in employee contributions based on sex, Senator Humphrey apparently assumed that the 1964 Act would have little, if any, impact on existing pension plans. His statement cannot, however, fairly be made the sole guide to interpreting the Equal Pay Act, which had been adopted a year earlier; and it is the 1963 statute, with its exceptions, on which the Department ultimately relies. We conclude that Senator Humphrey's isolated comment on the Senate floor cannot change the effect of the plain language of the statute itself.

III

The Department argues that reversal is required by *General Electric Co. v. Gilbert*. 429 U.S. 125. We are satisfied, however, that neither the holding nor the reasoning of *Gilbert* is controlling.

In *Gilbert* the Court held that the exclusion of pregnancy from an employer's disability benefit plan did not constitute sex discrimination within the meaning of Title VII. Relying on the reasoning in *Geduldig* v. *Aiello*, 417 U.S. 484, the Court first held that the General Electric plan did not involve "discrimination based upon gender as such." The two groups of potential recipients which that case concerned were pregnant women and nonpregnant persons. "While the first group is exclusively female, the second includes members of both sexes." 429 U.S., at 135. In contrast, each of the two groups of employees involved in this case is composed entirely and exclusively of members of the same sex. On its face, this plan discriminates on the basis of sex whereas the General Electric plan discriminated on the basis of a special physical disability.

In *Gilbert* the Court did note that the plan as actually administered had provided more favorable benefits to women as a class than to men as a class. This evidence supported the conclusion that not only had plaintiffs failed to establish a prima facie case by proving that the plan was discriminatory on its face, but they had also failed to prove any discriminatory effect.

In this case, however, the Department argues that the absence of a discriminatory effect on women as a class justifies an employment practice which, on its face, discriminated against individual employees because of their sex. But even if the Department's actuarial evidence is sufficient to prevent plaintiffs from establishing a prima facie case on the theory that the effect of the practice on women as a class was discriminatory, that evidence does not defeat the claim that the practice, on its face, discriminated against every individual woman employed by the Department.[30]

In essence, the Department is arguing that the prima facie showing of discrimination based on evidence of different contributions for the respective sexes is rebutted by its demonstration that there is a like difference in the cost of providing benefits for the respective classes. That argument might prevail if Title VII contained a cost justification defense comparable to the affirmative defense available in a price discrimination suit. But neither Congress nor the courts have recognized such a defense under Title VII.

Although we conclude that the Department's practice violated Title VII, we do not suggest that the statute was intended to revolutionize the insurance and pension industries. All that is at issue today is a requirement that men and women make unequal contributions to an employer-operated pension fund. Nothing in our holding implies that it would be unlawful for an employer to set aside equal retirement contributions for each employee and let each retiree purchase the largest benefit which his or her accumulated contributions could command in the open market.[33] Nor does it call into question the insurance industry practice of considering the composition of an employer's work force in determining the probable cost of a retirement or death benefit plan. Finally, we recognize that in a case of this kind it may be necessary to take special care in fashioning appropriate relief.

IV

The Department challenges the District Court's award of retroactive relief to the entire class of female employees and retirees. Title VII does not require a district court to grant any retroactive relief. A court that finds unlawful discrimination "may enjoin [the discrimination] and order such affirmative action as may be appropriate, which may include, but is not limited to, reinstatement . . . with or without back pay . . . or any other equitable relief as the court deems appropriate." 42 U.S.C. § 2000e-5(g). To the point of redundancy, the statute stresses that retroactive relief "may" be awarded if it is "appropriate."

[30.]   Some *amici* suggest that the Department's discrimination is justified by business necessity. They argue that, if no gender distinction is drawn, many male employees will withdraw from the plan, or even the Department, because they can get a better pension plan in the private market. But the Department has long required equal contributions to its death benefit plan, see n. 19, *supra*, and since 1975 it has required equal contributions to its pension plan. Yet the Department points to no "adverse selection" by the affected employees, presumably because an employee who wants to leave the plans must also leave his job, and few workers will quit because one of their fringe benefits could theoretically be obtained at a marginally lower price on the open market. In short, there has been no showing that sex distinctions are reasonably necessary to the normal operation of the Department's retirement plan.

[33.]   Title VII and the Equal Pay Act govern relations between employees and their employer, not between employees and third parties. We do not suggest, of course, that an employer can avoid its responsibilities by delegating discriminatory programs to corporate shells. Title VII applies to "any agent" of a covered employer, 42 U.S.C. § 2000e(b), and the Equal Pay Act applies to "any person acting directly or indirectly in the interest of any employer in relation to any employee." 29 U.S.C. § 203(d). In this case, for example, the Department could not deny that the administrative board was its agent after it successfully argued that the two were so inseparable that both shared the city's immunity from suit under 42 U.S.C. § 1983.

In *Albemarle Paper Co.* v. *Moody*, 422 U. S. 405, the Court reviewed the scope of a district court's discretion to fashion appropriate remedies for a Title VII violation and concluded that "back pay should be denied only for reasons which, if applied generally, would not frustrate the central statutory purposes of eradicating discrimination throughout the economy and making persons whole for injuries suffered through past discrimination." *Id.*, at 421. Applying that standard, the Court ruled that an award of back-pay should not be conditioned on a showing of bad faith. *Id.*, at 422-423. But the *Albemarle* Court also held that backpay was not to be awarded automatically in every case. . . .

There can be no doubt that the prohibition against sex-differentiated employee contributions represents a marked departure from past practice. Although Title VII was enacted in 1964, this is apparently the first litigation challenging contribution differences based on valid actuarial tables. Retro-active liability could be devastating for a pension fund. The harm would fall in large part on innocent third parties. If, as the courts below apparently contemplated, the plaintiffs' contributions are recovered from the pension fund, the administrators of the fund will be forced to meet unchanged obligations with diminished assets. If the reserve proves inadequate, either the expectations of all retired employees will be disappointed or current employees will be forced to pay not only for their own future security but also for the unanticipated reduction in the contributions of past employees.

Without qualifying the force of the *Albemarle* presumption in favor of retroactive relief, we conclude that it was error to grant such relief in this case. Accordingly, although we agree with the Court of Appeals' analysis of the statute, we vacate its judgment and remand the case for further proceedings consistent with this opinion.

NOTES

1. A retirement plan which required women to retire at age 62 and men at age 65 was held to violate Title VII. Drewrys Ltd. U.S.A., Inc. v. Bartmess, 444 F.2d 1186 (7th Cir. 1971), *cert. denied*, 404 U.S. 939 (1971).

2. Consider the following questions in light of the Supreme Court's decision in *Manhart:*

(a) Can a private insurance company charge men and women different rates for the same pension benefit payout (on the theory that men do not live as long as women)?

(b) May an employer purchase an insurance plan from a private insurance company which provides for equal benefits for men and women even though the insurance company's cost estimates assume that it costs more to insure women than men? (Can the male employees file a charge under Title VII charging that the employer's contributions are lower for men than for women?)

(c) May an employer make equal contributions on behalf of men and women and purchase a pension program from a private insurance company that pays women less per month in benefits than men?

(d) Suppose men and women in *Manhart* were required to contribute the same amount, but women received less per month in pension benefits. Would this have violated Title VII?

3. Some of the aforementioned questions were considered by the First Circuit in EEOC v. Colby College, ___ F.2d ___ (1st Cir. 1978). Consider the opinion below and decide

whether you think that the views of court are consistent with *Manhart*. Is the suggestion by Chief Judge Coffin, relating to the redemption of "chits" by employees, a workable solution?

E. E. O. C. v. COLBY COLLEGE
First Circuit Court of Appeals
___ F.2d ___(1978)

ALDRICH, Senior Circuit Judge. Appellee Colby College is a private, coeducational liberal arts college, located in Waterville, Maine. Since 1935, with respect to annuities, and 1956 with respect to life insurance, it has insured most of its faculty, and a portion of its administrative staff, under a contributory pension plan with appellee Teachers Insurance Annuity Association (TIAA).[2] The plan also provides for decreasing term life insurance up to age 70. TIAA is a nonprofit, legal reserve life insurance company operating nationwide, and presently covering some 2800 educational institutions. It was founded in 1918 by The Carnegie Foundation for the Advancement of Teaching as a quasi-public service, and may offer special features for its unique clientele, but for the present purposes it in no way differs from any other legal reserve insurance company. This suit was brought by the Equal Employment Opportunity Commission (EEOC) against Colby as the result of a charge by a woman faculty member that she had been discriminated against on the basis of sex with respect to her annuity in violation of section 703(a)(1) of Title VII of the Civil Rights Act of 1964. Appellees TIAA and CREF are not charged with violation of Title VII, but were named as parties having an interest in the outcome of the litigation under F.R.Civ.P. 19(a).

Colby may quarrel with our shorthand statement that it insures its faculty with TIAA, but we quarrel even more with its contention that it is divorced altogether from the transaction and not to be charged with violation of Title VII because of the fact that TIAA makes separate contracts with the individual faculty members and other Colby employees. It is true that TIAA is the carrier, and that the insured employee looks solely to it for payment, but Colby is more than a broker, or other intermediary, that enables the parties to enter into the arrangement. As one district court has observed in a case presenting an identical challenge to the TIAA plan, an educational institution's adoption of TIAA "constitutes affirmative, active participation," without which "the challenged program could not operate." *Spirt v. TIAA*, S.D.N.Y., 1976 416 F.Supp. 1019, 1021, 1022. . . .

The eligibility and contribution formulas established by Colby are based upon the salary and position of the particular employee, and not in any degree on sex. The asserted discrimination is that the ultimate monthly annuity payments to women are smaller than those made to their male counterparts. This disparity results from the fact that TIAA, as do legal reserve companies generally, determines the amount of coverage it will

---

[2.]   Another carrier, appellee herein, College Retirement Equities Fund (CREF), presents no different questions and will be disregarded for the purposes of this opinion.

supply for a given premium by the use of mortality tables, segregated by sex. These tables are based upon the fact that, taken as a group or class, women have a greater life expectancy than men. Consequently, TIAA, in return for the total premium payment tendered by and on behalf of each individual future annuitant, provides smaller annuity payments to women employees of the same years in the plan, age and salary as men, because the women insureds, as a group, will live longer after retirement, and hence receive more payments, than the men.

The smaller individual annuity payment to women is not a chauvinistic distinction. The use of such mortality tables produces the converse situation in the case of life insurance. Since, as a group, the men will live a shorter time, the total group will pay fewer premiums before their policies mature. . . . Hence Colby's male employees, individually, receive smaller death benefits than their female counterparts. So far as any discrimination because of sex is concerned, however, there is no difference in principle between the annuity and the life insurance programs, except that one favors men as a class and the other women. For the balance of this opinion we will consider only the annuities, as to which women complain.

The district court found that as of any given moment, the actuarial value of TIAA's annuity contracts written on employees of the same age, salary, length of service, and hence premium contributions, was the same, regardless of the fact that the monthly payments were larger for men than for women. [5]   *Equal Employment Opportunity Commission v. Colby College,* D.Me., 1977, 439 F.Supp. 631, 634. This finding is not only not contested, it is assumed. The complaint is not that TIAA has been fudging mortality tables, but to the consequences of their use. The complaint is that if the male annuitant is to receive $120 a month on retirement at 65, so, under the Act, should the premium-equivalent female, even though on the basis of normal life expectancy she may expect to receive payments for twelve years, and he for ten.

Noting this actuarial equivalency, the district court held that there was no unlawful discrimination and dismissed the action. *Equal Employment Opportunity Commission v. Colby College,* ante. The court based this conclusion upon the fact that administrative interpretations of the Equal Pay Act, 29 U.S.C. § 206(d)(1), which qualifies the reach of Title VII, *see* 42 U.S.C. § 2000e-2(h) by providing that disparities in wages paid to employees of different sexes are not unlawful if the differential is "based on any other factor other than sex," had sanctioned plans such as Colby's where the employer's contributions are equal for both sexes, but benefits are unequal. *See* 29 C.F.R. § 800.116(d) (1976). The Commission appeals, relying on *Los Angeles Dep't of Water & Power v. Manhart,* 1978, 435 U.S. 702, decided by the Court subsequent to the district court's opinion. . . .

[5.]   In simple terms, and disregarding the interest factor, the present worth of a contractual obligation to pay $120 a month for, say, ten years, is the same as that to pay $100 a month for twelve.

Whether by accident, or design, *Manhart* brought to the Court the case that presented the fewest difficulties, and the most conspicuous discrimination, if discrimination there were. The female employees, obliged to suffer larger payroll deductions, and hence receive less take-home pay than their male counterparts, could point to an immediate and obvious disparity of treatment, and indeed did so, at great length, by affidavits and brief. They could well prefer bread on the table to pie in the sky, even though fairly costed. Had it wished to, we believe the Court could have found discrimination in this fact alone. However, it chose a different route, and we cannot reject the rationale of its decision because it could have taken another course.

Neither can we listen to TIAA's plaints that to decide this case in favor of the EEOC would require it to disregard actuarial experience in computing costs and benefits. The Court did not call for such. To the contrary, it said, perhaps as a result of spectres raised by a number of amici briefs filed by representatives of the industry, including TIAA, that it did "not suggest that the statute was intended to revolutionize the insurance and pension industries." 435 U.S. at 717. Had the Court done otherwise, it would have created a serious problem for companies required by law in nearly every state in which they do business to satisfy the local insurance commissioner that their practices are financially sound. We could not rule, however, that it would be impossible to frame a decision in favor of EEOC without offending that principle.

Most of all we reject appellees' contention based on the Court's statement that "[a]ll that is at issue today is a requirement that men and women make unequal contributions to an employer-operated pension fund." *Id.* Appellees would have us overlook the virtue of the common law that what is decided in one case, and, particularly as concerns inferior courts, what is said in one case, are guides for future cases where different, but comparable issues, are presented. We find the issues in the instant case highly comparable to *Manhart.*

If the statute's "focus on the individual" forbids an employer from treating women as a class with respect to annuities so as to require from them higher premiums, although they as a class receive more for their money, it is difficult to perceive a distinction that would permit a plan whereby women make contributions equal to those of men, but receive smaller monthly payments. The same would appear with regard to the Court's treatment of the Equal Pay Act. If the actuarial distinction arising from sex-segregated mortality tables failed to qualify as a "differential based on any other factor other than sex," in *Manhart,* one must ask how that same distinction can qualify here, especially since appellees, like the Department in *Manhart,* have presented no evidence that any factor other than sex was considered in arriving at the benefit differential.

Nor can we accept the argument that, because equal contributions are made, there is not, in fact, any discrimination. Appellee suggests that the college has done all it can do by making equal contributions on behalf of both men and women and that there is no employment discrimination simply because a woman happens to be able to buy a different annuity with her money than can a man with the same amount of money. Even aside from what we have already said about Colby being an active participant in the insurance and annuity plan, the fact is that the contributions are not made in the form of a payment with which the employee may do whatever he or she desires. Rather, the contributions may be used only to buy an annuity or life insurance policy with the foreknowledge that the woman's dollar can buy a different amount in those markets than can a man's.

This is not to say, in anticipation of our returning this case to the district court, that we do not foresee difficulties, possibly very great difficulties, that did not arise in *Manhart*, in light of the Court's caveat that the statute was not intended to revolutionize the industry. . . .

Like King Canute, neither the Congress nor a court can change the forces of nature. "As a class, women live longer than men." *Id.*, at 704. Manifestly, an insurance company cannot disregard this fact, any more than it can disregard age, or fail to require premiums and create reserves that will fund its total ultimate obligations in light of the expectancy of its policy holders. Regardless of what one individual woman may do in the way of paying in and taking out, if women in their totality are to take out more than their male counterparts, either they, or someone else, must pay in more. Even though an individual woman may prove to be shortlived, to add her to the group requires a larger premium contribution than if she had been a man.

There would seem, as a matter of mechanics, to be two ways of paying this female supplement. Although *Manhart* was decided below on summary judgment, and the only evidence was an affidavit from an actuary, who stated in part,

"[l]ife expectancy and mortality tables are universal throughout the western commercial world in separating male mortality rates from female mortality rates. . . . To my knowledge, no tables have yet been developed which measure life expectancy for annuity purposes on a unisex basis. . . ."

the thrust of the *Manhart* opinion envisaged a single rate, hereafter unisex rate, of sufficient size to pay for both sexes. The Court found it would be fair that "women as a class . . . be subsidized, to some extent, by the class of male employees." *Id.*, at 708-11. If the matter were open, we might have difficulty in seeing how this increased premium for every individual male employee is not based entirely on sex, *viz.*, simply on the presence of female employees. The direct sexual basis would seem emphasized by the only discussion we have found of a theoretical unisex table, which recognized that it would have to be at a variable rate. [10] The Court's conclusion that

---

[10.] Fellers and Jackson, "Noninsured Pensioner Mortality: The UP-1984 Table." 25 Proceedings, Conference of Actuaries in Public Practice, 456-59, 483-84 (1976), cited in brief for the United States and the EEOC as amici curiae at 24 n.20 & 27 n. 24. in *Los Angeles Dep't of Water & Power v. Manhart*, 1978. 435 U.S. 702. If a man whose premium has been (X) should find himself charged (X + W/4) because 25% of his co-employees are women, and (X + W/2) if

the subsidy would be fair did not address the issue of its sexual basis,[11] nor the fact that a variable subsidy would upset the widely desired practice of definiteness in pension plans. *See* n. 4, ante.

Another aspect not discussed by the Court in contemplating a male subsidy was its effect on plans already agreed to, in that increasing male contributions may constitute a breach of contract. . . . We may wonder whether this would lead to the employer itself having to absorb the difference. In the case of self-insurers, as in *Manhart,* this is a ready if not pleasant solution. It does not, even here, however, avoid other issues raised by unisex rates. . . .

We perceive, a further, two-headed problem. The *Manhart* court stated that "pension benefits, and the contributions that maintain them, are 'compensation' under Title VII." *Id.*, at 712 N.23. If the employer itself makes larger contributions on account of each female employee, this would seem discriminatory, and impermissible per se. But even if, by calculating a new unisex rate, the supplement is imposed upon the male employees, concededly each female employee ends up with a pension contract that is actuarially worth more than the one received by her male counterpart. In a sense this is not unequal compensation in the individual case because what she receives in dollars will depend upon her actual longevity as distinguished from her actuarial expectancy. We take the essence of *Manhart* to be that, although, to simplify, Title VII, as applied, requires all female employees to be given 12 chances to win $100, and men 10, this is not discriminatory against men because individual women may not realize on their better chances. The perfection of this approach, however, must be measured against the consequences if the plan permitted, as we note in the literature that some do, conversion, or surrender for a lump sum by the employee. In the case at bar the annuity plan does not afford the employee this right, but inequality would seem inescapable if the female employee could obtain a surrender value which, if fairly based on actuarial worth, must exceed her male counterpart's.

Whether, or how, unisex insurer-operated plans can be achieved without revolutionizing the industry we cannot resolve at this stage, and merely flag certain questions that occur to us. Prima facie, *Manhart* compels us to vacate the district court's dismissal of the complaint. However, some of the possible questions, including those adverted to in Chief Judge Coffin's concurrence, seem so serious that, without prejudice, we do not rule that *Manhart* requires a ruling on liability, in order to permit respondents to enlarge the record if they should see fit to do so.

Reversed and remanded.

women rise to 50%, he might ask how such extra deductions in his pay envelope were not based upon sex, even though it was not his sex, but that of his fellow employees.

[11.] The Court did refer to racial subsidy, at 709 N. 15, but without noting that there are no racial tables, and its reference's recital of the fact that at pension ages there is no appreciable life expectancy difference. Brief of the Society of Actuaries, et al., at 11 n. 10, in *Los Angeles Dep't of Water & Power v. Manhart*. 1978, 435 U.S. 702.

COFFIN, Chief Judge (concurring). I concur fully in the court's result and analysis, but I write to express my reservations about the opinion's tangential goal of commenting on problems created for future courts by *Manhart* and this holding. While I agree with the court that *Manhart's* rejection of sex-based actuarial tables extends to our situation, I am not sure that *Manhart* held that an employer could never offer a benefit plan using sex-based tables. . . .

The plan that is before us, as I see it, fails because it is as if a company paid its male and female employees equal salaries, but in the form of chits that could be redeemed only in a particular store which, the company knew, would give to one sex more for the same number of chits than to the other sex. That company could hardly claim that it was not discriminating between men and women. So here. Perhaps, however, once they turn their attention to the problem, the parties could work out a system permissible under *Manhart* that would eliminate the chit-like nature of the contributions through a set of genuine employee options or other features. If so, perhaps the system could legally include unequal, actuarially sound pension and life insurance benefits for participating men and women.

IX. Religious Discrimination

TRANS WORLD AIRLINES v. HARDISON
Supreme Court of the United States
97 S. Ct. 2264 (1977)

Mr. Justice WHITE delivered the opinion of the Court.

Section 703(a)(1) of the Civil Rights Act of 1964, Title VII, 42 U.S.C. § 2000e-2(a)(1), makes it an unlawful employment practice for an employer to discriminate against an employee or a prospective employee on the basis of his or her religion. At the time of the events involved here, a guideline of the Equal Employment Opportunity Commission (EEOC), 29 CFR § 1605.1(b), required, as the Act itself now does, 42 U.S.C. § 2000e(j), that an employer, short of "undue hardship," make "reasonable accommodations" to the religious needs of its employees. The issue in this case is the extent of the employer's obligation under Title VII to accommodate an employee whose religious beliefs prohibit him from working on Saturdays.

I

We summarize briefly the facts found by the District Court. 375 F.Supp. 877 (WD Mo.1974).

Petitioner Trans World Airlines (TWA) operates a large maintenance and overhaul base in Kansas City, Mo. On June 5, 1967, respondent Larry G. Hardison was hired by TWA to work as a clerk in the Stores Department at its Kansas City base. Because of its essential role in the Kansas City operation, the Stores Department must operate 24 hours per day, 365 days per year, and whenever an employee's job in that department is not filled, an employee must be shifted from another department, or a supervisor must cover the job, even if the work in other areas may suffer.

Hardison, like other employees at the Kansas City base, was subject to a seniority system contained in a collective-bargaining agreement [1] that TWA maintains with petitioner International Association of Machinists and Aerospace Workers (IAM). The seniority system is implemented by the union steward through a system of bidding by employees for particular shift assignments as they become available. The most senior employees have first choice for job and shift assignments, and the most junior employees are required to work when the union steward is unable to find enough people willing to work at a particular time or in a particular job to fill TWA's needs.

In the spring of 1968 Hardison began to study the religion known as the Worldwide Church of God. One of the tenets of that religion is that one must observe the Sabbath by refraining from performing any work from sunset on Friday until sunset on Saturday. The religion also proscribes work on certain specified religious holidays.

When Hardison informed Everett Kussman, the manager of the Stores Department, of his religious conviction regarding observance of the Sabbath, Kussman agreed that the union steward should seek a job swap for Hardison or a change of days off; that Hardison would have his religious holidays off whenever possible if Hardison agreed to work the traditional holidays when asked; and that Kussman would try to find Hardison another job that would be more compatible with his religious beliefs. The problem was temporarily solved when Hardison transferred to the 11 p. m.–7 a. m. shift. Working this shift permitted Hardison to observe his Sabbath.

The problem soon reappeared when Hardison bid for and received a transfer from Building 1, where he had been employed, to Building 2, where he would work the day shift. The two buildings had entirely separate seniority lists; and while in Building 1 Hardison had sufficient seniority to observe the Sabbath regularly, he was second from the bottom on the Building 2 seniority list.

In Building 2 Hardison was asked to work Saturdays when a fellow employee went on vacation. TWA agreed to permit the union to seek a change of work assignments for Hardison, but the union was not willing to violate the seniority provisions set out in the collective-bargaining contract, and Hardison had insufficient seniority to bid for a shift having Saturdays off.

A proposal that Hardison work only four days a week was rejected by the company. Hardison's job was essential and on weekends he was the only available person on his shift to perform it. To leave the position empty would have impaired Supply Shop functions, which were critical to airline

---

[1.]   The TWA-IAM agreement provides in pertinent part:
    "The principle of seniority shall apply in the application of this Agreement in all reductions or increases of force, preference of shift assignment, vacation period selection, in bidding for vacancies or new jobs, and in all promotions, demotions, or transfers involving classifications covered by this Agreement.
        . . . .
        "Except as hereafter provided in this paragraph, seniority shall apply in selection of shifts and days off within a classification within a department. . . ." App. 214.

operations; to fill Hardison's position with a supervisor or an employee from another area would simply have undermanned another operation; and to employ someone not regularly assigned to work Saturdays would have required TWA to pay premium wages.

When an accommodation was not reached, Hardison refused to report for work on Saturdays. A transfer to the twilight shift proved unavailing since that schedule still required Hardison to work past sundown on Fridays. After a hearing, Hardison was discharged on grounds of insubordination for refusing to work during his designated shift.

Hardison, having first invoked the administrative remedy provided by Title VII, brought this action for injunctive relief in the United States District Court against TWA and IAM, claiming that his discharge by TWA constituted religious discrimination in violation of Title VII, 42 U.S.C. § 2000e-2(a)(1). He also charged that the union had discriminated against him by failing to represent him adequately in his dispute with TWA and by depriving him of his right to exercise his religious beliefs. Hardison's claim of religious discrimination rested on 1967 EEOC guidelines requiring employers "to make reasonable accommodations to the religious needs of employees" whenever such accommodation would not work an "undue hardship," 29 CFR § 1605.1, 32 Fed.Reg. 10298 (1967), and on similar language adopted by Congress in the 1972 amendments to Title VII, 42 U.S.C. § 2000e(j).

After a bench trial, the District Court ruled in favor of the defendants. Turning first to the claim against the union, the District Court ruled that although the 1967 EEOC guidelines were applicable to unions, the union's duty to accommodate Hardison's belief did not require it to ignore its seniority system as Hardison appeared to claim. [4] As for Hardison's claim against TWA, the District Court rejected at the outset TWA's contention that requiring it in any way to accommodate the religious needs of its employees would constitute an unconstitutional establishment of religion. As the District Court construed the Act, however, TWA had satisfied its "reasonable accommodation" obligations, and any further accommodation would have worked an undue hardship on the company.

The Eighth Circuit Court of Appeals reversed the judgment for TWA. . . .

II

The Court of Appeals found that TWA had committed an unlawful employment practice under § 703(a)(1) of the Act, 42 U.S.C. § 2000e-2(a)(1), which provides:

[4.]   The District Court voiced concern that if it did not find an undue hardship in such circumstances, accommodation of religious observances might impose "a priority of the religious over the secular" and thereby raise significant questions as to the constitutional validity of the statute under the Establishment Clause of the First Amendment. 375 F.Supp., at 883, quoting Edwards & Kaplan, Religious Discrimination and the Role of Arbitration Under Title VII, 69 Mich.L.Rev. 599, 628 (1971).

"(a) It shall be an unlawful employment practice for an employer—

"(1) to fail to refuse to hire or to discharge any individual, or otherwise to discriminate against any individual with respect to his compensation, terms, conditions, or privileges of employment, because of such
individual's race, color, religion, sex, or national origin."

The emphasis of both the language and the legislative history of the statute
is on eliminating discrimination in employment; similarly situated employees are not to be treated differently solely because they differ with respect
to race, color, religion, sex, or national origin. This is true regardless of
whether the discrimination is directed against majorities or minorities. . . .

In brief, the employer's statutory obligation to make reasonable accommodation for the religious observances of its employees, short of incurring
an undue hardship, is clear, but the reach of that obligation has never been
spelled out by Congress or by Commission guidelines. With this in mind, we
turn to a consideration of whether TWA has met its obligation under Title
VII to accommodate the religious observances of its employees.

III

The Court of Appeals held that TWA had not made reasonable efforts
to accommodate Hardison's religious needs under the 1967 EEOC guidelines
in effect at the time the relevant events occurred. . . .

We disagree with the Court of Appeals in all relevant respects. It is our
view that TWA made reasonable efforts to accommodate and that each of
the Court of Appeals' suggested alternatives would have been an undue hardship within the meaning of the statute as construed by the EEOC guidelines.

A

It might be inferred from the Court of Appeals' opinion and from the
brief of the EEOC in this Court that TWA's efforts to accommodate were no
more than negligible. The findings of the District Court, supported by the
record, are to the contrary. In summarizing its more detailed findings, the
District Court observed:

"TWA established as a matter of fact that it did take appropriate action
to accommodate as required by Title VII. It held several meetings with
plaintiff at which it attempted to find a solution to plaintiff's problems.
It did accommodate plaintiff's observance of his special religious holidays. It authorized the union steward to search for someone who
would swap shifts, which apparently was normal procedure." 375
F.Supp., at 890-891.

It is also true that TWA itself attempted without success to find Hardison
another job. The District Court's view was that TWA had done all that
could reasonably be expected within the bounds of the seniority system.

The Court of Appeals observed, however, that the possibility of a variance from the seniority system was never really posed to the union. This is
contrary to the District Court's findings and to the record. The District
Court found that when TWA first learned of Hardison's religious observances

in April, 1968, it agreed to permit the union's steward to seek a swap of shifts or days off but that "the steward reported that he was unable to work out scheduling changes and that he understood that no one was willing to swap days with plaintiff". 375 F.Supp. at 888. Later, in March 1969, at a meeting held just two days before Hardison first failed to report for his Saturday shift, TWA again "offered to accommodate plaintiff's religious observance by agreeing to any trade of shifts or change of sections that plaintiff and the union could work out. Any shift or change was impossible within the seniority framework and the union was not willing to violate the seniority provisions set out in the contract to make a shift or change." 375 F.Supp., at 889. As the record shows, Hardison himself testified that Kussman was willing, but the union was not, to work out a shift or job trade with another employee. App. 76-77.

We shall say more about the seniority system, but at this juncture it appears to us that the system itself represented a significant accommodation to the needs, both religious and secular, of all of TWA's employees. As will become apparent, the seniority system represents a neutral way of minimizing the number of occasions when an employee must work on a day that he would prefer to have off. Additionally, recognizing that weekend work schedules are the least popular, the company made further accommodation by reducing its work force to a bare minimum on those days.

B

We are also convinced, contrary to the Court of Appeals, that TWA cannot be faulted for having failed itself to work out a shift or job swap for Hardison. Both the union and TWA had agreed to the seniority system; the union was unwilling to entertain a variance over the objections of men senior to Hardison; and for TWA to have arranged unilaterally for a swap would have amounted to a breach of the collective-bargaining agreement.

(1)

Hardison and the EEOC insist that the statutory obligation to accommodate religious needs takes precedence over both the collective-bargaining contract and the seniority rights of TWA's other employees. We agree that neither a collective-bargaining contract nor a seniority system may be employed to violate the statute, but we do not believe that the duty to accommodate requires TWA to take steps inconsistent with the otherwise valid agreement. . . .

Had TWA nevertheless circumvented the seniority system by relieving Hardison of Saturday work and ordering a senior employee to replace him, it would have denied the latter his shift preference so that Hardison could be given his. The senior employee would also have been deprived of his contractual rights under the collective-bargaining agreement. . . .

Title VII does not contemplate such unequal treatment. The repeated, unequivocal emphasis of both the language and the legislative history of Title VII is on eliminating discrimination in employment, and such discrimination is proscribed when it is directed against majorities as well as minorities. See pp. 2270-2271, *supra*. Indeed the foundation of Hardison's claim is that TWA and IAM engaged in religious *discrimination* in violation of § 703-(a)(1) when they failed to arrange for him to have Saturdays off. It would be anomalous to conclude that by "reasonable accommodation" Congress meant that an employer must deny the shift and job preference of some employees, as well as deprive them of their contractual rights, in order to accommodate or prefer the religious needs of others, and we conclude that Title VII does not require an employer to go that far.

(2)

Our conclusion is supported by the fact that seniority systems are afforded special treatment under Title VII itself. . . . 42 U.S.C. § 2000e-2(h). "[T]he unmistakable purpose of § 703(h) was to make clear that the routine application of a bona fide seniority system would not be unlawful under Title VII." *International Brotherhood of Teamsters v. United States, —— U.S. —— at ——*, 97 S.Ct. 1843 at 1863, 52 L.Ed.2d —— (1977). See also *United Air Lines, Inc. v. Evans, —— U.S. ——*, 97 S.Ct. 1885, 52 L.Ed.2d —— (1977). Section 703(h) is "a definitional provision; as with the other provisions of § 703, subsection (h) delineates which employment practices are illegal and thereby prohibited and which are not." *Franks v. Bowman Transportation Co., Inc.,* 424 U.S. 747, 758, 96 S.Ct. 1251, 1261, 47 L.Ed.2d 444 (1976). Thus, absent a discriminatory purpose, the operation of a seniority system cannot be an unlawful employment practice even if the system has some discriminatory consequences.

There has been no suggestion of discriminatory intent in this case. "The seniority system was not designed with the intention to discriminate against religion nor did it act to lock members of any religion into a pattern wherein their freedom to exercise their religion was limited. . . .

C

The Court of Appeals also suggested that TWA could have permitted Hardison to work a four-day week if necessary in order to avoid working on his Sabbath. Recognizing that this might have left TWA short-handed on the one shift each week that Hardison did not work, the court still concluded that TWA would suffer no undue hardship if it were required to replace Hardison either with supervisory personnel or with qualified personnel from other departments. Alternatively, the Court of Appeals suggested that TWA could have replaced Hardison on his Saturday shift with other available employees through the payment of premium wages. Both of these alternatives would involve costs to TWA, either in the form of lost efficiency in other jobs or as higher wages.

To require TWA to bear more than a *de minimus* cost in order to give Hardison Saturdays off is an undue hardship. Like abandonment of the seniority system, to require TWA to bear additional costs when no such costs are incurred to give other employees the days off that they want would involve unequal treatment of employees on the basis of their religion. By suggesting that TWA should incur certain costs in order to give Hardison

Saturdays off the Court of Appeals would in effect require TWA to finance an additional Saturday off and then to choose the employee who will enjoy it on the basis of his religious beliefs. While incurring extra costs to secure a replacement for Hardison might remove the necessity of compelling another employee to work involuntarily in Hardison's place, it would not change the fact that the privilege of having Saturdays off would be allocated according to religious beliefs.

As we have seen, the paramount concern of Congress in enacting Title VII was the elimination of discrimination in employment. In the absence of clear statutory language or legislative history to the contrary, we will not readily construe the statute to require an employer to discriminate against some employees in order to enable others to observe their Sabbath.

Reversed.

X.   Remedies for Employment Discrimination

CARTER v. GALLAGHER
United States Court of Appeals, Eighth Circuit
452 F.2d 315, 327 (1971)
Cert. denied, 406 U.S. 950 (1972)

On Petition For Rehearing En Banc.
GIBSON, Circuit Judge.

A panel of this court. . .sustained the order and opinion of the Honorable Earl R. Larson, District Court of Minnesota, finding that the employment practices and procedures for determining qualifications of applicants for positions on the Minneapolis Fire Department were racially discriminatory in violation of the Equal Protection Clause of the Fourteenth Amendment and the Civil Rights Act of 1870, 42 U.S.C. §1981, and approved a number of corrective practices ordered so as to eliminate all racially discriminatory practices; but disapproved that part of Judge Larson's order providing for absolute minority preference in the employment of the next 20 persons to be hired by the department. The case was brought as a class action and relief was extended to minority groups as a class.

The panel opinion, while sustaining most of Judge Larson's findings and orders granting affirmative relief, did not approve of the absolute preference in Fire Department employment to 20 minority persons who met the qualifications for the positions under the revised qualification standards established by the decree and held that the absolute preference order infringed upon the constitutional rights of white applicants whose qualifications are established to be equal or superior to the minority applicants. . . .

A petition for rehearing en banc by the appellees was granted but limited solely to the issue of the appropriate remedy. . . .

The fact of past racially discriminatory practices and procedures in employment by the Fire Department is accepted and clearly evidenced by the fact that of the 535 men in the Fire Department none are from minority groups. [2] We are thus here concerned only with the appropriateness of the remedy ordered by the District Court. The absolute preference of 20 minority persons who qualify has gone further than any of the reported appellate court cases in granting preference to overcome the effects of past discriminatory practices and does appear to violate the constitutional right of Equal Protection of the Law to white persons who are superiorly qualified.

The panel opinion has recognized the illegality of the past practices, has ordered those practices abandoned, and the affirmative establishment of nondiscriminatory practices and procedures. There is, as the panel pointed out, no claim or showing made that the plaintiffs were identifiable members of the class who had made prior applications for employment and were denied employment solely because of race. This latter situation could be remedied immediately by ordering the employment of such persons. However, in dealing with the abstraction of employment as a class, we are confronted with the proposition that in giving an absolute preference to a minority as a class over those of the white race who are either superiorly or equally qualified would constitute a violation of the Equal Protection Clause of the Fourteenth Amendment to the Constitution.

The defendants-appellants point out the mandatory requirements of the Minneapolis City and the Minnesota Veterans' Preference Act (Minnesota Statute § 197.45). These requirements however must give way to the Supremacy Clause of Article 6 of the United States Constitution.

Mr. Justice Black, in speaking for a unanimous court (although Mr. Justice Harlan concurred on the basis of the Fifteenth Amendment rather than on the Fourteenth) in Louisiana v. United States, 380 U.S. 145, 85 S. Ct. 817, 13 L. Ed. 2d 709 (1964), approved the suspension of Louisiana voting laws that had been administered discriminatorily against Negroes and held it was the affirmative duty of the district court to eliminate the discriminatory effects of past practices, stating, "We bear in mind that the court has not merely the power but the duty to render a decree which so far as possible eliminate the discriminatory effects of the past as well as bar like discrimination in the future." 380 U.S. at 154, 85 S. Ct. at 822. It is apparent that remedies to overcome the effects of past discrimination may suspend valid state laws. United States v. Mississippi, 339 F.2d 679 (5th Cir. 1964); United States v. Duke, 332 F.2d 759 (5th Cir. 1963).

Admittedly the District Court has wide power sitting as a court of equity to fashion relief enforcing the congressional mandate of the Civil Rights Act and the constitutional guarantees of the Equal Protection of the Law; and clearly, courts of equity have the power to eradicate the effects of past discriminations. Parham v. Southwestern Bell Telephone Co., 433 F.2d 421 (8th Cir. 1971). We are not here concerned with the anti-preference treatment section 703(j) of Title VII of the Civil Rights Act of 1964, 42

[2.] The total minority population of the Minneapolis area was 6.44 percent in 1970; black population 4.37 percent.

U.S.C. § 2000e-2(j)[3] as this class action is predicated under § 1981 of the old Civil Rights Act and the provisions of the Fourteenth Amendment. However, even the anti-preference treatment section of the new Civil Rights Act of 1964 does not limit the power of a court to order affirmative relief to correct the effects of past unlawful practices. United States v. IBEW, Local No. 38, 428 F.2d 144 (6th Cir.), cert denied, 400 U.S. 943, 91 S. Ct. 245, 27 L. Ed. 2d 248 (1970).

Although this case is not predicated upon Title VII of the Civil Rights Act of 1964 and most of the cases that have dealt with the issue of remedying past discriminatory practices along with prohibiting present discriminatory practices are under that Act, the remedies invoked in those cases offer some practical guidelines in dealing with this issue.

As the panel opinion points out most of these cases deal with discriminations to a specified individual who has been presently discriminated against on account of race, and the remedy is there easily applied as the individual who has been discriminated against can be presently ordered employed without running into the constitutional questions involved in granting preference to any one class over another. However, in United States v. Ironworkers Local 86, 443 F.2d 544 (9th Cir. 1971), cert denied, 404 U.S. 984, 92 S. Ct. 447, 30 L. Ed. 2d 367 (1971) the Ninth Circuit approved the district court decree ordering building construction unions to offer immediate job referrals to previous racial discriminatees and also approved a prospective order requiring the unions to recruit sufficient blacks to comprise a 30 percent membership in their apprenticeship programs. This was ordered in Seattle which had a black population of approximately 7 percent. See, United States v. Local No. 86, Int. Ass'n of Bridge S., D. and R. Ironworkers et al., 315 F. Supp. 1202 (W.D. Wash. 1970).

In Local 53 of Int. Ass'n of Asbestos Workers v. Vogler, 407 F.2d 1047 (5th Cir. 1969), the trial court ordered the immediate admission into the union of three Negroes who were racially discriminated against in their application for membership and voided a local membership rule that in effect made the union a self-perpetuating nepotistic group, specifically ordering the union to develop objective criteria for membership and prospectively ordering the alternating of white and Negro referrals.

[3.]   43 U.S.C. § 2000e-2(j) provides as follows:
         "Nothing contained in this subchapter shall be interpreted to require any employer, employment agency, labor organization, or joint labor-management committee subject to this subchapter to grant preferential treatment to any individual or to any group because of race, color, religion, sex, or national origin of such individual or group on account of an imbalance which may exist with respect to the total number or percentage of persons of any race, color, religion, sex, or national origin employed by any employer, referred or classified for employment by any employment agency or labor organization, admitted to membership or classified by any labor organization, or admitted to, or employed in, any apprenticeship or other training program, in comparison with the total number or percentage of persons of such race, color, religion, sex, or national origin in any community, State, section, or other area, or in the available work force in any community, State, section, or other area."

In United States v. Central Motor Lines, Inc., 325 F. Supp. 478 (W.D. N.C. 1970), the trial court issued a preliminary injunction requiring the motor carrier to hire six Negro drivers "promptly," (apparently within two weeks from the date of the order), and that any future drivers hired were to be in an alternating ratio of one black to one white.

Cases arising from Executive Order #11246, prohibiting all contractors and subcontractors on federally financed projects from discriminating in their employment practices, have also upheld plans which establish percentage goals for the employment of minority workers. See Contractors Association of Eastern Pa. v. Secretary of Labor, 442 F.2d 159 (3d Cir. 1971) (upholding the "Philadelphia Plan" requiring minority employment goals in the construction trades ranging from 19 percent-26 percent); Joyce v. McCrane, 320 F.Supp. 1284 (D.N.J. 1970) (requiring contractors to employ 30 percent-37 percent minority journeymen).

It is also appropriate to note that precedent from our own Circuit establishes that the presence of identified persons who have been discriminated against is not a necessary prerequisite to ordering affirmative relief in order to eliminate the present effects of past discrimination. In United States v. Sheet Metal Workers, Local 36, 416 F.2d 123 (8th Cir. 1969), we required substantial changes in union referral systems. In connection with this holding, Judge Heaney noted:

> "We recognize that each of the cases cited in n.15 to support our position can be distinguished on the ground that in each case, a number of known members of a minority group had been discriminated against after the passage of the Civil Rights Act. Here, we do not have such evidence, but we do not believe that it is necessary. The record does show that qualified Negro tradesmen have been and continue to be residents of the area. It further shows that they were acutely aware of the Locals' policies toward minority groups. It is also clear that they knew that even if they were permitted to use the referral system and become members of the union, they would have to work for at least a year before they could move into a priority group which would assure them reasonably full employment. In the light of this knowledge, it is unreasonable to expect that any Negro tradesman working for a Negro contractor or a nonconstruction white employer would seek to use the referral systems or to join either Local."
> Id. at 132.

It may also be pointed out that in actions under Title VII of the Civil Rights Act, 42 U.S.C. §2000e et seq., Congress has specifically granted authority to the trial courts to "order such affirmative action as may be appropriate, which may include . . . *hiring of employees*. . . ." 42 U.S.C. §2000e-5(g) (emphasis added).

None of the remedies ordered or approved in the above cases involved an absolute preference for qualified minority persons for the first vacancies appearing in an employer's business, in contrast to the remedy ordered in the

instant case. The absolute preference ordered by the trial court would operate as a present infringement on those non-minority group persons who are
equally or superiorly qualified for the fire fighter's positions; and we hesitate
to advocate implementation of one constitutional guarantee by the outright
denial of another. Yet we acknowledge the legitimacy of erasing the effects
of past racially discriminatory practices. Louisiana v. United States, *supra.*
To accommodate these conflicting considerations, we think some reasonable ratio for hiring minority persons who can qualify under the revised
qualification standards is in order for a limited period of time, or until there
is a fair approximation of minority representation consistent with the population mix in the area. Such a procedure does not constitute a "quota"
system because as soon as the trial court's order is fully implemented, all
hirings will be on a racially nondiscriminatory basis, and it could well be that
many more minority persons or less, as compared to the population at large,
over a long period of time would apply and qualify for the positions. However, as a method of presently eliminating the effects of past racial discriminatory practices and in making meaningful in the immediate future the
constitutional guarantees against racial discrimination, more than a token
representation should be afforded. For these reasons we believe the trial
court is possessed of the authority to order the hiring of 20 qualified minority persons, but this should be done without denying the constitutional
rights of others by granting an absolute preference.

Ideas and views on ratios and procedures may vary widely but this issue
should be resolved as soon as possible. In considering the equities of the
decree and the difficulties that may be encountered in procuring qualified
applicants from any of the racial groups, we feel that it would be in order for
the district court to mandate that one out of every three persons hired by
the Fire Department would be a minority individual who qualifies until at
least 20 minority persons have been so hired.

Fashioning a remedy in these cases is of course a practical question
which may differ substantially from case to case, depending on the circumstances. In reaching our conclusion in the instant case, we have been guided
to some extent by the following considerations:

(1)   It has now been established by the Supreme Court that the use of
mathematical ratios as "a starting point in the process of shaping a remedy"
is not unconstitutional and is "within the equitable remedial discretion of
the District Court." Swann v. Charlotte-Mecklenburg Board of Education,
402 U.S. 1, 25, 91 S. Ct. 1267, 1280, 28 L. Ed.2d 554 (1971).

(2)   Given the past discriminatory hiring policies of the Minneapolis
Fire Department, which were well known in the minority community, it is
not unreasonable to assume that minority persons will still be reluctant to
apply for employment, absent some positive assurance that if qualified they
will in fact be hired on a more than token basis.

(3)   As the panel opinion noted, testing procedures required to qualify
applicants are undergoing revision and validation at the present time. As the
tests are currently utilized, applicants must attain a qualifying score in order

to be certified at all. They are then ranked in order of eligibility according to their test scores (disregarding for present purposes the veteran's preference). Because of the absence of validation studies on the record before us, it is speculative to assume that the qualifying test, in addition to separating those applicants who are qualified from those who are not, also ranks qualified applicants with precision, statistical validity, and predictive significance. See generally, Cooper & Sobol, Seniority and Testing under Fair Employment Laws: A General Approach to Objective Criteria of Hiring and Promotion, 82 Harv. L. Rev. 1598, 1637-1669 (1969). Thus, a hiring remedy based on an alternating ratio such as we here suggest will by no means necessarily result in hiring less qualified minority persons in preference to more qualified white persons.

(4) While some of the remedial orders relied on by the plaintiffs and the Government ordered one to one ratios, they appear to be in areas and occupations with a more substantial minority population than the Minneapolis area. Thus we conclude that a one to two ratio would be appropriate here, until 20 qualified minority persons have been hired.

The panel opinion is adopted as the opinion of the court en banc with the exception of that part relating to the absolute preference.

The District Court properly retained jurisdiction pending full implementation of its decree and the remedy. Cause is remanded for further proceedings consistent with this opinion. . . .

[The concurring opinion of MATTHES, Chief Judge, is omitted.]

VAN OOSTERHOUT, Senior Circuit Judge (dissenting).

For reasons stated in Division V of the panel opinion in this case, reported at 452 F.2d 324, I dissent from the en banc mandatory determination that one out of three persons hired by the Fire Department shall be a minority person until at least twenty minority persons are hired. Such provision in my opinion is vulnerable to the same constitutional infirmity as Judge Larson's absolute preference provision. This court's minority preference provision will not discriminate against as many white applicants as Judge Larson's decree but it will still give some minority persons preference in employment over white applicants whose qualifications are determined to be superior under fairly imposed standards and tests.

Employment preferences based on race are prohibited by the Fourteenth Amendment. This case is distinguishable from Swann v. Charlotte-Mecklenburg Board of Education relied upon by the majority in that whites have no right to insist upon segregated schools, while white as well as Black applicants cannot be denied employment on the basis of race.

I agree that a court of equity has broad power to frame an appropriate decree but such power does not extend to establishing provisions which deprive persons of constitutionally guaranteed rights.

Present and future applicants for firemen positions are in no way responsible for past discrimination. Plaintiffs have not shown that any plaintiff now seeking employment has personally suffered as a result of past discrimination by being denied employment over a less qualified white person. Past general racial discrimination against Blacks under the circumstances of this case does not justify unconstitutional present racial discrimination against white applicants. The court should of course go as far as is constitutionally permissible to eliminate racial discrimination in employment of firemen. Substantial steps in that direction have been taken by other provisions of Judge Larson's decree and the panel opinion.

MEHAFFY, Circuit Judge, joins in this dissent.

NOTES

1. *Compare* NAACP v. Allen, 493 F.2d 614 (5th Cir. 1974), *with* Anderson v. San Francisco School District, 5 FEP Cas. 362 (N.D. Cal. 1972) (where it was held that "preferential treatment under the guise of 'affirmative action' is the imposition of one form of racial discrimination in place of another.")

2. In the cases involving quota or preferential hiring, the courts are often faced with the argument of "reverse discrimination" as seen in *Carter*. How should the courts deal with this problem? Can it be argued that any remedy which gives a preference to minority job applicants is violative of equal protection? The courts have tended to avoid this constitutional question by limiting preferential hiring orders. Usually, before an order for preferential hiring is issued, there must be a finding of a history of discrimination against a protected group or statistical evidence showing a pattern of gross discrimination; members of the preferred class are required to satisfy job related employment tests; the order is almost always temporary; the order is sometimes conditioned to take account of the availability of the preferred group in the geographic areas nearby the place of employment; and there is usually a finding that other available affirmative relief would be inadequate to overcome the present effects of the existing discrimination. *See generally* Edwards and Zaretsky, *Preferential Remedies for Employment Discrimination*, 74 Mich. L. Rev. 1 (1975).

3. The court-ordered preferential remedy (as distinguished from an "affirmative action program") has rarely, if ever, been used in the context of higher education.

4. A second type of court-ordered remedy involves a use of some form of fictional seniority. This alternative awards a person extra seniority either by replacing a departmental seniority system with plant-wide seniority, or by individual grants of seniority points. Fictional seniority of this sort is to be distinguished from the "retroactive seniority" awarded to identified victims of discrimination as part of the "make-whole" relief approved by the Supreme Court in its 1976 decision in Franks v. Bowman Transportation Company, 424 U.S. 747. Retroactive seniority places victims of discrimination in the position they would have been but for the identified discrimination, and therefore, theoretically at least, does not directly interfere with the vested seniority rights of non-minority persons. The courts in these cases have uniformly ruled that non-minority persons should not be entitled to gain an advantage over specific victims of discrimination even though the non-minority persons were not directly responsible for the unlawful discrimination. However, most courts have been unwilling to take the next step and award fictional seniority to minority persons who are not identified victims, either to give them some preference for future promotions or some special protection against layoffs. In such cases, the newly hired minority person is required to follow job progression rules established pursuant to existing facially neutral seniority systems. This is so even though it may be shown that the seniority system operates to perpetuate past discrimination by favoring non-minority persons who have the most service and thus are given the first right to bid on higher jobs and the greatest protection against layoff.

5. As alternative to fictional seniority and to retroactive seniority that might lead to the displacement of whites by blacks, some courts have approved of the concept of "front pay." This concept recognizes that, where victims of unlawful discrimination have been denied promotions which have been awarded instead to non-minority persons,

it may take years for the identified victims to achieve the place which they would have achieved absent the discrimination. This is so because the courts will never permit a discriminatee to bump or displace a non-minority person and it may be a number of years before vacancies occur into which the discriminatees can move. To overcome this problem, some courts have awarded discriminatees not only back pay but front pay at the higher job rate until the discriminatee actually achieves or is disqualified from the position which he had been denied. *See, e.g.,* Patterson v. American Tobacco Company, 12 FEP Cas. 314 (4th Cir. 1976); White v. Carolina Paperboard Corp., 16 FEP Cas. 44 (4th Cir. 1977); James v. Stockham Valves & Fittings Co., 15 FEP Cas. 827 (5th Cir. 1977).

6. In EEOC v. American Telephone & Telegraph Co., 14 FEP Cas. 1210 (3rd Cir. 1977), *cert. denied,* 46 U.S.L.W. 3799 (1978), the court upheld a consent decree which included an "affirmative action override" for promotion decisions. The company's bargained-for promotional system was a merit selection system in which management determined the best qualified employee, and seniority was only used to decide between two equally qualified candidates. The "override" provided that whenever a Bell Company was unable to achieve a target quota by applying normal selection standards, it had to pass over candidates with greater seniority or better qualifications in favor of members of the underrepresented group who were at least "basically qualified." It is noteworthy that the Supreme Court denied certiorari in *AT&T*. The case gives at least some implicit support to preferential remedies issued pursuant to court-approved "consent decrees," and also some support for preferential promotional schemes even where seniority is a factor.

XI.   Arbitration of Employment Discrimination Cases

ALEXANDER v. GARDNER-DENVER CO.
United States Supreme Court
415 U. S. 36 (1974)

POWELL, J., . . . [W]e must decide under what circumstances, if any, an employee's statutory right to a trial de novo under Title VII may be foreclosed by prior submission of this claim to final arbitration under the non-discrimination clause of a collective bargaining agreement.

I

In May 1966, petitioner Harrell Alexander, Sr., a black, was hired by respondent Gardner-Denver Co. (the company) to perform maintenance work at the company's plant in Denver, Colorado. In June 1968, petitioner was awarded a trainee position as a drill operator. He remained at that job until his discharge from employment on September 29, 1969. The company informed petitioner that he was being discharged for producing too many defective and unusable parts that had to be scrapped.

On October 1, 1969, petitioner filed a grievance under the collective bargaining agreement in force between the company and petitioner's union, Local No. 3029 of the United Steelworkers of America (the union). The grievance stated: "I feel I have been unjustly discharged and ask that I be reinstated with full seniority and pay." No explicit claim of racial discrimination was made.

Under Art. 4 of the collective bargaining agreement, the company retained "the right to hire, suspend or discharge [employees] for proper cause." Article 5, § 2, provided, however, that "there shall be no discrimination against any employee on account of race, color, religion, sex, national origin, or ancestry," and Art. 23, § 6(a), stated that "[n] o employee will be discharged, suspended or given a written warning notice except for just cause." The agreement also contained a broad arbitration clause.... Disputes were to be submitted to a multistep grievance procedure.... If the dispute remained unresolved, it was to be remitted to compulsory arbitration. The company and the union were to select and pay the arbitrator, and his decision was to be "final and binding upon the Company, the Union, and any employee or employees involved." The agreement further provided that "[t] he arbitrator shall not amend, take away, add to, or change any of the provisions of this Agreement, and the arbitrator's decision must be based solely upon an interpretation of the provisions of this Agreement." The parties also agreed that there "shall be no suspension of work" over disputes covered by the grievance-arbitration clause.

The union processed petitioner's grievance through the above machinery. In the final prearbitration step, petitioner raised, apparently for the first time, the claim that his discharge resulted from racial discrimination. The company rejected all of petitioner's claims, and the grievance proceeded to arbitration. Prior to the arbitration hearing, however, petitioner filed a charge of racial discrimination with the Colorado Civil Rights Commission, which referred the complaint to the Equal Employment Opportunity Commission on November 5, 1969.

At the arbitration hearing on November 20, 1969, petitioner testified that his discharge was the result of racial discrimination and informed the arbitrator that he had filed a charge with the Colorado Commission because he "could not rely on the union." The union introduced a letter in which petitioner stated that he was "knowledgeable that in the same plant others have scrapped an equal amount and sometimes in excess, but by all logical reasoning I . . . have been the target of preferential discriminatory treatment." The union representative also testified that the company's usual practice was to transfer unsatisfactory trainee drill operators back to their former positions.

On December 30, 1969, the arbitrator ruled that petitioner had been "discharged for just cause." He made no reference to petitioner's claim of racial discrimination. The arbitrator stated that the union had failed to produce evidence of a practice of transferring rather than discharging trainee drill operators who accumulated excessive scrap, but he suggested that the company and the union confer on whether such an arrangement was feasible in the present case.

On July 25, 1970, the Equal Employment Opportunity Commission determined that there was not reasonable cause to believe that a violation of Title VII of the Civil Rights Act of 1964 had occurred. The Commission later notified petitioner of his right to institute a civil action in federal court within 30 days. Petitioner then filed the present action in the United States District Court for the District of Colorado, alleging that his discharge resulted from a racially discriminatory employment practice in violation of § 703(a)(1) of the Act.

The District Court granted respondent's motion for summary judgment and dismissed the action. 346 F. Supp. 1012 (1971). The court found that the claim of racial discrimination had been submitted to the arbitrator and resolved adversely to petitioner. It then held that petitioner, having voluntarily elected to pursue his grievance to final arbitration under the nondiscrimination clause of the collective bargaining agreement, was bound by the arbitral decision and thereby precluded from suing his employer under Title VII. The Court of Appeals for the Tenth Circuit affirmed per curiam. . . . .

II

. . . . Congress created the Equal Employment Opportunity Commission and established a procedure whereby existing state and local equal employment opportunity agencies, as well as the Commission, would have an opportunity to settle disputes through conference, conciliation, and persuasion before the aggrieved party was permitted to file a lawsuit. In the Equal Employment Opportunity Act of 1972, Congress amended Title VII to provide the Commission with further authority to investigate individual charges of discrimination, to promote voluntary compliance with the requirements of Title VII, and to institute civil actions against employers or unions named in a discrimination charge.

Even in its amended form, however, Title VII does not provide the Commission with direct powers of enforcement. The Commission cannot adjudicate claims or impose administrative sanctions. Rather, final responsibility for enforcement of Title VII is vested with federal courts. The Act authorizes courts to issue injunctive relief and to order such affirmative action as may be appropriate to remedy the effects of unlawful employment practices. 42 U.S.C. § § 2000e-5(f) and (g) (1970 ed., Supp. II). Courts retain these broad remedial powers despite a Commission finding of no reasonable cause to believe that the Act has been violated. McDonnell Douglas Corp. v. Green [411 U.S., at 798-799] . . . . Taken together, these provisions make plain that federal courts have been assigned plenary powers to secure compliance with Title VII.

In addition to reposing ultimate authority in federal courts, Congress gave private individuals a significant role in the enforcement process of Title VII. Individual grievants usually initiate the Commission's investigatory and conciliatory procedures. And although the 1972 amendment to Title VII empowers the Commission to bring its own actions, the private right of action remains an essential means of obtaining judicial enforcement of Title VII. 42 U.S.C. § 2000e-5(f)(1) (1970 ed., Supp. II). In such cases, the private litigant not only redresses his own injury but also vindicates the important congressional policy against discriminatory employment practices. . : .

Pursuant to this statutory scheme, petitioner initiated the present action for judicial consideration of his rights under Title VII. The District Court and the Court of Appeals held, however, that petitioner was bound by the prior arbitral decision and had no right to sue under Title VII. Both courts evidently thought this result was dictated by notions of election of remedies and waiver and by the federal policy favoring arbitration of labor disputes, as enunciated by this Court in Textile Workers Union v. Lincoln Mills, 353 U.S. 448 (1957), and the *Steelworkers trilogy*. . . .

III

Title VII does not speak expressly to the relationship between federal courts and the grievance-arbitration machinery of collective bargaining agreements. It does, however, vest federal courts with plenary powers to enforce the statutory requirements; and it specifies with precision the jurisdictional prerequisites that an individual must satisfy before he is entitled to institute a lawsuit. In the present case, these prerequisites were met when petitioner (1) filed timely a charge of employment discrimination with the Commission, and (2) received and acted upon the Commission's statutory notice of the right to sue. . . . There is no suggestion in the statutory scheme that a prior arbitral decision either forecloses an individual's right to sue or divests federal courts of jurisdiction.

In addition, legislative enactments in this area have long evinced a general intent to accord parallel or overlapping remedies against discrimination. In the Civil Rights Act of 1964 Congress indicated that it considered the policy against discrimination to be of the "highest priority." Newman v. Piggie Park Enterprises, [390 U.S.] at 402. Consistent with this view, Title VII provides for consideration of employment-discrimination claims in several forums. See 42 U.S.C. § 2000e-5(b) 1970 ed., Supp. II) (EEOC); 42 U.S.C. § 2000e-5(c) (1970 ed., Supp. II) (state and local agencies); 42 U.S.C. § 2000e-5(f) (1970 ed., Supp. II) (federal courts). And, in general, submission of a claim to one forum does not preclude a later submission to another. See 42 U.S.C. § § 2000e-5(b) and (f) (1970 ed. Supp. II); McDonnell Douglas Corp. v. Green, supra. Moreover, the legislative history of Title VII manifests a congressional intent to allow an individual to pursue independently his rights under both Title VII and other applicable state and federal statutes.[9] The clear inference is that Title VII was designed to supplement rather than supplant, existing laws and institutions relating to employment discrimination. In sum, Title VII's purpose and procedures strongly suggest that an individual does not forfeit his private cause of action if he first

[9.]   For example, Senator Joseph Clark, one of the sponsors of the bill, introduced an interpretive memorandum which stated: "Nothing in Title VII or anywhere else in this bill affects rights and obligations under the NLRA and the Railway Labor Act. . . . [T]itle VII is not intended to and does not deny to any individual, rights and remedies which he may pursue under other Federal and State statutes. If a given action should violate both Title VII and the National Labor Relations Act, the National Labor Relations Board would not be deprived of jurisdiction." 110 Cong. Rec. 7207 (1964). Moreover, the Senate defeated an amendment which would have made Title VII the exclusive federal remedy for most unlawful employment practices. 110 Cong. Rec.. 13650-13652 (1964). And a similar amendment was rejected in connection with the Equal Employment Opportunity Act of 1972. See H.R. 9247, 92d Cong., 1st Sess. (1971). See H.R. Rep. No. 92-238 (1971). The report of the Senate Committee responsible for the 1972 Act explained that neither the "provisions regarding the individual's right to sue under Title VII, nor any of the other provisions of this bill, are meant to affect existing rights granted under other laws." S. Rep. No. 92-415, p. 24 (1971). . . .

pursues his grievance to final arbitration under the nondiscrimination clause of a collective bargaining agreement.

In reaching the opposite conclusion, the District Court relied in part on the doctrine of election of remedies. That doctrine, which refers to situations where an individual pursues remedies that are legally or factually inconsistent, has no application in the present context. In submitting his grievance to arbitration, an employee seeks to vindicate his contractual right under a collective bargaining agreement. By contrast, in filing a lawsuit under Title VII, an employee asserts independent statutory rights accorded by Congress. The distinctly separate nature of these contractual and statutory rights is not vitiated merely because both were violated as a result of the same factual occurrence. And certainly no inconsistency results from permitting both rights to be enforced in their respectively appropriate forums. The resulting scheme is somewhat analogous to the procedure under the National Labor Relations Act, as amended, where disputed transactions may implicate both contractual and statutory rights. Where the statutory right underlying a particular claim may not be abridged by contractual agreement, the Court has recognized that consideration of the claim by the arbitrator as a contractual dispute under the collective bargaining agreement does not preclude subsequent consideration of the claim by the National Labor Relations Board as an unfair labor practice charge or as a petition for clarification of the union's representation certificate under the Act. Carey v. Westinghouse Corp., 375 U.S. 261 (1964). Cf. Smith v. Evening News Assn., 371 U.S. 195 (1962). There, as here, the relationship between the forums is complementary since consideration of the claim by both forums may promote the policies underlying each. Thus, the rationale behind the election-of-remedies doctrine cannot support the decision below.[14]

We are also unable to accept the proposition that petitioner waived his cause of action under Title VII. . . . [W]e think it clear that there can be no prospective waiver of an employee's rights under Title VII. It is true, of course, that a union may waive certain statutory rights related to collective activity, such as the right to strike. These rights are conferred on employees collectively to foster the processes of bargaining and properly may be exercised or relinquished by the union as collective bargaining agent to obtain economic benefits for unit members. Title VII, on the other hand, stands on plainly different ground; it concerns not majoritarian processes, but an individual's right to equal employment opportunities. Title VII's strictures are absolute and represent a congressional command that each employee be free from discriminatory practices. Of necessity, the rights conferred can form no

---

[14.] Nor can it be maintained that election of remedies is required by the possibility of unjust enrichment through duplicative recoveries. Where, as here, the employer has prevailed at arbitration, there, of course, can be no duplicative recovery. But even in cases where the employee has first prevailed, judicial relief can be structured to avoid such windfall gains. . . . Furthermore, if the relief obtained by the employee at arbitration were fully equivalent to that obtainable under Title VII, there would be no further relief for the court to grant and hence no need for the employee to institute suit.

part of the collective bargaining process since waiver of these rights would defeat the paramount congressional purpose behind Title VII. In these circumstances, an employee's rights under Title VII are not susceptible for prospective waiver. . . .

The actual submission of petitioner's grievance to arbitration in the present case does not alter the situation. Although presumably an employer may waive his cause of action under Title VII as part of a voluntary settlement,[15] mere resort to the arbitral forum to enforce contractual rights constitutes no such waiver. Since an employee's rights under Title VII may not be waived prospectively, existing contractual rights and remedies against discrimination must result from other concessions already made by the union as part of the economic bargain struck with the employer. It is settled law that no additional concession may be exacted from any employee as the price for enforcing those rights. J. I. Case Co. v. NLRB, 321 U.S. 332, 338-339 (1944).

Moreover, a contractual right to submit a claim to arbitration is not displaced simply because Congress also has provided a statutory right against discrimination. Both rights have legally independent origins and are equally available to the aggrieved employee. This point becomes apparent through consideration of the role of the arbitrator in the system of industrial self-government.[16] As the proctor of the bargain, the arbitrator's task is to effectuate the intent of the parties. His source of authority is the collective bargaining agreement, and he must interpret and apply that agreement in accordance with the "industrial common law of the shop" and the various needs and desires of the parties. The arbitrator, however, has no general authority to invoke public laws that conflict with the bargain between the parties:

"[A]n arbitrator is confined to interpretation and application of the collective bargaining agreement; . . . He may of course look for guidance from many sources, yet his award is legitimate only so long as it draws its essence from the collective bargaining agreement. When the arbitrator's words manifest an infidelity to this obligation, courts have no choice but to refuse enforcement of the award." United Steelworkers of America v. Enterprise Wheel & Car Corp., 363 U.S. 593, 597 (1960). If an arbitral decision is based "solely upon the arbitrator's view of the requirements of enacted legislation," rather than on an interpretation of the collective bargaining

---

[15.]   . . . In determining the effectiveness of any such waiver, a court would have to determine at the outset that the employee's consent to the settlement was voluntary and knowing. . . .

[16.]   See Meltzer, Labor Arbitration and Overlapping and Conflicting Remedies for Employment Discrimination, 39 U. Chi. L. Rev. 30, 32-35 (1971); Meltzer, Ruminations About Ideology, Law, and Labor Arbitration, 34 U. Chi. L. Rev. 545 (1967). As the late Dean Shulman stated:
"A proper conception of the arbitrator's function is basic. He is not a public tribunal imposed upon the parties by superior authority which the parties are obliged to accept. He has no general charter to administer justice for a community which transcends the parties. He is rather part of a system of self-government created by and confined to the parties. He serves their pleasure only, to administer the rule of law established by their collective agreement." Shulman, Reason, Contract, and Law in Labor Relations, 68 Harv. L. Rev. 999, 1016 (1955).

agreement, the arbitrator has "exceeded the scope of the submission," and the award will not be enforced. Ibid. Thus the arbitrator has authority to resolve only questions of contractual rights, and this authority remains regardless of whether certain contractual rights are similar to, or duplicative of, the substantive rights secured by Title VII.

IV

The District Court and the Court of Appeals reasoned that to permit an employee to have his claim considered in both the arbitral and judicial forums would be unfair since this would mean that the employer, but not the employee, was bound by the arbitral award. In the District Court's words, it could not "accept a philosophy which gives the employee two strings to his bow when the employer has only one." . . . This argument mistakes the effect of Title VII. Under the *Steelworkers trilogy*, an arbitral decision is final and binding on the employer and employee, and judicial review is limited as to both. But in instituting an action under Title VII, the employee is not seeking review of the arbitrator's decision. Rather, he is asserting a statutory right independent of the arbitration process. An employer does not have "two strings to his bow" with respect to an arbitral decision for the simple reason that Title VII does not provide employers with a cause of action against employees. An employer cannot be the victim of discriminatory employment practices. . . .

The District Court and the Court of Appeals also thought that to permit a later resort to the judicial forum would undermine substantially the employer's incentive to arbitrate and would "sound the death knell for arbitration clauses in labor contracts." . . . Again, we disagree. The primary incentive for an employer to enter into an arbitration agreement is the union's reciprocal promise not to strike. . . . It is not unreasonable to assume that most employers will regard the benefits derived from a no-strike pledge as outweighing whatever costs may result from according employees an arbitral remedy against discrimination in addition to their judicial remedy under Title VII. Indeed, the severe consequences of a strike may make an arbitration clause almost essential from both the employees' and the employer's perspective. Moreover, the grievance-arbitration machinery of the collective bargaining agreement remains a relatively inexpensive and expeditious means for resolving a wide range of disputes, including claims of discriminatory employment practices. Where the collective bargaining agreement contains a nondiscrimination clause similar to Title VII, and where arbitral procedures are fair and regular, arbitration may well produce a settlement satisfactory to both employer and employee. An employer thus has an incentive to make available the conciliatory and therapeutic processes of arbitration which may satisfy an employee's perceived need to resort to the judicial forum, thus saving the employer the expense and aggravation associated with a lawsuit. For similar reasons, the employee also has a strong incentive to arbitrate grievances, and arbitration may often eliminate those misunderstandings or discriminatory practices that might otherwise precipitate resort to the judicial forum.

V

Respondent contends that even if a preclusion rule is not adopted, federal courts should defer to arbitral decisions on discrimination claims where: (i) the claim was before the arbitrator; (ii) the collective bargaining agreement prohibited the form of discrimination charged in the suit under Title VII; and (iii) the arbitrator has authority to rule on the claim and to fashion a remedy.[17] Under respondent's proposed rule, a court would grant summary judgment and dismiss the employee's action if the above conditions were met. The rule's obvious consequence in the present case would be to deprive the petitioner of his statutory right to attempt to establish his claim in a federal court.

At the outset, it is apparent that a deferral rule would be subject to many of the objections applicable to a preclusion rule. The purpose and procedures of Title VII indicate that Congress intended federal courts to exercise final responsibility for enforcement of Title VII; deferral to arbitral decisions would be inconsistent with that goal. Furthermore, we have long recognized that "the choice of forums inevitably affects the scope of the substantive right to be vindicated." U.S. Bulk Carriers v. Arguelles, 400 U.S. 351, 359-360 (1971) (Harlan, J., concurring). Respondent's deferral rule is necessarily premised on the assumption that arbitral processes are commensurate with judicial processes and that Congress impliedly intended federal courts to defer to arbitral decisions on Title VII issues. We deem this supposition unlikely.

Arbitral procedures, while well suited to the resolution of contractual disputes, make arbitration a comparatively inappropriate forum for the final resolution of rights created by Title VII. This conclusion rests first on the special role of the arbitrator, whose task is to effectuate the intent of the parties rather than the requirements of enacted legislation. Where the collective bargaining agreement conflicts with Title VII, the arbitration must follow the agreement. To be sure, the tension between contractual and statutory objectives may be mitigated where a collective bargaining agreement contains provisions facially similar to those of Title VII. But other facts may still render arbitral processes comparatively inferior to judicial processes in the protection of Title VII rights. Among these is the fact that the specialized competence of arbitrators pertains primarily to the law of the shop, not the law of the land. United Steelworkers of America v. Warrior & Gulf Navigation Co., 363 U.S. 574, 581-583 (1960).[18] Parties usually

---

[17.]   Respondent's proposed rule is analogous to the NLRB's policy of deferring to arbitral decisions on statutory issues in certain cases. See Spielberg Mfg. Co., 112 N.L.R.B. 1080, 1082 (1955).

[18.]   See also Gould, Labor Arbitration of Grievances Involving Racial Discrimination, 118 U. Pa. L. Rev. 40, 47-48 (1969); Platt, The Relationship between Arbitration and Title VII of the Civil Rights Act of 1964, 3 Ga. L. Rev. 398 (1969). Significantly, a substantial proportion of labor arbitrators are not lawyers. See Note, The NLRB and Deference to Arbitration, 77 Yale L.J. 1191, 1194 n.28 (1968). . . .

choose an arbitrator because they trust his knowledge and judgment concerning the demands and norms of industrial relations. On the other hand, the resolution of statutory or constitutional issues is a primary responsibility of courts, and judicial construction has proved especially necessary with respect to Title VII, whose broad language frequently can be given meaning only by reference to public law concepts.

Moreover, the factfinding process in arbitration usually is not equivalent to judicial factfinding. The record of the arbitration proceedings is not as complete; the usual rules of evidence do not apply; and rights and procedures common to civil trials, such as discovery, compulsory process, cross-examination, and testimony under oath, are often severely limited or unavailable. . . . And as this Court has recognized, "[a] rbitrators have no obligation to the court to give their reasons for an award." United Steelworkers of America v. Enterprise Wheel & Car Corp., 363 U.S., at 598. Indeed, it is the informality of arbitral procedure that enables it to function as an efficient, inexpensive, and expeditious means for dispute resolution. This same characteristic, however, makes arbitration a less appropriate forum for final resolution of Title VII issues than the federal courts. [19]

It is evident that respondent's proposed rule would not allay these concerns. Nor are we convinced that the solution lies in applying a more demanding deferral standard, such as that adopted by the Fifth Circuit in Rios v. Reynolds Metals Co., 467 F.2d 54 (1972). [20] As respondent points out, a standard that adequately insured effectuation of Title VII rights in the arbitral forum would tend to make arbitration a procedurally complex, expensive, and time-consuming process. And judicial enforcement of such a standard would almost require courts to make de novo determinations of the employees' claims. It is uncertain whether any minimal savings in judicial time and expense would justify the risk to vindication of Title VII rights.

[19.]   A further concern is the union's exclusive control over the manner and extent to which an individual grievance is presented. See Vaca v. Sipes, 386 U.S. 171 (1967); Republic Steel Corp. v. Maddox, 379 U.S. 650 (1965). In arbitration, as in the collective bargaining process, the interests of the individual employee may be subordinated to the collective interests of all employees in the bargaining unit. See J. I. Case Co. v. NLRB, 321 U.S. 332 (1944). Moreover, harmony of interest between the union and the individual employee cannot always be presumed, especially where a claim of racial discrimination is made. See, e.g., Steele v. Louisville & N. R. Co., 323 U.S. 192 (1944); Tunstall v. Brotherhood of Locomotive Firemen, 323 U.S. 210 (1944). And a breach of the union's duty of fair representation may prove difficult to establish. . . . In this respect it is noteworthy that Congress thought it necessary to afford the protections of Title VII against unions as well as employers. See 42 U.S.C. §2000e-2(c).

[20.]   In Rios, the court set forth the following deferral standard: "First, there may be no deference to the decision of the arbitrator unless the contractual right coincides with rights under Title VII. Second, it must be plain that the arbitrator's decision is in no way violative of the private rights guaranteed by Title VII, nor of the public policy which inheres in Title VII. In addition, before deferring, the district court must be satisfied that (1) the factual issues before it are identical to those decided by the arbitrator; (2) the arbitrator had power under the collective agreement to decide the ultimate issue of discrimination; (3) the evidence presented at the arbitral hearing dealt adequately with all factual issues; (4) the arbitrator actually decided the factual issues presented to the court; (5) the arbitration proceeding was fair and regular and free of procedural infirmities. The burden of proof in establishing these conditions of limitation will be upon the respondent as distinguished from the claimant." 467 F.2d, at 58.

A deferral rule also might adversely affect the arbitration system as well as the enforcement scheme of Title VII. Fearing that the arbitral forum cannot adequately protect their rights under Title VII, some employees may elect to bypass arbitration and institute a lawsuit. The possibility of voluntary compliance or settlement of Title VII claims would thus be reduced, and the result could well be more litigation, not less.

We think, therefore, that the federal policy favoring arbitration of labor disputes and the federal policy against discriminatory employment practices can best be accommodated by permitting an employee to pursue fully both his remedy under the grievance-arbitration clause of a collective bargaining agreement and his cause of action under Title VII. The federal court should consider the employee's claim de novo. The arbitral decision may be admitted as evidence and accorded such weight as the court deems appropriate[21]

The judgment of the Court of Appeals is Reversed.

NOTE

There have been some excellent scholarly treatments of the subject of arbitration of employment discrimination cases. Some of the works worth reviewing are: Coulson, *The Polarized Employee–Can Arbitration Bridge the Gap*, Proceedings of the Southwestern Legal Foundation Annual Institute on Labor Law (Oct. 26, 1977); Edwards, *Arbitration of Employment Discrimination Cases: A Proposal for Employer and Union Representatives*, 27 Lab. L.J. 265 (1976); Meltzer, *Labor Arbitration and Discrimination: The Parties' Process and the Public's Purposes*, 43 U. Chi. L. Rev. 724 (1976); Gould, *Labor Arbitration of Grievances Involving Racial Discrimination*, 118 U. Pa. L. Rev. 40 (1969); Platt, *The Relationship Between Arbitration and Title VII of the Civil Rights Act of 1964*, 3 Ga. L. Rev. 398 (1969); Sovern, *When Should Arbitrators Follow Federal Law?* In Proceedings of the 23rd Annual Meeting of the National Academy of Arbitrators 29 (BNA, Inc. 1970); Shaw, *Comment on "The Coming End of Arbitration's Golden Age,"* in Proceedings of the 29th Annual Meeting of the National Academy of Arbitrators 139 (BNA, Inc. 1976); St. Antoine, *Judicial Review of Labor Arbitration Awards: A Second Look At Enterprise Wheel and Its Progeny*, 75 Mich. L. Rev. 1137 (1977); Howlett, *The Arbitrator, The NLRB and the Courts*, in Proceedings of the 20th Annual Meeting of the National Academy of Arbitrators (BNA, Inc. 1967); Mittenthal, *The Role of Law in Arbitration*, in Proceedings of the 21st Annual Meeting of the National Academy of Arbitrators (BNA, Inc. 1968); Feller, *The Impact of External Law Upon Labor Arbitration*, in The Future of Labor Arbitration in America (Amer. Arb. Assoc. 1976); Edwards, *Labor Arbitration at the Crossroads: The "Common Law of the Shop" Versus External Law*, 32 Arb. J. 65 (June 1977).

[21.]   We adopt no standards as to the weight to be accorded an arbitral decision, since this must be determined in the court's discretion with regard to the facts and circumstances of each case. Relevant factors include the existence of provisions in the collective bargaining agreement that conform substantially with Title VII, the degree of procedural fairness in the arbitral forum, adequacy of the record with respect to the issue of discrimination, and the special competence of particular arbitrators. Where an arbitral discrimination gives full consideration to an employee's Title VII rights, a court may properly accord it great weight. This is especially true where the issue is solely one of fact, specifically addressed by the parties and decided by the arbitrator on the basis of an adequate record. But courts should ever be mindful that Congress, in enacting Title VII, thought it necessary to provide a judicial forum for the ultimate resolution of discriminatory employment claims. It is the duty of courts to assure the full availability of this forum.

CHAPTER 17

AFFIRMATIVE ACTION IN EMPLOYMENT

I. **Introduction**

Executive Order 11246, as amended by Executive Order 11375, 3 C.F.R. 169 (1974), prohibits federal government contractors (including universities and colleges) from engaging in employment discrimination of the sort prohibited by Title VII. Unlike Title VII, however, Executive Order 11246 requires contractors to take "affirmative action" to ensure that applicants are employed, and that employees are treated during employment, without regard to their race, color, religion, sex or national origin. Prior to 1978, the responsibility for enforcing the Executive Order for colleges and universities was delegated to the Office for Civil Rights in the Department of Health, Education and Welfare. Since October of 1978, pursuant to President Carter's "Reorganization of Equal Employment Opportunity Programs," *Reorganization Plan No. 1 of 1978,* the responsibility for enforcing the Executive Order has rested solely with the Office of Federal Contract Compliance Programs at the Department of Labor.

In the regulations issued by the Office of Federal Contract Compliance (OFCC), 41 C.F.R. §60-2.10 (otherwise known as "Revised Order No. 4"), an "affirmative action program" is defined as a:

set of specific and result-oriented procedures to which a contractor commits himself to apply every good faith effort. The objective of those procedures plus such efforts is equal employment opportunity. Procedures without effort to make them work are meaningless; and effort, undirected by specific and meaningful procedures, is inadequate. An acceptable affirmative action program must include an analysis of areas within which the contractor is deficient in the utilization of minority groups and women, and further, goals and timetables to which the contractor's good faith efforts must be directed to correct the deficiencies and, thus to achieve prompt and full utilization of minorities and women, at all levels and in all segments of his work force where deficiencies exist.

In 1972, the Office for Civil Rights at HEW issued *Higher Education Guidelines: Executive Order 11,246.* Excerpts from these *Guidlines* follow:

Nondiscrimination and Affirmative Action in the Executive Order

Executive Order 11246 embodies two concepts: nondiscrimination and affirmative action.

663

Nondiscrimination requires the elimination of all existing discriminatory conditions, whether purposeful or inadvertent. A university contractor must carefully and systematically examine all of its employment policies to be sure that they do not, if implemented as stated, operate to the detriment of any persons on grounds of race, color, religion, sex or national origin. The contractor must also ensure that the practices of those responsible in matters of employment, including all supervisors, are nondiscriminatory.

Affirmative action requires the contractor to do more than ensure employment neutrality with regard to race, color, religion, sex, and national origin. As the phrase implies, affirmative action requires the employer to make additional efforts to recruit, employ and promote qualified members of groups formerly excluded, even if that exclusion cannot be traced to particular discriminatory actions on the part of the employer. The premise of the affirmative action concept of the Executive Order is that unless positive action is undertaken to overcome the effects of systemic institutional forms of exclusion and discrimination, a benign neutrality in employment practices will tend to perpetuate the *status quo ante* indefinitely.

Who is Protected by the Executive Order

The *nondiscrimination* requirements of the Executive Order apply to *all* persons, whether or not the individual is a member of a conventionally defined "minority group." In other words, *no* person may be denied employment or related benefits on grounds of his or her race, color, religion, sex, or national origin.

The *affirmative action* requirements of determining underutilization, setting goals and timetables and taking related action as detailed in Revised Order No. 4 were designed to further employment opportunity for women and minorities. Minorities are defined by the Department of Labor as Negroes, Spanish-surnamed, American Indians, and Orientals.

Goals and Timetables

As a part of the affirmative action obligation, Revised Order No. 4 requires a contractor to determine whether women and minorities are "underutilized" in its employee work force and, if that is the case, to develop as a part of its affirmative action program specific goals and timetables designed to overcome that underutilization. (See Tab J) Underutilization is defined in the regulations as "having fewer women or minorities in a particular job than would reasonably be expected by their availability."

Goals are projected levels of achievement resulting from an analysis by the contractor of its deficiencies, and of what it can reasonably do to remedy them, given the availability of qualified minorities and women and the expected turnover in its work force. Establishing goals should be coupled with the adoption of genuine and effective techniques and procedures to locate qualified members of groups which have previously been denied opportunities for employment or advancement and to eliminate obstacles within the structure and operation of the institution (e.g. discriminatory hiring or promotion standards) which have prevented members of certain groups from securing employment or advancement.

The achievement of goals is not the sole measurement of a contractor's compliance, but represents a primary threshold for determining a contractor's level of performance and whether an issue of compliance exists. If the contractor falls short of its goals at the end of the period it has set, that failure in itself does not require a conclusion of noncompliance. It does, however, require a determination by the contractor as to why the failure occurred. If the goals were not met because the number of employment openings was inaccurately estimated, or because of changed employment market conditions or the unavailability of women and minorities with the specific qualifications needed, but the record discloses that the contractor followed its affirmative action program, it has complied with the letter and spirit of the Executive Order. If, on the other hand, it appears that the cause for failure was an inattention to the nondiscrimination and affirmative action policies and procedures set by the contractor, then the contractor may be found out of compliance. It should be emphasized that while goals are required, quotas are neither required nor permitted by the Executive Order. When used correctly, goals are an indicator of probable compliance and achievement, not a rigid or exclusive measure of performance.

Nothing in the Executive Order requires that a university contractor eliminate or dilute standards which are necessary to the successful performance of the institution's educational and research functions. The affirmative action concept does not require that a university employ or promote any persons who are unqualified. The concept does require, however, that any standards or criteria which have had the effect of excluding women and minorities be eliminated, unless the contractor can demonstrate that such criteria are conditions of successful performance in the particular position involved.

PERSONNEL POLICIES AND PRACTICES

An employer must establish in reasonable detail and make available upon request the standards and procedures which govern all employment practices in the operation of each organizational unit, including any tests in use and the criteria by which qualifications for appointment, retention, or promotion are judged. It should be determined whether such standards and criteria are valid predictors of job performance, including whether they are relevant to the duties of the particular position in question. This requirement should not ignore or obviate the range of permissible discretion which has characterized employment judgments, particularly in the academic area. Where such discretion appears to have operated to deny equality of opportunity, however, it must be subjected to rigorous examination and its discriminatory effects eliminated. There are real and proper limits on the extent to which criteria for academic employment can be explicitly articulated; however, the absence of any articulation of such criteria provides opportunities for arbitrary and discriminatory employment decisions.

Recruitment

Recruitment is the process by which an institution or department within an institution develops an applicant pool from which hiring decisions are made. Recruitment may be an active process, in which the institution seeks to communicate its employment needs to candidates through advertisement, word-of-mouth notification to graduate schools or other training programs, disciplinary conventions or job registers. Recruitment may also be the passive function of including in the applicant pool those persons who on their own initiative or by unsolicited recommendation apply to the institution for a position.

In both academic and nonacademic areas, universities must recruit women and minority persons as actively as they have recruited white males. Some universities, for example, have tended to recruit heavily at institutions graduating exclusively or predominantly non-minority males, and have failed to advertise in media which would reach the minority and female communities, or have relied upon personal contacts and friendships which have had the effect of excluding from consideration women and minority group persons.

In the academic area, the informality of word-of-mouth recruiting and its reliance on factors outside the knowledge or control of the university makes this method particularly susceptible to abuse. In addition, since women and minorities are often not in word-of-mouth channels of recruitment, their candidates may not be advanced with the same frequency or strength of endorsement as they merit, and as their white male colleagues receive.

The university contractor must examine the recruitment activities and policies of each unit responsible for recruiting. Where such an examination reveals a significantly lower representation of women or minorities in the university's applicant pool than would reasonably be expected from their availability in the work force, the contractor must modify or supplement its recruiting policies by vigorous and systematic efforts to locate and encourage the candidacy of qualified women and minorities. Where policies have the effect of excluding qualified women or minorities, and where their effects cannot be mitigated by the implementation of additional policies, such policies must be eliminated. . . .

Certain organizations such as those mentioned in Revised Order No. 4 may be prepared to refer women and minority applicants. For faculty and administrative appointments, disciplinary and professional associations, including committees and caucus groups, should be contacted and their facilities for employee location and referral used.

Particularly in the case of academic personnel, potentially fruitful channels of recruitment include the following:

a. advertisements in appropriate professional journals and job registries;

b. unsolicited applications or inquiries;

c. women teaching at predominantly women's colleges, minorities teaching at predominantly minority colleges;

d. minorities or women professionally engaged in nonacademic positions, such as industry, government, law firms, hospitals;

e. professional women and minorities working at independent research institutions and libraries;

f. professional minorities and women who have received significant grants or professional recognition;

g. women and minorities already at the institution and elsewhere working in research or other capacities not on the academic ladder;

h. minority and women doctoral recipients, from the contractor's own institution and from other institutions, who are not presently using their professional training;

i. women and minorities presently candidates for graduate degrees at the institution and elsewhere who show promise of outstanding achievement (some institutions have developed programs of support for completion of doctoral programs with a related possibility of future appointment);

j. minorities and women listed in relevant professional files, registries and data banks, including those which have made a particularly conscientious effort to locate women and minority persons.

It should be noted that a contractor is required to make explicit its commitment to equal employment opportunity in all recruiting announcements or advertisements. It may do this by indicating that it is an "equal opportunity employer." It is a violation of the Executive Order, however, for a prospective employer to state that only members of a particular minority group or sex will be considered. . . .

Policies which exclude recruitment at predominantly minority colleges and universities restrict the pool of qualified minority faculty from which prospective appointees may be chosen. Even if the intent of such policies may be to prevent the so-called "raiding" of minority faculty by predominantly white institutions, such policies violate the nondiscrimination provision of the Executive Order since their effect is to deny opportunity for employment on grounds relating to race. Such policies have operated to the serious disadvantage of students and teachers at minority institutions by denying them notice of research and teaching opportunities, assistantships, endowed professorships and many other programs which might enhance their potential for advancement, whether they choose to stay at a predominantly minority institution or move to a non-minority institution.

Minorities and women are frequently recruited only for positions thought to be for minorities and women, such as equal employment programs, ethnic studies, or women's studies. While these positions may have a particular suitability for minority persons and women, institutions must not restrict consideration of women and minorities to such areas, but should actively recruit them for any position for which they may be qualified.

Hiring

Once a nondiscriminatory applicant pool has been established through recruitment, the process of selection from that pool must also carefully follow procedures designed to ensure nondiscrimination. In all cases, standards and criteria for employment should be made reasonably explicit, and should be accessible to all employees and applicants. Such standards may not overtly draw a distinction based on race, sex, color, religion, or national origin, nor may they be applied inconsistently to deny equality of opportunity on these bases.

In hiring decisions, assignment to a particular title or rank may be discriminatory. For example, in many institutions women are more often assigned initially to lower academic ranks than are men. A study by one disciplinary association showed that women tend to be offered a first appointment at the rank of Instructor rather than the rank of Assistant Professor three times more often than men with identical qualifications. Where there is no valid basis for such differential treatment, such a practice is in violation of the Executive Order.

Recruiting and hiring decisions which are governed by unverified assumptions about a particular individual's willingness or ability to relocate because of his or her race or sex are in violation of the Executive Order. For example, university personnel responsible for employment decisions should not assume that a woman will be unwilling to accept an offer because of her marital status, or that a minority person will be unwilling to live in a predominantly white community.

Institutional policies regarding the employment of an institution's own graduates must not be applied in any manner which would deny opportunities to women and minorities. A university must give equal consideration to its graduate students regardless of their race or sex for future faculty positions, if the institution employs its own graduates.

In the area of academic appointments, a nondiscriminatory selection process does not mean that an institution should indulge in "reverse discrimination" or "preferential treatment" which leads to the selection of unqualified persons over qualified ones. Indeed, to take such action on grounds of race, ethnicity, sex or religion constitutes discrimination in violation of the Executive Order.

It should also be pointed out that nothing in the Executive Order requires or permits a contractor to fire, demote or displace persons on grounds of race, color, sex, religion, or national origin in order to fulfill the affirmative action concept of the Executive Order. Again, to do so would violate the Executive Order. Affirmative action goals are to be sought through recruitment and hiring for vacancies created by normal growth and attrition in existing positions.

Unfortunately, a number of university officials have chosen to explain dismissals, transfers, alterations of job descriptions, changes in promotion potential or fringe benefits, and refusals to hire *not* on the basis of merit or some objective sought by the university administration aside from the Executive Order, but on grounds that such actions and other "preferential treatment regardless of merit" are now required by Federal law. Such statements constitute either a misunderstanding of the law or a willful distortion of it. In either case, where they actually reflect decisions not to employ or promote on grounds of race, color, sex, religion or national origin, they constitute a violation of the Executive Order and other Federal laws. . . .

Promotion

A contractor's policies and practices on promotion should be made reasonably explicit, and administered to ensure that women and minorities are not at a disadvantage. A contractor is also obligated to make special efforts to ensure that women and minorities in its work force are given equal opportunity for promotion. Specifically, 41 CFR 60-2.24 states that this result may be achieved through remedial, work study and job training programs; through career counseling programs; through the posting and announcement of promotion opportunities; and by the validation of all criteria for promotion. . . .

Conditions of Work

A university employer must ensure nondiscrimination in all terms and conditions of employment, including work assignments, educational and training opportunities, research opportunities, use of facilities, and opportunities to serve on committees or decision-making bodies.

Intentional policy or practice which subjects persons of a particular sex or minority status to heavier teaching loads, less desirable class assignments, and fewer opportunities to serve on key decision-making bodies or to apply for research grants or leaves of absence for professional purposes, is in violation of the Executive Order.

Similarly, institutional facilities such as dining halls or faculty clubs have sometimes restricted their services to men only. Where such services are a part of the ordinary benefits of employment for certain classifications of employees, no members of such classifications can be denied them on the basis of race, color, national origin, sex, or religion. . . .

Back Pay

Back pay awards are authorized and widely used as a remedy under Title VII of the Civil Rights Act of 1964, the Equal Pay Act, and the National Labor Relations Act. Universities, like other employers, are subject to the provisions of these statutes.

This means that evidence of discrimination that would require back pay as a remedy will be referred to the appropriate Federal enforcement agency if the Office for Civil Rights is not able to negotiate a voluntary settlement with a university. At the direction of the Department of Labor, the Office for Civil Rights will continue to pursue back pay settlements only in cases involving employees who, while protected by the Executive Order, were not protected by the three statutes mentioned above at the time violation occurred. . . .

DEVELOPMENT OF AFFIRMATIVE ACTION PROGRAMS

Effective affirmative action programs shall contain, but not necessarily be limited to, the following ingredients:

1. *Development or reaffirmation of the contractor's equal employment opportunity policy*: Each institution should have a clear written statement over the signature of the chief administrative officer which sets forth the institution's legal obligation and policy for the guidance of all supervisory personnel, both academic and nonacademic, for all employees and for the community served by the institution. The policy statement should reflect the institution's affirmative commitment to equal employment opportunity, as well as its commitment to eliminate discrimination in employment on the basis of race, color, sex, religion and national origin.

2. *Dissemination of the policy*: Internal communication of the institution's policy in writing to all supervisory personnel is essential to their understanding, cooperation and compliance. All persons responsible for personnel decisions must know what the law requires, what the institution's policy is, and how to interpret the policy and implement the program within the area of their responsibility. Formal and informal external dissemination of the policy is necessary to inform and secure the cooperation of organizations within the community, including civil rights groups, professional associations, women's groups, and various sources of referral within the recruitment area of the institution.

The employer should communicate to all present and prospective employees the existence of the affirmative action program, and make available such elements of the program as will enable them to know of and avail themselves of its benefits.

3. *Responsibility for implementation*: An administrative procedure must be set up to organize and monitor the affirmative action program. 41 CFR 60-2.22 provides that an executive of the contractor should be appointed as director of EEO programs, and that he or she should be given "the necessary top management support and staffing to execute the assignment." (See the remainder of section 2.22 for details of the responsibilities of the Equal Employment Opportunity Officer.) This should be a person knowledgeable of and sensitive to the problems of women and minority groups. Depending upon the size of the institution, this may be his or her sole responsibility, and necessary authority and staff should be accorded the position to ensure the proper implementation of the program.

In several institutions the EEO officer has been assisted by one or more task forces composed in substantial part of women and minority persons. This has usually facilitated the task of the EEO officer and enhanced the prospects of success for the affirmative action program in the institution.

4. *Identification of problem areas by organization units and job classifications*: In this section the contractor should address itself to the issues discussed in sections I and II above. The questions involved in data gathering and analysis are treated in appendix J.

Once an inventory is completed, the data should be coded and controlled in strict confidence so that access is limited to those persons involved in administering and reviewing the Equal Employment Opportunity Program. Some state and local laws may prohibit the collection and retention of data relating to the race, sex, color, religion, or national origin of employees and applicants for employment. Under the principle of Federal supremacy, requirements for such inventories and recordkeeping under the Executive Order supersede any conflicting state or local law, and the existence of such laws is not an acceptable excuse for failure to collect or supply such information as required under the Executive Order.

5. *Internal audit and reporting systems:* An institution must include in its administrative operation a system of audit and reporting to assist in the implementation and monitoring of the affirmative action program, and in periodic evaluations of its effectiveness. In some cases a reporting system has taken the form of a monitoring of all personnel actions, so that department heads and other supervisors must make periodic reports on affirmative action efforts to a central office. In most cases all new appointments must be accompanied by documentation of an energetic and systematic search for women and minorities.

Reporting and monitoring systems will differ from institution to institution according to the nature of the goals and programs established, but all should be sufficiently organized to provide a ready indication of whether or not the program is succeeding, and particularly whether or not good faith efforts have been made to ensure fair treatment of women and minority group persons before and during employment. Reporting systems should include a method of evaluating applicant flow; referral and hiring rate; and an application retention system to allow the development of an inventory of available skills.

At least once annually the institution must prepare a formal report to OCR on the results of its affirmative action compliance program. The evaluation necessary to prepare such a report will serve as a basis for updating the program, taking into consideration changes in the institution's work force (e.g., expansion, contraction, turnover), changes in the availability of minorities and women through improved educational opportunities, and changes in the comparative availability of women as opposed to men as a result of changing interest levels in different types of work.

6. *Publication of affirmative action programs*: In accordance with 41 CFR 6-2.21(11), which states that the contractor should "communicate to his employees the existence of the contractor's affirmative action program and make available such elements of his program as will enable such employees to know of and avail themselves of its benefits," the Office for Civil Rights urges institutions to make public their affirmative action plans. University contractors should also be aware that affirmative action plans accepted by the Office for Civil Rights are subject to disclosure to the public under the Freedom of Information Act, 5 U.S.C. 552. Subject to certain exemptions, disclosure ordinarily will include broad utilization analyses, proposed remedial steps, goals and timetables, policies on recruitment, hiring, promotion, termination, grievance procedures and other affirmative measures to be taken. Other types of documents which must be released by the Government upon a request for disclosure include the contractor's validation studies of tests and other preemployment selection methods.

Exempt from disclosure are those portions of the plan which contain confidential information about employees, the disclosure of which may constitute an invasion of privacy, information in the nature of trade secrets, and confidential commercial or financial information within the meaning of 5 U.S.C. 552(b)(4). Compliance agencies also are not authorized to disclose the Standard Form 100 (EEO-1) or similar reporting forms or information about individuals.

7. *Developing a plan:* The Office for Civil Rights recognizes that in an institution of higher education, and particularly in the academic staff, responsibility for matters concerning personnel decisions is diffused among many persons at a number of different levels. The success of a university's affirmative action program may be dependent in large part upon the willingness and ability of the faculty to assist in its development and implementation. Therefore, the Office for Civil Rights urges that university administrators involve members of their faculty, as well as other supervisory personnel in their work force, in the process of developing an information base, determining potential employee availability, the establishment of goals and timetables, monitoring and evaluating the effectiveness of the plan, and in all other appropriate elements of a plan. A number of institutions have successfully established faculty or joint faculty-staff commissions or task forces to assist in the preparation and administration of its affirmative action obligations. We therefore recommend to university contractors

that particular attention be given the need to bring into the deliberative and decision-making process those within the academic community who have a responsibility in personnel matters.

Following the issuance of the *Higher Education Guidelines*, HEW received numerous critical comments from college and university officials who complained about the burdens imposed by the Executive Order. In response to these complaints, Peter E. Holmes, who was then Director of the Office for Civil Rights at HEW, issued the following in December of 1974:

MEMORANDUM TO COLLEGE AND UNIVERSITY PRESIDENTS

This Office, in October 1972, issued *Higher Education Guidelines* which set forth the compliance responsibilities of colleges and universities under the Executive Order. In the time during which the *Guidelines* have been in effect, OCR has been faced with determining the permissibility of many common practices designed to effect compliance with the Executive Order. The purpose of this Memorandum is to encourage resort to positive affirmative action steps by setting forth concrete examples designed to distinguish such positive steps from others which might conflict with nondiscrimination requirements.

At the outset, certain general principles should be made clear. Colleges and universities are entitled to select the most qualified candidate, without regard to race, sex, or ethnicity, for any position. The college or university, not the Federal Government, is to say what constitutes qualification for any particular position. No single appointment will be objected to where those not appointed are less well-qualified than the candidate actually selected.

   1. **Recruitment for Employment Vacancies Must Be Undertaken without Designation or Identification by Race, Sex, or Ethnicity.**

As defined on page five of the *Guidelines*, "[r]ecruitment is the process by which an institution or department within an institution develops an applicant pool from which hiring decisions are made." As indicated on page six of the *Guidelines*, a contractor must make an explicit statement of its commitment to equal employment opportunity in all recruiting announcements and advertisements, and it may do so by specifying that it is an "equal opportunity employer." There is a caveat:

    It is a violation of the Executive Order, however, for a prospective employer to state that only members of a particular minority group or sex will be considered.

A major purpose of the affirmative action provision of the Executive Order is to broaden the pool of applicants so that women and minorities will be considered for employment along with all other applicants. The affirmative action process must not operate to restrict consideration to minorities and women only. Acceptable nonrestrictive language designed to broaden the pool of applicants would be:

> The English Department of X University is subject to the requirements of Executive Order 11246 and is an affirmative action employer. All interested persons are encouraged to apply.

It would, however, be unacceptable to state that "women and minorities are preferred" or "this is an affirmative action position." Status as a member of any specific group should not be mentioned in any advertisement as preferred.

The type of announcement which identifies the category of applicants who will be considered on the basis of race and/or sex would be unacceptable because it has the effect of discouraging the candidacy of other categories of persons. Therefore, it would be unacceptable for an announcement to read:

> Pursuant to our affirmative action plan establishing goals for the employment of women and minorities, the English Department of X University is seeking to fill this position with a woman.

Of course, under the Executive Order, all employment advertising must contain a statement that the institution is an equal opportunity employer.

It has been suggested that a position might be designated on the basis of race or sex in order to meet an employment goal. This would be in violation of the nondiscrimination provisions of the Executive Order.

The following case represents an example of an improper interpretation of the affirmative action obligation:

> For the past four years, the Mathematics Department of X University has been operating under an affirmative action program. Although its goal for hiring women was established at 20 percent over a five-year period, during the past four years, each of four vacancies has been filled by a male. At an annual professional association conference, the department chairman informed a male applying for a fifth vacant position that he could not be given consideration regardless of his qualifications because Federal regulations require the department to fill the position with a woman.

The Mathematics Department has violated its equal employment opportunity obligations by designating the vacancy as a position for a woman, or as one in which a woman would be preferred, thereby excluding all other categories of applicants from consideration. Such action is forbidden by the Executive Order, and it is improper to suggest or to act on the assumption that Federal affirmative action provisions require that any particular position be filled by a woman or minority person.

The Mathematics Department has misunderstood the nature of goals. Goals are good faith estimates of the expected numerical results which will flow from specific affirmative actions taken by a college or university to eliminate and/or counteract factors in the university's employment process which have contributed to under-utilization of minorities and women in specific job categories or resulted in an adverse disproportionate impact in terms of promotion, compensation and training of currently employed minorities and women. They are not rigid and inflexible quotas which must be met. Nor should a university strive to achieve goals as ends in themselves, for "[n]o contractor's compliance status shall be judged alone by whether or not he reaches his goals and meets his timetables. Rather, each contractor's compliance posture shall be reviewed and determined by reviewing the contents of his program, the extent of his adherence to this program, and his good faith efforts. . . ." (41 Code of Federal Regulations, Sec. 60-2.14, known as "Revised Order No. 4")

The Mathematics Department must be able to demonstrate clearly that it has adhered to its affirmative action obligation by making a full and good faith effort to recruit and consider women for each of the five vacancies. If the Department is able to make this demonstration, its inability to meet its employment goal would not be deemed a violation of its affirmative action obligation. However, a failure by the Mathematics Department to make a sufficient good faith effort to recruit and consider women and minority candidates for the four earlier openings would constitute a violation of the Executive Order regulations.

As noted on page seven of the *Guidelines*, minorities and women are often sought to fill positions in women's and ethnic studies programs. Consider the following example, which would constitute a violation of the Executive Order:

A job description for a instructor position for a University's Black Studies Program, included, as job requirements, the ability to bring special insights to the course material and the ability to relate well to the large number of black students attracted by the program. The Dean of Arts and Sciences decided that only a black person could meet these requirements. When questioned by a white applicant, the Dean defended the selection of a black person on the grounds that race was a necessary element for the proper performance of the job.

While the university established job requirements to answer what it deemed as its special needs for the Black Studies Program, its actions amounted to giving exclusive consideration to candidates on the basis of race. Such action results in the restriction of the applicant pool and is a violation of the Executive Order.

In this case, the job requirements themselves (ability to relate to students, special insights, etc.) do not limit the applicant pool on the basis of race and do not by their own terms prohibit non-minorities from applying or being employed. However, it is the university's assumption that only a black person can meet the job requirements and serve as an instructor in a successful Black Studies Program which brings the university into violation of the Executive Order.

II. If an Institution Has Failed to Follow Its Affirmative Action Recruitment Procedure or if Its Recruitment Efforts Do Not Yield an Expanded Applicant Pool, the Recruitment Period for All Candidates May Be Extended.

The *Guidelines,* on pages 5-7, set forth a specific framework to which the recruitment process should conform. An institution or institutional department must develop a nondiscriminatory applicant pool from which hiring decisions are made, and failure to do so constitutes a violation of the Executive Order. Consider the examples which follow:

A. The Psychology Department of X University was given a period of two months to fill a vacancy on its clinical teaching staff. Prior to beginning its recruitment efforts, the Department received the unsolicited application of a qualified white male applicant, and made no further efforts to recruit for the position. Shortly before the two-month period was up, the nomination was sent to the Vice Chancellor for approval as a choice candidate. On the advice of the affirmative action monitoring committee, the Vice Chancellor rejected the nomination on the ground that the Department had failed to make adequate attempts to reach female and minority applicants, and required that the recruitment search be reopened and extended for another month.

The obligation to take specific steps to recruit applies even in instances where a university has not previously made a practice of active recruiting. Hence, even though it had received an unsolicited application from a person who was qualified, the Department's failure to recruit and consider women and minorities constitutes a violation of the Executive Order. In such case, further action is required under the Executive Order and the Vice Chancellor's decision to extend the period for recruitment does not amount to an abuse of the affirmative action process with respect to the Department's first choice, who will be subjected to greater competition for the job.

> B. In seeking to fill an academic position, the English Department took the recruitment steps required under its affirmative action plan. At the end of the recruitment period, during which time it had not received the applications of any women or minorities, the Department nominated one of the white male applicants as its first choice. Although the Vice Chancellor noted that good faith efforts to recruit women and minorities had been made, he required the Department to extend the recruitment period for another month during which period additional specified efforts were to be made to reach available women and minority applicants.

In carrying out an affirmative action plan, the period for recruitment may be extended, particularly where a utilization analysis indicates that the percentage of women and minorities recruited is substantially less than the percentage of qualified women and minorities available in the work force. In such cases, additional positive recruitment efforts may be undertaken to broaden the applicant pool to include qualified women and minorities. OCR would approve (but not require) the decision to keep open competition for the position. But it must be emphasized again that nothing in an affirmative action plan requires the employment of any specific number of women or minorities.

Thus, if the Department can demonstrate that it has taken all recruitment steps required under its affirmative action plan—and even though no (or very few) applications have been received from women and minorities—there would be no *requirement* that the recruitment period be extended, as in the following example:

> C. The Physics Department took all the affirmative recruitment steps called for by the university's affirmative action plan, and advertised the opening for several months. At the end of that time, no women and no minority candidates had applied and the recruitment procedure was concluded.

The Department was justified in ending the recruitment period, inasmuch as it had done everything possible to publicize the opening for a reasonable period of time.

III. Job Requirements Must Be Applied Uniformly to All Candidates without Regard to Race, Color, Sex, Religion, or National Origin.

The *Guidelines* stress the need for standardized employment practices that minimize the opportunity for arbitrary and/or discriminatory hiring decisions. It is not intended that affirmative action should result in a dilution of standards in order to attain the objectives of the Executive Order. Consider the example of the following institution, which violated the Executive Order:

> Because of the small size and location of X University, its History Department had experienced considerable difficulty in recruiting women and minorities for several teaching positions in the past. Consequently, the department chairman, with the support of his faculty and administration, waived the Ph.D. requirement for those women or minorities who wished to apply for the vacant Associate Professor position but retained the requirement for males or non-minorities applying for the same position and for all other positions.

The Executive Order does not require that job requirements be waived or lowered in order to attract women and minority candidates. Indeed, it expressly forbids differential standards based on race, color, sex, religion or national origin. Further, it requires that once valid job requirements are established, they must be applied equally to all candidates. It is discriminatory for such requirements to be applied selectively on the basis of race, color, religion, sex, or national origin. Thus, the history department must either waive the Ph.D. requirement for all applicants (without regard to race or sex) or maintain it for all applicants.

IV. A Job Requirement which Results in a Disproportionate Impact upon Minorities and/or Women Can Be Maintained Only if It Is Job-Related.

As the *Guidelines* make very clear . . . the Executive Order does not require an institution to eliminate or dilute legitimate employment standards by which to measure prospective employees. On the other hand, no standards or criteria which have, by intent or effect, worked to exclude women and minorities as a class can be utilized, unless the institution can demonstrate the necessity of such standards to the performance of the job in question. For example:

> X Law School has established a Teaching Fellows Program which is responsible for the administration of the law school's clinical practice program. The requirement for Teaching Fellows includes holding a graduate law degree as well as an LL.B. or J.D. Degree. In analyzing its workforce for its

affirmative action program, the law school learns that this job requirement disproportionately excludes blacks from consideration for the Teaching Fellows positions.

In order to continue the requirement for a graduate law degree, the law school must demonstrate that the requirement is related to successful job performance. If the law school is able to demonstrate that the skills and knowledge acquired through the advanced law degree are necessary for effective job performance, the job requirement can be maintained. On questions relevant to the validity of the requirement, the opinion or testimony of persons experienced in the conduct of legal aid clinics will be given substantial weight by HEW.

V. A University Is Required to Obtain Information on the Race, Sex, and Ethnic Identity of Applicants for Employment.

The Executive Order establishes the principle that Federal contractors, including colleges and universities, are required to collect and maintain data on the race, sex and ethnic identity of all applicants for employment.

The collection and analysis of such data is recognized as an essential means of providing both the institution and the Federal Government with the information necessary to monitor the compliance posture of the institution. In the case of universities and colleges, the collection of such data is particularly essential for the workforce analysis required by Revised Order No. 4. Each institution must adopt safeguards to ensure that such information cannot be used as a basis for discrimination.

Preserving the anonymity of applicants in the collection of applicant flow data can be accomplished by gathering the requisite race, sex, and ethnic data separately from the application form. Furthermore, applicants should be instructed not to identify themselves by name or number on this form. If the institution wishes to determine applicant response for a particular position, the data form may be coded by position, as long as it does not individually identify any applicant.

This document is intended to help clarify areas of confusion which have arisen during the implementation of contractor requirements set forth in the Executive Order regulations. . . .

NOTES

1. Does the Holmes *Memorandum* weaken the affirmative action obligation under the Executive Order? Does the *Memorandum* imply that a university may be compelled to hire a minority or female applicant when other applicants have *equal* qualifications?

2. The following articles and books offer useful insights and critical comments on "affirmative action" programs: Ahart, *A Process Evaluation of the Contract Compliance*

Program in Nonconstruction Industry, 29 Ind. and Lab. Rel. Rev. 565 (1976); Bell, *Book Review of Glazer's "Affirmative Discrimination: Ethnic Inequality and Public Policy,"* 25 Emory L. J. 879 (1976); Brest, *The Supreme Court, 1975 Term—Foreword: In Defense of the Antidiscrimination Principle*, 90 Harv. L. Rev. 1 (1976); Carnegie Council on Policy Studies in Higher Education, Making Affirmative Action Work in Higher Education: An Analysis of Institutional and Federal Policies with Recommendations (1975); R. Dworkin, Taking Rights Seriously (1977); Edwards & Zaretsky, *Preferential Remedies for Employment Discrimination,* 74 Mich. L. Rev. 1 (1975); Ely, *The Constitutionality of Reverse Racial Discrimination,* 41 Univ. Chicago L. Rev. 723 (1974); Flanagan, *Actual Versus Potential Impact of Government Antidiscrimination Programs,* 29 Ind. and Lab. Rel. Rev. 486 (1976); Glazer, Affirmative Discrimination: Ethnic Inequality and Public Policy (New York: Basic Books, 1975); Goldstein and Smith, *The Estimated Impact of the Antidiscrimination Program Aimed at Federal Contractors,* 29 Ind. and Lab. Rel. Rev. 523 (1976); Lester, *Labor Market Discrimination and Individualized Pay: The Complicated Cases of University Faculty,* in 1977 Industrial Relations Research Association Series, Equal Rights and Industrial Relations 197 (1977); Nash, *Affirmative Action Under Executive Order 11246,* 46 N.Y.U. L. Rev. 225 (1971); Note, *Executive Order 11246: Problems and Implications on Sex Discrimination in Employment in Higher Education,* 37 Albany L. Rev. 810 (1973); O'Neill, *Preferential Admissions: Equalizing the Access of Minority Groups to Higher Education,* 80 Yale L. J. 699 (1971); Posner, *The DeFunis Case and the Constitutionality of Preferential Treatment of Racial Minorities,* 1974 Sup. Ct. Rev. 1; Roche, The Blanacing Act: Quota Hiring in Higher Education (1974); Sandalow, *Racial Preferences in Higher Education: Political Responsibility and the Judicial Role*, 42 Univ. Chicago L. Rev. 653 (1975); Smith, Employment Discrimination Law, Cases and Materials 1023 (1978); Sowell, *Affirmative Action Reconsidered: Was It Necessary in Academia?*, in American Enterprise Institute for Public Policy Research, Evaluative Studies (1975); *Symposium—DeFunis: The Road Not Taken*, 60 Va. L. Rev. 917 (1974); *Symposium—Disadvantaged Students and Legal Education—Programs for Affirmative Action*, 1970 Toledo L. Rev. 277; U.S. Commission on Civil Rights, Federal Civil Rights Enforcement Effort—1974 (1975); and U.S. Dept. of Health, Education and Welfare, *Higher Education Guidelines: Executive Order 11246* (1972).

3. Not surprisingly, the enforcement of Executive Order 11246 in the area of higher education has been controversial. A number of critics, like Nathan Glazer, in Affirmative Discrimination: Ethnic Inequality and Public Policy 58-59, 75-76 (1975), have argued that:

> Affirmative action has developed a wonderful Catch-22 type of existence. The employer is required by the OFCC to state numerical goals and dates when he will reach them. There is no presumption of discrimination. However, if he does not reach these goals, the question will come up as to whether he has made a "good faith" effort to reach them. The test of good faith has not been spelled out. From the employer's point of view, the simplest way of behaving to avoid the severe penalties of loss of contracts or heavy costs in back pay . . . is simply to meet the goals. . . . [T]he nation is by government action increasingly divided formally into racial and ethnic categories with differential rights. The Orwellian nightmare ". . . all animals are equal, but some animals are more equal than others, . . ." comes closer. . . . Conceivably, there have been benefits as we have moved from nondiscrimination to soft affirmative action to harder goals and deadlines. But there have been losses, too.

One of the better overview studies of the problem, which includes an extensive analysis of numerous articles and books dealing with affirmative action in higher education, is Richard Lester's *Labor-Market Discrimination and Individualized Pay: The Complicated Case of University Faculty,* in Equal Rights and Industrial Relations, at 197 (IRRA 1977). The case in favor of affirmative action is ably summarized in the following article by Professor Herma Hill Kay.

II.   The Case in Favor of Affirmative Action

KAY, THE NEED FOR SELF-IMPOSED
QUOTAS IN ACADEMIC EMPLOYMENT*

* * * 1. There presently exists a nation-wide and, I think, uncontroverted dearth of women and minority professors in academic institutions. This statement applies to all levels of higher education, but it is most apparent at public and private prestigious research universities. This deficiency is due in part (particularly in the case of minority professors) to prior discrimination in college and graduate school admissions, but it is also due in part to the nature of the faculty hiring process.

2.   The current budgetary restrictions imposed on public universities and the decline in support for private universities, coupled with projected demographic changes in age distribution, will mean less entry-level hiring in the future.

3.   The move to raise or eliminate entirely the mandatory retirement age for existing faculty members, while salutary in many respects, will also tend to restrict entry-level hiring as well as promotions in the immediate future.

4.   National legislation enacted to redress discrimination in academic employment in 1972 has been ineffective. Title VII of the Civil Rights Act of 1964, amended in 1972 to apply to institutions of higher education, is a dead letter in individual cases brought against academic institutions. There is good reason to believe that Title IX (the Higher Education Amendments of 1972) will be interpreted not to apply to academic employment at all. The Executive Orders have been useful in establishing goals and timetables in some cases, but the lack of adequately trained staff and the lack of efficient investigative and enforcement authority have hampered many efforts.

Given those propositions, . . . the only feasible method I can foresee that will produce significant numbers of female and minority professors in the future is for academic institutions to leave positions unfilled while undertaking vigorous and determined searches for qualified candidates. Moreover, once these candidates are identified and hired, special support should be made available to them where necessary in the form of initially reduced teaching and committee assignments in order to enable them to have adequate time for research and publication. Care must be taken to assure fairness of process at the tenure review stage, and attention must be given to avoid salary inequity.

Now that I have summarized my argument, let me give you the supporting evidence. Here I wish to acknowledge my debt to three of my former students: . . . Elizabeth Thomas, D. Kelly Weisberg, and Hillary Kelley, all class of 1978.

---

* (Remarks delivered at Symposia on "The Quest for Equality," School of Law, Washington University at St. Louis, January 17, 1979). Reprinted by permission of Professor Herma Hill Kay and the Washington University Law Quarterly.

1.   A survey undertaken by the American Association of University Women (AAUW) of 600 four-year colleges and reported in the Chronicle of Higher Education on April 17, 1978, indicated that women now hold 16.5% of tenured positions (compared to 16% in 1973). They constitute 8% of full professors and 16% of associate professors. The study shows more tenured women at smaller institutions (28% at colleges enrolling less than 1000 students) and fewer at large institutions (14% where the student body exceeds 10,000). The pattern holds true for law schools as well. ABA data for 1975-76 showed women holding 8.9% of full-time faculty positions. Analyzed by Ms. Weisberg, however, these figures disclosed that the "top ten" law schools had an average of only 4.8% women on their faculties—slightly over half the national average. Women who hold the rank of full professor are 3.8% of the total—and 14% of them are law librarians. Moreover, these averages conceal the surprising fact that during 1975-76, 49% of all accredited law schools employed either no women at all or at most one woman.

Comparable figures for minority faculty members are difficult to obtain and contain probable reporting errors. The 1972-73 survey conducted by the American Council on Education indicated that minority faculty members numbered 2,580 or 5.5% of the total. These figures can be broken down into 1.84% Black, .55% Native American, .32% Mexican-Spanish surname, 1.8% Oriental, and .99% "other minority". The Annual Newsletter of the American Association of Law Schools distributed in February, 1976, showed 202 full-time minority group teachers and administrators out of a total of 5,337, or 3.78%. These figures break down into 2.52% Black, .03% Asian, .02% Chicano, .03% Puerto Rican, .02% other Hispanic-American, and 0% Native American.

It is generally agreed that the availability pools for women are larger than those for minorities. Even so, the discrepancies for women are not disappearing. Nor is this surprising. As the Carnegie Commission Report on Opportunities for Women in Higher Education pointed out in 1973, in a system with low faculty turnover, the hiring ratio set to achieve adequate utilization of women and, by extension, minorities would have to be much higher than the current availability pools in order to catch up by the end of the decade. Given existing patterns of faculty recruitment, such an effort is unlikely.

At most institutions, faculty hiring begins at the departmental level. The department's choice of a candidate at the Instructor or even the Assistant Professor level frequently is not subject to review by campus-wide faculty or administrative bodies, although the affirmative action officer usually must be satisfied that a good faith search was conducted for women or minority candidates. In most cases, the new appointee is either a graduate student who has recently completed or is in the process of completing the Ph.D., whose work is known primarily to his or her (usually white male) professors. In the case of law schools, a year or two of judicial clerkships or large law firm practice will add another source of evaluation (also largely by white males) to that of the home school teachers. Many complaints have been voiced about the "old boy network", but the institutional forces that maintain it in place are still present: the professors, judges and senior partners who know the candidates, whose judgment is sought out and given credence by their counterparts in other institutions are overwhelmingly white and male. The tendency to recognize intellectual power and unusual capacity for creative scholarship more easily in persons of one's own sex and race and who can be viewed most comfortably as one's proteges, is perfectly natural.

Moreover, appointments tend to be made singly, not in groups. Although each individual candidate is evaluated against the field, the competitive bidding among universities for "targets of opportunity" seems to bear more resemblance to the vying of college football coaches for a star high school quarterback than to the sober assessment of a scholar's potential. Asking a predominantly white male faculty to forego the appointment of a young white male "superstar" in order to continue the search for seemingly elusive female or minority candidates is not likely to succeed in the absence of a formulated plan voluntarily accepted in advance by that faculty.

2.   Surely I need not pause very long over the critical budgetary situation facing all but a very few institutions of higher education, nor call to the attention of this audience the increased difficulty of persuading able law graduates to choose teaching over practice. Cases like *Krotkoff v. Goucher College*, 585 F.2d 675 (4th Cir. 1978), which upheld the dismissal of a tenured female professor on grounds of financial exigency, are likely to become all too common. Goucher was supported in its defense by the American Council on Education and The American Association of University Professors as amicus curiae: both were evidently seeking to preserve the concept of tenure in situations viewed as more critical by refusing to assert it here. After all, without students to provide tuition and fees, and in the absence of large numbers of generous private donors, private colleges like private businesses must be able to go out of operation—department by department, if necessary. The situation of many publicly-financed institutions is different only in that the decision to cut back is made outside the ivory tower, rather than within.

3.   The elimination of the compulsory retirement age deserves slightly more extended comment. Federal law (The Age Discrimination in Employment Act Amendments of 1978) currently prohibits a mandatory retirement age of less than 70 for most employees. A special exemption permits a lower mandatory retirement age for "tenured employees" until July 1, 1982. The exemption was a compromise between those, including most of the major research institutions and the ACE, who wanted a total exclusion for faculty, and those, including the bill's sponsors and the AAUP, who thought professors should be treated like other employees. According to ACE's assistant general counsel, Laura Ford, higher education's case for different treatment rested on two points:[1]   first, the unique demographic warp created by the

---

1.   The Battle Over Mandatory Retirement, 59 Educational Record 204 (1978).

confluence of two factors: the expansive faculty hiring which took place in the late 1950's and 1960's has produced a "bulge" of recently-tenured faculty members in their middle forties who will not be retiring until the end of the century, and the decline in enrollments projected to begin in the early 1980's. Taken together, these two factors will produce a situation in which faculty turnover will be limited to death or retirement.

The second crucial difference for universities is the existence of tenure, coupled with a system of peer review which virtually precludes termination of faculty members for "cause". The bottom line is that universities can expect to face severe restrictions on faculty renewal in the near future—a term which, in this context, includes affirmative action through new hires.

Moreover, there is wide speculation that the university administrators, having won the battle of the exclusion, may be losing the war against mandatory retirement. Many faculty members, including those in the age cohorts affected by the exemption, feel the exemption is unfair. MIT has already announced that it will not rely on the exemption, but will immediately raise its retirement age to 70. While the AAU and the ACE have undertaken efforts to have the exemption extended beyond 1982, the AAUP seeks its elimination. Both efforts may be preempted by Congressman Pepper's anticipated attempt to eliminate the mandatory retirement age altogether for all employees. Taking account of these and other possibilities, proposals are currently under consideration for phased retirement plans that would permit senior faculty members to continue to teach at reduced loads and to enjoy support facilities in order to make available a portion of their FTE for new appointments.

4.   Legal remedies for individual plaintiffs charging discrimination in the academic context are virtually non-existent. After reviewing more than 60 reported cases in 1978, Elizabeth Thomas found only four in which plaintiffs had succeeded on the merits.[2] Subsequently, one of those cases was reversed, and another, involving a reverse discrimination suit by a white male, was vacated and remanded. Ms. Thomas's most significant conclusion, however, was not that the plaintiffs lost, but that the federal district courts, which have played the leading role in making Title VII effective in the industrial context, have failed abysmally in applying the same careful judicial scrutiny to academic cases. Nor has this contrast escaped the notice of some appellate courts. Judge Tuttle, sitting by designation in the First Circuit and participating in one of the four cases in which the plaintiff won, *Sweeney v. Board of Trustees, Keene State College*, pointed out that most female plaintiffs challenging sex discrimination in academia had lost, and then went on to observe (569 F.2d 169, 176):

---

2.   Sweeney v. Board of Trustees, Keene State College, 569 F.2d 169 (1st Cir. 1978), reversed, —— U.S. —— , 99 S.Ct. 295 (1978); Dyson v. Lavery, 417 F.Supp. 103 (E.D. Va. 1976); Mecklenberg v. Montana Board of Regents, 13 E.P.D. 11,438 (D. Mont. 1976) (class action); Cramer v. Virginia Commonwealth University, 415 F.Supp. 673 (E.D. Va. 1976) vacated and remanded, 580 F.2d 1047 (4th Cir. 1978) (Mem.).

... we voice misgivings over one theme recurring in those opinions: the notion that courts should keep "hands off" the salary, promotion, and hiring decisions of colleges and universities. This reluctance no doubt arises from the courts' recognition that hiring, promotion, and tenure decisions require subjective evaluation most appropriately made by persons thoroughly familiar with the academic setting. Nevertheless, we caution against permitting judicial deference to result in judicial abdication of a responsibility entrusted to the courts by Congress. That responsibility is simply to provide a forum for the litigation of complaints of sex discrimination in institutions of higher learning as readily as for other Title VII suits.

Sweeney was subsequently reversed per curiam by a 5-4 vote of the U.S. Supreme Court for failing to follow the precise standard of proof in Title VII cases established in *McDonnell Douglas Corp. v. Green,* 411 U.S. 792 (1973) and reaffirmed in *Furnco Construction Co. v. Waters,* 438 U.S.___, 98 S.Ct. 2943 (1978), both arising in industrial settings.

The failure of academic plaintiffs is not limited to white females. My own review of recent federal court decisions discloses failure on the merits in two cases involving a black woman suing predominantly white schools;[3] one case involving a black male suing a university that did not have either black students or black faculty prior to 1978,[4] and one case involving a white male suing a predominantly black college[5] —the latter example representing an apparently growing problem which is discussed in the Chronicle of Higher Education for December 11, 1978 at p. 3.

In one of these recent cases, *Geraldine Powell v. Syracuse University,*[6] a Second Circuit panel attempted to modify the position taken in its earlier opinion in *Faro v. New York University,* 502 F.2d 1229 (2d Cir. 1974), the leading case establishing a non-interventionist policy in academic cases. Quoting the earlier statement in *Faro* that (502 F.2d at 1231):

> Of all fields, which the federal courts should hesitate to invade and take over, education and faculty appointments at a University level are probably the least suited for federal court supervision[.]

Judge Smith noted that its effect in practice had been to render "colleges and universities virtually immune to charges of employment bias, at least when that bias is not expressed overtly." Noting that Congress, by extending Title VII to educational institutions in 1972 had "instructed us to be particularly sensitive to evidence of academic bias", Judge Smith quoted with approval Judge Tuttle's language from *Sweeney* (prior to its reversal) and concluded that (580 F.2d at 1154):

---

3.   Powell v. Syracuse University, 580 F.2d 1150 (2d Cir. 1978); U.S. v. University of Maryland, 438 F.Supp. 742 (D. Md. 1977).
4.   Scott v. University of Delaware, 455 F.Supp. 1102 (D. Del. 1978).
5.   Citron v. Jackson State University, 456 F.Supp. 3 (S.D. Miss. 1977).
6.   Note 3, supra.

It is our task, then, to steer a careful course between excessive intervention in the affairs of the university and the unwarranted tolerance of unlawful behavior. *Faro* does not, and was never intended to, indicate that academic freedom embraces the freedom to discriminate.

Judge Moore, the author of the *Faro* opinion, did not agree with the retreat. Concurring in the judgment that Syracuse had successfully rebutted Ms. Powell's prima facie case, he disclaimed the majority's "dicta" in these words (580 F.2d at 1157):

... Any reluctance of the federal courts to interfere with the decision-making process of universities does not come from an interest in promoting discrimination. Rather, such reluctance reflects the inability of the courts to perform "a discriminating analysis of the qualifications of each candidate for hiring or advancement, taking into consideration his or her educational experience, the specifications of the particular position open and, of great importance, the personality of the candidate." (citing *Faro* at 1232).

Despite Judge Moore's disclaimer, however, it is clear that courts can and do probe employment decisions in academia with the same skill they use in other settings. Although there are many who disagree with the outcome, few have faulted the detailed and careful review of the evidence provided by Judge Knox in *Sharon Johnson v. The University of Pittsburgh*, 435 F.Supp. 1328 (W.D. Pa. 1977). ...

[L]itigation by an individual faculty member must always be a last resort. In view of the inevitable discomfort for the plaintiff and his or her colleagues, the high cost of litigation, the time consumed in trial and trial preparation, the low chance of ultimate success, and the almost certain damage to the plaintiff's academic career even if success is attained, let alone the strains placed upon the defending institution, the path of individual litigation is not likely to be recommended.

I do not believe, however, that the problem of increasing the numbers of women and minority faculty members can be left to take care of itself through the normal recruitment processes. Despite the heightened sensitivity to the matter experienced by most white male professors, created in part by the paperwork made necessary by annual contract compliance reports, there still seems to be a gap between the abstract good intentions and the hiring decisions in particular cases. As I indicated at the beginning of my remarks, my view is that the least detrimental institutional way of closing this gap is for a department to decide in advance that faculty positions will be targeted for female and minority appointments. Advocates of affirmative action can then be reassured that the good will of their colleagues will not be worn thin by continuous reiteration of the argument each time a white male candidate is presented for consideration, and those whose chief concern is the maintenance—and indeed, the improvement—of intellectual

standards can undertake their search for qualified female and minority candidates on the assurance that different standards will not be applied to the
targeted appointments. In a work environment where intellectual and collegial interaction and respect is highly prized, the voluntary adoption of
such a policy would go far towards alleviating the present strains caused by
past societal neglect of the qualities and aspirations of women and minority
group members.

NOTE

In 1971, Peter G. Nash, then Solicitor of the Department of Labor, argued that
affirmative action could be reconciled with the ideal of nondiscrimination:

> Nondiscrimination and affirmative action are not mutually exclusive concepts
> designed to impale an employer upon the horns of a dilemma, but are wholly
> consistent and equally obtainable both in theory and in practice. The theory
> is best understood by acknowledgment of the fact that de facto discrimina-
> tion permeates American society despite our successes in combatting de jure
> discrimination. Thus, although an employer may not seek to discriminate,
> neutral employment policies may have the effect of discriminating against
> minorities. For instance, the recruitment policies of an employer determined
> not to discriminate may in the actual selection of job applicants have the
> effect of excluding minority persons unless a conscious effort is made to
> give the minority community notice of outstanding job vacancies. If this is
> not done, minority applicants will not appear to seek employment, and the
> employer will have no opportunity to place his nondiscriminatory selection
> policy into effect. In this situation, taking affirmative steps to broaden the
> recruitment base is wholly consistent with the employer's nondiscrimination
> obligation.
> [Nash, *Affirmative Action Under Executive Order 11,246*, 46 N.Y.U. L.
> Rev. 225, 230 (1971)]

Do you agree with Nash's appraisal? How about Professor Kay's suggestion that affirmative action will only work with "self-imposed quotas"? Are quotas permissible under
Title VII? Under Executive Order 11246? Under the Equal Protection clause?

III. The Legal Issues

Although affirmative action programs are designed to redress past
discrimination against minorities and women, it is nevertheless claimed that
the preferential treatment in favor of a particular race or sex conflicts with
the notion of equal opportunity. The court in Associated General Contractors of Massachusetts, Inc. v. Altshuler, 490 F.2d 9 (1st Cir. 1973), *cert.
denied.* 416 U.S. 957 (1974), recognized that this was a troublesome matter,
but concluded that:

> our society cannot be completely colorblind in the short term if
> we are to have a colorblind society in the long term. After cen-
> turies of viewing through colored lenses, eyes do not quickly
> adjust when the lenses are removed. Discrimination has a way of
> perpetuating itself, albeit unintentionally, because the resulting
> inequalities make new opportunities less accessible. Preferential
> treatment is one partial prescription to remedy our society's most
> intransigent and deeply rooted inequalities. 490 F.2d at 16.

The problem of the legality of affirmative action programs came into sharp focus in 1977 when the Fifth Circuit issued its opinion in Weber v. Kaiser Aluminum and Chemical Corp., 563 F.2d 216 (5th Cir. 1977). The *Weber* case was heard and decided by the Supreme Court during the 1978-1979 term and it no doubt will prove to be the landmark opinion in this area. Excerpts from the Fifth Circuit decision are printed below:

WEBER v. KAISER ALUMINUM AND CHEMICAL CORP.
Fifth Circuit Court of Appeals
563 F.2d 216 (1977)

GEE, Circuit Judge—In February 1974, Kaiser Aluminum & Chemical Corporation entered into a collective bargaining agreement with United Steelworkers of America, AFL-CIO (USWA), that significantly altered eligibility for on-the-job training to enter craft positions in all Kaiser plants. In an effort to increase the number of minority workers in the craft families, the 1974 Labor Agreement removed the requirement of prior craft experience for on-the-job training and established an entrance ratio of one minority worker to one white worker until the percentage of minority craft workers roughly estimated the percentage of minority population in the area surrounding each plant. Eligibility for training still rested on plant seniority but to implement their affirmative action goal it was necessary to establish dual seniority lists: for each two training vacancies, one black and one white employee would be selected on the basis of seniority within their respective racial groups. As predictable, black employees have been admitted to Kaiser's on-the-job training program with less seniority than their white competitors. One unsuccessful white bidder working at Kaiser's Gramercy, Louisiana, plant brought this class action on behalf of all persons employed by Kaiser at its Gramercy works who are members of the USWA Local 5702, who are not members of a minority group and who have applied for or were eligible to apply for on-the-job training programs since February 1, 1974. Mr. Weber alleged that by preferring black employees with less seniority for admission to on-the-job training, Kaiser and USWA were guilty of unlawful discrimination in violation of Title VII, 42 U.S.C. § § 2000e-2 et seq. (1970). The district court agreed and granted a permanent injunction against further use of the 1974 training eligibility quota. Although the 1974 Labor Agreement applies to all Kaiser plants and similar agreements were enacted through the aluminum industry, these facts pertain only to Kaiser's plant in Gramercy, Louisiana, and this action enjoined the use of the quota at that plant only. Kaiser and USWA supported by numerous amici curiae, bring this appeal asking us to hold that their training quota, which they say is mandated by valid executive action, does not violate Title VII and is justified by past societal discrimination even in the absence of past employment discrimination here.

Affirmative Relief or Reverse
Discrimination?

The case before this court today is unique in that the affirmative action complained of was not imposed by the judiciary; rather, this collective bargaining agreement was entered into to avoid future litigation and to comply with the threats of the Office of Federal Contract Compliance Programs (OFCC) conditioning federal contracts on appropriate affirmative action. [3] The case is also unique in that it presents a conflict between affirmative action dictated by the OFCC under Executive Order 11246 and preferential treatment prohibited by Title VII. . . .

The Supreme Court has never approved the use of a quota remedy to overcome employment discrimination, but circuit courts have repeatedly sanctioned judicially imposed quotas in certain factual circumstances. Prior to the 1972 amendments to Title VII, our circuit approved such a quota. Local 53, International Ass'n of Heat & Frost Insulators & Asbestos Workers v. Vogler, 407 F.2d 1047, 1 FEP Cases 577, 70 LRRM 2257 (5th Cir. 1969). Accord, United States v. International Brotherhood of Electrical Workers, Local 38, 428 F.2d 144, 149-59, 2 FEP Cases 716, 719-721 (6th Cir.), cert. denied, 400 U.S. 943, 91 S.Ct. 245, 27 L.Ed2d 248, 2 FEP Cases 1121 (1970); United States v. Sheetmetal Workers Local 36, 416 F.2d 123, 2 FEP Cases 127 (8th Cir. 1969). In 1972, a Senate amendment to overturn this case law and forbid the use of quota remedies was rejected two-to-one. Legislative History of Equal Employment Opportunity Act of 1972 at 1017, 1042-74, 1081, 1714-17 (1972). . . .

Quotas imposed to achieve the "make whole" objective of Title VII rest on a presumption of some prior discrimination. There can be no basis for preferring minority workers if there has been no discriminatory act that displaced them from their "rightful place" in the employment scheme. Several circuits have noted this distinction, holding that quotas or preferential treatment merely to attain racial balance of the work force are unlawful, while quotas to correct past discriminatory practices are not. . . .

Courts also have affirmed quota remedies imposed by federal affirmative action programs under the impetus of Executive Order 11246 and comparable state affirmative action programs. . . .

The affirmative action program mandated by 41 C.F.R. § 60-2 (Revised Order No. 4) for nonconstruction contractors requires a "utilization" study to determine minority and female representation in the work force. Goals for hiring and promotion must be set to overcome any "underutilization"

[3.]   Executive Order No. 11246 requires all applicants for federal contracts to refrain from employment discrimination and to "take affirmative action to ensure that applicants are employed, and that employees are treated during employment, without regard to their race, color, religion, sex or national origin." § 202(1), 3 C.F.R. 169 (1974), reprinted following 42 U.S.C. § 2000e (1970). The Executive Order empowers the Secretary of Labor to issue rules and regulations necessary and appropriate to achieve its purpose. He, in turn, has delegated most enforcement duties to the OFCC. See 41 C.F.R. 60-20.1 et seq.; 41 C.F.R. 60-2.24.

found to exist. The regulation then confuses things mightily by declaring that a goal shall not be considered a device for instituting quotas or reverse discrimination:

> [T]he purpose of a contractor's establishment and use of goals is to insure that he meet his affirmative action obligation. It is not intended and should not be used to discriminate against any applicant or employee because of race, color, religion, sex, or national origin.

41 C.F.R. §60-2.30. Attempts to distinguish a numerical goal from a quota have proved illusory, and most such goals suggested by the OFCC can fairly be characterized as quotas.

We must judge the legality of Kaiser's training ratio in light of both Title VII, with its "make-whole" objective, and Executive Order 11246, with its mandate for affirmative action that does not itself discriminate. . . .

Where admissions to the craft on-the-job training programs are admittedly and purely functions of seniority and that seniority is untainted by prior discriminatory acts, the one-for-one ratio, whether designed by agreement between Kaiser and USWA or by order of court, has no foundation in restorative justice, and its preference for training minority workers thus violates Title VII. We concur in the district court's opinion that however laudable the objective of training minority workers, Title VII clearly proscribes discriminating against minority workers. . . .

Appellants contend that if this racial quota is not sanctioned by Title VII it is sanctioned by Executive Order 11246 and regulations issued by the Office of Federal Contract Compliance (OFCC) mandating affirmative action by all government contractors. Indeed, the district court found that the 1974 collective bargaining agreement reflected less of a desire on Kaiser's part to train black craft workers than a self-interest in satisfying the OFCC in order to retain lucrative government contracts.

Appellees respond that because Kaiser has actively recruited black craft workers it has complied with the executive requirement of affirmative action and is not guilty of "underutilization." They argue that, properly interpreted, Executive Order 11246 would not require a racial quota in these circumstances and that the OFCC improperly threatened the withdrawal of all federal contracts unless this racial preference was enacted.

Executive Order 11246, with its implied mandate for affirmative action on the part of those who would supply the government with goods or services, has been upheld as valid executive action. Contractors Association of Eastern Pennsylvania v. Secretary of Labor, supra at 166-71, 3 FEP Cases at 399-403 (upholding the "Philadelphia Plan"); see also Farkas v. Texas Instruments, Inc., 375 F.2d 629, 1 FEP Cases 890, 71 LRRM 3154 (5th Cir.), cert. denied, 389 U.S. 977, 88 S.Ct. 480, 19 L.Ed.2d 471, 1 FEP Cases 894, 71 LRRM 3157 (1967). But executive orders may not override contradictory congressional expressions. In the famous challenge to executive power in Youngstown Sheet & Tube Co. v. Sawyer, 343 U.S. 579, 72 S.Ct. 863, 96 L.Ed. 1153 (1952), Justice Jackson divided executive orders into three categories: (1) those in which the President acts pursuant to express or implied authorization by Congress, as to which his authority is at a maximum; (2) those in which the President acts in the absence of congressional grant of authority and must rely upon his own independent powers; and (3) those in which executive action conflicts with the express or implied will of Congress and is most vulnerable to challenge.

> When the President takes measures incompatible with the expressed or implied will of Congress, his power is at its lowest ebb, for then he can rely only upon his own constitutional powers minus any constitutional powers of Congress over the matter. Courts can sustain exclusive presidential control in such a case only by disabling the Congress from acting upon the subject. Presidential claim to a power at once so conclusive and preclusive must be scrutinized with caution, for what is at stake is the equilibrium established by our constitutional system. [footnotes omitted].

343 U.S. at 638, 72 S.Ct. at 871. The Third Circuit first validated the Philadelphia Plan as valid executive action and then tested it for conflicts with congressional action, holding that "the Executive is bound by the express prohibitions of Title VII." 442 F.2d at 171-72, 3 FEP Cases at 404. The Third Circuit held that the general prohibition against discrimination found in sections 703(a), (h) and (j) did not prohibit the affirmative action imposed by the Philadelphia Plan, *given a finding of prior exclusionary practices* by the six trade unions controlling the work force.

Whether Kaiser has already met its affirmative action burden or not, we are unable to harmonize the more explicit language of section 703(d), which specifically prohibits racial classification in admission to on-the-job training programs, with the affirmative action imposed here. If Executive Order 11246 mandates a racial quota for admission to on-the-job training by Kaiser, *in the absence of any prior hiring or promotion discrimination,* the executive order must fall before this direct congressional prohibition.

We deny appellants relief, not unmindful of the delayed opportunities for advancement this will occasion many minority workers but equally aware of our duty, in enforcing Title VII, to respect the opportunities due to white workers as well. Whatever the merits of racial quotas—and the short-term and obvious benefits must not blind us to the seeds of racial animus such affirmative relief undeniably sows [17]—Congress has forbidden racial preferences in admission to on-the-job training programs, and under the circumstances of this case we are not empowered by the equitable doctrine of restorative justice to ignore that proscription.

AFFIRMED.

[17.]   Racial quotas also have been criticized for contributing to the Balkanization of this country by fostering "the dangerous notion that ethnic, racial or religious groups are entitled to proportional representation in all occupations."

In hindsight, one can see this was predictable. We wished to create a generalized, firm, but gentle pressure to balance the residue of discrimination. Unfortunately, the pressure numerical standards generate cannot be generalized or gentle; it inevitably causes injustice.

Dissenting Opinion

WISDOM, Circuit Judge, dissenting:—I respectfully dissent.

Today the Court grapples with the question whether, in a collective bargaining agreement, recognition of race for remedial purposes in employment practices is legal "affirmative action" or illegal "reverse discrimination". The majority does not assert race may never be considered in employment practices or in other racially tense areas. Over ten years ago this Court declared, "The Constitution is both color blind and color conscious". Where I differ from the majority is in my assessment of situations justifying reliance on race as a basis for decision-making. Here, the decision-making was by agreement between management and the union, presumably with the blessing of the legislative and executive branches of government but without benefit of the judicial branch. "Management and the government have been our [the unions'] partners in these endeavors [to eliminate discriminatory employment practices] and a great deal of credit must be given to them for the accomplishments of the past ten years." Bredhoff, Affirmative Action in a Declining Economy: Seniority and Incumbent Majority, in Federal Bar Association, An Equal Employment Opportunity Practice Guide, 118, 119 (1977). The third party beneficiaries of these joint endeavors and agreements are the disadvantaged minorities. . . .

A . . . ground for upholding the defendants' actions is that their program was required by Executive Order 11246, 30 Fed.Reg. 12319. This Executive Order requires federal contractors to take affirmative action to prevent low employment of women and minorities in their workforces, starting from the assumption that most disproportionately low employment is the result of discrimination—if not of the contractor involved, then of someone else. I disagree with the majority's view that if the Executive Order purports to legalize this program, the Executive Order is invalid. I believe, however, that the district court would have to determine whether this plan does in fact comport with the requirements of the Executive Order. Therefore, on this ground I would remand the case to the district court for further proceedings.

I do not disagree with the majority's conclusion that if a conflict between the Executive Order and Title VII exists, it should be resolved in favor of Title VII. But that weighty question of the allocation of power between the legislative and the executive branches of government need not be reached. Here, the two are not in conflict.

As the majority points out, affirmative action plans under the Executive Order have been held constitutional. See E.E.O.C. v. A.T.&T., 3 Cir. 1977, 556 F.2d 167, 14 FEP Cases 1210, aff'd, 1976, E.D.Pa., 419 F.Supp. 1022, 13 FEP Cases 392; Contractors Association of Eastern Pennsylvania v. Secretary of Labor, 3 Cir. 1971, 442 F.2d 159, 3 FEP Cases 395; Southern Illinois Builders Association v. Ogilvie, 7 Cir. 1972, 471 F.2d 680, 5 FEP Cases 229; Mele v. Department of Justice, 1975 D.N.J., 395 F.Supp. 592, 10 FEP Cases 1000, aff'd without opinion, 3 Cir. 1976, 532 F.2d 747, 16

FEP Cases 44. Cf. Associated General Contractors of Massachusetts v. Altshuler, 1 Cir. 1973, 490 F.2d 9, 6 FEP Cases 1013, cert. denied, 1974, 416 U.S. 957, 94 S.Ct. 1971, 40 L.Ed.2d 307, 7 FEP Cases 1160; Joyce v. McCrane, 1970 D.N.J., 320 F.Supp. 1184, 3 FEP Cases 111; Weiner v. Cuyahoga Community College, 1968 Ohio Ct. of Appeals, aff'd mem., 1969, 19 Ohio St.2d 35, 249 N.E.2d 907, 2 FEP Cases 30, cert. denied, 1969, 396 U.S. 1004, 90 S.Ct. 554, 24 L.Ed.2d 495, 2 FEP Cases 337 (similar state plans). For a history of the Executive Order and the response to it in Congress and the courts, see Comment, The Philadelphia Plan: A Study on the Dynamics of Executive Power, 39 U.Chi.L.Rev. 752 (1972).

The majority seeks to distinguish Contractors Ass'n of Eastern Pennsylvania by stressing the finding there that discrimination had existed in the industry. It should be noted that the parties involved in that case were the contractors; the groups discriminating were the crafts unions. The opinion is in fact directly in point in that respect because it involved actions of the non-discriminating parties.

The legal situation has changed significantly since that opinion. Congress has implicitly exempted the Executive Order from the constraints of Title VII. [22] See Comment, The Philadelphia Plan: A Study in the Dynamics of Executive Power, 39 U.Chi.L.Rev. 723, 751-57 (1972). Congress did so through three actions taken during consideration of the Equal Employment Opportunity Act of 1972, Pub.L. 92-261. At that time the regulations requiring affirmative action in the form of goals and timetables had been in effect for several years. The "Philadelphia Plan", the subject of the Associated Contractors decision, had been in effect for three years.

The legislation originally presented would have transferred the entire Executive Order enforcement program to the E.E.O.C. Congress eliminated that provision by an amendment offered by Senator Saxbe. In support of the amendment, the Senator stated:

> It has been the "goals and timetables" approach which is unique to the OFCC's efforts in equal employment, coupled with extensive reporting and monitoring procedures that has given the promise of equal employment opportunity a new credibility.

> The Executive Order program should not be confused with the judicial remedies for proven discrimination which unfold on a limited and expensive case-by-case basis. Rather, affirmative

---

[22.]   The predecessor of this Executive Order was mentioned in the 1964 Act in a section dealing with necessary reports, §709(d), 42 U.S.C. §2000e-8(d) (1970). It could be argued that the Order was protected by §1103, 42 U.S.C. §2000h-3 (1970), which is a saving clause for then existing authority for federal action.

    It could also be argued that the rejection in 1969 of the so-called Fannin Rider demonstrated Congressional approval of the Executive Order. The Comptroller General had declared the Philadelphia Plan illegal on the ground that it lacked standards needed to comply with rules regulating competitive bidding. Senator Fannin introduced a rider to an appropriations bill which would have denied all funds for any contracts held illegal by the Comptroller General. The debate made clear that the Philadelphia Plan was the target of the Rider. See Comment, The Philadelphia Plan, infra, 747-50.

action means that all Government contractors must develop programs to insure that all share equally in the jobs generated by the Federal Government's spending. Proof of overt discrimination is not required.

118 Cong. Rec. 1385 (1972). Another amendment which would have had substantially the same result as the original language was rejected by Congress. 118 Cong. Rec. 3367-70, 3371-73, 3959-65 (1972).

The most telling action was the rejection by the Senate of an amendment to § 703(j) of Title VII, offered by Senator Ervin. The Ervin amendment would have extended that section to read:

Nothing contained in this title *or in Executive Order No. 11246, or in any other law or Executive Order*, shall be interpreted to require any employer . . . to grant preferential treatment to any individual. . . . [Emphasis added.]

118 Cong. Rec. 1676 (1972). This amendment was viewed and debated as an attack on Philadelphia-type plans. See 118 Cong.Rec. 1664-65 (1972) (Sen. Javits). [23]

Finally, the section-by-section analysis of the amendments undertaken by the Senate Subcommittee on labor provided:

In any area where the new law does not address itself, or in any areas where a specific contrary intent is not indicated, it was assumed that the present case law as developed by the courts would continue to govern the applicability and construction of Title VII.

Subcomm. on Labor of the Senate Comm. on Labor and Public Welfare, Legislative History of Equal Employment Opportunity Act of 1972 at 1844 (1972). With the decision in Contractors Association before it, there can be little question that whatever was the status of that opinion before 1972, Congress ratified the Philadelphia Plan as consistent with Title VII.

The district court did not pass upon the validity and applicability of the Executive Order. There is a question whether Kaiser's extensive recruiting efforts before 1974 completely satisfied the requirements of the Executive Order. See 41 C.F.R. § 60-2.1 et seq. Furthermore, the regulations promulgated under the Executive Order disclaim any intent to impose a "quota". 41 C.F.R. § 60-2.-30. If the majority is right about the effect of Title VII on this litigation, apart from considerations of the Executive Order, then the disavowal in the regulations of quotas might be read in the same way. Those questions require the consideration of the trial court. Therefore, if I accepted the majority's position that Title VII, apart from the Executive Order, prohibited the conduct in question, I would still vacate the decision and remand it for further proceedings.

[23.] Senator Javits made clear the connection between the Philadelphia Plan and the Ervin Amendment:

"First, It would undercut the whole concept of affirmative action as developed under Executive Order 11246 and thus preclude Philadelphia-type plans."

18 Cong.Rec. 1665 (1972). The Contractors Association decision, which upheld the Philadelphia Plan, was printed in the Congressional Record at Senator Javit's request.

V.

"Reverse discrimination" is a question of great current concern. It has spawned an extensive literature, and caused heated debates, some between former allies. It is a troubling question. The color blind constitution, so eloquently invoked by the first Justice Harlan, has great appeal. A person's color should not be relevant to most decisions. This Court knows that acceptance of that principle did not come easily. At this stage in the history of eliminating racial discrimination, the use of a racial criterion because it is "benign" pulls us perilously close to self-contradiction. But in spite of our newly adopted equality, the pervasive effects of centuries of societal discrimination still haunt us. Kaiser and the United Steelworkers sought in a reasonable manner to remedy some of those effects in employment practices. Their actions may or may not be just to all its employees; they may or may not be wise; but I believe they are legal. Therefore, I respectfully dissent.

NOTE

On June 27, 1979, in a landmark decision, the Supreme Court reversed the Fifth Circuit decision in *Weber* and upheld the legality of voluntary affirmative action. (The Court's opinion will appear in the *Supplement.*)

CHAPTER 18

AGE DISCRIMINATION IN EMPLOYMENT

I. Introduction

As of July 1, 1977, it was estimated that 32.9 million persons, or 15.2% of the total population in the United States, were 60 years of age or older.[1] The 60-and-over group increased in size by approximately 15% from 1970 to 1977, as compared to a 6% increase in the size of the nation's population as a whole during the same period.[2]

Although older workers represent an ever-increasing proportion of the total population, they continue to suffer from unique forms of discrimination in the job market. The problem of age discrimination in employment arises in many situations because employers often assume that there may be an inverse correlation between work productivity and a worker's age; that is, it is often believed that older workers (especially those past fifty or sixty) are less likely to perform as well as they did at an earlier age. Stereotypical views are that older workers are highly prone to sickness and injury and, therefore, are more likely to be absent from work than younger workers; older workers are not as strong or alert as younger workers and, therefore, are unable to perform as many job tasks as well as younger workers, and older workers are more interested in retirement, vacations and holidays than younger workers and, therefore, are less motivated by work than are younger workers. In addition, it is also argued that older workers are relatively expensive to an employer, due to higher premium rates for life and health insurance payments, extra pay given to older workers for their experience or seniority, and lost productivity due to higher levels of absenteeism among older workers.

Finally, it has been asserted that it is unfair to limit the opportunities of the younger members of the work force by freezing them out of jobs being held by older workers who are simply biding their time until retirement. Not only are younger workers denied work opportunities, but it is also claimed that the employer is restricted from bringing in fresh talent and from implementing affirmative action programs where an employing institution is top-heavy with senior workers.

On the other side of the issue, there is the persuasive response that not *all* older workers should be forced into retirement or unemployment merely because some older workers are unable or unwilling to perform as well as younger workers. As for cost, many would agree that older workers, especially those with long seniority and unique skills, are well worth the extra

---

1. U.S., Dept. of Health, Education and Welfare, Administration on Aging, Office of Human Development Services, *Statistical Notes*, No. 2, August, 1978.

2. *Id.*

costs associated with their employment. Although it is often difficult to measure the real worth of "experience" on any given job, it is clear that in a number of working situations an experienced worker is more valuable to an employer than an employee with equal basic skills but only limited experience on the job. An employer cannot give a younger worker "experience" by training; only time on a job or in a trade or profession produces the kind of experience that is seen to justify premium pay for senior workers.

Discrimination against older workers also involves certain important public policy issues, several of which prompted Congress to pass the Age Discrimination in Employment Act of 1967. The House Labor Committee Report on H.R. 5383, 95th Congress, 1st Session, Rept. 95-527, Part I (1977), which preceded the adoption of the 1978 amendments to the ADEA, made the following significant observations with respect to the problem of forced retirement in employment.

Increasingly, it is being recognized that mandatory retirement based solely upon age is arbitrary and that chronological age alone is a poor indicator of ability to perform a job. Mandatory retirement does not take into consideration actual differing abilities and capacities. Such forced retirement can cause hardships for older persons through loss of roles and loss of income. Those older persons who wish to be re-employed have a much more difficult time finding a new job than younger persons.

Society, as a whole, suffers from mandatory retirement as well. As a result of mandatory retirement, skills and experience are lost from the work force resulting in reduced GNP. Such practices also add a burden to Government income maintenance programs such as social security.

In testimony before the Select Committee on Aging on March 16, 1977, Suzanne G. Haynes, Ph.D., of the National Heart, Lung, and Blood Institute, reported her research findings that the expected death rates in the third and fourth years after mandatory retirement were about 30 percent higher than expected. While more study of this issue is needed, Dr. Haynes agreed with Dr. Robert Butler, Director of the National Institute on Aging, who observes that the right to work is basic to the right to survive.

The committee has studied the arguments against reducing or eliminating mandatory retirement and while some have merit, the committee feels that they are far outweighed by the arguments against discrimination on account of age.

One concern expressed has been that reducing mandatory retirement would worsen the unemployment problem. This committee is very concerned about unemployment. However, as Congressman Paul Findley stated in testimony before this committee on June 2, 1977:

Our present system * * * of forcing retirees to give their jobs to younger people simply trades one form of unemployment for another. Nor does depriving older and still capable Americans of jobs make any more sense than discriminating in employment against blacks, women, or religious or ethnic minorities. . . .

A related argument has been that mandatory retirement is necessary to provide job opportunities for minorities and women. This argument overlooks the fact that women and minorities also grow old. Faced with what some have termed "double [or triple] jeopardy"—i.e., being old, a minority, and perhaps female—these persons need even more this protection against a possible added form of discrimination—on account of age. . . .

Some have expressed a concern over how management would terminate incompetent or unproductive employees without mandatory retirement. The committee believes that any successful employer must have methods of releasing employees incapable or unwilling to perform satisfactorily during the first 45 years of their work lives. If not, an additional few years shouldn't be a significant burden. . . .

The argument has also been made that older workers perform their jobs less well. Testimony to the committee cited the results of various research findings which indicate that older workers were as good or better than their younger coworkers with regard to dependability, judgment, work quality, work volume, human relations, and absenteeism; and older workers were shown to have fewer accidents on the job. As Congressman Pepper stated before our committee:

> The Labor Department's finding that there is more variation in work ability within the same age group than between age groups justifies judging workers on competency, not age.

Another interesting commentary on the problem of forced retirement is found in *Is Mandatory Retirement Necessary?*, a summary of a presentation by Jack Ossofsky published by the United States Department of Health, Education and Welfare (DHEW Publication No. (NIH) 78-1405):

> In an attempt to understand the dimensions of the problem of stereotyping, Louis Harris and Associates, in 1974, conducted an in-depth survey (with more than 4 thousand interviews) for the National Council on the Aging. The study, "The Myth and Reality of Aging in America," is the most definitive ever undertaken to determine the American public's attitude towards aging and the aged, as well as to document older Americans' views of themselves. (The *elderly, aged, older Americans,* or *aging* were defined as "those over age 65." The survey found that our thinking about aging is largely done in stereotypes, most of them inaccurate. The elderly were viewed as "stable," "warm," "friendly," and "seden-

tary." They were seen as incapable of learning, doing, or, even, wanting to do very much; they were seen as glad to be retired and freed from work's burdens.

Older people, strangely enough, despite having accepted some of the stereotypes that society has created, did not view themselves in the same way younger people did. Although on the one hand, older people, like the young, characterized the elderly as "not wanting to do very much," the older people polled did not include themselves in the category of "elderly"! They saw themselves as exceptions. When asked about themselves, these older people actually proved to be very active. According to the survey, 4 million older people would return to work, if given the opportunity to do so, full-time or part-time. Unfortunately, 87 percent of personnel directors interviewed indicated that they discriminate against older workers in hiring and firing.

Many of the elderly faced several problems, among them—health care, crime and economic stringency. But not all faced the same problems. There are 22 million elderly in the United States. Each one of these is an individual, different from every other. Also, not all the elderly are at the same chronological stage. Yet terms such as *elderly, aged, older Americans,* or *aging* lump all those over 65 together, not distinguishing the 70-year-old from the 100-year-old.

In general, studies of work situations indicate that when older workers are appropriately placed in their jobs, they function effectively, have greater stability, fewer accidents, and less time lost than most younger people. In each group of older people, a substantial number of persons were found performing at least at a level equal to the average level of their juniors. Approximately 20 studies now show that vocabulary, general information, and judgment may rise, but never fall, before, at, or around the age of 60.

Do we have a reason to keep mandatory retirement? Absolutely not. Compulsory retirement takes away older people's freedom— the freedom to work—or not to. The greatest loss in the older years is not the loss of vision, teeth, or hearing; it is the loss of the freedom to choose. Because of precedent, theory, and misconceptions of older people's capacities, we are disenfranchising a significant number of human beings, as well as wasting great human resources.

It is these considerations that have prompted the concern over age discrimination in employment. The materials that follow consider various constitutional and statutory provisions applicable to the problem.

II. Constitutional Issues

PALMER v. TICCIONE
United States Court of Appeals, Second Circuit
576 F.2d 459 (1978)

HAYS, Circuit Judge.

Appellant, Lois Palmer, commenced this action under 42 U.S.C. § 1983 (1970) for age discrimination in violation of the equal protection and due process guarantees of the Fourteenth Amendment. The district court granted the defendants' motion to dismiss for want of a substantial federal question. For the reasons stated below, we affirm the dismissal of the complaint.

I

The facts are undisputed. Appellant has been a teacher since 1943. She has been employed by the defendant Copiague Union Free District # 5 as a kindergarten teacher since the 1961-62 school year. She received tenure at the end of the 1963-64 school year. In February 1975, she reached the age of 70. On May 15, 1975, she met with defendant N. Paul Buscemi, the Copiague superintendent of schools. He informed her that she was to be retired at the end of the school year because she had reached the retirement age of 70. This decision was subsequently ratified by the Copiague school board, and the New York State Retirement System was directed to place Mrs. Palmer on retirement status as of August 25, 1975.

It is not disputed that appellant is willing and able to teach. Her performance as a teacher was rated satisfactory in each year of her employment. In the last evaluation, made just before she was retired in 1975, her principal recommended that she be rehired, "[s]ubject to review of compulsory retirement under New York State Education Law."

Appellant contends that retirement solely on the basis of her age violates her constitutional and state law rights. Essentially, she claims: that compulsory retirement at age 70 violates the equal protection clause; that it creates an irrebuttable presumption of incompetency based on age; that, as a tenured teacher, she is entitled to a hearing before termination; and that, in the alternative, the New York Education Law should be read to prohibit compulsory retirement or, if not, to require a hearing before termination.

II

Compulsory retirement systems have come under constitutional attack in several contexts. These equal protection and due process challenges have been rejected by this and other courts. The only exception is *Gault v. Garrison,* 569 F.2d 993 (7th Cir. 1977). In that case, the Seventh Circuit ruled that a retired teacher is entitled to a trial on her age discrimination claim. Because *Gault* involves a factual situation very similar to that of the instant case—the major difference is that the retirement age in *Gault* was 65, not 70—and because we disagree with the *Gault* holding, we think it appropriate to focus on this issue once again.

The ruling in *Gault* is premised on the implications of the Supreme Court's most recent decision in this area. In *Massachusetts Board of Retirement v. Murgia*, 427 U.S. 307, 96 S.Ct. 2562, 49 L.Ed.2d 520 (1976), the Court upheld a state law requiring the mandatory retirement of uniformed police at age 50. First, *Murgia* established that the proper standard for equal protection review in a case challenging a compulsory retirement statute is the rational basis test. *Id.* at 312-14, 96 S.Ct. 2562. Applying this standard, the Court found that forced retirement at age 50 did foster the purpose identified by the state; it assured the continued physical preparedness of the state's uniformed police. *Id.* at 314-16, 96 S.Ct. 2562. In *Murgia*, there had been a trial, and there was evidence in the record to support the conclusion that physical preparedness is rationally related to age.

As in the instant case, but unlike *Murgia*, *Gault* involved an appeal from an order dismissing the complaint. The *Gault* court assumed that the strongest justification for a retirement law for teachers is to remove those who are unfit. Working from that premise, it held that, absent an evidentiary showing, there was no reason to assume that there is any relationship between advancing age and fitness to teach. *Gault* distinguished *Murgia* as involving a question of whether physical fitness declines with age, and noted that there was evidence in the record to support the conclusion that it does. It contrasted this with the question whether teaching ability, which involves predominately mental skills, similarly declines with age. Absent an evidentiary showing, the court saw no reason to assume that it does; in fact, it speculated that the knowledge and experience necessary for teaching increases with age.[1]   Accordingly, it remanded for further proceedings to determine whether compulsory retirement of teachers at age 65 is rationally based. 569 F.2d at 996.

We decline to follow *Gault* for two reasons. First, while there is a valid distinction between the instant case and *Murgia*, we cannot distinguish the prior cases that have sustained compulsory retirement statutes for occupations that involve primarily mental skills. In *Johnson v. Lefkowitz*, 566 F.2d 866 (2d Cir. 1977), we upheld the constitutionality of § 70 of the New York State Retirement and Social Security Law (McKinney's 1971), which requires tenured civil servants to retire at age 70. In *Johnson*, the plaintiff had been dismissed from his position as senior attorney in the Real Property Bureau of the state's law department. In *Rubino v. Ghezzi*, 512 F.2d 431 (2d Cir.), *cert. denied*, 423 U.S. 891, 96 S.Ct. 187, 46 L.Ed.2d 122 (1975), we upheld the constitutionality of the mandatory retirement of state judges

---

[1.]   *Gault* also distinguished *Murgia* on another ground. It noted that, as between teachers and policemen, the consequences of lack of fitness differ substantially. If a police officer is not fit, his inability to perform could become a matter of life and death. Thus, a general, perhaps overly broad rule is justified to prevent such occurrences. If a teacher becomes unfit, however, the consequences are not so immediate. There is adequate time to effect his or her removal via appropriate procedural means. 569 F.2d at 996.

While this distinction has merit, we do not find it sufficiently persuasive in view of the considerations expressed below.

at age 70. And, in *Weisbrod v. Lynn*, 383 F.Supp. 933 (D.D.C. 1974), *aff'd,* 420 U.S. 940, 95 S.Ct. 1319, 43 L.Ed.2d 420 (1975), mandatory retirement of federal civil servants at age 70 was upheld as constitutional, even though the statute undoubtedly requires the retirement of some civil servants who are engaged in occupations that involve primarily mental skills. *Cf. Weiss v. Walsh,* 324 F.Supp. 75 (S.D.N.Y.1971), *aff'd,* 461 F.2d 846 (2d Cir. 1972), *cert. denied,* 409 U.S. 1129, 93 S.Ct. 939, 35 L.Ed.2d 262 (1973) (denial of state-endowed chair to college professor over 65 is not unconstitutional age discrimination).

Second, *Gault* too narrowly conceives the possible rational bases for a compulsory retirement statute. Unrelated to any notion of physical or mental fitness, a state might prescribe mandatory retirement for teachers in order to open up employment opportunities for young teachers—particularly in the last decade when supply has outpaced demand, or to open up more places for minorities, or to bring young people with fresh ideas and techniques in contact with school children, or to assure predictability and ease in establishing and administering pension plans. A compulsory retirement system is rationally related to the fulfillment of any or all of these legitimate state objectives. . . .

However, even if appellant was retired under a discretionary policy, the result would be the same. First, a discretionary retirement policy would still be rationally related to a legitimate state goal: it would further any of the purposes noted above, with the exception of those related to the maintenance of pension plans. Second, the *Johnson* case would still be on point. *Johnson* involved § 70 of the New York Retirement and Social Security Law (McKinney's 1971), a statute that is functionally equivalent to discretionary retirement. Subsection (c) provides that a civil servant may be retained beyond age 70 under certain conditions. If he or she is retained, however, he or she is subject to termination upon sixty days' notice. Johnson had been given two extensions and was then summarily retired. The court found no constitutional infirmity with that system. We find none in the instant case either.

We reach the same conclusion with regard to the due process attack on compulsory retirement as establishing an irrebuttable presumption. That claim is analytically very similar to the equal protection one. If the statutory classification is sustainable as rationally based, then it should not fall because it might also be labeled a presumption. . . .

Appellant also claims that she was entitled to a due process hearing before being retired. However, we can see no purpose for a hearing if appellant was retired under an across-the-board, mandatory retirement system. And even if a discretionary system was employed, we would be constrained to follow *Johnson, supra,* and deny this claim. In *Johnson,* we held that a hearing is not required because the benefits of holding such a hearing are outweighed by the burdens imposed upon the state by requiring a hearing in every case. 566 F.2d at 869. . .

IV

Today's decision is not intended as an endorsement of compulsory retirement for teachers or compulsory retirement in general. Rather, we are aware of the many older Americans who continue to be able and eager to work beyond age seventy. We are also aware of the debilitating effects that compulsory retirement has on many such individuals, with regard to their economic situation, their health, their outlook on life, and the continuing opportunities for fulfillment. However, in determining the desirability of compulsory retirement, these considerations must be weighed against the social goals that compulsory retirement furthers. This is precisely the type of clash of competing social goals that is best resolved by the legislative process. The federal courts should not second guess the wisdom or propriety of such legislative resolutions as long as they are rationally based.

Congress has recently considered this issue and, after extensive hearings, has amended the Age Discrimination in Employment Act of 1967. The amendments prohibit, with some exceptions, the compulsory retirement of people under seventy, and of federal employees at any age. The original Act requires the Secretary of Labor to make annual reports concerning the effects of the Act, taking into account demographic changes. The 1978 amendments impose on the Secretary the further duty of reporting, by 1981, on the effects of the amendments and the feasibility of extending their coverage. We note these developments because we are persuaded that they reinforce today's decision. There is no question but that the passage of the 1978 amendments to the Age Discrimination in Employment Act was the result of a process that was fair, deliberate, and well informed. Moreover, Congress has provided a mechanism for continually reassessing the effects and the wisdom of its actions on this issue. The superior ability of Congress to collect data and to resolve competing social goals, as well as the flexibility resulting from its ability to monitor the effects of its actions and to make adjustments accordingly, mark this issue as one which the Constitution has appropriately left to the legislative processes, both state and federal.

Affirmed.

NOTES

1. How can the courts reconcile the idea that an individual under the age of 65 or 70 should be judged on the basis of merit and not stereotypical thinking and the idea that an employee over a certain age should be presumed to be a liability to an employer? Do you agree with the judgment in *Palmer* that there is a "rational basis" to justify the mandatory retirement scheme at issue in the case? Which is the better decision, the one in *Palmer* or the opinion of the Seventh Circuit in Gault v. Garrison, 569 F.2d 993 (7th Cir. 1977) (which is cited and rejected by the court in *Palmer*)? *See also* Schmier v. Trustees of California State University and Colleges, 74 Cal. App. 3d 314, 141 Cal. Rep. 472, 16 F.E.P. Cas. 195, involving a California statute creating age-based mandatory retirement of a tenured college professor at age 67.

2. The court in *Palmer* follows the Supreme Court's holding in Massachusetts Board of Retirement v. Murgia, 376 F.Supp. 753 (D.Mass. 1974), *rev'd*, 96 S.Ct. 2564 (1976), holding that because age does not constitute a "suspect class" and that government employment is not a "fundamental interest," the validity of the statute is to be tested under

a rational basis standard. Justice Marshall, in dissent, argued that certain rights not "fundamental" and certain classes not "suspect" were, nevertheless, deserving of more protection than that traditionally afforded under the rational basis standard of review. Do you agree? Is age discrimination so different from race and sex discrimination that it should be regulated under a different standard of review?

3. In order for a plaintiff to bring a constitutional (equal protection) claim under 42 U.S.C. § 1983, it is necessary for the court to first find that the challenged rule was adopted pursuant to some "state action" or by some agency of the government. Therefore, many purely private colleges are not subject to actions of the sort brought in *Palmer.*

III. The Age Discrimination in Employment Act

A. Introduction

In order to promote the employment of older persons, Congress passed the Age Discrimination in Employment Act (ADEA) in 1967, 39 U.S.C. Sec. 621 *et seq.* The regulations interpreting the ADEA may be found at 29 CFR, Parts 850, 860. With a few minor exceptions, the prohibitions in the ADEA are identical to those of Title VII, except that "age" has been substituted for "race, color, religion, sex, or national origin." Not surprisingly, the case law under the ADEA has borrowed heavily from Title VII.

The Age Act makes it unlawful for employers, labor unions or employment agencies to discriminate against any individual on the basis of age. Examples of forbidden practices under the Act are segregating or classifying an employee in a way that would affect his status or employment opportunities, failing to refer an individual for employment because of age, or advertising in a way that indicates a preference or discrimination based on age. The Act applies to any employer affecting commerce and to any employer with 20 or more employees. Section 12 limits the prohibitions of the Act to persons who are at least 40, but less than 70 years of age. Employers are lawfully allowed to discharge older employees for good cause, to consider age where age is a bona fide occupational qualification and to be selective where the differentiation is based on factors other than age.

In 1978, Congress passed amendments to the Age Discrimination in Employment Act, Public Act 95-256, which greatly altered the legality of current employment practices, as follows:

(1) The amendments increased the protection of the Act from age 40 to age 70, instead of to age 65. When the Act was originally passed, there was almost no discussion as to why the upper limit was set at age 65; age 65 was chosen because it was customary. By 1977, some Congressmen sought to eliminate an upper age limit entirely. The age of 70 was selected as a compromise between not changing the original limit of 65 and removing the limit altogether. [3]

(2) The amendments raised the age of permissible mandatory retirement from 65 to 70. Under the original Act, an employer was allowed to

---

3. U.S., Bureau of National Affairs, Inc., Government Employee Regulations Report, No. 753, *1978 Age Discrimination Act Amendments,* April 3, 1978, Part 2, p. 3.

retire an employee involuntarily below the age of 65 so long as a pension or retirement plan provided for early retirement and the employer was merely observing the plan and the plan was not found to be a "subterfuge" to avoid the Act. Since many retirement plans were instituted before the passage of the Act, the courts had held that such plans were not a "subterfuge" and that early involuntary retirement was acceptable. This interpretation was upheld by the Supreme Court in United Air Lines v. McMann, 16 F.E.P. Cases 146, 98 S.Ct. 444 (1977). The 1978 Amendments reversed the *McMann* decision and prohibited the involuntary retirement of an employee pursuant to a seniority system or employee benefit plan until age 70.

(3) The 1978 Amendments made an exception to the above provision with respect to forced retirement in higher education. Colleges and universities may compel faculty to retire at age 65. However, this exemption will terminate on July 1, 1982. After that date, the general protection against involuntary retirement until age 70 will be extended to higher education.

(4) The amendments also permitted an exception for the retirement of executives. Employers will be able to involuntarily retire an employee at age 65 who is employed in a "bona fide executive or a high policy making position," if such employee is entitled to a retirement benefit equalling at least $27,000 annually.

(5) The amendments eliminated any maximum age for retirement for many employees of the federal government.

(6) The amendments permitted an ADEA plaintiff to have a jury trial for any issue of fact even though equitable relief is being sought.

(7) Finally, the amendments incorporated several procedural changes designed to strengthen and clarify the Act, including the tolling of the statute of limitations for up to one year while the Secretary of Labor attempts conciliation and the changing of the former requirement that an aggrieved person file a notice of intent to sue with the Secretary of Labor to a requirement that he file a "charge" with the Secretary.

B.   The Developing Law Under the ADEA

BUCHHOLZ v. SYMONS MFG. CO.
United States District Court, E. D. Wisconsin
445 F.Supp. 706 (1978)

MYRON L. GORDON, District Judge.

This is an action under the Age Discrimination in Employment Act, as amended, 29 U.S.C. §§621 et seq. Jurisdiction is based on 29 U.S.C. §622(b) and 28 U.S.C. §1331. The plaintiff claims to have been discharged from his employment with the defendant because of his age; the defendant claims that age was not a factor in the plaintiff's discharge, contending instead that he was terminated because of inadequate job performance. The plaintiff seeks back pay, lost benefits, damages for pain and suffering, liquidated damages pursuant to 29 U.S.C. §216, costs, and reasonable attorney's fees.

The case was tried to the court, and the parties have filed briefs on the merits. They have also submitted proposed findings of fact and conclusions of law. The testimony adduced at trial disclosed several key factual disputes. In this decision, which shall constitute my findings of fact and conclusions of law, pursuant to Rule 52(a), Federal Rules of Civil Procedure, these factual disputes have been resolved as indicated after a consideration of the conflicting testimony and the exhibits received into evidence.

LIABILITY

The plaintiff, Harold Buchholz, was employed by the Symons Manufacturing Company on March 1, 1959, in Chicago, where he and his wife then resided. Symons, an employer of more than 20 persons, manufactures, distributes, sells and rents concrete construction forms and accessories, and sells chemicals for concrete treatment and curing for use by contractors in pouring concrete buildings. Its headquarters are in Des Plaines, Illinois.

Mr. Buchholz served as an account manager responsible for sale and rental of Symons products in the Chicago area. As account manager, he was also required to act as liaison between the company and its customers, make collections, and to assist contractors with the application of Symons' products to the particular jobs.

From 1959 through 1969, Mr. Buchholz met or exceeded the sales quota assigned to him for each year. His sales volume and sales ranking among all Symons account managers for the years 1962 to 1969 was as follows:

YEAR	AMOUNT	NO. OF ACCT. MANAGERS	RANK
1962	$173,624.00	30	5
1963	218,797.00	37	5
1964	167,116.00	39	15
1965	334,741.00	47	3
1966	296,902.00	47	2
1967	305,068.00	44	2
1968	336,551.00	51	3
1969	368,180.00	45	6

Like account managers, Mr. Buchholz received a salary plus a commission on each sale to an account assigned to him whether or not his efforts contributed to making the sale.

On March 1, 1970, at the plaintiff's request, he was transferred from Symons' headquarters to Waukesha, Wisconsin, to become an account manager with the Wisconsin branch office. His immediate superior there, occupying the position of district sales manager, was Michael Nolan. Mr. Nolan's supervisor was Warren Senneke, the district manager. Mr. Senneke's supervisor was James Norris, the regional manager. Mr. Senneke and Mr. Norris worked at the Des Plaines headquarters.

Mr. Buchholz' sales record in Wisconsin for the years 1970-1972 was as follows:

YEAR	AMOUNT	NO. OF ACCT. MANAGERS	RANK
1970	$306,319.00	52	6
1971	359,412.00	65	7
1972	392,954.00	68	14

During these years, as in many previous years in Chicago, he received letters of commendation from John Imonetti, Symons' divisional marketing manager, and he was awarded bonuses for exceeding his sales quotas and for establishing new accounts.

At a meeting attended by Messrs. Nolan, Senneke, Norris and Buchholz on November 30, 1972, the plaintiff's performance as an account manager was criticized, and he was advised that four of his major accounts were being transferred to Mr. Nolan effective January 1, 1973. When Mr. Buchholz objected to the transfer of accounts, Mr. Norris stated: "Hell, you've only got four more years to go." As a result of subsequent written protests to Mr. Nolan and other Symons executives, one of the transferred accounts was returned to Mr. Buchholz.

After the November 30, 1972, meeting, the plaintiff's working relationship with Messrs. Nolan, Senneke and Norris was strained. His letters to them and other Symons management personnel were ignored, and he was left out of sales discussions and meetings. On several occasions prior to and after the November 30, 1972 meeting, Mr. Buchholz was compared to, and reminded of other retiring employees during conversations with Mr. Norris. Initially, Mr. Buchholz accepted references to his age and possible retirement as "good natured ribbing," but after the November meeting, the remarks became more pointed. In July, 1973, Mr. Buchholz requested and received information concerning early retirement benefits. However, when he discussed early retirement with Messrs. Norris, Senneke and Nolan at a meeting on September 4, 1973, he advised them that he had no intention of retiring.

On September 14, 1973 Mr. Nolan wrote a memorandum to Mr. Norris and Mr. Senneke recommending that Mr. Buchholz be retired at age 62, in February, 1974. The reason cited by Mr. Nolan for this recommendation was that Mr. Buchholz' customers were complaining "on an almost daily basis" of Mr. Buchholz' "lack of performance." Mr. Nolan also recommended that the plaintiff's territory be divided between himself and Craig Vanderbunt, a 22 year old Symons engineer assigned to the Waukesha office, because they were already servicing many of Mr. Buchholz' accounts.

On October 17, 1973, Mr. Buchholz met with Messrs. Nolan, Senneke and Norris in a tension-filled meeting at which he was told that fourteen of his accounts were being transferred to Mr. Vanderbunt because he "wasn't doing the job." He was told that he could continue as an account manager in Wisconsin without the transferred accounts (which constituted the bulk of his sales volume), that he could transfer to another territory if one were available, or that he could take early retirement.

On November 2, 1973, Mr. Buchholz met with Mr. Norris and James Carlson, Symons' personnel director, to discuss early retirement benefits. On January 10, 1974, Mr. Carlson's department forwarded retirement forms to be filled out by Mr. Buchholz. On January 16, 1974, Mr. Buchholz wrote to Mr. Carlson stating that the forms had been sent in error and that he had no intention of taking early retirement.

In late January, 1974, Mr. Buchholz was advised by telegram that all of his accounts were being transferred to Mr. Vanderbunt as of February 1, 1974, and that he should report to Mr. Norris' office in Des Plaines on January 31, 1974.

On January 31, 1974, Mr. Buchholz met with Mr. Norris and Mr. Carlson and reiterated his position that he had no intention of retiring early. He was then told that there was no suitable territory open for him and that because he was rejecting early retirement, he was terminated effective March 1, 1974. Mr. Buchholz responded by stating that his forced early retirement was "nothing but age discrimination." Mr. Norris' reply, according to the plaintiff, was "you're damned right it is."

On February 4, 1974, Mr. Carlson wrote a letter to Mr. Buchholz enclosing retirement forms and summarizing the reasons for his termination discussed at the January 31 meeting: "adverse customer reaction, ineffective job servicing, and a lack of technical understanding." Mr. Carlson also wrote that there were no "openings that do not require a greater technical insight than your current performance would indicate you possess."

The plaintiff introduced the testimony of two other former Symons employees concerning remarks made by Mr. Norris. Calvin Rudolph, an account manager who worked for Symons from 1950 until February 1, 1973, testified concerning the circumstances of his own early departure from the company. Mr. Rudolph testified that Mr. Senneke advised him that he was being retired early because "younger men were needed in the territory." The deposition of Robert Wilson, a former marketing manager and assistant to the president of Symons from 1962 to 1975, was admitted into evidence pursuant to Rule 32(a)(3)(C), Federal Rules of Civil Procedure. At the deposition, he testified that he overheard a conversation between Mr. Norris and Mr. Senneke in which Mr. Senneke said to Mr. Norris that they had disposed of Mr. Rudolph and now were going to get rid of Mr. Buchholz.

Mr. Norris testified at trial and denied making any of the remarks related above. The parties' evidence on these factual questions is in direct conflict. I have resolved the conflict in favor of the plaintiff, finding his testimony more credible.

The plaintiff has submitted certain statistical evidence to show a violation of the statute. I believe that the plaintiff has made out a substantial case of employment discrimination because of age with his other evidence, and thus the statistical evidence need not be considered.

It is not disputed that the plaintiff is an employee within the meaning of the act and that the defendant, an employer of more than 20 persons, is subject to the act. 29 U.S.C. §630. To establish a violation of the act, the plaintiff must show by a preponderance of the evidence that age was a factor in the decision to discharge him and that it in fact made a difference. *Laugesen v. Anaconda Company*, 510 F.2d 307 (6th Cir. 1975).

The plaintiff has, in my opinion, made a strong showing that the defendant's employees considered age in arriving at their decision to discharge the plaintiff and that age was the determining factor in that decision. I find that the statements attributed to Mr. Norris at the meetings on November 30, 1972 and January 31, 1974, were in fact made and that they are blunt admissions that the plaintiff was being discharged because of his age. The statement by Mr. Senneke during his conversation with Mr. Rudolph concerning the latter's early retirement, when considered in conjunction with the Norris-Senneke conversation overheard by Mr. Wilson, is convincing evidence that a plan to dispose of the older account managers had been devised.

At trial, the defendant attempted to establish that the plaintiff's forced early retirement was based on reasonable factors other than age or was for cause. 29 U.S.C. §623(f)(2) and (3). Evidence was introduced to show that the reason for Mr. Buchholz' termination was that customers were complaining of his failure to perform enough on-site servicing of his accounts and his lack of technical knowledge regarding the more complex projects for which Symons products were used. The defendant also attempted to show that the transfer of accounts from Mr. Buchholz was to increase sales.

Apart from Mr. Nolan's testimony regarding customer complaints, there is no written evidence of any customer complaint of Mr. Buchholz' performance as an account manager. The defendant did introduce two documents written by Symons personnel in which customer complaints are cited as reasons for taking action against Mr. Buchholz. The first is the September 14, 1973, memorandum from Mr. Nolan to Mr. Norris and Mr. Senneke. It is significant that in the same memorandum Mr. Nolan proposed a plan whereby Mr. Buchholz' territory would be divided between Mr. Vanderbunt and Mr. Nolan. Thus, Mr. Nolan stood to gain by painting a bad picture of Mr. Buchholz' performance. The second document was that prepared by Mr. Carlson on February 4, 1974, summarizing the reasons expressed at the January 31, 1974, meeting for discharging the plaintiff. This belated justification for the termination has minimal persuasiveness since it does not contemporaneously reflect the reasons which led to the plaintiff's termination. *Schulz v. Hickok Mfg. Co.*, 358 F.Supp. 1208, 1216 (N.D.Ga. 1973).

The claim of frequent customer complaints is clearly not reflected in the volume of Mr. Buchholz' sales to those customers. At the time of the November 30, 1972, meeting, the first occasion at which Mr. Buchholz was criticized by his superiors, Mr. Buchholz was exceeding his sales quota. He ultimately exceeded his quota for that year by $37,000. In fact, a few months later, on January 30, 1973, he received a letter from Mr. Imonetti praising him for working hard and doing "an excellent job" in 1972. It is also significant that Mr. Buchholz' younger replacement, Mr. Vanderbunt, had a poorer sales record than Mr. Buchholz' subsequent to the discharge, yet he remains an employee of Symons.

Under all the circumstances, I am not convinced that customer complaints motivated the defendant's termination of the plaintiff. Moreover, the plaintiff's claimed lack of technical knowledge was unmentioned in the letters from Mr. Nolan to Mr. Senneke and to Mr. Norris and was not substantiated by any objective pre-discharge evidence. Although inadequate performance and a lack of technical knowledge were cited to Mr. Buchholz as the reasons for his discharge, I am not persuaded that the reasons were actually relied upon, or that the defendant made a good faith, honest evaluation of the plaintiff's job performance. The preponderance of the evidence shows that age was the most important and determining factor in the defendant's decision to force the plaintiff into early retirement. I therefore find that the defendant violated the Age Discrimination in Employment Act by terminating the plaintiff because of age.

RELIEF

Back Pay and Benefits

The parties agree that the measure of back pay under the Age Discrimination in Employment Act is the amount the plaintiff would have earned but for the violation less the sum of unemployment benefits received plus income from other employment or amounts earnable with reasonable diligence. *Coates v. National Cash Register Company*, 433 F.Supp. 655 (W.D.Va. 1977); *Schulz v. Hickok Mfg. Co.*, 358 F.Supp. 1208 (N.D.Ga.. 1973).

The plaintiff claims that the amount of income he would have earned between March 1, 1974, and February 28, 1977, had he remained with Symons is $77,115.63. This figure represents the plaintiff's average income for the years 1968-1972, including both his base salary and commissions. The year 1973 was not included in the computation because it was during that year that the defendant began to transfer accounts from the plaintiff pursuant to the unlawful plan for his termination. From this sum the plaintiff would subtract the $6,626 received as unemployment compensation from the state of Wisconsin.

The defendant argues that the maximum the plaintiff may recover as back pay is $39,000, representing the sum of three years base salary, since an award including commission income would require the court to engage in conjecture. It is argued further that the plaintiff failed to make the required efforts to mitigate damages by diligently seeking employment elsewhere, and thus he is entitled to no award of back pay.

Addressing the latter argument first, I believe that Mr. Buchholz exercised reasonable diligence to secure alternate employment after his discharge. He sought employment through the Wisconsin Job Service and was interviewed for a sales position with several prospective employers. The positions he was offered would have provided only commission income or would have required relocation. At Symons, the plaintiff enjoyed a base salary of $13,000 and substantial commissions. A job which affords only commission income would not, in my judgment, be comparable with his position at Symons since it offers no certainty of reward. *Coates*, supra, at 662. Moreover, relocation for the three years of employment until Mr. Buchholz' planned retirement is not required as a reasonable effort to mitigate damages.

The defendant's argument that lost commission income cannot be included in an award of back pay is without merit. The plaintiff's annual income from commissions remained fairly constant from 1968 to 1972 and thus can be predicted with reasonable certainty. Therefore, the plaintiff will be awarded the difference between his back pay and unemployment compensation received, a sum of $70,489.63.

The plaintiff is also entitled to recover pension benefits computed as if he had been permitted to work until March 1, 1977, a sum of $432.54 monthly. Thus for the months of March through December, 1977, the plaintiff is entitled to pension benefits for a total of $3,892.86. The defendant will be enjoined to provide a like benefit to the plaintiff in the future or such amount as he would become entitled to under the Symons pension plan based on his length of service computed through March 1, 1977. The plaintiff claims reimbursement for health insurance expenses, but this claim is foreclosed by his concession at trial that he went uninsured after his discharge due to the high premiums quoted to him.

The plaintiff also claims a sum equal to three annual vacation periods to which he was entitled as an employee of 15 years. It is not clear, however, whether this amount is already included in the average yearly income used to compute the back pay award. The parties are directed to address this issue in the report to the court ordered below.

Liquidated Damages

Under 29 U.S.C. §626(b), where it is shown that an employer's violation of the act was willful, the plaintiff may recover "liquidated damages" in addition to back pay and benefits. In the statutory sense, such damages are in addition to back pay, not in lieu of it.

The purpose of an award of "liquidated damages" is to provide compensation for the more obscure items of damage resulting from the retention of the employee's pay by his employer. *Rogers v. Exxon Research and Engineering Co.*, 404 F.Supp. 324, 335 (D.N.J.1975), reversed on other grounds 550 F.2d 834 (3rd Cir. 1977). The measure of "liquidated damages" is the sum of "amounts owing" to the plaintiff as a result of the defendant's violation of the act. "Amounts owing" include unpaid wages and benefits but do not include damages for pain and suffering. *Rogers*, supra. Thus, the provision for "liquidated damages" effectively doubles the award of back pay and benefits.

For a violation to be willful, the plaintiff must show conduct that is intentional, knowing and voluntary, as distinguished from conduct that is accidental or unknowing. *Combes v. Griffin Television, Inc.*, 421 F.Supp. 841 (W.D.Okl.1976); *Hodgson v. Hyatt*, 318 F.Supp. 390 (N.D.Fla. 1970).

The statements made by Mr. Buchholz' superiors discussed previously in this decision established beyond a doubt that the unlawful discharge of the plaintiff was intentional, knowing and voluntary. Furthermore, there are no considerations of good faith as described in *Combes* to warrant less than a full award of "liquidated damages." Accordingly, an amount equal to the back pay award plus pension benefits withheld will be awarded to the plaintiff as "liquidated damages," as defined in 29 U.S.C. §626(b).

Damages for Pain and Suffering

Prior to trial the defendant moved to exclude evidence of pain and suffering relying on *Rogers v. Exxon Research & Engineering Co.*, 550 F.2d 834 (3rd Cir. 1977). I denied the motion based on my agreement with the lower court opinion in *Rogers*, reported at 404 F.Supp. 324 (D.N.J. 1975), and the decision in *Bertrand v. Orkin Exterminating Co.*, 432 F.Supp. 952 (N.D.Ill.1977). Accord, *Coates*, supra, at 664. My ruling was consonant with an earlier ruling of this court in an unreported opinion. *Wisniewski v. All-Star Insurance Corporation*, 76-C-662, decision and order dated January 14, 1977. I adhere to this position cognizant of the fact that the fifth circuit court of appeals recently joined the third circuit in disallowing pain and suffering damages. See *Dean v. American Security Insurance Co.*, 559 F.2d 1036 (5th Cir. 1977).

At trial, the plaintiff and his wife testified that the discharge adversely affected their marital relationship and created pressures which curtailed their social activities and vacation plans. The plaintiff also testified that the discharge resulted in emotional strain, causing loss of sleep. The plaintiff seeks $50,000 in damages for pain and suffering. In my judgment, an award of $7,500 for pain and suffering is appropriate.

CONCLUSION

To summarize, I compute the plaintiff's damages as follows: back pay in the amount of $70,489.63; pension benefits in the amount of $3,892.86; statutory liquidated damages in the amount of $74,382.49; and damages for pain and suffering in the amount of $7,500, for a total damage award of $156,264.98.

In accordance with the parties' stipulation, no award of compensation for reduced social security benefits or for reasonable attorney's fees and costs will be considered at this time. The parties will be ordered to file a status report within 30 days of this order informing the court of their progress in arriving at a stipulation on these remaining matters. Thereafter, a judgment will be entered in this case, encompassing all facets.

Therefore, IT IS ORDERED that the plaintiff recover from the defendant the sum of $156,264.98.

NOTES

1. As the *Buchholz* case illustrates, the remedies available to a successful ADEA plaintiff are wide ranging and flexible depending on the facts of the case. [29 U.S.C.S. § 626(b)]. A common remedy is back wages and fringes. The ADEA back pay formula is discussed in Coates v. National Cash Register Co., 433 F.Supp. 655 (W.D. Va. 1977).

Attorney fees and costs are usually awarded. *See* formula discussed in Rodriguez v. Taylor, 569 F.2d 1231 (3rd Cir. 1977). Reinstatement may be awarded. *See generally* Combes v. Griffin Television, Inc., 421 F.Supp. 841 (W.D.Okla. 1976). "Liquidated damages" are available when the defendant's violation is found to be "willful" as it was in the *Buchholz* case. In effect, the liquidated damages can double the amount plaintiff can win for back pay and lost pension benefits. Injunctive relief is available to remedy continuing wrongs and the scope of the injunction depends upon the scale of the employer's discrimination. Marshall v. Goodyear Tire & Rubber Co., 554 F.2d 730 (5th Cir. 1977). As the *Buchholz* case discusses, the courts are divided on whether compensatory damages are available for pain and suffering but two circuit courts of appeals have rejected requests for such damages. *See:* Rogers v. Exxon Research & Engineering Co., 550 F.2d 834 (3rd Cir. 1977) and Dean v. American Security Ins. Co., 559 F.2d 1036 (5th Cir. 1977). For *contra* district opinions in other circuits, see Bertrand v. Orkin Exterminating Co., 432 F.Supp. 952, 15 F.E.P. Cas. 21 (N.D. Ill. 1977); Coates v. National Cash Register Co., 433 F. Supp. 655 (W.D. Va. 1977). Punitive damages have been disallowed under the ADEA. Dean v. American Security Ins. Co., 559 F.2d 1036 (5th Cir. 1977). Also, damages for harm to professional reputation have not been permitted. Dubuque Communications v. American Broadcasting, 432 F.Supp. 543 (N.D. Ill. 1977). The opinion of the courts is that because the Act provides for liquidated damages, which may double plaintiffs' recovery for economic loss, compensatory and punitive damages were not intended by Congress. *See, e.g.,* Fellows v. Medford Corp., 431 F.Supp. 199, at 202 (D. Ore. 1977).

2. Will a university be required to employ an aged professor even if he or she is less competent than formally? The Act makes clear that "[i]t shall not be unlawful for an employer, employment agency, or labor organization . . . to discharge or otherwise discipline an individual for good cause." *See:* Anderson v. Viking Pump Division, Houdaille Industries, Inc., 545 F.2d 1127 (8th Cir. 1976). But is firing a humane way of terminating a professor after 30 to 40 years of distinguished teaching and research? If the university is to eliminate incompetent older professors, it likely must be done pursuant to a performance evaluation scheme so that the judgment to terminate an employee will withstand court challenge. Performance evaluations would thus probably have to be given to all faculty members because, presumably, an evaluation scheme limited to older faculty members would be a violation of the Act. The giving of regular faculty evaluations to tenured faculty members would carry the implied threat of the right of removal. What effect would such evaluations have on the tenure system?

3. Estimates of college enrollments for the decade 1978-1988 predict a 19% decrease in the number of high school graduates because of the low birth rate in the 1960s. The resulting reduction in college enrollments and tuition payments to universities and colleges, combined with possible taxpayer revolts against state funding of government services and inflationary costs, may mean severe financial emergencies for some colleges and universities over the next decade. Assuming that the required cut back in personnel (the chief item in any educational budget) could not be achieved by attrition or by the release of non-tenured faculty members, how would the necessary cuts be made among tenured faculty members? To what degree does the ADEA affect the university's ability to terminate older and presumably higher paid faculty members?

4. To the extent that senior faculty members have the authority to make the evaluations that determine who will be released, senior faculty members would, of course, be unaffected by financial exigency. But to the extent that authority in the college is hierarchical and the power to evaluate and make hiring and firing decisions rests with the administration, the problem may be a real one for older faculty members. The following non-university layoff cases may give some guidance. In Mastie v. Great Lakes Steel, 424 F.Supp. 1299 (E.D. Mich. 1976), the court distinguished between an employer's consideration of the extra costs of terminating one particular individual worker and an employer's generalized determination that older workers were more expensive to employ. The former does not violate the Act:

> However, the court appreciates that it would not be in the best interest of
> the defendant to terminate its younger employees where the company expects

long and beneficial employment from them. A company may consider a person's salary and fringe benefits in relation to other employees when faced with a reduction in force. The Act does not comtemplate that an employer must ignore employment costs or face possible ADEA violation charges. Both the legislative history and Department of Labor regulations tend to support the proposition that higher labor costs associated with the employment of older employees constitute "reasonable factors other than age" which an employer can consider when faced with possible termination of an older employee. [424 F.Supp. 1318]

However, the court continues:

The court readily concludes that an employer's arbitrary and across-the-board pronouncement that older workers are more expensive to employ than younger workers would be a flagrant violation of the Act. [Id., p. 1319]

The Eighth Circuit in Cova v. Coca-Cola Bottling of St. Louis, Inc., 574 F.2d 958, at 961 (8th Cir. 1978) suggested that "while ... the lack of fair formal evaluation procedures may cast doubt on the credibility of an employer's subsequent explanation of a discharge, we cannot agree such records are required as a matter of law by the Age Discrimination in Employment Act...." In Minstretta v. Sandia Corp., 15 F.E.P. Cases 1690, the court found age discrimination when the employer laid off employees age 52-64 based on a performance review that adversely affected that age group.

5. The courts have been somewhat divided on the applicability of Title VII proof guidelines to actions under the ADEA. In Cova v. Coca-Cola Bottling Co. of St. Louis, 574 F.2d 958, at 959, the Eighth Circuit indicated that:

... the guidelines set forth in McDonnell Douglas Corp. v. Green, 411 U.S. 792, 93 S.Ct. 1817, 36 L.Ed.2d 668 (1973), though specifically addressed to actions under Title VII of the Civil Rights Act of 1964, 42 U.S.C. § § 2000e, et seq., can be generally applied in age discrimination cases.

See also: Laugesen v. Anaconda, 510 F.2d 307 (6th Cir. 1975); Lindsey v. Southwestern Bell Telephone Co., 546 F.2d 1123 (5th Cir. 1977); Gabriele v. Chrysler Corp., 573 F.2d 949 (6th Cir. 1978), and Note, The Age Discrimination in Employment Act, 90 Harvard L. Rev., 383 (1976). However, in Marshall v. Goodyear Tire and Rubber, 554 F.2d 730, at 736 (5th Cir. 1977), the court observed that:

Because the aging process causes employees to constantly exit the labor market while younger ones enter, simply the replacement of an older worker by a younger worker does not raise the same inferences of improper motives that attend replacement of a black by a white person in a Title VII case.

Do you agree? All things being equal, is a discharged black employee more likely than not to be replaced by a white worker just as a discharged senior citizen is more likely to be replaced by a younger person? Should a different inference be drawn?

6. Often multiple reasons enter into an employer's decision not to hire an individual in the 40-to-70-year age bracket. in the Laugesen case, supra, the court discusses the proper jury instructions regarding the part age may play in an employer's decision that is adverse to plaintiff:

However expressed, we believe it was essential for the jury to understand from the instructions that there could be more than one factor in the decision to discharge him and that he was nevertheless entitled to recover if one such factor was his age and if in fact it made a difference in determining whether he was to be retained or discharged. This is so even though the need to reduce the employee force generally was also a strong, and perhaps even more compelling reason. It is because the instructions did not convey this necessary concept of the law to the jury that we are compelled to reverse and remand for a new trial. [510 F.2d 317]

7. The courts have indicated that they are not willing to merely accept the employer's statement of his reasons for not employing the plaintiff. In Hodgson v. First Federal Savings & Loan Association of Broward County, Florida, 455 F.2d 818 (5th Cir. 1972), the defendant bank asserted it had refused to hire plaintiff as a teller because she

was too fat. The Court found the bank had violated the ADEA partially because the defendant had not hired a single person within the protected age group for the job of teller although 35 persons had been hired for that position within approximately a year. In Minstretta v. Sandia Corp., 15 F.E.P. Cas. 1709, a violation of the ADEA was proved by statistical methods showing that age was a factor in promotion, salary increase and layoffs.

    8. The ADEA specifies that an employer lawfully may discriminate on the basis of age "where age is a bona fide occupational qualification reasonably necessary to the normal operation of the particular business." The proof of a bona fide occupational qualification is explained in Marshall v. Westinghouse Electric Corp., 576 F.2d 588 at 591 (5th Cir. 1978):

> . . . The establishment of a bona fide occupational qualification has been treated as an affirmative defense; the employer, therefore, carries the burden of persuasion. *Usery v. Tamiami Trail Tours, Inc.*, 531 F.2d 224, 227 (5 Cir. 1976). To establish a BFOQ an employer has the burden to demonstrate that he has a reasonable cause to believe that all or substantially all of a class of applicants would be unable to perform a job safely and efficiently. *Weeks v. Southern Bell Telephone & Telegraph Co.*, 408 F.2d 228 (5 Cir. 1969), and that the BFOQ is "reasonably necessary to the essence" of the business operation. *Diaz v. Pan American World Airways*, 442 F.2d 385 (5 Cir. 1971), *cert. denied*, 404 U.S. 950, 92 S.Ct. 275, 30 L.Ed.2d 267. *See also Hodgson v. Greyhound Lines, Inc.*, 499 F.2d 859 (7 Cir. 1974). Establishment of a BFOQ may, in some cases, permit an employer to discriminate along otherwise illegal lines without reference to an individual's actual physical condition at the terminal age. *Tamiami, supra* at 230. When an employer seeking to establish a BFOQ demonstrates that it is impossible or highly impracticable to deal with persons on an individualized basis, he may apply a generalized rule. *Weeks, supra* at 235 n. 5. The employer may carry its burden in those cases by establishing that some members of the discriminated-against class possess a trait precluding safe and efficient job performance that cannot be ascertained by means other than knowledge of the applicant's class membership. *Tamiami, supra* at 235; *Weeks, supra* at 235 n. 5.

The BFOQ cases appear to be inconsistent when safety to the public is involved. Under the bona fide occupational qualification exception, Greyhound Bus Lines was able to continue its practice of refusing to hire drivers for inter-city bus routes over the age of 35. Hodgson v. Greyhound Lines, Inc., 499 F.2d 859 (7th Cir. 1974), *cert. denied sub nom.*, Brennan v. Greyhound Lines, Inc., 419 U.S. 1122, 95 S.Ct. 805, 42 L.Ed. 2d 822 (1975). The court concluded that because of the overwhelming public safety factor involved in choosing drivers of public carriers:

> Greyhound need only demonstrate however a minimal increase in risk of harm for it is enough to show that elimination of the hiring policy might jeopardize the life of one more person than might otherwise occur under the present hiring practice. [499 F.2d at 863]

See also Usery v. Tamiami Trail Tours, Inc., 531 F.2d 224 (5th Cir. 1976). However, the Supreme Court has denied review of a case in which a 52-year-old test pilot successfully proved a violation of the ADEA because he was transferred to another position. The court held that the manufacturer was required to show it had a factual basis for believing that substantially all of its pilots over a certain age were incapable of performing the duties of a test pilot safely and efficiently. McDonnell Douglas Corp. v. Houghton, 553 F.2d 561 (8th Cir. 1977), *cert. denied*, 98 S.Ct. 506 (1977).

    9. Many states have laws prohibiting age discrimination and state agencies to enforce such laws. Section 633(b) of the ADEA provides that ". . . no suit may be brought . . . before the expiration of sixty days after proceedings have been commenced under the State law . . ." Does this mean an ADEA complainant *must* institute proceedings in a state

agency (assuming such an agency exists in the complainant's state) before beginning a suit in federal court? The Supreme Court has granted certiorari to review an Eighth Circuit decision that the statute requires the complainant to observe the waiting period if he elects to first file charges but that the statute does not require the filing of state charges as a jurisdictional prerequisite to an ADEA suit in federal court. Oscar Meyer & Co. v. Evans, 47 U.S.L.W. 2026, 17 F.E.P. Cas. 1119, *cert. granted,* 47 U.S.L.W. 3292.

10. The ADEA is discussed at length in the following articles: Note, *The Age Discrimination in Employment Act of 1967,* 90 Harvard L. Rev. 380 (1976); Note, *Procedural Aspects of the Age Discrimination in Employment Act of 1967,* 36 U. Pitt. L. Rev. 914 (1975); Note, *Age Discrimination in Employment,* 47 Southern Cal. Law Rev. 1311 (1974); Note, *The Right to Jury Trial Under the Age Discrimination in Employment and Fair Labor Standards Act,* 44 U. Chi. L. Rev. 365 (1977); Lopatka, *A 1977 Primer on the Federal Regulation of Employment Discrimination,* 1977 U. of Ill. L.F. 69; *Construction and Application of Age Discrimination in Employment Act of 1967,* 24 ALR Fed. 808 (1975); Levien, *The Age Discrimination in Employment Act: Statutory Requirements and Recent Developments,* 13 Duquesne L. Rev. 277 (1974).

CHAPTER 19

THE EQUAL PAY ACT

=====

CORNING GLASS WORKS v. BRENNAN
Supreme Court of the United States
417 U.S. 188 (1974)

MR. JUSTICE MARSHALL delivered the opinion of the Court.

These cases arise under the Equal Pay Act of 1963, 77 Stat. 56, §3. 29 U.S.C. §206(d)(1)[1] which added to §6 of the Fair Labor Standards Act of 1938 the principle of equal pay for equal work regardless of sex. The principal question posed is whether Corning Glass Works violated the Act by paying a higher base wage to male night shift inspectors than it paid to female inspectors performing the same tasks on the day shift, where the higher wage was paid in addition to a separate night shift differential paid to all employees for night work. In No. 73-29, the Court of Appeals for the Second Circuit, in a case involving several Corning plants in Corning, New York, held that this practice violated the Act. 474 F.2d 226 (1973). In No. 73-695, the Court of Appeals for the Third Circuit, in a case involving a Corning plant in Wellsboro, Pennsylvania, reached the opposite conclusion. 480 F.2d 1254 (1973). We granted certiorari and consolidated the cases to resolve this unusually direct conflict between two circuits. 414 U.S. 1110 (1973). Finding ourselves in substantial agreement with the analysis of the Second Circuit, we affirm in No. 73-29 and reverse in No. 73-695.

I

Prior to 1925, Corning operated its plants in Wellsboro and Corning only during the day, and all inspection work was performed by women. Between 1925 and 1930, the company began to introduce automatic production equipment which made it desirable to institute a night shift. During this period, however, both New York and Pennsylvania law prohibited women from working at night. As a result, in order to fill inspector positions on the new night shift, the company had to recruit male employees from among its

---

[1.] "No employer having employees subject to any provisions of this section shall discriminate, within any establishment in which such employees are employed, between employees on the basis of sex by paying wages to employees in such establishment at a rate less than the rate at which he pays wages to employees of the opposite sex in such establishment for equal work on jobs the performance of which requires equal skill, effort, and responsibility, and which are performed under similar working conditions, except where such payment is made pursuant to (i) a seniority system; (ii) a merit system; (iii) a system which measures earnings by quantity or quality of production; or (iv) a differential based on any other factor other than sex: *Provided,* That an employer who is paying a wage rate differential in violation of this subsection shall not, in order to comply with the provisions of this subsection, reduce the wage rate of any employee."

male dayworkers. The male employees so transferred demanded and received wages substantially higher than those paid to women inspectors engaged on the two day shifts. During this same period, however, no plant-wide shift differential existed and male employees working at night, other than inspectors, received the same wages as their day shift counterparts. Thus a situation developed where the night inspectors were all male, the day inspectors all female, and the male inspectors received significantly higher wages.

In 1944, Corning plants at both locations were organized by a labor union and a collective-bargaining agreement was negotiated for all production and maintenance employees. This agreement for the first time established a plant-wide shift differential, but this change did not eliminate the higher base wage paid to male night inspectors. Rather, the shift differential was superimposed on the existing difference in base wages between male night inspectors and female day inspectors.

Prior to June 11, 1964, the effective date of the Equal Pay Act, the law in both Pennsylvania and New York was amended to permit women to work at night. It was not until some time after the effective date of the Act, however, that Corning initiated efforts to eliminate the differential rates for male and female inspectors. Beginning in June 1966, Corning started to open up jobs on the night shift to women. Previously separate male and female seniority lists were consolidated and women became eligible to exercise their seniority, on the same basis as men, to bid for the higher paid night inspection jobs as vacancies occurred.

On January 20, 1969, a new collective-bargaining agreement went into effect, establishing a new "job evaluation" system for setting wage rates. The new agreement abolished for the future the separate base wages for day and night shift inspectors and imposed a uniform base wage for inspectors exceeding the wage rate for the night shift previously in effect. All inspectors hired after January 20, 1969, were to receive the same base wage, whatever their sex or shift. The collective-bargaining agreement further provided, however, for a higher "red circle" rate for employees hired prior to January 20, 1969, when working as inspectors on the night shift. This "red circle" rate served essentially to perpetuate the differential in base wages between day and night inspectors.

The Secretary of Labor brought these cases to enjoin Corning from violating the Equal Pay Act [8] and to collect back wages allegedly due female employees because of past violations. Three distinct questions are presented: (1) Did Corning ever violate the Equal Pay Act by paying male night shift inspectors more than female day shift inspectors? (2) If so, did Corning cure its violation of the Act in 1966 by permitting women to work

---

[8.]   The District Court in No. 73-29 issued a broadly worded injunction against all future violations of the Act. The Court of Appeals modified the injunction by limiting it to inspectors at the three plants at issue in that case, largely because of that court's belief that "Corning had been endeavoring since 1966—sincerely, if ineffectively—to bring itself into compliance." 474 F.2d 226, 236 (CA2 1973). Since the Government did not seek certiorari from this aspect of the Second Circuit's judgment, we have no occasion to consider this question.

as night shift inspectors? (3) Finally, if the violation was not remedied in 1966, did Corning cure its violation in 1969 by equalizing day and night inspector wage rates but establishing higher "red circle" rates for existing employees working on the night shift?

II

Congress' purpose in enacting the Equal Pay Act was to remedy what was perceived to be a serious and endemic problem of employment discrimination in private industry—the fact that the wage structure of "many segments of American industry has been based on an ancient but outmoded belief that a man, because of his role in society, should be paid more than a woman even though his duties are the same." S. Rep. No. 176, 88th Cong., 1st Sess., 1 (1963). The solution adopted was quite simple in principle: to require that "equal work will be rewarded by equal wages." *Ibid.*

The Act's basic structure and operation are similarly straightforward. In order to make out a case under the Act, the Secretary must show that an employer pays different wages to employees of opposite sexes "for equal work on jobs the performance of which requires equal skill, effort, and responsibility, and which are performed under similar working conditions." Although the Act is silent on this point, its legislative history makes plain that the Secretary has the burden of proof on this issue, as both of the courts below recognized.

The Act also establishes four exceptions—three specific and one a general catchall provision—where different payment to employees of opposite sexes "is made pursuant to (i) a seniority system; (ii) a merit system; (iii) a system which measures earnings by quantity or quality of production; or (iv) a differential based on any other factor other than sex." Again, while the Act is silent on this question, its structure and history also suggest that once the Secretary has carried his burden of showing that the employer pays workers of one sex more than workers of the opposite sex for equal work, the burden shifts to the employer to show that the differential is justified under one of the Act's four exceptions. All of the many lower courts that have considered this question have so held, and this view is consistent with the general rule that the application of an exemption under the Fair Labor Standards Act is a matter of affirmative defense on which the employer has the burden of proof.

The contentions of the parties in this case reflect the Act's underlying framework. Corning argues that the Secretary has failed to prove that Corning ever violated the Act because day shift work is not "performed under similar working conditions" as night shift work. The Secretary maintains that day shift and night shift work are performed under "similar working conditions" within the meaning of the Act.[13]   Although the Secretary

---

[13.] The Secretary also advances an argument that even if night and day inspection work is assumed not to be performed under similar working conditions, the differential in base wages is nevertheless unlawful under the Act. The additional burden of working at night, the argument goes, was already fully reflected in the plant-wide shift differential, and the shifts were made

recognizes that higher wages may be paid for night shift work, the Secretary contends that such a shift differential would be based upon a "factor other than sex" within the catchall exception to the Act and that Corning has failed to carry its burden of proof that its higher base wage for male night inspectors was in fact based on any factor other than sex. . . .

We agree with the Second Circuit that the inspection work at issue in this case, whether performed during the day or night, is "equal work" as that term is defined in the Act.[24]

This does not mean, of course, that there is no room in the Equal Pay Act for nondiscriminatory shift differentials. Work on a steady night shift no doubt has psychological and physiological impacts making it less attractive than work on a day shift. The Act contemplates that a male night worker may receive a higher wage than a female day worker, just as it contemplates that a male employee with 20 years' seniority can receive a higher wage than a woman with two years' seniority. Factors such as these play a role under the Act's four exceptions—the seniority differential under the specific seniority exception, the shift differential under the catchall exception for differentials "based on any other factor other than sex."

The question remains, however, whether Corning carried its burden of proving that the higher rate paid for night inspection work until 1966 performed solely by men, was in fact intended to serve as compensation for night work, or rather constituted an added payment based upon sex. We agree that the record amply supports the District Court's conclusion that Corning had not sustained its burden of proof. As its history revealed, "the higher night rate was in large part the product of the generally higher wage level of male workers and the need to compensate them for performing what were regarded as demeaning tasks." 474 F.2d, at 233. The differential in base wages originated at a time when no other night employees received higher pay than corresponding day workers, and it was maintained long after the company instituted a separate plant-wide shift differential which was thought to compensate adequately for the additional burdens of night work. The differential arose simply because men would not work at the low rates paid women inspectors, and it reflected a job market in which Corning could pay women less than men for the same work. That the company took advantage of such a situation may be understandable as a matter of eco-

---

"similar" by payment of the shift differential. This argument does not appear to have been presented to either the Second or the Third Circuit, as the opinions in both cases reflect an assumption on the part of all concerned that the Secretary's case would fail unless night and day inspection work was found to be performed under similar working conditions. For this reason, and in view of our resolution of the "working condition" issue, we have no occasion to consider and intimate no views on this aspect of the Secretary's argument.

[24.] In No. 73-29, Corning also claimed that the night inspection work was not equal to day shift inspection work because night shift inspectors had to do a certain amount of packing, lifting, and cleaning which was not performed by day shift inspectors. Noting that it is now well settled that jobs need not be identical in every respect before the Equal Pay Act is applicable, the Court of Appeals concluded that the extra work performed by night inspectors was of so little consequence that the jobs remained substantially equal.

nomics, but its differential nevertheless became illegal once Congress enacted into law the principle of equal pay for equal work.

III

We now must consider whether Corning continued to remain in violation of the Act after 1966 when, without changing the base wage rates for day and night inspectors, it began to permit women to bid for jobs on the night shift as vacancies occurred. It is evident that this was more than a token gesture to end discrimination, as turnover in the night shift inspection jobs was rapid. The record in No. 73-29 shows, for example, that during the two-year period after June 1, 1966, the date women were first permitted to bid for night inspection jobs, women took 152 of the 278 openings, and women with very little seniority were able to obtain positions on the night shift. Relying on these facts, the company argues that it ceased discriminating against women in 1966, and was no longer in violation of the Equal Pay Act.

But the issue before us is not whether the company, in some abstract sense, can be said to have treated men the same as women after 1966. Rather, the question is whether the company remedied the specific violation of the Act which the Secretary proved. We agree with the Second Circuit, as well as with all other circuits that have had occasion to consider this issue, that the company could not cure its violation except by equalizing the base wages of female day inspectors with the higher rates paid the night inspectors. This result is implicit in the Act's language, its statement of purpose, and its legislative history. . . .

To achieve this end, Congress required that employers pay equal pay for equal work and then specified:

> *"Provided,* That an employer who is paying a wage rate differential in violation of this subsection shall not, in order to comply with the provisions of this subsection, reduce the wage rate of any employee." 29 U.S.C. § 206(d)(1).

The purpose of this proviso was to ensure that to remedy violations of the Act, "[t]he lower wage rate must be increased to the level of the higher." H. R. Rep. No. 309, *supra,* at 3. Comments of individual legislators are all consistent with this view. Representative Dwyer remarked, for example, "The objective of equal pay legislation . . . is not to drag down men workers to the wage levels of women, but to raise women to the levels enjoyed by men in cases where discrimination is still practiced." Representative Griffin also thought it clear that "[t]he only way a violation could be remedied under the bill . . . is for the lower wages to be raised to the higher."

By proving that after the effective date of the Equal Pay Act, Corning paid female day inspectors less than male night inspectors for equal work, the Secretary implicitly demonstrated that the wages of female day shift inspectors were unlawfully depressed and that the fair wage for inspection work was the base wage paid to male inspectors on the night shift. The whole purpose of the Act was to require that these depressed wages be raised, in part as a matter of simple justice to the employees themselves, but also as a matter of market economics, since Congress recognized as well that discrimination in wages on the basis of sex "constitutes an unfair method of competition." Pub. L. 88-38, *supra,* § 2(a)(5).

We agree with Judge Friendly that

> "In light of this apparent congressional understanding, we cannot hold that Corning, by allowing some—or even many—women to move into the higher paid night jobs, achieved full compliance with the Act. Corning's action still left the inspectors on the day shift—virtually all women—earning a lower base wage than the night shift inspectors because of a differential initially based on sex and still not justified by any other consideration; in effect, Corning was still taking advantage of the availability of female labor to fill its day shift at a differentially low wage rate not justified by any factor other than sex." 474 F.2d, at 235.

The Equal Pay Act is broadly remedial, and it should be construed and applied so as to fulfill the underlying purposes which Congress sought to achieve. If, as the Secretary proved, the work performed by women on the day shift was equal to that performed by men on the night shift, the company became obligated to pay the women the same base wage as their male counterparts on the effective date of the Act. To permit the company to escape that obligation by agreeing to allow some women to work on the night shift at a higher rate of pay as vacancies occurred would frustrate, not serve, Congress' ends. . . .

The company's final contention—that it cured its violation of the Act when a new collective-bargaining agreement went into effect on January 20, 1969—need not detain us long. While the new agreement provided for equal base wages for night or day inspectors hired after that date, it continued to provide unequal base wages for employees hired before that date, a discrimination likely to continue for some time into the future because of a large number of laid-off employees who had to be offered re-employment before new inspectors could be hired. . . .

We therefore conclude that on the facts of this case, the company's continued discrimination in base wages between night and day workers, though phrased in terms of a neutral factor other than sex, nevertheless operated to perpetuate the effects of the company's prior illegal practice of paying women less than men for equal work. Cf. *Griggs* v. *Duke Power Co.,* 401 U.S. 424, 430 (1971).

The judgment in No. 73-29 is affirmed. The judgment in No. 73-695 is reversed and the case remanded to the Court of Appeals for further proceedings consistent with this opinion.

It is so ordered.

UNIVERSITY OF NEBRASKA v. DAWES
Eighth Circuit Court of Appeals
522 F.2d 380 (1975),
cert. denied, 96 S. Ct. 1112 (1976)

HEANY, Circuit Judge.

This action arises out of a suit for declaratory judgment brought by the Board of Regents of the University of Nebraska (University) seeking a determination of the rights and status of the parties under the Equal Pay Act of 1963, 29 U.S.C. § 206(d)(1). The essential issue is whether the University unlawfully discriminated against the male professional employees of the College of Agriculture and Home Economics when it sought to equalize salaries paid to the male and female employees of those colleges. The University established and put into effect a formula for determining a minimum salary schedule based on education, experience and merit for females then employed by the colleges but refused to put into effect the same formula for determining the minimum salaries of males then employed. We hold that this constituted unlawful discrimination and reverse the District Court.

In the spring of 1972, the University became aware of the problems encountered by the University of Wisconsin when it was investigated and found in violation of the Civil Rights Act of 1964. The University of Wisconsin was found to have unlawfully discriminated against women in setting salaries when it underwent a compliance review conducted by the United States Department of Health, Education and Welfare. The University, to avoid similar problems, determined to undertake a review of its salary structure and make such adjustments as necessary to eliminate salary discrimination based on sex in order to avoid the possible loss of federal funds. Directives were sent through administrative channels until they reached the Deans of the Colleges of Agriculture and Home Economics. These colleges referred the matter to a joint committee for study.

The committee, after intensive study, concluded that they could best determine whether inequities existed through a three-step process: first, identify comparable jobs; second, examine the salaries of the males and identify and assign a monetary value to the factors which went into determining their salaries; and third, compare the average male salary with individual female salaries based on a formula developed through the first two steps of the process.

In identifying comparable jobs, the committee decided that exact one-to-one comparisons were impractical. They determined that they could classify the employees according to whether they were Academic Research and Extension Specialist Staff or Extension Field Staff; *i.e.*, Specialist Staff or Field Staff.

In the second step, the committee determined that education, specialization, years of direct and related experience and merit were the factors which logically determined a male professional's salary. In order to assign a monetary value to these factors, the committee made a determination that

Doctors of Philosophy with no experience were being hired at $14,000. Of that $14,000, $8,000 represented the value of a Bachelor's degree, $2,000 represented the value of a Master's degree, $3,000 represented the value of a Doctor's degree and $1,000 represented the value of specialization. [2] The portion of salary allocated to education and specialization for each male was computed according to the above scale and totaled separately for the Specialist Staff and Field Staff. Those totals were then subtracted from the total salaries paid to the respective staffs. The remainders were considered to represent that portion of the total salaries attributable to experience and merit.

The committee then developed a formula to express the average value of experience and merit for each of the staffs. The committee assigned three points for each year of direct experience and one and one-half points for each year of related experience. The number of experience points for each male was calculated and totaled separately for each staff. The committee then divided the separate experience points of each staff by the respective total of the average individual annual performance ratings (merit) [3] which were based on a one-to-five scale with one indicating the highest level of achievement. The quotient gave the total "experience rating points" for the two staffs. The remainders representing the portion of salary attributed to experience and merit were then divided by the respective totals of the "experience rating points" which resulted in allocating $120.00 for each "experience point" of a member of the Field Staff and $106.00 for each "experience rating point" of a member of the Specialist Staff.

The committee was then in a position to set forth a formula by which it could compare an actual individual female salary with a hypothetical average male salary based only on education, specialization, experience and merit. The formula can be expressed as follows:

Field Staff

$$A + B + \frac{[(3 \times C + 1.5 \times D) \times \$120.00]}{[\qquad E \qquad]} = Salary$$

Specialist Staff

$$A + B + \frac{[(3 \times C + 1.5 \times D) \times \$106.00]}{[\qquad E \qquad]} = Salary$$

A = Education; B = Specialization; C = Years of Direct Experience; D = Years of Related Experience; E = Merit (individual annual performance rating).

The committee performed the calculations for each of the one hundred twenty-five females and determined that thirty-three of the female employees

[2.]   All Ph.D's were credited with $1,000 for specialization. The committee also credited personnel holding the position of County Agent Chairmen in the Field Extension Staff category with $1,000 for specialization although such personnel did not have Ph.D. degrees. The added amount in such cases represented administrative responsibility.

[3.]   The individual annual performance rating is a consensus of the ratings made by a professional employer's immediate supervisor. The annual performance ratings are kept on file by the University personnel office.

were receiving less than the formula salary. The difference between formula and actual salary was considered the amount necessary to equalize male and female salaries.[4]

The committee completed its work in April of 1972. The University, then faced with the problem of what to do with the committee's findings in budgeting salaries for the fiscal year beginning on July 1, 1972, decided to implement the committee's findings. Accordingly, effective July 1, the salaries of the thirty-three females were increased to the formula level. This "equalization" raise was to be effected prior to any other salary increases. The female professionals also received a $300.00 increase which had been mandated for male and female professionals by the legislature.

This process had a twofold effect: It established an "average"[5] male formula salary as the minimum salary for females and it left a number of males receiving less than the formula salary. In fact, of the two hundred seventy-two males whose salaries were used as the base, ninety-two of them received less than the formula. It is these males who contend that the University has violated the Equal Pay Act by not applying the formula to them.

A resolution of this case depends upon a proper application of the Equal Pay Act. 29 U.S.C. § 206(d)(1)[7] provides:

> No employer having employees subject to any provisions of this section shall discriminate, within any establishment in which such employees are employed, between employees on the basis of sex by paying wages to employees in such establishment at a rate less than the rate at which he pays wages to employees of the opposite sex in such establishment for equal work on jobs the performance of which requires equal skill, effort, and responsibility, and which are performed under similar working conditions, except where such payment is made pursuant to (i) a seniority system; (ii) a merit system; (iii) a system which measures earnings by quantity or quality of production; or (iv) a differential based on any other factor other than sex: *Provided,* That an employer who is paying a wage rate differential in violation of this subsection shall not, in order to comply with the provisions of this subsection, reduce the wage rate of any employee.

The University contends that the male employees of the class have failed to establish by a preponderance of the evidence, that the female employees were compensated at a different rate, that they were employed in the same establishment, and that they were engaged in jobs, the performance of which required equal skill, effort and responsibility. It further

---

[4.]   All of the committee's calculations were based on the 1971-1972 fiscal year salaries.

[5.]   We use the term "average" guardedly since it is not the true average of the males but rather a weighted average. The education attainment and specialization factors distort the "average."

[7.]   Congress amended the Fair Labor Standards Act, 29 U.S.C. § 213(a), effective July 1, 1972, so as to eliminate the exemption provision which had provided that the sex discrimination provision of the Equal Pay Act, 29 U.S.C. § 206(d)(1) would not apply to professional employees.

argues that the thirty-three female professionals received a one-time salary adjustment and that henceforth it will return to its traditional method of salary determination—individual negotiation considering education, experience, special skill, merit and market conditions (supply and demand). Thus, the University contends that there was no violation of the Act.

In our view, the defendant class has carried its burden of proof and has established that the members of the class were unlawfully discriminated against. [9] They proved that the University had established a minimum salary schedule for all presently employed female professionals in the Colleges of Agriculture and Home Economics and that at least thirty-three of that group were placed on that schedule. They further proved that at least ninety-two male professionals (having substantially equivalent education, experience and merit) were retained by the two colleges at a wage less than the minimum established for the females. This proof was sufficient to establish a violation of the Equal Pay Act.

It was the University, not the defendant class, that established the ground rules for determining whether women were being discriminated against. It determined the factors that were considered to be important for that purpose. It cannot now be heard to complain that some other additional factors must also be considered when the question is one of discrimination against the male employees who are being paid less than the formula minimum.

The University asserts that the "glaring fallacy" in the approach of the defendant class is that the formula does not represent the actual compensation paid to either male or female employees. It is in error in this assertion. On July 1, 1972, thirty-three women were placed on a step of the "salary schedule" consistent with their education, experience and merit rating solely because they were women and for no other reason—not because they had more administrative duties, taught more difficult subjects or worked harder and not because they were better teachers, researchers or field agents.[10]

It is, of course, true that there were and are male and female teachers who receive salaries in excess of those obtained by applying the formula. It may even be that a careful comparison of these professionals would uncover inequities as between the sexes, but we are not concerned with that problem on this appeal. It is not necessary to prove that all of the persons of one sex employed by a single employer are discriminated against to establish a violation of the law. It is sufficient to show that some are.

[9.] We agree with the University that the burden of proof rested on the defendant class even though the University had initiated the declaratory judgment action. *Reliance Life Insurance Co. v. Burgess,* 112 F.2d 234 (8th Cir. 1940).

[10.] The trial court found that on July 1, 1972, the average male was paid $1,337 per year above the formula and that the average female was paid only $744.00 above the formula. It concluded from these averages that there was no violation of the Equal Pay Act with respect to the men. The averages, if correct, would be largely irrelevant since all the females were paid at least the minimum set in the formula and ninety-two men who performed substantially equal work received less than that minimum.

We, of course, do not hold or imply that a University must establish salary schedules or even minimum salaries. We simply hold that when a University establishes and effectuates a formula for determining a minimum salary schedule for one sex and bases the formula on specific criteria such as education, specialization, experience and merit, it is a violation of the Equal Pay Act to refuse to pay employees of the opposite sex the minimum required under the formula.

In the light of our decision, the other points raised by the University are without merit and need no discussion. We express no opinion as to the merits of the University's Eleventh Amendment defense as the trial court did not rule on the issue. The decision of the District Court is reversed and the case is remanded for action consistent with this opinion.

NOTES

1. In Shultz v. Wheaton Glass Co., 421 F.2d 259 (3rd Cir. 1970), *cert. denied*, 90 S.Ct. 1696, the court ruled that, under the Equal Pay Act, "Congress in prescribing 'equal' work did not require that the jobs be identical, but only that they must be substantially equal. Any other interpretation would destroy the remedial purposes of the Act." *Id.* at 265.

2. Although the "substantial equality" test set out in *Wheaton Glass* is widely applied, it is not completely accepted by all circuits. *See* Hodgson v. Golden Isles Convalescent Homes, Inc., 468 F.2d 1256 (5th Cir. 1972). The courts will apply the Act to successive employees in a particular job, as well as to those holding jobs contemporaneously. In all cases, actual job content is the important consideration in determining equal or substantially equal work; the employer's job description does not control. *Compare* Brennan v. South Davis Community Hospital, 538 F.2d 859 (10th Cir. 1976), *with* Usery v. Columbia University, 15 F.E.P. Cas. 1333 (2nd Cir. 1977).

3. The defense to the Equal Pay Act which permits a "differential based on any factor other than sex" has generated litigation in a variety of situations. In Hodgson v. Robert Hall Clothes, Inc., 473 F.2d 589 (3rd Cir. 1973), *cert. denied*, 414 U.S. 866 (1973), the court held that the fact that the profit from the sale of men's clothes was greater than the profit from the sale of women's and children's clothes could justify a wage differential between male and female salespeople.

Although bona fide training programs can justify a wage differential, the courts have often required that the programs be formal. Schultz v. First Victoria National Bank, 420 F.2d 648 (5th Cir. 1969); Hodgson v. Behrens Drug Co., 475 F.2d 1041 (5th Cir. 1973), *cert. denied*, 414 U.S. 822 (1973). In addition, a training program may not be bona fide if qualified women are excluded from the program. Hodgson v. Security National Bank, 460 F.2d 57 (8th Cir. 1972).

4. Section 6(d)(1) of the Equal Pay Act provides that an employer who is paying a wage differential in violation of the Act may not reduce the wages of any employee in order to eliminate the differential. Thus, courts have required that the employer raise the wages of female employees to the level of male employees performing substantially equal work rather than lower the wages of the male employees. *See, e.g.,* Corning Glass Works v. Brennan, 417 U.S. 188 (1974).

5. The courts have held that the Supreme Court's decision in National League of Cities v. Usery, 426 U.S. 833 (1976), does not preclude the application of the Equal Pay Act to state and local governments. *See, e.g.,* Usery v. Allegheny County Institution District, 544 F.2d 148 (3rd Cir. 1976).

6. In Keyes v. Lenoir Rhyne College, 552 F.2d 579 (4th Cir. 1977), the court declined to order the College to produce confidential evaluations of faculty members during the trial of an equal pay suit. However, the court observed that:

In the present case the College asked that the confidentiality of the faculty evaluation records be protected, urging that the assurance of confidentiality enabled the College to receive honest and candid appraisals of the abilities of the faculty members by their peers. . . . [I]f the College had sought to justify any male-female disparity on the basis of these evaluations the plaintiff should have been granted the opportunity to use them to demonstrate that the explanation was pretextual. . . . Here, however, the College did not resort to the evaluations for that purpose, and . . . the district court's decision to protect these records from disclosure was not an abuse of its discretion." [*Id.* at 581].

CHAPTER 20

THE REHABILITATION ACTS

I. Introduction

NOTE, REHABILITATING THE REHABILITATION ACT OF 1973*
58 Boston U. L. Rev. 247-257 (1978)

I. Introduction

The Rehabilitation Act of 1973[1] represents a comprehensive federal response to the plight of the nation's handicapped.[2] The Act makes significant contributions in four distinct areas. First, in an attempt to promote "comprehensive and continuing State plans . . . for providing vocational rehabilitation services to handicapped individuals,"[3] the Act provides for federal coordination of and monetary assistance to state vocational rehabilitation programs.[4] Second, the Act encourages novel research on both the state and federal level into the myriad problems experienced by the handicapped.[5] Third, the Act establishes several new and innovative federal

---

   * Reprinted by permission of the Boston University Law Review.
1. 29 U.S.C. §§ 701-794 (Supp. III 1973).
2. Estimates of the number of handicapped persons within the United States vary. The U.S. Department of Labor recently fixed the number conservatively at twenty million. Employment Standards Administration, U.S. Dep't of Labor, Fact Sheet: Who Are the Handicapped? Another commentator estimates that the number is closer to twelve million. Note, Abroad in the Land: Legal Strategies to Effectuate the Rights of the Physically Disabled, 61 Geo. L. Rev. 1501, 1501 n.2 (1973).

   Previous federal legislation had been piecemeal in its approach to the problems experienced by the handicapped. *E.g.,* Architectural Barriers Act of 1968, 42 U.S.C. §§4151-4156 (1970) (eliminating structural impediments to public places); Urban Mass Transportation Assistance Act of 1970, 49 U.S.C. §§1601-1612, 1612(a) (1970) (increasing access to public transportation). At the time the Rehabilitation Act was passed, state law also failed to deal adequately with the problems of the handicapped. The few state laws that prohibited employment discrimination against the handicapped were inadequate, *see* Note, Equal Employment and the Disabled: A Proposal, 10 Colum. J.L. & Soc. Prob. 457, 459-65 (1974), and state tort law often discouraged handicapped individuals from becoming active members in their communities, *see* ten Broek, The Right to Live in the World: The Disabled in the Law of Torts, 54 Calif. L. Rev. 841 (1966). State statutes gave the least protection to the mentally disabled. *See* American Bar Foundation, The Mentally Disabled and the Law 207-49, 303-40 (rev. ed. S. Brackel & R. Rock 1971). For a general history of the treatment of the handicapped under state law, see Burgdorf & Burgdorf, A History of Unequal Treatment: The Qualifications of Handicapped Persons as a "Suspect Class" Under the Equal Protection Clause, 15 Santa Clara Law. 855, 861-99 (1975).
3. 29 U.S.C. §701(1) (Supp. III 1973).
4. *Id.* §§720-764.
5. *Id.* §§760-764 (state programs). On the federal level, the Act authorized the Secretary of Labor to conduct a study of the role of sheltered workshops in the rehabilitation of handicapped individuals. *Id.* §786. Sheltered workshops were developed to provide noninstitutionalized opportunities for employment, training and other rehabilitative services. In addition, the Rehabilitation Act Amendments of 1974 authorized a national conference to address the problems of the handicapped. Pub. L. No. 93-516, §§300-306, 88 Stat. 1631 (1974), *reprinted in* 29 U.S.C. §701 note (Supp. IV 1974). For background on the specific purposes of the conference, see S. Rep. No. 1297, 93d Cong., 2d Sess. 27-37, 49-53, *reprinted in* [1974] 4 U.S. Code Cong. & Ad. News 6399-409, 6421-25.

programs, such as a National Center for Deaf-Blind Youths and Adults[6] and federal mortgage insurance for rehabilitation facilities.[7]

The fourth major contribution of the Rehabilitation Act of 1973 is embodied in sections 503[8] and 504,[9] which together have far-reaching ramifications for large segments of the general public as well as for handicapped people. Section 503 provides that every employer doing business with the federal government under a contract for more than $2500 must take affirmative action to accommodate qualified handicapped individuals in all phases of employment. Section 504 prohibits discrimination against any qualified handicapped individual by any "recipient"[10] of federal financial assistance. . . .

II. Sections 503 and 504

A. *Administrative History*

In January, 1974, an executive order delegated to the Secretary of Labor the authority to prescribe and enforce rules and regulations implementing section 503.[11] Regulations promulgated pursuant to this authority became effective on June 11, 1974.[12] Under the regulations, the Department of

---

6. 29 U.S.C. §775 (Supp. III 1973).
7. *Id.* §773. The Act also established within the federal government an Interagency Committee on Handicapped Employees, whose primary task is to review the adequacy of hiring, placement and advancement opportunities for handicapped persons within the executive branch of government. *Id.* §791(a). Moreover, the Act created an interdepartmental Architectural and Transportation Barriers Compliance Board, *id.* §792(a), whose duties include enforcing the standards promulgated under the Architectural Barriers Act of 1968, 42 U.S.C. §§4151-4156 (1970). 29 U.S.C. §792(b)(1) (Supp. III 1973). The Board apparently is beginning vigorously to enforce the architectural barriers standards. *See* N.Y. Times, Dec. 20, 1977, at 14, col. 3 (city ed.); Helping the Handicapped, Time, Dec. 5, 1977, at 34.
8. 29 U.S.C. § 793(a) (Supp. III 1973), Section 503(a) provides in part: Any contract in excess of $2,500 entered into by any Federal department or agency for the procurement of personal property and nonpersonal services (including construction) for the United States shall contain a provision that, in employing persons to carry out such contract the party contracting with the United States shall take affirmative action to employ and advance in employment qualified handicapped individuals. *Id.* This provision also applies to subcontracts in excess of $2500 entered into by a prime contractor for the purpose of carrying out the federal contract. *Id.*
9. *Id.* §794. Section 504 provides in part: No otherwise qualified handicapped individual in the United States . . . shall, solely by reason of his handicap, be excluded from the participation in, be denied the benefits of, or be subjected to discrimination under any program or activity receiving Federal financial assistance. *Id.*
10. A "recipient" is any state or its subdivision, agency, institution, organization, or person who receives federal financial assistance, either directly from the federal government or through another recipient, 42 Fed. Reg. 22,678 (1977) (to be codified in 45 C.F.R. §84.3(f)).
11. Exec. Order No. 11,758, 39 Fed. Reg. 2075 (1974), *reprinted in* 29 U.S.C. §701 app., at 2069 (Supp. IV 1974).
12. 39 Fed. Reg. 20,566 (1974).

Labor's Office of Federal Contract Compliance Programs (OFCCP)[13] is solely responsible for the enforcement of section 503 and its regulations.[14]

Section 504's administrative history is more brief. The executive branch did not delegate its section 504 rulemaking authority until April 28, 1976. [15] The delegation of authority provided that federal departments and agencies possessing the power to provide federal financial assistance—labeled the "compliance agencies"—should promulgate and enforce rules and regulations consistent with the standards and procedures established by the Secretary of Health, Education and Welfare.[16] Twelve months later,[17] the Secre-

---

13.   Affirmative action programs based upon federal contracts are known as federal contract compliance programs. Until 1965, these contract compliance programs were enforced by so-called Presidential Committees. Office of Fed. Contract Compliance Programs, Employment Standards Administration, U.S. Dep't of Labor, Preliminary Report on the Revitalization of the Federal Contract Compliance Program 2-4 (1977). In 1965, President Johnson issued Executive Order No. 11,246, 3 C.F.R. 339 (1964-1965 Compilation), which created an affirmative action program for women, racial minorities and certain other groups, and gave authority for enforcing the Executive Order Program to the Department of Labor's new Office of Federal Contract Compliance (OFCC). Id., as amended by Exec. Order No. 11,478, 3 C.F.R. 214 (1973), Regional offices of the OFCC were responsible only to the national office of the OFCC. In 1969, the OFCC regional offices also became directly responsible to the Department of Labor's Employment Standards Administration regional administrators. In 1975, the OFCC was given the additional responsibilities of enforcing section 503 of the Rehabilitation Act and section 402 of the Vietnam Era Veterans' Readjustment Assistance Act of 1972, § 402, 38 U.S.C. § 2012 (Supp. IV 1974). At this time, the OFCC's name was changed to the Office of Federal Contract Compliance Programs (OFCCP). Office of Fed. Contract Compliance Programs, supra, at 2-4. A proposal currently exists to upgrade the status of the OFCCP within the Department of Labor by making the OFCCP regional offices independent of the Employment Standards Administration. This proposal would eliminate the present situation in which regional offices are directly responsible to two separate entities. Id. at 53-64.
14.   See, e.g., 41 C.F.R. §§60-741.2, .3(b), .25 (1977).
15.   Exec. Order No. 11.914, 3 C.F.R. 117 (1977).
16.   Id. §2, 3 C.F.R. at 118. Before 1969, the compliance agency was always the same agency that had awarded the contract that established coverage. The underlying theory was that, because equal opportunity obligations constituted a contractual obligation, those departments and agencies responsible for awarding and administering the contracts were in a better position to obtain compliance. In 1969, however, the "compliance agency system" replaced the previous "contracting agency system." The compliance agency system assigns contractors to agencies on an industry basis. In most cases, however, the compliance agency under the "compliance agency system" is the same agency as under the "contracting agency system." Office of Fed. Contract Compliance Programs, supra note 13, at 40-41.
       Recently, President Carter announced an executive reorganization plan that would merge the enforcement responsibility of the Executive Order Program under the OFCCP's jurisdiction. Office of the Assistant Secretary for Employment Standards, U.S. Dep't of Labor, Internal Memorandum: The President's Reorganization Plan (Feb. 1978). For a discussion of the rationale for this merger proposal, see note 13 supra. See also Office of Fed. Contract Compliance Programs, supra note 13, at 37-52.
17.   During this time, handicapped persons were exerting considerable pressure in an effort to hasten the rulemaking process. At least one plaintiff sought a court order to compel the Secretary of HEW to sign the pending regulations. See Cherry v. Mathews, 419 F.Supp. 922 (D.D.C. 1976). Groups of handicapped persons also staged sit-ins in federal offices throughout the nation. Hire the Handicapped, Newsweek, May 9, 1977, at 39.

tary of HEW signed the first—and, to date, the only—section 504 regulations,[18] which became effective on June 3, 1977.[19]

B.   *Coverage Prerequisites*

Section 503 and section 504 both specify two requirements that must
be satisfied in order to establish coverage. First, both sections protect only
"qualified handicapped individuals." [20] Regulations under the two sections
define a "handicapped individual" as any person who:

(1) has a physical or mental impairment which substantially limits one
or more of such person's major life activities, (2) has a record of such
impairment or (3) is regarded as having such an impairment.[21]

Thus, under both sections, "handicapped individual" is broadly defined
to include not only persons who have an actual present impairment,[22] but
also persons who have a history of or have been misclassified as having had a

---

18.   Secretary Califano signed the regulations on April 28, 1977. 42 Fed. Reg. 22,677 (1977).
Secretary Califano offered several reasons for the delay: (1) insufficient congressional guidance
regarding the issues raised by section 504; (2) a change in the presidential administration; and
(3) reluctance to sign the regulations without first ensuring that the regulations adequately
addressed the legitimate needs of the handicapped. U.S. Dep't of Health, Education and Welfare, HEW News 7-8 (Apr. 28, 1977).

19.   42 Fed. Reg. 22,676 (1977).

20.   *Compare* 29 U.S.C. § 793(a) (Supp. III 1973) *with id.* § 794.

21.   41 C.F.R. § 60-741.2 (1977) (section 503); 42 Fed. Reg. 22,678 (1977) (to be codified in
45 C.F.R. § 84.3(j)(1)) (section 504). Major life activities include, but are not limited to, ambu-
lation, learning, socialization and employment. 41 C.F.R. §60-741 app. A, at 441 (1977) (section 503); 42 Fed. Reg. 22,678 (1977) (to be codified in 45 C.F.R. §84.3(j)(2)(ii)) (section
504). The definition contained in the regulations is identical to the statutory definition. 29
U.S.C. §706(6) (Supp. IV 1974).
        Prior to 1974, the Rehabilitation Act defined "handicapped individual" as a person who had
a physical or mental disability that "substantially impaired" the individual's employability, and
who could "reasonably be expected to benefit in terms of employability from vocational
rehabilitation services." Rehabilitation Act of 1973, §7(6), 87 Stat. 355 (1973). Thus, a handicapped person was covered by the statute only if rehabilitation services could improve that
person's "employability." Because rehabilitation services often cannot improve the severely
handicapped person's "employability," this definition of "handicapped" excluded from the
Act's coverage those persons most in need of the Act's protection—the severely handicapped.
The 1974 Amendments to the Rehabilitation Act provided a new and broader definition of
handicapped individual, *see* text accompanying this note, which clearly encompasses the
severely handicapped.

22.   Two of the more controversial impairments are alcoholism and drug addiction. *See* Caring
for the Disabled, Boston Herald American, July 14, 1977, at 12, col. 6. The United States
Attorney General recently issued an opinion concluding that alcoholics and drug addicts are
covered by both sections of the Act. Letter from Attorney General Griffin Bell to HEW Secretary Califano (Apr. 12, 1977). The Departments of Labor and HEW have taken steps to implement this opinion. Office of Information, U.S. Dep't of Labor, Labor News (July 6, 1977)
(section 503), *reprinted in part* in Boston Herald American, July 6, 1977, at 3, col. 1; 42 Fed.
Reg. 22,686 (1977) (to be codified in 45 C.F.R. § 84 app. A, n.3) (section 504).

handicap.[23] Moreover, the definition protects all those who are perceived as having a handicap, regardless of whether an impairment actually exists. [24]

However, section 503 and section 504 necessarily have different definitions of the term "qualified." Section 503 by its terms only covers job applicants and employees of an employer who holds a section 503 contract.[25] For employers covered by section 503, the regulations define a "qualified" handicapped individual as a handicapped person "who is capable of performing a particular job, with reasonable accommodation to his or her handicap." [26] Section 504 defines "qualified" similarly in the employment context,[27] but the section's broader coverage requires a definition of "qualified" handicapped individuals in other contexts as well. For example, because the Department of Health, Education and Welfare extends federal financial assistance to educational institutions, section 504 regulations must also define "qualified handicapped individual" with reference to educational assistance.[28]

The second prerequisite to coverage under section 503 and section 504 identifies those parties who owe a statutory duty to qualified handicapped individuals. Section 503 imposes obligations only upon employers who satisfy three requirements. First, the employer must hold a federal contract.[29] Second, the contract must be for the procurement of personal property and nonpersonal services, including construction contracts. [30]

---

23. 41 C.F.R. § 60-741 app. A, at 441-42 (1977) (section 503); 42 Fed. Reg. 22,678 (1977) (to be codified in 45 C.F.R. §84.3(j)(2)(iii)) (section 504). This portion of the definition encompasses, for example, persons who have previously had a mental illness, a heart attack, or cancer. See 41 C.F.R. §60-741 app. A, at 441-42 (1977) (section 503); 42 Fed. Reg. 22,686 (1977) (to be codified in 45 C.F.R. §84 app. A, n.3) (section 504). The actual handicap need not continue to exist. If the person has a "record of such impairment," sections 503 and 504 both protect the individual. 41 C.F.R. §60-741 app. A, at 741 (1977) (section 503); 42 Fed. Reg. 22,678 (1977) (to be codified in 45 C.F.R. §84.3(j)(2)(iii)) (section 504).

24. 41 C.F.R. §60-741 app. A, at 442 (1977) (section 503); 42 Fed. Reg. 22,678 (1977) (to be codified in 45 C.F.R. §84.3(j)(2)(iv)) (section 504). The regulations recognize that other people's perceptions may themselves constitute a "physical or mental impairment that substantially limits major life activities. . . ." 42 Fed. Reg. 22,678 (1977) (to be codified in 45 C.F.R. §84.3(j)(2)(iv)(B)).

25. 29 U.S.C. §793(a) (Supp. III 1973).

26. 41 C.F.R. §60-741.2 (1977).

27. 42 Fed. Reg. 22,678 (1977) (to be codified in 45 C.F.R. §84.3(k)(1)).

28. Id. (to be codified in 45 C.F.R. §§84.3(k)(2)-(4)). For a discussion of the need to protect the handicapped in the area of educational opportunities, see Burgdorf & Burgdorf, supra note 2, at 868-83; Note, supra note 2, 61 Geo. L. Rev. at 1503 & nn.12-16. See also The White House Conference on Handicapped Individuals, Recommendations from the White House Conference on Handicapped Individuals with Special Attention to Massachusetts 36-41 (1977).

29. 41 C.F.R. §60-741.3(a)(1) (1977). The term "contractor" also includes a subcontractor who otherwise satisfies the jurisdictional prerequisites. Id. §60-741.2.

30. Id. §60-741.2. The term "government contract" does not include either agreements in which the contracting parties stand in an employer-employee relationship, or "federally assisted contracts." Id. The regional offices of the OFCCP find it particularly difficult to interpret this provision of the regulations. Interview with Margaret Joyce, Employment Opportunity Specialist for Region I of the OFCCP, in Boston, Mass. (Jan. 13, 1978).

   Based upon the "federally assisted contract" exception, the Department of Labor's solicitor for Region I opined that federal money disbursed to a local housing authority by the Department of Housing and Urban Development pursuant to a Consolidated Annual Contributions Contract did not constitute a section 503 contract. Id.

Third, the contractual amount must exceed $2500.[31] In contrast, section 504 applies to every recipient of federal financial assistance,[32] regardless of the amount of assistance received. Although section 503 applies only to holders of federal contracts, section 504 applies to recipients of grants, loans, contracts and other forms of financial assistance.[33]

C. Legal Obligations

Although section 504 regulates areas not covered by section 503,[34] both sections prescribe conduct within the area of employment practices.[35] In this context, the two sections impose upon the employer different legal obligations. Section 503 requires a covered employer to take "affirmative action" in the employment of handicapped individuals.[36] Section 504 prohibits "discrimination" against qualified handicapped individuals but imposes no additional affirmative action obligation.[37] Thus, the question whether federal money received is covered by section 503 or by section 504 may determine both the existence and the extent of the legal obligation owed by the employer.[38]

---

31.   41 C.F.R. §60-741.3 (1977).
32.   29 U.S.C. §794 (Supp. III 1973). See also 42 Fed. Reg. 22,678 (1977) (to be codified in 45 C.F.R. § 84.2).
33.   42 Fed. Reg. 22,678 (1977) (to be codified in 45 C.F.R. §84.3(h)).
34.   See, e.g., id. at 22,682-85 (to be codified in 45 C.F.R. §§84.31-.54) (protecting nonemployees in the educational, health, welfare and social services context).
35.   41 C.F.R. §60-741 (1977) (section 503); 42 Fed. Reg. 22,680-81 (1977) (to be codified in 45 C.F.R. §§84.11-14) (section 504). Handicapped persons have had great difficulty finding gainful employment. Studies demonstrate that the unemployment rates for the handicapped are significantly higher than the national rate. Employment Standards Administration, supra note 2; Note, supra note 2, 61 Geo. L. Rev. at 1512 n.78. Although handicaps may limit a person's employability, see text accompanying note 100 infra, many employers also have misconceptions regarding handicapped job applicants and employees that further constrict the job opportunities available to a handicapped person. Note, supra note 2, 12 Colum. J.L. & Soc. Prob. at 458 nn.6 & 7; Note, supra note 2, 61 Geo. L. Rev. at 1513 & nn.81-84. Professors ten Broek and Matson identified hostility and condescension as the two predominant employer attitudes that foster these misconceptions. ten Broek & Matson, The Disabled and the Law of Welfare, 54 Calif. L. Rev. 809, 809-16 (1966). An employer's typical fears include a belief that the employer's insurance premiums will increase, that considerable expense will be necessary in order to make accommodations for the handicapped, that safety records will be jeopardized, that handicapped employees will demand special privileges, and that handicapped workers will perform inadequately. Wolfe, Disability Is No Handicap for duPont. The Alliance Review (Winter 1973-1974) (U.S. Dep't of Labor reprint). A study conducted by the duPont Corporation indicates that these concerns are overstated or unfounded. Id.
36.   29 U.S.C. §793(a) (Supp. III 1973); 41 C.F.R. §60-741.1 (1977).
37.   29 U.S.C. §794 (Supp. III 1973); 42 Fed. Reg. 22,678 (1977) (to be codified in 45 C.F.R. §84.1).
38.   Distinguishing between a section 503 contract and a form of section 504 financial assistance is often difficult. Interview with Margaret Joyce, supra note 30. Moreover, coverage and enforcement of the two sections is not coordinated. Thus, even if the OFCCP determines that a particular form of federal aid is not covered by section 503, the financial aid in question is not necessarily covered by section 504. For example, insurance companies are currently contesting the issue whether section 503 covers federal insurance or reinsurance contracts. The position of the insurance companies seems to be that federal insurance and reinsurance contracts are not contracts for the "procurement of . . . nonpersonal services." 29 U.S.C. §793(a) (Supp. III 1973), within the meaning of section 503. Interview with Margaret Joyce, supra note 30. Yet section 504 regulations specifically exclude insurance contracts from coverage. 42 Fed. Reg. 22,678

The Rehabilitation Acts

An employer's obligations under section 503 depend upon the contractual amount involved. If the contractual amount is less than or equal to $2500, section 503 does not in any way regulate the employer's conduct.[39] If the contract exceeds $2500, section 503 imposes varying obligations. Section 503 regulations incorporate into every covered contract an affirmative action clause.[40] The clause requires the performance of several specific duties[41] and imposes upon an employer a general obligation to comply with all section 503 regulations.[42] Section 503 regulations also compel an employer to make a "reasonable accommodation" to the handicap of an employee unless the employer can demonstrate that the accommodation "would impose an undue hardship on the conduct of the contractor's business."[43] Additionally, an employer is required to review his personnel procedures to ensure that such procedures give careful and thorough consideration to the job qualifications of applicants and employees known to be handicapped.[44] The contractor must also review all physical and mental job requirements to make certain that, to the extent that these requirements disqualify otherwise qualified handicapped individuals, such requirements are job-related and "consistent with business necessity and the safe performance of the job."[45] Finally the employer is not permitted to reduce the compensation of a qualified handicapped individual because of the individual's possible outside source of disability insurance or benefit.[46]

If the federal contract in question exceeds $50,000 and is held by an employer with fifty or more employees, section 503 regulations impose additional obligations. In this case, the employer must develop and maintain

---

(1977) (to be codified in 45 C.F.R. § 84.3(h)). For the rationale supporting this specific exclusion, see 42 Fed. Reg. 22,685 (1977) (to be codified in 45 C.F.R. § 84 app. A, n.2). Thus, if the insurance companies prevail and insurance contracts are found not to be covered by section 503, such contracts will be totally exempted from the requirements of the Rehabilitation Act.

39.   41 C.F.R. §60-741.3(a)(I) (1977).

40.   *Id.* §60-741.23. The clause is deemed to be a part of the contract, regardless of whether it is expressly included in the document. *Id.* The contracting parties may incorporate the clause by reference. *Id.* §60-741.22. Paragraph (f) of the affirmative action clause, *reprinted in id.* §60-741.4, requires the covered contractor to include the affirmative action clause in every covered subcontract.

41.   Paragraph (d) of the affirmative action clause, *reprinted in id.* §60-741.4 requires the contractor to post conspicuous notices as prescribed by the OFCCP. Paragraph (e) of the affirmative action clause, *reprinted in id.* §60-741.4, requires the employer to inform each union with which the employer has a collective bargaining agreement that the contractor-employer has legal obligations under the Act.

42.   *Id.* §60-741.4 (paragraph (b) of the affirmative action clause).

43.   *Id.* §60-741.6(d); *see* text accompanying notes 97-103 *infra.*

44.   41 C.F.R. §60-741.6(b) (1977).

45.   *Id.* §60-741.6(c).

46.   *Id.* §60-741.6(e). However, federal law does not require that employers always pay handicapped workers wages equal to the wages that must be paid to nonhandicapped workers. 29 U.S.C. §214(c) (1970); 29 C.F.R. § 525 (1975). Thus, severely handicapped persons working in sheltered workshops usually do not receive federal minimum wages. Employment Standards Administration/Employment & Training Administration, 1 Sheltered Workshop Study: A Nationwide Report on Sheltered Workshops and Their Employment of Handicapped Individuals 64-95 (1977). *See generally id.* at 16-20, *But cf.* 41 C.F.R. §60-741.6(j) (1977) (contracts with sheltered workshops do not substitute for affirmative action within the contractor's own workforce).

a written "affirmative action program," setting forth the employer's policies and practices with regard to handicapped applicants and employees.[47] The contractor is required to review and update the affirmative action program annually,[48] and this program is also subject to review by the OFCCP.[49]

Section 504 requirements are somewhat different. Within the employment context, the duties owed to qualified handicapped individuals under section 504 are similar to those duties owed under section 503. For example, section 504 requires that the employer make a "reasonable accommodation" to handicapped applicants and employees and defines the accommodations that must be made in terms nearly identical to those contained in the section 503 regulations.[50] However, section 504 imposes no additional requirements on recipients of larger sums of money, and section 504 regulations thus impose no written affirmative action program obligation similar to that imposed under section 503.[51]

D. *Enforcement Procedures and Remedies*

The OFCCP is wholly responsible for enforcing section 503, regardless of which federal department or agency awarded the contract. In contrast, each department or agency providing federal financial assistance is responsible for enforcing section 504 with respect to the projects and programs funded by that particular agency.[52]

Sections 503 and 504 each utilize a complaint process, whereby any person who believes he was deprived of rights granted by the Act may file

47.   41 C.F.R. §60-741.5 (1977). The contractor-employer must develop a written affirmative action program for each facility. *Id.* §60-741.5(a). The contractor may request the Director of the OFCCP to "waive" the requirement for any of the contractor's facilities that are "in all respects separate and distinct from" federal contract work. *Id.* §60-741.3(a)(5); *see* text accompanying notes 111-12 *infra*. Absent a waiver, the contractor must develop the written affirmative action program within 120 days of the commencement of a contract that exceeds $50,000. 41 C.F.R. §60-741.5(a) (1977).

48.   41 C.F.R. §60-741.5(b) (1977). Unless the contractor holds other federal contracts that satisfy the $50,000 jurisdictional prerequisite, the legal obligation to maintain the written affirmative action program expires when the contract is completed. *See id.* §60-741.3(a)(2).

49.   The OFCCP may review an affirmative action program after receiving some indication that the program either does not exist or is inadequate. *See, e.g., id.* §§ 60-741.26(a), .28(a). Recently, however, one regional office of the OFCCP instituted a program whereby the office routinely contacted a contractor shortly after receiving notice that the contractor had been awarded a contract exceeding $50,000. This program is designed to prevent violations of the Act before they occur. Interview with Margaret Joyce, *supra* note 30.

50.   *Compare* 41 C.F.R. § 60-741.6(d) (1977) *with* 42 Fed. Reg. 22,680 (1970) (to be codified in 45 C.F.R. § 84.12).

51.   The two sets of regulations also differ in several other respects. Although section 503 regulations require only that the contractor review the job requirements to ensure that the requirements are "job related . . . consistent with business necessity and the safe performance of the job," 41 C.F.R. §60-741.6(c)(1) (1977), section 504 regulations provide that the contractor's use of an employment test or other selection criterion is valid only if "alternative . . . tests or criteria that do not screen out . . . as many handicapped persons are not shown by the Director [of HEW's Office for Civil Rights] to be available." 42 Fed. Reg. 22,680 (1977) (to be codified in 45 C.F.R. §84.13(a)(2)). Additionally, section 503 regulations require a more extensive review of personnel policies than the section 504 regulations require. *Compare* 41 C.F.R. §60-741.5 (1977) *with* 42 Fed. Reg. 22,680 (1977) (to be codified in 45 C.F.R. §84.11-(a)(3)).

52.   *See* text accompanying notes 13-16 *supra*.

a complaint with the appropriate compliance agency.[53] Aside from setting forth procedures with which the complainant must comply,[54] both sections state a preference for informal resolution of a complaint whenever possible[55] and grant to compliance agencies the powers necessary to investigate the complaint.[56] Under both sections, the time at which the right to judicial review attaches is unclear.[57] The possible existence of additional administra-

---

53.   41 C.F.R. §60-741.26 (1977) (section 503); 42 Fed. Reg. 22,685 (1977) (to be codified in 45 C.F.R. §84.61) (incorporating by reference 45 C.F.R. §80.7(b) (1976)) (section 504). During fiscal year 1977, the OFCCP received 2243 complaints. Of these, 886 (39.5%) alleged hiring violations; 832 (37.1%) alleged discharge violations; 123 (5.5%) alleged promotional violations; and 402 (17.9%) alleged miscellaneous other violations. Interview with Margaret Joyce, *supra* note 30.

54.   For example, the complaint must be filed within 180 days of the alleged violation. 41 C.F.R. §60-741.26(a) (1977) (section 503); 42 Fed. Reg. 22,685 (1977) (to be codified in 45 C.F.R. §84.61) (incorporating by reference 45 C.F.R. §80.7(b) (1976)) (section 504). Section 503 regulations authorize an extension of the filing date for "good cause shown." 41 C.F.R. §60-741.26(a) (1977). The OFCCP looks to at least two factors to determine whether the complainant has demonstrated good cause. First, using only the information supplied by the complainant, the OFCCP tries to evaluate the respondent's efforts to inform handicapped persons of the respondent's affirmative action obligations. Second, the OFCCP determines whether the complainant has made a "good faith effort" to pursue his legal rights. A good faith effort generally includes retaining a lawyer, exercising collective bargaining grievance procedures, and filing a complaint with either a state agency or a different federal agency. Interview with Margaret Joyce, *supra* note 30. Section 504 regulations also authorize extensions, although they do not state what test must be met in order to justify an extension. 42 Fed. Reg. 22,685 (1977) (to be codified in 45 C.F.R. §84.61) (incorporating by reference 45 C.F.R. §80.7 (1976)).

55.   *Compare* 41 C.F.R. §60-741.28(a) (1977) *with* 42 Fed. Reg. 22,685 (1977) (to be codified in 45 C.F.R. §84.61) (incorporating by reference 45 C.F.R. §80.7(d) (1976)). Often, an employer's collective bargaining agreement will contain procedures for informal resolution of complaints. Section 503 regulations require that, when the complainant is an employee of a contractor who has an internal grievance procedure, the OFCCP must initially refer the complainant to the respondent's grievance procedure. 41 C.F.R. §60.741.26(b) (1977). If no agreement that is satisfactory to the complainant has been reached within sixty days, then the OFCCP should resume the investigation. *Id.*

Most collective bargaining agreements include a provision for binding arbitration of those complaints that are not resolved by less formal procedures. U.S. Bureau of Labor Statistics, Dep't of Labor, Bull. No. 1822, Characteristics of Agreements Covering 1,000 Workers or More 64 (1974), and courts almost routinely affirm the arbitrator's award. *See* United Steelworkers v. Enterprise Wheel & Car Corp., 363 U.S. 593 (1960). However, arbitration awards resulting from complaints alleging violations of the Rehabilitation Act should be upheld only if the complainant finds the award satisfactory. *See* 41 C.F.R. §60-741.26(b) (1977). Thus, a union's decision not to arbitrate a handicapped member's grievance, *see, e.g.*, Vaca v. Sipes, 386 U.S. 171 (1967), would no longer be binding upon the complainant.

56.   *Compare, e.g.*, 41 C.F.R. §60-741.53 (1977) *with* 42 Fed. Reg. 22,685 (1977) (to be codified in 45 C.F.R. §84.61) (incorporating by reference 45 C.F.R. §80.6(c) (1976)) (right of access to contractor's or recipient's records during normal business hours); *and* 41 C.F.R. §60-741.51 (1977) *with* 42 Fed. Reg. 22,685 (1977) (to be codified in 45 C.F.R. §84.61) (incorporating by reference 45 C.F.R. §80.7(e) (1976)) (right to protect from future discrimination any person who files a complaint, testifies, assists, or otherwise participates in any activity relating to administration of the Act).

57.   Presumably, the Administrative Procedure Act, 5 U.S.C. §§551-706 (1970), will govern this question. Under this act, "final agency action for which there is no other adequate remedy in a court [is] subject to judicial review." *Id.* §704. Therefore, the determinative question is when an action by the OFCCP is "final." For example, under section 503 regulations, if the OFCCP's investigation results in a determination that no violation exists, or if the OFCCP after finding a violation "decides not to initiate administrative or legal proceedings," 41 C.F.R. §60-741.26-(g)(1) (1977), then the complainant has a right to appeal to the Director of the OFCCP. *Id.* The question whether such an appeal is necessary before judicial review attaches has not yet arisen.

tive enforcement methods available to the OFCCP under section 503[58] and to the compliance agencies under section 504 is also unsettled.[59]

The remedies for a violation of section 503 include withholding of progress payments,[60] termination of a federal contract[61] and debarment from the receipt of future federal contracts.[62] Moreover, the section 503 regulations authorize additional judicial remedies,[63] including injunctive

---

For a brief analysis of the problems involved in determining the right to judicial review under the Rehabilitation Act, see Note, Lowering the Barriers to Employment of the Handicapped: Affirmative Action Obligations Imposed on Federal Contractors, 81 Dick. L. Rev. 174, 189-90 (1977).

Courts are divided on the issue whether section 503 creates a private cause of action independent of the right of judicial review. *Compare* Drennon v. Philadelphia Gen. Hosp., 428 F. Supp. 809 (E.D. Pa. 1977); Duran v. City of Tampa, 14 Empl. Prac. Dec. ¶7799 (M.D. Fla. 1977), *with* Rogers v. Frito-Lay, Inc., 433 F.Supp. 200 (N.D. Tex. 1977); Wood v. Diamond Tel. Co., 440 F.Supp. 1003 (D. Del. 1977). *See also* Wright, Equal Treatment of the Handicapped by Federal Contractors, 26 Emory L.J. 65, 89-96 (1977). On the other hand, courts appear more consistent in holding that section 504 creates a private cause of action. *E. g.*, Leary v. Crapsey, 566 F.2d 863 (2d Cir. 1977); Lloyd v. Regional Transp. Auth., 548 F.2d 1277 (7th Cir. 1977); Gurmankin v. Costanzo, 14 Empl. Prac. Dec. ¶7519 (3d Cir.1977). Several explanations may underlie this conclusion. First, the language of section 504 is virtually identical to that found in other civil rights statutes under which courts have found a private cause of action. This similarity of language may support the inference that Congress intended to grant a private right of action under section 504. *See* 120 Cong. Rec. 30,534 (1974). Second, because no regulations existed under section 504 until recently, a private cause of action would not displace any administrative process and, indeed, may well be the only available method of enforcing section 504. However, as other federal departments and agencies promulgate section 504 regulations, this rationale for finding a section 504 cause of action may lose its validity.

58.   The national OFCCP has developed a new enforcement method called a "directed review." The directed review is designed to determine whether those contractors that are subject to the written affirmative action requuirement have fulfilled their responsibilities in this regard. Directed reviews are scheduled to commence in 1978. Interview with Margaret Joyce, *supra* note 30.

59.   For example, in its section 504 regulations, HEW incorporated by reference the administrative enforcement procedures already existing under Title VI of the Civil Rights Act of 1964, Pub. L. No. 88-352. §601, 78 Stat. 252 (codified at 42 U.S.C. §§2000d to 2000d-4 (1970)). 42 Fed. Reg. 22,685 (1977) (to be codified in 45 C.F.R. §84.61) (incorporating by reference 45 C.F.R. §§80.6-80.10, 81.1-81.131 (1976)). However, some of the enforcement procedures incorporated by reference are applicable only in the context of discrimination against women and racial minorities. *See, e.g.*, 45 C.F.R. §80.6(b) (1976). There is no indication whether HEW intends to modify these provisions to make them applicable in the context of the handicapped.

60.   41 C.F.R. §60-741.28(c) (1977). A formal hearing is required before this remedy can be invoked. *Id.* § 60-741.29(a)(2).

61.   *Id.* § 60-741.28((d). Termination may result in a revocation of all, or only a portion of, the federal contract. *Id.* A formal hearing is required prior to any termination remedy. *Id.* § 60-741.29 (a)(2).

62.   *Id.* §60-741.28(e). The Director of the OFCCP periodically distributes to all executive departments and agencies a list of all debarred, and therefore ineligible, contractors. *Id.* §60-741.31. Upon a showing that the contractor "has established and will carry out employment policies and practices in compliance with the affirmative action clause," *id.* §60-741.50, the Director may reinstate a previously ineligible contractor.

63.   *Id.* §60-741.28(b).

The OFCCP recently issued the first five administrative complaints under the section 503 regulations. U.S. Dep't of Labor, Labor News (Sept. 27, 1977); U.S. Dep't of Labor, Labor News (July 18, 1977). Judicial enforcement of administrative remedies has not yet been necessary; nor has a district court had occasion to fashion supplementary judicial remedies.

Although back pay is not specifically authorized by section 503 regulations, it would almost certainly be an available judicial remedy. Back pay may be necessary in order to ensure effective relief. *See* Albemarle Paper Co. v. Moody, 422 U.S. 405, 417-18 (1975). Such awards are available to other protected groups under similar circumstances. *See, e.g., id.* (back pay awarded to

relief. [64] Although the range of remedies available under section 504 regulations is still unsettled, section 504 does correspond to section 503 in authorizing the withholding or termination of, or the debarment from the future receipt of, federal financial assistance.

II. Section 504

A. Introduction

Section 504 of the Rehabilitation Act of 1973 prohibits discrimination under federal grants. The Act states:

> No otherwise qualified handicapped individual in the United States, as defined in Section 7(6) [29 U.S.C. § 706(6)], shall, solely by reason of his handicap, be excluded from the participation in, be denied the benefits of, or be subjected to discrimination under any program or activity receiving federal financial assistance. [29 U.S.C. § 794]

To implement Section 504, the Department of Health, Education and Welfare in 1976 adopted regulations which can be found at 45 C.F.R. § 84.1 *et seq.* These regulations broadly define a handicapped person as one who "(i) has a physical or mental impairment which substantially limits one or more major life activity, (ii) has a record of such an impairment, or (iii) is regarded as having such an impairment." [§ 84.3(j)] Thus Section 504 attempts to protect individuals from the adverse effects of handicaps which are actual *or* perceived, past *or* present, physical *or* mental. Section 504 applies only to "qualified" handicapped persons. With respect to employment, a qualified handicapped person is one ". . . who, with reasonable accommodation, can perform the essential functions of the job in question." [§ 84(k)(1)] With respect to higher education, a qualified handicapped person is one "who meets the academic and technical standards requisite

---

an "affected class" under Title VII of the Civil Rights Act of 1964); United States v. Duquesne Light Co., 13 Fair Empl. Prac. Cas. 1608 (W.D. Pa. 1976) (back pay awarded under Executive Order 11,246 Program); Bishop v. Jeleff Assoc., 308 F.Supp. 579 (D.D.C. 1974) (back pay awarded under Age Discrimination in Employment Act). Moreover, conciliation agreements between the agency and the parties to a complaint often include back pay awards. *See, e.g.,* U.S. Dep't of Labor, Labor News 3 (July 18, 1977); U.S. Dep't of Labor, Labor News (Jan. 10, 1976).

Compensatory damages are not specifically authorized by the regulations but should be awarded if back pay alone would not constitute a sufficient remedy. There is less justification for allowing an award of punitive damages. Although an award of punitive damages is not specifically prohibited under the regulations, such an award would not significantly aid enforcement of the Act; nor would such an award be necessary to compensate the complainant. However, courts have divided on the issue whether punitive damages are available under statutes that are similar in intent to the Rehabilitation Act. *See, e.g.,* Jackson v. Illinois Cent. Gulf R.R., 14 Empl. Prac. Dec. ¶7784 (S.D. Ala. 1977) (punitive damages not available under the Age Discrimination in Employment Act); Dean v. American Security Ins. Co., 429 F.Supp. 3 (N.D. Ga. 1976) (punitive damages available under the Age Discrimination in Employment Act).

64.   41 C.F.R. §60-741.28(b) (1977).
65.   42 Fed. Reg. 22,685 (1977) (to be codified in 45 C.F.R. §84.61)

to admission or participation in an institution's educational program or activity." A recipient of federal funds may not provide a handicapped person with "an aid, benefit, or service that is not as effective as that provided to others." [§ 84.4(b)(1)(iii)]

Section 504 has led to a great amount of litigation. The large number of federal grant recipients and the broad scope of the regulations, combined with judicial sympathy for the handicapped, has led to a great variety of affirmative remedies in many areas in addition to higher education: public transportation, United Handicapped Federation v. Andres, 558 F.2d 413 (7th Cir. 1977); hospital construction, NAACP v. Wilmington Medical Center, Inc., 426 F.Supp. 919 (D.C. Del. 1977); relocation of retarded to community based facilities, Halderman v. Pennhurst State School and Hospital, 446 F.Supp. 1295 (1977); prison vocational programs, Sites v. McKenzie, 423 F.Supp. 1190 (N.D. W. Va. 1976); and employment, Gurmankin v. Costanzo, 411 F.Supp. 982 (E.D. Pa. 1976), *aff'd* 556 F.2d 184 (3rd Cir. 1977).

B.   The Meaning of a Qualified Handicapped Individual

DAVIS v. SOUTHEASTERN COMMUNITY COLLEGE
United States Court of Appeals, Fourth Circuit
574 F.2d 1158 (1978)

K. K. HALL, Circuit Judge:

Frances B. Davis, a Licensed Practical Nurse ("LPN"), appeals from a final judgment entered against her in a civil action filed under the Civil Rights Act of 1871, 42 U.S.C. § 1983, and under Section 504 of the Rehabilitation Act of 1973, 29 U.S.C. § 794, ("the Act"). The Southeastern Community College ("college"), located in North Carolina, was the named defendant, and Ms. Davis complained that the college unlawfully denied her admittance to the college's Associate Degree Nursing Program ("program"), which would ultimately lead to certification as a Registered Nurse ("RN"), because of her admitted hearing disability.

Following a trial to the court, the district judge held: (1) that the plaintiff did not have to exhaust further administrative remedies as a precondition to suit; (2) that the plaintiff was not denied any constitutional or property rights, under either due process or equal protection clauses of the Constitution, [42 U.S.C. § 1983]; and (3) that the plaintiff, although plainly a "handicapped individual" within the meaning of 29 U.S.C. § 706(6), was not discriminated against within the strictures of 29 U.S.C. § 794. *Davis v. Southeastern Community College*, 424 F.Supp. 1341 (E.D.N.C. 1976). We affirm in part, and vacate in part and remand.

I.

PRIVATE RIGHT OF ACTION

Although the district court did not make a specific legal finding as to whether or not the plaintiff could pursue a private right of action under

Section 504 of the Act, we believe that such a finding was at least implicit, and was legally sound. On this point, we affirm, and we adopt the sound reasoning of the Seventh Circuit in *Lloyd v. Regional Transportation Authority,* 548 F.2d 1277, 1284-87 (7th Cir. 1977). *See also United Handicapped Federation v. Andre,* 558 F.2d 413, 415 (8th Cir. 1977); *Kampmeier v. Nyquist,* 553 F.2d 296, 299 (2nd Cir. 1977); *Hairston v. Drosick,* 423 F.Supp. 180 (S.D.W.Va.1976); *Sites v. McKenzie,* 423 F.Supp. 1190 (N.D. W.Va.1976). . . .

III.

THE SECTION 504 CLAIM

Our holding on the merits of plaintiff's Section 504 claim is rather narrow. We vacate and remand that portion of the district court judgment which has not been affirmed here, and hold that the college must reconsider plaintiff's application for admission to the nursing program without regard to her hearing disability. The college may consider such other relevant subjective and objective factors as it deems appropriate, consonant of course with a fair and essentially uniform application of those same subjective and objective factors utilized in the consideration of other candidates for enrollment in the nursing program. For instance, past academic performance would undoubtedly be a highly relevant factor governing admissibility to the nursing program.

We reach this result because the district court erred when it found that plaintiff was not "otherwise qualified" pursuant to Section 504 of the Act, 29 U.S.C. § 794, for admission to the college's nursing program.

The court below defined the key statutory terminology, "otherwise qualified," as contained in 29 U.S.C. §794, in their ordinary common meaning since, at the time the case was decided, there had not been any definitive interpretations of those terms. *Davis v. Southeastern Community College, supra,* at 1345, decided December 22, 1976. Thus, "otherwise qualified" was defined to mean that the plaintiff had ". . . to [be] otherwise able to function sufficiently in the position in spite of [her] handicap, if proper training facilities [were] suitable and available." *Id.* However, since plaintiff's hearing deficiencies would prevent her from safely performing the clinical training leading to her RN degree and would, after graduation, restrict her in the pursuit of her proposed profession, then in the district court's view she was not "otherwise qualified." *Id.*

Approximately six months after the district court decided *Davis,* on June 3, 1977, the regulations implementing Section 504 of the Act, promulgated by the Department of Health, Education and Welfare ("HEW"), became effective. 42 Fed. Reg. 22676 (May 4, 1977). Among these regulations, now embodied in 45 C.F.R. Part 84, is one which addresses the particular definitional problem presented on this appeal. Title 45 C.F.R. §84.3(k)(3) requires that:

> With respect to post-secondary and vocational educational services [an otherwise qualified handicapped person is one] . . .

who meets the *academic* and *technical* standards requisite to
admission or participation in the recipient's education program
or activity.
[Emphasis added.]
The official explanation provided by HEW for this definition indicates that:
> . . . both academic and technical standards must be met by appli-
> cants to these programs. The term 'technical standards' refers to
> all nonacademic admissions criteria that are essential to partici-
> pation in the program in question.

42 Fed.Reg. at 22687.

Thus, we hold the district court erred by considering the nature of the
plaintiff's handicap in order to determine whether or not she was "otherwise
qualified" for admittance to the nursing program, *Davis v. Southeastern
Community College, supra,* at 1345, rather than by focusing upon her
academic and technical qualifications as required by the newly promulgated regulations. We reach this result by applying the law which is in effect
at the time we render our decision, *Thorpe v. Housing Authority,* 393 U.S.
268, 281, 89 S.Ct. 518, 21 L.Ed.2d 474 (1969); *see also Cort v. Ash,* 422
U.S. 66, 95 S.Ct. 2080, 45 L.Ed.2d 26 (1975); *Bradley v. Richmond School
Board,* 416 U.S. 696, 94 S.Ct. 2006, 40 L.Ed.2d 476 (1974), and note that
other courts of appeals have been required to vacate and remand Section
504 cases to the lower courts for reconsideration in light of applicable
regulations which antedated their decisions. *See United Handicapped Federation v. Andre,* 558 F.2d 413, 416 (8th Cir. 1977); *Lloyd v. Regional
Transportation Authority,* 548 F.2d 1277, 1287-8 (7th Cir. 1977).

IV.

AFFIRMATIVE RELIEF

Since this case will be returned to the district court for further proceedings, we believe it would be appropriate, as guidance for the court
below, to briefly discuss plaintiff's claim that the district court also erred
by failing to consider that the college could be required to modify the
nursing program so as to accommodate the plaintiff and her hearing disability. Plaintiff bases her entitlement to such "affirmative relief" also
upon Section 504 of the Act, 29 U.S.C. §794, and upon certain designated
sections of the HEW regulations under Section 504.

The position of the college was relatively clear—it was not prepared,
from a faculty viewpoint, to adequately supervise and train the plaintiff
during her clinical training. Therefore, it could not modify its program
to compensate for plaintiff's hearing disability.

We believe the district court should give close attention, on remand, to
the regulations upon which plaintiff relies, which are cited in footnote 8
of this opinion, and especially to 45 C.F.R. §84.44(a), *Academic requirements,* which requires that:
> A recipient . . . shall make such modifications to its academic re-
> quirements as are necessary to ensure that such requirements do

not discriminate or have the effect of discriminating, on the basis
of handicap, against a qualified handicapped applicant or student.
* * * Modifications may include changes in the length of time
permitted for the completion of degree requirements, substitution of specific courses required for the completion of degree
requirements, and adaptation of the manner in which specific
courses are conducted.

and to 45 C.F.R. §84.44(d)(1), *Auxiliary aids*, which requires that:

A recipient . . . shall take such steps as are necessary to ensure that
no handicapped student is denied the benefits of, excluded from
participation in, or otherwise subjected to discrimination under
the education program or activity operated by the recipient because of the absence of educational auxiliary aids for students
with impaired sensory, manual, or speaking skills.

Additionally, precedent likewise supports the requirement of affirmative conduct on the part of certain entities under Section 504, even when
such modifications become expensive. *See e.g. United Handicapped Federation v. Andre*, 558 F.2d 413, 415-6 (8th Cir. 1977); *Lloyd v. Regional
Transportation Authority*, 548 F.2d 1277, 1281-84 (7th Cir. 1977); *Barnes
v. Converse College*, 436 F.Supp. 635, 637 (D.S.C.1977); *Hairston v. Drosick*, 423 F.Supp. 180, 184 (S.D.W.Va. 1976).

V.

OTHER CLAIMS—DAMAGES, DUE
PROCESS, AND EQUAL
PROTECTION

Both parties to this appeal presented other issues for our consideration.
For the reasons stated below, we decline to pass upon them.

The college complains that plaintiff's attempt to secure monetary
damages against it is precluded by the Eleventh Amendment immunity
accorded the state, and its institutions. The district court below did not
rule upon any damage request by the plaintiff, and indeed, ruled against
her. Plaintiff did not raise the damage question on appeal, and we thus
hold that any issue of damages could not, under any conceivable appellate
theory, be before us and decline to discuss it further.

The plaintiff also argued that the district court's decision, upholding
her exclusion from the nursing program, denied her due process of law and
the equal protection of the laws under the Fourteenth Amendment of the
United States Constitution. Because this appeal, thus far, has been disposed
of on nonconstitutional, statutory grounds, we have no need to reach the
constitutional questions which the plaintiff presented below. *See Gurmankin v. Costanzo*, 556 F.2d 184, 186 (3rd Cir. 1977); *Lloyd v. Regional
Transportation Authority*, 548 F.2d 1277, 1280 (7th Cir. 1977).

Accordingly, the judgment is
AFFIRMED in part; VACATED in part; and REMANDED. . . .

NOTES

1. The *Davis* case follows Lloyd v. Regional Transportation Authority, 548 F.2d 1277, 1284-87, in holding that the plaintiff does have a right of private action under Section 504. *In accord:* Doe v. New York University, 442 F.Supp. 522 (S.D.N.Y. 1978); Kampmeier v. Nyquist, 553 F.2d 296 (2nd Cir. 1977); Halderman v. Pennhurst State School and Hospital, 466 F.Supp. 1295 (1977); Leary v. Crapsey 566 F.2d 863 (2nd Cir. 1977); Drennon v. Philadelphia General Hospital, 427 F.Supp. 809 (E.D. Pa. 1977); and Barnes v. Converse College 436 F.Supp. 635, 638 (D.S.C. 1977).

2. Should a university be able to decide whether or not a handicapped person is able to pursue a certain occupation after graduation, for example a nursing career, and deny admission to a nursing program on that basis? If Ms. Davis is unable to be a surgical nurse because of her hearing problem, could she function in a doctor's office? Who should make that decision? Twenty-seven states and the American Council on Higher Education have asked the Supreme Court to review the *Davis* case. [47 U.S.L.W. 3318 *petition for cert. filed*, No. 78-711 (October 27, 1978)] The Supreme Court has been asked to decide if Section 504 requires institutions to admit handicapped persons if their disabilities make it impossible for them to "participate effectively in the educational program and the career to which it leads." *See also*: Chronicle for Higher Education, November 20, 1978, p. 10.

3. In its review of the *Davis* case, the Supreme Court has also been asked to decide if a person must exhaust his federal administrative remedies before filing a private law suit. On this point, it was held in *Lloyd v. Regional Transportation, supra*, in often quoted *dicta*, that:

> We expressly leave open as premature the question of whether, after consolidated procedural enforcement regulations are issued to implement Section 504, the judicial remedy available must be limited to post-administrative remedy judicial review. In any event, the private cause of action we imply today must continue at least in the form of judicial review of administrative action. And until effective enforcement regulations are promulgated, Section 504 in its present incarnation as an independent cause of action should not be subjected to the doctrine of exhaustion. . . . But assuming a meaningful administrative enforcement mechanism, the private cause of action under Section 504 should be limited to *a posteriori* review. [548 F.2d 1286]

The courts have been divided regarding the question of whether a handicapped plaintiff must exhaust the HEW administrative procedures. In Drennon v. Philadelphia General Hospital, 428 F.Supp. 809, a case factually similar to the *Duran* case, *infra,* an applicant with a history of epilepsy was denied employment, the court, at pages 816-817, observed that:

> The doctrine of primary jurisdiction had been developed by courts in order to avoid conflict between the courts and an administrative agency arising from either the court's lack of expertise with the subject matter of the agency's regulation or from contradictory rulings by the agency and the court. Under the doctrine, a court should refer a matter to an administrative agency for resolution, *even if the matter is otherwise properly before the court*, if it appears that the matter involves technical or policy considerations which are beyond the court's ordinary competence and with the agency's particular field of expertise.

See also: Doe v. New York University, 442 F.Supp. 522 (S.D.N.Y. 1978) in which plaintiff claimed the medical school's refusal to readmit her after psychiatric leave of absence constituted discrimination under Section 504. The court in *Doe* required exhaustion of the HEW administrative remedies even though it admitted "H.E.W.'s enforcement machinery in other areas of civil rights complaints is inefficacious, at best . . ." [422 F.Supp. 523]

More often, the federal courts have not required exhaustion or have not considered the issue and have given the handicapped plaintiff relief through a preliminary injunction under a Section 504 or other theory. Colleges, for example, have been ordered to provide interpreters for deaf students. Barnes v. Converse College, 436 F.Supp. 635 (D.C.S.C. 1977); Crawford v. University of North Carolina, 440 F.Supp. 1047 (M.D.N.C. 1977). *See generally:* Halderman v. Pennhurst State School and Hospital, 446 F.Supp. 1295 (1977); United Handicapped Federation v. Andres, 558 F.2d 413 (7th Cir. 1977); N.A.A.C.P. v. Wilmington Medical Center, Inc., 426 F.Supp. 919 (D.C. Del. 1977); Hairson v. Drosick, 423 F.Supp. 1012 (D.C. Wisc. 1975).

4. The regulations require any recipient of federal financial assistance to make their service as "effective" as that provided to others. [45 C.F.R. §84.4(b)(1)(iii)] In the *Davis* case, the college said that it was not prepared to modify its program and faculty responsibilities in order to be able to adequately supervise Ms. Davis. Who should bear the cost of providing services that are "equally effective" for the handicapped? The courts have put this responsibility upon the recipient, even though it may mean great expense for the recipient. *See:* Hairson v. Drosick, 423 F.Supp. 180 (S.D. W. Va. 1976). In Barnes v. Converse College, 436 F.Supp. 635, the Court ordered a small private college located in close proximity to a state supported school for the deaf to provide interpreter services for the plaintiff who was deaf. Noting that the defendant college is "justifiably concerned with the financial burden it ultimately must have to bear as a result of compliance with Sec. 794 [Section 504 of the Act] in the future," the Court said:

> Although the danger of future expenditures under this statute is not a proper consideration in this lawsuit, this court is most sympathetic with the plight of defendant as a private institution which may well be forced to make substantial expenditures of private monies to accommodate the federal government's generosity. Converse College is subject to regulation under 29 U.S.C. §794 because it receives federal financial assistance. None of this federal financial assistance, however, was given the Converse College for the purpose of providing auxiliary aids for the handicapped. No educational administrator needs to be reminded of the said fact that federal money means pervasive, bureaucratic federal control; and for pervasive, tyrannical bureaucratic federal control, the Department of Health, Education and Welfare knows no equal or superior. Converse College has been in the vanguard of educational institutions in this region which have developed programs and facilities for the handicapped. It is ironic that its students and benefactors may now be forced by the federal government to shoulder a substantial financial burden to provide special services for any handicapped person who should choose to go to Converse College. This is not to say that this court is not entirely sympathetic with the spirit of federal legislation which encourages the expansion of opportunities for the handicapped. This is merely to say that if the federal government, in all its wisdom, decides that money should be spent to provide opportunities for a particular group of people, that government should be willing to spend its own money (i. e. our taxes) for such purposes and not require that private educational institutions use their limited funds for such purposes.

> [436 F.Supp. 638-639]

Do you agree with the Court's view?

5. The decision in *Davis* was reversed by the Supreme Court in June 1979. The Court's opinion will appear in the *Supplement.*

C. The Importance of an Individualized Determination

DURAN v. CITY OF TAMPA
United States District Court
430 F.Supp. 75 (1977)

KRENTZMAN, District Judge. . . .

. . . The basis of the plaintiff's complaint alleges that the defendants violated both the plaintiff's fourteenth amendment due process rights and his rights pursuant to 29 U.S.C. § § 793 and 794 by failing to hire him for the position of policeman because of his history of epilepsy.

FACTS

In April, 1975, the plaintiff, who is a twenty-eight year old male, applied to the defendant, City of Tampa, for the position of policeman. Soon thereafter the City administered both a written and oral examination to the plaintiff and also gave him a polygraph test. The plaintiff satisfactorily completed all of the defendant's examinations. In October, 1975, the City placed the plaintiff's name on an eligibility list for the position of policeman. On December 19, 1975, the plaintiff was requested by the City to appear for a physical examination. Later that same day the defendant contacted the plaintiff and informed him that a physical examination would not be necessary because his past history of epilepsy would automatically exclude him from service as a policeman. The plaintiff attempted through several avenues to have the defendants reverse its decision but to no avail. The plaintiff filed this suit on August 26, 1976.

The plaintiff's history of epilepsy consisted of four episodes of grand mal seizures in 1958 and several petit mal seizures or blank staring episodes during 1959. The plaintiff has not experienced any seizures of either variety since 1959 and discontinued any medication related to epilepsy in July, 1966. . . .

The Supreme Court's analysis in *Cleveland Board of Education v. La Fleur*, 414 U.S. 632, 94 S.Ct. 791, 39 L.Ed.2d 52 (1974) can readily be applied to the plaintiff's case. In *La Fleur* the Court found the mandatory maternity leave policy under which a pregnant teacher in the Cleveland school system was forced to take maternity leave without pay at a period five months prior to delivery was a violation of her due process rights. The School Board in *La Fleur* argued that since "at least some teachers become physically incapable of adequately performing certain of their duties during the latter part of pregnancy", the mandatory maternity leave policy assured a physically capable instructor in the classroom and protected the health of the mother and her unborn child. *Id.* at 641, 94 S.Ct. at 797. The Court rejected such an argument and found that the mandatory cutoff dates established an irrebuttable presumption about the teacher's competence during pregnancy and could not pass muster under the due process clause. . . .

The City of Tampa Civil Service Board's Medical Standards lists as the principal objective of the standards to "select candidates for City employment who are physically fit and who can reasonably be expected to remain so." Given this noble purpose, the Board promulgated Standard K(4)(a) which states, "Not Acceptable for Group I, Epilepsy." The Board has further interpreted Standard K(4)(a) to automatically exclude from employment an applicant with a history of epilepsy even prior to medical examination. Thus, the Medical Standards have created an irrebuttable presumption to exclude all individuals from employment who have suffered from epilepsy.

The Court is of the opinion that the Medical Standards sweep too broadly and include within their ambit those individuals, like the plaintiff, whose history of epilepsy in no way infringes upon their present ability to perform the duties and tasks required by the position to which they have applied. Thus, the Court is of the opinion the absolute presumption established by Standard K(4)(a) as applied to the plaintiff is violative of his due process rights. At minimum, the due process clause mandates that the defendants provide the plaintiff with an individual determination of his medical status. . . .

NOTE

See also Gurmankin v. Costanzo, 411 F.Supp. 982 (E.D. Pa. 1976), *aff'd* 556 F.2d 184, in which the Court found the school district used the irrebuttable presumption that a blind teacher was incompetent and ordered defendant to permit Ms. Gurmankin to take the teacher's exam.

III. Section 503

Section 503 of the Rehabilitation Act requires federal government contractors to take affirmative action in hiring and promoting the handicapped. [29 U.S.C. §793] The Act requires prime contractors and their subcontractors who have contracts over $2,500 to "take affirmative action to employ and advance in employment qualified handicapped individuals."

The Labor Department regulations implementing Section 503, 41 C.F.R. §60-741 (1977), define "a handicap person" very broadly and in a way similar to the Section 504 regulations.

If a federal contractor comes within the $2,500 requirement, the contractor must recruit the qualified handicapped through personnel practices, outreach, notices and must make reasonable accommodations for the physical and mental limitations of a handicapped applicant, unless such an accommodation would provide an undue hardship related to business necessity. [§60-741.6(d)] A handicapped individual is "qualified" if he or she is "capable of performing a particular job with reasonable accommodation to his or her handicap." [§60-741.2]

Although Section 503 applies to all contractors with contracts over $2,500, only contractors or subcontractors with contracts of $50,000 or more and with 50 or more employees are required to prepare and update an affirmative action program annually. However, Section 503 does not require contractors to prepare or implement timetables or goals for the hiring of handicapped persons.

A complaint under Section 503 may be filed by any individual with the Director of the Office of Contract Compliance and the regulations outline an enforcement procedure emphasizing persuasion and conciliation, but also permitting the withholding of progress payments, contract termination and/or judicial action.

NOTES

1. To date, few cases have been litigated under Section 503. Most of the cases deal with the issue of the existence of a private cause of action and the courts are divided on this issue. "[I]ndependent federal litigation at the initiation of private individuals" is "inconsistent with the legislative scheme fashioned by Congress." Wood v. Diamond State Telephone Co., 440 F.Supp. 1003, 1010 (Del. 1977). *See also*: Moon v. Roadway Express, Inc., 439 F.Supp. 1308 (N.D. Ga. 1977); and Rogers v. Frito-Lay, Inc., 433 F.Supp. 200 (N.D. Tex. 1977). *But see* Drennon v. Philadelphia General Hospital, 428 F.Supp. 809 (E.D. Pa. 1977) (which allowed a private cause of action under Section 503 but stayed the action until plaintiff had exhausted her administrative remedies); and Duran v. City of Tampa, 430 F.Supp. 75 (M.D. Fla. 1977).

2. One of the many questions unresolved is the meaning of "a handicap" under the broad and vague definition given in the regulations. The handicaps involved in cases in which back pay has been awarded pursuant to conciliation settlements have included an intestinal infection, an injury to the right elbow, hypertension, anemia, alcoholism, and mental instability. See OFCCP Veterans and Handicapped Workers Program Operations Division, *Summary of Back Pay Cases* (available from U.S. Department of Labor, Employment Standards Adm., Office of Federal Contract Compliance Program, Room N-3402, New Dept. of Labor Bldg., Washington, D.C. 20210).

3. An employer must determine if the applicant's handicap is job related and, if so, if reasonable accommodations can be made which permit the applicant to work. So far there has been no litigation under §503 on the proof necessary that a handicap is job related. But it is likely the courts will require a careful consideration of the individual ability of the handicapped plaintiff and not a statistical survey of the capability of handicapped persons generally or unsupported presumptions as to the probable impact of a disability.

4. Another issue still to be answered by the courts is whether an employer may consider the danger to the handicapped applicant that might result from his employment—for example, an aggravation of a prior injury, or the possibility of increased absenteeism or increased insurance costs. *See:* Montgomery Ward & Co. v. Bureau of Labor, 28 Or. 747, 961 P2d 637, 639 (1977); Smith v. Olin Chemical Corp., 555 F.2d 1282 (5th Cir. 1977), considering the issue in a Title VII context.

5. Under the Act, a contractor has the duty to make "reasonable accommodation to the physical and mental limitations of an employee . . . unless such accommodation would impose an undue hardship. . . ." §60-741.6(d). How much accommodation is reasonable? If Section 504 is any guide to the interpretation of Section 503, the burden on the employer may be heavy (Barnes v. Converse College, 436 F.Supp. 635, a Section 504 case) or require accommodation to the detriment of other employees (Holland f. Bolling Co., 12 FEP Case 975 (Wash. Sup. Ct., 1976)).

IV. References for Sections 503 and 504

Wright, *Equal Treatment of the Handicapped by Federal Contractors,* 26 Emory L.J. 65 (1977); Lopatka, *A 1977 Primer on the Federal Regula-*

tion of Employment Discrimination, 1977 U. of Ill. L. Forum, 161-166; Guy, *The Rehabilitation Act of 1973—Its Impact on Employee Selection Practices,* Employee Relations L.J., Vol. 4, No. 1 (Summer, 1978); and Notes, *Rehabilitating the Rehabilitation Act of 1973,* Boston U. L. Rev., Vol. 58, March 1978, p. 247.

CHAPTER 21

THE FAMILY EDUCATIONAL RIGHTS AND PRIVACY ACT

The Family Educational Rights and Privacy Act, 20 U.S.C. §1232g (Supp. IV, 1974), often referred to as the Buckley Amendment because of the name of its principal sponsor, aims to protect the privacy of parents and students by giving a number of rights concerning students' past and present school records. 20 U.S.C. Sec. 1232(g). 45 C.F.R. 99.1 (1977). Educational institutions that fail to comply with the terms of the Act may face a loss of federal funds.

The Act has the following major provisions:

1.   Students must be given the opportunity to inspect and review their own educational records.

2.   The institution must provide an opportunity for a hearing if a student wishes to challenge information which is "inaccurate, misleading, or otherwise in violation of the privacy or other rights of the student."

3.   With specified exceptions relating to educational needs, "personally identifiable" information cannot be released to third parties without the prior written consent of the student or without a judicial order or subpoena. "Personally identifiable" information means the name, address, social security number, or personal characteristics or other information which would make the student's identity easily traceable.

4.   The Act does not require an institute of higher education to disclose to the student the financial records of the parent, confidential letters of recommendation written before the Act went into effect or recommendations with regard to which the student has signed a waiver of his right of access.

RIOS v. READ

United States District Court
73 F.R.D. 589 (E.D.N.Y. 1977)

[A class action was brought by Hispanic school children against school officials for violating their rights to equal educational opportunity, protected by the Fourteenth Amendment, by failing to provide programs, curriculum and teaching personnel adequate to remedy plaintiffs' English language deficiencies. The plaintiffs moved to compel answers to interrogatories requesting information tracing the progress of individual Hispanic students in both bilingual and regular school programs. The defendants objected to such discovery on the grounds that the Family Educational Rights and Privacy Act of 1974, 20 U.S.C. §1232g prohibited them from disclosing the names or other identifying information of individual students.]

751

MISHLER, Chief Judge.

This is a case of first impression involving §438(b)(2) of the General Education Provisions Act, popularly known as the Family Educational Rights and Privacy Act of 1974 (the "1974 Act"), 20 U.S.C. § 1232g(b)(2) (Supp. IV, 1974). . . .

Although much of the information sought by plaintiffs has been supplied by defendants, the names and other identifying characteristics on the test results, class schedules, bilingual identification cards, etc., were deleted by the school authorities. Unless they can trace the progress of the individual students from the initial testing for English language deficiencies through the bilingual or ESL instruction and the students' eventual participation in regular English language courses, plaintiffs contend, the mass of data provided by defendants is useless. Without identifying data, plaintiffs claim it is impossible to determine which students were evaluated as language deficient; whether the language deficient students received adequate English language training; and whether, despite the bilingual programs offered by defendants significant numbers of Spanish dominant students were academically disadvantaged by the defendants. . . .

THE FAMILY EDUCATIONAL RIGHTS AND PRIVACY ACT OF 1974

Section 438(b)(2) of the General Education Provisions Act, 20 U.S.C. § 1232g(b)(2) (Supp. IV, 1974), provides:

(2) No funds shall be made available under any applicable program to any educational agency or institution which has a policy or practice of releasing, or providing access to, any personally identifiable information in education records other than directory information, or as is permitted under paragraph (1) of this subsection unless—

(A) there is written consent from the student's parents specifying records to be released, the reasons for such release, and to whom, and with a copy of the records to be released to the student's parents and the student if desired by the parents, or

(B) such information is furnished in compliance with judicial order, or pursuant to any lawfully issued subpoena, upon condition that parents and the students are notified of all such orders or subpoenas in advance of the compliance therewith by the educational institution or agency.

In their response to interrogatories Nos. 12, 33, 51, 56, 59, 60 and document requests Nos. 3, 17 and 18, the defendants assert that the release of the names of pupils or other identifying data "is not authorized" by the 1974 Act. Two questions are posed by the defendant's objection. First, whether the 1974 Act, either by its terms or by virtue of the Congressional policy it expresses, bars disclosure of the pupils' names. Second, if the names must be disclosed, what type of notice must be given to the students and their parents, and whether an opportunity should be afforded for parents or students to object to disclosure.

Unfortunately, there is little guidance available to a court that must interpret this section of the 1974 Act. The entire 1974 Act itself, also known as the Buckley Amendment, after its principal sponsor, was offered as an amendment on the Senate floor to the bill extending the Elementary and Secondary Education Act of 1965. 120 Cong.Rec. S21487 (daily ed. Dec. 13, 1974) (joint remarks of Sen. Buckley and Sen. Pell). Since the amendments were not the subject of legislative committee inquiry, traditional legislative history in the form of hearings and reports is not available. Moreover, no decisions have been reported that interpret §438(b)(2) of the 1974 Act. Thus, we write on a largely clean slate.

The purpose of the 1974 Act is two-fold. The legislation is intended

> to assure parents of students, and students themselves if they are over the age of 18 or attending an institution or post-secondary education, access to their education records and to protect such individuals' rights to privacy by limiting the transferability [and disclosure] of their records without their consent. The Secretary of Health, Education, and Welfare is charged with enforcement of the provisions of the Act, and failure to comply with its provisions can lead to withdrawal of Office of Education assistance to the educational agency or institution.

120 Cong.Rec. S21487 (daily ed. Dec. 13, 1974) (joint remarks of Sen. Buckley and Sen. Pell). *See* Sen.Rep.No.93-1026, 93rd Cong., 2nd Sess. 186, *reprinted in* [1974] U.S.Code Cong. & Admin. News, p. 4250. The provision assuring privacy of student records, at issue in this case, was enacted in response to "the growing evidence of the abuse of student records across the nation." 121 Cong.Rec. S7974 (daily ed. May 13, 1975) (remarks of Sen. Buckley). [8] One study of record-keeping practices of school districts in various parts of the country found that:[9]

> Within many school systems, few provisions are made to protect school records from examination by unauthorized school personnel.
>
> Information about both pupils and their parents is often collected by schools without the informed consent of either children or their parents. Where consent is obtained for the collection of information for one purpose, the same information is often used subsequently for other purposes.

[8.] The remarks by Senator Buckley consist of a speech given by the Senator to the Legislative Conference of the National Congress of Parents and Teachers on March 12, 1975, in which he discussed the 1974 Act. On May 13, 1975, Senator Buckley inserted the text of his remarks in the Congressional Record.

[9.] Section 438(a)(1) of the 1974 Act deals with access to student records, providing in part:
 (a)(1)(A) No funds shall be made available under any applicable program to any educational agency or institution which has a policy of denying, or which effectively prevents, the parents of students who are or have been in attendance at a school of such agency or at such institution, as the case may be, the right to inspect and review the education records of their children. If any material or document in the education record of a student includes information on more than one student, the parents of one of such students shall have the right to inspect and review only such part of such material or document as relates to such student or to be informed of the specific information contained in such part of such material. Each educational agency or institution shall establish appropriate procedures for the granting of a request by parents for access to the education records of their children within a reasonable period of time, but in no case more than forty-five days after the request has been made.

Access to pupil records by non-school personnel and representatives of outside agencies is, for the most part, handled on an ad hoc basis. Formal policies governing access by law-enforcement officials, the courts, potential employers, colleges, researchers and others do not exist in most school systems.

Sensitive and intimate information collected in the course of teacher-pupil or counselor-pupil contacts is not protected from subpoena by formal authority in most states.

121 Cong.Rec. S7974 (daily ed. May 13, 1975). [10]

It is obvious, however, that the 1974 Act does not provide a privilege against disclosure of student records. The statute says nothing about the existence of a school-student privilege analogous to a doctor-patient or attorney-client privilege. Rather, by threatening financial sanctions, it seeks to deter schools from adopting policies of releasing student records. Moreover, a school is not subject to sanctions because it discloses "personally identifiable information" if it does so in compliance with a judicial order. Yet inquiry cannot end here because, although the 1974 Act does not by its terms limit discovery of school records under the Federal Rules of Civil Procedure, the Congressional policy expressed in this provision places a significantly heavier burden on a party seeking access to student records to justify disclosure than exists with respect to discovery of other kinds of information, such as business records. The remarks of Senator Buckley, quoted previously, emphasize strongly that students have substantial privacy and confidentiality interests in their school records, *see also* Sen.Rep.No.93-1026, 93rd Cong., 2nd Sess. 186-88, *reprinted in* [1974] U.S.Code Cong. & Admin.News, pp. 425-51, and that "there [is] clear evidence of frequent, even systematic violations of the privacy of students and parents by the schools through the unauthorized collection of sensitive personal information and the unauthorized, inappropriate release of personal data to various individuals and organizations." 121 Cong.Rec. S7975 (daily ed. May 13, 1975). These privacy violations are no less objectionable simply because release of the records is obtained pursuant to judicial approval unless, before approval is given, the party seeking disclosure is required to demonstrate a genuine need for the information that outweighs the privacy interest of the students. *See* Sen.Rep.No.93-1026, 93rd Cong., 2nd Sess. 187, *reprinted in* [1974] U.S.Code Cong. & Admin.News, p. 4251. [11]

[10.] This study was conducted by the Russell Sage Foundation in the late 1960's. The above-quoted remarks, according to Senator Buckley, represent the conclusions of a conference of prominent educators, lawyers and social scientists. 121 Cong.Rec. S7974 (daily ed. May 13, 1975).

[11.] This section of the limited legislative history of the 1974 Act provides in part:
    In approving this provision concerning the privacy of information about students, the conferees are very concerned to assure that requests for information associated with evaluations of Federal education programs do not invade the privacy of students or pose any threat of psychological damage to them. At the same time, the amendment is not meant to deny the Federal government the information it needs to carry out the evaluations, as is clear from the sections of the amendment which give the Comptroller General and the Secretary of HEW access to otherwise private information about students. The need to protect students' rights must be balanced against legitimate Federal needs for information.

In the present case, the plaintiffs have shown such a need. If the educational treatment of Hispanic children in Patchogue-Medford violates Title VI standards, it nonetheless would be impossible to prove unless the plaintiffs could trace the progress of the individual students. The need for records of individual student progress is particularly acute where the allegations concern the school district's methods of identifying language deficiency and evaluating the progress of students receiving bilingual training. It is impossible to determine, for example, if a student's English language problems were overlooked when he entered the school system unless examination is made of his subsequent academic progress and of the results of any language tests that were administered to him.

Furthermore, this action seeks to enforce Title VI of the 1964 Civil Rights Act and related regulations, as well as the fourteenth amendment. If the action had been brought by HEW, instead of the present plaintiffs, there is little doubt that government officials would have access to the school records. Section 438(b)(3) of the 1974 Act gives the Secretary of HEW access to student or other records in connection with the audit and evaluation of Federally-supported education programs, *or in connection with the enforcement of the Federal legal requirements which relate to such programs.* 20 U.S.C. § 1232g(b)(3) (Supp. IV, 1974) (emphasis supplied). *See* Sen.Rep. No.93-1026, 93rd Cong., 2nd Sess. 187, *reprinted in* [1974] U.S.Code Cong. & Admin. News, p. 4251. Moreover, on June 17, 1976, the Department of Health, Education, and Welfare issued final guidelines on the 1974 Act. These guidelines require, *inter alia*, that

(a) Nothing in section 438 of the Act or this part shall preclude authorized representatives of officials listed in § 99.31(a)(3) [12] from having access to student and other records which may be necessary in connection with the audit and evaluation of Federally supported education programs, or in connection with *the enforcement of or compliance with the Federal legal*

[12.] Section 99.31(a) of 45 C.F.R., 41 Fed.Reg. 24673 (1976) provides in part:

§ 99.31 *Prior consent for disclosure not required.*

(a) An educational agency or institution may disclose personally identifiable information from the education records of a student without the written consent of the parent of the student or the eligible student if the disclosure is—

(1) To other school officials, including teachers, within the educational institution or local educational agency who have been determined by the agency or institution to have legitimate educational interests;

(2) To officials of another school or school system in which the student seeks or intends to enroll, subject to the requirements set forth in § 99.34;

(3) Subject to the conditions set forth in § 99.35, to authorized representatives of:

(i) The Comptroller General of the United States,

(ii) The Secretary,

(iii) The Commissioner, the Director of the National Institute of Education, or the Assistant Secretary for Education, or

(iv) State educational authorities;

(4) In connection with financial aid for which a student has applied or which a student has received . . . .

(6) To organizations conducting studies for, or on behalf of, educational agencies or institutions for the purpose of developing, validating, or administering predictive tests, administering student aid programs, and improving instruction; *Provided,* That the studies are conducted

requirements which relate to these programs. 41 Fed.Reg.24674 (1976) (to be codified at 45 C.F.R. § 99.35(a)) (emphasis supplied) (footnote added). Thus, a school or school district could not rely on § 438 to avoid disclosure to government officials of information that might reveal its noncompliance with Title VI and related regulations. It follows that, in view of the significant role of private lawsuits in ending various forms of discrimination in school systems, § 438 should not serve as a cloak for alleged discriminatory practices simply because litigation to end such practices is initiated by private plaintiffs rather than the government.

Since we find plaintiffs are entitled to the student records that are the subject of this motion, the next issue is the right of the parents and students to receive notice and to make individual objections. Section 438 directs that an educational institution under judicial order to disclose student records must notify the parents and students of the order prior to compliance. The type of notice required, however, will depend on the circumstances of each case. The new HEW guidelines state that an educational institution may disclose personally identifiable information pursuant to judicial order provided it

> makes a *reasonable effort* to notify the parent of the student or
> the eligible student of the order or subpoena in advance of com-
> pliance therewith. . . .

41 Fed.Reg. 24673 (1976) (to be codified at 45 C.F.R. § 99.31(a)(9)) (emphasis supplied). Thus, where exceptionally large numbers of students are involved, it may be enough for a school or school district to publish the notice in a newspaper. This view is supported by a letter written on February 19, 1975, by the Assistant General Counsel for Education, Department of Health, Education and Welfare to the Department's General Counsel, describing the response to a query concerning § 438(b)(2)'s notice requirement.

(1) there is no legislative history as to whether publication would be adequate in the above-described circumstances; (2) we could not say as a matter of law that direct personal notice would be required in every case, absent regulations on the point; (3) however, at a minimum, some showing would have to be made that publication would be likely to reach the parents of the students, many of whom would presumably be of limited English-speaking ability; (4) the adequacy of the notice would depend on how reasonable it was under the circumstances.

---

in a manner which will not permit the personal identification of students and their parents by individuals other than representatives of the organization and the information will be destroyed when no longer needed for the purposes for which the study was conducted; the term "organization" includes, but is not limited to, Federal, State and local agencies, and independent organizations;

(7) To accrediting organizations in order to carry out their accrediting functions;

(8) To parents of a dependent student, as defined in section 152 of the Internal Revenue Code of 1954;

(9) To comply with a judicial order or lawfully issued subpoena; *Provided*, That the educational agency or institution makes a reasonable effort to notify the parent of the student or the eligible student of the order or subpoena in advance of compliance therewith; and

(10) To appropriate parties in a health or safety emergency subject to the conditions set forth in § 99.36.

In this case, involving several hundred students, appropriate notice could not be effected either by publication or by mail. The notice must be in both Spanish and English *see* Fed.Reg. 24672 (1976) (to be codified at 45 C.F.R. § 99.6(b)),[13] and it must describe the nature of this action, the parties, and the nature of the information that will be disclosed as a result of this court's order. In addition, the parents must be informed that on or before a date specified in the notice, prior to disclosure, they may bring to this court's attention any reasons why disclosure of their child's records should not be allowed.

We add this last requirement even though § 438(b)(2) does not mention the parents' right to a hearing. Under § 438(a)(2) of the 1974 Act, 20 U.S.C. § 1232g(a)(2) (Supp. IV, 1974),[14] however, which deals with the right of parents and students to inspect student records, provision is made for a hearing to challenge the content of the records in order to correct misleading or inaccurate data. Obviously, the right to inspect student records for inappropriate information is useless without an opportunity to contest the existence of such data in the record. It seems equally pointless to inform parents of the imminent disclosure of their childrens' records without affording at least some opportunity to contest the disclosure. We do not think Congress intended the right to notice of disclosure of school records to be less meaningful than the right to inspect for erroneous data.[15]

[13.] Section 99.6 of 45 C.F.R., 41 Fed.Reg.24671-72 (1976), provides as follows:
§ 99.6 *Annual notification of rights.*
   (a)   Each educational agency or institution shall give parents of students in attendance or eligible students in attendance at the agency or institution annual notice by such means as are reasonably likely to inform them of the following:
   (1)   Their rights under section 438 of the Act, the regulations in this part, and the policy adopted under § 99.5; the notice shall also inform parents of students or eligible students of the locations where copies of the policy may be obtained; and
   (2)   The right to file complaints under § 99.63 concerning alleged failures by the educational agency or institution to comply with the requirements of section 438 of the Act and this part.
   (b)   Agencies and institutions of elementary and secondary education shall provide for the need to effectively notify parents of students identified as having a primary or home language other than English.
[14.] Section 438(a)(2) provides as follows:
   (2)   No funds shall be made available under any applicable program to any educational agency or institution unless the parents of students who are or have been in attendance at a school of such agency or at such institution are provided an opportunity for a hearing by such agency or institution in accordance with regulations of the Secretary, to challenge the content of such student's education records, in order to insure that the records are not inaccurate, misleading, or otherwise in violation of the privacy or other rights of students, and to provide an opportunity for the correction or deletion of any such inaccurate, misleading, or otherwise inappropriate data contained therein and to insert into such records a written explanation of the parents respecting the content of such records.
[15.]   On the other hand, it does not follow that, in providing parents and students an opportunity to contest disclosure, we should adopt the sophisticated procedure suggested by HEW for challenging the existence of allegedly erroneous data in school records. For example, the HEW guidelines published in 41 Fed.Reg. 24673 (1976) (to be codified at 45 C.F.R. § 99.22)) envision an adversary proceeding including, if the parent or student desire, representation by counsel. In the context of a discovery proceeding under the federal rules, it should be sufficient that the parent or student has the opportunity to present to the court any specific reasons why disclosure of student records is undesirable or harmful to the student or his parents. This presentation should be in writing, particularly where the discovery involves large numbers of student records. . . .

BURDEN ON THE DEFENDANTS

The final objection of the defendants is that, even if the 1974 Act allows disclosure of identifying data in student records, compliance with a court order granting the requests for discovery places intolerable burdens on the school district. In the opinion of the defendants, the notice requirement, which would be the responsibility of the school district, will generate "great dissension and unrest" among parents. Moreover, the defendants claim that "[b]ecause of the multiplicity of records which reveal names or identities of students which are sought by plaintiffs, it would be onerous, burdensome and a practical impossibility to require the school district to devise some method to conceal the names of individual students by substituting numbers or some other coded identification because of the mass of documents involved." (Memorandum in Opposition to Plaintiffs' Motion to Compel Discovery, at 8).

Section 438 of the 1974 Act does not require an educational agency to conceal the names of individual students as part of an authorized disclosure of school records. Data collected by authorized representatives of HEW in connection with the enforcement of federal legal requirements, under § 438(b)(3), must be protected

> in a manner which will not permit the personal identification of students and their parents by other than those officials, and such personally identifiable data shall be destroyed when no longer needed. . . .

20 U.S.C. § 1232g(b)(3) (Supp. IV, 1974). *See* 41 Fed. Reg.24673 (1976) (to be codified in 45 C.F.R. § 99.31(a)(6)); 41 Fed.Reg. 24674 (1976) (to be codified in 45 C.F.R. § 99.35(b)). Although § 438(b)(2) does not mention the need for a protective procedure when disclosure to a private party is directed by court order, it would seem sensible to require in the disclosure order that the recipients of the student records avoid revealing the data to individuals unconnected with the litigation and destroy the data when it is no longer needed. But it is neither required nor necessary that the defendants redact the names of the students from the records and substitute neutral identifying information. Thus, this aspect of defendant's objections on grounds of burdensomeness is without merit.

The defendants' objection that the notice requirement creates an unreasonable administrative burden must be rejected for several reasons. In the first place, as mentioned earlier, under HEW guidelines the school district is only required to make a reasonable effort to notify parents of impending disclosure. Notice in this case can be effected by publication or other reasonable method chosen by the school district. Second, in class actions that seek to vindicate civil rights guaranteed by the Constitution or federal statute the cost or inconvenience to a party is less weighty a factor than in other cases since there is a substantial public interest in enforcing these rights. *See Burns v. Thiokol Corp.*, 483 F.2d 300, 304-05 (5th Cir. 1973); *Rios v. Enterprise Ass'n Steamfitters, Local 638,* 4 E.P.D. ¶¶7553, 7792 (S.D.N.Y.1971), *Cf. Parents Committee of Public School 19 v. Community School Board, N.Y.,* 524 F.2d 1138, 1143 (2d Cir. 1975) (action under Bilingual Education Act, 20 U.S.C. § 880b *et seq.* (Supp. IV, 1974)); *Maritime Cinema Service Corp. v.*

Movies En Route, Inc., 60 F.R.D. 587, 592 (S.D.N.Y.1973) (antitrust); *Rockaway Pix Theatre, Inc. v. Metro-Goldwyn-Mayer, Inc.,* 36 F.R.D. 15 (E.D.N.Y.1964) (Mishler, Ch. J.) (antitrust). Finally, even judged by the standards applicable to discovery in non-civil rights cases, the administrative burden on the defendants is not so great as to justify denying the plaintiffs relevant information. *See generally 4 Moore's Federal Practice* ¶ 26.56[1] (1976).

For these reasons, the plaintiffs' motion to compel answers to interrogatories is granted. Defendants are directed to respond, consistent with this opinion, to interrogatories Nos. 12, 33, 51, 56, 59, 60, and document requests Nos. 3, 17 and 18. Reasonable notice must be provided to the parents of the children whose names will be disclosed. . . .

APPENDIX

NOTICE TO PARENTS OF PUERTO RICAN AND OTHER HISPANIC STUDENTS WHO ATTEND OR HAVE ATTENDED SCHOOL IN THE PATCHOGUE–MEDFORD DISTRICT

The Puerto Rican and other Hispanic students and their parents named above have sued the Patchogue-Medford School District in federal court. The plaintiffs represent Puerto Rican and Hispanic children who are unable to benefit from their courses because of problems in understanding the English language. They claim that officials of the school district failed to provide adequate programs and qualified teachers for the bilingual education department. The school district denies the charges.

The plaintiffs seek to obtain evidence that they believe will support their case, including information contained in the records of Puerto Rican and Hispanic students. In response to a law called the Family Educational and Privacy Act of 1974, the federal court has ruled that, while the plaintiffs are entitled to examine these records, the parents first must be given an opportunity to object to disclosure of their children's records.

If no objections are made to disclosure, the information in the school records will be used only at the trial. During the trial, there should be no need to identify your child by name, address or parents. The law requires that personally identifiable data be destroyed when no longer needed.

The court will imply that you consent to disclosure of information in your children's school records unless you send a letter to the court indicating why you feel such disclosure would be harmful to you or your children. The letter must be received by the court before March 18, 1977, or you may appear in person on that day in Courtroom No. 5, in the federal courthouse in Brooklyn (see address below).

NOTES

1. The court in Rios v. Read states that "the Congressional policy expressed in [the Buckley Amendment] places a significantly heavier burden on a party seeking access to student records to justify disclosure than exists with respect to discovery of other kinds of information, such as business records." Nevertheless, it has been held that student records may be disclosed in appropriate circumstances and especially if needed as evidence in a criminal proceeding. See: In Re Grand Jury Subpoena Served N.Y. Law School 448 F. Sup. 822 (S.D.N.Y. 1978) and State v. Birdsall, 568 P.2d 1094 (Ariz. App., 1977). The privacy rights of the student may sometimes require *in camera* disclosure of the student record, or individual names may be deleted in subpoenaed student records, *see* Mattie T. v. Johnston, 74 F.R.D. 498 (N.D. Miss. 1976).

2. In addition to being a violation of statutory rights, a university's improper disclosure of a student's record may raise a claim under a state constitutional right of privacy. *See:* Porten v. University of San Francisco, 64 Cal. App. 3d 827, 134 Cal. Rptr. 389 (1976).

3. In *Rios v. Read,* the court permitted a class action by private plaintiffs but did not deal with the issue of whether the Buckley Amendment authorizes a private right of action. However, in Girardier v. Webster College, 563 F.2d 1267 (8th Cir. 1977), the court ruled that there was no private right of action under the Buckley Amendment.

4. As the *Rios* case indicates, the Family Educational Rights and Privacy Act was offered on the floor of Congress as an amendment to another educational bill. As a consequence, no legislative committee hearings and reports were made and, at the time, the educational community had no opportunity to respond to the proposed bill. Not surprisingly, a number of education administrators have expressed strong dissatisfaction with the Buckley Amendment. Typical of some of this criticism in the testimony given to The Privacy Protection Study Commission on November 11, 1976 by Gerald K. Bogin, former Vice President for Student Affairs at the University of Oregon:

> . . . Among those deliberative institutions in this society of ours the protection of privacy, a fundamental aspect of human dignity, should be cherished in the academic community. My experience suggests that privacy is cherished both in its lofty ideals and also in practice. However, I have an obligation to communicate to you that this history of the enactment of this legislation—or perhaps more appropriately—the lack of history and the attendant confusion and chaos created by our attempts to implement Public Law 93-380, the "Buckley Amendment," and its Regulations, have created problems more serious than those purported ills which were presumed to exist in American higher education before November of 1974. . . .

The current FERPA Regulations are a response to an impossible task. Congress in an unprecedented action intruded into the affairs of the colleges and universities of this country without even the courtesy of discussion. The legislative history on this legislation is embarrassingly meager. Officials within HEW have been helpful, they have been creative and as responsive as possible within the limitations imposed by the legislation. The uproar created throughout the country over these last two years is ample evidence that something is awry. I have not talked to any educational official who would deny that the issue of privacy is important; I have not talked to an educational official who was not in sympathy with the spirit of the legislation; I have not talked to an educational official who is content with the results, however, the human and monetary costs have been immense. I am not aware that any cost-benefit analyses were or have been conducted relative to the Family Educational Rights and Privacy Act. When I learn that Ohio State University spent $250,000 in an attempt to come into compliance, when I note that in 1974 Harvard University spent 60,000 staff hours on this effort, when I review my own activities and the activities of my staff for the last several years, I can only conclude that whatever benefits have accrued through this legislation, the benefits are vastly outweighed by the costs both in actual dollars and human agony which have been visited upon us. . . .

What I would suggest you consider is recommending repeal of the Family Educational Rights and Privacy Act and replacing it—if federal action is felt to be necessary—by legislation which would explicate the minimum requirements of an adequate policy. Such legislation should, for example, require institutions to publish their records policies, it should give students the right of inspection and correction, and hearings should be permitted to guarantee at least minimum due process rights. I would not recommend promulgation of anything more than the basic rudiments of an adequate policy. These few criteria could be written on the back of an envelope over coffee. I would urge that even this legislation not be enacted without adequate prior discussion with the higher education community. I would then place the burden on each higher education institution to develop its own policies which would be consistent with the legislation enacted, existing state legislation, and the peculiar character of the individual campus. There is really, in my judgment, no other alternative. It is an impossible, futile and very dangerous task to try and regulate all of the higher education institutions we have found in this country with this kind of legalistic rigidity.

Do you agree with this criticism? If so, how would you propose to amend the Act?

5. For some good commentaries on the FERPA, *see* Schatken, *Student Records at Institutions of Postsecondary Education: Selected Issues under the Family Educational Rights and Privacy Act of 1974,* 4 J. Coll. & U.L. 147 (1977); Note, *Federal Genesis of Comprehensive Protection of Student Educational Record Rights: The Family Educational Rights and Privacy Act of 1974,* 61 Iowa L.Rev. 74 (1975); Note, *The Buckley Amendment: Opening School Files for Student and Parental Review,* 24 Cath. U.L.Rev. 588 (1975). *See also* Project, *Government Information and the Rights of Citizens,* 73 Mich. L. Rev. 971 (1975), for a comprehensive survey of laws relating to government records and individual rights to privacy.

CHAPTER 22

STUDENT LOANS

I. Introduction

Government loan programs to benefit graduate students in specialized fields have been in effect since the years of the Second World War. Title II of the National Defense Education Act of 1958 (20 U.S.C. §§421-429, 1958), however, represented the first major commitment of federal funds to a program designed to make low interest loans available to large numbers of postsecondary students in need of finanacial assistance to continue their education. The terms of Title II provided for federal contributions of up to 90 per cent to loan funds which would be supplemented and administered by the institutions which the students attended. Not surprisingly, since the goals of the NDEA were closely tied to national defense, preference was originally given to borrowers with ability and interest in mathematics, science, engineering, and modern foreign languages. Among the terms of the act were "forgiveness" features providing for the cancellation of portions of the loan if the student followed his education with a teaching stint in public elementary or secondary schools.

In the mid-1960s Congress responded to the increasing financial pressure on low- and middle-income families faced with the rising costs of higher education by creating the Guaranteed Student Loan Program (also known as the Federal Insured Student Loan Program). Title IV of the Higher Education Act of 1965 (20 U.S.C. §§1071-1085, 1965) was designed to encourage loans to students from sources other than the federal government, including private financial institutions, state agencies, and the colleges, universities, and vocational schools which the students attended. Under the provisions of Title IV, the federal government or a corresponding state agency would insure long-term, low-interest student loans against default and pay interest supplements to the lending institutions. In addition, students whose families' adjusted annual income was less than $15,000 qualified for an interest subsidy while they were in school.

While the major outlines of the federal loan programs have remained the same over the years, new legislation has accompanied Congress' changing perception of the educational needs of the nation and the financial difficulties of students and their families. Appropriations for both programs have periodically been increased. As part of the Education Amendments of 1972, the NDEA loan provisions were recast as the National Direct Student Loan Program (20 U.S.C. 1087aa-1087ff, 1972), with new forgiveness features that recognized the need to encourage teachers of handicapped, disadvantaged, and preschool children. In 1972 and again under the Education Amendments of 1976 (20 U.S.C. 1088f-1(a) 1976), the Commissioner of Education was given greater authority to regulate and investigate the academic institutions which ultimately received the funds loaned to students under the GSLP. Income criteria for students qualifying for interest subsidies were relaxed under the Education Amendments of 1972 and finally removed under the terms of the Middle Income Student Assistance Act of 1978 (P.L.95-566, 1978).

Thus, by the late 1970s the federal government was allocating over $300 million a year to the National Direct Student Loan Program. More than $11 billion had been lent to students by other private and public agencies since the creation of the GSLP in 1965. Behind these billions of dollars, a complex web of legal relationships had developed among student borrowers, the educational institutions they attended, a variety of lending agencies, and the federal and state governments.

II. NDEA Loans and the Loyalty Oath

Following the enactment of the loan and grant provisions of the National Defense Education Act of 1958, a swirl of controversy arose regarding their loyalty oath and affidavit requirements. Section 1001(f) of Title X, 20 U.S.C. 581(f) read:

No part of any funds appropriated or otherwise made available for expenditure under authority of this Act shall be used to make payments or loans to any individual unless such individual (1) has executed and filed with the Commissioner an affidavit that he does not believe in, and is not a member of and does not support any organization that believes in or teaches, the overthrow of the United States Government by force or violence or by any illegal or unconstitutional methods, and (2) has taken and subscribed to an oath or affirmation in the following form: "I do solemnly swear (or affirm) that I will bear true faith and allegiance to the United States of America and will support and defend the Constitution and laws of the United States against all its enemies, foreign and domestic."

In protest over this section, several colleges and universities refused to participate in the program; more withdrew soon after it began. Other schools as well as individuals and organizations concerned with education expressed their displeasure in petitions, newspaper editorials, and letters to Congress. Criticism centered largely around the disclaimer affidavit. The issues are apparent in a letter from the American Association of University Professors introduced into the Congressional Record by Senator Wayne Morse on February 16, 1959 (105 Cong. Rec. 2364), and remarks made on the Senate floor on June 15, 1960 by Senator Thomas Dodd of Connecticut (106 Cong. Rec. 12666-68). The AAUP letter read as follows:

A Letter Sent to Members of the Senate Labor and Public Welfare Committee and the House Education and Labor Committee by the Officers of the American Association of University Professors

November 1, 1958.

Dear ——————: The American Association of University Professors has in mind petitioning the Senate Committee on Labor and Public Welfare of the 86th Congress to reconsider the requirement of section 1001(f), title X, of the National Defense Education Act of 1958, which reads:

"No * * * funds * * * shall be used to make payments or loans to any individual unless such individual (1) has executed and filed with the Commissioner an affidavit that he does not believe in, and is not a member of and does not support any organization that believes in or teaches the overthrow of the United States Government by force or violence or by any illegal or unconstitutional methods."

This disclaimer requirement, which will apply to large numbers of young people seeking loans, fellowships and grants to carry on their education, and to many teachers and to consulting experts, seems thoroughly harmful. It singles out persons in education as objects of suspicion; it imposes a "test oath" repugnant to our traditions; and it exposes those signing the affidavit to the possibility of perjury prosecutions resting on vague allegations or improper and intimidating inquiries about their conduct and their beliefs. * * *

The American Association of University Professors believes that the requirement which it opposes is subject to the following specific objections:

1. Vagueness: A person required to execute a disclaimer statement is given no guidance as to the organizations which are of the designated variety, and no definition of the support to such organizations which he must disclaim. We submit that it is a denial of the due process of law to compel an individual to gauge his conduct by such vague criteria, when criminal liability may turn on his action.

2. Unconstitutionality of the substance of the disclaimer: There is ground for grave question concerning the validity of requiring a disclaimer of the sort specified in the act, as a condition of enjoying governmental benefits. The justification which a majority of the U.S. Supreme Court held to be present with relation to the requirement of the Labor-Management Relations Act involved in *American Communications Association* v. *Douds*, 339 U.S. 382, is of doubtful applicability here. Moreover, the provision here in question is not in terms limited to knowing support of the specified type of organization; without such a limitation, the provision probably falls under condemnation of the view of the U.S. Supreme Court in *Wieman* v. *Updegraff*, 344 U.S. 183.

It is difficult to leave unquestioned legislation which borders so closely on unconstitutionality in a first amendment area, and which may well overstep the line.

3. The invidiousness of the requirement: A disclaimer requirement or test oath by its nature cannot fail to be invidious. If an individual refuses to sign, he raises a suspicion that he is unworthy of public trust or benefit. If he signs, he endorses the pertinency of the general suspicion about him and his kind which is embodied in the requirement. Social safeguards should be directed to specific dangers; they should not, as in this instance, take the form of inescapable and unwarranted derogatory implications directed toward a whole class of persons and all its members. . . .

Some of the remarks made by Senator Dodd are as follows:

I believe the Government has a legitimate right to require a disclaimer affidavit if it serves a sufficient purpose. Nor do I believe that students ought to feel abused, or put upon, or maligned, or discriminated against if they are asked to sign such an affidavit as one of the qualifications for receiving valuable public benefits. I believe that if they approached their Government for help in the proper spirit of humility and allegiance, they would be able to sign such an affidavit without any grave misgivings. But there is something about this affidavit which seems to me to violate good taste. It is unnecessarily officious.

For these reasons, I will support the elimination of this affidavit. But in doing so, I would also like to point out my opposition to a number of arguments which have been brought forth against the loyalty oath and the affidavit which, in my judgment, do not hold water.

These arguments are used interchangeably against both the oath of allegiance and the disclaimer affidavit. . . .

I am fairly well convinced that, in the present situation some of those who are behind the present proposal to repeal only the disclaimer affidavit really desire later to do away with the oath of allegiance and will attempt to do so when they think they can get away with that. . . .

Does section 1001(f) of this bill constitute an invasion of academic freedom? If it does, the only implication to be drawn from this assertion is that the U. S. Government has no right to ask a student to affirm loyalty or to renounce any ideology whatever, or any organization whatever, as a condition for participation in Government-sponsored programs. I reject this interpretation of academic freedom. Under appropriate circumstances, the Government has every right to require of a student, a teacher, or anyone else a pledge of loyalty and an assurance of opposition to those forces that would destroy our Government by force or violence. This is a basic allegiance from which no American is exempt.

The educators who have written to me on this subject generally take the position that the student's right to inquire freely, to satisfy his intellectual curiosity, to criticize his political system, is challenged by the loyalty oath and the affidavit. I think this argument is specious. Freedom of inquiry is not even remotely at issue here. The student who presently signs up under the national defense education loan program has the same academic freedom as all other students. He may inquire into anything he chooses; he may satisfy his intellectual curiosity to the full; he may criticize his Government to his heart's content. But as a willing participant in a Government program aimed at strengthening the Nation's defense, he must be willing to affirm basic loyalty to our country and certify his opposition to treasonable acts against it. . . .

Another argument made is the assertion that this act involves discrimination against the educational community. It is said that no other programs involving the extension of Government benefits require a loyalty oath and a disclaimer of disloyalty and that to level this requirement at the educational community alone is discriminatory and points the finger of suspicion at education.

There are three answers to this assertion. The first is that the aid given under the National Defense Education Act is not to be equated with other general Federal aid programs. In this instance, the educational community is treated differently because the nature of this program is different. The object of this program as I have said repeatedly before is, "to insure trained manpower of sufficient quality and quantity to meet the defense needs of the United States. . . ."

The second answer to the charge that this act is discriminatory against education is that there is a sound reason for the distinction between what is required of the beneficiary under the National Defense Education Act as opposed to the requirements of beneficiaries of the farm program, the FHA program, and the social security program which are most commonly cited as comparable examples.

Participation in the social security program requires a complete disclosure of one's income status and compulsory taxation irrespective of the wishes of the person involved.

Participation in the farm support program requires the farmer to put up his crop as collateral for the loan the Government gives him.

In the case of the FHA beneficiary, his house is collateral.

No such requirement is made of the student. The only collateral that the Government can hope for from him is his good faith, his loyalty, his patriotism, his devotion to the country which is educating him in the interests of its own defense. . . .

The third response to this point of discrimination is that in the field of education, unlike that of the farm program or the social security program or the housing program, a person's basic philosophy is of necessity a crucial element. Whether the farmer or the homeowner or the social security beneficiary as such is dedicated to our concept of government is irrelevant to the success of those particular programs. But whether the man or woman who is educated to enhance the contributions he can make to the defense of his country is loyal is of fundamental importance. . . .

Then we have the argument that this act discriminates against the needy students by setting up a double standard which requires loyalty oaths of the needy but leaves the other exempt and undefiled. This is rather a laughable argument coming from those supposedly trained in logic. It could be said with just as much sense that the Government sets up a double standard and discriminates against a large body of students when it finances the education of some and does not finance the education of others. The use of the word "discrimination" in this context obviously refers to the dictionary definition "an unfair or injurious distinction." It is a symptom of something seriously wrong with a segment of our educational community that they should protest against an oath of allegiance to their Government and a renunciation of its enemies on the grounds that it demeans such a student by requiring him to perform an odious, unfair, and injurious act.

Is it not truer to say that the Government under this act singles out the needy student in order to help him? Is it not truer to say that it singles him out for benefits rather than burdens, for preferment rather than mistreatment? And that the loyalty oath is merely an obvious necessity arising from this preferment?

The only group discriminating against the needy student so far as this issue is concerned are those few colleges which have abolished the loan program by which the needy students might have received an education in the college of their choice.

NOTES

1. Section 1001(f) should be understood in terms of the Cold War atmosphere which was prevalent in the late 1950s. The NDEA, which was enacted in the wake of American consternation over the launching of Sputnik, was itself conceived of as a weapon in the technological race against the U.S.S.R. The House Report accompanying the bill noted, "H.R. 13247 is designed to help our educational system meet the grave challenge of our time. Although the bill embraces a variety of approaches, its central purpose is to encourage improvement in the quality of education particularly with respect to those aspects which are most important now to national defense." H.R. Rep. No. 2157, 85th Cong., 2nd Sess. 2, reprinted in [1958] U.S. Code & Ad. News 4731, 4732.

2. The Supreme Court continued debating the constitutionality of loyalty oaths long after 1958. Many questions are worth asking in considering these provisions of the NDEA. Is an NDEA loan a right or a privilege? Should that distinction make a difference in assessing the constitutionality of the oath and affidavit requirements? Does the dis-

claimer pass the overbreadth test of Keyishian v. Board of Regents, 385 U.S. 589 (1967), which held that an affidavit requirement was invalid if it sanctioned "[m]ere knowing membership without a specific intent to further the unlawful aims of an organization"? 385 U.S. at 606. Does the oath meet the standard of constitutionality set forth in Cole v. Richardson, 405 U.S. 676, 686 (1972): "Since there is no constitutionally protected right to overthrow a government by force, violence, or illegal or unconstitutional means, no constitutional right is infringed by an oath to abide by the constitutional system in the future"?

3. For a contemporary viewpoint largely favorable to the provisions of § 1001(f), see Costanzo, *Loyalty Oath Affidavit,* 37 U. Det. L. J. 718 (1960). Later history of the oath can be found in Garsaud, *National Defense Education Act, Title II–Student Loan Program–Moving Toward the End of the First Decade,* 14 Loyola L. Rev. 79, 94-98 (1967-68). Loyalty oaths for faculty are discussed in Chapter 6.

4. In 1962 the affidavit, but not the oath, was eliminated from the act. See 20 U.S.C. 581 (f) (1) (1978).

III.   Guaranteed Student Loan Program: The Rights of the Parties

A.   The Student-Borrower and the School-Lender

DE JESUS CHAVEZ v. LTV AEROSPACE CORPORATION
United States District Court, N.D. Texas
412 F.Supp. 4 (1976)

MEMORANDUM OPINION AND ORDER
WILLIAM M. TAYLOR, Jr., Chief Judge.

Defendants LTV Aerospace Corporation and LTV Education Systems, Inc., have filed a motion to dismiss plaintiff's complaint for a) lack of subject matter jurisdiction, b) failure to state a claim upon which relief can be granted, and c) failure to allege the existence of necessary facts to comply with Rule 23, Federal Rules of Civil Procedure, with respect to plaintiff's class action allegations. . . .

Plaintiff, bringing this suit on her own behalf and on behalf of all others similarly situated, alleges that defendants violated 20 U.S.C. § 1071, *et seq.,* the Higher Education Act of 1965, which governs the terms and conditions of the federally insured student loan program. Plaintiff alleges that defendants charged plaintiffs for items not authorized by the statutes and regulations promulgated pursuant thereto; that defendants charged plaintiffs sums not applied to their tuition but rather passed on to the lenders, and that these charges exceeded the maximum interest rate allowable for their student loans; and that defendants passed on the costs of making the loan to plaintiffs in the form of higher tuition charges or otherwise in violation of the federal statutes. . . .

The basic issue to be decided is whether or not a private cause of action was created or exists under the terms of 20 U.S.C. § § 1071, et seq. While § 1082(a) provides for suits to be brought by or against the Commissioner of Health, Education and Welfare, neither the statutory language nor the legislative history provides an answer to the specific question at bar. Moreover, it appears that this is a case of first impression in the courts. Both parties have drawn analogies to other statutes which are silent with regard to the maintenance of a private cause of action. Some cases have interpreted various of these statutes as providing a private cause of action. *Gibson v. First Federal Savings and Loan Assoc. of Detroit*, 504 F.2d 826 (6th Cir. 1974), and *Partain v. First National Bank of Montgomery*, 467 F.2d 167 (5th Cir. 1972); and other cases have interpreted other similar statutes as not creating a private cause of action, *National Railroad Passenger Corp. v. National Association of Railroad Passengers*, 414 U.S. 453, 94 S.Ct. 690, 38 L.Ed. 2d 646 (1974) and *Cort v. Ash*, 422 U.S. 66, 95 S.Ct. 2080, 45 L.Ed.2d 26 (1975).

The Court is of the opinion that the proper statutory analysis is set out in *Cort v. Ash, ibid*. Justice Brennan, writing for a unanimous Court, stated that several factors are relevant in determining whether a private remedy is implicit in a statute not expressly providing one:

First, is the plaintiff "one of the class for whose *especial* benefit the statute was enacted," *Texas & Pacific Railroad Co. v. Rigsby*, 241 U.S. 33, 39 [36 S.Ct. 482, 484, 60 L.Ed. 874] (1916) (emphasis supplied)—that is, does the statute create a federal right in favor of the plaintiff? Second, is there any indication of legislative intent, explicit or implicit, either to create such a remedy or to deny one? See, e. g. *National Railroad Passenger Corp. v. National Association of Railroad Passengers*, 414 U.S. 453, 458, 460 [94 S.Ct. 690, 693, 694, 38 L.Ed.2d 646] (1974) (*Amtrak*). Third, is it consistent with the underlying purposes of the legislative scheme to imply such a remedy for the plaintiff? See, e. g. *Amtrak, supra; Securities Investor Protection Corp. v. Barbour*, 421 U.S. 412 (95 S.Ct. 1733, 44 L.Ed.2d 263]; *Calhoun v. Harvey*, 379 U.S. 134 [85 S.Ct. 292, 13 L.Ed.2d 190] (1964). And finally, is the cause of action one traditionally relegated to state law, in an area basically the concern of the States, so that it would be inappropriate to infer a cause of action based solely on federal law? Id. at 95 S.Ct. 2087-88, 45 L.Ed.2d at 36.

The plaintiff maintains, and the Court agrees, that plaintiff is indeed "one of the class for whose *especial* benefit the statute was enacted." Student borrowers were a primary concern of the Higher Education Act of 1965. The Commissioner of Education is directed, in the Act's Statement of Purpose, 20 U.S.C. § 1071, to encourage the creation of state and private non-profit loan insurance programs, to provide a federal program of student loan insurance for lenders and students without access to state and private non-profit programs, to pay an interest subsidy on qualified loans, and finally, to guarantee portions of certain loans. The entire program is based on the needs of the student borrower and exists for his benefit.

A violation of these regulations by a lending or educational institution works an injury on the class the Act intended to protect. Under the Act, and its regulations, members of the class have a right to be charged with a given interest rate (20 U.S.C. Section 1077(b); 45 C.F.R. Section 177.6(a)), to have their individual loan monies not applied to certain purposes (45 C.F.R. Section 177.6(2)), to have the loan charges limited to given services (45 C.F.R. Section 177.6(d)), and to repay the loan under certain conditions (20 U.S.C. Section 1077(c)). The class is possessed of specific rights in a given field of commerce.

The opinion in *Cort, supra*, 95 S.Ct. at 2090, 45 L.Ed.2d at 39, took notice of such statutory rights in discussing the second factor:

[I]n situations in which it is clear that federal law has granted a class of persons certain rights, it is not necessary to show an intention to *create* a private cause of action, although an explicit purpose to *deny* such cause of action would be controlling. (emphasis original)

Neither the language of the statute nor the legislative history shows an explicit congressional purpose to deny the plaintiff her cause of action. The transaction between the lender and student is regulated by a much broader law than is that of the borrower and lender in the traditional mercantile setting. The rights afforded the student borrower are correspondingly broader. The plaintiff being possessed of statutorily defined rights, the second factor in a *Cort v. Ash* analysis is answered by the undisputed finding that Congress made no explicit attempt to deny jurisdiction.

The third factor of consistency with the underlying purpose of the legislative scheme is achieved by implying a private remedy in the case at bar. The maintenance and regulation of interest subsidies and loan guarantees for student borrowers can and should be advanced by vigorous prosecution of claims such as plaintiff's claim, since obviously the Commissioner cannot investigate and prosecute every violation within his area of expertise.

Violations arising under the federal regulation of commerce are not "traditionally relegated to state law . . . ." *Id.*, 95 S.Ct. at 2088, 45 L.Ed. 2d at 36. Because the student loans are regulated, guaranteed, and, in many cases, subsidized, by the Federal Government, it is appropriate that a Federal forum determine the outcome of the instant claim on the merits. The fourth question asked in *Cort*, therefore, must be answered in favor of implying a private remedy. . . .

B.   The Government and the Private Lender

HICKS v. CALIFANO
United States District Court, N.D. Georgia
450 F.Supp. 278 (1977)

HOOPER, Senior District Judge.

I. STATEMENT OF THE CASE

Plaintiff as Trustee in Bankruptcy for North American Acceptance Corporation, filed a complaint on May 4, 1976 which was amended on November 3, 1976. Said complaint in Three Counts alleged that a contract of insurance existed between North American Acceptance Corporation and the defendants covering certain student loans, and that as a result of default by the borrowers of those loans plaintiff is entitled to Judgment against the United States in the amount of $279,264.31. . . .

The instant suit arose with respect to defendants' federal program of low interest insured loans to students in institutions of higher education pursuant to 20 U.S.C. § 1071, et seq.

In Count One plaintiff alleges the theory of estoppel against the government on the ground that the defendants knew, approved, and accepted the policy of disbursement before stamping "federally insured."

In Count Two plaintiff alleges that the issuance of insurance took place as of July 12, 1971, pursuant to "contract of insurance" signed on that date.

Count Three alleges that the conduct of defendants' agents constitutes an express waiver of the regulation contained in 45 C.F.R. 177.42(b) which provides

. . . unless expressly provided for, no disbursements made on a loan prior to the issuance of insurance shall be covered. . . .

II. GROUNDS ON MOTIONS FOR SUMMARY JUDGMENT

Plaintiff has moved the Court for summary judgment with respect to Count Two of his complaint, and alleges that the execution of a contract of insurance between the Office of Education and N.A.A.C. dated July 12, 1971 constitutes as a matter of law, the "issuance of insurance"; and, therefore, since the funds in question were disbursed in September, 1971, or thereafter, there was no violation of 45 C.F.R. § 177.42(b).

Defendants opposed plaintiff's motion for summary judgment and in addition filed a cross-motion for summary judgment alleging the following: (1) That 45 C.F.R. 177.42(b) was violated by the plaintiff in that disbursement occurred before issuance of insurance, and (2) that the issuance of insurance occurred when each particular borrower's application was stamped "federally insured" and not when the contract of insurance dated July 12, 1971 was executed, (3) that with respect to plaintiff's allegations in Count One of the complaint, estoppel could not be had against the government because it was acting in its sovereign capacity, and because agents of the defendants had no authority to waive the regulation in question, and (4) the Commissioner never "expressly provided for" a waiver of the regulation in dispute.

III. THE ISSUANCE OF INSURANCE

Plaintiff alleges that the date of the issuance of insurance was July 12, 1971, and that, therefore 45 C.F.R. § 177.42(b) was not violated. . . .

Three theories in support of this contention are asserted:

1—That the "contract of insurance" dated July 12, 1971 constituted a comprehensive commitment pursuant to 20 U.S.C. § 1079(b)(1). The Court rejects this contention and holds that the "contract of insurance" was not a certificate of comprehensive insurance since it did not insure all loans by the lender up to a specific amount during a specific period of time.

2—Alternatively, plaintiff asserts that the "contract of insurance" was a contract for the issuance of insurance for all proposed loans pursuant to 20 U.S.C. § 1079(a)(2). The Court also rejects this contention, as a careful reading of the contract will show it does not come within the provisions of §(a)(2) in regard to proposed loans or proposed lines of credit.

On the other hand, the Court accepts the argument of defendant that "federal loan insurance in the overwhelming majority of cases is conferred on an individual, loan by loan, basis. A lender will submit separate student loan applications and supporting documents to O.E. If the lender is eligible and the loan insurable (both conditions need be met), O.E. will at this time insure the loan."

"In lieu of issuing separate 'certificates' 20 U.S.C. § 1079(a) covering each loan (obviously a burdensome task), O.E. manifests its approval by stamping the loan application in the upper right hand corner. The stamp, a programmatic adaptation sanctioned by the regulations is virtually synonymous in intent and effect with the 'certificate' mentioned in the statute."

In connection with the same, the regulation under consideration by the Court states the following:

> (b) Each eligible lender with which the Commissioner has entered into an agreement pursuant to paragraph (a) of this section may make application to the Commissioner for Federal loan insurance in connection with each application for a loan which the lender has initially determined to be eligible for such insurance coverage. Upon receipt of such application, which shall be filed on such form and in such manner as may be determined by the Commissioner, the Commissioner shall determine whether or not the loan is insurable and if the loan is determined to be insurable, the Commissioner shall, by affixing to the application evidence thereof, advise the lender that the loan is insurable and the amount of insurance. The insurance shall extend to all disbursements made pursuant to the loan, except that unless expressly provided for, no disbursements made on a loan prior to the issuance of insurance shall be covered. 45 C.F.R. § 177.42(b).

Therefore, the Court denies the contention that the "contract of insurance" was issued on July 12, 1971 for all proposed loans in the future, but on the other hand, finds that the "contract of insurance" was merely an agreement between N.A.A.C. and O.E. recognizing that (a) N.A.A.C. was an eligible lender under the Act and that (b) if, in the future the Commissioner of Education should approve and issue insurance for any particular loan application submitted by N.A.A.C, N.A.A.C. will abide by all appropriate rules and regulations, including 45 C.F.R. § 177.42(b).

The third theory which plaintiff asserts under Count Two is that the "contract of insurance" was a contract "for all loans made thereunder", and that the stamping of "federally insured" by the government was at most a condition subsequent. A careful reading of the last sentence of 45 C.F.R. § 177.42(b) (quoted above) indicates clearly that the issuance of insurance (which this Court has determined as a matter of law to occur when the stamp "federally insured" is placed on the application) is a condition precedent to the coverage of any disbursements by the insurance issued by affixing of said stamp. Therefore, this Court denies plaintiff's third contention with respect to Count Two of his amended complaint.

WHEREFORE, this Court holds that "the contract of insurance" dated July 12, 1971 was not the issuance of insurance, that the issuance of insurance occurred as each particular application was stamped "federally insured", and that, furthermore 45 C.F.R. § 177.42(b) was violated by N.A.A.C.'s prior disbursements on the 95 loans in question. Therefore plaintiff's Motion for Summary Judgment on Count Two of his complaint as amended is hereby DENIED.

IV. ISSUE OF ESTOPPEL AGAINST THE GOVERNMENT

Plaintiff argues in Count One of his complaint

That the policy of disbursing money prior to the stamping of the application as 'federally insured' was known generally to agents of the Defendants and approved and accepted by them, thereby waiving the alleged 'insurance issuance before disbursement' requirement; and further that the Defendants should now be estopped from asserting the alleged 'insurance issuance before disbursement requirement.'

It is a generally recognized principle of law that estoppel cannot operate against the United States if the government is acting in its sovereign as opposed to its proprietary capacity. . . .

[I]n the case at bar, the government is acting in its sovereign capacity to confer a benefit upon the public and satisfy a well-recognized public need as opposed to acting as an ordinary citizen for a private insurance company. The legislative history of the 1965 Higher Education Act discloses that

It is well known that the financial burdens families now face, if they are to provide education for their children, are becoming increasingly heavy . . . The program proposed should make long-term credit for educational purposes available to every qualified college student in the Nation . . . The central objective of part B of title IV is to make loan insurance available to any college student who needs to borrow. *1965 U. S. Code Congressional and Administrative News*, pages 4059 to 4062.

An examination of the legislative history herein referred to (the details of which need not be discussed here) reveals ostensibly the sovereign nature of the government's function in providing insurance for loans to students for the purpose of higher education.

In the case of *Moody Nursing Home, Inc. v. David Matthews, Secretary of Health, Education and Welfare,* (No. C75-72, Northern District of Georgia, Atlanta Division, Jan. 10, 1977, Judge Freeman) the court restated the principle.

> The touchstone of whether the government is acting in its proprietary capacity or sovereign capacity is whether the government is entering into ordinary contractual relations with its citizens or whether it is seeking to enforce a public right or interest. In the latter instance the government is acting in its sovereign capacity, *U.S. v. State of Florida, Supra,* [5 Cir.] 482 F.2d at [205] 209; *U.S. v. Brady, Supra,* [D.C.] 385 F.Supp. [D.C.] at 1351, and would in most instances be immune from the application of estoppel principles.

Considering both the huge sums of money set aside under the Higher Education Act to insure student loans and the clearly stated public purpose for the same, this Court in applying the standard enunciated in the cases above, for determining sovereign versus proprietary capacity, is required to hold that the facts of the instant case can reflect none other than the government's acting in its sovereign capacity to provide a public benefit. Therefore, the defendants, having been deemed to have acted in their sovereign capacity, as a matter of law cannot be estopped by the acts of their agents.

V. NO EXPRESS WAIVER OF
THE REGULATION

Plaintiff contends in Count Three of his complaint as amended that the words "unless expressly provided for" contained in 45 C.F.R. § 177.42(b) allow for the Commissioner to waive the regulation found to be violated in the instant case. Furthermore, "plaintiff contends that the individual and collective actions of the defendants and their agents constituted such an express exception."

This Court rules that the language in the regulation, to-wit, "unless expressly provided for" is not satisfied by proof of conduct upon the part of the Commissioner or his agents from which it might be reasonably assumed that a waiver was made. On the other hand, only an express statement by the Commissioner that the regulation is being waived would satisfy the language "unless expressly provided for." However, plaintiff has not alleged either in his complaint as amended, or in his motion for summary judgment, or in his opposition to defendants' motion for summary judgment, that the Commissioner expressly made such statement. On the other hand, plaintiff contends that the *conduct* of "the defendants and their agents" satisfies the language "unless expressly provided for."

The Court disagrees with this contention. In the first place, as a matter of law conduct cannot be substituted for the regulation's requirement of an express waiver. Secondly, plaintiff has never asserted or argued that the Commissioner made such express statement. Thirdly, affidavits by Kenneth A. Kohl, Associate Commissioner, Office of Guaranteed Student Loans

(Nov. 9, 1976) and Edwin B. Parker, III, Acting Associate Commissioner of Education, Office of Guaranteed Student Loans (Apr. 21, 1977) show that the Commissioner of Education has never delegated his authority to waive statutory or regulatory requirements to subordinate employees of the Office of Guaranteed Student Loans. Plaintiff has not submitted to this Court any sworn affidavits or evidence to rebut the above mentioned affidavits.

It appears to this Court that in the instant case there is no genuine issue of material fact and that defendants are entitled to Judgment as a matter of law.

WHEREFORE plaintiff's motion for Summary Judgment is denied, and defendants' prayers for Summary Judgment are GRANTED. The Clerk is hereby directed to enter Judgment in favor of the defendants, dismissing this action.

C.   The Government and the School-Lender

KNOXVILLE BUSINESS COLLEGE v. BOYER
United States District Court, E.D. Tennessee
451 F.Supp. 58 (1978)

ROBERT L. TAYLOR, District Judge.

This action involves the administration of the Federal Insured Student Loan Program ["FISLP"] under Title IV, Part B, of the Higher Education Act of 1965, as amended, 20 U.S.C. § 1071 *et seq.* Plaintiff, Knoxville Business College ["the College"], is a privately owned vocational junior college of business located in Knoxville, Tennessee. On April 15, 1970, the College entered into a "Contract of Insurance" with the U. S. Commissioner of Education ["the Commissioner"] which provided that the Commissioner would insure (guarantee) all loans made to students by the College which were eligible for such insurance. Before the Court are loans made by the College to seven of its students in 1973 and 1974, which are now in default, and for which the College had filed claims to collect the amount of insurance granted on each loan. . . .

Lending Limit

As developed by the evidence at trial, the procedures used by the College to obtain insurance on a student loan were fairly simple. A student desiring to obtain a federally insured loan to attend the College completed an application form provided by the Commissioner to the College.

A college official helped the student with the form, approved the form and forwarded it to the Regional Office of the Office of Education in Atlanta. If the loan application was correctly completed and met the requirements for insurance, the Regional Office would stamp it in the upper right hand corner. The stamp reads across the top "FEDERALLY INSURED"; next it has a date; and, at the bottom it has a stamped signature of the Commissioner (or his designated officer). Below the stamp is a space for "Amount of Commitment", wherein an amount would be entered. The stamped application would then be returned to the College as notice that the loan had been insured on the date indicated on the stamp and for the amount entered beneath the stamp. When an application was incomplete or incorrect, it would be returned to the College with the mistaken entry underlined in red, so that the College could correct the error or withdraw the application.

Following this simple procedure, the College obtained federal insurance for student loans it made in 1970-72. In the early part of January 1973 the Commissioner sent a notice to all school lenders, including the College. The notice advised the College that "the Division of Insured Loans—through Evaluation Committee action—is placing a lending ceiling on all school contracts *to be effective during the coming fiscal year of each school."* . . .

On January 12, 1973, an officer of the Division of Insured Loans sent a letter to A. M. Luther, Jr., the Executive Vice President of the College, informing him that:

"We are pleased to inform you that the [Evaluation] Committee has approved the continuation of your school's Contract of Insurance for the next 12 months. In doing this the Committee stipulates that *your school is not to exceed $150,000 in new loan commitments during 1973."* (emphasis added).

Upon receipt of this letter the College was clearly put on notice that it would not receive federal insurance on student loans made in 1973 once the aggregate amount of those loans exceeded $150,000.

What happened in 1973 is a comedy of errors and reveals a sad state of affairs on the part of the Office of Education. Following the above-discussed process of sending loan applications to Atlanta and having them stamped as insured, the College obtained "federal insurance" on student loans totaling $482,154 during 1973. According to the testimony, neither the College nor the Regional Office attempted to keep a running total on the amount of the loans the Regional Office was approving as federally insured. The College argues that, when the stamp was placed on the application, which exceeded $150,000, the Commissioner thereby extended the limit to cover that additional loan. It appears that the Commissioner, in order to properly enforce the lending limit imposed on institutions, should have maintained a system (which he now has in effect), whereby he could monitor the loans and reject any applications which exceeded an institution's lending limit. However, he chose to rely on the institution to do its own self-monitoring and to not submit applications for loans once the lending limit had been reached. The Court cannot hold that such action on the part of the Commissioner was arbitrary or unfair. The College admits it had notice of the limit and, in the opinion of the Court, that is sufficient to make such limitation binding on it.

The authority of the Commissioner to impose such limits is clear, *Windsor v. Secretary of Health, Education and Welfare*, 550 F.2d 1203 (9th Cir. 1977), and the Contract of Insurance provided that the Commissioner would insure all eligible loans "[w]ithin such limits as may be set by him. . . ."

The Commissioner has done a computer analysis of the College's 1973 loans and determined that the College reached its lending limit on April 5, 1973. The Court holds that loans made by the College during 1973 that were made after April 5th could not be insured because of the lending limit imposed on the College. Therefore, five of the seven claims asserted herein by the College against the Commissioner for the collection of insurance are simply invalid. Those five loans were made during 1973, after April 5, and consist of the Coleman, King, Parkey, Begley, and Hendricks loans (approximately $6,703.70 total principal balance).

1974 Loans

The remaining two claims are based on loans made in 1974, the Melton and Meads loans, totaling approximately $2,722.90 in principal balance. While there has been some dispute as to whether the $39,220 in loans approved in 1974 were authorized, the preponderance of the evidence demonstrated that the College was never notified to stop lending in 1974. The evidence also showed that no lending limit was placed on the College during 1974. One witness spoke of an Office of Education officer referring to "back door notice" of a limit, but the proof failed to show even informal notice. The Court holds that the two loans made by the College in 1974 were properly submitted to the Commissioner for insurance and that he did insure those loans. Therefore, the College's claim for insurance on the Melton and Meads loans is to be paid by the Commissioner. . . .

NOTES

1. *Hicks v. Califano* seems to suggest that it is not the documents which pass between the government and the lender or the actions of the parties, but the "Federally Insured" stamp, which guarantees the loan. *Knoxville* appears to hold otherwise. Is this an accurate reading of the cases? How do you account for the difference?

2. Confusion over the administration of the GSLP has also arisen among branches of the government itself. See Jenkins, Statutory Comment, *Legislative-Executive Disagreement: Interpreting the 1972 Amendments to the Guaranteed Student Loan Program*, 10 Harvard J. on Leg. 467 (1973).

3. For a discussion of the ways in which federally subsidized loan programs have led to government regulation of academic institutions, see Jenkins, *Regulation of Colleges and Universities Under the Government Student Loan Program*, IV J. of Coll. and Univ. Law, (Fall 1976), 13.

4. Discussion of issues involving the NDEA loan programs can be found in Garsaud, *National Defense Education Act, Title II—Student Loan Program—Moving Toward the End of the First Decade*, 14 Loyola L. Rev. 79 (1967-68). The Internal Revenue Service policy of treating forgiven student loans as income is examined in Boe, *Cancelled Student Loans: For the Benefit of the Grantor?*, 39 Alb. L. Rev. 35 (1974).

IV. Loans Discharged in Bankruptcy or Defaulted

HANDSOME v. RUTGERS UNIVERSITY
United States District Court, D. New Jersey
445 F.Supp. 1362 (1978)

STERN, District Judge.

This case presents the question whether a state university may withhold transcripts and deny registration to a former student whose student loans have been discharged in bankruptcy. Not unmindful of the widespread abuse of the bankruptcy laws on the part of students, this Court holds that such thinly-veiled coercion on the part of a state university to compel repayment of loans duly discharged under the federal bankruptcy laws violates the Supremacy Clause and plaintiff's right to equal protection as guaranteed by the Fourteenth Amendment. Accordingly, the defendant is permanently enjoined from continuing those practices.

The facts here—perhaps more compelling than most—have been stipulated by the parties. Plaintiff Lynn Handsome attended Newark College of Arts & Sciences, a division of Rutgers University, from 1968 through 1974. While a student at Rutgers, she borrowed a total of $4,600 in the form of National Defense Student Loans and National Direct Student Loans. It is undisputed that, at the time she took out these loans, she had every intention of repaying them.

Beginning in 1973, plaintiff experienced serious health problems and was forced to undergo surgery. Finally, in January of 1975, her health had deteriorated to the point where it interfered with her academic performance and she was forced to withdraw from college.

In the meantime, payments on plaintiff's NDLS loans began to fall due. Because of her medical expenses, she found herself unable to meet her repayment obligations. Upon her default, the NDLS loan principal was accelerated, payment was demanded in full and, in July 1976, Rutgers obtained a default judgment against plaintiff in state court in an amount of $4,991.75 plus costs and interests.

In April 1977, plaintiff filed a petition for bankruptcy. The liabilities listed in her petition were in excess of $25,000—$7,000 representing medical expenses—and her assets totalled $368.85. Included in her schedule of creditors was Rutgers University, which made no objection to the discharge of her obligations in bankruptcy. On June 13, 1977, plaintiff was adjudicated a bankrupt.

In December 1977, plaintiff applied for readmission to Rutgers. By letter dated December 22, 1977, she was informed that the Scholastic Standing Committee had approved her readmission. However, it is the policy of the defendant to put "place hold" notices upon the records of all students who are more than three months delinquent in their debts to the university, precluding both their registration and the release of their transcripts. Accordingly, when plaintiff attempted to register on January 5, 1978, she was informed that such a notice had been placed on her records. Thus, not only was she prevented from registering, but she has been thwarted in her efforts to apply for admission to a Physician's Assistance Program, because she cannot supply the required transcripts.

It is at this point that plaintiff sought court intervention. On January 24, 1978 she filed the instant complaint alleging that Rutgers' actions violate the Constitution and the Bankruptcy Act, and she applied for temporary restraints. The Court issued a temporary restraining order, directing Rutgers to allow plaintiff to register. At issue now is whether this temporary restraining order should ripen into a permanent injunction, compelling defendant both to permit plaintiff to remain at the university and to release her transcripts so that she will be able to pursue her education elsewhere.

Prior to passing on the merits of plaintiff's claims, the Court will dispose of defendant's contention that there is no federal subject matter jurisdiction over the matter under either 28 U.S.C. § 1331 or 28 U.S.C. § 1343(3) and (4).

Defendant argues that this Court lacks federal question jurisdiction under 28 U.S.C. § 1331 because the requisite amount in controversy is lacking. Insofar as plaintiff can be said to be asserting a claim which arises under the Bankruptcy Act, it appears undisputed that this action "arises under" federal law. See Girardier v. Webster College, 563 F.2d 1267 (8th Cir. 1977). However, defendant claims that the amount in controversy should be measured by the amount of the discharged loans, which concededly is under $10,000. Plaintiff asserts that the amount in controversy is the value of her right to a college education, an amount which none could doubt must be in excess of $10,000.

While the question is not free from doubt among the Circuits, see generally, Earnest, The Jurisdictional Amount in Controversy in Suits to Enforce Federal Rights, 54 Tex.L.Rev. 527 (1976), it is clear that in the Third Circuit, intangible rights can be accorded a monetary value for purposes of meeting the amount in controversy requirement. Thus, in Spock v. David, 469 F.2d 1047 (3rd Cir. 1972), an action by political candidates to compel defendants to permit them to campaign on a military base, Judge Gibbons rejected the contention that the rights asserted were incapable of valuation. Noting that in actions seeking injunctive relief, "the measure of jurisdiction is the value of the right sought to be protected", id. at 1052, Judge Gibbons looked to the value of a political campaign and concluded that it must exceed $10,000. Here, the right to be protected is the right to a college education. None can dispute that by withholding plaintiff's transcripts defendant forces her to repeat the education she has undergone thus far. In reality, of course, the withholding of transcripts does more than merely force her to repeat elsewhere courses already taken at Rutgers. It is unlikely that any college or university will admit plaintiff without a transcript of her prior work, or would permit her to repeat for credit courses already taken elsewhere. The only purpose that Rutgers has for refusing transcripts is to recoup monies owed. This much was candidly admitted at oral argument. And certainly no one can dispute that the cost of such an education is well in excess of $10,000. Accordingly, this Court finds there is federal question jurisdiction.

In any event, because the constitutional claims asserted are substantial—indeed so substantial that the Court finds for plaintiff on the merits—it is clear that there is subject matter jurisdiction under 28 U.S.C. § 1343(3) and (4), which has no requirement that there be an amount in controversy. See Jones v. Alfred H. Mayer Co., 392 U.S. 409, 88 S.Ct. 2186, 20 L.Ed.2d 1189 (1968). There being a substantial constitutional claim under 42 U.S.C.

§ 1983 that defendant's actions violate the Fourteenth Amendment's Equal Protection Clause, this Court has pendent jurisdiction over the plaintiff's remaining claims under the Bankruptcy Act. *See Hagans v. Lavine*, 415 U.S. 528, 94 S.Ct. 1372, 39 L.Ed.2d 577 (1973).

Plaintiff's principal contention is that defendant's actions impinge upon the policies of the Bankruptcy Act and are, therefore, invalid under the Supremacy Clause. She relies primarily on the Supreme Court's decision in *Perez v. Campbell*, 402 U.S. 637, 91 S.Ct. 1704, 29 L.Ed.2d 233 (1971).

In *Perez*, plaintiffs, two bankrupts whose licenses had been suspended, attacked the constitutionality of a state statute which provided for the suspension of the driver's licenses of persons who had outstanding automobile accident judgments against them, notwithstanding that such judgments may have been discharged in bankruptcy. The Supreme Court framed the issue as follows:

> What is at issue here is the power of a State to include as part of [a] comprehensive enactment designed to secure compensation for automobile accident victims a section providing that a discharge in bankruptcy of the automobile accident tort judgment shall have no effect on the judgment debtor's obligation to repay the judgment creditor, at least insofar as such repayment may be enforced by the withholding of driving privileges by the State.

Id., at 643, 91 S.Ct., at 1708. Concluding that the sole purpose of the statute was to provide leverage for the collection of debts, the Supreme Court held the statute unconstitutional under the Supremacy Clause and overruled its decisions to the contrary. The Court stated that the purpose of the Bankruptcy Act is to give the debtor "a new opportunity in life and a clear field for future effort, unhampered by the pressure and discouragement of pre-existing debt," *id.*, at 648, 91 S.Ct., at 1710 [citations omitted]. The Court held that the statute "stands as an obstacle to the accomplishment and execution of the full purposes and objectives of Congress", *id.*, at 649, 91 S.Ct., at 1711 [citations omitted] and, thus, was invalid under the Supremacy Clause.

On the authority of *Perez* the lower courts have invalidated a rule providing for the suspension of municipal employees who have invoked the bankruptcy laws, *see Rutledge v. City of Shreveport*, 387 F.Supp. 1277 (W.D.La.1975), *appeal dismissed*, No. 75-1775 (5th Cir., September 14, 1976); *Matter of Loftin*, 327 So.2d 543 (La.App.1976); and a state statute providing for the suspension of the licenses of contractors who have been adjudicated bankrupts, *see Grimes v. Hoschler,* 12 Cal.3d 305, 115 Cal. Rptr. 625, 525 P.2d 65 (1974). *Compare Marshall v. District of Columbia Government*, 182 U.S.App.D.C. 105, 559 F.2d 726 (1977) (*Perez* does not proscribe police department's use of bankruptcy as a factor in evaluating applicant's fitness for employment). By contrast, the courts have refused to read *Perez* to proscribe discrimination against bankrupts on the part of purely private entities. *See Girardier v. Webster College*, 563 F.2d 1267

(8th Cir. 1977); *McLellan v. Mississippi Power and Light Co.*, 545 F.2d 919 (5th Cir. 1977) (*en banc*).

Of particular interest here is the Eighth Circuit's decision in *Webster College*. In *Webster College*, the defendant, a private college, refused to provide transcripts to plaintiffs, two former students whose student loans had been discharged in bankruptcy. Relying upon the decision of the Fifth Circuit in *McLellan v. Mississippi Power & Light Co., supra*, the Eighth Circuit refused to extend *Perez* to prohibit private institutions from coercing the repayment of debts which had been discharged in bankruptcy:

> The Bankruptcy Act, as now written, does not prohibit a private college's refusing to furnish transcripts to persons who have received a discharge in bankruptcy of their college loans.

563 F.2d 1276. Implicit in the rationale of the *Webster College* decision is that, while a private college is free to take such recourse, a public university would not be.[6] *See* Concurring Opinion of Bright, J., *id.*, at 1277 (noting the "anomalous result that a state school is obligated to furnish transcripts to a bankrupt former student . . . but a private school is not.")

Since defendant is a public university, we are not bound by the *Webster College* decision; if anything, it supports the result reached by this Court. However, it does not necessarily follow that *Perez* is dispositive of plaintiff's claim.

The state legislation at issue in *Perez* was designed not to protect the state as a creditor, but to protect third parties with unsatisfied tort judgments against bankrupts. Here, the state is itself a creditor, and its actions are designed to serve its own ends. On the face of it, it seems unfair to treat a public creditor differently from a private creditor, for both would seem equally justified in refusing to deal with someone who had defaulted on a debt *owed to it* in the past. However, while indeed it may be "anomalous" to treat private creditors differently from public creditors, it is the state—and not private parties—which is limited by the Supremacy Clause. While private parties are bound to observe only the letter of the law, the state may not by its actions "retard, impede, burden, or in any manner control, the operations of the laws . . . enacted by congress." *See McCulloch v. Maryland,*

[6.]   While this Court largely agrees with the Eighth Circuit's conclusion that *Perez* does not proscribe purely private discrimination against bankrupts, it must respectfully disagree with the result reached in the *Webster College* decision. At issue there was not a mere refusal to readmit former students whose student loans had been discharged in bankruptcy, but a refusal to release their transcripts. In concurrence, Judge Bright characterizes the interests at stake as, in effect, future interests which may be withheld for failure of consideration:

> Webster College, which has conferred upon now-bankrupt, former students an education represented by a degree, has taken no steps to penalize appellants in their use of knowledge gained in college . . . Rather, Webster College refuses further to enhance the benefits of those degrees by certification of the transcripts. *Id.* at 1277-78.

Surely, however, a student has some sort of a property interest in his transcripts, which reflect time, money and hard work. This Court cannot agree with the *Webster College* Court that even a private entity may withhold the debtor's property because the debt has been discharged in bankruptcy. Just as one might assume that a doctor could not withhold the medical records of a patient whose medical bills had been discharged in bankruptcy, a college should not be permitted to withhold a student's transcripts.

4 Wheat. 316, 436, 17 U.S. 316, 436, 4 L.Ed. 579 (1819) (Marshall, Ch. J.). There being no explicit provision in the Bankruptcy Act making it unlawful to discriminate against a bankrupt, private entities may lawfully refuse to deal with bankrupts. By contrast, the Supremacy Clause prevents a state from frustrating even the spirit of a federal law. Inasmuch as defendant, both by withholding plaintiff's transcripts and refusing to permit her to register, has transgressed upon the "fresh start" policies of the Bankruptcy Act, this Court must hold such actions violative of the Supremacy Clause.

The Court next addresses plaintiff's contention that defendant's actions violate her right to equal protection as guaranteed by the Fourteenth Amendment.[7] Since education is not a fundamental right, and since wealth is not a suspect classification, *see San Antonio School District v. Rodriguez*, 411 U.S. 1, 93 S.Ct. 1278, 36 L.Ed.2d 16 (1973), the Court need only determine whether the classification at issue here is reasonably related to a legitimate governmental interest. *See Reed v. Reed*, 404 U.S. 71, 76, 92 S.Ct. 251, 30 L.Ed.2d 225 (1971). However, on analysis, it is clear that defendant's actions cannot survive even this less lenient level of scrutiny.

The classification employed by Rutgers includes all persons who are more than three months delinquent in their debts to the school. As applied to persons who are not bankrupts, there is little doubt that this classification is legitimate, for the university has a legitimate interest in seeking repayment of valid debts. However, insofar as this classification includes bankrupts, it necessarily runs afoul of the Equal Protection Clause. The state cannot claim a legitimate interest in securing the repayment of loans discharged in bankruptcy, for, as we have already demonstrated, pursuit of such an interest is foreclosed by *Perez*. Moreover, defendant, as a state university, is under an obligation to treat its citizens alike. While it may, of course, discriminate on the basis of reasonable classifications such as academic performance, a citizen's status as a bankrupt is, *per force*, an impermissible criterion. This is not to say that defendant may not in the future validly decline to extend credit to one who has previously discharged his debts in bankruptcy, but it cannot deny a citizen so vital a privilege as an education on the basis of his status as a bankrupt.

Finally, plaintiff levels a statutory challenge to defendant's practices, claiming that they violate section 14(f) of the Bankruptcy Act, 11 U.S.C. § 32(f) (Supp.1977), which provides that:

An order of discharge shall—

.   .   .   .

(2) enjoin all creditors whose debts are discharged from thereafter instituting or continuing any action or employing any process to collect such debts as personal liabilities of the bankrupt.

[7.]   We reject out of hand defendant's contention that since it acts in a "proprietary" rather than a "governmental" capacity, it should not be regarded as an arm of the state. Rutgers is a state university, created pursuant to N.J.S.A. 18A-65 1 *et. seq.* Since, under certain circumstances, even private universities have been held to act "under color of state law", *see Braden v. University of Pittsburgh*, 552 F.2d 948 (3rd Cir. 1977) (*en banc*), *a fortiori*, defendant is bound by the Fourteenth Amendment.

Plaintiff would have the Court equate the phrases "any process" and "action" with the actions which are challenged here. However, it is clear from the legislative history of this provision, that the sole purpose of this section is to prevent creditors from taking *legal* actions against debtors; it does not proscribe actions which fall short of that. *See Girardier v. Webster College, supra*, at 1272-73; *Wood v. Fiedler*, 548 F.2d 216, 219 (8th Cir. 1977); 1 A Collier, Bankruptcy ¶ 14.69 (14th Ed.1976).

In holding defendant's practices unconstitutional, this Court in no way condones the abuse of the bankruptcy laws by students who, with little or no assets, take out loans with one eye on the bankruptcy laws and with no present intention to repay. However, as to students who have already discharged their student loans in bankruptcy—who, it should be noted, have undergone bankruptcy proceedings where the creditor has been given every opportunity to oppose the discharge and the Bankruptcy Judge was empowered to inquire into any allegations of fraud—this Court holds that the state may neither withhold the fruits of their prior education, nor thwart them in their attempts to seek a "fresh start" through a college education.

NOTES

1. Girardier v. Webster College, 563 F.2d 1267 (8th Cir. 1977), which is cited in *Handsome v. Rutgers University*, held that a private college could withhold transcripts from students whose loans had been discharged in bankruptcy. Concurring, Judge Bright suggested that the same result should apply in the case of a state university:

> Assuming *arguendo* that a public institution's refusal to issue a transcript is a state action conflicting with the purposes and provisions of the Bankruptcy Act and vulnerable under the Supremacy Clause, the court's rationale could lead to the anomalous result that a state school is obligated to furnish transcripts to a bankrupt former student but, until he or she pays the discharged educational loan, a private school is not.

> The *Perez* holding does not require such antithetical results. . . .

> A college transcript differs radically from the essential driver's license at stake in *Perez*. A student who obtains a degree from a college acquires not only the present benefit of that education, but also a fund of knowledge of lifelong value. In other words, it is not like purchasing an article of consumable goods that immediately is consumed or even durable goods with more lasting usefulness. Instead an education yields ever-continuing benefits. . . .

> Section 14 of the Bankruptcy Act speaks in terms of barring a creditor's affirmative action. The discharge bars ("enjoins") creditors whose debts are discharged from "instituting or continuing any action or employing any process to collect such debts as personal liabilities of the bankrupt." 11 U.S.C. §32(f) (1970). Additionally, *Local Loan Co. v. Hunt*, 292 U.S. 234, 244, 54 S.Ct. 695, 699, 78 L.Ed. 1230 (1934), emphasizes the underlying primary purposes of the Bankruptcy Act to give debtors a fresh start, "a new opportunity in life and a clear field for future effort, unhampered by the pressure and discouragement of preexisting debt."

> I agree with appellants that the above-cited code section and the fresh start principle of *Local Loan Co. v. Hunt* should be applied generously and broadly in favor of the bankrupt. But in my view, neither the statute nor the fresh start principle applies here.

> First, Webster College merely declined to confer any additional benefits upon the debtors by furnishing transcripts of their grades for the unpaid educational courses. Otherwise, it in no way coerced the debtors to pay the

discharged debts. Second, appellants have obtained far more than the fresh start contemplated by the Bankruptcy Act—they have obtained a head start because each has secured something of value that cannot be lost or taken away and which will give each appellant a continuing, lifelong economic benefit. No college, public or private, should be required to enhance such a benefit by issuing a transcript when it has not been paid for its services. The equities here lie with the college.

[563 F.2d at 1277-78]

Webster College was widely commented upon. See, for example: Note: *Bankruptcy—NDEA Loans—The Bankruptcy Act Does Not Prohibit a Private College from Refusing to Furnish Transcripts to Persons Who Have Received Discharges in Bankruptcy of Their College Loans*, 12 Ga. L. Rev. 143 (1977); Case Comment, *Post-discharge Coercion of Bankrupts by Private Creditors: Girardier v. Webster College*, 91 Harvard L. Rev. 1336 (1978); Comment, *Private College Can Refuse Transcript to Discharged Bankrupt for Non-Payment of Student Loan*, 29 Mercer L. Rev. 1169 (1978).

2. A provision of the Education Amendments of 1976 (20 U.S.C. § 1087-3, 1978) now prohibits the discharge of student loans in bankruptcy until five years after the date on which repayment is due to begin. The court can make an exception in cases which would "impose an undue hardship on the debtor or his dependents."

3. The rising rate of defaulted student loans has become a major concern of both the government and private lenders. By January, 1979, almost $1 billion in loans, representing more than 10 million borrowers under both the NDEA/NDSLP and the GSLP, had been defaulted (*New York Times*, Jan. 7, 1979). Much of the problem was attributed to the fact that the Office of Education lacked an efficient system for identifying and billing defaulters. Beefed up collection programs, involving court action as well as computer tracking by both federal and state governments, had begun to turn the tide somewhat in late 1978. Although some initial concern was expressed that involving private collection agencies would violate terms of the Privacy Act (5 U.S.C. 552a, 1978), in January 1979 the Office of Education announced that two such agencies had been hired in a pilot program to track down 94,000 debtors in the South and West (*New York Times*, Feb. 11, 1979).

4. A system of tuition tax credits is often proposed as an alternative or supplement to student loan programs. *See*, for example, the "Dissenting Views" of Representatives Ashbrook, Erlenborn, and Schuster appended to the House Report which accompanied the Middle Income Student Assistance Act (H.R. Rep. No. 95-951, 95th Cong., 2nd Sess. 46, reprinted in [1978] U.S. Code Cong. & Ad. News 6822, 6852):

We, too, are very concerned about the spiraling costs of higher education and the impact of these costs on middle income families. While we support the objective of H.R. 11274, we do not believe expansion of existing student aid programs is the best method to meet this objective and, therefore, oppose H.R. 11274 as reported by the committee.

We firmly believe that tuition tax credits are the simplest, most direct way to assist Americans in dealing with these costs, and therefore support these portions of the additional views which argue for the adoption of some form of tuition tax credit legislation.

Many tuition tax credit proposals have been introduced in both Houses of Congress. The Senate Finance Committee showed great wisdom recently in reporting, almost unanimously, one such proposal to the full Senate. We are pleased to note that the House Committee on Ways and Means has begun hearings on tuition tax legislation and urge them to expedite their consideration.

Many reasons were cited in the additional views why tuition tax credit legislation should be adopted. We would like to add that our support for tuition tax credits and opposition to H.R. 11274 does not in any way indicate a lack of support for lower income families. On the contrary, we believe that tuition tax credit legislation will serve to guarantee that no person be denied a college education on economic grounds alone. It would allow taxpayers to keep more of their earnings, instead of going through the morass of bureaucracy to obtain student aid.

The Internal Revenue Service already has the capability to process a tuition tax credit. No added bureaucracy is necessary. Compare this to the problems associated with processing student aid applications and one wonders why anyone could oppose the simplicity of a tax credit for tuition costs.

We believe that a tuition tax credit will help stimulate the diversity that has in the past characterized American education. The proportion of college students attending private colleges and universities has decreased in recent years due to the ever-expanding gap between tuition costs for private and public colleges. The freedom of choice of institutions is therefore being denied many students. Tuition tax credit legislation will help to promote freedom of choice.

We therefore oppose H.R. 11274 and urge our colleagues to strongly support tuition tax credit legislation.

CHAPTER 23

COPYRIGHT LAW REVISION OF 1976

Since it would be an impossible task to attempt to cover the law of copyright in a single chapter, the authors have decided instead to reprint the following article by Michael H. Cardozo. This article, which is reprinted here by permission of the National Association of College and University Attorneys, provides an excellent overview of the Copyright Law Revision of 1976 as it affects higher education.*

If the reader desires to obtain further information on copyright law, the best source available is the four-volume treatise, Nimmer On Copyright: A Treatise on the Law of Literary, Musical and Artistic Property, and the Protection of Ideas (New York: Matthew Bender, 1978). The reader may also wish to consider two other books by the same author: Nimmer, Copyright and Other Aspects of Law Pertaining to Literary, Musical and Artistic Works (West Publishing Co., 1971) (including the 1977 Supplement) and Nimmer, A Preliminary View of the Copyright Act of 1976: Analysis and Text (New York: Matthew Bender, 1977).

TO COPY OR NOT TO COPY FOR TEACHING AND SCHOLARSHIP: What Shall I Tell my Client?

MICHAEL H. CARDOZO**

This article began as an effort to provide for educators, scholars, students, and the administrators of the facilities they use, a simple, clear description of what they may, and may not, copy under the various provisions of the Copyright Law Revision of 1976[1] that deal with their concerns.[2] The effort failed for the reasons made obvious in the following pages. Briefly stated, the cause is the uncertainty of the language of the Act.

Even if a "simple, clear description" of what the members of the scholarly community may and may not copy under the new Act is too

---

*The article by Michael Cardozo first appeared in 4 J. Coll. & U.L. 59 (Winter 1976/77). Copyright ©1977 by the National Association of College and University Attorneys.

**LL.B., 1935, Yale. Private practice, Washington, D.C. Former Professor of Law, Cornell; former Executive Director, Association of American Law Schools. Former AALS representative to Ad Hoc Committee on Copyright Law Revision, Washington, D.C.

[1]General Revision of the Copyright Law, Public Law, 94-553, Oct. 19, 1976; 17 U.S.C. §§101 et seq. (1976).

[2]For general description of the Act, see Stedman, "The New Copyright Law: Photocopying for Educational Use" 63 AAUP Bull. 5 (1977); Am. Lib. Ass'n., Wash. Newsletter vol. 28, no. 13 (Nov. 15, 1976); C. Lieb, An Overview of the New Copyright Law (Ass'n. Am. Pub. 1976).

elusive, a fair description of the analytic process that the Act elicits may be feasible. This article tries to present such a description.

The Copyright Law Revision of 1976: A Warped and Illegible Slide Rule

An impressive coalition of educational and scholarly organizations established the Ad Hoc Committee on Copyright Law Revision in the early days of the effort to revise. Harold Wigren of the National Education Association chaired the Committee for its first thirteen years with patience, skill, and devotion. Right up to passage of the Act in 1976, the Ad Hoc Committee and members and staffs of the Congressional Committees struggled to find statutory language that would breach the impasse between the publishers and educators. Guidelines were produced at the eleventh hour that reflect more tenacity than triumph. As this article concludes, educators, scholars, librarians, and students will find scarcely greater clarity in the words of the 1976 revision, with its tortuous legislative history, than in the old act which had led Zechariah Chaffee to reflect in 1945 that:

> To require officials, judges and lawyers to work with a statute which is intricate and leaves many important points unsettled is like asking an engineer to do his calculations with a warped and illegible slide rule. [3]

If the lawyers who drafted the 1976 Act had merely failed to express the intent of Congress in clear and comprehensible terminology, and therefore were responsible for the uncertainty of these provisions, I would once more be ashamed of the lack of skill and sense of professional responsibility of members of my profession. In this case, however, the blame may be shared with the participants in the copyright system who, despite prolonged, monumental efforts, both adversary and amicable, could not reach a really helpful agreement on what Congress should do about copyright in education, scholarship, and libraries. As a result, the baffled members of the Senate and House Committees produced statutory language that gives legalistic comfort to practically everyone, but simple aid to no one. For what comfort it may give the layman seeking guidance in the Act: the law that describes their tax liability, The Internal Revenue Code, is worse.

Copyright Since 1909

In this age of xerography, teachers, research scholars, and students take material to a photo-copying machine every day to get or make copies for use in the classroom, the study, and the library. Most of the time they pay scant attention to the copyright status of the document to be duplicated. The Xerox Corporation, however, has recognized a responsibility to discourage the use of their copying machines for the infringement of a valid copyright. The

---

[3] Chaffee, "Reflections on the Law of Copyright: I," 45 Colum. L. Rev. 503, 514 (1945).

notice that accompanies the delivery of a Xerox copier states, "It is illegal
* * * to make copies of * * * copyrighted material of any manner or kind
without permission of the copyright owner." The Xerox Corporation, of
course, knows better. The officers of the Corporation know that it *is* legal to
make some copies of some copyrighted material. Presumably they asked their
lawyers to suggest an accurate, terse, and useful warning to accompany their
machines. It seems likely that, after they had heard their lawyers' response,
"You may make copies if * * * unless * * * ", they decided that the only
warning that would be safe, terse, and clear would be the inaccurate statement just quoted.

Now that Congress has enacted the first comprehensive revision since
1909 of the copyright laws of the United States, teachers, scholars, students,
and librarians are justifiably expecting to receive clear and terse guidelines
describing what may be copied, how many copies may be made, and what
may be done with the copies, without infringing the rights of copyright owners and incurring serious liability for damages. Unfortunately,
the longed-for guidelines, with the exception of a few categories of materials,
will have to be qualified by many admonitory "ifs" and subordinate "unless's". Some of the answers even require a temporal "maybe" because of
the existence and activities of the National Commission on New Technological Uses of Copyrighted Works (CONTU).[4]   That Commission's function
is to propose, before 1978, methods of reconciling authors' and publishers'
claims to protection of their works with the technological developments that
stem from computer and similar systems of information storage, retrieval,
and reproduction, as well as the burgeoning field of simple photocopying.

The copyright law is said to exist for the encouragement and reward of
individual creativity. It proceeds on the assumption that, if anyone may freely make copies of a work, the prospective creator of the work would be
discouraged from writing and recording ideas, thoughts, and compositions,
and publishing firms would be unwilling to print and distribute the written
works. Therefore humanity would be the poorer. Arguments over the
amount of protection needed by the creators and the publishers clouded the
effort to revise the 1909 stuatute,[5] and those arguments reached a crescendo
during the ten years preceding passage of the "General Revision of the Copyright Law" in 1976.[6]   To those who heard or read the recent arguments, it
would surely come as a great surprise that all the same things were said when
the 1909 Act was being drafted. In a 1905 message proposing a copyright
law revision Theodore Roosevelt said, "Our copyright laws * * * omit provision for many articles which, under modern reproductive processes, are
entitled to protection; they impose hardships upon the copyright proprietor
which are not essential to the fair practices of the public; they are difficult
for the courts to interpret and impossible for the Copyright Office to admin-

---

[4] Public Law 93-573, Dec. 31, 1974; 17 U.S.C. §201.
[5] 35 Stat. 1075 (1909).
[6] *Supra* note 1.

ister with satisfaction to the public"[7] The historic antagonism between those who rely on the constitution's copyright clause (Article I, section 8, clause 8) to protect them against infringement, and those who cite the First Amendment as permitting them to say or print anything, has been described as "irreconcilable" by Professor Melville B. Nimmer.[8] Although he concluded that copyright does not abridge First Amendment rights, the contesting partisans in the legislative battle from 1964 to 1976 fought to a standstill with cries of "amputation by fair use" on one side and "censorship by copyright" on the other.

Fair Use: A Judicial Doctrine Becomes Statutory

During the half century after the passage of the 1909 law, the courts ingeniously developed doctrines that were aimed at finding a middle way between "hardships upon the copyright proprietor" and "fair practices of the public." The recorded efforts of courts had started even earlier[9], as had their use of the words "fair use."[10] The "fair use" doctrine established the principle that a copyright is not infringed, and damages may not be assessed or further copying enjoined, if the material is to be "used" in ways that are "fair" to all concerned. At a very early stage in the writing of the recent revision, Congress decided to insert the doctrine of "fair use" into the Act, codifying what the judges had been holding during the past half century. The result of the codification effort is section 107 of the 1976 Act, captioned "Limitations on exclusive rights: Fair use." The caption demonstrates clearly that making copies for "fair use" without permission from the copyright owner does not infringe the "exclusive right" to make copies described in Section 106. (The texts of Sections 106 and 107 are reproduced on page 791).

Teachers, scientists, and research scholars who copy material for their studies and teaching normally do not seek permission from copyright proprietors. Some such material, of course, is not covered by copyright, possibly because it is "in the public domain," it was never copyrighted, or the copyright has expired. Regardless of the copyright status of the material, the typical copying of this kind involves a single copy of a portion of a printed work to be taken from a library to an office, classroom, or other working place. Also typical is the absence of profit motive, lack of intention to republish or display publicly, except possibly to quote phrases or sentences, and a spontaneity arising from an immediate need that would often be frustrated if the copyright owner had to be located and negotiation for

---

[7] Quoted by the Acting Librarian of Congress, John G. Lorenz, at Hearings on H.R. 2223. Before the Subcomm. on Courts, Civil Liberties and the Administration of Justice, House Comm. on the Judiciary, 94th Cong., 1st Sess., Pt. 1, at 91 (1975).

[8] Nimmer, "Does Copyright Abridge the First Amendment Guarantees of Free Speech and Press?" 17 U.C.L.A. Rev. 1180 (1970).

[9] See Folsom v. Marsh, 9 Fed. Cas. 342 (No. 4,901) (C.C.D. Mass. 1841), opinion by Justice Story; and Story v. Holcombe, 23 Fed. Cas. 171 (No. 13,497) (C.C.D. Ohio 1847), involving alleged infringement of Justice Story's "Commentaries on Equity Jurisprudence."

[10] Lawrence v. Dana, 15 Fed. Cas. 26 (No. 8,136) (C.C.D. Mass. 1869).

permission undertaken. The combination of no profit motive and no republication or public performance or display may be the key elements for fairness, as distinguished from infringement, in a teacher's or scholar's "typical" uses of copies.[11] Instances of copying that involve these elements have all the features of "fair use" as the judges designed the doctrine in their opinions. The most important challenge of the new Act is to discover if the way fair use has been defined in the Congressional codification of the doctrine in Section 107, and refined in several other sections of the Act, really conforms with the judicially designed doctrine.

Section 107 to the Act states that copying for "fair use" is not an infringement of a copyright. Following Section 107, there are five more sections captioned "Limitations on Exclusive Use," each permitting copying under different circumstances or of a different kind of work as an exception to the general rule that copying a copyrighted work without permission is an actionable infringement of the owner's rights. Starting with Section 113, there are six more sections defining the "scope" of the exclusive rights bestowed on the copyright holder, each section specifying limits on the power of the copyright owner to prevent copying or demand damages. Of all the sections immediately following Section 107, only Section 108 is of direct and exclusive interest to the university and college community, which includes teachers, librarians, scholars and students, plus the administrators who are responsible for the use or misuse of the institution's equipment such as photo-copiers, audio-visual machines, and computers. (The text of Section 108 is reproduced on the two pages following.)

The best drafted statute is the one that states in clear and simple language what people may or may not do. The language should be comprehensible to any literate person, not just to lawyers who specialize in the field. From the viewpoint of educators and librarians, it would have been a consummation much to be desired if Section 107 had included the words proposed by the educators' Ad Hoc Committee on Copyright Law Revision:

> Notwithstanding other provisions of this Act, non-profit use of
> a portion of a copyrighted work for non-commercial teaching,
> scholarship and research is not an infringement of copyright.[12]

Although the meaning of "use" in such a context is probably clear enough, an additional sentence stating, in the Ad Hoc Committee's proposed words, that "use" shall mean "reproduction, copying and recording; storage and retrieval by automatic systems capable of storing, processing, retrieving or transferring information, or in conjunction with any similar device, machine or process" would have made it clear that any of the typical kinds of copying, and any of the methods of storing material in computers and other kinds of electronic memories, would be permissible. Whether stated expressly in the Act or in the supporting legislative history, that is how the educational community wanted it to be interpreted.

---

[11] Wihtol v. Crow, 309 F.2d 777 (8th Cir. 1962).
[12] Hearings, *supra* note 7, Pt. 3, at 2056.

1976 General Revision of the Copyright Law
Sections 106, 107, 108

§ 106 Exclusive rights in copyrighted works

Subject to sections 107 through 118, the owner of copyright under this title has the exclusive rights to do and to authorize any of the following:

(1) to reproduce the copyrighted work in copies or phonorecords;

(2) to prepare derivative works based upon the copyrighted work;

(3) to distribute copies or phonorecords of the copyrighted work to the public by sale or other transfer of ownership, or by rental, lease, or lending;

(4) in the case of literary, musical, dramatic, and choreographic works, pantomimes, and motion pictures and other audiovisual works, to perform the copyrighted work publicly; and

(5) in the case of literary, musical, dramatic, and choreographic works, pantomimes, and pictorial, graphic, or sculptural works, including the individual images of a motion picture or other audiovisual work, to display the copyrighted work publicly.

§ 107. Limitations on exclusive rights: Fair use

Notwithstanding the provisions of section 106, the fair use of a copyrighted work, including such use by reproduction in copies or phonorecords or by any other means specified by that section, for purposes such as criticism, comment, news reporting, teaching (including multiple copies for classroom use), scholarship, or research, is not an infringement of copyright. In determining whether the use made of a work in any particular case is a fair use of the factors to be considered shall include—

(1) the purpose and character of the use, including whether such use is of a commercial nature or is for nonprofit educational purposes;

(2) the nature of the copyrighted work;

(3) the amount and substantiality of the portion used in relation to the copyrighted work as a whole; and

(4) the effect of the use upon the potential market for or value of the copyrighted work.

§ 108. Limitations on exclusive rights: Reproduction by libraries and archives

(a) Notwithstanding the provisions of section 106, it is not an infringement of copyright for a library or archives, or any of its employees acting within the scope of their employment, to reproduce no more than one copy or phonorecord of a work, or to distribute such copy or phonorecord, under the conditions specified by this section, if—

(1) the reproduction or distribution is made without any purpose of direct or indirect commercial advantage;

(2) the collections of the library or archives are (i) open to the public, or (ii) available not only to researchers affiliated with the library or archives or with the institution of which it is a part, but also to other persons doing research in a specialized field; and

(3) the reproduction or distribution of the work includes a notice of copyright.

(b) The rights of reproduction and distribution under this section apply to a copy or phonorecord of an unpublished work duplicated in facsimile form solely for purposes of preservation and security or for deposit for research use in another library or archives of the type described by clause (2) of subsection (a), if the copy or phonorecord reproduced is currently in the collections of the library or archives.

(c) The right of reproduction under this section applies to a copy or phonorecord of a published work duplicated in facsimile form solely for the purpose of replacement of a copy or phonorecord that is damaged, deteriorating, lost, or stolen, if the library or archives has, after a reasonable effort, determined that an unused replacement cannot be obtained at a fair price.

(d) The rights of reproduction and distribution under this section apply to a copy, made from the collection of a library or archives where the user makes his or her request or from that of another library or archives, of no more than one article or other contribution to a copyrighted collection or periodical issue, or to a copy or phonorecord of a small part of any other copyrighted work if—

(1) the copy or phonorecord becomes the property of the user, and the library or archives has had no notice that the copy or phonorecord would be used for any purpose other than private study, scholarship, or research; and

(2) the library or archives displays prominently, at the place where orders are accept-

ed, and includes on its order form, a warning of copyright in accordance with requirements that the Register of Copyrights shall prescribe by regulation.

(e) The rights of reproduction and distribution under this section apply to the entire work, or to a substantial part of it, made from the collection of a library or archives where the user makes his or her request or from that of another library or archives, if the library or archives has first determined, on the basis of a reasonable investigation, that a copy or phonorecord of the copyrighted work cannot be obtained at a fair price, if—

(1) the copy or phonorecord becomes the property of the user, and the library or archives has had no notice that the copy or phonorecord would be used for any purpose other than private study, scholarship, or research; and

(2) the library or archives displays prominently, at the place where orders are accepted, and includes on its order form, a warning of copyright in accordance with requirements that the Register of Copyrights shall prescribe by regulation.

(f) Nothing in this section—

(1) shall be construed to impose liability for copyright infringement upon a library or archives or its employees for the unsupervised use of reproducing equipment located on its premises: *Provided,* That such equipment displays a notice that the making of a copy may be subject to the copyright law;

(2) excuses a person who uses such reproducing equipment or who requests a copy or phonorecord under subsection (d) from liability for copyright infringement for any such act, or for any later use of such copy or phonorecord, if it exceeds fair use as provided by section 107;

(3) shall be construed to limit the reproduction and distribution by lending of a limited number of copies and excerpts by a library or archives of an audiovisual news program, subject to clauses (1), (2), and (3) of subsection (a); or

(4) in any way affects the right of fair use as provided by section 107, or any contractual obligations assumed at any time by the library or archives when it obtained a copy or phonorecord of a work in its collections.

(g) The rights of reproduction and distribution under this section extend to the isolated and unrelated reproduction or distribution of a single copy or phonorecord of the same material on separate occasions, but do not extend to cases where the library or archives, or its employee—

(1) is aware or has substantial reason to believe that it is engaging in the related or concerted reproduction or distribution of multiple copies or phonorecords of the same material, whether made on one occasion or over a period of time, and whether intended for aggregate use by one or more individuals or for separate use by the individual members of a group; or

(2) engages in the systematic reproduction or distribution of single or multiple copies or phonorecords of material described in subsection (d): *Provided,* That nothing in this clause prevents a library or archives from participating in interlibrary arrangements that do not have, as their purpose or effect, that the library or archives receiving such copies or phonorecords for distribution does so in such aggregate quantities as to substitute for a subscription to or purchase of such work.

(h) The rights of reproduction and distribution under this section do not apply to a musical work, a pictorial, graphic or sculptural work, or a motion picture or other audiovisual work other than an audiovisual work dealing with news, except that no such limitation shall apply with respect to rights granted by subsections (b) and (c), or with respect to pictorial or graphic works published as illustrations, diagrams, or similar adjuncts to works of which copies are reproduced or distributed in accordance with subsections (d) and (e).

(i) Five years from the effective date of this Act, and at five-year intervals thereafter, the Register of Copyrights, after consulting with representatives of authors, book and periodical publishers, and other owners of copyrighted materials, and with representatives of library users and librarians, shall submit to the Congress a report setting forth the extent to which this section has achieved the intended statutory balancing of the rights of creators, and the needs of users. The report should also describe any problems that may have arisen, and present legislative or other recommendations, if warranted.

Unfortunately, in the bill's final passage, and after due deliberation, Congress decided not to accede to the educators' pleas to write those words in or near Section 107. The result is that, in order to determine whether and how much copying is permissible for classroom teaching and scholarly research, of the kind described in the discarded proposal, the historic language that appears in Section 107 must be interpreted, dissected, analyzed and applied perspicaciously. The language is "historic" because it draws on all the encrustation of half a century of litigation and interpretation for its application in particular cases. In the final enactment, the language is substantially the same as Section 107 of H.R. 4347, introduced over ten years before. In adopting that language, the House Judiciary Committee made the following statement in both the 1966 and the 1976 reports on the legislation:

> The expanded statement of the fair use doctrine in amended Section 107 offers some guidance to users in determining when the principles of the doctrine apply. However, the endless variety of situations and combinations of circumstances that can arise in particular cases precludes the formulation of exact rules in the statute. We endorse the purpose and general scope of the judicial doctrine of fair use, as outlined earlier in this report, but there is no disposition to freeze the doctrine in the statute, especially during a period of rapid technological change. Beyond a very broad statutory explanation of what fair use is and some of the criteria applicable to it, the courts must be free to adapt the doctrine to particular situations on a case-by-case basis. *Section 107 is intended to restate the present judicial doctrine of fair use, not to change, narrow, or enlarge it in any way.* [13]

It is, of course, always good for Congress to tell what it intended to say in adopting particular statutory language. In reading the quoted statement, it should be especially pleasing to librarians, teachers, and scholars to know that Congress did not intend "to change, narrow, or enlarge" the "judicial doctrine of fair use" in any way, since the latest judicial precedent on fair use, the *Williams and Wilkins* case, discussed below, was not adverse to their position. Before librarians, teachers, scholars, and students, however, can be assured that all they need do to determine whether a particular work or excerpt may be copied is examine the judicial precedents on "fair use" and mull over the legislative history of Sections 107 and 108, it is worth reviewing the circumstances in which any extraneous statement may be used in interpreting the statutory language ultimately adopted by a legislature.

---

[13] H.R. Rep. No. 94-1476, 94th Cong., 2d Sess. 66 (1976); H.R. Rep. No. 2237, 89th Cong., 2d Sess. 61 (1966) (emphasis added). *See also* S. Rep. No. 93-983, 93rd Cong., 2d Sess. 116 (1974).

Statutory Interpretation: Plain Meaning versus Legislative History

Conventional wisdom in the legal profession holds that, when the "plain meaning" of a statute is clear from its express words, the courts may not look beyond "the words by which the legislature undertook to give expression to its wishes. [14] When the meaning of those words is not "plain", however, the courts consider themselves free to consult the legislative history, which includes the statements made by the various proponents of the legislation, by witnesses in hearings on the proposal, by the committees in the various houses of the legislature, and by the legislators on the floor of the legislature.

Usually, the lawyers for one or more of the litigating parties can be depended upon to show judges the ways in which the language of a statute is vague and uncertain. If the lawyers succeed, the judges are freed to examine the various parts of the legislative history. It is now a rare statute, particularly among those passed by the United States Congress, that does not require this kind of interpretation. Even when the court concludes that the language of the statute is "plain", and legislative history is not needed in the interpretation, the judges have felt free to check the legislative history to determine whether their conclusion concerning the clarity and certainty of the language is correct. [15] The judges are also aware of the frequency of "doctoring" of legislative history to prepare for an interpretation desired by interested persons and their counsel who find themselves frustrated in obtaining the exact statutory language they desire. They may resort to the preparation of draft portions of committee reports, and even statements to be delivered on the floor of the legislature, stating the "true" meaning of the statutory language as viewed by the writers or speakers. Some learned commentators have questioned the ethics of this practice, but it persists in the halls of Congress and other legislative bodies. [16] The practice is even openly admitted by proponents of various views. There is an express acknowledgement of the practice in a committee report on the Copyright Revision Act which quotes from a letter from representatives of educators and publishers: "We had originally intended to translate the agreement into language suitable for inclusion in the legislative report dealing with section 107." [17]

Despite these pitfalls of legislative history, it is clear under recent holdings that courts will not refuse to look beyond the "plain words" of the new Copyright Act. The Act's legislative history is voluminous, with many pages of testimony, innumerable memoranda and explanatory letters introduced at the hearings, and statements on the floor of both Houses of Congress. The highlights and meaning of this legislative history are discussed below.

---

[14] *United States v. American Trucking Ass'n,* 310 U.S. 534, 543 (1940).

[15] *Schmid v. United States,* 436 F. 2d 987 (Ct. Cl. 1971).

[16] F. Newman & S. Surrey, Legislation Cases and Materials 158 (1955).

[17] H. R. Rep. No. 94-1476, 94th Cong., 2d Sess. 67 (1976).

Interpretation Through Judicial Precedent: The Williams and Wilkins Case

A far more standard method of statutory interpretation is, of course, the citation of prior court decisions interpreting the same or similar language. Indeed, the key words of Section 107 of the 1976 Act come from a passage in the *Mathews Conveyor Co.* case decided in 1943.[18] The passage is quoted by Professor Melville Nimmer in his copyright treatise,[19] a work that, in turn, is constantly and justifiably quoted by the judges as the leading authority on the law of copyright.

A highly relevant judicial precedent appeared shortly before Congress passed the 1976 Act: the *Williams and Wilkins* case.[20] No other reported case so clearly raises the issues of fair use in the context of education and scholarship. That context involves copying that is not for republication, reprinting, or public performance, but is clearly to be used not-for-profit and only for research, scholarship or teaching.

The *Williams and Wilkins* case wended its way through the various courts while the Senate and House Committees were in the throes of drafting the Copyright Revision Act of 1976, leading everyone to hope that at last the judicial doctrine of fair use would be clarified by the wisdom of a congeries of federal judges. The consummation, however, was not realized. The sixteen judges who heard the case in the three levels of the courts split evenly, eight to eight, on the question of infringement as against fair use. The opinion of the majority of the middle court, the Court of Claims, had dropped the ball firmly back in the lap of Congress by refusing to terminate a common practice in the use of technologically sophisticated facilities, unknown when the 1909 Act was passed, and stating that proper resolution of the question was clearly a legislative matter. A commentator with wide experience in copyright law and practice has suggested that the court was implicitly recognizing "the doctrine that a long-standing custom and practice constituted 'fair use' per se" in the context of education and scholarship.[21] The United States Supreme Court only a few years before had refused to declare a widespread practice in the use of television broadcasts to be a copyright infringement or to establish a compromise rule that would accommodate conflicting policy claims, saying, "That job is for Congress."[22]

In the *Williams and Wilkins* case the copying involved material held in the National Library of Medicine, an institution established by the Federal Government to serve the needs of medical research. The library subscribed to thousands of periodicals and journals. The courts found that, in 1970, which was accepted as a typical year, the library responded to thousands of

---

[18] *Mathews Conveyor Co. v. Palmer Bee Co.*, 135 F. 2d 73, 85 (6th Cir. 1943).
[19] 2 M. Nimmer, Nimmer on Copyright, § 145, at 645 (1972).
[20] *Williams and Wilkins v. United States*, 487 F. 2d 1345 (Ct. Cl. 1973); *aff'd by equally divided ct.*, 420 U.S. 376 (1975).
[21] Rosenfield, "Customary Use as 'Fair Use' in Copyright Law," 25 Buff. L. Rev. 119, 131 (1975).
[22] *Fortnightly Corp. v. United Artists Television, Inc.*, 392 U.S. 390, 401 (1968).

requests from persons engaged in medical research and medical practice, asking for copies of articles and portions of articles in the journals in the library's collection. Some of the requests were in the form of "interlibrary loans," meaning that the requests were from other libraries rather than from individual doctors or scholars. Many of the requests came from persons doing research in the National Institutes of Health, the agency in which the library was administratively located. Other requests came from all parts of the country and from abroad. Copying was not wholly unlimited, as the library's system included standards for determining when it would accede to requests, although exceptions were frequently made.

The plaintiff, Williams and Wilkins Company, was the publisher of scholarly journals in the medical field. A very large number of copies of articles in those publications, all of which were covered by valid copyrights, were made by the library, all without the consent of the copyright proprietor. The findings of the courts were that all the copies were to be used in research, study, and practice, and were not reprinted or republished for any profit-making purpose. During 1970, the library filled over 85,000 requests for copies of journal articles, including those published by the plaintiff company. The authors of the articles were mostly scholars in biological and similar medical fields who expected and received no compensation for their writing. Nonetheless, the Williams and Wilkins Company published the various journals as part of its business, in which it intended to earn a profit. While there was no specific evidence in the case that some of the copies were for educators to use in classroom teaching, there is also no reason to believe that the complaint of the plaintiff Company, or the reasoning of the courts, would have been any different if that particular purpose had also been expressly demonstrated in connection with the copying.

The trial judge in the *Williams and Wilkins* case, who bore the title of "Commissioner" of the United States Court of Claims, found that under the 1909 Act the copying activities of the National Library of Medicine constituted an infringement of the rights of the plaintiff, the Williams and Wilkins Company, entitling the plaintiff to recover reasonable and entire "compensation" from the defendant, the United States Government. That decision was rendered on February 16, 1972. On November 27, 1973, the Court of Claims itself handed down its decision in the case, with a majority of four of the judges holding that the Commissioner was in error, since the activities of the National Library of Medicine, in the specific context of this case, were "fair use" and not an infringement. The other three judges dissented, agreeing in full with the Commissioner. The case was taken to the United States Supreme Court, which heard argument on December 17, 1974, and on February 25, 1975, announced that the Justices were split evenly, four to four, resulting in automatic affirmance, without opinions, of the Court of Claims' decision. Although such a result is somewhat inconclusive, the proponents of the "fair use" argument took heart from the fact that the Supreme Court had not overturned the Court of Claims' decision, leaving intact the conclusion that copying was fair use and the Williams and Wilkins Company could not collect for infringement.

The Williams and Wilkins Case Under the 1976 Act

Let us consider how the *Williams and Wilkins* case would have been re-solved had the 1976 revision been in force, with all its legislative history. Under the 1976 Act, the Williams and Wilkins Company would have had to start its argument by relying on Section 106, which states that "The owner of copyright * * * has the exclusive right to reproduce * * * the copyrighted work in copies," and would have had to claim a remedy under one of the remedial sections of the Act. For example, Section 504 makes "an infringer of copyright * * * liable for either * * * actual damages * * * or statutory damages." If the complaint seeks statutory damages, they would be between $250 and $10,000 for all infringements involved in the action. The Act also provides alternative remedies, but for purposes of this discussion the damage remedies will be sufficient. There is no doubt that the copying by the National Library of Medicine without permission of the Williams and Wilkins Company would have been an infringement of the latter's "exclusive right * * * to reproduce the copyrighted work in copies," unless some other section of the Act established a "limitation" on that right and removed the copying from the classification of "infringement."

The defendant, the United States, which controls the National Library of Medicine, would, of course, have defended against the Williams and Wilkins complaint by citing Section 107, which states that "Notwithstanding the provisions of Section 106, the fair use of a copyrighted work * * * for teaching, * * * scholarship, or research * * * is not an infringement of copy-right." An old fashioned legal scholar might feel that the argument could stop right there, on the grounds that the plain words of the statute per-mitted the very copying at issue, which was for teaching, scholarship, or research. As the discussion above indicates, however, there is little chance that judges would refuse to look beyond the "plain words" of Sections 106 and 107 to their legislative history.

A very significant element of the legislative history of Section 107 is the argument and decision of the *Williams and Wilkins* case while the Con-gressional committees were in the midst of revising the copyright law. The coincidence raises the question whether the legislative committees intended to conform or overrule the Court of Claims' application of the fair use doctrine, of which they were fully aware through testimony of many wit-nesses. The only direct clue to their intention is the repetition in 1976 of the statement from the 1966 House Report that no change in the "judicial doctrine of fair use" was intended.[23] Would the Committee members have repeated that statement after the *Williams and Wilkins* decision if they had thought that the outcome of the case, denying damages for infringement, distorted the doctrine as they understood it? It seems doubtful. Even if

---

[23]*See* text accompanying note 13, *supra.*

Section 107 is intended to be consistent with the *Williams and Wilkins* outcome, however, the second sentence of Section 107 provides warning that
much more must be examined in order to determine whether the National
Library of Medicine was making "fair use" of the plaintiff's works:

> In determining whether the use made of a work in any particu-
> lar case is a fair use the factors to be considered shall include:
> (1) the purpose and character of the use, including whether
> such use is of a commercial nature or is for nonprofit educa-
> tional purposes;
> (2) the nature of the copyrighted work;
> (3) the amount and substantiality of the portion used in rela-
> tion to the copyrighted work as a whole; and
> (4) the effect of the use upon the potential market for or value
> of the copyrighted work.

How does the legislative history of this sentence help to resolve the key
issue in this case, "What did Congress mean when it used these words?" The
Committee reports and the floor debates contain many pages of explanation
of the relevant provisions of the statute. The most important may be (1) the
statement quoted above from the report of the House Judiciary Committee
that "Section 107 is intended to restate the present judicial doctrine of fair
use, not to change, narrow, or enlarge it in any way;" (2) references to an
"Agreement on Guidelines for Classroom Copying in Not-for-Profit Educational Institutions" (set forth in full in the same House Report and in Appendix A to this article); and (3) references to "Guidelines for the Proviso
of Subsection 108 (g)(2)" (set forth in full in the Conference Report on the
1976 Act and in Appendix B to this article.)

The expressed intention of the House Committee to "restate" the
judicial doctrine of fair use, "not to change, narrow, or enlarge it in any
way," naturally sends us to the previous judicial decisions to determine how
the facts of the present case fit into that doctrine. The most recent decision,
of course, is the *Williams and Wilkins* case itself. The various opinions of the
judges in that case review practically all previous cases that seem relevant
and even seek to determine, from recent developments, what Congress
would expect. The majority opinion in the Court of Claims refers to the
1967 report of House Judiciary Committee[24] as "influential" in ascertaining
the existing law.[25] This emphasizes the relevance of the 1976 Act and its
legislative history as guides to the meaning of fair use even before the official
effective date of the new Act on January 1, 1978. Judge Oscar Davis' majority opinion quotes the "factors" that Section 107, then in draft stage, says
must be considered in determining if a particular use is fair.[26] Judge Davis
considers all those factors in some detail, and even discusses a few additional

---

[24] H.R. Rep. No. 83, 90th Cong., 1st Sess. (1967).
[25] *Williams and Wilkins v. United States*, 487 F. 2d 1345, 1361 (Ct. Cl. 1973).
[26] *Id.* at 1352. *See* text accompanying note 18, *supra*, for the derivation of the factors in Section
107.

ones. He concludes that the fair use doctrine applied to the facts, and summarizes the reasons as follows:

> [P]laintiff has not in our view shown, and there is no adequate reason to believe, that it is being or will be harmed substantially by these specified practices * * * .;
>
> [M]edicine and medical research will be injured by holding these particular practices to be an infringement;
>
> * * * and * * * since the problem * * * calls fundamentally for legislative solution or guidance * * * we should not, during the period before congressional action is forthcoming, place such a risk of harm upon science and medicine.[27]

The opinion emphasized the non-profit character of the copier and of the different persons requesting copies, which is the main point of the first factor found in Section 107. The court then called attention to "the nature of the copyrighted work"; the copied articles were "scientific studies" used by scientists and scholars in their scientific work. In considering the "amount and substantiality of the portion" copied "in relation to the copyrighted work as a whole," the court noted that the general practice of the National Library of Medicine was to furnish copies only of single articles in a journal, and to impose other restrictions on the quantity of copies and size of the copying.[28] After a lengthy discussion of the argument that the plaintiff had been financially hurt by the copying, the court concluded that "this record simply does not show a serious adverse impact, either on plaintiff or medical publishers generally, from the photocopying practices" involved in this case.[29]

If the majority opinion of the Court of Claims stood alone as the latest precedent on the meaning of "fair use," the copying done in the *Williams and Wilkins* case, and similar activities resembling the Library's practices in that case, would be fairly easy to fit in to the fair use doctrine. Guidelines adopting the majority's conclusions would be fairly easy to draft in a clear and helpful manner. Unfortunately, however, the four majority judges admitted that they were simply approving an established practice in library and scholarly circles, pending clarification by the legislative process. Also three judges of the very same court strongly disagreed with the result, four Justices of the United States Supreme Court indicated similar disagreement, and eminent commentators also expressed discordant views. For example, in a sentence reminiscent of Justice McReynold's anguished outcry, when some of the New Deal legislation was upheld forty years ago, that "the Constitution is gone,"[30] Professor Nimmer stated that "the *Williams & Wilkins* discussion carried to its logical extreme would largely undercut the entire law of copyright * * *."[31] He added that if the progress of the "useful

---

[27] *Williams and Wilkins v. United States, supra* note 25, at 1354.

[28] *Id.* at 1354.

[29] *Id.* at 1358.

[30] *Perry v. United States,* 294 U.S. 330 (1935).

[31] 2 M. Nimmer, Nimmer on Copyright. § 145 at 656.2 (1972).

arts" (the words from the U.S. Constitution) is promoted by granting copyright protection to authors, "such progress may well be impeded if copyright protection is largely undercut in the name of fair use." [32] Despite the
depths of legal scholarship that went into the opinions in the *Williams and
Wilkins* case, it led to profound disagreement among sixteen judges and equal
measures of praise and criticism by Professor Nimmer and other lawyers and
scholars. Consequently, it would be risky to rely on that case as demonstrating that its facts fit the statutory codification of the "judicial doctrine" of
fair use, even if the doctrine still stands without "change, narrowing or enlarging in any way." As already stated, however, no other case deals as
directly with the copying rights of educators and scholars.

If the answer cannot be found in court decisions on the "unchanged
judicial doctrine," resort must be had to the second available source of interpretation, namely, the legislative history of Section 107 and Section 108-
(g)(2). In 1976, that voluminous legislative history finally drew to a focus
in the two sets of "guidelines" previously cited and set forth in Appendices
A and B. These guidelines were the product of lengthy negotiations among
publishers, authors, teachers, scholars, scientists and their representatives,
usually lawyers. Although not drafted by members of the legislative branch,
they were officially incorporated into the legislative history of the Act by
being printed in the House and Conference Committee Reports with words
of approval by the members of the Committees. The guidelines for "classroom copying," addressed to Section 107, were accepted by the House
Committee as "a reasonable interpretation of the minimum standards of fair
use." [33] With certain "qualifications" the Conference Committee agreed that
the guidelines for "interlibrary arrangements", addressed to the "proviso"
subsection 108(g)(2), "are a reasonable interpretation of the proviso ***." [34]

Since the guidelines for Section 107 are addressed to "classroom copying", not significantly involved in the reproductions from the National
Library of Medicine, it may be more useful to look at the guidelines for
Section 108(g)(2). At the same time, the purpose served by Section 108
itself must be borne clearly in mind. As its caption indicates, it is a *limitation* on the exclusive right of the proprietor to make copies. Since Section
107 contains the "fair use" limitation, Section 108 must have been included
to provide some additional copying privileges. Phrases in Section 108 like
"systematic reproduction" and "concerted reproduction of *** multiple
copies * * * of the same material" are not limitations on fair use but describe limits to those *additional* privileges. The guidelines for any part of
Section 108 must be read in the light of this analysis.

The guidelines for section 108(g)(2) are addressed to "interlibrary
loans," which were involved in a substantial amount of the disputed copying
at the National Library of Medicine. In the interlibrary situation, the analysis starts with the statement, in the "plain words" of Section 108(g)(2), to

---

[32] *Id.*
[33] H.R. Rep. No. 94-1476, 94th Cong., 2d. Sess. 72 (1976).
[34] Conf. Rep. No. 94-1733, 94th Cong., 2d. Sess. 72 (1976).

the effect that a library is not to be prevented from "interlibrary arrangements * * * ," provided that those arrangements do not go beyond the limits in Section 108 itself as elaborated in the guidelines. Taking all of these sources of guidance into consideration, it may be concluded that a single copy may be made from time to time in response to a request from a library, if—

(1) there is no "purpose of direct or indirect commercial advantage;"

(2) the library where the copying is done is open to researchers who are not affiliated with the library's institution, as well as those who are;

(3) the copies bear a notice of copyright;

(4) the copying is not done at a library in such quantities "as to substitute for a subscription to or purchase of such work" (Section 108(g)(2), which means, according to the guidelines, no more than five copies of any one periodical, for one library within one year, if the article was published in the periodical within five years prior to the date of the request. The word "periodical" does not mean "issue of a periodical," but one title;

(5) the copying of articles is done at a library where the maker of the copies "has had no notice that the copy * * * would be used for any purpose other than private study, scholarship or research," and if the copying library has a conspicuous notice, in a form to be prescribed by the Register of Copyrights, warning about the rights of copyright proprietors; and

(6) above all, the library is not engaged "in the *systematic reproduction or distribution* of single or multiple copies" of most of the kinds of works found in research libraries (emphasis added).

The words "systematic reproduction or distribution," which appear in Section 108(g)(2) of the new Act, first came to light, without hearings, in late drafts of the Act, after it seemed possible that a decision in the *Williams and Wilkins* case would clearly declare that it is fair use to engage in extensive reproduction of single copies of library materials. No one really defined "systematic reproduction" any better than to say that it was evidently intended to reverse the result of such a Court of Claims decision.[35]   If the *Williams and Wilkins* kind of copying is "systematic," then it is not among the "limitations on the exclusive rights" of the copyright owner and may be an infringement, unless other language in the "guidelines" or elsewhere in the reports restores it as a limitation on the proprietor's rights. Fortunately for the educators, scholars, and librarians, there is such language; like so much of the Act and its history, however, a Delphic uncertainty taints its

---

[35]Testimony of Edmond Low for the American Library Association, Hearings, *supra* note 7, ser. no. 36, Pt. 1, at 184-204 (1975).

meaning with "amorphousness," the word applied by Barbara Ringer, the Commissioner of Copyrights. [36]

Section 108 itself says, in subsection (f)(4), that nothing therein "in any way affects the right of fair use as provided by section 107 * * *." In explaining Section 108 on the House floor on September 22, 1976, Representative Railsback, speaking for the subcommittee, said, "Libraries are subject to the 'fair use' doctrine of section 107." [37] Commissioner Ringer, testifying on this very question, warned the House subcommittee on October 9, 1975, that subsection (f)(4) "has already been, and certainly can be interpreted in different ways." [38] That was before the guidelines on the "proviso portion" of subsection 108 (g)(2) had been promulgated by agreement among the librarians and the publishers, and incorporated into the legislative history. Despite its grammatical distortion, the proviso portion makes clear the validity, under the fair use doctrine, of "interlibrary loans" that are not intended as a "substitute for a subscription to or purchase" of a work. Under the proviso, "interlibrary arrangements" that are not intended as a means of avoiding a sale are valid and do not become the "systematic reproduction" which so distresses the publishing industry. Being addressed only to "interlibrary arrangements," however, the guidelines for Section 108(g)(2) are of no help in the classification of copying, such as occurred so frequently in the National Library of Medicine, that was not initiated by a request from another library. For that kind of copying, the search for the answer reverts in a full circle back to the definition of the "unchanged judicial doctrine of fair use," which is where the effort to apply the new Act to the *Williams and Wilkins* facts began. Indeed, it is a paper chase without a happy ending.

Specific Examples of Fair Use

Some specific examples of copying for educational and scholarly purposes are impliedly or expressly permitted by the new Act, as refined by statements in the committee reports, particularly the guidelines. The educational community must first of all assume that any reproduction that resembles the kinds of copying that formed the basis of controversy in the *Williams and Wilkins* case is now—is still—fair use and not infringement. On that assumption, the conclusion follows that a single copy of a copyrighted work may be made in response to each request, especially from libraries, where the intended use of the copy is scientific, learning, scholarship, or any similar activity that does not involve reprinting, republication, or public "performance." To fall under this exemption, there should also be no evidence that the copies will be used directly in a profit-making context that would also be likely to detract from the copyright owner's expected returns. With these factors present, the outcome of the *Williams and*

---

[36] Hearings, *supra* note 7, Pt. 3, at 1801.
[37] 122 Cong. Rec. 1087 (daily ed., Sept. 22, 1976).
[38] Hearings, *supra* note 7, Pt. 3, at 1799.

Wilkins case should lead to the conclusion that the copying, even if large in the aggregate number of separate copies, is "within the judicial doctrine of fair use" codified in the 1976 Act.

The guidelines for Section 107 themselves state that they are "not intended to limit the types of copying permitted under the standards of fair use under judicial decision * * *." Despite its shakiness as precedent, the *Williams and Wilkins* case may be as reliable as some of the specific examples in the guidelines, because it is an existing judicial statement rather than legislative history. A judge confronted with a new copyright case might see an unexpected clarity in a relevant section of the new Act and invoke the traditional doctrine that extraneous statements in legislative history, even in committee reports, cannot vary the "plain language" of a legislative act; but that some judge would feel free to rely on the *Williams and Wilkins* opinions because decisions of courts are not "extraneous" as aids to interpretation.

Such judicial perspicacity, however, is hardly likely in this murky area, and the guidelines for Section 107, where they are specific, will probably be deemed reliable evidence of the fair use license intended by Congress. They describe the lower limits of fair use, as they are expressly characterized as the "minimums" that may be copied without infringement. Thus, a teacher who spontaneously decides one morning that the pupils in that day's class would benefit from seeing a poem that appeared in the local newspaper the day before, is clearly safe in making a few copies for the class if the poem is under 250 words, the pupils are not being asked to pay for a copy, and this is the first time the teacher has done this in the present term.

A more complex example is a chapter from a book. The guidelines expressly permit a "teacher" to make, or have a single copy made, of "a chapter from a book," to be used for scholarly research or teaching or preparation for teaching—

>   (1) *if* the copying is not to be used "to create or to replace or substitute for anthologies, compilations or collective works;" and
>   (2) *if* the chapter is not a "consumable" workbook, exercise, standardized test, or the like; and
>   (3) *unless* the copying is a substitute for the purchase of a book or a publisher's reprint; or
>   (4) *unless* the copying was directed by higher authority; or
>   (5) *unless* the same teacher is repeating the same copying in a subsequent term; and
>   (6) *as long as* the "student" is not being charged more than the actual cost of the copying.

The appearance of the words "teacher," "school," and "pupil" in the guidelines, except in the last sentence where "student" appears, would have created at least a modicum of doubt as to their applicability to higher education if the House Committee, in response to a protest by some representatives of university faculties, had not noted in its Report "that the Ad Hoc group [which nominally concurred in the guidelines] did include representatives of higher education." [39]

The teacher may also make or receive multiple copies of a chapter, limited, however, to one copy of the chapter per pupil in a course *if—*

(1) the chapter does not exceed "1000 words or 10% of the work, whichever is less, but in any event a minimum of 500 words;"

(2) the copying is done "at the instance and inspiration of the individual teacher;"

(3) "the inspiration and decision to use the work and the moment of its use for maximum teaching effectiveness are so close in time that it would be unreasonable to expect a timely reply to a request for permission;"

(4) the copying is "for only one course in the school;"

(5) not more than two excerpts are copied from the same author, nor more than three from the same collective work during one class term; and

(6) there are not more than "nine instances" of such multiple copying for one course during one class term;

and, of course, unless there exist any of the conditions in 3-6 of the previous paragraph applicable to a book.

The "but" clause in condition (1) above ("but in any event a minimum of 500 words") is from paragraph (ii) of "Definitions" in the guidelines. That clause defies rational parsing, and perhaps epitomizes the failure of efforts, despite the pressure from the Congressional committees, to close the gap between the educators' and the publishers' aims in the codification of "fair use." There is also no explanation whether, for example, the "nine instances" mentioned in condition 6 above refers to nine reproductions of a work in one course in one class term taught by one teacher, or by several teachers of the same course in a whole institution.

There has been one published effort to define the purpose and limits of the Section 107 guidelines, in the form of a letter to the editor of *The Chronicle of Higher Education* [40] signed by the Chairman of the Ad Hoc Committee and three law school professors, each representing higher education organizations. That letter states that "it is simply inconceivable that two teachers in different schools within a large university could lose the protection of the fair use doctrine when, perhaps even unbeknownst to each other, they use copies of the same excerpt * * * in teaching two widely different classes." The letter emphasizes that the guidelines are a statement of the "minimum scope" of the fair use doctrine, providing an assured "safe harbor" for any teacher who copies within their scope. The writers believe that the new Act is to be interpreted liberally in favor of copying for education and research. Unfortunately, the letter is extraneous legislative history,

---

[39] H.R. Rep. No. 94-1476, 94th Cong., 2d Sess. 72 (1976).
[40] *Chronicle of Higher Education*, p. 17, col. 1 (Nov. 15, 1976).

once removed, and a poor candidate for judicial contemplation as an aid to interpretation.

On the other hand, there is some internal legislative history that seems to support the claim that the 1976 Act should be interpreted liberally in favor of the educators' privilege to copy. Representative Robert Drinan, a member of the House Subcommittee, expressly stated on the House floor, that the purpose of some of the House amendments to the Senate version of S.22, which remained in the Act, was "to provide greater access to published materials by educators, librarians and the citizenry."[41] Representative Frenzel of Minnesota, not a member of the Subcommittee, while indicating that he supported the fair use portions of the Bill, said that he hoped "the courts will continue to construe 'fair use' as broadly as possible."[42]

In the face of this morass of interpretative guides, a teacher or librarian needing to copy a copyrighted work for classroom or research use may justifiably wonder how to determine, before any judges have spoken, whether the copying is "within the scope" of the guidelines, and even whether the guidelines are reliable guideposts. Must there be a questionnaire containing questions on every illustration, every "if" and every "unless" described in the preceding pages and equally applicable to several other specific illustrations in the guidelines? How else can the fairness of a particular copying be determined? If ever an action by Congress has portended a "chilling effect" on a legitimate activity, surely this Act and its guidelines are classic examples. Even a chief defender of the guidelines, who joined in their submission to the Committees and in the explanatory Letter to the Editor discussed above, has recognized that "some fundamental misreading of what Congress has done" began to surface before the ink was dry on the President's signature on the Act, potentially leading to "intimidation" of teachers and libraries from kinds of copying that the law actually permits.[43]

Fortunately, however, Congress has provided a measure of relief for members of the academic community in the form of several exculpatory clauses.

When Ignorance of the Law Does Excuse

When it was considering the fair use doctrine's relevance to the facts of the *Williams and Wilkins* case, the Court of Claims sought interpretive guidance from all possible sources, including the statements made by the Congressional committees during their consideration of the proposed copyright law revision. The court, writing before the 1976 House Report was published, cited the discussions in the 1966 House report, some of which are quoted above. The majority opinion states aptly that "the committee's observations are delphic."[44]   The same comment can certainly be made

[41] 122 *Cong. Rec.* 10880 (daily ed., Sept. 22, 1976).
[42] 122 *Cong. Rec.* 10882 (daily ed., Sept. 22, 1976).
[43] Newsletter, Nat'l. Ass'n. Col. & U. Bus. Officers (Dec. 1976).
[44] *Williams and Wilkins v. United States*, 487 F. 2d 1345, 1361 (Ct. Cl., 1973).

about the expressions of intention in the reports of 1976 and in the explanatory "guidelines" prepared so laboriously by representatives of the authors, publishers, and members of the educational community. All the great expressions that judges have used to report their confusion as to the meaning of particular statutes and other rules of law can be applied here: "Confusion now hath made his masterpiece,"[45] for instance, or "this case [involving copyright] calls not for the judgment of Solomon but for the dexterity of Houdini."[46] To ask librarians and users of library materials to determine whether a particular work may legally be copied under this statute is indeed like asking an ancient Greek-in-the-street to understand, without the help of priestly interpreters, the cryptic words of the Oracle at Delphi. One specialist with long experience in the field has only perceived "cloudiness in the crystal ball" that must be used to predict developments in fair use.[47] Even if librarians, scholars, teachers, and students could take time to study all the statutory language, committee reports, floor debates, and other extraneous statements constituting the legislative history of the 1976 Act, before determining whether a particular work could be legitimately copied, they would still end up in deep confusion. If, in addition, they have the opportunity to consult their lawyers for advice, they are likely to end up with nothing better than the statement of the Register of Copyrights, in testifying before the House Judiciary Committee in 1975:

> It is conceded that "fair use" is not susceptible to exact definition. Generally speaking, however, it allows copying without permission from, or payment to, the copyright owner where the use is reasonable and not harmful to the rights of the copyright owner.[48]

As already pointed out, there are a few situations where, under the plain statutory language, coupled with the legislative history, a particular work may clearly be copied without the permission of the copyright proprietor. Except for those specific situations, however, it may be so difficult to distinguish between the right to copy and the rights of the proprietor that the person who approaches a photocopying machine may have to put primary reliance on those sections of the Act providing that even if the rights of the proprietor are infringed, no damages can be exacted where evidence of good faith is present. Section 504 (c)(2)(i), for example, removes the liability for damages "in any case where an infringer believed and had reasonable grounds for believing that his or her use of the copyrighted work was a fair use under Section 107" whenever the inadvertent infringer was (a) an employee or agent of a non-profit educational institution, library, or archives; or (b) a non-profit institution, library, or archives

---

[45] Mr. Justice Jackson quoting from Shakespear's *MacBeth* in *Rice v. Rice*, 336 U.S. 674, 676 (1947).
[46] Mr. Justice Fortas dissenting in *Fortnightly Corp. v. United Artists Television, Inc.* 392 U.S. 390, 402 (1968).
[47] Stedman, "The New Copyright Law: Photocopying for Educational Use," 63 AAUP Bull. † (1977).
[48] Hearings, *supra* note 7, Pt. 3, p. 2055.

itself. Section 108 itself, in subsection (d)(1), provides that there is no infringement, and therefore no liability for damages, if (1) the proposed user appears unable to buy a copy at a fair price, (2) the user of the copy becomes its owner, (3) the library or archives where the work was copied "has had no notice that the copy or phonorecord would be used for any purpose other than private study, scholarship, or research," and (4) there is a clear warning that copyright law restricts reproduction, drafted under regulations issued by the Register of Copyrights and displayed prominently at the place where copies are made.

The 1976 House Committee report discussing the exculpatory provision for non-profit copiers in Section 504, stated that the burden of proof of lack of good faith would be on the party complaining of infringement.[49] If the copying is done in a profit-making facility, under certain other distinguishing circumstances, damages for infringement can be reduced to "not less than $100" whenever the infringer can prove that it had no knowledge that the copying would constitute an infringement of copyright. The most important ingredient in proving good faith in these cases is the conviction of the user that the copying has no commercial, profit-making motive, such as republication and sale, or conversely, lack of evidence that the only reason for the copying is to avoid the expense of obtaining advance permission.

Conclusion

We may have to conclude that the safest refuge of the harried scholar or librarian, standing in front of a purring photocopier and needing a copy of a copyrighted work that he holds in his hand, is to rely on the Act's express exculpation of the innocent copier who is free of profit motive. That is not a happy answer to the question, "What shall I tell my client?" Perhaps this analysis, however, provides some more helpful guidance through the analytical jungle. If so, it has served a better purpose than adding to the confusion. If, however, it has mostly delineated the uncertainties, the reason lies in the clash of policies and values in the interlocked world of communication and scholarship.

Throughout the hearings, negotiations, and court proceedings of the decade preceding the 1976 Act, the representatives of the copyright proprietors demonstrated that their concern about unrestricted copying for education and scholarship was loss of sales and profits for authors and publishers. While any copying for teaching and research, whether in schools, college and university libraries, or elsewhere, might reduce sales, the educational community argued that generally such copying either is not a substitute for purchases or, when it is, the public interest demands that it be permitted without fear of liability, within limits that are reasonable and practicable. By including the exculpatory provisions in the new Act, Congress showed that it accepted the education community's argument.

---

[49] H.R. Rep. No. 94-1476, 94th Cong., 2d Sess. 163 (1976).

For the librarians, and for scholars, teachers, and students making copies in non-profit educational institutions, the exculpatory provisions may be the only source of reliable license to copy particular works bearing a copyright notice. The complexity of the communications system of modern society is probably more to blame for the difficulty of drafting clear and simple guidelines than the fabled inability of lawyers to express rules in simple language. The tax experts who drafted the Tax Reform Act of 1969 similarly failed in the effort to find definitions when they tried to curtail the evil activities of some private foundations. The final text of the Act reveals that the effort to define "private foundation" was abandoned; Section 509 merely describes a few kinds of organizations that are *not* private foundations. The new Copyright Act, unfortunately, is even worse; it not only fails to define "infringement", but it sets forth a confusing mass of exceptions, starting with "fair use" and then proceeding with definitions and subdefinitions of actions that are, or are not, within that doctrine. Fortunately, among those subdefinitions is the exculpation of those who engage in innocent infringement. The innocent copier may be like the diplomat who violates the law but may not be arrested because the public interest in international communication transcends the value of punishing diplomats in local courts. "Copier's exculpation" will become the diplomatic immunity of the scholar and the librarian, because Congress has decided that the public interest in education and research transcends the authors' and publishers' need for financial compensation when copying is done for those purposes. The damages authorized by the Act will not be imposed when an offended copyright owner cannot show that the copier should have known that the copying, although it appeared to be reasonable, actually was not within one of the exceptions to the owner's "exclusive right," and that it in fact violated the law.

De facto ignorantia huius legis excusat innocentum; actual ignorance of this law does excuse the innocent.

APPENDIX A

In a joint letter to Chairman Kastenmeier, dated March 19, 1976, the representatives of the Ad Hoc Committee of Educational Institutions and Organizations on Copyright Law Revision, and of the Authors League of America, Inc., and the Association of American Publishers, Inc., stated:

You may remember that in our letter of March 8, 1976 we told you that the negotiating terms representing authors and publishers and the Ad Hoc Group had reached tentative agreement on guidelines to insert in the Committee Report covering educational copying from books and periodicals under Section 107 of H.R. 2223 and S. 22, and that as part of that tentative

agreement each side would accept the amendments to Sections 107 and 504 which were adopted by your subcommittee on March 3, 1976.

We are now happy to tell you that the agreement has been approved by the principals and we enclose a copy herewith. We had originally intended to translate the agreement into language suitable for inclusion in the legislative report dealing with Section 107, but we have since been advised by committee staff that this will not be necessary.

As stated above, the agreement refers only to copying from books and periodicals, and it is not intended to apply to musical or audiovisual works.

The full text of the agreement is as follows:

The purpose of the following guidelines is to state the minimum standards of educational fair use under Section 107 of H.R. 2223. The parties agree that the conditions determining the extent of permissible copying for educational purposes may change in the future; that certain types of copying permitted under these guidelines may not be permissible in the future; and conversely that in the future other types of copying not permitted under these guidelines may be permissible under revised guidelines.

Moreover, the following statement of guidelines is not intended to limit the types of copying permitted under the standards of fair use under judicial decision and which are stated in Section 107 of the Copyright Revision Bill. There may be instances in which copying which does not fall within the guidelines stated below may nonetheless be permitted under the criteria of fair use.

GUIDELINES

1. *Single Copying for Teachers*

A single copy may be made of any of the following by or for a teacher at his or her individual request for his or her scholarly research or use in teaching or preparation to teach a class:

A. A chapter from a book;

B. An article from a periodical or newspaper;

C. A short story, short essay or short poem, whether or not from a collective work;

D. A chart, graph, diagram, drawing, cartoon, or picture from a book, periodical, or newspaper;

II. *Multiple copies for Classroom Use*

Multiple copies (not to exceed in any event more than one copy per pupil in a course) may be made by or for the teacher giving the course for classroom use or discussion; *provided that:*

A. The copying meets the tests of brevity and spontaneity as defined below; *and,*

B. Meets the cumulative effect test as defined below; *and,*

C. Each copy includes a notice of copyright.

Definitions

Brevity

(*i*) Poetry: (a) A complete poem if less than 250 words and if printed on not more than two pages or, (b) from a longer poem, an excerpt of not more than 250 words.

(*ii*) Prose: (a) Either a complete article, story or essay of less than 2,500 words, or (b) an excerpt from any prose work of not more than 1,000 words or 10% of the work, whichever is less, but in any event a minimum of 500 words.

[Each of the numerical limits stated in "i" and "ii" above may be expanded to permit the completion of an unfinished line of a poem or of an unfinished prose paragraph.]

(*iii*) Illustration: One chart, graph, diagram, drawing, cartoon or picture per book or per periodical issue.

(*iv*) "Special" works: Certain works in poetry, prose or in "poetic prose" which often combine language with illustrations and which are intended sometimes for children and at other times for a more general audience fall short of 2,500 words in their entirety. Paragraph "ii" above notwithstanding such "special works" may not be reproduced in their entirety; however, an excerpt comprising not more than two of the published pages of such special work and containing not more than 10% of the words found in the text thereof, may be reproduced.

Spontaneity

(*i*) The copying is at the instance and inspiration of the individual teacher, and

(*ii*) The inspiration and decision to use the work and the moment of its use for maximum teaching effectiveness are so close in time that it would be unreasonable to expect a timely reply to a request for permission.

Cumulative Effect

(*i*) The copying of the material is for only one course in the school in which the copies are made.

(*ii*) Not more than one short poem, article, story, essay or two excerpts may be copied from the same author, nor more than three from the same collective work or periodical volume during one class term.

(*iii*) There shall not be more than nine instances of such multiple copying for one course during one class term.

[The limitations stated in "ii" and "iii" above shall not apply to current news periodicals and newspapers and current news sections of other periodicals.]

III. *Prohibitions as to I and II Above*

Notwithstanding any of the above, the following shall be prohibited:

(A) Copying shall not be used to create or to replace or substitute for anthologies, compilations or collective works. Such replacement or substitution may occur whether copies of various works or excerpts therefrom are accumulated or reproduced and used separately.

(B) There shall be no copying of or from works intended to be "consumable" in the course of study or of teaching. These include workbooks, exercises, standardized tests and test booklets and answer sheets and like consumable material.

(C) Copying shall not:

(a) substitute for the purchase of books, publishers' reprints or periodicals;

(b) be directed by higher authority;

(c) be repeated with respect to the same item by the same teacher from term to term.

(D) No charge shall be made to the student beyond the actual cost of photocopying.

Agreed MARCH 19, 1976.

Ad Hoc Committee on Copyright Law Revision:

By

SHELDON ELLIOTT STEINBACH.

Author-Publisher Group:

Authors League of America:

By IRWIN KARP, *Counsel.*

Association of American Publishers, Inc.:

By ALEXANDER C. HOFFMAN, *Chairman, Copyright Committee.*

APPENDIX B

Photocopying—Interlibrary Arrangements

INTRODUCTION

Subsection 108(g)(2) of the bill deals, among other things, with limits on interlibrary arrangements for photocopying. It prohibits systematic photocopying of copyrighted materials but permits interlibrary arrangements "that do not have, as their purpose or effect, that the library or archives receiving such copies or phonorecords for distribution does so in such aggregate quantities as to substitute for a subscription to or purchase of such work."

The National Commission on New Technological Use of Copyrighted Works offered its good offices to the House and Senate subcommittees in bringing the interested parties together to see if agreement could be reached on what a realistic definition would be of "such aggregate quantities." The Commission consulted with the parties and suggested the interpretation which follows, on which there has been substantial agreement by the principal library, publisher, and author organizations. The Commission considers the guidelines which follow to be a workable and fair interpretation of the intent of the proviso portion of subsection 108(g)(2).

These guidelines are intended to provide guidance in the application of section 108 to the most frequently encountered interlibrary case: a library's obtaining from another library, in lieu of interlibrary loan, copies of articles from relatively recent issues of periodicals—those published within five years prior to the date of the request. The guidelines do not specify what aggregate quantity of copies of an article or articles published in a periodical, the issue date of which is more than five years prior to the date when the request for the copy thereof is made, constitutes a substitute for a subscription to such periodical. The meaning of the proviso to subsection 108(g)(2) in such case is left to future interpretation.

The point has been made that the present practice on interlibrary loans and use of photocopies in lieu of loans may be supplemented or even largely replaced by a system in which one or more agencies or institutions, public or private, exist for the specific purpose of providing a central source for photocopies. Of course, these guidelines would not apply to such a situation.

GUIDELINES FOR THE PROVISO OF SUBSECTION 108(G)(2)

1. As used in the proviso of subsection 108(g)(2), the words ". . . such aggregate quantities as to substitute for a subscription to or purchase of such work" shall mean:

(a) with respect to any given periodical (as opposed to any given issue of a periodical), filled requests of a library or archives (a "requesting entity") within any calendar year for a total of six or more copies of an article or articles published in such periodical within five years prior to the date of the request. These guidelines specifically shall not apply, directly or indirectly, to any request of a requesting entity for a copy or copies of an article or articles published in any issue of a periodical, the publication date of which is more than five years prior to the date when the request is made. These guidelines do not define the meaning, with respect to such a request, of ". . . such aggregate quantities as to substitute for a subscription to [such periodical]".

(b) With respect to any other material described in subsection 108(d), (including fiction and poetry), filled requests of a requesting entity within any calendar year for a total of six or more copies or phonorecords of or from any given work (including a collective work) during the entire period when such material shall be protected by copyright.

2. In the event that a requesting entity—

(a) shall have in force or shall have entered in order for a subscription to a periodical, or

(b) has within its collection, or shall have entered an order for, a copy or phonorecord of any other copyrighted work, material from either category of which it desires to obtain by copy from another library or archives (the "supplying entity"), because the material to be copied is not reasonably available for use by the requesting entity itself, then the fulfillment of such request shall be treated as though the requesting entity made such copy from its own collection. A library or archives may request a copy or phonorecord from a supplying entity only under those circumstances where the requesting entity would have been able, under the other provisions of section 108, to supply such copy from materials in its own collection.

3. No request for a copy or phonorecord of any material to which these guidelines apply may be fulfilled by the supporting entity unless such request is accompanied by a representation by the requesting entity that the request was made in conformity with these guidelines.

4. The requesting entity shall maintain records of all requests made by it for copies or phonorecords of any materials to which these guidelines apply and shall maintain records of the fulfillment of such requests, which records shall be retained until the end of the third complete calendar year after the end of the calendar year in which the respective request shall have been made.

5. As part of the review provided for in subsection 108(i), these guidelines shall be reviewed not later than five years from the effective date of this bill.

CHAPTER 24

MISCELLANEOUS FEDERAL REGULATIONS

I.   Introduction

In late December 1978, the 6th Circuit Court of Appeals ruled that officials at the Veterans Administration possessed statutory authority to regulate the definition of full-time study for purposes of granting veteran's benefits, even though the definition adopted by the administrative agency might not be consistent with a college or university determination of full-time student status. The decision of the 6th Circuit, which appeared in Wayne State University, et al. v. Max Cleland, et al., Nos. 78-1141, 78-1142 (December 21, 1978), reversed a district court ruling invalidating certain V.A. regulations which altered the congressional definition of full-time study set out in 38 U.S.C. §1788(a)(4). The regulations, reported in 38 C.F.R. §21.4200 and 38 C.F.R. §21.4272, set out a specific formula using contact hours or seat-time by which the Veterans Administration could measure a "full-time" course. The appeals court found the regulations to be a rational and reasonable implementation of a uniform notion of "semester-hour."

The case arose when Wayne State University challenged the regulations which denied full-time educational assistance benefits to students in its Weekend College Program, even though the students paid full-time tuition and were considered full-time students at Wayne State. The university's challenge, and the reaction of several higher education associations to the 6th Circuit's decision, are indicative of a mounting concern about the federal government's increasing intrusion into the internal administration of institutions of higher education.

Some of the questions concerning the impact of federal regulation on higher education have already been explored, in theoretical terms in Chapter 13 and with respect to specific legislative enactments in Chapters 14-23. This chapter completes the analysis with a very general overview of several statutes and regulations which have impact on institutions of higher education. Some of the statutes are direct regulations of higher education; others are more general (in the nature of safety or welfare legislation) and may only have a limited impact on institutions of higher education. The materials here are not intended to be comprehensive; rather, the citations in this chapter should be viewed by the reader as a starting point for further study.

II.   Federal Aid to Education

The Federal government provides millions of dollars in higher education assistance each year. While some of the federal aid goes directly to institutions for their own improvement and research support, much of the support is channeled into programs to directly assist students in obtaining post secondary education.

In addition to being subject to requirements set out in the aid authorizing statutes, institutions receiving federal aid may be subject to regulations developed by the overseeing administrative agency, regulations in federal program manuals, guidelines and policy memoranda. Specific institutional requirements or suggestions may also be set out in grant award documents or contracts, administrative agency manuals, and Office of Management and Budget circulars. The legal weight of these many regulations varies with the issuing source and is a fertile area for challenge by institutions of higher education.

Enforcement of regulations for federal aid to higher education also varies with the program. While some regulations call for periodic agency audit and issuance of "audit exceptions" for funds not spent in compliance with the regulations, other programs call for limiting, suspending, or terminating federal aid to a noncomplying institution. (See Education Amendments of 1976, 20 U.S.C. 1088 f-1(a)(4)). One case has held that federal agencies are authorized to sue in court to obtain compliance. (See U.S. v. Institute of Computer Technology, 403 F.Supp. 922 (E.D. Mich. 1975).) Most often, an institution will have a right to a hearing before federal aid is cut off. (For examples, *see* 20 U.S.C. 1088 f-1; 20 U.S.C. 1232c(c); 45 C.F.R. 100a.495.)

Financial aid funds are distributed in a variety of ways; some as direct grants to students, some to institutions for their distribution as grants to students, and some to institutions to loan to students. The institution's specific responsibilities largely depend upon the program through which the aid is funded. However, the Buckley Amendment and non-discrimination regulations discussed earlier are umbrella requirements covering all financial aid programs.

A.   Higher Education Act of 1965

20 U.S.C. § 1001 et seq.

This act is the source of many postsecondary financial aid programs. It has a three-pronged focus providing: direct grants to states for the development of community service, continuing education and life-long learning programs (section 1001 et seq.); direct grants to institutions for such programs as library assistance (section 1021 et seq.); and direct financial aid grants to students or to institutions for distribution to students (section 1070 et seq.). The stated purpose of the act is to assist in making available the benefits of postsecondary education to qualified students in institutions of higher education. Many of the programs created by this act carry their own specific regulations:

- Sections 1070a, Basic Educational Opportunity Grants. Regulations at 45 C.F.R. § 190. (Direct educational grants to eligible undergraduate students based upon family income.)

– Sections 1070b, Supplemental Educational Opportunity Grants. Regulations at 45 C.F.R. § 176. (Supplemental grants to students of exceptional need who, for lack of such a grant, would be unable to obtain post-secondary education.)

– Sections 1070(c), Grants to States for State Student Incentives. Regulations at 45 C.F.R. § 192. (Incentive grants to states to assist them in providing grants to eligible students.)

– Section 1070(e), Assistance to Institutions of Higher Education. Regulations at 45 C.F.R. § 189. (Cost of education payments directly to institutions according to formula defined in the Act.)

– Section 1071, Guaranteed Student Loan Program (see Chapter 22). Regulations at 45 C.F.R. § 177. (Loan insurance and federal interest subsidy payments in order to assist federal, state, and private programs of low interest insured loans to students.)

– Section 1087aa, National Direct Student Loans. Regulations at 45 C.F.R. § 144. (Assists in the establishment and maintenance of funds at institutions of higher education for the making of low interest loans to students in need thereof to pursue study at the lending institution.)

– Section 1088. Regulations at 45 C.F.R. § 154, 155, 157, 159, 175, 176, 189, 190, 192. (General provisions relating to student assistance programs.) The most notable of these is section 1088b-1 (regulations at 42 Fed. Reg. 61043 (December 1, 1977), 45 C.F.R. § 178) detailing requirements for institutional and financial assistance information for students, and financial aid training programs. This Student Consumer Information Amendment is discussed further below.

– Section 1088f(1), Fiscal Eligibility of Institutions. Regulations at 45 C.F.R. § 168. (Auditing, financial responsibility and informational requirements.) Subpart (c) of this section authorizes the Commissioner of Education to suspend or terminate the program's eligibility status upon determination that the institution has engaged in substantial misrepresentation of the nature of its educational program, its financial charges, or the employability of its graduates.

Several cases construing financial aid regulations are: U.S. v. Institute of Computer Technology, 403 F.Supp. 922 (E.D. Mich. 1975) upheld injunctive order prohibiting institution's disbursement of $100,000 in B.E.O.G. awards because of inadequate records. The case also held that the United States may sue an institution for breach of contract under the B.E.O.G. Program. Windsor University v. Secretary of HEW, 550 F.2d 1203 (9th Cir. 1977)–held Commissioner of Education has broad discretion to impose dollar and time limitations in loan contracts made pursuant to Federal Insured Student Loan Program, 20 U.S.C. § 1082(a)(3), to protect the financial integrity and continued vitality of the loan program, especially where the lending institution is inexperienced. Girardier v. Webster College, 563 F.2d 1267 (8th Cir. 1977)–held the Bankruptcy Act does not prohibit a *private* college's refusing to furnish transcripts to persons who have received a discharge in bankruptcy of their college loans, but Handsome v. Rutgers Univ., the State University of New Jersey, 445 F.Supp. 1362 (D.N.J., 1978)–held that a *state* university may not withhold transcripts from and deny registration to a former student whose NDSL loans were discharged in bankruptcy.

B.   *College Work Study Program*

42 U.S.C. 2751-2756. Regulations at 45 C.F.R. § 175

This program is designed to stimulate and promote part-time employment of students in eligible institutions who are in need of the earnings from such employment to pay for their education. Section 2753 provides that grants can be made directly to institutions to assist in the operation of a work study program. Section 175.25(a) of the regulations requires the institution receiving a CWSP allocation to maintain a level of spending in its own scholarship and student aid programs in an amount not less than the average per year expenditure made during the three fiscal years preceeding the grant. The Commissioner may waive the requirement under special circumstances such as where an institution's inability to maintain the required expenditure level is due to a withdrawal of funds from outside sources or a decline in enrollment. Note that for public institutions, public appropriations are not considered an outside source. (45 C.F.R. 175.25(b)(1).)

C.   *Veterans' Readjustment Benefits Act of 1966*

38 U.S.C. § 1651 et seq. Regulations at 38 C.F.R. § 21.1020 et seq.

The general purposes of this educational assistance act, its amendments and regulations are to make service in the armed forces more attractive, to extend the benefits of higher education to qualified persons who might not otherwise be able to afford it, to provide vocational readjustment and restore lost educational opportunities to veterans, and to aid them in attaining the vocational and educational status which they might normally have obtained had they not served in the military. Although the student veteran receives benefits directly from the Veterans Administration, in order to make him eligible his institution is required to fulfill specified duties under the Act. The veteran receives benefits only if he is enrolled in a course approved by a designated state approval agency or by the Veterans Administration. Sections 1775 and 1776(b) of the Act require that the institution seeking approval submit to the state approval agency a certified copy of its catalog or bulletin. The Act specifies twelve types of information that the catalog must contain including: graduation standards, student conduct regulations, tuition refund policy, and course descriptions. In addition, as a condition of approval, the institution is required to maintain adequate records showing the progress of each veteran, previous educational training, appropriate credits given, and the training period proportionately shortened. Although section 1782 of the Act prohibits interference by the government with administrative functions of the school, section 1673 sets strict standards for the content of courses for which the agency will approve benefits, and sections 1784 and 1785 of the Act set out very specific requirements for monitoring and reporting by the institution. In addition to the full-time course definition requirements of the Act, institutions have also challenged the 85/15 and two-year rules of the Act which require disapproval of benefits if more than 85 percent of the students in a program have their charges paid for by the Veterans Administration, or if the course in which the veteran is enrolled has been offered by the institution for less than two years. *See* 38 U.S.C. § 1673(d), 38 U.S.C. § 1789.)

Recent cases discussing veterans assistance regulations are: Wayne State University, et al. v. Max Cleland, et al., Nos. 78-1141, 78-1142 (6th Cir. 1978)—upholding administrator's authority to promulgate course approval regulations. Cleland, et al. v. National College of Business, 435 U.S. 213 (1978)—upholding the 85-15 requirement, and two-year rule as not violating the Due Process Clause of the Fifth Amendment. Bob Jones University, et al. v. Johnson, 396 F.Supp. 597 (D.S.C. 1974), *affirmed,* 529 F.2d 514 (4th Cir. 1975)—upholding cutoff of G.I. benefits to students at fundamentalist religious institution which failed to comply with racial discrimination prohibition of Title VI. State of Colorado et al. v. Veterans Administration, 430 F.Supp. 551 (D. Colo. 1977)—held regulation requiring educational institutions to report change in student's status within 30 days did not result in exercise of control over the administrative functions of the school in violation of the statute. Letellier v. Cleland, et al. 437 F.Supp. 936 (S.D. Iowa 1977)—held student veterans do not have a constitutionally protected property or liberty interest in attending a particular institution that fails to meet Veterans Administration requirements for accreditation.

D. Health Professions Educational Assistance Act of 1976

42 U.S.C. § 292 et seq.
Regulations at 42 C.F.R. § 57; 45 C.F.R. § 16 and 149.

The act revises and extends the authorities of the Public Health Service Act providing assistance to schools and students of medicine, osteopathy, veterinary medicine, optometry, pharmacy, podiatry, public health, health administration, and allied health. The general purpose of the act is to insure the financial stability of health professions schools and to increase the health professional manpower supply. However, the statute's statement of policy and the legislative history indicate an intent to be fairly directive in legislating provisions that would correct the nation's geographic and specialty maldistribution of health professionals.[1] The act's provisions focus on providing assistance for training primary care general practitioners. The act also eliminates preferential treatment formerly granted to alien physicians and surgeons.

The general provisions under Part A (§ 292 et seq.) prohibit sex discrimination in admissions, regulate maintenance of records and audits, and

---

1. 1976 U.S. Code Cong. and Adm. News, p. 4947.

require shared schedule residency training positions for programs receiving federal assistance. Part B (§293 et seq.) authorizes federal grants for construction of health professions teaching facilities. Part C (§294 et seq.) provides loans, traineeships and scholarships to graduate students in health professions. Part D (§295 et seq.) provides specific grants for family medicine training, computer technology demonstration programs, and quality improvement grants for health professions schools. Eligibility requirements for grants under the various programs are very specific. For example, section 295f provides capitation grants to schools of medicine, osteopathy, and dentistry. The statute sets a formula multiplying the number of full-time students by a specified dollar figure. Other eligibility requirements include minimum enrollment levels for first year and primary care residency programs, and the operation of remote site training programs. The conditioning of grant awards upon satisfaction of the enumerated eligibility requirements indicates the federal government's willingness to aid only health professional programs of a certain size, quality, and educational objectives.

E.   Department of Energy Proposed Regulations

10 C.F.R. §455, 44 Fed. Reg. 1580 (January 5, 1979). National Energy Conservation Policy Act (NECPA), Pub. L. 95-619, 92 Stat. 3206

The regulations propose cost sharing grants for conducting technical assistance programs and for adopting energy conservation measures in schools, hospitals, units of local government, and public care institutions. Participation is voluntary, but under the rules, participating institutions would be required to undergo preliminary and regular audits of their energy conservation needs. An audit would precede any award of a technical assistance grant, and the institution would be required to take inexpensive conservation measures recommended in the audit before becoming eligible for the grant. The regulations specify actions which constitute energy-saving measures. Under Subpart G, §455.82 grants to schools, colleges, and hospitals must be matched by at least an equal share of non-federal funds.

Articles discussing the general implication of federal aid to higher education: Ford, *Constitutional Implications of Federal Aid to Higher Education*, I. J. Law & Ed. 513 (1972); and Smith, *Emerging Consequences of Financing Private Colleges with Public Money*, 9 Val. U.L. Rev. 561 (1975).

III. Protection of Student and Employee Rights

A.   Vietnam Era Veterans Readjustment Assistance Act of 1974

38 U.S.C. §2012, Regulations at 41 C.F.R. §60-250.

All educational institutions that are federal contractors and subcontractors in excess of $10,000 are required by this statute to take affirmative action to employ and advance at all levels of employment, including the executive level, qualified disabled veterans and veterans of the Vietnam era. Under the regulations, the contractor is required to enlist the assistance and support of recruiting sources such as: local Veterans' Employment Representatives, the V.A. Regional Office, the National Alliance for Businessmen, college veterans' counselors and national and local veterans' groups. 41 C.F.R. § 60-250.6. Veterans believing that a contractor has failed or refused to comply with the provisions of the act may file complaints with the Veteran's Employment Service of the Department of Labor. The Department of Labor may seek judicial enforcement, withhold progress payments, terminate a contract or debar from future contracts a contractor in non-compliance with its required affirmative action clause. 41 C.F.R. § 60-250.28.

B.   Education Amendments of 1976 (Student Consumer Information)

20 U.S.C. § 1088b-1, Regulations at 42 Fed. Reg. 61043 (December 1, 1977), 45 C.F.R. § 178.

In order to assist students and prospective students in making intelligent choices about funding their education, and to prevent them from undertaking student loan obligations without full knowledge of their obligations, the 1976 Education Amendments require student consumer information dissemination activities by institutions participating in administrative cost allowance programs under the Higher Education Act. The institution is required to distribute, through publicity and mailings to current and prospective students, information on the financial aid programs available, methods of aid distribution, means of application and eligibility requirements, rights and responsibilities of aid recipients, costs of attending the institution, refund policy, descriptions of academic programs, and the person(s) to contact for financial aid information. The institution is also required to have a full-time employee or group of employees available at the institution to assist students in obtaining financial aid information. The Commissioner of Education may waive the full-time employee requirement when the total institutional enrollment or the number of students on federal financial assistance is low. The regulations describe in detail the kind of information to be disseminated. For example, under rights and responsibilities of students, an institution is required to describe: criteria for continued eligibility, criteria for determining a student in good standing, the means of award payment, a sample student loan repayment schedule, and general terms and conditions of any employment provided as financial aid. (See 45 C.F.R. § 178.4(b).) The institution is required to maintain appropriate financial aid records for five years, and to perform institutional audits of transactions related to the use of administrative cost allowances. See 45 C.F.R. § 178.7 and § 178.8.)

For a general discussion of student consumer protection, see Consumer Protection and Higher Education—Student Suits Against Schools, 37 Ohio St. L.J. 608 (1976).

C. *Regulations for Protection of Human Subjects*

    1.   45 C.F.R. §46 (HEW)

        a.   Proposed rules for research involving children, 43 Fed. Reg. 31786 (July 21, 1978).

        b.   Research involving prisoners, 43 Fed. Reg. 1049 (January 5, 1978).

    2.   Research involving prisoners, (FDA) 43 Fed. Reg. 19417 (May 5, 1978), 21 C.F.R. §50.

    3.   Protection of Human Subjects (ERDA), 10 C.F.R. §745.1.

    4.   Protection of Human Subjects (NIH), 45 C.F.R. §1410.2.

    5.   Protection of Human Subjects—Procurement (HEW), 41 C.F.R. §3-4.5501.

The federal government has promulgated numerous regulations to insure the protection of human subjects from physical, psychological, and sociological risks in federally funded research projects. Although by and large the regulations are repetitive of each other, there is some variation depending upon the particular funding source and administrative agency responsible for oversight. Generally, no award is made to an individual researcher unless s/he is affiliated with an institution which can assume responsibility for the human subjects. Most of the regulations require that an Institutional Review Board review and approve the research, determine whether human subjects will be at risk and, if so, whether the risk is outweighed by the benefits of the research. The review board must also see that subjects are adequately protected and give informed consent, and it must perform periodic review of the research activity. The HEW regulations stipulate the terms to be included in informed consent and the contents of a required protection statement. 45 C.F.R. §46.103. The regulations even specify requirements for the composition of the Institutional Review Board. Part 46.122 authorizes the Secretary to impose additional conditions when determined to be necessary for the protection of human subjects. Other regulations cover the institution's executive responsibilities (*e.g.*, policy development, administrative assistance to IRBs, follow-up of board recommendations), maintenance of records, and coverage of subcontractors. Some of the regulations contain such vague language that they appear to give broad authority to the federal government to cut off funding at its discretion. For example, subpart 1 of the Proposed Rules for research involving children requires that the research be carried on only if the research methods are appropriate, the investigators are competent, the facilities are adequate, and the research procedures are designed to contribute vitally to generalized knowledge.

D.   Employee Retirement Income Security Act of 1974 (ERISA)

26 U.S.C. § 401 et seq., 29 U.S.C. § 1001 et seq., Regulations at 26 C.F.R. § 1, 11, 29 C.F.R. § 2509 et seq., § § 2601-2604, 28 C.F.R. § 4a.

ERISA, or the Pension Reform Act, alters both federal tax laws and federal labor laws in their regulation of retirement plans. By setting minimum standards to assure equitable character and financial soundness, the act seeks to protect interstate commerce and the interests of retirement plan participants and beneficiaries.

Employee benefit plans established and maintained by private postsecondary institutions or employee organizations are covered by the Act. Plans of public institutions are excluded as governmental plans. 29 U.S.C. § 1002(32), 26 U.S.C. § 414(d).

Employers, or employee organizations covered by the Act must appoint a plan administrator who is responsible for the preparation and filing of plan descriptions, annual and termination reports. Such reports must be filed with the Department of Labor, the Internal Revenue Service, the Pension Benefit Guaranty Corporation, and with those who participate in or benefit from the plan.

The Regulatory provisions of the act cover: information reporting and disclosure; participation and vesting; funding; fiduciary responsibilities; administration and enforcement.

Rules and regulations for these provisions appear at 29 C.F.R. § 2509, 2510, 2520, 2530, 2550, 2560.

The act provides special rules for teachers and employees of tax exempt educational organizations. Such plans may require that all employees be at least 30 years old and have completed one year of service in order to participate. 26 U.S.C. § 410(a)(1)(B), 29 U.S.C. § 1052(a)(1)(B)(ii). In addition, the rule regarding tax sheltered annuities for teachers and employees of tax exempt educational organizations allows the election of "catch up" provisions, i.e., higher contributions in later years to make up for relatively low contributions made in earlier years. 26 U.S.C. § 403(b), 26 U.S.C. § 415-(c)(4).

The enforcement provisions of the act provide the government, participants and beneficiaries with broad remedies. Criminal action may be brought for willful violation of the act. An individual may be fined up to $5,000 and/or imprisoned up to one year. An institution or employee organization may be fined up to $100,000. A participant or beneficiary may bring civil suit to recover benefits due, to enforce his/her rights under the plan, or to clarify rights to future benefits. The Secretary of Labor may also bring civil suit. A plan administrator who fails to comply with a government information request may be personally liable up to $100 per day for each day exceeding the 30-day compliance period.

For general discussions of ERISA requirements see: Am. Jur. 2d. New Topic Service, Pension Reform Act. Comment, *The Employee Retirement Income Security Act of 1974: Policies and Problems*, 26 Syracuse L. Rev.

539 (1975); Steen, *Employee Benefit Reporting After ERISA*, 36 Louisiana L. Rev. 867 (1976).

E.   Occupational Safety and Health Act of 1970

29 U.S.C. 651, Regulations at 29 C.F.R. § 1901, 42 C.F.R. § 80.

In order to "assure every man and woman in the nation safe and healthful working conditions and to preserve the nation's human resources, OSHA covered employers must meet OSHA safety and health standards including the act's posting and reporting requirements. Private educational institutions are covered by the act as employers engaged in a business affecting commerce. Public institutions are excluded from the federal program, but may be covered by state OSHA programs. In general, the act requires employers to comply with safety and health standards in the workplace and, where no specific standards exist, to maintain the workplace free from hazards. The government normally performs safety inspections without warrants, but if an employer objects, then an inspection warrant must be obtained. Employers are required to record and report job-related injuries and illnesses. In addition, they are responsible to take disciplinary action against employees who refuse to comply with the employer's safety standards. Employees themselves may initiate requests for OSHA inspections, and they must be notified of any violations discovered. Discriminatory action against employees asserting their OSHA rights is prohibited. The government may issue citations for violations of the act, its standards or regulations. Civil penalties range from up to $1,000 for each serious or non-serious violation to up to $10,000 for repeated or willful violations. Criminal penalties up to $10,000 and/or up to six months imprisonment may be imposed for very serious violations including those resulting in death.

A recent case involving a university and OSHA enforcement is: University of Pittsburgh of the Commonwealth System of Higher Education, OSHRC Docket No. 77-1290, April 4, 1978—vacated a citation for a non-serious violation issued to the University of Pittsburgh because the institution, although formerly a private school, is now a political subdivision of the State of Pennsylvania, therefore exempt from OSHA jurisdiction.

For articles on administration and enforcement of the act, *see:* Symposium, *Occupational Safety and Health,* 38 Law and Contemporary Problems 583 (1974); ABA Section of Labor Relations Law, *Occupational Safety and Health Law* (Proceedings of National Institute held in Washington, D.C., April 29-30, 1976).

F.   The Privacy Act of 1974

5 U.S.C. § 552a, Pub. L. 93-579, 88 Stat. 1896.

Although the Buckley Amendment (see Chapter 21) is probably the best known federal regulation affecting the records of higher educational institutions, the Privacy Act of 1974 may have significant impact on institutional records policies. The purpose of the act is to provide safeguards for an individual against the invasion of personal privacy, especially in the use of computer data and information obtained through research. The act requires federal agencies to permit an individual to inspect, copy, correct, and limit dissemination of information about himself. In addition, the act provides private right to sue for damages, as well as criminal penalties for willful violations. (Exemption from the requirements is granted only where there is important public policy need.)

Educational institutions are not federal agencies subject to the act simply because they receive federal monies. 5 U.S.C. 552a(a)(1). However, if an institution as a federal contractor assumes an agency function in operating a system of records, then the Privacy Act requirements apply to such a system. 5 U.S.C. §552a(m). The act defines conditions for records disclosure and access, requirements for accounting of disclosures, as well as recordkeeping and notice requirements.

Section 7 of Pub. L. 93-579 makes it unlawful for any federal, state, or local government agency to deny to any individual a right, benefit or privilege provided by law because of the individual's refusal to disclose his social security account number. This section of the act specifically applies to public institutions which, however, may require disclosure where the social security number is required by federal statute, or where the institution maintains "a system of records in existence and operating before January 1, 1975, if such disclosure was required under statute or regulation adopted prior to such date to verify the identity of an individual." If the social security number is requested, the institution must inform the individual whether the disclosure is mandatory or voluntary, by what statutory or other authority the number is solicited, and what uses will be made of it.

Cases construing Privacy Act requirements in institutions of higher education are: Ciba-Geigy Corp. v. Mathews, 428 F.Supp. 523 (S.D.N.Y. 1977)—held a university group diabetes program was not an "agency" whose records were subject to disclosure under §552 in that it had no independent authority to perform specific governmental functions. Department of the Air Force, et al. v. Rose, et al., 425 U.S. 352 (1976)—held nameless case summaries of honors and ethics hearings of U. S. Air Force Academy students could be disclosed to law review editors for research. Information was not exempted by §552(b)(2) from Freedom of Information Act requirements.

Articles discussing some implications of the Privacy Act are: Comment, *The Freedom of Information Act's Privacy Exemption and the Privacy Act of 1974*, 11 Harv. Civil Rights—Civil Liberties L. Rev. 596 (1976); Belair, *Agency Implementation of the Privacy Act and the Freedom of Information Act Impact on the Government's Collection, Maintenance and Dissemination of Personally Identifiable Information*, 10 John Marshall J. 465 (1977); Carter, Harris, Brown, *Privacy in Education: Legal Implications for Educational Researchers*, 5 J. of Law & Ed. 465 (1976); Cox, *A Walk Through Section 552 of the Administrative Procedure Act: The Freedom of Information Act; The Privacy Act; and The Government in the*

Sunshine Act, 46 U. of Cincinnati L. Rev. 969 (1977); Hulett, *Privacy and the Freedom of Information Act*, 27 Administrative L. Rev. 275 (1975).

G. Government in the Sunshine Act

5 U.S.C. 552b

Section 2 of Pub. L. 94-409 provides that:

"It is hereby declared to be the policy of the United States that the public is entitled to the fullest practicable information regarding the decision-making processes of the Federal Government. It is the purpose of this Act to provide the public with such information while protecting the rights of individuals and the ability of the Government to carry out its responsibilities."

Under the requirements of the act every portion of every meeting in a public institution where governmental business takes place shall be open to public observation. Agencies are required to give public notice in advance of such meetings, as well as to transcribe minutes of the open meetings and make them available to the public. Closed meetings are permitted for specified purposes such as personnel matters, collective bargaining, law enforcement and real estate transactions. However, Section 552b(f)(1) requires that the general counsel or chief legal officer of an institution publicly certify that in his/her opinion, pursuant to a relevant exemption to the act, the meeting may be closed to the public. Nevertheless, the agency must still maintain a transcript or recording, or minutes of the meeting. An individual may sue in federal court to set aside, enjoin, invalidate, or make records public of any agency action taken at a meeting held in violation of the act. 5 U.S.C. 552b(h). Many states have enacted their own state sunshine laws that apply to most public institutions.

For recent cases applying sunshine laws to universities *see*: Fain v. Faculty of the College of Law of the University of Tennessee, 552 SW2d 752 (Ct. App. Tenn. 1977)—law school faculty and faculty committee meetings held not subject to Tennessee Open Meetings Act T.C.A. §8-4401 et seq. Pope v. Parkinson, 363 NE2d 438 (App. Ct. Ill. 1977)—state open meetings act held not applicable to university Assembly Hall Committee Meetings. Greene, et al. v. Athletic Council of Iowa State University, et al., 251 NW2d 559 (Iowa 1977)—held athletic council of state university subject to state open meetings statute. Carl v. Board of Regents of the University of Oklahoma, 577 P2d 912 (Okla. 1978)—held admissions board of University of Oklahoma College of Medicine comes within the purview of state open meeting law. Student Bar Association Board of Governors, etc. v. Byrd, 239 SE2d 415 (N.C. 1977)—held state open meetings law does not require that meetings of law school faculty be open to public.

Useful articles are: Shurtz, *The University in the Sunshine: Application of the Open Meeting Laws to the University Setting*, 5 J. of Law and Ed. 453, (1976); Simon, *The Application of State Sunshine Laws to Institutions of Higher Education*, 4 J. of Coll. & U.L. 83 (1976/77).

IV. Regulation of Business or Commercial Practices

A.   Antitrust Laws

The Sherman Antitrust Act, 15 U.S.C. § § 1-7
The Clayton Act, 15 U.S.C. § § 12-27
The Robinson Patman Price Discrimination Act, 15 U.S.C. § § 13, 13a, b, and 21a
The Federal Trade Commission Act, 15 U.S.C. § § 41-58.

Property rights such as patents, copyrights, trademarks and names and the business transactions involving them are activities that might cause a private university to become involved in antitrust matters. Public institutions have been held exempt from federal antitrust laws under the exemption for governmental actions of state officials or agents. Saenz v. University Inter-scholastic League, 487 F.2d 1026 (5th Cir. 1973).

Section one of the Sherman Act prohibits every contract, combination or conspiracy in restraint of trade or commerce. The Clayton Act makes unlawful leases, sales or contracts of sale conditioned upon the lessee's or purchaser's agreement not to deal in the goods of a competitor. Exclusive contracts made in violation of the act may be declared null and void by the court. The Robinson Patman Act broadens the Clayton Act's prohibitions against discriminatory pricing in order to "curb all devices by which large buyers gained preferences over smaller ones by virtue of their greater pur-chasing power." However, the non-profit institutions exemption, 15 U.S.C. 13c, makes the Robinson Patman Act's prohibitions inapplicable to pur-chases of supplies for their own use by schools, colleges, universities, public libraries, churches, hospitals, and charitable institutions not operated for profit. The Federal Trade Commission Act makes unlawful any unfair method of competition, or any unfair and deceptive act or practice in commerce. The act does not apply to private non-profit or to public insti-tutions, but it does apply to proprietary postsecondary institutions.

For antitrust cases relating to higher education, *see*: Marjorie Webster Junior College v. Middle States Association, 432 F.2d 650 (D.C. Cir. 1970), *cert. denied*, 400 U.S. 965 (1970)—defendant's accreditation activities escaped antitrust liability as not undertaken with commercial motive, and at the heart of the concept of education itself; Jones v. National Collegiate Athletic Association, 392 F.Supp. 295 (D. Mass. 1975)—rule declaring a student ineligible to participate in N.C.A.A. sponsored intercollegiate hockey held not a violation of the Sherman Act; The Board of Regents of the University of Oklahoma v. National Collegiate Athletic Association, Okla-homa S.Ct., 1977-1 Trade Cases § 61, 288 (1977)—using "rule of reason test," court held N.C.A.A. bylaw limiting the number of coaches that a member institution may employ not a restraint of trade; Logan Lanes, Inc. v. Brunswick Corp., 378 F.2d 212 (9th Cir. 1967), *cert. denied*, 389 U.S. 898 (1967)—sales of bowling equipment at bowling lanes installed in student union used as part of physical education program held to be sales for the university's own use even though the bowling alley was self-sustaining.

For relevant discussions of antitrust legislation, *see:* Note, *Restrictive Practices in Accreditation of Medical Schools: An Antitrust Analysis,* 51 So. Calif. L. Rev. 657 (1978); Comment, *Proprietary Vocational School Abuses: Can the FTC Cure Them?* 24 Catholic University L. Rev. 603 (1975); Sullivan, Handbook of the Law of Antitrust (St. Paul: West, 1977); Wang, *The Unbundling of Higher Education,* 1975 Duke L.J. 53.

B.   *Internal Revenue Code of 1954*

26 U.S.C. § 1 et seq.

There are numerous tax code provisions, regulations, and procedures which apply to institutions of higher education. Some relate directly to the financial management of the institution, others require the taxable status of institutions in order to achieve broader social policy goals.

Section 501 of the code is a key provision for educational institutions in that it sets forth the requirements for exempt organizations. Private institutions may qualify for tax exempt status by meeting the requirements set out in I.R.C. § 501(c)(3).

(3) Corporations, and any community chest, fund, or foundation, organized and operated exclusively for religious, charitable, scientific, testing for public safety, literary, or educational purposes, or to foster national or international amateur sports competition (but only if no part of its activities involve the provision of athletic facilities or equipment), or for the prevention of cruelty to children or animals, no part of the net earnings of which inures to the benefit of any private shareholder or individual, no substantial part of the activities of which is carrying on propaganda, or otherwise attempting to influence legislation (except as otherwise provided in subsection (h)), and which does not participate in, or intervene in (including the publishing or distributing of statements), any political campaign on behalf of any candidate for public office.

A public institution may qualify for tax exempt status under L.R.C. § 115 as a political subdivision of the state, or it may qualify under the constitutional intergovernmental immunities doctrine. Private institutions qualifying for tax exempt status are also required to administer a racially non-discriminatory policy as to students. Rev. Rul. 71-447, 1971-2 C.B. 230 defines a non-discriminatory policy as one which "admits students of any race to all the rights, privileges, programs, and activities generally accorded or made available to students at that school." It also requires that the school "not discriminate on the basis of race in administration of its educational policies, admissions policies, scholarship and loan program and athletic and other school administered programs." This policy is reinforced in other Internal Revenue procedures. For example, Rev. Proc. 75-50, 1975-2, C.B. 587 sets forth guidelines and recordkeeping requirements for determining whether private schools that are applying for recognition of tax exempt status have racially non-discriminatory policies. The school is required to certify annually that it satisfies the requirements of the procedure.

Other tax law provisions regulate an institution's lobbying and political activities (*see* I.R.C. §501(h)), and tax on unrelated business income (*see* I.R.C. §501(b)). Section 117 and the regulations on the taxability of fellowships and scholarships (Treas. Reg. §1.117) may have great impact on how an institution administers its financial aid packages.

An important example of the use of tax laws to regulate antidiscrimination is: Bob Jones University v. Simon, 416 U.S. 725 (1974)—the court allowed the IRS to withdraw the university's preferential tax status because the university enforced a racially discriminatory admissions policy. However, a recent U.S. district court decision held that the IRS overstepped its power in denying tax exempt status to Bob Jones University because of its policy on interracial dating and marriage. Wall Street Journal, Feb. 14, 1979, at 1, Col. 5.

Useful discussions of federal tax policy and higher education are: *Alternatives to the University Property Tax Exemption*, 83 Yale L.J. 181 (1973); Burke, *Federal Taxation of State Colleges and Universities: Recent Developments Call for Reconsideration of the Theories of Exemption*, 4 J. Coll. and U. L. 43 (1976); Francis, *Federal Tax Problems of College and University Auxiliary Organizations*, 3 J. Coll. & U. L. 72 (1975); Hopkins, *Scholarships and Fellowship Grants: Current Tax Developments and Problems*, 3 J. Coll. & U. L. 54 (1975); Horvitz, *Tax Subsidies to Promote Affirmative Action in Admissions Procedures for Institutions of Higher Learning—Their Inherent Danger*, 52 Taxes 452 (1974); Sugarman and Mancino, *Tax Aspects of University Patent Policy*, 3 J. Coll. & U. L. 41 (1975); Symposium, *Federal Taxation and Charitable Organizations*, 39 Law and Contemporary Problems 1 (1975), includes Levi, *Financing Education and the Effects of the Tax Laws*, and Kirkwood and Mundel, *The Role of Tax Policy in Federal Support for Higher Education*; Symposium, *Federal Tax Issues Confronting Institutions of Higher Education*, 3 J. of Coll. & U. L. 1 (1976); Tucker, *Federal Income Taxation of Scholarships and Fellowships: A Practical Analysis*, 8 Ind. L. Rev. 749 (1975).

NOTES

1. For additional discussions of federal regulations and higher education, *see*:

Aiken (Part 1), Adams, Hall (Part 2), *Legal Liabilities in Higher Education: Their Scope and Management*, 3 J. of Coll. & U. L. 329 (1976).

Bender, *Federal Regulation and Higher Education* (American Association for Higher Education, ERIC/Higher Education Research Rpt. No. 1, 1977).

Faccenda, *Constitutional and Statutory Regulation of Private Colleges and Universities*, 9 Val. U. L. Rev. 539 (1975).

Gellharn, Boyer, *Government and Education: The University as a Regulated Industry*, 1977 Ariz. St. L. J. 569.

Kaplin, The Law of Higher Education (San Francisco: Jossey-Bass, 1978).

Lopati, Education and the Federal Government: A Historical Record (1975).

Oaks, *A Private University Looks at Government Regulation*, 4 J. of Coll. & U. L. 1 (1976).

Sky, *Rulemaking and the Federal Grant Process in the United States Office of Education*, 62 Virginia L. Rev. 1017 (1976).

Summerfield, Power and Process: The Formulation and Limits of Federal Educational Policy (McCutchan, 1974).

Winkler, *Proliferating the Federal Regulations: Is Government Now the Enemy?* Chronicle of Higher Education, December 13, 1976, p. 3, Col. 1.

2. Recent articles discussing the role of college and university legal counsel are:

Bealle, *Delivery of Legal Services to Administrators of Higher Education*, 2 J. of Coll. & U. L. 5 (1974).

Bickel, *The Role of College or University Legal Counsel*, 3 J. of Law & Ed. 73 (1974).

Corbally, *University Counsel–Scope and Mission*, 2 J. of Coll. & U. L. 1 (1974).

Epstein, *The Use and Misuse of College and University Counsel*, 45 J. of Higher Ed. 635 (1974).

McCarty, Thompson, *The Role of Counsel in American Colleges and Universities*, 14 Am. Bus. L. J. 287 (1977).

Orentlicher, *The Role of College or University Legal Counsel: An Added Dimension*, 4 J. of Law & Ed. 511 (1974).

Sensenbrenner, *University Counselor: Lore, Logic and Logistics*, 2 J. of Coll. & U. L. 13 (1974).

INDEX

Date Due